THE OXFORD COMPANION TO NEW ZEALAND MILITARY HISTORY

THE OXFORD COMPANION TO NEW ZEALAND MILITARY HISTORY

Edited by Ian McGibbon

With the assistance of
Paul Goldstone

OXFORD
UNIVERSITY PRESS

OXFORD
UNIVERSITY PRESS

540 Great South Road, Greenlane, PO Box 11-149, Auckland, New Zealand
Oxford University Press is a department of the University of Oxford.
It furthers the University's objective of excellence in research, scholarship,
and education by publishing worldwide in
Oxford New York
Athens Auckland Bangkok Bogotá Buenos Aires Calcutta
Cape Town Chennai Dar es Salaam Delhi Florence Hong Kong Istanbul
Karachi Kuala Lumpur Madrid Melbourne Mexico City Mumbai Nairobi
Paris Port Moresby São Paulo Singapore Taipei Tokyo Toronto Warsaw
with associated companies in Berlin Ibadan

OXFORD is a registered trade mark of Oxford University Press
in the UK and certain other countries

© Crown copyright 2000

First published 2000

All rights reserved. No part of this publication may be reproduced
stored, in a retrieval system or transmitted, in any form or by any
means, without the prior permission in writing of Oxford University
Press. Within New Zealand, exceptions are allowed in respect of any
fair dealing for the purpose of research or private study, or criticism
or review, as permitted under the Copyright Act 1994, or, in the case
of reprographic reproduction, in accordance with the terms of the
licences issued by Copyright Licensing Limited. Enquiries concerning
reproduction outside these terms and in other countries should be
sent to the Rights Department, Oxford University Press, at the above
address.

ISBN 0 19 558 376 0

Edited by Simon Cauchi
Cover design by Karen Trump
Text design by Polar Design
Typeset by Desktop Concepts Pty Ltd, Melbourne
Printed by Kyodo Printing Co. (Singapore) Pte Ltd

Front cover picture: Peter McIntyre, 'The alert at dawn—27th Machine Gun Battalion in Greece' [April 1941], oil on canvas, 562 x 700 mm, National Collection of War Art, 898/12, National Archives, Wellington.

Back cover picture: soldiers of the Canterbury Infantry Battalion in a trench on Walker's Ridge at Anzac, Gallipoli, in 1915 (*Weekly Press* Collection, Canterbury Museum, 7516).

Contents

Illustrations
vi

Maps
x

Preface
xii

Advisory Committee
xiv

Contributors
xv

Style Notes
xix

Military Nomenclature
xx

Military Ranks: Service Equivalents
xxi

Abbreviations
xxiv

Glossary of Maori terms
xxvi

The Companion: Alphabetical Entries
1

Appendix
628

Senior officers of the armed forces
628

Premiers and prime ministers
631

Ministers of defence-related portfolios
632

Heads of defence-related government departments
633

Index
635

Illustrations

A-4 Skyhawks practise refuelling in formation over Ohakea air base	3
An RNZAF Fairey Gordon light bomber is prepared for flight in 1940	7
Four New Zealand airmen serving in the Western Desert Air Force discuss an operation	12
New Zealand troops load water cans on to mules and donkeys in Tunisia in 1943	18
Antarctic support ship HMNZS *Endeavour* heads for Antarctica through heavy ice	20
One of 7th New Zealand Anti-Tank Regiment's 2-pounder guns in action in Libya in November 1941	25
Officers of the Armed Constabulary's Field Force at Parihaka in 1881	34
A New Zealand Sherman tank moves forward accompanied by infantrymen of 26th Battalion	37
Waiouru Military Camp in 1941	39
A New Zealand field gun in action in Flanders on New Year's Day 1918	42
The Australian Minister of Defence, Kim Beazley, and his New Zealand counterpart, Bob Tizard	47
The commander of New Zealand's 3rd Division, Major-General H.F. Barrowclough	53
Commodore Geoffrey Blake arrives to take over command of the New Zealand Squadron in 1929	58
New Zealand mounted riflemen prepare to move out on the South African veldt	62
RNZAF Hudson bombers are serviced at an island air base during the Pacific War	64
Bombing up one of 75 Squadron's Wellington bombers in England	66
The 58th Regiment on parade in Auckland in 1858	68
The Wanganui Marist Brothers School cadet unit on parade	77
General Duncan Cameron with a member of his staff and artillerymen at sunrise on the morning of the attack on Gate Pa in 1864	79
A New Zealand chaplain celebrates Holy Communion in the field at Messines, Belgium, in 1917	83
Major-General E.W.C. Chaytor with the commander of the 4th Turkish Army, Ali Bey Wahaby	84
A column of 'Massey's Cossacks' in Hanson Street in Newtown, Wellington, in 1913	90
A gun crew prepares to fire a 6-inch gun at Wellington's Fort Dorset in 1939	95
The gunboat *Pioneer* shells the Maori position at Meremere on the Waikato River in 1863	104
The proclamation of a requirement for registration for compulsory military service, 1911	111
Wellingtonians visiting the British battleship, HMS *Ramillies*, in January 1940	120
The commander of Creforce, Major-General B.C. Freyberg, addresses all the officers under his command at Suda Bay, Crete, on 29 April 1941	124
German paratroopers prepare to board their Junker Ju52 transports for the invasion of Crete	126
The light cruiser HMS *Dunedin* at Apia, Western Samoa, in January 1930	131
The first meeting of the Defence Council on 20 November 1964	138
The officers who attended the first meeting of the Council of Defence in 1907	141
Troops with field guns at Waimea in May 1898	149
A New Zealand soldier serving with the International Force East Timor at the border with West Timor	152

Illustrations

Members of 1NZEF sightseeing in Egypt during the First World War	153
Christchurch Home Guardsmen dig a shelter late in 1941	155
Trainee New Zealand airmen inspect the cockpit of a Spitfire at a training school in Canada	157
Members of 2nd/1st Battalion, RNZIR, alight from an RNZAF C-130 Hercules during an exercise	161
RNZAF airmen at a forward air base prepare for operational service a Corsair newly shipped from the United States in 1944	166
De Havilland Vampires, with their distinctive twin tail booms, were the RNZAF's first jet fighters	167
Troops of 30th Battalion have lunch during an exercise in Fiji in 1941	169
An encampment of the Forest Rangers about 1866	177
Peter Fraser arrives at Hawaii with Admiral Chester Nimitz and Vice-Admiral Ghormley in 1942	181
Lieutenant-General Sir Bernard Freyberg	182
A Westland Wasp HAS1 is secured on the flight deck of the Leander class frigate HMNZS *Waikato*	186
Anzac Cove	194
New Zealand troops resting in a trench on Walker's Ridge	196
Major-General A.J. Godley with members of his staff at Seatoun camp, 1912	201
New Zealand troops watch a column of Italian prisoners of war passing through Athens	204
Armed with a Steyr rifle, a New Zealand airman stands guard over an RNZAF C-130 Hercules	211
An RNZAF Iroquois helicopter lifts off a makeshift landing pad at Navua, Fiji	218
Wellington Home Guardsmen learn how to use a Lewis gun during their lunch hour in 1941	221
The hospital ship *Maheno*	228
A Schofield truck-tank undergoes a trial	237
A Semple tank	237
New Zealand infantrymen in a trench at Flers, France, in 1916	242
Captains L.M. Isitt and T.M. Wilkes with the De Havilland 4 light bomber in which they made the first flight over Mount Cook/Aoraki on 8 September 1920	247
New Zealand troops moving forward to the front line pass a divisional sign at Gambettola in 1944	248
New Zealand infantrymen cautiously approach a blown bridge across the Lamone River	252
A Jayforce patrol passes through a Japanese village	257
Admiral of the Fleet Viscount Jellicoe and officers of HMS *New Zealand* with members of the New Zealand Cabinet and officers of the New Zealand Military Forces	259
Lieutenant-Colonel Howard Kippenberger (with pipe) holds a staff conference in Egypt	264
The Kiwi Concert Party puts on a performance for New Zealand troops in the Volturno Valley, Italy	266
Kayforce's 16th Field Regiment in action up the Kap'yong Valley in April 1951	269
Part of the Arawa Flying Column pictured after an action against Te Kooti	271
Prime Minister David Lange discusses a battlefield simulation exercise	274
Peter Fraser meets with New Zealand troops in the Middle East in 1941	275
A Long Range Desert Group patrol pauses in the desert behind enemy lines	282
A New Zealand Vickers machine-gun in action at Minqar Qaim in July 1942	285
Major Peter McIntyre sketching at Cassino, Italy, in 1944	286
Pilots of 488 Squadron RNZAF return from a sortie during the Malayan campaign of 1941–42	290
A Canberra B2 of 75 Squadron, based at Singapore from 1958 to 1962, with one of 41 Squadron's Bristol Freighters	292
Plan of a pa destroyed by British forces on 18 March 1860 drawn by Lieutenant F.B. Mould RE	300
Kayforce Padre R.H. Rangiihu leads a Maori concert party	302
A party of Maori armed with traditional weapons	304
Members of 28th Maori Battalion prepare for action at Faenza in 1945 during the Italian campaign	310
An RNZAF P3 Orion attacks a submarine during an anti-submarine warfare exercise	312
Wounded New Zealanders are prepared for evacuation at Bir el Chleta, Libya, in 1941	314
A horse-drawn wagon of 9th (New Zealand) Station of the Mesopotamian Expeditionary Force's 1st Wireless Signals Squadron	318
The signals section of the Canterbury Engineer Volunteers takes part in an exercise	328
General Sir Bernard Montgomery inspects troops of 5th New Zealand Brigade in 1942	335
A New Zealand mortar crew loads its weapon at Colincamps on the Western Front in April 1918	337
Seamen are transported through the damaged streets of Napier following the earthquake	348
HMNZS *Achilles* undergoes a refit in Calliope Dock at Devonport naval base in 1943	353

Illustrations

The Japanese Naval Training Squadron in Wellington in 1932	355
New Zealand's gift battlecruiser, HMS *New Zealand*, arrives in Lyttelton Harbour in 1919	358
Seamen take part in gun drill on HMS *Philomel*	363
New Zealand troops arrive in Suez in December 1914	365
A recruiting poster for 2NZEF	367
A sketch of the repulse of a Maori counter-attack at Ohaeawai on 1 July 1845	371
Earthworks at Paterangi in 1864	378
Bush fighting: volunteers ambushed at Te Ngutu-o-te-Manu in 1868	381
A member of a German tank crew is taken prisoner by New Zealand troops	388
New Zealand transport south-east of Mersa Matruh in late June 1942	392
The passing out parade of the first all-New Zealand officer training unit at Taranto in 1945	398
Troops of New Zealand's 3rd Division landing on Nissan Island in 1944	409
General Dwight D. Eisenhower meets Air Marshal Sir Keith Park	411
Cases of comforts for New Zealand forces being packed and stacked for shipment	413
A Fairmile launch with the cruiser HMNZS *Leander*	415
A New Zealand mine clearance training team in Cambodia in 1993	416
Men of the New Zealand (Maori) Pioneer Battalion perform a haka in France in 1918	422
Captain Thomas Porter with a party of Ngaitai kupapa at Opotiki in 1870	429
Prisoners of war in Stalag 383, Germany, in 1945	432
Hauhau prisoners on a prison hulk awaiting transport to the Chatham Islands	435
Brigadier R.C. Queree in Egypt in October 1942	437
A Wellington Regiment field cooker being used to prepare a meal just 900 metres from the front line	440
Ceasefire Assembly Place Mike at St Paul's Mission, Rhodesia	449
The crew of HMS *Achilles* march through Auckland after their return in early 1940	451
The Royal Navy's Flying Squadron in Auckland Harbour in 1870	454
The RNVR contingent for service in the Royal Navy at the official farewell in Wellington for 2NZEF's Second Echelon	456
The Duke of York, later King George VI, inspects the New Zealand Permanent Air Force	460
A group of New Zealand nurses with the Minister of Defence, Frederick Jones, in Tunisia in 1943	469
Major-General Sir Andrew Russell inspects one of the Otago Regiment's battalions	472
A 64-pounder gun mounted *en barbette* at Kaiwharawhara, Wellington, as a result of the 1885 Russian scare	474
Seamen and marines from HMS *Dunedin* with Mau prisoners in January 1930	476
Walter Nash addresses the SEATO meeting held in Wellington in March 1959	482
The Premier, Richard Seddon, at a review of the Canterbury Volunteers	485
A New Zealand gunner's cartoon which appeared in *Chronicles of the N.Z.E.F.* in 1917	488
New Zealand mounted riflemen watering their horses before the action at Richon le Zion	491
The Imperial Camel Corps during a halt in their advance in the Sinai Desert	492
Two New Zealand Bren gunners of 23rd Battalion fire on targets during the Italian campaign	497
RNZAF Warhawks being serviced at an airfield in the islands	502
Members of 2NZEF take part in an impromptu game of rugby in Egypt in 1940	507
A pre-war review of the RNZAF at Rongotai, Wellington	508
The frigates HMNZS *Waikato* and *Wellington* refuelling from the fleet supply tanker HMNZS *Endeavour* during exercises off the Australian coast in 1988	515
Major William Mair reads a proclamation to his Arawa kupapa contingent at Kaiteriria	519
An artist's depiction of the 'surrender' of Wiremu Tamihana Te Waharoa	525
An artist's depiction of the death of Major Gustavus von Tempsky	527
A squad of Territorials of 7th Battalion (Hawke's Bay–City of Wellington's Own), RNZIR, in 1976	530
Auckland's spar torpedo boat	534
Aerospace CT4-B Airtrainers at the RNZAF's Central Flying School, Wigram	535
An RNZAF C-130 Hercules landing at McMurdo air strip in Antarctica	538
The departure of the troopship *Aquitania* from Wellington in May 1940	542
The British Army's 65th Regiment on parade at New Plymouth in 1861	545
American troops take a rest during a route march around Wellington's Oriental Bay in 1942	551
Lieutenant Charles Upham is congratulated by his platoon sergeant	553

Illustrations

Members of V Company's 6th Platoon board one of 9 Squadron RAAF's Iroquois helicopters	562
The Te Awamutu Cavalry Volunteers on parade at the opening of the Main Trunk railway at Puniu	567
Canterbury Engineer Volunteers practise bridge building about 1900	568
Flight Lieutenant Sidney Wallingford with his Moth seaplane	574
New Zealand troops moving forward in landing barges at Vella Lavella	575
Land girls assist with farm work during the visit to New Zealand in 1943 of Eleanor Roosevelt	584
The burial of Brigadier-General F.E. Johnston in Belgium in 1917	588
German guns captured during the New Zealand Division's successful attack on Messines	595
Brigadier N.W.M. Weir inspects the Hutt Valley Battalion of the Home Guard	597
Troops have a meal within 200 metres of the enemy at La Signy Farm on 6 June 1918	607
New Zealand and British infantrymen moving forward with Mark V tanks near Grévillers	609
Women sorting donated items for despatch to the troops at the front	613
Female munitions workers	616
WAACs operating a range finder on 21 January 1943	621
A female soldier serving with the New Zealand contingent in the International Force East Timor in November 1999	622
Troops and staff outside a YMCA facility in France during the First World War	626

Maps

Map 1	The principal RNZAF bases	4
Map 2	Australia Station, showing successive changes of boundaries	45
Map 3	The theatre of conflict during the Boer War, South Africa, 1899–1902	60
Map 4a	Coast defence sites at Auckland	96
Map 4b	Wellington harbour defences	97
Map 4c	Lyttelton's defences	99
Map 4d	Coast defence sites at Dunedin	99
Map 5	Areas of conflict during Confrontation, 1963–66	113
Map 6	The German assault on Crete, May 1941	125
Map 6a	The Maleme sector, 20 May 1941	125
Map 7	Movement of New Zealand expeditionary forces in August–December 1914	173
Map 8a	Gallipoli, showing the Allied landings in April and August 1915	192
Map 8b	The Anzac sector at Gallipoli, April–December 1915, with the axes of advance during the August offensive	193
Map 9	Greece, April 1941	206
Map 10	The Gulf War theatre of operations, January–February 1991	212
Map 11a	The Italian theatre of operations, 1943–45	250
Map 11b	The Cassino area, February–March 1944	251
Map 12	The BCOF's zone of operations in Japan, 1946–48	257
Map 13	The Korean theatre of operations, 1950–53	268
Map 14	The Japanese invasion of Malaya, December 1941–February 1942	289
Map 15	Malaya during the Emergency, 1948–60	293
Map 16	The principal Maori tribes, battles, and sieges during the Musket Wars, 1807–39	341
Map 17	Boundaries of the New Zealand Station	370
Map 18a	Bay of Islands, 1845–46	372
Map 18b	Taranaki, 1860–61	375
Map 18c	Waikato, 1863–64	376
Map 18d	East Coast region, 1866–72	380
Map 19a	The North African theatre of operations, 1940–43	389
Map 19b	The Crusader offensive, November 1941	390
Map 19c	The Battle of El Alamein, October–November 1942	394
Map 20	The Pacific theatre, 1941–45	405
Map 21	The ANZAM region following the Radford–Collins agreement of 1951	439
Map 22	Sinai–Palestine campaign, 1916–18: area of operations	493
Map 23	The Solomons theatre of operations, 1942–45	503

Maps

Map 24	Operational commands in the South and South-west Pacific, 1942–45	504
Map 25	New Zealand's military organisation in 1912	528
Map 26	South Vietnam, 1965–72: area of operations	563
Map 27a	The Western Front, showing the front line in April 1916	599
Map 27b	The Somme, July–November 1916: area of operations and movement of the front line	601
Map 27c	Flanders, 1917: area of operations and movement of the front line	603
Map 27d	Amiens–Arras sector, 1918: area of operations and movement of the front line	608

Preface

War has played a key role in the development of New Zealand society during much of the last millennium. The Maori who migrated to New Zealand at least seven centuries ago were a warlike people. Growing numbers and pressure on resources soon led to inter-tribal conflict, which left its mark on the landscape in the form of fortified pa. The insertion of Europeans into this picture after 1769 provided a new element, especially new weaponry, which led to even more devastating wars. The early years of the Colony of New Zealand were notable for two periods of warfare, in which Maori and Pakeha fought Maori, though relations since 1872 have been marked by an absence of military conflict. In the first half of the twentieth century a quarter of a million New Zealanders, men and women, Maori and Pakeha, were sent overseas in support of the British Empire and Commonwealth which provided the framework of New Zealand's security. More than 28,000 of them died, mainly in fighting with Germans, a people living on the other side of the globe. Although since 1945 New Zealand has lost less than a hundred persons in battle, war or the threat of war has continued to be a very significant influence on society.

For all the centrality of war to the New Zealand experience, there is a curious lack of interest among scholars in the impact of war on New Zealand. The study of New Zealand's wars has been overwhelmingly dominated by state-funded efforts, especially following the Second World War. The official history of the 1939–45 conflict, running to forty-eight volumes, is the largest publishing venture undertaken in New Zealand. Reinterpretations or revisions have been conspicuous by their absence, except in occasional ephemeral and often inaccurate television documentaries. Tellingly, only two major works have appeared on the main element of New Zealand's First World War effort, 1NZEF, in the last seventy-five years. This contrasts sharply with the position in Australia, where Australia's role in the First World War has been the subject of much debate and publishing. New Zealand has lacked either a war college or a national war museum which might have provided a focus for historical reassessment of such matters. While this situation may change with the developing defence studies programme at Massey University, for the time being New Zealand's war history has a relatively limited and narrowly focused historiographical base.

The *Oxford Companion to New Zealand Military History*, another largely state-funded effort, is an attempt to demonstrate the central place of war in New Zealand's history. It is inevitably concerned with the campaigns and battles which have involved New Zealand, and with the leading personalities who have shaped New Zealand's military history. But a very broad approach has been taken in defining the influences and events which have had a bearing on New Zealand's approach to war. An attempt has been made to go beyond the merely military to the impact of war on society generally, as (for example) in language, literature, religion, and popular culture. New Zealand had its own wars up until the early 1870s, but since then war has been something that has taken place elsewhere, notwithstanding occasional incursions by enemy raiders and for a period in the 1940s a fear of invasion. New Zealand has been outward-looking in military matters, and for more than a century it conceived of itself as an integral part of the British Empire and later British Commonwealth. It fought its wars within a British context, and many New Zealanders made their careers in the British services, some with great distinction. British officers played key roles in the development of all three New Zealand services. An attempt has been made in this work to convey the complexity and richness of New Zealand's military tradition, which of course has both Maori and European strands. The role of women is not overlooked, though the essentially masculine nature of New Zealand's military activities (until recently) ensures that their representation in this volume is relatively limited.

Preface

The selection of the topics to be included presented problems. A list was circulated among those with expertise in military history, and further subjects have been added as the project proceeded. Readers may find that topics they expected to find are subsumed within general entries. For example, instead of providing separate entries on the various First World War battles, a general entry **Western Front** encompasses them all. This arrangement is facilitated by the index, which allows easy identification of relevant material on any particular subject. The selection of personalities to be included was necessarily somewhat idiosyncratic. In general, the focus has been on those who were influential in determining the shape of New Zealand's military or defence activities, who commanded substantial forces, who won the highest decorations and in some cases lesser honours, who wrote the histories of New Zealand's military activities, and who gained prominence in other than military fields but whose military service was interesting. It is recognised that many distinguished and gallant acts go unmentioned in this Companion.

This work seeks to bring together diverse information from a variety of often conflicting sources. Two important aids to its production must be given particular acknowledgment. The *Oxford Companion to Australian Military History*, which covers so much similar ground (because of the close similarity of the military experience of the two countries in the twentieth century at least), provided many valuable signposts. It often proved difficult to find a different way of putting things from their succinct summaries. The *Dictionary of New Zealand Biography* was also an indispensable help. Many of the personalities featuring in this Companion are also to be found in the Dictionary. Our interest has been more narrowly focused on the military careers of such people than is the case in the Dictionary's treatment of them, and details about their non-military careers should be sought there. We made a policy of not having the author of a Dictionary entry write the entry for the same person in the Companion.

In the preparation of this work we have received help from many quarters. I am indebted to Linda Cassells, Oxford University Press's New Zealand representative until 1999, for her assistance in getting the project off the ground and ongoing support; to the Ministry of Defence for contributing to the project in the form of funds for an assistant and for its hospitality; to the New Zealand Defence Force, and in particular John Crawford, the Deputy Director (History), for assistance, especially in making service personnel records available; and to the members of the Advisory Committee, and particularly its chairman, Professor David McIntyre, who provided much-appreciated support and advice. Associate Professor Jeffery Grey of the Australian Defence Force Academy was also helpful and encouraging. Responsible for about 40 per cent of the text, the sixty-seven contributors have been vital to the completion of the project, and I am grateful for their cooperation. Within the Department of Internal Affairs, Dr Jock Phillips, Dr Claudia Orange, Ross Somerville, and Shirley Williams have all played important supportive roles; Louise Buckingham was very helpful with biographical data and Tairongo Amoamo with Maori–English definitions, while the Historical Branch's administrative assistant, Kathryn Hastings, assisted in a myriad of ways, especially in photograph procurement. My thanks to my other colleagues in the Historical Branch and the Dictionary of New Zealand Biography, for their fellowship, understanding, and assistance. I acknowledge with thanks the assistance of Ian Wards, Professor David McIntyre, Ray Grover, and John Crawford in reading the manuscript and making many helpful suggestions. Dr Vincent Orange, Commander Richard Jackson, Commander Denis Fairfax, Wing Commander Kevin Baff, and Lieutenant-Commander Peter Dennerly were among those who kindly read particular articles.

The help of Caroline Carr and her Defence Library staff and Defence public relations officer John Seward is especially acknowledged, along with the staff of the National Archives, the Alexander Turnbull Library, particularly Joan McCracken, Walter Cook, and John Sullivan of its Photographic Section, and the Kippenberger Military Archive and Research Library, Waiouru. Brian Lockstone and Philip O'Shea made available photographs from their collections; and my thanks also to Sir John White, Marie Penrice, the *Evening Post*, the *New Zealand Herald*, Fletcher Challenge, the National Archives, the Alexander Turnbull Library, the Hawke's Bay Museum, the Wellington Museum, New Zealand Police Centennial Museum, the Canterbury Museum, the Imperial War Museum, the Australian War Memorial, the Canadian National Archives, and the Queen Elizabeth II Army Memorial Museum for permission to publish photographs. Finally I am indebted to my assistant, Paul Goldstone. His enthusiastic and dedicated help throughout the course of this three-year project has contributed greatly to its completion.

In the production of the volume, Simon Cauchi did a sterling job in the preparation of the text for publication. I am grateful to him for picking up numerous inconsistencies and improving the text in many places. Peter Rose, Oxford University Press's Academic Publisher, was very supportive in all stages of the project, and his experience and guidance in the latter stages was especially useful. The contribution of Cathryn Game, Karen Trump, and other staff at OUP Melbourne is also acknowledged.

ICM

Advisory Committee

Professor W. David McIntyre OBE (Chair)

Professor James Belich

Mr John Crawford

Mr Wira Gardiner

Mr Ray Grover

Lieutenant-Colonel Glyn Harper RNZAEC

Mr Gerald Hensley CNZM

Mr William Matson

Dr Vincent Orange

Dr Jock Phillips

Dr Christopher Pugsley

Ms Jane Tolerton

Contributors

Andy Anderson, a Feilding-based freelance historian, is a co-author of *The Golden Age of New Zealand Flying Boats*.

Dr Laurie Barber, the recently retired Professor of History at the University of Waikato, is the author of thirteen books and a Fellow of the Royal Historical Society.

Dr John Battersby, a historical adviser to the Crown on Treaty of Waitangi claims, is a graduate of Massey University. His PhD thesis examined the first fifteen years of New Zealand's involvement in the United Nations.

Dr James Belich is Professor of History at the University of Auckland. His books include *The New Zealand Wars*, *'I Shall Not Die': Titokowaru's War*, and *Making Peoples*. He wrote and presented a five-part television documentary series on the New Zealand Wars which screened in 1998.

Trevor Bentley, who holds master's degrees from both Auckland and Waikato universities, is a doctoral candidate at the latter. He is the author of *Pakeha Maori: The Extraordinary Story of the Europeans who Lived as Maori in Early New Zealand*.

Peter Boston, a doctoral candidate at Victoria University of Wellington, has published essays in *Japan and New Zealand—150 Years,* and has written for the *Dictionary of New Zealand Biography*. He is a researcher for the Treaty of Waitangi Unit at Victoria University's Stout Research Centre.

Dr Stephen Clarke, a graduate of the University of New South Wales' Australian Defence Force Academy, is preparing a history of the New Zealand Returned Services' Association at the Historical Branch, Department of Internal Affairs.

Les Cleveland is an honorary Research Fellow in Victoria University of Wellington's School of Political Science and International Relations. A former infantry soldier in the Second World War, he is the author of numerous articles and books about popular culture and occupational folklore, including *Dark Laughter: War in Song and Popular Culture*.

Peter Cooke is a graduate of Massey University. In 1996 he formed the Defence of New Zealand Study Group and edits its journal *Forts & Works*. He is the author of the forthcoming *Defending New Zealand: Ramparts on the Sea 1850–1950*.

Elizabeth Cox, who holds a master's degree in history from Victoria University of Wellington, is a research officer at the Waitangi Tribunal. She has previously worked for both the Dictionary of New Zealand Biography unit and Auckland University Press.

John Crawford, a graduate of the University of Canterbury, is the New Zealand Defence Force's historian. He has published works on various aspects of New Zealand's military history, including *To Fight for Empire: An Illustrated History of New Zealand and the South African War*.

Grant Crowley, the group general manager of a large intellectual property firm, served thirty years in the Regular and Territorial Forces of the New Zealand Army, reaching the rank of colonel. He holds a degree in history from Massey University.

Lieutenant-Commander Peter Dennerly is the Curator of the Royal New Zealand Naval Museum at Devonport, Auckland.

Dr David Dickens, a graduate of Victoria University of Wellington, is the Director of that university's Centre for Strategic Studies.

Ellen Ellis, a freelance historian and archivist, was photographic researcher for *To Fight for Empire: An Illustrated History of New Zealand and the South African War*.

Denis Fairfax is a retired naval officer and graduate of the universities of Otago and St Andrews. He is the

Contributors

author of *Navy in Vietnam* and *The Basking Shark of Scotland*, and is preparing a bibliography of New Zealand naval history.

David Filer has published two pictorial books on New Zealand military history, *Kiwis in Khaki* and *Home and Away*, as well as articles on military issues. He has researched and produced television documentaries on historical subjects, including 'Freyberg V.C.' and 'Our People, Our Century'.

Aaron Fox is a Teaching Fellow in history at the University of Otago. He is a PhD candidate with research interests in New Zealand military, diplomatic, and environmental history.

Dr Ross Galbreath was a scientist in the Department of Scientific and Industrial Research before becoming a freelance historian. His published works include *DSIR: Making Science Work for New Zealand, Themes from the History of the Department of Scientific and Industrial Research, 1926–1992*.

Dr Bryan Gilling is a Senior Research Associate in Victoria University of Wellington's Treaty of Waitangi Research Unit. A specialist in nineteenth century race relations, he was formerly Senior Historian in the Office of Treaty Settlements.

Dr Frank Glen, a retired military chaplain and graduate of the University of Waikato, is the editor of the *New Zealand Journal of Military History* and a Fellow of the Australian Institute of History and Arts. His publications include *For Glory and a Farm*.

Dr Ashley Gould, a historical researcher based in Wellington, is a graduate of Massey University. He is an authority on the repatriation of New Zealand soldiers following the First World War.

Dr Christina Goulter, a Senior Lecturer at the British Joint Services Command and Staff College, was Visiting Associate Professor of Strategy at the US Naval War College from 1994 to 1997. Her publications include *A Forgotten Offensive: Royal Air Force Coastal Command's Anti-Shipping Campaign, 1940–1945*.

David Grant, a Wellington-based historian, is the author of a number of works, including *Out in the Cold: Pacifists and Conscientious Objectors in New Zealand during World War II*. He was John David Stout Research Fellow at Victoria University of Wellington in 1999.

David Green has been Editor/Historian in the Historical Branch, Department of Internal Affairs since 1987. He has written a short history of New Zealand for the 1995 *New Zealand Official Yearbook*, a dozen entries for the *Dictionary of New Zealand Biography*, and a *Guide to Style* for historians which was published in 1998.

Dr Jeffrey Grey is Associate Professor of History at University College, Australian Defence Force Academy. Among numerous books, he is the author of *A Military History of Australia* and co-editor of the *Oxford Companion to Australian Military History*.

Ray Grover is a former Director of the New Zealand National Archives. His publications include *Another Man's Role*, *New Zealand* (a volume in the World Bibiographical Series) and *Cork of War: Ngati Toa and the British Mission*.

Bradford Haami, a journalist by training, is the Maori Cultural Adviser to the Maori Natural History Gallery at the Auckland War Memorial Museum. He was Maori Fellow in the Historical Branch, Department of Internal Affairs, from 1996 to 1998. His publications include *He Waiata Onamata: Songs from the Past*.

Dr Glyn Harper, the commanding officer of the New Zealand Army's Military Studies Institute, holds a PhD from the University of New England. He served as an education officer in the Australian Army from 1988 to 1996 before transferring to the New Zealand Army. His published works include *Kippenberger: An Inspired Commander*.

Paul A. Harrison has been a military aviation historian for thirty years, and has published several books on the RNZAF, including *Send for the Artist*. He is a co-author of *The Golden Age of New Zealand Flying Boats*. From 1992 to 1998 he was the RNZAF's Public Relations Officer.

Alan Henderson, a graduate of the University of Auckland and the Australian National University, is preparing a history of the Royal New Zealand Artillery. His publications include *The Quest for Efficiency: The Origins of the State Services Commission*.

Gerald Hensley CNZM was Secretary of Defence from 1991 to 1999. A graduate of the University of Canterbury, and later a fellow at Harvard University's Centre for International Affairs, he was New Zealand's High Commissioner in Singapore before heading the Prime Minister's Department from 1980 to 1987.

Dr Richard S. Hill, who holds a DLitt from the University of Canterbury, is the Director of the Waitangi Research Unit at Victoria University of Wellington's Stout Research Centre. His publications include the first three volumes of *The History of Policing in New Zealand*.

Megan Hutching is the oral historian at the Historical Branch, Department of Internal Affairs, and National Secretary of the Women's International League for Peace and Freedom, Aotearoa Section. She has written on women's peace activities, but most recently about post-Second World War British migrants to New Zealand.

Commander Richard Jackson, a former serving officer in the Royal New Zealand Navy, is Deputy Naval Corporate Relations Manager. He is a graduate of the US Naval Academy, Maryland, Victoria University of Wellington, and the Joint Services Staff College, Canberra.

Dr Peter Lineham, a Senior Lecturer in Massey University's School of History, Philosophy, and Politics, is based at the university's Albany Campus in Auckland. His most recent book is *Bible and Society*.

Brian Lockstone is an airline executive. He is a member of the Royal Aeronautical Society and an Associate of the Chartered Institute of Transport. He is co-author of several works, including *The Golden Age of New Zealand Flying Boats*, and edits journals of the Aviation Historical Society of New Zealand.

Dr John E. Martin, a Senior Lecturer in History at Victoria University of Wellington, has published widely on political, rural, and labour history, including *People, Politics and Power Stations: Electric Power Generation in New Zealand 1880–1998* and *Holding the Balance: A History of New Zealand's Department of Labour 1891–1995*.

Errol Martyn was until 1996 employed in the airline industry. Now a full-time researcher on aviation history, he is the author of *For Your Tomorrow*, the first volume of a trilogy covering New Zealanders who have died in military aviation since 1915.

W. David McIntyre OBE, Emeritus Professor of History, Canterbury University, was educated at Peterhouse, Cambridge, the University of Washington, Seattle, and the London School of Oriental and African Studies. His twelve books on Commonwealth and New Zealand history include the strategic trilogy *Rise and Fall of the Singapore Base*, *New Zealand Prepares for War*, and *Background to the Anzus Pact*.

Fiona McKergow is a social history curator at the Science Centre and Manawatu Museum in Palmerston North. Her research interests include the history of clothing and textiles in New Zealand.

Dr Malcolm McKinnon, currently Editor, Millennium Project at the Alexander Turnbull Library, is a former history lecturer at Victoria University of Wellington. He is the author of *Independence and Foreign Policy: New Zealand in the World Since 1935* and editor of *New Zealand Historical Atlas/Ko Papatuanuku e Takoto Nei*.

Denis McLean CMG was Secretary of Defence from 1979 to 1988 and New Zealand's Ambassador in Washington from 1990 to 1994. After being a Fellow at the US Institute of Peace in 1994–95, he spent the following three years as Warburg Professor of International Relations at Simmons College, Boston. He is the author of *The Long Pathway, Te Ara Roa*.

Dr Gavin McLean is a Senior Historian in the Department of Internal Affairs' Historical Branch. His publications include *The Southern Octopus: The Rise of a Shipping Empire*, *Local History: A Short Guide to Researching, Writing and Publishing a Local History*, and *Wellington: The First Years of European Settlement 1840–1850*.

Deborah Montgomerie teaches history at the University of Auckland. Author of a number of articles about the experience of women in New Zealand during the Second World War and co-editor of *The Gendered Kiwi*, she is currently at work on a book-length study of New Zealand women at war.

Dr Brian O'Brien, an editorial officer in the *Dictionary of New Zealand Biography* unit, holds a PhD in English literature from the University of Otago and is a former tutor both there and at Victoria University of Wellington.

Dr Claudia Orange OBE is General Editor of the *Dictionary of New Zealand Biography* and acting Chief Historian, Department of Internal Affairs. She has produced several works on the Treaty of Waitangi and on early New Zealand and twentieth century race relations, including *The Treaty of Waitangi*.

Dr Harry William Orsman CNZM was from 1960 to 1993 Reader in English Language and Literature at Victoria University of Wellington, which awarded him a LittD in 1997. His publications include *The Dictionary of New Zealand English* and *A Dictionary of Modern New Zealand Slang*.

Phillip O'Shea LVO, KStJ, the New Zealand Herald of Arms Extraordinary, is Executive Officer (Honours) in the Department of the Prime Minister and Cabinet. He designed the various insignia of the New Zealand Orders. His publications include *Honours, Titles, Styles and Precedence in New Zealand* and *An Unknown Few*.

Dr Jock Phillips is acting General Manager, Heritage Group, in the Department of Internal Affairs. He was previously Chief Historian. He is the author of *A Man's Country?* and with Chris Maclean *The Sorrow and the Pride: New Zealand War Memorials*. He is also the joint editor of a book of soldiers' diaries from the First World War.

Nigel Prickett, the E. Earle Vaile Archaeologist at the Auckland War Memorial Museum, has carried out fieldwork on both Maori and European fortifications. His PhD topic was 'The Archaeology of a Military Frontier: Taranaki, New Zealand, 1860–1881', and he has published numerous papers on nineteenth century defence works.

Wing Commander David Provan has been Director of the RNZAF Museum and Commanding Officer of the RNZAF Research and Studies Department since 1993. Previously he served from 1960 in weapons and engineering specialisations, latterly in senior RNZAF training and manning positions.

Contributors

Dr Christopher Pugsley, a former New Zealand Army officer and freelance historian, is a Senior Lecturer in History at the University of New England. An authority on the First World War, he is the author of *Gallipoli: The New Zealand Story* and *On the Fringe of Hell: New Zealanders and Military Discipline in the First World War.*

Dr Roberto Rabel, a Senior Lecturer in History at the University of Otago, is preparing the official history of the political and diplomatic aspects of New Zealand's involvement in the Vietnam War. His publications include *Between East and West: Trieste, the United States and the Cold War 1941–1954.*

Dr Geoffrey Rice is an Associate Professor in the University of Canterbury's History Department. He was general editor of the second edition of the *Oxford History of New Zealand*. His publications include *Black November: The 1918 Influenza Epidemic in New Zealand* and *Ambulances and First Aid: St John in Christchurch.*

Bernard Robertson is Editor of the *New Zealand Law Journal,* the *New Zealand Law Reports,* and the *New Zealand Courts-Martial Appeals Reports.* Before coming to New Zealand he was a Supply and Secretariat Officer (Barrister) in the Royal Navy and subsequently a Metropolitan Police officer in London.

Dr James Rolfe lectures in international relations in Victoria University of Wellington's Department of Political Science. His publications include *Defending New Zealand: A Study of Structures, Process and Relationships* and *The Armed Forces of New Zealand.*

Monty Soutar, a Lecturer in Massey University's School of Maori Studies, has a particular research interest in the area of Maori participation in war. Of Ngati Porou and Ngati Awa descent, he is the chief researcher for the C Company, 28 Maori Battalion Oral History Project.

Richard Stowers is a freelance historian whose publications include *Kiwi versus Boer: The First New Zealand Mounted Rifles in the Anglo-Boer War 1899–1902* and *Forest Rangers*. His *New Zealanders to the Anglo-Boer War 1899–1902* was published in 1999.

Dr John Subritzky is a policy officer in the Ministry of Foreign Affairs and Trade, Wellington. A graduate of the universities of Auckland and Cambridge, he is the author of *Confronting Sukarno: British, American, Australian and New Zealand Diplomacy in the Malaysian–Indonesian Confrontation.*

Richard Taylor, an Education Officer in the New Zealand Army, is a graduate of Waikato and Massey universities. He has published *Tribe of the War God, Comrades Brave,* and *A Favoured Few,* in addition to a range of articles on aspects of New Zealand politics and military history.

Malcolm Thomas, a senior graphic designer at GP Print, researches and collects New Zealand and Allied cloth insignia and uniform distinctions. He is the co-author of *New Zealand Army Distinguishing Patches 1911–1991.*

Jane Tolerton is a freelance historian based in Wellington. Her publications include a biography of Ettie Rout, *Ettie.* She is the co-author of an oral history of New Zealand soldiers in the First World War.

John Tonkin-Covell is a member of the staff of the Military Studies Institute. He is the co-author of *Freyberg: Churchill's Salamander.*

Dr Ann Trotter ONZM, Emeritus Professor of History, Otago University, is a graduate of the universities of New Zealand and London and a specialist on the international history of East Asia. Her publications include *Britain and East Asia 1933–1937* and *New Zealand and Japan 1945–1952.*

Susan Upton holds a master's degree from Victoria University of Wellington. A former researcher for the *Dictionary of New Zealand Biography* unit and the Historical Branch, she is preparing a history of women and alcohol.

Ian Wards served with 2NZEF as a gunner in the Middle East and Italy during the Second World War and then became a research historian in the War History Branch. He was later Chief Historian in the Historical Publications Branch. His publications include *The Shadow of the Land: A Study of British Policy and Racial Conflict 1832–1852.*

Style Notes

Entries are arranged in alphabetical order up to the first punctuation in the headword. The surnames of people (e.g. **Phipps, Peter**) are printed in bold at the beginning of articles, followed by given names. Titles and ranks, but not post-nominal letters denoting honours and awards, have been included in biographical headwords. Ranks are the highest attained by the individual. In the case of individuals with knighthoods parentheses have been used to indicate that the name used with it is the second or third given name, for example, **Goddard, Sir (Robert) Victor**. Pseudonyms or nicknames are printed in inverted commas within brackets, for example **Thornton, Lieutenant-General Sir Leonard Whitmore ('Bill')**. The names of other entities, such as departments, organisations, and events, are printed in bold (e.g. **Greece**). Readers will note that any initial definite articles have been deleted from these headwords.

Cross-references are indicated by a star before the word or by the use in parentheses of 'see' followed by the entry title in capitals. Occasionally, 'See also' is used to inform the reader of related subjects that may be of interest. Place names in the text and on the maps have been given their English names; brief quotes within the text have not been sourced. Where appropriate, references for further reading have been included at the end of entries. These are not necessarily the sources upon which the entry is based.

Maori words are used in accordance with conventions in New Zealand, ie are not italicised, even though they are in essence foreign words (in so far as they do not follow English conventions in regard to plurals). Reference should be made to the Glossary of Maori Terms.

Contributors' names are to be found at the end of their entries. Those without such attribution, about 60 per cent of the text, were prepared by the volume editor with the help of his assistant.

Military Nomenclature

Military organisations are established on hierarchical lines, with units of steadily increasing size under correspondingly higher-ranked officers.

The basic naval unit is the ship, the crew of which depending on size is usually divided into watches or divisions. When grouped, several small warships form a flotilla and larger ships a squadron. Squadrons may be grouped as a fleet, usually commanded by a vice-admiral or an admiral. Until 1967 the Royal Navy's area of operations was divided into stations, i.e. East Indies Station, Australia Station. The United States Navy uses a system of area commands, such as the Pacific.

The smallest army component is the section, comprising ten men under an NCO. There are three sections in a platoon, which is usually commanded by a lieutenant, and three platoons in a company, commanded by a major. These are sub-units. The smallest unit is the battalion, which groups four companies under a lieutenant-colonel. A brigade comprises three battalions, with supporting arms, including close support artillery, and is normally commanded by a brigadier. Groupings larger than brigades are formations, the basic one being the division, consisting of three brigades along with other arms in support and under a major-general. Two or more divisions may be grouped to form a corps, a lieutenant-general's command. The largest formations are the army, grouping several corps, and the army group, comprising several armies. The hierarchical progression is therefore: section–platoon–company–battalion–brigade–division–corps–army–army group.

This basic framework has been varied at times during the twentieth century. During the First World War, for example, there were four battalions in a brigade, and, for a time, the New Zealand Division comprised four brigades. At the beginning of that war brigades were commanded by colonels. The terms 'battalion group' or 'brigade group' refer to infantry battalions or brigades which have been augmented with units beyond their normal establishment. Different nomenclature is used for mounted and armoured divisions and artillery. The former have troops instead of platoons, squadrons instead of companies, and regiments instead of battalions. Artillery was organised in brigades before and during the First World War; these were later designated as field regiments. An artillery regiment has as its basic unit a troop of four guns, commanded by a captain. There are two troops in a battery, which is commanded by a major, and three batteries in a field regiment, commanded by a lieutenant-colonel.

In the British military system, different arms of service are grouped in corps, for example the Royal New Zealand Corps of Signals, or regiments. A regiment may have a number of battalions or may encompass a whole arm, such as the Royal Regiment of New Zealand Artillery. This is in direct contrast to the usage in the United States, where a regiment has a precise meaning as a unit equivalent to a British brigade.

In the air force, the basic unit is the flight of four aircraft, commanded by a flight lieutenant. There are three flights in a squadron, which is commanded by a squadron-leader. Two or more squadrons may form a wing under a wing commander, and two or more wings form a group, under a group captain. In practice air force organisation has varied greatly: a squadron can have as few as three aircraft, and most RNZAF post-war squadrons have been commanded by wing commanders.

Military Ranks: Service Equivalents

Commissioned officers

Navy	Army	Air Force
Admiral of the Fleet	Field Marshal	Marshal of the RAF
Admiral	General	Air Chief Marshal
Vice-Admiral	Lieutenant-General	Air Marshal
Rear-Admiral	Major-General	Air Vice-Marshal
Commodore	Brigadier	Air Commodore
Captain	Colonel	Group Captain
Commander	Lieutenant-Colonel	Wing Commander
Lieutenant-Commander	Major	Squadron-Leader
Lieutenant	Captain	Flight Lieutenant
Sub-Lieutenant	Lieutenant	Flying Officer
Ensign	Second Lieutenant	Pilot Officer

Warrant and non-commissioned officers

Navy	Army	Air Force
Warrant Officer	Warrant Officer Cl 1	Warrant Officer
	Warrant Officer Cl 2	
Chief Petty Officer	Staff Sergeant	Flight Sergeant
Petty Officer	Sergeant	Sergeant
Leading Rating	Bombardier/Corporal	Corporal
	Lance-Bombardier/Lance-Corporal	

Note: A Midshipman is an RNZN officer under training. In the RNZAF persons at the same stage are referred to as Pilots under Training, and in the Army as Officer Cadets.

Military ranks

BADGES OF COMMISSIONED RANK IN THE NEW ZEALAND ARMED FORCES

RNZN		NZ ARMY		RNZAF
Vice-Admiral		Lieutenant-General		Air Marshal
Rear-Admiral		Major-General		Air Vice-Marshal
Commodore		Brigadier		Air Commodore
Captain		Colonel		Group Captain
Commander		Lieutenant-Colonel		Wing Commander
Lieutenant-Commander		Major		Squadron-Leader
Lieutenant		Captain		Flight Lieutenant
Sub-Lieutenant		Lieutenant		Flying Officer
Ensign		Second Lieutenant		Pilot Officer

Military ranks

BADGES OF NON-COMMISSIONED RANK IN THE NEW ZEALAND ARMED FORCES

RNZN		NZ ARMY		RNZAF	
Warrant Officer		Warrant Officer Class 1		Warrant Officer	
		Warrant Officer Class 2			
Chief Petty Officer		Staff Sergeant		Flight Sergeant	
Petty Officer		Sergeant		Sergeant	
Leading Rating		Bombardier ········ Corporal		Corporal	
Able Rating		Lance-Bombardier ········ Lance-Corporal		Leading Aircraftsman	

xxiii

Abbreviations

AFC	Air Force Cross	EEZ	Exclusive economic zone
ANZAC	Australian and New Zealand Army Corps	EPS	Emergency Precautions Scheme
		FPDA	Five Power Defence Arrangements
ANZAM	Australia, New Zealand, and Malaya	GBE	Knight Grand Cross of the Order of the British Empire
ANZUS	Australia, New Zealand, United States	GOC	General Officer Commanding
ANZUK	Australia, New Zealand, United Kingdom	GHQ	General Headquarters
		GSO	General Staff Officer
AOC(-in-C)	Air Officer Commanding(-in-Chief)	HDML	Harbour defence motor launch
BCOF	British Commonwealth Occupation Force	HQ	Headquarters
		HMAS	His or Her Majesty's Australian Ship
C-in-C	Commander-in-Chief	HMNZS	His or Her Majesty's New Zealand Ship(s)
CAS	Chief of (the) Air Staff		
CB	Companion of the Order of the Bath	HMS	His or Her Majesty's Ship(s)
CBE	Companion of the Order of the British Empire	KBE	Knight Commander of the Order of the British Empire
CDF	Chief of Defence Force	KCMG	Knight Commander of the Order of St Michael and St George
CDS	Chief of Defence Staff		
CGS	Chief of (the) General Staff	MBE	Member of the Order of the British Empire
CIGS	Chief of the Imperial General Staff		
CMG	Companion of the Order of St Michael and St George	MC	Military Cross
		MM	Military Medal
CMT	Compulsory military training	NAC	National Airways Corporation
CNS	Chief of Naval Staff	NCO	Non-commissioned officer
CRA	Commander Royal Artillery	NMR	National Military Reserve
CRE	Commander Royal Engineers	NZANS	New Zealand Army Nursing Service
DCM	Distinguished Conduct Medal	NZC	New Zealand Cross
DFC	Distinguished Flying Cross	NZDF	New Zealand Defence Force
DSC	Distinguished Service Cross	NZEF	New Zealand Expeditionary Force
DSO	Companion of the Distinguished Service Order	NZMC	New Zealand Medical Corps
		NZMR	New Zealand Mounted Rifles Brigade
EATS	Empire Air Training Scheme	NZR	New Zealand Regiment

Abbreviations

NZRB	New Zealand Rifle Brigade	RNZN	Royal New Zealand Navy
NZRNVR	New Zealand Royal Naval Volunteer Reserve	RNZNR	Royal New Zealand Naval Reserve
NZRSA	New Zealand Returned Services' Association	RNZNVR	Royal New Zealand Naval Volunteer Reserve
OBE	Officer of the Order of the British Empire	RSA	New Zealand Returned Services' Association
ONS	Organisation for National Security	SAS	Special Air Service
POW	Prisoner of war	SEATO	South East Asia Treaty Organization
RAF	Royal Air Force	TAF	Territorial Air Force
RBL	Rifled breech loading	UN	United Nations
RFA	Royal Fleet Auxiliary	US	United States
RFC	Royal Flying Corps	USS	United States Ship
RN	Royal Navy	VC	Victoria Cross
RNAS	Royal Naval Air Service	WAAC	New Zealand Women's Auxiliary Army Corps
RNVR	Royal Naval Volunteer Reserve	WAAF	New Zealand Women's Auxiliary Air Force
RNZA	Royal New Zealand Artillery		
RNZAC	Royal New Zealand Armoured Corps		
RNZAF	Royal New Zealand Air Force	WWSA	Women's War Service Auxiliary
RNZIR	Royal New Zealand Infantry Regiment	YMCA	Young Men's Christian Association

Glossary of Maori Terms

In keeping with Maori usage, Maori words do not take an s to denote plural form. In references to hapu and iwi, the words 'Nga', 'Ngai', 'Ngati', and 'Te' mean 'the', which is dropped.

haka	action dance
hapu	clan, sub-tribe
hui	meeting
huia	bird, the tail feathers of which are highly prized
iwi	major tribe, nation
kainga	village, settlement
kupapa	neutral, government-supporting Maori during the New Zealand Wars
mana	authority, prestige, integrity, honour
marae	communal meeting area, village common
mere	short flat club, sometimes of greenstone
pa	fortified village, stronghold, stockade
Pakeha	European, a foreigner
piupiu	flax kilt
rangatira	chief
taiaha	staff of hard wood
tapu	sacred, forbidden, confidential, taboo
taua	war party, expedition
tiki	neck pendant
waka	canoe
whanau	family, genus
whare	house

A

Abyssinia (Ethiopia) was a victim of Italian dictator Benito Mussolini's dreams of recreating a Roman Empire in Africa. After being invaded by Italian forces on 3 October 1935, it appealed to the ★League of Nations for help. Neither Great Britain nor France, the League's leading members, were prepared to use force, the former partly because of the dangerous effect the loss of any British capital ships might have on its ★Singapore strategy. Nevertheless, the crisis led the British authorities to take a number of precautionary measures, in case war with Italy should eventuate. When approached, New Zealand did not hesitate in making available one of the ★cruisers of the ★New Zealand Division of the Royal Navy for deployment in the Indian Ocean. As a result, HMS *Diomede* left Auckland on 21 October 1935 for Aden, where she served with the 4th Cruiser Squadron until February 1936. Her replacement in the division, HMS *Achilles*, later served with the 2nd Cruiser Squadron at Gibraltar from April to July 1936. By this time, however, the League of Nations was moving towards acquiescence in Italy's subjugation of Abyssinia, a course firmly opposed by the Labour government which had taken office in Wellington in December 1935. In arguing against the lifting of economic sanctions that had been imposed on Italy, New Zealand publicly disagreed with the British government's approach, a notable development in the evolution of New Zealand's international position. New Zealand refused to recognise Italy's conquest of Abyssinia. (See APPEASEMENT)

Active service When deployed for operations, armed forces personnel are deemed to be on active service. In this condition they are subject to a disciplinary regime more stringent than that pertaining during training or on ordinary service in New Zealand.

Agent Orange, a mixture of herbicide chemicals 2,4D and 2,4,5T, was the most common defoliant used in the ★Vietnam War. It was sprayed over large areas of South Vietnam in an attempt to deny the Vietcong both the cover of forest foliage and crops. During the late 1970s controversy arose over the alleged harmful effects to servicemen's health of Agent Orange, a term which came to denote all herbicides and insecticides used by Allied forces in Vietnam. There is no recorded instance of New Zealand troops being exposed to aerially sprayed Agent Orange, though they certainly operated in areas that had been defoliated, and insecticides were widely used around the principal New Zealand base at Nui Dat. During the late 1970s Vietnam veterans in the United States and Australia began seeking compensation for the supposed adverse effects of their exposure, pointing to higher rates of cancers among veterans and birth defects in their children. Some New Zealand veterans joined a class action against American chemical companies, which as a result of an out-of-court settlement in 1984 led to New Zealand veterans as a group receiving $750,000, which was disbursed through a trust. Nonetheless, the issue remains an emotive one, and further claims for compensation have since been made by veterans in all three countries. Although an Australian Royal Commission in 1985 found no link between ill health and herbicides, an American inquiry nine years later (*Veterans and Agent Orange: Health Effects of Herbicides used in Vietnam*) did accept that there was a relationship between some cancers and exposure to Agent Orange. Apart from the issue of compensation, New Zealand veterans are entitled to a

Air Department

war disability allowance, which is granted on a case-by-case basis. There is no onus on them to prove that their particular war-related illness or disability was caused by Agent Orange, and they are invariably given the benefit of any doubt (see WAR PENSIONS). In 1990 a parliamentary select committee dismissed allegations that New Zealand chemical companies manufactured Agent Orange that was later used by the Americans in Vietnam. In 1999 an inquiry under Sir Paul Reeves concluded that there was no probable link between Agent Orange and birth defects of children and grandchildren of Vietnam veterans. (See SHELL-SHOCK)

Air Department, established on 1 April 1937, took over from the Department of Defence responsibility for the administration and financial control of the *Royal New Zealand Air Force. Unlike the later-established *Navy and *Army Departments, it did not encompass the service itself, though there was to be little difference in practice. An Air Secretary headed the department, which also included responsibility for civil aviation. The RNZAF-oriented functions of the department were incorporated within the Ministry of Defence on 1 January 1964, with the Air Secretary becoming Deputy Secretary of Defence (Air). A Department of Civil Aviation took charge of civil aviation.

Air force bases The first air bases in New Zealand were perhaps the tents and rough sheds erected by the *Walsh brothers on Auckland's Orakei Beach in 1915. These supported their New Zealand Flying School's seaplane, which trained pilots for service in the *First World War. Henry *Wigram constructed the Canterbury Aviation Company's field at Sockburn in 1916 with a similar aim. Advising the government on aviation policy immediately after the war, Colonel A.V. *Bettington recommended concentrating land planes at Sockburn and flying boats at Auckland. Although his report bore little immediate fruit, the acceptance of gift aircraft from the British government in 1920 led to several machines being stationed at Sockburn. On the formation of the Permanent Air Force in 1923, the Canterbury Aviation Company's assets were acquired with the assistance of a £10,000 gift by Wigram. The aerodrome, named after Wigram in recognition of his generosity, became New Zealand's first military aviation establishment. In 1925 the site of a flying boat base was secured at Hobsonville, but financial constraints delayed construction of facilities for two years. Wigram and Hobsonville remained the sole air force stations until work started on new bases in 1937. The facilities at both were expanded between 1934 and 1936, with the building of new hangars, workshops and accommodation.

In his report on the air aspects of New Zealand's defence in 1936, Wing Commander R.A. *Cochrane proposed a new station to house two squadrons of medium bombers for the defence of New Zealand's territory and communications. In the event, the government decided in 1937 to build two new stations—at Whenuapai, near Hobsonville, and at Ohakea in the Manawatu. A year later it added a station at Woodbourne, near Blenheim, for a regular squadron. After the outbreak of the *Second World War, the need to increase RNZAF training and to train aircrew for the RAF under the *Empire Air Training Scheme demanded expansion of all these stations. Many more had to be created or converted from civil airfields. This was the job of the Aerodrome Services Branch of the Public Works Department (PWD), headed before the war by E.A. Gibson, the Aerodrome Engineer at the head office of the Public Works Department. Mobilised in 1939, he became the RNZAF's Director of Works and was replaced in the PWD by D.O. Haskell. During the six-year conflict the Aerodrome Services Branch works programmes encompassed no less than thirty-nine RNZAF stations in New Zealand and four in the Pacific. Nineteen aerodromes were built and ten extended. Nearly 400,000 square metres of accommodation and hangarage were built in New Zealand. In all fifty-two kilometres of runways were laid down, including 11 kilometres of 45-metre-wide concrete strips. By 1943 there were fifteen main aerodromes and seventy-nine other landing grounds in New Zealand.

The pre-war stations provided the core of this expanded service. Whenuapai housed reconnaissance, transport, and other operational units; it was the main departure and arrival point for aircraft flying to or from overseas. At Hobsonville there was limited aircrew training and considerable ground-crew training, while the major task of assembling aircraft delivered by sea was also undertaken. For most of the war the main function at Ohakea was advanced aircrew training, though many other types of unit spent some time there. Flying training on both single and twin-engined aircraft began at Woodbourne in late 1939, but from mid 1942 only single-engined pilot training was carried out there. Some fighter squadrons formed and trained at Woodbourne. Flying training, both single- and multi-engined, was Wigram's basic function. Many of the subsidiary wartime stations rivalled these main stations in size and importance. Elementary flying training at Harewood and Taieri, aircrew selection and ground training at Rotorua and Delta (near Blenheim), work at stores and repair depots around the country, and even at Air Headquarters in Wellington—all played their part in supporting an RNZAF swollen from 756 to 41,907 personnel in five years.

The role and size of individual stations varied greatly from early 1942 as the emphasis switched from training to the defence of New Zealand, and as

Air force bases

A-4 Skyhawks practise refuelling in formation over Ohakea air base (*RNZAF, OH98/481*)

demands for trained aircrew changed. The relocation of training units to the South Island, and the urgent need to build fighter and bomber airfields in the face of the threat of Japanese invasion, resulted in much building and expansion of stations in the mid-war years. Whenuapai and Ohakea were given concrete runways for heavy American bombers. New airfields were constructed at Seagrove and Te Pirita, and existing stations such as Gisborne and Palmerston North were enlarged. Most RNZAF units in the South Pacific operated from American bases, although some New Zealand stations and field headquarters were established at these bases for administrative reasons. These included RNZAF Stations Bougainville, Espiritu Santo, Guadalcanal, New Georgia, and Halavo Bay, and Field HQs Green Island, Emirau, Los Negros, Jacquinot Bay, and Piva. The RNZAF itself controlled stations in Fiji: Nadi and Nausori airfields, and the seaplane base Lauthala Bay. Nadi, used from 1939 originally for reconnaissance, was greatly enlarged in mid 1942 as a transit stop for large American aircraft on the South Pacific reinforcement route. At the same time Nausori was enlarged as the base for RNZAF patrol bombers. The RNZAF Stations Tonga and Norfolk Island were also used by patrol bombers.

By mid 1944 the decreasing requirement for replacement aircrew, and the improved strategic situation in the Pacific, had greatly reduced training requirements. Elementary flying training at Taieri and Ashburton ceased in October 1944, the latter station closing completely after only two years of existence—it had been hastily established as part of the 1942 reorganisation of the RNZAF. Other units relocated or closed as their *raison d'être* diminished.

The RNZAF emerged from the war far larger, in every respect, than was necessary or affordable in peace. Demobilisation rapidly released most personnel, though some found, to their dismay, that they were retained to sort out the vast amount of care-taking and disposal needed to settle the RNZAF into a new shape. By the end of 1946 only Whenuapai, Hobsonville, Ohakea, and Wigram remained as active flying stations in New Zealand, with Lauthala Bay in Fiji still supporting seaplanes. Woodbourne and Taieri were retained with skeleton staffs. Most stores and repair depots were closing down, except for Te Rapa and Weedons. At this time the remaining New Zealand units took on the roles that most, in essence, still retain. Whenuapai was the main transport base. Hobsonville became the ground trade training centre and

Aircraft, RNZAF

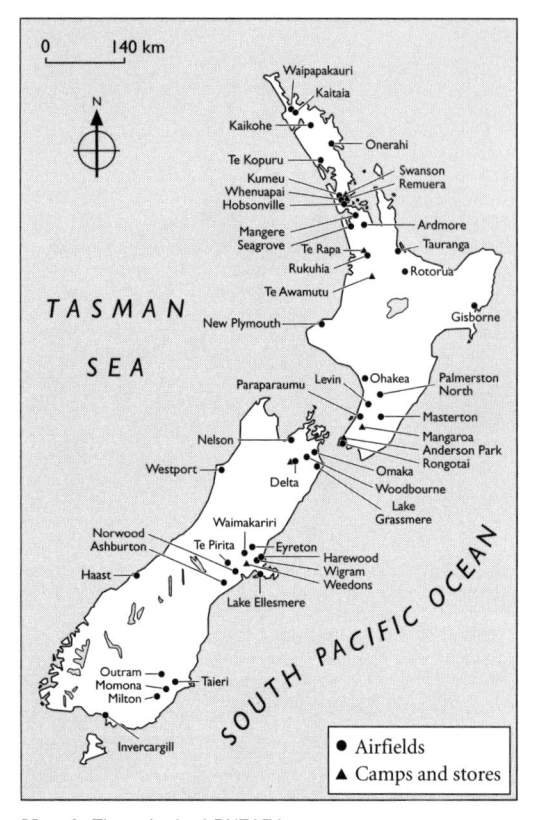

Map 1 The principal RNZAF bases

also supported seaplane operations. Te Rapa became the northern stores depot, and Weedons the southern. Ohakea was largely devoted to bomber and fighter units. Shelly Bay, the only post-war addition to the list of RNZAF stations, was taken over from the RNZN in 1946 to support RNZAF HQ in Wellington. Woodbourne was established as the sole RNZAF Repair Depot from 1949, with ground training functions being assumed subsequently. Wigram retained its largely flying training role, again with some ground trade training. Taieri was reformed in 1950 to undertake initial aircrew training.

Taieri closed in 1959, and in the following year Weedons was incorporated in Wigram's organisation. Hobsonville was amalgamated with Whenuapai as RNZAF Base Auckland in 1965, the term 'Base' having replaced 'Station' in that year. Lauthala Bay closed in 1967, with the departure of the Sunderland flying boats from service. The RNZAF's physical make-up thereafter stayed the same for two decades, until major reviews of the structure and resources of the armed forces forced changes in the interests of efficiency and cost saving. In 1988 an independent consultancy examined all aspects of the use of Defence resources, from personnel to land use and logistic support. It recommended a phased programme of relocation and closures which would have left the RNZAF retaining only Ohakea, Woodbourne, and Wigram. Although these proposals were not immediately followed, Te Rapa eventually closed in 1992 and Shelly Bay in 1995. The 1991 Defence review had meanwhile set in motion a process which led to the decision, in 1993, to close Wigram. The alternative of closing Woodbourne was deemed too costly because of the need to relocate 1 Repair Depot. Flying training moved to Ohakea and ground training to Woodbourne in 1993 and 1995 respectively, with Wigram finally closing in September 1995. Today the RNZAF has bases at Auckland, Ohakea, and Woodbourne, with a small area of Wigram retained by Defence for the RNZAF Museum. Auckland houses Air Command and supports transport and maritime operations, with the Army occupying much of Hobsonville. All flying training is performed at Ohakea, which remains the RNZAF's strike base. Woodbourne is the home of 1 Repair Depot and the integrated Ground Training Wing, which includes recruit training, officer training and trade training. Operation of the Depot was contracted to Air New Zealand and Safe Air Ltd in mid 1998.

DAVID PROVAN

Aircraft, RNZAF New Zealand's first military aircraft was a Blériot XI-2 monoplane. A gift from the United Kingdom–based Imperial Air Fleet Committee, formed by business and political interests to stimulate military aviation in the British Empire, it was intended to form the nucleus of an aviation service in New Zealand. 'Britannia', as the aircraft was christened, had been specially modified for long-distance flights. It was unloaded in Wellington in September 1913. An 80 h.p. Gnome rotary engine gave the 390-kilogram craft a 'guaranteed speed' of more than 112 km/h. After making several flights at the Auckland Exhibition in 1914, it was stored in a specially constructed building at Mount Cook Barracks pending the return of New

Table 1 Aircraft Flown by the RNZAF

Aircraft type	Total aircraft	In service
Bomber aircraft		
Baffin, Blackburn	29	1937–42
Canberra B2, English Electric	9	1958–62
Aircraft hired from RAF for 75 Sqn while based at Singapore		
Canberra B12, English Electric	11	1959–70
Fairey IIIF general purpose/bomber	3	1929–39
Gordon I/II, Fairey day bomber	41	1939–43
Also used for training and drogue-towing		
Harpoon, Lockheed PV-2	4	1945
Four delivered of 48 on order at war's end		

Aircraft, RNZAF

Hudson III/IIIA/V/VI, Lockheed	94	1941–48
Twelve converted to C-63 transports, also used for target towing, training		
Ventura PV-1/Lexington B-34	39	1943–46
Vildebeeste II/III/IV, Vickers	39	1935–44
Also used for training		
Vincent, Vickers	62	1939–44
Also used for training		
Wellington I, Vickers	30	1939–40
Transferred to RAF		

Captured aircraft

Messerschmitt Bf 109E-4	1	
Shipped from Great Britain in 1941–42 for display and technical training. Broken up around 1948		
Mitsubishi A6M3 22 Zero-Sen	1	1945
Captured from Japanese forces on Bougainville and brought to NZ		

Communications/miscellaneous aircraft

Auster J/5 and 7C Antarctic	7	1947–70
J/5 for forestry patrols, 7C for service with Antarctic Flight		
Beaver, De Havilland Canada DHC-2	1	1956–60
Acquired for Antarctic Flight. Crashed Beardmore Glacier in January 1960		
De Havilland 4 light bomber	2	1919–29
Gift from UK		
De Havilland 9 day bomber	4	1923–29
Only three of 4 received flown		
De Havilland 50A 5-seater communications aircraft	1	1927–30
Express, De Havilland 86	3	1939–46
Acquired from Union Airways for training, reconnaissance duties		
Fox Moth, De Havilland 83	1	1943–48
Acquired for communications flying from Air Travel (NZ) Ltd		
Gull, Percival	1	1939–40
Three-seater owned by Air Department		
Hawk, Miles M2	4	1939–43
Impressed from aero clubs for training and communications		
Magister, Miles M14A	2	1939–46
Monospar ST-25, General Aircraft	1	1939–41
Light twin-engined aircraft used for communications		
Moth Minor, De Havilland 94	5	1940–49
Light civil aircraft used for communications and training		
Otter, De Havilland DHC-3	1	1960–63
Bought in 1960 to replace Beaver. Never flown in Antarctica		
Porterfield 35W	1	1939–46
Ex aero club		
Puss Moth, De Havilland 80A	4	1931–46
First bought in 1931, then sold. Reacquired with others in 1939		
Sportster, Rearwin	4	1942–46
Ex aero clubs		
Staggerwing, Beech C-17L	1	1939–46
Impressed for communications flying		
Vega Gull, Percival	1	1939–46
Ex aero club		
Waco light aircraft	3	1939–46
Ex clubs and Mount Cook Airlines		
Whitney Straight, Miles M11A	3	1939–46
Wicko GM1 Foster-Wickner light aircraft	1	1939–42

Dive and torpedo bomber aircraft

Dauntless, Douglas SBD-3/4/5	68	1943–44
Avenger, Grumman TBF-1/1C	48	1943–59
After 1945 used for drogue-towing, transport, aerial top-dressing trials		

Fighter aircraft

Buffalo, Brewster	approx 23	1941–42
Flown by 488 Squadron during defence of Singapore		
Corsair, Chance Vought F4U-1/1D/FG-1	424	1944–48
Fighter Mark III/J type, Bristol F2B	7	1921–38
Grebe, Gloster	3	1927–38
Two single-seaters, 1 two-seater		
Kittyhawk/Warhawk, Curtiss P-40E/K/M/N	297	1942–46
Also 4 destroyed before being brought on charge		
Meteor III, Gloster	1	1946–50
Mustang IV, North American P-51D	30	1945–57
Vampire Mark 52 and FB5, De Havilland	47	1951–72
Eighteen Mark 52 bought new, remainder from RAF		

Fighter bomber/attack aircraft

Hurricane, Hawker IIB	9	1942
Used briefly by 488 Squadron in Singapore/Java		
Mosquito FB6, De Havilland 98	89	1947–55
Skyhawk, McDonnell Douglas A-K/A-G	19	1970–
Ten A-4K new, 9 A-4G from RAN		
Venom FB1, De Havilland DH112	12–16	1955–58
Hired from RAF and flown by 14 Squadron, Singapore		

Helicopters

Iroquois, Bell UH-1D/H	15	1966–
Two additional UH-1H bought from US Army		
Seasprite, Kaman SH-2F	4	1998–
To be replaced by later SH-2G		
Sioux, Bell 47G	13	1965–

Aircraft, RNZAF

Wasp, Westland	8	1966–
Embarked in RNZN ships, 2 extra bought for spares		

Maritime/flying boats

Catalina, Consolidated PBY-5/PB2B-1	56	1943–53
PB2B-1 was built by Boeing		
Cutty Sark, Saro A-17M	1	1930–36
Trainer also used for communications		
Orion, Lockheed P-3B	6	1966–
Five new, one bought from RAAF		
Singapore III, Short	3	1941–43
Sunderland V, Short	16	1953–67
Walrus, Supermarine	11	1943–47
First aircraft embarked in HM ships on *New Zealand Station, later models used by RNZAF for training		

Training aircraft

Airtourer, Aerospace T6/2	4	1970–95
Used for flight grading and basic training of army pilots and ATC cadets		
Airtrainer, Pacific Aerospace Ltd CT/4B	19	1976–99
Airtrainer, Pacific Aerospace Ltd CT/4E	13	1998–
Improved model of CT/4B		
Avro 504K	12	1921–30
Avro 626	4	1935–43
Avro 652A Anson I	23	1942–52
Canberra, English Electric T.13	2	1960–70
Also several borrowed from RAF for RNZAF at Singapore		
Devon, De Havilland 104	30	1948–81
Used for navigation, signalling training, and transport		
Harvard II/IIA/IIB/III, North American	202	1941–77
Hind & Hind Trainer, Hawker	63	1940–44
Also used for second-line operations		
Macchi, MB339CB	18	1991–
Moth/Moth Major, De Havilland 60G/M	28	1929–43
Six purchased new, remainder impressed in 1939		
Oxford, Airspeed I/II	299	1938–52
Skyhawk, McDonnell Douglas TA-4K/G	5	1970–
Four TA-4K, one TA-4G acquired from RAN		
Strikemaster Mark 88, BAC 167	10	1972–91
Tiger Moth, De Havilland 82A	335	1939–56
Tomtit, Hawker	4	1931–40
Vampire T.11, T.55 trainers, De Havilland 115	11	1951–72

Transport aircraft

Aerovan, Miles	2	1949–50
Attached to the Research & Development Flight, 42 Squadron		
Andover, Hawker Siddeley C1	10	1976–98
Bought from the RAF		
Anson XII, Avro	2	1946–52
Used by British High Commission		
Beech B200 King Air	3	1998–
Boeing 727-22QC	3	1981–
Passenger/cargo version of airliner		
Consul, Airspeed	6	1947–54
Converted from Oxford trainers		
Douglas C-47/47A/47B	49	1943–77
Douglas DC-6	3	1961–68
Bought from Empire Airways Ltd		
Dragon, De Havilland 84	2	1939–43
Acquired from Union Airways Ltd and used as trainers		
Dragon Rapide/Dominie, De Havilland 89	14	1939–53
First 5 acquired from Cook Strait Airways Ltd in 1939		
Friendship 120, Fokker F27	3	1980–92
Bought from Air New Zealand. Used as navigation/electronic training aircraft		
Freighter Mark 31NZM, Bristol B170	12	1951–77
Golden Eagle, Cessna 421C	3	1981–90
Hastings, Handley Page C3	4	1952–66
Hercules, Lockheed C-130H	5	1965–
Lodestar, Lockheed	9	1943–47
Sunderland, Short III	4	1944–48
Bought from the RAF		

Zealand's first military pilot, Lieutenant W.W.A. *Burn, who was learning to fly in the United Kingdom. After the outbreak of hostilities in 1914, it left New Zealand lashed to one of 1NZEF's *troopships; its destination was the Royal Flying Corps, with which it served as a trainer.

Since the *First World War nearly 2900 aircraft of about eighty different types have been employed by New Zealand armed forces (excluding those allocated to the seven 'New Zealand' squadrons in the RAF during the *Second World War). The total is evenly split between aircraft with an offensive/defensive role and those involved in support, such as transport and training aircraft. There is also a roughly equal split between British and American manufacture of aircraft, though more of the latter entered service because of wartime demands from 1941 to 1945. (See table 1.) The RNZAF became a significant air force in its own right during the 1939–45 conflict, with the acquisition of large numbers of fighters, bombers, transports, and trainers. (See BOMBER AIRCRAFT; FIGHTER AND FIGHTER-BOMBER AIRCRAFT; HELICOPTERS; TRAINING AIRCRAFT; TRANSPORT AIRCRAFT)

BRIAN LOCKSTONE

An RNZAF Fairey Gordon light bomber is prepared for flight in 1940. While the pilot receives final instructions, two airmen on the lower wing prepare to crank the aircraft's engine into life (*RNZAF*)

Airmen, New Zealand, in the First World War Adventurous young New Zealanders were naturally attracted to aviation from its earliest days, and many hundreds made their way into the Allied air services. About 250—those already studying or working in Great Britain or Australia, and others who had made their own way there early in the war—eagerly enlisted in the Royal Flying Corps (RFC), the Royal Naval Air Service (RNAS) or the Australian Flying Corps (AFC), Australia being the only Dominion to possess its own air arm. Continuous expansion resulted in regular calls for volunteers from the imperial forces to serve as aircrew. The ★New Zealand Expeditionary Force also proved a significant source throughout 1917 and 1918, in Europe and the Middle East. Some NZEF volunteers actually arrived via the imperial forces, men such as Major Keith ★Park, who transferred from the NZEF while at ★Gallipoli and finally to the RFC when in France.

Two private schools undertook elementary pilot training in New Zealand, the ★Walsh brothers' New Zealand Flying School (NZFS) on seaplanes at Kohimarama, from December 1915, and Henry ★Wigram's Canterbury (NZ) Aviation Company with landplanes at Sockburn, from August 1917. A creditable total of 253 had taken their 'ticket' by the Armistice, the majority with the Canterbury Aviation Company during 1918. Nearly 90 per cent sailed for Britain to undergo further training, almost all eventually being commissioned. However, many arrived late in the war and fewer than seventy-five had graduated by its end. Although the Canterbury Aviation Company's output outweighed that of the NZFS by more than two to one, its later start meant that only a handful of its pupils flew operationally.

Though a very modest-sized contribution (perhaps 700 ground and aircrew in all, about half of whom saw operational service), the New Zealanders enjoyed a success that was quite disproportionate to their number. At least twelve commanded their own squadrons, including Majors Keith ★Caldwell, Roderick ★Carr, Arthur ★Coningham, Cuthbert Maclean, and Park, all of whom would later achieve air rank and serve with distinction in the ★Second World War. Maclean was one of three to reach the rank of lieutenant-colonel and went on to command a wing.

Caldwell, the second NZFS graduate, had by 1917 justifiably established himself as one of the most widely respected fighter (or 'scout') pilots on the ★Western Front. In 1918, through astute leadership, he rapidly established 74 ('Tiger') Squadron as a premier fighting unit. An excellent pilot but indifferent shot, he was never once wounded in an extraordinarily long and vigorous combat career. Captain Ronald ★Bannerman, fighting from February 1918, enjoyed rapid and spectacular success, becoming the highest-scoring New Zealander, with fifteen aircraft and a balloon credited as destroyed. Captains Harold Beamish, Clive Collett, and Malcolm McGregor were other outstanding fighter pilots. Collett's career included experimental work at Orfordness, where, in January 1917, he carried out the first parachute descent from an RFC aircraft. Over England in 1916, Captain Alfred ★Brandon achieved fleeting fame hunting Zeppelins, aiding in the destruction of L15 and L33. Elsewhere, Royal Naval Air Service bomber pilot Captain Euan Dickson completed more than 180 raids, thought to be a First World War record, while Reginald Kingsford flew with the Independent Force, a precursor to Bomber Command, and wrote two books based on his experiences. Most experienced of all was pre-war pioneer pilot Captain 'Joe' Hammond, who took his 'ticket' in 1910. Extensive test-flying work followed early war duty in France, but he died in a flying accident in September 1918, while with the British Air Mission in the United States. In the Russian campaign of 1919 (see RUSSIAN INTERVENTION), Carr earned a DFC executing a daring airfield attack, while Lieutenant Samuel Dawson, in July 1918 a participant in the first carrier-launched air strike, was lost flying from HMS *Vindictive* and became New Zealand's last air force death of the 1914–19 fighting.

Casualties were relatively high, more than seventy losing their lives by the Armistice, 40 per cent through flying accidents—a reflection of poor training, ignorance and pressure to replace losses with the inadequately qualified. Nearly thirty were captured or interned on being forced down through battle damage or mechanical failure. Ten others died by the end of 1919 while awaiting demobilisation. Of those who survived, some gained precious permanent commissions in a substantially reduced RAF, and a few played significant roles in the Second World War. The majority, however, returned to their homeland, never again to engage in aviation. A handful did continue flying, giving 'joyrides' or attempting with rare success to establish more viable commercial ventures. A small group became flying instructors or secured positions in the fledgling New Zealand air force, their experience and knowledge being further called upon in the Second World War.

ERROL MARTYN

Airmen, New Zealand, in the RAF in the Second World War The close relationship which existed between New Zealanders and the RAF well before the ★Second World War explains why New Zealand was able to make a significant contribution to the RAF from day one of the war, and why, in 1939, there were more New Zealanders serving in the RAF than men from any of the other Dominions. The second feature of New Zealand's participation in the air war is the generosity the New Zealand government demonstrated in its provision of personnel. Not only was the Dominion content to have its manpower subordinated to British command, but it also met all the aircrew quotas required of it under the ★Empire Air Training Scheme, even during periods in the war when New Zealand was threatened by Japan or suffered acute manpower shortages at home.

Although most of the 700 New Zealand airmen who had served in the RFC, RNAS, and RAF were repatriated after 1918 (see AIRMEN, NEW ZEALAND, IN THE FIRST WORLD WAR), a number remained in the RAF, and some would play key roles in the next war. Close ties between the RAF and the New Zealand Air Force were established. A scheme for secondment of New Zealand officers to the RAF for fixed terms was introduced, and by 1925 New Zealand officer cadets were also being sent to Great Britain for four-year periods. During the next decade, other New Zealanders made their own way to Britain to join the RAF, so that by 1935 there were about 100 New Zealanders serving in the British force, mainly as pilots. At this stage, the RAF having begun its expansion programme, a special request was made to New Zealand for the provision of pilots to serve in the RAF, and a number of schemes were developed to this end during 1937. The first involved the top fifteen pilot trainees from basic training in New Zealand being sent to Britain on short-service commissions with the RAF, after which they would return to New Zealand to serve in the ★Royal New Zealand Air Force. A second scheme called for the yearly training of twenty-five pilots for service with the RAF. As the situation in Europe deteriorated, another scheme for the training of 1000 New Zealand pilots per year was introduced in the summer of 1939. The cost of passages to Britain for New Zealanders who wanted to serve in the RAF would be met by the New Zealand government. Once war began, New Zealand further increased its commitment by joining the Empire Air Training Scheme.

As a result of the inter-war programmes, 550 New Zealanders were already serving in the RAF in September 1939. The first 'New Zealand' squadron (75) was formed around a nucleus of sixteen New Zealanders who had been sent to Britain to take delivery of the first of thirty Wellington bombers on order for the New Zealand government and who were immediately placed at the disposal of the RAF. The first of the Dominion units in the RAF, 75 Squadron regularly headed the monthly totals for operational sorties, and equally regularly headed the loss tables, to the extent that it became known as the 'chop squadron'. Another six New Zealand squadrons were later formed, three in Fighter Command, two in Coastal Command, and one more in Bomber Command. The contributions of each of these squadrons, and of the many New Zealanders who served in non-'New Zealand' squadrons, is most easily appreciated when set in the context of each Command's operations.

In spite of an expansion programme lasting five years, which gave priority to bomber production, Bomber Command was not prepared for long-distance bombing operations in 1939. Together with fears of German retaliatory attacks on Britain, this meant that for the first six months of the war it was limited to attacks on purely military objectives. The bombing policy changed in May 1940, after the *Luftwaffe* bombed Rotterdam and the invasion of the Low Countries changed the British strategic outlook. Bombing attacks on Germany were initially directed against oil plants and rail communications, with the dual objectives of damaging enemy war industry and disrupting German logistics in support of the enemy forces. The first major raid was carried out on 15 May on oil plants in the Ruhr, with half of 75 Squadron forming part of the eighty-strong force. Poor bombing accuracy, faulty navigation, and the small size of the bombs limited the effectiveness of this attack, and of similar attacks over the following month. Aircrew loss rates were often in excess of 11 per cent (at a time when the Air Ministry considered 6 per cent the maximum sustainable loss rate).

While these operations were being undertaken, other New Zealanders were involved in the Battle for France. A lack of aircraft hampered the RAF's effectiveness in this campaign; apart from three squadrons of Hurricanes, those available were mostly obsolete types like the Bristol Blenheim and the Fairey Battle. The Battle squadrons suffered particularly heavy casualties, over half of the aircraft being lost within the first two days of operation (11–12 May); half the New Zealanders in these squadrons were killed. The Hurricane pilots, meanwhile, were tested to the limits of their endurance, as they had to fulfil multiple roles, including escorting bombers, strafing enemy columns, and defending Allied areas. As the situation became critical, with the Germans threatening to cut the Allied forces in two, the RAF squadrons were used to try to halt the German movement and to protect the retreating Allied forces. During the intense battles which occurred up to the time of the evacuation from Dunkirk, many New Zealanders distinguished themselves, and some were to become household names only a few months later during the Battle of Britain. One of them, Air Vice-Marshal K.R. ★Park, as commander of 11 Group, was in charge of fighter patrols over the Dunkirk area, and won admiration for the way in which he flew his Hurricane over the beaches in order to see first-hand what was happening. His observations led him to increase fighter cover from one to two squadrons, thus achieving at least localised air superiority over Dunkirk. Without this fighter protection, embarkation of the BEF 'would have been well-nigh impossible', its commander later noted. The *Luftwaffe* suffered some of its heaviest casualties during this period of the Battle for France.

The RAF was not permitted a breathing space to recoup its losses and reflect on the lessons learnt in France for it was immediately involved in the Battle of Britain. The battle was significant for New Zealand in a number of respects. First, the heaviest fighting fell on 11 Group, still under Park's command. Second, a large number of New Zealanders were involved in the heaviest fighting, and a sizeable number lost their lives. Finally, coming on top of the heavy casualties incurred in France and in Bomber Command up to that point, the Battle of Britain exacerbated an already critical shortage of aircrew, particularly pilots, in the RAF. As a result New Zealand, like the other participants in the Empire Air Training Scheme, doubled its aircrew training efforts.

Most accounts of the battle rightly point to the enormous contribution to the British victory made by the integrated air defence system, the first of its type in the world, the intelligence network which served Fighter Command, and the skill and bravery of all the aircrew involved. However, Park's contribution is not always acknowledged. A brilliant leader and operational commander, he had what Clausewitz called *coup d'oeil*, the ability to take things in at a glance and so to make sense quickly of the chaos of the battlefield. From early morning until late afternoon throughout the four-month battle, Park worked tirelessly in his operations room before flying off in his Hurricane to visit the various stations in his Group, to 'see how the squadrons and pilots were standing up to it'. He had an 'hour by hour' appreciation of the battle. Sensitive to the *Luftwaffe*'s every move and change of tactic, he was able, in almost every instance, to anticipate the enemy's intentions and respond by altering the disposition of his fighter forces. He positioned his squadrons so that the German aircraft were engaged as soon as they entered British airspace.

Park claimed after the war that the battle was won only by the very narrowest of margins, and that Britain came close to losing the battle a number of times during the heaviest period of fighting, between mid August and the first week of September 1940. The magnitude of his task is obvious from the respective orders of battle: Fighter Command, with 644 fighters available for operations, faced two *Luftwaffe* groups comprising 2600 aircraft, 760 of them single-engined. Moreover, 11 Group could call on only twenty-five of the Command's fifty-two squadrons. In just one fortnight, between 23 August and 6 September, Park lost 295 aircraft and 103 pilots (plus 128 wounded), a rate which clearly could not be sustained for long.

With such unfavourable odds, victory depended on force multipliers, one of which was the skill and brav-

Airmen

ery of his pilots. Many were New Zealanders. At the start of the battle, there were sixty New Zealand pilots in Fighter Command. By the end of October, this number had risen to ninety-five (the third highest national component after British and Poles). In all, 127 New Zealanders took part in the battle. Especially prominent were C.F. ★Gray and A.C. ★Deere. During the battle, eighteen New Zealanders in Fighter Command lost their lives. Although Fighter Command bore the brunt, the other Commands also contributed to the victory. Of the 1495 RAF aircrew killed between 10 July and 31 October, 449 were fighter pilots, 718 were Bomber Command aircrew engaged in attacks on Channel ports and enemy airfields, and 280 were from Coastal Command, employed mainly on anti-invasion patrols. In total, forty-seven New Zealand airmen died during the period of the battle.

For both sides, the outcome of the Battle of Britain had immense strategic consequences. Hitler, like Napoleon, had to accept Britain's continuing interference with his plans on the Continent, while the *Luftwaffe*'s losses, 1733 aircraft and 2662 aircrew (including some of the most experienced pilots), were never recouped, with immense strategic consequences. For Britain, survival ensured a platform from which the Allies would re-enter the Continent in 1944. The RAF's losses, 1017 fighter aircraft and 248 other types, were quickly made up by an aircraft industry which had expanded threefold between 1939 and 1941. However, a lack of experienced aircrew remained a constraint on operations after the Battle of Britain.

The RAF was paying the price for the failure during the 1930s to expand its training organisation sufficiently. Pilot training failed to keep pace with aircraft production. A lack of suitable training sites, qualified instructors, and training aircraft (because production was concentrated on bomber aircraft) meant that the RAF had entered the war with a deficiency of about 1200 pilots. Since training under the EATS scheme did not commence until April 1940, the chronic crew shortages of the summer and autumn continued into 1941. When asked, with the other Dominions, to increase its output of aircrew, New Zealand responded immediately.

The RAF's pre-war underestimation of its manning requirements was exacerbated by the enormous change in Britain's strategic position in 1940. The fall of France placed greater pressure on all Britain's fighting services, not merely the RAF. For instance, with the Royal Navy unable to perform all the tasks required of it in the Home Waters, Atlantic, Mediterranean, and Far East, one of its traditional roles, blockade, was handed to the RAF in the spring of 1940. Pre-war industrial intelligence assessments of Germany established that, apart from oil imports, her dependence on high-grade Swedish iron ore was her Achilles heel, since virtually every part of the German fighting machine depended upon steel produced from it. Cutting these supplies could, it was reasoned, bring Germany's war-waging capability to a halt. Thus, from May 1940 RAF Coastal Command mounted an anti-shipping campaign which claimed 366 enemy vessels by the end of the war, and caused an estimated 10 per cent fall in German steel production during 1944–45. Although a sound complementary strategy to Bomber Command's offensive, it was never viewed in that light, and did not receive sufficient resources until the last year of the war. Largely for this reason, aircrew loss rates were high, often exceeding those of Bomber Command. Most of the 5863 aircrew killed while serving in Coastal Command were from the anti-shipping squadrons.

Among the nine squadrons which would ultimately form the anti-shipping component of Coastal Command was a New Zealand unit, 489 Squadron. Because of manpower shortages and the low priority accorded maritime aviation, it did not form until August 1941 and became operational only in the spring of 1942. When operations over the North Sea and off the Norwegian coast began, it was compelled, like other anti-shipping units, to use aircraft discarded by Bomber Command. When purpose-designed weaponry and tactics were employed, in combination with more suitable aircraft, the toll on enemy shipping rose substantially after the end of 1943. During the course of the war 489 Squadron accounted for thirty-three enemy vessels.

New Zealanders also took part in Coastal Command's most publicised role, anti-submarine operations. The seventh, and last, of the New Zealand squadrons, 490, was formed in March 1943 and began operations from West Africa in July. Other New Zealanders were scattered among the other anti-submarine squadrons, most of them joining their units just as the Battle of the Atlantic became critical in 1942. During the worst month, June, 124 vessels were sunk. Losses for the whole year were double those in 1941 (1006 as compared with 496). The seriousness of the situation was such that by mid 1942, anti-shipping resources were diverted to anti-submarine work. For example, in May, a detachment of 489 Squadron's aircraft was sent to the south-west of England to conduct anti-submarine patrols.

Another peak of U-boat activity in the Atlantic occurred during the first five months of 1943, the 100 or so submarines constantly on patrol being nearly double the figure for 1942. However, as the year progressed the tide turned against the submarines for two main reasons: the widespread introduction of ASV (air to surface vessel) radar and the availability of greater numbers of very long-range aircraft, such as the B-24 Liberator and B-17 Fortress. By the end of 1943, eleven squadrons were equipped with these types of aircraft. During 1943 ninety submarines were sunk by Coastal Command, as compared with twenty-eight in 1942. In total, Coastal Command sank 166 U-boats during the war.

The benefits of having these aircraft, equipped with the latest ASV radar, in the anti-submarine role were not appreciated by everyone at the time. Bomber Command's commander Sir Arthur Harris wanted all long-range aircraft and radar development to be devoted to the bomber offensive, going so far as to describe Coastal Command as an 'obstacle to victory', because the resources devoted to it prevented his Command from delivering the decisive blow. Fortunately for the Allies, the ensuing doctrinal debate within the RAF was decided in favour of Coastal Command. Harris's anxiety to see his Command expand in size was finally alleviated in 1943 as its front-line strength rose from 380 heavy bombers in March to about 500 three months later. Even so, he demanded additional aircraft, claiming they were needed to carry out an effective campaign against the enemy's industrial heartland, the Ruhr.

Running from March to July 1943, the Battle of the Ruhr comprised forty-three major attacks on German targets, mostly cities. The most cost-effective way to undermine Germany's industrial production, Harris believed, was to cause 'dislocation' in its industrial cities by 'dehousing' the labour force. Such attacks would also, secondarily, cause damage to industrial plants and the communications which served them. Post-war bombing surveys show that these 1943 attacks did not prevent the growth of German industrial production. They did, however, place constraints on it, preventing even larger increases than occurred. This outcome was achieved at a high price. During the Battle of the Ruhr, more than 6 per cent of raiding aircraft failed to return. Since most New Zealand bomber aircrew were scattered throughout the squadrons, their losses were of similar proportions. During the battle twenty-eight New Zealanders lost their lives while serving with 75 Squadron, which took part in all the major raids and suffered particularly heavy losses at the end of May and during June.

By the beginning of 1944, the battle for air superiority was turning in the Allies' favour. This was due mainly to the introduction of long-range American escort aircraft, such as the P-38 Lightning and P-51 Mustang. However, the RAF had contributed to the air superiority battle by undertaking offensive fighter sweeps over France and the Low Countries after Fighter Command's victory in the Battle of Britain. Forty-eight of the sixty-nine fighter squadrons were regularly engaged in this work, and two of the units were the New Zealand squadrons, 485 and 486. Together, the two squadrons claimed 144 enemy aircraft in operations up to the end of the war.

Meanwhile important lessons on inter-service cooperation being learnt in North Africa and Italy would contribute greatly to the ultimate Allied victory. Allied successes in the ★North African campaign during 1942 had been achieved by having the land forces working in close concert with the Western Desert Air Force. Air power played a decisive role in the Western Desert, not only in support of land operations but also in securing sea lines of communication, upon which the supply of war materiel was entirely dependent. However, Allied success came only after a lengthy learning process, and institutional resistance to army cooperation only grudgingly dissipated.

The Western Desert Air Force was created in October 1941, after a succession of Allied reversals in the North African campaign had pointed to the need for improved air–ground cooperation. One of the keys to German successes in this period was the *Luftwaffe*. Its effective control of the Mediterranean meant that British resupply operations had to go via the Cape and the Suez Canal, and enemy aircraft based in Libya were able to attack RAF airfields in Egypt. During 1941, the RAF had few resources to counter enemy air superiority, mostly obsolete aircraft such as Gladiator biplanes and Blenheims. It was also apparent that the squadrons lacked the necessary support services to cope with the mobility of desert war. Largely on the initiative of the new AOC-in-C, Middle East, Air Marshal Arthur Tedder, RAF units were reorganised in the face of many obstacles, not least from within the RAF. Some in the Air Ministry were loath to take resources away from the bomber offensive and regarded army cooperation aviation as a retrograde step for the RAF. Many in the Army, meanwhile, pointed to the recent campaigns in ★Greece and ★Crete as proof that the RAF's main function should be to provide the Army with a constant air 'umbrella'. The only means of preventing air attack on Allied land forces, Tedder warned, was to win command of the air, which demanded offensive action, often well beyond the immediate battlefield. In short, the RAF in North Africa had two objectives: to beat the *Luftwaffe* and then to go into battle against the enemy's surface forces.

Tedder appointed Air Vice-Marshal Arthur ★Coningham, a New Zealander who had made his career in the RAF after the ★First World War, to head the new Western Desert Air Force (WDAF). Coningham quickly developed a reputation for understanding the battlefield and the support required by the Army. On taking up his appointment, he co-located his WDAF headquarters with that of the 8th Army, and thereafter they moved together. The principles of air support

11

Airmen

Four New Zealand airmen serving in the Western Desert Air Force discuss an operation during the latter stages of the North African campaign (*War History Collection, Alexander Turnbull Library, F-3042-1/4-DA*)

were defined more clearly for the benefit of both air and land forces, and fighter sections were organised on the 'leapfrog' principle, with two operations headquarters, one forward and one rear, so as to maintain continuity in spite of the 'see-sawing' nature of the desert war. Meanwhile, medium bombers operated day and night against enemy lines of communication (both land and sea) and airfields.

The New Zealand contribution to the WDAF increased steadily. By the end of 1941, there were about 300 New Zealanders in North Africa, most of them pilots. None of the New Zealand squadrons served in this theatre, and New Zealanders were scattered throughout the various squadrons which comprised the WDAF. Among the WDAF's first achievements was its effective support of the Crusader offensive in November 1941, in which hundreds of enemy tanks, aircraft, and other equipment were destroyed by air attacks. Its next major challenge came in protecting highly vulnerable troop and armoured columns during the Allied retreat to El Alamein in the first months of 1942: a measure of its success was the fact that only six men and one vehicle were lost to enemy air attack. The WDAF played a key role in defeating Rommel's bid to reach Alexandria in August 1942, the German commander complaining that 'the continuous and heavy attacks of the RAF absolutely pinned down my troops … and made impossible any safe deployment or advance'. Allied air power was, in Rommel's opinion, the deciding factor in the closing stages of the North African campaign.

Allied victory in the North African campaign owed much to the successful defence of Malta. The island was recognised by both sides as the key to any Mediterranean strategy, since German supplies transported to North Africa via Italy had to travel within range of aircraft operating from it. Malta became the focus of Axis attention as early as June 1940, and aerial attacks on Malta continued through to the early months of 1943.

Pitted against the Italian and German assault was a handful of RAF squadrons, equipped at the beginning with obsolete biplanes. What the defenders lacked in equipment, they made up for with courage and tenacity. Among the personnel on Malta were 198 New Zealand airmen, while two of the three air commanders during this period were also New Zealanders, Air Vice-Marshal F.H.M. Maynard and Park.

So effective were the RAF's anti-shipping operations from Malta by the end of 1941 that Hitler ordered the deployment of a major part of the *Luftwaffe* (*Luftflotte* 2) to Sicily to obtain air supremacy in the area. From December 1941, when 250 long-range bombers and about 200 fighters were available, the *Luftwaffe* mounted increasingly heavy assaults on the island, reaching a climax in April with nearly 7000 tons of bombs being dropped. When Park took command during the summer of 1942, invasion seemed imminent. A system of forward interception, similar to that used during the Battle of Britain, which he immediately introduced, soon showed results, as the German assault began to weaken in July. With the balance now swinging in British favour, Park stepped up the attacks on enemy shipping, inflicting severe losses during the crucial months of September and October and forcing the *Afrika Korps* to curtail its operations because of fuel shortages. That only 3300 of 10,000 tons of fuel dispatched during October safely reached North African ports was a major reason for Rommel's defeat at El Alamein.

Once North Africa was cleared, the lessons learnt were applied in the ★Italian campaign. Techniques of close air support were perfected, after an initial hesitant start in Sicily. Once again, New Zealand airmen were represented throughout the Italian campaign, and five squadrons were commanded by New Zealanders. The cumulative lessons learnt from the Mediterranean theatre were then applied in Europe, and the preparations for ★D-Day were almost as important as the operations after 6 June 1944. The importance of gaining air superiority before a land battle was one of the most important lessons driven home in the Mediterranean. Consequently, a major effort was expended on counter-air operations. In these operations prior to D-Day, 487 (New Zealand) Squadron played an important part, having been transferred to the 2nd Tactical Air Force from Bomber Command in mid 1943. As one of six Mosquito-equipped squadrons, it attacked enemy airfields. Other operations in preparation for D-Day included the all-important attacks on rail targets in France, Belgium, and Germany, designed to prevent the enemy's easy reinforcement of the front line. In April 1944, 75 Squadron began attacking rail communications, and most of its raids were soon being directed against such targets.

During D-Day, and the critical establishment period up to September 1944, New Zealanders were involved across the board, serving in Bomber, Coastal, and Transport Commands, the 2nd Tactical Air Force, and the Air Defence of Great Britain (as the Fighter Command structure based in the United Kingdom was now known). This involved about 3850 New Zealanders, including those who were in the six New Zealand squadrons based in Europe. Some were to play prominent roles. Coningham was made field commander of the Allied Expeditionary Air Force. Building on his successes in the Mediterranean, his tactical air forces played a key part in maintaining air supremacy (not merely air superiority) over the battlefield and prevented enemy reinforcements from reaching the forward areas. Three New Zealand squadrons (485, 486, and 487) share in the credit, as they formed part of the 2nd Tactical Air Force during this period. Another New Zealand unit, 488 Squadron RAF, also made a significant contribution during 1944 in a night-fighter role.

Coastal Command's role during the D-Day period was to prevent enemy submarines and surface vessels from interfering with the invasion fleet and subsequent resupply operations. The main effort was concentrated on the lower English Channel because of the proximity of U-boat forces based in the Bay of Biscay and the serious threat posed by German torpedo boats (especially E- and R-boats) and midget submersibles. So successful were Coastal Command's patrols that no submarines entered the invasion area on 6 June, and enemy torpedo-boat activity was largely limited to night-time. The submersible threat never materialised, as an insufficient number of craft were ready in time. Among the squadrons engaged in these invasion patrols was 489 (New Zealand) Squadron, which claimed a number of vessels, including a large E-boat depot ship and a minesweeper.

Over land, New Zealanders with Bomber Command were involved in a number of different roles in support of D-Day operations. The main focus was enemy communications. Heavy attacks were launched against rail centres throughout the Normandy area, especially at Caen and St Lô, forcing the Germans to use already heavily congested roads, which were attacked by aircraft of the 2nd Tactical Air Force. Other bombing attacks were launched against enemy airfields in Belgium and the Netherlands. These attacks, which continued well into August, succeeded in reducing to a minimum *Luftwaffe* fighter operations over France. The most controversial use of Bomber Command's aircraft, however, came with close battlefield support. Heavy bomber support was sought by the Army as a means of laying down a weight of bombardment which would have been impossible with field artillery alone. Harris's objections were overruled, and

between D-Day and mid August 1944 Bomber Command dropped nearly 20,000 tons of bombs on German troop concentrations. Involved in all these bombing operations, 75 Squadron lost nineteen aircraft with their crews (126 men) during the Normandy campaign. The cost to Bomber Command as a whole had been heavy between April and September 1944, with the loss of 11,580 men.

The losses in this period added weight to Harris's argument that his forces should not be diverted from the 'primary task' of bombing Germany and prompted him to pay scant attention to directives issued to him in September which required Bomber Command to concentrate its efforts against oil and communications targets. Post-war analyses, including those undertaken by the United States Strategic Bombing Survey and its British equivalent, concluded that attacks on these target systems did hasten the end of the war and that more effort should have been devoted to them at an earlier point (1943 and not 1944). By 1945, most of the *Luftwaffe* was tied to the ground because of a lack of fuel, and all aspects of German industry were affected by the rapidly declining oil supplies. The collapse of German industry had started, not only because of direct attacks on plants, but because industries were being starved of their most basic fuel, coal, which was transported chiefly by rail. For example, many steel industries in the south of Germany were compelled to stop production at the end of December 1944 because their coal supplies had been cut off.

However, Bomber Command's area attacks were also having an important impact on German industry by the last year of the European war. Such attacks placed a ceiling on production, as indicated by the German aircraft industry. Although planned production figures called for an output of 80,000 aircraft in 1944, the actual figure achieved was 40,000. Area bombing had an important impact also because it compelled the Germans to divert potential front-line resources to the defence of the Reich. Some two million soldiers and civilians were involved in anti-aircraft defence in 1944. Thirty per cent of total gun output and 20 per cent of heavy ammunition was destined for anti-aircraft use. The effects of the area bombing campaign, whether direct or indirect, must be balanced against the enormous human cost. Of the 125,000 aircrew who entered service with Bomber Command, over 47,000 were killed on operations (as well as 8000 during training). Another 2000 died while working as ground crew, as a result of enemy action, accidents, or ill health, caused by servicing aircraft in appalling weather conditions.

These losses were staggering (45.6 per cent in total), but few serious historians of the Second World War claim that the sacrifice was not necessary. Perhaps the best way to assess Bomber Command's efficacy during the war as a whole is to ask how well the Germans would have performed had there been no bomber offensive. Even when Germany came under the full weight of the combined bomber offensive in the closing stages of 1944 and early 1945, the Germans were not only fighting on two fronts but were also able to launch an offensive in the Ardennes.

It was in acknowledgment of the continuing threat posed by Germany that New Zealand kept sending its full quota of aircrews to the European theatre in spite of acute manpower shortages. New Zealand's difficulties in meeting its home defence and production requirements and a twenty-squadron force planned for operations in the South-west Pacific were made apparent to London. The prospect of even a partial withdrawal of New Zealand forces from Europe before Germany had been defeated alarmed the British authorities, but the New Zealand government accepted advice that the European theatre should have priority, as it had done ever since the beginning of the ★Pacific War. This stance was broadly supported by the public, though for a brief period at the end of 1941 and in early 1942 Japanese advances had caused nervousness. Some New Zealand airmen destined for service in the RAF in Britain had been handed white feathers at embarkation points. The notion that such men were abandoning New Zealand in her time of need was dispelled as it became evident that New Zealand airmen fighting in Europe, especially in Bomber Command, were suffering heavy losses.

Although most New Zealanders who served in the RAF did so in Europe, a sizeable number were involved in operations in South-east Asia against the Japanese. More than 400 New Zealanders took part in the ★Malayan campaign of 1941–42. Most were to be found in the ten RAF squadrons based in the peninsula, but some were in 488 Squadron RNZAF and 1 Airfield Construction Squadron. All the units were poorly equipped, which reflected the fact that the Far East had not been considered a strategic priority in pre-war planning. Nevertheless, all fought bravely with whatever obsolete and obsolescent aircraft they possessed, and 488 Squadron was one of two defending Singapore up until the time it fell in February. Other New Zealanders flew bombing and anti-shipping missions against the Japanese landings, and those in two Vildebeeste squadrons (36 and 100) fought with great gallantry in the face of overwhelming odds. During one action, on 26 January 1942, over half of the force dispatched to oppose the Japanese landings at Endau, on the Malayan east coast, were shot down.

Most of the New Zealanders involved in these operations were safely evacuated to Australia, but a number who had gone on to Java were ultimately taken prisoner. Meanwhile, others were involved in the fighting retreat from Burma, which came under attack first on 23 December 1941. The air defence of Burma was provided by just thirty-seven assorted British and American aircraft. One unit, 67 Squadron, was manned almost entirely by New Zealanders, and was heavily involved in the air battles over Rangoon in December, and again in the last week of January 1942. By the end of February, the fall of Rangoon was imminent, and the squadrons were withdrawn to India. Throughout 1942, the air force re-equipped, and personnel were supplemented by crews recently trained under the Empire Air Training Scheme. By the end of the year, 250 New Zealanders were serving in the India Air Command. Scattered throughout about fifteen RAF squadrons, these men were involved in offensive action against the Japanese, which began with the first Arakan campaign in December 1942. A number of squadrons supported Wingate's Chindit operations, which commenced in February 1943, and all the units were involved, to a greater or lesser extent, in the battle to achieve air superiority over Burma. This effort included night bombing raids on Japanese air bases. The success of the counter-air campaign was demonstrated by the fact that the Japanese kept most of their air forces in rear areas.

Air superiority was finally achieved at the end of 1943, after the receipt of additional aircraft, including seven squadrons of Spitfires. New Zealand participation in the air effort had also increased, and seven of the fighter squadrons were commanded by Dominion pilots. The fighter force played a critical role in the next offensive action against Arakan in February 1944. In the clash between the Allied and Japanese land forces, victory would be achieved only if lines of supply could be kept open. The Allies achieved this through air resupply. As the Japanese had lost control of the air, they were compelled to retreat. New Zealand aircrew (thirty-five in total) flew in the Dakota squadrons responsible for the air supply of the Allied divisions.

During March, the RAF's main role was to support Wingate's second expedition behind Japanese lines. This entailed dropping a divisional-sized force, with its equipment, and heavy machinery to clear airfields. This effort provided vital experience for the next, and most important, airlift operation: the relief of Slim's 14th Army and the reinforcement of Imphal and Kohima, which had become the focus of a Japanese offensive. If the Japanese had secured this area of northern Burma, they would have been in a position to disrupt communications with China and interdict supplies to General Stilwell's forces, which were attacking from the north. The Imphal and Kohima battles reached a climax in June 1944, and thereafter the RAF harassed the retreating Japanese forces. Nearly 150

New Zealand pilots flew in the Dakota, Spitfire, Hurricane, and Beaufighter squadrons involved in the 1944 ★Burma campaign. Some sixty-eight other New Zealanders were involved in complementary air action, including bombing raids on Rangoon and anti-submarine patrols in the Indian Ocean, protecting Allied shipping en route to Indian ports.

By the end of the year, the Allied forces were on the offensive throughout South-east Asia. The closing stages of the Burma campaign coincided with Park's tenure as Commander-in-Chief, Allied Air Forces. He took over in February 1945, and was instrumental in increasing air supply to land forces, so that during March 1945 nearly 90,000 tons of supplies were being flown into Burma.

As soon as the Allied forces went on the offensive in the Far East, Britain began planning in earnest for the war against Japan. Once Germany was beaten, the plan was to form a Commonwealth Task Force in the South-west Pacific using those RNZAF personnel who had served in Europe. However, at the Quebec Conference in September, this decision was overturned, and the Air Ministry informed the New Zealand Chief of Air Staff, Air Vice-Marshal L.M. ★Isitt, that all New Zealand aircrews would operate in the South and South-west Pacific under the direct control of General Douglas MacArthur. By this time, there were already sixteen RNZAF squadrons operating in the Southwest Pacific under US operational control (see SOLOMONS CAMPAIGN).

Once Germany was defeated, further attention was given to utilising RAF resources against Japan. There were plans for 75 Squadron to take part in the strategic bombing of Japan, as part of a twenty-squadron bomber force contributed by the RAF. At the beginning of July 1945, the US Chiefs of Staff agreed that an initial force of ten squadrons could be stationed on the Ryukyu Islands. The other New Zealand unit earmarked to go to the Pacific was 489 Squadron, again in an anti-shipping role. However, by the time final arrangements were made, changes in the strategic situation in the Pacific were such that the New Zealand contribution was considered superfluous. Neither unit made it to the Pacific, and 489 Squadron was disbanded a week before the end of the war. In fact, very few RAF personnel, British or Dominion, who had served in Europe were sent to the Far East or the Pacific. An acute shortage of shipping meant that most plans to redeploy squadrons after the European war were shelved.

With the exception of 75 Squadron (whose name was transferred to the RNZAF in 1946), the New Zealand squadrons were all disbanded by September 1945 and the many thousands of New Zealanders who served in other RAF units were all rapidly demobilised, leaving only a small number, as after the previous world war, to seek permanent careers in the RAF. In all, 12,078 had served in the RAF, of whom 3285 (27 per cent) had died and about 500 had been taken prisoner of war, mostly in the European theatre. They had formed part of a huge Dominion contribution to the RAF: in 1943 thirty-two (23 per cent) of the RAF's 140 squadrons were Dominion and Allied, and in Bomber Command the proportion was even higher at twenty (32 per cent) out of sixty-three. Harris was perhaps the only senior British commander to have questioned this situation, when he complained in early 1943 about the 'ever increasing tendency to alienise or Dominionise the RAF'. New Zealand's contribution to the European war was generally appreciated and acknowledged within higher defence circles. Sir John Slessor, Air Member for Personnel in 1945, summed up the views of many when he praised the New Zealander as 'a magnificent type who fits well into the RAF organisation'. In noting 'countless … acts of almost superhuman bravery' among the aircrews, Tedder was equally laudatory: the New Zealander, he observed, 'perhaps more than most, has a way of regarding such things as all in a day's work'. At the end of hostilities, the Air Council conveyed the following message to the New Zealand government:

> [New Zealanders] have brought honour to their country and to the Royal Air Force by their gallant service in all theatres of war. With great foresight you developed your training organisation, you became a ready partner in the Empire Air Training Plan which was to lay the foundations of our air supremacy; in all this you held nothing back, but gave to the limit of your power.

New Zealanders could rightly claim that they played a significant part in the air war—a war which proved to be decisive in the overall Allied effort.

H.L. Thompson, *New Zealanders with the Royal Air Force*, 3 vols (War History Branch, Wellington, 1953–59).

CHRISTINA GOULTER

Allen, Colonel Sir James (10 February 1855–28 July 1942), who oversaw New Zealand's huge military effort during the ★First World War, was an effective and innovative Minister of Defence. Born in Australia, but taken as a child to Dunedin, he became a successful businessman in that city after being educated in England. In 1887 he entered Parliament, where he soon demonstrated his interest in defence issues. From 1891 until 1912 he served in the ★Volunteer Force and later ★Territorial Force, his final appointment being as Coast Defence Commander of the Otago Military District (1911–12). He was also a stalwart of the National Defence League and Navy League. In W.F. ★Massey's first ministry (1912–15), he held the Defence portfolio, in addition to Finance and Education, and formed an effective partnership with the GOC, Major-General A.J. *Godley, though the personal relationship between them remained cool. Allen was supportive of the organisational changes, centred on the Territorial Force and *compulsory military training, already underway when he took office. He made improvements to the CMT scheme, encouraged preparations for the possible dispatch of an expeditionary force overseas, and recognised the potential importance of aviation. Under his guidance, the first real efforts were made towards *Australian–New Zealand defence cooperation. He was also the father of the New Zealand navy. Long an opponent of existing subsidy arrangements for naval defence, he looked to establish a naval force in New Zealand which might cooperate closely with the Royal Australian Navy. After sometimes acrimonious discussions with Winston Churchill, the First Lord of the Admiralty, in 1913, Allen secured British agreement to his proposed scheme, resulting in the acquisition, on loan, of the old cruiser HMS *Philomel* as a training ship for the New Zealand Naval Forces, which were constituted in 1914. Allen's role was greatly expanded with the outbreak of the First World War and the creation of the *New Zealand Expeditionary Force. As Minister of Defence in the coalition government established in August 1915, he worked tirelessly to sustain New Zealand's effort overseas, was responsible for the introduction of *conscription in 1916, and took steps to provide for the welfare of returned servicemen. His efforts were not without controversy among an increasingly war-weary public, and he bore much criticism for administrative shortcomings at Trentham Military Camp in particular. His administration of the Defence Department was intensely scrutinised by an independent commission in 1918, and he was vindicated by its report. For much of the last two years of the war Allen, who was knighted in 1917, was effectively New Zealand's war leader, for both Massey and his coalition partner Sir Joseph Ward were often absent overseas together attending imperial discussions in London. From 1920 to 1926 Allen was New Zealand's High Commissioner in London, and also represented New Zealand at the *League of Nations in Geneva during that period. He was a member of the Legislative Council from 1927 to 1942.

Allen, Colonel Sir Stephen Shepherd (2 August 1882–4 November 1964) first came to New Zealand, where his father had acquired a large estate near Morrinsville, in 1892. He had been born in Staffordshire, England. After being educated at Cambridge University, he began practising law in Morrinsville in 1907, and became a significant landowner in his own right. He was commissioned in the local *Territorial Force unit, the 6th (Hauraki) Regiment, in 1911; as C Company's commander, he initiated the military career of B.C. *Freyberg, then practising as a dentist in Morrinsville, by persuading him to become a subaltern in the company. Joining 1NZEF in 1915, Allen was a company commander in the Auckland Battalion at *Gallipoli. With his patrician bearing, his English accent, and a pronounced lisp, 'Old Steve' was a source of considerable merriment among his men, though they always respected his courage and leadership. While serving on the *Western Front, he was slightly wounded three times, and once, at Passchendaele, more seriously. From January 1917 until the Armistice he commanded the 2nd Battalion, Auckland Regiment; and for most of the time his brother Robert did the same for the regiment's 1st Battalion. Allen was appointed a DSO for his efforts at Passchendaele, and added a bar soon after his return to the front from convalescence in England, when in February 1918 he led his battalion in a successful counter-attack on the Somme. He was made a CMG in 1919. Back in New Zealand after the war, he published in 1920 an account of his battalion's service in France. He remained active in the Territorial Force, commanding the 1st Infantry Brigade from 1920 to 1925 and the Hauraki Regiment from 1926 to 1928. In 1920 he became part of covert measures to deal with a possible 'bolshevistic outbreak' when he was asked by the government to prepare a force in the Hamilton area. After succeeding Major-General Sir George *Richardson as Administrator in Western Samoa in 1928, he had the difficult task of dealing with a nationalist movement, the Mau, which deliberately challenged the authority of his administration. His attempt to uphold the law led to an incident in December 1929, in which a number of Samoans, including the high chief Tamasese Leolofi, were killed by police gunfire; following the arrival of HMS *Dunedin* at Apia soon afterwards, he mounted a 'war in the bush' to suppress the Mau, which had been declared a seditious organisation. His measures appeared to be successful when the Mau, in March 1930, came out of the bush and agreed to disperse. Allen resigned from his position in 1931, and two years later was made a KBE for his services. Back in New Zealand, he was again active in the Territorials, commanding the 1st Infantry Brigade from 1933 to 1937. When the *Second World War began, he was in England and secured a commission in the British Army. When consulted by Prime Minister Peter *Fraser about Freyberg's fitness for command of 2NZEF in November 1939, he enthusiastically endorsed his former subaltern, under whose command he was now serving as Staff Captain, Salisbury Plain Area. In

March 1940 Allen became 2NZEF's Military Secretary, and he helped administer the Second Echelon in the United Kingdom. He later served in ★Greece and ★Crete, and was mentioned in dispatches. His career with 2NZEF came to an end when, convinced that undertakings regarding his appointment as Base Commander in Egypt had not been fulfilled, he expressed himself intemperately to Freyberg. He relinquished his position in July 1941 and returned to the United Kingdom, where he served in the Ministry of Home Security in Birmingham until late in 1942.

Andrew, Brigadier-General Albert William (28 March 1866–16 July 1941). A young officer in the New Zealand ★Volunteer Force in Christchurch, Andrew became in 1886 the first New Zealander to take advantage of a scheme which offered commissions in the British Army to officers of colonial defence forces. After passing the demanding examination set by the imperial authorities, he was commissioned in New Zealand as a junior officer in the Devonshire Regiment in September 1886, and served with it in India. Two and a half years later, he transferred to the Indian Army. During the ★Boer War, he was seconded to the New Zealand Military Forces, and commanded the Sixth and Tenth New Zealand Contingents. An accomplished linguist, he took an interest in military affairs and published several books on military matters. Perhaps the most significant was his progressive *Cavalry Tactics of To-Day*, which drew on his experiences in South Africa. During the ★First World War, he capably led an Indian Army infantry brigade group in ★Mesopotamia. He was made a CMG and mentioned in dispatches five times. After retiring from the Indian Army in 1920, he took up residence in Christchurch.

JOHN CRAWFORD

Andrew, Brigadier Leslie Wilton (23 March 1897–8 January 1969) won a ★Victoria Cross in 1917. A railway clerk, he lied about his age to enlist in the ★New Zealand Expeditionary Force in 1915. Eight days after joining the 2nd Battalion, Wellington Regiment, at the Somme in September 1916, he was wounded in the neck. The actions which led to his decoration took place on 31 July 1917, when his battalion attacked La Basseville. Commanding a section, he captured a German machine-gun post, before stalking and bombing a second machine-gun. During a reconnaissance forward, he came across yet another German machine-gun position, which he also destroyed. He was commissioned in March 1918, and after the war secured a commission in the ★New Zealand Staff Corps. Apart from a two-year officer exchange in India, he occupied various administrative posts until the ★Second World War, when he was seconded to 2NZEF. As commander of 22nd Battalion he was a strict disciplinarian, earning the nickname 'February' among his men for his habit of handing out 28-day detentions. After seeing little action in ★Greece, his battalion was evacuated to ★Crete in April 1941. Ordered to hold the vital Maleme airfield and the neighbouring hill, Point 107, 'at all costs', he was forced to spread his companies out, leaving a reserve of only one platoon and a few tanks. After losing touch with his companies after the German assault began on 20 May 1941, he appealed unsuccessfully for support to a neighbouring battalion and to his superior, Brigadier James ★Hargest. A counter-attack by his reserve failed, and believing, incorrectly, that three of his companies had been overrun, he pulled back from his positions on Hill 107, allowing its occupation by the enemy. After the war he drew much criticism for his actions, which led inexorably to the loss of the island; slightly wounded by shrapnel, imbued with a First World War conception of tactics, and under intense attack from the air, he was not the only New Zealand commander to have difficulty in adjusting to the novel conditions that arose on 20 May; nor did he receive adequate support. Following the evacuation from Crete, he commanded 22nd Battalion in the early stages of the ★North African campaign. During the Crusader offensive in late 1941 he temporarily took over 5th Brigade following Hargest's capture, and succeeded in ambushing a German force at Menastir on 3 December. However, the divisional commander, Major-General B.C. ★Freyberg, had lost faith in Andrew after the débâcle on Crete, and in February 1942 he was returned to New Zealand, where he commanded the Wellington Fortress Area. In 1946 he was a member of the Victory Contingent to London, and later commanded the Central Military District until his retirement in 1952.

Anglo-Japanese Alliance was a key element in New Zealand's strategic situation in the first two decades of the twentieth century. First concluded in 1902, and renewed in 1905 and in 1911, the arrangement allowed the British government to concentrate imperial naval forces against the rising threat from Germany nearer home. Its value to the British Empire in the ★First World War was immense. Although the New Zealand government's attitude to its conclusion had been positive, by 1911 there were fears that the New Zealand immigration laws, which excluded Japanese (and other Asians), would be compromised by the alliance. Nevertheless, the importance of the arrangement to the Empire strategically was recognised. When the treaty came up for renewal in 1921, because of the British Empire's weakness in the Pacific, New Zealand strongly favoured its continuation, but

Animals

New Zealand troops load water cans on to mules and donkeys in Tunisia in 1943 (War History Collection, Alexander Turnbull Library, F-3062-1/4-DA)

had to be content with a watered-down version in the form of the Four Power Pact signed at Washington on 13 December 1921. (See JAPANESE THREAT)

Animals have played an important role in New Zealand's military history. Although their use in the ★New Zealand Wars was restricted by the roadless and rugged nature of the terrain, with preference being given to more efficient water transport, large numbers of draught animals were pressed into service. In the Waikato campaign, for example, the British Army employed 1946 horses and 728 bullocks. While bullocks were preferred because they required less forage and care, it was the horse that emerged as the most important military animal not only as a riding and draught animal but also as a symbol of military prestige. The quality of New Zealand horses and the supposed inherent horsemanship of New Zealanders were powerful factors in shaping ideas about national character, the image of 'rough riding' colonials being reinforced by the experience of the ★Boer War. Some 8000 horses were sent to South Africa from New Zealand during the conflict. Volunteers for the early contingents were expected to provide their own mounts, while others were either obtained from patriotic gifts or purchased by the government. These horses were given no time to acclimatise in South Africa, and they suffered from the long treks; the troops preferred captured Boer ponies for their hardiness.

In response to the increasing need for horses for the New Zealand Military Forces, a system of acquiring and caring for military horses had been created before the ★First World War. The New Zealand Veterinary Corps and a Remount Branch were established in 1907, and preparations were put in train to meet the estimated war-time requirement of 18,637 horses. After the outbreak of the First World War more than 1400 horses were donated by citizens, and another 9300 were purchased by Department of Agriculture stock inspectors. Mounted riflemen generally provided their own horses, receiving payment for them at market values. A Remount Depot was established at Palmerston North (later moved to Upper Hutt) where horses were checked and classified before being sent overseas. In all, nearly 10,000 horses were transported overseas before shipments were stopped in December 1916.

There was not much need for horses at ★Gallipoli, with the Mounted Rifles Brigade fighting there as infantry. The little Egyptian donkeys used by the Field Ambulance proved invaluable in carrying wounded and water, a contribution that was immortalised in ★Moore-Jones's painting of *The Man with the Donkey*. Despite the small size of the Anzac enclave, nearly 2000 pack mules were needed to carry ammunition and supplies. Initially unpopular because of their cantankerous temperament, these animals were soon respected by the soldiers for their stoic ability to carry heavy loads in the most appalling conditions, and they played a significant role in all New Zealand's First World War campaigns. Considerably less popular as pack animals were the Indian and Egyptian camels employed by the New Zealand Mounted Rifle Brigade in the *Sinai–Palestine campaign to carry water and equipment; they were slow and difficult to handle, even though they were well adapted to desert conditions. Stretcher-bearing cacolet camels were used by the brigade's field ambulance, but the wounded were often tormented by their slow, jolting gait. Two companies of New Zealanders rode camels with the Imperial Camel Corps until June 1918, when they were reconstituted as a horse-borne mounted machine-gun squadron.

Some New Zealand horses accompanied the New Zealand Division to the *Western Front, though the division's requirements for up to 6000 animals were mainly met by imperial remount depots. The large trains of horses and mules made an obvious target for enemy bombardment. To meet the danger from gas, masks were supplied for horses and mules. On the Western Front horses were susceptible to mange, which flourished in the cold, muddy conditions, as well as suffering injury from shards of metal hidden in the mud. Most New Zealand horses were sent to the Middle East to meet the Mounted Rifles Brigade's requirement for nearly 4000 mounts. Desert conditions were harsh, and a riding horse had to carry a rider, weapons, ammunition, forage, and water—a load of about 127 kilograms. Their endurance was notable, even when water became scarce. Mounted riflemen considered that 'of all the horses gathered from the four corners of the earth, our Colonial horses are second to none'. Close bonds were formed between horse and rider. The excellent horsemanship of the mounted riflemen and the proficiency of the New Zealand Veterinary Corps ensured that remarkably few horses were lost. After three years' active service, one squadron of mounted rifles still had 60 per cent of its original complement. Despite their sterling service, all but three of the horses had to be left behind when the troops were repatriated at the end of the war because of the cost of shipping and risk of disease. Many New Zealanders preferred to destroy their horses rather than allow them to be sold into a miserable existence in Egypt.

Even though New Zealand slowly mechanised its army in the 1930s, pride of place still lay with the horsed regiments of mounted rifles. As late as 1941, the Army had a requirement for 4000 horses, but by 1942 mounted rifles regiments had been equipped with armoured vehicles. Other animals were to have their uses during the conflict. A few American-trained dogs were sent to the 3rd Division engaged in the *Solomons campaign to detect Japanese infiltrators and track snipers, though they were never used in action. In Tunisia and Italy a company of mules attached to the 2nd New Zealand Division proved useful in carrying supplies in the mountainous terrain. In New Zealand a lack of radios led to the formation of a Carrier Pigeon Service operated by the *Home Guard in 1942.

Inevitably mechanisation made redundant the military use of most animals, and in 1946 the Remount Branch and the New Zealand Veterinary Corps were abolished. Animal involvement in the armed forces continues in several forms, not least as mascots, which are assumed to embody the spirit of a unit. It was natural that soldiers would take favoured pets on service, usually dogs, in spite of official disapproval. Far away from home, soldiers gathered an amazing collection of pets, acquired locally or from other units. Pets as mascots tended to achieve quasi-official status, a bull-terrier of a battalion in the Second World War even being accorded the rank of lieutenant-colonel. While dogs have been the most popular mascots, soldiers have claimed all kinds of creatures as their own, including magpies, monkeys, donkeys, and snakes. Animals are still used in operational roles. Dogs, with their acute senses of hearing and smell, are an invaluable asset for security or tracking. During the *Malayan Emergency, Alsatian and Labrador dogs were attached to the New Zealand battalion to track communist insurgents. In 1967 the RNZAF Police Dog Handler Section was established at Whenuapai to provide security for aircraft on the ground. The section continues to safeguard RNZAF installations and aircraft, track intruders, help apprehend violent offenders, undertake detection of drugs or explosives, instruct RNZAF and other service personnel on the uses of military dogs, and perform at public displays.

Antarctica, military involvement in New Zealand's formal involvement in the Antarctic dates from 1923, when the territory known as the Ross Dependency was placed under its jurisdiction, but it was to be thirty-three years before a presence was established there. In December 1956 HMNZS *Endeavour* carried a team of scientists under the leadership of Sir Edmund Hillary to the continent to establish Scott Base. This step had been prompted by New Zealand's involvement in the International Geophysical Year and the Commonwealth Trans-Antarctic Expedition, but in March 1957 it was decided to establish a permanent presence. An American base had already been established at McMurdo Station, and the American programme in the Antarctic (Operation Deep Freeze) was supported through Christchurch and Lyttelton. Since 1958, when New Zealand allowed the United States to base facilities in New Zealand in connection with Operation Deep Freeze, there has been close cooperation between the New Zealand and American

Antarctic support ship HMNZS *Endeavour* heads for Antarctica through heavy ice (*RNZN, PN4915*)

programmes. On 1 December 1959 New Zealand signed the Antarctic Treaty, pledging to use the continent for peaceful purposes only. Measures of a military nature, such as the establishment of military bases or fortifications, the carrying out of military exercises, or the testing of weapons, were prohibited. The treaty did however permit the use of military personnel and equipment for scientific or other peaceful purposes.

Until 1971, when RNZAF Hercules took over the role, New Zealand's Antarctic presence depended on an annual summer resupply by *Endeavour*. American flights south from Christchurch had begun as early as December 1955, transporting American and New Zealand cargo and personnel to the airfield on sea ice at McMurdo, and the first RNZAF flights took place in October 1965. Currently there are about 150 American and New Zealand flights out of Christchurch annually in support of Operation Deep Freeze and the New Zealand Antarctic Programme. Helicopter personnel were sent to support the US Navy helicopter squadron at McMurdo, and since 1985 an Iroquois helicopter of the RNZAF has been stationed there. Army cargo-handling teams have spent the summer at McMurdo since 1972. Other New Zealand defence personnel serve in the Antarctic in a variety of support roles, including environmental work, construction and maintenance, base support, and fire-fighting. The US Navy's long link with Christchurch came to an end in February 1998, when the New York National Guard took over responsibility for flights to McMurdo.

Anti-aircraft weapons New Zealand's first anti-aircraft weapons were machine-guns employed in a makeshift anti-aircraft role during the ★First World War. The Lewis and Vickers machine-guns were supplemented by Stokes ★mortars, firing upon German aircraft with time-fused bombs. The first true anti-aircraft guns were four 3-inch 20-cwt guns acquired in 1936 and stationed at Auckland and Wellington. In January 1941 the 14th Light Anti-Aircraft Regiment was formed for service with the 2nd New Zealand Division, though too late for deployment to ★Greece and ★Crete. It was equipped with thirty-six Bofors 40 mm light anti-aircraft guns, which could each fire 150 rounds per minute against low-flying aircraft. The weapons were also used in both North Africa and Italy to support ground troops, to mark inter-unit boundaries, and in an anti-tank role. The regiment operated until October 1944 when, with the threat from the air declining, it was disbanded to provide reinforcements for the infantry. Bofors guns also equipped the 29th Light Anti-Aircraft Regiment, which served in the ★Solomons campaign. With all its available 3-inch guns and four Bofors guns having been sent to Fiji, New Zealand was left without air defence at the onset of the ★Pacific War. By July 1942 the situation had been transformed, with 134 Bofors guns and sixty-eight 3.7-inch heavy anti-aircraft guns in place to defend important sites. In 1943 the Auckland anti-aircraft defences amounted to twenty-four 3.7-inch guns, twenty-eight Bofors guns, and seventeen searchlights. Plans for New Zealand to be defended by more than 600 guns, searchlights, and radar, requiring an establishment of more than 20,000 men and women, were eventually shelved. By the time that the government had accepted 'that the dangers of air attack of any kind at the present time are negligible' in 1943, there were 450 anti-aircraft guns in the country.

After the war anti-aircraft regiments were based at Auckland, Wellington, and Christchurch, and a light anti-aircraft regiment was assigned to the field forces. The last two anti-aircraft regiments were disbanded in 1961, and New Zealand was without anti-aircraft weapons until 1997, when French Mistral short-range heat-seeking missiles were acquired.

Anti-invasion defences New Zealand has only once faced the possibility of imminent invasion. After Japan precipitated the ★Pacific War in December 1941, a state of readiness, 'Alert 2', which acknowledged the danger of invasion while rating it 'unlikely within next 8 days', was instituted. Although the government did not call for the immediate return of 2NZEF from the Middle East, its commander, Major-General B.C. ★Freyberg, was told on 27 December 1941 to expect no reinforcements for the time being. The 1st Army Tank Brigade, which had been raised in August for the Middle East, was held back for home defence, and in December reorganised into one emergency tank battalion and two infantry battalions. For much of the next year the only reinforcements to leave New Zealand would go to the garrisons in the South Pacific. As the Allied situation in the western Pacific deteriorated in early 1942, the preparation of anti-invasion defences assumed top priority, even though the ★Chiefs of Staff soon decided that an early invasion was unlikely (see PACIFIC WAR). The options available to an invader had been considered by the government's military adviser, General Sir Guy ★Williams, prior to Japan's entry to the war. The Japanese, he decided, would seek a base in the Bay of Islands or Marlborough Sounds; coast defences were rapidly installed in these localities, as well as at other minor ports considered of value to enemy shipping. At this time the home defence forces consisted of one brigade in each district, with a fourth (7th Brigade) added in 1940 for the Army Reserve. In accordance with Williams's advice, three additional brigades were raised in January 1942. All seven were enlarged with artillery and armour to brigade group size. By the middle of the year the South Island's division (5th Division) had reached full strength with the 3rd, 10th and 11th Brigade Groups. The Northern Military District's 1st Division had the 1st and 12th Brigade Groups, and the Central Military District's 4th Division the 2nd and 7th Brigade Groups. The call-up of the ★Territorial Force and the integration of the ★National Military Reserve raised eighteen more battalions, bringing the total available to forty-four. The ★Home Guard also entered camp; by April enrolment in the Guard was compulsory for men up to fifty years of age. The fortress concept was applied to five harbours—the Bay of Islands and Dunedin being added to Auckland, Wellington, and Lyttelton. Each was classed as a defended port backed by fortress troops. In the event of an invasion some of the divisional troops in the vicinity would be deployed within the fortresses, while the rest remained mobile to harry the invader. Each of the three district headquarters was instructed to prepare emergency defence works to slow down the enemy. These included beach defences, anti-tank ditches, and road blocks; civil aerodromes not required for operational purposes were to be rendered unusable. In March 1942 £100,000 was voted for such activities, and the amount rose to £503,768 within a year. Near most ports, beaches where landings were possible were defended with pillboxes covering barbed wire and sometimes anti-tank ditches. Around 250 concrete pillboxes of differing designs were hastily built. Anti-tank ditches 4.5 metres wide ringed such places as Tauranga and Timaru, as well as the three big ports. In case the Japanese should secure a beachhead, several hundred roadblocks were readied in each military district to cut crucial routes. There were many types, including concrete blocks to take large logs or rail irons across bridges, 'dragons teeth' or old railway wagon axles for wide roads, and rail lines sunk vertically into city streets. Around the main cities 'stop lines' of blocks and ditches were prepared to impede the enemy's advance, and the mobile forces practised delaying actions.

To ensure the security of the fortresses' command and communications, work began on underground headquarters at Auckland, Wellington, and Lyttelton, though only the first-named was completed. A start was also made with underground facilities in the suburb of Khandallah to protect the capital's essential communications. In mid 1942 the Army began strengthening bridges that would be required to move its 16-ton tanks (on a 7-ton transporter) to meet an invader; these were mainly on secondary routes between railheads and likely tank operating areas especially in north Auckland, Waikato, Taranaki, Manawatu, central Hawke's Bay, and on the Canterbury plains. Air raid shelters were prepared in cities. As well as purpose-designed underground shelters, existing rail tunnels and concrete basements were reclassified as air raid shelters. Many large firms and municipalities prepared trench or 'pipe' shelters for their staff. In the end, public shelters (excluding many erected in schools and hospitals) were prepared for 60,000 people in Auckland, 29,000 in Wellington, 12,000 in Christchurch and 33,000 in Dunedin. Even the inland city of Hamilton provided shelters for more than 6000 people. More than 244,000 booklets on how to build a domestic shelter were produced. All shelter designs were tested with bomb blasts in Kaituna late in 1942. Government subsidies for public air raid shelters had committed £965,000 to New Zealand's thirteen largest towns by March 1943.

Passive defence against attack was favoured for its cost-effectiveness. Smoke defence barrages as a means of hindering air raids were promoted because of a shortage of anti-aircraft guns. The production of chemicals for the smoke pots started in Auckland and Dunedin, and trials of garden incinerators, factory smokestacks, domestic chimneys, and scrub fires to create a 'fog' over the harbour were conducted in the Hutt Valley. The camouflage of economic and military targets also got underway later in 1942. That applied to Arapuni dam was particularly extensive, including decoy roads and dummy trees. Blackout and lighting restrictions imposed on domestic and motor vehicle lights were largely aimed at hindering shelling or bombing of coastal towns. Bulk oil installations received an extensive programme of splinter-proofing against air raid damage: 149 tanks in the main ports were treated at a cost of £290,000. The four underground fuel tanks dug in cliffs behind Devonport naval base from 1943—at a cost of £323,500—were also partly an anti-raid measure.

Anti-nuclearism

In conjunction with government departments, the military authorities also gave attention to requirements in the event of a successful Japanese landing. Under the heading Denial of Resources, essentially a 'scorched earth' approach, they aimed to deny any useful resources to the invading forces. Plans were adopted in February 1942 to destroy or render inoperable bridges and factories, port and communication facilities, and water and power utilities. They were to be 'selective, ruthless, carefully planned in advance and rigorously applied in practice'.

The Allied position had so improved by November 1942 that 'Alert 2' was officially lifted. By this time, however, troops on beach defence had already been stood down, and the home defence divisions were demobilised in mid 1943. The removal of the defence works, including 1063 roadblocks, started as early as November 1943. (See COAST DEFENCES)

PETER COOKE

Anti-nuclearism New Zealand's approach to nuclear matters was not at first characterised by hostility. Lord Rutherford's role in splitting the atom, the involvement of New Zealanders in the Manhattan Project, a sense of relief that the ★atomic bomb had brought the ★Pacific War to an abrupt end (obviating the need for New Zealand participation in any invasion of Japan)—all played their part in shaping attitudes. Possible peaceful uses of nuclear energy, especially for electric power generation, were foreseen. But increasingly the threat posed by nuclear weapons, especially after the development of the first thermonuclear (hydrogen) bombs in 1952, overshadowed such attitudes. From the late 1950s a small but increasingly vocal anti-nuclear movement emerged. A Campaign for Nuclear Disarmament, imitating a British organisation, was established (see ANTI-WAR MOVEMENTS).

Nuclear issues were brought to the fore by a series of developments in the early 1960s. After the Soviet Union in 1961 breached a moratorium on nuclear testing (in place since 1958), the United States resumed testing. The scale of the weapons worried many New Zealanders, whose unease was increased by the 'awesome glow' in the night sky following one American test in 1962. The announcement that France intended to initiate a testing programme in its territories in eastern Polynesia provided an even more direct focus for public concern. The Prime Minister, K.J. Holyoake, responded in 1963 by announcing that New Zealand had no intention of ever acquiring nuclear weapons and that they would not be stored in New Zealand. His government subsequently signed the 1968 Non-Proliferation Treaty. Nevertheless, New Zealand continued to frame its security policy within a Western framework which was, from the mid 1950s, founded on nuclear deterrence. Allied warships were able to visit New Zealand without hindrance, despite the possibility that they were carrying nuclear weapons. Visits by nuclear-powered warships were, however, suspended for a period until an appropriate indemnity scheme was introduced.

Growing opposition within the Labour Party to visits by nuclear-armed vessels ensured that the Labour administration from 1972 to 1975 avoided them altogether. Anti-nuclear feeling during this period was stimulated by France's continued testing at its site at Mororoa Atoll. As a protest the government sent the frigates HMNZS *Otago* and *Canterbury* to the testing zone with a Cabinet minister on board in 1973. It also took a case to the International Court of Justice. Although concern in New Zealand was alleviated by the French decision to conduct its tests underground in future, the anti-nuclear movement was boosted by the confrontational approach adopted by the National administration led by R.D. Muldoon in the late 1970s. Ship visits were promoted as an essential element in New Zealand's alliance relationship with the United States. A series of visits by nuclear-powered vessels drove the point home, providing a focus, from 1976, for protest action by flotillas of small craft which attempted to block the ships' entry into ports. The anti-nuclear movement was boosted still further by the great increase in tension between the two superpowers, the United States and the Soviet Union, from the late 1970s.

Anti-nuclearism became the basis of New Zealand's approach to security during the Labour ministry of David ★Lange. The question of ship visits was brought to a head during the USS ★*Buchanan* affair in 1985. Although the immediate issue was nuclear armament capability, the question of safety in relation to nuclear propulsion also assumed importance. The American response to New Zealand's refusal to accept the *Buchanan* visit introduced a nationalistic element to the issue, which the government played hard: little New Zealand was being bullied by a great power. Latent anti-American feelings were brought to the fore. Hostility to France was even more intense, following the ★*Rainbow Warrior* affair in 1986. Although the government insisted that its anti-nuclear policy was not for export, this was not a position supported by many New Zealanders, who felt, unrealistically, that the world should follow their country's lead. Lange in particular denounced nuclear deterrence as the basis of Western security. The passage of legislation in 1987 effectively banning both nuclear weapons and nuclear-propelled ships from New Zealand waters, and any involvement of the New Zealand armed forces with nuclear weapons generally, ensured the end of New Zealand's participation in the ★ANZUS alliance.

With public opinion firmly on the side of the government's anti-nuclear stance—though awkwardly also in favour of retaining New Zealand's membership of ANZUS—the opposition National Party, in 1990, came into line. This made it impossible for the National government elected soon afterwards to restore the alliance relationship with the United States, and the impasse continued throughout the 1990s. An independent Special Committee on Nuclear Propulsion, which in 1992 found that nuclear-powered ships were relatively safe, was quietly ignored. Anti-nuclear sentiment was mostly directed against France, which continued to test at Mororua. After a protest flotilla headed to the test zone in 1995, the government reluctantly sent a ship, HMNZS *Tui*, to give logistic and moral support. Once again an attempt was made to restrain France by reopening New Zealand's case against French testing in the International Court of Justice, but the outcome was unsatisfactory. The end of French testing in 1996 removed the issue from the agenda.

Anti-nuclear activists meanwhile were directing their attention to nuclear weapons generally. Not content with the huge reductions in the superpower arsenals following the end of the ★Cold War, they now aimed at the complete abolition of such weapons. To this end they promoted the World Court Project, which had been initiated by Harold J. Evans, a former participant in the Japanese war crimes trials of the late 1940s and a retired New Zealand magistrate. This culminated in the International Court of Justice being asked by the World Health Organization for an advisory opinion on the legality of nuclear weapons. The outcome was a partial victory, with the court determining that the use of nuclear weapons was illegal but possession of them was not. Anti-nuclear efforts subsequently were subsumed within the Abolition 2000 campaign. (See ANTI-WAR MOVEMENTS; DISARMAMENT)

Anti-submarine warfare The submarine established itself firmly as a major weapon of naval warfare during the ★First World War. Accepting that the key to combating it was a system that required its detection underwater, the Allied Submarine Detection Investigation Committee endorsed a concept of using a transducer to generate a high-frequency pulse of sound through the water and listening for its echo. The time taken for the echo to return would indicate the range of the underwater target. By the time this system, then known as 'Asdic' (today Sonar), was fully developed in 1920, the war had ended, but it was to play a vital role in the ★Second World War. The anti-submarine battles of this conflict, in which New Zealanders were heavily involved (see ROYAL NAVY IN THE SECOND WORLD WAR, NEW ZEALANDERS IN), left an indelible impression on the Allied navies. The defeat of the German submarine campaign was the fundamental 'enabler' for Allied victory, given the central importance to the Allied war effort of freedom to use the sea. As the ★Cold War developed in the late 1940s, the Western powers were faced with the same challenge: a hostile continental power with a large submarine fleet. With access to German submarine designs and technology, the post-war Soviet Navy was able to develop new, fast submarines, a threat which demanded a quantum leap in both tactics and technology on the part of the Allied navies. Hence the Admiralty gave priority in its post-war planning to the global defence of shipping, in conjunction with the Commonwealth navies. This focus was reflected in New Zealand's defence planning: the RNZN's main role would be anti-submarine warfare. It would take responsibility, with the RAN, for the protection of shipping in the ★ANZAM region against the threat posed by Soviet conventional submarines operating from bases in the northern Pacific. To this end, New Zealand purchased six Loch class ★frigates from the Royal Navy. The anti-submarine role also underpinned New Zealand's later purchase of two Type 12 and the first Leander class frigates. In order to maintain experience in anti-submarine warfare tactics, New Zealand and Australia agreed to meet the operating costs of a British submarine division based in Sydney. From 1949 to 1965 the 4th Submarine Division operated 'A' class and 'T' class submarines, and a generation of New Zealand naval officers gained experience of submarine operations through year-long attachments, many gaining their 'Dolphins' as a mark of submarine qualification.

As the threat evolved from fast, snorkel-equipped diesel-electric boats to nuclear-powered submarines with anti-ship missiles, anti-submarine warfare techniques had to be refined. Ever since the First World War, it had been accepted that, although the oceans are opaque to light and radio waves, sound was the best medium for transmissions through water. Since low frequency sound travels further, with less loss of signal strength, the Western navies concentrated during the 1950s and 1960s on developing higher-powered and lower-frequency active sonars. The Type 177 search sets in HMNZS *Otago* and *Taranaki* were a good example of the mid-1950s sonars. The Graseby 750 refitted into the RNZN's Leander class frigates is an early-1980s medium-range sonar. Nevertheless detection ranges remained limited. Although the new sonars had theoretical ranges of sixteen kilometres and more, their 'unalerted' detection ranges were in reality only a few thousand metres, inside the firing range of contemporary Soviet torpedoes. Even variable-depth sonars, lowered over the stern of a frigate in order to get the transducer into optimum water conditions (such as the Type 199 sonar on HMNZS *Southland*), did not greatly increase detection ranges.

The advent of nuclear-powered submarines dramatically changed the anti-submarine warfare problem, since they had no need to surface or 'snort' (use a snorkel tube) to run diesels and recharge batteries, while they could achieve submerged speeds similar to those of modern surface escort ships. The early nuclear-powered submarines were noisy, however, and this led to a new emphasis on passive sonar. Designed to pick up, and gain an accurate awareness of direction from, low-frequency noises, a passive sonar consists of an array of hydrophones, up to a kilometre long, carried in a neutrally buoyant 'tail' streamed from the stern of the anti-submarine warship. The towing ship needs to be quiet itself, which generally means operations at low speeds. To reduce transmitted noise from her own engines, the ship's propulsion system has to be specially mounted. The RNZN's first towed array was an experimental model built by the Defence Scientific Establishment in the mid 1970s and streamed from the research ship HMNZS *Tui*. Subsequently an FMS15 towed array was purchased from the United Kingdom in 1990 and used in operation trials from *Tui*. Its prime function was area surveillance, providing, with support from appropriate signal processing and plotting systems, a 'picture' of major noise sources, including merchant ships, over several hundreds of square kilometres. Because of the inherent need for wide-area surveillance around New Zealand, the Anzac class frigates were fitted with a winch suitable for a towed array installation. Passive sonars are also useful against modern conventional submarines, which, while very quiet when running on battery, have to snort regularly, rendering them both noisier and vulnerable to radar detection.

Thus contemporary anti-submarine warfare doctrine embraces team work and the complementary capabilities of different systems. Towed array ships can conduct wide-area surveillance by passive sonar, supported by maritime patrol aircraft with search radar and sonobuoys. In the 'midfield', towed array frigates can investigate and attack contacts with their own anti-submarine helicopters, while in the inner zone, close to the convoy or task group (where the background noise from the escorted ships is high), frigates and helicopters with active sonars search for enemy submarines that come within torpedo firing range. Submarines, too, have a role in anti-submarine warfare, though generally they would be used to patrol enemy choke points (focal points for sea traffic) and would operate independently of surface and air anti-submarine units. However, both the British and American navies have experimented with their nuclear-powered attack submarines in direct support of task forces, an approach which demands specialised communications and careful management of the 'waterspace'.

The RNZN ceased to be a specialist anti-submarine warfare navy in the early 1970s, when the arrival of the Leander class frigates HMNZS *Waikato* and *Canterbury* emphasised its general purpose operational approach. The modern frigates are valued for their command and control, surveillance and gunfire support capabilities, while the new generation of naval helicopters also enhances the frigates' surface combat role. Contemporary anti-submarine warfare systems in the RNZN—hull-mounted sonars and ship-launched ★torpedoes—are primarily for self-defence. In addition the anti-submarine warfare potential of the RNZAF's P3 Orions was reduced when Project Rigel II was cancelled in the mid 1980s, leaving the aircraft with their original 1966-vintage anti-submarine equipment. However, their value for anti-submarine warfare operations will be improved by the modernisation of their sensors under Project Sirius.

RICHARD JACKSON

Anti-tank weapons New Zealand troops first fought tanks near Bapaume on 31 August 1918, 18-pounder field guns of the New Zealand Division beating off an attack by German AV7 tanks. During the early part of the ★Second World War, the anti-tank defences of the 2nd New Zealand Division were provided by a regiment of forty-eight (later increased to sixty-four) 2-pounder cannon. For its time the 2-pounder was a good weapon, but from 1941 heavier armour on German tanks rendered the gun increasingly ineffectual. Two-pounders were mounted upon trucks (known as portees) in order to improve their mobility, but such a tactic left the crew exposed to enemy fire, and casualties were high. The effective range of the 2-pounder was considered to be about 400 metres, but New Zealand crews often opened fire at extreme ranges of 1500 metres. As a stopgap measure, old 18-pounder guns were used to supplement the 2-pounder guns. Desperate circumstances also forced the use of 25-pounder artillery pieces as anti-tank guns. It was not until the battle at Minqar Qaim in 1942 that more powerful 6-pounder guns were received by the anti-tank regiment, with 2-pounders being assigned to new anti-tank platoons in the infantry battalions. In February 1943 the anti-tank batteries were re-equipped with extremely powerful 17-pounder guns. Reorganised in 1944, the anti-tank regiment was equipped with M10 tank-destroyers (see ARMOUR). For home defence 2-pounder and later 6-pounder guns were considered adequate.

The first anti-tank weapon for infantry was the Boys anti-tank rifle, one being assigned to each infantry platoon in 1940. Nothing more than a large-calibre rifle, it

One of 7th New Zealand Anti-Tank Regiment's 2-pounder guns in action in Libya in November 1941 (*War History Collection, Alexander Turnbull Library, F-9608-1/4-DA*)

was virtually useless against enemy tanks. Infantry anti-tank weapons were supplemented by mines, grenades, and even Molotov cocktails, but it was not until 1943 that infantry platoons were equipped with an effective anti-tank weapon, the PIAT. A simple tube projecting a hollow-charge shell, it gave the infantry good defence against armour at very close ranges, and remained in service until 1953 when the Army re-equipped with 3.5-inch rocket launchers, descendant of the famous 'bazooka'. Also obtained were the more substantial 120 mm BAT L1 recoilless rifles, which were in turn replaced by 106 mm recoilless rifles in 1960. These gave way to the Carl Gustav anti-tank weapon, a reliable and robust Swedish-made recoilless rifle, in 1967. The Carl Gustavs were supplemented in the 1970s with M72 lightweight 'throw-away' anti-tank rockets. At present the New Zealand Army has no modern anti-tank weapons.

Anti-war movements It would be difficult to call opposition to war a 'movement' in the early years of the twentieth century. Members of the Society of Friends, Christadelphians, and Seventh Day Adventists opposed war for different reasons, as did some Fabians and socialists, and individuals within organisations such as the National Council of Women, and very small groups such as the Auckland Peace Association, established in 1899. While these people may have had different motivations (religion, socialism, conscience), they did have ideas in common: they called for arbitration instead of war, general disarmament, and the abolition of secret diplomacy leading to secret treaties.

Although New Zealand wasted no time in sending a contingent to fight in South Africa in 1899 (see BOER WAR), not all New Zealanders supported involvement in the war. At the National Council of Women conference in Dunedin in 1900, Wilhelmina Sherriff Bain, among others, spoke against the war; she and the Council were vilified by Dunedin's mayor and other worthies for their stance, which was consistent with previously stated positions. The Council had passed resolutions deploring war and advocating arbitration since its establishment in 1896.

The introduction of *compulsory military training for boys and men under the Defence Act 1909 (see DEFENCE ACTS) prompted the establishment of groups such as the Anti-Militarist League and the National Peace Council (NPC) in Christchurch, and the New Zealand Freedom League in Auckland. While these groups were ostensibly only opposed to compulsory military training, they argued that military training inculcated a spirit of militarism in young men and boys which would make them more amenable to war should one occur. The NPC, for example, had the repeal of the compulsory clauses of the Defence Act as its major focus, but it also supported the principle of arbitration and advocated the appointment of a Minister of Peace rather than of Defence. Its most influential member was Baptist lay-preacher Charles Mackie, who had an important role in the establishment of the Council and was its secretary until shortly before his death in 1943.

The NPC, the Society of Friends, the Canterbury Women's Institute, and the Freedom League all publicly declared their opposition to the *First World War in 1914. It was an unpopular stance—the NPC suspended all its public work because 'war fever' was too 'acute'. However, Mackie and other members often attended sittings of military service boards and courts martial dealing with *conscientious objectors. Much opposition was framed as opposition to *conscription, rather than the war itself, but peace groups were also established. These included branches of international organisations such as the Women's International League for Peace and Freedom (WILPF) and the International Fellowship of Reconciliation which were both established in New Zealand in 1916. WILPF called for a negotiated settlement to end the war.

During the inter-war years there were a number of organisations, such as the League of Nations Union, the Student Christian Movement, and the International Council of Women, which, while not primarily anti-war, considered war to be wrong. A pacifist group, the No More War Movement, whose members were committed to pacifism 'in the search for a new socialist-oriented world order', was established in 1928. Its early efforts were concentrated on repeal of the compulsory military training legislation. Among its members were Lincoln Efford, Muriel and John Morrison, Alfred Page, and, after her son's death, Sarah Saunders Page.

The New Testament interpretation of God as a god of love, combined with the social gospel approach to Christianity which taught that the kingdom of God

Anti-war movements

could be established on Earth, and that Christians should strive for changes in society that would help to establish that kingdom, provided a framework within which some pacifists could espouse their beliefs. In 1936 Archibald *Barrington and Ormond *Burton established the Christian Pacifist Society (CPS), which remains active sixty years later. Methodist pacifists ran and organised the society during its formative years. It was open only to communicants of a Christian church, and members were obliged to sign a covenant which contained a clause stating that they would refuse even to render non-combatant service should a war ensue. Because of the public image of Burton and Barrington and the publicity which they were able to generate, the CPS was a significant peace group in New Zealand despite its small membership. It held poster parades, as well as street meetings with members of the Peace Pledge Union (PPU) in the late 1930s, and worked to convert the churches to the pacifist cause. Members actively opposed involvement in the *Second World War, and the street meetings continued despite the continual arrests of speakers. Although the arrests gave much-needed publicity, their cause was hopeless. Detention in camps or prisons of the younger activists in the PPU and the CPS meant that in 1941 the CPS's attention turned towards helping conscientious objectors and lobbying the authorities for their fairer treatment.

In 1949 the Peace and Anti-Conscription Federation was established in Wellington in response to the proposed reintroduction of compulsory military training. Ormond Burton had always argued that anti-conscription agitation was necessarily against war because conscription for military service 'is an act of preparation for war, and is therefore an act of war'. After the CMT referendum in August 1949, the Peace and Anti-Conscription Federation was renamed the New Zealand Peace Council. The Council tried to widen its membership in the 1950s and began to publish a weekly newspaper, *Peace*. One of its first activities was to circulate an international petition against nuclear weapons—20,000 signatures were collected in New Zealand. It also opposed New Zealand's involvement in the *Korean War, though with little effect in a *Cold War atmosphere in which its efforts were officially denounced as communist-inspired.

The dropping of the atomic bombs by the United States on Hiroshima and Nagasaki in 1945 provided a new focus for anti-war groups, one which has taken up the energies of many campaigners ever since. In 1949 the Soviet Union exploded its first *atomic bomb, followed by Great Britain in 1953, and hydrogen bombs were soon being developed and tested. In 1951 the Maori Women's Welfare League had passed a resolution opposing *nuclear weapons testing, and in the election year of 1957 in Auckland the Society of Friends circulated a petition to Parliament against the manufacture and testing of nuclear weapons. (Around 11,000 signatures were gathered.) After a convention on nuclear disarmament in August 1959, the New Zealand Council for Nuclear Disarmament was founded, changing its name to the Campaign for Nuclear Disarmament (CND) in 1960.

Meanwhile the French government had begun to plan atmospheric nuclear tests in the Pacific, and was undeterred by a formal protest by New Zealand in 1963. Nor did it sign the partial Nuclear Test Ban Treaty concluded in August that year. When it began the atmospheric tests above Moruroa Atoll in July 1966, there were about 400 groups in New Zealand publicly decrying the tests. At this time CND was campaigning to make the southern hemisphere a nuclear-free zone; it collected more than 80,000 signatures for a petition demanding 'No Bombs South of the Line'. Influenced by the United States, which had said that such a zone would compromise *ANZUS commitments, the government declined to act on the petition.

New Zealand involvement in the *Vietnam War provided a new focus for anti-war activities in the mid 1960s. In March 1965 the Peace for Vietnam Committee was founded in Auckland as a result of a public meeting called by various peace groups and unions. Anti-war groups were also established in other towns and cities, including the Wellington and Dunedin Committees on Vietnam. There were also university-based groups, such as the Vietnam Youth Action Committee and the Auckland Committee on South-east Asia, which organised 'teach ins' about the situation in Vietnam. Most of these were umbrella groups made up of activists who had not previously been involved in the peace movement and groups such as the CPS and WILPF. Various public activities were organised: in 1968 the Peace, Power and Politics in Asia conference was held in Wellington at Easter, and in 1970 there began a series of 'mobilisations'—street marches against the war held simultaneously throughout the country.

With the end of New Zealand's military involvement in Vietnam in 1972, the attention of peace activists returned to nuclear issues. The Pacific Peoples' Anti-Nuclear Action Committee, based in Auckland, was active in opposing all nuclear activities in the Pacific. With the resumption of visits to New Zealand ports by nuclear-powered ships from the United States Navy after 1975, a Peace Squadron was formed in Auckland, and soon afterwards in other ports. Members sailed to confront the warships and submarines as they entered port. A petition against the ship visits circulated by WILPF collected 330,000 signatures. Nevertheless the number of visits increased: between mid 1983 and July 1984 there were seven, compared with six in the previous eight years. Protest mounted. In April 1983 Australian activist Helen Caldicott had toured New Zealand publicising the effects of the arms race between the United States and the Soviet Union and drawing people's attention to the effects of a nuclear war. More than 300 neighbourhood peace groups were set up in the early 1980s. These influenced many municipal councils to declare themselves nuclear-free zones. Three private member's bills, which would have made New Zealand a nuclear-free zone, were introduced to Parliament between 1982 and 1984. It was the prospect of a defeat of the government over the 1984 Bill which ostensibly led to Prime Minister R.D. Muldoon calling a snap election in which his party was heavily defeated. The aspirations of anti-nuclear activists were fulfilled by the Labour government which took office as a result (see ANTI-NUCLEARISM).

For most of the twentieth century, actively working for peace has been an unfashionable and unpopular occupation, with only small groups of people speaking and writing about compulsory military training, conscription, and pacifism. Since the Vietnam War, the idea of social peace—which includes issues of domestic as well as international violence, indigenous rights, and the inequities of the world's economic system—has come to occupy the minds and actions of those who are peace activists.

G. Hanly (ed), *Peace is More Than an Absence of War* (New Women's Press, Auckland, 1986); E. Locke, *Peace People: A History of Peace Activities in New Zealand* (Hazard Press, Christchurch, 1982); M. Hutching, 'Mothers of the World: Women, Peace and Arbitration in Early Twentieth-Century New Zealand', *NZ Journal of History*, vol 27, no 2 (1993).

MEGAN HUTCHING

ANZAC is the acronym for Australian and New Zealand Army Corps, the formation created in December 1914 by grouping the Australian Imperial Force and ★New Zealand Expeditionary Force stationed in Egypt under the command of Lieutenant-General William Birdwood. Initially the term 'Australasian Corps' had been mooted for this force, but there was a reluctance among both Australians and New Zealanders to lose their separate identities completely. The acronym itself was probably devised at Birdwood's headquarters by a New Zealand clerk, Sergeant K.M. Little, for use on a rubber stamp. Some time later it was taken on as the telegraph code word for the corps. Consisting of the 1st Australian Division and the ★New Zealand and Australian Division (under Major-General A.J. ★Godley), the corps made its operational debut at ★Gallipoli on 25 April 1915. The small cove where Australian and New Zealand troops landed was quickly designated 'Anzac', and the word was soon being used to describe all Australian and New Zealand soldiers who fought on the peninsula, and eventually any Australian or New Zealand soldier. On the ★Western Front there were two Anzac corps, with the New Zealand Division serving in II ANZAC Corps until early 1918. During the ★Sinai–Palestine campaign the combined Australia and New Zealand Mounted Division was more commonly called the Anzac Mounted Division. A new Anzac Corps was briefly formed during the campaign in ★Greece in 1941, while New Zealand and Australian infantry companies combined to form an Anzac battalion during the ★Vietnam War. As an adjective the word was soon being used to describe items ranging from biscuits to buttons. Shrewd entrepreneurs saw the commercial advantages of the term, but there was strong popular opposition to such exploitation. On 31 August 1916 the word 'Anzac' was protected by law to prevent its exploitation for business or trade purposes. Anzac continues to denote both a distinctive nationalistic spirit of sacrifice and courage and a sense of Australian and New Zealand community of interest. Whereas in New Zealand the word retains its connotation of Australian–New Zealand kinship, there has been a tendency in Australia to take the NZ out of the acronym, and to use the word to denote purely Australian endeavour in the ★First World War. In both Australia and New Zealand ★Anzac Day, on 25 April, is the main day of remembrance for the fallen in all wars.

Anzac Day is held on 25 April each year to commemorate New Zealanders killed in war and to honour returned servicemen and women. The ceremony itself has been continually adapted to the times, but has also steadily acquired extra layers of symbolism and meaning. A typical commemoration begins with a march by returned service personnel before dawn to the local war memorial. Military personnel and returned servicemen and women form up about the memorial, joined by other members of the community, with pride of place going to the war veterans. A short service follows with a prayer, hymns (including Kipling's 'Recessional' or 'Lest We Forget'), and a dedication which concludes with the last verse of Laurence Binyon's 'For the Fallen':

They shall not grow old, as we that are left grow old:
Age shall not weary them, nor the years condemn.
At the going down of the sun and in the morning
We will remember them.

The Last Post is then played, followed by a minute's silence and Reveille. A brief address follows, after which the hymn 'Recessional' is sung. The service concludes with a closing prayer and the singing of the National Anthem. Another ceremony takes place later that morning, with returned service personnel wearing

Anzac Day

their medals, and marching behind banners and standards. The veterans are joined by other community groups, including members of the armed forces, the ★Red Cross, ★cadets, and veterans of other countries' forces. The march proceeds to the local war memorial, where another service takes place, including the laying of wreaths by various organisations and members of the public. This service is a less intimate and emotional ceremony than the dawn service, but serves as a more public commemoration. The speech, usually by an important dignitary, serviceman, or returned serviceman or woman, tends to be of a conservative nature, with much stress on nationhood and remembrance. After these services, many of the veterans retire to the local RSA club or hotel, where they enjoy coffee and rum (in the case of the dawn service) and 'unwind' after an emotionally and, for elderly veterans, physically exhausting event. At the end of the day, the ceremony of the 'Retreat' is performed.

The first public recognition of the landings at ★Gallipoli took place on 30 April 1915, after news of the dramatic event had reached New Zealand. A half-day holiday was promptly declared for government offices, flags were flown, and patriotic meetings were held around the country. Descriptions of the landings (and casualty lists) were eagerly read, while newspapers gushed about the heroism of the New Zealand soldiers. From the outset, public perceptions of the landings at Anzac Cove were imbued with strong feelings of national pride. The eventual failure of the Gallipoli operation enhanced its sanctity in the public mind; the courage and sacrifice of the New Zealand soldiers in adversity was highlighted (see NATIONAL IDENTITY AND WAR). Demands for some form of remembrance on the anniversary of the landing on the peninsula, both as a public expression of grief and as a means of rallying support for the war effort, were soon being heard. A half-day public holiday was gazetted on 5 April 1916, and church services and recruiting meetings were proposed. Among the growing body of returned servicemen, however, such an approach was an anathema—'the boys don't want to be split up among twenty or thirty different churches on Anzac Day, and it is certain they don't want to go to a meeting to hear people who haven't been there [to war] spout and pass resolutions'. Instead, returned servicemen preferred a public service conducted by an army chaplain. From the beginning, returned servicemen claimed 'ownership' of the commemoration. In the event, commemorations were marked by processions of returned and serving service personnel, followed by church services and public meetings at town halls. Speeches extolled national unity, imperial loyalty, remembrance of the dead, and the need for young men to volunteer (★conscription was imminent). Large crowds attended the commemorations, 2000 at the Anzac Day service in Rotorua, for example. In London the landing day was marked by a procession of 2000 Australian and New Zealand troops and a service at Westminster Abbey. New Zealand soldiers in Egypt commemorated the day with a service and the playing of the Last Post, followed by a holiday, including sports. In August 1916, after lobbying by returned soldiers, the use of the word ★'Anzac' was prohibited for trade or business purposes, further enshrining the Anzac myth and the sacredness of the commemoration.

A similar pattern of 25 April processions of servicemen, church services, and public meetings continued for the rest of the war. These were generally organised by the New Zealand Returned Soldiers' Association (see VETERANS' ASSOCIATIONS) in cooperation with local authorities. The ceremony was an opportunity to stimulate patriotism, in which the righteousness of the war and New Zealand's place as part of the British Empire were stressed. However, after the war the service quickly lost its patriotic function, becoming more explicitly a remembrance of the war dead. Gradually standardised after the war, the ceremony was essentially a re-enactment of a military funeral. It would be conducted around a bier of wreaths and a serviceman's hat, with a firing party with heads bowed and a chaplain to read the words from the military burial service. Three volleys would be fired by the guard, and the Last Post played, followed by a prayer, hymn, and benediction. Nevertheless, there was continual adaptation of the service. The funeral bier in halls was replaced by public ★war memorials as these were erected throughout the 1920s. The move to Anzac Day commemorations at public war memorials rather than in town halls or churches signified an increasing secularisation of the ceremony. Despite occasional protests from churches, it was RSA leaders, servicemen, and local politicians who increasingly made the speeches, rather than clergymen. The laying of wreaths became more central to the ceremony, while fewer speeches were made and hymns sung. On the other hand, the presence of the uniformed members of the armed forces in many places became accepted as part of the march and service. Gradually throughout the 1920s the Anzac Day service became less and less akin to a mournful funeral.

The day itself was not marked as a public holiday until 1921. Peace was celebrated from 19 to 21 July 1919, but no official day of commemoration for the war was at first instituted. The government was prepared to move St George's Day to 25 April and declare that day to be a government holiday. However, the public was not greatly excited by government holidays, which in the main were religious observances or patriotic occasions, while Dominion Day, the self-styled 'National Day', possessed no emotional appeal. While not an official holiday, Anzac Day had already acquired a strong appeal among the public. Not until 1920 did the government respond to RSA lobbying for 25 April to be declared a holiday. Although legislation was passed which made Anzac Day a public holiday, with hotels and banks closed and race meetings prohibited, this did not meet RSA demands for the day to be 'Sundayised'. In 1922 the government backed down and 25 April became a full public holiday as if it were a Sunday.

Throughout the 1920s and 1930s, Anzac Day was marked with varying degrees of public enthusiasm. Common themes in the speeches were New Zealand nationhood, national unity, imperial loyalty, sacrifice, and a desire for peace. While some of a left-wing bent and members of *anti-war movements criticised the commemoration as militarist, most New Zealanders regarded the day as sacred—an expression of sorrow rather than an opportunity to glorify war. During the Depression Anzac Day provided a forum to extol the ideals of unity and selflessness. As the international situation deteriorated in the 1930s, Anzac Day speeches increasingly focused on the need for defence preparations and the importance of not forgetting past lessons. The numbers of marchers increased, too, during the late 1930s, perhaps because returned servicemen, as they aged, became more interested in commemorating their war experiences through public ritual. Anzac Day began to take on the characteristic of an annual reunion for many returned servicemen. This was exemplified by the 1300-strong contingent of New Zealand returned servicemen which participated in the Anzac Day ceremony in Sydney in 1938. It was from Australia that the dawn parade, commemorating both the time of the initial landings at Gallipoli and the routine dawn 'stand-to' in the trenches, was introduced to New Zealand for Anzac Day in 1939. The cold and darkness breaking into sunrise added to the symbolism of the occasion.

Anzac Day assumed new relevance during the *Second World War. Public interest in the day increased, though crowds were not encouraged to gather in 1942 as a security precaution. The commemorations predictably focused on the current war, with appeals for people to follow the 'spirit of Anzac'; the links between the 'first Anzacs' and personnel now serving or recently returned were stressed. Thus Anzac Day became the day of commemoration for all the wars in which New Zealanders had taken part, and returned servicemen and women from the Second World War joined the parades alongside their older counterparts. This wider focus was encompassed in 1949 legislation, which also specifically protected the holiday from becoming 'Mondayised'.

Attendance at Anzac Day ceremonies peaked during the 1950s. In 1957 there were 6000 people at the dawn service at Auckland. Anzac Day seemed at this time to reflect the ideal of New Zealand as a united community. Returned service personnel now spanned two world wars, making participation in the day intergenerational. Anzac Day also seemed to reflect Maori–Pakeha unity through shared war experiences. The commemoration of 25 April also continued to serve its principal purpose as an expression of public grief, a sense of loss assuaged by the notion that loved ones had not died in vain, and that the 'Anzac spirit' would live on, renewed each year at Anzac Day. Nevertheless, there was dissent over the religious aspect of the service. Roman Catholics were prevented by their own rules from attending ecumenical services, but RSA proposals to remove religion from the ceremonies altogether were firmly resisted by Protestant churches, already unhappy at what they felt was the overly secular nature of services. Not until 1965 did the churches resolve their differences, until which time many Roman Catholic or Jewish returned service personnel had simply not attended Anzac Day ceremonies.

During the 1960s substantial changes occurred in Anzac Day commemorations. Calls to liberalise Anzac Day, unthinkable in the early 1950s, became increasingly vocal, given impetus by the apparent double standard of returned servicemen and women enjoying their traditional Anzac Day 'booze up' while the general public was denied access to entertainment in hotels or cinemas. The commemoration itself was also modified. The afternoon citizens' service was gradually moved to mid morning, while the popularity of the dawn service increased. Time, too, had changed the nature of the day, from one of mourning to one of commemoration. These shifts led the RSA in 1965 to recommend liberalisation of the afternoon of Anzac Day, and this was done two years later. In 1967 Anzac Day became associated with protest when two members of the left-wing Progressive Youth Movement in Christchurch laid a wreath protesting against the *Vietnam War (and were subsequently convicted of disorderly behaviour). Further incidents followed at subsequent Anzac Days, as protesters sought to bring attention to their anti-war cause. With the end of the Vietnam conflict, such protest faded away in the mid 1970s, but in 1978 renewed controversy arose when a women's group laid a wreath in memory of women killed and raped in war. During the 1980s other lobby groups—feminists, gays, anti-nuclear and peace activists, Maori radicals—all laid wreaths at the Anzac Day services. Anzac Day had become more than a commemoration of New Zealand war dead and war service; it was increasingly being used to make statements about war and society. While bewildering to many returned servicemen, such controversies breathed fresh relevance into the day. Increasingly

Anzac Day was regarded as an appropriate day on which to debate defence and war-related issues—ex-servicemen and politicians used such platforms to speak out on the anti-nuclear policy during the 1980s.

In the meantime Anzac Day had undergone a renaissance, with increasingly large numbers of young people attending the services. The burgeoning mood of nationalism evident in the 1980s found partial expression in Anzac Day, which had always been an opportunity to celebrate the alleged foundation of a New Zealand national identity at Gallipoli. A combination of external influences (such as the ★ANZUS crisis and ★anti-nuclearism) and a series of books, plays, and documentaries reinforced the association of war and national identity in the public eye. The 75th anniversary of the Gallipoli landings in 1990 (coinciding with the 150th anniversary of the signing of the Treaty of Waitangi) attracted immense interest. An official delegation, led by the Governor-General and including a Gallipoli veteran, and a host of Australian and New Zealand tourists attended an emotional Anzac Day dawn service at Gallipoli. Since that time many New Zealanders have made the 'pilgrimage' to Gallipoli for Anzac Day, with nearly 3000 Australians and New Zealanders being present in 1997. Once regarded by many as an implicit glorification of war, Anzac Day was now almost universally seen as a repudiation of war and a celebration of New Zealand's national identity.

Anzac Day continues to enjoy unusual reverence in a country where emotional public rituals are otherwise absent. It has come to celebrate values that many New Zealanders consider either distinctive or admirable about their nation—mateship, unity, courage, self-sacrifice, loyalty—in addition to its traditional commemorative function. Indeed, such has been the atmosphere of national unity engendered by Anzac Day that some have called for it to become the day of national commemoration in place of Waitangi Day (which has often been marked by protest and division). In 1996, Prime Minister Jim Bolger suggested, without eliciting much enthusiasm, that Anzac Day have the dual function of commemorating the war dead and celebrating nationhood. Other proposed changes, such as that in 1997 to allow shops to open on Anzac Day morning, have been firmly resisted by the RSA. Despite this, Anzac Day will continue to be redefined by each succeeding generation, especially as the last of the Second World War veterans gradually pass away in the early twenty-first century.

M.R. Sharpe, 'Anzac Day in New Zealand, 1916–1939: Attitudes to Peace and War' (MA thesis, University of Auckland, 1981); S.J. Clarke, 'The One Day of the Year: Anzac Day in Aotearoa/New Zealand 1946–1990' (MA thesis, University of Otago, 1994).

ANZAM Between 1949 and 1971 New Zealand was involved in an evolving Commonwealth defence planning arrangement known as ANZAM. The product of Australian initiative, the ANZAM machinery emerged from discussions in Melbourne between a British service planning team, the Australian Defence Committee, and the New Zealand ★Chiefs of Staff in August 1949. Although uneasy at Australian dominance of the proposed arrangements, New Zealand agreed to participate on the understanding that there would be no distraction from its primary defence effort of preparing to carry out its ★Middle East commitment.

ANZAM was concerned with planning for the protection of wartime sea communications in the ANZAM area, covering the eastern Indian Ocean, Malaya and Thailand up to the Kra Isthmus, Indonesia and the area south of the equator and west of the Cooks (156°W). The name ANZAM derived from the area—Australia, New Zealand and Malaya. The contingency planning was carried out by the Australian defence machinery in Melbourne with appropriate representation of the British and New Zealand military authorities who, for this purpose, joined the Australian Defence Committee to form the ANZAM Defence Committee. This was a service-level arrangement which did not commit the respective governments.

It was also agreed in 1949 that ANZAM would provide the framework of command in the region in wartime. Operations would be directed by the ANZAM Chiefs of Staff, which would comprise the Australian Chiefs of Staff and representatives of both the New Zealand and British Chiefs of Staff. Again, the committee would function through the Australian higher defence machinery. All these arrangements were kept secret—even the name ANZAM was classified—though New Zealand Prime Minister Sidney Holland several times caused a stir in London and Canberra—and Wellington—by inadvertently alluding to ANZAM publicly in the early 1950s.

The perceived need for coordination of ANZAM planning with that of the American military authorities led to a meeting at Pearl Harbor in February 1951, from which emerged the ★Radford–Collins agreement affecting the extent of the ANZAM area. Nevertheless, ANZAM planning for the protection of wartime sea communications remained relatively undeveloped; in 1952 it was dismissed by a New Zealand officer as largely a paper organisation. ANZAM received a new lease of life, however, with the decision to establish a ★British Commonwealth Far East Strategic Reserve, control of which would be an ANZAM responsibility. In 1955 the three governments agreed that ANZAM should plan for the defence of Malaya in situations short of global war, but its efforts in this direction were hindered by the unforthcoming attitude of the United

States, whose support was considered essential to any successful defence of the peninsula. As a result ANZAM planning focused primarily on supporting ★SEATO. It also provided a planning forum for dealing with ★Confrontation issues as well. The ANZAM Chiefs of Staff Committee, as the ANZAM Defence Committee was renamed in 1967, continued to meet until 1971, when ANZAM was superseded by the ANZUK arrangements.

ANZUK Force The Australian, New Zealand and United Kingdom Force was formed on 1 November 1971 with the coming into effect of the ★Five Power Defence Arrangements. It comprised the small forces which the three countries agreed to sustain in Malaysia and Singapore. New Zealand contributed 1RNZIR, the infantry battalion serving in ★28th British Commonwealth Infantry Brigade, which now became 28th (ANZUK) Brigade, a frigate, and 41 Squadron RNZAF, as well as logistic personnel for the ANZUK Support Group. The ANZUK troops continued to train for possible ★SEATO deployments. Following Australia's decision to withdraw its forces, the force was disbanded on 31 January 1974. New Zealand's troops in Singapore then came under the command of ★New Zealand Force South East Asia.

ANZUS The mutual security treaty between Australia, New Zealand, and the United States, known as the 'Anzus Pact', was signed on 1 September 1951 and came into force in April 1952. It was, primarily, a response to the ★Cold War. First, both Great Britain (the former mother country of the Anzac nations) and the United States (their new-found ★Second World War protector) had identified the Soviet Union as a potential enemy. They anticipated that in a third world war the Soviet Union would drive simultaneously into western Europe and the Middle East. Britain would have to defend the Middle East to protect its oil supplies, the Suez Canal, and airfields from which the Soviet Union could be bombed. To achieve this Britain looked for support from Australia and New Zealand, but both were cautious about making commitments without an American guarantee of their security in the Pacific in order to (as it was said) 'bolt the back door' (see MIDDLE EAST COMMITMENT). Second, with the extension of the Cold War into Asia, Britain wanted Anzac support in fighting communist guerrillas in Malaya and for a possible defence of ★Hong Kong against the newly created Chinese People's Republic. Both Dominions sent modest air transport units in 1949–50. Third, the outbreak of the ★Korean War in 1950 intensified American efforts to sign a 'peace of reconciliation' with Japan, formally terminating the Second World War, and to ensure its Western alignment in the Cold War. But Australia and New Zealand feared future Japanese resurgence and would not sign the peace treaty unless they got an American security guarantee. China's intervention in the Korean War in December 1950 induced great urgency for the United States, and the Pacific Security (ANZUS) Treaty was drafted in Canberra in February 1951 with the American negotiator, John Foster Dulles.

The treaty was regarded, at the time, as a step towards a more comprehensive regional security system—a 'Pacific Pact' to match the North Atlantic Treaty. The main provision was that the three parties would consult if their metropolitan territories, island territories, or forces, vessels, or aircraft were attacked in the 'Pacific area'. An attack would be treated by each party as 'dangerous to its own peace and safety'. (This was a phrase from the Monroe Doctrine and weaker than the North Atlantic Treaty's attack-on-one-is-an-attack-on-all principle). The parties also undertook to maintain their 'individual and collective' ability to resist. No treaty organisation was created, but provision was made for a ministerial council. The treaty was to remain in force indefinitely.

Britain's exclusion marked a 'parting of the ways' and Winston Churchill, who returned to power shortly after the signing, tried hard to get Britain associated in some way, but was rebuffed. However, the British and French campaigns against communist guerrillas in Malaya and Indo-China and the overriding fear that China might intervene in South-east Asia, as it had done in Korea, led to Western cooperation. Staff consultations took place in the years 1951–53 between Britain, France, the United States, Australia, and New Zealand to study the problem of deterring China. These led on, after the French defeat at Dien Bien Phu, to the Manila Pact of 1954 and the creation of ★SEATO in 1955. The formation of the ★British Commonwealth Far East Strategic Reserve in 1955 meant ending the Middle East commitments in favour of a joint British–Australian–New Zealand force in Malaya and Singapore.

The Anzac nations were, thus, in a position of dual dependence. ANZUS was not an exclusive relationship but, in reality, a backstop. The Anzacs deployed alongside the British and the Americans in the Thai–Laos border area in 1962; they assisted the British during ★Confrontation with Indonesia from 1963 to 1966. They supported the Americans with troops in South Vietnam between 1962 and 1972 while the British held aloof (see VIETNAM WAR). Thus close military and diplomatic relationships developed between Washington, Canberra, and Wellington. Anzac officials had entrée to the White House and the Pentagon; there was close intelligence-sharing, and preferential equipment procurement. When the British withdrew from 'East of Suez' in the 1970s, Australia and New Zealand kept

31

Appeasement

some forces in Malaysia and Singapore until the late 1980s. ANZUS was regularly described as the 'keystone' of defence policy. Under the American nuclear umbrella Australia and New Zealand could avoid large defence expenditures and keep their forces small, yet feel secure.

The ANZUS triangle was breached in 1985 when the Labour government, led by David ★Lange, adopted a 'nuclear free' policy. As it embarked on an aggressive domestic policy of restructuring in the direction of free-market economics, the government appeased the party's left wing by excluding from New Zealand ports vessels which were nuclear armed, or propelled, or, even, 'capable'. After an ageing US Navy destroyer was denied entry (see BUCHANAN AFFAIR), the US government declared ANZUS 'inoperative' in respect of New Zealand and suspended the defence guarantee. In 1987, the new policy was embodied in law in the New Zealand Nuclear Free Zone, Disarmament, and Arms Control Act. While Australia strengthened its bilateral relationships with both partners, New Zealand found itself treated by the United States as a 'friend, not ally' at the very moment when the Cold War (the alliance's prime motivation) ended.

In the 1990s, 'Nuclear-Free New Zealand' became a bipartisan policy and something of an icon of national identity. However, the National government elected in 1990 sought to restore relations with the United States. In 1991 Prime Minister Jim Bolger had a corridor meeting with President George Bush during a conference and in 1993 President Bill Clinton promised to review the stand off. Early in 1994, the so-called 'Clinton thaw' began with a lifting of barriers to high-level defence talks. The US Commander in the Pacific and the Assistant Secretary of State visited New Zealand, and the Chief of Defence Staff and the Minister of Foreign Affairs visited the United States. When, in 1995, the Prime Minister went to the White House (the first such high-level visit for eleven years), the President hoped that they would meet 'perhaps one day again as allies'. Very close relations with the United States were restored, but the 'unfinished business' caused by the exclusion of nuclear-propelled ships under the nuclear-free legislation remained a barrier to the full restoration of the alliance.

R.L. Harry, 'Treaty between Australia, New Zealand and the United States of America', *Australian Outlook*, vol 35, no 2 (1981); W.D. McIntyre, *Background to the Anzus Pact: Policy-Making, Strategy and Diplomacy, 1945–55* (Canterbury University Press, Christchurch, 1995).

W. DAVID McINTYRE

Appeasement was the term given to the approach adopted by the British and French governments in dealing with attempts by Germany and Italy in particular to change the status quo in the 1930s. In effect, political concessions were made to buy peace in a way that seemed to compromise principles. Although in part driven by perceptions of the British and French armed forces' lack of preparedness for war relative to a rearmed Germany, appeasement also stemmed from British Prime Minister Neville Chamberlain's belief that conciliation could moderate the demands of the dictators. It reached its apogee at the 1938 Munich conference, which led to the dismemberment of Czechoslovakia. New Zealand, privately in imperial councils and publicly at the ★League of Nations, consistently opposed such an approach, though it enjoyed the advantage of isolation from the scene of any conflict likely to arise from a firm stance. Appeasement was abandoned in 1939 when Great Britain and France not only gave assurances of support to Poland but also stood by them when Germany invaded on 1 September, thereby precipitating the ★Second World War. In the aftermath of the war, the dangers of the discredited appeasement approach became a favourite argument of those who advocated a firm stance against perceived aggressive tendencies in the Soviet Union, and underlay the onset of the ★Cold War.

Ardagh, Brigadier Patrick Augustine (30 August 1891–6 April 1944) was born at Ngapara in North Otago and practised medicine in Christchurch before joining 1NZEF on the ★Western Front in January 1917. As the regimental medical officer of 1st Battalion, Auckland Regiment, he won an MC for his courage in evacuating and treating wounded soldiers under fire, despite himself being wounded on three occasions. His exemplary conduct near Crèvecoeur in October 1918 in treating wounded under fire for thirty-six hours led to his being recommended for a VC; he was instead made a DSO. After serving in the ★Territorial Force between the wars, he returned to active service in August 1940 to head the surgical section of 2NZEF's 2nd New Zealand General Hospital. After commanding 1st New Zealand Casualty Clearing Station, he became Assistant Director of Medical Services of the 2nd New Zealand Division in May 1942. The efficient and rapid evacuation and treatment of wounded in the ★North African campaign owed much to his administrative skills. From February 1943 he was Deputy Director of Medical Services of XXX Corps, with which he served in Tunisia and the ★Italian campaign. Highly regarded by 8th Army commander General Sir Bernard Montgomery, he was made a CBE in 1943. In 1944 he went to England to prepare for ★D-Day, but his health had been undermined by constant strain and he succumbed to illness.

Armed Constabulary In May 1867, about three years after the suppression of the Kingite resistance to the Crown, a new armed structure was needed for the colony of New Zealand; the imperial government had withdrawn the last of its actively operational troops, and the military settlers on confiscated land were obliged to serve the Crown only until the end of the year. However, the colonial government believed that the backbone of Maori armed resistance to state authority had been broken. Even the conquered areas, therefore, could be occupied by coercive forces that were less expensive and disruptive than armies: remaining 'pacification' tasks could be carried out by a body of armed constables able to operate both as soldiers and police. This would serve as a core organisation around which militia, volunteers, provincial police, special constables, and 'loyalist' (★kupapa) Maori elements would coalesce whenever a threat to the fabric of the state, whether Maori or non-Maori, was perceived. Armed constabularies were common in British and other colonies that had large numbers of resistant indigenous subjects. They were designed to be transitional, the ultimate goal being that of police forces benignly (and therefore cheaply) controlling societies which were largely self-disciplining. The provincial police forces in New Zealand had evolved from the Armed Police established in the 1840s during the first wave of Maori 'rebellion', partly modelled—as with most constabularies of the empire—on the overtly coercive Irish Constabulary.

On 10 October 1867 Defence Minister Colonel Theodore ★Haultain's Armed Constabulary Act passed into law, and Lieutenant-Colonel Thomas ★McDonnell was appointed founding head of the new body. Establishing a genuine police (albeit semi-military in orientation) proved difficult, and lack of progress led to McDonnell's replacement by Lieutenant-Colonel G.S. ★Whitmore in March 1868. Though the new commandant's personality was abrasive, he was a military officer of great organisational talent. This proved essential when in mid 1868 the force was transformed into a purely military organisation, a tactical response to the armed Maori resistance to state authority led by warrior chiefs ★Titokowaru on the western seaboard of the North Island and ★Te Kooti on the eastern. In this final phase of the ★New Zealand Wars, much of the fighting on the Crown side was conducted by men who were sworn constables. The colony's initial striking ('Field') force, placed under McDonnell, was hastily cobbled together at Patea. Amid disorganisation, severe losses to the 'rebels' occurred, and after the Crown's defeat at Titokowaru's headquarters at Te Ngutu-o-te-manu, the police-troops of the Armed Constabulary's 5th Division mutinied. The unit was disbanded, McDonnell dispensed with, and all armed constables placed under full military discipline. Whitmore (soon to be a full colonel) now personally took over all colonial forces as, in effect, commander-in-chief. He decreed that all newcomers to the fighting forces were to come within the Armed Constabulary purview, and began to enlist and train a 'better class' of men. Taking advantage of the European monopoly on steamship travel by rapidly switching his troops from seaboard to seaboard, Whitmore showed considerable military prowess in preventing the 'rebels' making anything more than short-term gains. Moreover, severe defeats were inflicted on the forces of the resistant chiefs, such as those of Te Kooti at Ngatapa. But they remained uncaptured—indeed the last shots of the wars were not fired until 1872—and so in 1869 the 'war policy' ministry fell. Its successor's conviction that the backbone of the rebellion had finally been broken, and that the rebel forces no longer posed any serious danger to state or settlers, left the Armed Constabulary in an uncertain position.

The new administration, led by William Fox, determined that the Armed Constabulary should 'demilitarise', reverting to its role as primarily an armed *police* force. Having stripped Whitmore of his position, ostensibly on health grounds, in August 1868, Donald ★McLean, the Defence Minister, appointed as Commissioner of Armed Constabulary St John Branigan, who had founded Otago Province's acclaimed paramilitary police force and whose advice on the Armed Constabulary's future had strongly influenced Fox. The 'great demilitariser' established in practice (as opposed to the theoretical position of the 1840s) the first centrally controlled police force with a colony-wide mandate. A body of 'ragged and war-worn soldiers' would be turned into a 'small but highly trained Force' of disciplined paramilitary police. Branigan aimed to concentrate his force on a small number of defensive frontier posts, to avoid offensive measures, and eventually to reduce a 2000-strong body to 600 elite men. Those constables who survived an intensive culling process were to be trained and disciplined at a depot at Mount Cook in Wellington, supplemented by 'superior' recruits from other paramilitary Australasian forces attracted by good pay and conditions. Demilitarising tendencies were embodied in the Armed Constabulary Amendment Act of September 1869.

By mid 1870 the Armed Constabulary had been reduced to a total of 776 all ranks, increasing numbers of whom were engaged in labouring on public works. Colonial Treasurer Julius Vogel's plans to open up the frontier with grandiose development schemes were seen, *inter alia*, as the key to suppressing Maori insurrectionary activities. Such works, including building roads and bridges and draining swamps, could be carried out by armed constables concurrently with patrolling and surveillance. Where no provincial police

Armed Constabulary

Officers of the Armed Constabulary's Field Force at Parihaka in 1881. The commanding officer, Major J.M. Roberts, is seated in front, sixth from the left (*Alexander Turnbull Library, G-179521-1/1*)

were stationed, as in Poverty Bay, the armed constables carried out civil duties in addition to their semi-military policing duties. As pacification of the countryside became more apparent, the 'best' men were increasingly placed on civil duties. Branigan employed very few Maori police. The Native Contingents patrolling the Urewera borders (the 'Arawa Flying Column') worked alongside the Armed Constabulary but were not formally part of it. Among other things, this would change after Branigan lapsed into insanity in early 1871. Branigan had shown signs of wanting to take the demilitarisation process too far, too fast, for his political masters, even McLean. With his replacement by a military man, William Moule, it was confirmed that the armed police would continue to be a viable 'standing army' with a capacity for rapid mobility to meet emergencies. During 1874–75 the hundred or so members of the Flying Column were incorporated into the Armed Constabulary, leading to its first significant Maori membership since demilitarisation. By March 1875 'race problems' were so quiescent that Moule gained permission to go on long-term leave. Acting Commissioner William Lyon, another military officer, further slowed down the demilitarisation process. But the sight of armed policemen playing a key role both in McLean's conciliatory Maori policies—he was also Native Minister—and on public works only highlighted the anachronistic nature of a sizeable 'occupation police'.

Meanwhile in 1870 a financial crisis for Auckland Province offered the central government the opportunity to pursue its objective of rationalising the policing structure in New Zealand: it took over the policing function in Auckland, all of whose provincial constables had been absorbed into the Armed Constabulary by 1 June. The presence of a regional civil police within the Armed Constabulary accelerated its evolution away from overt towards benign coercion. In 1873, for example, permission was gained for a departure in Auckland District from the system of transferring police rapidly between stations, a practice which had been established early in the colony to prevent familiarity with the populace. Outside the Auckland region the Armed Constabulary, by this time, was increasingly referred to as the 'Field Force' to distinguish its constables from the provincial civil police. The central government's long-standing aspiration to base all policing services as well as its 'standing army' on the Constabulary became reality with the abolition of the provinces in 1876. Arrangements for a new combined military–police force, planned to total about 430 police and 350 soldiers, were completed in July 1877. Given the option, most provincial constables joined the new organisation's Police Branch, together with 109 members of the Armed Constabulary who had been doing police and quasi-police duties. Very few of the Maori Armed Constabulary men were among them, leaving the bulk of the Maori personnel in the military wing. The new organisation, headed by Moule, was called the New Zealand Constabulary Force, the omission of the word 'armed' reflecting the gradual process of demilitarisation of control of the populace by the state. Yet so evocative was the old Armed Constabulary name that it continued to be used frequently for the Force, or sometimes its military wing (also called, informally, the Field Force at first). Its use at times in official communications helped to further confuse the nomenclature issue. Although they would operate jointly in the event of any danger to the state, the new organisation's policing and military wings remained operationally separate. The latter, the Reserve Division, was superimposed upon the colony-wide network of police districts. The soldier–police continued much as before: drilling, training, carrying out public works, and surveilling conquered Maori populations.

John Sheehan, the Defence Minister in Sir George ★Grey's 'radical' government of 1877–79, anxious to end 'McLeanite' influences, quickly forced Moule to resign from his positions as both commissioner and acting head of the colony's defence bureaucracy. On 1 January 1878 Whitmore replaced him as Commissioner of Constabulary, despite being a member of Grey's ministry, while Lieutenant-Colonel H.E. Reader became acting Under-Secretary for Defence. In continuing to 'demilitarise' control of the colony, the authorities differentiated even more clearly between the two coercive wings of the state, enshrining this in separate seniority lists. In 1878 Whitmore withdrew all issue firearms from foot police, so that henceforth weapons would only be available to police constables in emergencies (although protests led to the reissue of revolvers). As a result of another of the periodic ★Russian scares in that year, reinforced by the growing official perception

Armed Constabulary

that the colonial frontier was well on the way to being 'tamed', the Constabulary's military wing had begun to focus on meeting threats from external rather than internal enemies. In 1883, the Constabulary built its last defensible military post against Maori attack; in the same year, the Reserve Division's name was officially changed to Field Force.

Meanwhile the fall of Grey brought down the politician-bureaucrat Whitmore. In December 1879 Reader had the Commissionership of Constabulary added to his responsibilities. He soon struck problems, as a recession in the economy led, from 1880, to a series of redundancies and reductions in rank and pay that adversely affected morale. This was especially so among the military component of the Force, whose pay and conditions had been worse than those of the police from the outset. Moreover, there was no compensatory military 'glamour' for the military, given the success of the Crown's policy of conciliation, marked for example by the 1881 surrender of the Maori King. The only sizeable mobilisation occurred that year when more than 1500 Constabulary men and other troops advanced upon 'passive resistance' chief Te Whiti o Rongomai's ★Parihaka settlement—to be welcomed with gifts by singing women and children. This did not prevent arrests, mass expulsions, and the sacking of the village, but a dashing military operation it certainly was not. Henceforward, potentially problematic 'native areas' in Taranaki and elsewhere, hitherto monitored from soldier–police garrisons that the Maori inhabitants considered provocative, would be controlled under a 'one-policeman policy'. Coercive backup would be called in only when justified by the reports of the sole-charge local constable's surveillance. In fact the Constabulary Force constables never did experience much 'field action', though they were sometimes used to control European populations, as for example when the Armed Constabulary was deployed to Westland to prevent sectarian disorder among Irish miners in 1868. The Reserve/Field troops did little but toil away in backblock areas. But at least this provided employment. In a time of depression-induced retrenchment, indeed, the Constabulary Force could be very selective. Maori soldier–police were especially vulnerable to cuts, although the final colonial police to remain outside the Constabulary—twenty-nine 'Native Constables' attached to Resident Magistracies—were transferred to the Police Branch in 1882.

In 1880 imperial harbour defence expert Colonel P.H. ★Scratchley had recommended the provision of an artillery-based coastal defence force to protect the colony against attack by an external enemy. Not until 1885, under the influence of yet another Russian scare, was action taken along these lines, Scratchley's plans having by this time been modified by the Governor, Major-General Sir William ★Jervois. These developments complemented the state strategy of lessening coercive control over the New Zealand population: troops would normally be oriented towards meeting the threat from external aggressors. In fact, it was deemed no longer appropriate for a single organisation to discharge both police and defence functions, and the establishment of a distinct standing army was under contemplation. Withdrawing from the interior, leaving civil police to fill any resulting vacuums, many of the soldier–police were soon busily engaged in mounting guns at the four main ports. Plans for separate artillery, torpedo, and engineering units within the military wing of the Constabulary Force were announced in April, and responsibility for the reorganisation was placed in the hands of Whitmore, who became the first commander of the New Zealand Forces on 27 April 1885. In July Major Walter ★Gudgeon replaced an ill Reader as Commissioner of Constabulary on an acting basis, but following Reader's death later in the year Whitmore assumed both the Commissionership and the Under-Secretaryship for Defence in addition to his command of the forces. In the event of war it was envisaged that the permanent military core would need to be supplemented by other forces, and in 1886 the government sought to establish such support by offering retirees from the Constabulary Force the opportunity to take up land at special settlements. As with the ★military settlers of the 1860s, such soldier–police would become soldier–farmers in case the frontier was not yet fully tamed. But in general terms the frontier was deemed to be effectively pacified by this time. The Constabulary Force, established to handle the transition from overtly coercive to benign social control, had served its purpose. By May 1886 all the remaining Field Force troops had left the 'Maori districts', and parliamentary action was underway to formalise the separation of army and police. The ★Defence Act created the ★Permanent Militia, which was in effect the old Field Force of the Constabulary Force in its recently remodelled form, while the Police Force Act turned the now largely unarmed civil police into the New Zealand Police Force. The legislation still linked the two organisations together both in theory (allowing for troops to assist the police in an emergency and vice versa) and in practice (police recruits were to be taken entirely from the military, for example). Moreover, Whitmore, soon to be promoted to major-general, was not only the ranking military officer and defence bureaucrat in the colony but also, briefly, the founding Commissioner of the New Zealand Police Force. But substantively, from 1 September 1886 the military and police were separate entities in New Zealand. The New Zealand Constabulary

Armed merchant cruisers

Force, and therefore the Armed Constabulary (however defined), had come to an end.

R.S. Hill, *The History of Policing in New Zealand, Volume 2: The Colonial Frontier Tamed, New Zealand Policing in Transition, 1867–1886* (GP Books, Wellington, 1989).

RICHARD S. HILL

Armed merchant cruisers For centuries belligerent powers had impressed merchant ships into their lines of battle whenever war broke out. That became less profitable from the mid nineteenth century after the development of the steam-powered armoured warship greatly enlarged the widening gulf between the fighting qualities of purpose-built warships and converted merchant ships. Nevertheless, the exploits of fast commerce raiders during the American Civil War and the Spanish–American War encouraged many governments to subsidise merchant vessels suitable for conversion to auxiliary cruisers. Fitted with six or eight 6-inch guns and rudimentary fire control equipment, auxiliary cruisers served most major navies in each world war. In both conflicts German ships operating as disguised commerce raiders claimed victims in New Zealand waters using mines and gunfire (see ENEMY OPERATIONS IN NEW ZEALAND WATERS). Allied armed merchant cruisers performed more conventional trade protection duties, freeing regular cruisers for fleet duties. New Zealand did not operate any armed merchant cruisers during the ★First World War, but the *Aotearoa*—the Union Steam Ship Company's planned consort for the trans-Pacific liner *Niagara*—was completed as HMS *Avenger*. She was sunk by *U-69* in June 1917.

Although submarines had sunk many armed merchant cruisers in 1917–18, Great Britain continued to subsidise liners between the wars and to maintain stocks of suitable guns at depots around the world. So, when war broke out in 1939, the Union Company's 18-knot trans-Tasman liner *Monowai* proceeded to Devonport dockyard for conversion. The decks of the 10,852-ton ship had been designed to take guns, and the weapons had been sent out to New Zealand, but despite those preparations the conversion took from October 1939 until August 1940. When completed *Monowai* mounted eight turn-of-the-century 6-inch guns, two 3-inch and six 20 mm anti-aircraft guns, some machine-guns and eight ★depth charges. Radar and a couple of extra 20 mm guns were added in June 1942. She had a crew of 366. *Monowai* was the best known of the armed merchant cruisers on the ★New Zealand Station, but three others each spent a few months here in 1940–42—HMS *Hector*, HMCS *Prince Robert*, and HMS *Ascania*.

Monowai escorted convoys, helped HMS *Achilles* to search for German auxiliary cruisers, and patrolled to Ocean and Nauru islands when time permitted. Occasionally she also carried small drafts of troops. Most of the time the work was uneventful. *Monowai*'s only casualties occurred on 30 December 1941 in the placid Hauraki Gulf; a gun-crew error led to a cordite charge blowing the breech of the Port No. 1 gun back into the gun-crew, killing four men and injuring several others. Barely more than a fortnight later *Monowai* had her only contact with an enemy warship. On the afternoon of 16 January 1942 she had just started escorting the troopship *Taroona* back from Fiji when, sixteen kilometres south-west of Suva, shells began exploding around her. The aggressor was the Japanese submarine *I-20*, which had surfaced to use her 5.5-inch deck gun after missing with torpedoes that *Monowai*'s captain, G.R. Deverell, at first mistook for explosions from a high-level air attack. The Japanese captain also probably got more than he bargained for when *Monowai* replied with her 6-inch guns. He crash-dived just as the last of *Monowai*'s twenty-three rounds found the range. Neither ship suffered damage in the brief exchange.

By late 1942, with surface raiders practically eliminated, the Admiralty withdrew the vulnerable armed merchant cruisers to quieter waters away from the submarine threat and began converting them for other duties. In April 1943 *Monowai* left Auckland for the United Kingdom, where she was paid off on 18 June. Converted into an assault landing ship for the British Ministry of War Transport, she served as a troopship until 1946, when she entered dockyard hands for a lengthy refit for a return to the trans-Tasman passenger run.

R.J. McDougall, *New Zealand Naval Vessels* (GP Books, Wellington, 1989); T.D. Taylor, *New Zealand's Naval Story* (A.H. & A.W. Reed, Wellington, 1948).

GAVIN McLEAN

Armistice Day, 11 November, commemorates the end of hostilities on the ★Western Front with the signing of the Armistice at 11 a.m. on 11 November 1918. Although eventually overshadowed by ★Anzac Day, it was marked solemnly in New Zealand until the 1960s, with a two-minute silence being observed at 11 a.m. It remains the major commemorative event in the United Kingdom.

Armour New Zealand troops first received armoured support on the ★Western Front during the Battle of the Somme in 1916. Four tanks supported their attack on Flers on 15 September, the first time such weapons had been used in action. They became a standard support element in the next two years, but the formation of a New Zealand tank battalion was forestalled by the end of the war. Little attention was given by the New

Armour

A New Zealand Sherman tank moves forward accompanied by infantrymen of 26th Battalion at Zagonara in the Senio sector during the final stages of the Italian campaign in 1945 (*War History Collection, Alexander Turnbull Library, F-9151-35mm-DA*)

Zealand military authorities to armour between the world wars. Not until March 1939 did New Zealand acquire its first armoured vehicles, six Bren Gun Carriers. An open-topped lightly armoured carrier vehicle, mounting a Bren light machine-gun, the ubiquitous Bren Gun Carrier (later called Universal Carrier) was developed as a scout vehicle and general carrier for armoured units and as a carrier for platoons of infantry battalions. As Bren Gun Carriers slowly arrived in New Zealand, they equipped the mechanising mounted rifle regiments, which were retitled as Light Armoured Fighting Vehicle (LAFV) Regiments in January 1942 (see MOUNTED RIFLES). Armoured forces in New Zealand were rapidly expanded; during the course of 1942 about 400 Stuart tanks and 255 Valentine tanks in the country, along with various types of scout cars and armoured cars, entered service with the home forces.

New Zealand's first armoured unit was the Divisional Cavalry Regiment of the 2nd New Zealand Division, which was equipped with South African–made Marmon–Herrington armoured cars in February 1940. These were replaced in October 1941 by the mechanically unreliable Mark VI light tanks, carrying only machine-guns. The regiment's need for a capable reconnaissance vehicle was finally met in July 1942 by fast little M5 Stuart or 'Honey' light tanks. One was converted to a command vehicle for divisional commander Lieutenant-General Sir Bernard *Freyberg; it carried extra radios and a dummy cannon. Powerful Staghound armoured cars replaced the Bren carriers and Stuarts in July 1943 in preparation for the *Italian campaign. However, there being little need for fast armoured cars in the slow grind up the Italian peninsula, the Divisional Cavalry was converted to an infantry battalion at the end of 1944.

The decision to form an armoured brigade for service with the 2nd New Zealand Division in the Middle East was made in July 1941. The 1st New Zealand Army Tank Brigade was established in October 1941 at Waiouru, soon after receiving its first batch of twenty Valentine tanks. The threat of Japanese invasion, however, ensured that the brigade was never sent overseas, despite Freyberg's calls for it in August 1942 after his infantry had suffered from a lack of British armoured support. The brigade was eventually broken up to provide reinforcements for the Middle East; its remnant served with 3rd Division in the *Solomons campaign as a Valentine-equipped independent tank squadron, seeing action only at Nissan Island in September 1944.

In the Middle East, the armoured problem was resolved by the conversion in late 1942 of 4th New Zealand Infantry Brigade to an armoured brigade. After several months training on a few Crusader and Grant tanks, 4th New Zealand Armoured Brigade began to receive new Sherman medium tanks. Fast and reliable, with thick armour and a stabilised 75 mm gun and usually two machine-guns, the M4 Sherman was the first British or American tank that could engage German tanks on a relatively equal footing, despite the disadvantage of a high silhouette. At full strength, the brigade possessed about 160 Shermans. The 4th Armoured Brigade served with the 2nd New Zealand Division in Italy, where the rugged terrain and static nature of the operations limited the effectiveness of tanks. Mud, mines and well-camouflaged German positions exacted a heavy toll on the New Zealand tanks, and the Shermans were mainly used as infantry support weapons or as mobile artillery. To meet the threat of the heavily armoured German Tiger tanks some Sherman tanks were rearmed with more powerful 17-pounder cannon in December 1944. From June 1944 the 7th Anti-Tank Regiment was equipped with M10 tank destroyers—a 3-inch cannon on a Sherman chassis—which were used, like the Shermans, in an infantry support role. The 4th Armoured Brigade was disbanded in December 1945.

In 1948 New Zealand armoured units were organised into three armoured regiments, and an armoured car regiment. Training was undertaken at the Royal New Zealand Armoured Corps School at Waiouru. Although no armoured units were sent to the *Korean War, regular force members of the RNZAC crewed a 'Kiwi tank' in a British armoured regiment. In New Zealand, units were equipped with Second World War–era Valentine tanks, augmented by eleven Centurion tanks in 1953. A fourth armoured regiment, Queen Alexandra's Armoured Regiment, was established in 1958. There was a gradual reduction in the armoured forces throughout the 1960s, and by 1963 the armoured regiments had been reduced to squadrons. M41 Walker Bulldog light tanks replaced the last of the ageing Valentines in 1960. The introduction of M113

37

Army camps

armoured personnel carriers in 1970 brought about a reorganisation of armoured units, with two reconnaissance squadrons re-forming as APC squadrons, and two armoured squadrons amalgamating to form a 'cavalry' squadron of M41 tanks and M113s. The seventy-eight M113s have been the mainstay of New Zealand's armoured forces. Essentially an aluminium box able to carry ten fully equipped troops, the M113 has proved to be an extremely reliable machine. Most New Zealand M113s mount a small turret with two machine-guns. Despite rebuilding in 1982, the M113 APC is considered obsolete, and extra armour had to be urgently acquired before these vehicles could be deployed in Bosnia–Herzegovina with New Zealand's peace-keeping company during the 1990s. Twenty-six small, fast Scorpion light tanks were acquired in 1982 for reconnaissance and fire support, and to provide a basic level of tank training. Plagued with technical problems, they were phased out in 1998.

Army camps have traditionally been the tents or bivouacs and horse lines of an army, either on campaign or during training. Camps are usually sited for their proximity to good communications and open areas for training, though some ★fortifications and ★coast defences have become army camps after their original function of fortified defence has lapsed. Most camps in New Zealand have been temporary affairs, usually annual training camps for ★Volunteer Force and later ★Territorial Force units on leased farms, racecourses, or showgrounds. Mobilisation camps during war have also tended to be of a temporary nature under canvas at racecourses, showgrounds, or parks. Over time wooden barracks and amenities have been erected, followed by drains, roads, and water supply. More permanent camps have acquired properly constructed barracks, offices, workshops, storehouses, training areas, and other facilities. The first permanent camps were established at Mount Cook in Wellington and Point Britomart in Auckland, which housed units of the ★British Army in New Zealand. Semi-permanent camps with wooden barracks were established at Otahuhu and Onehunga during the ★New Zealand Wars. Following the departure of the British regiments, the Mount Cook Barracks became the headquarters of the ★Armed Constabulary and later ★Permanent Militia. In 1892 the dilapidated condition of the barracks led to an outbreak of typhoid, which killed nine soldiers. The site at Mount Cook continued to grow, with the Permanent Militia in 1901 taking over the neighbouring prison to serve as a store and barracks.

In 1914 temporary camps were established at racecourses, parks, or showgrounds for the mobilisation of the ★New Zealand Expeditionary Force. Reinforcement camps for the force were established at Trentham (Upper Hutt), Featherston (Wairarapa), Narrow Neck (Takapuna), Avondale (Auckland), and Awapuni (Palmerston North). The principal camp, at Trentham, was rendered more suitable because of its rail link and proximity to Wellington, the Hutt River nearby, and the facilities of the racecourse and rifle ranges. By mid 1915 there were about 8000 men there, mostly under canvas. The crowded conditions led to epidemics of pneumonia, measles, and meningitis, causing the deaths of thirty-three soldiers. As a result the camp was reorganised; drains were dug and more permanent facilities erected. By 1918 the camp accommodated 4500 men in wooden huts. In the Middle East 1NZEF's first base was at Zeitoun, ten kilometres from Cairo. From 1916 the main camp was in England, at Sling on the Salisbury plains. A dreary, lonely camp of wooden huts, it was distinguished only by the New Zealand badges carved into the chalk hillsides. By 1917 Sling Camp had reached its limit of 4000 men, and subsidiary camps were established at Brocton (Staffordshire), Boscombe (Dorset), Grantham (Lincolnshire), and Ewshot (Hampshire). Closer to the front line New Zealand troops were either billeted with French civilians or accommodated in tented camps.

After the ★First World War the Mount Cook Barracks remained the principal headquarters, depot, and barracks for the New Zealand Military Forces. However, in 1931 the military authorities were forced to relocate the depots, workshops, and barracks from Mount Cook to Trentham following the decision to build the National Museum and War Memorial on the Mount Cook site. Trentham was upgraded and expanded to become the army's principal depot and training camp. In 1920 the industrial school at Burnham (thirty-five kilometres south of Christchurch) was acquired as an ordnance depot, and a small permanent camp for an ordnance depot and houses for permanent staff was established at Ngaruawahia.

When the ★Second World War began, plans were in train to establish mobilisation camps in each of the three military districts—at Burnham, Trentham, and Papakura. Work on constructing cookhouses, stores, and barracks began immediately. Trentham was upgraded and expanded, while new camps were established at Papakura and Burnham. While the Papakura Camp was being constructed, its overflow was accommodated at an expanded Ngaruawahia Camp. A camp was also planned for Waiouru, which with its surrounding area of uninhabited tussock land was an ideal site for mechanised manœuvres and artillery firing. Construction began in June 1940. The first stage, including a hospital, chapels, theatre, and other facilities to make life more bearable in the bleak surroundings, had been completed within six months. Overseas, 2NZEF's principal camp was at Maadi, twelve kilometres south of

Army camps

Cairo, which by 1941 had become a prefabricated town, complete with sports and welfare facilities. Prefabricated huts gradually replaced tents at Helwan (used until mid 1941) and other smaller camps.

In New Zealand the decision to expand the Territorial Force in 1940 led to more camps being established at racecourses and showgrounds around the country. Full mobilisation in December 1941 saw even more parks, schools, racecourses, and showgrounds pressed into service as camps, and by 1942 there were hundreds of army camps. At Whangarei, for example, there were army camps at forty-two sites, with nearly 3000 buildings. From June 1942 American troops were camped in the greater Auckland and Wellington areas. Most camps were concentrated in Northland, Auckland, Palmerston North, Wellington, Blenheim, and south of Christchurch. Work on a major camp at Linton, just south of Palmerston North, chosen for its central location, began in February 1942; by the end of the war it had 182 permanent buildings and more than a thousand barrack huts.

After the Second World War the New Zealand Army was based at five major camps—Papakura, Waiouru, Linton, Trentham, and Burnham—with smaller camps at Fort Cautley (Takapuna), Hopuhopu (Ngaruawahia), Fort Dorset (Wellington), and Addington (Christchurch). Waiouru was the army's principal base after the war. Training facilities, including most Army Schools, were gradually concentrated there from 1950, and most of the recruit training under the ★compulsory military training and later National Service schemes was undertaken at Waiouru. There was a continual aggregation of land in the vicinity of Waiouru, the size of the training area eventually reaching 36,000 hectares by the 1970s. The place of Waiouru as the 'home' of the ★New Zealand Army was underscored by the establishment of the Queen Elizabeth II Army Memorial Museum there in 1978. Trentham served as the principal administrative base, while Linton housed support and engineer units. The 1st Battalion, New Zealand Regiment (later 1st Battalion, RNZIR) was stationed at Terendak Camp in Malaya from 1961, which it shared with other Commonwealth units. From September 1971 the battalion was based at the Dieppe Barracks in Singapore. In all the camps there was a gradual move towards better accommodation, draughty wooden dormitory-style barracks being replaced by twin- or three-storeyed accommodation blocks of hollow-block construction. Welfare and sporting facilities were improved and family housing was established at the camps.

A major restructuring of army camps began in the late 1980s. The Resource Management Review of 1988 recommended a rationalisation of army property, at a

Waiouru Military Camp in 1941 (*Waiouru Army Museum, 1988.1045*)

Army Department

time when many buildings, of prefabricated wartime vintage, had become very run down. At the same time, the imminent return of 1RNZIR from Singapore demanded accommodation for about 700 men and their families. Linton was therefore substantially upgraded, with 146 houses and six barracks blocks being built. There was a reshuffling of other units among the camps, with the general approach being to concentrate field units and headquarters together at either Linton or Trentham. Virtually all the remaining army properties were sold over the next decade, including Papakura, which was vacated in 1991.

There are currently four army camps: Burnham, Linton, Trentham, and Waiouru. Some army units, most notably the *Special Air Service, are based at RNZAF Hobsonville (see AIR FORCE BASES). Burnham, occupying 520 hectares, has about 1000 soldiers and 900 dependants. Trentham continues to serve as the principal depot and administrative base of the New Zealand Army, the New Zealand Land Command having been stationed there since 1998. With most regular units stationed at it, Linton is the principal base of the New Zealand Army; it houses about 1700 personnel. A further 900 are accommodated at Waiouru, the principal training establishment, which has most *army schools and the Officer Cadet School. Smaller bases dotted around the country serve as depots for Territorial units.

Army Department, formally constituted on 30 November 1950, included both the *New Zealand Army and those public servants responsible for its administration and financial control. It had previously existed in de facto form since November 1937, when an Army Board assumed responsibility for command and control of the Army and the Under-Secretary of Defence became the Army Secretary. The term Army Department came into general use during 1938 in place of Department of Defence. The department was subsumed within the Ministry of Defence on 1 January 1964, at which time the Army Secretary became the Deputy Secretary of Defence (Army). (See DEFENCE, DEPARTMENT OF; DEFENCE, MINISTRY OF)

Army Educational and Welfare Service (AEWS) Education for New Zealand soldiers (apart from military education undertaken as part of their training) began in 1915, with the *YMCA running lectures and classes to stimulate mental activity and assist in their eventual rehabilitation into civilian life. A comprehensive education programme was implemented in England in 1918. Educational programmes were also organised for soldiers in Egypt, France, and on *troopships. Classes were held in a wide variety of subjects ranging from civics and history to woolclassing and mechanical engineering. Education programmes for soldiers were not re-established until the *Second World War, with the Workers' Educational Association holding infrequent lectures for the army personnel in New Zealand. At the urging of the Director General of Education, Dr Clarence Beeby, an education scheme to maintain the morale of otherwise bored soldiers and assist with their rehabilitation was developed. The Army Educational and Welfare Service was duly established in 1942. It offered study and vocational training courses, ran a library service, and produced a current affairs bulletin. Educational services were also offered to the RNZAF and RNZN. Overseas, AEWS was designated the New Zealand Education and Rehabilitation Service. It continued to operate after the Second World War, running continuing education programmes and cultural activities for the three services. Not until the 1970s were its remaining educational and welfare functions taken over by the *Royal New Zealand Army Education Corps.

Army schools are the principal institutions where soldiers are trained. The primary focus of most schools is to teach particular technical skills relating to one particular corps, while some schools provide initial training for Regular Force cadets or teach skills applicable for higher levels of command. The development of an effective system of instruction was a stop–start affair in New Zealand. In an attempt to raise the standard of *Volunteer Force officers and NCOs, a School of Instruction was established in 1885 at Mount Cook in Wellington, but it was closed three years later. From 1902, a new school offered brief courses in specialist subjects such as garrison artillery, infantry drills, and engineering, but it, too, only lasted three years. A form of army school emerged at Trentham Military Camp during the *First World War, preparing men for service with 1NZEF. At the front, the need for specialised training led to the establishment in France of a series of divisional schools in such subjects as gas, machineguns, sniping, and tactics. They were staffed by experienced officers and NCOs, often those recovering from illness or injury. Schools were also attached to the main training camps in England, the most important being at Sling on the Salisbury Plains. Although a Central School of Instruction was established at Trentham after the war, it soon fell victim to economies in 1921, and continued only in a curtailed form as the Small Arms School. As the international situation deteriorated, a new attempt to establish an effective school was made in 1937, with the establishment of the Army School of Instruction at Trentham. By the outbreak of war two years later, it had 543 students, including 172 RNZAF recruits, who were being taught a variety of technical and staff subjects as well as basic recruit training. During the ★Second World War, signals, administrative, drill, small arms, forest and jungle warfare, and other wings were added to the school. In 1941 a separate School of Artillery was established at Fort Dorset and Trentham, followed by an Armoured Fighting Vehicle School at Waiouru, and a Tactical School at Wanganui to train junior officers and NCOs in company-level tactics. After training many thousands of soldiers, these schools were closed in 1944. New Zealand troops overseas received specialist training at a number of schools in the Middle East, which imparted skills ranging from motor mechanics to cookery.

A substantial reorganisation of Army training followed the end of hostilities in 1945, and the focus shifted from Wellington to Waiouru. Between 1948 and 1950 the Army School of Instruction was replaced by eleven separate schools: the Tactical School, responsible for staff and tactical training; the Regular Force Cadet School, responsible for basic training of young regular recruits, either as instructors or soldier-tradesmen; the Armoured School; the School of Artillery; the School of Infantry; the School of Signals; the School of Army Administration; the Medical School (located at Burnham); the School of Military Engineering (Linton); the Royal New Zealand Army Service Corps School; the Royal New Zealand Electrical and Mechanical Engineers School, teaching mechanics, fitters, welders, armourers, and other trades. Some new schools have been established and others closed in the ensuing half-century. Currently there are thirteen army schools, divided between the Army Logistics Centre (at Trentham) and the Army Combat Centre (at Waiouru).

Artillery The first artillery used in New Zealand was ordnance acquired by Maori tribes from European traders or shipwrecks. The stubby, large-calibre, short-range carronade (made by the Carron Iron Founding and Shipping Company in Scotland) was especially popular. Such weapons bestowed mana on their owners and were useful for both defensive and offensive purposes. For example, in 1832 Nga Puhi assembled a siege train of eleven guns for their campaign against Ngai Te Rangi, who themselves possessed several carronades.

Artillery was first used by the ★British Army in New Zealand during the Northern War of 1845–46, with the British dragging an artillery train of nine cannon (including three 32-pounders) thirty kilometres to batter Ruapekapeka Pa for two weeks. In the early 1850s an assortment of cannon were mounted at Point Britomart in Auckland as defence against a possible Maori attack; no other artillery existed in the colony. A major technological leap was the introduction of rifled breech-loading Armstrong guns, which were first brought to New Zealand in 1861. These weapons possessed superior range and accuracy to the previous smooth-bored muzzle-loading cannon. Three 6-pounder Armstrong guns were used at Rangiriri and at Orakau, though with little impact on the Maori entrenchments. At Gate Pa the British artillery train included one 110-pounder and two 40-pounder Armstrong guns, firing more than 3000 kilograms of shot and shell at the pa to little effect. The British Army left its cannon behind in New Zealand, and they were taken over by the ★Volunteer Force artillery corps and the ★Armed Constabulary. Nothing else was done to acquire artillery until 1878 when twenty-two 7-inch and 64-pounder guns were obtained for harbour defence. These were supplemented by 6-inch and 8-inch RBL guns and Nordenfelt and Hotchkiss quick-firing guns ordered following the Russian scare of 1885 (see COAST DEFENCES). Some 9-pounder Armstrong guns were acquired for the field artillery in 1886. Although the artillery was described by Lieutenant-Colonel F.J. ★Fox in 1893 as being in a 'terribly bad state', little was done until 1900, when the Volunteer artillery batteries were equipped with 15-pounder quick-firing field guns. Their limited range and ability to fire only by line of sight meant that these weapons were already obsolescent.

In 1911 modern 18-pounder field guns and 4.5-inch howitzers were acquired. With advanced recoil systems, they could fire more quickly, at greater ranges, and with greater accuracy than their predecessors. Complex sighting devices made possible accurate indirect fire with these weapons. A quick-firing gun, with a range of 5600 metres, the 18-pounder was the heaviest weapon of its type at the time. The 4.5-inch howitzer fired a 16-kilogram high explosive shell up to 6300 metres. Three batteries of four 18-pounders and a battery of 4.5-inch howitzers were taken overseas by 1NZEF in 1914, and went into action for the first time at ★Gallipoli. With their ability to fire over the razor-backed hills, the howitzers proved particularly effective, whereas the 18-pounders' flat trajectory limited their effectiveness because of crest clearance problems. Moreover, their shrapnel fire was unsuitable for cutting barbed wire or demolishing trenches; not till August 1915 could New Zealand's 18-pounder batteries fire high explosive shells, though ammunition supply remained severely limited.

Modern artillery tactics were developed on the ★Western Front. In defence, pre-planned barrages were fired by artillery on to the approaches to friendly trenches in response to 'S.O.S.' flares from defending infantry. Gunners also reacted to intelligence from infantry or forward observation posts, dropping concentrations of shells on any enemy that were spotted. The most important tactical innovation of the ★First World War was the 'creeping barrage', in which

Artillery

A New Zealand field gun in action in Flanders on New Year's Day 1918 (*RSA Collection, Alexander Turnbull Library, PA1-f-091-0402*)

'curtains' of high explosive and shrapnel were programmed to move across the battlefield in timed 'lifts', cutting barbed wire and neutralising the enemy defenders. Eighteen-pounders were used for the immediate covering barrage, while 4.5-inch howitzers bombarded enemy artillery and special targets. The attacking infantry followed the barrage as closely as possible to deal with the defenders still dazed or inside their bunkers. Further barrages protected the infantry as they consolidated their gains. The scale and complexity of artillery barrages was demonstrated during the Messines offensive in 1917: the New Zealand creeping barrage employed twenty 'lifts' as well as continuous counter-battery and standing barrages. More than 160,000 shells were fired in support of the operation. Scientific improvements dramatically improved the performance of artillery. From 1917 improvements to the 18-pounders increased their range, while new percussion fuses greatly increased the lethality of high explosive shells as well as reducing the churning up of the ground caused by the bombardments. Accurate surveying and meteorology allowed for 'predicted fire', in which a bombardment would fall on an enemy without the warning provided by 'registration' shots. New Zealand artillerymen were employing these new techniques with good effect by the end of the war.

After the First World War, New Zealand acquired heavy artillery in the form of 6-inch howitzers and 60-pounder guns, and 3.7-inch mountain howitzers. In the 1930s the artillery was slowly mechanised, horses being replaced with rented civilian vehicles, and the cannon receiving pneumatic tyres. Eighteen-pounders and 4.5-inch howitzers continued to provide the mainstay of the New Zealand artillery. Training opportunities were limited, and when New Zealand entered the ★Second World War it was with obsolescent ordnance.

Only in 1940 did the 2nd New Zealand Division replace its old 18-pounders and 4.5-inch howitzers with the most famous of New Zealand's artillery pieces, the rugged, dependable, and accurate 25-pounder. Mounted on a circular base plate for firing, which allowed a 360° traverse, it could throw an 11-kilogram high explosive shell up to 11,500 metres. A limber carried ammunition and other ancillaries. Its versatility was demonstrated by its effective use as an anti-tank weapon. The 2nd New Zealand Division had seventy-two of these weapons, organised in three regiments of three batteries. Under the direction of the CRA, Brigadier Reginald ★Miles, the New Zealand Divisional Artillery was shaped into a formidable instrument. Miles's influence was especially significant in the development of barrage schemes. Nevertheless, the capability of the artillery was hindered in the early stages of the ★North African campaign by several tactical requirements, apart from a general shortage of ammunition. In the first place, it was necessary to site the 25-pounders well forward to serve as dual role anti-tank/field artillery. While grappling with enemy tanks, the field artillery was distracted from its task of providing the close support of attacking infantry. This was particularly evident during the Crusader offensive of 1941, in which enemy tanks inflicted heavy losses on the field artillery. Second, the emphasis in the early part of the North African campaign upon brigade-level operations made difficult the coordination of the whole division's artillery. Not until mid 1942 did changing tactical approaches and the onset of positional warfare at El Alamein allow these problems to be overcome. Under the command of Brigadier C.E. *Weir, the control of artillery was increasingly centralised, thereby augmenting the firepower that could be brought to bear at any particular point. Creeping barrages were redeveloped to deal with the problem of breaching Axis fortified zones. By First World War standards, the barrages at Alamein were thin, though effective in suppressing the enemy defences and in guiding the assaulting troops; an important innovation was the use of Bofors anti-aircraft guns firing tracer to mark boundaries. The desirability of bringing crushing fire from the whole Divisional Artillery to bear on a fleeting or unexpected target led to the development of the 'quick barrage' or 'stonk' (a quick concentration according to a prearranged pattern) and the 'murder' (massed fire on a single pinpoint target). These firing procedures were subsequently adopted by the 8th Army. The combination of radios and streamlined procedures increased the effectiveness of artillery even further. By 1943 the fire of six artillery regiments could be brought down on a target within two minutes. Survey, flash-spotting, and sound-ranging troops (replaced towards the end of the war by radar) assisted in plotting the location of enemy batteries for counter-battery fire. The weight of artillery increased during the war, with a corresponding tendency to rely upon methodical attacks preceded by crushing artillery barrages. At Cassino the infantry assault was supported by about 900 guns, firing 4 million kilograms of shells. In the Pacific 25-pounders and a battery of 3.7-inch mountain howitzers supported the 3rd New Zealand Division.

From 1942 5.5-inch guns had provided medium artillery support for the 2nd New Zealand Division, but it was only in the 1950s that these powerful guns replaced the venerable 60-pounders and 6-inch howitzers in New Zealand. From 1951 to 1953 a field artillery regiment provided close support to Commonwealth infantry during the *Korean War; its 25-pounders fired more than three-quarters of a million shells. Although artillery tactics remained unchanged, improved radio communications greatly increased the responsiveness of the artillery to infantry requests for support. From October 1951 the regiment's effectiveness was increased by the use of VT-fused (vicinity or variable-timed fuse) shells, which burst at a set distance above the ground to deadly effect on troops below.

The most important improvement in artillery was the introduction of reliable lightweight radios, which allowed for faster and more flexible support. From 1963 L5 Italian-designed pack howitzers began to replace the 25-pounders, which finally went out of service in 1977. During the *Vietnam War, 161st Battery at first used L5 howitzers, but these were replaced by heavier, more robust, and longer-ranged American M2A2 (also designated M101A1) howitzers in 1967. In contrast to previous wars, the artillery was usually deployed by Chinook helicopters to forward fire bases, providing direct support for Australian and New Zealand infantry and harassing likely Vietcong positions and routes. In 1986 the Hamel Light Gun, a 105 mm British-designed Australian-manufactured piece, was introduced to replace the 105 mm howitzer. Computerised artillery systems and global positioning systems, introduced in 1989 and 1997 respectively, promise to revolutionise artillery.

Atomic bomb There was a small New Zealand involvement in the British and American programmes which led to the development of the atomic bomb. New Zealanders, being British subjects (there was then no separate New Zealand nationality), were easily accepted, when required, into the British teams involved in the secret atomic research. When British teams were first admitted to the American 'Manhattan' project late in 1943, one New Zealander working in Great Britain was included. R.R. Nimmo was well known to the British scientists leading the teams— they had all, Nimmo included, been students of Ernest Rutherford, the New Zealander who had pioneered atomic physics.

The Rutherford connection assisted further New Zealand involvement as well. When Ernest *Marsden, a Rutherford student and now New Zealand's wartime Director of Scientific Developments, saw several of his old classmates in Washington in December 1943, he guessed what was going on and brashly offered New Zealand scientists to assist the project. He was initially warned off, but a few months later, when more scientists were needed to maintain credible British contributions to the Anglo-Canadian Montreal project as well as the Manhattan project, his offer was taken up. With the approval of the Prime Minister, Peter *Fraser, and the *War Cabinet, a small number of scientists and engineers were seconded from the New Zealand radar development programme, which was then tapering off. Thus in July 1944 two New Zealand scientists, R.M. Williams and G. Page, went to the Manhattan project. They joined the same group as Nimmo, working at Berkeley and Oak Ridge on the electromagnetic separation of uranium-235. The rest

Australasian naval agreements

went to Montreal: C.N. Watson-Munro, K.D. George, and an engineer, W.W. Young, went in July 1944, and J.G. Fergusson and another engineer, A.H. Allen, in April 1945. In the relatively small Montreal project the New Zealanders made a significant contribution to the design and construction of its heavy-water reactors. It was clear, however, that the Montreal project would not contribute to the production of an atomic bomb for use in the war; Canada and especially Britain were looking to their post-war atomic capabilities.

The Manhattan project culminated in August 1945 with the Hiroshima and Nagasaki bombs which ended the *Pacific War, but the Montreal project continued. Several more New Zealand scientists were sent there. However, in 1946 Britain set up its own atomic energy research establishment at Harwell and withdrew most of its team from the Montreal project. Several of the New Zealanders, including Watson-Munro and Fergusson, went on to Harwell with them, and more were sent from New Zealand. Marsden envisaged his scientists returning to establish an atomic research programme in New Zealand. Clearance for the necessary secret information to be passed from Britain was even written into the latter's *modus vivendi* agreement with the United States in 1948. But the New Zealand government was never convinced and jibbed at the cost. Other countries (including Australia) with similar involvement in the wartime atomic projects moved to exploit the experience gained for defence or industrial purposes, but New Zealand did not. Many of New Zealand's 'Manhattan' scientists ended up in positions in Australia, among them Watson-Munro, who was appointed Chief Scientist and oversaw the construction of Australia's first nuclear reactor near Sydney.

R.A. Galbreath, 'The Rutherford connection: New Zealand scientists and the Manhattan and Montreal Projects', *War in History*, vol. 2, no. 3 (1995).

ROSS GALBREATH

Australasian naval agreements At London in 1887 the Australian colonies, New Zealand, and the United Kingdom agreed on the basis of cooperation in the provision of naval defence in the South Pacific. The agreement sought to balance the Admiralty's desire for control over all the Empire's naval resources and the colonies' demands for increased local naval defence provision coupled with a reluctance to relinquish control over any forces they might fund. Under the provisions of the Colonial Naval Defence Act 1865, several Australian colonies, but not New Zealand, had developed embryonic naval forces, which were strictly local in character though under Admiralty control, a situation which Victoria in particular found irksome. By the early 1880s, the colonies were demanding better naval provision on the *Australia Station, and were prepared to contribute to the cost—an important concession for they had hitherto insisted that *imperial defence was a British responsibility. From 1884 attempts were made to reconcile the British and Australasian requirements, with protracted negotiations between the Commander-in-Chief of the Australia Station, Rear-Admiral Sir George Tryon, and the colonial governments forming the basis of the eventual resolution of the matter.

Under the agreement Great Britain would provide additional vessels—five second-class cruisers and two torpedo-boats—for the Australia Station, with the colonies paying the interest on their capital cost and their annual maintenance. The total liability of the colonies was limited to £126,000 per annum, to be apportioned on a population basis calculated annually. New Zealand's share came to about £21,000. From the Admiralty's viewpoint the advantages of securing colonial contributions to naval defence were offset by the limitations imposed on the movement of the new vessels: they could not be removed from the Australia Station without the permission of the colonial governments. New Zealand, moreover, was willing to contribute only on the understanding that two of the Station's vessels should be stationed in New Zealand waters in peacetime.

The agreement, which was for ten years, came into effect with the arrival in Sydney of the *Australian Auxiliary Squadron in 1891. By the time of its expiry Admiralty distaste for its deployment limitation had increased markedly, for it ran completely counter to the blue-water principles now dominant in British naval thinking. A squadron restricted to the Australia Station could not contribute to the offensive action required to secure and hold command of the seas. Australia and New Zealand, for their part, had grown steadily more anxious about perceived inadequacies in the strength of the forces on the Australia Station. A new ten-year agreement concluded in 1903 provided for a strengthened seagoing fleet on the station to replace the Auxiliary Squadron and also training opportunities for Australian and New Zealand seamen. Three of the squadron's third-class cruisers would be set aside for this latter purpose. The two colonial governments (the Commonwealth of Australia and New Zealand) would make a direct financial contribution to the Australian Squadron, with New Zealand's share being one-twelfth of the annual running costs (up to a limit of £40,000) and Australia's five-twelfths. One drill ship and one cruiser would be stationed in New Zealand waters. The three drill ships and one cruiser were to be manned by Australians and New Zealanders on a population-based ratio, and provision was made for the training of officers, with New Zealand getting two naval cadetships and Australia eight. Branches of the Royal Naval Reserve would also be established in Australia and New Zealand. The Admiralty could draw satisfaction not only from the increased colonial financial contributions but also from the colonies' more flexible approach to deployment. The Squadron would be able to freely operate in the East Indies and China Stations if necessary.

New Zealand was satisfied with the agreement. It easily filled the 144 places allocated to it in the drill ships, and several New Zealanders took up cadetships. Unlike in Australia, where discontent with the arrangement soon grew, New Zealand was happy with the subsidy system, and in 1908 increased its payment to £100,000. But agreement among the parties in 1909 to create a Pacific Fleet led to a change of approach by Australia in favour of developing a local navy, which spelt the end of the 1903 arrangements. (See NEW ZEALAND DIVISION OF THE ROYAL NAVY)

I. McGibbon, *The Path to Gallipoli: Defending New Zealand 1840–1915* (GP Books, Wellington, 1991).

Australia–New Zealand Agreement ('Canberra Pact') Signed on 16 January 1944, the agreement was the main outcome of a conference of Australian and New Zealand delegations in Canberra. The need for coordination of the two countries' policies had been demonstrated during the course of the ★Second World War, but the real motivating force behind the meeting was a desire by both governments to have their views heard on the post-war settlement. To their dismay, neither had been consulted about the Cairo Declaration of 1 December 1943, outlining the great powers' intentions regarding the post-war disposition of the Japanese Empire. The Australians drafted the agreement, which the New Zealanders, led by Prime Minister Peter ★Fraser, readily accepted. It included a range of matters, both civil and military. The latter, which were heavily influenced by the recent Japanese advance into the South Pacific, included agreement to establish a zone of defence, covering the island territories in an arc to the north of Australia and New Zealand. The agreement was received without enthusiasm by the British, while American authorities, angered by its tone, became less cooperative over war planning. In the event, the promise of a closer Australia–New Zealand partnership in defence and other matters went largely unfulfilled. Provisions for consultation broke down during consideration of the contribution of ground forces for Korea in 1950, and ★Australian–New Zealand defence cooperation remained on an ad hoc basis. The zone of defence proposal was subsumed within arrangements made with the British for regional defence planning known as ★ANZAM. Not until the 1970s did the agreement undergo something of a revival, as Australia and New Zealand again moved closer in defence matters, though as a symbol of earlier cooperation rather than as a prescription for the future.

Australia Station was the administrative term for the British naval command which encompassed New Zealand from 1859 to 1913. In the early years of the colony Royal Navy vessels which visited New Zealand

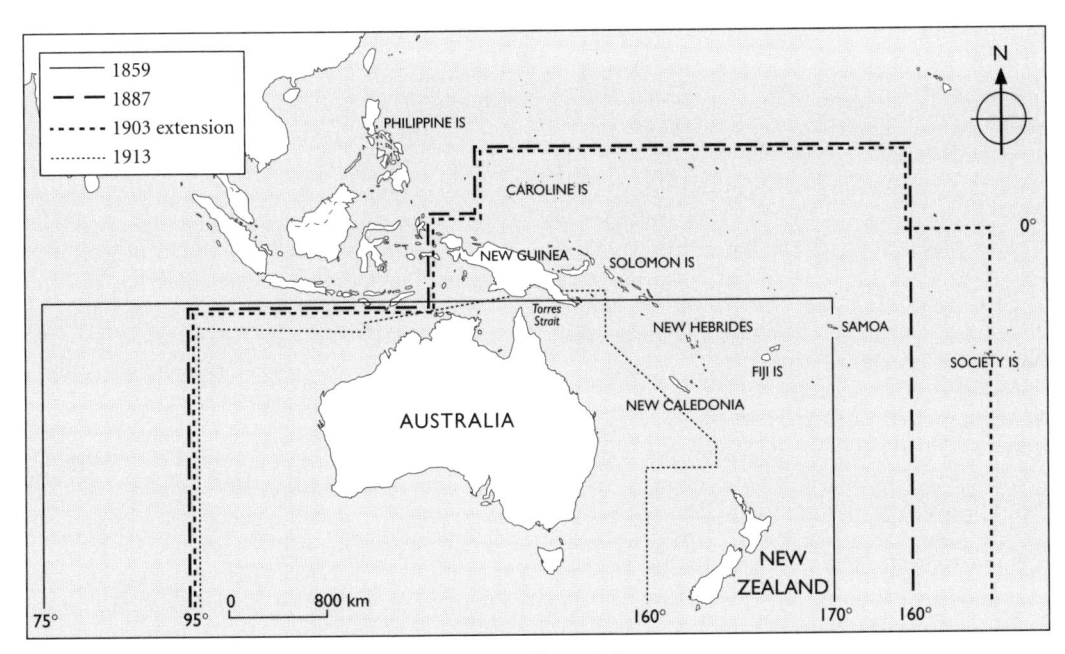

Map 2 Australia Station, showing successive changes of boundaries

were part of the squadrons on the East Indies and China Station, which had bases variously at Bombay, Trincomalee (1909–45), and Hong Kong. The establishment of the Australia Station, with naval vessels permanently stationed at Sydney, reflected the growing extent of British naval activity in the South Pacific. It was modified from time to time to increase its extent, especially to the north of Australia and New Zealand. Originally under a commodore, it was raised to a rear-admiral's command in 1884. In 1913, it was reduced to exclude New Zealand, and became the responsibility of the Royal Australian Navy. From then until 1921, when a separate ★New Zealand Station was established, New Zealand and its surrounds were part of the China Station.

J. Bach, *The Australia Station: A History of the Royal Navy in the South West Pacific 1821–1913* (New South Wales University Press, Sydney, 1986).

Australian Auxiliary Squadron In accordance with the Australasian Naval Agreement of 1887, the British government earmarked five Pearl class cruisers and two Rattlesnake class torpedo-boats then under construction to reinforce the strength of the ★Australia Station. These vessels, when completed, formed the Australian Auxiliary Squadron, which arrived in Sydney in 1891 and came under the command of the commander-in-chief of the Station. Normally two of the cruisers and one torpedo-boat were placed in reserve, while the others operated in the same fashion as the other warships on the Station. Two of the cruisers were stationed in New Zealand waters in peacetime. Along with the Australian colonies, New Zealand paid a proportion, determined on a population basis, of the interest on the capital cost of the squadron, and of its annual running costs. The terms of the agreement prevented the deployment of the vessels beyond the boundaries of the Australia Station without the approval of the governments of the Australian colonies and New Zealand. This occurred only once when HMS *Wallaroo* was deployed to China during the Boxer Rebellion. With the negotiation of a new Australasian Naval Agreement in 1903, the squadron went out of existence, and the ships had all returned to Great Britain for disposal by 1906. (See 'P' CLASS CRUISERS)

Australian–New Zealand defence cooperation The word ★Anzac is symbolic of close cooperation between New Zealand and Australian troops on the battlefield. Australians served in the Waikato during the New Zealand Wars (see NEW ZEALAND WARS, AUSTRALIAN INVOLVEMENT IN), and they even formed a composite unit with New Zealanders during the ★Boer War, but it was at ★Gallipoli, in a situation of shared adversity and mutual dependence, that the relationship flowered. C.E.W. Bean, the Australian official historian, evoked the Anzac spirit in his description of the first three days' fighting: 'As brothers they died; their bodies lay mingled in the same narrow trenches; as brothers they were buried.' Later, New Zealand and Australian divisions, for a time, formed an ANZAC Corps on the ★Western Front, and an Anzac Mounted Division fought the Turks in ★Sinai–Palestine. Although the opportunities for Anzac cooperation were more limited during the ★Second World War, New Zealand and Australian troops shared the same battlefields in ★Greece and ★Crete and the ★North African campaign. In Greece, an ANZAC Corps was revived briefly. In 1942 New Zealand naval forces formed part of an Anzac squadron, albeit under American command. During the ★Korean and ★Vietnam Wars New Zealand gunners enjoyed a close relationship with the Australian infantrymen whom they supported; in the latter Anzac infantry battalions were also formed.

Such easy cooperation had its roots in the many similarities between the backgrounds of the two countries' troops. The dominant cultures in both Australia and New Zealand shared a common heritage. Settled mainly by emigrants from the United Kingdom during the nineteenth century, they developed similar institutions and attitudes within a British framework. Geographical location alone ensured a broad similarity of outlook on the world and of strategic perspective. New Zealand and Australia have long regarded each other as natural allies. In 1901 New Zealand's Premier, Richard Seddon, insisted that his country 'would give her heart's blood in defence of Australia'. But this apparent concordance of interests did not ensure that close cooperation on the battlefield was replicated in the two countries' approach to defence matters in peacetime until the latter part of the twentieth century. Anzac was not merely a symbol of unity; it also denoted the separate nationalisms of Australia and New Zealand so powerfully boosted by their efforts at Gallipoli. Developed largely on an ad hoc basis, the defence relationship between the two countries was characterised by suspicion, competition, irritation, and indifference. Occasional attempts to improve it only served to highlight problems.

Before the creation of the Australian Commonwealth in 1901 New Zealand was one of the larger of a group of seven Australasian colonies. Although defence cooperation in this period was not regarded as urgent because of the lack of a significant threat to the South Pacific, New Zealand did take part in the efforts to improve naval strength in the region which culminated in the Australasian Naval Agreement of 1887.

Australian–New Zealand defence cooperation

The Australian Minister of Defence, Kim Beazley, and his New Zealand counterpart, Bob Tizard, converse with soldiers of their two countries during an Anzac exercise in New Zealand in 1989 (*NZDF*)

After the Australian federation in 1901 New Zealand was reduced to the status of smaller neighbour. A desire to avoid being overshadowed by Australia now influenced New Zealand's approach to defence issues. Better, it was felt in Wellington, to be dominated by mother rather than older brother. In these circumstances the role of junior partner in Australasian ventures was not appealing to New Zealand authorities. A competition in imperial patriotism was evident, as New Zealand sought to upstage its larger neighbour.

Strategic considerations also inhibited cooperation. So long as both were allies of the same great power there was no incentive to get closer. Both looked to that power to prevent any serious threat from developing in the South Pacific on a scale that would demand cooperation between them. There was, too, a distaste at first in New Zealand's Liberal government for the approach adopted by Australia in regard to naval affairs, and an unwillingness to consider a cooperative venture to produce an Australasian naval force.

Convinced that such a development would weaken the British naval power on which both countries ultimately depended, Prime Minister Sir Joseph ★Ward maintained that New Zealand's future destiny was 'as distinct from that of Australia as is daylight from dark'. Not until the change of government in 1912, and the advent of the Australian-born Colonel James ★Allen as Minister of Defence in William ★Massey's Reform administration, was there a shift in New Zealand's stance. Australia and New Zealand, Allen insisted, were 'brothers in the Pacific'. He was determined that the New Zealand naval forces he set about creating should cooperate closely with their Australian counterparts. He envisaged common training methods, the use of the Royal Australian Naval College for the training of New Zealand officers, and regular joint exercises. But the outbreak of the ★First World War prevented the realisation of these objectives.

Military cooperation was also encouraged at this time. Both countries had introduced territorial

Australian–New Zealand defence cooperation

schemes, which demanded not only a more professional officer corps in each but also a larger number of officers. The establishment of the Royal Military College at Duntroon met this need, with New Zealand participation important to its viability. Ten of the forty-one cadets of the foundation intake in 1911 were New Zealanders—beginning an association of great importance to the capacity of the two countries' armies to cooperate on the battlefield. An exchange of officers was instituted, and the New Zealand commanding officer, Major-General A.J. ★Godley, visited Australia for talks with his counterpart, Brigadier-General J.M. Gordon, who had served briefly in New Zealand's ★Armed Constabulary about thirty years before. These discussions were the genesis of the modern defence relationship between the two countries. The two commanders considered the formation of a joint expeditionary force and possible action in the South Pacific in the event of war, but plans to meet every two years were overtaken by the First World War. Although the joint expeditionary force did not get off the ground, the two countries' expeditionary forces were closely associated in Egypt, and a ★New Zealand and Australian Division was established for service at Gallipoli.

Between the wars, the promise of 1912–18 was not fulfilled. Although the two countries presented an Anzac front on the strategic issue of the fate of the ★Anglo-Japanese Alliance in 1921, the pre-war developments were not sustained. Financial problems intruded. As a cost-saving measure, New Zealand refrained from sending cadets to Duntroon between 1921 and 1934. The 'main fleet to ★Singapore' strategy, which underlay both countries' approach to security in this period, seemed to reduce the need for local cooperation. Both countries focused on their primary partner, rather than upon each other. As late as 1938 they were finding out what the other was doing in defence through London. Only occasionally were attempts made to get closer, the most notable one being initiated by the Australian Prime Minister, J.A. Lyons, in 1933. Apologising for 'appearing somewhat in the role of a salesman with goods to offer for sale', he offered a number of suggestions for improved cooperation. Australia saw advantage, at this time, in having New Zealand utilise Australian sources of supply; it would help to build up industrial resources in South Pacific, though at the expense of New Zealand accepting higher costs for Australian, as opposed to British, defence goods and services. A visit to Wellington by the Australian Minister of Defence, Senator George Pearce, in late 1934 led to some minor cooperative measures being adopted, but New Zealand generally resisted the Australian initiative, if only because of the adverse financial implications of utilising Australian supplies.

New Zealand soon became more amenable to closer ties, in part because of the growing doubts about the security position in the South Pacific as British capacity to implement the Singapore strategy declined, in part because of the emergence of individuals who favoured cooperation. For example, Major W.G. ★Stevens, who became Secretary of the ★Organisation for National Security in 1937, was convinced that the fates of the two countries were 'inextricably bound up'. It was put to Lyons in September 1938 that cooperation was 'not as good as is desirable'. But this time it was the turn of the Australians to be unenthusiastic. The perceived left-wing political complexion of the New Zealand government, a lesser concern for coordination because of greater resources, a lack of immediate advantage for Australia in supply cooperation (now that the slack in Australian production lines had been taken up by Australia's own rearmament programme), Lyons's death—all played a part in Australia's procrastination. Some progress was made at the ★Pacific Defence Conference in April 1939, but generally the results were disappointing from Wellington's point of view. Exchanges of information had been agreed, but in mid 1939 there was 'no machinery or regular arrangements of any kind' for consultation on defence matters.

New Zealand and Australia adopted similar approaches at the outset of the Second World War, though not without a mini-crisis in relations over the announcement of their respective expeditionary forces, and there was considerable cooperation in supply matters, yet their relations were strained by developments following Japan's entry into the war. The two countries found themselves in different American command areas. More significantly, New Zealand failed to follow Australia's lead in withdrawing its troops from the Mediterranean theatre for service in the South Pacific. Nevertheless the two countries were drawn together by a desire to assert a South Pacific right to be heard on the post-war settlement in the Pacific, and signed the ★Australia–New Zealand Agreement in January 1944. This provided, among other things, for the institution of a zone of defence in the islands to the north of the two countries, continuous consultation on defence issues, and attention to the problems of inter-operability of forces. However, the defence aspects of the agreement were destined to remain a symbol rather than a prescription for cooperation, never being given serious attention after the war.

After the Second World War, old influences reasserted themselves. Once again New Zealand and Australia gave differing emphases to post-war requirements. Whereas New Zealand formally accepted the ★Middle East commitment, Australia would do no

48

more than agree to consider the position at the time of an emergency and would not give priority to the Middle East over Malaya. New Zealand once again preferred to deal with the British, partly because British sources of supply were cheaper and partly because of a revived fear in Wellington of Australian domination. In 1947 Prime Minister Peter *Fraser described some Australian proposals for defence planning as savouring 'of a form of "Australian Imperialism"'. Nevertheless the common interests of New Zealand and Australia were emphasised by their membership of a number of multilateral arrangements, including *ANZAM, *ANZUS, and *SEATO. Ad hoc cooperation between the two countries' armed forces was relatively easy. From 1956 New Zealand increased its use of both naval and military training facilities in Australia, with military cadets now attending the Officer Cadet School at Portsea in addition to Duntroon. In 1959 contingents began participating in each other's exercises, and this was put on an annual basis from 1962. A naval exchange scheme was implemented in 1957.

Not until the late 1960s was the impetus towards closer cooperation given a decisive boost by a number of developments. First, the prospective demise of the British military presence in the Pacific region forced New Zealand, in particular, to reassess its approach to security (which till then had been essentially to participate in a British framework with the Americans as the backstop). Australia and New Zealand notably agreed, in 1969, to retain their forces in Malaysia–Singapore even after the departure of British forces. Second, the United States enunciated the Nixon or Guam Doctrine, which placed emphasis on self-help among the United States' allies. Third, the demise of the *forward defence strategy inevitably focused antipodean attention closer to home. Finally, economic influences were driving the two countries closer together. These developments encouraged the formalisation of defence links between the two countries, beginning with an agreement on supply cooperation in 1969. A joint consultative committee on defence cooperation was established three years later. In 1977 the process was furthered by the creation of the Australian–New Zealand Defence Policy Group and a Defence Supply Working Group. Officials were now charged with seeking ways of improving cooperation within a political framework provided by now regular meetings of the two countries' ministers of defence. Although supply cooperation faltered in the late 1970s, the problems were addressed in a new agreement in 1983.

Australian–New Zealand defence cooperation was given a fillip by the effective withdrawal of New Zealand from ANZUS in the late 1980s following the USS *Buchanan* affair. Notwithstanding the major divergence of strategic approach between the two countries—Australia stuck firmly to ANZUS—they have continued to broaden the cooperation between them. New Zealand found itself more reliant on Australia for a range of assistance, especially in the training and exercise fields. The number of New Zealanders attending training courses in Australia doubled, and by 1988 70 per cent of New Zealand's overseas training was being carried out in Australia. New Zealand's involvement in September 1989 in the Anzac Frigate project, described as the 'litmus test' of the relationship, was the most spectacular manifestation of Anzac cooperation, recalling the Australasian Naval Agreement of a century earlier. More recently, New Zealand agreed to station a squadron of A-4K Skyhawks at Nowra in New South Wales, to assist in the RAN's training programmes. During the 1990s the term Closer Defence Relations was coined to emphasise the increasingly integrated nature of the two countries' defence programmes. The possibility of a unified force was even raised by the Australian Minister of Defence, Robert Ray, in 1991, though such an outcome seems unlikely in the absence of a major threat.

I. McGibbon, 'Australia–New Zealand Defence Relations to 1939', in Keith Sinclair (ed), *Tasman Relations, New Zealand and Australia, 1788–1988* (Auckland University Press, Auckland, 1988); I. McGibbon, 'The Australian–New Zealand Defence Relationship since 1901', in *Revue Internationale d'Histoire Militaire*, No. 72 (Australian Commission of Military History, Canberra, 1990).

Awatere, Lieutenant-Colonel Arapeta (25 March 1910–6 March 1976) was an outstanding, if controversial, commander of the 28th (Maori) Battalion during the *Second World War. Born at Tuparoa, he was of Ngati Porou. After attending Te Aute College and Victoria University College, he found employment as a civil servant until enlisting in 2NZEF in November 1939. Commissioned in March 1940, he left New Zealand for the Middle East with reinforcements for 28th (Maori) Battalion in the following November. From June 1941 he was the battalion's intelligence officer, and a year later became a company commander. For his determined leadership of the attack on Point 209 in Tunisia on 26 May 1943, during which he was wounded, he was awarded an MC. From November 1944 he commanded the battalion in the final stages of the *Italian campaign. His outstanding conduct during a difficult operation near Faenza on the night of 14–15 December led to his being made a DSO. Renowned for his violent bent, Awatere was apt to use his fists to punish erring subordinates. He was reputed to be less than scrupulous in his adherence to the rules of war. Interviewed for a 1995 television

Awatere

documentary, a member of the Maori Battalion recalled an incident in which Awatere had allegedly had a group of German prisoners executed after holding them overnight. Although this allegation went unrebutted, no documentary evidence has since come to light to corroborate it. Moreover, there is no evidence that Awatere was ever disciplined for such conduct. Rumours that he was quietly removed from command by divisional commander Lieutenant-General Sir Bernard ★Freyberg appear unfounded, for he was still commanding the Maori Battalion at the end of the war. In 1946 he was a member of the New Zealand contingent which participated in the Victory Parade in London. Following his return to New Zealand, he devoted himself to the welfare of Maori, and in 1962 was elected to the Auckland City Council. Convicted of murdering his mistress's lover in 1969, he was still in prison when he died.

B

Babington, Lieutenant-General Sir James Melville (31 July 1854–15 June 1936). The son of a British cavalry officer, Babington joined the 16th Lancers in 1873, and by 1892 had succeeded to its command. During the ★Boer War, he commanded a mounted column which included the 4th New Zealand Contingent. In late 1901 he was appointed as Commandant of the New Zealand Forces, with the rank of major-general (see COMMANDANTS). Like his predecessors Colonels F.J. ★Fox and A.P. ★Penton, he found that his efforts to implement substantial military reform were blocked by the Premier, R.J. ★Seddon. The colony's forces did improve under his command, but Babington's annual reports reveal his frustration at the slow rate of progress. Strongly resisting Seddon's claim that the Boer War experience had demonstrated the utility of amateur soldiers, he tried unsuccessfully to have the ★Volunteer Force replaced by a smaller, better trained, partially paid force. Declining the offer of an extension, he returned to England in September 1906. For his colonial service, he was subsequently made a CMG. In 1907 Babington retired from the British Army; he was made a CB. On the outbreak of the ★First World War, he was recalled to active service; he commanded the 23rd Division in France and Italy, thereafter XIV Corps, and finally the entire British Army in Italy. His war service was recognised with a knighthood and several foreign decorations.

STEPHEN CLARKE

Baker, Lieutenant-Colonel Frederick (19 June 1908–1 June 1958). Of Nga Puhi descent, Baker rose steadily in the ranks of the civil service after joining the Public Works Department in 1924. He served in the ★Territorial Force and was commissioned in 1929. During the ★Second World War, he embarked in January 1940 as an officer in 28th (Maori) Battalion, and commanded the battalion's reinforcement company in ★Greece; although captured, he succeeded in escaping to ★Crete, where he was wounded during the subsequent battle for the island. Evacuated to Egypt, he became a company commander in 25th Battalion but rejoined the Maori Battalion in May 1942 as second-in-command. Two months later he became commander, only to be badly wounded in the face at El Alamein in November. He was later made a DSO for his leadership in this battle. After recovering in New Zealand, he became Director of Rehabilitation in December 1943. In this capacity, he oversaw the repatriation of more than 100,000 ex-servicemen, taking a particular interest in the rehabilitation of Maori ex-soldiers. In 1954 he became a Public Service Commissioner.

Bands are an important part of the ceremonial life of armed forces. Musicians have historically served in armies and on ships to provide both music for entertainment and a beat for soldiers on the march; in battle they served as stretcher bearers. Bugles are also used for signalling, and reveille is still sounded at all ★army camps. Bands also provide music for social occasions, such as balls. Most importantly, bands reflect the prestige and honour of their unit, and traditionally bandsmen have worn particularly splendid uniforms (usually at the unit's own expense), while drums and other instruments are adorned with the unit crest and ★battle honours.

The first band in New Zealand was that of the 58th Regiment, which arrived in April 1845. Other British regiments also brought their bands, which proved popular as entertainment for the civilian population.

Volunteer brass bands attached themselves to various corps of the ★Volunteer Force, the first probably the band of the Taranaki Militia and Rifle Volunteers, formed in 1858. Among other early volunteer bands was the Artillery Band, formed at Auckland in 1864, which survives today as the Band of the Royal New Zealand Artillery. The creation of the ★Territorial Force brought unit bands under much closer Defence control, and bands were restricted to twenty-five members of military age. During the ★First World War bands were raised at military camps and by each battalion, some of the latter being pipe bands. Bands continued to be associated with Territorial units in the inter-war period, and in 1937 the Royal New Zealand Air Force Band, a Territorial-based unit, played for the first time. Royal Marines, stationed in New Zealand as part of the ★New Zealand Division of the Royal Navy, formed their own band. In the ★Second World War bands were formed by brigades, and given an expanded role as dance bands. With a number of prominent band personalities in them, these bands attained a high standard. The only full-time band was the Central Band of the RNZAF, established in 1940, which undertook numerous tours and participated in patriotic parades and fund-raising activities for the war effort.

After the war a variety of base or station bands and bands attached to Territorial units existed on an entirely volunteer basis. The exception was the Royal Marine Band of the RNZN, which was active until the late 1950s. From the 1960s there were determined efforts by the Treasury to reduce the number of bands with Territorial regiments and air force stations. In 1964 Army bands were reorganised in line with the wider reorganisation of the Army, and the number of bands was reduced to seven. These economies resulted in an outcry from communities which suddenly lost a band with a long affiliation with their locality. Currently each of the Territorial battalions of the ★New Zealand Army possesses a brass or pipe and drum band. The Central Band of the RNZAF was re-formed out of the Hutt Valley Military Band as an RNZAF Territorial unit in 1952, with members drawn from professional musicians and music students from the Wellington area. It consists of sixty-five musicians, including a full symphonic band, a brass quintet, a swing band, a jazz combo, a saxophone ensemble, and an eight-person herald fanfare ensemble. The Band of the RNZN is a full-time branch, and its members must complete naval training in addition to performing music. It maintains brass, woodwind, and percussion sections, with a strength of twenty-seven musicians and an officer. A brass band and a pipe band were raised as part of the 1st Battalion, New Zealand Regiment, until 1957; the bandsmen were originally volunteers from the battalion, but from 1961 accomplished musicians were recruited directly into the band. In April 1964 it was renamed the Band of the New Zealand Army, and in the following year a school of music was established at Burnham Military Camp. The band has earned an excellent reputation, especially for its marching prowess, through popular concerts, displays at state and public occasions, and participation in military tattoos both in New Zealand and overseas. Bands continue to provide an important contribution to the ceremonial functions of the armed forces, and are an essential component of the armed forces' relationship with the wider community.

Bannerman, Air Commodore Ronald Burns (21 September 1890–2 August 1978) was the highest-scoring New Zealand fighter ace of the ★First World War. After learning to fly at the ★Walsh brothers' flying school in Auckland, he proceeded to England in 1917 and was commissioned in the Royal Flying Corps. Flying single-seat fighters on the ★Western Front, he quickly made his mark, shooting down six German aircraft in a month and earning a DFC and bar. By the end of the war, he was credited with fifteen 'kills'. Between the world wars, he practised law in Gore. Accepting a temporary commission in the RNZAF in September 1940, he served as a ground instructor and administration officer at bases in New Zealand. From 1943 to 1945 he was Air Member for Personnel on the Air Board. He was made a CBE in 1945.

Barrington, Archibald Charles (8 May 1906–4 March 1986). A clerk from Marton, Barrington was active in the Workers' Educational Association and a lay preacher in the Methodist Church. In April 1936 he and Ormond ★Burton founded the New Zealand Christian Pacifist Society. During the ★Second World War he campaigned actively against war, and was arrested on a number of occasions for obstruction and other offences. In March 1941 an anti-war speech in Wellington led to his being sentenced to one year's imprisonment. He helped establish the Riverside alternative life-style community at Moutere during the war, and was a leading figure in the ★anti-war movements. His brother Benjamin rose to the rank of brigadier in 2NZEF.

Barron, Wing Commander James Fraser (9 January 1921–20 May 1944) was a leading New Zealand bomber pilot of the ★Second World War. A clerk from Dunedin, he enlisted in the RNZAF in July 1940 and reached England as a sergeant pilot shortly after his twentieth birthday. He was posted to the Stirling bomber–equipped 15 Squadron, with which he flew thirty-five operational sorties. He was commissioned in March 1942 and awarded a DFM. He served briefly as an instructor before returning to active operations with 7 (Pathfinder) Squadron. He soon earned a DFC, and was made a DSO in February 1943 for pressing home a mission against Cologne despite heavy flak. In February 1944, at the age of only twenty-three, he became commander of 7 Squadron. He gained a bar to his DSO after a raid on an airfield at Nantes in France. On his seventy-seventh sortie, he was killed when his aircraft was involved in a mid-air collision with another bomber.

Barrow, Thomas Abram (16 July 1897–16 September 1967) was the first and longest-serving Secretary of the *Air Department. Born in Dobson, he joined the public service in 1919, and was Chief Accountant in the Public Works Department when appointed as Air Secretary in 1937. He collaborated with Wing Commander R.A. *Cochrane in developing the RNZAF as a separate service, and after the outbreak of the *Second World War was involved in the negotiation, in Ottawa, of the *Empire Air Training Scheme. Shortly after his retirement in 1954, he was made a CBE.

Barrowclough, Major-General Sir Harold Eric (23 June 1894–4 March 1972) was one of New Zealand's most illustrious citizen soldiers. Born in Masterton and educated at Otago University College, he enlisted as a private in 1NZEF in January 1916, but was commissioned four months later. As commander of an infantry company in the New Zealand Rifle Brigade, he distinguished himself on the Somme in September 1916, and was awarded an MC. After recovering from a serious wound in the back suffered in June 1917, he commanded reserve battalions in England. When he returned to the *Western Front in 1918, he again commanded a company. As commander, from June 1918, of the 4th Battalion, New Zealand Rifle Brigade, he displayed considerable skill and bravery, being made a DSO for his part in driving back a German counter-attack near Havrincourt Wood in September 1918. On 4 November 1918, in one of the most dramatic episodes in New Zealand military history, his battalion scaled the ramparts of Le Quesnoy and accepted the surrender of the German garrison. While practising law in Dunedin after the war, he continued to be interested in military matters as a *Territorial Force officer. In 1930 he became commander of the 3rd Infantry Brigade, but resigned when he moved to Auckland in the following year. By this time he had become disillusioned by the declining state of the military forces, reflected in the suspension of *compulsory military training in 1930. In an effort to counter this decline, he was subsequently instrumental in re-forming the Defence League (see DEFENCE LOBBY GROUPS), which sought in the late 1930s to encourage defence preparedness. Realising that war was inevitable, he offered his services to the Army again in August 1939. In March 1940 he left New Zealand with 2NZEF's Second Echelon as commander of the 2nd New Zealand Division's 6th Brigade. A hard taskmaster, he was rewarded by its creditable performance during the ill-fated *Greece campaign. Barrowclough's only involvement in the *North African campaign was during the Crusader offensive in November 1941. Given the task of taking Sidi Rezegh, he did not allow heavy losses to deter him from pressing home his attack against strong enemy defences, but on 30 November most of his brigade was overrun by German armour. For this action, he received a bar to his DSO. As a result of the urgent need to bolster New Zealand's home defences following the onset of the *Pacific War, a somewhat reluctant Barrowclough was returned to New Zealand in early 1942. Having been earmarked by 2NZEF's commander, Major-General B.C. *Freyberg, as a potential divisional commander, he was duly given command of the Northern Division covering what was considered the most vulnerable area. When New Zealand began preparing a division for offensive purposes in the Pacific in August 1942, Barrowclough was the obvious choice as commander, and in November he became GOC 2NZEF in the Pacific. Faced with operating within an American command framework, he insisted upon being given a charter similar to that earlier given to Freyberg as 2NZEF commander (see FREYBERG'S CHARTER). After serving at first in a garrison role in *New Caledonia, his force moved forward to take part in the *Solomons campaign in August 1943. Despite his strong, even stern, personality, he got along well with his American superiors, not least because of his tactful manner in dealing with them. By his own admission his role was more an administrative than an operational one, as compared with his counter-

The commander of New Zealand's 3rd Division, Major-General H.F. Barrowclough, in his command post during the Solomons campaign (*Waiouru Army Museum, 1992.2052*)

part, Freyberg, in the Mediterranean. Nevertheless, he commanded his division (and supporting American and Fijian units) in three successful amphibious assaults (Vella Lavella, Treasury Islands, and Green Islands). Much to his disappointment his division, which had never been brought to full strength, was disbanded after months of uncertainty in 1944; its manpower was needed to both reinforce 2NZEF in Italy and sustain industrial production in New Zealand. Barrowclough did his best to ensure fair treatment of officers of his force when they joined the division in the Mediterranean. He was also involved in consideration of a possible New Zealand role in the war against Japan when fighting ended in Europe. After the war Barrowclough resumed his legal career and was Chief Justice of New Zealand from 1953 to 1966.

Base Records was established in 1915 to meet the greatly expanded needs of the military forces for accurate personnel records following the formation of 1NZEF. A branch of the Adjutant-General's Branch in the Department of Defence, it checked pay rolls from all 1NZEF units, handled allotments and remittances, maintained personnel files, kept records of casualties, and stored soldiers' wills. By 1918, 230 clerks, most of them female, were employed in this work. Between the wars Base Records lost its status as a separate branch, but with the establishment of 2NZEF in 1939 a Pay, Accounts and Base Records Office was established in the *Army Department. By 1943 it had about 580 staff. Since the *Second World War Base Records, now located at Trentham Military Camp, has assumed responsibility for RNZAF and RNZN personnel files as well. Sadly many of the files have been purged to save space, resulting in much historically valuable material being lost. Nevertheless, the more than 300,000 personnel files, many of them containing medical records, constitute a unique record of the social and physical composition of the male population of the country during two periods in particular.

Bassett, Lieutenant-Colonel Cyril Royston Guyton (3 January 1892–9 January 1983), a bank officer who enlisted in 1NZEF in August 1914 and became a sapper in the New Zealand Divisional Signal Company, is the only signaller to have won the *Victoria Cross. He was so honoured for his distinguished conduct during the August 1915 offensive at *Gallipoli, laying and repairing telephone lines under continuous enemy fire. Self-conscious about his decoration—the only VC awarded to a 1NZEF soldier during the campaign—he noted later that 'All my mates ever got were wooden crosses'. Evacuated sick from the peninsula on 13 August 1915, he did not rejoin his unit until it was engaged on the *Western Front, where he was wounded twice. After the war he returned to banking. Recalled to duty in July 1940, he served as the commander of Northern Military District signals until December 1943.

Batchelor, Sergeant Eric (29 August 1920–) was the only New Zealander to be awarded a DCM and bar in the *Second World War. A farm worker from Waimate, he was a Territorial soldier before enlisting in 2NZEF in June 1940. He served with 23rd Battalion in the *North African campaign, and was wounded at both Fort Capuzzo in November 1941 and El Alamein in October 1942. He played a conspicuous part in the fighting at Takrouna, especially in reconnoitring enemy positions. His first DCM recognised his leadership in a successful attack on a German strongpoint near Florence in July 1944. Five months later, at Celle, his platoon destroyed three strongpoints in a spirited attack. During the following night, he and three others made their way to what they thought was their company HQ, only to find a large force of Germans there. After a spirited action, nineteen enemy POWs were taken. For this exploit Batchelor was awarded a bar to his DCM. He returned to New Zealand and was demobilised in 1945, but later went to London with both the 1946 Victory Contingent and the 1953 Coronation Contingent.

Battle honours are ceremonial recognition of a unit's or ship's active participation in a particular battle or campaign. Battle honours are carried by RNZN ships, RNZAF squadrons, and Army infantry and mounted rifle regiments. Artillery and Engineers units have only one battle honour—'Ubique' ('Everywhere'). By the same logic service units are assumed to be present in greater or lesser strength at every action, so their particular commemoration is deemed unnecessary. Battle honours may be worn on the unit's *colours. They are passed down to the unit's descendants, so preserving a strong sense of tradition and pride. The battle honours of New Zealand troops in general appear at the War Memorial Museum in Auckland, at the *National War Memorial at Wellington, and in the debating chamber in the Parliament Buildings.

The first battle honour awarded to a New Zealand unit went to the Taranaki Militia for its participation in the action at Waireka in 1860. The battle honour 'New Zealand' is currently carried by certain units of the *New Zealand Army. Further battle honours were awarded in 1907 to volunteer corps which sent more than twenty men to the *Boer War, the unit descendants in the New Zealand Army still holding the honour 'South Africa'. The distribution of battle honours in the *First World War was complicated by the fact that *Territorial Force regiments provided only a proportion of their strength to the *New Zealand Expeditionary Force. After long adjudication by a committee and approval by the British War Office to ensure conformity with British regiments, battle honours were issued to Territorial Force regiments in 1926. Most infantry regiments were awarded thirty honours, while mounted rifles regiments received about ten. Battle honours for the New Zealand Army after the *Second World War were decided by a committee chaired by Major-General Sir Howard *Kippenberger, and were issued to Territorial regiments in 1957 according to the extent of their members' participation in actions—some infantry regiments were awarded up to fifty-seven honours. In 1964, there was a further reorganisation of battle honours with the wholesale amalgamation of regiments. The regular 1st Battalion, Royal New Zealand Infantry Regiment received battle honours at that time. In 1972 it received the battle honour 'South Vietnam 1967–70', the last to be awarded to an army unit.

Ships of the RNZN also carry the battle honours of former ships of the Royal Navy of the same name. For example, HMNZS *Endeavour* bears the battle honour 'Cadiz 1596', the oldest such honour in the New Zealand services. Similarly RNZAF squadrons' battle honours include those awarded to units in the RAF, as in the case of 75 Squadron, whose battle honour 'Home Defence 1916–1918' dates from before any New Zealand association with that squadron.

Baxter, Archibald McColl Learmond (13 December 1881–10 August 1970). An Otago farm labourer, Baxter was a committed socialist pacifist when the *First World War began. When conscripted in November 1916, he sought unsuccessfully to be classed as a conscientious objector. After being held at Trentham, he and thirteen other *conscientious objectors were sent overseas with the 28th Reinforcements in July 1917. When increasingly brutal attempts to break their resistance failed, Baxter with two others was dragged into the front line itself. Sent to hospital in April 1918, he was dubiously diagnosed as insane, and sent home four months later. His account of his wartime treatment, *We Will Not Cease*, published in 1939, is perhaps the best-known New Zealand pacifist text. He was the father of the leading New Zealand poet James K. Baxter.

Begg, Colonel Charles Mackie (13 September 1879–2 February 1919) was one of the first officers to be commissioned in the newly formed New Zealand Medical Corps. He commanded the New Zealand Field Ambulance at *Gallipoli. During the offensive on Chunuk Bair in August 1915, he assumed the appointment of Assistant Director of Medical Services of the *New Zealand and Australian Division. In October 1916, as Deputy Director of Medical Services, he became the chief medical officer of II ANZAC Corps on the *Western Front, a position he would also hold in XXII Corps in 1918. His organisation of the evacuation of wounded at Messines in 1917 was exemplary, but at Passchendaele later in the year evacuation arrangements collapsed as a result of rushed planning and appalling weather. He died of influenza and acute pneumonia immediately after the war.

Bell, Arthur Wilbraham Dillon (5 April 1856–28 May 1943) played a major role in developing New Zealand's *coast defences. After secondary education in Christchurch and entering the civil service in 1874, he went to England for five years, where he gained considerable engineering experience. Returning to New Zealand, he joined the Public Works Department and was employed as an assistant engineer in Dunedin. When the last of the *Russian scares propelled the government into hasty action in 1885, he was appointed Resident Engineer of Defences, and worked under the guidance of Major Henry *Cautley to install the available guns and others ordered from the United Kingdom. From February 1888 until his resignation in early 1893, he was responsible, as Engineer for Defences, for the completion of the scheme. The remainder of his career as an engineer was spent in Western Australia.

Bennett, Lieutenant-Colonel Sir Charles Moihi (27 July 1913–26 November 1998). A Ngati Whakaue of Te Arawa, Bennett attended Te Aute College and Canterbury University College before working as a schoolteacher. After enlisting in 2NZEF in November 1939, he left New Zealand as a platoon commander in 28th (Maori) Battalion in the following May. He was the battalion intelligence officer during the *Greece and *Crete campaigns, and commanded a company during the fighting in North Africa in late 1941. As commander of B company, he performed well at the Battle of El Alamein in October–November 1942, and temporarily commanded the battalion when its commanding officer was wounded. From January 1943 his command was made permanent. He was made a DSO for his leadership during the fight for Point 209 in Tunisia. In April 1943 his active service came to an end when he stood on a mine at Takrouna in April 1943, inflicting serious wounds that would have him in and out of hospital for years. After the war he worked briefly in the *War History Branch before joining the Department of Maori Affairs. He was New Zealand High Commissioner in Kuala Lumpur from 1959 to 1963, and President of the New Zealand Labour Party from 1973 to 1976. He was knighted in 1975.

Berendsen, Sir Carl August (16 August 1890–12 September 1973) was the government's chief civilian defence adviser before the *Second World War. Born in Sydney, he had come to New Zealand as a boy and won a public service cadetship, joining the Education Department in 1906 and later serving in the Labour Department. He was a member of the Samoa Expeditionary Force in 1914–15, and was called up for 1NZEF in 1917, though by accident or design—the Army authorities thought the latter—he did not leave New Zealand until shortly before the end of the war, and arrived in England just in time to take part in the Victory Parade. In 1926 he was appointed as Imperial Affairs Officer in the Prime Minister's Department, and quickly became a key adviser on international affairs. When New Zealand's two cruisers were sent to Western Samoa in an attempt to overawe the Mau, he went along as the Prime Minister's representative. As head of the Prime Minister's Department from early 1935, he found the first Labour government's supportive approach to the *League of Nations much to his liking, and drafted proposals put forward by New Zealand for its reform in 1936. The Western democracies' *appeasement of the European Fascist dictatorships appalled him, and would strongly influence his approach to international affairs after 1945. He was conscious that New Zealand's security ultimately rested upon the British Commonwealth's position, which would be determined in Europe, yet at the *Pacific Defence Conference in April 1939 he produced a critique of British plans for the *Singapore strategy which the British representative described as a 'real broadside'. During the early part of the war, Berendsen was involved, as chief adviser to Peter *Fraser, in several important military matters, including the appointment of Major-General B.C. *Freyberg as commander of 2NZEF and the inquiry into Freyberg's command after the evacuation from *Crete. In 1943 Berendsen became the first New Zealand High Commissioner in Canberra, and was involved in the conclusion of the *Australia–New Zealand Agreement. Minister (later Ambassador) in Washington from 1944 to 1952, he was a member of the New Zealand delegation to the 1945 San Francisco Conference from which emerged the *United Nations, and he was knighted the following year. An early advocate of a strong stand against the perceived aggressive approach of the Soviet Union in the *Cold War, he went so far as to describe the Soviet leadership as 'international thugs and gangsters'. He greatly applauded New Zealand's rapid response to the United Nations' call for assistance in the *Korean War, and opposed appeasement of Communist China after its intervention. A security relationship with the United States seemed to him essential to New Zealand, and in 1951 he helped finalise the text of the Pacific Security (*ANZUS) Treaty, which he described as the 'greatest gift that the most powerful country in the world can offer to a small comparatively helpless group of people'; he signed both it and the Japanese Peace Treaty on New Zealand's behalf in September 1951.

Berlin airlift A manifestation of the developing *Cold War, the Berlin airlift was the Western powers' response to the imposition by the Soviet Union of a land and water blockade of Berlin on 25 June 1948 (made total on 10 July). Operation Plainfare, the British contribution to the airlift, involved most of the RAF's transport resources, as well as seconded Sunderland flying boats and a mixture of civilian aircraft on contract. As a token of New Zealand's support for the Allied stance, three three-man RNZAF aircrews, drawn from 41 Squadron, were made available. From September 1948 they operated out of Lübeck in north-west Germany, flying RAF twin-engine Dakota transports to and from Berlin, 260 kilometres to the south-east. For most of their 473 sorties the cargo was coal, with evacuees being carried out on the return flights. By the time of the last, on 11 August 1949, the New Zealanders had transported 1577 tonnes of coal to the city. Meanwhile RNZAF officer Group Captain R.J. ('Nugget') Cohen, who was on secondment to the RAF, was making a significant contribution to the planning and control of the airlift in the headquarters which controlled the British element of the Anglo-American operation. Although the crisis greatly increased international tension (nuclear-configured B29 bombers were deployed from the United States to Great Britain during its course as part of the Allied deterrent), it also demonstrated the Western powers' resolve, in the face of which the Soviet Union eventually backed down, lifting the blockade in September 1949. By this time more than 2.3 million tonnes of supplies had been airlifted to the city, with the British share being just over half a million tonnes in 175,682 sorties.

PAUL HARRISON

Best, Elsdon (30 June 1856–9 September 1931) wrote one of the few works on pre-European Maori warfare in New Zealand. From Tawa, near Wellington, he joined the *Armed Constabulary in the 1870s, and served in Taranaki, including at *Parihaka. He began to take an increasing interest in Maori culture, and was a founding member of the Polynesian Society in 1892. After serving as government mediator in the Urewera, he held a position at the Dominion Museum from 1910. Although his large corpus of work has since been criticised for its evolutionary and racial assumptions, it remains of significance in New Zealand ethnography. In his book, *The Pa Maori*, published in 1927, he described *Maori traditional warfare and Maori reaction to the introduction of firearms in the early nineteenth century.

Bettington, Group Captain Arthur Vere (12 June 1881–2 August 1950) was the first of a series of British officers to advise the government on air policy between the world wars. His early service included participation in the ★Boer War as a member of irregular forces commanded by his father. He subsequently served with the Johannesburg Mounted Rifles in the Zulu War of 1906. He learned to fly in 1912, and after the outbreak of the ★First World War was commissioned in the RFC. He commanded 48 Squadron from March to August 1917. His service brought him three mentions in dispatches and, in 1919, appointment as a CMG. When he arrived in New Zealand in March 1919 to become Aviation Adviser to the New Zealand government, he brought with him two Bristol fighters and two De Havilland trainers. A detailed report which he presented in June on the 'Aerial Defence of New Zealand' provided a blueprint for the creation of a seven-squadron air force, covering personnel, equipment and bases. In strongly urging that the local air forces should be capable of fitting into the wider 'Empire Air Force', he endorsed the existing basis of New Zealand's defence strategy, based on close cooperation with the United Kingdom. Nevertheless, his proposals foundered in the face of government caution and parsimony. Nothing had been achieved when he left New Zealand in September 1919, and his report, which was soon mislaid, had no lasting influence. He was commander of RAF forces in Ireland in 1922, but was seriously injured in a flying accident. After serving as Air Attaché in South America from 1923 to 1928, he retired in 1931, but was recalled for special duties in the ★Second World War.

Bibliographies There is only one bibliography specifically devoted to listing sources of material on New Zealand military history—*The New Zealand Army, A Bibliography* (Hope Farm Press, New York, 1961), compiled by C.E. Dornbusch. Even at the time it was recognised to be less than complete, and is now well out of date. The *New Zealand National Bibliography*, issued monthly by the National Library of New Zealand, includes military-oriented items appearing in New Zealand, while earlier publications are listed in the *New Zealand National Bibliography to the Year 1960* (Government Printer, Wellington, 1969–85), edited by A.G. Bagnall. H.O. Roth's *Pacifism in New Zealand: A Bibliography* (University of Auckland Library, Auckland, 1966) covers works on an important subtheme in New Zealand's military history.

Birks, Lieutenant-General Anthony Leonard (30 December 1941–   ). A Wellingtonian by birth, Birks began his military career in 1959. After graduating from the Royal Military Academy, Sandhurst, he served in the New Zealand Regiment in Malaysia. He spent two periods in South Vietnam, the first, in 1968, as liaison officer with the 1st Australian Task Force; two years later, he was attached to an American field force headquarters. After attending the Australian Army Staff College at Queenscliff, commanding 2nd/1st battalion, RNZIR at Burnham and 3rd Task Force (1985–90), and undergoing further study at the Royal College of Defence Studies in the United Kingdom in 1990, he became Chief of General Staff in 1992. In this capacity, he oversaw a reshaping of the ★New Zealand Army which saw combat units strengthened and manœuvre warfare doctrine adopted. He also encouraged the establishment of the ★Military Studies Institute. Later, as Chief of Defence Force (1995–99), he had to contend in particular with the difficult problems arising from the need to re-equip all three services and with gender issues brought to the fore by some well-publicised cases of discrimination against servicewomen. On the former, he achieved considerable success in relation to the Army and RNZAF at least; on the latter, he decreed a policy of zero tolerance of discrimination. With a view to ensuring that maximum resources could be devoted to training activities, he also instituted measures to ensure that the overhead costs of developing operational forces were kept to a minimum. He was appointed a CB in 1994.

Black market Illicit trading in goods and services has been a concomitant of war since time immemorial. A shortage of goods, whether through breakdowns of supply or through rationing, inevitably opens the way for shrewd operators to meet demand. Among New Zealand troops serving overseas alcohol, stolen or looted army goods, and souvenirs were popular black market items, while at home evasion of rationing was common. In the ★First World War soldiers dealt on the black market behind the lines at markets often run by deserters. In New Zealand the absence of any tight economic regulations meant a black market did not develop, though scarce goods were subject to profiteering by legitimate traders. Members of 2NZEF in the ★Second World War were little different from their predecessors. They took advantage of a flourishing black market in Cairo, while during the ★Italian campaign such activities reached unprecedented proportions. The abundance of war materiel, the chaos created by the war, and the disparity between the incomes of Italian and Allied personnel provided ideal conditions for black marketeering. Similarly an artificially pegged exchange rate and the shortage of consumer goods ensured that there was an active black market in Japan in the immediate aftermath of the war. A minority of members of both ★Jayforce and

57

★Kayforce were involved in various 'rackets' or in selling stolen supplies. In New Zealand itself during the Second World War the introduction of strict economic controls created a black market in rationed goods. Petrol was particularly vulnerable to such trading, but as the war dragged on black marketeering spread to other goods where there were shortages, such as stockings, eggs, and fruit.

Blake, Vice-Admiral Sir Geoffrey (16 September 1882–23 July 1968) was the most able of the British naval officers who commanded the New Zealand naval forces between the world wars. He entered the Royal Navy as a cadet in 1897. During the ★First World War, he served in the flagship of the Grand Fleet, HMS *Iron Duke*. For his services as her Gunnery Control Officer during the Battle of Jutland in 1916, he was mentioned in dispatches and made a DSO. After serving as Naval Attaché in Washington (1919–21) and commanding the battleship HMS *Queen Elizabeth* (1921–23), he spent six years on the staff of the Naval War College and the Royal Naval Staff College, directing the latter in 1926–27. His subsequent service as Chief of Staff of the Atlantic Fleet was recognised by his appointment as a CB in 1929. In that year, he was seconded to the ★New Zealand Division of the Royal Navy. His roles were threefold: he was First Naval Member of the Naval Board, Commodore Commanding the New Zealand Squadron, and commanding officer of HMS *Dunedin*. Increasing economic problems confronted him with the difficult problem of maintaining the division's activities with a shrinking budget. The most important event during his tenure was *Dunedin*'s deployment to Western Samoa in January 1930 to bolster the New Zealand administration there. Marines and seamen from his ship scoured the bush in an unsuccessful attempt to round up members of the Mau, a nationalist movement. Following his reversion to the Royal Navy in 1932, he was Fourth Sea Lord for three years before taking command of the Mediterranean Fleet's Battle Cruiser Squadron in 1936. He was made a KCB in 1937. A boating accident led to his being invalided out of the navy in 1938, but his career resumed following the outbreak of the ★Second World War. He was an able assistant to the First Sea Lord and an additional member of the Board of Admiralty in 1940. From 1942 to 1945 he played an important role in Anglo-American naval coordination as a liaison officer at the headquarters of the American naval forces in Europe.

Commodore Geoffrey Blake arrives to take over command of the New Zealand Squadron in 1929 (*W. H. Raine Collection, Alexander Turnbull Library, C-24257-1/2*)

Boer War was the first overseas conflict to involve New Zealand troops. Fought between the British Empire and the Boer South African Republic (Transvaal) and its Orange Free State ally, it was the culmination of long-standing tensions in southern Africa. Although Transvaal had been annexed by the British Crown in 1877, it had secured a limited form of independence after defeating local imperial forces in a series of engagements during the Transvaal Revolt or First Boer War of 1880–81. An influx of thousands of mainly British *uitlanders* (foreigners) into the Transvaal after the discovery of gold there in 1886 destabilised the Boer state. Tension grew with Transvaal's refusal to grant the *uitlanders* citizenship, and was greatly exacerbated in 1895 by the privately organised Jameson Raid which ended in a fiasco when an *uitlander* uprising in Johannesburg failed to materialise. Perhaps hoping for intervention by European powers, Transvaal resisted British demands, and by mid 1899 both sides were preparing for war. Although the rights of the *uitlanders* were the immediate issue, the conflict was rooted in British determination to dominate South Africa and equally strong Boer determination to resist the extinction of their independence.

With war seemingly imminent, New Zealand offered its support. On 28 September 1899 its Premier, R.J. ★Seddon, asked Parliament to approve the offer to the imperial government of a contingent of mounted rifles and the raising of such a force if the offer were accepted. The British position in the dispute with the Transvaal was 'moderate and righteous', he maintained. He stressed the 'crimson tie' of Empire which bound New Zealand to the 'Mother-country' and the importance of a strong British Empire for the colony's security. Amid emotional scenes, the proposition was overwhelmingly endorsed—only five members voted against it—and within days the offer had been accepted by the authorities in London. Seddon proudly proclaimed Parliament as the first legislature in the Empire to offer assistance. Hundreds of men applied to serve in the contingent, membership of which was restricted to those already serving in New Zealand's tiny regular forces and the ★Volunteer Force. By the time that war began on 11 October, after a Boer ultimatum over the deployment of British troops in South Africa had been ignored by London, a 215-man contingent was already encamped in the Wellington suburb of Karori while the Defence Department sought frantically to gather together its equipment and horses. Ten days later, it was given a tumultuous send-off from Wellington. A huge crowd heard Seddon proclaim that New Zealanders 'would fight for one flag, one Queen, one tongue, and for one country—Britain'.

Under the command of Major A.W. ★Robin, the contingent reached South Africa on 23 November after an 'ocean race' across the Indian Ocean with contingents from Australian colonies, a contest it won by a few days. Despite having received only rudimentary training, the New Zealanders were immediately sent north to join Lieutenant-General Sir John French's Cavalry Division in northern Cape Colony. They had their first engagement with Boers on 9 December, and at Jasfontein nine days later their first hard fight. When he succumbed, on 28 December, to wounds he received at the latter, Private George Bradford earned the dubious distinction of being the first New Zealand soldier to lose his life in an overseas conflict; he was also the first to be taken POW, for he died while in Boer hands.

The highly mobile and well-armed Boer forces began the war by attacking the British possessions of Natal and the Cape Colony, and laying siege to the towns of Kimberley, Mafeking, and Ladysmith. In December 1899 they inflicted a series of defeats on imperial forces in what became known as 'Black Week', leading the British government to send the Empire's two most famous generals to South Africa. Field Marshal Lord Roberts became commander-in-chief with General Lord ★Kitchener as his chief of staff. News of the British reverses—and the obvious political advantages of jumping on the jingoistic bandwagon—induced the New Zealand government to raise a Second Contingent, which left for South Africa in February 1900. A Third Contingent was largely organised and paid for by a committee of prominent Christchurch citizens and other members of the public. This contingent, which sailed from Lyttelton in mid February 1900, was followed a month later by the Fourth Contingent, raised on a similar basis by a committee of Dunedin citizens. Both were known as 'Rough Riders', because they mainly comprised good horsemen and marksmen who were not members of the Volunteer Force.

Particularly in its early stages, New Zealand's involvement in the war enjoyed overwhelming public support in New Zealand. Large sums were raised to organise and equip the Third and Fourth Contingents and to provide comforts for the New Zealand troops. Public donations towards the colony's war effort exceeded £113,000. Most Maori supported the war and many expressed a wish to serve in South Africa, but were, at least in theory, barred from serving there by the British policy of not employing 'native' troops in the conflict (see MAORI AND THE BOER WAR). There was very little active opposition to New Zealand's participation. It was confined to a small group of radical members of Parliament, religious leaders, and others who condemned the war as an aggressive act of imperialism designed to seize control of the Transvaal's gold mines. Such views had little

Boer War

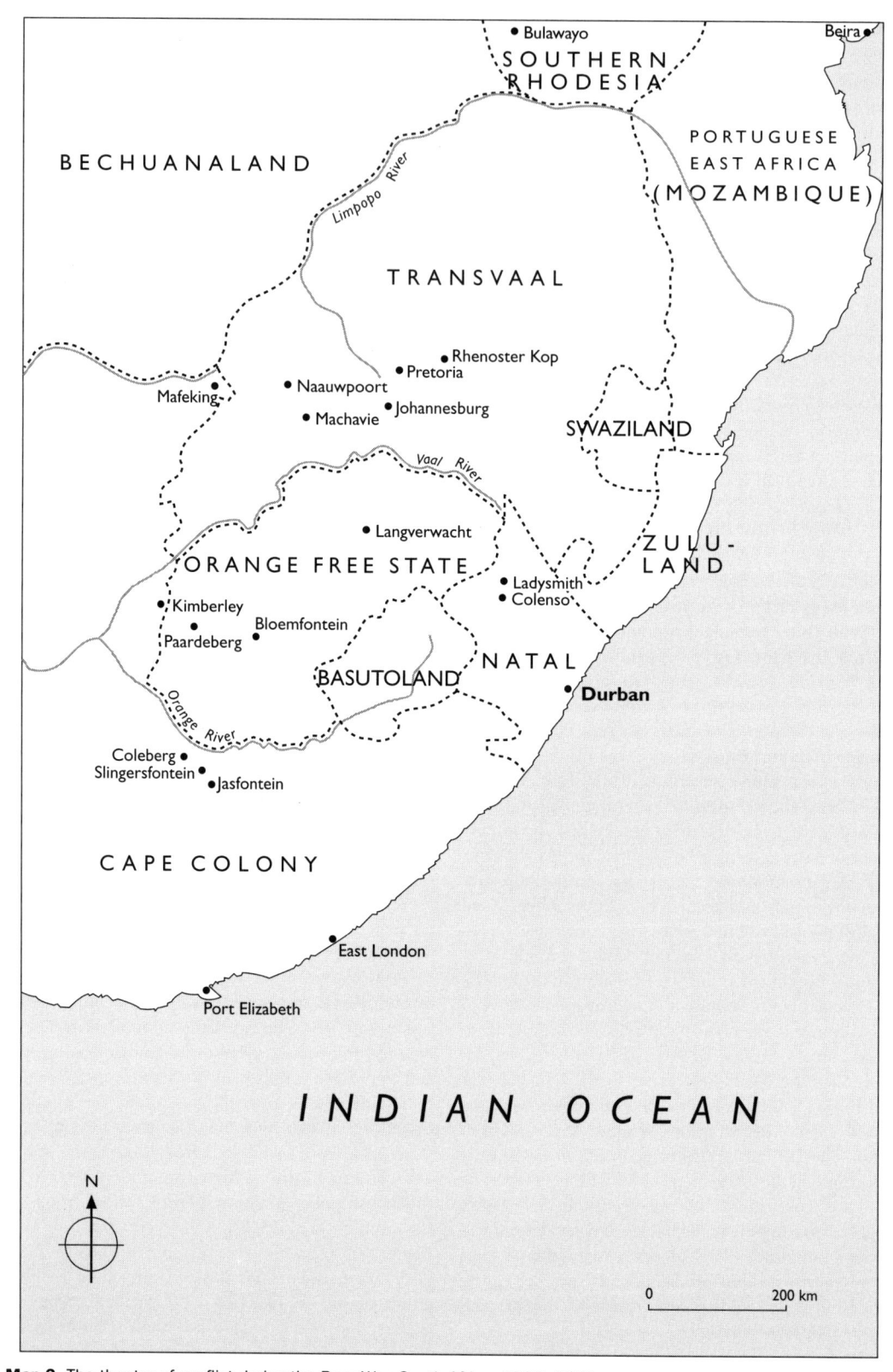

Map 3 The theatre of conflict during the Boer War, South Africa, 1899–1902

impact on public opinion; indeed New Zealand's political leaders and the community in general were rather intolerant of opposition to the war.

A detachment from the First Contingent distinguished itself when, on 15 January 1900, it smashed a Boer attempt to seize a hill overlooking the contingent's camp at Slingersfontein. In recognition of its gallant conduct the site of the action was renamed New Zealand Hill. At the end of that month, the now reinforced and reorganised British forces took the offensive. A mounted force which included the New Zealand contingent relieved Kimberley on 15 February. Soon afterwards Roberts decisively defeated the Boers at Paardeberg and the siege of Ladysmith was lifted. On 13 March the New Zealanders were among the British forces which entered Bloemfontein, the capital of the Orange Free State. For rescuing a wounded comrade during a Boer ambush near the city, Private Henry Coutts was awarded one of four scarves knitted by Queen Victoria for presentation to colonial soldiers who performed acts of bravery.

In mid May 1900 the first three New Zealand contingents were organised into one regiment under Robin's command. They took part in the advance through the Transvaal to Johannesburg and Pretoria, which were both in British hands by early June. Orange Free State and Transvaal were annexed to the British Empire on 28 May and 25 October 1900 respectively. By late November, when Kitchener succeeded Roberts, it was widely believed that the war was virtually over. The last conventional battle of the war took place on 29 November at Rhenoster Kop, east of Pretoria, when imperial forces rather foolishly and unsuccessfully attacked a Boer force occupying a very strong position. Men of the Second and Third Contingents—those of the First Contingent were in the process of being repatriated—showed considerable bravery and had five men killed and twenty-one wounded in this action.

From late 1900 those Boers who were determined to continue resisting British rule split up into smaller commandos. Abandoning their heavy equipment to improve their mobility and adopting guerrilla tactics, they retained control of most of the countryside in the former Boer republics. Roberts and later Kitchener responded to this development by forming numerous mobile columns to seek out and destroy the Boer commandos. To remove sources of support for the Boer resistance, agricultural supplies and livestock were also removed or destroyed and Boer civilians rounded up and incarcerated in concentration camps. The Second and Third New Zealand Contingents spent the final months of their service in South Africa on such anti-guerrilla operations, which involved arduous treks interspersed with sniping, ambushes, and skirmishes with a skilful and elusive enemy.

Meanwhile New Zealanders were also serving elsewhere in the Fourth and Fifth Contingents, which had arrived in the theatre in April–May 1900. The Fifth had been raised following a British initiative in February 1900 to meet a shortage of mounted troops. Its expenses (as with all subsequent contingents) were met by the imperial authorities. It was originally intended that the men, who were enlisted on one-year terms of engagement (in contrast to the open-ended terms of their predecessors), would serve with British mounted rifles regiments, but in the event the Contingent was kept together. With the Fourth Contingent, it entered the conflict through Beira in Portuguese East Africa. A group of volunteers from the contingents were formed into the 1st New Zealand Battery, which was equipped with six 15-pounder guns. Congestion on the railway linking Beira with Rhodesia meant that the contingents had to spend several weeks at camps where malaria and dysentery were rife. The New Zealanders spent more than two months making an arduous journey by rail and on horseback to Bulawayo in Rhodesia and thence to Mafeking. Between August 1900 and May 1901 they fought many skirmishes and conducted a series of arduous marches during operations against Boer commandos in the western Transvaal. The most successful action was the capture of General De La Rey's artillery and supply column with 135 men on 24 March 1901. Near Naauwpoort on 28 January 1901 Farrier Sergeant-Major W.J. ★Hardham became the only New Zealander to be awarded the ★Victoria Cross during the war, for rescuing a wounded comrade under fire.

In December 1900, the New Zealand government agreed to replace the First Contingent and provide 300 men to reinforce the other contingents. Later, after men of the Second and Third Contingents had protested about the length of their service, it was decided that this new contingent should replace the first three New Zealand contingents. Arriving in South Africa in March 1901, the Sixth Contingent was soon involved in a series of long treks through northern Transvaal. It formed part of one of the elite highly mobile formations employed by Kitchener throughout South Africa to attack Boer commandos and to respond to enemy actions. During its service in South Africa the contingent was involved in operations in the former Boer republics and in Natal, covering about 5000 kilometres on horseback or foot. During such operations men would spend 11 or 12 hours alternately riding and leading their horses. Generally men had to sleep in the open and survive on inadequate rations, which consisted mainly of hard army biscuits and bully beef. Support arrangements for the mobile columns with which the New Zealanders served were inadequate. As a result, men often had to serve in ragged uniforms that were infested with lice. At the end of June 1901 the men of the Sixth Contingent staged a 'general strike' in protest at the failure to replace their worn-out uniforms. The harsh conditions were especially hard on the horses. Like all the New Zealand contingents, apart from the Seventh, the Sixth had taken a full complement of horses with it to South Africa (some of the more than 8000 New Zealand horses sent during the conflict). Wastage was high: during April 1901, for example, two were killed in action, ninety-five had to be destroyed, and forty-five died.

New Zealand's Seventh Contingent, which was intended to replace the Fourth Contingent, reached South Africa in May 1901. Within twelve days of landing it had its first significant clash with the enemy. It had some success with dawn raids on Boer laagers (camps), which were an important feature of British tactics in the latter part of the war. By late 1901 the number of Boer guerrillas who were still active had been substantially reduced, though thousands of the most determined and effective fighters were still in the field. In an effort to crush the remaining Boer forces, and in response to criticism of their policies, the British military and civilian authorities in South Africa adopted a new three-pronged strategy. First, Boer civilians were no longer to be rounded up and placed in insanitary concentration camps, where thousands had died of disease. Instead they were to be left in the countryside, where the guerrillas would have to take responsibility for them. Second, protected areas were established which were guarded by lines of blockhouses linked by barbed wire entanglements. By the end of the war, more than 8000 blockhouses had been built in lines which stretched 6000 kilometres across South Africa. Third, 'new-model' drives were organised, in which British columns established a cordon of men right across an area and then moved forward, sweeping the Boers ahead of them towards blockhouse lines. At the beginning of February 1902, the Seventh Contingent formed part of one of the elite mounted columns employed in the new-model drives.

During the second of the new-style drives in the eastern Orange Free State, General Christiaan De Wet decided to break through the British cordon at Langverwacht Hill, a point on the line held by the Seventh Contingent. The New Zealand line consisted of small posts of five or six men in small trenches or sangars. On the night of 23–24 February a picked force of guerrillas overwhelmed one of the New Zealand posts, then turned left and advanced up the hill destroying each of the posts in turn in ferocious close-quarter fighting. The Boers succeeded in opening up a gap through which most of their force was able to escape. The New Zealanders, who were reported to have 'displayed great gallantry and resolution', lost twenty-four men killed and forty-one wounded—a very high pro-

New Zealand mounted riflemen prepare to move out on the South African veldt (*NZ National Archives, WA250*)

portion of the eighty men engaged. Despite this setback, the drive was a qualified success, with fifty guerrillas killed and nearly 800 taken prisoner.

In January 1902 New Zealand agreed to a British request for an additional contingent to serve in South Africa. The thousand-strong Eighth Contingent was commanded by Colonel R.H. ★Davies, one of the outstanding New Zealand officers to emerge during the war. New Zealand's political leaders, military personnel, and public were all concerned about the way previous New Zealand units had on many occasions been split up and lost their national identity. Seddon and Davies impressed upon Kitchener and his staff New Zealand's strong desire for the Eighth Contingent to be kept intact and possibly combined with other New Zealand Contingents to form a column. Kitchener was not prepared, at least officially, to compromise his ability to deploy the forces under his command as he saw fit, but the contingent did operate as a separate entity. After disembarking in South Africa in mid March 1902, the Eighth Contingent took part in a major drive against Boer guerrillas. In mid April sixteen men were killed and eleven seriously injured in a rail accident at Machavie in the Transvaal. With their situation increasingly desperate, the Boers were at last induced to come to terms. A peace treaty was concluded on 31 May 1902. Two final large contingents from New Zealand, the Ninth and Tenth, arrived in South Africa too late to see any significant action. On 4 June 1902 Lieutenant Robert McKeich became the last New Zealander to be killed in action in the war when he was shot in an unfortunate clash with a group of Boers who did not know of the peace treaty.

During the war New Zealand sent nearly 6500 men to South Africa, almost half of them in the last three contingents, which were all more than a thousand strong. New Zealanders also served in the war with other colonial forces or with the British Army, though their numbers cannot be accurately established. In all, seventy-one members of the contingents were killed in action or died of wounds (including three former members who had joined other units), twenty-six were accidentally killed, and 133 died of disease (more than half from typhoid fever). New Zealand sent medical officers with each of its contingents and at least thirty New Zealand nurses served in South Africa during the war. As part of efforts to improve conditions at concentration camps, twenty women primary school teachers were sent from New Zealand to South Africa in 1902.

The New Zealand contingents were highly regarded. *The Times History of the War in South Africa*, for instance, concluded that the New Zealanders were, after they had gained some experience, 'on average the best mounted troops in South Africa'. In many ways the South African war set the pattern for New Zealand's later involvement in the two world wars. Specially raised units, consisting mainly of volunteers, were dispatched overseas to serve with forces from elsewhere in the British Empire. The success enjoyed by the New Zealand troops fostered the idea that New Zealanders were naturally good soldiers, who required only a modicum of training to perform creditably. The war also strengthened New Zealanders' sense of a national identity, which centred on the physical and military capabilities of the New Zealand male. At the same time the war enhanced the ties of sentiment and shared interests which bound New Zealand to Great Britain and the other parts of the British Empire.

D.O.W. Hall, *The New Zealanders in South Africa 1899–1902* (War History Branch, Wellington, 1949); J. Crawford with E. Ellis, *To Fight for Empire: An Illustrated History of New Zealand and the South African War, 1899–1902* (Reed, Auckland, 1999).

JOHN CRAWFORD

Bomber aircraft, RNZAF Although RNZAF personnel with 75 (New Zealand) Squadron flew Wellington, Lancaster, and Stirling medium and heavy bombers from Great Britain during the ★Second World War, the RNZAF itself has operated only dive, light, and medium bombers. None of the thirty Vickers Wellington medium bombers ordered in 1937 reached New Zealand. The Hudsons and Venturas which equipped RNZAF ★squadrons during the ★Pacific War were light and medium bombers used largely for reconnaissance. Between 1958 and 1970 the RNZAF developed a tactical bomber capacity, with 14 and 75 Squadrons flying two versions of the Canberra in New Zealand and South-east Asia. With the departure of the last of the Canberras in 1970, the RNZAF reverted to a single-seat fighter-bomber role.

The principal RNZAF bomber aircraft have been:

Avenger, Grumman (3-seat torpedo-bomber). Wingspan 16.5 m; length 12.2 m; armament up to 3 x .3-inch and one .5-inch machine-guns, 2000 lb bombs; maximum speed 445 km/h; range 1450 km; power 1 x 1700 h.p. Wright Cyclone radial engine.

The Avenger was used by 30 and 31 Squadrons in the ★Solomons campaign in 1944. After their replacement by Corsairs, many were converted to drogue towers. After the war some were used in early aerial top-dressing trials. The Avenger ended its service days with the RNZAF in 1959 towing aerial targets for Vampires at Ohakea.

Baffin, Blackburn (2-seat biplane torpedo-bomber). Wingspan (upper mainplane) 13.66 m (lower mainplane) 13.71 m; length 11.7 m; armament 2 x .303-inch machine-guns, up to 2000 lb bombs; maximum speed 218 km/h; range 700 km; power 1 x 660 h.p. Bristol Pegasus radial engine.

Bomber aircraft

RNZAF Hudson bombers are serviced at an island air base during the Pacific War (NZ National Archives, AIR118/72b)

The Baffin, designed as a biplane torpedo-bomber for the ★Fleet Air Arm, was offered to New Zealand when it was superseded by the Fairey Swordfish. Twenty-nine were obtained to equip the TAF's new coastal reconnaissance squadrons. Allocated to squadrons in Auckland, Wellington, and Christchurch from 1937, they were among the first RNZAF machines to see operational service after the outbreak of the Second World War. They were later replaced by Vincents.

Canberra, English Electric (2-seat tactical bomber). Wingspan 19.5 m; length 20 m; armament 8000 lb bombs; maximum speed 865 km/h; range 6000 km; power: 2 x Rolls Royce Avon turbojets.

The Canberra, the RNZAF's first jet bomber, was obtained to meet the RNZAF's requirement for a tactical bombing and interdiction capacity. Although the aircraft was being built under licence in Australia, New Zealand was deterred from utilising this source by cost; instead it ordered thirteen British-built aircraft (including two trainers) in 1957. This decision was influenced by the fact that 75 Squadron in Malaya had been equipped with hired Canberras, which it employed in ★Malayan Emergency operations during the late 1950s. New Zealand's new aircraft were operated by 14 Squadron with great success between October 1959 and July 1970, in New Zealand and overseas. Two were lost in accidents and one was returned to the manufacturers with cracks in its main spar. The remainder were sold to the Indian Air Force when the RNZAF replaced them with the A-4 Skyhawk.

Dauntless, Douglas (Single-seat dive-bomber). Wingspan 12.5 m; length 9.8 m; armament 2 x .5-inch machine-guns, 1 or 2 x .3-inch machine-guns, up to 1600 lb bombs; maximum speed 408 km/h; range 730 km; power 1 x Wright Cyclone radial engine.

The Dauntless was used by the US Navy as a carrier and land-based dive-bomber during the Pacific War. Of the sixty-eight which served in the RNZAF during 1943–44, the first twenty-three were Guadalcanal veterans, SBD-3 models used by 25 Squadron for training at Seagrove, near Auckland. Eighteen SBD-4s (later replaced by SBD-5s) were flown by 25 Squadron in the Solomons campaign. However, the aircraft's operational service with the RNZAF lasted only from March to May 1944.

Hudson, Lockheed (5-crew light bomber). Wingspan 20 m; length 13.5 m; armament 5 x .303-inch machine-guns, 1600 lb bombs; maximum speed 394 km/h;

range 3450 km; power [Marks III, IIIA] 2 x 1200 h.p. Wright Cyclone radial engines, [V, VI] 2 x 1200 h.p. Pratt & Whitney Twin Wasp radial engines.

During the early years of the Second World War, the two-engine Hudson, with its distinctive twin fins and rudders, was the only modern aircraft available to the RNZAF for home and regional defence. Hudsons could claim several firsts: the first RNZAF aircraft to go into action, the first RNZAF aircraft to shoot down an enemy aircraft (on 2 April 1943), and the first to attack a submarine. In all ninety-four were delivered. As they were progressively replaced by the larger, faster Lockheed Ventura from 1943, they were transferred to secondary roles. Twelve were converted to carry twelve passengers each, as well as about 850 lb of freight. They were pressed into service with 40 Squadron on regular services between Whenuapai and forward units in the Pacific. Others joined the gunnery training school at Ohakea and a utility flight at Guadalcanal where duties included target towing. Three, painted in colourful orange and black markings, stood on search and rescue duties, while others served at the Air Navigation School at Wigram until 1949.

Ventura, Lockheed (4–5-crew medium bomber). Wingspan 20 m; length 15.7 m; armament 2 x .5-inch machine-guns, 6 x .303-inch machine-guns, 3000 lb bombs; maximum speed 500 km/h; range 2650 km; power 2 x 2000 h.p. Pratt & Whitney Double Wasp radial engines.

Developed by Lockheed from the Lodestar airliner, the Ventura had a troubled entry into the RNZAF. Faster and heavier, with more complex systems than the Hudson, it demanded careful handling and additional training for crews accustomed to the relatively docile Hudson. Once the aircraft was mastered, however, it produced outstanding results for squadrons in the Pacific. The first were taken into action by 1 Squadron from Guadalcanal in October 1943, joining the fighter squadrons in the assault on Bougainville and Rabaul. Later twenty-three US Army versions of the Ventura (B-34), with glazed rather than solid nose, were obtained by the RNZAF, but were used mainly in training units because of their indifferent condition and non-standard equipment.

Vildebeeste, Vickers (3-seat biplane). Wingspan 14.2 m; length 11.2 m (Mark IV 11.5 m); armament 1 x Vickers .303-inch machine-gun, 1 x .303-inch Lewis machine-gun, 1000 lb bombs; maximum speed 227 km/h; range 2000 km; power 1 x 620 h.p. Bristol Pegasus radial engine, [IV] 1 x 825 h.p. Bristol Perseus engine.

The Vildebeeste was the first genuine bomber to serve with the RNZAF. Eight were ordered in 1933 for coastal defence and reconnaissance purposes, and the first arrived in 1935. One conducted an extensive aerial survey of the South Island in 1937–38. From 1940, twenty-seven former RAF Vildebeestes arrived from Britain to supplement the RNZAF's meagre front-line aircraft strength, and many served in the general reconnaissance squadrons before the arrival of the Hudsons. Several carried early radar sets. One was dispatched to Fiji. Most ended their days at training schools in 1943–44. Some were used as target towers.

Vincent, Vickers (3-seat biplane general purpose bomber). Wingspan 14.2 m; length 11.1 m; armament 1 x Vickers .303-inch machine-gun, 1 x .303-inch Lewis machine-gun, 1000 lb bombs; maximum speed 227 km/h; range 2000 km; power 1 x 620 h.p. Pegasus radial engine.

Developed as a general-purpose machine, the Vincent entered service with the RNZAF in 1940, when the first of sixty-two ex-RAF machines were received. They were allocated to the reconnaissance squadrons, and conducted long-range patrols over the maritime approaches.

BRIAN LOCKSTONE

Bombs Although aerial bombing emerged as a significant form of warfare during the ★First World War, New Zealand did not acquire any substantial quantity of bombs until the late 1930s, following Group Captain R.A. ★Cochrane's report on RNZAF requirements. Along with thirty Wellington medium bombers, standard high explosive (HE) and small practice bombs were ordered from Great Britain, and work began on the necessary bomb storage facilities at Wigram, Hobsonville, Ohakea, and Whenuapai. The bombs were eventually received, but not the Wellingtons, which were made available to the RAF for operations in Europe. Part of New Zealand's bomb reserves were later transferred to Fiji as part of measures to deal with the Japanese threat. Since the ★Second World War the RNZAF has continued to hold only HE and practice bombs. Incendiary, napalm, nuclear, chemical, special munitions, and other such bombs have never formed part of its armoury. Once New Zealand began acquiring American equipment in the late 1960s, there was a shift to American sources of supply. Current stocks include 1000 lb Mark 83 bombs for strike aircraft, 500 lb Mark 82 bombs for strike aircraft and as depth bombs (earlier 350 lb depth charges having been withdrawn), 25 lb BDU 33 practice bombs to simulate low drag bombs, and 5 lb Mark 106 practice bombs to simulate high drag bombs. The Mark 83 and 82 series bombs are assembled for use as either low drag or high drag weapons by the fitting of a conical tail unit (low drag) or a snake eye tail unit (high drag). High drag is used for a low-level attack and allows the bomber aircraft to clear the target before the bomb explodes. When used as a depth bomb, the Mark 82 is

Bombing up one of 75 Squadron's Wellington bombers in England (*War History Collection, Alexander Turnbull Library, F-1191-1/2-DA*)

fitted with a modified snake-eye tail unit and a special fuse. The upgraded Skyhawk weapon systems now in use allow the Mark 83 bomb to be used as a laser-guided bomb. As dramatically demonstrated during the ★Gulf War, the old iron high explosive bomb can now be delivered very accurately on a target and at a considerably lower cost than sophisticated missiles.

B.R. ANDERSON

Bonifant, Brigadier Ian Lambert ('Bonny') (3 March 1912–7 May 1994) was a leading citizen soldier of the ★Second World War. Born in Ashburton, he was a stock agent and a Territorial officer when he enlisted in 2NZEF in September 1939. His first action was with the Divisional Cavalry in ★Greece, from which he later escaped to ★Crete in a caique. He commanded a squadron of light tanks during the Crusader offensive in North Africa. From September 1942 he commanded 25th Battalion; he was wounded during its assault on the Miteiriya Ridge during the Battle of El Alamein. His aggressive leadership was rewarded by appointment as a DSO. After his recovery, he commanded the Divisional Cavalry in Tunisia and the early part of the ★Italian campaign. As commander, from March 1944, of 6th Brigade, he had the task of taking Cassino; that he failed owed much to the conditions in which the New Zealanders found themselves fighting, though his inexperience as a brigade commander was probably also a factor. After furlough in New Zealand, he returned to Italy to command 5th Brigade in the last four months of the campaign. His effective leadership earned him a bar to his DSO. After the war he became a regular soldier, but soon found peacetime soldiering not to his liking and resigned. He later resided in Australia, and died in Sydney.

Boxer, Air Vice-Marshal Sir Alan Hunter Cachemaille (1 December 1916–26 April 1998) was a prominent expatriate officer in the RAF. Hastings-born, he was the son of a noted surgeon from the ★First World War and long-serving president of the New Zealand RSA. He gained a commission in the RAF in 1939, and served for three years in Training Command before joining Bomber Command. He won a DFC in 1943, and was made a DSO in the following year. From March 1944 he commanded 161 (Special Duties) Squadron, which was involved in supporting resistance movements in German-occupied Europe and rescuing Allied pilots and escaped prisoners. He flew Halifax bombers to Warsaw to drop supplies to the Polish Home Army during the uprising in 1944. In 1949 he was seconded to the United States Strategic Air Command, and during 1950–51 he flew with 92nd Bomber Group in the Far East. In August 1950, during the ★Korean War, he became the first non-American to lead a Super fortress group into action over North Korea. Back in the United Kingdom in 1952, he served in a variety of staff posts before taking command, in 1956, of 7 Squadron, whose Valiant bombers were part of Great Britain's nuclear deterrent. After commanding the RAF station at Wittering in 1958–59, he held high staff positions in Bomber Command Headquarters and in the Ministry of Defence until his retirement in 1970. He was appointed a CB in 1968 and a KCVO two years later.

Braithwaite, Brigadier-General William Garnett (21 October 1870–15 October 1937) was one of a group of British officers who oversaw the reorganisation of New Zealand's military forces before the ★First World War and went on to serve with distinction in 1NZEF. After attending Sandhurst, he was commissioned in the Royal Welch Fusiliers in 1891, and served in the ★Boer War. In 1911 he was seconded to the New Zealand Military Forces. As Chief of the General Staff, he played a key role in the development of the new ★Territorial Force. After the outbreak of the First World War, he became General Staff Officer responsible for operational planning in 1NZEF. He was the ★New Zealand and Australian Division's operations officer at ★Gallipoli, and briefly commanded the New Zealand Infantry Brigade. From 1916 he commanded the 2nd New Zealand Infantry Brigade on the ★Western Front. His performance during the New Zealand Division's operations on the Somme in 1916 and at Messines in 1917 demonstrated considerable competence, and he temporarily commanded the division in both December 1916 and July 1917. When his brigade suffered appalling losses during the unsuccessful attack on Passchendaele on 12 October 1917, he demanded that the attack be discontinued. A later attack upon Polderhoek Chateau in December 1917 was also repulsed with heavy losses. Shortly after, ill and exhausted, he was evacuated to England. A thorough professional, energetic and bluntly critical of those that failed to meet his standards, he was also noted for his sense of humour and concern for the welfare of his men. Following his evacuation, he severed his connection with the New Zealand forces, and when he returned to service later in 1918 it was as a staff officer in a British corps. After the war he continued his career in the British Army until his retirement in 1925.

Brandon, Lieutenant-Colonel Alfred de Bathe (21 July 1883–19 June 1974) was the first New Zealand airman to be made a DSO. Born in Wellington, the son of a Wellington mayor in the 1890s, he was educated in Wellington and the United Kingdom before joining his father's legal firm in Wellington. Active in both the ★Volunteer and ★Territorial Forces, he was lieutenant-colonel commanding the 5th (Wellington) Regiment in 1915 when he resigned to go to England to learn to fly at his own expense. He joined the Royal Flying Corps in December 1915, and received his honour for his attacks on German Zeppelins raiding targets in eastern England in the following year. He was possibly instrumental in the destruction of the first Zeppelin brought down on 31 March 1916—there remains some question as to whether artillery batteries were responsible—and helped destroy another on the night of the following 23–24 September. Apart from the DSO, his exploits won him a MC and three mentions in dispatches; he rose to the rank of major. A flying accident in March 1917 left him severely injured. He returned to New Zealand in 1919 as a staff officer to Colonel A.V. ★Bettington, and helped draft his report, after which he returned to the law.

Bridge, Colonel Cyprian (7 June 1807–7 July 1885) was a senior British officer during the Northern War, whose watercolour paintings have left an enduring image of the conflict and British Army and Maori life in New Zealand. Commissioned in the 58th Regiment in 1825 and promoted to major in 1842, he proceeded to Australia with his regiment in 1844 and was sent across the Tasman in the following year. He commanded the regiment in the campaign against Hone ★Heke and ★Kawiti, fighting at Puketutu in May 1845 and subsequently leading an expedition against Kapotai Pa. In July 1845 he led one of the ill-fated storming parties at Ohaeawai, an operation he knew to be ill considered. He was Resident Magistrate in the Bay of Islands until 1851, and was promoted to command the 58th Regiment in 1854. He retired when his regiment returned to England four years later. His journal and a collection of his watercolours is held by the Alexander Turnbull Library in Wellington. A nephew, Rear-Admiral Sir Cyprian Bridge, commanded the ★Australia Station in the 1890s.

Bridson, Commander Gordon (2 December 1909–6 December 1972) was a leading citizen seaman of the ★Second World War. Born in Wellington, he enlisted in the Auckland Division of the New Zealand Royal Naval Volunteer Reserve in 1927 while working as a sales representative, and was soon commissioned. Called up in April 1940, he was one of a group of RNVR personnel sent to the United Kingdom for service in the Royal Navy in the following month. For more than a year, he commanded a minesweeper-trawler (HMS *Walnut*) in convoy escort operations in the English Channel, service which earned him a DSC. Late in 1941 he set off for New Zealand in command of the RNZN's new corvette HMNZS *Kiwi*, and he subsequently commanded her in the ★Solomons campaign as part of the 25th Minesweeping Flotilla. His most dramatic moment of the war came on the night of 29–30 January 1943 when *Kiwi*, with HMNZS *Moa*, destroyed the Japanese submarine *I-1*, a spirited action which ended when he rammed and sank the much larger and more heavily armed enemy vessel. For this exploit, he was made a DSO and awarded a US Navy Cross. After serving from May 1944 as Naval Officer in Charge first at Dunedin, then at Lyttelton, he was demobilised in 1946.

British Army in New Zealand The British Army and all its component parts are an essential element of New Zealand history. From its colonial beginnings in 1840 to at least the end of the ★Second World War in 1945 the British Army, in some form or another, played a vital part in the development of New Zealand. The British government's decision to acquire the sovereignty of New Zealand by treaty owed much to the state of the Army. Prior to 1840 New Zealand had been regarded by successive governments as independent, although there had been attempts by the nearest British colony, New South Wales, to secure the interests of its traders by imposing order through the use of its military and naval resources. These had ranged from a sergeant's guard, sent to recapture escaped convicts, to a detachment from 50th Regiment which took part in

British Army in New Zealand

the 1834 punitive expedition of HMS *Alligator* (see EARLY MAORI–EUROPEAN CONFLICT). However, because (to save expense) the British government was trying to control its rapidly expanding empire without augmenting its armed services, it had become a feature of policy that when New Zealand was added it would be with the consent of the indigenous Maori tribes. Moreover, that consent would be formalised by a treaty which would signify the acquisition of sovereignty and ward off any objections by France and the United States, which both had interests in the South Pacific. The Royal Navy, supreme on the oceans, and not the Army would then safeguard the new possession.

In the event the policy worked with regard to foreign interference, but failed to maintain order internally. At this time there were 103 battalions in the British Army, of which only twenty-one were in the United Kingdom. Canada, South Africa, the Indies, India, and Australia absorbed the bulk of the remainder, with their military and administrative leaders insisting that they required more, not fewer, troops. With political power in Great Britain balanced uneasily between Whigs and Tories and a budget yet without the benefit of income tax, augmentation was not an option. Instead, existing troop allocations were combed for spare companies, with Australian colonies under particular scrutiny. Consideration was even given to stationing in New Zealand waters a naval vessel with 100 marines, but the Admiralty objected on the grounds that this would be tantamount to increasing the Army at the expense of the Royal Navy. However, it was found that there were five regiments in the New South Wales command and that their only purpose was to control convicts. A great military establishment with a major-general at its head could not be defended on any grounds of sound policy. By 1846, after much debate, the decision had been made that there would be a military establishment of 2000 in New Zealand led by a major-general. Thus Major-General G.D. ★Pitt became on 8 October 1847 the first general officer commanding in New Zealand. The Duke of Wellington, the Commander-in-Chief, had earlier warned that this would be just the beginning. An official British Army establishment now existed in New Zealand rather than occasional urgent but temporary detachments from New South Wales, such as the first, from 80th Regiment, which had come with Major Bunbury in April 1840. Although the first two Governors, Captains Hobson and FitzRoy, were naval officers, British army officers soon predominated in the development of the new colony. There is space to look at only two early examples.

Major Thomas Bunbury, 80th Regiment, has the distinction of having been the first officer commanding in New Zealand. He was a fairly typical officer of the period, having bought his promotion step by step to his final rank of lieutenant-colonel. His great virtue may have been his common sense and reliability, clearly demonstrated during his first important task, that of gaining adherents to the Treaty of Waitangi in the South Island. That he proclaimed British sovereignty over Stewart and South Islands is now a largely forgotten quirk of history. His greatest contribution may have been that he warned British authorities that Maori could become a foe much more formidable than missionaries and others had reported. Major Matthew Richmond, 96th Regiment, was sent to Wellington in July 1843 as Police Magistrate and chief government agent for all the southern districts. As such he commanded troops, played a leading role in negotiating with Maori and settlers over the Hutt Valley land, was involved with disturbances in Wanganui

The 58th Regiment on parade in Auckland in 1858 (*Alexander Turnbull Library, F-152177-1/2*)

and Nelson, and in general terms was closely identified with the attempt to ensure that the imposition of European government was not accompanied by conflict. He was frequently vilified by New Zealand Company settlers as an obstacle between them and the possession of land. Governor George ★Grey found him insufficiently compliant and banished him to Nelson as Resident Magistrate. Like so many army officers, he had served in the ★Militia, in Wellington, with the rank of lieutenant-colonel. It would be difficult to overstate the influence that this patient, sensible officer had on the early development of Wellington, Wanganui, and Nelson.

Army personnel added greatly to cultural development, and much of our knowledge of both landscapes and personalities comes from the sketches and watercolours of men such as Colonel Cyprian ★Bridge and Lance-Sergeant J. Williams of 58th Regiment, and the Royal Engineer Captain G. Bennett, who brought the art of hachuring to New Zealand at the very beginning of its existence. Major-General Robley's work on the Maori moko (facial tattoo) is of exceptional value, as are his sketches and paintings of much to do with Maori protocol and the nature of pa defences. Lieutenant-Colonel C.E. ★Gold left a series of invaluable panoramas, studies of untouched tree and vegetation growth, haka actions, and contemporary military camps. Some soldiers, such as Lieutenant-Colonel E.A. Williams and J.O. Hanley, gained a wide circle of interest through the reproduction of their sketches in the *Illustrated London News*. Many of the officers' sketch books have survived, all regiments being represented, and without their work much less would be known about both the countryside from the beginning of European colonisation and about the indigenous tribes.

The Army played a major part in the financial affairs of the colony, and consequently in the development of the infrastructure of all the settlements. Until early 1844 military detachments were financed by their parent headquarters in New South Wales, but at the end of 1843 a Commissariat, or Military, Chest was established in New Zealand. A Deputy Acting Commissary-General, P. Turner, appointed from New South Wales, assumed control of the Chest. The duties of Commissariat officers, who, although subject to military law and discipline, were governed by the Lords Commissioners of the British Treasury, included not only the payment of all strictly military dues but also payment for public works undertaken by the local authority. Thus, to take two early examples, the stone wall around the Auckland barracks and the Wellington–Porirua road were constructed by soldiers getting, in addition to their normal allowances, extra pay according to scales set by the Treasury. In both cases Maori—chiefs with their slaves or men from nearby tribes—gave assistance, paid by the Military Chest on a strict scale. The good will and camaraderie between Maori and soldiers was a notable feature of these public works. The Military Chest was funded by the British Treasury in either bills or specie and until British troops were withdrawn in the 1860s was often overdrawn and the subject of disputes between the colonial government and London and New South Wales.

The British Army was responsible for establishing many of the systems and protocols that exist to this day, often in a modified form. The first Governor, Hobson, was also the first commander-in-chief. His responsibilities as such were meticulously set down in the Queen's Regulations for the Army. The main difference between that day and the present is that until self-government in military matters was achieved in 1870 with the departure of the last imperial troops, the Governor as commander-in-chief in and over New Zealand acted on the advice of a British minister of the Crown, whereas after 1870 the Governor (and from 1917 the Governor-General) has acted only on the advice of a New Zealand minister. Now, as in 1840, all commissioned officers swear an oath of loyalty to the reigning monarch, but since 1953 the Queen has also been Queen of New Zealand. The British Army Act of 1881 allowed self-governing colonies to legislate for their forces serving overseas, but until New Zealand's Army Act 1950 severed all direct links, the relevant British Act, subject to some modifications, actually governed New Zealand troops, both overseas and locally. That meant that New Zealand services were subject to King's Regulations as stipulated in the Army Act 1881 and it was not until the Second World War that the vital modification voiding the ★death penalty was made. The legal connections were reinforced by the part played by British Army officers in the development of the New Zealand military forces. From 1892 officers were seconded to serve as Commandant, a process which reached its apogee with the advent of Major-General A.J. ★Godley in 1910 with thirteen British officers to take in hand the development of the new ★Territorial Force and greatly enhance the professionalism of the New Zealand military establishment. The lasting effect of this century-long association with the British Army, its traditions, and its regulations has been a marked compatibility between New Zealand and British armed forces, evident to the present day in, say, peace enforcement in Bosnia-Herzegovina (see PEACE-KEEPING). Apart from the many inevitable similarities of the British and New Zealand legislation, the single remaining link dating back to 1840 is that the Letters Patent of the Governor-General appoint him or her as commander-in-chief in and over New Zealand, a provision considered sufficiently covered by

British Army in New Zealand

the authority of New Zealand ministers of the Crown. Thus it can be established that the connection with the British Army has been as important to the development of the ★New Zealand Army as has been the Westminster tradition to government. Facing a new century, both are now under careful scrutiny because of changes in national and international requirements.

Table 2   British Infantry Regiments in New Zealand

Regiment	Dates
12th (East Suffolk) Regt of Foot	1860–67
14th (Buckinghamshire) Regt of Foot	1860–66
18th (Royal Irish) Regt of Foot	1863–70
40th (Somersetshire) Regt of Foot	1860–66
43rd (Monmouthshire) Light Infantry	1863–66
50th (Queen's Own) Regt of Foot	1863–67
57th (West Middlesex) Regt of Foot	1861–67
58th (Rutlandshire) Regt of Foot	1845–58
65th (Yorkshire North Riding) Regt of Foot	1846–65
68th (Durham) Light Infantry	1864–66
70th (Surrey) Regt of Foot	1861–66
80th (South Staffordshire) Regt of Foot	1840–44
96th (Manchester) Regt of Foot	1843–46
99th (Lanarkshire Volunteers) Regt of Foot	1844–47

All told, a total of fourteen regiments, in the case of the 80th (South Staffordshire) Regiment a detachment only, served in New Zealand between 1840 and 1870 when the last regiment, the 18th (Royal Irish), departed. (See table 2.) Of these, all except the 80th wore 'New Zealand' on their ★battle honours. In 1957 eight of these regiments were amalgamated, but their battle honours were taken over by the amalgamated regiment. Only the 18th Regiment, in New Zealand from 1863 to 1870, with its battle honours, has entirely disappeared, being disbanded on the creation of the Irish Free State in 1922. Little is written about the effect of the New Zealand experience on these regiments, and it remains a fruitful area of study for the future. However, conflicts with Maori during the ★New Zealand Wars presented many potential lessons in a type of warfare that was new to the officers of the time. One thing was certain, the myth that one hundred soldiers could defeat any Maori opposition was soon exploded, but perhaps it was fortunate that the Maori so-called rebels, never more than 1000-strong at any one time, made the tactical mistake of bottling themselves up in their fortified pa rather than concentrating on purely guerrilla tactics. For, however lacking in military expertise many of the investments of pa now seem, these strongholds inevitably fell or were abandoned in the long run. Maori war parties attacking in sudden and deadly affray and then disappearing into the fastness of the bush would have imposed more serious difficulties. Governor Grey recognised the danger of such Maori tactics when he summed up the future need for troops in 1849 by stressing that Maori were addicted to war, were well armed, and were the equal of European troops. They were good tacticians and availed themselves of the advantages afforded by their wilds and fastnesses, carrying no baggage, and attended by their women carrying potatoes on their bodies and digging fern roots.

New Zealand was the first country in the South Pacific to have a detachment of Royal Artillery. There had certainly been a few pieces scattered around the country before this, either in bartering for land as by J. Blenkinsop in Cloudy Bay or for means of control through display, like Thomas ★McDonnell's nine-gun battery of 6- and 12-pounders together with two 24-pounders at Hokianga. The French Nanto-Bordelaise Company at Akaroa, better supported for colonisation than the British New Zealand Company, had the first 'official' battery, but this was not off-loaded from the French warship stationed there until 1849. When Governor FitzRoy's urgent request for artillery for use in his confrontation with Hone ★Heke was discussed in London, it was found incredible that there were not even a couple of howitzers in the New South Wales command. Arrangements were immediately made to rectify this situation and the first detachment of Royal Artillery was sent to New Zealand via Sydney in January 1846. This began a long and mutually fruitful association between New Zealand and the Royal Artillery.

Military action against the Maori and the creation of a separate British Army command in New Zealand were responsible for vital changes in the imperial structure of the Army. The most important of these changes was the 'tour' of units, or the manner in which they were shuffled throughout the Empire, and the changes to the regulation governing expiry of service and settlement in the several colonies. From mid 1845 the size and make-up of the forces in New Zealand was much discussed by the Colonial Secretary, the Secretary for War, the Board of Ordnance, and the Commander-in-Chief. As well as actual military needs, the means of fulfilling the policy requirements of the colony were closely debated. Thus a Deputy Quartermaster-General was appointed to sort out the New Zealand Company's land claims while at the same time actual troop dispositions were being discussed. The normal process was for the regiments, or battalions, to have five years in England for every ten years abroad, but it was proving impossible to maintain either this or the sequence of colonial possessions in which the regiments were rotated. The new establishment in New Zealand greatly exacerbated the situation. Various remedial proposals were circulated among London officials, many of them rejected by the Commander-in-Chief, the Duke of Wellington, who wanted to ensure that the most suitable serving men were not discharged in the colonies to become settlers on advantageous terms. The final solution was that only soldiers serving in Australia and New Zealand could obtain their discharge in order to remain as settlers. New South Wales had already passed on to the Colonial Secretary a comment by a select committee of its Legislative Council to the effect that New Zealand was afforded protection by depriving New South Wales of the troops to which it was fairly entitled, and probably did not greatly benefit from the new ruling, but New Zealand settlement was indeed affected. British soldiers were in fact already seeking release in New Zealand. Colonel McCleverty in the southern district reported that NCOs and men, usually of good character and possessing trade and other skills, wanted to get their discharge either gratuitously or by purchase to become settlers. Many had been employed on roads or other public works and had accumulated savings with a view to buying land, leading generally to habits of economy, industry, and sobriety. Some had already grown vegetables and pastured cattle on unoccupied land. They would form a valuable class of settler and a good militia, although the regiment would lose its best-behaved men—echoing precisely the Duke of Wellington's fear. Major-General Pitt, in the northern district, in the following year suggested that two or three hundred men could purchase their discharge to become settlers. Such reduction would not be as obvious to Maori as the embarkation of a similar number of men, and there would be no real decrease in the European population or numbers available for service should the need arise. Grey agreed, and soldier settlement became a part of land settlement schemes that included occupation of confiscated Maori land as a means of keeping the peace (see MILITARY SETTLERS). As well as providing small farmers who also worked at the many unskilled and semi-skilled tasks of the new settlements, the Army from its officer corps yielded valuable leaders in most walks of civilian life, in the Militia, the Mounted Police, the larger rural communities, and in politics. Some carried on the tradition of military service, the most outstanding example being that of the Russell family, members of which served in early military operations, in politics, and as farmers, providing a divisional commander in the ★First World War and a distinguished battalion commander in the Second.

The experience of serving officers must not be overlooked, for there are many examples of the influence they had both in New Zealand and in London. Two examples can give an indication of this. In the Wellington area, officers questioned the legality of court-martialling Maori rebels at the instigation of Governor Grey. Later, Major-General Duncan ★Cameron so strongly reported his distaste for operations against Maori that led to land confiscation, on the grounds that it was against the long-term interests of both races, that he was given an equal share in the responsibility of authorising them. In politics, although serving officers could play no active part in national politics until they had sold their commissions or retired on half pay, the very nature of their leading role in society gave them considerable influence. A notable example may be found in the activity of Captain T.M. ★Haultain, who commanded a division of ★Fencibles and was the first in New Zealand to be accused of arranging block voting when, thanks largely to Fencibles' votes, he was elected to the first Auckland Municipal Council. Later, he commanded a Waikato militia regiment and then entered national politics to become the Minister of Colonial Defence responsible for the location of military settlers.

The importance of the military presence to the social life of both settlers and Maori cannot be exaggerated. Charlotte Brontë would have found ample material for her gentle but probing analysis of the effect of the redcoats on the crinolines at the balls and functions of the new towns. Many Maori observed and learned; even the phlegmatic Colonel Henry ★Despard was moved to record that it was astonishing to see the perfect good fellowship that existed between the troops and their Maori allies. For the soldiers themselves discipline was extremely rigid and the class system of the day was unrelenting. Initially defaulters were imprisoned in the town jails, but those suffering long sentences were transported to Australian convict stations. Sentences now appear outrageous: insubordination could result in imprisonment for life, a fate suffered by one unfortunate who had thrown a mess tin at an officer. Wellington had forbidden all officers to speak directly to a private soldier, and all communication had to be through an NCO. Perhaps the contrast between the restrictions of a soldier's life and the evident freedom of a settler was an important factor in the popularity of soldier settlements. Clearly, then, in very many aspects of New Zealand life, as in its renowned military tradition, the British Army played a greatly significant and enduring part.

I. Wards, *The Shadow of the Land: A Study of British Policy and Racial Conflict in New Zealand 1832–1852* (Historical Publications Branch, Wellington, 1968).

IAN WARDS

British Commonwealth Far East Strategic Reserve

, established in 1955, was a response to the problems of defending Malaya against possible external attack from Chinese forces. First mooted two years before, it was intended to provide the forces needed to implement the preferred ★ANZAM defence strategy, which was based on holding positions on the narrow isthmus of the Malayan peninsula (the so-called Songkla Line)—an operation which demanded immediately available forces. Since these positions were in Thailand, they could not be occupied until after that country was invaded. It was hoped in 1953 that the ★Korean War armistice would release forces which could be redeployed to Malaya—an approach which New Zealand firmly resisted. The reserve consisted of an infantry brigade (★28th British Commonwealth Infantry Brigade), air force squadrons, and a naval carrier group. New Zealand's agreement to make a contribution to the reserve coincided with the shift of the focus of its global war planning from the Middle East—the ★Middle East commitment—to South-east Asia. It provided an SAS unit, which was replaced in 1958 by an infantry battalion, 14 Squadron RNZAF (redeployed from ★Cyprus), half a long-range air transport squadron (later the full 41 Squadron), and two frigates (and another if necessary in an emergency). As the United States' strategic concept for the defence of South-east Asia took precedence, the emphasis of planning for the use of the reserve soon shifted from the defence of Malaya under ANZAM to participation in ★SEATO operations. To this end, training exercises involving reserve forces were held in Thailand at regular intervals. Without prejudice to these preparations for external defence, the reserve was also, as a secondary objective, available for operations against communist insurgents in Malaya during the ★Malayan Emergency, and New Zealand forces were used in this role in the late 1950s. Following the attainment of independence by Malaya, the Anglo-Malayan (later Malaysian) Defence Agreement of 1957, with which New Zealand was associated two years later, provided the basis for the continued stationing of the reserve in that country. Its deployment as part of SEATO, of which Malaya was not a member, became somewhat problematical, but in the event the issue never had to be faced. New Zealand units from the reserve did, however, take part in ★Confrontation and the ★Vietnam War. In 1966 14 Squadron was withdrawn to New Zealand, and the naval contribution was reduced to one frigate. The reserve continued in existence until 1971, when an ★ANZUK Force was established.

I. McGibbon, 'The Defence of New Zealand 1945–1957', in Sir Alister McIntosh et al, *New Zealand in World Affairs*, vol I (Price Milburn, Wellington, 1977).

British Commonwealth Forces, Korea (BCFK), established in December 1950, was responsible for the administration and non-operational control of the British Commonwealth ground forces—British, Australian, New Zealand, Canadian, and Indian—which took part in the ★Korean War as part of the United Nations Command. Lieutenant-General Sir Horace Robertson, the Commander-in-Chief of the ★British Commonwealth Occupation Force in Japan, which provided most of the Commonwealth units' logistic support, became Commander-in-Chief, BCFK as well. Not until mid 1951 was BCFK's separate identity in Japan enhanced by the establishment of a separate small BCFK headquarters distinct from BCOF headquarters, though BCOF continued to provide a range of support to BCFK. Costs were apportioned on a pro rata basis according to the numerical strength of the national contingents in Korea, in New Zealand's case amounting to approximately 5 per cent. BCFK line of communication and logistic support units in South Korea and Japan were often composite in nature. At the end of 1951 New Zealanders comprised 3 per cent of BCFK's 5300 personnel. They included a signals troop, which was based in Seoul, and individuals serving in a range of BCFK composite units. After the conclusion of the Japanese Peace Treaty, BCFK assumed those Korean support functions previously provided by BCOF. BCFK was finally disbanded on 1 July 1956, at which point support arrangements in Japan were wound up and the Commander-in-Chief, British Far East Land Forces, in Singapore assumed responsibility for the non-operational requirements of the residual Commonwealth units in Korea (until their withdrawal in 1957).

British Commonwealth Occupation Force (BCOF) Following the capitulation of Japan in August 1945, agreement was reached with the United States on the deployment of a British Commonwealth force as part of the occupation. Great Britain, Australia, New Zealand, and India all agreed to contribute infantry brigades. These forces arrived in Japan between February and May 1946, substantially after their American counterparts. Together with separate air forces and shore-based naval personnel, the British Commonwealth Occupation Force numbered 36,000 men and women at its peak. New Zealand contributed both troops and airmen (see JAYFORCE).

In keeping with its conception of the changing nature of Commonwealth arrangements in the Pacific region, Australia assumed a leading role in the establishment of the force. This was reflected in the appointment of an Australian officer, Lieutenant-General John Northcott, to command the force, though he was almost immediately replaced by Lieutenant-General H.C.H. (later Sir Horace) Robertson, whose tenure lasted until November 1951. Robertson reported to the Joint Chiefs of Staff in Australia, which met in Melbourne and comprised the Australian Chiefs of Staff Committee with British, New Zealand, and Indian representation. Australia also supplied many of the headquarters personnel.

Both Britain and India withdrew their forces from BCOF in 1947, and New Zealand did so in late 1948. Australia continued to maintain the force, though its size steadily diminished. Plans were in train to withdraw the remnants of BCOF by the end of 1950, but the outbreak of the ★Korean War gave it a new lease of life. Australian forces in Japan were soon made available to the United Nations Command in Korea. BCOF assumed a key role in the support of the Commonwealth forces deployed in Korea, with Robertson becoming their non-operational commander. Following the peace settlement with Japan, BCOF's residual functions were assumed by the ★British Commonwealth Forces, Korea.

Brown, Brigadier-General Charles Henry Jeffries (8 May 1872–8 June 1917) was one of three New Zealand brigadier-generals killed in the ★First World War. Christchurch-born, he enlisted with the Denniston Rifle Volunteers in 1900, joined the ★New Zealand Staff Corps in 1911, and was seconded to 1NZEF in 1914. At ★Gallipoli he took command of the Canterbury Battalion in May 1915 but was badly wounded a month later. He did not return to active service with the NZEF until April 1916 after hospitalisation in England. He was an active and successful commander of 2nd Battalion, Auckland Regiment, during the New Zealand Division's operations on the Somme in September 1916. From February 1917 he commanded the 1st New Zealand Infantry Brigade. He was killed by a sniper while inspecting ground taken by his brigade in the successful attack on Messines.

Brown, Sergeant Donald Forrester (23 February 1890–1 October 1916) was 1NZEF's first Victoria Cross winner on the ★Western Front. After enlisting in October 1915, he joined 2nd Battalion, Otago Regiment. His posthumous decoration recognised a series of gallant actions during the New Zealand Division's operations on the Somme, beginning with the attack on Flers on 15 September 1916. Three times he charged and destroyed enemy machine-gun positions, while generally encouraging his men as they contended with heavy artillery bombardment by the enemy.

***Buchanan* affair** of 1985 precipitated a crisis in New Zealand's relations with the United States which led to the unilateral suspension by Washington of the United States' obligations under the ★ANZUS treaty, and the downgrading of New Zealand's status from ally to 'friend' of the United States. Despite strong anti-nuclear sentiment within the Labour Party, the Labour administration of David ★Lange initially appeared to respond positively to an American request in December 1984 for a ship visit. The United States authorities nominated USS *Buchanan*, a conventionally powered destroyer, and resisted a New Zealand request, which became public through a leaked report to the press, for a vessel of the Oliver Hazard Perry class, which was clearly incapable of carrying nuclear weapons. Under intense pressure from anti-nuclear activists, the Labour Cabinet thereupon made an about-face. At issue was the question of whether the ship was carrying nuclear weapons. The American government had refused to diverge from its long-standing policy of neither confirming nor denying the presence of nuclear weapons on American naval vessels, a stance which it maintained was essential for operational purposes but which also, perhaps more importantly, left an element of ambiguity for allied governments obliged to take account of domestic anti-nuclear sentiment in dealing with ship visits. The New Zealand government made clear that it would determine that the ship was not nuclear capable, to use Lange's term, before allowing the visit to proceed. Because the *Buchanan*'s ASROC anti-submarine weapon system was capable of delivering nuclear depth charges, port access was refused on 4 February 1985. The *Buchanan*'s proposed visit was cancelled amid bitter recriminations. The American authorities, with some justification, believed that the New Zealand government had acted in bad faith by allowing preparations to proceed so far before baulking, while the New Zealand government for its part maintained that American officials had misunderstood the terms on which New Zealand was willing to accept a visiting warship. (See ANTI-NUCLEARISM)

Buckley, Air Commodore Maurice William (3 August 1895–3 November 1956), a sheep farmer in north Otago, joined the Royal Naval Air Service in 1916 and served in the Eastern Mediterranean theatre. Back in New Zealand, he had been a Territorial airman for three years when, in 1926, he secured a permanent commission in the New Zealand Military Forces. He was an instructor at Wigram, and later commander both there and at Hobsonville. On exchange with the RAF when the ★Second World War began, he was involved in the formation, using Wellington bombers earlier ordered for the RNZAF, of 75 Squadron, which he commanded from April 1940 as it took part in bombing raids on Germany. After commanding an RAF station in 1941, he reverted to the RNZAF late in the year and commanded Northern Group at Whenuapai for about two years, during which it became the hub of a major RNZAF effort in the ★Solomons campaign. His role in that campaign became more direct when, in November 1943, he took command of 1 (Islands) Group. After serving as Deputy Chief of the Air Staff (1944–46) and as the RNZAF's liaison officer in London, he retired in 1951. He was made a CBE in 1946.

Burma campaign Although no New Zealand units took part in the fighting in Burma during the ★Pacific War, a substantial number of New Zealanders were involved there while serving with RAF squadrons or with the Indian Army. In particular, 67 Squadron RAF was manned almost completely by RNZAF personnel on secondment. Formed at Singapore in April 1941, and equipped with obsolete Brewster Buffalos, it was later transferred to Burma, and was the only RAF squadron in the country when Japan entered the war. With a squadron from the American Volunteer Group ('Flying Tigers') from China, it accounted for many raiding Japanese aircraft in the first three months of the conflict, and managed to delay the Japanese advance to some extent. Reinforcement squadrons arrived late in January, and effective operations were mounted against overwhelming odds until the fall of Rangoon on 7 March 1942. Thereafter Japanese pressure became so great that all the RAF squadrons pulled back into India. New Zealanders serving with the RAF continued to take part in the Burma campaign during the next three years. In 1943 there were 300 New Zealand airmen in the theatre, including 200 pilots. Air Marshal Sir Keith ★Park commanded the Allied air forces in South-east Asia from February 1945.

From early 1942 New Zealand met requests for specialist officers for service with the Indian Army, with 2NZEF in the Middle East providing twenty-six (who transferred to British forces for the purpose). During 1943–44, two large parties of engineer officers, forty-six in all, were seconded to the Indian Army from New Zealand itself. Many of them assisted with the provision of facilities on the Burma–India border, in support of General Slim's 14th Army, which defeated the Japanese attempt to invade India at Imphal and Kohima and eventually drove them out of Burma. Most of the twenty-seven New Zealand cadets appointed to commissions in the British or Indian Armies probably also served in Burma.

Burn, Lieutenant William Wallace Allison (17 July 1891–30 July 1915) was New Zealand's first qualified military pilot. Australian by birth, he was an enthusiastic cadet during his secondary schooling in Christchurch. Commissioned in the new ★New Zealand Staff Corps in 1911, he served as the adjutant of a ★Territorial Force unit before being selected, while in England in 1912, to undergo training as a pilot. By the time he returned to New Zealand in 1914, the government had shelved plans to develop an air capacity, and he served as an area officer in Auckland. With the outbreak of the ★First World War, he was seconded in early 1915 to the Indian Army for service in ★Mesopotamia with the Royal Flying Corps. He undertook a number of missions over Turkish lines in an unreliable Caudron aircraft. On 30 July 1915, while serving as an observer, he went missing in action; he and his pilot were probably killed by hostile Arabs after crash-landing.

Burrows, Brigadier James Thomas (13 July 1904–10 June 1991) was a schoolteacher from Christchurch before the ★Second World War. An enthusiastic sportsman, he represented Canterbury at rugby, cricket, and boxing, and was an All Black in 1929. He also commanded his school's cadet unit. Enlisting in 2NZEF in September 1939, he went overseas as a junior officer in 20th Battalion. He rose quickly to command the battalion temporarily on ★Crete, before taking over permanently in December 1941. He was in temporary command of 4th Brigade during the breakout at Minqar Qaim, and subsequently led his battalion in the disastrous battle at Ruweisat Ridge (during which he was briefly captured), before overseeing its conversion to an armoured unit in Egypt. From March 1944 he commanded 5th Brigade at Cassino, 6th Brigade in the advance on Florence, and 5th Brigade again in late 1944 during the fighting on the Adriatic coast. He had the distinction of being the only New Zealand officer to command all three of the division's infantry brigades. Released from 2NZEF in December 1944 to become Rector of Waitaki Boys' High School, he continued his military career by commanding a ★Territorial Force brigade before rejoining the Regular Force in 1950, and taking command of the Southern Military District. He spent a year in South Korea from November 1953 commanding ★Kayforce and was later Army Liaison Officer in London. He retired in January 1960, and later published his memoirs.

J.T. Burrows, *Pathway Among Men* (Whitcombe & Tombs, Christchurch, 1974).

Burton, Second Lieutenant Ormond Edward (16 January 1893–7 January 1974) was an able and courageous soldier who became one of New Zealand's leading pacifists. In the front line at Gallipoli in 1915, Armentières and the Somme in 1916, Messines and Passchendaele in 1917, and the Somme in 1918, he was wounded three times, and awarded an MM. After the fighting at Bapaume in 1918, he was awarded the Médaille d'Honneur avec Glaives en Argent. Regarding this modest French decoration, he said if his commanding officer had not been absent it would have been a DCM; others claim it should have been a VC. Always a committed practising Christian, he had volunteered in 1914, seeing the war as a crusade. He joined the Field Ambulance, but the death of a friend, reinforced by a feeling that 'it was the infantryman who stood the brunt of battle', induced him to seek a transfer to the infantry, and he joined the 2nd Battalion, Auckland Regiment. His abilities at, and fascination with, patrolling in no man's land under the noses of German sentries led to his appointment in due course as Scout Sergeant. Although a natural leader, he did not go on an officer training course until late in 1918, having earlier turned down an opportunity because it would have meant missing Messines—an unwillingness to miss action which was also evident at Passchendaele when he deserted the 2nd Auckland B team (left out of battle personnel) to participate in the New Zealand attack on 4 October 1917. He attended a 'Soldiers' and Workmen's Council' chaired by Major-General Sir Andrew ★Russell for the purpose of raising morale, and was commissioned to write a brief history of the New Zealand Division. Returning to New Zealand, he briefly served as Assistant Vocational Officer, while preparing the official history of the Auckland Regiment, which was published in 1922. He later published a short account of the division in 1935, and a year later the more substantial *The Silent Division, New Zealanders at the Front, 1914–1919*. The outcome of the Paris Peace Conference and reconsideration of his faith had meanwhile led him to become an uncompromising pacifist, who went to prison for his principles during the ★Second World War. On 4 September 1939 Burton, who had helped found the Christian Pacifist Society of New Zealand five years before, was arrested when he spoke out against war outside Parliament. Thereafter he suffered increasingly heavy prison sentences and dismissal from the Methodist Church for his continuing defiance of the law (see ANTI-WAR MOVEMENTS). But his identification with the Cromwellian Ironside tradition persisted, whatever the battlefield he volunteered for. He continued attending ★Anzac Day parades, saluted 'in reverence' from the prison garden overlooking Wellington harbour the departure of a troop convoy, and was unimpressed by the performance of 2NZEF in ★Greece and ★Crete.

RAY GROVER

Butler, Captain George Edmund (15 January 1872–9 August 1936) was an official war artist during the ★First World War. Born in England, he emigrated to New Zealand with his family while still a child. After studying art in Wellington and Sydney, he returned to Europe to establish himself as a successful artist. Reasonably well known and an expatriate New Zealander, he was seen by 1NZEF's War Museum Committee as an appropriate artist to depict the activities of the New Zealanders on the ★Western Front. He began work in September 1918 with the rank of honorary captain, and spent two months preparing a series of watercolour sketches. His landscapes are starkly realistic portrayals of desolate terrain and destroyed buildings in which humans are reduced to impersonality. From late November 1918 he was commissioned to paint portraits of senior 1NZEF officers. He also worked on a number of large oil paintings, which were later purchased by the New Zealand government. His works are part of the war art collection held by the National Archives in Wellington. (See WAR ART)

C

Cadets Cadet service was a feature of secondary schooling for boys in New Zealand for more than a century. Although the first unit was established in 1864, at Dunedin High School, it was not until the ★Boer War that such activities became prominent. The number of cadets greatly expanded, a development which reflected the militaristic ethos of the time. Cadet service, it was believed, would help to avert 'racial decay'. The virtues of military drill were extolled: it 'opens the heart, it expands the chest and lungs, it improves the figure and carriage, and increases the muscular power. Mentally it encourages manliness. It teaches the duty of obedience.' From 1902 the cadet corps were given official encouragement when they were placed under the control of the Education Department. Teachers became officers, while cadets were equipped with miniature rifles and wore a uniform of a glengarry cap and a blue jumper. By 1908 there were more than 15,000 cadets. In the following year cadet service was made compulsory for all boys. From ages twelve to fourteen they would be junior cadets before graduating to the senior cadets for another four years. However, the junior cadets were discontinued in 1912 in favour of physical education for both boys and girls. Administered by the Defence Department, the senior cadets were considered an important part of the ★compulsory military training scheme. They had to undergo sixty-four hours of drill and rifle-shooting annually, with a view to ensuring that when they entered the ★Territorial Force they would already possess basic military skills. When the ★First World War began, there were 25,000 senior cadets. In 1921 cadet units were formed into battalions and affiliated to local Territorial regiments. During the 1920s they reached a high level of efficiency. The first Sea Cadet unit (originally known as the Boys' Naval Brigade) was established in 1928 with the support of the Navy League. When compulsory cadet training was abandoned in 1930, cadet units continued within secondary schools only on a voluntary basis. Although most secondary schools continued to maintain cadet corps, the number of cadets dropped by half. In order to give prospective airmen some background knowledge and training before enlistment, an Air Training Corps (ATC) was formed in March 1941 and grew rapidly. By 1944 9300 boys aged between sixteen and eighteen were involved. The corps's value ensured its continuation after the war. In 1950 it became part of the RNZAF.

In 1948 school cadet corps, the ATC, and the Sea Cadets were brought together in the New Zealand Cadet Force, a joint service agency to oversee their day-to-day administration. With support from their parent services, which regarded the cadets as an effective way of introducing boys to compulsory military training, cadet corps flourished. By 1960 there were more than 60,000 cadets, most in secondary school units. Most units held week-long camps, and specialist artillery, intelligence, signalling, and machine-gun sections were formed. As in the 1920s, rifle shooting competitions between schools were popular.

In the early 1960s service support for cadets began to wane. In part this was attributable to the administrative burden which the scheme imposed on the services, but it also reflected the movement away from a citizen soldier orientation of the Army, which undercut the preliminary training aspect of the cadets. School-based cadets were cut back to a ceiling of 20,000 in July 1964. When asked whether they wanted to continue in the scheme, more than half of the

The Wanganui Marist Brothers School cadet unit on parade (*Tesla Studios Collection, Alexander Turnbull Library, G-16929-1/2*)

schools withdrew, further reducing the cadet force. Changing attitudes within society continued the process. Cadets became less popular, especially among teachers. By 1970 there were only thirty-seven units, down from 139 in 1963. Although inclined to disestablish the cadets altogether, the government was dissuaded by the RSA, the Navy League, and community and cadet groups. Instead it reorganised them. The cadets were removed from their parent services, though the armed forces continued to provide administrative support, uniforms, and specialist instruction. Henceforth local communities and schools provided primary support. For the Sea Cadets and the ATC, which had the Navy League and the Air Cadet League respectively to fall back on, the impact of these changes was not especially damaging. Army cadet units based in secondary schools, on the other hand, fared much worse, sharply declining. Although the opening of cadets to girls in 1978 briefly arrested the overall decline of the cadet movement, there were only 3653 cadets, mostly in ATC units, six years later. The trend was reversed in the late 1980s, however, as adolescents and their parents responded positively to an increased emphasis on adventure pursuits and on citizenship and leadership training. An Army-based New Zealand Cadet Corps was formed in 1986. Like the Sea Cadets and the ATC, it is a community-based rather than school-based youth organisation. There are currently around 4000 cadets in 100 units.

Caldwell, Air Commodore Keith Logan (17 October 1895–28 November 1980) was a leading New Zealand airman of the ★First World War. A Wellingtonian by birth, he learned to fly at the ★Walsh brothers' flying school at Kohimarama before travelling to England at his own expense to enlist in the Royal Flying Corps. From July to November 1916 he flew BE2 observation aircraft with 8 Squadron on the ★Western Front. Transferring to 60 Squadron, which was equipped with Nieuport fighter planes, he earned a reputation as an aggressive pilot. By September 1917 he had secured nine 'kills' and been awarded an MC. From April 1918 he commanded 74 Squadron, earning the nickname 'Grid', the New Zealand nickname for bikes, which he used to refer to aircraft. When during a dogfight his aircraft lost control after a mid-air collision, he climbed on to one wing to balance his stricken aircraft; holding a wing strut with his left hand and controlling the joystick with his right, he was able to crash-land the aircraft, saving himself by leaping out just before it struck the ground. By the end of the war, such exploits had earned him a DFC and bar and the Belgian Croix de Guerre. He took up farming at Cambridge after the war. He also joined the Territorial Air Force, which he commanded from 1930. With the outbreak of the ★Second World War, he returned to active duty as a temporary officer in the RNZAF, and was engaged in a variety of training and administrative posts in New Zealand until May 1945, when he became Air Officer Commanding RNZAF at London. He was made a CBE in 1945.

Calliope Dock Construction of a large graving (or dry) dock at Devonport on Auckland's north shore was begun by the Auckland Harbour Board in 1884. Named after HMS *Calliope*, like Calliope Point, it was opened on 16 February 1888. By a coincidence, one of the Royal Navy's two warships in attendance was a later HMS *Calliope*. At this time the graving dock was the largest in the southern hemisphere, able to take a ship of up to 152 metres in length. The naval authorities already had an interest in the area, with a small piece of land set aside for naval stores (see NAVAL BASES). In 1899 an agreement between the harbour board and the Royal Navy ensured that, for an annual subsidy of £2950, the latter would have priority use of the dock. Before the ★First World War the dockyard was increased in size; new workshops and a deep-water jetty were constructed. After 1918 little work was done on the dockyard until the arrival of Leander class ★cruisers on the ★New Zealand Station. A new agreement between the naval authorities and the Auckland Harbour Board on 22 December 1936 transferred the dockyard, with the exception of the graving dock itself, to the Royal Navy. Renamed HM Dockyard, Devonport (and HMNZ Dockyard, in 1941), it underwent a period of expansion which accelerated markedly after the onset of the ★Pacific War, and undertook a considerable amount of wartime work repairing Allied warships. Throughout the post-war period it kept pace with the increasing technological sophistication of naval vessels. In 1987 the Ministry of Defence acquired the graving dock from the Auckland Harbour Board. But, as part of an efficiency drive in the early 1990s, HMNZ Dockyard was leased to a British firm, Babcocks, for a ten-year period from 1 August 1994.

Cameron, General Sir Duncan Alexander (probably 19 December 1808–7 June 1888) was the most important Pakeha military commander of the ★New Zealand Wars. Considered by colleagues 'the finest soldier in England', he was derided by headstrong New Zealand colonists as the 'old woman in uniform', vitriol which has long impaired his reputation in New Zealand. He was in fact an able commander, who combined thoroughness and caution with a willingness to take bold initiatives when necessary. Beginning his military career in 1825 in the 42nd Highlanders (Black Watch), he rose to command the Highland Brigade in the ★Crimean War, an experience which left him determined not to repeat that campaign's logistical disasters. In 1861 he was appointed to command the imperial forces in New Zealand, with the local rank of lieutenant-general. Constantly seeking a decisive victory, he warmly supported Governor Gore Browne's plan to invade the Waikato, but was greatly frustrated when Browne's successor, Sir George ★Grey, postponed the operation, a step which immediately and permanently soured the relationship between Grey and his field commander. Cameron's capture of Katikara on 4 June 1863 temporarily halted the renewed fighting in Taranaki. Returning to Auckland, he advanced south into the Waikato on 12 July with a large force. He successfully led the 14th Regiment in person at Koheroa, and was recommended for the ★Victoria Cross. His painstaking advance upriver to Ngaruawahia, during which two substantial pa at Meremere and Rangiriri were taken, earned him appointment as a KCB. On 21 February 1864, in a tactic described as 'little short of brilliant', he outflanked the strongly fortified Paterangi defensive line to attack the Maori supply base at Rangiaowhia, incurring minimal casualties, forcing the abandonment of the fortifications, and ending any possibility of sustainable Maori independence. On 29 April 1864, his massive initial assault on Gate Pa, near Tauranga, was repulsed with heavy losses, though the defenders evacuated the pa during the following night. This costly action was followed by a subsequent victory at Te Ranga. His cautious, redoubt-based Wanganui campaign in early 1865 led to Maori contempt for the 'Lame Seagull'. Despite achieving his objective, he returned to Auckland complaining that he and his men were being misused in fighting a war for settlers' benefit. He resigned from his command in February 1865 and left New Zealand six months later. In 1868 he became Governor of the Royal Military College, Sandhurst, and retired in 1875 in the rank of general, having been made a GCB in 1873.

Cameron's careful approach stemmed from his respect for Maori fighting methods and pa systems. He was constantly hampered by extended supply lines vulnerable to guerrilla attack and quickly gained a wariness of fortified pa, leading to his successful outflanking manœuvre at Paterangi and his tactic of patrolling in strength at the incomplete Te Ranga. Yet he was unable to inflict a final defeat on his opponents,

General Duncan Cameron (leaning against the centre of the gun carriage wheel) with a member of his staff and artillerymen at sunrise on the morning of the attack on Gate Pa in 1864. In front is a Coehorn mortar (*Alexander Turnbull Library, F-17924-1/2*)

and eventually concluded that seeking such an outcome was an unworthy role for British troops. Although Grey's calumnies and the memorable 'Lame Seagull' sobriquet have long besmirched his reputation, he was an able, courageous, and independent-minded commander who, in New Zealand, came up against a redoubtable and resourceful enemy.

BRYAN GILLING

Carey, Major-General Robert (12 December 1821–25 January 1883), a leading British staff officer during the Taranaki War of 1860–61, published one of the earliest accounts of the fighting. Commissioned in the 40th Regiment in 1839, he took part in the Afghan War of 1841–42. He arrived in New Zealand in August 1860 as the Deputy Adjutant General on the staff of the commander of the imperial forces, Major-General T.S. ★Pratt. A capable officer, he helped develop the sapping tactics which proved effective in the fighting, and was appointed a CB for his services. He was disenchanted by the readiness of the settlers in New Plymouth to use the imperial forces to advance their own ends, an attitude which was reciprocated by the settlers, who dubbed him 'Robin Redbreast' because of his red staff-coat and portly figure. His *Narrative of the Late War in New Zealand*, published in London in 1863, exaggerated the extent of British success during the conflict, though acknowledging Maori skill in bush fighting. Carey later served on the staff of Lieutenant-General Duncan ★Cameron in the Waikato War, and, after returning to the United Kingdom, was promoted to the rank of major-general in 1869. He attended the Staff College, and was later Deputy Judge Advocate General.

Carr, Air Marshal Sir (Charles) Roderick ('Roddy') (31 August 1891–15 December 1971) was one of a number of New Zealanders who achieved high rank in the RAF. Born at Feilding, he served in the ★Territorial Force in 1914, before making his way to the United Kingdom. After attending a number of ballooning courses, he secured a commission in the Royal Naval Air Service and learned to fly at the RNAS Flying School. For nearly two years from July 1916 he served on the staff of the flying school both in England and in France. He transferred to the RAF in April 1918, and commanded 91 Squadron at Tangmere from June 1918 to March 1919 before serving in the RAF HQ in the North Russian Expedition, for which he was awarded a DFC. With no further RAF posting after October 1919, he secured employment as Lithuania's Chief of Air Staff in 1920 and went as a pilot with Ernest Shackleton's

Casualties

Antarctic Expedition in 1921–22, though no flights were made. In September 1922 he gained a short-service commission in the RAF, and four years later a permanent commission. In 1928 he was awarded an AFC for a long-distance flight from England to the Persian Gulf. After holding an instructional post from 1929 to 1933, he spent a year as Adjutant of the RAF Depot, Middle East. After his return to England in 1934, he underwent training in naval aviation before becoming Senior Air Force Officer on HMS *Eagle* in 1937. He commanded a flying training school in 1939, and after the outbreak of war went to France with the Advanced Air Striking Force. After the withdrawal of the BEF, he was AOC in Northern Ireland until December 1940. From July 1941 until February 1945 he commanded Bomber Command's 4 Group, and was mentioned in dispatches in 1944. He was Deputy Chief of Staff (Air) at Supreme HQ Allied Expeditionary Force (SHAEF) and commanded the base air forces in South-east Asia before his final posting as AOC Air HQ, India in 1946–47. He was made a KBE in 1945.

Casualties are the total losses suffered by a military unit. The term 'casualty' encompasses all those who become ineffective through death, injury, illness, or capture. Casualties inflicted by the enemy are described as being incurred in action; the remainder as incurred on active service. The latter can vary widely, ranging from motor accidents to drownings and, in one recorded instance, a mauling by a tiger. Casualty figures are seldom accurate, especially in the immediate aftermath of battle when accurate counting of losses is almost impossible. Nor do early casualty returns take into account deaths arising from war wounds or impaired health often years afterwards. (See table 3.)

J. Studholme, *Some Records of the New Zealand Expeditionary Force* (Government Printer, Wellington, 1928); 'Statement of Strengths and Losses in the Armed Services and Mercantile Marine in the 1939–45 War', *Appendix to the Journal of the House of Representatives*, 1948, H-19B.

Cautley, Colonel Henry (1838/39–9 February 1918) played an important role in the development of New Zealand's nineteenth century harbour defences. Born at Shoreditch, England, he secured a commission in the Corps of Royal Engineers in 1859. In the late 1870s he served as an instructor in fortification at the Military College and in 1881 reported on the defences of the Falkland Islands. After overseeing the fortification of Cork Harbour, he commanded part of Gibraltar's defences before being appointed, in 1883, to take charge of New Zealand's defence works, largely at the instigation of the Governor, Major-General Sir William ★Jervois. He worked closely with Jervois to modify the scheme previously proposed by Colonel P.H. ★Scratchley. In January 1885 he set out a two-stage programme, but this was upset by the onset in March of the last and most intense of the periodic ★Russian scares. For several months he worked tirelessly to install the heavy guns already on hand in the colony, the urgency of the situation leading to some departure from his earlier plans that would prove awkward when it came to completing the defences. He completed his engagement in June 1885 and returned to England. His name was given to Fort Cautley, on Auckland's North Head. (It was transferred to the Narrow Neck military camp in 1958.) During the late 1880s he was stationed at Aldershot.

Censorship was imposed in New Zealand during both world wars with two aims: to deny the enemy information of military importance, and to maintain civilian morale and suppress internal opposition to the war effort. Prior to the ★First World War, there was no censorship of war news—the imperialistic press rarely questioned the British Empire's cause in the ★Boer War, though there was often strong criticism of the British Army. However, concerns about German espionage and the need to safeguard information about ship movements were instrumental in bringing the need for censorship of telegraph and wireless communications to the fore. When war began in 1914, regulations were imposed to control overseas mail and telegrams and to ban the advertising of shipping movements in the press. Since New Zealand newspapers depended on already-censored cables

Table 3	Casualties	
Conflict	Total casualties	Total dead
BOER WAR	398	230
FIRST WORLD WAR	59,483	18,166
Gallipoli	7473	2721
Western Front	47,902	12,483
Egypt–Sinai–Palestine	1786	640
UK, other places, at sea	853	—
SECOND WORLD WAR	36,038	11,625
Greece	2504	291
Crete	3818	671
North Africa	13,990	2989
Italy	8924	2003
Pacific	442	203
RAF/RNZAF	4979	4149
RN/RNZN	800	573
Merchant Marine	233	110
KOREAN WAR	115	35
MALAYAN EMERGENCY	38	15
CONFRONTATION	1	—
VIETNAM WAR	224	37

from London, the censorship of newspapers was not at first thought necessary. Censorship was directed against internal enemies of the war effort, such as pacifists and socialists; anti-war literature was confiscated and distributors of this material were prosecuted for subversion under the War Regulations. Soldiers' mail was censored by their officers.

Censorship was reintroduced in August 1939, when the government asked newspapers to suppress reference to the small force departing New Zealand for garrison duty on ★Fanning Island and censorship of telegrams by the Post and Telegraph Department began. Draft regulations for wartime censorship, which had been in existence since February 1939, came into effect on 1 September 1939. Mail to or from New Zealand was screened, and all airmail, letters for servicemen, and letters bound for countries under enemy occupation were scrutinised. Mail from or to 2200 suspect names was also watched. Any information thought likely to be useful to the enemy, such as the names of ships and their ports of call or discussion of military formations, was excised from the letters. There were numerous complaints about political censorship, and censors had to draw a fine line between criticism of the government and undermining the war effort.

Censorship of the press was controlled by the Director of Publicity, J.T. Paul, a former journalist and Labour Party stalwart. Publication of material deemed prejudicial or subversive was illegal. 'Reasonable and temperate discussion in good faith' of war measures was not considered subversive. Even so, the criteria for censorship of the press were broader than those applied in Australia or even Great Britain, and led to allegations of political censorship. In the main, relations between Paul and newspaper editors were harmonious enough, and censorship instructions were generally obeyed. However, there were occasional difficulties, such as over the ban on news of the 'widely known' deployment of 2NZEF to Greece. During 1941 and 1942 censorship of news relating to defence in New Zealand was tightened up considerably, with publication of any information considered to be of even the remotest use to the enemy being banned. This harsh regime backfired somewhat, since it left the public misinformed and suspicious. When coverage of industrial trouble and news of shortages were censored, there were allegations of the abuse of the censorship regulations for political purposes by the Labour Party. Press coverage of the ★furlough affair, for example, was suppressed, and full details were not revealed to the public until after the war. The government also suppressed literature held to be prejudicial to the war effort or subversive or intended to cause dissatisfaction, and it prosecuted the distributors of such material. The main targets were the small Communist Party and pacifist movement. From February 1940 communist propaganda against the war was restricted, and from May 1940 the communist newspaper *People's Voice* was banned, along with the left-leaning *Tomorrow*. Distributors of communist and pacifist pamphlets were also considered to be subversive and from mid 1940 were prosecuted. Illegal pamphlets continued to appear, however, until 1941 when the Communist Party changed its attitude to the war following Germany's attack on Russia. Pacifist literature was also seized during the war. A Social Credit newspaper, *Democracy*, was suspended in 1942 for opposing war loans. In general, newspaper proprietors understood the need for some measure of censorship, though they often complained that its exercise was excessive.

Army censorship was designed to suppress any information about military operations or likely to be harmful to morale. Letters and parcels were censored by the soldier's unit before being sent on to field censor sections at base, where items were further scrutinised. About 8 per cent of all mail—nearly 20,000 letters and parcels monthly—was censored. In the process a vast quantity of illicit, captured, or stolen material, including even machine-guns and live shells, was intercepted. The censorship regime was quickly dispensed with at the end of the war. No censorship of servicemen's mail has been deemed necessary in New Zealand's campaigns after 1945.

Centre for Strategic Studies With the study of security issues not traditionally enjoying high priority in New Zealand's universities, public debate on such matters has tended to be unfocused and led by lobby groups pushing particular lines. In an attempt to remedy this situation, the Centre for Strategic Studies was established at Victoria University of Wellington in September 1993, with former diplomat Terence O'Brien as director. The Ministry of Foreign Affairs and Trade, the ★New Zealand Defence Force, the Ministry of Defence, and the Asia 2000 Foundation are all involved in the funding of the centre, which operates under the direction of a management committee comprising eminent academics, military leaders, and civil servants. It hosts visiting overseas fellows, arranges seminars, encourages publication of studies of security matters, and participates actively in discussions with similar bodies, particularly in the Asia–Pacific region. In January 1994 it became a member of the Council for Security Cooperation in Asia Pacific (CSCAP). The centre's credibility was damaged in 1999 with the ousting of O'Brien, amid allegations that the Minister of Defence, Max Bradford, had engineered his departure because of his criticisms of the government's defence policy.

Chaplains

Chanak crisis arose suddenly in September 1922 as a result of Turkish successes in a war with Greece which threatened to overturn the arrangements for the peace settlement with Turkey. Under the Treaty of Sèvres, a neutral zone surrounding the Dardanelles Strait between the Aegean Sea and the Black Sea had been established. In accordance with these provisions, a battalion of British soldiers plus some French and Italians had been stationed at Chanak (Çannakale), a small town on the Asiatic side of the Dardanelles Narrows. The presence of this small force became of international moment as the Turkish forces swept towards Chanak. Public opinion in Great Britain and elsewhere was aroused by a massacre of Christians following the occupation of Smyrna (Izmir). Deciding that the Turks must be halted, the British government dispatched telegrams to the Dominions asking if they would join Britain in taking a stand against Turkey. That to New Zealand arrived at Government House on the evening of 16 September 1922, when fortuitously Prime Minister W.F. ★Massey and six other ministers were present at a social occasion. The Governor-General, Lord ★Jellicoe, consulted Massey, the ministers then met, and a message offering a contingent was sent that very evening. It was received in London within fourteen hours of the British telegram's dispatch. The decision was confirmed by the full Cabinet on the following Monday, and subsequently overwhelmingly supported in Parliament. Enlistment began immediately, and an enthusiastic response was forthcoming throughout the country. By 28 September more than 13,000 men had come forward, as well as 394 nurses. Within days, however, the crisis subsided, after the Turks refrained from attacking Chanak. The affair had demonstrated that the imperial patriotism of New Zealanders remained undiminished despite the ★First World War toll. Indeed the chance of another round with the victors of ★Gallipoli was probably a motivation for many. The crisis was important in the evolution of the Commonwealth, for the other Dominions had not been so forthcoming as New Zealand. Indeed, the response made clear that Dominion support could not be taken for granted in London in the event of war involving the British Empire.

A. Ross, 'The Chanak Crisis', *New Zealand's Heritage*, vol 6, pt 77 (1973).

Chaplains have marched with armies ever since Constantine the Great's campaign against the Persians in the fourth century. A form of chaplaincy, known as the Eusebian model, emerged from this early alliance between the Roman state and the church: the clergy would participate in a just cause but would confine themselves to fighting a theological battle through prayer. Chaplaincy in New Zealand has been clearly identifiable with this model. Non-combatant, it is responsible for the conduct of Christian ordinances and the maintenance of the spiritual morale and welfare of those who serve their nation within the profession of arms. Four chaplains were with the 12,000 imperial troops involved in the ★New Zealand Wars, and about twenty served with the various ★Militia and ★Volunteer Force units. One lost his life: Reverend John Whiteley was murdered in 1869 while visiting an armed settlers' outpost in Taranaki. Maori chaplains, usually lay readers of the Wesleyan or Anglican missions, offered prayers before and during battle. The Hauhaus set apart individuals as tohunga (priests) to support the warriors with prayers and incantations. After 1872 colonial clergy remained attached to Volunteer units and the ★Armed Constabulary. When New Zealand decided to send troops to the ★Boer War, the churches pressed the government to appoint chaplains, and five were eventually sent—the first to serve overseas. Under the army reorganisation of 1911, a Chaplains Department was established as part of the ★Territorial Force. During the ★First World War 140 chaplains and more than 100 ★YMCA secretaries from nine denominations served overseas with the ★New Zealand Expeditionary Force, while fifty chaplains in New Zealand ministered to those in the training camps. Eight chaplains lost their lives on active service. Between the world wars strong pacifist sentiment in New Zealand society generally and the churches in particular hindered the recruitment of clergy for the Chaplains Department. When on the outbreak of the ★Second World War difficulties were experienced in filling chaplaincies in 2NZEF, welfare officers from the YMCA and Anglican Church Army were appointed as de facto chaplains—a practice which continued throughout the war whenever chaplains were unavailable. By November 1941 a number of them had become prisoners of war, along with sixteen chaplains. During captivity chaplains continued their ministry where possible. In all, 161 chaplains served overseas, with a further hundred remaining on garrison duty in New Zealand. One chaplain and one Church Army worker were killed in action. The chaplains distinguished themselves by their courage under fire: of the seven British Commonwealth chaplains who were appointed DSOs, three were New Zealanders. Nineteen chaplains served with ★Jayforce from 1945 to 1948. Perhaps the most significant long-term contribution of the Second World War chaplaincy was the fostering of ecumenical unity—an approach which can nevertheless be traced to the New Zealand Wars. In 1940 2NZEF commander Major-General B.C. ★Freyberg instituted the 'one unit one chaplain' policy, under which each chaplain (except Roman

Chaplains

A New Zealand chaplain celebrates Holy Communion in the field at Messines, Belgium, in 1917 (RSA Collection, Alexander Turnbull Library, G-12781-1/2)

Catholics) ministered to a unit. This experience helped foster church union among the Protestant churches after the war, with many of the wartime chaplains taking a leading role in furthering social, political, and ecumenical reform within their churches. Congregations were swelled, at least in the first two decades after the war, by returned servicemen and their families. The Royal New Zealand Army Chaplains Department was established in 1947, and the first Regular Force chaplains were appointed. Non-regular chaplains served in the *Korean War, but in subsequent overseas campaigns—the *Malayan Emergency, *Confrontation, and the *Vietnam War—regular chaplains filled the overseas appointments. Four were involved in New Zealand's *peace-keeping operations in Bosnia–Herzegovina (1995–96) and Bougainville (1994 and 1997–98).

Regular chaplains were employed in the New Zealand Naval Forces from the outset. With the establishment of the *New Zealand Division of the Royal Navy in 1921, James R. Beaufort was appointed chaplain on HMS *Philomel*. As the only permanent defence chaplain, he also ministered to military and later air force personnel in the Auckland area, as did his successor, G.T. Robson. With the outbreak of the Second World War, Robson oversaw the appointment of additional Anglican or Roman Catholic chaplains to ships and bases in New Zealand. After the formation of the RNZN ten chaplains, mainly Anglicans loaned by the Royal Navy, served on New Zealand warships. Eight chaplains of the RNZNVR were also employed in New Zealand. A New Zealander serving as a chaplain aboard the British battleship HMS *Prince of Wales* lost his life because he remained with wounded when his ship was sunk by the Japanese in December 1941. Naval chaplains, including Harry Taylor (who had been made a DSO while serving as a chaplain in 2NZEF), went to Korea with New Zealand frigates during the Korean War and later to Malayan waters. The RNZN currently has three permanent chaplains (including the first woman to hold the position of Principal Naval Chaplain) at Devonport naval base, supported by four reserve chaplains.

The first chaplains were appointed to the RNZAF in 1940. They wore RNZAF uniform but army chaplains' insignia badges. During the Second World War more than thirty full-time chaplains and twenty-four officiating clergy were appointed. Chaplains who served with the squadrons in the Pacific were assisted by YMCA secretaries and, like their army associates, some found time to restore Christian missions close to RNZAF bases. After the Second World War, RNZAF chaplains served in Malaya, Singapore, and Fiji.

83

Chaytor

Chaplains in all three branches of the armed forces serve within the terms of the Geneva Convention as non-combatants and have no authority of command. The RNZN follows the sixteenth century British naval tradition insofar as its chaplains are considered to be of equal rank to whomever they are addressing or being addressed by. New Zealand Army chaplains do not hold military rank, but are designated by an ecclesiastical equivalent; for example, a Chaplain Class 2 is equivalent to a lieutenant-colonel. An Honorary Colonel Commandant is normally a former senior serving chaplain. Usually there is one chaplain to every 800 to 1000 servicemen and women. RNZAF chaplains hold honorary rank ranging from flight lieutenant to group captain.

Chaplaincy within the *New Zealand Defence Force is coordinated by the Principal Defence Force Chaplain. The Anglican, Presbyterian, Roman Catholic, Methodist, and Baptist Churches and the Salvation Army are represented on the Chaplains' National Advisory Committee, which provides ecumenical appointments in the Regular and Territorial Forces, of which there are about thirty altogether.

J.B. Haigh, *Men of Faith and Courage: The Official History of New Zealand's Army Chaplains* (Word Publishers, Auckland, 1983).

FRANK GLEN

Chaytor, Major-General Sir Edward Walter Clervaux (21 June 1868–15 June 1939) was an outstanding New Zealand commander of the *First World War. The son of a Marlborough runholder, he was born at Motueka and began his military career in the *Volunteer Force in 1886. Having been an officer in the Marlborough Hussars (later Marlborough Mounted Rifles Volunteers) from 1889, he volunteered for service in the *Boer War and left with the Third (Rough Riders) Contingent early in 1900. Although invalided home after suffering a bad leg wound at Reit Keil on 26 May, an action for which he was mentioned in dispatches, he went back to South Africa in 1902 in command of the South Island Regiment of the Eighth Contingent. Back in New Zealand, he gained a permanent commission in September 1902, and served as Assistant Adjutant-General until going to Great Britain in 1907 as the first New Zealand officer to attend the Staff College at Camberley, where he excelled. From 1910, he was successively Director of Military Training and Education, commander of the Wellington Military District, and, just before the *First World War began, Adjutant-General. In this last-named capacity, he was heavily involved in the raising of both the Samoa Expeditionary Force and 1NZEF's Main Body, leaving New Zealand with the latter in October 1914. While serving as AAG and QMG in the *New Zealand and

Major-General E.W.C. Chaytor with the commander of the 4th Turkish Army, Ali Bey Wahaby, who was captured by the Anzac Mounted Division (*Australian War Memorial, B00088*)

Australian Division at *Gallipoli, he was seriously wounded in the right arm, an injury which probably prevented him from succeeding Major-General A.J. *Godley as divisional commander later in the year. In November 1915, after his recovery, he took command of the Mounted Rifles Brigade, which remained in Egypt to form part of the Australian and New Zealand (Anzac) Mounted Division when the rest of 1NZEF deployed to France in 1916. From April 1916 he also commanded 1NZEF in Egypt. An effective staff officer and daring tactician, he earned the ironic nickname 'Terrible Ted' from his troops because of his quiet nature. His brigade helped inflict a decisive defeat on the Turks at Romani in August 1916 after launching a counterstroke against the Turkish flank. After the Battle of Rafa in January 1917, in which his confidence and tactical acumen were conspicuous, the commander of the Desert Column, Lieutenant-General Sir Philip Chetwode, described him as 'by far the best man of the lot … a better soldier than any of them, with a real eye for ground and a fight'. During the First Battle of Gaza, Chaytor took his brigade around the Turkish positions and was about to take Gaza from the rear when ordered to withdraw. From April 1917 he commanded the division—the only time a New Zealander has done so at this level in an Anzac force—in a series of successful actions, including two raids into Jordan in early 1918. In September 1918 he commanded a combined force including British, Jewish, and Indian troops—Chaytor's Force—in a crossing of the Jordan on a 30-kilometre front, which led to the capture of Amman and the taking of more than 10,000 prisoners. His services during the war were recognised by his appointment as a CB and a KCMG; he was also mentioned in dispatches seven times. He was made a KCVO in 1920. After becoming GOC of the New Zealand Military Forces in December 1919, he oversaw a major reorganisation which reduced the ★Territorial Force to more manageable proportions and created three ★military districts. However, limited funds prevented him from extending the scope of the ★compulsory military training scheme. When the ★Chanak crisis of 1922 briefly raised the possibility of war with his old foe, he oversaw hasty preparations, soon suspended, for the dispatch of another expeditionary force. After his retirement in 1924, he resided in London until his death.

Checketts, **Wing Commander John Milne ('Johnny')** (20 February 1912–) was a leading New Zealand fighter ace of the ★Second World War. A mechanic from Invercargill, he enlisted in the RNZAF in October 1940. During his initial flying instruction in New Zealand, he was rated below average as a pilot, but was nevertheless commissioned and sent to England. Further training was followed by a posting to 485 (New Zealand) Squadron. More than a year elapsed before he secured his first confirmed 'kill', in May 1943, while flying with 611 Squadron. From July 1943 he commanded 485 Squadron with great success, and was awarded a DFC. On one day he personally shot down three German fighters. Shortly after claiming his thirteenth German aircraft on 6 September 1943, he was himself shot down. Despite severe burns he managed to evade capture with the assistance of the French resistance and, after several weeks on the run, returned to England aboard a fishing boat. In November 1943 he was made a DSO. After a period as an instructor, he was given command of a wing in time to take part in the ★D-Day operations. By the time his operational career ended in September 1944, he had fourteen confirmed victories. He spent the rest of the war in a staff position analysing fighter tactics. Reverting to the RNZAF in 1945, he occupied various posts, including command of 5 (Flying Boat) Squadron at Fiji and of Ohakea air base, until 1955, when he resigned to start an aerial top-dressing business. More recently he has been actively involved with the RNZAF Museum at Wigram.

V. Orange, *The Road to Biggin Hill: A Life of Wing Commander Johnny Checketts* (Mallinson Rendel, Wellington, 1987).

Chemical weapons The stalemate on the ★Western Front during the ★First World War prompted Germany to initiate the use of lethal gas in warfare, in contravention of the Hague Convention then in force. On 22 April 1915, during the Second Battle of Ypres, poisonous chlorine gas was released to envelop the Allied lines, causing heavy casualties. The British retaliated with their first gas attack in September, at Loos, though fickle winds sent much of the green cloud of chlorine drifting back into their own trenches. Though horrific in inflicting slow death by suffocation, chlorine gas and phosgene—also utilised extensively after its introduction by Germany in December 1915—proved to be of limited tactical utility after the development of practical gas masks. Rudimentary masks were improvised by the Allies almost immediately after the first German chlorine attack, and a few months later the improved 'P Helmet' was issued in anticipation of the use of phosgene.

By the time the New Zealand Division was deployed to France in April 1916, Allied precautions against gas attack were well developed. A divisional gas officer and staff were appointed, and a Divisional Gas School set up to instruct in the use of the P Helmets. The division was subjected to an attack by tear-gas shells on 20 September 1916 during the Battle of the Somme, and in the following February the New Zealand sector of the line at Fleurbaix, near Armentières, was bombarded with phosgene. By now the division was equipped with the highly effective small box respirators, but on this occasion some of the front-line troops were taken by surprise; there were forty casualties and five deaths. The division suffered its first mustard gas (bis (2-chloroethyl) sulphide) attack in July 1917 during the Third Battle of Ypres. This agent had been introduced by the Germans only a few days before, and its effects were as yet poorly understood; initially, Allied casualties were heavy. Mustard gas—in fact an oily liquid delivered by artillery shells and atomised by an explosive charge—was not only fatal when inhaled but also caused severe blistering on contact with the skin, and temporary or sometimes permanent blindness; it would remain difficult to counter, and for almost a year the Germans enjoyed a monopoly on its use. The delivery of gas by artillery shells was more precise than the discharge of gas cylinders at the front line. Gas shells (both lethal and tear gas) were issued to the New Zealand Divisional Artillery during the Battle of the Somme and used by New Zealand gunners for the first time on 12 September 1916. Subsequently the division fired gas shells at Messines and Passchendaele.

In 1930 the New Zealand government, along with Great Britain, ratified the 1925 Geneva Protocol prohibiting gas and bacteriological warfare. Nevertheless, several states reserved the right not to be bound if at war with an enemy not subject to the protocol, and to reply in kind to any chemical or biological attack. Indeed, Japan and the United States would not ratify the protocol until the 1970s. Japan used mustard gas extensively in China from 1937, and Italy, despite being a party to the protocol, waged large-scale chemical warfare in 1935–36 during its invasion of *Abyssinia. Between the wars all the major powers continued the development and production of more lethal chemical agents. Most work focused on phosgene and variants of mustard gas, but German scientists developed the nerve agents tabun and sarin, which interrupt the nervous system, causing spasms and rapid death. It is likely that German reluctance to use these weapons in the *Second World War was based mainly on the mistaken assumption that the Allies had produced similar nerve gases and could respond in kind.

In New Zealand an Emergency Precautions Committee had reported in July 1936 on the need for preparations against poison gas. Over the next two years, Army experts trained small numbers of civilians in anti-gas precautions, and 1500 gas masks for civilian use were distributed to three depots. After the outbreak of war in Europe in 1939, the government decided against the provision of gas masks for the public, although in 1941 additional gas masks were obtained for emergency workers in the main centres, along with small numbers of decontamination units. The early Japanese successes in the *Pacific War lent urgency to gas precautions. In March 1942, 250,000 gas masks for civilian use were ordered from a Christchurch firm, but shortages of rubber delayed production and masks were made available only to 'front-line' staff of the *Emergency Precautions Scheme. By the time the *National Service Department issued its handbook, *War Gases: Decontamination and Protection Measures*, in August 1942, and gas masks were becoming available in larger numbers, Japanese advances had been checked; most of the civilian gas masks were put into storage.

After the war, German stocks of nerve gas were captured by the Western Allies and the Soviet Union, and the development of these agents and other chemical weapons proceeded rapidly. Herbicides were adapted for military use, most notably 2,4,5T, or *Agent Orange, used widely in Vietnam as a defoliant; its by-product dioxin was subsequently suspected of causing cancer and psychological problems in exposed service personnel and civilians, and genetic defects in their offspring.

In post-war New Zealand, as elsewhere, military and civil defence precautions against chemical and biological weapons were absorbed within the concept of NBC (nuclear–biological–chemical) defence. The *frigates of the RNZN have incorporated NBC protection and decontamination systems since the commissioning of HMNZS *Otago* in 1960. NBC defence capabilities were revived within the *New Zealand Army in the late 1980s in response to the proliferation of chemical and biological weapons. The New Zealand medical teams deployed to Bahrain during the 1991 *Gulf War received nerve agent protection tablets and frequently donned their NBC suits because of the launching of Iraqi Scud missiles (which in the event were conventionally armed).

The need for progress in the control of chemical weapons had long been apparent when the end of the *Cold War made a far-reaching treaty feasible. In 1993 the United Nations Conference on Disarmament finally secured agreement on a new Chemical Weapons Convention. Successive New Zealand governments have promoted the control of chemical weapons. In 1988 New Zealand withdrew its sole reservation to the 1925 Geneva Protocol, relinquishing its right to respond in kind against chemical attacks. New Zealand applied for membership of the Conference on Disarmament in 1988 and was admitted as a full member in 1996. The Chemical Weapons (Prohibition) Act 1996 implements the Chemical Weapons Convention in New Zealand, empowering international inspectors to access private facilities, and providing for import and export controls on certain chemicals. Chemical weapons, easily manufactured from common industrial and agricultural chemicals, remain appealing to rogue states and terrorists; they pose a permanent danger requiring long-term vigilance.

ALAN HENDERSON

Chiefs of Staff are the professional heads of the armed services. They hold the highest rank in their respective services, which they command under the Chief of Defence Force. They are the principal advisers to the Minister of Defence for their particular service. The first New Zealand chief of staff was Colonel A.W. *Robin, who was appointed as Chief of the General Staff and First Military Member of the Council of Defence in 1907 (see DEFENCE COUNCIL). In 1910 the position of CGS was terminated with the appointment of a General Officer Commanding the Forces, who became the professional head of the military forces. It re-emerged in 1912, however, and has remained in existence ever since, though termed 'Chief of the Staff' between 1919 and 1924. From 1931 the positions of GOC and CGS were for the first time held by the same officer. This arrangement came to an end in November 1937 with the establishment of an Army Board and abolition of the GOC position. The incumbent, Major-General J.E. *Duigan, in his other capacity as CGS, became First Military Member of the board.

Initially the professional head of the *New Zealand Division of the Royal Navy was the First Naval Member of the Naval Board, who was also, awkwardly, Commodore (later Rear-Admiral) Commanding, the New

Zealand Squadron, a role which made it difficult for him to fulfil his responsibilities ashore. This problem was not overcome until 1938, when Rear-Admiral H.E. Horan was appointed Chief of Naval Staff and First Naval Member, with a commodore assuming command of the New Zealand Squadron. The first Chief of the Air Staff, Wing Commander R.A. *Cochrane, was appointed in 1937, and he became First Air Member of the Air Board.

After the departure of Godley with the *New Zealand Expeditionary Force in October 1914, the positions of GOC/CGS have been held by New Zealand officers. This was a reflection of the large number of relatively senior and experienced officers who were available as a result of the New Zealand effort in the *First World War. The situation in the New Zealand Naval Forces was quite the opposite, and British officers on loan from the Royal Navy filled the position until 1960, when Rear-Admiral Peter *Phipps became the first RNZN officer to be appointed CNS. In the case of the RNZAF, a New Zealander, Air Vice-Marshal L.M. *Isitt, became CAS as early as 1943, though British officers were again used to fill the position between 1951 and 1956.

Recognition of the desirability of coordination led to the establishment of the Chiefs of Staff Committee in 1933. At this stage it comprised the GOC and the Rear-Admiral Commanding, with the Minister of Defence in the chair. It was not very active, however, and did not meet at all in 1934. A major appreciation of New Zealand's defence position was produced in March 1935, and the deteriorating international situation led to the committee's role increasing in importance in the late 1930s. By 1937 the Minister had virtually withdrawn from participation, because of a lack of time to attend regularly, and from May 1938 the senior chief of staff by appointment filled his role as deputy chairman.

The *Second World War greatly enhanced the importance of the COS Committee. It had become an integral part of the *Organisation for National Security, whose head, Foss *Shanahan, served as its secretary, and it had assumed a much-increased workload in dealing with the problems of coordinating New Zealand's war effort. After the war it was accepted as having responsibility for advising the government generally on important defence questions and on questions with joint service implications. A Joint Planning Committee, consisting of the three service directors of plans, was established in September 1946 to support it, though it did not become fully effective until the 1950s, when full-time plans officers were appointed. From March 1954 the COS Committee, which had previously operated on an ad hoc basis, began meeting on a more or less regular basis every Monday afternoon providing there was enough business. A number of other subcommittees also reported to the COS Committee, the most important of which was the Joint Intelligence Committee. A *Defence Secretariat eventually provided an administrative framework for this incipient joint service organisation.

During the early 1950s two of the COS Committee's three members were British officers on loan. This proved awkward at times as New Zealand became more involved in military planning with the Americans, since the United Kingdom was excluded from ANZUS. On one occasion Major-General W.G. *Gentry, the CGS, was sent to a meeting because he was the only 'New Zealand' chief of staff available. Later one of the Chiefs of Staff became Military Adviser to SEATO and ANZUS, necessitating much time away from New Zealand attending meetings. In 1960 this problem was overcome by the appointment of Major-General Sir Stephen *Weir as Chief Military Adviser to the government. He sat as a full member of COS Committee when matters with external implications were being discussed. (In practice he attended all meetings.) The COS did not like the fact that Weir tendered advice to the government without the brake of responsibility for implementation, but the arrangement proved short-lived, the appointment lapsing in 1961. As part of a major reorganisation of higher defence machinery, an Independent Chairman of the COS Committee was appointed in 1963. Vice-Admiral Phipps assumed the position, the title of which was soon changed to Chief of Defence Staff (see DEFENCE, MINISTRY OF). The COS Committee continued in existence as a committee of the *Defence Council until the further defence reorganisation in 1990. (See DEFENCE, HIGHER ORGANISATION OF)

Chute, General Sir Trevor (31 July 1816–12 March 1886) commanded imperial forces during the *New Zealand Wars. Commissioned in the Ceylon Rifles in British India in 1832, he rose to command the British 70th Regiment seventeen years later. During the Indian Mutiny of 1857–58, he led a flying column. He arrived in New Zealand with his regiment in 1861, and for two years was stationed at Auckland before crossing the Tasman to take command of the imperial forces in Australia. In August 1865, he succeeded Lieutenant-General Sir Duncan *Cameron as commander of the forces in New Zealand. When fighting resumed in south Taranaki four months later, he led a 620-strong force in an attempt to break Maori resistance. In contrast to Cameron's evident reluctance to prosecute the war vigorously, he undertook an active campaign of 'bush-scouring'. His troops laid waste Maori villages and cultivations, both 'rebel' and 'loyal' alike, destroying seven pa and twenty-one villages. To highlight the

Civil community

dominance of his forces, he embarked on an inland 'forest march' from Patea to New Plymouth. Although no hostile Maori were encountered, his troops nearly starved before making a triumphal entry to the provincial capital. With the withdrawal of imperial forces underway, he returned to Australia in 1867 to resume command of the garrison there. For his services, he was made a KCB.

Civil community, assistance to As a formed, trained, disciplined body, disposing of considerable technological resources, the armed forces assist the community in various ways, both in emergencies and as a matter of routine. Since 1971 they have had statutory responsibility to provide not only assistance to the civil power either in New Zealand or elsewhere 'in time of emergency or disaster' but also 'such public services' as the government may require. They also represent the Crown at numerous official ceremonies, and add much to the cultural life of the country at parades, concerts, and shows. This non-military assistance has in recent years been highlighted with a view to encouraging public acceptance of defence funding allocations. In 1996–97 6 per cent of the defence vote was devoted to this purpose.

The most striking example of military assistance by the New Zealand armed forces in an emergency occurred in 1931 in the aftermath of the *Napier earthquake. Since the *Second World War the armed forces have been routinely involved in civil defence preparations, and armed forces personnel have participated in all major New Zealand disaster relief operations, such as, for example, the Tangiwai rail disaster of 1953 and the foundering of the ferry *Wahine* in 1968. They have regularly been called out to assist with the rescue of people in flood-stricken areas. Military personnel were involved in the grisly search for bodies and wreckage following the Erebus disaster in 1979, and six years later in rescuing survivors from the stricken Soviet cruise liner *Mikhail Lermontov*. During and after Cyclone Bola in 1987, nearly a hundred Army personnel with thirty vehicles took part in civil defence operations on the East Coast, in which engineers cleared roads and operated a raft service across the Wairoa River, while other Army personnel provided water purifiers, meals, and medical assistance. The armed forces have also given limited assistance during droughts, such as that which afflicted Marlborough in 1998. Disaster relief has also been provided to countries as far afield as Zaire, to which C-130 Hercules transport aircraft flew urgent relief supplies and *Red Cross personnel following the mass exodus of refugees from Rwanda in 1994. Most external disaster relief, however, has focused on Pacific Islands, and emergency assistance following cyclones has been a recurring task of the armed forces, with the aim of replenishment and rehabilitation. The most important contribution made to disaster relief in the Pacific was to Western Samoa following Cyclone Ofa in 1990.

Search and rescue is perhaps the most high-profile of the armed forces' routine activities in support of the community. Flights for this purpose began during the Second World War originally to find missing Allied airmen. The service was maintained after the war by 5 Squadron RNZAF, which made frequent flights in search of stricken or missing vessels. Search and rescue and mercy flights by its Short Sunderland flying boats occupied about a fifth of the squadron's flying time. Since the mid 1960s, most of the search and rescue work by the RNZAF has been borne by P3 Orion maritime surveillance aircraft. Search and rescue capacity was augmented by the acquisition of Iroquois helicopters. By the 1970s as many as 100 search and rescue missions were being flown annually, and about sixty people (around half of whom are trampers or climbers) rescued, annually. Ships of the RNZN are also available for search and rescue operations, as when HMNZS *Monowai* joined merchant ships, RNZAF Orions, and a French naval vessel to rescue yachts caught in atrocious weather in 1993, saving twenty-one lives. Army personnel, too, have often been involved in mountain rescue operations, usually by undertaking ground searches for missing trampers or climbers and providing transport, communications, and rations for police and volunteer search parties. Search and rescue remains an important secondary role for the armed forces. Since the 1980s, as civilian emergency services have gradually acquired rescue helicopters or search aircraft of their own or contracted the role out to private companies, the participation of the armed forces in such operations has decreased. Even so, they remain the only body able to provide the expertise and equipment necessary for many types of operation. Similar to rescue operations are mercy flights or medical evacuation from Pacific Islands. These were maintained until 1997, when a specialist air ambulance was contracted to fulfil the role previously undertaken by the Sunderlands or Hercules aircraft. The Army also assists with casualty evacuation, mostly involving vehicle accidents on the Desert Road, and the Navy's hyperbaric centre provides treatment for divers suffering decompression sickness.

Military assistance is provided to the police on a regular basis. Army ordnance specialists have investigated bomb hoaxes and disposed of explosives, involving about 150 hours annually. During the 1980s the RNZAF flew up to 300 hours each year on anti-cannabis operations. The RNZN's diving team provides routine assistance to the police in searches for

Civil power

evidence or missing persons: examples include naval divers' investigations of the sunken *Rainbow Warrior* in 1986 (see *RAINBOW WARRIOR* AFFAIR) and involvement in searches for evidence of homicide in the deep waters of the Marlborough Sounds in 1998. Other defence personnel are frequently involved in evidential searches on land, while the Army provides training for the police Armed Offenders Squad. Firefighting assistance by Army personnel, RNZAF helicopters, and service firefighters has been provided on a regular basis. Other assistance to government departments or local authorities includes bridge building and dental care in isolated areas. Civilian scientific programmes are supported on a regular basis, the most important being the Antarctic programme (see ANTARCTICA, MILITARY INVOLVEMENT IN). Routine assistance is provided in transporting scientists and supplies to outlying islands.

During the 1990s the armed forces began providing assistance to the civil community through training and unemployment relief. Up to 1000 unemployed civilians per annum have been given adventure training by all three services as Limited Service Volunteers with a view to building up their self-confidence and gaining skills. Other young adults receive more specialised training, such as woodcraft, at Trentham Military Camp.

The armed forces fulfil an important ceremonial role for the state, flying visiting dignitaries, providing guards of honour and ★bands for important state occasions, and carrying out gun salutes to mark important dates. Military police have assisted police during Royal tours, and catering staff are seconded to Parliament and other locations. An important ceremonial role of the armed forces is the provision of aides-de-camp to the Governor-General and visiting dignitaries. RNZN vessels make 'showing the flag' visits to other countries, as well as taking part in the Waitangi Day commemorations. The RNZAF has provided occasional air shows for the public, with that on 29 March 1958 to mark the RNZAF's 21st anniversary attracting 120,000 spectators. Aerobatic performances by RNZAF jets have thrilled the public at numerous events, such as the low-level fly-pasts at the opening of the Museum of New Zealand/Te Papa in 1998. Military bands provide displays and music at almost all important public occasions, and perform at concerts, parades, and marches at regular intervals around the country. ★Anzac Day in particular is an opportunity for the three services to parade and reinforce the links between the armed forces and the wider community. Other ceremonial support given by the New Zealand armed forces includes commemorations of battles overseas, such as at Gallipoli in 1990 and Cassino in 1994. (See CIVIL POWER, AID TO; HYDROGRAPHIC SURVEYING; INDUSTRIAL DISPUTES, USE OF ARMED FORCES IN; RESOURCE PROTECTION)

Civil power, aid to Although the maintenance of law and order within New Zealand is the responsibility of the police, the armed forces represent a source of potential support in the event of a situation arising beyond the capacity of policing resources. Before 1886 the distinction between police and military functions was blurred by the dual roles of the ★Militia (which could be called out by a magistrate) and the ★Armed Constabulary. Even after that date, when two separate forces were established, the police role of the military lingered. In the Defence Act 1886 the ★Permanent Militia was charged with assisting the police in the event of any 'sudden or extraordinary disturbance'. As late as 1907 permanent militiamen were still performing occasional routine street duties as policemen (while, reciprocally, police were trained in the forts and regarded as a military reserve). Provision for the military forces to act as police survived revision of the Defence Act in 1909. Section 17 of the new Act empowered the government, in the event of a sudden or extraordinary disturbance, to order the whole or part of the Permanent Force to act 'either in aid of or as a Police Force'.

There were both legal and practical obstacles to the use of non-regular service personnel in aid of the civil power. Only after they had been declared to be on actual service could ★Volunteer Force units be used, and their community-based composition left their reliability open to question. For these reasons, the option of using Volunteer personnel in an individual capacity as special constables was preferred. The first instance of Volunteer personnel being used in this role occurred in 1879 when strife erupted in Christchurch between Irish nationalists and Orangemen. During the 1890 Maritime Strike numerous Volunteers were sworn in, in Christchurch, Dunedin, Greymouth, and probably Wellington. They supplemented the limited resources of the Permanent Militia, which was involved from the outset of the strike at Wellington and later Lyttelton. Initially they joined police in guarding the wharves at Wellington, but later confined their involvement mainly to routine duties which released police for strike duty. To the extent that these coercive resources allowed the employers unimpeded use of non-union labour, the armed forces were involved in a strike-breaking operation, even if their ostensible focus was on law and order.

The armed forces performed a similar, though much more extensive, role during a major waterfront dispute in Wellington, which erupted in October 1913 and spread to other ports. So inadequate did police

Civil power

A column of 'Massey's Cossacks' in Hanson Street in Newtown, Wellington, in 1913 (*S.C. Smith Collection, Alexander Turnbull Library, G-48777-1/2*)

resources appear to be to deal with the situation which arose in Wellington that Governor Lord Liverpool feared the 'necessity for extraordinary action'. The Prime Minister, W.F. ★Massey, wanted to use members of the Royal New Zealand Artillery, the main regular component of the armed forces, to take the place of police on the streets, unarmed, thereby releasing the police to operate on the wharves. Despite the 1890 precedent and statutory authority for such action, the military authorities resisted this approach. Colonel E.S. ★Heard, the acting Commandant of the New Zealand Military Forces, urged the government to act on the principle that if the troops were called out to aid the police, they would do so 'armed and prepared to use their weapons'—in short as a last resort. As an alternative to Massey's proposal, Heard offered to provide indirect military assistance in reinforcing police resources by the enlistment of special constables. ★Territorial Force squadron commanders from the various military subdistricts were called together, and ordered, in their private capacity assisting the police, to ascertain who in their districts would be available to go to Wellington as special constables. These names were given to local police, who organised and dispatched them. The military forces also provided assistance in quartering and organising the mounted specials (who became known as 'Massey's Cossacks'), when they reached Wellington; their barracks became the focus of rioters' hostile attention. Although commanded by Colonel Stuart ★Newall, the mounted specials were effectively under the direction of his younger deputy, Colonel A.H. ★Russell. Foot specials were also recruited, with the military authorities again playing a significant part and Territorials again to the fore in leadership roles. In Auckland and Christchurch, there was similar covert military assistance, though recruitment of mounted specials in Auckland was generally arranged by the Farmers' Union.

The local naval forces, then under Admiralty control, were also drawn into the fray. The unexpected arrival in Wellington on 28 October of HMS *Psyche* had had a calming effect—Liverpool would later claim that it forestalled an attempt to proclaim a provisional government. Her commander agreed to land a company with a Maxim gun if requested by the government 'in case of very urgent necessity' (i.e. if the Riot Act was read), but in the event no such action was required, though men were drilled on the wharves. In Auckland HMS *Pyramus*, by providing patrols on the wharves in support of non-striking workers, had a similar intimidatory effect on strikers there.

In both 1890 and 1913 the military forces had been drawn into actions designed to achieve the government's political objectives. In short, their role went beyond merely supporting the police in restoring the peace. After the ★First World War, the Defence Department was covertly involved in a number of precautionary measures, including the development of an intelligence system. Equipment and supplies were organised for distribution to civilian authorities as part of contingency arrangements to deal with the possibility of civil unrest and strikes. In the event, direct action was not required, and the threat of unrest subsided in 1921, not to be revived until a decade later under the impact of the Great Depression. When riots occurred in Auckland in April 1932, a twenty-three-strong detachment of New Zealand naval personnel and Royal Marines marched up Queen Street to the Town Hall armed with rifles and clubs. They were later reinforced by RNVR personnel and airmen from Hobsonville air base. Naval personnel were again deployed the next day when disturbances spread to other parts of Auckland, and they were joined by nearly a hundred Waikato Mounted Rifles personnel who had been urgently railed to Auckland. The latter marginally distanced themselves from the military by removing their badges. Armed naval and military guards were maintained at key points for a few weeks afterwards. These events demonstrated the lack of any legislative basis for the use of armed forces in such circumstances. The ★Public Safety Conservation Act 1932 subsequently provided for a proclamation of emergency in situations in which the 'public safety or public order' was likely to be imperilled. Under such a proclamation, non-regular elements of the armed forces could be used for law and order or other purposes.

During the state of emergency proclaimed in 1951 as a result of the waterfront dispute, the possibility of the strikers' violently opposing use of armed forces personnel on the wharves led the army to hold unobtrusively in readiness some parties armed with rifles, though neither ammunition nor bayonets were issued to the troops. In the event, none of these parties had to be deployed. (See INDUSTRIAL DISPUTES, USE OF ARMED FORCES IN)

During its more than fifty years in force—it was repealed in 1987—the Public Safety Conservation Act was never invoked for law and order purposes. The statutory provision for military personnel to be used in a policing role ended with the repeal of the Defence Act in 1950. Since 1971 statutory authority has existed for the armed forces to be made available, at police request, for assistance in an emergency beyond the capacity of the police to deal with using their own resources. Under this legislation the armed forces provided transport assistance for policing operations in removing protesters from Bastion Point in 1978; army engineers demolished their structures. A more prolonged and substantial involvement in support of the police occurred in 1981, when the tour of a South African rugby team deeply divided the country and led to large-scale protests aimed at disrupting games. The Ministry of Defence was reluctant to be involved at all, and sought to act as discreetly as possible. At first military assistance was confined to transport and other logistic support, but after protesters forced the cancellation of a game at Hamilton the government authorised an increased Defence commitment. An Iroquois helicopter was made available for rapid deployment of police, army engineers installed barbed wire on approaches to and even inside rugby grounds as crowd control measures, and bomb disposal personnel were kept on standby. Facilities were provided for police riot training. The RNZAF made more than 800 flights in support of the policing operations. At no time, however, were military personnel used in a confrontational role with protesters, though they were sometimes subjected to verbal abuse. In 1984 off-duty sailors assisted police in quelling a riot in Auckland's Queen Street, their intervention being called for by junior police officers on the spot; they acted as individuals, however, under the provisions of the Police Act 1958 and Crimes Act 1961. (See also CIVIL COMMUNITY, ASSISTANCE TO)

J. Crawford, 'Overt and Covert Military Involvement in the 1890 Maritime Strike and 1913 Waterfront Strike in New Zealand', *Labour History*, no 60 (1991); R.S. Hill, *The Iron Hand in the Velvet Glove, The Modernisation of Policing in New Zealand 1886–1917* (Dunmore Press: Palmerston North, 1995); W.D. McIntyre, *New Zealand Prepares for War: Defence Policy 1919–39* (University of Canterbury Press, Christchurch, 1988); M. Pedersen, 'Aid to the Civil Power: The New Zealand Experience' (MA thesis, Massey University, 1987).

Civil–military relations There are two main facets to the relationship between the armed forces and society: specifically the means by which the armed forces are controlled, and, more generally, the perception by the community of the armed forces. The latter is important because ultimately public opinion, as reflected by political parties in Parliament, determines the size of the appropriations made for defence, and hence the size and shape of the armed forces. It also has a bearing on the willingness of men and women to enlist in the services.

In democratic societies there is a principle of firm civil control of the armed forces. In New Zealand's case, this depends on both constitutional arrangements and conventions. The armed forces are under

Civil–military relations

the Commander-in-Chief, who is the Governor-General, but policy in regard to them is set by the government through the Cabinet and departmental structure (see DEFENCE, HIGHER ORGANISATION OF). The armed forces are charged with carrying out the lawful orders of the civil authority. There is a convention that they stay out of the political arena.

In situations where judgment must be exercised there is scope for conflict between civilian and military perspectives. Nevertheless, serious disputes between ministers and their military advisers have been rare. Richard *Seddon quarrelled with the Commandant, Colonel F.J. *Fox, over the state of the *Volunteer Force in 1893. More recently Major-General K.L. *Stewart and Prime Minister Sidney Holland had a row in 1950 when the newly elected National government appeared unwilling to proceed with the measures needed to speed up New Zealand preparations to meet the *Middle East commitment. In 1987 there was conflict between the Chief of Defence Staff, Air Marshal David *Crooks, and the Prime Minister, David *Lange, over New Zealand's response to the military coup in Fiji on 14 May 1987 (see FIJI COUPS).

There have been instances of soldiers entering the political arena. In 1938 four senior serving *Territorial Force officers issued a statement which criticised government policy and were retired for their pains (see FOUR COLONELS' REVOLT). There were echoes of this affair in the public statement issued in October 1985 by sixteen retired service chiefs, criticising the government's approach to defence, especially with regard to *ANZUS. They were dismissed by Lange as 'geriatric generals' and later as 'unreconstructed military neanderthals'. In 1997, a Territorial Force officer who spoke out about the inadequacy of government policy during an *Anzac Day address was rebuked by the Chief of General Staff.

Only rarely have constitutional questions been raised or conventions challenged. The Governor, Lord Glasgow, enraged Seddon in 1894 by privately criticising the government's approach to defence provision and demanding that it take action to remedy deficiencies, an intervention which earned him a reprimand from the Colonial Office in London. Shortly after the outbreak of the *First World War in 1914, a later Governor, Lord Liverpool, also had a disagreement with his Prime Minister, W.F. *Massey, over the dispatch of the Main Body of the *New Zealand Expeditionary Force. Uncertainties about the whereabouts of the German Eastern Asiatic Squadron had led to the departure of the force being postponed on 25 September. The available naval vessels were palpably inadequate to protect the ten-troopship convoy from such a threat. After news of the German squadron's bombardment of Papeete on 22 September indicated that it was well to the north-east of New Zealand, however, the Admiralty urged that there be no further delay in sending the force across the Tasman to link up with the AIF. Probably in an effort to get around Massey's political difficulties, Liverpool on 4 October offered to take responsibility as Commander-in-Chief of the New Zealand Military Forces for the immediate dispatch of the force, but desisted when Massey indicated that he would resign. In the event, the force did not leave New Zealand until 16 October, accompanied by the Japanese battlecruiser *Ibuki*.

Among the public, the armed forces have generally been perceived favourably. Before the First World War they enjoyed patriotic support among a population strongly influenced by imperialist ideology and by conceptions of the glory of war. Civil–military relations were tempered, though, by popular distrust of professional soldiers as being contrary to New Zealand's 'democratic' way of life; imperial officers sent to assist with the New Zealand defence forces were frequently attacked as an unwanted military caste by a press which extolled the virtues of a citizen army. Although this liberal attitude remained strong throughout the twentieth century, New Zealanders generally accepted the need for *conscription twice in wartime, and *compulsory military training for significant periods. In spite of the bloody experience of the First World War, the armed forces continued to enjoy high esteem, not least because of the high proportion of the male population which had served in them in the recent conflict. This was reinforced by the *Second World War experience, during which New Zealand itself was threatened with invasion, and all available men were mobilised or served in the *Home Guard or *Emergency Precautions Scheme. The Returned Services' Association assumed a prominent, essentially conservative, role in support of the armed forces. Nevertheless there was a countervailing left-wing strand of public opinion, led by pacifists and members of the labour movement (who resented the involvement of armed forces, however covertly, in industrial disputes) (see INDUSTRIAL DISPUTES, USE OF ARMED FORCES IN). The high prestige enjoyed by the armed forces in the community persisted after the Second World War, as they undertook a number of combat tasks in support of New Zealand's interests. But New Zealand's involvement in the *Vietnam War negatively affected the attitudes of the post–Second World War generation, and this was publicly reflected in a hostile reaction to New Zealand artillerymen returning from Vietnam in 1971—the only time that returning New Zealand troops have been so received. Military involvement in the policing of the 1981 Springbok rugby tour of New Zealand, a very divisive community issue, enhanced such negative perceptions in the eyes of some. More recently a minority have argued that New Zealand does not need defence forces at all, but a poll conducted in 1997 found that 72 per cent of the population considered it important for New Zealand to possess strong and effective armed forces.

Of the parties, the National Party has traditionally been regarded as more sympathetic to the defence forces than its main rival, the Labour Party. The latter, in its early days, reflected labour movement suspicion of the forces, though its views moderated as it came to power in the 1930s when Fascism was on the march. After the Second World War it so reversed its early stance that it undertook a peacetime commitment to send an expeditionary force to the Middle East in the event of war. Notwithstanding general support for the armed forces, National and Labour governments in peacetime have tended to be parsimonious of resources, with the result that defence appropriations have steadily fallen. To counter this trend, the armed forces have emphasised the assistance provided to the community in peacetime and have actively sought to cultivate public interest in defence issues (see CIVIL COMMUNITY, ASSISTANCE TO).

Clark, Lieutenant Russell Stuart Cedric (27 August 1905–29 July 1966) was a leading war artist in the *Second World War. Originally from Christchurch, he worked as a commercial artist and art teacher in Dunedin before moving to Wellington in 1939 to work as an illustrator for the *New Zealand Listener*. Called up in 1942, he was at first given the dull work of signwriting and illustrating army books and pamphlets. In 1943 he was appointed official war artist in the Pacific. Over a period of nine months during 1944 he sketched the day-to-day activities of New Zealanders serving with the 3rd Division in the *Solomons campaign, making the finished watercolours after his return to Wellington. Some 110 works, faithfully recording the ordinary life of New Zealand troops in the Pacific, are lodged in the war art collection in the National Archives in Wellington. After the war Clark lectured at the Canterbury University College School of Art, and was a noted sculptor and painter.

Clark-Hall, Air Marshal Sir Robert Hamilton (21 June 1883–9 March 1964). A Londoner, Clark-Hall entered the Royal Navy in 1897. While serving as a midshipman on the China Station, he took part in the relief of Peking following the Boxer Rebellion in 1900. In 1911 he learned to fly, and his experiments with aircraft as a possible fighting machine were later described as 'possibly the most dangerous and gallant exploits in pre-war flying'. He transferred to the Royal Naval Air Service in 1913, and commanded the aircraft-carrier HMS *Ark Royal* during the *Gallipoli campaign. For his war services, which included commanding the RNAS's 1 Wing in France in 1917–18 and serving as the Grand Fleet's Fleet Aviation Officer in 1918–19, he was made a CMG and a DSO. After the war he secured a permanent commission in the RAF. He commanded the RAF in the Mediterranean from 1925 to 1929, was Director of Equipment at the Air Ministry, and finally was AOC Coastal Area before retiring at his own request in 1934 (in which year he was appointed a KBE) and emigrating to New Zealand. In 1936 the Air Ministry considered appointing him as air adviser to the New Zealand government, but opted instead for Wing Commander R.A. *Cochrane. After war broke out in 1939 Clark-Hall, at the age of fifty-six, volunteered to serve in the RNZAF. Temporarily relinquishing his rank of air marshal, he was commissioned as a wing-commander and given command of RNZAF Harewood. He commanded Southern Group in 1943–44 before serving as AOC 1 (Islands) Group, the RNZAF effort in the *Solomons campaign, in 1944–45. He retired from the RNZAF in 1946.

Clifton, Brigadier George Herbert (18 September 1898–13 March 1970). Born at Greenmeadows, near Napier, Clifton entered the Royal Military College at Duntroon in 1915. After being commissioned in the *New Zealand Staff Corps in 1918, he was attached to the British Army in India for two years, and was awarded an MC while serving on the North-west Frontier. From 1921 he was a staff officer with various *Territorial Force units in New Zealand, aside from twice attending engineering and staff courses in the United Kingdom. Posted to 2NZEF in 1940, he served as brigade major with 5th Brigade before becoming, in September, Commander Royal Engineers, of the 2nd New Zealand Division. During the retreat in *Greece, he commanded an improvised rearguard of engineers and artillery, an independent role he relished, and was made a DSO for his oversight of demolition policy. He earned a bar to his DSO when, as Chief Engineer of XXX Corps (from October 1941), he led a large convoy to resupply the New Zealand division during its first action in the *North African campaign as part of the Crusader offensive. From February 1942 he was an active and demanding commander of 6th Brigade, and was briefly taken prisoner when it was overrun by German tanks at El Mreir in July 1942. He was less fortunate when, on 4 September, he was captured for a second time while undertaking a reconnaissance near the front. His demeanour impressed *Afrika Korps* commander General Erwin Rommel, who interrogated him soon after his capture; Rommel queried the New Zealanders' presence in a European war, asking if they were 'in it for the sport'. Clifton managed to escape, but was retaken after walking for six days in the desert. Held in Italy, and later Germany, as a prisoner of war, he was badly wounded during another escape attempt in 1943. Not until March 1945, on his ninth attempt, was he successful. His various escape efforts were recognised by a second bar to his DSO. After the war he served on the headquarters staff of the ★British Commonwealth Occupation Force in Japan, as the ★New Zealand Army's liaison officer in London (1949–52), and finally as commander of the Northern Military District (1952–53). After his retirement he became a successful sheepfarmer.

G. Clifton, *The Happy Hunted* (Cassell & Co Ltd, London, 1952).

Closer defence relations see AUSTRALIAN–NEW ZEALAND DEFENCE COOPERATION

Clouston, Air Commodore Arthur Edmund (7 April 1908–1 January 1984) was one of New Zealand's most talented airmen. Born in Motueka, he was inspired to take private flying lessons by Kingsford Smith's flight to New Zealand in 1928; in 1930 he sold his business and went to the United Kingdom to seek a short-service commission in the RAF. With some difficulty—he suffered from high blood pressure—he achieved this objective through the assistance of Keith ★Park, and was quickly recognised to be a natural pilot. When his commission ended in 1935, he became a civilian test pilot with the Royal Aircraft Establishment at Farnborough. He was awarded an AFC in 1938 for testing the effect of barrage balloon cables on aircraft. During the late 1930s, he became well known in New Zealand through his participation in international air races and long-distance flights. In 1938 he made the longest non-stop flight yet achieved when he flew non-stop (apart from fuelling/rest stops) from the United Kingdom to New Zealand and back, covering the 41,600 kilometres in just under eleven days, and in the process breaking the record for the fastest flight between London and Sydney. Recalled to the RAF with the outbreak of the ★Second World War, he continued to serve as a test pilot with the Experimental Section at Farnborough. His desire for a more active role was partly alleviated by occasional opportunities for action against enemy raiders after test aircraft were armed, and he secured one victory. For his work on the development of airborne searchlight work while serving with the Directorate of Armament Development from November 1940, he was awarded a DFC. In 1943–44 he served in Coastal Command as commander of the Liberator-equipped 224 Squadron. For his service, which included an apparently successful attack on a U-boat in July 1943, he received a bar to his DFC and was made a DSO. He commanded the RAF base at Langham from February 1944 until the end of the war, and then a communications wing in Germany. Appointed to a permanent commission in the RAF after the war, he was sent to New Zealand in 1947 for a two-year attachment to the RNZAF, during which he commanded Ohakea air base. He was commandant of the Empire Test Pilots' School (1950–53), Air Officer Commanding Singapore (1954–57), and commandant of the Aeroplane and Armament Experimental Establishment at Boscombe Down (1957–60). He published an account of his wartime flying activities, *Dangerous Skies*, in 1954, and was made a CB in 1957.

Coast defences Coast or harbour defences were an integral part of New Zealand's military establishment until the 1950s. Ninety-nine forts and batteries (including heavy anti-aircraft) were established with many other outposts servicing minefields or detection devices. Many were manned for just a few months, but some filled the role unchanged for more than seventy years—making them among the longest-serving defence facilities in the country. Coast defence had three main phases of activity: 1885–1900, 1910–18, and 1935–46. That the installations never fired a shot in anger is a measure of their success: reconnaissance of New Zealand ports by enemy ships and planes showed their vulnerability as economic and population centres. Coast defences were a response to the country's isolation and the price of preparedness.

Settlements at both Auckland and Wellington built batteries soon after they were founded. The New Zealand Company may have mounted three 18-pounders from the immigrant ship *Adelaide* on Somes Island in Wellington as early as 1840. The French Pacific squadron was not the only concern: fear of Maori waka taua (war canoes) grew after the ★Wairau massacre in 1843. Barracks started on Auckland's Te Rerenga-ora-iti point in December 1840 soon became Fort Britomart, and sprouted a few cannon to guard the commercial harbour. A short-lived battery was dug in behind earthworks on Flagstaff Hill overlooking Wellington's inner anchorage in July 1843, with another partially completed above Pipitea Point. The ★New Zealand Wars tended to keep the settlers' focus inwards, but successive war scares to the 1870s influenced thinking on coast defence.

External defence was reviewed in 1852 following French expansion in the Pacific. The ★Crimean War led to the preparation of plans for coast batteries for Auckland and Wellington, but all that could be afforded was a low parapet at Fort Britomart. In 1859, Britomart was again upgraded with revetted embrasures and sixteen guns. No progress was made with batteries for the other ports, including Lyttelton. Dur-

Coast defences

A gun crew prepares to fire a 6-inch gun at Wellington's Fort Dorset in 1939 (*Waiouru Army Museum, 1992.256*)

ing the American Civil War, the possibility of war between the British Empire and the Union caused tension. A Confederate raider even targeted Yankee whalers in New Zealand waters. Unsuccessful attempts to obtain guns for coast defence were made by both the central government and that of Canterbury Province in 1865. In the late 1860s old naval cannon were issued to a few Volunteer units which had been formed to provide particular ports with some defence, but these guns were never permanently installed. Planning for New Zealand's external defences intensified in 1871 as a result of fears that war in Europe would involve the British Empire. Within a year, no fewer than five major reports dealt with the subject, laying down the basics of what was done a decade later. Premier Julius Vogel had sought information from London about the newly developed underwater mine for protecting harbours. Defence Minister Donald ★McLean raised the possibility of floating batteries, only to have the Admiralty dismiss it. Captain F.W. Hutton, a geologist who had served in the British Army, toured the main ports and recommended modern rifled guns at each port, including Nelson. His preferred sites were close to inshore anchorages and burgeoning wharfage. Lieutenant-Colonel John Cargill, the commander of the Dunedin Militia District, favoured mines and guns mounted on disappearing carriages. The Director of Works for Fortifications at the War Office, Colonel W.F.D. ★Jervois, though, preferred defences to be placed closer to the heads to keep an enemy from reaching still water. Following Vogel's request, he had assessed New Zealand's requirements from a distance using charts. All these experts saw a problem in the manning of the many guns or new technology proposed because there were virtually no trained professional soldiers in New Zealand. The colony's evident vulnerability to hostile raiders was exploited by David Luckie, the editor of the *Daily Southern Cross* in Auckland, who caused a minor panic when he published an account in 1873 of an overnight assault on Auckland and its new-found wealth by a fictitious Russian cruiser *Kaskowiski* (see HOAXES). Heavy coast defence guns were only acquired after a real Russian war scare—in 1878. Following a report by a British Royal Commission examining the defences of all the Australasian colonies on New Zealand's requirements (which benefited from Jervois's 1871 report), Premier George ★Grey agreed on 4 May to spend £17,600 on twenty-two rifled muzzle-loading (RML) guns. Although shipped to the four main ports in October, the guns were not mounted because the war scare had subsided.

During the early 1880s mounting tension between the British and Russian empires led many people to urge the mounting of the guns. Colonel P.H. ★Scratchley had (with Jervois) been advising the Australian colonies on their defence programmes, and was brought to New Zealand in 1880 to advise on putting

Coast defences

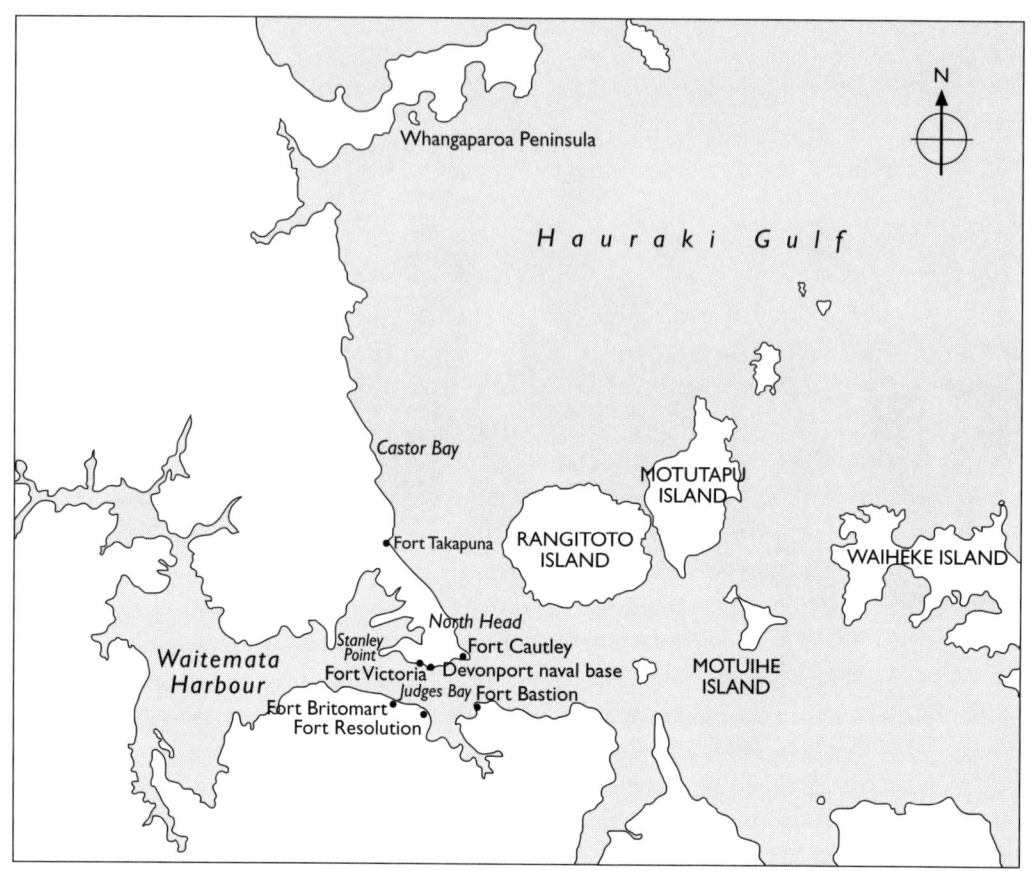

Map 4a Coast defence sites at Auckland

its defences in order. A sum of £9000 was voted to make a start with implementing his proposals, and in 1882 four (of twelve proposed) spar ★torpedo boats were ordered. After being appointed as Governor of New Zealand a year later, Jervois advised the government to continue with Scratchley's programme, and Major Henry ★Cautley was brought out from England in late 1883 to oversee the works. Jervois himself later proposed modifications to Scratchley's scheme: the inclusion of Bluff Harbour in the ports to be defended and changes to the plans at both Wellington and Lyttelton. He also suggested augmenting the RMLs with new breech-loading (BL) guns, and converting New Zealand's ten best merchant steamships into armed cruisers. Stage one of his three-year programme would involve installing thirteen 8-inch and ten 6-inch BL 'disappearing guns' at a cost of £205,000; mounted on pivoting hydropneumatic carriages, these pieces, when fired, recoiled into their pits where, out of harm's way, they were reloaded before being slowly raised to fire again.

The orderly implementation of Cautley's scheme was prevented by the onset in March 1885 of the sharpest of the recurrent ★Russian scares. ★Armed Constabulary personnel hurried to the ports in March to install twenty of the '1878' RML guns in temporary works. The earthen fortifications they threw up were redolent of the field redoubts which had characterised the New Zealand Wars. The RMLs were mounted on the same headland sites planned for the permanent forts under Cautley's scheme, which made the job harder for Cautley's successor, Major Tudor Boddam, when construction started in 1886. The permanent works were completed from the late 1880s, with the new ordnance (thirteen BL 8-inch guns, ten BL 6-inch Armstrong guns, and 20 quick-firing 6-pounders) arriving from 1887. The main forts were a standard design for two 6-inch gun pits, or a single 8-inch pit, usually with underground magazines, crew bomb-proofs, and infantry defences. Most of the RML guns remained in support. Batteries were concentrated at Auckland's North Head, Wellington's Miramar Peninsula, and Otago's Taiaroa Head, each supported by detached RML batteries. Ripapa Island in Lyttelton Harbour became the only island fort in New Zealand, later criticised as offering too compact a target. Otago had two potential targets to

Coast defences

Map 4b Wellington harbour defences

defend: Dunedin city which could be bombarded from the south, and Port Chalmers close to the harbour mouth. In 1888–93 existing works were remodelled and more batteries added, directed by A.W.D. ★Bell of the Public Works Department. Late in the 1890s new works were added on Auckland's Mt Victoria, at the Botanical Gardens in Wellington, and on Otago's Harrington Point. Responding to the new menace of fast motor torpedo boats, 12-pounder quick-firing guns were added at all the main ports except Lyttelton. The BL 6-inch guns were sent to the United Kingdom, unnecessarily, for strengthening. (See table 4.)

By the 1890s coast defence was an integrated system. Batteries were coordinated by a fire commander, who was in telephone contact, protected by infantry positions. Submarine minefields, covered by quick-firing guns and searchlights, were ready to be laid. (Submarine mining was considered integral to coast defence.) Facilities were established in Auckland, Wellington, and Otago. Auckland's depot was particularly extensive, spread between Bastion Point and North Head. Wellington's was at Shelly Bay and Mahanga Bay, and Dunedin's at Deborah Bay. The minefields were surveyed, but there was always a shortage of mine-laying boats. Submarine mining was scrapped in 1908.

With over £645,000 spent on coast defences by 1904 enthusiasm for more construction waned. The RML weapons were taken out of commission. Attention turned to developing ★defence schemes, reorganising the military forces, and defending cable stations and coaling facilities. Two 12-pounders were mounted on rail wagons and sent to patrol Westport's coaling wharves from 1910. Two batteries (of newer Mark VII 6-inch) were added in Auckland and Wellington in 1911. The latter were near the harbour mouth, at Point Dorset.

Coast defences

Table 4 Coast Defence Fixed Guns 1885–1901

AUCKLAND

Fort Cautley/North Head	1 × 64-pounder RML gun (1885), 3 × 7-inch RML guns (1885, reduced to 2 1888), 3 × 8-inch BL guns (1887–88), 2 × 12-pounder QF guns, 3 × 6-pounder QF guns, 2 × searchlights
Fort Resolution	2 × 64-pounder RML guns (1885)
Fort Victoria	4 × 64-pounder RML guns (1885, removed 1891), 1 × 8-inch BL gun (1899)
Fort Takapuna	2 × 6-inch BL guns (1887), 2 × 6-pounder QF guns, 2 × searchlights
Fort Bastion	2 × 6-inch BL guns (1889), 1 × 6-pounder QF gun, 1 × searchlight

WELLINGTON

Fort Ballance/Gordon	2 × 64-pounder RML guns (1891, in the Low Battery, but replaced by 2 × 6-pounder QF guns in 1897), 2 × 7-inch RML guns (1885, one removed 1894), 2 × 6-inch BL guns (1886, 1894), 1 × 8-inch BL gun (1893), 2 × 12-pounder QF guns, 2 × 6-pounder QF guns, 1 × searchlight
Fort Buckley	2 × 64-pounder RML guns (1885), possibly 1 × 6-pounder QF gun
Halswell Pt Battery	1 × 64-pounder RML gun (1885), 1 × 7-inch RML gun (1885), both replaced by 1 × 8-inch BL gun (1889), 1 × 6-pounder QF gun
Fort Kelburne	2 × 6-inch BL guns (1889), 1 × 3-pounder QF gun
Kau Pt Battery	1 × 8-inch BL gun (1891)
Gardens Battery	1 × 7-inch RML gun (1896, possibly not mounted)

LYTTELTON

Spur Pt Battery	1 × 64-pounder RML gun (1885)
Battery Pt Battery	2 × 7-inch RML guns (1885), 1 × searchlight
Ft Jervois, Ripapa Is	2 × 6-inch BL guns (1889), 2 × 8-inch BL guns (1889), 2 × 6-pounder QF guns
Erskine Pt Battery	1 × 7-inch RML gun (1891)

OTAGO

Fort Taiaroa	3 × 64-pounder RML guns (1885), 1 × 7-inch RML gun (1893), 1 × 6-inch BL gun (1889), 1 × 6-pounder QF gun
St Clair Battery	1 × 7-inch RML gun (1885), 1 × 6-pounder QF gun
Lawyers Head Battery	1 × 7-inch RML gun (1885)
Ocean Beach/Central Battery	2 × 6-inch BL guns (1889)
Harrington Pt Battery	1 × 7-inch RML gun (1898). A second 7-inch RML gun was installed in 1903.

(Not all guns and searchlights remained installed for the full period.)

During the ★First World War, New Zealand's coast defences were activated. Garrison Artillery Territorials were mobilised for a time, but a chronic manpower shortage, coupled with growing confidence in the strategic situation in the Pacific, soon led to their stand-down. Torpedo nets curtained the dry docks and the examination service (and batteries) oversaw all ship movements. Most quick-firing guns were reshuffled (some as defensive weapons for merchant ships) and cordite gave the disappearing guns greater accuracy. Despite no new batteries being built in the war years, the deterrent value of the defences was probably, paradoxically, at its greatest.

In the 1920s, all the 1880s 'disappearing guns' were struck off the books and most were melted down. On the other hand the 4-inch secondary armament of the recently scrapped HMS ★*New Zealand* was sent out to the Dominion. With rising global tensions in the late 1930s, however, coast defences were reinvigorated and expanded. Old sites were upgraded for 12-pounder and 4-inch guns. Three-gun counter-bombardment batteries were begun for modern guns on Motutapu Island in the Hauraki Gulf, Wellington's Palmer Head, and Lyttelton's Godley Head, and all were upgraded during the ★Second World War. Field guns were hurriedly obtained for beach defence in September 1939. Up to twenty mobile medium guns also stood sentinel at Godley Head, Great Barrier Island, Bay of Islands, and Marlborough Sounds, some serving well into 1942. The defences of the main ports were boosted

Coast defences

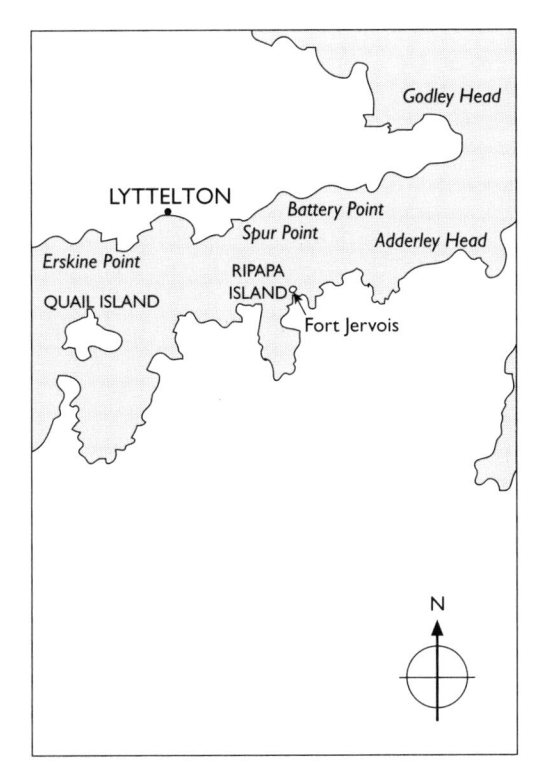

Map 4c Lyttelton's defences

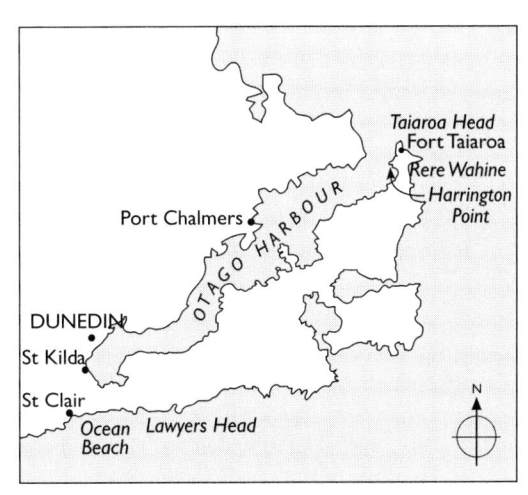

Map 4d Coast defence sites at Dunedin

with new 6-inch Mark VII close-defence batteries. Even old 6-inch disappearing guns were revived in Lyttelton and Otago harbours.

With the onset of the ★Pacific War in December 1941, and the fall of Singapore two months later, near-panic attended the question of harbour defences. Field and anti-tank guns, including captured Italian First World War pieces, scanned the horizon. In 1943–44 twin 6-pounder guns were installed as anti–motor torpedo boat measures in both Auckland and Wellington. On the advice of General Sir Guy ★Williams, secondary harbours were designated minor ports worthy of defence. Weapons for these batteries were British 6-inch guns originally intended for arming merchant ships, and ex-US Navy 5-inch pieces. New batteries were built at sixteen harbours in 1942–43, with the British guns (some with searchlights) being sent to Whangaroa, Bay of Islands (two sites), Napier, Marlborough Sounds (five sites), Nelson, Akaroa, Timaru, Bluff, and Manukau (a 4.7-inch gun), and the American equipment going to Whangarei, Gisborne, Wanganui, Oamaru, Westport, Greymouth, and New Plymouth (155 mm field guns). Four 9.2-inch batteries had been proposed in the 1930s, yet they received the go-ahead only in the heat of 1942. Based on modified British designs, they involved an incredible volume of excavation and construction work. Each battery was built for three guns but, for economy, only two were mounted. The battery planned for Lyttelton was cancelled in 1943. Slow progress prevented Waiheke's and Wright's Hill's guns being serviceable before the war ended, and only one 9.2-inch gun (Whangaparaoa's No. 3) was proof-fired during the hostilities. Radar changed the way New Zealand's batteries observed their targets. Previously equipped with depression range finders and plotting tables, many batteries were progressively linked to radio direction finding from 1941, using New Zealand–made sets (see SCIENCE AND TECHNOLOGY). New Zealand–made autosights developed at the University of Auckland were fitted to many guns. During the war, New Zealand garrisons also had a coast defence role in Fiji, Tonga, ★New Caledonia, and Norfolk and ★Fanning Islands. Altogether more than forty guns, overlooking seven anchorages, were installed or served. New Zealand's responsibility for Suva continued into the late 1950s.

The threat of air attack led to anti-aircraft defences being hurriedly added from 1942. Heavy concrete emplacements were built for batteries of four static 3.7-inch guns. Auckland started twelve, Wellington six, and Lyttelton, Dunedin, and Nelson one each. These were clustered around air bases and defended waterfronts, but their expense led to a simplified earthen version for mobile guns. A number were dual-role emplacements, allowing fire against ships as well as aircraft. There was also a return to the concept of defensive minefields and physical barriers against submarines and fast surface craft. Extended defence posts involved the navy as much as the Army. Minefields were laid in Whangaroa, Hauraki Gulf (two), Bay of Islands (three), Great Barrier Island (two), Wellington, and Akaroa, and were

Coast defences

planned for Lyttelton and the Marlborough Sounds (two). Detection devices were installed to detect unseen enemy movement, and booms and piles to obstruct it. Extended defences were an important part of the fleet anchorages planned for the Hauraki Gulf and Marlborough Sounds; some were started before the US Pacific Fleet was sent elsewhere.

At their peak in mid 1943, New Zealand's coast defences covered twenty-one harbours with seventy-three pieces of artillery at 24-hours readiness. Almost 3500 men and women manned them. Most batteries were reduced to care and maintenance status in late 1943, after which a skeleton crew offered a slow rate of fire at ten minutes readiness. The German raider *Adjutant* in 1941 regarded Wellington harbour as being barred, ironically, by the searchlights sweeping the entrance. The guns defending Gisborne and Napier, the only ports entered by an enemy vessel, would not have been much use: they had been dismounted a month before the German submarine *U-862* ventured into them in January 1945. (See table 5.)

Fixed defences were continued after the war, based around the 9.2-inch batteries, 3.7-inch dual-role batteries, and twin 6-pounder AMTB guns. With a growing realisation, however, that these defences were impotent in a missile and jet age, the coast defence function was reviewed in 1956 and the units disbanded the following year. All equipment was eventually scrapped.

PETER COOKE

Table 5 Coast Defence Fixed Guns in Service during the Second World War

AUCKLAND (9th Heavy Regiment, RNZA)

North Head	2 × 6-inch (1911, transferred to Whangaparaoa 1941, then back to North Head after the war), 2 × 4-inch (1941), 4 × 6-pounder guns, 6 × searchlights
Takapuna	6 × 4-inch guns (1937–40, two later moved to North Head, two to Tonga), 2 × searchlights
Motutapu Is	3 × 6-inch (1938), 2 × searchlights
Castor Bay	2 × 6-inch guns (1941), 2 × searchlights
Bastion Pt	1 × twin 6-pounder guns, 2 × 12-pounders from Rangitoto Is in 1941 (where they had been for a few months), 3 × searchlights
Motuihe Is	2 × 4-inch guns (1942)
Whangaparaoa	2 × 9.2-inch guns (1945), 2 × 6-inch guns (1941), 2 × searchlights
Waiheke Is	2 × 9.2-inch guns (not mounted before end of war)

WELLINGTON (10th Heavy Regiment, RNZA)

Fort Dorset	2 × 6-inch guns (1911), 4 × 4-inch guns (1936, of which 2 moved to Gordon Point), 4 × 12-pounder guns, 7 × searchlights
Palmer Head	3 × 6-inch guns (1937, 1943), 4 × searchlights
Gordon Pt/Ft Ballance	2 × 4-inch (1941), 1 × twin 6-pounder guns, 2 × 75 mm QF guns, 4 × searchlights
Fort Opau	2 × 6-inch guns (1942)
Wright's Hill	2 × 9.2-inch (not serviceable before the end of war)

LYTTELTON (11th Heavy Regiment, RNZA)

Fort Jervois	1 × 6-inch gun (1889)
Battery Pt	2 × 4-inch guns (1939), 2 × searchlights
Godley Head	3 × 6-inch (1941) (2 × Mark VII 6-inch guns in Taylor Battery removed when the first of three Mark XXIVs was mounted in Godley Bty in December 1941), 2 × searchlights

OTAGO (11th Heavy Regiment, RNZA)*

Harrington Pt	2 × 15-pounder (later 6-pounder) guns, 1 × searchlight
Taiaroa Hd	1 × 6-inch gun (1889, replaced in 1944)
Rere Wahine	2 × 6-inch guns (1942, one removed to Taiaroa Head in 1944), 2 × searchlights
St Kilda/Tomahawk	2 × 6-inch guns (1942)

*13th Heavy Regiment briefly in 1943

(Total number of guns available at each site at any one time. Searchlights include mobile mounts. Minor ports are excluded.)

Coastwatchers, service and civilian personnel whose task it was to keep a 24-hour watch for enemy ships and aircraft, were a link in the intelligence chain. Under a scheme drawn up by the Royal Navy, and extensively reorganised just before the ★Second World War, about sixty stations were established around the New Zealand coast, with others eventually at the Chatham Islands, Pitcairn Island, Norfolk Island, the Kermadecs, and the subantarctic Auckland and Campbell islands (called the 'Cape Expedition'). Those in New Zealand itself were supplemented from 1941 by sixteen radar coastwatching stations. After the outbreak of war coastwatching was extended to the Pacific Islands to the north of New Zealand. When the ★Pacific War began, there were fifty-eight stations spread between Western Samoa, Tonga, the Cook Islands, Fiji, the Gilbert and Ellice Islands, the Phoenix Islands, Tokelau, and ★Fanning Island, and more were established in 1942 and 1943. A typical station had a radio operator, one or two soldiers, a radio to communicate with headquarters, and a number of lookout posts. Reports on passing ships and aircraft and on meteorological conditions were transmitted from these Pacific coastwatching stations to parent stations, which in turn sent messages on to Suva. Important messages were then sent on to the intelligence centres in Auckland and Honolulu. Although the stations were serviced by three small vessels of the Public Works Department, the naval authorities had overall responsibility for the scheme. Coastwatchers were a mixture of service personnel, civilian government officials (especially from the Post and Telegraph Department), and local volunteers. Personnel put up with the tedium of staring out at sea for long periods, making meteorological reports, and maintaining their radio equipment. Many coastwatchers were aided by island inhabitants, but it was an isolated and often lonely experience. For those keeping post in the 'front line' of the Gilbert group, there was also the risk of capture by the Japanese. Seven who were captured on Butaritari in the Gilbert Islands in December 1941 were taken to Tokyo (probably the first Allied POWs to be seen in Japan) and spent the remainder of the war in a Japanese POW camp. Seventeen captured by the Japanese in the rest of the Gilberts in August and September 1942 were not so fortunate. Together with five civilians, they were beheaded by the Japanese at Tarawa in October 1942. By giving coastwatchers military rank from December 1942, it was hoped to reinforce their right to treatment as POWs when captured. Among New Zealanders serving with Australian coastwatchers in the Solomons group, Major D.G. Kennedy distinguished himself by waging a mini-guerrilla war against the Japanese occupiers of New Georgia and rescuing downed airmen. Most of the coastwatching stations were closed down in 1944, and the last of the coastwatchers returned to New Zealand two years later.

O.A. Gillespie, *The Pacific* (War History Branch, Wellington, 1952); D.O.W. Hall, *Coastwatchers* (War History Branch, Wellington, 1951).

Cochrane, Air Chief Marshal the Hon. Sir Ralph Alexander (24 February 1895–17 December 1977) was the key adviser of the New Zealand government on air force development in the late 1930s. The son of a Scottish peer, he joined the Royal Navy in 1912, and served in the Royal Naval Air Service as a test pilot and airship captain during the ★First World War. After the war he gained a permanent commission in the RAF and spent a considerable part of the 1920s in the Middle East. After serving on the directing staff of the RAF Staff College and at the Air Ministry, and attending the ★Imperial Defence College, he was sent to New Zealand in 1936 to advise the Labour government on air defence policy. In his report, which he wrote while on the voyage across the Pacific to New Zealand and presented in December 1936, he endorsed the ★Singapore strategy as the basis of New Zealand's defence policy, and recommended a range of air force measures to improve New Zealand's capacity to deal with enemy raiders. These included acquiring two squadrons of bombers and giving attention to forward defence possibilities in the Pacific Islands to the north. His report was accepted by the government, and, as he had proposed, the RNZAF was constituted as a separate service in April 1937. Despite his rather aloof and aristocratic manner, he was invited to stay on as New Zealand's first Chief of the Air Staff. During the next two years, he oversaw the construction of aerodromes at Whenuapai and Ohakea, the creation of aircrew training schemes, and the ordering of thirty Wellington medium bombers from the United Kingdom. He also developed an extensive air defence scheme for the Pacific Islands, but lack of resources and the likely vulnerability of airfields north of Suva eventually prevented its implementation. Following his reversion to the RAF in 1939, he held a series of staff appointments in the United Kingdom in intelligence and training. From 1942 until 1945, he commanded first 3, then 5 Group, Bomber Command, and played an important role in the bomber offensive against Germany, developing long-range precision bombing at night. His forces' feats included the destruction of the Möhne and Eder dams in 1943 (the Dambuster raid) and of the battleship *Tirpitz* in 1944. He was made a KBE in 1945. As commander of Transport Command from 1945 to 1947, he oversaw the repatriation of thousands of troops, liberated prisoners of war, and civilians. The final postings of his career were as commander of Flying Training Command (1947–50) and Vice Chief of

Cold War

the Air Staff (1950–52). He was made a KCB in 1948 and a GBE two years later.

Cold War The onset of the Cold War has been dated to the Bolshevik revolution in Russia of 1917 and the establishment of the Communist International in 1919. But as both an inter-state and an ideological contest a later date is preferable. The major capitalist democracies—the United States and Great Britain—allied with the Soviet Union to defeat Nazi Germany and Japan in 1941–45. But with victory came discord: not 'hot' war, but not peace either—a 'cold' war, as it was termed. Just over forty years later, with the disintegration of communist power in the Soviet Union and its sphere of influence, the Cold War ended.

Throughout the Cold War, international tension waxed and waned, being greatest between 1948 and 1953, 1958 and 1962, and 1979 and 1983; least during the post-Stalin 'thaw' of the mid 1950s, the heyday of détente in the early 1970s, and the *glasnost* era from 1985. But hostility and suspicion between Cold War antagonists was the rule throughout: intelligence gathering and espionage, diplomatic manœuvring, and strategic planning never ceased.

The historiography of the Cold War has mirrored the conflict. Were the United States and its allies reacting to Soviet and communist expansion? Was the Soviet Union reacting to the United States' ambition to establish a global capitalism? These questions dominated the approaches taken by historians during the conflict, but recent historiography has been more even-handed.

New Zealand's alignment and participation in the Cold War was determined by the decision of the 1940s Labour government to back the United States and Great Britain (*that* concord was crucial) in their disagreements with the Soviet Union. The decision was questioned, though not overturned, by the Left, with communists and others claiming that Labour had rejected both peace and socialism. Thereafter, the story of New Zealand's involvement in the war echoes that of many small states in the Western alliance, such as Norway, Denmark, and the Netherlands. Like them, New Zealand remained aligned; like them, the alignment was qualified in a number of ways. The most persistent qualifications were these: a preference (especially in the Labour Party) for social and economic rather than military solutions to Cold War problems, for détente rather than hostility, for nuclear weapons test bans rather than testing; caution in the expenditure of either financial or human resources in support of Cold War operations; national attitudes and concerns, including the influence of Australia and Britain, fear of Japan in the 1950s, and antipathy to nuclear weapons 'too close to home' in the 1970s and 1980s.

Regarded as a war, the Cold War was New Zealand's most protracted 'military' engagement. As the adjective suggests, however, open combat was the exception not the rule. New Zealand was involved in Cold War-related combat operations only between 1950 and 1953 (★Korean War), 1949 and 1960 (★Malayan Emergency) and 1965 and 1972 (★Vietnam War).

The 'front line' of the Cold War in the 1940s lay across Europe and the Middle East. New Zealand provided crews for the ★Berlin airlift of 1948–49 and in its ★Middle East commitment pledged in advance to send forces to that region in the event of open war with the Soviet Union. Although these commitments were easily accepted in New Zealand, the introduction of ★compulsory military training to back up the latter aroused controversy. Asia was another 'theatre' of the conflict. The communist victory in the Chinese Civil War led New Zealand to accept commitments to assist in the defence of ★Hong Kong, and it continued to recognise the defeated Nationalist regime, based on Taiwan, even after Britain had recognised the new communist government in Beijing. New Zealand also gave military support to anti-communist South Korea, albeit under United Nations auspices, when the communist North invaded, and its troops came into open conflict with Chinese communist forces. Although resisting American pressure to be joined to Japan in a Cold War alliance, it did ally with the United States (in ★ANZUS) in 1951, and in doing so committed itself to American Cold War policy in Asia. At home, a number of public servants were removed from what were regarded as sensitive positions, while in 1951 watersiders were lambasted by the government for industrial action which could only benefit the country's enemies.

In 1954 the United States sought support in its effort to stop a communist takeover in Vietnam. When Vietnam was partitioned, it promoted an anti-communist front, leading to the establishment of ★SEATO. Although New Zealand joined this front, it put more effort into the Colombo Plan, which sought to combat the spread of communism by improving living standards in Asian countries. It also contemplated recognition of the communist Chinese regime, but the United States demurred.

In the late 1950s tension between the Cold War adversaries escalated as both sides enhanced and enlarged their nuclear weapons arsenals. New Zealand supported the West, but opinion was particularly exercised about atmospheric ★nuclear weapons testing. Cold War tensions over other issues—the Chinese offshore islands, Antarctica, the former Belgian Congo, the building of the Berlin Wall, the deployment of missiles by the United States in Turkey and by the Soviet Union in Cuba—saw New Zealand supporting Western positions in forums such as the United Nations, while at the same time welcoming negotiated solutions, especially the 1963 Partial Test Ban Treaty.

In Asia New Zealand forces had helped to defeat a communist insurgency in British-ruled Malaya and to keep Laos neutral. The outcome of the brutal demolition of communist influence in Indonesia in 1965 was welcomed. In that year New Zealand had been (reluctantly) drawn by the United States into a protracted, controversial, and ultimately unsuccessful war to stop a communist takeover of South Vietnam. In 1972 New Zealand followed the United States lead in disengaging from Vietnam and pursuing détente with both the Soviet Union and China (which had been openly at odds with each other since the early 1960s). A mission was reopened in Moscow and diplomatic relations established with China.

Soviet–American (but not Sino-American) tension revived in the later 1970s. The United States combated communist activity in the disintegrating Portuguese empire, including East Timor, which was invaded by Indonesia in 1975. New Zealand accepted the fait accompli. United Vietnam remained a Soviet ally, and Prime Minister R.D. Muldoon highlighted Soviet naval activity in the Pacific and Indian oceans. In 1978 Vietnam invaded both Laos and Cambodia, but was not stopped by the United States. SEATO had died; New Zealand supported ASEAN, an association of non-communist South-east Asian nations, and still had troops in Singapore. New Zealand supported United States opposition to the Soviet invasion of Afghanistan in 1979 but avoided a trade boycott. Simultaneously (but, it seems, coincidentally) the Soviet Ambassador in Wellington, Vsevelod Sofinsky, was expelled for clandestinely donating money to a New Zealand organisation, the Socialist Unity Party.

As in the late 1950s, so in the late 1970s and early 1980s, the Soviet Union and the United States both planned to enhance their nuclear arsenals, thereby reigniting a peace movement world wide. For New Zealanders there was a South Pacific focus. Initially provoked by French nuclear testing, from 1975 it was directed more at the United States' nuclear presence in the region. Reinforced by world trends, the New Zealand movement exploded in size in the early 1980s.

The fourth Labour government's 1985 breach with the United States over banning port visits by nuclear-powered or nuclear-armed ships (see *BUCHANAN AFFAIR*) distanced New Zealand from its Cold War allies. This occurred even though the government stressed that the dispute was issue-specific—that it was a pro-peace, not a pro-Soviet government policy. Unconvinced, the United States suspended its ANZUS obligations to New Zealand. Nevertheless, the depth of sentiment in New Zealand was such that the National Party also adopted Labour's 'anti-nuclear' stance in 1990. By then, with Soviet control having collapsed in east and central Europe, the Cold War was approaching its end. The Berlin Wall came down in 1989. The demise of the Soviet Union itself at the end of 1991 completed the process. Some commentators saw the massive build-up of the American nuclear arsenal in the 1980s as a crucial factor, given that the Soviet Union proved unable to match it. But the collapse of Soviet power probably owed more to Eastern European resentment of Soviet domination, and to internal factors, in particular, the declining ability of the Soviet system to meet its citizens' needs, and the loss of legitimacy on the part of the country's governing Communist Party.

MALCOLM McKINNON

Colonial Defence Act 1862, which came into effect on 5 May 1863, provided for 'the internal Defence of the Colony'. It authorised the raising of the first permanent military force in New Zealand, a ★Colonial Defence Force of up to 500 men, at a cost of not more than £30,000 per annum. It was repealed when the Armed Constabulary Act came into force on 1 November 1867.

Colonial Defence Committee Established in London in 1885, the Colonial Defence Committee was a response to concerns about the coordination of the imperial resources for defence purposes. Comprising representatives of the Colonial Office, the War Office, and the Admiralty, and with a Royal Engineers officer, Captain G.S. Clarke, as its permanent secretary, it gathered information on the various colonies' defence resources—the first time this had been done systematically—and provided advice on a wide range of local defence matters affecting Great Britain's colonies, especially ★coast defences. The colonies were supposed to submit their ★defence schemes, updated annually, for review by the CDC, though it was more than ten years before New Zealand fulfilled this requirement. In the late 1890s, in response to the British Empire's declining strategic position, the CDC began to emphasise the importance of seapower as the fundamental basis of the colonies' security and the possible contributions that colonies could make to ★imperial defence even when not threatened themselves in a war involving the British Empire. It eventually became a subcommittee of the more wide-ranging ★Committee of Imperial Defence established in 1902.

Colonial Defence Force, the first permanent New Zealand military force, was established under the ★Colonial Defence Act 1862. Limited by statute to no more than 500 men, and probably never exceeding 375 men in practice, it was a response to the conflict that

Colonial naval activities

had begun in Taranaki in 1860 (see NEW ZEALAND WARS). Both Maori and European men were eligible to enlist for terms not exceeding three years. Under regulations issued in September 1864, ordinary troopers were paid 7s 6d a day (as compared with 2s a day for a called-out ★Militia private), but were required to provide their own uniform and horse, and meet 'the whole expense of subsistence for themselves and their horses'. Divisions were formed in Auckland, Wellington, and Napier, and a detachment was also stationed at Wanganui. Major-General T.J. ★Galloway commanded the force from 1863 to 1865. The Auckland Division saw considerable action in the Waikato and Bay of Plenty, while the troops at Napier and Wanganui were involved in some minor skirmishes. The force was replaced in November 1867 by the ★Armed Constabulary, to which many of its members transferred.

Colonial naval activities The Colonial Naval Defence Act of 1865 empowered colonial legislatures to raise, at their own expense, naval forces for local defence purposes, and to man them either with personnel made available from the Royal Navy or locally recruited crews. Although New Zealand did not emulate Victoria in establishing a formal naval organisation until nearly half a century after the legislation came into effect, it had already, by 1865, acquired a number of small craft for ★New Zealand Wars operations. A flotilla of small craft was deployed against rebel Maori, in at least one case with telling effect. This incipient naval activity began as early as 1846, during fighting in the Wellington area. Because of the importance of the Paremata Harbour to the insurgents under the Ngati Toa chief ★Te Rangihaeata, a blockhouse was built at the entrance to the harbour and a small flotilla was raised to check the movement of canoes carrying supplies and reinforcements. The 'Porirua Navy' included a pinnace and two whaleboats from HMS *Calliope*, together with a longboat (salvaged from the wrecked barque *Tyne*), whose purchase, for £100, constitutes New Zealand's first naval procurement. Converted by *Calliope*'s carpenters, she mounted a 12-pounder carronade in her bow and a small brass swivel gun and was protected above the waterline with copper plating and layers of bedding. Under the command of Midshipman H.F. McKillop RN, these craft were used to reconnoitre the Maori pa at Pauatahanui and to observe the movements of Maori canoes on the harbour. The gunboat's weapons were fired in anger on 17 July 1846, when she ventured too close to the shore and only just managed to drive off Maori trying to board her. Although McKillop later played up the role of his 'navy', its impact on the campaign against Te Rangihaeata was limited. The gunboat was later sent to Wanganui, where it was damaged by its own firing in May 1847.

During the fighting that erupted in Taranaki in the early 1860s, another colonial armed vessel, the *Caroline*, mounting a 32-pounder, plied between Manukau and New Plymouth as a dispatch boat and guard ship. A much greater naval effort was mounted during the campaign in the Waikato in 1863–64, in support of both operations and logistics. Wider and deeper in the

The gunboat *Pioneer* shells the Maori position at Meremere on the Waikato River in 1863 (*Alexander Turnbull Library, PUBL-0033-1864-093*)

mid 1860s than it is today, the Waikato River was ideal for riverine operations. Steamers could potentially deploy as far south as the native village of Pukerimu (Cambridge) and Te Rore (General Sir Duncan ★Cameron's eventual base and staging post) on the tributary Waipa River, between Ngaruawahia and Pirongia. The first gunboats were purchased by the colonial government with a view to supporting the planned invasion of the Waikato from the end of the Great South Road at Queen's Redoubt (Pokeno) south along the river. Of the nine steamers which served on the Waikato River during the period 1863–70, only three—*Avon*, *Pioneer*, and *Koheroa*—did so during the campaign itself from July 1863 to April 1864. They were supported by four armoured barges and a number of smaller barges. This small flotilla was commanded by the Commodore of the ★Australia Station, Sir William Wiseman. The paddle steamer *Avon*, the first to be purchased, had been constructed in Glasgow as the *Clyde*, shipped to New Zealand in pieces, and reassembled at Port Lyttelton. After being acquired by the colonial government in November 1862, she was modified for service at Onehunga by the installation of iron plates along the bulwarks and down to the water line. Displacing 43 tons, and nearly 18 metres in length, she mounted a single 12-pounder Armstrong breech-loading gun in her bow. Two days after she was towed from Onehunga to Port Waikato on 25 July 1863, she steamed south to the junction of the Mangatawhiri Stream and the Waikato River, where she was tied up until her first engagement two weeks later. The gunboat *Pioneer* was the first warship to be built for the New Zealand government. After her construction in Sydney, she was towed to New Zealand by HMS *Eclipse* and also modified at Onehunga, with the installation of two iron gun turrets, each mounting a 12-pounder Armstrong. (These turrets can still be seen in Mercer and Ngaruawahia.) Larger than *Avon*, she was able to carry 500 men in light order. She arrived in Port Waikato on 3 October 1863. She was followed by *Koheroa*, which arrived on the Waikato near the end of the campaign in February 1864. She, too, was built in Sydney, but was then shipped to New Zealand in pieces in late 1863 and assembled at Port Waikato. About twenty-seven metres long, she was armed with two 12-pounder Armstrongs. Meanwhile, the government had also converted four small coastal sailing cutters as troop and cargo barges—*Ant*, *Midge*, *Chub*, and *Flirt*. Each was armour-plated, armed with a 12-pounder Armstrong and a 4.4-inch Coehorn mortar, and manned by a crew of seven.

The gunboats *Avon* and *Pioneer* took part in the investment and capture of Meremere pa (October 1863) and the capture of Rangiriri (November 1863), and at least one member of the former's crew was killed. In both actions the boats were used to reconnoitre and shell Kingite positions and to land forces in the rear of the enemy. Together with the barges, they thereafter supported the supply chain linking the Great South Road with Cameron's advance, and were used to ferry Maori prisoners of war and British wounded northward. During this phase of the campaign, the flotilla operated from a shipyard in Ngaruawahia, which included a smithy, a carpenter's shop, light repair facilities, and a storage depot. After the end of the fighting, it was reorganised as the Waikato Transport Service. Another four steamers were purchased for it, and it was used to support the European settlement of the Waikato.

The Waikato Flotilla's contribution was crucial to the outcome of the campaign. Before *Pioneer*'s advent, the protection of Cameron's logistic chain from Whangamarino Redoubt to Auckland required no less than 80 per cent of his total forces: for every soldier at the front there were another four engaged in convoy escort duties and counter-insurgency patrolling. Once *Pioneer* was available many of these latter troops could be redeployed to the front because the supplies could be moved more easily and quickly by water. While these operations proceeded, other colonial vessels were used outside the Waikato River. For example, the paddle steamer *Sandfly*, armed with two 12-pounder Armstrong guns and with a twenty-two-man crew, operated in the Firth of Thames between 1863 and 1865. In April 1864 she bombarded Maori retreating along a beach at Tauranga. With the end of the fighting the various craft were dispensed with, and it was not until the 1880s that the colony again acquired war vessels, four spar ★torpedo boats.

S.D. Waters, *The Royal New Zealand Navy* (War History Branch, Wellington, 1956).

RICHARD TAYLOR

Colour patches are a cheap and secure means of battlefield identification among troops all wearing identical uniforms. Although they were adopted in 1915 by 1NZEF's New Zealand Native Contingent and New Zealand Rifle Brigade, they did not come into widespread use until the New Zealand Division was deployed on the ★Western Front in the following year. Following the British practice, the New Zealanders used two-inch square geometric woollen colour patches for its infantry brigades and other units, with different colours denoting arm of service or New Zealand district. They were worn on the back below the collar by the 1st, 2nd, and 4th Infantry Brigades and on both sleeves by the 3rd New Zealand (Rifle) Brigade and New Zealand Infantry Reserve units. Subsequently patches were introduced for field artillery, trench mortar, machine-gun, and employment

Colours

companies as well as the Cyclist Corps. Members of the New Zealand Mounted Rifles Brigade in the Middle East wore rectangular patches on both sides of their felt hats within the middle fold of the hat band (puggaree). All 1NZEF colour patches were discontinued in 1919. Although mobilisation regulations drawn up in 1929 and 1935 made provision for elaborate schemes of patches, very few units wore patches between the world wars. The Wellington Regiment adopted the black woollen patches in 1930 as a dress distinction to perpetuate associations with the New Zealand Rifle Brigade. Mounted rifles and infantry units of Central Command wore green and red patches respectively to be worn on both sleeves one inch below the shoulder. In 1939 a new scheme of patches was introduced for 2NZEF, consisting of a large 'Basic Shape' identifying arm of service, such as artillery or infantry, worn four-and-a-half inches below the shoulder on both sleeves. Superimposed on this was a khaki 'Unit Shape' identifying the unit, such as battery or battalion, in which the bearer served. Above these the 'Formation Patch' showed the formation, such as brigade, to which the wearer's unit was attached. This scheme was issued to troops of the First Echelon while they were en route to the Middle East in early 1940. Problems with supply and laundering, and its complex nature, led to the scheme being replaced on 2 September 1940 with a white-on-black New Zealand cloth title to be worn above the formation patch (see SHOULDER TITLES). Men of the New Zealand infantry brigades that served overseas in the Pacific theatre wore colour patches on the right side of their ★lemon-squeezer puggarees. These were similar to the 1NZEF designs. In mid 1943 New Zealand cloth titles in black-on-khaki for the 3rd New Zealand Division and red-on-khaki for 2NZEF(IP) personnel were introduced. On the home front reinforcement drafts wore the large 'Basic Shape' and men of the 1st New Zealand Army Tank Brigade's battalions wore one-inch square patches on both sleeves. After 1945 9th New Zealand Brigade Group, part of the ★British Commonwealth Occupation Force in Japan, used diamond-shaped patches worn two-and-a-half inches below the shoulder on both sleeves. When a BCOF patch was introduced, it was worn on the right sleeve above the diamond. Shortages during the occupation forced the use of locally made silk embroidered diamond patches; although frowned upon by authorities, silver wire BCOF patches and New Zealand titles were popular with troops for their 'best' uniforms. New Zealand soldiers deploying overseas more recently have retained the white-on-black NEW ZEALAND slip-on title and adopted the patches of the formations to which they were attached, such as 1st Commonwealth Division in Korea. When the Australian and British forces left Singapore in the early 1970s, ★New Zealand Force South East Asia introduced a formation patch of a white kiwi and diamond on a black square. From 1963 to the mid 1970s the last 'scheme' of cloth patches was used by the ★New Zealand Army's Field Force in New Zealand. Component groups were identified by red, black, green, and blue circular patches. More recently, New Zealand personnel serving in the Multinational Force and Observers in the Sinai and United Nations ★peace-keeping missions have worn the insignia of these organisations, but often with the New Zealand Force South East Asia Kiwi patch as an unofficial means of identification. This practice was formalised with the adoption officially of a similar round kiwi insignia, which was first used by the contingents sent to Bosnia–Herzegovina from 1994 to 1996.

M. Thomas and C. Lord, *New Zealand Army Distinguishing Patches 1911–1991* (Privately published, Wellington, 1995).

MALCOLM THOMAS

Colours Until the late nineteenth century Colours had an important role in battle, serving to signify unit positions or to rally or inspire soldiers. Today their function is largely ceremonial. They are seen as embodying the traditions and pride of units. New Colours are dedicated in elaborate ceremonies, while old Colours or the Colours of disbanded regiments are laid up at churches, cathedrals, or museums. Colours are generally purchased at the unit's expense.

Maori use of flags for war was considerable. Pai Marire adherents in particular flew a variety of pennants and flags, usually with religious motifs such as crosses, moons, and stars. ★Te Kooti's flag *Te Wepu* ('the whip'), 15.8 metres in length, featured a mountain and a bleeding heart to signify the loss of Maori land. Although carried by various corps, ★Volunteer Force Colours were not standardised. Probably the first were presented by the 'Ladies of New Plymouth' to the Taranaki Militia and Volunteers in 1861. It was not until 1913 that a formal system of Colours, following British precedents, was adopted for infantry regiments of the recently established ★Territorial Force, providing for a 1143 mm by 914 mm silk Colour with a gold fringe and tassels. Since then, each regiment has carried two Colours: the Sovereign's (King's or Queen's) and its Regimental. Initially the Great Union ('Union Jack') with the name or number of the regiment in gold in the centre, the former is now based on a New Zealand flag. Regimental Colours are dark blue or green, bearing the regimental crest surrounded by a wreath of fern leaves and ★battle honours. Mounted rifles regiments (and their descendants as armoured squadrons) have carried guidons (a smaller flag with a swallow tail) since 1928. The guns of the Royal Regiment of New Zealand Artillery are assumed to be their

Colours, but a standard is flown for ceremonial occasions. All units of the ★New Zealand Army use 1828 mm by 914 mm flags in the unit's colours for identification purposes, while pennants are also flown from the vehicles of senior officers.

The Queen's Colour carried by the RNZN for ceremonial purposes ashore was first presented in 1924. It is a silk White Ensign with the Royal Cipher superimposed. At the inception of the New Zealand Naval Forces in 1914, it was accepted that New Zealand warships should carry the Royal Navy's White Ensign, which had been in use since 1864. At the Battle of Jutland in 1916 HMS ★*New Zealand* wore the New Zealand national flag in addition to the White Ensign, as did New Zealand warships in the ★Second World War. Ships of the RNZN continued to wear the White Ensign until 1968, when a New Zealand White Ensign, similar to the New Zealand national flag but on a white background, was adopted. The White Ensign is worn by a ship when underway at sea and during daylight hours in harbour. Following the British tradition, New Zealand warships never lower their Colours in salute to a foreign warship unless that ship has already done so. A variety of pennants, standards, and flags are occasionally flown to signify the presence of a senior officer or the head of state.

The RNZAF carries a Queen's Colour of light blue, with a Union flag in the upper left corner, the Southern Cross, and the Royal Cipher. It was presented by the Queen in 1953. Each squadron carries a light blue standard bearing its badge and battle honours. An RNZAF Ensign, consisting of a light blue flag with a Union flag in the upper left corner and a roundel with the letters 'NZ' in the centre, is also flown at stations and bases.

Command and control Command is the basis of military organisation. It is the authority exercised by the commander over the formation, unit, or individual directly subordinated to him or her, and should not be confused with control, which is a more indirect form of authority, exercised through a subordinate. When applied to higher formations, the terms differentiate between the operational direction (command) and the political, administrative, and financial management (control). In the ★Korean War, for example, the Commonwealth forces were under the operational control of the Commander-in-Chief, UN Forces and the operational command of a US Army corps commander; their non-operational control was the responsibility of the Commander-in-Chief, ★British Commonwealth Forces, Korea.

Commandants During the last quarter of the nineteenth century it became common practice in the British settler colonies to appoint seconded officers from the imperial army as commanders of their military forces (commonly referred to as 'commandants', though the term had no statutory authority in New Zealand until 1900). The colonies wanted up-to-date professional advice to secure their defences. Initially London simply supplied the officers, but increasingly came to view them as a means of ensuring that colonial forces developed along uniform lines with an eye to their future involvement in ★imperial defence. Mainly for financial reasons, New Zealand long resisted the pressure to appoint an imperial officer, despite its forces being without a commander throughout most of the 1870s and 1880s. However, the Liberal government came to power in 1891 with a commitment to defence reform; its top priority was the appointment of a British officer as commandant.

The system began badly. The first British officer to command the New Zealand forces, Colonel F.J. ★Fox, who arrived in 1892, soon became embroiled in a protracted quarrel with the Premier, R.J. ★Seddon. Fox's inexperience and uncompromising stance exacerbated the dispute, which culminated in the cessation of his command in 1894. The authorities in London were alarmed by the affair, fearing that it would endanger the system of imperial military appointments. So concerned was the War Office that a retired general, William Fielding, was informally requested to look into the matter while visiting New Zealand on private business. The Fox fiasco forced the War Office to adopt a policy designed to ensure the appointment of more experienced and conciliatory officers to such colonial positions in future. This new policy was evident in the selection of Fox's successor, Colonel A.P. ★Penton, in 1896, after the New Zealand government had decided to give the system a second chance in the face of relentless pressure from the Governor, Lord Glasgow. Though by no means trouble-free, the commands of Penton and his successor, Major-General J.M. ★Babington, were tranquil by comparison with that of Fox.

The common perception of British officers serving as commandants in other colonies, based largely on conjecture, has been one of imperial agents conspiring to implement policies more favourable to London than to their colonial masters. While the officers who came to New Zealand were certainly imperialistic and to some extent 'briefed' in London, it is too simplistic to suggest that they followed a predetermined imperial agenda; nor does the evidence support such a charge. In reality the commandants recommended reforms based on their own assessment of New Zealand's defence requirements, albeit one which by 1900 envisaged an imperial role for the colony's forces. This independent stance is evident from the fact that their advice was not infrequently criticised by the London-

Commands

based ★Colonial Defence Committee. At the 1902 Colonial Conference in London, furthermore, Seddon criticised the system because of the varying advice which his government had received from successive commandants. In short, the distance from London and the absence of a coordinated system of imperial defence enabled the commandants in New Zealand to march largely to their own drum.

The one recommendation that successive commandants did urge in common was the need for reform of the antiquated ★Volunteer Force. They criticised its unwieldy size and called for a smaller, more effective force, ideally one based on a partially paid system underpinned by stricter enforcement of discipline. The practice of officer election was particularly deplored as 'utterly subversive of discipline'. The commandants were professional officers accustomed to the ways of the British Army, whereas the Volunteer Force was more akin to a social institution than a military one. However, the government blocked the commandants' endeavours for fear of the political repercussions of substantial reform. Given this opposition, the commandants could only seek to alleviate some of the worst deficiencies in the existing force, paying particular attention to training and military education. They also attempted to develop a command structure and improve defence administration, with mixed results. By the time of Babington's departure in 1906, New Zealand's defence capability had improved, although the amateur Volunteer system did not lend itself to the professional requirements of a modern army, which seemed increasingly necessary as the international situation became more threatening.

The record of imperial commandants in New Zealand is, above all, characterised by contentious ★civil–military relations. Before 1900 confusion was caused by the use of the title 'Commandant', which implied a certain status and range of responsibilities that were not provided for in the ★Defence Act. Even after the position was given a statutory basis, and its responsibilities were defined, in 1900 the commandant's powers remained considerably less extensive than those enjoyed by their counterparts in other colonies. Nevertheless, successive commandants in New Zealand claimed powers that ignored the constitutional and political realities of self-government. The problem was that their previous experience as regimental commanders had not adequately fitted them for dealing with the political intricacies of high command. In addition, a prejudice against politicians, particularly when fortified by a disdain for the parochial tone of colonial society, was hardly useful baggage for a commandant. The government, for its part, was not blameless either. Political patronage was rampant in the forces. Apart from his aversion to British officers, furthermore, Seddon administered the Defence Department in an autocratic manner that reflected his nickname 'King Dick'. Mostly the system was at fault, not simply because of an inherent conflict between the goals of the commandant and the government but also because it concentrated all the strains of reform on the former. Whether aggressive or easy-going in imposing outside values, the commandant was too obviously the target for disgruntled soldiers or politicians. Politically isolated, he was easily jettisoned, as Fox discovered. The experience of other colonies indicates that civil–military conflict was inherent in this system of imperial military appointments.

The problematic position of commandant in New Zealand was finally resolved only by its abolition in late 1906 as part of a major restructuring of defence administration. The decision to replace the commandant with a Council of Defence followed developments in Great Britain (see DEFENCE COUNCIL). The new system proved a failure in New Zealand, however, and the government reverted to the practice of appointing an imperial officer as commandant in 1910. Under Major-General A.J. ★Godley, who was given powers denied to his predecessors, the Volunteer Force was replaced by a ★Territorial Force during four years of substantial military reform which reflected the greater sense of anxiety about the international situation than had previously existed. The office of commandant continued in existence until 1937, although after Godley's departure in 1914 it was held by New Zealand officers only. These latter experienced no significant problems in their dealings with their political masters, other than the perennial one of obtaining sufficient resources to meet requirements.

I. McGibbon, *The Path to Gallipoli: Defending New Zealand 1840–1915* (GP Books, Wellington, 1991).

STEPHEN CLARKE

Commands, New Zealand Army The division of the Army into functional commands rather than geographically based ★military districts began in 1964 when the ★New Zealand Army was divided into a Field Force of operational formations (a combat brigade group, a reserve brigade group, and a logistics support group) and a smaller Static Support Force responsible for administration, ★army camps, stores, and training. This dual division of responsibilities was further refined in 1970: Field Force Command at Auckland was responsible for operational units and Home Command, based at Wellington, for training and other support functions. As part of a move away from the functional commands, the Army in 1979 was formed into a 'framework force' based on three task-force regions under a New Zealand Land Forces HQ. However, this was found to lack definition and tended to mix support and training functions with operational units. A further reorganisation in 1984 brought the Army back essentially to the 1964–79 organisation with a Land Force Command, with headquarters at Takapuna, controlling operational units, and a Support Command at Trentham responsible for training and base support. Yet another reorganisation occurred in 1998, with the two commands being merged into New Zealand Land Command at Trentham, which has responsibility for Force troops (such as the *Special Air Service) at Hobsonville, 2nd Land Force Group at Linton, 3rd Land Force Group at Burnham, and the Army Training Group at Waiouru.

Commemorative contingents The first New Zealand troops to proceed overseas did so to represent their country on the occasion of the 60th jubilee of Queen Victoria's reign in 1897. A fifty-four-strong contingent, including twenty Maori soldiers, was dispatched to London. The pageant itself, marked by appropriate imperial pomp and glamour, was paralleled by a series of processions and tournaments in New Zealand, which helped spark a revival of interest in the *Volunteer Force. During the following five years, similar contingents left New Zealand at regular intervals. Seventy-three mounted riflemen were sent across the Tasman to take part in ceremonies marking the creation of the Commonwealth of Australia at Sydney in January 1901—the first occasion when troops from all the Australasian colonies were brigaded together. They were followed later in the year by a 214-man contingent, again with substantial Maori involvement, for the opening of the Federal Parliament at Melbourne. After the former ceremony, a contingent of British and Indian troops which had also participated visited New Zealand on a tour that was notable for spectacular military parades and much patriotic speech-making. In 1902 a contingent of 122 *Boer War veterans and thirty-two Maori soldiers went to London to take part in events related to King Edward VII's coronation. Similar contingents were also sent to the coronations of King George VI and Queen Elizabeth II, in 1937 and 1953 respectively. Following both world wars large contingents of New Zealand soldiers marched at victory parades in London. More recently, parties of *New Zealand Defence Force personnel have been sent overseas to take part in commemorative events relating to the world wars, such as, for example, *Anzac Day at *Gallipoli and anniversaries of important battles in the *Second World War. Returned servicemen and women have also been involved in these more recent commemorations.

Committee of Imperial Defence was the British Empire's central advisory and coordinating organ in security matters in the first four decades of the twentieth century. Originally created in 1902, but reconstituted in May 1904, it represented a flexible group of advisers to the British Cabinet on issues of *imperial defence. The only permanent member was the Prime Minister, who was normally its chairman, and those invited to take part in its deliberations included ministers and senior military and civilian officials. The *Colonial Defence Committee, which had advised New Zealand and the other colonies on *coast defences, was subsumed within the CID structure, which comprised a substantial number of both ad hoc and standing committees dealing with particular aspects of defence. Dominion high commissioners in London were usually invited to attend CID meetings when matters relating to their country were being discussed, and Dominion leaders, when also in London, often took part in the discussions. CID papers sent to Dominion capitals assisted Dominion defence authorities in local preparations. The CID was served by a small but influential secretariat under, for much of its existence, Lieutenant-Colonel Sir Maurice *Hankey. New Zealand established a New Zealand section of the CID in 1933, though it did not operate on the same basis as the British organisation—the Prime Minister was not its chairman—and it was never as influential (see ORGANISATION FOR NATIONAL SECURITY).

Commonwealth Liaison Mission, Korea, was established in 1957 at the time of the withdrawal of the last of the British Commonwealth forces from South Korea. Fourteen-strong, and headed by a British brigadier, it was designed to demonstrate by its presence at UN Command HQ the Commonwealth's continued support for the Republic of Korea and the *United Nations' objectives in Korea. It represented the United Kingdom, Australia, and New Zealand—Canada had its own arrangements—on the Military Armistice Commission, which oversaw the armistice arrangements agreed in July 1953. A New Zealand officer served in the mission until 1971. (See KOREAN WAR)

Compulsory military training The first calls for some form of compulsory military training in peacetime in New Zealand arose during the *Boer War, which highlighted the Empire's military weakness and shattered the Victorian sense of complacency. Japan's defeat of Russia in the war of 1904–05 enhanced New Zealand fears, especially after British battleships were withdrawn from the Pacific to face the growing threat posed by Germany's expanding fleet. In 1906 a National Defence League was formed to campaign for CMT. Assisted by a strongly imperialist press, it cleverly manipulated popular fears of the *yellow peril and racial degeneration. At the same time the New Zealand government was being pressed to adopt some form of CMT by its military advisers, who pointed to

Compulsory military training

the continued inefficiencies of the ★Volunteer Force and the apparent failure of the British voluntary Territorial Army scheme. During the Imperial Defence Conference in London in 1909, Prime Minister Sir Joseph ★Ward reluctantly accepted the necessity to reform the New Zealand Military Forces. At his request, the Chief of Imperial General Staff, General W.G. Nicholson, proposed a scheme which called for the creation of a ★Territorial Force of 30,000 men. Since there were only 10,356 Volunteers in 1909, CMT seemed the only way of providing the necessary manpower. Growing international tension ensured that there was little opposition to the passage of a new ★Defence Act, which required all boys from ages twelve to fourteen to undergo fifty-two hours of teacher-supervised physical training annually as Junior Cadets—a provision which was dropped in 1912 (see CADETS). From age fourteen the boys would, as Senior Cadets, be given elementary drill and rifle practice under military control until, at age eighteen, they would become part of a General Training Section. Each would then be liable to serve at least sixty days (including an annual seven-day camp) in their local Territorial unit over the ensuing three years, before being posted to the Reserve until they turned thirty. It was intended that those not posted to a Territorial unit would be attached to rifle clubs. This arrangement was modified in 1910, after the government accepted a recommendation by the visiting Field Marshal Lord ★Kitchener that the upper limit for compulsory training, either in the Territorial Force or General Training Section, should be raised to twenty-five.

The task of implementing the scheme fell to Major-General A.J. ★Godley. Registration of all men aged between fourteen and twenty inclusive started in 1911, with those who were physically fit being posted directly to their local Territorial unit from June. The number of men available for service almost exactly matched the requirements for the Territorial Force, with the result that the General Training Section was not introduced. Men classified as not being fully fit—about 35 per cent of the registered total—were posted to rifle clubs for rifle training. Some 5 per cent of men were found to be unfit for any service, while those from isolated areas were exempt from CMT. Although no Maori men were required to serve, they were not prevented from volunteering for the Territorial Force. Although the military authorities could exempt men on religious grounds, there was no provision for ★conscientious objectors. By 1914, 4811 men had been convicted for breaches of the Defence Act. They faced loss of civil rights and fines. Determined to make the scheme work, the government from 1913 approved the military detention of defaulters who refused to pay their fines. Nevertheless, the relatively small number of dissenters—Godley dismissed them as 'cranks, faddists and conscientious objectors'—did not disrupt the development of CMT, with attendance at the annual camps averaging 82 per cent. By 1914 there were 57,322 men or boys serving under the provisions of the Defence Act. Although the CMT scheme remained in operation during the ★First World War, it was severely affected by the departure of many members of the Territorial Force with 1NZEF, not least by the introduction of ★conscription in 1916. The rapid turnover of recruits, the labour demands of the economy, and a lack of trained officers and NCOs made the scheme increasingly doubtful, and late in 1917 compulsory training was curtailed. Annual camps were subsequently suspended.

During the 1920s CMT remained an attenuated affair. Although the GOC, Major-General Sir Edward ★Chaytor, proposed a General Training Section for eighteen- and nineteen-year old recruits, to be followed by three years' part-time Territorial service, including an annual eleven-day camp, little was done because of the financial difficulties which soon beset the government. Costs were cut by bringing the Territorial Force's peace establishment down to 20,000, and reducing the annual intake by about 40 per cent by not posting men who lived more than an hour from a drill centre. Until 1926 obligatory training was limited to twelve half-day and whole-day parades and twelve evening drill sessions; thereafter all Territorials were obliged to attend six days' training in camp, six half-day parades, and twelve drills. Renewed financial problems led to suspension of obligatory service altogether in June 1930. During the ensuing decade there was little support for its reintroduction, despite calls for such a course by the National Defence League in 1938. During the ★Second World War, conscription was again imposed on all men of military age.

Not until 1950 was a new scheme of compulsory training instituted. In the immediate aftermath of the Second World War, the Army authorities had envisaged some form of compulsory service being necessary if a new expeditionary force was to be raised. As the international situation deteriorated with the onset of the ★Cold War, the government was increasingly sympathetic towards such an approach, though Prime Minister Peter ★Fraser doubted its political feasibility. With the crisis deepening, he sought advice from the British authorities in 1948 as to how best New Zealand could contribute to a Commonwealth war effort against the Soviet Union. The only way New Zealand could play the role proposed for it—an immediate deployment of forces in the Middle East—was by having its planned expeditionary force ready for departure at the outset of a war, in contrast to the year taken to dispatch 2NZEF in 1939–40 (see MIDDLE EAST COMMITMENT).

Compulsory military training

G. R.

MILITARY TRAINING.

DOMINION OF NEW ZEALAND.

NOTICE AS TO MILITARY TRAINING.

NOTICE IS HEREBY GIVEN that every male inhabitant of New Zealand who, on the 1st day of March, 1911, had attained the age of fourteen years or upwards, but had not attained the age of twenty-one years, and who is a British subject and has resided in New Zealand for at least six months, IS HEREBY REQUIRED before 7 p.m. on the 2nd day of June, 1911, to fill in a prescribed form of registration in respect of military training under the Defence Acts, and to post or deliver the same to the Area Sergeant-Major of the territorial area in which the applicant for registration resides.

Forms of registration may be obtained at any Post Office or Police Station. No postage is required where the form is posted as aforesaid.

Any person to whom this notice applies who fails to take any step necessary to secure his registration as aforesaid is liable to a fine of FIVE POUNDS, and shall not be eligible for employment in any branch of the Government Service.

Dated at Wellington, this 10th day of April, 1911.

GEO. FOWLDS,
Acting Minister of Defence.

The proclamation of a requirement for registration for compulsory military service, 1911 (*Alexander Turnbull Library, Eph-D-ARMY-1911-01*)

Compulsory military training

Only compulsory training would make this possible. Armed with the views of the British Chiefs of Staff, Fraser set about achieving this objective. Resistance within the Labour Party led to a referendum on the issue being held on 3 August 1949. The government campaigned vigorously for a favourable vote, playing upon public apprehension of communist aggression and labelling opponents as tools of the Communist Party. With the opposition National Party, the Returned Services Association, and most newspapers also strongly in favour of CMT, and trade unions inhibited by the anti-communist mood, the outcome was hardly surprising: 533,016 people voted for compulsory military service, with 152,443 against.

Under the Military Service Act 1949 all eighteen-year-olds had to register within a fortnight of their birthday. The roughly 80 per cent who were fit for service were posted to one of the three services, usually the one of the recruit's choice. The Army's annual intake of 8000 recruits received their whole-time training at Papakura, Linton, Burnham, or more usually Waiouru, where training began in May 1950. A shortage of Regular Force instructional staff meant that whole-time training had to be limited to ten and a half weeks. The recruit was then posted to his local Territorial unit, with which he served part-time for twenty days annually during the next three years before being posted to the Reserve. RNZAF recruits (about 950 annually) received fourteen weeks' whole-time training. Since this was considered inadequate to train airmen to the required level of technical efficiency, more intensive part-time training was needed subsequently. Recruits had the choice of either joining a Territorial Air Force squadron for five years of part-time service (consisting of a two-week camp and sixteen parades annually) or undergoing three years' part-time service (of twenty days 'on the job' annually) with the Territorial Air Force Supplement. Naval recruits (about 330 annually) were trained at HMNZS *Tamaki* for fourteen weeks, followed by three years' part-time service, consisting of seven days' sea training and thirty-nine parades annually, with the RNZNVR.

In 1951 training was extended to twenty-year-olds (eighteen- and nineteen-year-olds having already been called up). Intended to bring the Army to a state of war readiness by 1954, this change left the Territorial Force over-strength by a third, with attendant training and administrative difficulties, to alleviate which the class of twenty-year-olds were released from further training obligations after only a year's part-time service. By 1955 the CMT scheme was in full operation, with about 10,000 eighteen-year-olds annually receiving military training, and receiving the relatively low pay of eleven shillings and sixpence per day while in uniform. The number of recruits placed great demands upon the voluntary Territorial Force officer corps and NCO cadre, and from April 1956 Territorial part-time training was reduced to allow for officer and NCO training and administration. Nor were the RNZN or RNZAF satisfied with the scheme, because the relatively short periods of training were inadequate for the development of technical crews, and in 1957 both services withdrew from the scheme, having by this time trained 6221 airmen and 1992 naval reservists. On the other hand, the CMT scheme was very effective in providing a steady flow of recruits for the Territorial Force. But even the Army experienced difficulties, as an increasing population produced more men than it either needed or could handle effectively. The reduction of the Territorial Force to 23,000 compounded the problem, as did the need to form a Regular Force battalion in 1957, exacerbating the shortage of instructional staff for CMT. From 1957 the intake age was progressively increased from eighteen to twenty years of age. This had the effect, in the short term, of reducing the numbers commencing CMT from 7100 to 5600 annually, as well as ensuring that more mature recruits were available. However, the long-term problem of an oversupply of recruits remained unresolved until, in 1959, the Labour government under Walter Nash discontinued the scheme altogether, having decided that it was 'a waste of time, money, and personnel'. This was strongly opposed by ex-Army officers, the National Defence League, and the National Party, which accused Nash's administration of having 'smashed the Territorial Army'. Indeed, the voluntary system soon proved insufficient and Territorial strength fell far below establishment. The National government formed by Keith Holyoake in late 1960 proved receptive to calls for the introduction of a selective service scheme. The National Military Service Act 1961 made provision for 2000 men annually to be balloted from a pool of 20,000 twenty-year-old men. The first balloted recruits began their fourteen weeks' initial training at Waiouru and Burnham in May 1962. They were then posted to Territorial units for three years, during which they had to serve twenty days annually, before serving for three years in the Reserve. In 1964 the numbers of men balloted was increased to 3000 annually. National Service never became a controversial issue in New Zealand, unlike in Australia, which had a similar scheme but with a liability for overseas service (under which 19,000 national servicemen were sent to Vietnam). Nevertheless, the selective basis of the scheme—only an unlucky 15 per cent of young men were obliged to serve—ensured that it was never popular in spite of claims by the Army that national servicemen acquired training in 'citizenship'. Pledged to repeal the 'birthday lottery', the Labour Party moved quickly once it won office in 1972. National Service was abolished on 31 December 1972, by which time 23,319 national servicemen had completed their obligations under the scheme. Although calls for the reintroduction of some form of national service are occasionally made, usually as a cure for alleged social ills since such a step no longer has any defence rationale, they elicit little public support.

Confrontation was a conflict which developed in 1963 between Indonesia and the new state of Malaysia backed by Commonwealth allies. Its origins lay in Great Britain's plans to divest itself of formal empire in Southeast Asia. This would be achieved by federating the then Crown colonies in Borneo (Sabah and Sarawak), the protected state of Brunei, and the self-governing colony of Singapore with Malaya, which had been independent since 1957. Formal agreement providing for a federation of greater Malaysia was reached between London and Kuala Lumpur in November 1961. Both parties agreed to establish the new state by 31 August 1963. Despite relinquishing sovereignty, the British were guaranteed the continued use of their bases at Singapore by the Malayan Prime Minister, Tunku Abdul Rahman.

These plans for a greater Malaysia were strongly opposed by neighbouring Indonesia and its charismatic president, Achmed Sukarno. He complained, with particular emphasis on the continued British military presence at Singapore, that London's grant of independence was not sincere. Sukarno reasoned that Malaysia, by virtue of its intended close relationship with Britain, would become a British satellite, ultimately serving to perpetuate, rather than end, European domination of the region. In addition, opposition to Malaysia conveniently buttressed the President politically, since engaging nationalist fervour against Britain distracted Indonesian public opinion from the appalling state of the nation's economy. It came as no surprise, therefore, when the Indonesian foreign minister, Dr Subandrio, declared on 20 January 1963 that Indonesia would henceforth pursue a policy of *Konfrontasi* (Confrontation) against Malaysia.

Sukarno was limited in his options for opposing Malaysia. Although equipped with modern weapons from Moscow, the Indonesian armed forces were not capable of prevailing in an open engagement with the British. Instead, Sukarno decided to encourage and support subversive movements already existing in Borneo. If allowed to develop into a major insurgency, the British might eventually be worn down into abandoning the objective of greater Malaysia altogether. By the end of 1963, this strategy increasingly involved Indonesian army regulars, posing as guerrillas, crossing the border from Kalimantan to attack the security forces in Borneo and then quickly retreating to the safety of Indonesian territory.

The British responded to Confrontation in a two-pronged manner. In order to deter the Indonesians from mounting an open attack on Malaysia, substantial air and naval forces were deployed in and around Singapore. The main concern for British military planners throughout the conflict, however, was containing the insurgency in Borneo. Here the security forces were in an impossible situation. They were required to defend a frontier of approximately 1600 kilometres, in extremely dense jungle and against an enemy who could retreat to the safety of Indonesian Kalimantan. Increasingly frustrated, Major-General Sir Walter Walker, director of operations in Borneo, requested permission to pursue the guerrillas across the border. After considerable debate, London finally agreed in April 1964. The objective of cross-border operations, code-named Claret, was to wrestle the initiative from

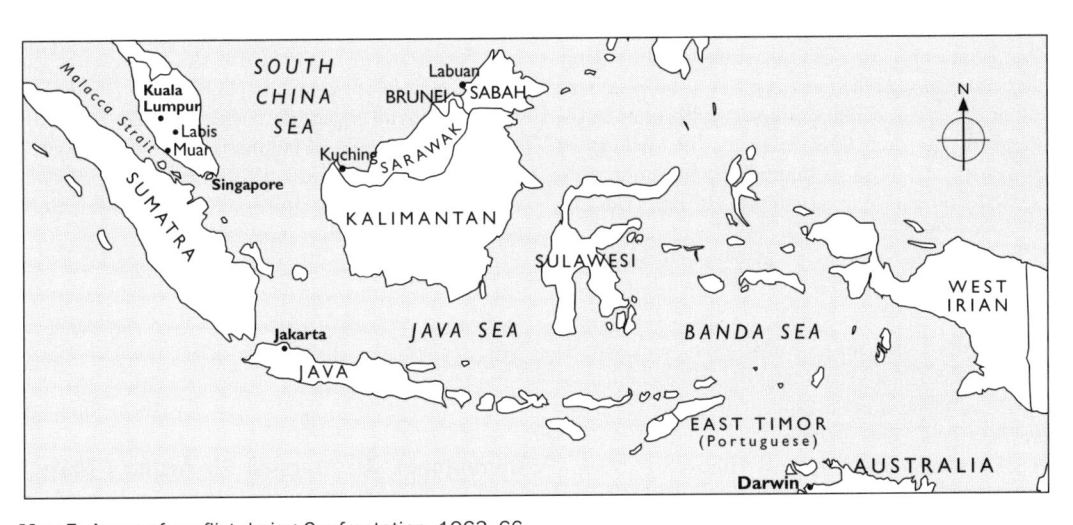

Map 5 Areas of conflict during Confrontation, 1963–66

the enemy. Accordingly, starting in May that year, predominantly SAS troops, operating in groups of four, regularly patrolled territory immediately across the border. When a patrol discovered enemy guerrillas moving towards Borneo, it would arrange for them to be ambushed as they crossed the border.

This strategy, both regarding deterrence and military operations, was remarkably successful in containing the insurgency to a low level of conflict. Nonetheless, it required a considerable deployment of Britain's limited resources and manpower. By early 1965, for example, Britain had more than 60,000 servicemen deployed in the region, together with a surface fleet of more than eighty warships, including two aircraft-carriers. It was not surprising, therefore, that, starting in December 1963, repeated requests were made by the British for New Zealand (and Australia) to send combat forces into Borneo to assist in containing the insurgency.

In responding to these requests the National administration led by K.J. Holyoake had to weigh carefully certain countervailing policy considerations. On the one hand, there was no disagreement that Malaysia should be supported. In both official and public eyes, Indonesia had committed clear and frequent acts of aggression against the new state. On the other hand, however, Wellington was eager to avoid New Zealand becoming embroiled in a major war with Indonesia. Policy-makers realised that, in the event of considerable bloodshed, New Zealand's relations with its closest Asian neighbour could be poisoned for generations to come. Consequently, the government initially refused to send troops into Borneo, arguing that British and Malaysian forces already stationed there were sufficient to deal with the problem.

Deeply frustrated by the failure of Confrontation to make any real headway, Sukarno decided in mid 1964 to intensify it by extending military operations to the Malay peninsula. On 1 September, ninety-eight Indonesian paratroopers landed just north of Labis in Johore. One of the few available Commonwealth units in the area was 1st Battalion, RNZIR, which, with Wellington's permission, was used to hunt down the infiltrators, most of whom surrendered without a struggle. Later, on 29 October, the New Zealanders were involved in a similar operation to capture a small amphibious force which had landed at the mouth of the Sungei Kesang River north-west of Muar. In addition to these activities, the RNZAF's 14 Squadron, consisting of six Canberra bombers, was deployed to Singapore, where it remained as part of the Commonwealth's air power deterrent until the end of Confrontation.

Sukarno responded to these failures by substantially increasing the flow of insurgents crossing the border into Borneo. With Britain's military resources stretched to almost breaking point, the New Zealand government believed it could no longer decline the genuine appeals for assistance coming from London. On 1 February 1965 the Prime Minister announced that a small ★Special Air Service detachment, together with the 1RNZIR, would be deployed in Borneo as soon as possible. In addition, New Zealand crews would man two former Royal Navy minesweepers, renamed HMNZS *Hickleton* and *Santon*, which would join the frigate HMNZS *Taranaki* in patrolling Malaysian waters around the Malacca Strait.

During late February the 1st Ranger Squadron NZSAS, comprising about forty men under the command of Major W.J.D. Meldrum, began its tour of duty. They were replaced by a similarly sized detachment, commanded by Major R.S. Dearing, in October the same year. Both detachments took part in Claret operations alongside Britain's 22nd Regiment SAS. 1RNZIR, commanded by Colonel R.M. Gurr, was not deployed in Borneo until May 1965, when it relieved a Gurkha battalion in Sarawak. In a series of skirmishes, it inflicted substantial losses on the enemy without suffering any fatal casualties. Relieved during October, 1RNZIR returned to its base in Malaya. By the time it was redeployed to Borneo in May 1966, Confrontation had all but ended.

On 1 October 1965 a group of army officers made an unsuccessful attempt to seize power in Jakarta, but the uprising was ruthlessly crushed by troops loyal to Major-General Suharto. This event heralded a major transformation in Indonesian politics. Increasingly, Sukarno became a paper President, with real power being exercised by Suharto and the army establishment. These generals, concerned with restoring economic stability and suppressing the Indonesian communist party, were determined quietly to abandon Sukarno's radicalist agenda, particularly the Confrontation. As a result, military activity in Borneo by Indonesian insurgents subsided drastically after the coup. During its second deployment, for example, 1RNZIR did not engage the enemy at all. On 11 August 1966 representatives of Indonesia and Malaysia signed a peace treaty in Bangkok. Hostilities were officially at an end. 1RNZIR completed its withdrawal from Borneo in October the same year.

R. Gurr, *Voices of a Border War: A History of 1 Royal New Zealand Infantry Regiment 1963 to 1965* (Privately published, Melbourne, 1995); W.D. Baker, *Dare to Win: The Story of the New Zealand SAS* (Lothian Publishing Company, Melbourne, 1987).

JOHN SUBRITZKY

Coningham, Air Marshal Sir Arthur ('Mary') (19 January 1895–30 January 1948) was, after Keith ★Park, New Zealand's most prominent expatriate officer of the ★Second World War. Although born in Brisbane, he grew up in Wellington. He went to German Samoa with the Samoa Expeditionary Force in August 1914, and later served with the ★New Zealand Expeditionary Force at Gallipoli from June to October 1915, before typhoid led to his repatriation to New Zealand in October. Travelling to England at his own expense in March 1916, he joined the Royal Flying Corps and underwent flying training. From December 1916 he was a fighter pilot with 32 Squadron on the ★Western Front. He did not achieve his first 'kill' until 11 July 1917, but followed it with three more in the ensuing nine days. These successes earned him a MC. His streak of victories continued when in late July he claimed yet another three victories, for which he was made a DSO. Wounded in his last engagement and suffering from the effects of stress, he was sent to England to recover. By this time he had acquired the nickname 'Maori', a reference to his New Zealand origins, which duly became corrupted to 'Mary'. From March 1918 he commanded 92 Squadron. By the Armistice, he had flown 176 patrols, personally destroyed nine enemy aircraft, and shared in the destruction of four, service which was recognised by the award of a DFC in June 1919.

Coningham secured a permanent commission in the RAF after the war, and spent much of his time in the Middle East. He commanded a squadron charged with maintaining order in Iraq. In October–November 1925, he led three DH-9a two-seater biplanes from Helwan (near Cairo) to Kaduna (Nigeria), a round trip of more than 10,000 kilometres, for which he was awarded an AFC in 1926; the value of that route for sending aircraft to Cairo from Great Britain and the United States would be fully realised during the Second World War. At the outset of that conflict, he was commanding Bomber Command's 4 Group, which he led through the first two years of the bomber offensive against Germany; for this service he was made a CB in July 1941. But it was in the Middle East that he made an even greater mark. Dispatched to Egypt in July 1941 to command 204 Group, later the Western Desert Air Force, he forged a powerful ground attack instrument which was to play a vital role in the ★North African campaign. He was appointed a KCB in November 1942. The doctrine of inter-service and Allied cooperation which he championed was put to good effect when he commanded what became the 1st Allied Tactical Air Force in Tunisia, Sicily, and Italy during 1943. In January 1944, he took command of the 2nd Tactical Air Force, with responsibility for the air support of the invasion of France (see D-DAY). He remained in this post for the rest of the war, and in January 1946 was made a KBE. After commanding Flying Training Command, he retired from the RAF at his own request in August 1947. Five months later, he was killed when the airliner in which he was crossing the Atlantic crashed into the sea north-east of Bermuda.

V. Orange, *Coningham* (Methuen, London, 1990).

Connolly, Lieutenant-Commander Phillip George (14 November 1899–13 February 1970) was a wartime naval officer who later became Minister of Defence. Born in Dunedin, he gained his first taste of military service in the ★Territorial Force in 1917. Later, as a merchant seaman, he joined the Otago Division of the Royal Naval Volunteer Reserve in 1928. After being mobilised in 1940, he was dispatched to the United Kingdom for service with the Royal Navy. He commanded the trawler/minesweeper HMS *Deodar*, which was involved in escorting convoys in the English Channel. For this service he was awarded a DSC and a mention in dispatches. In August 1941, he took command of the minesweeper HMS *Moa*, and set out for New Zealand, which he finally reached in April 1942 after spending a period on patrol in Fiji. He resigned his commission at the beginning of 1943 to stand successfully for Parliament as a Labour candidate in that year's general election. As Opposition spokesman on defence in the 1950s, he opposed ★compulsory military training. From 1957 to 1960 he held the Defence portfolio in the Labour government led by Walter Nash, in which capacity he oversaw a major review of defence policy. CMT was abolished and steps were put in train to develop a more readily available military force based on a regular battalion. He retired from politics in 1963.

Conscientious objectors Unlike Australia, New Zealand made no provision in the 1909 legislation which authorised ★compulsory military training for exemption from military service on grounds of conscientious belief. When the new scheme came into operation in 1911, a defiant few rallied against it. Apprentices in Christchurch's Addington Workshops formed the core of the socialist Passive Resisters' Union (PRU) and agitated against 'boy conscription' (all males between fourteen and twenty were required to register). Three major Christian-based movements also emerged to oppose CMT—the Christchurch-based National Peace Council, the Anti-Militarist League with branches throughout New Zealand, and the Freedom League in Auckland. Members of these groups defied police raids—and in one case a sedition charge—to advise young men against carrying out their military training obligations. In the first year less than 20 per cent of Canterbury's eligible youth attended training, and by June 1913 more than 3000 men (including senior cadets) had been convicted for failing to attend parades or camps. An amendment to the legislation in 1912 had permitted the military detention of objectors who

Conscientious objectors

refused to pay their fines. Defaulters were held at military facilities at Point Halswell, Otago, North Head, and Ripapa Island. Although dismissed by the Commandant, Major-General A.J. *Godley as a 'hopeless minority', the defaulters proved a troublesome problem, not least when thirteen boys went on a hunger strike at Ripapa Island, but not one that seriously hindered the implementation of the new defence scheme.

With the introduction of *conscription in 1916, conscientious objection quickly became a contentious public issue. The National Register the previous year had indicated that a substantial minority classified themselves as objectors, whether on religious or political grounds. In the Military Service Act, provision was made for the exemption of members of religious bodies which had, before the outbreak of war, declared military service 'contrary to divine revelation', so long as they were prepared to provide 'alternative' non-combatant service in New Zealand or overseas. Under these restrictive provisions—only Quakers, Christadelphians, and Seventh-day Adventists were eligible—only seventy-three objectors had been offered exemption by war's end (of whom sixty accepted). Although generally unsympathetic to conscientious objectors (a reflection of the public mood), the Military Service Boards which examined the 'consciences' of those seeking exemption did soften the effect of the legislation in practice. At the suggestion of the Defence Department, they offered non-combatant service to those who were considered 'genuine' in their objections but ineligible for exemption. Between September 1917 and October 1918 170 men went overseas on this basis. The remainder of the 'genuine' objectors were eventually imprisoned, joining those who had refused service but who were not considered genuine. The latter included Christian pacifists, Irish, Maori, and political and humanitarian defaulters. They faced a tough, carefully regulated plan of punishment. After a short period in detention and a month's imprisonment—designed to break the resolve of the weaker men—they faced a court martial at Trentham Military Camp, where they were sentenced to from eleven to twenty-four months' hard labour. On completion of their sentence they would be either sent to the front or reimprisoned if they still refused to enlist. Most were exemplary prisoners, but conditions in the jails were oppressive. Conversation was often forbidden, labour in quarries was back-breaking, and solitary confinement was imposed on recalcitrants. By April 1918, 188 men were doing hard labour in various parts of the country. Fourteen of the more 'troublesome', including Archibald *Baxter and two of his brothers, were dispatched to Great Britain. When they refused to carry out gardening work at Sling Camp, they were placed in solitary confinement, and an attempt was made to break their spirits. In the end, ten were sent to Étaples Camp in France, where they were warned that they would 'inevitably be shot' if they refused to submit. Several became stretcher bearers, and three were sentenced to hard labour. Four who remained intransigent were subjected to harsh treatment at the front, including repeated sentences of Field Punishment No. 1 (see DISCIPLINE) and assaults. Only Archibald Baxter and Mark Briggs held out, two of the others having by March 1918 become bearers. Beatings and food deprivation eventually led to Baxter's collapse, and he was hospitalised in Boulogne. Diagnosed as a 'melancholic', he was eventually quietly repatriated in August 1918.

When the war ended three months later, 273 objectors remained in prison in New Zealand, and the last of them were not released until November 1920, the Cabinet having decided that it would be unfair to release defaulters before all the soldiers had returned home. All defaulters—including Paddy Webb, later a prominent Labour politician—lost their voting rights for ten years and were barred from working for government or local bodies. With peace, the issue of conscientious objection lost salience, only to be revived in the late 1920s when several pacifists objected to compulsory military training, for which they were heavily fined and lost civil rights for ten years. The suspension of compulsory training in 1930 removed the problem.

When conscription was reintroduced in June 1940 following Allied reverses in the *Second World War, the government contained a number of men who had actively opposed conscription in the previous conflict. Provisions for exemption on grounds of conscience were wider in scope than those of 1916. Although only Quakers and Christadelphians were allowed exemption as of right, individuals had the right to seek exemption by persuading one of twenty-seven appeal boards that they held the absolute belief that war was wrong. The boards could allow appeals outright, allow them conditionally (in which case the appellant was liable to non-combatant service), or dismiss them. To Prime Minister Peter *Fraser's dismay, and the Returned Services Association's anger, more than 5000 men applied for exemption on conscience grounds. Of 3000 appeals heard by the appeal boards throughout the country, 20 per cent were allowed and 40 per cent dismissed, with the remainder being allowed conditionally. There were regional variations, however, for only 14 per cent of appeals were allowed in Auckland in contrast to 35 per cent in Christchurch. Exempted objectors remained in the community, but were not allowed to earn more than an army private and were subject to strict manpower provisions.

The process had replicated that of the First World War in producing a group of determined defaulters.

Nearly 70 per cent of those with conditional exemption refused to serve in any capacity. Including men who had had their appeals dismissed but refused to serve or had refused to participate in the process at all, there were 803 defaulters. Five broad types were represented: fundamentalist Christians such as members of the Christian Assembly, Jehovah's Witnesses, Brethren, and Seventh-day Adventists, by far the most numerous; Christian pacifists from orthodox churches, mainly Methodists; non-religious objectors who based their stance on a variety of ethical reasons; a handful of 'political' objectors opposed to the war on the grounds that it was a capitalist abomination; and an even smaller number of apolitical men of varying personal integrity who acknowledged little sense of responsibility or loyalty to their fellows and for whom self-interest was the main driving force. The earliest defaulters were confined in military compounds until they were transferred to purpose-built compounds in the countryside, of which Strathmore Camp, at Whenaroa between Rotorua and Taupo, was the first. Further camps were built at Hautu, adjacent to the prison near Turangi, Whitanui and Paiaka in the Horowhenua, and Balmoral in North Canterbury. Some 'trusted' defaulters were sent to a series of smaller, unfenced camps.

Strathmore and Hautu inmates were employed in developing pumice lands for returned servicemen, grubbing thistles and fern, cutting scrub, digging drains, building tracks, and planting trees. The work was repetitive and monotonous, and many of the men doubted the value of their labour. At Whitanui and Paiaka the work was even more mundane. With sharp hoes, they weeded the endless rows of flax that grew on the adjacent Moutoa swampland for rope mills at Foxton. Punishments were prison-like, with loss of privileges being imposed for minor infractions. Disobedience meant a spell in the camp lock-up on bread and water rations and possibly a change of camp. Persistent offenders were sent to the 'Red' punishment huts at Hautu, where they were confined for all but half an hour each day in a tiny hut for up to ninety days at a stretch. In winter they froze. As defaulter resistance hardened, the government in May 1942 authorised camp supervisors to send refractory inmates to prison for the duration of the war. All that was required was for the supervisor to advise a magistrate in open court that he wanted a defaulter removed; there was no inquiry to determine guilt or innocence and no right of appeal. By May 1945 there were fifty-eight defaulters in prison, and the last of them would not be released until a year later. Although more than 7000 New Zealanders had signed church-based petitions calling for defaulters' release during 1943 and 1944, the government held its hand until 1945, when a special tribunal reviewed the status of 476 men (those who had not protested) and granted conditional exemption to 283 of them. However, none were released until after the war, and recalcitrants not until 1946. All military defaulters were deprived of their civil rights for ten years and banned from working in the public service. The camps were quickly torn down.

When compulsory military training was again introduced following a referendum in 1949, provision was made for a register of conscientious objectors. A three-person Conscientious Objection Committee which reviewed each case could determine that a person was unconditionally exempt or liable for call-up for non-combatant duties. Those whose applications were dismissed were transferred to the National Service register; failure to carry out their training obligations resulted in fines or directed employment at pay no better than that of an army private—the limit also set for the pay of conscientious objectors, of whom there were 358 (out of more than 83,000 men found fit for CMT between 1950 and 1958). A similarly small minority were exempted from compulsory training under the selective National Service scheme between 1961 and 1972. Because the Army's manpower requirements were amply provided for under the latter scheme, there was little incentive to deal harshly with resisters, and most appeals against service were allowed. The fact that the ★Territorial Force was never called up for active service before compulsory training ended in 1972 further reduced the significance of conscientious objection as a public issue.

P. Baker, *King and Country Call: New Zealanders, Conscription and the Great War* (Auckland University Press, Auckland, 1988); D. Grant, *Out in the Cold: Pacifists and Conscientious Objectors in New Zealand during World War II* (Reed Methuen, Auckland, 1986).

DAVID GRANT

Conscription New Zealanders have been compulsorily subjected to active military service in three periods—during the ★New Zealand Wars, from 1916 to 1918, and from 1940 to 1945. Under the Militia Act 1858, all men were required to register, and in various districts in the North Island were called out for active service against rebel Maori during the 1860s. In the ★First World War, the ★New Zealand Expeditionary Force was initially raised and sustained by voluntary enlistment. The number of men coming forward during 1915 declined significantly, however, and the expansion of the NZEF in early 1916 prior to its deployment on the ★Western Front compounded the problem. Public calls for conscription to be introduced, drawing strength from a growing feeling that there should be equality of sacrifice, were reinforced by the revelation, in a national register taken in late

Conscription

1915, that 40 per cent of those eligible to enlist in the NZEF were not prepared to do so. After trying unsuccessfully to stimulate voluntary enlistment during 1916, the government eventually followed its British counterpart in introducing conscription. The first ballots for conscripts, under the provisions of the Military Service Act, began on 16 November 1916. New Zealand's experience diverged significantly from that of Australia at this point, since attempts to introduce conscription there failed when the proposition was twice rejected in referenda.

Balloting for conscripts was used at first to make up the shortfall of volunteers in each district, and even a year later only 30 per cent of those joining 1NZEF were conscripts. From August 1917, however, all those entering camp in New Zealand as reinforcements were conscripts. At the outset all men aged between twenty and forty-six had been divided into two divisions, the first comprising those who were unmarried or recently married and the second, all the rest. Balloting was at first confined to the First Division, but in October 1917 it was extended to the Second Division (for married men without children). The greater social impact of conscripting Second Division men had, during 1917, led to agitation, led by a Second Division League, for better pay, pensions, and allowances, which bore fruit in substantially increased separation allowances and widows' pensions. Fathers with one or two children were soon being conscripted. However, most of the 55,000 married men called up were still either in the process of entering camp or training in New Zealand when the war ended in November 1918.

About three weeks after being called up, a conscript underwent an Army medical examination, at which stage 65 per cent of them were found to be unfit for overseas service. Of those who were passed fit, a substantial proportion would also later be found to be unfit before reaching the front line. Those whose fitness could be rectified were sent to camp at Tauherenikau for the purpose. Four (later nine) Military Service Boards heard appeals against service which were made by roughly half those called up on grounds of hardship, public interest, or religious objection. Without clear guidelines or precedents, board members tended to approach their task as defenders of conscription, and rejected most appeals. By the war's end 32,270 men (out of 135,000 called up) had gone through the process to join 1NZEF, but they were far outnumbered by the nearly 70,000 who served with it as volunteers.

Conscription ensured a steady flow of reinforcements to the training camps and on to the front line in the latter part of the war. It was primarily responsible for ensuring that the New Zealand Division was arguably the strongest division on the Western Front in 1918. Australia, by contrast, faced great difficulty in keeping its formations up to strength on a purely voluntary basis. While in this respect the New Zealand scheme was successful, it was not without critics in New Zealand itself, though opposition was largely confined to militant Labour, some Maori, and tiny groups of pacifists. Militant unions went out on strike in November 1916 and April 1917 in protest against conscription, but without achieving any change of policy. Anti-conscriptionists found themselves isolated by public opinion and persecuted by a government quick to use its powers to silence them. Only Waikato Maori (still resenting their experience a half-century earlier) mounted effective resistance, as a result of which it was not until May 1918 that conscription was applied to them and then not very effectively. (See MAORI AND THE FIRST WORLD WAR)

Elsewhere there were individual cases of resistance. Men sought to avoid being balloted for conscription by failing to register. Others defaulted after being balloted. By August 1917 more than 5500 men had failed to respond to their call-up. Conscientious objection was only recognised on narrow religious grounds, and some men resisted all attempts to force them to undertake military service.

The ★Second World War experience replicated that of the First World War in that 2NZEF was initially raised on the basis of voluntary enlistment. This was hardly surprising, given that the Labour Party, traditionally opposed to conscription, was in power. Indeed the Cabinet included four men who had been imprisoned for anti-conscription activities in the earlier conflict. The government had rejected plans to introduce a national register in February 1939. Although the initial response to the call for volunteers for 2NZEF was favourable, problems in finding sufficient manpower for the Second Echelon foreshadowed the need for compulsion. Despite the best efforts of local authorities, patriotic societies, and groups such as the RSA, men of military age were noticeably less willing to volunteer than their fathers or uncles had been in 1914; many waited for what they felt was the inevitable introduction of conscription. Although the 20,000 men who had volunteered by January 1940 were barely sufficient to fill 2NZEF's three echelons, the government remained firmly against conscription. Not until the Allied disasters of May 1940 was it impelled to act, in the face of strong public demand. Under the Emergency Regulations Amendment Act of 31 May 1940, it was empowered to make regulations requiring people to place themselves and their property at the disposal of the government for securing the defence of New Zealand and the efficient prosecution of the war. A few days later an emergency Labour Party conference overwhelmingly endorsed the government's assumption of these wide-ranging powers. Only pacifists and the small Communist Party (until June 1941) continued to oppose conscription. Most New Zealanders were resigned to compulsory service. Ironically, the May 1940 crisis boosted volunteering, bringing the number of volunteers to 38,399 by the end of that month. It was clear, however, that volunteering could not provide the constant flow of sufficient manpower to meet the requirements of a growing war effort. The National Service Emergency Regulations establishing conscription were proclaimed on 18 June 1940. Volunteering for army service ceased on 22 July 1940, though entry to the other two services remained voluntary. The *National Service Department assumed the formidable task of registering, investigating, balloting, and examining the estimated 400,000 men of military age. Registration of men aged between nineteen and forty-five began in August 1940. As in the First World War, there were two basic categories—single men and married men, who were allotted to the First and Second Divisions respectively. These two classes were further subdivided according to age and, in the case of the Second Division, number of children. Men over forty were not liable for overseas service. Only Maori, members of the armed forces, prison inmates, the permanently unfit, and the mentally unsound were exempt. Following medical examination a system of statutory District Manpower Committees and Armed Forces Appeal Boards considered appeals against conscription on the basis of hardship, essential employment, and conscientious objection. The vast majority of appeals were on grounds of public interest or hardship—*conscientious objectors accounted for only 2 per cent. The essential criteria for the appeal committees was the appellant's worth to the war effort. Those engaged in work listed as essential had their appeals allowed.

To bring the *Territorial Force up to strength, 16,000 men were called up for Territorial service immediately, to be followed by a further 33,700 men a month later. Ballots for overseas service in December 1940 and March 1941 called up another 23,000 men. Between March and August 1941 the remainder of the First Division were called up without ballot, augmented by 11,000 eighteen-year-olds, to whom the compulsory provisions had now been applied. This raised another 11,000 for the ballot in June 1941, after which the entire First Division of unmarried men had been called up. The onset of the *Pacific War in December 1941 further exacerbated manpower problems. The first ballot of the Second Division men took place in January 1942, and compulsion was applied to the *Home Guard and the *Emergency Precautions Scheme. All men between eighteen and sixty-five not already in these groups, or in the armed forces, were enrolled in the EPS. From April it was compulsory for all men between thirty-five and fifty to serve in the Home Guard. By the end of 1942, 160,000 married men had been balloted and virtually all men of military age had been called up. When in December 1942 married men aged forty-one to forty-five were called up, their lack of physical fitness and high rates of appeal ensured that their service was deferred. Between 1943 and 1945 another 29,000 men, mainly young men turning eighteen, were called up, bringing the total number of conscripts to more than 312,000.

Overall only 52 per cent of men called up were fit enough for overseas service, though another 30 per cent were found to be suitable for home defence. Of the fit men, 27 per cent were granted indefinite postponement from service. After medical examination and appeals, fewer than half of the men called up actually saw service, and the final ballots of middle-aged married men yielded to the forces less than one-fifth of the total called up. By late 1942 virtually all fit men had been called up, and the Appeal Boards turned to weeding out soldiers from the camps for essential farm work which had suffered from the withdrawal of so much labour into the Army. By April 1944 more than 30,000 men had been released from the Army back into industry. At this point the role of the Appeal Boards changed once again. To meet the shortage of reinforcements for 2NZEF they reassessed fit men held back in essential industry, a 'comb out' which yielded another 8153 men for military service before the war ended.

The conscription of such a large number of men from industry into the armed forces inevitably created a manpower crisis. As early as November 1941 the withdrawal of 13 per cent of the male working population from the workforce had begun to disrupt the economy. The massive increase in the numbers needed for home defence and to increase production after Japan's entry to the war led to the extension of compulsion to labour as well. From January 1942 the Minister of National Service was empowered to declare certain industries as essential, and to direct certain classes of people into those industries. Workers were unable to terminate (or have their employment terminated) without the permission of a District Manpower Officer. The number of essential industries grew rapidly as the government sought to harness civilian productive capacity to the war effort, ensuring that by 1944 they were employing 40 per cent of the labour force. From February 1943 all men up to the age of sixty and women between eighteen and forty and not in the armed forces were required to register at their local manpower office for possible direction into essential work. Effectively all adult New Zealanders had been conscripted for the war effort, and by the war's end 150,000 people had been directed into essential industry. Because manpower regulations were implemented with reasonable leniency, there was a high level of compliance and relatively few prosecutions. Not until the end of the war in Europe did conscription begin to wind down. The Appeal Boards ceased their 'comb out' of fit men from industry, and manpower regulations began to be relaxed, with the last industrial manpower regulations being withdrawn on 29 June 1946.

P. Baker, *King and Country Call: New Zealanders, Conscription and the Great War* (Auckland University Press, Auckland, 1988); N.M. Taylor, *The Home Front*, 2 vols (Historical Publications Branch, Wellington, 1986).

Convoys The convoy, a long-established concept of naval warfare whose value was reaffirmed during both world wars, is a means of protecting merchant ships from attack by enemy warships. The sailing of merchant ships in a group under close escort is both a defensive and offensive tactic. It not only ensures that these vulnerable vessels are shielded from enemy raiders, both surface and underwater, but also forces the enemy, in attacking them, to expose its forces to counteraction from the convoy escorts. The first convoy involving New Zealand forces left Wellington on 15 August 1914, when two ★troopships, escorted by HMS *Philomel* and two ★'P' class cruisers, set off to occupy German Samoa. On 16 October 1914 the ★New Zealand Expeditionary Force departed from Wellington in a convoy of ten troopships escorted by the Japanese battlecruiser *Ibuki*, the British cruiser HMS *Minotaur*, and two 'P' class cruisers; joining up with the twenty-eight troopships carrying the Australian Imperial Force at Albany, Western Australia, it proceeded across the Indian Ocean to Egypt. During the transit, one of the combined convoy's escorts, HMAS *Sydney*, sank the German raider *Emden*. Reinforcement drafts for 1NZEF were thereafter carried in troopships which were independently routed, without escorts. A reluctant Admiralty, in 1917, belatedly accepted the need for a convoy system in the Atlantic theatre to combat the German submarine menace, and it soon proved successful in reducing shipping losses.

A similar pattern was evident during the ★Second World War. Between the wars an incipient worldwide shipping control system, linked to geographic naval stations, had been maintained. Under this system, the New Zealand Naval Board was responsible for issuing routing instructions to merchant ships, maintaining a plot of Allied and neutral ships, and controlling the operations of ★cruisers on the ★New Zealand Station. As in the ★First World War, convoy arrangements were instituted to convey 2NZEF to Egypt. The first echelon left Wellington and Lyttelton on 5 January 1940 aboard six troopships, escorted by the battle-

Wellingtonians visiting the British battleship, HMS *Ramillies*, part of the convoy escort for 2NZEF's First Echelon in January 1940 (*War History Collection, Alexander Turnbull Library, G-7123-1/4-DA*)

ship HMS *Ramillies* and the cruisers HMAS *Canberra* and HMS *Leander*. Four troopships carrying the Second Echelon followed on 2 May and three with the Third Echelon on 27 August, both convoys having cruisers as escorts and being joined by Australian troopships off Australia. The direct escort of specific ships, particularly those bound for Canada with personnel for the ★Empire Air Training Scheme, was also instituted during 1940 because of the threat posed by German raiders. Trans-Tasman convoys were introduced after Japan's entry to the war, but after the RNZN's converted coasters proved unsuitable as ocean escorts the practice was terminated, vessels being independently routed instead.

Although New Zealand's naval framework was altered following the onset of the ★Pacific War—New Zealand became part first of the Anzac Area, then of the ★South Pacific Area—the naval staff in Wellington retained their protection of shipping duties. From March 1943 the Americans changed the naval control of shipping structure to a number of 'Sea Frontiers', the New Zealand Sea Frontier encompassing the area between 160°E and 130°W and north to 25°S. The New Zealand naval authorities were responsible for the safe conduct and routing of all coastal shipping, shipping to and from adjacent sea frontiers, and routine shipping in support of military operations. However, the Japanese submarines that penetrated New Zealand waters did so only for reconnaissance, and, as in much of the Pacific area, shipping in the New Zealand Sea Frontier was generally sailed independently. Only off the east coast of Australia was an interlocking convoy system introduced between June 1942 and 1944 to meet the threat from Japanese submarines.

The most important convoy system in the Second World War, as in the First, was that in the North Atlantic. Numerous New Zealanders were involved in this vital theatre with British naval and air forces, and the *merchant marine. They served on Royal Navy escort vessels, in *Fleet Air Arm squadrons, and as aircrew in RAF Coastal Command squadrons, in the operations which finally overcame the German U-boat menace. New Zealand personnel played similar roles in the great convoy battles in the Arctic and the Mediterranean. New RNZN escort ships on their delivery voyages to New Zealand worked their passage as additional escorts for outward-bound Atlantic convoys. While the RNZN has not had the need to institute convoys since the end of the Second World War, the concept of convoy remains an important option for maritime forces; indeed, it was applied for neutral shipping in the Persian Gulf during the Iran–Iraq 'tanker war' in 1985–88. The RNZN retains its naval control of shipping function, with the RNZNVR responsible for maintaining the necessary skills.

RICHARD JACKSON

Corner Committee see DEFENCE COMMITTEE OF ENQUIRY

Corvettes Novelist Nicholas Monsarrat immortalised the corvette as the archetypal *Second World War convoy escort. Misused in the Victorian Royal Navy to describe large steam warships, the word *corvette*—French for sloop—resurfaced during the Second World War to describe small escorts based on a commercial whalecatcher design. It remains an elastic term, generally applied to escort vessels of about 1000 tons.

HMNZ ships *Kiwi*, *Moa*, and *Tui* were multi-purpose minesweepers, anti-submarine escorts, and training vessels. They were called 'trawlers', 'minesweepers', and 'corvettes' at varying times by the Naval Board but will be treated as corvettes here, since their capabilities lifted them well above trawlers of the Castle class. They displaced 607 tons standard, were 47.6 metres long, and shipped one 4-inch gun, light AA guns, and forty depth charges. They could reach fourteen knots. After completing trials in late 1941, the trio had very active careers in the Pacific, where they escorted convoys, bombarded shore positions, and took part in 'barge-busting'. On the night of 29 January 1943, in an epic surface action off Guadalcanal, *Kiwi* and *Moa* detected, forced to the surface, and then drove ashore the larger, more heavily armed Japanese submarine *I-1* (1970 tons standard, one 5.5-inch gun and lighter pieces, six torpedo tubes). During this tough fight at close quarters, the New Zealanders used every weapon aboard and *Kiwi* rammed the *I-1*. *Kiwi*'s Leading Seaman C. Buchanan, the only fatality, won the United States Navy Cross for his bravery during this action. On 19 August of the same year *Tui*, assisted by American aircraft, sank the 2198-ton *I-17* with depth charges and gunfire forty miles south-west of Noumea Bay. This was partial revenge for the Japanese air raid that sank *Moa* while refuelling at Tulagi on 7 April 1943, killing five men and injuring fifteen others including the captain, Lieutenant-Commander Peter *Phipps. After helping to clear local minefields, both surviving corvettes had long post-war careers. *Kiwi*, a training ship in 1948–49 and 1951–56, was broken up in 1964. *Tui* served as a training ship from 1952 to 1955, then as an oceanographic ship between 1956 and 1967, finally going for scrap two years later.

In June 1943 the Royal Navy offered the RNZN two modified Flower class corvettes, *Arabis* and *Arbutus*. They featured greater hull flare and sported a stylish clinker screen on the funnel, but otherwise shared the virtues and vices of the earlier Flowers, which were renowned for their liveliness in heavy seas. They displaced 980 tons standard, were 63.5 metres long, and could make sixteen knots. Armament was a single 4-inch gun, eight 20 mm anti-aircraft guns, a Hedgehog mortar, and depth charges. *Arabis* escorted convoys in the Pacific. *Arbutus* grounded off Fiji on the delivery voyage on 7 October 1944 and was not ready for service until the end of April 1945, after which she served as a radio and radar maintenance ship for the British Pacific Fleet. In early 1946 both swept mines in New Zealand waters. *Arabis* was paid off that year, but *Arbutus* remained in commission until 1948 when both sailed to the United Kingdom in April to provide crews for the Loch class *frigates. They were scrapped three years later, the Royal Navy's last Flowers.

R.J. McDougall, *New Zealand Naval Vessels* (GP Books, Wellington, 1989)

GAVIN McLEAN

Courlander, Lance-Corporal Roy Nicholas (6 December 1914–1 June 1979) is the only New Zealand soldier known to have collaborated with the enemy in the *Second World War. A Londoner by birth, he came to New Zealand by way of the New Hebrides in the 1930s and volunteered for 2NZEF in 1939. He was serving with 18th Battalion when he was captured in *Greece. Early in 1942 he was taken to Germany and held in a prisoner of war camp near Marburg. His ingratiating behaviour led to his being selected for transfer, in June 1943, to a special camp at Genshagen, near Berlin, where he became an enthusiastic participant in efforts to form a British Free Corps. In addition to the inducement of better living conditions than pertained in the ordinary camps, he may have been influenced by anti-Soviet sentiments (his step-father was of Lithuanian descent). He made propaganda broadcasts and recruiting visits to POW camps wearing a Waffen-SS uniform. During one such visit, an enraged New Zealander struck him, and in retribution was almost beaten to death by accompanying Germans. When the British Free Corps was formally established in April 1944, it had only eight members; ultimately it would reach a peak strength of twenty-seven. Realising that Germany's defeat was inevitable, Courlander had, in the meantime, escaped with a companion, after joining an SS war correspondents' unit in Brussels. He was slightly wounded by Allied fire in the process. When he was court-martialled in England in 1945, he insisted that he had joined the Free Corps to gather information from within, but the evidence of his active involvement was compelling. He was sentenced to fifteen years' imprisonment, and was returned to New Zealand. Nevertheless a review of his case later led to his sentence being reduced to nine years, and he was released in 1951.

T.J. Rowe, 'Kiwi Defector? Lance Corporal Roy Courlander of the British Free Corps', *New Zealand Army Journal*, No. 20 (1998).

Cowan, James (14 April 1870–6 September 1943) wrote the official history of the ★New Zealand Wars. The son of a farmer and veteran of the conflict, he was born in Auckland and brought up on a farm which encompassed part of the site of the Battle of Orakau. He became a fluent speaker of the Maori language, and was increasingly interested in Maori history and culture, especially after taking a publicity post in the Tourist Department's head office. He published a number of works on the Maori, before in 1917 seeking a commission to write an account of the wars, pointing to the urgency of recording the recollections of the veterans before they all passed away. An initially reluctant government relented in early 1918, and Cowan laboured for the next three and a half years on the project. Much of this time was spent visiting the various sites, and talking to surviving veterans, and his account makes good use of oral history long before that ancient form of history again became popular. One of the few New Zealand official war historians to have been able to speak the language of the two adversaries he was writing about, Cowan was determined to do 'even justice to both sides', and his history is notable for its sympathetic, sometimes sentimental treatment of the Maori part in the wars and for its detailed battle descriptions. Published in two volumes in 1922–23, his history remained the standard work on the subject for more than sixty years, and was twice reprinted. He subsequently wrote *The Maoris in the Great War*, the official history of the Maori contingent in the ★First World War, which was published in 1926.

J. Cowan, *The New Zealand Wars: A History of the Maori Campaigns and the Pioneering Period*, 2 vols (Government Printer, Wellington, 1922–23).

Cox, Major Sir Geoffrey Sandford (7 April 1910–) was a war correspondent and 2NZEF staff officer. Born in Palmerston North, he went to Oxford University as a Rhodes Scholar in 1932. Taking up a career in journalism, he represented the London newspapers *News Chronicle* and *Daily Express* during the Spanish Civil War and the Russo-Finnish War. He would later publish accounts of his experiences in *Countdown to War, A Personal Memoir of Europe 1938–40* (1988) and *Eyewitness, A Memoir of Europe in the 1930s* (1999). After reporting on the French and Belgian campaigns in 1940, he enlisted in the British Army, passed through an officer training unit, and after being commissioned transferred to 2NZEF. While serving as a junior intelligence officer in the 2nd New Zealand Division's headquarters, he took part in the campaigns in ★Greece and ★Crete (where he published the *Crete News*) and the Crusader offensive of late 1941. In June 1942 he was appointed First Secretary in the newly established New Zealand Legation in Washington. Not until May 1944 did he rejoin the New Zealand division, assuming the appointment of divisional intelligence officer, a role which he likened to being the editor of a busy news service. Discharged from 2NZEF immediately after the war, he resumed his career in the United Kingdom and was later knighted for his services to journalism. He wrote a number of accounts of 2NZEF's operations in the Mediterranean theatre: *The Road to Trieste* (1946), *The Race for Trieste* (1977), and *A Tale of Two Battles* (1987). (See WAR CORRESPONDENTS)

Crawford-Compton, Air Vice-Marshal William Vernon (2 March 1915–2 January 1988) was one of the most highly decorated New Zealand pilots of the ★Second World War. Born in Invercargill and educated in New Plymouth, he worked his passage to England on a tramp steamer (after initially setting out in a ketch) in 1939 and joined the RAF as a ground mechanic. After pilot training, he was posted to a fighter squadron late in 1940, and quickly earned a reputation as a fearless and skilled pilot. Although temporarily grounded by a broken wrist suffered in a crash landing in April 1942, he had taken his tally of victories to seven by the end of 1942, and had been awarded a DFC and bar. When he returned to flying after his accident, he shot down two German aircraft even before being officially posted. He commanded 64 Squadron from the end of 1942 to July 1943. Shortly after being made a DSO, he went to the United States to lecture on aerial tactics, and did not return to England until April 1944. He then commanded 145 (Free French) Fighter Wing during the ★D-Day operations and afterwards in France. By the end of hostilities he had flown 517 missions, including 483 in Spitfires, making him one of the most experienced Allied fighter pilots of the war. He was awarded a bar to his DSO in 1945. After briefly visiting New Zealand in 1945, he took up a permanent commission in the RAF. His subsequent appointments included Air Attaché in Oslo, command of RAF Bruggen, Germany, Senior Air Staff Officer (1963–66), and command of 22 Group, Training Command. He was made a CBE in 1957 and a CB in 1965, and retired in 1969.

Crete Crete's central position in the eastern Mediterranean, 100 kilometres from southern Greece and 320 kilometres from Libya, made the island of potentially great strategic value, a fact initially recognised by both German and British high commands as early as mid 1940. From Crete's airfields at Maleme, Heraklion, and Retimo the British could pursue an aggressive strategy in the Balkans, and in particular threaten the Romanian oilfields at Ploesti, vital for the German war effort. Suda Bay on Crete's northern coastline was also the largest harbour in the Eastern Mediterranean, though it had very limited port facilities. Conversely for the Germans, possession of Crete could secure for the *Luftwaffe* an excellent base from which to launch air attacks on Egypt and the Suez Canal. It would also further secure the Mediterranean flank of the forthcoming invasion of Russia (Operation Barbarossa). In November 1940 Winston Churchill had informed the Australian and New Zealand Prime Ministers that the loss of Crete 'would be a military and political disaster of the first order'. However, Crete was accorded a low priority by General Wavell, the C-in-C Middle East, whose scarce resources were necessarily committed to campaigns in Greece and North Africa. With the collapse of Greece in April 1941, the holding of Crete seemed to offer to the British the opportunity to neutralise the effects of the Greek débâcle. But resources were still insufficient. Coming at a time of Axis success in North Africa, with a revolt also underway in Iraq, the timing of the campaign in Crete could hardly have been worse from the British perspective.

Crete is 260 kilometres long west to east and only sixty kilometres across at its widest point. Whereas the south is mountainous, the northern coast is gently sloping. Geography dictated that Crete's three main airfields—and its only major harbour—faced the enemy forces now ensconced in Greece. These facilities were connected by a single narrow road. Telephone communications between these vital centres were equally poor. Great Britain had been given permission by Greece to garrison Crete in May 1940, and had established a small force at Suda Bay in the following November, but it was only in April 1941 that serious defence preparations began. Wavell still lacked the capacity to reinforce Crete apart from some fighters and anti-aircraft guns. However, from Greece came the bulk of the evacuated 2nd New Zealand Division and 19th Australian Brigade, most of the troops carrying little more than their personal weapons. It was believed at the time that Crete was an assembly point for their return to Egypt after Greece, and it was not until 30 April 1941, only twenty days before the air-borne invasion, that Major-General B.C. ★Freyberg and his staff learned that the New Zealand troops were to play an active role in the defence of Crete. Freyberg was to be Creforce's GOC and Major-General Edward ★Puttick the temporary commander of the New Zealand division.

Freyberg faced a most difficult challenge. His troops lacked the most basic type of equipment: entrenching tools without which it is impossible to prepare defensive positions (the steel helmet became the main digging tool), base plates for mortars, tripods for machine-guns, sights for artillery pieces and even the most simple communications equipment. Many of the troops on Crete were support personnel, and the 11,000 Greek troops were poorly trained and equipped. Some extra materiel, including some obsolete tanks, were received from Egypt, but despite frantic appeals from Freyberg, Crete remained a pauper's campaign.

Despite these shortcomings, the Allies had one great advantage—the accurate intelligence as to enemy intentions which was provided by ★ULTRA. So fully were German plans revealed by this intelligence that Churchill, in London, was tempted by the prospect of inflicting a decisive defeat on the Germans. The extent to which Freyberg was aware of the nature of the intelligence he was receiving remains a matter of debate. On one side, it is contended that Freyberg, given the foreknowledge offered by ULTRA, should have been able to dispose his forces in such a way as to achieve Churchill's objective. This argument focuses on the seeming pre-eminence which Freyberg accorded to a possible sea-borne invasion, with ultimately fatal consequences, despite clear evidence from ULTRA sources that the airfields would be the Germans' primary targets. Freyberg's son, in his 1991 biography of his father, suggested, unconvincingly, that Freyberg was constrained from redeploying his forces the better to protect the airfields because of the danger of compromising the intelligence source. On the other side, the possibility that Freyberg was aware of the source of ULTRA is dismissed. It is maintained that he properly placed considerable weight on the danger of a sea-borne landing, perhaps after the seizure of a port by paratroopers. In these circumstances he prudently deployed his forces to meet both the threat to the airfields and that of a landing

Crete

The commander of Creforce, Major-General B.C. Freyberg, addresses all the officers under his command at Suda Bay, Crete, on 29 April 1941 (*Australian War Memorial, 069892*)

from the sea. The problem of the airfields could, of course, have been nullified by their destruction, but Freyberg was prevented from taking this course by Wavell, pursuing the vain hope that he would be able to fly in badly needed but non-existent aircraft.

Brigadier James ★Hargest's 5th New Zealand Brigade was responsible for protecting the airfield at Maleme in the north-west. The dual nature of the brigade's objectives—to defend the airfield as well as the beaches in its sector—left it seriously 'strung out'. In light of the expected enemy preponderance in air power and the lack of effective communications between units of the brigade, this was a serious problem. A particularly important role was allotted to 22nd Battalion, which was responsible for defending the airfield itself, though given no jurisdiction over RAF personnel and anti-aircraft guns within its area. The fact that the ground immediately west of Maleme airfield was left undefended was, in time, to prove a crucial disadvantage. Positioned about five kilometres east of 5th Brigade on the Galatas Plain was 10th NZ Brigade, under Colonel H.K. ★Kippenberger. This unit, which consisted of a composite battalion of service troops and gunners, the New Zealand Divisional Cavalry, and two Greek regiments, had the task of holding a defensive position facing west. West of 10th Brigade at Canea was 4th NZ Brigade under the command of Brigadier L.M. ★Inglis. Despite having only one heavy

vehicle this unit was designated as Creforce's mobile reserve force. Defending Suda Bay, which could be crucial to a sea-borne invasion, was the Marine Naval Base Defence Organisation, a force of mainly marines and naval personnel under the command of Major-General E.C. Weston. In the central Retimo sector 19th Australian Brigade (Brigadier G.A. Vasey) was deployed at Georgeoupolis, with a further two Australian battalions and two Greek regiments covering the airfield at Retimo. At the eastern end of the island the British 14th Brigade protected the airfield at Heraklion.

On 25 April 1941, Hitler issued Directive 28 which ordered the *Luftwaffe* in Greece to occupy the island of Crete with the object of using it as an air base from which to launch attacks against British forces in the eastern Mediterranean. Overall responsibility for Operation MERKUR, as the attack was code-named, lay with General Alexander Löhr, the commander of the IVth Air Fleet. General Kurt Student's highly trained XI Air Corps, consisting of an assault regiment and the three parachute regiments of 7th Air Division, would make the ground assault. With three rifle regiments from the 5th and 6th Mountain Divisions and sundry other troops held in reserve, there were more than 22,000 men available for the operation. The German plan provided for an initial two-wave assault by both paratroops and glider-borne infantry. The first, in early morning, was designed to capture Maleme airfield and

124

Crete

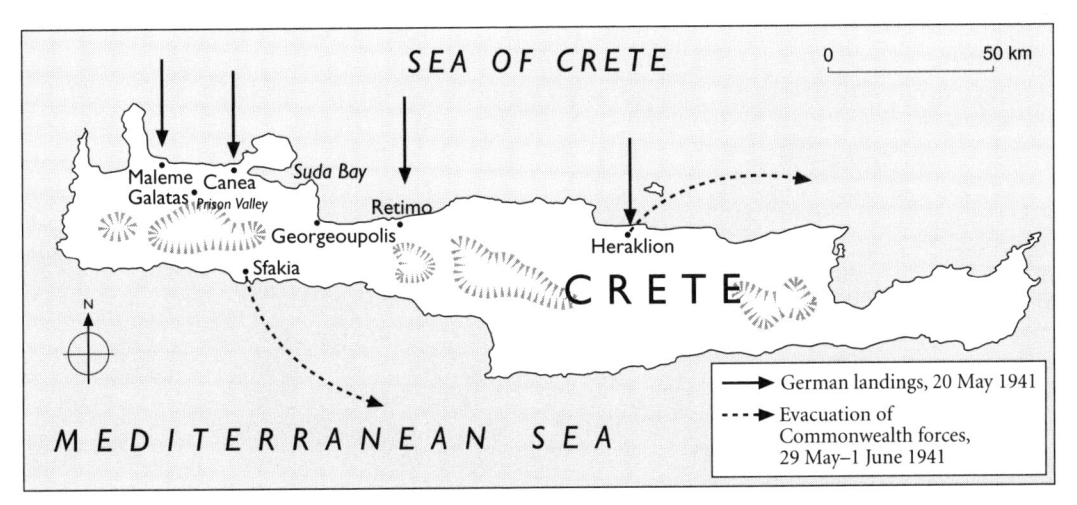

Map 6 The German assault on Crete, May 1941

the defensive positions around Canea and Suda Bay; in the afternoon, the second would seize the airfields of Retimo and Heraklion. With all three airfields in German hands by nightfall, the landing of reinforcements would begin the next day. With further reinforcements arriving by sea, the mopping-up phase could begin. Air support was to be provided by General Wolfram von Richthofen's VIII Air Corps, which had available 650 aircraft. An important factor in German planning was the need for a swift victory because of the impending Operation Barbarossa, for which VIII Air Corps in particular was urgently required in Poland. Barbarossa imposed other restrictions upon Merkur—planning was hasty and reconnaissance poor. Like the New Zealand defenders, Crete was to be an exercise in improvisation for the Germans. The major difference was that the Germans had plentiful equipment.

The invasion of Crete began after dawn on 20 May 1941 with a furious aerial bombardment and strafing which was completely unopposed in the air, the last remnants of RAF fighter cover having been withdrawn the previous day. When shortly after 8 a.m. the first wave of air-borne troops appeared, a breakfasting Freyberg was moved to comment that they were right on time. Landing on or near the defenders' concealed positions at Maleme and about Canea and Galatas, the Germans suffered appalling losses, as many gliders were shot down or broke up on landing. Many of the parachutists were picked off as they drifted down under their parachutes; others were slaughtered before they could recover their heavier weapons from containers dropped with them; others again were killed by armed Cretans (who would later suffer terrible retribution for this intervention). Even so, survivors were

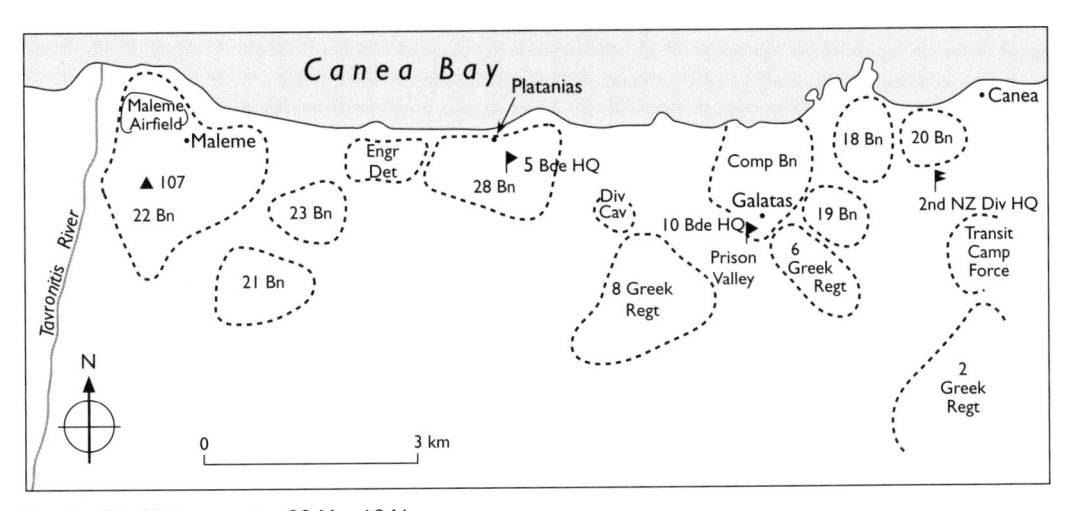

Map 6a The Maleme sector, 20 May 1941

125

German paratroopers prepare to board their Junker Ju52 transports for the invasion of Crete (*War History Collection, Alexander Turnbull Library, F-1313-1/2-DA*)

able to establish a foothold in the Prison Valley southwest of Galatas, threatening communications with 5th Brigade. The need for a spirited counter-attack was apparent to Inglis, who began readying 4th Brigade for such action. But the divisional commander, Puttick, was reluctant to commit his reserve in broad daylight under air attack and with the possibility of sea-borne invasion at any time (and Freyberg concurred with his decision). It was not till after dark that a weak counter-attack was launched, only to stall in confusion. An even more serious threat was posed by gliders landing in the dry riverbed of the Tavronitis, west of Maleme airfield. The Germans who secured a lodgment there were soon threatening the airfield. By afternoon the situation was sufficiently serious for the commander of 22nd Battalion, Lieutenant-Colonel L.W. ★Andrew, to request Hargest to commit the brigade reserve, 23rd Battalion, in a counter-attack. Mistakenly believing 23rd Battalion to be heavily engaged against paratroopers in its own battalion area, Hargest refused. Left to his own devices, Andrew then committed his battalion reserve—two tanks and 14th Platoon—but the counter-attack, at 5.15 p.m., collapsed when the tanks broke down during the attack. The respective failures of Puttick and Hargest to respond vigorously to the developing situation by committing their reserves were serious errors of judgment (and contrasted sharply with the rapid action taken in the other sectors).

Despite the lethargy in the Maleme sector, the German position at nightfall on the first day remained tenuous. The second wave had gone in as planned in the Retimo and Heraklion sectors, but had met with fierce and effective resistance—and immediate counter-attacks which forced the Germans on to the defensive. Neither airfield had been taken, though the defenders had been effectively cut off from the battle to the west. At Maleme the New Zealanders were still resisting strongly, and the German officers on the spot were conscious of their vulnerability to a vigorous counter-attack. It had become apparent that the number of Allied troops on Crete had been grossly underestimated. An atmosphere of despair pervaded the German headquarters in Athens. Student was convinced that the invasion had failed, and that Germany was on the verge of a humiliating defeat. But overnight the position was transformed by New Zealand command errors. At about 6 p.m. Andrew, mistakenly believing that his two forward companies had been overrun, decided to withdraw 22nd Battalion from its positions on Hill 107 overlooking the airfield. Hargest had at first concurred—'If you must, you must'—but then ordered two companies forward to reinforce 22nd Battalion, one of which briefly reoccupied Hill 107 before withdrawing. When the other failed to make contact in the darkness—it had been sent from the more distant 28th Battalion—it also withdrew. Andrew pulled his battalion back to 21st Battalion's positions to the east. (The abandoned forward companies of 22nd Battalion were later able to extricate themselves as well.) The possibility of 21st and 23rd Battalions making an immediate counter-attack was considered but rejected. Their commanders' misjudgment was compounded by Hargest's lethargy. Instead of taking control of the situation, he remained at his headquarters, five kilometres to the rear, and acquiesced in his subordinates' inaction, contrary to Freyberg's intent.

At dawn on 21 May, the Germans discovered, to their surprise and relief, that Hill 107 was unoccupied. Consolidating their hold on Maleme airfield, they were able to land about forty transport aircraft under fire during the afternoon of the 21st. Although the airfield was soon littered with wrecked aircraft, vital reinforcements and supplies were now available to the beleaguered paratroops. The Allied response to this dangerous situation was affected by the assumption that a sea-borne attack was still imminent. When during the afternoon, a conference of the senior New Zealand and Australian commanders determined that a counter-attack should be mounted that night, only two battalions, the 20th and 28th (Maori), were allotted to the task, and they could not move until an Australian battalion had relieved the 20th Battalion. The New Zealanders were confronted with the need to advance the six kilometres from the start line to the airfield across broken terrain in the dead of night to avoid attacks from the air. From the beginning, things went terribly wrong. The late arrival of the relieving Australian battalion because of German bombing delayed the attack by four hours. Despite great courage on the part of the troops—this action contributed to Captain Charles ★Upham's winning his first Victoria Cross—the two battalions were unable to reach the airfield. At dawn they found themselves exposed to devastating German air attack. It proved impossible to consolidate their advanced positions, and by afternoon they had retreated to their start line. The failure of this counter-attack, Creforce's last hope of recovering the lost positions, determined the fate of the island. It was a case of far too little far too late. The only good news for Freyberg that night was that the Royal Navy, forewarned by ULTRA, had intercepted an enemy flotilla of nineteen caiques, two steamers, and an Italian light destroyer carrying reinforcements and heavy equipment for the German forces on Crete. The convoy was dispersed, and about 400 Germans were drowned (many less than was assumed at the time). For the Royal Navy, these operations proved very expensive in ships and lives, as the *Luftwaffe* mounted determined daylight bombing attacks on its retreating forces.

Meanwhile 5th Brigade's position had become increasingly vulnerable, as the German troops in the Prison Valley threatened to cut it off. On 23 May it pulled back to a new line near Galatas. Now reinforced with fresh mountain troops landed at Maleme, the Germans drove eastward. The New Zealanders, exhausted by the continual bombing and strafing, buckled as infantry assaults were launched on the Galatas line on 25 May. Although a famous counter-attack ordered by Kippenberger drove the Germans out of Galatas briefly, the situation remained precarious, with some units having disintegrated. On the 26th a new defensive line was established west of Canea, but that position, too, under continual air attack and threatened with outflanking, became untenable. The confusion was exacerbated when Freyberg, at this point, reorganised his command structure, placing Weston over Puttick. When during the evening of 26 May Vasey and Hargest requested a withdrawal by their respective brigades, Weston could not be located. With Weston absent, Puttick ordered Vasey and Hargest to retreat to a new line south of Suda Bay at 42nd Street, orders from Freyberg to hold arriving too late. In the confusion the reserve force of British troops was left behind, most of whom were later to be taken prisoner.

By 26 May, with no reinforcements available, dwindling supplies, exhausted troops, and constant enemy air attack, the commanders on the spot were convinced that Crete was lost. That morning Freyberg urged an immediate decision on withdrawal to save at least part of his command. However, there was a reluctance in London to accept the inevitable—General Wavell had been reminded that 'victory was essential and that he must keep hurling in reinforcements'. In the absence of any sensible orders Freyberg began preparations for an evacuation from Sfakia that night. (It was not until the evening of the 27th that Freyberg received the order from Wavell to evacuate.) On the 27th German attacks on the line at 42nd Street were repelled by a spirited counter-attack by 5th Brigade, while the remainder of the 2nd New Zealand Division began the long, arduous route marches over the mountains to the evacuation beaches at Sfakia. A group of commandos under Colonel Laycock and Vasey's 19th Australian Brigade covered the retreat. Not realising at first that the bulk of Creforce was retreating across the island to Sfakia, General Julius Ringel, now commanding the German ground effort, threw most of his troops eastwards towards Retimo, which surrendered on 30 May. Further east still about 6000 troops were successfully evacuated from Heraklion on 29 May (though many were killed in subsequent bombing attacks on their ships). Evacuations from Sfakia had begun after dark on 28 May, continuing for three further nights. During this anxious period the New Zealand Prime Minister Peter ★Fraser was visiting Cairo. When it seemed that the evacuation would cease on the night of 30–31 May, he prevailed upon Admiral Sir Andrew Cunningham, the Commander-in-Chief of the Mediterranean Fleet, to make one last effort on the following night, pointing out that such a large loss of men would be 'a crushing disaster for our country and its war effort'. As a result, another 3700 men were rescued on the 31st, bringing to 16,500 the total of men evacuated (about half the Commonwealth troops on Crete at the beginning of the battle).

The weakening of German air attacks, as a result of the redeployment of forces north for Operation Barbarossa, ensured that shipping losses during the Crete evacuation were less than feared at the outset. On 1 June the exhausted remnants of Creforce, about 6500 men, formally surrendered; hundreds took to the hills rather than enter captivity, many later escaping by submarine or fishing boat. Some hid on the island for years and took part in partisan fighting, but most were eventually captured. (See RESISTANCE IN EUROPE, NEW ZEALANDERS AND)

The cost of the battle for Crete was very high for all parties involved. Total losses for the Allies numbered 15,743, of whom 1751 had been killed or died of wounds. New Zealand had lost 671 killed and 967 wounded, while another 2180 had become prisoners of war. During the operations around Crete, three of the Royal Navy's cruisers as well as six destroyers were sunk, and more than 2000 naval personnel were killed. German losses, too, were very heavy—about 3300 killed and 3400 wounded. Crete was, as Student lamented, the 'graveyard of the paratroops'. They would not be used in a similar role again. Many Cretan civilian hostages were executed as reprisals for partisan attacks and for the alleged mistreatment of German prisoners during the campaign, and guerrilla warfare would continue for the next four years.

In the aftermath of the battle Freyberg's performance came under scrutiny from both above and below. Some of his own subordinates went behind his back to raise doubts at the highest levels. Hargest, for example, expressed to Fraser the view that Freyberg was responsible for the loss of Crete and should be replaced. Inglis, sent as Freyberg's emissary to report to an angry Churchill on the loss of Crete, denounced Freyberg's performance as tactically inept. Coming on top of concerns about Freyberg's role in the fiasco in Greece, these damaging comments left Fraser inclined, for a time, to sack the general. However, with both Wavell and his successor, General Auchinleck, strongly defending him, Freyberg survived this inquiry. Other senior officers were less fortunate—there was a reshuffling of command positions within 2NZEF, with many being returned to New Zealand.

Crete was a major defeat for the Allied cause. Churchill's last-minute scheme for Crete to become a base to threaten the German southern flank was hopelessly unrealistic given the weakness of British power. ULTRA intelligence could not compensate for inadequate resources and hasty preparations. Yet short-term defeat was never inevitable—it was the desperate gamble of Student to reinforce Maleme while the New Zealand senior commanders wavered that prevented an outstanding British victory. The consequences of the battle were less decisive. Crete was a major propaganda victory for the Germans, but British power in the Mediterranean was not destroyed. Even before the end of the battle, German forces were being diverted away to the north. Far from representing the first step in a concerted German campaign to oust British forces from the Mediterranean, the seizure of Crete was regarded by Hitler as a necessary precursor to Operation Barbarossa. Crete became a strategic backwater.

Crete holds a special place in the public imagination of New Zealanders. There a scratch force made up largely of New Zealanders and Australians came tantalisingly close to inflicting Germany's first land defeat of the war. It was a tragedy and serious defeat for the Allies but by only the narrowest of margins.

D. Davin, *Crete* (War History Branch, Wellington, 1953); L. Barber and J. Tonkin-Covell, *Freyberg: Churchill's Salamander* (Century Hutchinson, Auckland, 1989).

GLYN HARPER

Crichton, Sergeant James (15 July 1879–22 September 1961) won a ★Victoria Cross in the ★First World War. Irish-born, he served for five years in the Cameron Highlanders, during which he took part in the ★Boer War, before emigrating to New Zealand, where he lived at Auckland as a cable-joiner. Enlisting in 1NZEF, he was an Army Service Corps baker on the ★Western Front until May 1918, when he transferred to 2nd Battalion, Auckland Regiment. His decoration resulted from his actions during the crossing of the Scheldt River on 30 September 1918. A wound in the foot did not prevent him from accompanying his unit in rushing a stone bridge across the river. With his platoon cut off and under fire, he volunteered to take a message back to his company headquarters, which he did by swimming across the river and traversing bullet-swept open ground. When he rejoined his hard-pressed platoon, he defused a bomb under the vital bridge, before making another dash back to his unit headquarters to inform them the bridge was safe. He was still recovering from his wounds when the war ended. In 1937 he accompanied the Coronation Contingent to the United Kingdom.

Crimean War Because of the time taken for communications to pass between Europe and New Zealand, news of the outbreak of war between a British–French–Turkish coalition and Russia did not reach the colony until 9 July 1854, more than three months after the event. Although the main theatre of conflict was in the Crimean Peninsula, there was both a Baltic and a Pacific dimension to the war. The Russians had established a naval base at Petropavlovsk on the Kamchatka Peninsula, and Russian warships were believed to be operating in the Pacific. An unsuccessful attempt was made by an Anglo-French fleet to seize Petropavlovsk, which was later abandoned by the Russians. The small Russian naval forces in the region withdrew into the sanctuary of the Amur River, where they were bottled up for the duration of the war. No Russian ships ventured into the South Pacific, but the colonial authorities in New Zealand took some measures to deal with the threat. Colonel R.H. ★Wynyard, as temporary Administrator of the government (in the absence of the Governor) authorised himself as commander of the imperial troops in the colony to build earthworks to protect a battery earlier installed at Auckland's Britomart Point as a precaution against attack by rebel Maori. Early fears were soon allayed, however, and no further defence measures were taken before the war ended in March 1856. New Zealand, Wynyard noted at this time, remained 'a Colony perfectly helpless as regards an external foe'. (See RUSSIAN SCARES)

I. McGibbon, *The Path to Gallipoli: Defending New Zealand 1840–1915* (GP Books, Wellington, 1991).

Crooks, Air Marshal David Manson (8 December 1931–). Born at Rangiora, Crooks joined the RNZAF in 1951 and within six years was a pilot in 14 Squadron, then stationed in Singapore. He subsequently served in the ★Defence Secretariat, commanded the Flying Training School at Wigram, attended the Royal College of Defence Studies in England, and commanded Ohakea and Whenuapai bases. He was then successively Director of Strategic Policy at Defence HQ (1976–77), AOC RNZAF Operations Group (1978–80), and Deputy CAS (1980–83). As Chief of Air Staff from 1983 to 1986, he grappled with the problem of sustaining New Zealand's air strike capacity, eventually securing a substantial modernisation programme for the Skyhawks. He was made a CB in 1985. When he became Chief of Defence Staff in 1986, he faced problems of low morale and loss of purpose among the armed forces in the aftermath of the ★ANZUS dispute. A defence review sought to chart a new direction within the constraints imposed by the new situation. His uneasy relationship with the government was exacerbated, and ★civil–military relations were sorely tested, by consideration of New Zealand's response to the first of the ★Fiji coups of 1987. The recriminations over this troubled process continued into the 1990s. After his retirement later in 1987, Crooks remained active in air force matters, presiding over both the RNZAF Association and the RNZAF Museum Trust Board.

Cruisers The largest warships to form part of the New Zealand naval forces, cruisers emerged as a natural progression from the screw frigates of the mid nineteenth century with the roles of commerce protection and scouting for the battlefleet. They were the smallest vessels capable of independent action. During the ★Second World War, their commerce protection function was assumed by the new frigates and sloops and they developed into (and remain) the key element of the anti-aircraft defence of the aircraft-carrier group. (See table 6.)

New Zealand's association with cruisers began with the Australasian Naval Agreement of 1887, under which New Zealand paid a subsidy towards the cost of the five-cruiser-strong ★Australian Auxiliary Squadron. It was not until July 1914 that New Zealand, under the terms of the ★Naval Defence Act 1913, acquired its own cruiser, the ageing Pearl class vessel HMS *Philomel*, which had been first commissioned in 1891 and spent most of her life in African waters. She was borrowed from the Royal Navy, with New Zealand meeting her operating costs. Envisaged as a training ship, she was on her shakedown cruise when the outbreak of the ★First World War became imminent. Returning to Wellington, she was readied for war service, not an easy task given her poor material condition. She was formally transferred to Admiralty control on 3 August. Her mainly British crew was augmented by fifty-nine members of the Royal Naval Reserve and volunteers. With two other ★'P' class cruisers, she formed part of the escort for the Samoa Expeditionary Force, which sailed from Wellington on 14 August (see SAMOA, NEW ZEALAND'S MILITARY ROLE IN). After the successful completion of this task, she helped escort the Main Body of the ★New Zealand Expeditionary Force as far as Albany, West Australia. During the following two years she was deployed in the Middle East theatre, initially in the eastern Mediterranean, where a landing party sustained New Zealand's first naval casualties when it encountered a body of Turks. Later, and for most of the time, she served in the Persian Gulf, a naval backwater except briefly in 1916 during operations in ★Mesopotamia. Generally, *Philomel* was engaged in keeping the peace among local inhabitants and maintaining a British presence. Her condition was so poor, however, that the decision was eventually taken to return her to New Zealand; she was paid off in Wellington in March 1917 and was reduced to the role of depot ship under a care and maintenance party. Her armament was removed and installed in merchant ships. During 1918–19 her personnel provided equipment and advice to the fishermen who undertook the task of sweeping mines laid by the German raider *Wolf*. Presented to New Zealand by the British government, she was made sufficiently seaworthy in 1921 to get her to Auckland, where she became the depot ship of the ★New Zealand Division of the Royal Navy—a role she fulfilled until January 1947. The

Cruisers

Table 6 Cruisers in the New Zealand Naval Forces

Ship	Length (metres)	Displacement (tons)	Speed (knots)	Complement	Armament
Philomel	85	2575	17	220	8 × 4.7-inch guns 8 × 3-pounder guns 2 × 14-inch torpedo tubes
Chatham	139	5400	25.5	475	8 × 6-inch guns 1 × 3-inch gun 4 × 2-pounder guns 2 × 14-inch torpedo tubes
Dunedin Diomede	144	4700	29	450	6 × 6-inch guns 3 × 4-inch guns 12 × 21-inch torpedo tubes
Achilles Leander	169	7030	32	550	8 × 6-inch guns 8 × 4-inch guns 4 × 2-pounder guns 8 × 21-inch torpedo tubes
Gambia	169	10,830	32	920	12 × 6-inch guns 8 × 4-inch guns 10 × 2-pounder guns 20 × 20 mm guns 6 × 21-inch torpedo tubes
Bellona Black Prince Royalist	156	7400	30	550	8 × 5.25-inch guns 8 × 40 mm guns 12 × 2-pounder guns 10 to 12 × 20 mm guns 6 × 21-inch torpedo tubes

name *Philomel* was then transferred to the ★Royal New Zealand Navy's shore establishment at Devonport.

During 1919 Prime Minister W.F. ★Massey negotiated the loan of another training cruiser, the Southampton class coal-burner HMS *Chatham*. Following her arrival in New Zealand in January 1921, she embarked on a tour of the Dominion's ports which had the dual objectives of showing her to the people and encouraging recruiting for naval service. From July to October 1921 she was engaged on the first of several visits to islands in the South Pacific, during which her limitations as a coal-burner were apparent. With a range of only 7400 kilometres, she often had to steam at very low speeds to conserve fuel during extended passages in the islands. This regular programme of local and Pacific cruises was varied occasionally by joint exercises with units of the Royal Australian Navy. *Chatham*'s service with the New Zealand Division came to an end in May 1924 with the arrival of the Royal Navy's Special Service Squadron, which included her replacement HMS *Dunedin*. She left a lasting memory in the form of the Chatham Cup, New Zealand's premier national soccer trophy, which was presented by the ship's company.

Named after the South Island city, *Dunedin* was the first of two 'D' class cruisers obtained for the New Zealand Division under similar terms to those that had pertained for *Philomel* and *Chatham*. Her sister ship *Diomede* arrived in New Zealand in January 1926. The mobility of these oil-burning warships was improved by the hire of the tanker RFA *Nucula* from the Admiralty. Both ships operated in a similar fashion to *Chatham*, with periodic refits in the United Kingdom and occasional interruptions to routine. In 1928 both were dispatched to Western Samoa to provide support to the administration beset by nationalist agitation, and *Dunedin* returned there in early 1930, after further trouble. Both ships were involved in relief efforts following the devastating ★Napier earthquake in 1931. In 1935 *Diomede* spent five months based at Aden, where she had been deployed to supplement British forces during the crisis over the Italian invasion of ★Abyssinia, before proceeding to England in early 1936. She was followed to England by *Dunedin* in 1937.

The crews of *Diomede* and *Dunedin* commissioned the replacement cruisers for the New Zealand Division, the most modern yet to serve with it. The Leander class HMS *Achilles* was less than three years old when it replaced *Diomede* in 1936, and went initially to serve with a cruiser squadron at Gibraltar. In April 1937 she was joined in the division by HMS *Leander*, which had as her first task to represent the Dominion's

The light cruiser HMS *Dunedin* at Apia, Western Samoa, in January 1930 (*Penrice Collection*)

naval forces at the Spithead Review in honour of the coronation of King George VI. One of *Leander*'s tasks in 1938 was to carry the New Zealand ★Chiefs of Staff on a visit to the Pacific Islands to assess possible defence measures there. When the ★Second World War began, *Leander* was retained in New Zealand waters, after a brief trip with personnel to garrison the cable landing point at ★Fanning Island. *Achilles*, in accordance with plans, sailed even before the conflict began to join the Royal Navy's America and West Indies Station; in December she took part in the Battle of the ★River Plate. In February 1940 she returned to New Zealand, and *Leander* was deployed to the Middle East, initially as part of the escort of 2NZEF's Second Echelon. Her most notable action was the sinking of the Italian raider *Ramb I* in the Indian Ocean in February 1941. With the outbreak of the ★Pacific War, both cruisers were deployed in the South Pacific (the intention that *Achilles* would join Force Z at Singapore being altered by that force's rapid destruction by Japanese shore-based aircraft off the coast of Malaya). Both were engaged in the ★Solomons campaign. *Achilles* was heavily damaged by a bomb on 5 January 1943, and twenty-one casualties were sustained. She proceeded to England for repairs, and was not recommissioned until May 1944, work having been delayed by an explosion. Meanwhile *Leander* had also suffered major damage. While on patrol with Task Force 18 off the island of Kolombangara in July 1943, she was heavily damaged by a torpedo hit amidships during an engagement with a Japanese force. There were forty-three casualties. Superb damage control allowed her to reach Tulagi, where she was sufficiently repaired to proceed to Auckland. Because the repairs were beyond the capacity of the facilities there, she was repaired in Boston, Massachusetts, and, in May 1944, reverted to the Royal Navy.

With both cruisers undergoing lengthy repairs, New Zealand negotiated the loan of a near-new Fiji class cruiser to replace *Leander*. HMNZS *Gambia* was commissioned in September 1943 with the majority of her crew coming from *Achilles*. After working up at Scapa Flow, she was employed in the Atlantic on patrols against blockade runners until the end of 1943, and early the following year joined the British Eastern Fleet's 4th Cruiser Squadron at Trincomalee. When the now-repaired *Achilles*, which had been recommissioned with most of *Leander*'s crew, also joined the Fleet in September 1944, *Gambia* proceeded to New Zealand but rejoined the Fleet early in 1945. Both cruisers were actively involved in the final operations against Japan. *Gambia* had the distinction of firing the last rounds of the war against mainland Japan when she bombarded a steel works; she was present at the formal Japanese surrender in Tokyo Bay. She also fired the last shots of the war when an air attack was made on the Fleet after the Emperor's capitulation announcement on 15 August. Her service with the RNZN came to an end in early 1946—as did that of *Achilles*. The New Zealand government had decided to replace them with modern improved Dido class light cruisers.

The RNZN's new cruisers were HMNZS *Bellona* and *Black Prince*. The latter was placed in reserve, while *Bellona* carried out a similar programme to that followed by the pre-war cruisers. In 1952 she visited the United Kingdom—the first of what had been intended to be an annual trip by one or other cruiser to help maintain operational efficiency—and thereafter she was placed in reserve. *Black Prince* attended the Coronation Review at Spithead in June 1953, and was involved in earthquake disaster relief in the Greek islands during her return voyage. She subsequently escorted the royal yacht *Gothic* during Queen Elizabeth II's first visit to New Zealand. After visits to the Pacific Islands and the Far East, she was placed in reserve in 1955, and eventually reverted to the Royal Navy in 1961. A recommissioned *Bellona* left New Zealand in October 1955 with many young ratings among her crew, a situation which had given rise to one of the most memorable signals in New Zealand naval history: 'Ratings drafted to Bellona for passage to UK should be vice trained men'. She was replaced by another improved Dido class vessel, the recently modernised HMNZS *Royalist*, which was working up in the Mediterranean when the ★Suez crisis erupted. For a time it seemed likely that she would become involved, the British authorities being anxious to utilise her anti-aircraft capabilities. In the event, the New Zealand government declined to allow her participation, and she proceeded to New Zealand. Deployed in the Far East, she took part in ★Malayan Emergency and ★Confrontation operations, and spent a brief period with the United Nations Command off Korea. Periodic deployments to the Far East Station continued, interspersed with the traditional Pacific Islands cruises. While returning from her last deployment to the Far East in November 1965, she suffered a total steam failure near the Solomons Islands and had to be towed most of the way back to Auckland. She was paid off in July 1966. The RNZN's involvement with cruisers came to an end when she was returned to the Royal Navy in late 1967.

R.J. McDougall, *New Zealand Naval Vessels* (GP Books, Wellington, 1989).

PETER DENNERLY

Crump, Brigadier Stanley Herbert (25 January 1889–13 July 1974) was affectionately known as the 'Father of the Army Service Corps'. Born in Wellington, he began his career in 1914 as a junior officer in the ★Territorial Force. From 1915 to 1919 he served in 1NZEF both on the ★Western Front and in the ★Sinai–Palestine campaign. He commanded the ASC element of the NZ Mounted Rifle Brigade in Egypt in 1917. After the war, he became a regular soldier when he was commissioned in the ★New Zealand Staff Corps in 1923. He was responsible for the organisation, training, and administration of supplies and transport in the inter-war period. From 1932 to 1939 he was Director of Supplies and Transport. He was made an OBE in 1939. Seconded to 2NZEF, he departed with the First Echelon in January 1940. From his arrival in Egypt he was 2nd NZ Division's Commander NZASC, serving in that capacity in every theatre in which the division operated. He combined energy, resourcefulness, and an uncompromising approach with considerable organisational and command skills. Nowhere were these attributes more in evidence than during the New Zealand division's long and difficult left hook at Mareth, its successful support being one of the most impressive logistic feats of the ★North African campaign. For his efforts during the war he was made a DSO in 1943, and a CBE two years later. From June to September 1947, he commanded ★Jayforce, and in 1948–49 was on the staff of BCOF Headquarters; he was New Zealand's representative on the Disposals Board in Japan. Following his retirement in 1949, he was Colonel Commandant of the RNZASC for the following eight years.

GRANT CROWLEY

Cyprus In October 1952, 14 Squadron RNZAF deployed to Cyprus. This was designed to allow New Zealand more effectively to fulfil obligations undertaken in 1949 in the event of a war with the Soviet Union which would have led to most of New Zealand's available military forces being committed in the Mediterranean theatre (see MIDDLE EAST COMMITMENT). Based at Nicosia and equipped with Mark 9 Vampire jet fighters, 14 Squadron undertook training with NATO forces, mobility exercises to Africa, and goodwill visits around the Middle East. In April 1955, as a result of the shift of focus of New Zealand's defence strategy to South-east Asia, it was transferred to Singapore, where it became part of the ★British Commonwealth Far East Strategic Reserve. Following an outbreak of ethnic conflict between the majority Greeks and minority Turks, a contingent of New Zealand policemen served with a UN ★peace-keeping force in Cyprus from 1964 to 1967.

D

D-Day, the staff term for day of operation (D stands for day), is usually associated with the Allies' invasion of Western Europe on 6 June 1944, an operation which marked the opening of the long-awaited Second Front in Europe. Operation Overlord, an amphibious assault involving nearly 6000 ships and 199 air force squadrons, secured a lodgment in German-occupied Europe on the coast of Normandy, France, and by 5 July 1944 one million men were ashore. There were no New Zealand units among the invasion force, which comprised mainly American, British, and Canadian troops, but numerous New Zealanders nevertheless took part in Overlord as members of the Royal Navy, the Merchant Navy, and the RAF. Many of the 4700 New Zealanders serving in the Royal Navy were present, commanding or crewing landing craft or motor torpedo boats, serving in the escorting warships, troopships, and supply vessels, or flying missions over the area as part of the ★Fleet Air Arm. One of New Zealand's leading literary figures, Denis ★Glover, commanded a landing craft, and later wrote about his experience. Another New Zealander serving in the Royal Navy, Auckland-born Rhodes Scholar Lieutenant-Commander G.L. Hogben, was right at the heart of invasion decision-making as a member of the Admiralty meteorological team whose weather forecast played a crucial role in the timing of the onslaught. There were nearly 6000 New Zealanders serving in the RAF in June 1944, many of whom were involved, directly or indirectly, in providing air support to the landing forces. The most prominent was Air Vice-Marshal Arthur ★Coningham, commanding the 2nd Tactical Air Force, which provided close air support to the invasion force and included three 'New Zealand' squadrons, 485, 487, and 488. Another New Zealand squadron, 486, also took part in the initial stages of Overlord. A New Zealand pilot was the first to shoot down an enemy aircraft during the landings. A senior 2NZEF officer, Brigadier James ★Hargest, who was present as an official New Zealand observer with the British 50th Division on D-Day, was later killed by a shell on 12 August 1944.

Davies, Major-General Richard Hutton (14 August 1861–9 May 1918) was the first New Zealander to command a division on active service. Born in London and educated in England, he emigrated to New Zealand as a young man. He was working as a surveyor in Taranaki when he began his military career in the ★Volunteer Force in 1893. He commanded the Hawera Mounted Rifles from 1895 to 1899. Joining the Defence Department as a staff officer in October 1899, he assumed responsibility for the instruction of mounted rifles Volunteers in the North Island but was almost immediately posted to the First Contingent sent by New Zealand to the ★Boer War. He proved a capable and popular company commander, and was soon given increased responsibilities. In May 1900 he commanded the Third (Rough Riders) Contingent for four weeks. Transferring to the Rhodesia Field Force, he commanded two squadrons, and later the whole, of Fourth Contingent. He was made a CB in 1901. After briefly returning to New Zealand, he again embarked for South Africa in February 1902 as commander of the Eighth Contingent, which served as an operationally discrete unit—the first such New Zealand force to do so overseas—though the war ended too soon for it to take part in more than a few skirmishes. He then commanded the Auckland Military District until his appointment, in December 1906, as Inspector-General of the New Zealand Military Forces and member of the Council of Defence. Convinced of the inevitability of war, he condemned the volunteer system as inefficient and advocated its replacement with ★compulsory military training. His scathing report of 1909 was suppressed by the Prime Minister, Sir Joseph ★Ward. Although his outspoken approach was criticised in some quarters, his persistent advocacy of defence reform helped pave the way for changes foreshadowed in the ★Defence Act 1909. With the intention of preparing him to succeed Major-General A.J. ★Godley as GOC, he was sent to the United Kingdom, where he was attached for a year to the 2nd Cavalry Brigade. His performance so impressed the British authorities that they offered him a four-year appointment as commander of 6th Infantry Brigade. In 1914 he commanded it in France as part of the British Expeditionary Force, and was mentioned in dispatches for his actions at Mons. With the New Zealand government's agreement, he transferred to the British Army in February so that he could take command of a division. After three months' rest to recover from ill health which had forced his evacuation from France, he assumed command of the 20th (Light) Division. He was again mentioned in dispatches in January 1916, but the strain once more proved too great and he was evacuated to England at the end of that year. In poor health, he commanded a number of base camps in England until ending his own life.

Davin, Major Daniel Marcus (1 September 1913–28 September 1990) was a prominent New Zealand war novelist. A Southlander by birth, he was educated at Otago University and, after winning a Rhodes scholarship in 1935, at Oxford. When the ★Second World War began, he joined the British Army but transferred to 2NZEF after being commissioned in May 1940. He took part in the campaigns in ★Greece and ★Crete, and was badly wounded in the latter. From May 1943 to July 1944 he was 2nd New Zealand Division's Intelligence Officer. In the latter stages of the war, he was an intelligence officer in the War Office in London. Remaining in Great Britain, he became assistant secretary at the Clarendon Press and, resuming his literary career, wrote a number of novels and short stories with his early Southland background or war as themes, perhaps the best known being *For the Rest of Our Lives* (see LITERATURE AND WAR). He was also the author of the acclaimed New Zealand official war history *Crete*, which appeared in 1953. Despite the book's reception, he claimed later that its preparation had 'ended all desire he might have had to become a historian'.

K. Ovenden, *A Fighting Withdrawal: The Life of Dan Davin, Writer, Soldier, Publisher* (Oxford University Press, Oxford, 1996).

Davis-Goff, Commodore George Raymond (24 September 1905–30 May 1987) was the outstanding product of the naval training system instituted in New Zealand after the ★First World War. Born in Renwicktown, Marlborough, he entered the ★New Zealand Division of the Royal Navy in the first draft of boy trainees in 1921. By 1931 he had attained the rank of petty officer and was later promoted to torpedo gunner—becoming the first New Zealander to achieve warrant rank in the New Zealand Naval Forces. Serving in HMS *Achilles*, he was mentioned in dispatches for his role in the Battle of the ★River Plate and was commissioned in May 1941—the first New Zealander to reach commissioned rank from the lower deck. After serving in Atlantic and Arctic convoys, he returned to New Zealand and was torpedo officer in HMNZS *Leander* when she was torpedoed in July 1943, later overseeing the repairs in Boston. He spent the rest of the war in HMNZS *Gambia* with the British Pacific Fleet. In August 1945 he commanded the first party of New Zealanders to land in Japan after the surrender. He was awarded a DSC for his part in the operations against Japan. After the war, he occupied a series of staff posts, underwent staff training in England, and from 1951 was executive officer in HMNZS *Bellona*. A colourful officer—one of his subordinates described him as 'a buccaneer type person'—he commanded the frigate HMNZS *Hawea* during her deployment with the UN Command in the latter stages of the ★Korean War; this service, which mainly involved constant patrolling and shore bombardments, earned him a bar to his DSC. In 1953 he became the first RNZN officer to reach captain's rank from the lower deck. After heading the New Zealand Joint Services Liaison Staff in Canberra, he became the first New Zealander to serve as Naval Officer-in-Charge, Auckland. He was made a CBE in 1958, and retired in the following year.

Death penalty Military forces throughout history have used the death penalty as a means of enforcing ★discipline. The British forces were no exception; the system of military law established by the Army Act 1881 included seventeen offences punishable by death. In addition to treachery and mutiny, soldiers could be executed for cowardice, desertion, sleeping on sentry duty, or leaving a post. New Zealand servicemen when on 'actual service' were subject to this system of law by the provisions of the ★Defence Act 1886, which specifically proscribed the infliction of corporal punishment, 'except death or imprisonment', on any member of the New Zealand forces. New Zealanders who served in the ★Boer War were subject to the Army Act, though no sentences of death were passed on them. The application of the Army Act to New Zealand's military forces, with some modification in relation to terms of imprisonment but not to the death penalty provisions, was confirmed in the Defence Act 1909. Members of the New Zealand naval forces were subject, by the Naval Defence Act 1913, to the British Naval Discipline Act 1866 and the Naval Discipline (Dominion Naval Forces) Act 1911; these also included provision for the death penalty to be applied for a range of offences.

In contrast to New Zealand, Australia had legislated to modify the application of the death penalty—a step which had its roots in nineteenth century legislation of the Australian states. The Australian Defence Act 1903, in applying the Army Act to Australian forces, made a significant reservation in relation to the death penalty. Not only was the number of offences subject to the death penalty restricted to four but also the carrying out of any sentence was subject to confirmation by the Governor-General of Australia. The Australian naval forces were covered by a similar provision in the relevant naval legislation.

Although an adequate legal basis already existed for the application of the Army Act 1881 to 1NZEF during the ★First World War, specific statutory authority was provided in the Expeditionary Forces Act 1915. The only modifications again related to imprisonment. Of the twenty-eight members of 1NZEF sentenced to death, twenty-three had their sentences commuted or quashed after review; five sentences were confirmed and carried out. Those executed were Private Frank Hughes (25 August 1916), Private J.J. Sweeney (2 October 1916), Private John Braithwaite (29 October 1916), Private John King (19 August 1917), and Private Victor Spencer (24 February 1918). Sweeney and King (an assumed name) were Australians, who had the misfortune to be serving in 1NZEF, rather than in the Australian Imperial Force. The latter served under the terms of the 1903 Australian legislation, which in practice prevented any of the 121 death sentences inflicted on its members during the First World War from being carried out. All but one of the five New Zealand soldiers were court-martialled and executed by the New Zealand divisional authorities for the crime of desertion. The odd one out was Braithwaite, who was sentenced to death (along with three Australians) for mutiny at Blargies North Military Prison in Rouen in 1916. Braithwaite went before the firing squad, while the Australians had their sentences commuted to two years' hard labour.

Partly because they were not publicised at the time (outside army orders), partly because of a general public acceptance of the death penalty as a basis for military discipline and as the punishment for the civil crime of murder, these executions attracted little attention at the time. Not until the mid 1980s did they become a matter of controversy, especially as a reflection of growing interest in Great Britain in the more than 300 executions of British troops during the First World War. Some in both countries have called for the executed soldiers to be pardoned on the grounds that the courts martial were superficial or that the men were suffering from ★shell-shock. In New Zealand the government, supported by the NZRSA, resisted such pressure, arguing that the executions must be judged according to the conditions of the time rather than the social and emotional predilections of the present. While harsh punishment, the executions were an application of the law of the time. Moreover, there is little evidence that any of the New Zealanders who suffered this fate were afflicted by shell-shock, apart from Spencer, who claimed to have been blown up by a shell and may have been debilitated by his service at ★Gallipoli (which might perhaps have mitigated his sentence). It has not been demonstrated that the law was misapplied; nor has new evidence come to light that calls into question the verdicts, as opposed to the confirmation of the sentences. Nevertheless, continuing publicity about the cases led to the appointment, in 1999, of retired Court of Appeal judge Sir Edward Somers to review all the cases involving death sentences in 1NZEF. His report, released in October 1999, dismissed the idea of a pardon for the men, noted that they were all suffering from some disorder, and suggested a statement in Parliament to the effect that they were brave men and victims of the war. However, in 2000, the Labour-led government resolved to 'pardon' the soldiers.

In the ★Second World War, New Zealand ensured that the Australian precedent was followed in relation to the 2nd New Zealand Expeditionary Force. The Expeditionary Force Emergency Regulations 1940 applied the Army Act to all members of the force while out of New Zealand but provided that no sentence of death should be carried out 'without the concurrence of the Governor-General'. New Zealanders attached to the RAF and other air forces were, by the provisions of the Air Force Act 1937, subject to those forces' disciplinary provisions 'in all respects', while naval personnel serving in the Royal Navy remained subject, as previously, to British naval discipline. In all three services, therefore, the death penalty was available as punishment, but between the wars amendments to the British legislation had left only mutiny and treachery as punishable by death. There were only four executions for military offences—three for mutiny and one for treachery—by the British forces in the Second World War. No New Zealanders are known to have been sentenced to death.

The New Zealand Army Act 1950 and the Royal New Zealand Air Force Act 1950 finally cut New Zealand's links with the British disciplinary legislation for those two services. They both included provision for the death penalty for treachery or mutiny. In keeping with the British system which it replaced, this legislation prescribed life imprisonment as the maximum penalty for the crimes of cowardice or desertion. New Zealand naval personnel remained subject to the British naval discipline regime until the passage of the Armed Forces Discipline Act 1971. The death penalty was not finally removed from New Zealand's system of military discipline until 1989, at which time its application for the crime of treason (the only death penalty offence for civilians) was also ended.

C. Pugsley, *On the Fringe of Hell: New Zealanders and Military Discipline in the First World War* (Hodder & Stoughton, Auckland, 1991); 'Braithwaite, John', *Dictionary of New Zealand Biography*, vol III (Auckland University Press/Department of Internal Affairs, Auckland, 1996).

Deere, Wing Commander Alan Christopher

(12 December 1917–21 September 1995) was a leading New Zealand fighter ace of the ★Second World War. A law clerk from Wanganui, he joined the RAF in 1937 and three years later was stationed with 54 Squadron in France. His aptitude for aerial combat was demonstrated in his first dogfight, on 19 May 1940, when two enemy aircraft fell victim to his cannon. By the end of the month he was an ace, having made seven 'kills'. He survived being shot down near Dunkirk and a mid-air collision during the Battle of Britain, escaping the latter with minor burns despite a parachute malfunction (he landed in a cesspool). With justification he would later entitle his memoirs, published in 1959, *Nine Lives*. His exploits in 1940 won him a DFC and bar. He commanded 602 Squadron in 1942 and the Wing at Biggin Hill in the following year. By the time he was ordered to ground duties in September 1943, he had accounted for twenty-one enemy aircraft. He was made a DSO in 1943 and an OBE two years later. After the war he held a variety of posts in the RAF until his retirement in 1967.

Defence, Department of

was the main instrument of defence administration from 1863 to 1937. Before 1863 military matters, such as the keeping of annual militia lists, were handled by the Colonial Secretariat. When in August 1859 Captain H.C. Balneavis was appointed as Deputy Adjutant-General for Militia and Volunteers, the Militia and Volunteer Office so established also operated through the Colonial Secretariat. The Colonial Defence Office, which assumed responsibility for defence matters in July 1863, continued for some time to have close links to the Colonial Secretariat as well. William Seed was the first Under-Secretary for Colonial Defence. Subsequent Under-Secretaries, usually military officers, often doubled as de facto commandant of the forces, but with the greater formalisation of New Zealand's defence machinery in the last two decades of the nineteenth century the relationship between the civilian and military component of the Department became an issue. While the Commander of the Forces had statutory responsibility for the forces, he did not control the resources upon which they depended. Despite vigorous efforts to change this situation by Major-General J.M. ★Babington, the Commandant from 1901 to 1906, who insisted that the system meant 'much unnecessary work and friction', the Premier, R.J. ★Seddon, adamantly opposed any change which would give greater control to the Commandant. He looked instead to co-location of the Commandant and the Under-Secretary in the same building to help improve the relationship between them. The abolition of both positions under the arrangements for a Council of Defence which pertained from 1907 to 1910 resolved this problem. Even after this system was superseded in 1910 by the appointment of Major-General A.J. ★Godley as GOC of the New Zealand Military Forces, the failure to appoint a new Under-Secretary ensured that there would be no resumption of the earlier friction. Under his successor, Major-General A.W. ★Robin, the Department made its greatest effort in supporting the ★New Zealand Expeditionary Force in Europe from 1914 to 1919. With the creation of the ★New Zealand Division of the Royal Navy in 1921, a separate Navy Office was established to administer naval policy. In November 1930 an Under-Secretary for Defence was again appointed, mainly with a view to searching out potential economies in defence spending. Henry Turner held the position until the Department was replaced in 1937 by three separate service departments (see NAVY DEPARTMENT; ARMY DEPARTMENT; AIR DEPARTMENT).

Defence, higher organisation of

Arrangements for the higher command and control of the armed forces are detailed in the ★Defence Act 1990. The Governor-General is Commander-in-Chief in and over New Zealand and is authorised 'in the name and on behalf of the Sovereign to continue to raise and maintain armed forces' for a variety of purposes. The Minister of Defence has 'the power of control of the New Zealand Defence Force'. That control is exercised through the Chief of Defence Force (CDF), who not only 'commands the armed forces' but also is 'the principal military adviser' to the government. This makes explicit the relationship between the political and uniformed professional leaders. Until 1990 (when the existing defence legislation was revised), the Minister of Defence's powers were explicitly defined as being 'political control of the Ministry', which did 'not mean command of the Armed Forces'. Now that command by the CDF is made explicit, that explanation is apparently no longer necessary.

Although the individual services generally operate independently of each other, there is an overall command and control structure, working through the Headquarters of the ★New Zealand Defence Force and a separate, primarily civilian, Ministry of Defence headed by the Secretary of Defence (see DEFENCE, MINISTRY OF). This higher defence organisation provides advice to the government, sets broad policy directions for and commands the armed forces, and establishes the way defence funding is used. The dual organisation has been in place since the major defence reorganisation of the late 1980s. Advice on wider defence policy matters is the responsibility of the Secretary of Defence as the government's principal civilian adviser. In recognition of the importance of the military component to defence advice, the Secretary's advice has to be formulated in consultation with the Chief of Defence Force. Although the CDF's advice role is theoretically limited to military matters, in practice it is almost impossible to differentiate between the kinds of advice that might be given by the Secretary and by the CDF. The system can only work effectively if the two officials and their departments work closely together.

The Ministry of Defence is small, comprising only about seventy people in total. It has three main operating divisions involved in policy matters. The Policy and Planning Division provides advice on defence policy goals, capabilities, and relationships, and on the enhancement of regional security. The Acquisition Division is responsible for the management of procurement of new defence capability, including project investigation, quality assurance, equipment selection, and the negotiation and execution of contract arrangements. The Evaluation Division provides independent external evaluations of NZDF management functions and systems, outputs and programmes, and policies and practices for resource management. It also reviews the management of equipment procurement projects.

The Headquarters of the NZDF, with about ninety military and 250 civil staff, is considerably larger than the Ministry of Defence. It needs to be, for the range of functions it undertakes is considerably greater, but it is still a small organisation at about 2 per cent of the total strength of the NZDF (uniformed and civilian) and very small when compared with its counterparts in other countries. The main 'policy' branches are those dealing with strategic policy and force development. The operations, resources, and personnel branches deal with policy issues at a more immediate working level than the other two. The CDF has a strategic policy adviser, who is responsible for providing 'competent and timely policy advice on matters affecting New Zealand's international defence relations'. The Development Branch advises the CDF on medium- to long-term development of the NZDF in terms of organisation, capabilities, and doctrine.

A ★Chiefs of Staff Committee comprises the CDF and the individual service Chiefs of Staff. The Deputy Chief of Defence Staff (DCDS) is an associate member of this committee, which has only limited terms of reference. It is advisory, and its functions, duties, and powers are determined by the CDF. Members are entitled to have their dissenting and varying opinions conveyed to the Minister of Defence by the CDF, who will add such advice 'as the Chief of Defence Force considers appropriate'. There is close consultation and coordination between the Ministry of Defence and the Defence Force, to the extent in some areas that they act as one organisation. This is a partial return to the diarchic structure of the 1970s and 1980s. Both organisations are based in the same building and, in recognition of the need for close cooperation, elements of the NZDF Force Development Branch work alongside the Ministry's Policy Branch. At the highest level there is an Office of the Chief Executives, which 'brings together many aspects of the two organisations' activities'; the two chief executives and their advisers hold a regular weekly meeting. A Defence Policy Committee exists to ensure that each organisation is formally aware of the other's position, and a Defence Evaluation Board coordinates programming and reviews of the NZDF carried out by the Ministry of Defence. There are also functional activities, such as public relations, which are shared. As well, ad hoc project teams are formed and dissolved according to specific needs, and there is constant consultation between officials from each organisation. In the late 1990s this dual higher defence organisation was being questioned on the grounds, apparently, that the duplication of activities between the Ministry of Defence and the NZDF was not efficient. Nevertheless, it seems likely that this broad structure will provide the basis of the country's higher defence organisation for some time to come. There may be some amalgamation of functions between the Ministry of Defence and the Headquarters of the NZDF, but the overall model of a professional uniformed officer working with a senior civilian policy adviser will remain into the future.

J. Rolfe, *Defending New Zealand: A Study of Structures, Processes and Relationships* (Institute of Policy Studies, Wellington, 1993); J. Rolfe, *The Armed Forces of New Zealand* (Allen & Unwin, Sydney, 1999).

JAMES ROLFE

Defence, Ministry of There were two main influences behind the establishment of the Ministry of Defence in 1963. First, the need for more effective arrangements to coordinate the activities of the three service departments had become apparent. The

Defence, Ministry of

The first meeting of the Defence Council on 20 November 1964. From the left, standing: A.D. McIntosh (Secretary of External Affairs), D.W.A. Barker (Deputy Secretary of the Treasury), Rear-Admiral R.E. Washbourn (CNS), D.J. Eyre (Minister of Defence), Air Vice-Marshal I.G. Morrison (CAS), Major-General L.W. Thornton (CGS); seated are J.K. Hunn (Secretary of Defence) and Vice-Admiral Peter Phipps (CDS) (*NZDF*)

existing system, based on the ★Defence Secretariat in the Prime Minister's Department, had evolved largely around the personality and skills of Foss ★Shanahan, and his departure in 1955 had left a significant gap. Second, and more important, financial imperatives increasingly pointed the way towards rationalisation and integration of the functions of the service departments. Pressure on New Zealand's defence funds was being imposed by the need to re-equip New Zealand's forces in the late 1950s at a time when cheaper war surplus materiel was no longer available.

The driving force behind the reorganisation of New Zealand's defence machinery was the Minister of Defence, Dean ★Eyre. He developed proposals for the creation of a fourth department, which would bring together the civil administrations of the three services and incorporate the Defence Secretariat. This approach was endorsed by the Royal Commission on the State Services in 1962, and on 5 November of that year the Cabinet approved the creation of a coordinating body along these lines. A Secretary of Defence and an Independent Chairman of the ★Chiefs of Staff Committee were to be appointed, and an officials committee established. Jack ★Hunn became Secretary of Defence on 8 July 1963, just after Vice-Admiral Peter ★Phipps took up his appointment as Independent Chairman, a title which was soon changed to Chief of Defence Staff.

Even at the time of its decision to establish the new department, which was soon designated the Ministry of Defence, the Cabinet had looked to a further restructuring to establish a unitary department. One of Hunn's first tasks, therefore, was to examine the feasibility of this course. His recommendation in favour of a unitary department was approved by the Cabinet on 29 October 1963, and came into effect on the following 1 January. A statutory basis for the new organisation was provided by the ★Defence Act of 17 November 1964, legislation that was developed amid much controversy within the defence hierarchy. A ★Defence Council was created. Awkwardly the existing Service boards, with the minister in the chair, remained in existence, a reflection of the successful rearguard action fought by the services to mitigate the effect of the new structure on their independence.

The reorganisation was completed in 1971. The Secretary of Defence, J.F. ★Robertson, an expert in the theory of organisational restructuring, and the Chief of Defence Staff, Lieutenant-General L.W. ★Thornton, played a significant role in developing a new approach to the reorganisation. This stressed the importance of minimising service resistance by fully involving the services in the process as partners rather than as adversaries. A new scheme was developed under which the service boards would be abolished but the services themselves would retain their separate existence. Command of the armed forces would be vested in the Defence Council but would be exercised by the Chief of the Defence Staff through the three Chiefs of Staff, who would remain the heads of their respective services. On this basis, a diarchic system evolved in which the Secretary of Defence took responsibility for administration and the Chief of Defence Staff for command and control of the armed forces. Integrated personnel and support branches were created, and the services were reshaped to fit the new structure. Of the services, the most affected was the Army: its long-standing district structure was replaced by a Field Force Command and a Home Command. In 1971, these changes were embodied in a further Defence Act which came into effect on 1 April 1972.

The diarchic system fell victim to the reforms of the 1980s, which were driven partly by an ideological requirement for a split between policy and provision and partly by a desire on the part of the government for the availability of contestable advice. The outcome was the reconstitution of the Ministry of Defence as a small policy-making organ, and the establishment of a separate ★New Zealand Defence Force, responsible for the command of the armed forces (see DEFENCE, HIGHER ORGANISATION OF).

Defence Act provides the statutory basis for the maintenance of armed forces in New Zealand. The first such legislation, 'An Act to amend and consolidate the Laws relating to the Militia, Volunteers, and Permanent Militia' of 31 July 1886, addressed the need to establish a small professional force to man the ★coast defences which had been hastily thrown up following the Russian scare the previous year. Together with a separate Police Act, it provided for the separation of police and military functions hitherto carried out under the ★Armed Constabulary and its successor, the New Zealand Constabulary Force. A ★Permanent Militia was created from the latter's Field Force. The roles of the Governor, the ★Militia, and the ★Volunteer Force in New Zealand's defence scheme were clarified, and provision was made for the enrolment of volunteers for 'special or emergent service or public danger', who would be deemed to be on actual service and liable to the provisions of the imperial Army Act 1881. An amendment to the Defence Act in 1900 provided a statutory basis for the responsibilities of the Commandant of the Defence Forces, which had earlier been brought into question during Colonel F.J. ★Fox's tenure as Commandant. It also authorised the establishment of an ★Imperial Reserve, in which volunteers could subject themselves to the liability to serve overseas, though the scheme was never implemented. Another amendment passed in 1906 established the Council of Defence. These measures were consolidated in the Defence Act 1908.

This earlier legislation was overhauled in 1909. 'An Act to make Better Provision for the Internal Defence of New Zealand' on 24 December 1909 authorised a major reorganisation of New Zealand's military forces. It provided for the replacement of the Volunteer Force by the ★Territorial Force, and for ★compulsory military training as the basis for manning the new force. The abolition of election of officers was an important step towards improving professionalism. Substantial amendments soon modified the Act's provisions, including the replacement of the Council of Defence by a Commandant and the extension of the age of eligibility for CMT to twenty-five in 1910. A 1912 amendment concerned punishments for evasion of military training. The Act was repealed with the passage of the New Zealand Army Act on 1 December 1950.

A new Defence Act, 'An Act to establish the Ministry of Defence and to provide a unified defence policy for the better defence of New Zealand', was passed on 17 November 1964. Apart from formally establishing the Ministry of Defence, it established a ★Defence Council, defined the responsibilities of the Chief of Defence Staff and Secretary of Defence, and clarified the position of the three service boards in the new structure. Further reorganisation of the higher defence framework, including in particular the abolition of the service boards, was formalised by a new Defence Act on 12 November 1971. This structure was replaced nineteen years later with the separation of the ★New Zealand Defence Force from the Ministry of Defence. On 1 April 1990 the changes were given statutory backing by another Defence Act which, apart from constituting the NZDF, defined the responsibilities of the Minister of Defence, Chief of Defence Force, and the Secretary of Defence, and the relationship of the CDF with the three service ★Chiefs of Staff. (See DEFENCE, HIGHER ORGANISATION OF; DEFENCE, MINISTRY OF)

Defence Committee of Enquiry (Corner Committee) Anxious to formulate a new direction for New Zealand's defence policy to offset the effects of the ★ANZUS dispute arising from the ★*Buchanan* affair, the Labour government constituted a Defence

Defence construction

Committee of Enquiry in late 1985. Chaired by former Secretary of Foreign Affairs F.H. Corner, with Dr Kevin Clements, Diane Hunt, and Major-General B.M. *Poananga as members, it was charged with ascertaining the attitudes of New Zealanders towards defence and security issues. Perhaps to the surprise of the Prime Minister, David *Lange, the committee, after wide consultation and extensive polling, reported in July 1986 in a sense which implied criticism of his government's policy. It noted, in particular, that a substantial majority of the population favoured both New Zealand's membership of ANZUS and a nuclear-free policy, but that confronted with the incompatibility of these two approaches a clear majority (52 per cent) preferred a return to an operational ANZUS with the acceptance of ship visits on the previous 'neither confirm nor deny' basis. Lange's distaste for the findings was reflected in a terse exchange with Corner in which he queried various aspects of the committee's report.

Defence and Security: What New Zealanders Want, Report of the Defence Committee of Enquiry July 1986 (Wellington, 1986).

Defence construction began with the building of the first Maori pa (see MAORI DEFENCE WORKS). During the *New Zealand Wars British and colonial forces built roads, redoubts, and blockhouses in various parts of the North Island, while the Vogel works scheme of the 1870s was undertaken in part for internal security purposes (see FORTIFICATIONS). New Zealand's most substantial defence construction effort in the nineteenth century developed the *coast defences from 1885. Drill halls, rifle ranges, and barracks provided the beginnings of a defence infrastructure. During the *First World War, construction was largely confined to some barracks at Trentham, Featherston, and other camps about the country. Development of aerodromes and of the naval base at Devonport were the most important construction projects of the period between the world wars. Such efforts were greatly expanded during the *Second World War, with the institution of a major programme of barracks, road, and aerodrome construction. Until 1941 this work was carried out by the Public Works Department along largely traditional lines, contracting private firms to implement specific projects. This approach proved inadequate following the outbreak of the *Pacific War and the urgent need for additional fortifications and barracks for the mobilised home defence forces. As a result authorisation procedures for defence construction were streamlined at the beginning of 1942, with local military commanders being given greater latitude to initiate works. The appointment, in March 1942, of James Fletcher as Commissioner of Defence Construction was of crucial importance. Given the power to stop any construction, let contracts, and direct or commandeer any labour or materials as necessary, he went about his task with great energy and determination, overseeing a massive expansion of defence construction. In 1943 the government created the Ministry of Works, with Fletcher as its head, and regulation of defence construction gradually eased. By far the greatest amount of defence construction was carried out in the development of *Army camps, starting with the mobilisation camps at Trentham, Papakura, and Burnham, and eventually covering about 6900 hectares in all. From 1942 this work was expanded to include the construction of facilities for American forces in the Auckland and Wellington areas. The building of a camp for 20,000 American soldiers at Paekakariki in six weeks was a particularly notable achievement. Most of the camps were prefabricated huts, nearly 29,000 of which were constructed during the war. Other important works included gun emplacements, anti-aircraft positions, and coastal defences. Road building and improvement, especially on the strategically important roads connecting with Waiouru, was undertaken. A hundred aerodromes with 280 kilometres of runway were either constructed or improved in New Zealand and in the Pacific during the war. Overall, about £50 million of construction work was carried out—equivalent to the construction of seventeen towns complete with electricity, sewerage, drainage, and water supplies.

Defence construction was drastically scaled back after 1945. Most of the various camps and bases were dismantled or turned over to civilian use. Other facilities dating from the war (such as those at Waiouru and Linton) remained the basis of the defence infrastructure well into the 1980s. There was, however, sporadic defence construction, essentially the replacement of wartime prefabricated huts with more permanent facilities. The most significant defence construction since the Second World War has been at Linton Camp. While the services have undertaken some of this recent construction themselves, most is tendered out to private contractors.

Defence Council The first Council of Defence, established on 5 January 1907, brought New Zealand into line with changes in army direction in the United Kingdom. The Minister of Defence presided over five officers: three military members (the Chief of the General Staff, the Adjutant and Quartermaster-General, and the Inspector-General of the Forces), a Finance member, and a Secretary. Each member was responsible for a specific area of the headquarters of the military forces. The Council did not prove particularly effective as a system of administration. Differences of

Defence Council

The officers who attended the first meeting of the Council of Defence in 1907: (from left) Colonel R.H. Davies (Inspector-General), Colonel R.J. Collins (Finance member), Colonel W.H. Webb (Secretary), Colonel A.W. Robin (CGS) (*New Zealand Graphic and Ladies Journal*)

opinion between its president, Sir Joseph ★Ward, and the military members over the contentious issue of ★compulsory military training no doubt influenced the government's attitude. By 1909 the Council had withered as new members were not appointed to replace the Inspector, the Adjutant, and the Secretary, all of whom had either gone to Great Britain or retired. Convinced that the system was 'far from a success', Colonel A.W. ★Robin, the CGS, urged—and the visiting Lord ★Kitchener strongly endorsed—the appointment of a major-general to command the forces. The government accepted this proposal, and the Council lapsed when Major-General A.J. ★Godley took up his duties on 7 December 1910.

A new Council of Defence was instituted by the first Labour government to oversee the work of the ★Organisation for National Security. Designed as an advisory and coordinating body, rather than as an administrative entity, it had the Prime Minister as president and comprised the Minister of Defence, the three ★Chiefs of Staff, the head of the Prime Minister's Department, and such other members as the Prime Minister might decide. It convened for the first time on 8 July 1937, and met at relatively frequent intervals until the outbreak of the ★Second World War. From February 1940 it was superseded by the Cabinet Committee on Defence, though the Chiefs of Staff continued to attend. The Council of Defence was reconstituted as an advisory body on 3 July 1946 with a similar membership as before the war, except that officials now participated in a consultative capacity only. It was fairly active in 1947, after which meetings became sporadic. The council lapsed with the fall of the Labour government in 1949.

The incoming National administration was persuaded to continue the arrangement by creating a Defence Committee, which had its first meeting on 26 June 1950 and which from February 1951 was known as the Defence Council. Like its predecessor, it brought together ministers and officials. Some initial uncertainty about the status of officials was resolved in 1952, with their formal exclusion from membership. Meetings became increasingly irregular, and were convened mainly to hear visiting overseas defence officials. A Cabinet Committee on Defence established in 1955 largely usurped the Council's role, and by 1959 it was regarded as defunct.

A new Defence Council, established as a result of the reorganisation of New Zealand's higher defence machinery in the 1960s (see DEFENCE, MINISTRY OF), held its first meeting on 20 November 1964. Responsible for the control and administration of the

Defence lobby groups

armed services, it was more akin to the 1907–10 Council than to the more recent councils, with the Minister of Defence again presiding. The Secretary of Defence, the Chief of Defence Staff, and the three service Chiefs of Staff sat as full members, while the Secretary of External Affairs and the Secretary to the Treasury were coopted members. Until 1971, the system was complicated by the continued existence of Naval, Air, and Army Boards, each also presided over by the Minister of Defence and subordinate to the Defence Council. The Council provided an effective means of coordinating defence activities until it was abolished in 1990 after a further reorganisation of New Zealand's higher defence machinery.

Defence lobby groups are a means of exerting pressure on the government on defence issues. Although the New Zealand public tends towards apathy on defence matters in peacetime, a number of influential organisations have from time to time made an appearance. The first was a branch of the British-based Navy League formed at Auckland in 1896 with the stated aim of mobilising public support for the Royal Navy and educating the public about the necessity for British naval superiority. Although enjoying a low profile in New Zealand until 1904, the Navy League thereafter grew rapidly as the Anglo-German naval race awakened public concern. Popular and respectable, it campaigned tirelessly on the need for further naval armaments and imperial patriotism, organised patriotic occasions such as the annual Trafalgar Day, and disseminated propaganda chiefly aimed at children. Always insisting that it was above party politics, it was most influential before the ★First World War. During the ★Second World War it was active in providing comforts to sailors. Later renamed the New Zealand Navy League, it concentrated after 1945 on supporting the Sea Cadets. More recently it has shifted its focus back to the educative role, though without attaining great influence in the 1990s.

A far more radical defence pressure group was the National Defence League. Founded in 1906 by W.B. Leyland and W. Lane, it sought to influence public opinion in favour of ★compulsory military training. Aggressively militarist and imperialist in tone, it played on fears of invasion and racial degeneration. Like the Navy League, it claimed to be above party politics, though its membership was predominantly conservative. With its aims having been met in the ★Defence Act 1909, it was wound up in 1910, but was revived after the First World War, under the presidency of Major-General Sir Andrew ★Russell, with a view to encouraging the government to maintain effective armed forces. It made little headway and was virtually moribund by the early 1930s. However, the deteriorating international situation led to its re-emergence later in the decade, though it never achieved great influence with a Labour government unenthusiastic about military matters. A further attempt to revive it in the 1950s to support compulsory military training came to nothing.

More recently, lobbying on defence issues has been generally restricted to individual retired servicemen, ★veterans' organisations (especially the NZRSA), and members of what has come to be known as the peace movement. Perhaps predictably, the RSA has been supportive of New Zealand's traditional approach to defence, based on participation in alliances, and has consistently advocated greater defence spending. On the other side, a myriad of groups have questioned the role of New Zealand's armed forces, both generally and in specific situations such as the ★Vietnam War, called for changes in New Zealand defence policy, or focused attention on broader security matters, such as nuclear proliferation. Some have been broad-based coalitions of groups, like the Campaign for Nuclear Disarmament; others have scrupulously avoided indicating the extent of their membership. 'Just Defence', which was active in lobbying against the decision to acquire Anzac class frigates in the late 1980s, falls into this latter category, gaining considerable publicity for views which may have represented the opinions of a very small group. Manufacturers who saw opportunities in the frigate project for New Zealand industry provided another lobby group on this issue.

Defence reviews are major studies of New Zealand's defence requirements carried out by the government and those agencies responsible for New Zealand's external security. They traverse the strategic environment and New Zealand's place in it, New Zealand's defence philosophy and strategy, equipment requirements, and the financial implications of the proposed policy. Although reports on New Zealand defence requirements have been produced almost from the inception of the colony, the practice of officers of different services jointly reviewing policy dates from 1934–35. Carried out periodically since the ★Second World War, defence reviews have tended to have a direct political purpose, perhaps to justify a new government's change of focus or direction or to introduce a new force structure. In recent times attempts to formalise the process have not been completely successful. From 1989 the Ministry of Defence was charged with producing an annual defence assessment, but completion of the initial efforts proved difficult and it was decided that the assessments should be biennial. Even this proved difficult, however, and the long-delayed 1996 assessment was the last to be carried out in the decade. Since 1957 the outcomes of reviews and assessments have from time to time been published in parliamentary white papers. There have been nine of the latter over the last forty years, the most recent, in 1997, setting out an investment plan to rebuild New Zealand's defence capabilities.

Defence schemes The first Defence Scheme, a detailed mobilisation plan, was prepared in 1897. This was New Zealand's belated response to British urging of such action over the previous decade. It was intended that all the self-governing colonies should submit their schemes to the *Colonial Defence Committee in London for comment, and that the schemes would be updated annually. However, New Zealand only revised its scheme at intermittent intervals in the early part of the twentieth century.

Defence Secretariat During and following the *Second World War, the need for coordination of New Zealand's defence effort had increased the importance of the *Chiefs of Staff Committee, and led to the establishment of a number of subordinate joint service committees. To service this growing machinery the Defence Secretariat was created within the Prime Minister's Department in 1949. Several service officers were seconded to it to be secretaries of the various joint committees. They functioned under the general supervision of Foss *Shanahan, who was a deputy secretary in the Prime Minister's Department. Although responsible to the Prime Minister, the Secretariat dealt directly with the Minister of Defence on service matters. It provided a service input to matters going before the Cabinet and was charged with ensuring the coordination of defence matters generally. Nevertheless its influence owed much to the personal qualities and standing of Shanahan, as became apparent following his departure in 1955. The need for a more effective means of coordination was one of the driving forces behind the establishment in 1963 of the Ministry of Defence, to which the Defence Secretariat was transferred (see DEFENCE, MINISTRY OF).

Denvir, Second Lieutenant John (5 May 1913–11 March 1973), a Glaswegian by birth, came to New Zealand as a boy. When the *Second World War began, he immediately enlisted in 2NZEF, and was posted to 20th Battalion. Taken prisoner of war in *Greece in May 1941, he succeeded in escaping from Marburg camp in the following December and made his way to the Slovenian capital, Ljubljana. After concluding that an attempt to reach neutral Turkey would be futile, he joined a partisan band. So effective a fighter did he prove that he rose to command first a company, later a battalion (2nd Battalion, 4th Slovenian National Freedom Shock (Ljubo Sercer) Brigade).

For a successful attack on a train in August 1943 he would later be awarded a DCM on the recommendation of the British liaison officer with the partisans. In September a bullet shattered the bones in his right arm—the fourth time he had been wounded in action. Known by the partisans as 'Frank', Denvir was given the honorary rank of lieutenant in the National Freedom Army, and later promoted to brigade commander, also an honorary rank. In January 1944, he was evacuated to Italy for hospital treatment, and subsequently repatriated to New Zealand after being commissioned in 2NZEF and awarded the Soviet Medal of Valour—the only member of the New Zealand forces to be so honoured. During a visit to Yugoslavia in 1955 he received the honorary rank of major in the Yugoslav Army, as well as several Yugoslav decorations.

J. Caffin, *Partisan* (Collins, Auckland, 1945).

Depth charges New Zealand was too isolated during the *First World War to be troubled by enemy submarines. Even during the inter-war years none of the *sloops on the *New Zealand Station carried depth charges. That changed drastically in the 1939–45 conflict when the government imported large quantities of depth charges. The most common weapon, the British *Second World War Mark VII, was a simple high-explosive-filled drum, pierced centrally by a hollow tube which carried a priming charge at one end and a pressure fuse and detonator at the other. The charge could be set to detonate by hydrostatic pressure. Charges were dropped from stern-mounted traps or rails. Typical RNZN converted anti-submarine minesweepers carried about twenty to fifty depth charges, Fairmile and HDML *patrol craft twelve and eight respectively. The Fairmiles' small Y-guns hurled pairs of charges either side of the ship. Depth charges were also adapted for delivery by aircraft, and the RNZAF acquired a stock of these weapons to replace its unsatisfactory anti-submarine bombs.

Because escorts lost asdic/sonar contact whenever they passed over their submerged target while manoeuvring to drop charges, Allied navies developed ahead throwing weapons (ATW) such as Hedgehog, which equipped the *corvettes HMNZS *Arabis* and *Arbutus*. This 24-spigot mortar fired contact-fused projectiles 183 metres ahead of the escort. The projectiles carried a 16-kilogram charge of Torpex. Success rates for Royal Navy ships using Hedgehog rose from 7.5 per cent in late 1943 to 28 per cent in late 1944.

Squid and the Mark 10 packed an even bigger punch. Squid entered Royal Navy service in 1943–44. This three-barrel, 12-inch mortar fired time-fused 177-kilogram bombs set automatically from a depth recorder. Unlike Hedgehog, direct hits from this big bomb were not necessary for kills. The British rated it twice as effective as Hedgehog, Squid ships achieving a 60 per cent success rate by early 1945. New Zealand's Loch class *frigates each mounted two.

Squid's post-war successor, the Mark 10, known unofficially as Limbo, was also a triple-barrelled weapon. Pitch- and roll-stabilised and loaded pneumatically, it could throw its 179-kilogram charges up to 1000 metres. The frigates HMNZS *Otago*, *Taranaki*, and *Blackpool* carried two Mark 10s and *Waikato* one, but by the time HMNZS *Canterbury* was commissioned in 1971 lightweight Mark 44 homing *torpedoes had replaced the mortars. The RNZN retired the Mark 10 during the 1980s. New Zealand frigates no longer mount depth charges, but the SH-2F and G Super Seasprite shipboard helicopters can carry the Mark 11 depth charge as well as other weapons. (See ANTI-SUBMARINE WARFARE)

GAVIN McLEAN

Despard, Major-General Henry (1784/5?–30 April 1859) commanded the imperial troops in the Northern War of 1845–46. His military career began in 1799, when he was commissioned as an ensign in the 17th Regiment. He took part in several campaigns in India between 1808 and 1818, and had reached the rank of lieutenant-colonel by 1829. After serving as inspecting officer in Bristol, he was sent to Sydney in 1842 to command the 99th Regiment. Following the outbreak of fighting in the Bay of Islands in March 1845, he crossed the Tasman with two of his regiment's companies in response to an appeal for assistance from New Zealand's Governor. He reached the scene of conflict in June as a temporary colonel at the head of more than 600 imperial troops. The ensuing campaign highlighted his personal and tactical deficiencies: quick-tempered, obstinate, and inflexible, he had little time for the Maori, his own allies included, and underestimated their martial capacity. At Ohaeawai, on 1 July, apparently infuriated by a rebel sortie, he made the mistake of ordering an assault on a pa whose defences remained intact despite several days' bombardment of them; half the 200-strong attacking force were killed or wounded before he called the operation off. Ten days later the now-deserted pa was occupied and destroyed. In December Despard led a much augmented force against a pa on a formidable hilltop position at Ruapekapeka, south of Kawakawa, which the rebels had fortified during a five-month break in the fighting. After his ally Tamati Waka *Nene (who described him as a 'very stupid person') counselled against an immediate attack, Despard laid siege to the pa. The subsequent fall of Ruapekapeka on Sunday 11 January 1846—perhaps while its defenders were at divine worship at the rear (though they may have been trying to draw the defenders into an ambush)—ended the war. After returning to New South Wales, Despard was made a CB for his services in July 1846. He was promoted to the rank of major-general and retired from the Army eight years later, and returned to the United Kingdom.

RICHARD TAYLOR

Disarmament is the reduction by states of their level of armaments, either unilaterally or more generally as the result of international agreements. The ultimate goal of such measures is often depicted as complete, multilateral abolition of weapons and the means of their deployment, but in practice the aim is generally to reduce arsenals to a less threatening level. The process is also associated with measures to control the development of new weapons or the deployment of existing weapons. Disarmament is therefore usually regarded as encompassing arms control, or arms limitation, as well as arms reduction.

New Zealand's first involvement with disarmament negotiations occurred in 1921 with its representation, as part of the British Empire Delegation, at the Washington Conference on Naval Arms Limitation. Sir John Salmond, on behalf of New Zealand, took part in discussions leading to agreement on a framework for security in the Pacific and on limitations of naval power to be deployed by the great powers. As a result, the British battlefleet was substantially reduced, with the New Zealand gift battlecruiser HMS *New Zealand* being one of the casualties. The conference also resulted in a prohibition on the construction of fortifications in a large part of the Pacific, designed to keep the British Empire, the United States, and Japan at arm's length from each other.

Further attempts to reduce naval arms took place at conferences in Geneva in 1927 and London in 1930. The former failed when the United States and British Empire deadlocked over the number of cruisers they were to be allowed. New Zealand's approach to both conferences was characterised by concern to prevent any derogation of British capacity to protect the long sea routes upon which it depended. To this end it strongly supported the Admiralty, with Lord *Jellicoe in 1927 adding the weight of his reputation as a member of New Zealand's delegation. (New Zealand's efforts to secure Jellicoe's services again at London in 1930 were foiled by the British Labour government, which was determined to secure an agreement even at the expense of big cuts in British cruiser strength.) Although unhappy with the resulting treaty, New Zealand used the bargaining power that the need for its ratification provided to ensure that there was not a complete shutdown of work on the strategically more important Singapore naval base (see SINGAPORE STRATEGY). By the time a further naval conference

Disarmament

was held in London in 1936 the emphasis had shifted to rearmament, and only weak limitation measures were agreed. In 1930 New Zealand had signed the Geneva Protocol banning the use of chemical and bacteriological weapons—a measure that had been prompted by the use of gas by both sides during the ★First World War.

Since the ★Second World War the main focus of disarmament and arms control has been on nuclear weapons, especially as the size of the American and Soviet nuclear arsenals increased during the ★Cold War. Although New Zealand did not have such weapons, and the government in 1963 would proclaim New Zealand's intention not to acquire them, it had an interest in the arms race because of the threat which a nuclear conflict would pose to the security of all states. From the late 1950s, moreover, a small but often vociferous lobby group called for nuclear disarmament (see ANTI-NUCLEARISM). New Zealand's firm adherence until the 1980s to the Western framework of security, which was based on nuclear deterrence and ★ANZUS, constrained its approach to such issues, but intensifying Cold War tensions in the early 1980s increased the influence of the 'peace movement'. During the 1984–90 Labour administration, New Zealand not only withdrew from participation in ANZUS but also rejected nuclear deterrence as the basis of Western security. The government, perhaps seeking to deflect left-wing criticism of its hardline economic strategy, campaigned actively against nuclear weapons, though claiming that New Zealand's nuclear-free policy was not for export. A Minister of Disarmament and Arms Control was appointed in 1987. The main thrust of the Labour policy was continued by the National and National-led coalition governments of the 1990s—a situation foreshadowed by the National Party's adoption of the nuclear-free policy prior to the general election in 1990.

As a state without nuclear weapons, and far from the main areas of conflict, New Zealand has had no direct influence on the most important disarmament and arms control talks—the bilateral negotiations between the United States and the Soviet Union (and its successor the Russian Federation) on strategic weapons. It has, however, been supportive of these powers' efforts to limit the growth of their nuclear arsenals and more recently, especially since the end of the Cold War and the collapse of the Soviet Union, to reduce the number of warheads on both sides. New Zealand's involvement in disarmament negotiations since the Second World War has been largely confined to the ★United Nations, and to four main forums. First, in the UN General Assembly and in particular its First Committee, New Zealand has regularly co-sponsored resolutions, including a joint effort with Australia calling for a comprehensive nuclear test ban. Although Cold War influences limited the effectiveness of such action until the late 1980s, a more constructive approach has been possible since then. The second forum was the Geneva-based Conference on Disarmament, established in 1978 as result of the UN Special Session on Disarmament. The conference, which reports annually to the UN General Assembly, succeeded earlier conferences from 1961 and included the five declared nuclear-weapons states (United States, Soviet Union, France, Great Britain, and China) and more than thirty other states. Although not a member, New Zealand was able to participate as an observer from 1984, devoting its attention in particular to such issues as ★chemical weapons, a nuclear test ban, and negative security assurances. In 1996 it was accorded full membership, along with twenty-two other states. The conference, which holds three sessions a year, operates on the basis of consensus—an approach which left little scope for progress on the most difficult issues until the end of the Cold War. Another forum has been provided by the UN Disarmament Commission, which was established in 1982 by the Second Special Session on Disarmament. Comprising all members of the United Nations, it is a deliberative body which makes recommendations to the UN General Assembly on all aspects of disarmament. Again, a lack of consensus during the Cold War ensured much 'sterile discussion' in the commission. New Zealand sought to improve the commission's functioning in the late 1980s. Finally, New Zealand has taken part in several seminars on disarmament issues organised by the UN Regional Centre for Peace and Disarmament in Asia and the Pacific in Kathmandu.

New Zealand's interest in arms control measures was reflected in its signature of the 1968 Nuclear Non-Proliferation Treaty, under which it pledged not to develop nuclear weapons. This measure was regarded as central to curbing the spread of nuclear weapons, and at a review conference held in 1995 New Zealand agreed to the treaty remaining in force indefinitely, despite some agitation against such a course by anti-nuclear activists on the grounds that it legitimised possession of nuclear weapons by the five declared nuclear powers. By 1999 there were 186 signatories to the treaty, though several important states, including India, Pakistan, and Israel, remained outside its ambit. New Zealand strongly supported the Comprehensive Test Ban Treaty, which was concluded in 1996 (though not yet in force). It was also prominent in the establishment of the South Pacific Nuclear Weapon Free Zone in 1985.

Although nuclear issues have dominated the disarmament and arms control agenda, attention has also been given to non-nuclear weapons, especially in the more constructive post–Cold War atmosphere of the

Discipline

1990s. New Zealand added its voice to calls for the conclusion of conventions covering the elimination of both chemical and bacteriological weapons, the reduction of conventional arsenals, and more recently the banning of anti-personnel landmines.

R. Alley, 'The Awesome Glow in the Sky: New Zealand and Disarmament', in M. McKinnon (ed), *New Zealand in World Affairs, Volume II: 1957–1972* (New Zealand Institute of International Affairs, Wellington, 1991).

Discipline, the means by which control and order are exercised over members of the armed forces, is the basis of effective military organisation. It serves to maintain law and order among armed forces so that they can carry out their tasks effectively and unencumbered by indecision. It derives from two basic sources—external rules imposed on all service personnel and internal motivation leading to self-discipline. Formal military discipline imported into New Zealand from the British Army and Royal Navy sat uneasily with settlers' conceptions of autonomy. Hence a robust sense of democratic rights was evident within the ★Volunteer Force, where election of officers and the voluntary part-time nature of the service prevented any real discipline being imposed. The ★Boer War experience encouraged the belief in New Zealand that formal discipline was less important than self-reliance and initiative. Despite the creation of the ★Territorial Force, the introduction of ★compulsory military training, and a concomitant tightening of discipline under the supervision of regular imperial officers, large numbers of New Zealanders did not find themselves subject to the full rigour of military discipline until the ★First World War. During both world wars the formal disciplinary apparatus was reinforced by informal mechanisms, such as knowledge that a serviceman's conduct could become well known in the small communities to which he would eventually return.

From the moment they enlisted, service personnel were subject to a regime which monitored their every move. Drill, military protocols such as saluting, and ★uniforms were designed to inculcate instinctive patterns of obedience and discipline that allowed military commanders to command and control those under them. The seemingly ludicrous bureaucratic process of military life was fundamental to discipline. It was also necessary because military units generally operate in areas independent of normal support facilities.

Those who strayed outside the web of military discipline often found themselves subject to sanctions codified in the Army Act 1881, various Queen's or King's Regulations, and Special and Routine Orders. The enforcement of discipline without undue delay was not only intended to punish the offender but also to serve as a deterrent to others. An important factor in the process of military discipline was command. It was the serviceman's commanding officer who, for summary offences, judged and awarded a sentence. Despite proposals during the ★Second World War to establish special permanent military courts, the principle was retained that a soldier should be tried by officers from his own unit.

In general, punishments meted out during the First World War were harsher than those meted out during the Second World War. At the front, a desire not to 'let down one's mates' often played a larger role in ensuring effective discipline than it did in at the rear, where most acts of ill discipline were observed. Most breaches were brief absences from camp or drunkenness. This was particularly the case during the Second World War, with mass drunkenness occurring when entire units were taken out of the line and given leave en masse. Breaches of discipline that directly attacked the fabric of military order and discipline received particularly heavy punishment. For example, threatening or striking an officer was punished by a lengthy sentence of penal servitude.

Most breaches of discipline were dealt with by a simple warning, and officers were instructed to admonish first-time offenders for minor breaches of discipline. Although officers and NCOs were normally not permitted to abuse their subordinates, the exigencies of ★active service, coupled with the undesirable administrative requirements of formal punishment, more often than not led to swift, unofficial, corporal punishments being handed out for minor offences. More serious breaches of discipline were dealt with summarily by commanding officers; punishments ranged from loss of pay or additional duties to confinement to barracks (CB) (generally for personnel based away from the front) or field punishment (FP) of up to twenty-eight days (generally at the front, when it was impracticable to transfer the offender to the rear base). Intended to be a deterrent, field punishment was deliberately severe. It was to provide a short, sharp shock to the offender, who until 1924, if sentenced to Field Punishment No. 1, was detained with hard labour, lost pay and privileges, and was bound in irons or tied to a pole.

More serious breaches of discipline were tried by courts martial of three officers acting as judge and jury. About 2745 New Zealand troops were court-martialled during the First World War, 2683 during the Second World War, and 112 (about 3 per cent of the New Zealand troops in the theatre) during the ★Korean War. Punishments were more severe for offences committed while on active service (or closer to the front line). For example, a soldier absent from parade at a rear camp could expect several days' CB and loss of pay, whereas a soldier absent before going into the front line was regarded as a deserter, and could face the ★death penalty (though imprisonment with hard labour for a lengthy term was the norm and the death penalty was effectively removed as an option in the Second World War).

Serious lapses in discipline occurred more frequently during the immediate post-war periods. After the First World War there were brief riots and strikes in New Zealand camps, and absences without leave reached epidemic proportions. Similarly after the Second World War, discipline proved difficult to maintain once the war was over. 'Swanning off' became common and ★black market rackets thrived.

During both world wars troops flouted rules regarding saluting and uniforms, another reflection of New Zealand egalitarianism. Nevertheless, most New Zealand soldiers stoically obeyed the plethora of orders and restrictions. There was also a high degree of internal, unofficial self-discipline—dubbed 'mateship' (the comradeship common to all armies and not confined solely to Anzacs). A tacit understanding was evident between the ranks and commanders such that misdemeanours were frequently overlooked and a high degree of latitude was allowed in dress and protocol; however, those in the ranks in return were expected to be effective in combat. Although this understanding worked well for most of the Second World War, there were signs of it breaking down in the ★furlough affair of 1943 and in the ★Italian campaign in 1944. A combination of exhaustion and lax discipline allowed by unit commanders led to serious problems that extended to criminal behaviour, such as looting. Dress was allowed to become peculiarly individualistic until a crackdown was ordered by 2NZEF commander Lieutenant-General Sir Bernard ★Freyberg in August 1944: 'It is now impossible', he complained, 'to know when going along the roads whether a man is an Italian or a New Zealander.'

Disciplinary problems have diminished from the late 1950s with peacetime conditions and the shift away from a citizen-based Army. The modern ★New Zealand Defence Force takes pride in its professionalism. As the composition of the NZDF has changed, especially as more women have been recruited, old methods of instilling discipline have altered, to the extent that during 1999 an NCO was court-martialled and found guilty for verbally abusing a recruit during initial training.

C. Pugsley, *On the Fringe of Hell: New Zealanders and Military Discipline in the First World War* (Hodder & Stoughton, Auckland, 1991); J. McLeod, *Myth and Reality: The New Zealand Soldier in World War II* (Reed Methuen, Auckland, 1986).

Dittmer, Brigadier George (4 June 1893–11 August 1979) was the uncompromising first commander of 28th (Maori) Battalion. Born in Hawke's Bay, he was a masseur when he enlisted in 1NZEF in August 1914. He served with the Auckland Battalion at ★Gallipoli, and was commissioned in the field in June 1915. While serving on the ★Western Front, he won an MC at Messines, and was wounded at Passchendaele. After the war, he secured a commission in the ★New Zealand Staff Corps and served in various appointments in the Northern Military District until the ★Second World War. Assuming command of the Maori Battalion in November 1939, he quickly stamped his personality on it, insisting upon the highest standards of discipline and drill. He led it during the ill-fated campaigns in ★Greece and ★Crete, and was made a DSO for his service in the latter. After being wounded during the Crusader offensive in North Africa in November 1941, he was briefly taken prisoner when the field ambulance at which he was being treated was overrun. He led a group of about thirty soldiers in an escape, travelling 130 kilometres back to Allied lines. When he returned to New Zealand in 1942, he was made commander of the 1st Brigade, and then 1st Division. In September 1943 he took command of the Fiji Military Forces. Relinquishing this position shortly after the war, he served as commandant of Papakura Camp and commander of the Central Military District before retiring in 1948.

Divisions, New Zealand Army A division is commonly held to be the smallest strategic unit able to be deployed independently and the largest tactical unit employed in battle. Combining all the arms of an army, it consists of between 20,000 and 30,000 men, is usually commanded by a major-general, and is logistically self-sufficient. In the ★First World War New Zealand initially contributed troops to an improvised formation, the ★New Zealand and Australian Division. However, in early 1916 1NZEF had grown to more than 30,000 men, and its commander, Major-General Sir Alexander ★Godley, sought permission from Wellington to form them into a New Zealand division—a course that was also being urged by the British authorities. Despite some doubts (mainly because of the increased scale of reinforcements and extra supporting troops that would be required for a division), the government responded positively. After a month's training under its commander, Major-General Sir Andrew ★Russell, the division was sent to the ★Western Front in April 1916. The New Zealand Division consisted of three infantry brigades (1st Infantry, 2nd Infantry, and 3rd New Zealand (Rifle) Brigades), each of four battalions. The infantry were supported by four 'brigades' of artillery, three field engineer companies, three field ambulances, as well as machine-gun and mortar companies. This organisation changed in 1917 with the addition of a fourth infantry brigade, an innovation that Russell had opposed. In February 1918 the 4th Brigade was disbanded to provide reinforcements for the other three infantry brigades. Meanwhile, the brigade of mounted rifles had been involved in the ★Sinai–Palestine campaign as part of the Australian and New Zealand (Anzac) Mounted Division, which from April 1917 was under the command of Major-General E.W.C. ★Chaytor.

New Zealand's principal army contribution during the ★Second World War was 2nd New Zealand Division, which followed the standard British pattern with an additional battalion to allow for the inclusion of a Maori unit. Commanded by Major-General B.C. ★Freyberg, it contained three brigades of infantry (4th, 5th, and 6th), three regiments of field artillery, an anti-tank regiment, a divisional cavalry regiment, engineers, field ambulances, and other supporting troops. This divisional organisation changed over time, with, for example, a regiment of anti-aircraft artillery being added in mid 1941. Following the defeats at Ruweisat Ridge and El Mreir in 1942, 4th Brigade was withdrawn for conversion to an armoured brigade (with an attached British armoured brigade replacing it in the division in the meantime). In the event, 4th (Armoured) Brigade proved something of a luxury in Italy, where conditions placed a premium on infantry. A shortage of reinforcements eventually forced a reorganisation: the anti-aircraft regiment was disbanded, the anti-tank artillery reorganised, and the machine-gun battalion and divisional cavalry re-formed as infantry battalions, which became part of a newly formed 9th Infantry Brigade. Thus 2nd New Zealand Division ended the war with the unusual structure of an armoured brigade and three infantry brigades.

Three divisions were raised in New Zealand for home defence during the Second World War. Formed in the three ★military districts—Northern, Central, and Southern—they followed no standard pattern, though usually consisting of a strong infantry brigade and a weaker brigade with mounted rifles or light armour. In May 1942 they were retitled 1st Division (based at Whangarei), 4th Division (Palmerston North), and 5th Division (Burnham). Placed on a cadre basis as the danger of invasion receded in 1943, they gradually withered away. Another division, the 3rd, was raised in Fiji in May 1942 from the two brigades (8th and 14th) forming the garrison there (see FIJI, NEW ZEALAND FORCES IN). Returning to New Zealand in August 1942, it was augmented, though never to full establishment. With two infantry brigades and various artillery regiments, it was deployed to ★New Caledonia in November 1943 under the command of Major-General H.E. ★Barrowclough. A projected third infantry brigade had to be broken up to provide reinforcements. After limited involvement in the ★Solomons campaign, the division was disbanded in September 1944 in favour of sustaining 2nd Division in Italy.

One further divisional structure was developed by New Zealand following the onset of the ★Cold War in the late 1940s. Designed to fulfil commitments undertaken in 1949—the ★Middle East commitment—it consisted of an augmented infantry division similar to 2nd Division in 1945, i.e. including an armoured brigade. ★Compulsory military training was introduced to provide the necessary manpower. The CGS doubled as the divisional GOC. This concept underlay the Army's planning for more than a decade, even though the commitment was shifted to South-east Asia in 1955 and international developments made a large-scale conflict in which it might be needed less likely. During the 1960s, as attention focused on the provision of a logistically self-supporting brigade group, the division faded away.

Dog Tax rebellion was one of a number of occasions in the late nineteenth century when military force was used to police dissident Maori communities. The imposition of a tax on dogs in 1881, mainly as a financial disincentive to dog ownership, upset many Maori dog owners, who regarded it as intrusive and discriminatory. When in April 1898 Maori at Waima, near Hokianga, indicated that future attempts to enforce the tax would be resisted, there were fears among the local non-Maori population of a full-scale rebellion. The Premier, R.J. ★Seddon, ordered the dispatch of troops to the area. Under the command of Lieutenant-Colonel Stuart ★Newall, a force equipped with field guns set out for Waima on 5 May. No resistance was encountered, however, as the 'ringleaders' were arrested.

Douglas, Major Sir Arthur Percy (15 October 1845–30 September 1913) was a prominent defence administrator at the end of the nineteenth century. Born in Devon, England, he entered the Royal Navy as a cadet in 1858 and during his fifteen years' naval service became an expert in gunnery. He retired in the rank of lieutenant. From 1873 to 1876 he was instructor to the Naval Artillery Volunteers in Liverpool. After emigrating to New Zealand in 1877, he farmed in the Rangitikei area. His skills as a gunner lay behind his attendance at a 'sort of council of war' convened by the Governor, Sir William ★Jervois, in early 1885, when fears of attack by Russian raiders were exacerbated by the ★Pendjeh crisis. As Naval Staff Officer until August 1885 he helped oversee the subsequent hasty preparations to defend New Zealand's main ports, but relinquished the post once the crisis subsided. From April 1885 he was Vice Commodore of

Troops with field guns at Waimea in May 1898, the last occasion military forces were deployed in response to Maori dissidence (*Alexander Turnbull Library, F-18760-1/2*)

the colony's fifteen-corps-strong Naval Artillery Volunteers, a position he held for eighteen years. Douglas was also involved in efforts to improve the standard of officers in the colonial forces: he was secretary of the short-lived Council of Military Education from 1886 to 1888, and from 1888 sat on the board which considered candidates for commissions in the ★Volunteer Force. In August 1887 he was appointed a major and became Staff Officer of Artillery and Inspector of Ordnance Stores and Equipment in the ★Permanent Militia, in which capacity he served until taking command of the Permanent Militia at Lyttelton in 1891. In that year he succeeded to a baronetcy. During a dispute with Colonel F.J. ★Fox in 1894, Premier Richard ★Seddon was tempted to appoint Douglas as Commander of the Forces but in the end, in June 1895, made him Under-Secretary for Defence. Douglas's assertive performance in this role irritated successive Commanders of the Forces. He was heavily involved in preparing New Zealand contingents for the ★Boer War, later recalling the 'incessant work night and day' that outfitting the first had required. With his health impaired, he took sick leave in September 1902 and went to the United Kingdom, from where he cabled his resignation in March 1903. In 1909 he published a survey, *The Dominion of New Zealand*, which included a useful account of the evolution of New Zealand's defence policy. He died of injuries received in a train crash in Yorkshire.

Duigan, Major-General Sir John Evelyn (30 March 1883–9 January 1950). Originally from Wanganui, Duigan worked his passage to South Africa as a sixteen-year-old to take part in the ★Boer War. Enlisting in a colonial volunteer unit, he was seriously wounded at the siege of Wepener in April 1901 and later returned to New Zealand. In 1902 he went back to South Africa as an officer in the 10th New Zealand Contingent, but saw no further action. In 1903 he secured appointment to the Permanent Force. After being commissioned two years later, he underwent specialist engineering training in England in 1906 and 1908, and in 1912 was sent to the Staff College at Quetta in India. Seconded to 1NZEF in November 1914, he served briefly as a staff officer before a nervous breakdown forced his repatriation to New Zealand. He returned to active service as commander of the New Zealand Tunnelling Company on the ★Western Front in 1916. From January 1917 he occupied a series of staff positions, including an unhappy period at New Zealand Division HQ, until his health again deteriorated. Thereafter he was effectively sidelined in positions as an instructor, first at Aldershot, then in the United States. For his services he was made both a CB and a DSO. Despite his rather patchy war record, he rose steadily in the inter-war military forces. An efficient staff officer in New Zealand, he was given the Northern Command in 1930. In April 1937 he became General Officer Commanding and Chief of the General Staff (though the former position was soon abolished), an elevation which probably owed much to his willingness to fall in with the Labour government's requirements. He was a member of the Council of Defence established in 1937. Senior *Territorial Force officers were unimpressed with his performance in the period leading up to the outbreak of war in September 1939. They strongly resisted his plans to bring the Army's organisation, based on an infantry division and three mounted rifles regiments, into line with the limited numbers available under the voluntary system of enlistment for the Territorial Force; the answer, in their eyes, lay in the reintroduction of *compulsory military training to provide the necessary manpower. Duigan did not prove a forceful CGS in dealing with his political masters, and Army preparations for war lagged. Although aspiring to command 2NZEF, he was not seen as a credible candidate by either the government or the military hierarchy and had to be content with the consolation prize of an extension of his term as CGS. During 1940 his administrative capacities were tested to the full with the dispatch of 2NZEF, the introduction of *conscription, and the expansion of the Territorial Force for home defence. In late 1940 he attended conferences in Singapore and New Delhi before visiting 2NZEF in the Middle East. His health again suffered from the strain, eventually forcing him to relinquish his post in May 1941.

Duigan, Sidney (4 November 1918–11 October 1997), was involved in the Resistance in German occupied France during the *Second World War. Born in Wanganui, she was educated at Woodford House and the University of Cambridge. In 1937 she moved to France, where she studied at the Sorbonne. When war began, she joined the French Red Cross, and was nursing in Calais when captured by the Germans. Escaping from an internment camp, she made her way to Vichy France where she continued to work with the Red Cross. She also took part in Resistance activities and was briefly arrested on suspicion of being a spy. She was always reticent about her wartime activities in later life, but her contribution to the Resistance was recognised by the award of a Croix de Guerre after the war. She married a Russian exile, Vladimir Koreneff, in 1946, and they returned to New Zealand. She was later editor of the *Wanganui Herald* and one of the first women to be ordained as a priest in the Anglican Church in New Zealand.

Early Maori–European conflict Known contact between Europeans and New Zealand's earlier immigrants, the Maori, began violently when the expedition of Abel Janszoon Tasman was attacked on 19 December 1642; four Dutch sailors were killed. During the exploratory visits, from 1769, of European scientific vessels, notably those of James Cook and Dumont d'Urville, Maori–European relations were generally cordial, though some violent incidents were caused by mutual fear and misunderstandings. In the first such instance, on 8 October 1769, a Maori was shot and killed when one of Cook's sailors probably mistook his challenge for a threatening action. Nervous sailors shot several more the next day, and at Matau-a-aanui (Cape Kidnappers) an attempt to kidnap one of HMS *Endeavour*'s boys resulted in three Maori dead. As *Endeavour* sailed around the coast misunderstandings about challenges or gifts resulted in further deaths. The toll was not one-sided: on a later expedition ten members of the crew of HMS *Adventure* were killed and eaten at Queen Charlotte Sound. French explorer Marion du Fresne's probable desecration of tapu led to his murder along with twenty-six of his crew at the Bay of Islands in 1772. The French retaliated, burning villages and killing about 200 local inhabitants.

In the wake of the explorers came European traders, whalers, and sealers. Relatively amicable Maori–European relationships soon developed, as Europeans traded small quantities of iron for timber (for masts and spars), flax (for sails), food and water, and sexual favours. Even so there were violent incidents, particularly when musket-armed European sailors retaliated against what they saw as theft or threatening behaviour, or when Europeans were attacked for iron or revenge (utu). In the south unscrupulous sealing and whaling captains took advantage of musketless Maori communities, which in turn led to several revenge attacks against isolated gangs of sealers, the worst incident occurring in Otago in 1817 when the *Sophia* was attacked. A village and canoes were burnt in retaliation. Renegades also had an impact on local communities from time to time, the most notable example being the depredations of the *Venus* in 1806. Greed, misunderstandings, theft, and insults to chiefly mana invited violent retaliation: in 1808 the shipwrecked crew of the *Parramatta* were killed by inhabitants they had previously cheated. The flogging of a Whangaroa Maori chief by the crew of the *Boyd* in 1809 led to the seizure of the ship and the massacre of its crew and passengers. In retaliation several whaling ships sacked a pa (mistakenly that of a friendly chief), massacring about sixty men, women, and children.

Despite the *Boyd* incident, the European–Maori relationship tended to become more stable during the 1820s and 1830s. The European desire for flax, food, women, and whaling stations and the Maori need for muskets and mana opened the way for a cooperative, if not always friendly, relationship. Outside of the principal anchorages of Kapiti and the Bay of Islands, sporadic violence still occurred. In 1834 the most spectacular incident of Maori–European conflict followed the shipwreck of the *Harriet* on the Taranaki coast. The castaways were attacked, and the survivors taken captive. As a result of the intervention of HMS *Alligator*, the captives were eventually released after a number of confused violent incidents. Europeans also became embroiled in the inter-tribal ★Musket Wars. The most celebrated incident of European involvement in Maori affairs was the conveyance of ★Te Rauparaha to Banks Peninsula by the *Elizabeth* in 1830.

East Timor

European traders were occasionally involved in the fighting, as at Nga-Motu in 1832, but on the whole the stations of European traders and missionaries were treated as neutral.

East Timor is the largest ★peace-keeping operation undertaken by New Zealand, involving all three services. A former Portuguese colony, East Timor was invaded by Indonesia in 1975 following Portugal's virtual abandonment of the territory in the previous year. Indonesia's annexation, which was resisted by a sizeable proportion of the indigenous population, was recognised only by Australia, and the United Nations continued to regard Portugal as the legal authority in the territory. Despite a prolonged guerrilla conflict, Indonesian control seemed unshakeable until the collapse of Indonesia's economy in 1997 and the departure of its long-serving President, Hari Suharto. Suharto's successor, President B.J. Habibie, offered to allow the inhabitants of East Timor to determine their future status in a referendum. This was held on 30 August 1999, amid much violence instigated by Indonesian-supported militia groups. Despite the intimidation, an overwhelming majority opted for independence, an outcome which provoked a militia rampage in which many people were killed. With Australia to the fore, an International Force East Timor (INTERFET) was formed and, with the sanction of the United Nations and the reluctant agreement of the Indonesian government, was deployed in the territory from 20 September. New Zealand actively supported this development. Public opinion in New Zealand had long sympathised with East Timorese aspirations, not least because of the murder of a New Zealand citizen during a massacre in Dili in 1991. The New Zealand frigate HMNZS *Te Kaha* joined an international naval force in the vicinity of the island, and was joined in the theatre by the supply ship HMNZS *Endeavour*. *Te Kaha* was later relieved by HMNZS *Canterbury*. The RNZAF played a major part in the transport of the New Zealand Army's contribution to INTERFET, which eventually included forces from sixteen countries under the command of an Australian general. A company-sized New Zealand infantry unit and an SAS detachment were deployed initially, after a brief period of training in Darwin. They were followed later by the remainder of a battalion group–sized force based on 1st Battalion, RNZIR, which had hastily incorporated men and women from other corps. Iroquois helicopters were also made available. The Senior National Officer, New Zealand Force East Timor, Brigadier Martyn Dunne, was appointed as Commander Dili Garrison. By December 1999, 830 New Zealand soldiers were taking part in the operation as members of INTERFET; one had been killed in an accident (New Zealand's first fatal casualty in a peace-keeping operation). The INTERFET deployment was

A New Zealand soldier serving with the International Force East Timor at the border with West Timor in late 1999 (*NZ Army, OH99-1567-83*)

made without any significant clashes with Indonesian troops, who were soon withdrawn from the territory, and a vaunted challenge by the militia groups did not eventuate. The episode had, however, soured relations between Australia and Indonesia in particular, and had reawakened fears in Australia about security in the area. For New Zealand, the prospect of a prolonged deployment highlighted the limited capabilities of the Army, and seemed to bear out the arguments of those who called for a refocusing of defence expenditure away from such capital items as frigates and combat aircraft to the upgrading of the Army's capabilities, an approach which overlooked the importance of sea and air power in providing the framework for the East Timor intervention. During February 2000 INTERFET personnel donned the blue UN helmet after control of the operation passed from Australia to the UN Transition Administration in East Timor.

Egypt, New Zealanders in New Zealand troops were stationed in Egypt in both world wars. A British protectorate from December 1914, and nominally independent but under virtual British occupation in the ★Second World War, Egypt was of vital strategic significance to the British Empire. Since 1869 the Suez Canal had been the principal route between Great Britain and much of the Empire, including New Zealand. When it came under threat following Turkey's entry to the ★First World War on the side of the Central Powers in November 1914, the Australian and New Zealand troops then en route to Europe were the most readily available troops for bolstering its defences, and they were disembarked in Egypt. The New Zealanders established themselves at Zeitoun ten kilometres from Cairo and began training (see ARMY CAMPS). For most of the troops it was their first overseas experience, and sightseeing was an early preoccupation for many, with visits to the Pyramids and the Sphinx, and to the cosmopolitan city of Cairo. Reflecting the aggressively self-confident and racialist culture from which they hailed, the New Zealanders viewed the local inhabitants—'Gyppos'—as corrupt and licentious. They were encouraged in their attitudes by the tone set by their commander, Major-General Sir Alexander ★Godley: in a Special General Order on 30 November 1914 he noted that Egyptians 'belong to races lower in the human scale'. Attempts to deter men from using prostitutes by shaming them and to prevent drunkenness by establishing wet canteens in camp were only partially successful. Discipline remained a major problem for the force. The most notorious example was the Wazza riot on 2 April 1915: drunk and bored Australians and New Zealanders ran amok in the brothel district of Cairo, assaulting Egyptians, smashing and burning buildings, and engaging in a running battle with the military police.

When the bulk of 1NZEF left for Europe in April 1916, a brigade of mounted rifles remained to take part in the ★Sinai–Palestine campaign, with its base headquarters at Cairo. Returning from Palestine at the end of 1918, the brigade was stationed at Ismailia. In March 1919 it was used to help crush nationalist disturbances, during which Egyptians were beaten indiscriminately and houses damaged. Most New Zealanders were glad to leave for home in July 1919.

New Zealanders returned to Egypt in February 1940. The need to boost the British presence there as a deterrent to the Italians had led to the decision that 2NZEF should follow in the footsteps of its predecessor. The New Zealanders were based at Maadi and at Helwan south of Cairo. Many delighted in the opportunity to explore the environs during their leaves, as their fathers and uncles had done. Relations with Egyptians were not much better than in the First World War, and were usually restricted to 'booze and bints'. The authorities were aware of the dubious attractions of Cairo: one of those responsible for 2NZEF's administration noted later that they 'always felt that they were sitting on a volcano, and heaved a sigh of relief each morning if nothing out of the way had happened in Cairo the evening before'. To fight the problems arising from drunkenness and boredom, welfare facilities were established at Maadi, while in September 1940 a New Zealand Forces Club was established at Cairo. The club was extremely popular among New Zealand and Allied troops. Although drunkenness outside the club proved a problem, Freyberg considered a certain amount of disorder at the Club to be preferable to soldiers going to disreputable bars. Like their First World War predecessors, 2NZEF troops frequented the brothels, in one week alone 2164 New Zealanders using the preventative ablution centre in the 'Berka' brothel area of Cairo. The city's brothels were placed off limits in August 1942, but soldiers continued to use prostitutes, and ★venereal disease remained a problem for 2NZEF. It

Members of 1NZEF sightseeing in Egypt during the First World War (*Waiouru Army Museum, 1988.1268*)

was not all booze and bints, however. On one tense occasion all New Zealand troops at Maadi were deployed in Cairo to prevent King Farouk deserting to the Italians: they stood shoulder to shoulder round his palace, alternately facing towards it or away from it, until the crisis passed.

As in the First World War, most of the New Zealand troops were eventually deployed to Western Europe, the bulk of 2NZEF going to Italy in 1943. All that remained in Egypt was the training and administrative base at Maadi. The last members of 2NZEF were repatriated from Egypt in February 1946, leaving behind an obelisk at Maadi (since destroyed) as a reminder of their presence.

For a time after the Second World War it appeared that New Zealanders might repeat the Egyptian experience yet again. The *Middle East commitment, undertaken in 1949, was predicated on a war with the Soviet Union which never materialised, and extensive plans for the deployment once again of most of New Zealand's available combat forces to Egypt were never implemented. Not until 1982 were New Zealand servicemen again deployed on Egyptian soil as part of the Multinational Force and Observers, though several officers served there with the UN Truce Supervision Organization from 1956 (see PEACE-KEEPING).

Elliott, Second Lieutenant Keith (25 April 1916–17 October 1989) won a *Victoria Cross at Ruweisat Ridge in 1942. A farmer from Mangamaire in the Wairarapa, he had his first taste of action as a lance-corporal in 22nd Battalion during the fighting in *Greece and *Crete. In the latter he was wounded in the arm while stalking German paratroopers. Late in 1941, during the *North African campaign, he was briefly a prisoner of war after 5th Brigade HQ was overrun. His VC recognised his efforts after his battalion suffered a similar fate at Ruweisat Ridge on 15 July 1942. Although hit in the chest, he led his men on a successful breakout. In subsequent fighting he led a bayonet charge across 500 metres of open ground which resulted in the capture of an anti-tank gun, machine-guns, and fifty prisoners. He followed this exploit by destroying another machine-gun post, despite having been shot in the thigh. A third wound, this time to his knee, did not prevent him from assisting in wiping out yet another machine-gun post. Although commissioned in May 1943, he was repatriated to New Zealand soon afterwards. Discharged from 2NZEF in December 1943, he later became an Anglican priest and a *Territorial Force chaplain. In 1954 he attended the unveiling of the Alamein Memorial in Egypt.

K. Elliott and R. Adshead, *From Cowshed to Dog Collar* (A.H. & A.W. Reed, Wellington, 1967).

Elworthy, Marshal of the Royal Air Force Sir Samuel Charles, Baron (23 March 1911–4 April 1993), as an RAF officer, achieved the highest rank held by a New Zealander in any armed service. Born in South Canterbury, he was sent to England in 1924 to attend Marlborough College. He went on to graduate in law from Cambridge University in 1933. After briefly serving in an auxiliary squadron, he gained a permanent commission in the RAF in 1936. From 1938 to 1940 he was personal assistant to the AOC-in-C of Bomber Command, before taking command of 82 Squadron in December 1940. For his Blenheim-equipped squadron's successful low-level bombing attacks against German shipping and targets in occupied Europe, he was awarded both an AFC and a DFC and appointed a DSO in 1941. From 1942 he was closely involved in the planning of the bomber offensive against Germany as group captain in charge of operations at Bomber Command headquarters. He finished the war as senior staff officer of 5 Group. Among his post-war activities was involvement in the planning of the British invasion of Egypt during the 1956 *Suez crisis. Thereafter, he was successively commandant of the RAF Staff College (1957–59), Deputy Chief of the Air Staff (1959–60), and Commander-in-Chief of British forces in the Middle East (1960–63), in the last-named capacity dealing with a threatened Iraqi invasion of Kuwait in 1961. In 1963 he became Chief of the Air Staff, and four years later was elevated to Chief of the Defence Staff. With his four-year term being dominated by cuts to the British forces, he likened his role to that of a 'military undertaker'. Following his retirement, he held a number of prestigious appointments, including Constable and Governor of Windsor Castle and Lord Lieutenant of London. He was created a life peer in 1972 and a Knight of the Garter five years later. He retired to Timaru in 1978.

Emergency Precautions Scheme An Emergency Precautions Committee (part of the New Zealand Section of the *Committee of Imperial Defence) was formed in 1935 to coordinate a national response to natural disaster or enemy attack. However, little was done until 1939, when a booklet was issued to municipal authorities on the framework to be adopted in the event of an emergency. Emergency preparations were accelerated with the crisis of mid 1940. Emergency Precautions Regulations were introduced in July, giving local bodies statutory authority to administer emergency schemes in their areas, while overall administration of the scheme passed from the Department of Internal Affairs to the *National Service Department. The structure reflected the assumption that the primary threat to New Zealand, so long as

Emergency Precautions Scheme

Christchurch Home Guardsmen dig a shelter late in 1941 (*War History Collection, Alexander Turnbull Library, F-481-1/4-DA*)

British arms were not defeated in the main theatres, was 'hit-and-run' raids. Local bodies formed a central executive, with sections for such aspects as supply, medical arrangements, law and order, public utilities, works, and fire. These sections comprised representatives from relevant organisations including hospital boards, fire brigades, Boy Scouts, and the ★Red Cross. Enlistment of volunteers began in mid 1940, with all British subjects being eligible for enrolment.

From October 1941 the government took an increasingly forward role in the preparations, a process which was further accelerated by the onset of the ★Pacific War and the possibility of invasion. The EPS was now brought fully under central government control. To provide sufficient auxiliary policemen, fire-watchers, and wardens, compulsion was introduced on 23 January 1942 for all men aged between eighteen and sixty-five not already in the armed services. Women were allowed to volunteer, and once enrolled could not resign. For civilians not in EPS work, instructions were issued in June 1941 on such matters as fire precautions and first aid. City councils also encouraged households to keep fire-fighting equipment, such as buckets of sand, and emergency stores of food.

EPS medical units formed first aid posts and advanced dressing stations at schools and public buildings, usually run by Red Cross or St John Ambulance volunteers. Law and order units enrolled auxiliary police for extra policing and traffic duties in an emergency. To improve coordination of fire-fighting a separate Emergency Fire Service was formed in March 1941 from the fire brigades and auxiliary fire sections, with auxiliary fire units paid and uniformed. The most familiar EPS personnel were wardens, the backbone of the EPS. Wardens, organised into blocks, areas, and districts, were charged with reporting damage, assisting emergency services, cordoning off dangerous areas, and preventing confusion and panic. They also policed the blackout, with wide powers, including the right to enter private property. Lighting restrictions had been introduced in March 1941. On 12 December 1941 the blackout was extended even further, with windows covered and external lights disconnected or shaded, particularly those near the sea or in the main cities. Cars, too, were expected to shade their headlights. Most people took the blackout seriously, particularly in early 1942, but there was an element of irritation at 'busybody' wardens vigilant to douse any light. From July 1942 the restrictions began to ease, and by 1943 lighting had been restored. It was wardens who organised the weekend and night-time fire-watches of people at buildings in the four main cities against the threat of fire from an incendiary attack. Fire-watches began in October 1941. In December they were extended to 24-hour watches over city buildings; by April 1942 there were 11,875 people in Wellington doing shifts watching for fires. Fire-watching was an imposition increasingly resented, and in December 1942 the government ordered that it should cease.

Empire Air Training Scheme

Although little had been done to protect people or property from bombing in the early part of the war, this changed after 7 December 1941. A frantic programme of air raid shelter construction was set in train. Within ten days of Pearl Harbor, Christchurch had nearly a kilometre of community trenches. At first it was expected that only the main cities would be likely targets, but from January 1942 the EPS expanded the digging of air raid shelters to the main towns, and the Japanese air attack on Darwin in February hastened construction even further. By September 1942 Auckland city could accommodate 58,000 people in public air raid shelters. In Wellington parks and vacant lots became sites for air raid shelters, even Parliament's grounds being dug up for shelters. The burst of air raid shelter building tailed off as the fortunes of war changed, and in October 1943 it was decreed that the shelters were no longer necessary. Similarly, the EPS began planning for evacuation of the main cities in the event of an invasion, though the government maintained the 'stay put' policy that the decision to evacuate should be left to the military, not the EPS. Nevertheless, art works and treasures were taken out of the cities, and EPS supply controllers issued plans for food reserves.

By late 1942 there was general fatigue with the civil defence effort. EPS duties were disruptive of normal life. In February 1943 the scheme was considerably reduced, and on 1 January 1944 placed on a peacetime basis. Virtually all civilian New Zealanders were involved in the EPS to some extent, with nearly 40,000 people in 'front line' units. The scheme was beset by inexperience and administrative problems, in particular the propensity for forming committees or extra layers of authority. Nevertheless, it proved valuable in a number of minor natural disasters during the war, and would have done so had New Zealand suffered an enemy incursion.

N.M. Taylor, *The Home Front*, 2 vols (Historical Publications Branch, Wellington, 1986).

Empire Air Training Scheme (also known as the British Commonwealth Air Training Plan) was the primary source of advanced training for Commonwealth aircrews for the Royal Air Force during the *Second World War. The foundation of this vast air training plan, which contributed hugely to the Allied success in the conflict, was laid in the mid 1930s when the British, Canadian, Australian, and New Zealand governments discussed ways of coordinating aircrew training in case of war. At that time New Zealand, like the other Dominions, was providing small numbers of personnel for short-service commissions in the RAF. In May 1939 the Air Ministry in London approved a New Zealand proposal to train annually 600 pilots and 650 observers and air gunners for the RAF in addition to its own requirements. Additional British payments for the pilots offset the cost of the 100 Tiger Moth aircraft that were ordered to meet this expanded task. A factory at Rongotai was established to assemble the new aircraft. Before the end of 1939 new flying training schools had been established at Woodbourne, Taieri, and New Plymouth (which moved to Ashburton in 1942) to supplement that at Wigram; an observers' and air gunners' school was set up at Ohakea, and a flying instructors' school at Mangere.

With the outbreak of war in September 1939, the British government gave urgent attention to the problem of meeting British air force requirements, and on 26 September 1939, largely at Canadian and Australian urging, outlined its proposed solution to the Dominions. An estimated 20,000 pilots and 30,000 other aircrew would be needed annually, but Great Britain, from its own resources, could only provide 44 per cent of the numbers required. Moreover it lacked the space available to create the necessary facilities, which would in any case be vulnerable to German attack. The Dominions, it was proposed, should meet the manpower shortfall, with shares being divided on the basis of population ratio. Fifty flying training schools would be needed. Half of them would be for advanced training, and these would be concentrated in Canada. Difficult negotiations followed at a conference in Ottawa in October, at which New Zealand was represented by the Chief of the Air Staff, Group-Captain H.W.L. *Saunders, and the Air Secretary, T.A. *Barrow. In the face of alternative proposals, they firmly insisted upon a population-based ratio which entailed New Zealand providing about 3000 trainees per annum, and argued strongly that as many pilots should be fully trained in New Zealand as possible, if only to use the facilities recently established there. Under the terms of the agreement of 17 December 1939, New Zealand would provide per annum 880 fully trained pilots for the RAF. In addition, it would train 520 pilots to an elementary standard and 546 observers and 936 air gunners (soon to be combined as wireless operator/air gunners) to an initial stage, all of them completing their training in Canada. Apart from paying a share (8.08 per cent) of the total cost of the Canadian training, New Zealand was confronted with a substantial expansion of training facilities in New Zealand. In practical terms this meant establishing an organisation to allow 144 pilots to begin elementary training every four weeks, along with 80 pilots for advanced training and 116 other aircrew for initial training. Additional training schools were set up at Whenuapai and Harewood. Training aircraft were supplied by Britain, as a result of which Oxfords, Ansons, and Harvards were progressively delivered to New Zealand during the war.

Enemy aliens

there was a further modification of New Zealand's contribution, with the training of an additional 130 observers, the first increased draft leaving for Canada in the following January.

Japan's entry into the war did not have any marked effect on New Zealand's contribution to the EATS, despite the need to increase training in New Zealand for local defence. Because of the threat of invasion in the North Island, all flying training there was relocated to the South Island. There was only a slight reduction—forty-eight pilots per annum—in the number of trainees sent to Canada. However, in mid 1942, modifications to New Zealand's contribution were necessary as the demand for trained personnel in Europe began to lessen. A large surplus was beginning to accumulate in the United Kingdom. Under a new agreement negotiated in June 1942 (which extended the scheme's duration a further two years to March 1945), EATS flying training courses were increased in length to twelve weeks to improve the standard of training. New Zealand's commitment lessened: it would henceforth send 450 partially trained pilots and 1391 observers/air gunners to Canada, as well as providing 730 fully trained pilots to the RAF. By February 1944 the position with regard to aircrew availability in operational areas in Europe had further improved to such an extent that the EATS scheme was reduced by 40 per cent. Even so, by June 1944 the backlog of New Zealand pilots awaiting training was such that the New Zealand government suspended the dispatch of pilots to Canada until May 1945. In the event, no more were sent. At the end of 1944 it was agreed that New Zealand should cease sending any personnel to Canada, and halt the dispatch of fully trained pilots to the United Kingdom. The EATS scheme came to an end on 31 March 1945, by which time 131,553 Commonwealth personnel had graduated. Of the 7002 New Zealanders involved, 1764 of whom were subsequently commissioned, 2220 were pilots, 829 navigators (bombardier), thirty navigators (wireless operator), 724 navigators, 634 air bombers, 2074 wireless operator/air gunners, 48 wireless operator/air gunners (with no bombing or gunnery school training), and 443 air gunners. Thirty-one New Zealanders were fatally injured during training.

J.M.S. Ross, *Royal New Zealand Air Force* (War History Branch, Wellington, 1955).

PAUL HARRISON

Trainee New Zealand airmen inspect the cockpit of a Spitfire at a training school in Canada (*War History Collection, Alexander Turnbull Library, F-1193-1/2-DA*)

Each of the Dominions was anxious that its own personnel should be employed in RAF squadrons which had a distinctive association with it. This was reflected in Article XV of the agreement, which provided for the formation of Dominion squadrons within the RAF. Although it was intended that Dominions would supply ground crews for these squadrons, New Zealand had little capacity to do so, and its 'Article XV' squadrons were supported by mainly RAF personnel. The lack of New Zealand officers with sufficient experience meant they were initially commanded by RAF regular officers, which sometimes rankled with New Zealand pilots who preferred to be commanded by one of their own. The RAF had also insisted on the right to disperse graduates of the EATS to non-'Article XV' squadrons to cover combat losses, with the result that most New Zealanders involved in the air war in Europe served with ordinary RAF squadrons. In all, seven 'New Zealand' squadrons (485–490 and 75) were formed. (See AIRMEN, NEW ZEALAND, IN THE RAF IN THE SECOND WORLD WAR)

Even before the first New Zealand trainees—fifty pilots, forty-four observers, and seventy-five wireless operators—arrived in Canada in October 1940, Germany's successful onslaught in Western Europe had impelled the British government to seek ways of increasing the output of the EATS. New Zealand hastened the full development of its training organisation, and in September agreed to both expand the size of pilot training courses and reduce their duration from eight to six weeks. This increased New Zealand's quota of fully trained and partially trained pilots per annum to 1480 and 850 respectively. British pressure in January 1941 to further reduce the course length to five weeks was resisted, and the eight-week duration was restored in February 1942. From September 1941,

Enemy aliens, wartime treatment of At the outset of the ★First World War, New Zealand followed imperial precedents in dealing with enemy aliens. Under the War Regulations Act 1914, they could be interned at the discretion of the Minister of Defence. About 4000 Germans and 2000 Austro-Hungarians,

157

Enemy aliens

regardless of whether they had gained British naturalisation, were classified as enemy aliens; males of military age who were considered to be a 'security threat' were interned. A heavy-handed government approach led to about 450 aliens, mainly Germans, being interned on Somes Island and Motuihe Island. However, government policy had less impact on aliens than mounting public hysteria, stemming from anti-German sentiment which pre-dated the war, reports of German atrocities, and reaction to long casualty lists. Distaste for German sympathisers, reports of German spies, fears that German agents would poison water supplies or spread disease—all affected the public mood. An Anti-German League led the crusade to combat the supposed German threat. New Zealanders of German descent suffered from abuse and harassment, and several buildings owned by Germans were burned, including a Lutheran church. The passing of the Alien Enemy Teachers Act 1915, which forced the dismissal of Professor G.W. von Zedlitz from Victoria University College, reflected the frustrated and vindictive atmosphere of the time. In Northland the war heightened existing antipathy towards Dalmatian gum-diggers. Despite supporting Serbia, an ally, they found themselves classified as enemy aliens. Rumours abounded of a planned revolt, and the Dalmatian community was harassed.

In conformity with developments in Great Britain, the government established an Alien Enemies Commission in June 1915 to investigate the loyalty of enemy aliens. Public unease remained, however, and feelings were easily inflamed, as by the apparent desertion from 1NZEF of Private W.P. Nimot (a soldier of German descent) to the enemy in June 1916. Soldiers with foreign-sounding names came under suspicion, and those of German or Austro-Hungarian descent were either discharged from 1NZEF or removed from the front line. Official treatment became progressively harsher and more systematic during the war. By September 1915 any alien could be interned, while from 1916 businesses of enemy aliens had to be licensed. Under the Registration of Aliens Act 1917, all aliens—more than 8000—had to be registered with the police. A major source of resentment was the fact that aliens were exempt from conscription. Many Dalmatians were anxious to prove their loyalty, but bureaucratic inertia and divisions within the Dalmatian community prevented anything being done, until in June 1918 John Cullen was appointed to take charge of enemy aliens for compulsory home service. A worse man for the position could not have been appointed—he was intolerant and tactless. In June 1918 strikes broke out among the Dalmatian workers, leading to arrests and internment. Although the last internees were released in February 1919, hostility towards enemy aliens lingered for a long time.

With war looming in the late 1930s the New Zealand authorities again found themselves considering the problem of enemy aliens. From 1937 the Aliens Committee of the ★Organisation for National Security began preparing for action on the outbreak of war. The Alien Control Emergency Regulations, which came into force on 4 September 1939, required all aliens, including naturalised German-born New Zealanders, to register with the police. By 1940 about 2000 enemy aliens had been registered, and forty-five Germans and Italians considered to be pro-Nazi or pro-Fascist had been interned at Somes Island. Both government and public attitudes to enemy aliens were relatively benign until the war situation deteriorated sharply in mid 1940. Reports of a 'fifth column' at work in New Zealand brought calls for the internment of all enemy aliens, and in Auckland a 'sixth column' proposed vigilante action against enemy aliens. Public anxiety and the need to screen enemy aliens more thoroughly led to changes in the administration of enemy aliens in October 1940. Fifteen Alien Authorities were established to inquire into 2341 enemy aliens, who were to be classified into five categories. An Aliens Appeal Tribunal reviewed contentious cases. Most enemy aliens were prohibited from owning weapons, maps, or radios, and restrictions were placed upon their movements. Many, such as Italian fishermen at Island Bay, Wellington, were placed under close surveillance. Men considered to be a security risk were interned; ninety Germans, twenty-nine Italians, and twenty-nine Japanese were held on Somes Island by 1942. Because of the possibility of a Japanese attack, they were moved to Pahiatua in 1943, but returned to Somes Island in the following year. Most of the Japanese and two Thais were repatriated via Australia in 1943, a process that was marred by an air crash at Whenuapai in August which killed twelve. In dealing with internees, the authorities adhered scrupulously to international conventions, and they were subject to monitoring by the Swiss Consul.

In classifying aliens by their original nationality, the regulations adversely affected the position of ★refugees from enemy states. While recognising that political or Jewish refugees were sympathetic to the Allied cause, both the government and the public remained suspicious of them. Proposals for a separate classification for refugees were firmly declined. Although aliens were not liable for service, by 1942 they were allowed to join the ★Emergency Precautions Scheme and ★Home Guard. Considerable resentment was caused by the perception that aliens were setting up businesses and taking jobs from New Zealanders disadvantaged by military service, as a result of which aliens' ability to purchase land was restricted in March 1942. While enemy aliens did not face the almost hysterical First

Enemy operations

World War levels of harassment, their position was uncomfortable. They also had to contend with an insensitive and often incompetent officialdom, which even interned several Jewish refugees with Nazis on Somes Island.

Enemy operations in New Zealand waters

During both world wars New Zealand suffered intrusions by enemy warships whose purpose was to disrupt trade and cause a dispersal of Allied forces. Although the German East Asiatic Squadron had plans in 1914 to prey on Australian and New Zealand trade, it was not able to implement them. Not until 1917 did a German warship enter New Zealand waters. The German armed merchant cruiser *Wolf*, commanded by Captain Karl August Nerger, laid twenty-five mines off the Three Kings Islands on the night of 25–26 June and thirty-five mines off Farewell Spit two nights later. Both minefields would later claim victims. The merchant ship *Port Kembla* struck a mine off Farewell Spit on 18 September 1917, and the inter-colonial steamer *Wimmera* went down off North Cape on 26 June 1918 with the loss of twenty-six lives. The *Wolf* also captured, plundered, and sank the steamer *Wairuna*, outward bound from Auckland, and the schooner *Winslow* in the Kermadec Islands in June 1917. Although *Wolf* was the only German vessel to enter New Zealand waters during the ★First World War, there was one other brief German military operation in its vicinity. This involved Count Felix von Luckner, the captain of another raider, *Seeadler*, who had been captured in the Fiji Islands in August 1917 and brought to New Zealand where he was held on Motuihe Island. With ten others, including five interned German naval cadets and one civilian, he seized the camp commandant's launch and made off into the Bay of Plenty. Boarding the scow *Moa*, the escapees hoisted the German ensign and headed north-west. However, they were soon recaptured in the Kermadecs.

During the ★Second World War the German Navy again sent raiders into the South Pacific. The first to make its mark was the *Orion* (Captain Kurt Weyher), which spent seven hours on the night of 13–14 June 1940 laying 228 mines across several approaches to Auckland in Hauraki Gulf. Five days later one of them accounted for the mail steamer *Niagara*, which was carrying 136 passengers as well as half New Zealand's small-arms ammunition (intended to help replenish Great Britain's supplies after the Dunkirk evacuation) and £2.5 million worth of gold bullion. No lives were lost in this incident, but five men were killed later when their minesweeper hit one of the mines. On 20 August 1940 *Orion* intercepted *Turakina* in the Tasman Sea, about 400 kilometres from Cape Egmont. *Turakina*'s broadcast of a raider warning signal led to a one-sided gun duel in which some Germans were wounded; thirty-five of *Turakina*'s crew were killed and twenty made prisoner. This was the first engagement ever fought in the Tasman Sea and the closest to New Zealand in either world war. Although HMNZS *Achilles* was immediately dispatched to the scene of action, *Orion* escaped into the vastness of the ocean.

Joined by *Komet* (Captain Robert Eyssen) and the supply ship *Kulmerland*, *Orion* returned to New Zealand's vicinity later in the year, patrolling the trade routes to the east from 6 to 24 November without success. They were heading north to Nauru when, on 25 November, they came upon and sank the small steamer *Holmwood* en route from the Chatham Islands to Lyttelton. Their presence remained unknown because the *Holmwood* refrained from sending a raider warning signal. This proved costly for the motor-liner *Rangitane*, which had left Auckland that morning and might otherwise have been recalled; she was intercepted by the raiders about 450 kilometres from East Cape. *Rangitane* did successfully transmit a warning signal, but was ruthlessly shelled for her pains. Six of her 111 passengers, including four women, and five crew members were killed or mortally wounded. After the survivors had been taken off, *Rangitane* was sunk by a torpedo, and the raiders escaped from the scene before the arrival of *Achilles*. Most of the prisoners were later landed on Emirau Island in the Bismarck Archipelago; more than 150 Europeans, many of them New Zealanders, were later conveyed to France aboard the German merchantman *Ermland* and spent the rest of the war in German prisoner of war camps. *Komet* returned to New Zealand waters in the second half of June 1941. While her consort, the captured whale-chaser *Adjutant*, laid small minefields of ten mines each in the entrances to both Wellington and Lyttelton harbours on successive nights, she fruitlessly patrolled the trade routes east of Wellington. Neither minefield claimed any victims, and their existence was only revealed by captured German documents after the war. None of the mines have been located.

Despite the relative proximity of her forces, Japan did not mount any serious operations in New Zealand waters during the Pacific War. The first known Japanese intrusion was by the submarine *I-25* (Commander Masaru Obiga) which approached New Zealand from the direction of Tasmania. Entering Cook Strait, she sent her aircraft on a pre-dawn reconnaissance flight over Wellington harbour on 8 March 1942. Proceeding up the east coast, *I-25* used its seaplane to reconnoitre both Hauraki Gulf and Auckland harbour before heading north towards Fiji. On 24 May 1942 a similar reconnaissance of the Auckland area was carried out by *I-21*, which had come south from Fiji and subsequently proceeded to Sydney to join other

Japanese submarines in launching a raid on Sydney harbour six days later. There is evidence of further submarine visitations during 1943 and 1944, though none have been confirmed.

The last enemy warship to operate in New Zealand waters was *U-862* (Captain Heinrich Timms), during a three-month operational cruise in Australian waters from the German base at Penang. A type IXD2 boat carrying a crew of sixty-four, she passed down the east coast of New Zealand from 7 to 21 January 1945. The submarine made close inspections of Gisborne and Napier harbours, and unsuccessfully attacked a merchant ship off the latter. Members of the crew were astonished at the seeming lack of any sense of threat in the New Zealand towns at this late stage of the war, but there is no truth in claims that some of them were put ashore to milk Hawke's Bay cows. *U-862* was heading for Wellington when a message was received recalling her to Jakarta. She continued round the South Island and proceeded south of Australia. The unplanned nature of her intrusion (and hence lack of radio messages about it) helped to ensure that the submarine's movements in New Zealand waters were not revealed by Allied signals intelligence sources, and it passed unnoticed in New Zealand at the time.

R. Alexander, *The Raider "Wolf"* (Angus & Robertson, Sydney, 1968); S.D. Waters, *The Royal New Zealand Navy* (War History Branch, Wellington, 1956); D. Stevens, *U-boat Far from Home: The Epic Voyage of U 862 to Australia and New Zealand* (Allen & Unwin, St Leonards, NSW, 1997).

Ensor, Wing Commander Maechel ('Mick') Anthony (5 January 1922–27 December 1994) was one of New Zealand's most successful anti-submarine airmen. From Rangiora, he began pilot training in the RNZAF in August 1940 and a year later was posted to the RAF's Coastal Command. It was while flying with 500 Squadron in January 1942 that he first came to notice, winning a DFC for a determined attack on three German supply ships in the North Sea, in which he flew so low that the airscrew of his starboard engine struck the sea. Anti-submarine patrols over the Atlantic occupied the squadron's attention during the rest of the year, and by October he had earned a bar to his DFC for four attacks on U-boats. After his squadron moved to Tafaraoui in Algeria, he made yet another attack on an enemy submarine north of Algiers on 15 November 1942. His aircraft was caught in the blast of the explosion which destroyed the German vessel, but he managed to gain enough height for his crew and himself to bale out; of the four men aboard, two died as a result of this incident. For this exploit he was made a DSO. After spending six months as a staff officer at Coastal Command headquarters, he returned to flying duties in August 1943, and was assigned to 224 Squadron. Two months later he had the misfortune to damage a Free French submarine which was operating in the wrong area. From January 1945 he commanded the squadron, and he sank his last U-boat on 5 May 1945. His anti-submarine successes were recognised with the award of a bar to his DSO. Ensor remained in the RAF after the war. He took part in the ★Berlin airlift, served with the US Navy on attachment, was awarded an AFC in 1954, and occupied various staff jobs before retiring to Christchurch in 1967.

V. Orange, *Ensor's Endeavour* (Grub Street, London, 1994).

Exchanges play an important role in providing military personnel with opportunities to gain both direct professional expertise and experience of other military systems. They are particularly valuable in New Zealand's case because of the limited availability of command experience at high levels or in specialist areas. Exchanges between British and colonial units were advanced as useful in encouraging cooperation during the 1897 Colonial Conference in London. However, New Zealand authorities at first saw the small size of the New Zealand permanent forces as an obstacle to such activities, and it was not until 1909 that the first exchanges involving New Zealand military personnel occurred. New Zealand officers from the Permanent Force underwent instruction in England, while British officers were seconded for staff and instructional duties in New Zealand. Exchanges with Australia began in 1913, but were soon brought to a halt by the outbreak of the ★First World War. In the inter-war period New Zealand officers were posted to the Indian Army to gain command experience. The close relationship between the British and New Zealand armies was continued after the ★Second World War, with New Zealand officers being attached to British units, while British officers gave instruction in specialist areas such as artillery or signalling. Exchanges between the RNZAF and RAF were inaugurated in 1947, and involved several senior officers annually. RAF officers held important posts in the RNZAF such as Deputy Chief of the Air Staff and Director of Technical Services, while New Zealand staff held positions at RAF commands and schools. A similar system of exchanges also existed between the RNZN and the Royal Navy, with New Zealand officers being attached to the Royal Navy to gain experience of higher levels of command. In the 1950s RNZN frigates were exchanged with British frigates to allow the former experience operating with larger forces in the Mediterranean.

Since the 1970s there have usually been about forty New Zealand officers and NCOs on exchange postings overseas at any one time. These longer-term arrangements have been supplemented by a number of more

Members of 2nd/1st Battalion, RNZIR, alight from an RNZAF C-130 Hercules during an exercise in 1985 (*NZ Army*)

transient arrangements, such as the 'Tasman' unit exchanges between the Australian and New Zealand armies, first instituted in 1962, under which units of up to 200 personnel have been exchanged each year to participate in exercises. Such exchanges were extended to American and British units in 1974 and 1978 respectively. Defence links with Australia were further extended in 1979 when a short-term exchange programme was implemented, with up to forty personnel annually being exchanged for short periods. However, exchanges with the United States were suspended in 1985 as a result of the ★ANZUS dispute.

Exercises or manœuvres are simulated operations or rehearsals intended to train soldiers, test and evaluate their performance, and improve preparation for actual wartime operations. They usually take the form of mock battles with umpires adjudging casualties and the success of operations. The first exercises began with annual camps of the ★Volunteer Force, and were designed to acquaint volunteers with field work, even if many appear to have resembled a day out, complete with civilian spectators to view the excitement. A more professional approach was apparent after the arrival of Major-General A.J. ★Godley in 1910. More rigorous camps were held, and officers underwent regular 'staff rides' in which, by a combination of maps and rides across the countryside, they devised and solved tactical problems.

The importance of realistic and hard training was reinforced during the ★First World War. In 1917, for example, the New Zealand Division exercised for more than a month in preparation for its attack at Messines over ground chosen for its resemblance to that which would have to be traversed on the day. Exercises were also held in March 1918, with the emphasis upon open warfare. Between the world wars exercises were limited to annual camps (often cancelled because of financial constraints) and TEWTs (tactical exercises without troops), in which officers conducted hypothetical operations on maps, in an area of countryside, or on a sand table sculptured to represent terrain. The first divisional-level exercise for the 2nd New Zealand Division took place in April 1940, though the lack of equipment detracted from its value. The 'Sidi Clif' exercises in late 1941 were particularly important in developing mobile doctrine for the desert, but crucially no British tanks (which New Zealanders would rely on in action) participated in the exercise. Exercises conducted in Syria in 1942 were an important step in the development of the division, particularly in regard to the use of ★artillery. General Sir Bernard ★Montgomery's appointment as commander of the 8th Army in late 1942 led to an increased emphasis upon realistic exercises, and the El Alamein offensive was notable for the thorough and realistic exercises conducted beforehand. Such intensive rehearsals set a pattern that was followed for the rest of the war. Exercises were also

161

staged in New Zealand and the Pacific during the ★Second World War, the most important being the 'Battle of the Kaimais' in October 1942, a jungle warfare exercise held by 3rd New Zealand Division in preparation for its deployment to the Pacific.

Since the Second World War exercises, especially with overseas forces, have been fundamental to the effectiveness of New Zealand's small services. During the 1950s the Army had to be content with annual camps and large-scale officer exercises, while the RNZN trained with British and Australian navies in ★anti-submarine warfare, usually in biannual exercises in the Far East. The RNZAF stationed a fighter squadron at ★Cyprus in the early 1950s, partly to provide aircrew with the opportunity of working alongside allies in regular exercises. During the 1960s the number of joint exercises with allies increased. The annual Tasman exchange exercises between the New Zealand and Australian armies began in 1962 (and continue today). The RNZN conducted about five major exercises annually, most with the British and Australian navies in anti-submarine warfare, including the annual Longex/Auckex exercises in New Zealand waters. The RNZAF trained on a regular basis with the RAAF. By the 1970s joint exercises had become a standard feature of New Zealand defence preparations. The Tropic series of exercises in the South Pacific and the Taiaha Tomak annual exercises involving New Zealand and Malaysian forces were instituted in the late 1970s. Exercises also tended to become increasingly large and complex, the Tasmanex exercises of 1979 for example involved twenty-six ships from four navies. Exercises with American forces became more important, with Pacific Pack (an annual exchange with American land forces), Triad (a regular command exercise for the ANZUS partners), and Rimpac (a major naval exercise for Western forces near Hawaii).

The suspension of New Zealand's participation in the ★ANZUS alliance in the mid 1980s badly affected the ability of New Zealand forces to exercise with its allies. It has prevented New Zealand forces taking part in major exercises with their Australian counterparts when American units are involved, though Australia has been willing, at some considerable additional expense to itself, to conduct separate exercises with New Zealand forces. In 1985 the ★New Zealand Defence Force mounted a tri-service exercise in the Cook Islands—the biggest of its type by the New Zealand forces since 1945—to demonstrate a self-reliant capacity. Four years later, in Exercise Golden Fleece, 7800 troops in New Zealand rehearsed an intervention on the mythical Pacific island of 'Colchis'. The suspension of defence links with the United States hit the RNZN and RNZAF particularly hard, the former being forced, for example, to run its own control of shipping exercises or rely upon the Australians. The ability of the armed forces to exercise was further curtailed by severe budgetary constraints in the 1990s. Currently New Zealand forces exercise on a regular basis with Australian forces, and also take part in the exercises of allies in Asia and Canada. Even though their equipment has often been antiquated, New Zealand personnel have generally performed creditably in joint exercises with allies.

Eyre, Dean Jack (14 May 1914–) was the driving force behind the establishment of the Ministry of Defence. After serving in the RNVR during the ★Second World War, he entered Parliament in 1949 and gained Cabinet status five years later. He briefly held the Defence portfolio in 1957, and regained it after the National Party's victory in the 1960 general election. An activist minister, he was determined to achieve greater integration of the three services' activities to cut overhead costs and free up funds for re-equipment programmes which were becoming urgent as New Zealand's Second World War surplus materiel became obsolete. Often remarking on his feeling of driving 'a three-wheeled coach', he concluded that a new coordinating department of state was necessary. Although he secured Cabinet's agreement to this course in November 1962, he soon went further to propose a unitary ministry incorporating the three services. Despite strong service opposition, he was able to achieve this goal in 1964. He was the first chairman of the ★Defence Council established later that year. On security issues, he firmly supported New Zealand's alliance-based policy, and saw no alternative to the contribution of combat forces to the American-led coalition in the ★Vietnam War, though he was overseas when Cabinet in May 1965 decided to send an artillery battery. After retiring from politics in 1966, he was New Zealand's High Commissioner in Canada from 1968 to 1973.

F

Fairbrother, Brigadier Monty Claude (21 September 1907–16 February 1997) oversaw the Second World War official history project after the death of Major-General Sir Howard ★Kippenberger in 1957. Carterton-born, and working as a clerk in Masterton, he began his military career in 1925, when he became a member of his local ★Territorial Force unit, the Hawke's Bay Regiment, in 1925. From 1931 to 1936 he was aide-de-camp and secretary to the Administrator in Western Samoa. He first became associated with Kippenberger when, in September 1939, he joined 20th Battalion as a junior officer. After serving with it in ★Greece, and on the staff of 2nd New Zealand Division in 1941–42, he became brigade major in Kippenberger's 5th Brigade. In 1943 he commanded successively 21st, 23rd, and 28th (Maori) Battalions. Another spell on the divisional staff in 1944 was followed by command of 26th Battalion during the last eight months of the ★Italian campaign. His wartime relationship with Kippenberger lay behind his appointment as associate editor in the ★War History Branch in 1946. He was Editor-in-Chief from 1957 to 1963, a largely administrative role. Still a Territorial officer, he commanded 2nd Infantry Brigade between 1951 and 1956, and was later honorary colonel of the Hawke's Bay Regiment. He was also an associate member of the Army Board from 1955 to 1960, and later chairman of the War Pensions Board (1963–75). He was made a CBE in 1956.

Falklands War New Zealand was not directly involved in the British–Argentinian conflict which occurred in 1982 following the occupation of the Falkland Islands, a British colony, by Argentine troops. However, during a visit to the United Kingdom Prime Minister Robert Muldoon offered to make available a New Zealand frigate to relieve a similar British vessel operating in the Royal Navy's Task Group in the Indian Ocean so that the latter could be deployed to the South Atlantic. Some in New Zealand criticised this action as a throwback to the era of supporting Great Britain through thick and thin. A desire to enhance New Zealand's position in trade negotiations with Britain was a more likely explanation for Muldoon's offer, which reputedly was made during a dinner. HMNZS *Canterbury* was duly deployed to the Indian Ocean in May 1982, she and HMNZS *Waikato* thereafter alternating in the role. *Waikato* returned for another three-month deployment with the Task Group in mid 1983. A number of New Zealanders serving with British forces saw action in the war, with at least one being killed in action.

Fanning Island, a small atoll just north of the equator, was important during the first half of the twentieth century as a landing point for the cable linking New Zealand with the United States. In September 1914 the German cruiser *Nürnberg* landed an armed party on the island to cut the cable and destroy installations there. With this in mind, New Zealand undertook in August 1930 to send a garrison to the island in the event of war. This commitment led to the New Zealand regular force being increased by 150 men in April 1939. On 30 August 1939 a thirty-two-strong detachment (A Company, Permanent Force) left New Zealand for the island aboard the cruiser HMS *Leander*. In March 1941 the garrison was reinforced by another platoon and the crew for a 6-inch gun. A few months later four signallers arrived to establish a coastwatching service (see COASTWATCHERS). For

Featherston incident

the men, ultimately numbering 113, it was a lonely and uncomfortable vigil, broken only by periodic reliefs from New Zealand. In May 1942 the United States took over responsibility for the garrison.

Featherston incident On 25 February 1943, forty-eight Japanese prisoners of war and one New Zealand guard died following a stand-off at the Featherston prisoner of war camp in the Wairarapa. From a New Zealand perspective, the incident remains one of the most controversial wartime encounters between New Zealand and Japan, and highlights the cultural gap which existed between the two belligerent nations. Japanese servicemen captured by United States forces arrived in New Zealand in August 1942. Neither the New Zealand government nor the Army received adequate warning about the transfer, forcing hasty renovations to the former ★First World War army camp at Featherston. By 16 February 1943, the camp housed 855 prisoners, mainly from the Imperial Work Force and naval units. In compliance with the Geneva Convention, the Work Force personnel maintained their compound, but the remaining prisoners became increasingly recalcitrant in the weeks leading up to the incident. A suicide plot by several naval personnel came to the attention of the camp authorities, while some prisoners allegedly planned to overpower the guards. On the morning of 25 February matters came to a head. A group of approximately 250 naval ratings in No. 2 compound refused to parade for work. The Camp Adjutant, Lieutenant James Malcolm, and a Japanese officer, Sub-Lieutenant Adachi, attempted to negotiate for two hours. The guards arrived, encircling the prisoners, who sat on the alluvial ground of the compound. Nishimura, another officer, was removed by the guards and Adachi retreated among the prisoners. Eventually, Malcolm fired two shots, the second hitting Adachi in the shoulder. When the prisoners surged forward throwing stones and improvised weapons, the guards opened fire. Within twenty seconds, thirty-one Japanese lay dead, and another ninety-one were wounded, of whom seventeen died. Ten New Zealanders were injured by the barrage of stones and one, caught in the cross-fire, subsequently died. Concern about Japanese reprisals against Allied prisoners of war influenced the reaction of both the government and the military authorities to the incident. A military Court of Inquiry sat at Featherston from 2 to 10 March 1943. The Imperial POW Committee in London edited the New Zealand report on the shootings to diminish any possible propaganda value to the Japanese authorities. The final report emphasised the guards' necessity to protect themselves, and that firing stopped at the earliest available opportunity. Moreover, incitement by Adachi and Nishimura, the inquiry claimed, underlay the 'mutiny'. Accordingly, the Army made plans to court-martial both officers, but dropped them when questions arose about the applicability of existing legislation to mutiny by POWs and it was realised that a trial would disrupt a now-settled camp life. In effect, the Army refused to accept any responsibility for the incident. However, the hasty construction of the Featherston Camp, and inadequate staffing, had hindered attempts to establish a smooth camp regime. More importantly, the guards at Featherston and their captives held dramatically different cultural values. For the New Zealanders, the camp provided their first direct contact with Japanese. Wartime propaganda did not weigh in favour of good camp relations. Although the New Zealand government, unlike its Japanese counterpart, had ratified the Geneva Convention in 1934, only a fragmentary translation of its contents was available to the prisoners before the incident. Moreover, under the Japanese Military Field Code 1941, the prisoners equated physical capture with spiritual death, leaving them ostracised by both the state and their families. New Zealand official understanding of this issue came too late.

M. Nicolaidi, *The Featherston Chronicles: A Legacy of War* (HarperCollins, Auckland, 1999).

PETER BOSTON

Fencibles were a specially raised corps of army pensioners sent to New Zealand to augment British military resources in the newly established colony. Their arrival arose from Governor George ★Grey's advice to London in February 1846 that he would need at least 2500 men to secure British supremacy in New Zealand. Faced with the problem of funding a rapidly expanding empire from an inadequate tax base—there was no income tax—the British government looked to means of meeting Grey's requirements without augmenting the Army, which was deemed politically impossible. The answer seemed to be to transfer a further 900 troops from the New South Wales command to reinforce the 1100 already in New Zealand and send 500 army pensioners from the United Kingdom. The latter would be recruited from the existing Fencibles corps organised throughout the British counties by Colonel A.M. Tulloch and numbering about 20,000 men. The idea of an overseas corps of pensioners had developed from an earlier correspondence between E.G. Wakefield and the Secretary of State for the Colonies, Earl Grey. Wakefield had added to Prince Eugene's early eighteenth century notion of a cordon of soldier settlers to defend Austria against invasion from Turkey by using Patrick Matthew's published work on recruiting emigrant settlers for the defence of new colonial possessions. This work, *Emigration Fields*, made particular reference to New Zealand. Governor

Grey was instructed to prepare two or three village sites for the reception of what was to be known as the Royal New Zealand Fencibles Corps. The men, who would be accompanied by their wives and children, were to be given an acre (0.4 hectare) of land and a house or hut. As the discharged soldiers had for so long been under the care of their officers, they had little initiative of their own and made poor settlers. Therefore they would be accompanied by staff officers on permanent pay, who would be granted four hectares of cleared land, 16.2 hectares of uncleared land, and a house. As Auckland, the colony's capital, would always need to be defended, Earl Grey suggested that the Fencibles' villages be located in that vicinity. It was first thought that, to save expense, the corps would be shipped to New Zealand by the Royal Navy. When this proved impractical, transport was provided by chartered vessels. As well, an adequate supply of building materials for the cottages and implements for the gardens was to be sent and, to overcome the probable lack of engineers in the colony, a detachment of engineers was added. The high degree of care taken in providing for the corps was in marked contrast to the lack of concern for New Zealand Company emigrants. The corps was to be financed by the British government from a medley of sources, for Parliament was not asked to vote supply. Governor Grey was authorised to draw on the British Treasury, through the Military Chest, for what monies he required at his end and, in England, the raising, equipping, and transporting costs were to be met by the Army vote. Eventually British expenditure was to be recouped from profits from the sale of Crown land in New Zealand. This convenient but impractical system of accounting led to much heated discussion, particularly after the New Zealand Company debts were charged to the colony; it was not until 1868, about ten years after all the Fencibles had become civilians, that both governments decided to drop all claims and counter-claims, and the Fencibles' debt, amounting to nearly £68,000, was no longer an issue.

In New Zealand Governor Grey did not feel bound by Earl Grey's stipulation that the Fencibles would be best sited with the defence of Auckland in mind. However, after flirting with the notion of settlements at Kerikeri on missionary land, at the Bay of Islands, or to the north of Warkworth, he decided that sites near Auckland, which would benefit from the necessary public works, would have the best chance of economic success. Panmure, named after Fox Maule, the Secretary of State for War and soon to become the 2nd Baron Panmure, was chosen as the central village; its site was 14.5 kilometres from Auckland. Three further villages, each about eight kilometres from Panmure, were selected: Onehunga, Otahuhu, and Howick (the second title of Earl Grey). Unfortunately for the men not even the site for the first village had been decided before the first ship, the *Ramillies*, arrived on 5 August 1847; they were kept on board ship for a month until temporary accommodation was prepared. In all ten shipments between 1847 and 1852 brought 695 men to the colony, along with 1887 wives and children. The men were mostly Army pensioners, though some were from the Royal Marines and a few were seamen from the Royal Navy. Many were Irish and Roman Catholic, but most of the English shires were represented. The level of literacy was low and addiction to drink among both men and women was common. Governor Grey considered the plan for the cottages sent by Ordnance too expensive and replaced it with his own plan. This exchanged the single cottage for each family, of two lined rooms and a large loft, for a double unit, unlined and without foundations, wooden floor, or loft. The records are unclear but it appears that sergeants had single cottages. Officers were more lavishly housed in four-roomed bungalows. Until the first cottages were ready, large accommodation sheds were built.

The Fencibles were called out only once for actual military service. On 17 April 1851, in the face of a suspected Maori attack on Auckland, 164 officers and men occupied a crest above Mechanics Bay, while others defended ferries, portages, and footways near the villages. However, no attack eventuated. For the rest of the time, besides improving their cottages and acre plots, Fencibles built roads to connect the villages, cut and sawed timber, and carried out a range of public works. They had signed on for a period of ten years and all had completed their service by 1859. Their military service was of no consequence, and as settlers they lacked initiative and drive. Their major benefit would be derived from their families and the establishment of a considerable number of small, landed proprietors in a fertile country.

IAN WARDS

Fenian riots When news of the execution of three Irish nationalist 'Fenians' at Manchester reached the gold mining settlements on the West Coast in early 1868, sectarian tensions between Irish Catholics and Protestants were inflamed. As demonstrations and protest marches swelled, incited by a vitriolic local press, several hundred special constables were sworn in and a volunteer rifle corps was formed. The arrest of seven Hokitika 'Fenians' further angered the Catholics. Fearing a possible insurrection, the government on 1 April ordered seventy members of the ★Armed Constabulary under the command of Lieutenant-Colonel Thomas ★McDonnell to proceed to Hokitika. On the following day there was rioting near Westport in what was termed, with much exaggeration, the Battle of Addison's Flat, but cooler heads eventually prevailed.

Fighter and fighter-bomber aircraft

The 'Hokitika Seven' were given light sentences, and in May the situation had quietened to the extent that the Armed Constabulary men were able to return to their pacification duties in the North Island. Eleven years later, clashes between Catholics and Orangemen at Timaru and Christchurch led to the dispatch of fifty Armed Constabularymen to the former and the swearing in of ★Volunteer Force personnel as special police, but the tumult quickly died away. (See CIVIL POWER, AID TO)

R.S. Hill, *The History of Policing in New Zealand, Volume 2: The Colonial Frontier Tamed, New Zealand Policing in Transition, 1867–1886* (GP Books, Wellington, 1989).

Fighter and fighter-bomber aircraft, RNZAF

Most fighters flown by the RNZAF have had dual roles of pure day fighter and fighter-bomber/ground attack. Apart from three Gloster Grebe 1920s biplane fighters purchased as advanced trainers, the first to be obtained were US-built Curtiss P-40 Kittyhawks. These were released to New Zealand from British orders for local defence purposes in 1942, at a time when Japanese carrier air groups ranging through the Pacific and Indian Oceans raised the possibility of serious aerial attack on New Zealand for the first time. Since fighters are severely limited without a supporting early warning system based on radar, much effort was expended by the RNZAF, with support from the Department of Scientific and Industrial Research and the New Zealand Post Office, to develop radar-based systems.

From 1943 until the end of the war RNZAF fighter squadrons were actively engaged in support of American forces in the ★Solomons campaign. For a country the size of New Zealand, waging an air war with single-engine fighters over an area the size of Western Europe was an extraordinary feat of organisation and technical prowess. Supply lines stretched thousands of miles. The fighters were shipped from the United States to New Zealand or island bases where they had to be stripped of protective coatings, assembled, and test-flown. Once received, the aircraft had to be maintained in a difficult climate, with frequent shortages of spares. Tropical-weight flying suits and flying helmets seemed always to be in short supply. Operations, and ferrying of aircraft to and from the rear, were conducted over hundreds of kilometres of ocean with limited communications and navigation aids, patchy search and rescue facilities, and incomplete weather forecasting.

Six squadrons took the P-40 into action during the ★Pacific War. The RNZAF evolved a practice where aircraft were allocated to servicing units, which supplied the squadrons on a daily basis as required. The aircraft were shipped to New Zealand, then flown into the combat area via Norfolk Island and Espiritu Santo in the New Hebrides, escorted by Hudson bombers providing

RNZAF airmen at a forward air base prepare for operational service a Corsair newly shipped from the United States in 1944. RNZAF roundels have already been painted on the fuselage and will soon be applied over the US markings under the starboard wing (*RNZAF, 4875*)

navigational support. By mid 1943 it was clear that the P-40 was past its prime as an air superiority fighter, although it enjoyed considerable support as a fighter-bomber. Given that the RNZAF was operating under US Navy command, it turned to that service for a replacement. The United States agreed to supply Chance-Vought F4U Corsairs. The first of more than 400—the most of any single type employed by the RNZAF—began entering service in May 1944. Thirteen squadrons flew the hefty aircraft with its distinctive gull-shaped wing. The RNZAF was preparing to transfer a four-squadron fighter wing using the latest Corsairs to the former Netherlands East Indies when the war ended. Had it continued into 1946, the Corsairs would have been replaced by North American Mustangs.

With the war's end, ★Lend-Lease was terminated and major supply arrangements were cancelled—although too late to halt the first thirty Mustangs already on the water to New Zealand. These were placed in storage until issued to the new TAF fighter squadrons between 1948 and 1957. In 1946, the RAF loaned a Gloster Meteor jet fighter to the RNZAF for familiarisation, while the first jets to serve with squadrons, Vampires, arrived in 1952, and were used by 14 and 75 Squadrons in a day fighter/ground attack role. Former RAF Vampires were obtained to replace the Mustangs in the TAF squadrons. When in 1952 14 Squadron was posted to ★Cyprus, it flew Vampires hired from the RAF. It transferred to Singapore in 1955 to fly RAF Venoms. During the 1960s the RNZAF switched to a tactical bombing/interdiction role, but in 1970 it reverted to a single-seat fighter-bomber role with the purchase of A-4 Skyhawks. This role seemed

Fighter and fighter-bomber aircraft

De Havilland Vampires, with their distinctive twin tail booms, were the RNZAF's first jet fighters. Surplus RAF Vampire FB5s purchased in the 1950s included NZ5671, which is depicted at Ohakea air base in its RAF camouflage and with 75 Squadron markings on its tail booms (*RNZAF*)

set to continue into the new century with the National-led coalition government's decision, in 1998, to replace the Skyhawks with twenty-eight F-16s leased from the United States; however, the Labour–Alliance administration which took office in December 1999 wasted little time in cancelling the deal.

The principal RNZAF fighter and fighter-bomber aircraft have been:

Corsair, Chance-Vought and Goodyear (Single-seat fighter). Wingspan 12.5 m; length 10.2 m; armament 6 x .5-inch machine-guns, 1000 lb bombs; maximum speed 680 km/h; range 1790 km; power 1 x 2250 h.p. Pratt & Whitney Double Wasp radial engine.

The RNZAF operated three versions of the Corsair, whose unusual 'bent wing' shape was designed to provide sufficient room for the large propeller required by the Double Wasp engine and short main undercarriage legs. The first went into action with 20 Squadron on Bougainville in 1944. As Japanese aerial opposition had been largely eliminated, the Corsairs were used for close air support as the fighting moved from the central Solomons to New Britain and New Ireland. As deliveries built up, Corsairs were allocated to the fighter operational training units, the Central Fighter Establishment, and the Central Flying School. By the end of the war, seventeen had been lost to enemy action and about 130 written off in accidents. The survivors were flown back to New Zealand. Twenty-four were shipped to Japan aboard the British aircraft-carrier HMS *Ocean* when 14 Squadron was dispatched to form part of the ★British Commonwealth Occupation Force. Four were destroyed in crashes and the remainder were burned in a spectacular funeral pyre before the squadron returned to New Zealand. The remaining RNZAF Corsairs in New Zealand were flown to Rukuhia to join the rows of surplus aircraft for scrapping in the 1950s and 1960s. One RNZAF Corsair survives in an airworthy condition in Great Britain.

Kittyhawk/Warhawk, Curtiss (Single-seat fighter). Wingspan [P-40E] 11.3 m; length 9.7 m; armament 6 x .5-inch machine-guns, 1000 lb bombs; maximum speed 603 km/h; range 1072 km; power 1 x 1150 h.p. Curtiss Wright Allison engine.

The P-40 was the RNZAF's first modern fighter. While not enjoying the reputation of the Spitfire, Mustang, or Thunderbolt, it was a capable low- and medium-level performer, and more than 14,000 were produced during the Second World War. According to US practice, only the P-40E was called Kittyhawk; the other versions were known as Warhawks. New Zealand acquired both Kittyhawks and Warhawks. The former were retained in New Zealand (along with US P-40s formerly used in Tonga and the New Hebrides) for training purposes, and the latter were employed on operations in the Solomons campaign. The P-40N had its RNZAF fighter-bomber operational debut on 7 March 1944, when twenty from the Fighter Wing at Torokina, staging through Green Island, attacked Rabaul with 500 lb bombs. The majority of strikes thereafter were in the Rabaul area. As Corsairs became available, the surviving P-40s were returned to New Zealand to second-line units. Most were scrapped after the war at Rukuhia. One RNZAF P-40E has been restored to flying condition.

Mosquito, De Havilland (2-seater fighter bomber). Wingspan 13.8 m; length 12.3 m; armament 2 x 20 mm cannon, 4 x .303-inch machine-guns, 2500 lb bombs; maximum speed 665 km/h; range 2250 km; power 2 x 1635 h.p. Rolls Royce Merlin engines.

In Europe, 487 (New Zealand) Squadron RAF became a leading exponent of the Mosquito fighter-bomber—the 'wooden wonder'—between 1943 and 1945, playing a prominent part in several famous low-level raids. Planning to equip three regular squadrons with Mosquitos, the RNZAF acquired eighty-nine after the Second World War. The first arrived at Ohakea in January 1947. The three squadrons never eventuated, and only about twenty-two of the Mosquitos were ever used. The rest were placed in storage at Woodbourne until they were scrapped. The type lasted in squadron service with 75 Squadron until 1952, when the arrival of the first Vampires and a reversion in role to day fighter/ground attack made them redundant.

Mustang, North American (Single-seat fighter). Wingspan 11.2 m; length 9.8 m; armament 6 x .5-inch machine-guns, 2000 lb bombs or 8 rockets; maximum speed 700 km/h; range 2700 km; power 1 x 1450 h.p. Packard Merlin engine.

Only thirty of an intended 370 Mustangs had arrived in New Zealand when the war ended in 1945 and the re-equipment of the RNZAF with them was cancelled. They were placed in storage at Hobsonville, then at Ardmore. Reactivated in 1951 for four TAF fighter squadrons, they saw only brief service before being withdrawn in 1955. Several crashed in TAF service. The Mustang ended its RNZAF days with 42 Squadron, towing targets for Vampires at Ohakea. One complete airworthy RNZAF Mustang is still flying in the United States.

Skyhawk, McDonnell Douglas (Single-seat fighter-bomber). Wingspan 8.4 m; length 12.3 m (TA-4K 13 m); armament 2 x 20 mm cannon, up to 7500 lb missiles, bombs, and rockets; maximum speed 1141 km/h; range 3250 km; power 1 x 9300-lb thrust Pratt & Whitney turbojet.

The Skyhawk was the RNZAF's main strike weapon in the last three decades of the twentieth century. The first fourteen (A-4Ks and TA-4Ks) arrived in 1970 and joined 75 Squadron. They were supplemented by a further ten (A-4Gs and TA-Gs) purchased from the RAN in 1984. More advanced avionics were installed in the fleet under Project Kahu in the late 1980s. In 1984 2 Squadron was re-formed to operate initially the RAN-origin aircraft. In 1991 the squadron deployed to the RAN's air station at Nowra, New South Wales, where it provides training for RAN ships against air threats and is allocated an operational role in the defence of northern Australia. The squadron is also responsible for Skyhawk conversion training.

Vampire, De Havilland (Single-seat fighter). Wingspan 11.6 m; length [Mark 52] 9.4 m, [T11] 10.5 m; armament 4 x 20 mm Hispano cannon, 2000 lb bombs; maximum speed 855 km/h; range 1840 km; power 1 x 3100–3500-lb thrust DH Goblin turbojet.

The twin-boom Vampire was the RNZAF's first operational jet aircraft. Eighteen Mark 52s arrived in 1951 and 1952. After assembly and test flying at Hobsonville, they joined 14 Squadron at Ohakea in the day fighter/ground attack role. The Mark 52 had no RAF equivalent, being an export version. Eight ex-RAF versions (FB5), generally similar but with differing radios and more powerful engines, later arrived to supplement the Mark 52. When the RNZAF decided to replace the TAF squadrons' Mustangs, a further twenty-one ex-RAF aircraft were obtained. Six Vampire trainers (T55), with heavily framed cockpit canopies similar to that of the Mosquito, arrived with the Mark 52s, and five new models (T11), with clear canopies, were delivered in 1955 and 1956. When 14 Squadron was posted to Cyprus, 75 Squadron took over its Vampires in New Zealand and 14 Squadron used Vampires hired from the RAF. Vampire flying dwindled with the arrival of Canberra bombers for 14 Squadron, the handful in use being flown by the jet conversion unit. In 1957 and 1958 75 Squadron won wide acclaim for performances by its precision aerobatics team, flying Vampires. When the squadron returned from Singapore in 1962, it re-equipped with the Vampire, which stayed in service until replaced by the Skyhawk in 1970.

Venom, De Havilland (Single-seat fighter). Wingspan 12.7 m; length 10 m; armament 4 x 20 mm cannon, 2000 lb bombs; maximum speed 923 km/h; range 1730 km; power 1 x 4850-lb thrust DH Ghost turbojet.

Venoms were flown by 14 Squadron during its tour of duty in Singapore from 1955 to 1958. Developed from the Vampire, the Venom retained its predecessor's distinctive twin-boom configuration and armament. However, a new wing was developed to take advantage of its more powerful engine. The Venom gave sound service during the *Malayan Emergency, and was flown by 14 Squadron to many parts of South-east Asia.

BRIAN LOCKSTONE

Fiji, New Zealand forces in Fiji's strategic importance to New Zealand's defence was recognised by Lord *Jellicoe in his 1919 report on Pacific defence requirements. It sat astride the shipping routes between Australasia and the United States, and was well placed to serve as a base for an attack on New Zealand by the most likely enemy, Japan. Nothing could be done to fortify it, however, because of an agreement reached at the 1921–22 Washington Conference, which prohibited fortifications in a wide area of the Pacific. Not until 1938 did the New Zealand service authorities begin to give close attention to the islands' defences. Preparations finally got underway in 1939, with the cost of the construction of defence installations being divided between Fiji (which was a Crown colony), New Zealand, and the United Kingdom. Upon the outbreak of the *Second World War the Fiji Defence Force (FDF) consisted of a single weak territorial battalion raised from local European and Fijian volunteers and equipped by New Zealand. In October 1939 five New Zealand officers and NCOs arrived at Suva to instruct the Fijian battalion, followed shortly by another four to advise on the construction of a coastal battery of two 4.7-inch guns. Ten more New Zealand personnel were sent to assist the FDF in early 1940. In June 1940 preparations were begun to send a brigade group from New Zealand to Fiji. Known as 'B Force', 8th Brigade departed New Zealand in late October 1940, at which time New Zealand took formal responsibility for the defence of the group. Both Fijian and New Zealand forces came under the command of Brigadier W.H. Cunningham.

Troops of 30th Battalion have lunch during an exercise in Fiji in 1941 (*K. A. Hendry Collection, Alexander Turnbull Library, PAColl-5645-014*)

The FDF was expanded with the raising of a regular battalion (1st Battalion, FDF), which was integrated into the brigade.

The situation was transformed in December 1941 with Japan's entry into the war. A second brigade (14th) was sent from New Zealand, but this was still felt to be inadequate to meet what was believed to be an imminent Japanese assault, and the FDF was steadily expanded, most of the officers and NCOs for the Fijian units being seconded from 2NZEF (Pacific Section). By mid 1942 the FDF consisted of five coastal artillery batteries, three infantry battalions, and three independent commando units.

The requirements of garrisoning Fiji, preparing for home defence, and maintaining an expeditionary force in the Middle East proved beyond New Zealand's means. After some discussion with the United States, it was agreed in May 1942 that the United States would take over responsibility for the group, which occurred formally on 30 June 1942. Once American troops began to arrive, most of the 3rd Division (formed in Fiji) had returned to New Zealand, but about 500 2NZEF officers and NCOs posted to the FDF remained, along with another 1000 New Zealanders in coastal and anti-aircraft units. All New Zealanders in Fiji were grouped under the title, Fiji Section, 2NZEF, and a New Zealander, Colonel J.G.C. Wales, took command of the FDF. His task was not easy: although under the operational command of the Americans, he was dependent on New Zealand for supplies, officers, and NCOs, and required the cooperation of the British Governor of Fiji.

Both the need to bring the miscellany of Fijian units being created together and the expectation that the FDF would assume a role outside Fiji lay behind the establishment of a Fijian brigade group in November 1942, with the title of the FDF changing to Fiji Military Forces (FMF). At this time there were 211 New Zealand officers and 1340 other ranks with the FDF or with the remaining anti-aircraft units. The expansion of Fijian forces required more New Zealand personnel, and another 300 officers and NCOs from 2NZEF were seconded to the FMF. By August 1943 the FMF had attained a peak strength of 8513, of whom 808 were New Zealanders.

As the Allies went over to the offensive in the Pacific, the question of deploying Fijian forces outside Fiji came to the fore. A special party of twenty-three Fijian commandos under seven New Zealand officers and NCOs had been sent to Guadalcanal in the Solomon Islands in December 1942 where they performed well, gaining a reputation for bushcraft. This

Fiji coups

led to an American request for more Fijian troops, and in April 1943 the 1st Commando, Fijian Guerrillas (including a Tongan platoon), and the 1st Battalion, with New Zealand officers and NCOs, landed at Guadalcanal. In July 1943 the 1st Commando began operations in New Georgia, earning the accolades of American commanders before being withdrawn the next month. The 1st Battalion had spent a quiet nine months coastwatching and training at Guadalcanal and on Kolombangara Island when in December 1943 it was moved to Bougainville, being assigned the role of protecting the recently established air bases there. Over the next five months, in a campaign of ambushes and patrols in thick jungle, heavy casualties were inflicted upon the Japanese. In May the 1st Battalion was joined by the 3rd Battalion on Bougainville, where it was to conduct amphibious operations against the Japanese. During one of these actions Corporal Sefanaia Sukanaivalu won a posthumous ★Victoria Cross. In July 1944 both battalions were returned to Fiji. Intensive training of the FMF continued, with the possibility of their being sent to Burma in 1945, but the war ended before any decision was made. In all fifty-seven members of the FDF/FMF were killed or died overseas during the Second World War, including nine New Zealanders seconded from 2NZEF (Pacific Section). Demobilisation began on 1 September 1945 and was completed by March 1946.

R.A. Howlett, *The History of the Fiji Military Forces, 1939–1945* (Whitcombe and Tombs, Christchurch, 1948); O.A. Gillespie, *The Pacific* (War History Branch, Wellington, 1952).

Fiji coups The overthrow of the Fijian government of Timoci Bavadra by soldiers led by Lieutenant-Colonel Sitiveni Rabuka in May 1987 confronted New Zealand with a difficult problem in determining an appropriate response, in the solving of which ★civil–military relations were severely strained. The New Zealand government was taken by surprise by the coup on 14 May, despite New Zealand's long-standing and close association with the Royal Fiji Military Forces. Indeed, there were several New Zealand instructors and advisers in Fiji at the time as part of the ★Mutual Assistance Programme. The frigate HMNZS *Wellington*, en route to Fiji on a scheduled visit, was after some hesitation allowed to proceed to Suva, where she docked on 16 May (and remained until the 23rd). HMNZS *Canterbury* was also later deployed from Cairns to the vicinity of Fiji. On 18 May Prime Minister David ★Lange, somewhat injudiciously, stated publicly that he would consider a request for assistance in transporting Fijian forces involved in peace-keeping in the Middle East, forty-seven Fijian officers undergoing training in New Zealand, and the commander of the Royal Fiji Military Forces (then in Australia) back to Fiji. The situation was greatly complicated by the hijacking, on 19 May, of an Air New Zealand jumbo jet at Nadi airport. The government's response to this new crisis has been the subject of much controversy since 1987. To the dismay of his military advisers, Lange seemed to favour dispatching a C-130 Hercules to Fiji with a ★Special Air Service detachment to free the hostages. The military authorities were worried by the implications of possible resistance by the Fijian armed forces to this initiative. When they sought a clear definition of the mission, Lange apparently somewhat cavalierly expanded it to protecting New Zealand's interests in Fiji. The resolution of the hijacking within hours forestalled further conflict over the matter by removing the need for immediate military action (though Lange wanted the SAS detachment to remain on standby in case New Zealand diplomatic personnel were threatened). The hydrographic survey ship HMNZS *Monowai* was dispatched to Fiji in case New Zealand nationals had to be evacuated, reaching Suva on 28 May after breaking down en route. However, on 1 June the Fijian authorities ordered her to leave after two New Zealand soldiers had been briefly detained, allegedly for spying. When four months later the Fijian military forces staged a second coup, *Monowai* was again sent to Fiji, though evacuation of New Zealand nationals again proved unnecessary. In the meantime, New Zealand's assistance to Fiji under the Mutual Assistance Programme had been suspended; it would not be resumed until 1992.

Fiji Expeditionary Force The dispatch of New Zealand soldiers to Fiji in 1920 was the first peacetime deployment of New Zealand forces overseas (apart from ★commemorative contingents). It was precipitated by a strike among Indian indentured labourers and sugar-cane farmers. Determined to break the strike, but fearing violence, the Governor of Fiji sought military support from Wellington to back his limited police resources. Convinced that it was 'no ordinary strike'—anti-British feeling was thought to lie behind it—Prime Minister William ★Massey had no hesitation in complying with the request, and the New Zealand government steamer *Tutanekai* was hastily fitted out for the purpose of carrying a small expeditionary force 'as a precautionary measure for [the] safety of [the] white population'. Fifty-six regular soldiers, mainly members of the RNZA, were quickly gathered together from camps throughout New Zealand. Under the command of Major Edward ★Puttick, they departed on 5 February, taking with them a 12-pounder gun (for mounting on the *Tutanekai*) and a dozen machine-guns. Waterside workers and stokers, who opposed the apparent strike-breaking purpose of the expedition, made some difficulties before being assured that the security of the 5000-strong European population was the main consideration. The force reached Suva on 12 February, one day after a minor riot had occurred there. After the troops had landed and marched to the town hall, where they were billeted, a section was immediately sent up the Rewa River by launch to reinforce police. The situation became even more tense when another confrontation with police took place between Suva and Rewa on 14 February, during which one Indian was mortally wounded. Small parties were dispatched to reinforce police outposts at short notice, while others patrolled the roads in cars, but at no stage did the New Zealanders come into direct conflict with the strikers. The arrival of a British sloop further bolstered the local authorities, and the strike petered out. A small permanent Fijian military force was established, using arms and ammunition provided by the New Zealand force. The troops left for home on 18 April 1920, leaving Massey, with characteristic exaggeration, to boast that New Zealand had 'saved Fiji from a disaster'.

Film and television, war in Among the earliest films to be screened in New Zealand were images of New Zealand troops preparing to depart for the ★Boer War. During this conflict, silent films like 'Our Boys in South Africa' reflected the jingoistic mood of the time. When war broke out in 1914, cinema—by now the country's dominant form of popular entertainment—was again to the fore in shaping opinion. Imported 'hate' films such as *Lust of Ages* depicted the alleged barbarism of the German people. However, the conflict did not inspire any home-grown fictional or semi-documentary films relating to the war, as occurred in Australia. In an attempt to provide a New Zealand perspective on the fighting on the ★Western Front, the government arranged for a British cameraman to be attached to the New Zealand Division late in 1917. It was not until 1925 that the first war film was made in New Zealand. Rudall Hayward drew extensively from James ★Cowan's official history *The New Zealand Wars* in producing *Rewi's Last Stand*, in which the captured British hero, a member of the ★Forest Rangers, ends up at the siege of Orakau, where the Maori heroine dies in his arms. The film was notable for the emphasis placed on historical accuracy, albeit within a romantic and Eurocentric framework. Hayward again drew inspiration from Cowan's work in subsequently producing *The Te Kooti Trail*, which depicted the pursuit of the Maori guerrilla ★Te Kooti during the latter stages of the ★New Zealand Wars. Nevertheless American and British films, among them such war stories as the popular *Beau Geste* and the compelling *All Quiet on the Western Front* (initially banned), continued to dominate cinema fare in New Zealand between the world wars. The only talking New Zealand movie with a war theme made in this period was Hayward's remake of *Rewi's Last Stand*, which was released in 1940.

The propagandist influence of cinema did not escape the government upon the outbreak of the ★Second World War, and a series of short films exhorting the public not to be wasteful were screened. A cinematography unit was formed in 2NZEF early in 1941. News films such as the 1941 'The Prime Minister in the Middle East' and 'Country Lads' were also made, but it was not until after the creation of the National Film Unit that regular news films were produced in New Zealand for New Zealand audiences. 'Weekly Reviews', up to twenty minutes long, covered all aspects of New Zealand's war effort from dive-bombers in the Pacific to farm production. New Zealand servicemen were depicted as either heroic or cheerful, accompanied by a stridently patriotic commentary and stirring music. Footage of New Zealanders in 'action' was usually staged. 'Weekly Reviews' (renamed 'Pictorial Parade' from 1952) continued to be produced after the war, and periodically covered military subjects, including the conflicts in South-east Asia, though their tone was much more neutral than in the Second World War features. National Film Unit cameramen twice visited Korea to film activities of New Zealand servicemen during the ★Korean War. 'Pictorial Parade' ran until 1972, by which time television had become the dominant news medium. In 1983 the 'Weekly Reviews' were used as a basis for the National Film Unit's production 'War Years'. Such news material dominated New Zealand cinematography about war in the thirty years after the end of the Second World War. With no substantial indigenous film industry, New Zealand film-goers had to be content with overseas films, which often portrayed New Zealand servicemen in action, as for example in *The Dam Busters* (1954), *Mosquito Squadron* (1968), and *Battle of Britain* (1943, 1969). When another New Zealand-made war movie finally appeared in 1983, it followed Hayward's lead in drawing its theme from the New Zealand Wars. *Utu* displayed some features common to other New Zealand movies, including the brooding, violent 'man alone'. Another war film shot in New Zealand at this time, though not a New Zealand production, *Merry Christmas Mr Lawrence* (1984), dealt with British prisoners of the Japanese. In 1991 New Zealand film-makers at last turned their attention to ★Gallipoli. Based on Maurice Shadbolt's play, *Once on Chunuk Bair* recounted the efforts of a heroic Colonel Connolly who was eventually killed by British shells on the summit of Chunuk Bair. Despite its strongly nationalistic perspective, the film failed to elicit any strong emotional reaction from New Zealand audiences, partly no doubt because its low budget prevented any realistic depiction of the fighting. More recently, Second World War themes have been addressed. *Absent Without Leave* (1993) told the story of a conscript deserting from the Army to be with his young wife. In Gaylene Preston's popular *War Stories Our Mothers Never Told Us*, seven women candidly recalled their experiences of the war. Despite occasional (and notable) successes, New Zealand filmmaking has always struggled. Successful movies have appealed to an international audience or struck an obvious emotional (and nationalistic) chord with the New Zealand public. The experience of war, while a central feature of New Zealand national identity, is difficult to film in a country lacking any substantial film industry and having limited resources. Big-budget war movies such as the Australian productions *Gallipoli* or *The Light Horsemen* have always been beyond New Zealand's means.

The introduction of television in 1960 brought a new element to war cinematography in New Zealand. Early news coverage of war in South-east Asia was both incidental and uncritical. Not until the late 1960s did television become an increasingly critical news medium. The current affairs programme 'Gallery' was strongly criticised by the Minister of Defence, David Thomson, for what he alleged was unbalanced coverage of the ★Vietnam War. Shocking televised images of the war, such as of the summary execution of a Vietcong soldier during the Tet offensive in 1968 or a naked child fleeing a napalm attack, induced strong emotional responses to the war. Television's perceived role in undermining public support at home for the American effort in Vietnam lay behind restrictive controls placed on the medium during subsequent conflicts. During the ★Falklands War of 1982, for example, the British government strictly censored all news reports from the South Atlantic. Media coverage of the US-led coalition's operations in the 1991 ★Gulf War was confined to carefully controlled 'Press Pools', though a different perspective was provided by CNN's coverage from Baghdad (see WAR CORRESPONDENTS). Some television programmes depicting war have been produced in New Zealand. The 1977 miniseries 'The Governor', which was based on the life of Governor George ★Grey, included re-enactments of New Zealand Wars battles. A documentary, 'Gallipoli, the New Zealand Story', was produced to mark the 70th anniversary of the Gallipoli campaign in 1985. Narrated by Lieutenant-General Sir Leonard ★Thornton, it was well received by an audience increasingly aware of the campaign's importance in the shaping of New Zealand national identity. Other such attempts at 'anniversary' documentaries have been less successful. The six-part 'New Zealand at War', produced by the commercial television production company Communicado to mark the fiftieth anniversary of the end of the Second World War, was perhaps the best example of how not to make such a programme, even though it enjoyed good viewer ratings. Communicado determinedly excluded historians from any significant role its production, and the documentary is riddled with errors, naïve assertions, and misuse of film resources. More modest, and historically accurate, documentaries such as 'The Betrayal' (1996) and 'Journey to Arras' (1997) have highlighted previously overlooked aspects of New Zealand's military history, while several documentaries on New Zealand's involvement in Vietnam have been screened. The most recent major documentary series attempted by New Zealand television has been the six-part 'The New Zealand Wars', written and narrated by the historian James Belich. Although some of Belich's assertions have been challenged by other historians, and the presentations were somewhat flat and repetitive, his portrayal of the conflict proved extremely popular and stimulated considerable public debate about the New Zealand Wars.

Findlay, Air Commodore James Lloyd (6 October 1895–17 March 1983) was one of the small group of officers responsible for the development of New Zealand's air force between the wars. The son of a prominent politician and lawyer, he went to the United Kingdom in 1912 to attend the Imperial Service College. With the outbreak of the ★First World War, he secured a commission in the East Surrey Regiment. While serving on the ★Western Front, he was awarded an MC before being wounded during the opening stages of the Battle of the Somme in July 1916. He transferred to the Royal Flying Corps in March 1917, and later gained a commission in the RAF. After being demobilised in 1921, he returned to New Zealand, where he was commissioned in the New Zealand Permanent Air Force in 1923 as a pilot instructor. He commanded the Wigram air base for twelve years from 1926 apart from a period spent on attachment to the RAF in 1930–31. From 1938 to 1941 he was again with the RAF on an exchange posting; he commanded 48 Squadron and later Hooton Park Station. After he returned to New Zealand in July 1941, he served as a staff officer and commanded the Central Group before proceeding to Washington in 1943 to become head of the New Zealand Joint Staff Mission, a post he held for more than a decade. He was made a CBE in 1944.

First World War As part of the British Empire, New Zealand was formally involved in the First World War (also often referred to as the Great War) by King George

First World War

V's declaration of war on Germany on 4 August 1914. This was the culmination of a crisis which had erupted in Europe following the assassination of Archduke Franz Ferdinand of Austria–Hungary on 28 June 1914. A chain reaction of mobilisations prompted by the alliance structure then pertaining and the imperatives of existing war plans was set in motion, and made more menacing by the rapid concentrations made possible by railroads, leading inevitably to a confrontation between the Central Powers (Germany and Austria–Hungary) and the Franco-Russian entente. Faced with the prospect of war on two fronts, Germany was driven by the need to deal rapidly with the French before the Russians could bring their power to bear in the east. This would be accomplished by a massive wheeling movement against France, embodied in the Schlieffen Plan, which was launched immediately (see WESTERN FRONT). The resulting German violation of neutral Belgium on 2 August precipitated the British Empire's intervention, though more fundamentally the British response derived from its long-standing determination to ensure that Germany did not dominate continental Europe.

News of the outbreak of war was received in Wellington at 1 p.m. on 5 August 1914. It was announced by the Governor, Lord Liverpool, on the steps of Parliament to a crowd of 15,000 people. In Europe popular enthusiasm for the war had been evident in all the great powers, and New Zealanders caught the mood. New Zealand's emotional response to the outbreak of war was a reflection of the Dominion's close ties with Great Britain. With New Zealanders regarding themselves as British and Britain as 'Home', the crisis prompted a public clamour in favour of assisting Britain in its moment of crisis. The strongly militarist atmosphere of the time and feelings of moral outrage at the aggression of the Central Powers against smaller countries also contributed to the general ardour with which most New Zealanders entered the war. But behind such sentiments lay a solid foundation of national self-interest. Both New Zealand's economic prosperity and security were at stake. New Zealand was dependent on the availability of the British market for the sale of the wool, frozen meat, and dairy products which dominated its economy. Anything which threatened this market threatened New Zealand's livelihood. An island state in the Pacific, New Zealand had become increasingly aware of its dependence on the British security framework for not only the preservation of its physical integrity but also the protection of its trade on the long haul to the British market. The perceived German threat to that framework had already induced it, in 1909, to make the offer which resulted in the battlecruiser HMS ★*New Zealand* being added to the British battlefleet and to introduce ★compulsory military training. New Zealanders were conscious, moreover, that defeat for the British Empire might lead to a settlement in which their sovereignty could be compromised or extinguished. In these terms Britain's war was New Zealand's war.

In the circumstances New Zealand's pledge of assistance was as inevitable as it was immediate. One of its first actions was to send an expeditionary force

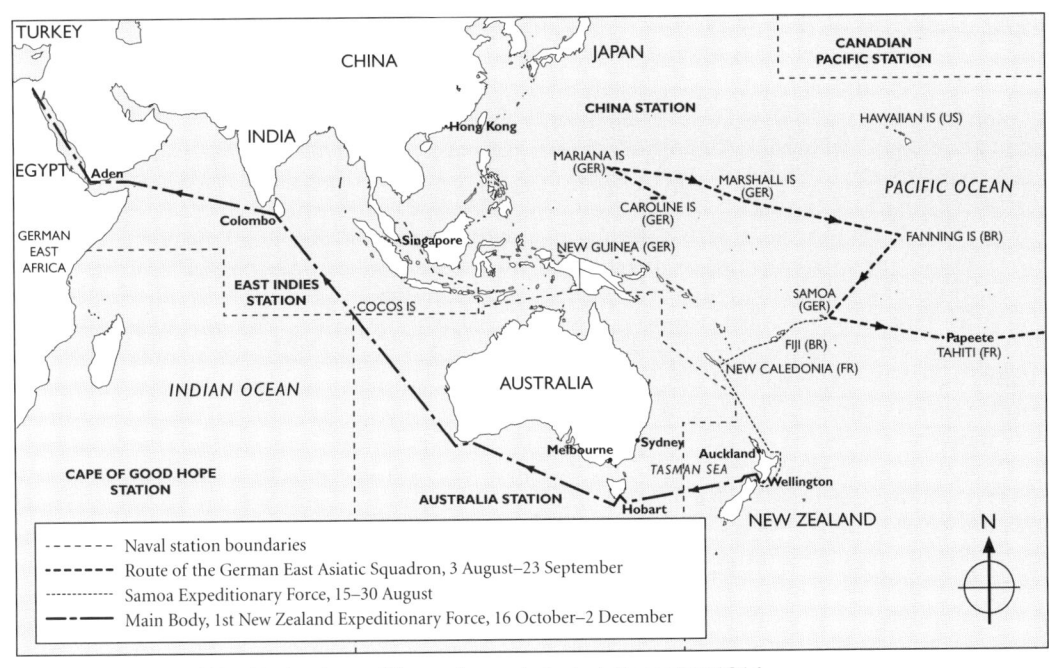

Map 7 Movement of New Zealand expeditionary forces in August–December 1914

First World War

to capture German Samoa, an objective which was achieved on 29 August 1914 (see SAMOA, NEW ZEALAND'S MILITARY ROLE IN). Even before the outbreak of war the provision of a much larger force for service in the main theatre of conflict had been foreshadowed in Parliament by Prime Minister W.F. *Massey. After 5 August, preparations were rapidly put in hand. This response, which entailed sending New Zealand troops to the other side of the globe, was assisted by the absence of any direct threat in the Pacific region. On 23 August Japan entered the war on the side of the Allies, ensuring Allied naval dominance in the Pacific. The Japanese quickly set about capturing German territories north of the equator. After a delay while an adequate escort was provided, the Main Body of the *New Zealand Expeditionary Force left New Zealand on 16 October (see CIVIL–MILITARY RELATIONS). The intention that it should fight in France was overtaken by events. The entry of the Ottoman Empire into the war on the side of the Central Powers on 5 November changed the strategic picture, and the New Zealand and Australian troops were disembarked in Egypt to complete their training and if necessary assist in its defence.

New Zealand's strategy in the war thereafter was to sustain 1NZEF as its main contribution to the common effort, while also keeping up the food production that was so vital to the survival of Britain. Reinforcement drafts left New Zealand at regular intervals throughout the next four years. The manpower requirements of 1NZEF were secured by the introduction of *conscription late in 1916. New Zealand troops took part in the *Gallipoli campaign before being deployed on the *Western Front, while a mounted rifles brigade participated in the *Sinai–Palestine campaign. A small number of New Zealanders also served with British naval and air forces (see AIRMEN, NEW ZEALAND, IN THE FIRST WORLD WAR; ROYAL NAVY IN THE FIRST WORLD WAR, NEW ZEALANDERS IN).

New Zealand, then, played a small but useful part in the British Empire's war effort, and its essential war aim was achieved with the defeat of Germany and its allies in late 1918. Its security, both physical and economic, was ensured by the victory. Superior Allied seapower had made any significant danger to New Zealand's territory remote, at least after the defeat of the German squadron in the Pacific at the outset. Only the triumph of the German High Seas Fleet in the North Sea confrontation with the British Grand Fleet might have changed the picture, but the Battle of Jutland in 1916, the main clash between the two fleets, had not affected the strategic position. As predicted by its defence advisers before the conflict, New Zealand had suffered no more than raider incursion: an armed merchantman laid mines in its waters in 1917 (see ENEMY OPERATIONS IN NEW ZEALAND WATERS). Despite the efforts of German submarines, which brought matters to a crisis in 1917, Britain's supply routes had never been severed. New Zealand farmers enjoyed the benefits of relatively good prices for their produce under commandeer arrangements (see WAR ECONOMY). But the price of security was high: more than 18,000 New Zealanders were killed while serving overseas.

On the home front, most New Zealanders supported the war. The initial response was one of giddy enthusiasm. Alleged (and sometimes actual) German atrocities fired indignation and anger towards all things German, and a campaign arose in the main newspapers to root out anything possibly contaminated by German *kultur*. This public hysteria was heightened by casualty lists. People of German descent became the target of abuse and harassment, while rumours abounded of German spies and conspiracies. As the war dragged on, casualty lists dampened martial ardour. With a long-drawn-out struggle now likely, newspaper editorials preached the necessity of greater sacrifices if the war were to be won. Despite public opprobrium, 69 per cent of men eligible for military service had not volunteered by 1916; only with conscription was New Zealand able to maintain its war effort. By 1917 there was a definite sense of war-weariness; the war remained in a stalemate while the casualty list and food prices continued to rise. In July 1917 there were calls for New Zealand's military commitment to be reduced, and opposition began to the conscription of married men. Heavy losses at Passchendaele in October of that year created despondency, and there was frustration at the length of time being taken in bringing to bear the resources of the United States, which had entered the war in the previous April. Nevertheless, newspapers remained sure of ultimate British victory and there were no calls to bring New Zealand troops home.

The war had a major impact on constitutional arrangements within the British Empire, and affected New Zealand's international status. Tentative moves had been made before the war towards involving the Dominions in imperial decision-making, and the process was accelerated by their contribution to the imperial war effort. An Imperial War Conference was called in 1917 and an Imperial War Cabinet established. These developments were seen by the Dominions as foreshadowing a more cooperative post-war imperial system. After the war, the process continued with the Dominions signing the Treaty of Versailles and becoming members of the *League of Nations in their own right. It culminated in the Balfour Declaration of 1926, which established the equal status of Britain and its self-governing Dominions, and the Statute of Westminster of 1931, which embodied the principle in law.

The First World War seemed to have further strengthened the British Empire. Not only were the resources of the Empire successfully marshalled in the common cause but also the Empire had further extended its territory. German territories in Africa and the Pacific had been acquired, albeit as mandates of the League of Nations. By contrast, rival empires in Europe were in disarray: dismembered Germany was in the throes of revolutionary ferment, the ramshackle Austro-Hungarian Empire had collapsed into a plethora of smaller states, the Ottoman Empire had also been dismembered, Russia was racked with civil war following the Bolshevik coup in November 1917 which had led to its early withdrawal from the war, France was exhausted.

Although it was not immediately apparent, the war had seriously undermined the British Empire's strategic position, and with it the security system upon which New Zealand relied. New potential rivals outside Europe had emerged, in particular the United States and Japan, while the creation of a fundamentally antagonistic communist power in Russia was a new and unstable ingredient in international relations. With its financial position seriously weakened by the war, Britain found it impossible to sustain the level of armaments required to protect its worldwide empire. Its position was further weakened by the termination of the ★Anglo-Japanese Alliance in 1921. Increasingly Britain relied on political action to maintain the status quo, an approach which fell apart in the 1930s.

At first sight the prolonged and costly conflict did not affect New Zealand attitudes to war. When in 1922 a new conflict with Turkey seemed in the offing during the ★Chanak crisis, thousands of men rapidly came forward to form a new expeditionary force. Nevertheless the heavy toll of lives and the seemingly futile nature of many of the battles, especially on the Western Front, affected opinion in New Zealand, as in other Commonwealth countries. Pacifism was boosted. The war also had a marked influence on the development of a distinctive New Zealand national identity, with Gallipoli assuming a central place in New Zealanders' perceptions of themselves as warriors (see NATIONAL IDENTITY AND WAR).

I. McGibbon, *The Path to Gallipoli: Defending New Zealand 1840–1915* (GP Books, Wellington, 1991).

Fisken, Flying Officer Geoffrey Bryson (17 February 1915–) was the leading British Commonwealth air ace against the Japanese. Originally from Gisborne, he was a farm worker in the Wairarapa when he enlisted in the RNZAF in March 1940. After gaining his wings, he was sent to Singapore and eventually posted to 243 Squadron. Despite flying a Brewster Buffalo that was outclassed by its opponents, he managed to down six Japanese aircraft, and possibly another two, during the ★Malayan campaign. Wounded in an engagement on 1 February 1942, he was evacuated from Singapore just before it fell. Back in New Zealand, he was commissioned and subsequently posted to 14 Squadron. While serving at Guadalcanal in mid 1943, and flying a Kittyhawk named 'Wairarapa Wildcat', he destroyed another five Japanese aircraft. Exhausted and ill, he was repatriated to New Zealand in August 1943, and discharged on medical grounds.

Five Power Defence Arrangements In 1967 Australia and New Zealand were confronted by the prospect of the imminent departure of their British partner from the ★British Commonwealth Far East Strategic Reserve in Malaysia and Singapore. The British government indicated that, as part of a general retraction of British power from east of Suez, half the British forces in those countries would be pulled out by 1971, with the rest following within five years. After prolonged discussions, the Australian and New Zealand governments agreed, in 1969, to sustain their presence in Malaysia and Singapore even after the withdrawal of the British forces. A change of government in Great Britain in 1970 led to a change in British plans: it was agreed that a small British force, comparable in size to those of Australia and New Zealand, would remain in place. On this basis, a new defence arrangement was negotiated to replace the Anglo-Malaysian Defence Agreement, which terminated on 31 October 1971.

The Five Power Defence Arrangements, which came into effect on 1 November 1971, were not a formal treaty but rather an exchange of letters which established a broad framework. Britain, New Zealand, and Australia separately concluded agreements with both Malaysia and Singapore. Under the arrangements the five governments made clear their intention to consult together in the event of a threat developing against either Malaysia or Singapore 'for the purpose of deciding what measures should be taken jointly or separately'. A Joint Consultative Council was established. The letters also provided the basis for the continued stationing in Malaysia and Singapore of forces by the three outside powers, which were now grouped as the ★ANZUK Force, and for cooperation between the forces of the five powers. An Integrated Air Defence System (IADS) was created, with an Air Defence Council providing a coordinating forum. Two New Zealand officers have served in the IADS headquarters since its inception.

Australia determined in 1973 to withdraw its ground forces from Singapore (RAAF units remained in Malaysia until 1988), after which Britain decided to follow suit. Following the demise of the ANZUK Force

Fleet Air Arm

in January 1974, New Zealand's troops remained in place as part of the *New Zealand Force South East Asia for another fifteen years. The FPDA, balanced by bilateral cooperative programmes with Indonesia and Thailand, remained an important element in New Zealand's defence policy as a basis for cooperation with Malaysia and Singapore in the 1990s. It provides a framework for *exercises, in which all three arms of the *New Zealand Defence Force take part. Army units of up to battalion strength have been deployed regularly to Malaysia and Singapore to take part in brigade-level exercises with the FPDA partners. New Zealand frigates and 75 Squadron RNZAF are also deployed to the area regularly to participate in exercises. To facilitate New Zealand participation in FPDA activities and its *Mutual Assistance Programme, a small New Zealand Defence Support Unit (South East Asia) has been stationed in Singapore since the disbandment of New Zealand Force South East Asia.

Fleet Air Arm Because of its limited resources, New Zealand has never sought to develop any substantial naval aviation capability. The *cruisers of the *New Zealand Division of the Royal Navy and later the *Royal New Zealand Navy carried floatplanes for reconnaissance purposes, but New Zealand's main contribution in this field was made within the auspices of the Royal Navy's Fleet Air Arm during the *Second World War. Prior to July 1939, when the Admiralty opened the Air Branch (as the Fleet Air Arm was officially known between 1937 and 1953) to volunteers from the Dominions, a few New Zealanders had joined the Royal Navy independently and trained as naval aviators. Under the new scheme only three New Zealanders had sailed for the United Kingdom by the time of the disastrous Norwegian campaign of April 1940, in which about 30 per cent of the Fleet Air Arm's strength was lost, and which highlighted the need for much larger numbers of aircrew. New Zealand offered twenty candidates a month for the air branch of the RNVR. The first draft of these 'Scheme F' personnel—obtained by seeking volunteers from the RNZAF—left in July. At the Admiralty's request, the following two drafts were larger. The fifth draft, of eighteen, had the misfortune to be captured by the German raiders *Orion* and *Komet* when the *Rangitane* was lost shortly after leaving New Zealand; thirteen were eventually released on parole on Emirau Island, but five ended up as *prisoners of war in Germany. From December 1940 to October 1941 the monthly drafts were raised to forty men. Scheme F was suspended between March and August 1942 because of a temporary oversupply of aircrew in the United Kingdom. When it resumed, the number of volunteers that could be obtained from this source was reduced by the RNZAF's increased requirements for aircrew in New Zealand as a result of the *Pacific War. The RNZN was forced to recruit potential candidates directly.

On reaching the United Kingdom, the New Zealanders entered HMS *St Vincent*, the Fleet Air Arm's initial training school at Gosport, Hampshire. After learning to fly, the trainees undertook operational conversion in 'second line' squadrons before being assigned to fighter, torpedo bomber, or reconnaissance specialties. From 1941 many of the New Zealanders completed their training in the United States after the United States Navy opened its air training system to the Fleet Air Arm; several were killed while training. Because training courses for pilots took eighteen months and for observers twelve months, it was not until late 1941 that the first Scheme F personnel began reaching the operational squadrons. Most of the pilots then had to master the risky art of landing on the deck of an aircraft-carrier, which remained the crux of the naval aviator's art. Some of the first New Zealanders to reach front-line squadrons flew Albacores with 826 Squadron in support of forces engaged in the *North African campaign, while at least seven flew Swordfish and Albacores from Malta in defence of *convoys.

In all, 1066 New Zealanders were selected for Scheme F, of whom 738 were eventually commissioned. By May 1944, the peak month, 456 were serving in the 7000-strong Fleet Air Arm—7 per cent of its strength. New Zealand aircrew played a major part in the air operations of the British Pacific Fleet against Japan in the last nine months of the war (and one, Sub-Lieutenant T.C.G. McBride, was the last New Zealander killed as a result of enemy action in the Second World War). Nineteen New Zealanders rose to command Fleet Air Arm squadrons. One of them, Lieutenant-Commander A. *Richardson, was killed in August 1944 while leading his Hellcat squadron against the German battleship *Tirpitz* ensconced in a Norwegian fiord; his fleet commander recommended him unsuccessfully for a posthumous *Victoria Cross. Richardson was one of the more than 150 New Zealanders killed in naval flying operations.

After the war the New Zealand naval authorities gave some consideration to acquiring a light aircraft-carrier for the RNZN, but this aspiration quickly faded as resource limitations became apparent. A handful of New Zealanders flew with the Royal Navy or the Royal Australian Navy during the *Korean War, one commanding a squadron on HMAS *Sydney*. The RNZN's naval aviation at present is confined to the helicopters carried by its Leander and Anzac class *frigates. With their capacity to drop *depth charges, these have a much more significant role than did the floatplanes carried by the pre-war cruisers.

S.D. Waters, *The Royal New Zealand Navy* (War History Branch, Wellington, 1956).

RICHARD JACKSON

Forest Rangers were formed as a specialist 'bush-fighting' corps by Lieutenant William Jackson at Papakura on 10 August 1863 with the intention of scouring the Hunua Ranges for hostile Maori forces. Volunteers, mainly local farmers and miners, enlisted for three months. Their pay, at eight shillings a day, was significantly better than that of British or other colonial troops. They were armed with Callisher and Terry breech-loading carbines and revolvers, and many later carried long-bladed bowie knives. Their first action was a skirmish at Lusk's Clearing, near Mauku, on 8 September 1863.

In November 1863 the Forest Rangers were re-formed into two companies, under Captains Jackson and Gustavus von ★Tempsky; the latter had been an ensign in the original company. Jackson remained in overall command. From this time the Forest Rangers were also referred to as Jackson's Forest Rangers or Von Tempsky's Forest Rangers. Under these new arrangements about 100 men were enlisted at five shillings per day for three years' service, after which they would be entitled to a land grant in the Waikato. The relatively high pay and irregular character of the unit encouraged a collection of men from Great Britain, Germany, Australia, New Zealand, Denmark, Jersey, and the United States; there were even two African-Americans, who were 'as good as any white man', wrote Jackson, 'and more sober than most'. The Forest Rangers were again in action at Paparata, in the Hunua Ranges, on 13 December 1863. They marched south with the forces which invaded the Waikato and fought in the sharp action at Waiari, Mangapiko, on 11 February 1864. They distinguished themselves in actions at Rangiaowhia and Hairini in February 1864, before playing a major role in the Battle of Orakau. Following this action, both Jackson and von Tempsky were promoted to the rank of major. Garrison duties in the Waikato followed, with the Forest Rangers settling on their land grants. In March 1865 a company of Forest Rangers under von Tempsky was moved to Wanganui. It was in action at Kakaramea, near Patea, in May, and again at Weraroa, near Wanganui, two months later. In September the Forest Rangers refused to embark for service in the Bay of Plenty after their pay was cut. Men who refused to accept the new conditions were court-martialled, along with von Tempsky who had refused to serve under Major James Fraser. Captain Charles Westrup, who thereupon took command of the company, led it during operations on the East Coast. The Forest Rangers took part in actions at Pukemaire, near East Cape in October 1865, and at Waerenga-a-Hika,

An artist's depiction of an encampment of the Forest Rangers about 1866. Gustavus von Tempsky is at far left (*Fletcher Challenge Art Collection*)

Poverty Bay, a month later. When Major-General Trevor ★Chute invaded Taranaki in early 1866, a reinstated von Tempsky and a company of Forest Rangers accompanied him. They fought many engagements, including Okotuku, Te Putahi, Otapawa, Ketemarae, and Waikoko in January–February, before being virtually all struck off pay by a cost-conscious government. After the unit was officially disbanded on 30 October 1867, many of its members enlisted in the ★Armed Constabulary, particularly No. 5 Division. There were, in all, approximately 365 Forest Rangers, with no more than about 100 serving at any one time. The difficult conditions, especially the strain imposed by the need for constant alertness in the bush, ensured a high attrition rate, with men continually seeking their discharge. By the time of disbandment only a few of those originally enlisted were still serving.

R.W. Stowers, *Forest Rangers* (Richard Stowers, Hamilton, 1996).

RICHARD STOWERS

Forsyth, Sergeant Samuel (3 April 1891–24 August 1918) was awarded a posthumous ★Victoria Cross for his actions while serving with 1NZEF on 24 August 1918. A Wellingtonian by birth, he had served with the New Zealand Engineers for nearly four years when he was attached to the 2nd Battalion, Auckland Regiment, in August 1918. On the 24th, his battalion made an early morning advance on Grévillers, during which he was conspicuous in rushing a number of the German outposts. As dawn broke, his company came under heavy machine-gun fire. Despite being wounded, he made his way to a nearby British tank, which he led into action against the machine-gun posts. Although the tank was knocked out, he re-formed the tank crew and with some of his men continued the attack, eventually forcing the enemy to withdraw. He was killed by a sniper later in the day.

Fortifications

Fortifications European settlers in New Zealand built over 200 redoubts, stockades and blockhouses for the defence of settlements as well as for military action against Maori. In the 1840s, stockades and blockhouses generally protected civilian settlements. In the 1860s and 1870s these and redoubts were also used to hold confiscated land, and a few British Army field redoubts in Taranaki took the fight to the enemy.

No doubt influenced by the central role of Maori fortifications and recent attacks on ships, early visitors threw up temporary stockades, such as in the Firth of Thames in 1801. A 'fortress mentality' became widespread, however, after the 1843 ★Wairau massacre. Wellington's magistrate sanctioned two small forts as places of rendezvous, and Mt Cook was levelled for barracks. The landward defences of Auckland's prominent Britomart Barracks, occupied in 1841 (see COAST DEFENCES), were strengthened and St Paul's Church barricaded. Nelson built the stockade Fort Arthur and the French settlers in Akaroa started three blockhouses.

When fighting flared in 1845 (see NEW ZEALAND WARS), virtually all the fledgling civilian settlements threw up some defences, laying the foundation for the use of forts for internal order. Settlers fled to the blockhouses during ★Heke's and ★Kawiti's attack on Kororareka. A redoubt, Fort Ligar, was started west of Auckland, and after the war a 'loopholed scoria wall' was built around Albert Barracks, south-east of the town. Wellington's measures were, however, the most extensive response. More redoubts were built in April at both ends of the town, and the following year a chain of five stockades guarded New Zealand's first military road, cut to subdue the Porirua area. This road led to the most castle-like fort, the Paremata Barracks, built in stone in 1847. Two storeys high, it had turrets from which small cannon could be fired and loopholes for troops to use their muskets. The locally made lime was, however, no match for Wellington's 1848 earthquake, after which the edifice was reduced to a storehouse. With stockades also erected in Karori, Pauatahanui, Taita, and the Hutt, Wellington threw up at least seventeen defensible works and batteries in the period 1843–47. Wanganui's brief campaign in 1847 produced four stockades.

The campaigns from 1860 saw dozens of defensible outposts established to hold territory and protect settlements, particularly in Taranaki, Waikato, the Bay of Plenty, and the Urewera. Taranaki had sixty-five (through two wars) and the environs of Auckland around forty-four even before the invasion of the Waikato, where they sprouted as Cameron's forces advanced and then stood sentry along the confiscation line (aukati). Auckland's included ten blockhouses at Ponsonby, Karangahape Road, Freemans Bay, Grafton, Parnell, and Newmarket, and the Fencible posts in Howick, Panmure, Otahuhu, and Onehunga. Blockhouses were also prefabricated in Otahuhu and shipped in sections to frontier posts.

New Plymouth was similarly ringed with nine outposts and Marsland Hill entrenched. Wellington, in contrast, only added two blockhouses to its earlier works. The tactical field redoubt grew in importance: Major-General T.S. ★Pratt progressively built eight redoubts as his troops advanced against Te Arei pa near Waitara, then invested the pa with old-fashioned sapping. As the threat to Wanganui from ★Titokowaru developed in 1868, many homes were fortified. Defence Minister T.M. ★Haultain issued to militia districts plans for a 'Redoubt Military' with a blockhouse in one corner. Many were thrown up, and some from previous campaigns reoccupied. Rangitikei got ten, with a similar number north of Wanganui. *Hints on House Defence, Blockhouses, and Redoubts* was published by an imperial officer of Wanganui's garrison. Military redoubts became the sanctuary in new towns. ★Armed Constabulary posts were still being built up to 1874 in the Waikato, and long used along telegraph routes such as that from Napier to Taupo. Some redoubts were reoccupied during the 1881 ★Parihaka incident in Taranaki and the 1883 Kawhia action. Even the Cape Egmont lighthouse was fortified.

Civilian structures were fortified—many isolated farmsteads or public houses in the 1860s; a sawmill in Cabbage Bay, Coromandel; even churches (in Opotiki, Papakura, Mauku, Pirongia, and Pukekohe). Farmer David Strachan of Okoia, Wanganui, loopholed a nearby cave as a defensible refuge. As late as 1882 Josiah Firth built a three-story concrete lookout and loopholed sanctuary at Matamata. Colonel T.R. ★Mould, the Royal Engineers officer most associated with Taranaki and Auckland fortifications, also designed a 'defensive' police station/courthouse for Kohekohe in 1862.

In 1891 New Zealand's last earthwork redoubt was built in Wellington—to protect the rear of coast defence forts. This and Auckland's Panmure Fencible Redoubt were still listed in the Defence Scheme and being used for field training as late as 1908.

Three types of fortification were in use, though many were a mix of all elements:

Stockade—rough-hewn poles or squared posts dug into the ground as a palisade. Sometimes these were neatly capped and loopholed, or surrounded by a ditch. Howick's was unusual: stockaded with sheets of loopholed iron. Some Maori pa were renovated for colonial garrisons, and ★kupapa forces also built European-style stockades.

Redoubts consisted of a ditch in front of a high parapet, presenting a near-vertical face up to fourteen feet high. Engineers borrowed the Maori technique of reinforcing the parapet sodding with ferns. The trace (shape) was usually square or rectangular with at least two flanking bastions. A shape unique to New Zealand had a bastion at each corner but covering only one side. Queens Redoubt (Pokeno) was the largest redoubt with sides 100 yards long.

Blockhouses were defensible bullet-proof buildings, usually made of wood with walls filled with gravel. A number in Auckland were of brick; iron was also used. Many were two storeys, the upper sometimes overhanging the lower in 'New England' style. A blockhouse would often sit inside a redoubt (Wanganui's Westmere camp had seven) or its walls would form part of the stockading.

PETER COOKE

Forward defence In a general sense forward defence has been the basis of New Zealand's defence philosophy since its inception. The preservation of the wider security framework was seen as the key to its own security, given its own lack of physical capacity to defend itself. During the first century of New Zealand's existence, forward defence was pursued within the context of ★imperial defence, an approach which led to New Zealand troops being deployed on the other side of the globe in two world wars, on the principle that Great Britain was the first line of New Zealand's defence. In a more specific sense, the first manifestation of forward defence thinking in New Zealand occurred in 1852, when Governor George ★Grey suggested that, in the event of war between the British and French empires, New Zealand should dispatch a force to seize Tahiti. He envisaged the use of a 4000-strong force of Maori with European officers. A similar approach can be discerned in New Zealand's involvement in capturing German Samoa in 1914, and in garrisoning islands in the South Pacific during the ★Second World War.

The term 'forward defence' came to define New Zealand's defence policy in South-east Asia during the 1950s. The stationing of New Zealand troops in that region as part of Commonwealth defence arrangements was advanced as a means of keeping communism as far from New Zealand's shores as possible. Initially New Zealand's attention concentrated on Malaya, which Prime Minister Sidney Holland in 1955 described as 'the gateway' to Australia and New Zealand, and 'about the last place we can make a stand without coming into our own territory'. A contribution was made to the ★British Commonwealth Far East Strategic Reserve. However, the need to align policy with the United States, because of that power's central importance to the Western stance in the region, ensured that New Zealand's focus was drawn northward, and ★SEATO became the basis of planning for operations in the region. During the mid 1960s New Zealand was drawn reluctantly into involvement in the ★Vietnam War. With the withdrawal of the British from South-east Asia in the late 1960s, New Zealand and Australia at first envisaged a continued military role in Malaysia, but this approach in turn was undercut by the United States' own withdrawal from Vietnam and enunciation of the Guam or Nixon Doctrine. The Sino-American *rapprochement* in the early 1970s heralded the demise of forward defence in South-east Asia, though the last New Zealand forces were not withdrawn until 1989. By then the scope of New Zealand's defence activities had been more directly oriented towards the South Pacific. The concept of dealing with threats well before they might threaten New Zealand directly continues to underlie New Zealand's approach to international affairs, the emphasis in the 1990s being on diplomatic rather than military means.

Four Colonels' revolt was the most open defiance of authority by officers in New Zealand's military history. In 1937 the Army was in a parlous state, with obsolete equipment, low morale, and a strength less than half that provided for in the unit establishments. With a view to overcoming existing deficiencies, the Chief of the General Staff, Major-General J.E. ★Duigan, introduced plans to reorganise the Army away from the divisional concept which had underlain preparations since the ★First World War. The effective disbandment of regiments, which were to be reduced to 'Composite' or 'Fortress' battalions, and the retirement of so many experienced officers did nothing for morale within the ★Territorial Force. Nor did the inept handling of the issue by Duigan and the Minister of Defence, Frederick ★Jones, help the situation. Four Territorial Force colonels, R.F. Gambrill, N.L. Macky, A.S. Wilder, and C.R. Spragg, had become increasingly frustrated and disillusioned with the state of the force. Having exhausted all permitted avenues of protest, they were confronted by a conflict of loyalties between what they saw as their duty as citizens and their obligations as army officers. On 19 May 1938 they issued a public manifesto denouncing the deficiencies in the Territorial Force. In doing so, they consciously broke Army Regulations, paragraph 443 of which forbade communication with the press except with special permission.

The colonels received much support from newspapers, National Party politicians, and, privately, other army officers, including the commander of the New Zealand Division in the First World War, Major-General Sir Andrew ★Russell. Duigan and Jones, embarrassed by this open challenge, declined to give the recalcitrant colonels further opportunity for publicity by court-martialling them. Instead Duigan effectively sacked them by posting them to the Reserve List on 13 June 1938. Although the 'four colonels' revolt' increased public awareness of the appalling state of the Army, the government had no option but to deal quickly and firmly with such an open breach of ★discipline. The affair caused some problems in filling appointments in 2NZEF in late 1939. Two of the colonels, Macky and Wilder, later served as battalion commanders in 2NZEF, with the latter retiring in the rank of major-general after further service in New Zealand. (See CIVIL–MILITARY RELATIONS)

LAURIE BARBER

Fox, Colonel Francis John (20 September 1857–27 February 1902). Born in Ireland, Fox was commissioned as a lieutenant in the Royal Artillery in 1876. Over the next fifteen years, active service in India, Natal, and Egypt was followed by staff appointments in England. When in 1891 the New Zealand government requested an imperial officer to take charge of the colony's military forces, Fox actively sought the War Office's nomination, perhaps because his brother was already in New Zealand. Despite having the relatively junior rank of captain, he arrived in New Zealand in 1892 with impressive references and the high expectations of the authorities in London to begin his five-year term (see COMMANDANTS). He was given the local rank of lieutenant-colonel, but was later appointed as a colonel in the New Zealand Militia as well. Fox's term has come to symbolise the civil–military conflict endemic to such imperial appointments in colonial forces. The origin of the trouble lay in the uncompromising nature of Fox's inaugural report on the New Zealand forces submitted in 1893, after he had insisted on inspecting every corps in the colony. His naming of inefficient officers (who became known as 'Fox's Martyrs') and calls for the disbandment of inefficient corps might have been justified militarily; but they were an anathema to the Minister of Defence and Premier, R.J. ★Seddon, because of their political implications. In accusing Seddon of playing politics and refusing to take responsibility for the colony's defence until his recommendations were approved and he had been given extensive powers as Commandant, Fox demonstrated his political naïvety. A Colonial Office official later complained that he had begun 'by putting a pistol at the Minister's head, and dictating to him in an absurd manner'. Convinced that Fox's inexperience and uncompromising attitude had precipitated the crisis, the authorities in London re-evaluated their selection policy for such appointments. Even so, Seddon had not helped matters by his autocratic and sometimes underhand method of dealing with Fox. Things came to a head in March 1894 when Fox sought a release from his contract. The mysterious leaking to the press of his resignation letter, along with a list of complaints against Seddon, exacerbated the situation, as did the intervention of the Governor, Lord Glasgow, a retired naval officer, on Fox's behalf. Fox's close relationship with the Leader of the Opposition, W.R. Russell, whose daughter he married in February 1895, undoubtedly left Seddon suspicious of political collusion. Although outraged by Fox's conduct, Seddon refused to accept Fox's resignation. But Fox forced the issue by pointing out that his appointment was *ultra vires*, there being no statutory provision for a Commandant. After some negotiation, he accepted a lesser role as Military Adviser and Inspector of the Forces, positions which he held until 30 November 1896. Having retired from the imperial army in May 1894, he remained in New Zealand and took up farming in Canterbury. With the outbreak of the ★Boer War, he was subjected to one final humiliation when Seddon rejected his offer to serve with one of the New Zealand contingents, leading him to resign his Militia commission in disgust in October 1900. Sixteen months later he succumbed to tuberculosis.

STEPHEN CLARKE

Fraser, Peter (28 August 1884–12 December 1950) was New Zealand's war leader during the ★Second World War. A Scot who emigrated to New Zealand in 1910, he became prominent in the trade union movement and was elected to the executive of the newly formed New Zealand Labour Party in 1916. Although not a pacifist—he had served in the Seaforth Highlanders, a Territorial regiment, in Scotland—he became an implacable opponent of ★conscription during the ★First World War, which led to his being sentenced to a year's imprisonment for sedition. He was a member of Parliament from 1918 until his death. Although his responsibilities in the first Labour government initially lay in the health and education fields, he was deputy Prime Minister and a member of the Council of Defence established in 1937. He became more involved in matters relating to New Zealand's security when Prime Minister M.J. ★Savage's health deteriorated in 1939, and was the key figure in the determination of New Zealand's war effort. While in the United Kingdom in November 1939 for important talks with the British authorities, he interviewed Major-General B.C. ★Freyberg and recommended him for command of 2NZEF.

Fraser became Prime Minister in April 1940 after Savage's death. Over the ensuing five years, he proved an able leader. His clear grasp of strategy and recognition of New Zealand's needs as a small ally, his determination to express New Zealand's views on matters

Peter Fraser arrives at Hawaii with Admiral Chester Nimitz and Vice-Admiral Ghormley in 1942 (*War History Collection, Alexander Turnbull Library, F-2002-1/4-DA*)

important to it, and his political skills were amply demonstrated as he grappled with the problems of defining New Zealand's role in the conflict and best using its limited resources. This became an acute problem after the onset of the ★Pacific War. Fraser was largely instrumental in ensuring that 2NZEF remained in the Mediterranean theatre for the duration of the war. After some initial difficulties, relating especially to the deployment of 2nd New Zealand Division in ★Greece, he established a good working relationship with Freyberg. Despite his experience in the previous conflict, he did not hesitate to support the introduction of conscription in 1940. His strong practical focus was matched by an idealistic desire to promote an effective post-war security organisation. At the San Francisco Conference in 1945, he fought hard to secure a ★United Nations Organization in which small powers could have confidence, but was disappointed by the outcome.

After the war, Fraser reluctantly accepted the implications of the onset of the ★Cold War. By 1948 he had been persuaded that the Soviet Union was embarked on an aggressive course, and he strongly supported measures to meet the contingency of outright war. He agreed that, in such an eventuality, New Zealand should concentrate most of its forces in Egypt within ninety days of the outbreak of the war. This timescale could not be met without the introduction of ★compulsory military training. Characteristically, he threw himself behind this ★Middle East commitment despite its political disadvantages for him as leader of a party traditionally opposed to compulsion. After his government fell in December 1949, he remained as Leader of the Opposition until his death. He strongly supported New Zealand's involvement in the ★Korean War.

M. Clark (ed), *Peter Fraser, Master Politician* (Dunmore Press, Palmerston North, 1998).

Freyberg, Lieutenant-General Sir Bernard Cyril, Baron (21 March 1889–4 July 1963) was New Zealand's most important twentieth century military figure. Although born in England, he spent his formative years in New Zealand, after emigrating to the colony with his family in 1891. The nickname 'Tiny' bestowed on him as a child would stick with him for the rest of his life, despite the fact that he stood over 1.8 metres tall. Although Freyberg's paternal roots lay in Germany, his great-grandfather and grandfather both served in the Russian Army, the former taking part in the Battle of Borodino. His grandfather married an Englishwoman and emigrated to Great Britain shortly after the end of the Napoleonic Wars. Apart from a period in the school cadets at Wellington College, Freyberg's military career began in the small provincial town of Morrinsville, where he was practising as an

Freyberg

Lieutenant-General Sir Bernard Freyberg (*War History Collection, Alexander Turnbull Library, F-17933-1/4*)

assistant dentist. In 1912 he became a junior officer in the local ★Territorial Force company, but was unsuccessful in an application to join the ★New Zealand Staff Corps. From January 1913, while based in Levin, he was a lieutenant in a senior cadet company, and was one of Massey's Cossacks in 1913. In the following year he went to the United States and thence to Mexico, where he may have been involved briefly in that country's civil war. With the outbreak of the ★First World War he lost no time in making his way to London.

With the assistance of Major G.S. ★Richardson, a New Zealand staff officer in London, he secured a commission in the newly formed Royal Naval Division. He became an enthusiastic company commander in the Hood Battalion, writing at the time that he was 'in this with all my heart'. Among his fellow officers were Arthur Asquith, a son of the British Prime Minister, and the poet Rupert Brooke. After taking part in the unsuccessful attempt to defend Antwerp, he proceeded with his Division to the Mediterranean, where it was committed to the ★Gallipoli operation. A pre-war New Zealand swimming champion, Freyberg swam ashore at Bulair to light diversionary flares during the initial landing, for which exploit he was made a DSO. Wounded at Helles, he later returned to command the Hood Battalion until the evacuation, broken only by hospitalisation in Egypt for another serious wound. In 1916 Freyberg transferred to the British Army. Although posted to the Royal West Surrey Regiment, he remained seconded to the Naval Division, with which he served on the ★Western Front from May 1916. For his bravery in an assault on the village of Beaucourt sur l'Ancre late in the First Battle of the Somme, described by one general as 'probably ... the most distinguished personal act in the war', he was awarded a ★Victoria Cross. He was also badly wounded, and spent months recovering in England. When he returned to the front, he became reputedly the youngest general in the British Army when he was given command of a Territorial brigade in the 58th Division. He was again evacuated to England after a shell landed at his feet, inflicting the most severe of the nine wounds he suffered during the war. 'I only know it wasn't my fault I am alive,' he wrote when it was all over. From January 1918 Freyberg commanded one of 29th Division's brigades. On the day the war ended he was typically in the van of the Allied advance, seizing a bridge at Lessines one minute before the Armistice came into effect. For this exploit, he was awarded a second bar to his DSO (the first having been gained in 1917). With five mentions in dispatches and appointment, in 1917, as a CMG, he emerged from the war as one of the Empire's most decorated heroes.

Granted a regular commission in the Grenadier Guards in early 1919, Freyberg settled down with difficulty to peacetime soldiering. His wounds continued to trouble him, but he gradually recovered, his convalescence being helped by a visit to New Zealand in 1921. His friendship with the Asquiths and Churchills, and the writer James Barrie, and his marriage, in 1922, to Barbara McLaren, provided him with social connections; his public profile was heightened by candidacy for Parliament and attempts to swim the English Channel, both unsuccessful. After several staff appointments, he commanded the 1st Battalion, the Manchester Regiment, from 1929 to 1931, during which he demonstrated a keen interest in the welfare of his men, especially the standard of their rations. His ideas on unit logistics were published in a treatise, *A Study of Unit Administration*, in 1933. With further staff appointments, including two years in the War Office, promotion to the rank of major-general at the age of forty-five, and appointment as a CB in 1936, Freyberg was seemingly on the path to high command. His hopes were soon to be shattered, however, when a medical examination prior to his embarking to take up a posting in India indicated a heart defect. As a result he was forced to retire from the British Army in October 1937.

Freyberg's career was revived by the outbreak of the ★Second World War. He was given command of the Salisbury Plain Area, helping organise the British Expeditionary Force. He also offered his services to the New Zealand government. By the time he met Peter

★Fraser, the acting Prime Minister, in November 1939, he had managed to secure a revision of his medical grading that would permit him to serve overseas. After his appointment as commander of both 2NZEF and the 2nd New Zealand Division, he visited New Zealand. When he left Wellington with 2NZEF's First Echelon, he took with him a charter setting out his position as the commander of a small national contingent that would serve within a British command framework—an important difference from the arrangements for 1NZEF in 1914 (see FREYBERG'S CHARTER). Freyberg's first task was to establish a base for his division in Egypt, and then to concentrate his force. After the diversion of the Second Echelon to Britain, he joined it there from June to September 1940 to oversee its involvement in anti-invasion preparations during the Battle of Britain. When he returned to Egypt, he faced difficulties in concentrating his dispersed units. The whole division was not finally brought together until early 1941. Freyberg also had to contend with the diffidence with which he was regarded, as an outsider, by some of the senior officers in the division. These problems were both exacerbated and alleviated by the division's role in the ill-fated campaigns in ★Greece and ★Crete in 1941. During these operations Freyberg's record was mixed. In Greece he performed particularly well during the retreat and evacuation of the Allied forces. As commander of Allied forces in Crete, he faced a very difficult task because of the inadequacy of the forces available, especially in heavy weapons and in air support. Nevertheless, so detailed was the intelligence available about German intentions, through ★ULTRA sources, that British Prime Minister Winston Churchill saw the opportunity to inflict a crushing defeat on the Germans. Freyberg's failure has generated one of the most significant areas of dispute in New Zealand's military historiography. Essentially it turns on the degree to which Freyberg overestimated the threat from a seaborne landing and allowed his anxieties in this regard to inhibit his response to the German capture of the key airfield at Maleme. Some British historians have tended to criticise his inflexibility and lack of mental agility in assessing the intelligence information being fed to him. At the time, Freyberg faced an inquisition by Fraser into his conduct of the two campaigns. Fraser's receptiveness to criticisms by several of Freyberg's subordinates, including Brigadier James ★Hargest, was heightened by his own anger at misunderstandings over the dispatch of the division to Greece in the first place. The support Freyberg received from his British superiors helped overcome this crisis, and thereafter he maintained a good working relationship with the New Zealand government. Perhaps aware that he had let slip a great opportunity, he remained extremely sensitive about the Crete operation until the end of his life.

Notwithstanding the criticism of him by some officers, Freyberg's performance in Greece and Crete had helped overcome much of the earlier reticence among his subordinates, who came to admire his personal characteristics, not least his energy. He was later described by one of his subordinates as 'kind, considerate, gentle, compassionate, always ready to listen, always approachable'—and exasperatingly reluctant to criticise errant subordinates (a product perhaps of his consciousness of the stress of active service on relatively inexperienced individuals). Among the troops, Freyberg's standing was enhanced by his willingness to share their privations during the evacuations. His concern for their welfare was demonstrated by his establishment of a series of recreational clubs in Egypt, and later Italy, which were overseen by his wife.

The benefits of this formative period, and the intensive training regime which Freyberg instituted, were reaped during the ★North African campaign, in which the New Zealanders participated in the ensuing two years. During this fighting Freyberg, who was promoted to lieutenant-general in early 1942, led the division skilfully through many difficult and sometimes disastrous situations, himself being always well to the fore. The risks he took were amply demonstrated when he was seriously wounded during the fighting at Minqar Qaim in 1942, giving Churchill further reason to describe him, in the following year, as 'the salamander of the British Empire'. Freyberg found himself at odds with the brigade-focused tactics adopted by the British high command, but these problems were overcome with the arrival of General Sir Bernard ★Montgomery as commander of the 8th Army. Freyberg's important part in the ensuing climactic battle of El Alamein was recognised in his immediate appointment as a KCB (he had been made a KBE earlier in the year). During the pursuit of the enemy forces across North Africa, Freyberg led the New Zealanders on a series of left hooks to turn the Germans out of their successive defence lines; he would later be criticised for his excessive caution at Tebaga Gap. The surrender of an Italian field marshal and two German generals to him in Tunisia in May 1943 provided a fitting finale to the campaign.

Freyberg's performance in the ★Italian campaign, his last, has since become a matter of controversy because of the bombing of the monastery at Monte Cassino, the German bastion south of Rome. Although he favoured the obliteration of the monastery, believing (apparently incorrectly in retrospect) that it was being used by the Germans for military purposes, the decision was not his alone to take, and his superiors certainly shared the responsibility. Temporarily com-

Freyberg's charter

manding the New Zealand Corps, but conscious of his responsibilities as a national commander, he had committed the New Zealanders to the operations at Cassino, in February–March 1944, with doubts about their ability to break through at this point, and had characteristically set firm limits as to the casualties that would be sustained in the attempt. He quickly called off the assault when it bogged down amid the rubble of the township. Interrupted only by six weeks' hospitalisation after being injured in an aircraft accident in September, Freyberg's performance as commander in Italy reflected both his experience and the now formidably efficient team which he led. This was evident in the division's 400-kilometre advance in the last three weeks of the war, which involved repeated river crossings and the taking of 30,000 German prisoners of war. These skilfully executed operations earned Freyberg a third bar to his DSO. He kept a cool head when, at Trieste, the New Zealanders found themselves in a briefly troubling confrontation with Yugoslav partisans, eager to secure the city.

In 1946 Freyberg, who had relinquished command of 2NZEF and the division in November 1945, became the first New Zealand–raised person appointed as Governor-General of New Zealand. In this capacity, he farewelled yet another New Zealand expeditionary force in 1950—that to serve in the *Korean War. During his term, which ended in 1952, he took a strong personal interest in the work of the *War History Branch in preparing the official history of New Zealand's part in the Second World War. Appointed a GCMG in 1946, he was raised to the peerage five years later. Baron Freyberg of Wellington, New Zealand, and of Munstead in the County of Surrey spent a decade as Deputy Constable and Lieutenant-Governor of Windsor Castle, before succumbing to the rupture of one of his Gallipoli wounds.

The immense pride which Freyberg's exploits in the First World War inspired among New Zealanders was reinforced by his performance as commander of their troops in the Second. His ability as a tactician was matched by a capacity to get the best out of the mainly amateur soldiers he commanded; his disdain for danger, exemplified in his many decorations, his evident concern for their welfare, and his proficiency in the skills of soldiering all helped inspire confidence throughout 2NZEF. Overcoming the disadvantage of being an outsider initially, Freyberg forged a unit which acquitted itself with distinction in hard-fought campaigns. With some hiccups, he also surmounted the problems of commanding a small national contingent within a much larger coalition.

P. Freyberg, *Bernard Freyberg V.C., Soldier of Two Nations* (Hodder & Stoughton, London, 1991); W.G. Stevens, *Freyberg V.C., The Man 1939–45* (A.H. & A.W. Reed, Wellington, 1965); L. Barber and J. Tonkin-Covell, *Freyberg: Churchill's Salamander* (Century Hutchinson, Auckland, 1989).

Freyberg's charter was a document given to 2NZEF's commander, Major-General B.C. *Freyberg, on 5 January 1940 setting out his responsibilities in relation to the New Zealand government. It addressed the problem that Freyberg would have in serving two masters—his British military superiors as a divisional commander within a British operational framework and the New Zealand government as the commander of a small national force which was not part of the British Army. Whereas in the *First World War 1NZEF had been made available for use as determined by the imperial authorities, in 1939 the Labour government led by Michael *Savage considered such an approach inconsistent with New Zealand's status as a self-governing Dominion. While Freyberg would operate in accordance with the directives of his commander-in-chief, he would have the right to communicate directly with the government in Wellington and the commander-in-chief 'in respect of all details leading up to and arising from policy decisions'. Although personal qualities ultimately counted for more than formal instructions in determining Freyberg's relations with his British superiors, his charter proved useful on occasions. In August 1940, he used it to resist attempts to detach a number of elements of his division to support operations against the Italians in Cyrenaica. In early 1941 he ran into difficulties with the New Zealand government over his failure to advise it of his doubts about the proposed deployment of New Zealand and other Allied forces to *Greece. Misunderstandings were resolved following the *Crete campaign, and he thereafter kept Wellington fully advised of planned operations. By late 1942 British commanders were also becoming more accustomed to the arrangement, and to Freyberg's responsibilities as a national commander. During the *Italian campaign, some problems were experienced when Freyberg came under the command of US 5th Army commander General Mark Clark at Cassino, who was less conscious of Freyberg's responsibilities to the New Zealand government. In the Pacific 3rd Division commander Major-General H.E. *Barrowclough was issued with a charter similar to Freyberg's, though more narrowly focused, in November 1942: while under the operational command of a British or American officer, he was 'expressly authorised' to contact the government 'regarding the proposed employment of your troops if in your opinion the operations you are required to undertake might unjustifiably imperil your command'. He never had call to assert this right during his division's participation in the *Solomons campaign in 1943–44.

RICHARD TAYLOR

Frickleton, Captain Samuel (1 April 1891–6 August 1971) won a *Victoria Cross on the *Western Front in 1917. Born in Scotland, he emigrated to New Zealand to work as a coal miner on the West Coast. Enlisting in 1NZEF, he served briefly at *Gallipoli before being returned to New Zealand as medically unfit in November 1915. In the following April he re-enlisted, and was posted to the 3rd Battalion, 3rd New Zealand (Rifle) Brigade, at the end of the year. At Messines on 7 June 1917 he rushed ahead into the artillery barrage, despite being slightly wounded, to destroy with hand grenades two enemy machine-gun posts that were inflicting heavy casualties. Later in the battle he was severely gassed, an injury that would cause recurring illness during 1918. He was commissioned in March 1918. Following his return to New Zealand, he joined the *New Zealand Staff Corps, with which he served until 1927.

Friendly fire is the term used for accidental hostile action against one's own or Allied forces—a common occurrence in the confusion of war, and one which has become much more likely in the twentieth century with the introduction of more powerful, complex, and longer-ranged weapons. Mistaken identity is an ever-present danger, and is particularly so in the case of ground support by aircraft. Because of the need for precision in dealing with a number of variables, artillery is also susceptible to friendly fire incidents. The use of an incorrect charge, the application of mistaken map coordinates, the effect of wear and tear on gun barrels, faulty aiming—all can lead to artillery rounds falling on the infantry forward of the guns.

New Zealand forces have been involved in innumerable friendly fire incidents. The New Zealanders' efforts to capture Chunuk Bair at *Gallipoli were, for example, hindered by shells fired by British warships standing off the battlefield. On the *Western Front infantry were frequently on the receiving end of British or New Zealand artillery fire which dropped short, as, for example, during the disastrous attack on Bellevue Spur during the Battle of Passchendaele. It was even more common for infantry to rush ahead into the covering barrage, preferring to risk friendly artillery fire than German machine-guns. The worst friendly fire incident was during the Battle of Messines when a staff error led to New Zealand and British artillery opening fire on the men of 4th Australian Division in the belief that they were counter-attacking Germans. It took several hours to sort out the confusion, by which time the Australian brigade had suffered 1450 casualties from the combined Allied and German fire. There were many instances of mistaken identity during the *Second World War, especially because of the greater use of air power. Large white stars were painted prominently on vehicles to aid in recognition from the air during the *Italian campaign. During the crossing of the River Sangro in 1943, New Zealand troops shot down an American fighter-bomber after it had strafed New Zealand transport. During the *Korean and *Vietnam Wars there were incidents of drop-shorts by New Zealand gunners, which killed Canadian and Australian infantrymen. In 1999 the revelation of a long-covered-up incident in Vietnam, involving the accidental shooting of an NCO, led to the resignation from the *New Zealand Army of the platoon commander at the time, Roger Mortlock, by then a brigadier. The RNZN's most celebrated friendly fire incident occurred in 1954, when the frigate HMNZS *Black Prince*, during an exercise off the coast of Australia, accidentally landed several shells in the New South Wales town of Nowra, fortunately without causing any injuries.

Frigates served as the 'eyes of the fleet' in Nelson's day, but the term developed its modern meaning during the *Second World War when the Royal Navy applied it to its new River class long-range anti-submarine escorts. In 1947–48 all surviving British corvettes, sloops, and escort destroyers were re-rated as frigates. New Zealand had operated sloops between the wars and two modified Flower class corvettes since 1944, but acquired its first true frigates in 1948 when it purchased six Royal Navy Loch class ships. It did so on the recommendation of the Chief of Naval Staff, Commodore G.W.G. Simpson, a wartime submariner, who believed that submarines would be the main naval threats in future conflicts.

Successors to the Rivers, the Lochs were specially adapted for *anti-submarine warfare. The main armament, sited before the bridge, was two Squid three-barrel anti-submarine mortars. These trainable, forward-throwing weapons were an enormous advance on the lightweight Hedgehog thrower or conventional depth charge racks, which required a ship to pass over a submerged submarine before pressing home its attack. Gun armament was weak, a single 4-inch gun forward and a mixture of 2-pounder pom-pom, 40 mm and 20 mm AA guns (later six 40 mm guns in *Rotoiti* and *Pukaki*). There was nothing fancy about these rugged, cheap little ships. Their hulls were simplified for mass construction and their reciprocating engines developed a maximum speed of 19.5 knots, adequate for the early 1940s, but deficient by the late 1940s. They were 1435 tons standard and 93.7 metres long, and had a crew of about 114 men.

The Lochs reached New Zealand in two batches in 1949. After some parochial dithering over nomenclature they took the names of local lakes—HMNZS *Hawea, Kaniere, Pukaki, Rotoiti, Taupo*, and *Tutira*.

Frigates

Although overshadowed by the cruisers and outclassed by the later Type 12s, the Lochs nevertheless served actively. Beginning with *Pukaki* and *Tutira*, all operated off Korea between July 1950 and March 1954, *Rotoiti* and *Hawea* making two deployments (see KOREAN WAR). They escorted ships, enforced blockades, bombarded shore positions, and landed raiding parties. On the night of 19–20 February 1952 *Taupo* helped foil an invasion of the island of Yang-Do by sinking 10 sampans full of troops, in the process suffering minor damage from a near-miss from shore batteries. While heading home in October 1951 *Rotoiti* confronted Chinese pirates who had captured the British merchant ship *Hupeh* off the Yangtze River. After *Rotoiti* located the ship and fired starshells, the pirates agreed to be landed on an island, leaving the *Hupeh* and her crew free to sail on to Hong Kong. Several collisions and minor groundings rounded out the Lochs' Korean adventures.

The Lochs' duties took them from the tropics to the Antarctic. In 1950 *Taupo* and *Hawea* participated in a six-month exchange with Royal Navy Mediterranean frigates. A year later crews from *Taupo* and *Kaniere* worked as strike-breakers during the waterfront dispute. In 1957–58 *Pukaki* and *Rotoiti* acted as weather ships for the British government's hydrogen bomb tests off Christmas Island, the medical consequences of which were still being debated in the 1990s. *Kaniere*, *Pukaki*, and *Rotoiti* all had tours of duty on the Far East Station, which would also become an important station for later vessels. From 1961 until 1965 *Rotoiti* and *Pukaki*, based at Dunedin during the summer season, ventured south to serve as weather picket ships for Operation Deepfreeze.

The RNZN defended the six-frigate force concept until the mid 1960s, but in practice seldom had six at sea. *Taupo* and *Tutira* were paid off after returning from Korea in 1952 and 1951 respectively. *Kaniere* spent the last five years as an alongside training ship. By 1965 only *Rotoiti* and *Pukaki* were still active, albeit restricted to sheltered waters. *Rotoiti* was paid off on 6 August 1965. All went to Hong Kong ship-breakers.

A Westland Wasp HAS1 is secured on the flight deck of the Leander class frigate HMNZS *Waikato*. While carrying RNZN markings, the Wasps were operated by the RNZAF's 3 Squadron, which provided servicing personnel (*RNZN, PN3716*)

Frigates

Taupo and *Tutira*, unmodernised and unused for almost a decade, were towed away in October 1961, followed by *Hawea* and *Pukaki* in November 1965. Last to go were *Rotoiti* and *Kaniere*, sold in September 1966 and towed north in January 1967.

High-speed submarines had made the Lochs obsolescent even before they joined the RNZN. Throughout the late 1940s and the 1950s the British converted destroyers into high-speed frigates and designed new classes, the most successful of which, the Type 12 group (Whitby, Rothesay, and Leander classes), were also built for Australia, New Zealand, India, South Africa, Chile, and the Netherlands. Of about 2150 tons standard, the Whitbys and Rothesays used a raised forecastle, a highly seaworthy hull, and powerful steam turbines to offer a maximum service speed of about 30 knots. Armament was a twin 4.5-inch Mark 6 dual-purpose mount forward, a light anti-aircraft gun aft, anti-submarine torpedo tubes, and two Mark 10 anti-submarine mortars, the so-called 'Limbo', an improved Squid. In October 1956 New Zealand ordered two Rothesays. These 'nuclear-age' warships took the names of New Zealand provinces. HMNZS *Otago*, completed in 1960, had been ordered as HMS *Hastings*, but HMNZS *Taranaki*, completed in 1961, was a fresh order. The ships were more extensively air-conditioned than their British counterparts and in 1962–63 were converted at Devonport dockyard to mount the navy's first anti-aircraft missile system, the Short Seacat.

New Zealand's next frigates were improved Type 12s, the Leander class. Ironically, the country had played an important part in the evolution of this design. An earlier RNZN request for a fully air-conditioned, helicopter-carrying Rothesay had led to HMS *Leander*, a general-purpose frigate. On a slightly modified Rothesay hull, the 2350–2500 ton Leanders added long-range radar, two 20 mm AA guns, Seacat, and a light helicopter, the Westland Wasp H.A.S. Mark 1—and dispensed with the Bofors, the unsuccessful heavy torpedo tubes, and one mortar. HMNZS *Waikato* was commissioned in 1966 and a second, broad-beamed Leander, HMNZS *Canterbury*, followed in 1971. Between 1966 and *Canterbury*'s completion, the RNZN maintained its four-ship frigate force (imposed on it by budget problems during the mid 1960s) by hiring the British Whitby, HMS *Blackpool*.

Unlike the Royal Navy, the RNZN never reconstructed its Rothesays to carry Wasps, so by the late 1970s *Otago* and *Taranaki* were causing concern. In 1978–79 the four-ship force became 'three and a bit' when *Taranaki* landed its anti-submarine mortars and Seacat to become a resource protection and training vessel. The old ship was to have been converted to gas turbine propulsion at Devonport from April 1982. Perhaps mercifully, the 1981 British defence cuts enabled the RNZN to buy two Royal Navy Leanders instead. HMS *Dido* (1963), renamed HMNZS *Southland*, arrived in 1983 after a short refit. HMS *Bacchante* (1969), renamed HMNZS *Wellington*, sailed for New Zealand in late 1982 and spent from January 1983 until July 1986 in dockyard hands. Decommissioned in 1982 and 1983 respectively, *Taranaki* and *Otago* were scrapped at Auckland in 1983–84 and 1987.

The purchase of the British Leanders was a stopgap measure. *Southland*, an overspecialised anti-submarine conversion, was a dubious bargain, chosen mainly for her ADAWS5 command computer system despite some recognised deficiencies. The government cancelled a long refit planned for 1988, the Australians ceased supporting her Ikara anti-submarine missile system in 1991, and she went to the Philippines for scrap in late 1996, after being effectively non-seagoing from mid 1994. By early 1997 crew shortages had *Waikato*, partly disarmed, alongside at Devonport. The RNZN poured millions into refitting the later broad-beamed *Wellington* and *Canterbury*, installing anti-submarine torpedo tubes instead of mortars and (applying lessons learnt from the Royal Navy's experience in the ★Falklands War) enlarging the hangars for bigger helicopters that were in the event never acquired. They were also fitted with the British NAUTIS command system and new long-range radars. In the late 1990s Phalanx close-in weapons replaced the obsolete Seacat and the ships began another refit to take the Kaman Seasprite helicopter. *Canterbury* is expected to close the New Zealand Leander story in 2005.

For four decades the Type 12s, improved or otherwise, symbolised the RNZN; they appeared on recruiting posters and at Waitangi Day ceremonies, and showed the flag around the globe. *Canterbury*, for example, represented New Zealand at the Silver Jubilee Royal Fleet Review at Spithead in 1977, and sixteen years later attended the Battle of the Atlantic commemorations, while *Waikato* participated in American VJ Day ceremonies in Hawaii in 1995. In May 1987 *Wellington*, heading for Suva when the first Fijian coup took place, was later ordered out of the port by the new regime; *Canterbury* was diverted to stand by the islands. That year *Canterbury* and *Southland* made the RNZN's first port calls to China. The ships have exercised with vessels from allied navies, made port visits, escorted HMY *Britannia* in New Zealand waters, and rescued seafarers, for example two Malay fishermen rescued by *Wellington* from the South China Sea in September 1995. The ships have experienced several berthing mishaps and engineering problems. Unlike the Lochs, the Type 12s never fired a gun or missile in anger, but they have participated in three high-profile events. *Otago* made international headlines in July 1973 when the Labour government sent her to protest against French atmospheric nuclear testing at Moruroa Atoll. *Canterbury* followed, also supported by HMAS *Supply*. Nine years later the National government controversially sent a frigate to the Indian Ocean patrols in order to free a British ship for service in the Falklands War; *Canterbury* and *Waikato* alternated on these duties in 1982–83. In late 1995–96 *Wellington*, followed by *Canterbury*, joined the Multinational Interception Force in the Persian Gulf (see GULF WAR). Rather than being paid off in late 1999 as planned, *Wellington* continued in commission into 2000 as a training ship.

During the 1980s the RNZN had been evaluating Leander replacements. Unlike the 1950s and 1960s, New Zealand no longer automatically looked to frontline British designs. Because Australia was known to be looking for a follow-on frigate for its FFG7 programme, New Zealand joined its neighbour in a joint fleet replacement programme. After rejecting the more capable (and more expensive) British Type 23, the partners shortlisted the Dutch Royal Schelde M-type and the German Blohm and Voss MEKO 200 design, settling on the slightly less capable but cheaper German ship, whose flexible, modular design, based on an earlier one for Argentina and Nigeria, serves the Portuguese, Turkish, and Greek navies. With gas turbines and increased automation, they would require a crew of only 160, as compared to the Leander's 260. But technical specifications were only part of the story. No warship purchase had ever generated such strong political debate. Block obsolescence of the RNZN frigate fleet had given its critics a two billion dollar target. The country had banned visits by nuclear-armed or nuclear-powered warships, and New Zealand's economy had been undergoing radical restructuring since 1984. Anti-defence feeling and the 1987 international sharemarket collapse hardened opposition to the new frigates. Criticism was made on economic, social, and defence grounds (aircraft and offshore patrol vessels having their advocates, just as submarines had had in the early 1980s). Although many within the ruling Labour Party opposed the programme, the government agreed on 14 August 1989 to join Australia in building the MEKOs at Transfield Shipbuilding's Williamstown yard in Victoria. Australia ordered eight ships and New Zealand two, retaining an option on a further two. A major 'selling' point for the deal was the expectation that New Zealand businesses would win at least $800 million worth of work prefabricating modules for the ships. By early 1997, 407 New Zealand businesses had gained work, which ranged from the construction of superstructures at Whangarei to electronic switching gear at Hamilton.

The RNZN's first gas turbine frigates dropped the provincial names initiated by the Type 12s. HMNZS *Te Kaha* ('Strong') was launched in July 1995 and joined the fleet two years later; HMNZS *Te Mana* ('Authority') was launched in May 1997 and commissioned in 1999 to replace *Wellington*. They displace 3195 tons standard. An LM2500 gas turbine and MTU diesels propel them at 27 knots. A single 5-inch gun, eight Seasparrow short-range missiles, anti-submarine torpedo tubes recycled from the Leanders, and the Kaman Seasprite SH-2G medium helicopter form the armament, although these 'baseline' ships (as they are euphemistically styled) lack the helicopter haul-down system fitted to the Australian ships, having instead a different, harpoon grid system. The ships have often been criticised for being beyond the means of the New Zealand economy, yet in 1995 *Combat Fleets of the World* considered that 'the New Zealand version will be more offshore patrol vessel than combatant'.

That assessment could not take the political heat out of the frigate project. During 1996–97 most political parties lined up against the MEKOs. In late 1997 the RNZN even inspected second-hand US Navy FFG7s, but the 1997 Defence white paper, published just days after the option for the third and fourth MEKOs expired, rejected further orders in the short term at least. This effectively cut the frigate force to three ships after 1998 when the semi-operational *Waikato* was stricken. A question mark hangs over the replacement for *Canterbury* (due to be retired c. 2005) and/or restoration of the four-ship force.

R.J. McDougall, *New Zealand Naval Vessels* (GP Books, Wellington, 1989).

GAVIN McLEAN

Fulton, Brigadier-General Harry Townsend

(15 August 1869–29 March 1918) was one of three New Zealand brigadier-generals killed in action during the ★First World War. The son of a lieutenant-general, he emigrated with his family to Otago as a boy. His military career began in April 1887 when he was commissioned in the Dunedin City Guards. In 1892 he joined the Argyll and Sutherland Highlanders, and then the Indian Army; he took part in operations on the North-west Frontier, including those at Malakand and Tirah. On leave in New Zealand when the ★Boer War began, he was attached to the 4th Contingent sent by the colony to South Africa, and was severely wounded at Ottoshoop. Returning to India, he served for a time as second-in-command of a Gurkha battalion. Back in New Zealand, he was a member of the Samoan Expeditionary Force raised in August 1914. During 1915, he took command of infantry reinforcements at Trentham; these would later be constituted as the New Zealand Rifle Brigade. Fulton took the brigade to Egypt, where it was involved briefly in the ★Senussi campaign before proceeding to the ★Western Front as part of the New Zealand Division.

Brusque in manner, punctilious by nature, and a stickler for discipline with a strong distaste for the use of bad language, he led an increasingly effective brigade, which performed well on the Somme and at Messines. After a period of rest in England, he briefly commanded the reserve brigade at Sling before returning to the Rifle Brigade on 27 March 1918. On the following day he was mortally wounded by a shell which scored a lucky hit on the cellar in which his headquarters was located at Colincamps.

Furlough affair was the most prolonged act of collective insubordination in New Zealand's military history. From late 1942 the continued presence of 2NZEF in the Mediterranean had become increasingly questioned in New Zealand. When in May 1943 it was determined that 2nd New Zealand Division should take part in the forthcoming ★Italian campaign, the need for the 'old hands' to be given a rest was recognised. Despite the serious reservations of the Chief of the General Staff, Lieutenant-General Edward ★Puttick, and the commander of 2NZEF, Lieutenant-General Sir Bernard ★Freyberg, the ★War Cabinet decided that 6000 men of the first three echelons were to be returned home on extended leave or furlough. The first, the 'Ruapehu' draft, were returned to New Zealand in July 1943. Although a three-month furlough was envisaged, the period was extended until early 1944 because of a combination of shipping difficulties and political manoeuvring. In the meantime the furlough draftees had returned to civilian life. Many became increasingly resentful at what they perceived as a lack of sacrifice within New Zealand, with many apparently able-bodied young men still not having been called up. This sense of bitterness among many furlough draftees led to public outbursts, which were censored by an increasingly embarrassed government. By the time the government had determined that certain classes of furlough draftees—mainly married men with children, Maori, and medically unfit—would not go back overseas, a mere 1637 furlough draftees were required to report to mobilisation camps in January 1944. Once in camp a large proportion of these draftees made it clear that they were not prepared to embark for a second time while medically fit men who had not served remained in the country. In the event, only 663 men embarked on 12 January; the rest were placed under open arrest at Trentham, Linton, Burnham, and Papakura. The government suppressed news of the mutiny, but with such large numbers of troops involved it became widely known. Even though courts martial began convicting defaulters for desertion from late January, passive resistance at army camps continued. Forced to negotiate with the ringleaders late in February, the government made important concessions, with the result that 250 defaulters embarked for overseas. However, the bulk of the defaulters remained defiant, and in early April their sentences for desertion were quashed by the Court of Appeal. A frustrated government then dismissed the 'rebels' without discharge privileges; they lost their entitlement to rehabilitation benefits and future employment in the public service. The situation was made worse by the fact that a second furlough draft was due to return overseas in May 1944. On mustering in camps, it had also become infected with the dissent. Further defaulters were dismissed for misconduct and insubordination. In September 1944 the furlough scheme was discontinued in favour of a replacement scheme in which soldiers with more than three years' service overseas were returned to New Zealand. Ultimately the government had to accept that there were limits to its authority if it was not to use force against recalcitrant soldiers who had widespread public sympathy. In 1945 the furlough mutineers had their discharge privileges restored.

F.L.W. Wood, *Political and External Affairs* (War History Branch, Wellington, 1958); N.M. Taylor, *The Home Front*, 2 vols (Historical Publications Branch, Wellington, 1986); J. McLeod, *Myth and Reality: The New Zealand Soldier in World War II* (Reed Methuen, Auckland, 1986).

G

Gallipoli The Gallipoli campaign, in which New Zealand made its first major effort during the ★First World War, had its origins in the stalemate which had developed on the ★Western Front by the end of 1914. Following the initial free-flowing operations, the opposing sides found themselves facing each other along a line of trenches which stretched from Switzerland to the Belgian coast. The power of the defence having already made its impact felt, statesmen in both camps were at a loss as to how to proceed. In these circumstances the need for an alternative approach was patent.

On the Allied side the search for an alternative was encouraged by the opportunities presented by superior seapower. With the German High Seas Fleet contained in the North Sea, the possibility of launching amphibious attacks on the enemy was particularly evident to the British First Lord of the Admiralty, Winston Churchill. Impatient to use British naval resources, he advanced a series of proposals, among them an assault on the Dardanelles—the nearly fifty-kilometre-long strait separating the Aegean Sea from the Sea of Marmara, which at its narrowest point, the Narrows, was less than two kilometres wide. The object would be to pass a force into the Sea of Marmara and threaten the capital of Germany's ally the Ottoman Empire. Constantinople, which guarded another narrow waterway, the Bosphorus, into the Black Sea, was very vulnerable to seaward attack. Such action had precedents: in 1807 a British squadron had forced the Narrows only to be becalmed and eventually forced to retreat before it could attack Constantinople. As recently as the Italo-Turkish War of 1911–12, an Italian force had attacked the Dardanelles and penetrated as far as the defences of the Narrows. Even before the Ottoman Empire entered the war on 31 October 1914, the possibility of a Greek–Russian assault on the Dardanelles had been canvassed. Once hostilities began, Churchill had wasted no time in ordering a bombardment of the forts guarding the Narrows. This operation, carried out before Great Britain formally declared war on the Ottoman Empire, merely reminded the Turks of the threat to the Dardanelles, and impelled them to improve the defences, especially by the laying of minefields.

In London strategic issues were from November 1914 in the hands of the War Council, whose chief members were the Prime Minister, H.H. Asquith, the Secretary of War, Lord ★Kitchener, and Churchill. The last-named urged an attack on Gallipoli at its first meeting on 25 November. This was rejected—pre-war studies had indicated that such an operation would be too risky—but the issue was soon brought back to the foreground by developments in the war. With the Turks advancing northwards in the Caucasus, Russia appealed for action to relieve the pressure. The need was fleeting—Russian forces soon drove the Turks back—but impetus had been given to Churchill's concept of an attack on Turkey. The tempting idea of inducing the Balkan states to join the Allies and attack Austria–Hungary from the south-east, never more than an illusion, was also influential. A campaign in the Eastern Mediterranean might, moreover, encourage Italy to enter the war on the Allied side. These considerations were reinforced by the limited nature of the intended action. Despite the strong reservations of the commander of the Eastern Mediterranean Squadron (Vice-Admiral Sackville Carden), Churchill proposed a naval attack on the forts guarding the Narrows. His plan had the attraction of not requiring any substantial military forces for its implementation. Nor would it entail any diminution in Britain's naval position in the vital North Sea, since only older battleships would be used. The War Council approved the proposal on 15 January 1915.

The naval attack began on 19 February. Despite delays caused by bad weather, the outer defences, based on forts on both European and Asian coasts at the entrance to the strait, had been overcome within a week. Attention then switched to the intermediate defences, consisting of minefields guarded by batteries of mobile field guns and howitzers. In London meanwhile the War Council had agreed to provide some military forces to support these operations: on 15 February it decided to send out the 29th Division, the only regular division not committed to the British Expeditionary Force in France. Churchill also dispatched the Royal Naval Division, a hotchpotch of Royal Marine and other units raised from surplus sailors. Later, when the decision to send the 29th Division was reversed (temporarily as it transpired), it was decided to deploy to Mudros on the Aegean island of Lemnos the Australian and New Zealand troops which had, since December, been training in Egypt (see NEW ZEALAND EXPEDITIONARY FORCE); because of a lack of transport, only one Australian brigade was deployed for the time being. The French government, meanwhile, had also decided to deploy to Mudros a specially composed division. All these troops were regarded as garrison forces which might occupy the forts (and later Constantinople) when the naval attacks had been successfully completed. A military assault on the Dardanelles was not envisaged. General Sir Ian ★Hamilton was appointed to command the Mediterranean Expeditionary Force, as these disparate forces were designated.

By the time that Hamilton arrived in the Eastern Mediterranean on 17 March, the slow progress of the naval operations had raised doubts about the likelihood of success by these means alone. A sustained attempt to subdue the forts and guns guarding the intermediate defences was made on 18 March, but this proved disastrous when six of the sixteen capital ships taking part struck mines, and three were lost. The minefields remained as a barrier to progress. Within four days the commanders on the spot, Hamilton and Vice-Admiral John de Robeck (who had replaced Carden on 16 March), had shifted the emphasis of the operations from a purely naval to a military orientation, a change in which London eventually acquiesced. An opposed landing was now proposed, with a view to capturing the Kilid Bahr plateau, high ground immediately to the west of the Narrows. From here the positions on both sides of the strait dominating the sea approaches could be neutralised, allowing the naval operation to proceed. The forces at Hamilton's disposal, about 75,000 strong, were not in any state to carry out such a plan immediately, such an eventuality not having been foreseen. So that the necessary arrangements could be made, the French division, the Royal Naval Division, and the 29th Division were all transported to Egypt, where all but one brigade of the Australian and New Zealand Army Corps, commanded by Lieutenant-General William Birdwood, were still located. The ANZAC comprised the 1st Australian Division (Major-General W.T. Bridges) and the composite ★New Zealand and Australian Division commanded by 1NZEF commander Major-General Sir Alexander ★Godley, which included the New Zealand Infantry Brigade (Brigadier-General F.E. ★Johnston).

Over the ensuing month Hamilton prepared his plan for the landing—not an easy task given the rugged nature of much of the peninsula's coastline. He chose as his main focus the southern part of the Gallipoli peninsula at Cape Helles and Sedd el Bahr. While the 29th Division landed there on five separate beaches, a subsidiary landing would be made by the ANZAC about twenty kilometres up the coast, north of Gaba Tepe. The Australians and New Zealanders would seize the southern part of the Sari Bair ridge before advancing across the peninsula to Maidos, from where they would mount a threat to the Kilid Bahr plateau from the rear. The French division would meanwhile make a temporary landing on the Asian shore at Kum Kale to prevent Turkish gunners there bombarding the troops landing at Helles. To divert Turkish attention, the Royal Naval Division would make a feint attack at Bulair, at the narrow neck of the peninsula. This was a demanding task for a force which had evolved in an ad hoc fashion, was barely sufficient for its initially envisaged garrison role, and was not fully equipped, especially in ammunition. There was much improvisation in the weeks preceding the implementation of the plan, and little time to practise the landings. But a certain complacency, based on a disparaging assessment of Turkish fighting qualities, and a lack of forcefulness on Hamilton's part hindered efforts to overcome the most serious deficiencies.

The landings were originally scheduled to take place on 23 April, but weather conditions led to a delay of two days. The first ashore were to be the ANZACs, who had moved forward to Lemnos in early April. The 3rd Australian Brigade would land before dawn and advance to Gun Ridge. Following them, the 2nd Australian Brigade would occupy the Sari Bair ridge as far as Hill 971. The 1st Australian Division's remaining brigade would land by 9 a.m. as divisional reserve. With the covering force in place, the New Zealand and Australian Division would then land, and the drive across the peninsula would begin. From Lemnos, the troops would be carried to the landing zone on

Gallipoli

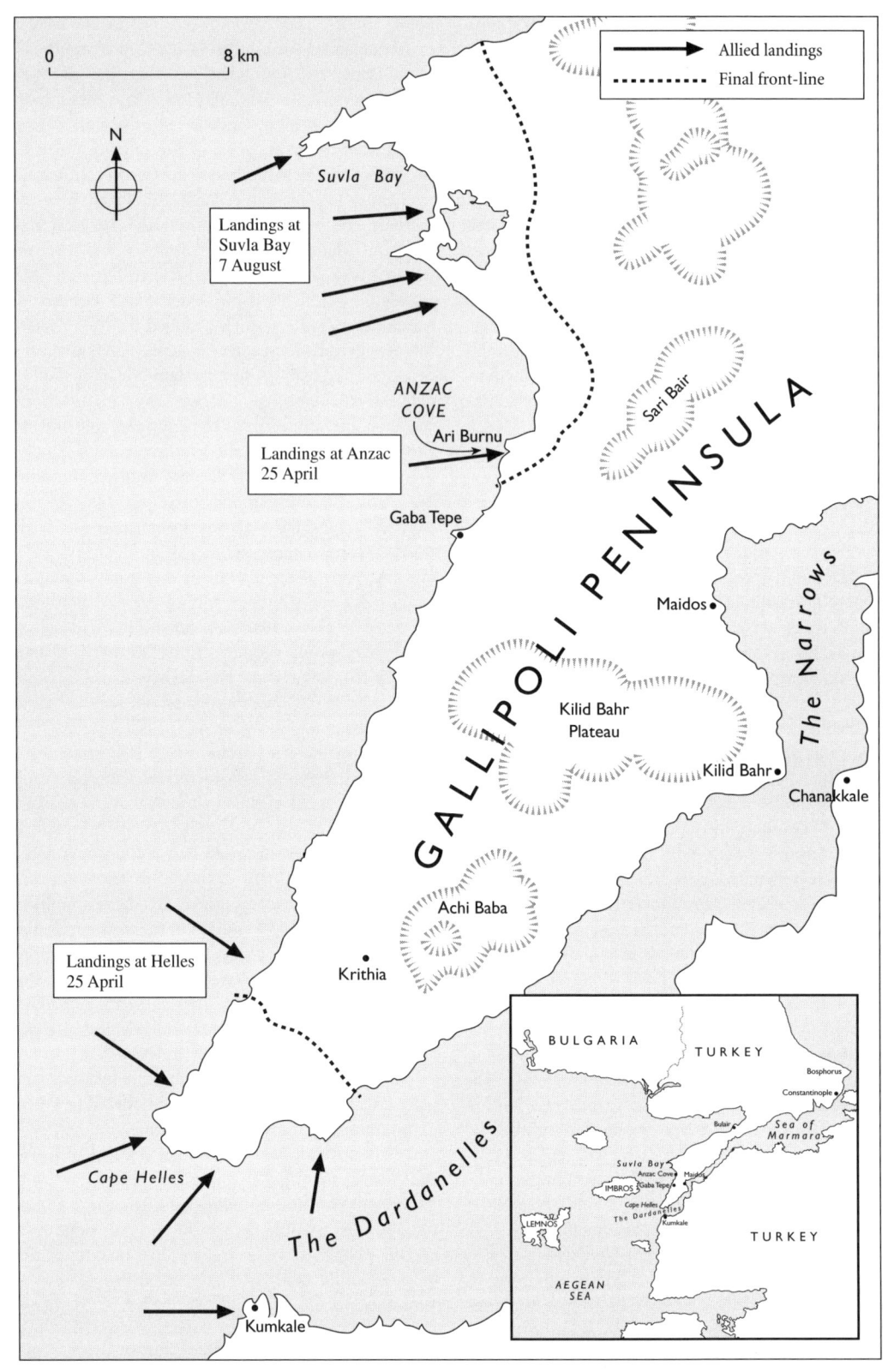

Map 8a Gallipoli, showing the Allied landings in April and August 1915

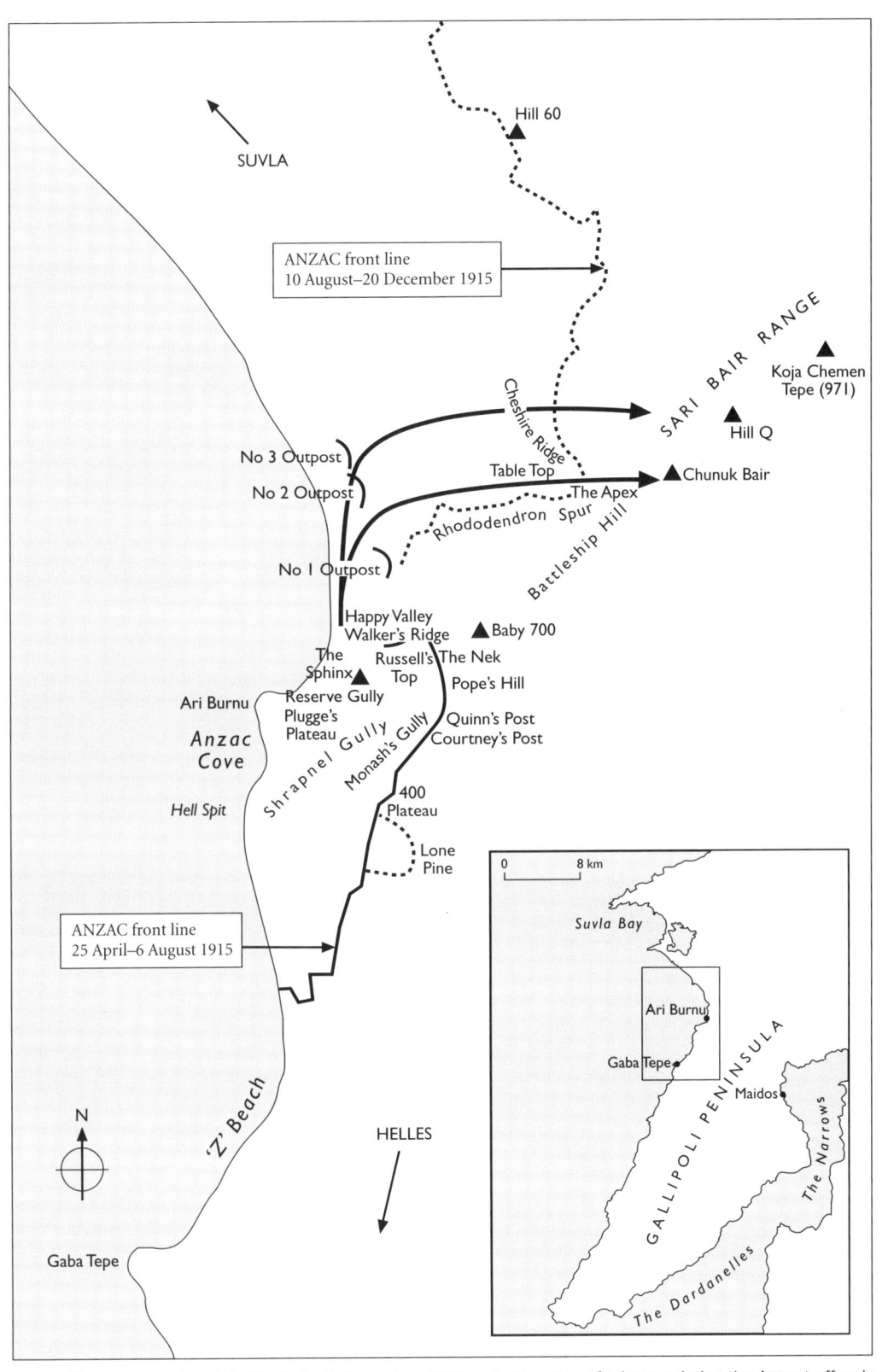

Map 8b The Anzac sector at Gallipoli, April–December 1915, with the axes of advance during the August offensive

Gallipoli

Anzac Cove (*Alexander Turnbull Library, C-5519*)

warships (in the case of the 3rd Brigade) or on merchant ships, loaded into ships' boats and towed inshore by steamboats, and eventually rowed to the beaches. They would come ashore on a 2700-metre front with their left south of Ari Burnu on what was later dubbed Brighton Beach.

Even if all had gone to plan on the 25th, the force would have struggled to secure its objectives, especially within the time allotted. But the plan was thrown into disarray even before the troops began landing. The Australian spearhead was mistakenly directed about two kilometres north of the envisaged landing place, nearer to Ari Burnu at what was later named Anzac Cove and on a much narrower front than envisaged in the plan. The reasons for this have been hotly debated over the last eighty years, with tides, faulty navigation by the landing fleet, belated changes of orders all being canvassed. An unauthorised alteration of direction northwards by one of the midshipmen commanding a steamboat, which pulled the whole line of tows in this direction, is the most likely explanation. As a consequence the troops, on landing, found themselves confronted with far more formidable natural terrain immediately inland than they would have faced at the originally planned landing place. As they pushed inland through this difficult country of tangled ravines and spurs, the various units were split up and inextricably mixed. Only a few small, uncoordinated parties managed to reach the objective, Gun Ridge. These problems were compounded by delays in landing the remainder of the 1st Australian Division, the last of which reached shore four hours behind schedule. In the meantime, the first elements of the New Zealand and Australian Division had also begun landing soon after 9 a.m., and they became intermixed with units of the Australian division.

These developments were made more serious by the defenders' vigorous response. In the landing zone itself there had only been two Turkish infantry companies and an artillery battery. Although these units used their dominating position to inflict substantial casualties on the invaders, they were too few to prevent the Australians from landing and pushing inland. However, exercising near Hill 971 was the 19th Division, based at Maidos and commanded by Mustafa Kemal Bey. Using his initiative Kemal rapidly deployed these forces to meet the threat posed by the ANZACs, units being thrown into battle as soon as they reached the position. A counter-attack in mid morning drove the Australians back from the 400 Plateau. Kemal then turned his attention to the left of the ANZAC position, where New Zealand troops had joined the Australians in the front line. A fierce struggle ensued for the Baby 700 feature, but by evening the ANZACs had been forced back from it and the Nek. In this fighting about one in five of the 3000 New Zealanders who landed on the first day became casualties. The Turks had succeeded in securing the high ground. Far from rapidly gaining their initial objectives on Gun Ridge, the ANZACs found themselves in danger of being pushed back into the sea.

The situation at the main British landing site at Helles, where the landings had begun at dawn, was equally unpropitious. Tactical success was gained at two of the beaches, though unimaginative leadership ensured that it was not exploited. At the main landing points the 29th Division suffered heavy losses in securing a precarious lodgment, a major achievement in itself. Many men were killed, especially at V Beach, where the improvised landing craft, the transport *River Clyde*, had been run ashore. The results fell far short of the first-day objectives. Not until the 26th were the Turks finally driven back and the remainder of 29th Division landed. On this second day, the first units of the Royal Naval Division came ashore. This division had carried out the planned feint at Bulair on 25 April. In this operation, which had little effect on the enemy, Bernard ★Freyberg, a lieutenant-commander in the Hood Battalion, distinguished himself for the first time, by swimming ashore to light flares with a view to misleading the Turkish defenders. A French brigade also landed during the 26th. The rest of the French division had landed at Kum Kale the previous day, but it was soon withdrawn and deployed at Helles as well. When, however, the British and French troops sought to advance towards Achi Baba on 28 April, they were held and then driven back by a strong Turkish counter-attack.

Meanwhile, at Anzac, the crisis had been surmounted. On the first night the situation had looked so dangerous that Birdwood had recommended evacuation, but this had been rejected by Hamilton, who was conscious that there was no means of carrying out such a plan. He could only urge the ANZACs to dig in. As they did so the position was gradually made more secure. Gaps in the line were plugged by further units of the New Zealand and Australian Division as they came ashore. As soon as possible, the original landing units were pulled out of the line and reorganised. Eventually Birdwood was able to establish two divisional sectors: the New Zealand and Australian Division took responsibility for the line north of Courtney's Post, and the 1st Australian Division south of it.

These preparations were timely, for from the 27th Kemal, having received reinforcements, began to intensify the pressure on the besieged ANZACs. The deployment in the enclave of four RND battalions at Anzac Cove bolstered the defences and allowed the reorganisation of the 1st Australian Division. It also raised the possibility of forcing back the besiegers. An attack aimed at seizing the Baby 700 feature was eventually mounted on the evening of 2 May by the New Zealand and Australian Division, with the RND battalions in support. But the plan was too ambitious. Poorly prepared and coordinated—the Otago Battalion in particular failed to make its start-line in time—the assault failed.

The main operational focus remained at Helles, where the British and French forces were soon reinforced. From Egypt came the 29th Indian Brigade, followed by the 42nd Division. Another French division also arrived. But these deployments were matched by the build-up of Turkish forces. After a major Turkish attack had been defeated on 1–2 May, the Allies prepared to launch a new drive on the village of Krithia on the rising heights of Achi Baba. To further bolster the Allied strength, two ANZAC brigades, including the New Zealand Brigade, were taken out of the line at Anzac and redeployed to Helles, along with one New Zealand and four Australian field batteries which had not managed to get ashore at Anzac. The Allied plan, which was based on an unimaginative frontal assault in daylight, was put into effect on 6 May. The advancing troops were soon brought to a halt, an outcome that was repeated on the following day. Heavy losses were sustained without any indication that a breakthrough was possible. The New Zealand Brigade was detailed to take part in an attack on 8 May, wheeling on the stalled 29th Division. The New Zealanders had little time to prepare, and their attack went in behind a weak artillery bombardment at 10.30 a.m. The Wellington Battalion, on the left, got the furthest forward, advancing several hundred metres before being brought to a halt. Ordered to renew the attack at 5.30 p.m., the New Zealand troops again suffered heavily as they struggled across the Daisy Patch. The Australian brigade, suddenly ordered to advance as well, could make no progress either. The three-day operation, later designated the Second Battle of Krithia, had cost the Allies 6500 men in gaining about half a kilometre of ground of no major significance. The New Zealand Brigade lost more than 800 men in this ill-conceived attack.

As Hamilton was sent further reinforcements—the 52nd Division arrived in early June—the Dardanelles Committee (as the War Council had been retitled following the reconstitution of Asquith's government) considered the options. Was the land operation, which was still far short of achieving its first-day objectives, to be continued or was it to be shut down and the troops withdrawn? Political considerations made the latter course unpalatable. In the event, it was decided to persist, and to bolster Hamilton's force still further. Despite the outcome of the previous two attacks, Hamilton agreed to a further attempt being made at Helles. By now the situation was even less advantageous for the attacker, since an elaborate trench system would have to be overcome. By the use of heavy bombardment, a series of attacks in June and July made

Gallipoli

New Zealand troops resting in a trench on Walker's Ridge (*E.S. Gibson Collection, Canterbury Museum, 10209*)

small gains, at the cost of 12,000 British and French casualties. The Turks merely pulled back up the slope and prepared to meet the next onslaught.

The more the situation at Helles seemed permanently stalemated, the more attention focused on the position at Anzac. Early in May reinforcements had arrived in the form of the New Zealand Mounted Rifles Brigade (Brigadier-General A.H. ★Russell) and the 1st Australian Light Horse Brigade, which had left their horses in Egypt. The RND battalions were withdrawn. On 19 May the ANZACs, now relatively well organised, faced a fierce onslaught by more than 40,000 Turks. In the New Zealand sector, the troops defending Russell's Top beat off repeated attacks from the Nek, while the Australians did the same further south. No man's land was left strewn with an estimated 10,000 casualties, including 3000 dead. After this Turkish disaster (their worst of the campaign) and a brief truce which allowed some of the dead to be buried, the two sides were left in a state of deadlock in this area as well. They faced each other, sometimes only metres apart, in a state of increasing discomfort. Searing heat and the swarming flies (made worse by unburied corpses in no man's land) tormented the men, conditions exacerbated by water shortages. Disease, especially dysentery, flourished in the insanitary conditions among men already debilitated by weeks of inadequate food. These physical problems were compounded by the psychological pressures stemming from the consciousness that no place in the tiny perimeter was safe from artillery fire. With the Turks overlooking them, snipers were an ever-present hazard.

In the southern part of the front at Anzac, the trench system offered no more prospect of a breakthrough than at Helles. However, in the rugged terrain at the northern end of Anzac the front was less clearly defined. It was marked by a series of outposts. The possibility of outflanking the Turks through this area was recognised at an early stage by Birdwood. While the futile attacks continued at Helles, Hamilton began preparing an offensive at Anzac, using further reinforcements which the Dardanelles Committee on 7 June had agreed to provide. These amounted to three additional divisions, to which Kitchener added two more late in the month, bringing the number deployed to a total of thirteen divisions. During July London's commitment to Gallipoli increased, as a consequence of the disasters which befell the Russians at the hands of the Austro-German offensive launched on 13 July.

Hamilton's plan envisaged two columns advancing on to the Sari Bair Range, with a view to capturing the key high points of Chunuk Bair, Hill Q, and Hill 971 (Koja Chemen Tepe) during the night of 6–7 August. A diversionary attack by the Australians would distract Turkish attention from the assault. At dawn on the 7th, an attack launched by the New Zealanders from Chunuk Bair in conjunction with an Australian attack from Russell's Top against the heavily fortified position at the Nek would complete the capture of the whole ridge as far as Hill 971. It was another complicated plan, requiring strict adherence to timetables to pull it off. With no room at Anzac for further troops, Hamilton determined to use his additional forces, grouped as IX Corps, by landing at Suvla Bay, to the north of Anzac, as well. This operation was initially conceived in terms of supporting the assault on the Sari Bair Range. However, the intervention of the lacklustre and timid IX Corps commander, Lieutenant-General Sir Frederick Stopford (a long-retired officer who had been foisted on Hamilton by Kitchener because of his seniority), ensured that the establishment of a base became the primary objective, with support of the assault on the Sari Bair Range left dependent on the situation.

The offensive opened on 6 August with diversionary attacks at both Helles and Anzac's Lone Pine. Predictably, the former was a costly failure. While savage fighting at Lone Pine (seven Australian VCs were won there) did induce the movement of Turkish reserves, this proved counterproductive, for the troops so moved were better placed to intervene on the Sari Bair Range when that position's importance became apparent. As soon as night fell, two covering forces moved out to capture the foothills through which the assaulting columns would move to secure their objectives. On the right, the New Zealand Mounted Rifles Brigade and Otago Mounted Rifles had secured their objectives by 1 a.m. The plan thereafter came unstuck. Proceeding up separate *deres* (valleys), the two elements of the right assaulting column, which consisted of Johnston's New Zealand Infantry Brigade and an Indian mountain battery, were supposed to rendezvous on Rhododendron Spur before moving up on to the summit of Chunuk Bair. At dawn Johnston was still waiting at the Spur for part of his column to come up; when ordered to attack immediately he did so half-heartedly and was repulsed by the comparatively weak Turkish forces on the summit. Meanwhile the left assaulting column, made up of British and Indian troops, had also failed to seize its objective after becoming lost in the rugged terrain in the darkness. Although the timetable had thus been completely thrown out, the planned dawn attack at the Nek went in even though there was to be no converging attack from Chunuk Bair. The 3rd Australian Light Horse Brigade was in effect sacrificed by Birdwood in the forlorn hope that the attack might help the assaulting columns up on to their objectives by distracting the enemy.

The overall plan had depended upon speed, to ensure that the troops on the summits could consolidate their positions before the Turks could deploy their reserves in response. The delays had fatally compromised the whole offensive, though on the 8th a glimmer of hope was provided when Johnston's column found Chunuk Bair unoccupied and the Wellington Battalion moved quickly on to the summit. But the position was enfiladed by Turks on other high points, and after dawn they prevented significant reinforcements getting up to join the Wellingtons. Not until after dark did the Otago Battalion and the Wellington Mounted Rifles join them. A further attempt to seize Hill Q was made on 9 August, but once again the whole enterprise was fatally compromised by a lack of coordination. Even so, a small force of Gurkha soldiers managed to reach the top of Hill Q, but were unable to consolidate their position before falling back after being hit by friendly naval gunfire. By this time the weight of Turkish pressure was beginning to make itself felt, as reinforcements arrived. In desperate fighting, the New Zealanders on the summit of Chunuk Bair held off the Turks for two days. But on 10 August a massive Turkish counter-attack settled the issue. The British battalions which had relieved the New Zealanders on Chunuk Bair the previous night were swept away. The British forces on the approaches to Hill Q were also driven back.

The seizure of the summits of Chunuk Bair and Hill Q were impressive tactical achievements, and the Gurkha and New Zealand troops involved distinguished themselves by their steadfastness at a critical moment. But by the time the summits were gained, it was already too late: Turkish reserves were converging on the area in numbers that spelt doom for the whole enterprise. There was no chance of the British getting sufficient forces up on to these positions (even if they had been immediately available), and supplying them, in time to consolidate the positions before the inevitable Turkish counter-attack. Even if the positions had been held, it is by no means certain that the Allies could then have pushed on towards the Narrows: the ANZACs themselves had proved that troops holding the high ground could face difficulties in dislodging determined defenders. In reality, the outcome of the offensive had been determined by the failure to secure the Sari Bair heights on the first night, but the performance of IX Corps underscored the failure. Two divisions were ashore by midday on 7 August, but, despite limited resistance from Turkish forces in the vicinity, they failed to take decisive action to seize the commanding heights in the area. When they did finally move forward to do so, they were forestalled by hastily deployed Turkish reserves. To be sure, Stopford's orders had emphasised the establishment of a base, but his lack of drive was apparent and he was soon replaced. The conditions in which the British troops found themselves also played a part in the failure to seize the opportunity presented by the successful landing. Godley bemoaned the fact that all that had been gained at Suvla was 'five hundred acres of bad grazing land'.

Fighting in the Anzac–Suvla perimeter continued throughout the rest of August, and the New Zealand and Australian Division suffered significant casualties in a series of attacks on features of doubtful tactical importance, especially at Hill 60. In mid September the weary New Zealanders were withdrawn to Lemnos for rest and reorganisation. By the time they returned to Anzac in November, the future of the campaign had been determined. In London Hamilton's demands for more men in the aftermath of the failure of the August offensive had brought into question the utility of persisting at Gallipoli, especially in light of needs both on the Western Front and at ★Salonika. General Sir Charles Monro, who replaced Hamilton on 15 October, soon proposed evacuation. Kitchener visited Gallipoli in November, and endorsed Monro's recommendation. After a storm ravaged the peninsula in late

November and caused many deaths among the exposed troops on both sides, the authorities in London reluctantly agreed to evacuate Suvla and Anzac. In a well-planned operation which contrasted sharply with those mounted earlier in the campaign, the withdrawal was carried out successfully on 19 and 20 December. It was soon decided to evacuate Helles as well. This was completed on the night of 8/9 January, again almost without casualties.

The Gallipoli campaign was a costly failure. While it is possible to point to moments when tactical developments offered the promise of success, the outcome was determined by strategic factors. Essentially there were not enough men available at the crucial moments. Hamilton launched the campaign with five divisions against a roughly comparable Turkish force which enjoyed the advantage of operating on interior lines. The rough parity was sustained as the campaign progressed with the thirteen Allied divisions eventually facing fourteen Turkish divisions. The half-hearted approach in London, until July 1915, ensured that the Allied build-up was always too little too late. Inadequate leadership played a part in the Allied failure, and many men were sacrificed in futile attacks on strong positions, especially at Helles.

The campaign had no significant effect on the outcome of the war. This could only be resolved where the main enemies confronted each other—on the Western Front—and the prospect of a Balkan coalition forming to lead a mighty offensive from the south-east was illusory, if only because of the pitiful state of the Balkan armies. Moreover, there was no certainty that the Turks would necessarily have capitulated had their capital come under threat from Allied naval forces. In pursuit of this chimera, 120,000 British and 27,000 French troops became casualties. Of the 7500 New Zealand casualties, there were 2721 dead—one in four of those who landed. Australia's 26,000 casualties included 8000 fatalities. Nevertheless, the fighting at Gallipoli was always less murderous than on the Western Front, where most of the Australians and New Zealanders would shortly head.

The campaign holds a special place in both Turkey and Australia and New Zealand. For the Turks, whose casualties probably numbered as many as 250,000, including 87,000 dead, it was the beginning of a process of national revival. The Turkish hero of Gallipoli, Kemal, would eventually, as Kemal Atatürk, become the founding President of the Turkish Republic. In the South Pacific the campaign helped bolster a sense of national identity, albeit within a British framework, in both countries. At the time of the landing, New Zealanders at home had thrilled to learn that their men were taking part in the top league—a sense of exhilaration that was soon tempered by the arrival of long casualty lists. There was pride that 1NZEF had performed well in difficult conditions. The institution of *Anzac Day, the day of the landing, ensured that the campaign would retain a special significance in both antipodean societies. The joint defence of the Anzac perimeter provided a strong sentimental underpinning to the relationship between Australia and New Zealand in the remainder of the century. 'Anzac' became the lasting label for trans-Tasman cooperation.

F. Waite, *The New Zealanders at Gallipoli* (Whitcombe & Tombs Ltd, Wellington, 1921); C. Pugsley, *Gallipoli: The New Zealand Story* (Reed, Auckland, 1998).

Galloway, General Thomas James (1800–15 September 1881) was the first commander of a New Zealand regular force. He entered the British Army as an ensign in 1821 and took part in the suppression of an insurrection in Jamaica in 1831. By 1854 he had risen to command the 70th Regiment, which was involved in Indian Mutiny operations. He arrived in New Zealand with the regiment in 1861. In September 1863 he was appointed to command the newly formed *Colonial Defence Force, in addition to his responsibilities (assumed the previous July) as commander of the Militia and Volunteers in the Auckland Province. These services were performed without remuneration. Galloway commanded the colonial forces during the Waikato campaign. An important redoubt at Wairoa was named after him. He resigned from both his colonial positions in February 1865, and immediately returned to the United Kingdom. His services were rewarded with a 324-hectare land grant near Hamilton. He was Colonel of the 70th (Surrey) Regiment from 1874, and was promoted to the rank of general three years later.

Gentry, Major-General Sir William George (20 February 1899–13 October 1991). London-born, Gentry arrived in New Zealand with his family in 1910 and six years later entered the Royal Military College, Duntroon, as an officer cadet. After graduating in December 1919, he had a two-year attachment to the Indian Army, which included active service on the North-west Frontier. Back in New Zealand, he held a variety of staff appointments, between spells in the United Kingdom for staff and engineering instruction. He attended the Staff College at Camberley in 1938, and was still in England when the *Second World War began. After serving briefly with the British Expeditionary Force in France, he proceeded to Egypt to join 2NZEF. He was the 2nd New Zealand Division's chief administrative officer (AAQMG) for a year, before becoming GSO1 in October 1942. His calmly efficient contribution to the Battle of El Alamein was recognised by his appointment as a DSO. He commanded 6th Brigade in the latter stages of the *North African campaign, after which he returned to New Zealand to become Deputy CGS. In June 1944 he headed back to the Mediterranean to command first the New Zealand troops in Egypt and then 9th Brigade in the last three months of the *Italian campaign, earning a bar to his DSO. Following the war he represented the *Chiefs of Staff in Melbourne, before again becoming Deputy CGS in 1946. After attending the *Imperial Defence College in 1948, he was heavily involved, as Adjutant-General from 1949 to 1952, in the development of New Zealand's capacity to meet its *Middle East commitment. As CGS from April 1952, he continued this task, while becoming increasingly involved in planning for the defence of South-east Asia. He was New Zealand's military representative in *ANZUS and other Allied planning consultations until his retirement in 1955. Although he had been made a CBE in 1950 and a CB in 1954, he had to await the advent of a Labour government before being belatedly made a KBE in 1958, along with his predecessor Major-General K.L. *Stewart. National ministers, it seems, had long memories of the disagreements which had characterised the development of Army policy in 1950. He was Honorary Colonel of the RNZIR from 1964 and 1967.

S. Mathieson (ed), *Bill Gentry's War, 1939–1945: Letters Edited by Sally Mathieson* (Dunmore Press, Palmerston North, 1996).

George Cross (GC) is the non-combatant or civilian counterpart of the *Victoria Cross. Instituted by Royal Warrant dated 24 September 1940, it is awarded 'for acts of the greatest heroism or of the most conspicuous courage in circumstances of extreme danger'. In the British 'order of wear' of decorations and medals, it ranks second to the VC and before all other honours from the Crown. Between 1940 and 1999, when it ceased to be available for award to New Zealanders, two New Zealand servicemen were awarded the George Cross, both posthumously: Lance-Corporal David *Russell, 22nd Battalion, 2NZEF, for gallant and distinguished services while a prisoner of war in German hands in Italy prior to 1945, and Sergeant Murray Ken Hudson, 7th Battalion, RNZIR, for saving life during a live grenade–throwing exercise at Waiouru Military Camp in October 1974. On the GC's institution, holders of the Medal of the Order of the British Empire for Gallantry, instituted in 1922 and commonly known as the Empire Gallantry Medal (EGM), were required to exchange their award for the GC. From 1971 holders of the Albert Medal (AM) were treated and regarded as holders of the GC. Instituted in 1866 and reorganised in 1867 and 1877 into two classes for saving life on both land and at sea, this award had always been understood to be the civilian equivalent of the VC, although it did not enjoy a very high precedence. The status of the AM had become even more vague when the EGM, which ranked junior to it, was replaced by the GC. New Zealand's first Albert Medallist was Trooper James Werner Magnusson of the New Zealand Mounted Rifles, a Swedish citizen, who received the award posthumously for saving life during the sinking of the troopship *Transylvania* in the Mediterranean in May 1917. Randolph Gordon Ridling, a lieutenant in the New Zealand Rifle Brigade, was awarded an AM in 1919 for saving life during a live grenade–throwing exercise at Brocton Camp, Stafford, England. The medal was also awarded to Stoker First Class Donald William Dale, RNZN, in 1943 for playing a leading role in rescuing four workers trapped after an explosion in HMNZS *Achilles* while she was docked at Portsmouth undergoing a refit. In 1999 the GC was replaced by a new *New Zealand Cross as the premier non-combatant or civilian award for acts of bravery by New Zealanders. (See HONOURS AND AWARDS)

P.P. O'Shea, *An Unknown Few: The story of those holders of the George Cross, the Empire Gallantry Medal, and the Albert Medals associated with New Zealand* (Government Printer, Wellington, 1981).

PHILLIP O'SHEA

Germ warfare The deliberate transmission of disease has a long tradition in warfare, but the direct use of microbes as weapons was essentially theoretical when the 1925 Geneva Protocol prohibited the use of bacteriological (along with chemical) weapons. Nevertheless, the potential of such weapons had been recognised for some time. Indeed, in April 1918, following the revelation of the incursion by the German raider *Wolf* the previous year, Captain P.H. *Hall-Thompson, Naval Adviser to the New Zealand government, had warned of the possibility of such an intruder using an aircraft to spread anthrax or other germs. Not until the late 1930s did the development of biological weapons begin in earnest. Japan established a major research and production programme involving a variety of bacteria, viruses, and biologically derived toxins, and some of these weapons were used in China. Great Britain and the United States collaborated closely on the development of biological weapons, focusing mainly on anthrax and botulinus toxin; anthrax-based weapons were produced on a large scale. In comparison, Germany's biological weapons programme was very limited. Neither Germany nor the Allies resorted to bacteriological weapons during the *Second World War.

In the decades after the war, advances in molecular biology and microbial genetics enabled the development of more virulent and drug-resistant strains of microbes. In 1968 Britain introduced to the UN Disarmament Committee a draft Biological Weapons Convention that separated the control of biological agents from ★chemical weapons, on which negotiations were deadlocked. In 1969 the United States decided unilaterally to destroy all its biological weapons, and agreement was reached with the Soviet Union in April 1972 that neither country would develop, produce, stockpile, or acquire such weapons. This cleared the way for progress on the Biological Weapons Convention, which came into force in 1975. Subsequently the Soviet Union was suspected of supplying fungal-based T_2 toxins to North Vietnam and collaborating in their use in Laos, and Soviet forces probably used such toxins in Afghanistan. The break-up of the Soviet Union uncovered further breaches of the convention, including the production of gene-modified variants of the smallpox and marburg viruses. Following the 1991 ★Gulf War, UN inspectors confirmed the existence of an extensive biological weapons programme in Iraq. These revelations emphasised the need to develop a verification regime for the Biological Weapons Convention. Unfortunately, the small-scale facilities capable of producing some biological weapons are easily concealed. New Zealand representatives have been active in the discussions seeking to establish the necessary verification measures.

Some toxins and bacteria are lethal in much smaller inhaled doses than chemical agents, including nerve gases. It is possible to protect operational military personnel from a range of current biological threats. New Zealand personnel deployed to Bahrain during the Gulf War, for example, were issued with NBC (nuclear–biological–chemical) suits and vaccinated against anthrax. But the protection of civilian populations against these indiscriminate weapons would be virtually impossible in the face of attacks with genetically engineered biological agents known only to the aggressor.

ALAN HENDERSON

Gilbert, Brigadier Sir William Herbert Ellery ('Bill') (20 July 1916–26 September 1987). Born in Wanganui, Gilbert graduated from the Royal Military College, Duntroon, in 1937 and was posted to the Royal New Zealand Artillery. He served with coastal batteries at Auckland before being seconded, in 1940, to 2NZEF, in which he held a number of artillery and staff appointments, including GSO2 of 2nd New Zealand Division. He commanded 6th Field Regiment from November 1943, and his efforts to support the infantry at Cassino earned him appointment as a DSO. His abilities as a staff officer were to the fore as GSO1 of the division from November 1944. After serving as New Zealand's military representative in Canberra immediately after the war, he became Director of Plans and Military Intelligence in Army HQ, Wellington, in 1948. During the early 1950s he was involved with his Allied counterparts in various military planning exercises for the defence of South-east Asia. In 1956, while serving as the Army's liaison officer in London, he was appointed as the first director of the New Zealand Security Intelligence Service. At the end of his twenty-year tenure, in 1976, he was made a KBE, at which time he added William to his forenames.

Gillies, Sir Harold Delf ('Giles') (17 June 1882–10 September 1960) was one of the greatest war surgeons New Zealand has produced. A native of Dunedin, he attended Cambridge University before becoming a surgeon at St Bartholomew's Hospital in London. When the ★First World War began, he offered his services to the ★Red Cross. While serving on the ★Western Front, he became aware of the many soldiers suffering from jaw and facial wounds, and pressed for the creation of a specialist facility to deal with them. When such a ward was established at Aldershot early in 1916, he was soon practising his 'strange new art' on thousands of hideously disfigured and burned soldiers. The techniques developed by a process of trial and error became the basis of modern plastic surgery. In October 1917, for example, Gillies devised the tube pedicle flap, whereby a tube of live skin increases blood supply to a skin graft. In that year the hospital was moved to a larger establishment, the Queen's Hospital at Sidcup. More than 11,000 major facial operations had been carried out by the end of the war. Gillies was made a CBE in 1920, and he subsequently established himself as a noted cosmetic surgeon. He was knighted in 1930. During the ★Second World War he provided much valuable advice to 2NZEF surgeons, and arranged for the training of several doctors in plastic surgery.

Girls' War, a conflict fought in March 1830 between northern and southern Nga Puhi, had its roots in inter-hapu rivalry and competition for European trade at Kororareka. It was precipitated by a fight among some high-born young Maori women, including the wives of a European whaler, Captain W.D. Brind. This minor incident led to threats and posturing between the girls' tribes, which resulted in more serious fighting after someone was accidentally shot. The northern Nga Puhi under Ururoa and southern Nga Puhi under Kiwikiwi clashed at Kororareka. Although the battle itself was largely inconclusive, Kiwikiwi retreated to Otuihu. The subsequent peace negotiations, in which missionaries Samuel Marsden and Henry Williams served as intermediaries, left Kororareka in the hands of the northern Nga Puhi. However, intermittent hostilities among Nga Puhi for control of the town continued for another seven years. (See MUSKET WARS)

Glover, Lieutenant-Commander Denis James Matthews (10 December 1912–9 August 1980), a leading poet, was decorated for his part in the Normandy landings on *D-Day, 6 June 1944. He was born in Dunedin, and was an English lecturer at Canterbury University College before the *Second World War. A keen yachtsman, he volunteered for the navy in September 1941, and was sent to Great Britain for service with the Royal Navy early the following year. He served in the destroyer HMS *Onslaught*, which was involved in the escort of Arctic convoys, including the ill-fated PQ17. He wrote about his experience under enemy attack in his 'Convoy Conversations', published in *Penguin New Writing* in early 1943. Commissioned in January 1943, he served in the commando raiders HMS *Dundonald* and *Dinosaur* before beginning training, in October of that year, for the Normandy landing. In that operation he commanded a landing craft, part of the 200th Flotilla, which landed commandos at Ouistreham. For his efforts on the day of the landing, and later, he was awarded a DSC. Later in the year he published a personal account of the operation, *D-Day*, some of which he wrote while his landing craft was hauled up on a Normandy beach after being damaged. He returned to New Zealand on leave in November 1944, and was eventually demobilised a year later. From 1947 until 1953, when he was dismissed for disobeying an order, he was a member of the RNZNVR's Canterbury Division, and was involved in training CMT personnel.

G. Ogilvie, *Denis Glover: His Life* (Godwit, Auckland, 1999).

Goddard, Air Marshal Sir (Robert) Victor (6 February 1897–21 January 1987) was an RAF officer who was New Zealand's Chief of the Air Staff during the *Second World War. Born at Harrow, he joined the Royal Navy in 1910, and served in the Grand Fleet for the first year of the *First World War before transferring to the Royal Naval Air Service. He transferred to the RAF in 1918. He read engineering at Cambridge University in the early 1920s, and later commanded a bomber squadron in Iraq before becoming, in 1935, Deputy Director of Intelligence in the Air Ministry in London. In 1940 he served as Senior Air Staff Officer in the BEF's GHQ in France. After another stint at the Air Ministry as Director of Military Co-operation in 1940–41, during which he made a significant contribution to the development of the concept of close air support of ground forces, he arrived in New Zealand to take up the post of CAS. His two-year tenure proved particularly busy because of the onset of the *Pacific War; he was in overall command of RNZAF operations in the *Solomons campaign, while at the same time overseeing the RNZAF's important contribution of trained men for the RAF effort in the European theatre. From 1943 to 1946 he was in charge of administration at Air Command, South East Asia at RAF HQ in New Delhi. He held a liaison post in Washington, and then sat on the Air Council as Member for Technical Services while commanding the Empire Flying School until his retirement in 1951. He was made a CBE (1940), a CB (1943), and a KCB (1947). His later years were marked by increasing eccentricity (he spent much time investigating flying saucers). His memoirs, *Skies to Dunkirk*, were published in 1982.

Godley, General Sir Alexander John (4 February 1867–6 March 1957) commanded 1NZEF during the *First World War. Born at Gillingham, Kent, he was educated at Haileybury College before winning a place at the Royal Military College, Sandhurst, in 1885. In the following year he was commissioned in the Royal Dublin Fusiliers. Much of his time was spent with horses—he trained polo ponies to boost his income—and he was an enthusiastic huntsman. In 1896 he was promoted to captain and appointed as adjutant of the Mounted Infantry at Aldershot. Volunteering for a mounted infantry force sent to suppress a rebellion in Mashonaland in 1896–97, he gained some limited command experience in the field. He was attending the Staff College at Camberley when the *Boer War became imminent, and gave up his studies to take part. He was sent to South Africa to help raise two irregular mounted regiments, and later served as adjutant in one of them under Colonel Robert Baden-Powell. He took part in the defence of Mafeking before becoming Lieutenant-Colonel Herbert Plumer's chief

Major-General A.J. Godley (centre) with members of his staff at the Territorial camp at Seatoun, Wellington, in March 1912. (*Curry Collection, Alexander Turnbull Library, F-53157-1/2*)

staff officer. Back in the United Kingdom, he was serving as a staff officer in the 2nd Division at Aldershot when offered the post of Commandant of the New Zealand Military Forces. Although not the New Zealand government's first choice for the position, he had excellent credentials, having had experience of the command of 'colonials' in South Africa and of mounted infantry and staff work. He left for New Zealand conscious that he was passing up the opportunity to command a regular infantry brigade and that the posting might not help his career—'one might in the Antipodes be out of sight and out of mind'. He had been influenced in his decision by the prospect of working with the 'magnificent material' provided by the New Zealand mounted infantry and by a sense of duty. He also had a connection with New Zealand—his uncle, John Robert Godley, had founded the Canterbury settlement. After travelling by way of Canada, the United States, and Australia, and observing military educational activities in those countries, he took up his duties in Wellington in December 1910.

Godley's first task in New Zealand was to implement the new defence scheme upon which the government had 'rather lightheartedly embarked'. He noted later that it was 'quite evident that the New Zealand Parliament ... had passed their universal service law with very little idea of how it was to be put into practice'. Accepting recommendations made by Lord *Kitchener, who had visited New Zealand earlier in the year and had briefed him before he left England, he set about establishing the *Territorial Force, assisted by fourteen British officers who were loaned to New Zealand. Part of his task was to sell the *compulsory military training scheme to the public, for which he made a promotional tour throughout the country, recalling later that it was a 'curious and most interesting' experience akin to standing for Parliament. It is a measure of Godley's considerable skills as an administrator that the new system was introduced so quickly and with so little difficulty. He drew much satisfaction from the endorsement of his efforts by the Inspector-General of the Oversea Forces, General Sir Ian *Hamilton, in 1914. Alive to the value of cooperation with Australia, Godley visited that country in both 1912 and 1913. Talks with his Australian counterpart covered a range of issues, including the possibility of forming a joint expeditionary force. From 1912 Godley developed an effective professional relationship with Minister of Defence Colonel James *Allen, a staunch advocate of military reform. His efforts were recognised by his appointment as a KCMG in 1914.

Put to the test in August 1914, Godley's achievement came through with colours flying. Apart from dispatching a force to capture German Samoa, New Zealand was able to advise London on 7 August that an 8000-strong force would be ready to sail 'in about four weeks' (though, in the event, it did not leave until 16 October because of naval escort problems). Godley went with it as GOC of the *New Zealand Expeditionary Force, and his ability as an administrator and trainer of men was again in evidence in Egypt. He kept a tight rein on his troops, coming down severely upon acts of indiscipline and insisting upon the highest standards. With a realistic attitude towards drinking and *venereal disease among the troops, he established wet canteens in the camps and quietly arranged for VD treatment centres. He commanded the *New Zealand and Australian Division at *Gallipoli, and like most generals of the time had difficulty in coming to terms with the conditions not only of modern warfare generally but also of the battlefield at Anzac. He has been unfairly criticised for failing to keep sufficient control of his forces during the offensive in August 1915, thereby allowing the impetus of the attack on Chunuk Bair to be lost; in reality such control was impossible in the terrain and blame for the failure of the offensive cannot be laid at the door of any inadequacy of command on his part. Although he constantly toured the trenches, and was concerned for the welfare of his troops, he did not endear himself to them; nor did he feel the need to court popularity. Tall, austere, aloof, he was unfairly perceived to have an uncaring attitude. This was not helped by a myth that, during the earlier training in Egypt, Godley's wife had told him to 'Make them run again, Alec!' as they struggled through the sand in searing heat. In November 1915 he relieved Lieutenant-General William Birdwood as commander of the Australian and New Zealand Army Corps, and oversaw its evacuation from the peninsula. He was made a KCB for his services at Gallipoli.

Godley commanded II ANZAC Corps on the *Western Front from June 1916 until January 1918, when it lost its Australian component and was retitled XXII Corps. He remained GOC of 1NZEF, and from October 1916 to March 1918 had the New Zealand Division as part of his corps. He was a competent, if unimaginative, commander in a theatre which offered little scope for independent action by corps commanders: the army commanders called the shots when it came to major operations and plans. His corps's first major attack, at Messines in June 1917, was a resounding success, though high casualties in its latter stages (no fault of Godley's) took the gloss off it. When committed to the ensuing Third Battle of Ypres, however, it was, like other corps, able to make little progress in terrain and weather conditions that grew steadily worse. During 1918 Godley's corps performed well in operations on the Marne, at Amiens, and finally at Valenciennes just before the Armistice.

From a New Zealand perspective, most interest has centred on his role in the fiasco at Passchendaele on 12 October 1917, some contending that he should have sought a delay in the operation because of the quagmire in which his troops were struggling and the inability to ensure an adequate artillery barrage. Certainly Godley was remiss in failing to ascertain the conditions at the front (though he was by no means atypical in this regard among corps commanders of the time). For all his professionalism as an administrator, he did not run a tight ship as a corps commander, and the performance of his headquarters left much to be desired at a time when coordination was essential. Moreover, he was overconfident that the Australians and New Zealanders would succeed where his other troops had failed three days earlier. Given that the men on the spot, Major-Generals ★Russell and Monash, did not reveal any misgivings about the impending operation, his duty was clearly to ensure that his corps fulfilled its part in what was a two-army operation. Responsibility for the disaster lay with the Commander-in-Chief, Field Marshal Sir Douglas Haig, and 2nd Army commander General Sir Herbert Plumer, whose plan for a rapid succession of attacks allowed for little flexibility or adequate preparation. Nevertheless, the failure at Passchendaele and the heavy losses severely dented Godley's reputation among the New Zealand Division and with the public at home. He later suffered the indignity of being compared unfavourably with the commander of the Australian Imperial Force in the New Zealand Parliament. The New Zealand government, nevertheless, stood firmly behind him, and he resisted his inclination to resign as commander of 1NZEF.

Following the Armistice Godley held a number of prestigious appointments. He was Military Secretary to the Secretary of State for War from 1920 to 1922 before spending two years in command of the British Army of the Rhine. After serving as GOC Southern Command (1924–28), he was Governor of Gibraltar until his retirement in 1933. When appointed as a GCB in 1928, he chose the figure of a New Zealand soldier as a bearer for his coat of arms. He was gratified by his reception when he revisited New Zealand in 1934–35. Although, perhaps unfairly, his reputation as a field commander does not stand high in New Zealand, he was a crucial element in the success of 1NZEF, not least because of the training programme which he oversaw in the three years before its formation. He brought to New Zealand military preparations a professionalism which had never hitherto existed, and the system he instituted remained essentially in place for half a century. Surprisingly perhaps, no biography of him has yet appeared. There are rich sources available for such a work: after his death a collection of his papers was acquired by the New Zealand government to supplement others earlier donated by him, and it is now lodged in the National Archives in Wellington.

Sir A.J. Godley, *Life of an Irish Soldier, Reminiscences of General Sir Alexander Godley G.C.B., K.C.M.G.* (John Murray, London, 1939).

Gold, Major-General Charles Emelius (6 January 1809–29 July 1871) commanded the British forces during the initial fighting in Taranaki in 1860. He purchased a commission in the 65th Regiment of Foot in 1828, and spent until 1841 on garrison duty in the Americas. He arrived in New Zealand with his regiment in early 1847, and for most of the next eleven years commanded a detachment at Wellington, an uneventful sojourn which allowed him to indulge his hobby of painting. From November 1858 he was the senior British officer in the colony. As commander of the forces, he took a 200-man detachment to New Plymouth in March 1860, and was confronted with the difficult task of ensuring its safety against a foe which soon proved far more adept and determined than had been anticipated. The Maori's unwillingness to deliver themselves up for a conventional battle proved frustrating. His conduct did little to inspire confidence among the settlers, especially when he appeared to leave a beleaguered detachment of colonial troops to its fate at Waireka. He was further vilified by the settlers for the defeat at Puke-to-kauere. Although there were mitigating factors in each of these incidents—his apparent inaction for two months was, for example, the result of orders by the Governor, who feared intervention by outside Maori forces—Gold earned a reputation for feebleness and ineffectiveness. He was promoted to the rank of major-general in June 1860, but two months later was superseded in command of the forces at Taranaki by Major-General Thomas ★Pratt. In financial embarrassment, he appears to have left New Zealand secretly in early 1861.

Gradation lists contain details of seniority and appointments of officers of the three services. The *Army List* was the first to appear in New Zealand—in 1864, following the establishment of the ★Colonial Defence Force. It was updated at regular intervals, at first annually but later twice or more a year. From early in the twentieth century, it was being issued quarterly, and prior to the ★First World War contained brief details of those officers who had been on ★active service. During the world wars, separate lists were prepared for 1NZEF and 2NZEF. The first *Navy List* was published in 1922, and an *Air List* was produced from 1937. The lists, which also contain information on honorary appointments such as colonels of regiments and corps, are valuable research tools for historians and others seeking information on the careers of particular officers.

Grant, Lieutenant John Gildroy (26 August 1889–25 November 1970) was a *Victoria Cross winner on the *Western Front. A builder from Hawera, he enlisted in 1NZEF in June 1915 and joined the 1st Battalion, Wellington Regiment, in Egypt just before it was sent to France in April 1916. He received his decoration for his exemplary conduct on 1 September 1918, as the New Zealand Division advanced in the vicinity of Bapaume. When his battalion attacked German machine-gun positions on a hill, Sergeant Grant and Lance-Corporal C.T. Hill, undeterred by intense enemy fire, rushed the guns, leaping into the machine-gun post in the centre of the German defences to destroy it. Grant then eliminated the surrounding posts in a similar manner. After subsequently attending an officer cadet school in England, he was commissioned shortly before his discharge from 1NZEF in 1919.

Gray, Group Captain Colin Falkland (9 November 1914–1 August 1995) was the highest-scoring New Zealand fighter ace of the *Second World War. His first attempt to join the RAF, in 1937, failed on medical grounds, but after improving his fitness by working as a sheep musterer he secured a short-service commission in January 1939. Serving with 54 Squadron in France, he downed his first enemy aircraft on 25 May 1940 over Dunkirk. During the Battle of Britain his squadron, defending the approaches to London, was in the thick of the action. His many victories earned him a DFC (to which he would add a bar a year later). From September 1941 he commanded 616 Squadron. Stationed in the Mediterranean theatre during 1943, he commanded first a squadron, then a wing, and added another thirteen victims to his tally. Back in England in 1944, he commanded a fighter wing which operated over north-west Europe. In all he destroyed twenty-seven enemy aircraft, shared one 'kill', and probably destroyed or damaged another twenty-two. After the war he served in various posts in the RAF before retiring to New Zealand in 1961.

C. Gray, *Spitfire Patrol* (Random Century, Auckland, 1990).

Greece The brief Greek campaign in April 1941 was the 2nd New Zealand Division's first major operation as a complete entity, and its first against German forces. Together with British and Australian formations, it was deployed ostensibly to assist a small, weak state faced with extinction by the Axis powers but in reality as part of an ill-conceived effort to open a major Allied front in the Balkans. While the evident demonstration of solidarity with a victim of aggression had some short- and long-term benefits, the wider political objective had no hope of achievement. The campaign itself was predictably a complete failure militarily, with the Allies being expelled from the Greek mainland. (Their subsequent operations in *Crete, which is part of Greece, are covered in a separate entry.) The Allied intervention's strategical effects were no more favourable: not only did it fail to create a Balkan front but also, more seriously, the diversion of resources had adverse consequences for the Allied position in North Africa. As in *Gallipoli twenty-six years before, New Zealand troops were committed to an enterprise in the Mediterranean which owed much to Churchill's strategic vision; as at Gallipoli, they had to be evacuated in due course. But Greece differed from Gallipoli insofar as the Allies set about a task which had no hope of success from the outset, whereas the earlier campaign foundered not in its conception but in its execution.

As part of efforts to bolster the resolve of anti-Fascist forces in Europe following the abandonment of its *appeasement strategy, Great Britain had offered Greece a unilateral guarantee of support against aggression on 13 April 1939. When Greece was attacked by Italy on 28 October 1940, this undertaking was invoked and limited British air support (five RAF squadrons) was provided. Also among the troops sent to Greece from Egypt (without 2NZEF HQ's knowledge) as part of Barbarity Force was a section of 9th New Zealand Railway Survey Company. The Greeks defeated the initial Italian thrust, and drove the invaders back into Albania, where a stalemate developed, but the likelihood of German assistance to its Axis ally changed the picture. The protection of the oilfields in Romania from possible attack by British bombers based in Greece, but more fundamentally the need to secure the southern flank of the planned

New Zealand troops, distinctive in their desert-style helmets, watch a column of Italian prisoners of war passing through Athens (*War History Collection, Alexander Turnbull Library, F-1005-1/4-DA*)

German invasion of the Soviet Union, pushed Germany towards intervention.

Following a British decision in January 1941 to make an offer of substantial assistance to Greece, General Wavell, the C-in-C, Middle East Command, had talks in Athens, at which Greek concern over the adequacy of the support was expressed. An inadequate force, the Greeks feared, might only attract a German attack, without being able to provide effective resistance. Britain hoped, however, to build a Balkan front against the Germans to include Yugoslavia, Greece, and Turkey. To this end, Foreign Secretary Anthony Eden and the Chief of the Imperial General Staff, General Sir John Dill, had been sent to the Middle East. At a conference in Athens on 22 February with the Greek commander-in-chief, General Alexandros Papagos, they persuaded the Greek government reluctantly to accept a British reinforcement at a strength well below that which the Greeks considered necessary. It was planned to send three divisions (the Australian 6th and 7th Divisions and the 2nd New Zealand Division), a Polish brigade, and an armoured brigade. These troops, the British finally planned, would be deployed on the Aliakmon line. Situated south of Salonika, this was potentially a position of some strength because of its mountainous nature. It was hoped that Greek troops redeployed from Macedonia would reinforce the British force, but the Greek authorities were understandably loath to relinquish so much of their territory as such a redeployment would entail (including the important port of Salonika). They preferred a forward line roughly on the Greek–Bulgarian border covering both the Rupel Pass and Salonika—the Metaxas line. This fundamental difference of outlook was never satisfactorily resolved.

The New Zealand government was first informed of the plan to deploy the New Zealand division to Greece on 26 February. Within hours, concurrence had been signalled to London. Behind this rapid decision lay recognition of the general objective of British policy, a sense of moral duty to the Greeks, and awareness of Australian involvement. There was acceptance, too, that the project was militarily feasible, based on the assumption that 2NZEF's commander, Major-General B.C. ★Freyberg, had been consulted, and had endorsed it. This misunderstanding derived from the fortuitous arrival of a cable from Freyberg just two days before stating that 2nd New Zealand Division, having now been concentrated with the arrival of 2NZEF's Second Echelon from the United Kingdom and brought up to war scale in both equipment and transport, had reached a state where it could be released for a fully operational role with confidence if the British so requested. Freyberg had in fact learnt of the proposed deployment to Greece from Wavell on 17 February, and had expressed agreement with it. He later claimed to have asked Wavell whether the New Zealand government agreed to the deployment and to have been told that it did. It would be only after the campaign that the Prime Minister, Peter ★Fraser, learned that privately Freyberg had never considered the operation feasible, indeed believed that it violated every principle of war.

Second thoughts were soon in evidence in Wellington, as more information was received. The limited scale of the deployment in relation to the objective was now apparent—as was the fact that Australia and New Zealand would be providing the bulk of the British forces in Greece. There was concern that these troops should be properly supported. These antipodean doubts were in fact shared by Churchill and his Cabinet in London, but the outcome of further diplomacy essentially forced their hand. When Eden and Dill returned to Athens early in March, they found a very different atmosphere to that existing on 22 February. Contrary to British (though not Greek) understanding of the previous agreement, Greek troops in Macedonia had not been withdrawn to the Aliakmon line, a movement which the Greek authorities insisted was to await Yugoslavia's response to Allied overtures. The entry of German troops into Bulgaria on 1 March now ruled out any such redeployment, in Greek eyes. The British rejected Greek calls for the arriving British troops to be deployed piecemeal forward in Macedonia. A compromise was reached, in which three Greek divisions and seven unattached battalions—twenty-three battalions in all, mostly newly formed, rather than the previously envisaged thirty-five—would be provided for the Aliakmon line. Two days later the British War Cabinet approved the revised plan. They were influenced by the approval of the plan by both Dill and the British military commanders in the Middle East—and by the apparent concurrence of the two Dominion commanders, Freyberg and Lieutenant-General T.A. Blamey, both of whom were led to believe, incorrectly, that the whole RAF strength in the Eastern Mediterranean (twenty-three squadrons) would be available to provide support. (In the event, only ten squadrons were deployed in Greece by mid April.)

When asked to assent to the use of New Zealand's troops in the revised plan, the New Zealand War Cabinet recognised that an already 'highly dangerous and speculative' plan had been replaced by one 'obviously much more hazardous'. There was a possibility of German forces reaching the Aliakmon line before the New Zealanders, and even if this danger was avoided the Axis forces would have the advantage of interior lines and predominant air power. Despite the dangers, the Cabinet agreed that the proposed deployment must

Greece

Map 9 Greece, April 1941

proceed unless militarily quite impossible. The information at its disposal indicated that the military commanders on the spot still considered the operation feasible. (Freyberg's doubts were not known in Wellington at this time, and indeed the contrary impression was provided by the British advice.) The moral issue, in any case, seemed to leave little alternative. The New Zealand ministers were unaware that professions of hope about Yugoslavia's and Turkey's possible attitudes were quite contrary to Eden's own opinion, or that the Greek government had been initially hesitant to accept British help. Like its Australian counterpart, the New Zealand government urged upon the British the need for the preparation of evacuation plans—in advance of the New Zealand division landing in Greece.

Even before New Zealand had assented to the new plan, New Zealand troops had begun redeploying to Greece as part of W Force or Lustreforce, as the Commonwealth force had been designated by the Greeks and British respectively. The first elements sailed from Alexandria on 6 March. They were followed by 6th Australian Division, but plans to send 7th Australian Division and the Polish Brigade had to be amended when Rommel, on 31 March, launched a counter-attack in Libya and threatened Tobruk. In its final form, W Force therefore comprised 2nd New Zealand Division, 6th Division, and the British 1st Armoured Brigade—considerably weaker than the originally contemplated force, itself unbalanced and weak for the task. This mainly Dominion force, which was commanded by the British General Sir Henry Maitland Wilson (who had served as a staff officer in the New Zealand Division on the ★Western Front), was deployed on the as-yet-unprepared Aliakmon line. The New Zealanders were allocated a 24-kilometre-wide sector with their right flank resting on the coast. Convinced that he had too few men to hold this position for any length of time against a full-blooded attack, and worried by the possibility of the Aliakmon line being outflanked to the west, Freyberg gave particular attention to the Mount Olympus pass about twenty kilometres in his rear. While 4th and 6th Brigades installed themselves on the Aliakmon line, 5th Brigade, which began arriving in the area on 31 March, was given the task of guarding the pass. Two companies of the 27th (Machine Gun) Battalion and the armoured cars of the New Zealand Divisional Cavalry were deployed forward of the Aliakmon line. The British 1st Armoured Brigade was dispersed on the plain as well. Occupying the high ground on the left would be the Greek 12th Division, while another Greek formation, 20th Division, would hold the ground nearer the Yugoslav frontier. The 6th Australian Division was supposed to take over the Greek 12th Division's sector, but only its 16th Brigade had reached the front by 6 April and was ordered to deploy in the Veroia pass area.

From the German perspective, the Allied position had obvious weaknesses. Numerically the Allies were at a serious disadvantage. Planning for the invasion, code-named Operation Marita, had begun in November 1940. The Germans had potentially available twenty-seven divisions, well balanced, combat-experienced, and operating on interior lines. Against this array stood a force of eighteen Greek divisions, most of which were deployed in Albania, poorly served with transport, supported by a two-division strong Commonwealth force being supplied from Egypt (albeit without the danger of serious naval interference, in light of the severe reverse inflicted by the Royal Navy on the Italian fleet off Cape Matapan). In the skies the Allies were completely outnumbered: whereas the Germans had 800 aircraft available, and about 300 Italian aircraft in support, the Allies had 80. These German advantages in materiel were enhanced by the problems of coordination of effort which existed on the Allied side, with Papagos in overall command of the Allied forces, and the influence of political requirements. The deployment of Allied forces offered opportunities to the Germans. Because of the Greek insistence on clinging to their gains in Albania and holding the Metaxas line, most of the Greek forces were at the western extremity of the front or formed a thin shield on the frontier in the east, where four divisions were deployed on the Bulgarian border; the British Commonwealth forces supported by two weak Greek divisions, on the other hand, were concentrated south of Salonika, where they were vulnerable to being outflanked by German forces moving through Yugoslavia and entering Greece via Monastir. Wilson had endeavoured to counter this latter danger. Among other steps, he deployed part of 27th (Machine Gun) Battalion to Amindaion as part of a detachment including artillery and armour. These dispositions were rendered significant by events in Belgrade, where on 25 March the government, under German pressure, had adhered to the Tripartite Pact, only to be overthrown in a *coup d'état* two days later (briefly reviving Allied hopes of a Balkan front). Germany reacted vigorously to this unexpected development, and both Greece and Yugoslavia were invaded on 6 April. The latter would capitulate eleven days later.

Attacking from Bulgaria, the Germans easily broke through at the western end of the Metaxas Line. Although they were held for a few days in the central sector, they outflanked the position by moving through Yugoslavia and within three days were threatening Salonika. By this time another German thrust was bearing down on the Monastir Gap. The need for a

Greece

shortening of the Allied line was apparent, and between 8 and 10 April 4th and 6th Brigades pulled back to the Servia Pass–Mount Olympus area. It was intended that the Monastir Gap should be covered by Mackay Force, as it was designated after its commander, Major-General I.G. Mackay, comprising the original Amindaion detachment, 6th Australian Division less 16th Brigade, and the 1st Armoured Brigade (with whom two troops of the New Zealand Divisional Cavalry were serving). Papagos also determined to redeploy the Greek forces from the right flank of Mackay Force to its left—a difficult process because of the terrain and the Greek lack of motorised transport. When German forces invaded Greece in strength in the Monastir sector on 10 April, the Divisional Cavalry became the first New Zealand unit to engage the enemy in Greece.

Although the Allies successfully withdrew from the Aliakmon line, the overall situation was so unpromising that evacuation plans were already under consideration among Wavell's staff. A further withdrawal to the vicinity of Thermopylae was contemplated—and initiated by General Wilson during the night of 13–14 April. Such a step became more urgent as advances by the German 40th Corps in the Greek sector on the left opened the way for an outflanking drive through Grevena to Larisa. To meet this danger Savige Force, comprising the Australian 17th Brigade, some armour, and the New Zealand 25th Battery, 4th Field Regiment, was hastily deployed at Kalabaka. Further to the southwest, the German 18th Corps attacked New Zealand positions in three places in the period 14–16 April. At the Servia Pass and at Mount Olympus the enemy were held by 4th and 5th Brigades respectively. But the third attack, on the coast above the Platamon Tunnel, produced a threatening situation, as 21st Battalion was forced to give ground after German troops moved through rugged terrain to outflank it. Falling back about seventeen kilometres to the western end of the Pinios Gorge (or Vale of Tempe), it was subsumed within a brigade group (Allen Force) based on a hastily deployed 16th Brigade. This force had the vital task of holding the Germans while the three New Zealand brigades and Savige Force were withdrawn—one which it successfully accomplished, though it was eventually forced into precipitate withdrawal through rugged terrain. By the time the Germans entered Larisa on the 19th, the Allied troops had escaped to the south. However, 21st Battalion, after seriously delaying the German advance in the Pinios Gorge, was outflanked and eventually dispersed.

The Australians and New Zealanders, now fighting (since 12 April) as an ANZAC Corps under the Australian commander Blamey, fell back across the Thessaly plain behind a series of rearguards to naturally strong positions in the vicinity of Thermopylae. Two Australian and two New Zealand (5th and 6th) brigades were deployed, with 4th Brigade in reserve. However, the collapse of Greek resistance in western Greece, following the appearance of German forces in the rear of the Western Macedonian Army, meant that the left flank of the Thermopylae position was exposed. On 21 April the decision was taken to evacuate W Force from Greece. Units began to be pulled out of the Thermopylae position, and the first embarkations aboard Royal Navy warships took place on the night of 24–25 April. They continued over the ensuing five nights, covered first by 6th Brigade and the New Zealand artillery (which defeated a German armoured thrust at Thermopylae) and then by 4th Brigade. Despite being ordered to leave for Egypt immediately, Freyberg stood fast, not leaving until five days later. His presence would become more important following the departure of Wilson and Blamey on 26 April, and he was left with the difficult task of overseeing the final stages of the evacuation. The situation became threatening when German paratroops seized the narrow Corinth isthmus connecting the main part of Greece with the Peloponnese peninsula, cutting off 4th Brigade from the evacuation points in the Peloponnese. Withdrawal plans had to be altered at short notice, and 4th Brigade was eventually taken off beaches west of Athens. The bulk of 6th Brigade was successfully evacuated from Monemvasia on the night of 28–29 April. Stray detachments which had gone to Kalamata were mostly taken prisoner, though not before Sergeant Jack *Hinton performed deeds which won him the *Victoria Cross. The last evacuations by the Royal Navy took place on the night of 30 April–1 May. More than 50,000 had been taken off, but 14,000 men were forced to surrender. Many, including possibly 400 New Zealanders, escaped in small parties and made their way to Crete by small boats in due course. In addition to the prisoners, W Force had lost about 900 men killed during the brief campaign. New Zealand casualties were 291 killed, 387 wounded, and 1826 prisoners.

Throughout the campaign the German dominance in the air had placed the Allies at a major disadvantage. On the first day a devastating attack had been mounted by the *Luftwaffe* on the port of Piraeus, and the damage was magnified by the explosion of a ship laden with ammunition. This was to have adverse effects on W Force's supply throughout the campaign. At the front the outnumbered RAF had suffered from a lack of adequate airfields and communications difficulties. German air attacks made movement down the narrow defiles during the day highly dangerous. Despite incessant air attacks the New Zealand troops had performed extremely well in their first major action. Although not trained for the mountainous conditions in which they found themselves, and quickly forced into a delaying-action role, they adapted quickly, and generally retained good battle discipline. Some deficiencies apparent in leadership were to be expected in units exposed to the confusion of battle for the first time.

The Allied intervention in Greece failed in its immediate objective. No front in the Balkans emerged, and the Germans occupied the whole of mainland Greece with relative ease. Moreover, the diversion of resources to Greece may have prevented the completion of the campaign in North Africa by the occupation of Tripoli, with serious long-term consequences as the landing of German forces through this port soon bolstered the Axis position. The contention that the need to cover his flank by subjugating Yugoslavia and Greece caused a fatal delay in Hitler's timetable for the invasion of Russia, leading to eventual failure to capture Moscow before the onset of winter, is not supported by the evidence of German preparations for Operation Barbarossa, though the need to keep a substantial German force in the Balkans was a disadvantage as the campaign in Russia developed. The New Zealand government remained convinced that the deployment was necessary, even claiming that it 'would take the same course again in the same circumstances', but it probed the British decisions retrospectively in a series of questions to the British Chiefs of Staff about the strategy and tactics involved. There were also recriminations between Fraser and Freyberg, the former angered that the field commander's doubts about the operation's viability had not been conveyed to Wellington before the division was deployed. Following the ensuing disaster in Crete, he conducted an inquiry into Freyberg's fitness as a divisional commander.

W.G. McClymont, *To Greece* (War History Branch, Wellington, 1959).

Grey, Sir George Edward (probably 14 April 1812–19 September 1898) was Governor of New Zealand during both periods of the *New Zealand Wars. His long-standing positive reputation as a military commander rests almost entirely on self-serving reports of his own achievements and barefaced, often falsified, denigration of opponents, subordinates, and even supporters. Born into a military family during the Peninsular War, he was commissioned in the 83rd Foot in 1830 and saw active service in Ireland. In advanced study at Sandhurst, he gained an endorsement detailing his 'superior merit and talents', but, disenchanted with military life, he commanded small exploratory expeditions into western Australia in 1837–39 and was, briefly, Resident Magistrate at Albany. After being appointed Governor of South Australia in 1841, he sold his commission. As Governor of New Zealand from 1845 to 1853, his first task was to deal with hostilities in the far north which had begun under his predecessor, Robert FitzRoy. He took active command of the successful siege at Ruapekapeka, but failed to gain a conclusive victory. After sensibly withdrawing, he indulged his growing addiction to gilding the lily at the expense of FitzRoy and the missionaries. In 1846, he incensed Wellington Maori with unnecessary violence, then bullied others further north, threatening to 'conquer' the entire region. Sporadic warfare erupted where there had been none. To curb the fractious *Te Rangihaeata, he deceitfully imprisoned the elderly *Te Rauparaha. In 1847 Grey mounted a farcical, ineffectual expedition from Wanganui against Te Mamaku, whom he had provoked. Throughout, he never permitted his professional officers independent action.

In 1861 after serving in the Cape Colony Grey, who had been made a KCB in 1848, was reappointed to the New Zealand governorship to deal with the renewed warfare besetting the colony. While offering peace, he simultaneously sought imperial reinforcements and began a military road south from Auckland into the Waikato. Maori were provoked into renewed hostilities. His strategy of invading the Waikato in July 1863 was aimed at crushing opposition from Kingite Maori and developing a colonial force of *military settlers largely rewarded with confiscated land. His over-optimism and haste led to conflict with the more deliberate commander of the forces, General Duncan *Cameron. Grey's most publicised field command was at Weraroa, near Wanganui. In early 1865 Cameron had rendered the well-defended pa strategically irrelevant, considering it too strong for a frontal assault. Grey dithered for months, but when he finally attacked on 20 July using colonial and Maori troops, his botched encirclement allowed the remaining defenders to escape. Grey trumpeted his 'great victory', a self-assessment universally accepted until recently, and denigrated Cameron and the regulars. Grey was relieved in 1868, largely because of his procrastination over the withdrawal of imperial regiments. His reputation is almost entirely attributable to his abilities in dissembling and personal self-aggrandisement: his lies sometimes reached breathtaking proportions. Without his voluminous propaganda, his erratic and maladroit generalship would have been exposed more clearly and rapidly than it was. Grey later returned to New Zealand, and entered politics. The ministry which he formed in 1877 was responsible for ordering the guns which formed the basis of the harbour defences hastily installed during the 1880s.

BRYAN GILLING

Gudgeon, Lieutenant-Colonel Walter Edward (4 September 1841–5 January 1920) was born in London, and emigrated to New Zealand as a boy. He was a farm manager near Wanganui when conflict in the area led to his taking up arms in 1865. After serving briefly in the Wanganui Bushrangers, he became second-in-command of the Wanganui Native Contingent and was soon commissioned. He took part in the fighting in southern Taranaki in 1865–66 before returning to farming after accidentally wounding himself. He rejoined the Native Contingent when the war with ★Titokowaru began. As a sub-inspector in the ★Armed Constabulary, he was involved in operations against both ★Te Kooti and Titokowaru in 1869. Subsequently, he would apparently write two books (they were published in the name of his father) on the conflict—*Reminiscences of the War in New Zealand* (1879) and *The Defenders of New Zealand* (1887). He commanded a redoubt at Runanga on the route between Taupo and Napier, and later the Armed Constabulary in the Poverty Bay district. He was subsequently the Resident Magistrate in the Wairoa. Back in Taranaki, he took part in the 'invasion' of ★Parihaka in 1881, built a substantial redoubt at Manaia, and oversaw road-building by his Field Force personnel. In 1885, he and his men were concentrated at Wellington because of a Russian scare, and were involved in the hasty construction of defences at the port. From 1885 to 1888 he was Acting Under-Secretary of Defence to assist the overcommitted Secretary, Major-General G.S. ★Whitmore. He was Commissioner of the Police Force from 1887 to 1990, a Judge of the Native Land Court in the 1890s, and from 1898 until his retirement in 1909 British Resident and later Resident Commissioner in the Cook Islands. He was made a CMG in 1901. He served briefly as a censor of telegraphic messages following the outbreak of the ★First World War in 1914.

Gulf War Iraqi forces invaded and occupied neighbouring Kuwait on 2 August 1990. Historic claims to Iraqi sovereignty over the sheikhdom were advanced in justification of this blatant aggression by one member of the ★United Nations against another, but Iraq's action was precipitated by a dispute over oil, not only the price being offered on the world market but also control of an oil field which straddled the two countries' borders. Iraqi dictator Saddam Hussein gambled that the international community would acquiesce in Iraq's action. He expected American policy-makers to be inhibited by the American public's apparent reluctance to become involved in hostilities in the wake of their country's defeat in the ★Vietnam War—the so-called post-Vietnam syndrome—especially when confronted with the prospect of high casualties.

Iraq's resort to force challenged the existing basis of international order, as defined in the United Nations Charter. Its irredentist claim awakened memories of pre-1939 international relations. Of more immediate moment, however, was the threat which it posed to the economic security of the Western industrialised nations. Their dependence on oil left them unwilling to countenance the prospect of Iraq's having control over the bulk of the world's supplies of this vital commodity. Iraq's efforts to develop a nuclear capability were, moreover, threatening to destabilise the Middle East and to undermine international efforts to contain the proliferation of nuclear weapons.

The United States led the international response to the crisis. Diplomatically, it secured the UN Security Council's condemnation of the invasion and the imposition of economic sanctions on Iraq. Militarily, it implemented Operation Desert Shield, the massive and rapid deployment of American and other forces in Saudi Arabia, which appeared threatened. Eventually twenty-eight states participated in the coalition, involving more than half a million troops. Once this build-up was complete, a more forceful response to Iraq's defiance of the United Nations became possible. In a further resolution on 29 November 1990, the Security Council authorised member states to use 'all necessary means' to liberate Kuwait. A deadline of 15 January 1991 was set for Iraq's withdrawal. This was the first time since the ★Korean War in 1950 that the UN Security Council had authorised the use of force to meet aggression.

Immediately following the Iraqi invasion of Kuwait New Zealand denounced Iraq's action, and sent an RNZAF C-130 Hercules transport aircraft to Egypt with a load of milk powder. Together with an RNZAF Boeing 727, it carried out a number of evacuation flights, conveying expatriate refugees formerly resident in Kuwait back to their homelands. On the issue of removing Iraq from Kuwait, however, the New Zealand response was less forthright. Although lip service was paid to the United Nations, the Labour administration was unable to act. In part this reflected a government in disarray—Mike Moore took over as Prime Minister a month after the invasion with a general election in the offing—and the practical difficulties involved in making any contribution, given that the armed forces had been firmly oriented towards operating in the relatively benign South Pacific. Factional divisions within the Cabinet prevented any move to overcome these difficulties. Ideological distaste for the fact that the United States was leading the coalition tended to override the principles of collective security which earlier Labour governments had been eager to assert. Not until a National government took office under Jim Bolger did New Zealand at last make a firm, albeit

Gulf War

Armed with a Steyr rifle, a New Zealand airman stands guard over an RNZAF C-130 Hercules on an airfield in Saudi Arabia during the Gulf War in 1991 (*RNZAF*)

non-combatant, commitment. On 3 December 1990, it was announced that two C-130 Hercules and a thirty-two-person Army medical team would be sent to join the coalition forces.

The RNZAF commitment began with the departure of the Hercules on 20 December. Forty-six personnel (later increased to sixty) of 40 Squadron were involved. As in the Korean War, New Zealand's forces operated in close cooperation with British forces. Integrated with the RAF unit at Riyadh, the New Zealand airmen carried out a variety of tasks, including conveying ammunition and troops, spare parts, and mail. On 19 January they were joined in the theatre by the 1st New Zealand Army Medical Team, which was integrated into the United States Navy's 6th Naval Fleet Hospital in Bahrain. A further medical team, the New Zealand Defence Force Medical Contingent, soon followed. Arriving on 5 February 1991, it was located at the RAF hospital at Al Muharraq. This twenty-strong tri-service team brought to 112 the number of New Zealand service personnel committed to the coalition. Significantly, this was the first major conflict involving the United Kingdom or the United States during the twentieth century in which New Zealand did not commit combat troops. As in previous wars, some New Zealanders served with British forces: Whangarei-born Air Marshal Sir Kenneth Hayr, as second-in-command of RAF Strike Command, was responsible for coordinating and directing British air operations, including logistic support.

The coalition's military action against Iraq, Operation Desert Storm, had opened on 16 January 1991, immediately after the deadline expired. Saddam sought desperately but unsuccessfully to divide the coalition by launching missile attacks on Israel in the hope of provoking Israeli retaliation. Despite his predictions of a bloodbath, the conflict proved a complete mismatch. For thirty-nine days, the coalition's air forces ravaged Iraq and softened up the Iraqi ground forces deployed in defensive fashion around Kuwait City. A massive armoured left hook launched by the coalition on 24 February rapidly outflanked and destroyed these forces. By the time a truce came into effect, the Iraqi armed forces had been completely

Gulf War

Map 10 The Gulf War theatre of operations, January–February 1991

defeated in one of the most lopsided victories in history. But the temptation to go forward to occupy Iraq itself was resisted (unlike the United Nations' response to a similar situation in Korea in 1950).

The coalition suffered remarkably few casualties during Desert Storm, and the New Zealand medical teams were not required to handle any battle casualties. Nor were there any casualties among the New Zealand personnel involved, all of whom had been withdrawn by the end of April 1991. Once fighting began, 'peace' activists sought to mobilise New Zealand public opinion against the action, insisting that UN action should have been confined to economic sanctions and suggesting that Iraq had legitimate historical claims to Kuwait 'province'. Their efforts were conspicuously unsuccessful, and the fighting ended before a planned day of demonstration against the war.

New Zealand service personnel were involved in two aspects of post-hostilities operations against Iraq. First, from June 1991 until late 1998 they took part in the activities of the UN Special Commission on Iraq, established to oversee the destruction of Iraq's weapons of mass destruction and long-range missiles and capacity to produce them. The initial contribution of medical personnel was later supplemented by administrative and communications personnel, bringing the total number involved to eleven. In February 1998 a 23-man ★Special Air Service detachment and two RNZAF aircraft were dispatched to the region to support efforts to ensure that Iraq complied with UN resolutions. Second, New Zealand naval personnel have participated in the Multinational Interception Force deployed in the Arabian/Persian Gulf to ensure that economic sanctions against Iraq are not breached. From late 1995 HMNZS *Wellington*, *Canterbury*, and *Te Kaha* all spent periods with the force as did, in 1999, a specialist boarding party.

J. Crawford, *In the Field of Peace: New Zealand's Contribution to International Peace-support Operations: 1950–1995* (New Zealand Defence Force, Wellington, 1996).

H

Hall-Thompson, Admiral Percival Henry (5 May 1874–6 July 1950) commanded the first New Zealand naval vessel to serve overseas in wartime. Born in England, he entered the Royal Navy in 1887 and by 1913 had reached the rank of post-captain. Appointed as Naval Adviser to the government and commander of HMS *Philomel*, New Zealand's new training cruiser, he arrived in New Zealand in June 1914, and hoisted his pendant on *Philomel* on 15 July. The outbreak of war less than three weeks later interrupted plans for developing the New Zealand Naval Forces, and *Philomel*, with only a handful of New Zealanders in her crew, was transferred to Admiralty control. Hall-Thompson took her to Samoa as part of the escort of the Samoa Expeditionary Force, and then to the Middle East with 1NZEF (see CRUISERS). His operational service ended when she returned to Wellington in March 1917 and was decommissioned. For his services, he was made a CMG. He continued to serve as Naval Adviser until 1919, establishing a cordial relationship with the Minister of Defence, Colonel Sir James ★Allen. During 1918 he organised sweeping operations to deal with mines laid in New Zealand waters by the raider *Wolf* in June 1917—a possibility he was slow to accept. Although he prepared several schemes for the development of the New Zealand Naval Forces, these were superseded soon after his departure by the advice tendered by Admiral of the Fleet Lord ★Jellicoe. A short account of *Philomel*'s wartime activities by Hall-Thompson was published in the official history *The War Effort of New Zealand* (1923). Returning to the Royal Navy, he commanded a battleship and from 1923 to 1926 was First Naval Member of the Australian Naval Board. He subsequently commanded both a battle squadron in the Atlantic Fleet and the Reserve Fleet before retiring in 1932.

Hamilton, General Sir Ian Standish Monteith (16 January 1853–12 October 1947) was the commander of the British forces at ★Gallipoli. Commissioned in the British Army in 1872, he took part in numerous small imperial wars in the late nineteenth century. After a long stint in India, he became Commandant of the Musketry School at Hythe in 1898. During the ★Boer War, he commanded a column and was later Lord ★Kitchener's chief of staff. He was made a KCB in 1900. In the first decade of the twentieth century, he occupied positions of increasing importance in the army hierarchy, including Military Secretary at the War Office in 1902, GOC Southern Command from 1905 to 1909, and Adjutant-General in 1909. He led a military mission to observe the Japanese military operations in the 1904–05 Russo-Japanese War. Literate and charming, he was one of the most influential military thinkers of his day, writing extensively on tactics. From 1910 he was Commander-in-Chief, Mediterranean Command, as well as Inspector General of the Oversea Forces. In the latter capacity, he visited New Zealand in 1914, and observed the first divisional camps of the new ★Territorial Force. He was most impressed by the preparations New Zealand was making under the guidance of the Commandant, Major-General Sir Alexander ★Godley, even if he had to suppress his personal distaste for ★compulsory military training. When the ★First World War began, he initially commanded Central Force in Great Britain, designed to repel a possible German invasion, before being appointed, in March 1915, to command the Mediterranean Expeditionary Force. When it was decided to land a force on the Gallipoli peninsula to open the way for the fleet through the Dardanelles, he had only a month to organise a major amphibious operation with a scratch staff. The resources available were clearly insufficient, though he never indicated any concern on this score in the lead-up to the landings on 25 April 1915. A bold plan was developed but it could not be carried out with the means available. Once the troops were ashore he had little influence over the fighting except to order the troops to dig in. His remote style of leadership did not help—he rarely visited the peninsula—and the entire operation suffered from chronic disorganisation. He was out of touch with the reality of a stalemated campaign. In November 1915 he was relieved of his command, and was never given another. In 1920 he published an account of the campaign, *Gallipoli Diary*. He was Lieutenant of the Tower of London from 1918, and active in veterans' affairs between the world wars.

Hankey, Lieutenant-Colonel Sir Maurice Pascal Alers, Baron (1 April 1877–26 January 1963) was a key figure in the coordination of *imperial defence as the Secretary of the *Committee of Imperial Defence from 1912 to 1938. He also served as Secretary of the British War Cabinet from 1916 to 1918 and as Secretary of the Cabinet from 1919 to 1938, and was Secretary-General of all the Imperial Conferences between the world wars. These offices allowed him to wield enormous behind-the-scenes influence in the formulation of defence policy. He visited Wellington in November 1934, after attending Victoria's centenary celebrations and having discussions on defence with Australian leaders. The British government had determined that his visit to the South Pacific should be used to inform the Dominions of current defence plans. A strong advocate of the *Singapore strategy, he found much scepticism about it in Australia but a much more sympathetic audience in New Zealand, where the limited resources available for defence provided few options other than the existing strategy. He outlined the current British programme, focused on building up Great Britain's air defences, and emphasised the need for care in dealing with Japan until Singapore's defences were ready. He endorsed New Zealand's six-year programme of rearmament and sought to encourage the New Zealand authorities to prepare to provide reinforcements for the base in the event of war. His reassuring remarks bolstered New Zealand confidence in the Singapore strategy at a time when the situation in Europe was beginning to raise doubts about its long-term viability. Hankey was raised to the peerage in 1939. During his career, his services had also been recognised by his appointment as a GCB, a GCMG, and a GCVO.

S.W. Roskill, *Hankey, Man of Secrets, 1877–1963*, 3 vols (Collins, London, 1970–74).

Hanson, Brigadier Frederick Melrose Horowhenua ('Bull') (9 July 1895–15 July 1979) commanded the New Zealand Divisional Engineers for most of the *Second World War. Born in Levin, he lied about his age to secure a place at the Royal Military College, Duntroon, in 1915 but was expelled for misconduct in October 1917. Enlisting in 1NZEF, he was posted to the 1st Battalion, Wellington Regiment, and served on the *Western Front, where he was promoted to sergeant and awarded a MM in September 1918. Between the world wars he established himself as a public works engineer and as a leading expert on road-building. Joining 2NZEF in 1939, he was given command of 7th Field Company. During the ill-fated campaign in *Greece, he led a rearguard of engineers which delayed the German advance by blowing up roads and bridges. In the ensuing battle for *Crete, he was 2nd New Zealand Division's temporary CRE, and took part in the celebrated bayonet charge at 42nd Street. As CRE, substantively from October 1941, he was responsible for the defences constructed by the division in Egypt. During the Battle of El Alamein, his engineers played a vital role in clearing paths through the minefields; while inspecting progress in the front line, he captured a German machine-gun post. For the remainder of the *North African campaign, he reconnoitred the tracks used by the division and oversaw the construction of roads and de-mining. For his bravery and quick thinking in the attack on Axis positions at Wadi Akarit on 6 April 1943, he was made a DSO. In the *Italian campaign, where his engineers played an even more important role, he continued to provide innovative leadership. His use of mobile bridging during the final Romagna campaign in 1945 was masterly and contributed greatly to the speed of the division's advance. This exploit earned him a bar to his DSO. A determined, strong-willed commander, he had a penchant for leading from the front, which led to his being wounded three times during the course of the war. After the war he became Commissioner for Public Works, and was an associate member of the Army Board from 1952 to 1955.

Hardham, Major William James (31 July 1876–13 April 1928) was the first New Zealand serviceman to win the *Victoria Cross and the only one to do so in the *Boer War. A blacksmith, rugby player, and member of the *Volunteer Force, he enlisted as a farrier sergeant-major in the 4th Contingent, which left New Zealand for South Africa in March 1900. The action which led to his decoration took place on 28 January 1901. He was among a party of New Zealanders who were ambushed by Boers at Naauwpoort in the Transvaal. While the group scattered for cover, he galloped back under fire to rescue a wounded countryman, bringing him out safely. During the ★First World War, he served with the Wellington Mounted Rifles, rising to the rank of major. He was later active in the RSA.

Hargest, Brigadier James (4 September 1891–12 August 1944) was one of the original brigadiers in 2NZEF. A Southland farmer and Territorial sergeant, he volunteered for 1NZEF in August 1914. He served, and was wounded, at ★Gallipoli as a junior officer in the Otago Mounted Rifles. Later, on the ★Western Front, he commanded a company in the Otago Regiment's 2nd Battalion. During the operations on the Somme in September 1916, he won an MC by rallying the remnants of the battalion and stabilising the line after a failed attack had inflicted heavy casualties. As commander of the battalion from September 1918, he earned a reputation for courage, daring, and organisational ability; his services were recognised by his appointment as a DSO. During the first decade after the war, while farming near Invercargill, he commanded a ★Territorial Force battalion and later the 3rd Infantry Brigade. From 1931 he was a member of Parliament. Following the outbreak of the ★Second World War, Hargest sought a senior appointment in 2NZEF. However, a medical board found that he was unfit for service overseas because of the lasting effect of ★shell-shock which he had suffered late in the previous war. The acting Prime Minister, Peter ★Fraser, to whom Hargest appealed (despite the fact that they were on opposite sides of the political divide), ignored military advice in ensuring that Hargest was duly appointed to command the 5th Infantry Brigade, which departed with the Second Echelon in May 1940. Because of the possibility of an invasion of the United Kingdom, the echelon was diverted there, with the result that it was not until March 1941 that he joined the rest of 2nd New Zealand Division just before its deployment to ★Greece. His brigade performed well, especially in its delaying action at Olympus Pass. During the ensuing campaign in ★Crete, he was given the responsibility of holding the western sector of the New Zealand defences, including the vital Maleme airfield. The deployment of his brigade was faulty, which allowed German paratroopers to gain a foothold on the airfield on 20 May 1941. As the battle turned against the New Zealanders, Hargest sat at his headquarters seemingly oblivious to the disaster unfolding before him. That night he acquiesced in the retreat of the battalion holding positions covering the airfield—a decision which contributed to the loss of the island. Back in Egypt after the battle, he blamed Creforce commander, Major-General B.C. ★Freyberg, for the débâcle, going behind his back to complain privately to the Prime Minister about his performance. His own actions did not come under critical scrutiny, however, and he was awarded a bar to his DSO for his service in Greece and Crete. During the Crusader offensive in November 1941, he again proved incapable of meeting the demands of brigade command. Having placed his headquarters on an exposed airfield, he failed to ensure its defence, with the result that it was overrun by German armour on 27 November. He was among the 700 men taken prisoner. After tunnelling out of the camp for captured senior officers in which he was held near Florence, Italy, in March 1943, he and another New Zealand officer, Brigadier Reginald ★Miles, made their way to Switzerland. Hargest received yet another bar to his DSO for this exploit, and was later made a CBE. He recounted his escape in his *Farewell Campo 12*, first published in 1945. While serving, at his own suggestion, as New Zealand's observer with British forces in the Normandy campaign (see D-DAY), he was wounded in June 1944, and killed by shellfire two months later.

Hart, Brigadier-General Herbert Ernest (13 October 1882–5 March 1968). Born at Taratahi in the Wairarapa, Hart was a clerk in Carterton when he enlisted in the 9th Contingent for the ★Boer War. The contingent arrived too late to see action before the war ended, and Hart, now a lance-sergeant, returned with it in August 1902. Subsequently qualifying as a lawyer, he was active in the ★Volunteer Force, and later the ★Territorial Force. He volunteered for service in 1NZEF in August 1914, and was appointed as second-in-command of the Wellington Infantry Battalion. On 27 April 1915 he was wounded while stemming a dangerous Turkish attack at Walker's Ridge, Anzac, and did not return to ★Gallipoli until September. From this time he commanded the Wellington battalion. In March 1917 he took command of 4th New Zealand Infantry Brigade, then being formed from reinforcements in England. Following the brigade's disbandment in January 1918, he took over 2nd New Zealand Infantry Brigade, but almost immediately was severely wounded by gas, and had to be evacuated to England. After commanding the New Zealand reserves at Sling Camp, he returned to France in July 1918 to command the 3rd New Zealand (Rifle) Brigade. Discharged from 1NZEF in 1919, he resumed his legal career, and until 1925 was an active Territorial, commanding the 2nd New Zealand Infantry Brigade. After serving as Administrator of Western Samoa from 1933 to 1935, he was appointed Deputy Controller of the Imperial War Graves Commission, serving in the Middle East until 1943 from a base in Jerusalem.

Hassett, Major-General Ronald Douglas Patrick (27 May 1923–) played a key role in the establishment of the Queen Elizabeth II Army Memorial

Museum in 1978. He was born in Wellington and began his military career as a cadet at Duntroon in February 1941. After graduating from a shortened course in December 1942, he was commissioned in the Royal New Zealand Artillery and later seconded to 2NZEF. He took part in the *Italian campaign in 1944–45 as a junior officer in the 2nd New Zealand Division's 5th Field Regiment and later in the Divisional Artillery HQ. After the war he occupied various staff and training posts at Army HQ in Wellington and served with the Army liaison staff in London before being made Chief Instructor at the School of Artillery at Waiouru in 1951. He took part in the *Korean War as second-in-command of 16th Field Regiment in the second half of 1952, and was mentioned in dispatches. During the 1960s he served with *28th British Commonwealth Infantry Brigade in Malaya, as an instructor at the New Zealand Staff College, and as Deputy Quartermaster-General. He was made a CBE in 1970. After attending the Royal College of Defence Studies in 1971, he was successively Assistant CDS (Policy), Deputy CDS, and, from 1976, CGS in Defence HQ. During his two-year term as CGS he launched 'Operation Heritage' to develop an army museum, a project which was successfully brought to fruition just before he retired in November 1978. He has since been active in the direction of the Museum, presiding over its Executive Management Committee from 1992 to 1996 and overseeing the construction of the Kippenberger Pavilion. He was appointed a CB in 1978.

Haultain, Theodore Minet (1817–18 October 1902). After attending Sandhurst, Haultain was commissioned in 1834 in the 39th Regiment, with which he served for ten years in India before returning to Great Britain in 1847. Two years later he arrived in New Zealand in charge of a detachment of *Fencibles. After commanding at Onehunga, and later Panmure, he resigned from the army in 1857 to take up farming. In the following year he won a seat in the House of Representatives, but lost it in 1860. With the outbreak of fighting in Taranaki, he found himself helping to establish a defence force for Auckland, and was appointed lieutenant-colonel of the 1st Battalion, Auckland Militia. He became involved in the Waikato campaign of 1863–64 as commander of the 2nd Regiment, Waikato Militia. Although the task of these colonial troops was essentially to guard the lines of communication of the imperial troops who did most of the fighting, Haultain did take part in operations against Rewi *Maniapoto at Orakau in 1864. In February 1865 he was promoted to colonel commandant of the Waikato Militia, and set about installing his troops as *military settlers on confiscated land in the Waikato. By this time, however, he had been returned to Parliament, and he soon resigned his command to concentrate on politics. Although strongly opposed to the *self-reliant policy espoused by Frederick Weld, he would, ironically, be obliged to make it a practical reality as Minister for Colonial Defence in the Stafford ministry from October 1865 to June 1869. He was instrumental in the creation in 1867 of the *Armed Constabulary, the precursor of the New Zealand standing army, but it was not yet fully established when fighting broke out in southern Taranaki in the following year. After the Armed Constabulary was defeated by *Titokowaru in September 1868, Haultain went to Patea to reorganise and reinforce the demoralised government forces. Titokowaru's victory at Moturoa on 7 November and *Te Kooti's raid on Poverty Bay on 10 November precipitated a major crisis for the government. However Haultain, a skilled organiser, was able to juggle his resources to meet the threats. The Armed Constabulary and *kupapa defeated Te Kooti at Ngatapa in December 1868 before being rapidly brought back to south Taranaki to face Titokowaru. By January 1869 both Te Kooti and Titokowaru were fugitives. By the time that Haultain retired from politics in 1871 the last imperial troops had been withdrawn and the *New Zealand Wars had petered out.

Heaphy, Major Charles (probably 1820–3 August 1881). A civilian soldier during the *New Zealand Wars, Heaphy became the first member of a colonial force to win the *Victoria Cross. Born in London, he trained as an artist at the Royal Academy before proceeding to New Zealand as an artist and draughtsman for the New Zealand Company in 1839. After surveying and exploring in Wellington, Nelson, and the West Coast, he became Auckland provincial surveyor in 1858. (His numerous maps, paintings, and drawings provide a valuable record of early colonial New Zealand.) He gained *militia experience in Nelson and then, from 1859, as a private in the City Company of the Auckland Rifle Volunteers. As conflict approached, he enlisted for active service, winning a lieutenant's commission in June 1863 and captaincy of the Parnell Company in August. In July, his unwilling militia erected St John's Redoubt at Papatoetoe. His extensive knowledge of the country then led to his being employed as both a military surveyor and a guide. He participated in surveying the new military road being driven south from Auckland towards the heart of the Waikato, and in charting river channels for the military steamers being deployed. He was also attached to Lieutenant-Colonel M.G. *Nixon's flying column as a guide from September 1863 and to Lieutenant-Colonel Sir Henry Havelock's from January 1864. While encamped on the Mangapiko before Paterangi, the 40th Regiment had a bathing party ambushed on 11 February 1864. In his only command of regular troops, Heaphy led about a dozen soldiers of the 50th Regiment to help isolate the ambushers. Once the attackers were cornered in the old Waiari pa, he went to the aid of a wounded soldier trapped in overgrown entrenchments under heavy fire. Although lightly wounded three times himself from virtually point-blank range, he managed with assistance to attend to, then retrieve, the man, fighting off their attackers. Two others were killed in that attempt. He subsequently tried to relieve another trapped group and guided stretcher parties. A recommendation by Governor Sir George ★Grey that he be awarded the Victoria Cross failed because regulations limited the award of the decoration to regular servicemen. When Heaphy applied on his own behalf, supported by Havelock, General Duncan ★Cameron, and Grey, the imperial authorities relented. The Royal Warrant for the Victoria Cross was changed on 1 January 1867 to allow its award to members of colonial forces. Already promoted retrospectively to the rank of major for his 'distinguished services in the field', Heaphy received the decoration on 11 May 1867. His active service had ended in March 1864, when he became chief surveyor for the central government, with particular responsibility for the survey of the confiscated Waikato lands. He was later the first Commissioner of Native Reserves and a Native Land Court judge.

BRYAN GILLING

Heard, Colonel Edward Severin (7 March 1863–28 February 1944). The son of a Royal Artillery assistant surgeon, Heard was born at Kamptee in Madras, India, and obtained a commission in the Northumberland Fusiliers in 1883. He took part in the Hazara campaign on India's North-west Frontier in 1888, and was a 'Special Service Officer' in South Africa during the early part of the ★Boer War, later being staff officer in charge of intelligence in the Cape Colony. After the conflict, he was Professor of Military Topography at the Staff College, Camberley. He was one of a group of imperial officers that were brought to New Zealand by the new Commandant, Major-General A.J. ★Godley, in December 1910. As Director of Military Training and Education in the New Zealand Military Forces, Heard had a key role in the introduction of the new ★Territorial Force scheme in 1911. From 1912 he was also Chief of the General Staff. While temporary Commandant during Godley's absence overseas in 1913, he resisted the idea of employing military personnel to maintain law and order during the waterfront strike in Wellington, but provided support to 'special constables' who were organised unofficially by Territorial Force commanders (see CIVIL POWER, AID TO). His secondment to the New Zealand forces ended in July 1914.

Heke Pokai, Hone Wiremu (c. 1808–6 August 1850). Hone Heke Pokai of Kaikohe was the first Maori leader forcibly to challenge the post-1840 shift in the balance of power between Maori and Pakeha in northern New Zealand. He provoked and played a leading role in the Northern War of 1845–46, which delayed but could not reverse European ascendancy. He attended a mission school, where he was described as a 'daring impudent fellow', and married a daughter of ★Hongi Hika in 1837 after showing leadership qualities during Nga Puhi military expeditions in the 1830s. In 1840 Heke was the first chief to sign the Treaty of Waitangi. But the consequences for Bay of Islands Maori were soon seen as negative: trade followed the capital to Auckland, and was further stunted by new customs duties. The execution for murder of Maketu in 1842 made it clear that chiefly authority now rested with the British Crown. Heke opposed this unanticipated transfer of power in a traditional way, through a series of challenges. He repeatedly felled the flagstaff at Kororareka which flew the British flag. On the fourth occasion, in March 1845, this involved an alliance with Te Ruki ★Kawiti to defeat the British troops who were now garrisoning the town, and open warfare broke out. Heke built a pa at Puketutu, Te Kahika, from which he engaged in trials of strength with the warriors of Tamati Waka ★Nene, who supported Governor Robert FitzRoy. On 8 May, a British assault on this stronghold was defeated by the coordinated forces of Heke and Kawiti. A month later, Heke suffered a significant defeat when he unsuccessfully attempted to recapture his new pa, Te Ahuahu, from Waka Nene in the largest battle involving Nga Puhi during the Northern War. Severely wounded, he took no part in Kawiti's defeat of the British at Ohaeawai on 1 July. After peace negotiations came to nothing, the new Governor, George ★Grey, took up Kawiti's challenge to attack him at a new fighting pa at Ruapekapeka. Heke and sixty warriors joined Kawiti's force shortly before the British occupied Ruapekapeka. A week later, Heke and Kawiti told Nene that they were making peace, and Grey subsequently pardoned them. Their casualties had been significant, as had been the strain of warfare on the tribal economy.

DAVID GREEN

Helicopters, RNZAF The RNZAF came late to helicopters with the arrival, in 1965, of the Bell G-47 Sioux, the standard British and American light observation machine, which was generally similar to the civilian model widely used in aerial work around New Zealand. The Bell Iroquois followed a year later and soon became a familiar sight and sound with its distinctive 'thump-thump' rotor noise. The RNZN acquired the diminutive Westland Wasp for its Leander class ★frigates. During 1998–99, these were

An RNZAF Iroquois helicopter lifts off a makeshift landing pad at Navua, Fiji, to deliver a load of supplies to an inland village following a hurricane (RNZAF)

replaced by three US-built Kaman SH-2F Seasprite, which were in turn soon replaced by five later model SH-2Gs.

The principal RNZAF helicopters have been:

Iroquois, Bell (2-seat medium transport helicopter). Rotor diameter 14.6 m; length 12.8 m; load 11 fully equipped troops or 6 stretchers; maximum speed 230 km/h; range 533 km; power [UH-1H] 1 x Lycoming 1400 shaft h.p. engine derated to 1100 shaft h.p.

The RNZAF has used two models of the standard US Army Bell Iroquois, known universally as the 'Huey' (a name derived from the UH of its model numbers). The first five (UH-1Ds) were delivered to 3 Squadron at Hobsonville from June 1966. Nine of the more powerful UH-1H models were received in 1970. The helicopters have been widely used around New Zealand, by the New Zealand forces in Singapore, and in many South Pacific island states on exercises and disaster relief operations. They have been used for several seasons in the Antarctic, painted bright orange and known as 'Orange Roughies'. Several, similarly painted, served with the Truce Monitoring Force in Bougainville in 1998–99. White-painted Hueys have also been flown by the Multinational Force and Observers in the Sinai, though these aircraft were never taken on RNZAF strength.

Sioux, Bell (2-seat light helicopter). Rotor diameter 10.4 m; length 8.3 m; maximum speed 174 km/h; range 430 km; power 1 x Lycoming 260 shaft h.p. engine or 1 x Lycoming TV0-435 of 280 h.p.

From 1965 to 2000 thirteen Bell Sioux helicopters were flown by 3 Squadron. Their roles included battlefield liaison, visual reconnaissance, and medical evacuation.

Seasprite, Kaman (3-seat naval helicopter). Rotor diameter 13.5 m; length 16 m; maximum speed 256 km/h; range 885 km; power [SH-2G] 2 x General Electric T700-GE-401 engines each of 1723 shaft h.p.

The standard small-ship US Navy helicopter, the Seasprite won a spirited competition to replace the veteran Westland Wasp in RNZAF shipboard service in 1997. Serving with the RNZN (though attached to 3 Squadron RNZAF), and armed with Maverick missiles, *torpedoes, and *depth charges, they have *anti-submarine warfare and transport roles.

Wasp, Westland (2-seat naval helicopter). Rotor diameter 9.8 m; length 12.3 m; maximum speed 212 km/h; range 518 km; power 1 x Rolls Royce (Bristol Siddeley) Nimbus 1050 shaft h.p. (de-rated to 710 shaft h.p.) engine.

In the thirty years from 1965, eight of the tiny Wasps operated aboard RNZN frigates. They had a limited offensive role with torpedoes and depth charges.

BRIAN LOCKSTONE

Henderson, Lance-Bombardier James Herbert ('Jim') (26 August 1918–   ). Born at Motueka, Jim Henderson served in 2NZEF as a gunner, and was wounded and taken prisoner at Sidi Rezegh in December 1941 during the *North African campaign. His left leg later had to be amputated while he was being held in a camp in Italy. Following his liberation in 1943, he wrote an earthy account of his experiences which proved immensely and enduringly popular: first published in 1945, *Gunner Inglorious* is now in its eleventh edition. The *War History Branch commissioned him to prepare two official unit histories: *RMT: Official History of the 4th and 6th Reserve Mechanical Transport Companies* (1954) and *22 Battalion* (1958). In 1978 he published *Soldier Country*, a collection of wartime anecdotes. This was based on material contributed to the regular column, 'Unofficial History', which he produced in the NZRSA's newspaper *RSA Review* for more than forty years. A popular radio personality—his programme 'Open Country' ran for fourteen years from 1961—and author of numerous books on non-military subjects, he was made an MBE in 1984.

GRANT CROWLEY

Hensley, Gerald Christopher Philip (4 December 1935–   ) was the government's chief civilian defence adviser during the 1990s. Born in Christchurch and educated at the University of Canterbury—his masters thesis was on the withdrawal of imperial forces from New Zealand in the late 1860s—he began his career in the Department of External Affairs. From 1976 to 1980 he was New Zealand High Commissioner in Singapore, before becoming permanent head of the Prime Minister's Department. Following the change of government in 1984, his position became increasingly difficult because of his association with the now-repudiated approach of the previous administration led by R.D. Muldoon. This culminated in his appointment, in 1987, as Coordinator for Domestic and External Security, in effect sidelining him. Not surprisingly, perhaps, the Labour government baulked at his proposed appointment as Secretary of Defence in 1990, and it was not until after its fall later that year that he became Chief Policy Adviser in the Ministry of Defence. He was Secretary of Defence from 1991 to 1999. As the principal architect of the 1991 Defence white paper, he developed the concept of ★self-reliance in partnership, which underlay the National government's approach to defence in the post-ANZUS environment. This shifted the focus of New Zealand strategy back to a more traditional stance, and emphasised cooperation with allies and a wider perception of New Zealand's interests than had pertained in the period 1984–90.

Herrick, Chief Officer Ruth Hermione (19 January 1889–21 January 1983) was New Zealand's leading female naval personality of the ★Second World War. Born at Ruataniwha of a prominent Hawke's Bay land-owning family, she spent much of her early life in London, where she was educated. During the ★First World War, she was secretary to the head of the Nursing Division at the New Zealand Stationary Hospital at Walton-on-Thames. A schoolteacher, she was heavily involved in the New Zealand Girl Guide movement between the world wars, beginning a twenty-nine-year stint as Chief Commissioner in 1934. She became director of the newly established ★Women's Royal New Zealand Naval Service in 1942, and held the position until 1946. She successfully developed the service from scratch, not only establishing the shape of the new organisation along the lines of a similar service in the United Kingdom but also recruiting and training its members. Recruits were carefully selected, for she set very high standards. Her contribution was recognised by her appointment as an OBE in 1946; she would later be promoted to a CBE for her services to the Girl Guides. Three of her brothers were killed in action while serving with the RAF in the Second World War; two others served in the Royal Navy, one of them, Lieutenant-Commander L.E. Herrick, later commanding HMNZS *Pukaki* in the ★Korean War while seconded to the RNZN.

Hesselyn, Squadron-Leader Raymond Brown ('Hess') (13 March 1921–14 November 1963) was one of the most successful New Zealand fighter 'aces' of the ★Second World War. A native of Invercargill, he joined his local ★Territorial Force unit in 1937, but in 1940 transferred to the RNZAF. After training in Canada, he was seconded to the RAF and posted to 34 Squadron. In March 1942 he flew a Spitfire off HMS *Eagle* to the embattled island of Malta, where he joined 249 Squadron. Over the next four months he claimed twelve enemy aircraft, successes which earned him a DFC and bar. Returning to the United Kingdom, he was a pilot instructor until posted back to an operational squadron in 1943. By the time he was shot down over France and made a POW on 3 October 1943, he had taken his tally of confirmed victories to eighteen. Although his several attempts to escape from prison camp were unsuccessful, they earned him appointment as an MBE. After the war he secured a permanent commission in the RAF, and became a squadron-leader in Fighter Command HQ.

P. Brennan, R. Hesselyn, and H. Bateson, *Spitfires Over Malta* (Jarrolds, London, n.d. [1942]).

Hinton, Sergeant John Daniel (17 September 1909–28 June 1997) won the VC during the 2nd New Zealand Division's ill-fated campaign in ★Greece. A driver with the Public Works Department, he had enlisted in 2NZEF in September 1939, and served in 20th Battalion. In April 1941, he found himself among a large force of British and New Zealand troops awaiting evacuation at Kalamata. When an attack by a German reconnaissance group developed, and a retreat was ordered, Hinton shouted 'To hell with this! Who will come with me?' and charged two German field guns. He killed the crews with hand grenades before storming two houses, killing the Germans inside. He was then shot in the stomach. Following his recovery, he was taken to Germany, where he was liberated in April 1945. After the war he managed hotels. With the death of Charles ★Upham, he was New Zealand's last surviving VC winner.

G. McDonald, *Jack Hinton V.C.: A Man Amongst Men* (David Ling, Auckland, 1997).

Hoaxes A number of hoaxes have been perpetrated in New Zealand over defence matters, either by newspapers or, in one case, by a confidence trickster. On 17 February 1873 the Auckland *Daily Southern Cross* published a detailed report of the intrusion of a Russian warship, the *Kaskowiski* ('Cask of Whisky'), which had used a newly invented disabling gas to seize a British warship in the harbour and had then landed detachments to occupy key points in the city. After demanding one and a half million roubles, the Russian vessel had slipped away leaving the city threatened by the guns of the captured British warship. With only a paltry sum having so far been found, the paper reported, it seemed that the city was doomed to be burned when the *Kaskowiski* returned. The report caused a sensation, with people besieging the newspaper office and some concealing their valuables. The *Daily Southern Cross*'s editor had hoped to remind readers of the vulnerability

Holland

of the port to a raider, but it was to be five years before anything was done to put the defences in order.

The *Wanganui Herald* was responsible for a similar hoax in April 1885, when it published a detailed account of an unsuccessful Russian attack on Wellington. Both sides were reported to have suffered serious casualties. The story, which did not have the giveaways of its *Daily Southern Cross* predecessor, caused considerable excitement in Wanganui. On the following day, the *Herald*'s rival, the *Wanganui Chronicle*, published an equally fictitious account of the lynching of the *Herald*'s editor by a crowd angered by the joke played on them.

A more significant hoax was perpetrated in 1942 when New Zealand faced a real threat, as opposed to an imagined one. In March 1942 Sidney Gordon Ross, a just released convict with a record of false pretences offences, told a Cabinet minister that he had been approached by enemy agents. He subsequently convinced the lacklustre head of the Security Intelligence Bureau, Major Keith Folkes, a loaned British officer, that Nazi agents landed from a submarine had developed a fifth column organisation which aimed at sabotage and even assassination of members of the *War Cabinet. Ross toured the North Island with SIB agents at public expense. It was not until plans were set in train to arrest the conspirators, and military assistance was sought, that the Prime Minister's suspicions began to develop. Once the police were belatedly invited to investigate the matter, the hoax was quickly exposed. Folkes's performance had been demonstrably incompetent, and he was dismissed in February 1943.

I. McGibbon, *The Path to Gallipoli: Defending New Zealand 1840–1915* (GP Books, Wellington, 1991); F.L.W. Wood, *Political and External Affairs* (War History Branch, Wellington, 1958).

Holland, Major Francis George Leopold (20 July 1884–?) was a liaison officer with the American force which invaded the Gilbert and Ellice Islands in 1943. Born at Feilding, he was a schoolteacher in the Wanganui area from 1902 to 1911 before spending two years in Germany. During the *First World War, he was commissioned in the Royal Field Artillery Special Reserve and served at *Salonika. He joined the education service of the Gilbert and Ellice Islands in 1922, and was Superintendent of Education from 1931. He escaped from the islands before the Japanese occupied them in 1942, and joined the US forces as a liaison officer in the New Hebrides. The Tarawa invasion force which he accompanied comprised US Marines who had spent the previous months in New Zealand recuperating from their Guadalcanal ordeal. From his twenty-year experience of Tarawa, he warned that on the day planned for the US landing in November 1943 the tides would be at their lowest. This advice was rejected by the US commander, Rear-Admiral H.W. Hill, with disastrous consequences. More than 1000 marines were killed and 2000 wounded during the landings on Betio Island. After the war Holland was District Commissioner at Abemama.

Home Guard Formed in 1940, the Home Guard became an important element in New Zealand's home defence preparations during the *Second World War. Taken under Army control in 1941, and made compulsory in 1942, it reached its peak of efficiency and size in 1943. Its advent in New Zealand was the result of an upsurge of popular patriotism encouraged, as so often in New Zealand history, by developments in Great Britain. There, the fall of France had prompted the raising of Local Defence Volunteers (soon to be renamed the Home Guard). Unofficial militia units began appearing in a number of New Zealand towns as early as May 1940. These so-called 'private armies' were already being considered by the newly formed *National Service Department when, in July, the Dominion Farmers' Union pressed the government to form a Home Guard type of force. On 2 August the *War Cabinet approved the creation of the Home Guard as part of a short-lived Emergency Defence Corps, which included the *Emergency Precautions Scheme and the Women's War Service Auxiliary. Within a few weeks, all males over fifteen were invited to enrol. No upper age limit was set. Twelve hundred townships or suburbs set up Home Guard training centres under a recruitment committee. Generally run by local authorities, these were responsible to the National Service Department. Hamlets and rural communities raised enough men for at least a platoon (twenty-five or more men), which became the basic Home Guard unit. Companies of 100 to 200 men—the largest unit—appeared in most towns and city suburbs. There were small units in Stewart Island and the Chathams, and members of Parliament even formed two platoons. Home Guard platoons were attached to the Army's area offices and reported to commanders in the three *military districts. Major-General Robert *Young was appointed Dominion Commander of the Home Guard.

By the end of the year, 50,000 men had taken the oath, and four months later the Guard's strength stood at 98,600. Volunteers had 'to be physically capable of carrying out the training', though no fitness tests were imposed. Initially the government absolved itself from any liability for injury suffered on Home Guard duty. Guardsmen were required to attend evening and weekend parades. They were promised uniforms but had to be content with 'Home Guard' armbands. After the first 2600 Army rifles had been issued to the Guard

Home Guard

early in 1941, it was realised at Army HQ that available surplus stocks were insufficient to arm the now 65,900-strong force. After appeals to civilians to loan their .303 rifles 'for the duration' had met with little success, all civilian rifles were impressed. This produced 16,000 useable weapons, which were supplemented with 12,100 service rifles. Priority in the allocation of scarce equipment was given to Home Guard units in the minor ports, such as New Plymouth, Gisborne, or Timaru, where they reinforced the meagre ★National Military Reserve units. Everywhere, the scarcity of military equipment led to improvisation. Shovels were many guardsmen's best friend. Some made dummy guns incorporating a wooden ratchet to enliven exercises. Recipes for 'jam tin bombs' and Molotov cocktails were distributed. Heliographs made from car headlights blinked Morse code from hilltops. In Hamilton an Awake New Zealand campaign urged all civilians to defend their hearths with home-made bombs, though the Army authorities soon prohibited such devices. Although the Army was supposed to assist with training the Home Guard, it had insufficient resources for this task, and its courses concentrated on teaching Home Guardsmen how to train themselves. From April 1941 a capitation was paid for administration. For each 'reasonably fit' man—about 75 per cent of the total—who fulfilled minimum parade attendance requirements, his unit received one shilling a quarter.

The Home Guard both inherited and created second-line units. Transferred from the NMR in November 1940, Guards Vital Points (known as GVPs) watched over strategic bridges, tunnels, oil tanks, internees, and power and radio stations. Emergency Traffic Police detachments were formed in February 1941 to control civilian traffic. Bowser Guards protected the Army's reserve fuel stocks, stored in closed petrol stations. Coastwatchers within New Zealand also became Home Guardsmen. In mid 1941 the burgeoning Home Guard was organised into battalions: by July there were 157, each nominally of 776 men and based on a structure of three companies of four platoons each. Fortress battalions also had a support company. Generally named after the locality, some battalions took names like Gonville, Somes, Bush, Flagstaff, Lakes, and Levels. Many with very scattered sub-units never operated as a battalion, while some, especially in cities, were tight, cohesive formations.

Soon, however, the huge numbers involved (101,659 in July 1941) and the lack of uniformity

Wellington Home Guardsmen learn how to use a Lewis gun during their lunch-hour in 1941 (*Evening Post Collection, Alexander Turnbull Library, C-24255-1/2*)

Home Guard

prompted calls for greater control. Military Adviser General Sir Guy ★Williams, bringing to bear his knowledge of the British experience, recommended that the Home Guard remain part-time and voluntary, that commissions be issued to Home Guard officers, and that it develop its own administrative structure. When another of his recommendations, that the Home Guard be brought under Army control, was implemented on 1 August 1941, twenty-eight group offices were formed. Each liaised between their handful of battalions and the relevant area or fortress HQs. Capitation rose to £1 a year for 20 hours a month training.

The role of the Home Guard was to patrol isolated coastlines, oppose landings until the Army arrived, and delay the enemy with moveable obstructions. Defence of their localities was always the Home Guard unit's job, but in 1943 this static defence role evolved to include protection of places a 'considerable' distance from Guardsmen's homes (possibly as much as 30 kilometres). Even so, they were not permitted to take offensive action other than limited counter-attacks to 'restore the local situation'. Despite the transfer to the Army, there was a lingering suspicion that the Guard would merely be used to supply manpower to other defence units. The lack of uniforms (only 7300 had been issued by February 1942) and undersupply of arms further undermined morale, and helped account for the 40 per cent drop in the strength of fit Guardsmen in the second half of 1941. This problem of motivation disappeared with the onset of the ★Pacific War. A greater sense of urgency permeated Home Guard activities as the Allied situation in the Pacific theatre deteriorated. The Guard's status was enhanced by the disbandment, in January 1942, of the NMR; it became the second line of defence behind the ★Territorial Force. It inherited many of the less fit reservists as well as a number of mounted troops. Volunteers became liable for full-time paid call-up on 28 January. For instance, Gisborne mobilised small numbers of Guardsmen for nightly duty, in week-long shifts, on 16 May. For a month, they manned the beach pillboxes, relieving 8th Independent Company. Mangonui also mobilised a beach observation post. Many other guardsmen did weekend or longer stints digging trenches, erecting roadblocks, or relieving weary Territorials. Enrolments rose when Home Guardsmen were exempted from compulsory service in the EPS, but compulsion was extended to the Guard itself in March 1942, at first generally, but later being limited to men between the ages of thirty-five and fifty. This brought the total roll to 109,200 by October 1942.

Many Guardsmen were disgruntled by their service. They felt let down by broken promises of uniforms and arms and unhappy about their perceived role. In the face of calls for a committee of inquiry, which were backed by the Opposition, the government empowered the defence committee of the ★War Council, under William Perry, to tour the country hearing grievances over the Guard's status, equipment, and conditions of service. However, its recommendations for a number of improvements and increases in equipment had little effect in the face of resistance by the Army authorities. In June a reorganisation created nine new battalions and, over a few months, sixteen weak ones were subsequently amalgamated. This reduced the muster to 136 battalions, now divided into two categories. Only the A-priority battalions were brought up to strength with conscripts. They also received more and better equipment, though all battalions now had two full-time logistics staff each. Specialist units were added in 1942. Opotiki and Te Karaka had earlier deployed mounted units; Ngati Porou formed a mounted regiment. Members of the ★Maori War Effort Organisation called for more Maori units in the Bay of Plenty. Many mounted sub-units were authorised in all Home Guard groups: by September forty-seven battalions had a mounted troop attached. Ultimately there were eighty-nine mounted troops. Artillery was issued to priority Home Guard battalions late in 1942, once spare guns had been released from Territorial units. Dunedin had raised a Home Guard artillery unit in 1941; now sections (two guns) or troops (of four or more) were attached to thirty-one battalions. By June 1943 these units had seventy-six field guns, a mix of old 18-pounders, 4.5-inch howitzers, and, for five battalions, captured Italian 65 mm guns. In addition four beach defence batteries were regarded as Home Guard units, while many Guardsmen relieved searchlight operators and, in smaller defended ports, coast artillery gunners. The Guard also furnished aerodrome defence units. Small units, misleadingly named guide platoons, were authorised in March 1942 to prepare for guerrilla warfare should New Zealand be occupied by the Japanese. By mid 1943, 102 17-men platoons had been formed, each with a secret bush hideout stocked with sufficient supplies to support one month's operations. Some Waikato guides exercised with US Marines, imparting to them bush warfare techniques. Secrecy surrounded their activities. Only the guides themselves and a liaison officer knew where their caches were, and fake bases were created. The Home Guard also provided an administrative home for units engaged in other roles, such as the RNZN's bomb disposal units. Two hundred scientists working on defence matters were given the protection of its uniform.

In September 1942 the twenty-eight Home Guard groups were superseded by thirty-three zones, each of which had three to five Home Guard or Territorial battalions. By early in 1943, when equipping had reached an advanced stage and training had improved, the Guard was confident of its ability to fight alongside the Territorial Force. More than 96,800 Guardsmen in 136 infantry battalions had been provided with uniforms and they were armed with 63,000 rifles of varying makes (including 40,000 imported from America), 3400 various pieces of equipment, including recycled machine and submachine-guns, and anti-tank rifles and 3-inch mortars. Guide platoons and mounted troops added 11,411 men to Division I. With just over 11,000 Division II traffic police, sentries, and air observers, they brought the total strength to 119,000 (with another 4000 listed as unfit). In all, 7.5 per cent of the New Zealand population were involved in the Home Guard, compared with 3.7 and 1.4 per cent in Britain and Australia respectively.

During 1943 the improving war situation in the Pacific brought into question the continued need for the Home Guard. In June it was deemed to be in reserve, and units were urged to grow vegetables or help unload cargo ships. Although men were still required to attend quarterly parades, capitation ceased in September. The Guard was finally disbanded in December. Although never required to fight, it had provided a clear demonstration of the 'nation at arms' and a certain reassurance to a population conscious of the absence of most of New Zealand's trained fighting men in distant theatres.

PETER COOKE

Homosexuality and the military Until 1986 homosexual acts were illegal in New Zealand, and the armed forces determined their policy accordingly. During the world wars, New Zealand servicemen found to have committed acts of an 'indecent or unnatural kind' were imprisoned for up to two years before being ignominiously discharged. Although military disciplinary legislation from 1950 provided for sentences of up to two years for 'disgraceful conduct', in most instances offenders were quietly discharged without prosecution. When the Homosexual Law Reform Act decriminalised homosexuality in 1986, the armed forces were specifically exempted from its provisions. It was not until 1993, following the passage of the Human Rights Act and examination of the practice in other Western armed forces, that formal discrimination against homosexual personnel in the armed forces was removed, without any controversy (in marked contrast to the position in the United States). The sexual relations, orientation, and activities of service personnel were deemed to be 'a normal part of adult life and primarily a private matter'.

Hong Kong, defence of Communist victories in the Chinese Civil War in 1949 brought into question the security of the British colony of Hong Kong. The British government was determined to resist any Chinese attempt to seize the colony, and sought assistance from both Australia and New Zealand. While the former concluded that resistance would be futile, but nevertheless provided four harbour defence launches, New Zealand offered three frigates for use in the colony's defence if required. From mid September 1949 three vessels were accordingly kept at one month's notice for service with the British Far East Squadron in case of hostilities. New Zealand also offered to make available a flight of transport aircraft and four Mosquito fighter-bombers with eight crews and the necessary ground staff. The latter were not accepted because of their unsuitability for operations in Hong Kong, but from September 1949 to November 1951 a detachment from 41 Squadron RNZAF served with the British Far East Air Force in Singapore, making regular flights to Hong Kong. In the event, the arrival of Chinese Communist forces on the Hong Kong border in mid October 1949 passed without incident, and Chinese sovereignty over Hong Kong was not finally restored until 1997, in accordance with treaty agreements.

Hongi Hika (c. 1772–3 March 1828) was the first Maori leader to master the use of muskets in intertribal warfare. He thereby changed radically the scale and nature of these conflicts, and his Nga Puhi tribal confederation achieved unprecedented military success. Among many other talents, Hongi also had artistic ability and an intellect which enabled him to learn to write English in a few days. About 1807, he narrowly escaped with his life from the Battle of Moremonui, in which Nga Puhi were defeated by Ngati Whatua when they took too long to reload the muskets they had recently begun to acquire. Several of Hongi's relatives were killed and he was both obliged and motivated to seek revenge. By 1815, he was the recognised leader of the 'northern alliance' of Nga Puhi centred on his kainga of Waimate. Campaigns against Far North iwi showed Hongi that the key to the successful use of the shoddy muzzle-loaders then available was to deploy them in large enough numbers to both terrify opponents and compensate for the deficiencies of individual weapons. He set about obtaining muskets from Europeans, who visited the Bay of Islands in increasing numbers after a Church Missionary Society mission was established under his protection in 1814. Hongi was soon able to assemble guns with 'accuracy and ingenuity'; he had 'an evident predilection' for such mechanical work. While the missionaries generally refused to sell

Honours and awards

muskets directly, they provided iron tools which were used in large-scale cultivation of potatoes and other crops that were traded for muskets. The fields were worked by slaves captured in southern expeditions, some led by Hongi, from 1818. Hongi also visited England and Sydney in 1820 to buy arms. His return with up to 500 muskets (as well as a suit of armour and a steel helmet which he wore to further demoralise his enemies) re-established his lead in the northern arms race.

In the early 1820s, many hundreds of warriors left the Bay of Islands each year on expeditions against southern tribes which as yet had few firearms. By distributing his muskets, Hongi was able to combine most of Nga Puhi's factions for campaigns which lasted several months—probably the first time this had ever happened. While his organisational role was crucial, other chiefs retained independent control of their forces in battle, sometimes with near-disastrous results. Nevertheless, in 1821 Ngati Paoa of Tamaki and Ngati Maru of Hauraki were overcome, and the following year Waikato were overwhelmed at Matakitaki, near Pirongia. In 1823, Te Arawa were surprised and defeated on Mokoia Island, Rotorua, after canoes were hauled overland from the coast. In each case, victory was eventually won through the terrifying effect of massed firepower deployed in a disciplined fashion—for example controlled volleys—combined with the use of more traditional tactics such as flying wedges (kawau maro). Hongi exhibited his leadership qualities and personal bravery on several occasions. Many of the vanquished fled, beginning a pattern of migration and warfare which was to transform the demography of the North Island by the 1830s and facilitate European settlement in the 1840s.

In 1825, Nga Puhi won a satisfying (albeit incomplete) revenge victory over Ngati Whatua in the battle of Te Ika-a-ranga-nui. Hongi scoured Waikato for the survivors. But by now the balance of power was shifting against Nga Puhi as other iwi also acquired many muskets and learned to use them effectively. In 1827, Hongi moved to Whangaroa, both to assert his ancestral rights in the area and to punish the inhabitants for harassing valued European settlers. Ngati Uru were easily defeated in a battle notable for Nga Puhi's deployment of artillery, but Hongi was gravely wounded by a musket ball which passed through his chest. He lived for another year, planning expeditions he was unable to mount, notably the capture of Kororareka, a port increasingly popular with visiting Europeans. Both Nga Puhi and their enemies feared retributive expeditions, but the cycle of warfare in the north had ended with his death.

DAVID GREEN

Honours and awards New Zealand's royal honours system, like its constitutional status, has gradually evolved since 1840. Until 1975 honours and awards were almost entirely British. In that year a distinctive New Zealand honour, the Queen's Service Order (QSO), with an associated medal, the Queen's Service Medal (QSM), was instituted to supplement British honours. In 1987 the Order of New Zealand (ONZ) was instituted and is the highest honour in the gift of the Queen of New Zealand. By 1995 the majority of honours and awards were New Zealand–based and in January of that year the Prime Minister, J.B. Bolger, appointed an Honours Advisory Committee to review the system. The committee proposed that British honours for meritorious services, gallantry, and bravery should cease and be replaced by a third distinctive order and a new series of gallantry and bravery awards. The New Zealand Order of Merit, of five levels, was instituted in May 1996, and details of the proposed gallantry and bravery awards were announced in May 1998 and formally instituted in 1999.

Meritorious services: Since the nineteenth century the services of New Zealand military personnel have been recognised by appointments as knights, companions, officers, or members in the various British orders of chivalry, namely the second (KCB) and third (CB) classes of the military division of the Order of the Bath, the second (KCMG) and third (CMG) classes of the Order of Saint Michael and Saint George, and since 1917 four of the five classes of the military division of the Order of the British Empire (KBE, CBE, OBE, MBE) and associated British Empire Medal (BEM). The honour of Knight Bachelor was also conferred on several senior Army officers. These British honours were replaced by the New Zealand Order of Merit, instituted in 1996. Military personnel are eligible for all five levels of the Order (Knights and Dames Grand Companions (GNZM); Knights and Dames Companion (KNZM, DNZM); Companions (CNZM); Officers (ONZM), and Members (MNZM)). Additional appointments are usually contemplated for military operational services. The ONZ has an ordinary membership limited to twenty persons living at any one time. Although military personnel are eligible, none have been appointed to date. The QSO and QSM are essentially civilian honours. However, Cadet Force officers and several military personnel have been awarded the QSM for non-military or community-based services.

Gallantry awards: From the ★Boer War until 1996 New Zealand military personnel were eligible to be considered for the various British awards for acts of gallantry performed in war and war-like or combat operations. Apart from the first and fourth levels of awards—the ★Victoria Cross (VC) and Mention in Dispatches—the level of the other awards was based on the

Honours and awards

rank of the individual and not the action. Several of the awards had a dual purpose in that they could be awarded both for acts of gallantry and meritorious or distinguished services. Until 1979 only the VC and Mention could be granted posthumously. It is now acknowledged that many posthumous Mentions during the ★First and ★Second World Wars might have merited a more senior decoration had the individual survived. These anomalies have been removed from the British system and do not exist in the New Zealand system.

In 1999 Queen Elizabeth II instituted four New Zealand Gallantry Awards to recognise acts of gallantry by members of the ★New Zealand Defence Force and certain support personnel while deployed on war or war-like operations, including ★peacekeeping. These combatant awards are for acts which do not necessarily involve the saving of life. Bars may be awarded for further acts and all may be awarded posthumously. The premier gallantry award is the Victoria Cross for New Zealand. The New Zealand Gallantry Medal replaces the previous fourth-level awards, the Mention in Dispatches and Commendations, which were denoted by a small ribbon emblem. The awards and criteria, with the British awards they replace, are listed in table 7.

Table 7 New Zealand Gallantry Awards

Level I
Victoria Cross for New Zealand
For most conspicuous gallantry, or some daring or pre-eminent act of valour or self-sacrifice, or extreme devotion to duty, in the presence of the enemy or of belligerents.
Replaces Victoria Cross

Level II
New Zealand Gallantry Star (NZGS)
For acts of outstanding gallantry in situations of danger.
Replaces Distinguished Service Order, Distinguished Conduct Medal, Conspicuous Gallantry Medals (naval and flying)

Level III
New Zealand Gallantry Decoration (NZGD)
For acts of exceptional gallantry in situations of danger.
Replaces Distinguished Service Cross, Military Cross, Distinguished Flying Cross, Air Force Cross, Distinguished Service Medal, Military Medal, Distinguished Flying Medal, Air Force Medal

Level IV
New Zealand Gallantry Medal (NZGM)
For acts of gallantry.
Replaces Mention in Despatches, Commendations for Brave Conduct and Valuable Service in the Air

Bravery awards: Four New Zealand Bravery Awards, instituted in 1999, replaced the four levels of British awards previously available to New Zealand civilians and those military personnel for which military awards were inappropriate. The awards are for acts of bravery in saving or attempting to save life. Bars may be awarded for further acts and all may be awarded posthumously. The new ★New Zealand Cross (NZC) is the premier award for acts of bravery and replaces the British ★George Cross. It is almost identical in design to the original New Zealand Cross. As early as 1885 it was proposed that that award should be modified so that it could be awarded for acts of bravery by civilians. The awards and criteria, with the British awards they replace, are listed in table 8.

Table 8 New Zealand Bravery Awards

Level I
New Zealand Cross
For acts of great bravery in situations of extreme danger.
Replaces George Cross

Level II
New Zealand Bravery Star (NZBS)
For acts of outstanding bravery in situations of danger.
Replaces George Medal

Level III
New Zealand Bravery Decoration (NZBD)
For acts of exceptional bravery in situations of danger.
Replaces Queen's Gallantry Medal (formerly appointments to the Order of the British Empire and awards of the British Empire Medal for gallantry), Air Force Cross, Air Force Medal

Level IV
New Zealand Bravery Medal (NZBM)
For acts of bravery.
Replaces Commendations for Brave Conduct and Valuable Service in the Air

The Royal Red Cross was instituted in 1883 for award to nurses serving with the armed forces who display special devotion to duty. Later the criteria were extended also to cover exceptional acts of bravery. In 1915 a second class or Associate level (ARRC) was instituted. The first New Zealand nurse to receive the RRC was Matron Janet Wyse Mackie Williamson in 1901 for services during the Boer War. Matron Evelyn Gertrude Brooke is one of a hundred nurses and the only New Zealand nurse to receive the RRC (1917) and bar (1919). In 1996 the RRC and ARRC were replaced by appointments to the New Zealand Order of Merit or an appropriate gallantry or bravery award.

Honours and awards

The Distinguished Service Order, instituted in 1886, for award to officers for meritorious or distinguished services, leadership, and gallantry while in combat was first conferred on New Zealand officers in 1900 during the Boer War. Four appointments were made during the ★Korean War and the last in 1955 to a New Zealand officer with the Fiji Infantry Regiment in Malaya. A British review resulted in this decoration being reconstituted in 1995 as an award for command leadership in combat with its gallantry provisions being embodied in a new second-level award, the Conspicuous Gallantry Cross (CGC). The CGC also replaced the DCM and CGM.

In addition to the George Cross, New Zealand military personnel have been awarded the George Medal and the Queen's Gallantry Medal. Prior to the institution of the QGM, they also received appointments to the Order of the British Empire and awards of the British Empire Medal 'for gallantry'.

Campaign Medals: The first New Zealand campaign medal was the New Zealand Medal instituted in 1869 for award to British forces involved in operations against Maori during the wars of 1845–47 and 1860–66. The medal was extended to local units in 1871 for personnel who served during the 1860–66 period and had actually been under fire in any engagement. Those who performed conspicuous or distinguished service in the field though not under fire also qualified. The design of the medal was unusual and a departure from others of the period in that it had a distinctive fern frond suspender, and the years of service, of which there were twenty-eight variations, were recorded in relief on the reverse of the medal. Medals issued to local units were usually undated. Colonel R. McGregor, 58th Regiment, is the only known recipient of the medal dated 1846–65, which is now in the Napier Museum.

Troops of the New Zealand Contingents in the Boer War received the Queen's South Africa Medal, to which twenty-six clasps were sanctioned. Most received the medal with up to a maximum of five clasps, though there are some with six, seven, and eight clasps. Approximately 170, including nurses, also received the King's South Africa Medal with two clasps. Those who served in the First World War were eligible for the 1914–15 Star, British War Medal 1914–18, the Mercantile Marine War Medal 1914–18, and the Victory Medal 1919. Although New Zealand military personnel did not qualify for the 1914 Star, at least four New Zealanders, two nurses, Colonel R.H. ★Davies, and Major G.S. ★Richardson, who were attached to British forces after the outbreak of war and served on the continent in 1914, received this medal. The proposal that there should be a Gallipoli Star (originally to be called the ANZAC Star) for those members of the Australian Imperial Force and 1NZEF who served at ★Gallipoli was put forward by Lieutenant-General Birdwood in October 1917. King George V approved the idea the following month. However, by August 1918 when the design of the star and the conditions for award had been finalised, and stocks of ribbon forwarded to New Zealand and Australia, the proposal was reviewed by the British government following criticism from both members of Parliament and the media in the United Kingdom, who were uneasy about British and other forces of the Empire being ineligible for the star. After consultation with the Australian and New Zealand governments, the British War Cabinet agreed that the 1914–15 Star would be awarded to all personnel who had served at Gallipoli. In 1967 the Australian and New Zealand governments jointly agreed to issue an ANZAC Commemorative Medallion (which was not designed to be worn) to all veterans and the next of kin of veterans who had served at Gallipoli. Living veterans were also issued with a small lapel badge based on the design of the large medallion. A small number of New Zealand officers who were attached to the Indian Army immediately after the First World War received the India General Service Medal (1908) with clasps WAZIRISTAN 1919–21 and MAHSUD 1919–20.

Eight campaign stars, eight clasps, and two medals were instituted for the Second World War; New Zealand personnel, including those who served in the Merchant Navy, were eligible for all of them. In addition, a distinctive medal, the New Zealand War Service Medal 1939–45, was instituted in 1948 for personnel who completed between twenty-eight days' and six months' service either overseas or with the armed forces or ★Home Guard in New Zealand. Service in the Korean War was recognised by the issue of either the Korea Medal or the United Nations' Service Medal with clasp KOREA, or both. The New Zealanders who served in Korea only after the armistice were in 1998 retrospectively awarded the New Zealand General Service Medal with clasp KOREA 1954–57 (in bronze). During the two post–Second World War decades, New Zealand personnel served alongside forces from other Commonwealth countries in both the ★Malayan Emergency and the ★Confrontation. This service was recognised by the award of the General Service Medal (Army and RAF) 1918–62, the Naval General Service Medal 1915–62, and the General Service Medal 1962, each with an appropriate clasp. In 1968 a New Zealand Royal Warrant established the Vietnam Medal (which is of the same design as Australia's Vietnam Medal); New Zealand personnel deployed in South Vietnam during the ★Vietnam War received either this medal or the South Vietnamese Campaign Medal (actually a star), or both.

Honours and awards

The New Zealand General Service Medal was instituted by Royal Warrant in 1992 and amended in 1997. It is awarded in silver for war and war-like operations and in bronze for peace-keeping operations. The medal has been issued in silver for activities in Kuwait (see GULF WAR) and in bronze for the Sinai, Iraq, Peshawar, Somalia, Mozambique, the Arabian Gulf, and Bougainville operations. The institution of this medal and the move away from sharing Commonwealth-wide medals has enabled previously unrecognised service to be accorded medallic recognition. In 1997 the medal with clasp MALAYA 1960–64 (in silver) and the medal with clasp KOREA 1954–57 (in bronze) were approved. Service with 2NZEF (Japan) or ★Jayforce in Japan was recognised in 1995 with the institution of the New Zealand Service Medal 1946–49. New Zealand personnel have been involved with most United Nations peace-keeping operations and have received the appropriate United Nations Service Medal or United Nations Special Service Medal. The New Zealand Defence Force contingent which joined the Commonwealth Force to monitor the Rhodesian elections were awarded the Commonwealth-wide Rhodesia Medal 1980.

Long service awards: The ★New Zealand Army, RNZN, and RNZAF have always enjoyed close ties with their British counterparts, from which they evolved and developed. From the time of their formation they decided to make use of the various long service awards issued to personnel in the British Army, Royal Navy, and RAF. The authority for the awarding of the medals to New Zealand personnel was provided either under New Zealand regulations issued pursuant to a British Royal Warrant or by letter indicating that the King had approved New Zealand personnel being eligible for them. In addition, several distinctive New Zealand Army medals were instituted under local, rather than Royal, authority, but by 1931 these medals had been discontinued. The awards were the New Zealand Militia Long Service and Good Conduct Medal (1887–1898), New Zealand Long and Efficient Service Medal (1887–1931), New Zealand Volunteer Service Medal (1902–1911), and the New Zealand Territorial Service Medal (1911–1931).

During the early 1980s the various British Royal Warrants, the basis of authority for awards to New Zealand personnel, were reviewed, and in 1985 Queen Elizabeth II signed distinctive New Zealand Royal Warrants (retrospective to 1 December 1977) for the New Zealand Meritorious Service Medal (originally an Army medal, it was extended to all NCOs in the RNZN and RNZAF), the New Zealand Army Long Service and Good Conduct Medal, the RNZN Long Service and Good Conduct Medal, the RNZAF Long Service and Good Conduct Medal, the Royal New Zealand Naval Reserves Officers' Decorations (RD and VRD), and the RNZNVR Long Service and Good Conduct Medal. The words 'New Zealand' have always appeared on the first two medals; otherwise the awards are identical in design to the corresponding British awards. In 1985 long and efficient service of regular force officers, serving on or after 1 December 1977, was recognised by the institution of the New Zealand Armed Forces Award. Long service awards are now generally for fifteen years' service with a clasp for each additional fifteen years' service, or ten years in the case of Territorials. There are several military awards, currently under review, which are made under New Zealand regulations issued pursuant to British Warrants, viz: the Efficiency Decoration (ED), the Efficiency Medal, the Air Efficiency Award, and the Cadet Forces Medal. Members of the New Zealand Defence Force are also eligible for one of three medals for marksmanship, viz: the Queen's Medal for Champion Shots of the NZ Naval Forces (instituted by NZ Royal Warrant in 1958, retrospective to 1955, and identical in design to the British Naval Good Shooting Medal 1903–14), the King's, later Queen's, Medal for Champion Shots in the Military Forces (a British medal awarded in New Zealand since 1923), and the Queen's Medal for Champion Shots of the Air Forces (a British medal, instituted in 1953, awarded under New Zealand regulations). Prior to the availability of these medals, a range of unofficial or local good shooting medals were issued.

Memorial awards: The next of kin of New Zealand personnel, like those of other British Empire forces, killed during the First World War or who died of wounds or disease attributed to the war were issued with a large bronze Memorial Plaque instituted in 1918 (affectionately known as the 'Dead Man's Penny') bearing the name of the deceased in relief, together with a Memorial Scroll. All those who served in 1NZEF also received a Certificate of Honourable Service. In 1947 King George VI sanctioned a New Zealand Memorial Cross, based on the Canadian Memorial Cross instituted for the First World War, for issue to the next of kin of those New Zealanders who died while on active service with New Zealand or other Allied forces. The New Zealand Memorial Scroll, identical to that issued to other British Empire or Commonwealth forces and similar in design to that issued for the 1914–18 conflict, was issued in limited numbers to the next of kin of New Zealand military personnel who died during the Second World War. In 1960 Queen Elizabeth II sanctioned the issue of a second New Zealand Memorial Cross to the next of kin of personnel who have died while on active service in various post–Second World War operations.

PHILLIP O'SHEA

Hospital ships

Hospital ships 'Reading the newspapers only gives a very small idea of what our men are putting up with … All the men that we have on board are, apart from wounds, just wasted away and broken down for want of food and rest.' This diary entry by First Officer John Duder of the hospital ship *Maheno* brings home the horrors of modern industrialised warfare and helps to explain why the hospital ships are New Zealand's best-remembered requisitioned merchant ships of the ★First World War. In 1915, as the ★Gallipoli campaign got underway, the New Zealand government requisitioned two of the Union Steam Ship Company's newest passenger liners, the *Maheno* and *Marama*, for service as hospital ships. After being fitted out for her new role at the company's Port Chalmers workshops, the *Maheno* arrived off the crowded beach at Anzac Cove on 26 August 1915. With the benefit of their experience with the *Maheno*, the workshop staff transformed the *Marama* in just twenty-three days, removing most internal walls and fittings to permit the installation of 600 beds and the construction of storerooms and offices for the medical staff. The *Marama* sailed from New Zealand in December 1915. Painted white, bearing three large red crosses and green stripes, both ships carried many little luxuries paid for by public subscription.

During the next four years they would make seventeen voyages back to New Zealand in addition to many shorter trips, carrying in all about 47,000 wounded and sick servicemen. It was often hot, dangerous work. *Maheno* was a heavy coal-eater and in September 1915, while off Malta, some of her firemen and trimmers, worked past breaking point, went on strike, for which they received three months' imprisonment. Despite the threat of guns and submarines, neither ship was hit, though the surgeons, nursing staff, and civilian crews spent considerable time within sight and sound of the firing line and worked under dangerous and unpleasant conditions. The *Marama*'s wartime role is commemorated by Otago University's Marama Hall. During the ★Second World War, the New Zealand government requisitioned the Union Company's old liner *Maunganui* in January 1941 for conversion into a hospital ship, primarily to serve the needs of 2NZEF. HMNZHS *Maunganui* made many trips between Suez and New Zealand and finished the war serving with the British Pacific Fleet's Fleet Train. After transporting the New Zealand contingent to the official victory celebrations in London, she returned to Wellington in August 1946 and was paid off, New Zealand's third and last hospital ship.

GAVIN McLEAN

The hospital ship *Maheno* (*John Dickie Collection, Alexander Turnbull Library, G-17141-1/2*)

Hotham, Admiral Sir Alan Geoffrey (3 October 1876–10 July 1965) commanded the first cruiser to serve with the ★New Zealand Division of the Royal Navy. From a family with an illustrious naval background—one of his forebears had been raised to the peerage for his naval services in the eighteenth century and his own father would reach the rank of admiral of the fleet—he entered the Royal Navy as a cadet and later became a gunnery specialist. He secured his first command, the destroyer HMS *Aurora*, just before the ★First World War. After serving with the Harwich Force, he took command in 1915 of HMS *Comus*, which soon after joined the Grand Fleet's 4th Light Cruiser Squadron. Hotham was mentioned in dispatches for his service during the Battle of Jutland in 1916. In December of that year he became Assistant Director of Naval Equipment at the Admiralty, and from October 1917 he was Director of the Trade Division. He was made a CMG in 1919. Relinquishing his naval staff post in 1920, he was appointed to command HMS *Chatham* and took her to New Zealand, arriving in January 1921. He was the first Commodore Commanding, the ★New Zealand Station, and also the first First Naval Member of the New Zealand Naval Board, which was established in March 1921. His seagoing duties limited his capacity to oversee the administrative side of his responsibilities during the next three years. Appointed a CB in 1923, he reverted to the Royal Navy in the following year with the departure of *Chatham* from New Zealand. He was an adviser to the New Zealand delegation at the 1926 Imperial Conference in London. After serving as Director of Naval Intelligence from 1924 to 1927, he retired from the navy in 1929 and for the next twenty-seven years was a member of the Port of London Authority. He was advanced to a KCMG in 1938. A gifted musician, he always took a piano with him to sea.

Hughes, Colonel John Gethin ('Jacky') (13 March 1866–23 July 1954) was the first New Zealand serviceman to be made a DSO. Born at Bluff, he first joined the ★Volunteer Force in 1884 as a member of Timaru's volunteer artillery unit. From 1891 to 1897 he was a member of F Battery in Napier, ending up as battery commander. In 1898 his unit was transformed into the Napier Guards Rifle Volunteers, shortly before he became adjutant and captain of the 3rd Battalion, Wellington (East Coast) Rifle Volunteers. In October 1899 he departed for South Africa in New Zealand's 1st Contingent to the ★Boer War. Although he went as a trooper, he was commissioned in the field shortly after arriving in South Africa. His decoration resulted from his courageous conduct during the defence of what later was christened New Zealand Hill, near Slingersfontein. He was later mentioned in dispatches as well. His outstanding conduct led to his being commissioned in the New Zealand Militia and appointed as Assistant Staff Officer to the Commandant following his return to New Zealand early in 1901. In the following year, he went back to South Africa as an officer in the 10th Contingent. He thereafter held a number of staff and instructional appointments in New Zealand until he was transferred to the ★New Zealand Staff Corps in 1910. He left New Zealand in October 1914 with the Main Body of 1NZEF as its commander's Assistant Military Secretary. At ★Gallipoli, he served in this capacity in the headquarters of the ★New Zealand and Australian Division until June 1915, when he assumed command of the Canterbury Battalion. During the August offensive his battalion lost its way during the initial night attack, and suffered heavy losses in the attempt to take Chunuk Bair when caught in the open by a Turkish battery. His health having deteriorated, he was evacuated from the peninsula in October, and eventually repatriated to New Zealand in mid 1916. For his service at Gallipoli this popular though not very well-educated officer was made a CMG and mentioned in dispatches. His military career ended in 1917.

Hulme, Sergeant Alfred Clive (24 January 1911–2 September 1982) won a ★Victoria Cross for a series of courageous actions on ★Crete. A farm labourer from Nelson, he had enlisted in 2NZEF in January 1940 and become a sergeant in 23rd Battalion by the time the Germans invaded the island. During the fighting at Maleme airfield on 20 and 21 May 1941 he led groups of men in attacks on the German paratroopers. He also took a conspicuous part in the counter-attack on Galatas village on 25 May, clearing an important enemy position with hand grenades. Throughout this period he ruthlessly hunted down German snipers, either alone or in the company of several other New Zealanders and sometimes disguised as a German paratrooper. In all, he is believed to have killed more than thirty snipers during these forays. While stalking yet another sniper on 28 May, he was severely wounded in the arm and had to be evacuated to Egypt. Repatriated to New Zealand, he was discharged from 2NZEF as medically unfit in February 1942, but was subsequently called up for home service between April 1942 and September 1943.

Hunn, Jack Kent (24 August 1906–14 June 1997) was appointed Secretary of Defence in 1963, the first to hold the position following the reorganisation of the New Zealand higher defence arrangements (see DEFENCE, MINISTRY OF). He brought to the post outstanding administrative credentials—he had been an innovative Secretary of Maori Affairs from 1960—

Hydrographic surveying

but no background in military or foreign policy formulation. His period at Defence was marked by much controversy, which was exacerbated by his pugnacious approach. Although he successfully initiated the process of reform, his efforts fully to integrate the armed forces within the ministry fell foul of service resistance, especially by the Army, and government procrastination. More significantly, he strongly advised the government against the commitment of combat forces to the conflict in South Vietnam, putting himself offside with not only the service ★Chiefs of Staff but also the government's external affairs advisers. The revelation of his views thirty years later, by which time events had proved many of them justified, would receive considerable prominence, and establish him in the public mind as a far-sighted and courageous campaigner against the disastrous involvement in Vietnam. At the time his arguments failed to prevent an already very reluctant government from committing a token force in Vietnam. Disillusioned by the ill feeling engendered by this debate and by his difficulties in asserting the role of the Secretary of Defence, Hunn took early retirement late in 1965.

Hydrographic surveying The French and Dutch navies established hydrographic offices in the seventeenth century, but the Royal Navy waited until 1795. By then the realisation that it was losing more ships through grounding than through enemy action made the creation of the office of the Hydrographer of the Navy essential. The work of James Cook, George Vancouver, and Dutch, French, and Spanish explorers in mapping the New Zealand coast pre-dated that administrative reform, but from then on surveying would be led by the Royal Navy, which issued the first catalogue of New Zealand charts in 1839, supplemented by the work of local authorities and others. Many Royal Navy ships charted New Zealand's waters during the course of other duties, but three systematic surveys made the greatest contribution to local cartography. The first, the 'Great Survey of New Zealand', was carried out by HMS *Acheron* and *Pandora* between 1849 and 1855. HMS *Penguin* conducted the second between the late 1890s and the early 1900s, and the third was done by HMS *Endeavour* from 1937 until the outbreak of war in 1939.

Accurate maps are important for navies but they are also crucial for merchant vessels and recreational sailors. Charting New Zealand's rough waters and indented coastlines is a significant undertaking. Not until February 1997 was the plan of Pickersgill Harbour—the last portion of any chart in current use directly attributed to Cook—finally replaced when the RNZN Hydrographer issued a new chart for Dusky Sound, based on 1994–95 work by HMNZS *Monowai*, *Tarapunga*, and *Takapu* updating *Acheron*'s and *Pandora*'s 'Great Survey of New Zealand' of nearly 150 years earlier.

Hydrographic surveying has continued to make use of increasingly sophisticated technology. Cook used the traditional lead during his 'running surveys'; echo-sounders entered service between the world wars; but after 1945 RNZN ships acquired new sonars, large powered boats, and Wasp helicopters to assist their work. By the late 1990s HMNZS *Resolution*'s suite included a Swathe multibeam echo-sounder and the highly accurate satellite-guided Differential GPS (Global Positioning System). The accuracy of a sounding could be plotted to within 30 centimetres. The 1990s brought other changes. When Land Information New Zealand was designated as the National Hydrographic Authority, regulatory functions were removed from the RNZN, which now had to compete for hydrographic survey and charting contracts.

The new RNZN sought its own survey ship after 1945. It requested a seventh Loch class frigate, *Loch Craggie*, then awarded the Leith shipbuilder, Henry Robb Ltd, the contract to build a new vessel from unused Bay class components. Robb began work, but early in 1953 the government cancelled the deal, leaving the RNZN to rely on the ex-Australian River class frigate *Lachlan*, which it had taken over on short-term loan in 1949. HMNZS *Lachlan*, painted in traditional Royal Navy survey colours of white hull and superstructure and buff funnel, would give New Zealand very long service. The ship gained a helicopter deck in 1966. When the need for a replacement arose in the early 1970s, the RNZN again had to accept a hand-me-down, the redundant 1960 Cook Islands service passenger–cargo ship *Moana Roa*. Acquired in late 1974, this vessel, renamed HMNZS *Monowai*, needed expensive reconstruction. The conversion, in Scotland, took longer than anticipated, and *Monowai* was finally commissioned late in 1977; the harbour defence motor launch HMNZS *Paea* had to help fill the gap in the period 1975–78. In 1987 *Monowai* became the first RNZN ship to take women crew to sea. Like their British counterparts, New Zealand survey ships are normally unarmed in peacetime but in 1980 *Monowai* acquired two 20 mm guns for fisheries EEZ enforcement and also later supported RNZN mine countermeasures work. For inshore work the RNZN did better, acquiring new craft in 1980, the 92-ton, steel-hulled HMNZS *Tarapunga* and *Takapu*, which replaced the existing survey motor launches, formerly harbour defence motor launches of the same names.

In late 1996 New Zealand cashed in on post–★Cold War US Navy cutbacks by acquiring cheaply the Stalwart class USS *Tenacious*, a towed array general oceanographic surveillance ship. Taking the name of

Hydrographic surveying

Cook's ship, this vessel was commissioned in February 1997 as HMNZS *Resolution*. Completed in 1989, the 1614-ton (light displacement) ship lacks the helicopter decks of *Lachlan* and *Monowai* and is capable of only a very modest 11 knots, but she offers a new, highly seaworthy hull and major crewing reductions over *Monowai* (laid up 1998). *Resolution* is also configured to replace HMNZS *Tui*, the 1963-built former USS *Charles H. Davis* (1200 tons), which had been on loan to the RNZN since 1970 as a replacement for the former Bird class *Tui*. *Tui* (laid up 1995) worked mainly on underwater acoustics (submarine detection), but supported science and industrial research and also contributed to the RNZN's hydrographic charts.

R.J. McDougall, *New Zealand Naval Vessels* (GP Books, Wellington, 1989); S. Natusch, *The Cruise of the 'Acheron'* (Whitcoulls, Christchurch, 1978).

GAVIN McLEAN

Imperial and Commonwealth conferences

The Colonial Conferences, 1887–1907, Imperial Conferences, 1911–37, and Commonwealth Prime Ministers' Meetings, 1944–69, provided New Zealand's first window on the world. They were the first international gatherings where New Zealand was represented. Although intended primarily for political, constitutional, and trade consultations, they were also occasions for strategic discussions and the making of ★imperial defence arrangements.

The origin of the conferences went back to 1869, the year of the 'garrisons crisis' caused by Great Britain's decision to withdraw the last imperial troops from the self-governing colonies. New Zealand was in the forefront of demands for new forms of imperial and intercolonial consultation such as representation in the Westminster Parliament, an Imperial Congress, colonial diplomatic representation in London, or conferences of the self-governing colonies. These demands were all rejected. Unofficial conferences that met in London in 1869–70 and 1871 failed to advance these ideas. At this time, Henry Sewell, who had been the first Premier, put forward the idea that if New Zealand became independent it could provide better for its defence by treaty.

It was not until 1887, on the occasion of Queen Victoria's Golden Jubilee, that the first Colonial Conference was called. Five years of negotiation about increasing the Royal Navy's presence in Australian and New Zealand waters were brought to completion in the ★Australasian Naval Agreement providing for the first of a series of naval subsidies in support of an ★Australian Auxiliary Squadron. At the second Colonial Conference, held at the time of Victoria's Diamond Jubilee in 1897 (there had been a trade conference in Ottawa in 1894), the naval subsidies were renewed and, after the conference, Cape Colony also offered a subsidy. A proposal for exchanging army units was discussed in general terms. By the time of the next conference, in 1902, at the time of the coronation of King Edward VII, expeditionary forces from the self-governing colonies had taken part in the ★Boer War. Seddon now proposed the general adoption of a New Zealand scheme for creating an ★Imperial Reserve, comprising forces specifically designated for service overseas, but the proposal was not followed. Natal and Newfoundland offered modest naval subsidies. It was also agreed that the conferences should be institutionalised and held at four-year intervals.

At what proved to be the last Colonial Conference, in 1907, decisions were made to style as 'Dominions' those colonies with responsible government and to hold quadrennial Imperial Conferences of Prime Ministers. The original Dominions were Canada, Australia, New Zealand, Newfoundland, Cape Colony, Natal, and Transvaal. (The last three joined with the Orange Free State in 1910 to form a single Dominion, the Union of South Africa.) On defence, it was agreed that Dominion representatives might be called to attend the ★Committee of Imperial Defence when their interests were involved. The British explained their recent creation of a General Staff and suggested that an ★Imperial General Staff should be formed, which could be called on to advise Dominion governments. The British also wanted the Dominions to provide torpedo boats and submarines for their defence, but the Australian delegate talked of an Australian-controlled local naval force. A similar idea for a local navy was under consideration in Canada.

Before the Imperial Conferences began, a special Imperial Defence Conference was held in London in

1909. A Dreadnought-building race between Britain and Germany had prompted a new development in the naval subsidy idea. New Zealand had offered to pay for the cost of a Dreadnought-type ship (two if needed). The British were now willing to accept the principle of Dominion navies, but suggested each should be based on a 'Fleet Unit' (made up of one battlecruiser, three cruisers, six destroyers, and three submarines) and conditions of service permitting full naval careers for the officers and other ranks. Australia went ahead and agreed to buy a battlecruiser as flagship of an Australian navy. New Zealand suggested that its battlecruiser should be flagship of the China Squadron, which should visit Dominion waters and also include New Zealanders among its crews (see NEW ZEALAND, HMS). The British hoped that the Australian fleet unit, along with the Royal Navy's East Indies and China Squadrons, would be the nucleus of an Empire Pacific fleet. Australian hopes that New Zealand would contribute to an Australasian fleet unit were dashed when New Zealand preferred that its infant Dominion naval force should be a division of the Royal Navy. The British outlined their progress in creating the Imperial General Staff, to which Dominion army officers might be attached, and the Dominions agreed to adopt British army organisation and doctrine.

The first Imperial Conference met in 1911. As the British wished to renew the *Anglo-Japanese Alliance, the Dominions were consulted by calling their representatives to join the Committee of Imperial Defence for the discussions. The sequence of four-yearly meetings was interrupted by the outbreak of war in 1914, but in 1916 Prime Minister Lloyd George decided to call an Imperial Conference and also invite representatives from India. In addition to the Imperial War Conferences (as they were called) in 1917 and 1918, there were more intimate meetings of Prime Ministers, known as Imperial War Cabinets, where the war situation was discussed.

In the 1917 Conference the New Zealand representatives criticised British naval neglect of the Pacific, and it was agreed that the Admiralty would draw up plans for post-war Pacific defence. A scheme based on the principle of a unified navy was presented in 1918. It envisaged an Imperial Naval Authority to exercise overall control (on which Dominions' representatives would sit), and Dominion Naval Boards to control recruiting, training, and dockyards locally. This proposal was rejected. Instead, in 1919 Admiral of the Fleet Lord *Jellicoe was sent to the Dominions and India to advise them individually on naval defence. His proposals for the Pacific provided the main theme of imperial defence discussions at the Imperial Conferences that were held, at increasing intervals, over the next two decades—in 1921, 1923, 1926, 1930, and 1937.

While the prime topics at the Imperial Conferences were political cooperation and constitutional status—culminating in the Statute of Westminster of 1931 making the Dominions as independent as they wanted to be—important defence matters were tackled in simultaneous meetings of the Committee of Imperial Defence. Here Japan (though still an ally) was identified in 1921 as the most likely enemy in the Pacific and a new Empire Pacific Fleet with a major new dockyard at Singapore was proposed. The British government balked at the cost of the new fleet, but decided to build the Singapore naval base to service the Main Fleet when it needed to operate in the Pacific. This was announced at the 1921 Imperial Conference during discussions about the renewal of the Anglo-Japanese Alliance. The base was to be a place of concentration for the fleet in the defence of the Empire east-of-Suez for which Dominion contributions were sought (see SINGAPORE STRATEGY).

The need for the Singapore base was seen as more urgent after the Washington treaties and the ending of the Anglo-Japanese Alliance. At the 1923 Imperial Conference appropriations for site preparations were announced. New Zealand offered an initial contribution of £100,000, but this was not actually used because Britain's first Labour government cancelled the project in 1924. The base was renewed on a smaller scale after Labour lost office and at the 1926 Imperial Conference the British were able to announce a £2 million contribution from the Federated Malay States. The New Zealand Prime Minister, Gordon Coates, discussed options for a New Zealand contribution while at the conference, and a £1 million contribution was announced in the following year. The second Labour government in Britain slowed down the project and sought Dominion endorsement for this at the 1930 Imperial Conference. Here George Forbes, the New Zealand Prime Minister, emerged as the most vocal opponent, claiming that Pacific Ocean security depended on the Singapore base and that New Zealand regarded its contribution as an insurance policy. After using New Zealand's ratification of the London Naval Treaty as leverage, he acquiesced when the British reaffirmed that the base would eventually be completed. In meetings with the Chiefs of Staff Committee, a New Zealand representative indicated that the Dominion was contemplating creating a branch of the Committee of Imperial Defence and the possibility of stationing a New Zealand battalion in Singapore or elsewhere.

Within the next few years the strategic situation was revolutionised by Japan's occupation of Manchuria in 1931, its attack on Shanghai in 1932, Adolf Hitler's coming to power in Germany in 1933, and Italy's invasion of *Abyssinia in 1935. Rearmament commenced, and the (now infrequent) Commonwealth meetings

Imperial and Commonwealth conferences

were warned of Britain's overextension. During Prime Ministers' Meetings at the time of the Silver Jubilee in 1935, Dominion leaders were made aware of the need for a new naval standard. This should allow the fleet to act on the defensive and as a deterrent in the Far East, while at the same time maintaining sufficient strength in home waters to contain Germany. In the event, this standard could never be met.

During the Imperial Conference of 1937, which coincided with the coronation of King George VI, New Zealand was outspoken in criticising British *appeasement of Germany, Japan, and Italy and in demanding assurances about the dispatch of the fleet to Singapore. The Dominion was also a sceptical supporter of an Australian scheme for a Pacific non-aggression pact. The British were concerned to warn the conference that, as well as being threatened at both ends of the Empire, it had recently lost its security in the 'centre' because of Italy's incursion into Africa. However, the Dominions were assured that the security of Britain and of Singapore were the 'keystones' of Imperial defence and that no fears in the Mediterranean would deter the dispatch of a fleet to the Far East.

Shortly after the end of the 1937 Conference Japan went to war with China and a little over two years later the *Second World War broke out in Europe. A conference (called the Dominion Ministerial Visit) was convened in October 1939 when the British reiterated their promise to send a fleet to the Far East, but said they could not 'tether' one there before war broke out in the region. During this conference New Zealand announced that it would send an expeditionary force to the Middle East. Consultation in wartime was continuous, mainly by daily exchange of cables and occasional prime ministerial visits to London, when Dominion leaders were invited to attend the British War Cabinet. In 1943 there was talk of an Imperial Conference, but, instead, in 1944 the first of a series of informal Commonwealth Prime Ministers' Meetings was held. Here the impending Allied invasion of Europe was discussed. The Australians proposed the creation of a Commonwealth Secretariat.

Over the first two post-war decades there were Commonwealth consultations nearly every year and, at simultaneous meetings with the Chiefs of Staff Committee, defence arrangements in the Middle East, South-east Asia, and the Pacific were discussed. In 1946, the first post-war British strategic review identified the Soviet Union as the most likely threat. The principle of regional responsibility for defence was agreed and a system for exchanging services liaison staffs was arranged. There were informal discussions of a revised strategic review at the time of the royal wedding in 1947. In 1948 the attendance of newly independent India, Pakistan, and Ceylon induced a change of atmosphere. The British felt they could not divulge intelligence derived from the United States in the full meetings, so separate discussions were held with representatives of the old Dominions. The British sought help in defending the Middle East in a future war with the Soviet Union, and New Zealand responded by offering to send an army division, five air squadrons, and surplus naval forces (see MIDDLE EAST COMMITMENT).

In 1949, the special Prime Ministers' Meetings that arranged for India's continued membership as a republic also discussed maintaining unity in the *Cold War. During a unique Foreign Ministers' Meeting in Colombo in 1950, there was general talk about the possibility of a Pacific Pact to match the Atlantic Pact. In the 1951 Prime Ministers' Meeting, the *Korean War and the Japanese Peace Treaty were discussed. Australia and New Zealand made it clear that they were seeking an American security guarantee— an aspiration that bore fruit in the *ANZUS Treaty later in the year. Meetings held in 1953, at the time of the coronation, discussed the Korean War armistice talks. In the meetings of 1955 and 1956 Britain's progress in testing an H-bomb (in which they were assisted by Australia and New Zealand) were discussed and arrangements were made for the creation of the *British Commonwealth Far East Strategic Reserve in Malaya.

The *Suez crisis of 1956 marked a watershed in Commonwealth consultation. The British government deliberately avoided frank consultation with its old partners. Australia and New Zealand were the only members to offer moral, but not military, support. Thereafter, as issues relating to decolonisation came to dominate Commonwealth meetings, defence issues became less relevant. In 1957 Ghana, the first black African member, attended. In 1961 South Africa quit at the same time as Cyprus, the first small state, joined. Henceforth there was a permanent non-white majority. In 1964 and 1965 the future of Rhodesia dominated the meetings and arrangements were made to create the Commonwealth Secretariat, which took over from Whitehall the arranging of future meetings. The Wilson government, elected in 1964, began the 'Withdrawal from East of Suez', which was completed in the mid 1970s. Although a remnant of the old-style defence cooperation lingered on in the *Five Power Defence Arrangements, the Commonwealth had long ceased to be a defence organisation. The Commonwealth Heads of Government Meetings (CHOGMs), held every two years from 1971, discuss defence only in terms of global trends, international disarmament endeavours, and *peace-keeping.

J.E. Kendle, *The Colonial and Imperial Conferences, 1887–1911* (Longman, London, 1967); H.D. Hall, *Commonwealth* (Van

Nostrand Reinhart, London, 1971); W.D. McIntyre, *The Commonwealth of Nations 1869–1971* (University of Minnesota Press, Minneapolis, 1977).

W. DAVID McINTYRE

Imperial defence was the basis of New Zealand's defence strategy for more than a hundred years. At one level it denoted a system designed to protect the far-flung British Empire; at another, it was the framework for coordination of effort between the United Kingdom and its self-governing colonies of settlement (later Dominions) which evolved in the second half of the nineteenth century. The former centred increasingly upon the role of seapower, and the need for a navy capable of preserving the sea lanes between the imperial centre and the outlying colonies. The latter assumed increasing importance as Great Britain's capacity to provide this seapower was challenged by potential rivals. Britain looked to the self-governing colonies to assume some of the burden of defending the worldwide empire, a proposition which raised issues of control of forces provided, especially among the larger, more assertive colonies. A conflict between centralists and localists developed, especially in relation to naval activity. The *Boer War emphasised the value of colonial contributions on land to the general effort, and prompted New Zealand to advance the concept of an *Imperial Reserve.

Imperial defence, as it evolved in the early twentieth century, was founded on three basic assumptions: that the Royal Navy was the heart of the system, and must be sustained in a position of pre-eminence; that the Dominions must, behind this shield, meet their own requirements for local defence, accepting that so long as the Royal Navy had not lost command of the seas the scale of attack on them would be within their capacity to meet successfully; and that in time of war the Dominions should assist in the general defence of the Empire. So long as major potential enemies lay in Europe, imperial defence was effectively provided by a powerful but distant navy, concentrated to protect the United Kingdom (the essential foundation of the system). To send a powerful force to the South Pacific for example, an enemy would have to expose its own homeland to a force sitting astride its sea routes to the wider world.

Britain's declining ability to sustain the naval supremacy it had enjoyed in the nineteenth century, and the emergence of potential enemies outside Europe, brought into question the concept of imperial defence, particularly between the world wars after the termination of the *Anglo-Japanese Alliance. Although British naval power proved insufficient to protect South-east Asia in 1941–42, the concept of imperial defence underlay the ultimately successful British Commonwealth effort in the *Second World War. Imperial defence, in modified guise as Commonwealth defence cooperation, continued to underlie New Zealand's approach to defence after the war. In 1949 it committed itself in advance to participation in another Commonwealth defence effort (see MIDDLE EAST COMMITMENT), but Britain's decline as a world power, changes in weaponry, and decolonisation undermined the concept of imperial defence during the 1950s. Vestiges of it lingered on in South-east Asia until Britain's withdrawal in the early 1970s.

Imperial Defence College was established in London in 1927 to provide higher education for senior service officers and members of the civil service. The Dominions were also invited to send small numbers of officers to undergo the one-year course in classes which ranged between twenty and thirty-two before the *Second World War. The officers examined general issues of defence strategy, organisation, and international affairs, as well as focusing on specific issues of *imperial defence which had been referred to the college by the British authorities. Five New Zealand military officers attended the college before the Second World War, along with one civilian (in 1939). After the college reopened in 1946, New Zealand sent one or two officers (and three in 1964 and 1966) to attend it in most years. By 1967 thirty-seven had graduated from it, many going on to hold senior positions in the New Zealand armed forces or civil service. The post-war courses no longer involved examining specific contemporary problems, but a new development was the introduction of visits first to various countries of relevance to their defence studies and later also to industry. The college was renamed the Royal College of Defence Studies in 1971.

Imperial General Staff As a means of ensuring the coordination of the military resources of the Empire, the possibility of forming an Imperial General Staff (IGS) was raised at the Colonial Conference in London in 1907. In each Dominion, it was envisaged that a section or 'local headquarters' would study, in consultation with the Chief of the Imperial General Staff, the respective local defence problems. Following agreement by the Dominion governments, the proposal was implemented in 1909. All officers performing general staff duties throughout the Empire became members of the IGS, though still responsible to their own governments. A New Zealand Section of the IGS was designated within the General Headquarters in Wellington. From April 1912, there was also an Oversea Dominions Section of the IGS in the War Office in London, upon which Colonel A.W. *Robin represented New Zealand until he was relieved in December

235

1913 by Major G.S. ★Richardson. They provided useful reports to Wellington on a range of defence matters. With the outbreak of the ★First World War, the representation lapsed. The designation 'New Zealand Section of the IGS' ended in 1919. Although the system was not revived, a vestige of it remained in the 'Imperial' in the title of the British Army's chief of staff, the CIGS, until 1964.

Imperial gift aircraft Following the ★First World War, the British government offered Commonwealth governments unused surplus military aircraft for use in creating their own air forces. When New Zealand was offered 100 unused machines in 1919, it accepted thirty-five, though only twenty-nine were received in 1920—twenty Avro 504K trainers and nine De Havilland 9 light bombers. Two of the Avro 504Ks were retained by the military authorities, and the remainder were lent to the private aviation companies then beginning to flourish. Sent to the Canterbury Aviation Company at Sockburn (later Wigram), the two Avros joined four other military machines (two Bristol F2B Fighters and two De Havilland 4 light bombers) which had been brought to New Zealand by Colonel A.V. ★Bettington, when he visited the Dominion to advise on air requirements in 1919. These six aircraft formed the basis of the New Zealand Permanent Air Force set up in 1923. The early aircraft saw hard service as training machines. One DH 4 became the first aircraft to fly over the summit of Mt Cook/Aoraki on 8 September 1920. Most of the 'gift' aircraft were broken up in the late 1920s.

BRIAN LOCKSTONE

Imperial Reserve was a New Zealand initiative aimed at harnessing colonial support for ★imperial defence and assisting planning by providing some certainty of availability, in contrast to the ad hoc nature of the colonial contributions to the ★Boer War. In May 1900 the Premier, R.J. ★Seddon, proposed the formation of an 'Imperial and Colonial Reserve Force', which would consist, in New Zealand's case, of ordinary members of the ★Volunteer Force. Enlisted for a set term (Seddon thought five years), they would meet certain training obligations. The British government, it was proposed, would pay for the equipping of the force (with the colony concerned meeting the interest costs on the capital charge) as well as three-quarters of the running costs, such as pay and capitation. Seddon had in mind a 10,000-strong Reserve in New Zealand, including 2000 Maori. Subsequent consideration by Parliament led to a tightening of the concept: legislation in October 1900 provided for a 2000-man Reserve, restricted to field artillerymen and mounted riflemen who would be engaged for three years. New Zealand's share of running costs would apply only to those incurred within New Zealand, and Parliament would retain control over its liability for service. Although the proposal was welcomed in London—the Colonial Secretary lauded it as 'the first organised effort of the people of a great self-governing Colony to create a force which shall be available for service wherever the Empire may require it'—there were doubts about the financial and control aspects of the proposed force. When Seddon pressed the idea at the Colonial Conference in 1902, he found Canada and Australia unsupportive, and eventually withdrew it. Some desultory consideration of the proposal continued for a few more years, but Seddon lost interest in it, especially in light of practical objections raised in London, where the idea was seen as imposing a 'certain liability' for an 'uncertain benefit'.

I. McGibbon, *The Path to Gallipoli: Defending New Zealand 1840–1915* (GP Books, Wellington, 1991).

Improvised weapons The use of improvised weapons in New Zealand dates from the earliest days of the colony—a 5.5-inch mortar designed and cast in Sydney for service in New Zealand was employed at Ruapekapeka during the Northern War of 1845–46—but it was only during the ★Second World War that they were developed on any scale. Lacking an industrial base to mass-produce weapons of its own, New Zealand was forced to adopt stopgap measures. Numerous attempts were made by inventors to develop weapons based on surplus items or from easily accessible materials that might be produced at workshops without the need for great technical skill. Most such weapons were made by enthusiasts for the ★Home Guard, and included home-made mortars and grenade launchers. Many of these improvised mortars, bomb throwers, or adapted shotguns would probably have been more dangerous to the user than to an invading enemy, but some reflected considerable ingenuity and engineering skill and received serious attention from the government.

The most well-known New Zealand improvisation was the Semple Tank. Work on a prototype began in June 1940 at the Public Works Department workshops at Temuka. Another two models were built at the Addington Railway workshops. Essentially a mild steel box on a caterpillar tractor, with corrugated steel added to the front to increase protection, it mounted five machine-guns, and had a maximum speed of ten kilometres per hour. However, it was vulnerable and unwieldy, and useful only as a moveable strongpoint for beach defence. Semple tanks were also used for public parades, probably doing little to instil public confidence. In November 1942 the Army returned the Semple tanks to the Public Works Department, and in March 1943 they were converted back to tractors.

Industrial disputes

A Schofield truck-tank undergoes a trial in the presence of members of the War Cabinet and Army officers at Trentham Military Camp in December 1940 (*Alexander Turnbull Library, C-24256-1/2*)

A Semple tank (*War History Collection, Alexander Turnbull Library, C-14276-1/2*)

The Schofield truck-tank was another, less hasty improvisation. Two experimental models were built at General Motors at Petone in 1940. An armoured Chevrolet truck, with the track suspension from a universal carrier for cross-country movement, the design, after initial promise, was shelved as priority went to the production of universal carriers. The second model was sent to England for evaluation in 1943, where tank experts were impressed with the innovative dual wheel/track design. However, there were more conventional half-track vehicles available, and development of the Schofield truck-tank was abandoned.

The lack of automatic weapons for home defence encouraged Philip Charlton successfully to develop an automatic rifle adaptation of obsolete Lee-Metford and Lee-Enfield rifles in 1941. Civilian-owned rifles were commandeered by the government and sent to Morrison's Motor Mowers Ltd, Hastings, for conversion. About 1500 Charlton rifles were made, and production of them was also undertaken in Australia. Parts for about 10,000 were produced. By 1943 the supply of obsolete rifles had dried up, and the urgency had been lessened by the arrival of large quantities of Bren light machine-guns. Production of Charltons was halted, and the rifles were stored at Palmerston North, where most were destroyed in a fire after the war. The shortage of automatic weapons was also met by a submachine-gun designed by Alan Mitchell, the most remarkable feature of which was its astonishing rate of fire, about 1800 rounds per minute. However, development of the weapon was too slow for it to go into production before the war ended. Mitchell also designed a machine-gun with a rate of fire of 6600 rounds per minute, but it was unusable because of its violent recoil. Although New Zealand inventors proved themselves capable of producing effective and unique designs with few resources, the development of promising weapon designs was always hamstrung by New Zealand's lack of industrial development.

Industrial disputes, use of armed forces in

Traditionally the armed forces have been reluctant to become involved in industrial disputes. Initially their

Industrial disputes

role was conceived as aiding the authorities in dealing with disorder which arose from conflict between strikers and scab labour (see CIVIL POWER, AID TO). Immediately after the ★First World War some contingency planning was carried out for the provision of covert military assistance, along the lines of the 1913 intervention, to civilian organisations preparing to deal firmly with industrial unrest. In the event these plans did not have to be implemented, and it was not until the ★Second World War that service personnel were again involved in industrial disputes, this time in a more direct role. Rather than protecting scab labourers, they themselves in effect became the scab labourers, being used as substitute labour. The first such instance occurred during the Second World War state of emergency. In January 1945 troops were ordered to man dairy factories in Waikato when dairy workers went on strike. The temporary employment of service personnel in agricultural work and a range of related activities declared to be 'urgent work of national importance' had been authorised by the Army Board under the Emergency Regulations in 1943, but the absence of specific provision for dairy factories brought into question the legality of the government's action in deploying the troops in this instance, especially when several soldiers refused to work in the factories. A new Army Board order was duly made encompassing dairy factories.

In peacetime, there was no provision for involvement of troops in industrial disputes, except when a state of emergency was in existence. Such a situation required the invocation of the ★Public Safety Conservation Act, Section 2 of which allowed the proclamation of a state of emergency in the event of action which threatened to interfere with the supply and distribution of 'food, water, fuel or light or with the means of locomotion' and so to deprive the community of the 'essentials of life'. Determined to break the power of the Waterside Workers' Union, the National government of Sidney Holland resolved to use these provisions when a waterfront dispute arose in 1950. Similar action had been taken across the Tasman the previous year during a miners' strike, and as in Australia a split in the labour movement allowed the watersiders to be effectively isolated. A state of emergency was briefly proclaimed in September 1950 but a settlement forestalled the use of the armed forces. This merely heralded a much more serious confrontation early in the following year. A new emergency was proclaimed on 22 February after a further stopwork or lockout, depending on which side of the divide one stood. Regulations providing the government with far-reaching powers came into force on the 26th. Each chief of staff was empowered to order members of their respective services to carry out temporary employment in relation to the dispute. Servicemen started work on wharves at Auckland and Wellington on 27 February. This action soon extended to Timaru and other ports and to other sectors of the economy, including shipping, freezing works, cool stores, and mining, as other workers supported the watersiders. The government used the ★Cold War as justification for its actions, claiming that the strike was merely an extension of that conflict to New Zealand.

An improvised system of control emerged. Essential suppliers' committees were set up at the ports where servicemen were involved. Chaired by mayors, with service representatives as members, they were responsible for maintaining the supply of essential foodstuffs and services to their local communities. Service personnel were available merely as a labour force for this purpose. The committees had no executive power over them. Of the services the Army, with its three-district structure, was the best placed to meet the community needs. In Auckland overall command of service operations was placed in the hands of the commander of the Northern Military District, who chaired a working committee established under the local Emergency Suppliers' Committee. A combined services headquarters was established at the district headquarters to coordinate the work of the services, and the commander was assisted by a committee of senior naval and air officers in the area. An RNZN officer (later an RNZAF officer) commanded the service personnel engaged at Auckland. In Wellington, there was an Action Committee, chaired by the General Manager of the Wellington Harbour Board, which met daily to carry out the directions of the local Emergency Suppliers' Committee. Service representatives then arranged the distribution of personnel to ships and other tasks. The commander of the Central Military District chaired a Services Committee, which coordinated the services' work. Similar ad hoc forms of control were instituted at the other ports.

By the end of March 1951 there were approximately 3200 regular service personnel engaged, 43 per cent of whom were from the RNZAF. (No non-regular servicemen were involved.) Air force personnel worked in freezing works and cool stores, loading out carcasses into Army trucks. Three hundred naval personnel worked on Auckland wharves, but 200 had to be withdrawn to man about twenty coastal vessels. Ratings from HMNZS *Taupo* and *Lachlan* mined coal on the West Coast. From 14 March women were also deployed, the first being eighteen Wrens who took over a cafeteria and tea stands at Auckland wharves, thereby releasing RNZN cooks for other duties. The peak manning figures for each service (not necessarily at the same time) were: RNZN 930, Army 1170, RNZAF 1425.

The service personnel initially went about their unusual tasks with gusto. The greater speed with which they worked as compared with the watersiders—some estimates were as high as 100 per cent—drew considerable comment, though the fact that they worked shorter days and handled easier cargoes tended to be overlooked. In all, servicemen handled 778,193 tons of cargo during the emergency. They generally did all that was expected of them, one of the few exceptions being when some airmen refused to unload race horses, contending that horse racing was not essential to the community in an emergency. Two men were killed in accidents: a naval rating at Westport and a soldier employed in the hold of an overseas vessel at Wellington.

The services inevitably suffered a loss of operational efficiency as personnel were diverted to industrial duties. Training programmes were disrupted. Most normal RNZAF activities came to a standstill, with the exception of *compulsory military training and apprentice training. All annual leave between February and May was deferred. The RNZN's planned programme was also upset. *Taupo* and HMNZS *Bellona*, which had been exercising with the RAN, were recalled, and *Lachlan* suspended surveying operations. All Army activities were ruthlessly pared, and on 13 March 1950 CMT was suspended until further notice.

As the dispute dragged on, service enthusiasm steadily waned. There was growing resentment at the apparent failure to apply sufficient pressure to get the watersiders back to work and a feeling that the armed forces were being used 'as a political instrument'. The government perceived political advantages in the situation, for the watersiders had soon found themselves largely isolated. The Federation of Labour had not supported them (the watersiders were members of the rival, and more radical, Trade Union Congress) and the Labour Party chose to sit on the fence. In the end the watersiders were forced to accept defeat, the emergency regulations were revoked on 26 July 1951, and the government won a snap election on 1 September with an increased majority. Service personnel directly involved would later receive a gratuity of five shillings a day for their efforts during the emergency, while all other members of the armed forces, including those serving with ★Kayforce, received two shillings a day.

Between 1969 and 1983 the services mounted seven separate operations (Operation Pluto) to convey passengers across Cook Strait because of industrial disputes involving the ferries. The first, in November 1969, was initiated by the Railways Department, which in effect with Cabinet approval leased an RNZAF Hercules. The uncertain legal position regarding such usage of the armed forces had been clarified by the time of the next intervention, two years later. Under the terms of the ★Defence Act 1971, the Minister of Defence could authorise the use of the armed forces to perform a public service when he considered it 'in the public interest to do so'. Pluto 2 involved 308 flights over a five-day period; 1448 passengers and 737 vehicles were transported. Another dispute led to a further 355 flights during two stoppages in February 1979. The government also initiated Operation Pluto in 1976, 1980, and 1983, when illegal strikes arising from the visits of American warships halted ferry sailings. In each instance, the Army took responsibility for freight and passenger handling at the terminals in Wellington and Woodbourne, while the RNZAF provided Hercules, Bristol Freighters, or Andovers for the flights. Non-essential users were discouraged by the imposition of a substantial surcharge on the normal fare. In 1981 a trans-Tasman Pluto operation was mounted in conjunction with the RAAF when a strike disrupted air services between Australia and New Zealand.

Other instances of service personnel being used in this role have included a dispute at Oakley Psychiatric Hospital in 1971 and a Christchurch firefighters' stoppage in 1975, in both cases relatively brief and uncontroversial interventions. In 1997 900 NZDF personnel served as temporary prison warders during an industrial dispute involving prison staff.

M. Pedersen, 'Aid to the Civil Power: The New Zealand Experience' (MA thesis, Massey University, 1987).

Industry The Colonial Ammunition Company (CAC), established in 1885 by Major John Whitney, was New Zealand's first defence industry. Difficulties in procuring ammunition from Great Britain during that year's Russian scare had pointed to the need for a local source of supply. Production of cartridges for the New Zealand Military Forces began at the Mount Eden factory in 1886, and two years later the CAC established a factory at Footscray, Victoria, to meet the ammunition requirements of Australian colonial forces. By 1897 the CAC was producing more than a million cartridges annually for the New Zealand forces, though the ammunition was considered 'very unreliable and gave general dissatisfaction'. The output had increased sevenfold by 1914. Although there was no other defence industry in New Zealand at this time, saddlery and uniforms were obtained from local suppliers.

In the ★First World War it was apparent that procurement of military equipment was beyond the capacity of the Defence Department. A Ministry of Supply was established in 1915. The Minister of Supply, Arthur Myers, accepted that New Zealand's lack of an industrial base precluded any major industrial war effort. While the CAC increased its production, other manufacturing efforts were mainly confined to boots

Industry

and uniforms for 1NZEF. In contrast, Australia had made considerable progress in establishing its own defence industry by 1918.

New Zealand's industrial potential in time of war again came under scrutiny in the late 1930s. It was decided in 1938 to establish a Ministry of Supply (based on the Department of Industries and Commerce) as soon as war began, and stockpiling of essential supplies was commenced. With the outbreak of war Daniel Sullivan became Minister of Supply, and Controllers of various branches of industry were appointed to supervise and regulate New Zealand's ★war economy. It was expected that New Zealand's war industry would be similar to that of the previous conflict: the production of woollen cloth, clothing, and boots, and a relatively small output of small-arms ammunition. The first priority was the provision of food (particularly butter, cheese, and meat, but also fruit and vegetables) to Britain and later United States forces in the Pacific. Most sectors of the economy simply converted existing production over to wartime uses. The clothing industry, for example, produced more than a million battledress suits as well as blankets, boots, and greatcoats by the end of the war, while production of civilian clothing fell. Similarly, the building industry shifted production away from housing to the construction of aerodromes, camps, depots, and fortifications. Expenditure on ★defence construction rose from £3 million in 1939 to nearly £18 million in 1942. Whereas most war production was simply the manufacturing of existing items for a military purpose, the government deliberately created a linen flax industry in 1940 to meet urgent demands for linen fabric. Seventeen factories were built to process linen flax to meet British war needs.

Even before the war New Zealand could not meet its military equipment requirements from either British or Australian sources, both of which were devoted to their own country's rearmament programmes. New Zealand, it was clear, had no choice but to try to meet its own needs from local resources, and this became even more urgent with the onset of the ★Pacific War in December 1941. Small-arms ammunition was not a major problem. By 1940 two million small-arms cartridges a month were being produced by the CAC. Concern about the factory's security led to its transfer to Hamilton in April 1942. At its peak production, more than 1200 people were producing 74 million rounds annually. For other armaments, there were only two plants in New Zealand capable of large-scale production—the Ford Motor Company and the General Motors Company. These plants depended on small-scale workshops for specialised production of parts—a dispersion which was to prove a major obstacle to expanding production. Nevertheless, the output of the two plants was impressive, given the improvised nature of the work. The Ford Motor Company factory at Lower Hutt produced more than 5.5 million hand grenades and mortar bombs with the assistance of British and Australian experts. At the General Motors factory at Petone Bren gun carriers were assembled, with parts imported from Australia and Canada; an initial batch had been manufactured at the Petone railway workshops. By the time production of Bren gun carriers ceased in December 1943, about 1170 had been built. The other major defence industry was boat building and repair undertaken at engineering firms, boat-building yards, and railway workshops. Thirteen Castle class minesweepers based on trawler designs, twelve Fairmile anti-submarine boats, and 443 tugs, barges, and other small craft were built for the RNZN, the RNZAF, and American forces in the Pacific. Other war production was of small, relatively simple items such as water bottles, fire-fighting equipment, mortars, and steel helmets; about 10,000 Sten submachine-guns were manufactured at school workshops in Hawke's Bay. Radios were also supplied to the Eastern Group Supply Council in India. By 1943 more than 270 contractors were supplying war materiel. New Zealand's industrial war production was a considerable achievement for a country with a complete absence of heavy industry, a small and decentralised light industrial sector, a relatively unskilled workforce, and a paucity of raw materials.

Given New Zealand's lack of heavy industry and tiny defence base, it is not surprising that no defence industry developed after 1945. The government continued to purchase ammunition from the CAC until 1965, when a cheaper source of supply from Australia was preferred. In contrast to Australia, there was little emphasis on self-sufficiency in New Zealand, though the value of building up sources of supply in the South Pacific was regularly acknowledged by ministers and officials and underpinned the 1983 memorandum of understanding with Australia on defence supply. Defence-related manufacturing in New Zealand was long confined to limited 'one-off' orders. In the 1980s Pacific Aerospace Corporation at Hamilton, for example, built CT4 Airtrainer aircraft for the RNZAF, and two hydrographic inshore survey vessels were built at Whangarei for the RNZN. Clothing, rations, and 'off the shelf' items were also supplied to the New Zealand armed forces by local contractors.

During the 1990s New Zealand's defence industry received a big boost from its participation in the Anzac frigate project. The agreement signed in 1989 provided for A$585 million worth of defence contracts to be awarded to New Zealand firms, which were also given the right to compete on equal terms with Australian firms in bidding for Australian defence contracts.

Some fared very well under this regime, and there was disappointment among manufacturers and workers alike when the government, in 1998, determined not to take up the option of obtaining further Anzac frigates. Other firms have moved into wider defence markets: Oscmar and Marine Air Systems, for example, successfully developed electronic products such as battlefield simulation systems. Participation in the defence arena has benefited New Zealand industry generally, by increasing awareness of the importance of quality assurance. Firms have gained experience in a highly competitive market and access to new technologies. In 1999 New Zealand companies exported $100 million worth of defence-related products.

J.V.T. Baker, *War Economy* (Historical Publications Branch, Wellington, 1965).

Infantry, soldiers who fight on foot, have throughout history constituted the backbone of most armies. In modern times the 'foot-sloggers' have been equipped with increasingly deadly weapons and adopted new tactics; they are more likely to drive or fly on to the battlefield than to march, as in the past. But their fundamental role of closing with and destroying the enemy and seizing and holding terrain remains unchanged. During the twentieth century the basic unit of organisation for infantry was the battalion, commanded by a lieutenant-colonel, and organised into companies (commanded by captains or majors) and platoons (commanded by lieutenants). Initially a somewhat looser structure existed in the *Volunteer Force. In 1895 corps had been linked in battalions, with six to eight in each. This tended, however, to be a paper organisation: few corps met the establishment laid down, and the battalions were merely assortments of cyclists, Rifles, Highlanders, and Guards. The creation of the *Territorial Force in 1911 completely changed the picture, and brought New Zealand into line with British organisational structures. The motley Volunteer battalions were replaced by sixteen (later increased to seventeen) 1000-man battalions formed on a strict territorial basis. In 1913 the initial eight-company composition was changed to a four-company organisation, with each company having 227 men formed in four platoons of four sections each. A section of two machine-guns was attached to the battalion headquarters. Tactics at the time were based on opposing lines of infantrymen engaging in a fire-fight until one side gained the ascendancy and concluded matters with a bayonet charge. Training was limited mainly to musketry and drill, and infantrymen were not expected to display much initiative or intelligence.

An infantry brigade of four battalions (Otago, Canterbury, Wellington, and Auckland) formed part of the *New Zealand Expeditionary Force in 1914. There was further expansion of the infantry from reinforcements in Egypt in early 1916, with second battalions of the Otago, Canterbury, Wellington, and Auckland regiments forming the 2nd Infantry Brigade. Another four battalions raised in New Zealand during 1915 were designated 3rd New Zealand (Rifle) Brigade. This brought the New Zealand Division up to an establishment of twelve battalions. A fourth infantry brigade was created in 1917, its units becoming the third battalions of the Otago, Canterbury, Wellington, and Auckland Regiments. However, this brigade was disbanded in 1918 to provide reinforcements for the other three brigades. This allowed the New Zealand Division to maintain four-battalion brigades at a time when their British counterparts were reduced to three.

As every infantryman knew, it was the infantry who bore the brunt of the fighting. A stanza of the poem 'The Infantry', by P.J. Jory, which was published in *New Zealanders at the Front* in 1917, summed it up for them:

They're writin' in the papers of a scientific war,
An' not of winnin' it by men but by machines—
Mechanical devices are the ones wot's goin' to score
An' new inventions wot'll give the Germans beans;
But when it comes to rootin' out the cunnin' wily 'Un,
The infantry must do it with the bay'nit an' the gun!

Casualties among the infantry were extremely heavy. Even relatively successful or minor operations could decimate a battalion, and prolonged fighting could effectively destroy it. The 2nd Battalion, Canterbury Regiment, for example, suffered 746 casualties in the fighting on the Somme in 1916. Of the 14,817 men of 1NZEF who died as a result of enemy action, 11,967 were infantrymen. Their losses were exacerbated by the relatively unsophisticated assault tactics made in the early part of the war. Going over the top could be a deadly affair given the ascendancy of enemy defensive firepower. Even in 'quiet' periods the front line was a dangerous place because of artillery bombardments. The infantry manning the trenches suffered steady losses. By 1917 infantry were using new techniques to overcome enemy machine-guns and artillery. Technological developments such as *mortars, grenades, and Lewis light machine-guns (and their increasing availability) allowed for the development of flexible tactics based around mutually supporting groups of machine-gunners and 'bombers'. The platoon was now regarded as the smallest tactical unit, comprising two rifle sections, a Lewis gun section, and a bombing section. Battalions were supported by machine-gun platoons, mortar batteries, and—from 1918—attached field guns. By 1918 an infantry battalion had become a highly specialised unit of scouts, machine-gunners, bombers, and marksmen.

241

Infantry

New Zealand infantrymen in a trench at Flers, France, in 1916 (Alexander Turnbull Library, F-66895-1/2)

After the war, the number of battalions in New Zealand was reduced to twelve in 1922—a configuration which remained until 1937, when the regiments were combined to form either 'Composite' or 'Fortress' battalions. In 1928 one of the four rifle companies in each battalion was re-formed as a machine-gun company, and motorcycle, sniper, and mortar platoons were added to each battalion's strength in the 1930s. By the ★Second World War an infantry battalion consisted of three rifle companies and a support company of machine-guns and mortars, with a war establishment of about 776 men. This organisation was retained during the war for New Zealand service, but battalions of 2NZEF adhered to British organisational structures. The infantry of 2nd New Zealand Division were organised into nine battalions, numbered 18 to 26, initially three from each military district, with an additional battalion, the 28th (Maori), to accommodate the desire for a separate Maori unit. In 1942 three battalions were converted to armoured regiments (see ARMOUR), which left the Division deficient in infantry during the ★Italian campaign. The 27th (Machine Gun) Battalion and the Divisional Cavalry were converted to infantry battalions in 1944–45. Each battalion comprised four rifle companies of three platoons, and each platoon of thirty-six men comprised three sections. There was also a support company of six platoons: signals, anti-aircraft, mortar, carrier, pioneer, and administrative. Battalions were augmented with a platoon of eight anti-tank guns in June 1942 and a machine-gun platoon in 1944; the pioneer and anti-aircraft platoons were disbanded. Although varying throughout the war, the establishment was generally about 750 men. The battalion's firepower came from its Bren light machine-guns, each rifle section having one. These were often augmented by 'unofficial' weapons, usually captured German machine-guns. Nonetheless, the battalion's 350 or so riflemen, armed with bolt-action rifles, were the mainstay of the unit, and bore a disproportionate share of the casualties. In all, 3931 of the 5624 members of 2NZEF who died as a result of enemy action were infantrymen. More than forty battalions had meanwhile been raised for the home defence of New Zealand by mid 1942, and six battalions formed part of 3rd New Zealand Division, which participated in the ★Solomons campaign.

The post-1945 Army in New Zealand was organised into an infantry division of nine battalions with a view to fulfilling the ★Middle East commitment. Each battalion had an establishment of 933, organised in four companies of three platoons each, with a support company of anti-tank weapons, mortars, and assault pioneers. Following the shift of New Zealand's focus from the Middle East to South-east Asia in 1955, infantry training changed from a desert to a jungle orientation. Ambushing and patrolling skills became the main concern. For service in Malaya a regular battalion was raised. A battalion now consisted of two, three, or four rifle companies, with a support company of machine-guns, mortars, signals, anti-tank, and assault pioneer platoons. The establishment was 39 officers and 714 men, which has remained the basic organisation to the present. In 1964, with the formation of the Royal New Zealand Infantry Regiment, the nine Territorial infantry battalions were reduced into six. All seven infantry battalions, including that in Malaya, were numbered as battalions of the one regiment. Between 1967 and 1971 infantry companies from 1RNZIR in Malaya took part in the ★Vietnam War, integrated with Australian troops in an Anzac battalion. In the 1970s changing strategic circumstances led to a shift in emphasis away from jungle warfare towards an airmobile light infantry battalion, with the Territorial battalions forming the nucleus of a skeleton infantry brigade. In 1974 a second regular battalion (designated 2nd/1st Battalion) was formed. In a further restructuring in 1992 the two regular battalions became the basis of a light infantry brigade, which would be rounded out by the Territorial Force. As a result the six Territorial infantry battalions were reorganised as infantry training depots to provide additional companies for the regular force battalions and to form a composite Territorial battalion. A 250-strong reinforced infantry company was sent to Bosnia-Herzegovina between 1994 and 1995 (see PEACE-KEEPING).

Influenza pandemic The last months of the ★First World War coincided with the severe second wave of the world's deadliest pandemic of modern times, the misleadingly named 'Spanish influenza', which killed an estimated 25–30 million people in 1918–19. One theory links the severity of this pandemic to chemical warfare in 1918, suggesting that widespread use of mustard gas on the ★Western Front caused a mild 'normal' virus to mutate suddenly into a 'killer-flu'. The first New Zealand soldiers to die from 'Spanish flu' were members of the 40th Reinforcement on the troopship *Tahiti*, which caught the start of the severe second wave at Sierra Leone in August 1918; more than seventy men died at sea or in hospitals in England. Another 252 soldiers died from influenza in France and Palestine, while 281 died in camps in New Zealand. Featherston was worst hit, with 177 deaths (including eighteen Maori soldiers) in November, at a death rate of 22.6 per thousand, one of the worst locality rates in New Zealand. By comparison, the civilian population lost 6091 Europeans and 2160 Maori in November–December 1918—nearly half the total of New Zealand soldiers killed in the 1914–18 conflict.

The Army played a significant role in helping New Zealand to cope with the 'Spanish flu'. Teams of medical orderlies were sent from Awapuni Camp to smaller North Island towns such as Dannevirke and Ngaruawahia, while army beds and blankets were used to set up temporary influenza hospitals in Wellington. Major T. McCristell, the Director of Equipment and Ordnance Stores at Defence HQ, was later hailed by relief workers as 'our Napoleon' for organising these hospitals so quickly. News of the Armistice on 11 November 1918 reached most New Zealand towns just as the epidemic was spreading, and many places went ahead with long-planned processions and celebrations despite alarming reports of deaths in Auckland. The resulting crowds helped to spread infection from towns to rural areas. Yet New Zealand was better able to cope with this epidemic which struck in wartime than it would have been if it had occurred in peacetime: ★Red Cross, St John Ambulance, and other wartime organisations swiftly transformed themselves into epidemic relief committees.

German Samoa, under New Zealand military administration, suffered one of the world's worst death rates in the pandemic (a fifth of the population died) owing to a neglect of quarantine by the acting medical officer at Apia and the refusal by the military administrator, Colonel Robert ★Logan, of all offers of assistance from American Samoa (where there were no influenza deaths).

G.W. Rice, *Black November: The 1918 Influenza Epidemic in New Zealand* (Allen & Unwin/Historical Branch, Wellington, 1988).

GEOFFREY RICE

Inglis, Major-General Lindsay Merritt ('Whisky Bill') (16 May 1894–17 March 1966) was one of New Zealand's most prominent citizen soldiers. Born in Mosgiel, he graduated from Otago University with a law degree before enlisting in 1NZEF in 1915. He served on the ★Western Front from 1916 to 1918, initially in the 3rd New Zealand (Rifle) Brigade. During the New Zealand Division's attack on the Somme on 15 September 1916, he was for much of the day the only surviving officer in the most exposed section of the front line; for his efforts in stabilising the situation, he was awarded an MC. From March 1917 he was a company commander in the New Zealand Machine Gun Battalion. Between the wars Inglis, who was a lawyer in Timaru, was active in the ★Territorial Force, commanding a regiment (1926–30) and later a brigade (1930–36). With the outbreak of the ★Second World War, he immediately volunteered for 2NZEF, and left New Zealand in command of 27th (Machine Gun) Battalion. As commander of 4th Brigade at ★Crete, he recognised the need for an immediate counter-attack once German forces had seized the vital Maleme airfield, but was restrained by higher command. His conduct after the battle was disloyal and unprofessional. Sent to London to report on what had transpired, he laid the blame for the island's loss at the door of Creforce commander, Major-General B.C. ★Freyberg, who was not in a position to respond to the charges. Nevertheless, he continued to serve under Freyberg in the ★North African campaign, leading his brigade with success during the breakthrough to Tobruk in late

243

Intelligence

1941 (for which he was made a DSO) but spoiling this effort by failing effectively to organise his brigade's defences, with disastrous consequences. At Minqar Qaim in June 1942, he won a bar to his DSO for his 'brilliant leadership' while temporarily commanding the 2nd New Zealand Division during its dramatic breakout. During the next two months he performed without great distinction in the same capacity, as the division suffered a series of disasters, mainly because of the failure of British armour to support New Zealand infantry. After a period of brigade reorganisation at Maadi and sick leave in New Zealand, he returned to 4th Armoured Brigade in March 1944. His role in the ★Italian campaign was relatively undistinguished, not least because of the lack of opportunities for brigade-level action. A drinking problem—from which his nickname among the troops derived—may also have affected his capacity. Overlooked several times as temporary divisional commander, he finally sent an insulting letter to Freyberg, for which he was sent home to New Zealand. Following the defeat of Germany, he was employed by the Allied Control Commission for Europe as director of the Military Government Courts and, from 1947 to 1950, as Chief Judge of the Commission's Supreme Court in the British zone of occupation in Germany. He was made a CBE in 1944 and a CB four years later.

Intelligence, military concerns the gathering of information likely to be of use against an enemy, and the withholding of information likely to be injurious to one's own side from the enemy. The former is termed intelligence collection or espionage in the widest sense; the latter is security intelligence or counter-intelligence. The means by which intelligence gathering or counter-intelligence is carried out may involve the use of agents, the interception of various forms of communications, the application of technical means, or a mixture of these. It should be noted that reconnaissance by military formations is an adjunct of intelligence activity. In the nineteenth century, agents, codes, and mail interception were the means most closely associated with intelligence. During the twentieth century, there was a spectacular rise in technical intelligence gathering, which augmented, rather than replaced, more traditional means. This rise was accompanied by a huge growth in the amount of intelligence obtainable, leading to problems in collation and analysis, and making it more difficult at times to sort out the most useful information. Line-of-sight reconnaissance rose into the sky and then into space, accompanied by developments in photographic imagery, while burgeoning communications interception mined a fertile seam by technically complex means. A trend towards greater up-to-the-minute intelligence collection had begun. Needless to say, these posed complications for counter-intelligence.

In New Zealand, intelligence gathering came from two streams: the centuries-old tradition of using spies by Maori fighting chiefs, and the use of agents by the British naval and military authorities. During the ★New Zealand Wars, quite extensive use was made of agent intelligence by both sides. Examples of Maori activity in this field included the use by Kingite chiefs of a code for certain communications or the collection by ★Titokowaru's men of information before the attack on Turuturu-mokai redoubt. On the British side, intelligence use ranged from an accurate threat assessment before Kororareka to Governor ★Grey's used of agents like Morgan, Gorst, Whiteley, and Volkner, the last-named being one of the few spies to be caught and punished for his activity. Local inhabitants, officials, traders, and missionaries were used, as well as military personnel, like Sergeant William Marjouram of the Royal Artillery, who undertook a spy mission with Robert Parris before hostilities opened in Taranaki in 1860.

During the ★First World War, the intelligence arrangements in the New Zealand Division in France and the New Zealand Mounted Rifles Brigade in the Middle East became reasonably sophisticated. By mid 1918, for instance, the New Zealand Division had an extensive battlefield intelligence organisation, the 'New Zealand Intelligence Service', an elaborate structure from the GSO3 (Intelligence) down to brigades and battalions, with thirty-man intelligence platoons deployed with each battalion. Naval intelligence activities were facilitated by the appointment of a Naval Intelligence Officer in Wellington on 4 August 1914. The practice of intercepting radio signals from enemy warships at sea began almost immediately, with New Zealand radio stations assisting in tracking the progress of the German East Asiatic Squadron across the Pacific prior to the battles of Coronel and the Falkland Islands. This involved close cooperation with naval intelligence authorities in Australia, Hong Kong, and Canada, and with the Admiralty in London. Radio stations established at Awarua, Wellington, Auckland, and Awanui were an integral part of an interception effort maintained throughout the war. An Admiralty Intelligence Centre was established in Wellington under the control of the Naval Intelligence Officer. Another dimension of this naval intelligence effort was the setting up of an extensive system of reporting officers in New Zealand and the Pacific Islands. In both these roles the provision of technical assistance and skilled personnel by the Post and Telegraph Department and the Customs Department was vital.

Between the wars the naval intelligence organisation continued through the agent-based reporting

Intelligence

officer system and further refinements in wireless intelligence using Post and Telegraph stations. The reporting officers, both in New Zealand and in the Pacific Islands, were from a variety of backgrounds, though generally civilian officials of the local administration. In New Zealand they were the collectors of customs at the ports; in the islands they could be resident commissioners, comptrollers of customs, or consuls. The accumulation of extra duties by the local New Zealand naval intelligence officer, who had now become the Staff Officer (Operations & Intelligence), left him overloaded at the outbreak of the ★Second World War.

The ★Organisation for National Security was the government umbrella organisation formed to prepare the War Book. It also had an intelligence dimension overseen largely by the Chiefs of Staff Committee and the Secretary of the ONS. From 1937, there were moves afoot in the direction of coordinating intelligence through a combined services intelligence organisation, although nothing effective was done until late in 1940. There were also plans for a sizeable coastwatching system, although they had not moved very far by 1939.

Intelligence was not accorded any real priority in New Zealand during the war. Minuscule resources were allocated to it, and actions tended to be reactive to operational developments, like the activity of the German raiders in 1940–41 and the onset of the war with Japan. A Central War Room and a Combined Intelligence Bureau was set up in Wellington late in 1940. The latter was essentially an outgrowth of naval intelligence. The CIB did not function well, and it was not until a successor organisation came into being towards the end of 1941 that real progress was made. The new Combined Operational Intelligence Centre, under a Director of Naval Intelligence, was an attempt to pull together the threads of intelligence from all sources to brief the ★Chiefs of Staff with a stream of timely operational intelligence. This involved the production of a variety of intelligence summaries and, for a period, the provision of daily intelligence notes on the operational situation. The Army proved to be less committed to the venture and the RNZAF, after a slow start, moved off on its own tangent, leaving the COIC as mainly a naval organisation. The naval signals intelligence 'Y' section (see below) was of special significance in its work, and it played a useful role in gathering maritime intelligence. An unfortunate incident occurred in 1941, when some COIC intelligence summaries fell into the hands of a German raider after the merchantman *Nankin* was captured at sea. Although this information was passed to Tokyo, it is unlikely to have been of great value to the Japanese high command. (There is no substance to later claims that these summaries contained explicit references to ★ULTRA intelligence or to the fact that Japanese naval ciphers had been broken by the Allies.) The COIC maintained close links with the Royal Navy's Far East Combined Bureau, the RAN in Melbourne, the US Navy's intelligence organisations in Melbourne and Honolulu, and the Royal Canadian Navy.

Signals intelligence played a vital role in Allied success in the Second World War, nowhere more so than in the ULTRA intelligence obtained from intercepted German signals traffic. New Zealand's effort in this field was centred on the RNZN's 'Y' organisation, which under Lieutenant H. Philpott coordinated the interception of enemy signals by the new high-frequency direction-finding (H/F D/F) stations at Awarua, Waipapakauri, Musick Point, and Tamavua (in Fiji). This initiative depended on a close working relationship with the Post and Telegraph Department, under whose auspices the bulk of the wireless operators for interception work were obtained. The station at Awarua may have had a role in the location of the German raider *Admiral Graf Spee* early in the war. The New Zealand H/F D/F stations located enemy submarines off Sydney before the famous harbour raid in 1942, although the RAN authorities failed to heed the warnings. Following the move of the British Far East Combined Bureau from Singapore to Colombo, the RNZN 'Y' organisation further developed its links for operational purposes with the US Navy. In late 1942 a radio-fingerprinting (REB) station was set up near Blenheim, operating on the H/F D/F stations' network. This station's targets were Japanese submarines. Along with the H/F D/F stations, it provided the 'Y' organisation with useful operational intelligence until May 1944. A small Army 'Y' Special Section at Nairnville Park in Johnsonville was set up by Lieutenant Ken MacKenzie in 1942 with the dual purpose of intercepting illicit communications from within New Zealand (a function which soon fell away) and monitoring Japanese traffic overseas. There was a degree of contact and cooperation between the RNZN's 'Y' organisation and the Army's 'Y' section, although much of Nairnville's intercepted product seems to have gone to the US Navy's intelligence centre in Melbourne, the British–Australian Allied Intelligence Bureau, and General Douglas MacArthur's Central Bureau in Brisbane. This inter-Allied cooperation in signals intelligence was based on the British–American (BRUSA) and Holden agreements, which paved the way for further collaboration in the post-war period as well.

By contrast, New Zealand coastwatching had a patchy record. Despite there being too few stations for the enormous length of coastline, constant efforts were made to reduce the number of stations. Although

Intelligence

coastwatching stations were maintained by all three services and some other agencies, and were supplemented by a rudimentary Air Observer Corps organisation and radar posts, they generally failed to spot intruding enemy vessels. The one exception was a small German vessel which laid mines off Wellington's Port Nicholson in 1941; when reported by the local coastwatching posts, its presence was dismissed by the Naval Officer in Charge, Wellington. At least three intruding enemy submarines (two Japanese and one German) and one surface raider (the *Orion*) went almost unobserved by coastwatching posts: reconnaissance aircraft from the Japanese submarines were noted, and one submarine was seen (even if two sighting reports were dismissed). To be fair, the authorities had to contend with many bogus reports, but the level of surveillance on the New Zealand coast was inadequate.

Coastwatching stations set up on New Zealand possessions like the Chathams, the Kermadecs, and the Auckland Islands also functioned as weather reporting stations. New Zealand took responsibility for coastwatching in a variety of Pacific Islands, some of which were British possessions (see COASTWATCHERS). Reporting to the Navy Office in Wellington, and coordinated in radio networks through a Controller of Pacific Communications in Fiji, these posts provided a useful stream of operational sighting reports.

Counter-intelligence in New Zealand was initially a police responsibility, but perceived deficiencies led the government to set up a separate security service under Army control, using Great Britain's MI5 as a model. The new agency, always understaffed, was at odds with the Police from the outset. There was friction between the Director of the Security Intelligence Bureau, Major Kenneth Folkes, and the Police Commissioner. The former's access to the Prime Minister, together with his energy and somewhat bizarre personality, made him unpopular with local officials, while his agency's probings were resented. A security fiasco in which the bureau was deceived by a confidence trickster (see HOAXES) gave the Police Commissioner an opportunity to engineer Folkes's dismissal. The Commissioner's brother replaced him. As a result, the SIB, an Army intelligence body, now came under the control of the Police, a state of affairs that continued until 1945. A reasonably effective port security organisation was developed.

A number of field security sections were established by 2NZEF during the war. In the Middle East, one was at Maadi in Egypt and another operated with 2nd New Zealand Division in ★Greece, North Africa, and Italy. Four others were set up in New Zealand, and a ★New Zealand Intelligence Corps was established. One of these field security sections went with 3rd Division to participate in the ★Solomons campaign, while the other three were attached to the Northern, Central, and Southern Military Districts. A further field security unit was later formed to go to Japan with ★Jayforce. Some useful interrogations of Japanese POWs were conducted at Featherston POW camp. ★Home Guard units had intelligence officers and intelligence sections. A lack of maps led to these units carefully making their own highly detailed local maps. For a time, fear of a fifth column led to the setting up of commando-type units under Home Guard control as a security measure.

In the Mediterranean theatre 2nd New Zealand Division had a divisional intelligence officer (the GSO3(Intelligence)), an intelligence officer, and an intelligence section. There were intelligence officers and intelligence sections at brigade and battalion levels. In practice, the most important work, designed to ascertain enemy positions, was done at division and battalion level, with the brigade sections operating as conduits between the two. Robin Bell, Paddy Costello, Geoffrey ★Cox, and Dan ★Davin were outstanding senior intelligence officers in 2nd New Zealand Division. Specialists in POW interrogation and aerial photograph interpretation were added to divisional intelligence in the latter part of the war. The 3rd New Zealand Division in the Pacific had a similar intelligence set-up.

The RNZAF intelligence organisation was almost non-existent at the beginning of the war. It expanded with the formation of an Air Intelligence section, within the Combined Operational Intelligence Centre, which developed rapidly in 1942. The establishment of 1 Islands Group, with its operational squadrons and attached intelligence personnel, gave added impetus to the development of RNZAF intelligence capacity. By mid 1944 there were intelligence officers scattered through Allied air headquarters in the Pacific Islands, and personnel in each of seventeen RNZAF squadrons. There was a rotational personnel exchange system in operation between the now separate Air Intelligence Department in Wellington and the forward area, which gave RNZAF intelligence a sharp focus on operational intelligence. By the end of the war, the RNZAF's air intelligence organisation was sufficiently impressive for South East Asia Command to contemplate the RNZAF running an intelligence directorate to support the Commonwealth Air Task Force in the war against Japan, but the end of hostilities removed any such prospect.

Individual New Zealanders served in a variety of intelligence organisations overseas, including the 8th Army's intelligence formations, the Australian coastwatching organisation (Donald Kennedy in the Solomons, for example), the RAN in Melbourne, the Allied Intelligence Bureau, the Royal Navy's establishment in Colombo, and the Special Operations Executive in Europe (John ★Mulgan, among others). Half the personnel of the ★Long Range Desert Group were New Zealanders, engaged in behind-the-lines reconnaissance and sabotage.

With the end of hostilities, there was an abrupt rundown of the New Zealand intelligence organisations. The three services continued to support separate intelligence organisations until the late 1960s, when they were brought together under what was to become the Directorate of Defence Intelligence. The ★Malayan Emergency, the ★Confrontation with Indonesia, and the ★Vietnam War meant a certain amount of intelligence activity for the ★New Zealand Army. The formation of the New Zealand ★Special Air Service in the 1950s saw a revival and development of special operations skills, including long-range reconnaissance. The signals intelligence effort continued after 1945, with New Zealand becoming a party to the United Kingdom–United States (UKUSA) signals intelligence agreement of 1947–48. Both the RNZN and the RNZAF contributed personnel to the post-war signals intelligence activity. The New Zealand Combined Signals Organisation looked after signals interception. In 1977 it was reorganised as the Government Communications Security Bureau (GCSB). The development of a small, essentially analytical intelligence body began in 1949 with the Joint Intelligence Organisation, which became the Joint Intelligence Bureau four years later, the External Intelligence Bureau in 1975, and the External Assessments Bureau (EAB) in 1988. The Special Branch of the Police looked after internal security until 1956, when a new security agency, the Security Intelligence Service (SIS), was set up under Brigadier H.E. ★Gilbert. Although not under military control, the GCSB, SIS, and EAB have a good leavening of former military personnel among their staff. Coordination of intelligence activities in New Zealand is provided by the Domestic and External Security Secretariat.

JOHN TONKIN-COVELL

Isitt, Air Vice-Marshal Sir Leonard Monk (27 September 1891–21 January 1976) was the first New Zealander to serve as Chief of the Air Staff. The son of a member of Parliament, he was born in Christchurch, and received part of his education in England. His military experience was in the ★Territorial Force from 1911. He served with 1NZEF in Egypt and France during the ★First World War. Badly wounded on the Somme in 1916, he was hospitalised in England and, following his recovery, joined the Royal Flying Corps. Granted a permanent commission in the New Zealand Military Forces in 1919, he provided refresher courses for former RAF pilots. A variety of posts in the embryonic air force between the world wars included command of the bases at Wigram and Hobsonville. He was attached to the RAF in 1926–27. In 1937 he became one of the inaugural members of the New Zealand Air Board, with responsibility for personnel issues. After attending the ★Imperial Defence College in England,

Captains L.M. Isitt and T.M. Wilkes with the De Havilland 4 light bomber in which they made the first flight over Mount Cook/Aoraki on 8 September 1920 (*RNZAF*)

Italian campaign

he was posted to Canada in 1940 to represent New Zealand on the supervisory board of the *Empire Air Training Scheme and on various purchase and supply bodies. After serving as Air Attaché in the New Zealand Legation in Washington in 1942, he established the RNZAF headquarters in London before returning to New Zealand to become Deputy Chief of the Air Staff. As Chief of the Air Staff from July 1943, he oversaw the RNZAF's massive expansion to meet the needs of the *Solomons campaign. His skills as an administrator were reflected in the efficient training and replacement systems put in place to support this commitment. Given the RNZAF's substantial role in the *Pacific War, it was fitting that he should represent New Zealand at the Japanese surrender ceremony aboard USS *Missouri* in Tokyo Bay in September 1945. Following his retirement from the RNZAF in 1946, shortly after being made a KBE, he took a leading role in commercial aviation.

New Zealand troops moving forward to the front line pass a divisional sign at Gambettola in 1944 (*War History Collection, Alexander Turnbull Library, F-7695-35mm-DA*)

Italian campaign from 1943 to 1945 is New Zealand's only major theatre of war not shared with Australian troops. As the *North African campaign, in which both South Pacific Dominions had been involved, drew to its successful conclusion, Allied strategists were undecided as to the future direction of the war. Anxious to engage German forces in Europe immediately with seasoned troops from North Africa and eliminate Italy from the war, British commanders strongly advocated the opening of an Italian front. They were also attracted by the opportunities that a successful Italian campaign would open up in the Balkans. Their American counterparts, on the other hand, were less convinced about the possible benefits of an invasion of Italy. Although favouring an immediate invasion of France, they eventually acquiesced in an Italian commitment, though the strategic aims were fundamentally opportunistic and a compromise. Not until May 1943 was agreement reached between Churchill and Roosevelt to delay the invasion of France until 1944 and instead to invade Italy, beginning with Sicily. British and American forces took the island in July–August 1943.

As the British and Americans haggled over strategy, the Germans moved sixteen divisions into Italy under the command of Field Marshal Albert Kesselring. When Italy surrendered on 8 September 1943, they were well placed to react immediately and vigorously to seize control of most of the country, though not to prevent the lodgment on the Italian mainland of the US 5th Army (under General Mark Clark) and the 8th Army (under General Sir Bernard *Montgomery). The 2nd New Zealand Division soon joined the latter, landing on Italian soil in October 1943—an event which had been preceded by much soul-searching in Wellington, as the New Zealand authorities sought to determine the appropriate place for their country's continued contribution to the Allied war effort.

Determining the focus of New Zealand's war effort, Pacific or Mediterranean, had been a difficult issue for New Zealand ever since the *Pacific War began in December 1941, especially after Australia withdrew its forces from the Middle East to defend its homeland. There had been a consensus, however, that New Zealand's troops should remain with 8th Army until victory had been achieved in North Africa, at which point their future deployment would be reconsidered. As the North African campaign drew to a close, the New Zealand government resisted Churchill's pleas for the division to be made available for the planned invasion of Sicily. The only New Zealand personnel participating in that brief campaign were those serving in the RAF and Royal Navy. When the issue became pressing in May 1943 Prime Minister Peter *Fraser, after some initial indecision, set about securing approval for the retention of the division in the Mediterranean, skilfully persuading both the Cabinet and Parliament to accept that course. It was agreed that long-service members should be given furlough in New Zealand. There followed a long period of reorganisation for the division in Egypt, during which the 5th and 6th Brigades were reunited with 4th Brigade, now equipped as an armoured brigade with Sherman tanks. Reinforcements were absorbed, new equipment issued, and the men given warm clothing suitable for the Italian winter before the division embarked at Alexandria for Italy.

By November the bulk of the division had concentrated at Bari, which was to become the principal base for New Zealand troops in Italy for the remainder of the war. In the meantime the Allied drive up the Italian peninsula had become bogged down before the Gustav Line, in the east marked by the line of the Sangro River and in the west by the Garigliano and Rapido Rivers. The New Zealanders' first task was to cross the Sangro, in preparation for which they began entering the line on 14 November 1943. A few days later New Zealand tanks were in action at Perano, on the river's southern bank, as the division closed up to the river in preparation for the main attack. This went in at 2.45 a.m. on the 28th, with the two New Zealand infantry brigades fording the river and seizing the steep hills beyond at a cost of 150 casualties. For the next few days the advance continued against light opposition. With the fall of Castelfrentano on 2 December, the New Zealanders seemed about to break through the Gustav Line, but German reinforcements were able to establish positions just to the north of Orsogna. On the morning of 3 December New Zealand infantry entered the town but were driven out by tanks, dashing hopes of a quick forcing of the Gustav Line. With its maze of gullies and steep ridges, the area was well suited to defence; the New Zealanders' difficulties were compounded by the ubiquitous mud. On 7 December a more deliberate attack on Orsogna and the Sfasciata Ridge to the north-east was made by 5th and 6th Brigades. Although some gains were made, counter-attacking German tanks and infantry rendered the forward positions untenable, forcing a partial withdrawal early the next morning. Another attack was made on the morning of the 15th to the north-east of Orsogna. After a two-day battle the New Zealanders were still unable to penetrate the Germans' improvised defences. Although 5th Brigade made some ground to the north of the town on Christmas Eve, a stalemate had developed. The number of casualties (particularly among the infantry) and the cold, muddy conditions were taking their toll on the troops' morale, reflected in a platoon's refusal to advance on the 24th. For another three weeks the New Zealanders clung to their hard-won positions. It was a tense, miserable period as the two sides harassed each other, and the engineers laboured to construct and repair roads. Not until January 1944 were the New Zealand troops withdrawn, having suffered 1634 casualties in two months' fighting.

With the Italian front bogged down, the Allied high command decided on a daring operation to break the deadlock, taking advantage of Allied command of the seas surrounding the Italian peninsula. The plan envisaged Clark's 5th Army breaking through the Gustav Line in the west while, simultaneously, the US VI Corps landed behind the German line at Anzio. For this operation 2nd New Zealand Division would come under Clark's command. Its role would be to exploit the breakthrough by driving up the Liri Valley towards Rome. In mid January 1944 the New Zealanders moved across the Apennines to the Volturno area, where they were to prepare for action. However, the offensive did not go to plan: the 5th Army's attack was a costly failure, faltering before the immensely strong German position at Cassino, while VI Corps at Anzio, far from trapping a retreating enemy, soon found itself contained by rapidly redeployed German forces. In early February the New Zealanders were drawn into the Cassino inferno as part of the newly formed New Zealand Corps under Lieutenant-General Sir Bernard ★Freyberg, consisting of their division, 4th Indian Division, and supporting American and British artillery. In Freyberg's absence, Brigadier-General Howard ★Kippenberger became temporary commander of the New Zealand division. Far from driving through a broken enemy, he was confronted with the problem of breaking one of the strongest positions on the German front.

The Gustav Line rested securely on a line of mountains, which was broken only by a ten-kilometre gap at the Liri Valley. The mouth of this strategic valley was overlooked by Monte Cassino, a steep 500-metre high hill topped by the great Benedictine monastery. Below Monte Cassino lay the sheer promontory of Castle Hill, and then the town of Cassino and the Rapido River. The forbidding natural features had been strengthened by demolitions, minefields, flooding, and fortifications, which had allowed the German defenders of Cassino to withstand the attacks of an American corps for nearly three weeks. Although not confident about the task given him by Clark, Freyberg did not dissent, though, conscious of his responsibilities as a national commander as well as a corps commander, he resolved to limit the number of casualties that the New Zealand division would incur. With Clark having rejected a proposed turning movement through the mountains to the north of Monte Cassino, he had no alternative but to mount a frontal attack as previously. He hoped that a heavy aerial bombardment would open the way for the hapless infantry. Convinced that the Germans would not fail to utilise such a commanding feature as the monastery (an assumption which in retrospect proved to be incorrect), he insisted that the building had to be bombed. His request was approved at the highest level, by Commander-in-Chief General Sir Harold Alexander. Freyberg was informed that the air bombardment would take place on 15 February, a full day and a half before his corps could attack. Planning to move the corps's timetable forward to take advantage of the bombing was still in train when the bombing of the monastery began. The operation, which would engender much post-war controversy, proved to be counter-productive: reduced to rubble, the monastery became an even more effective fortress.

Italian campaign

Map 11a The Italian theatre of operations, 1943–45

Italian campaign

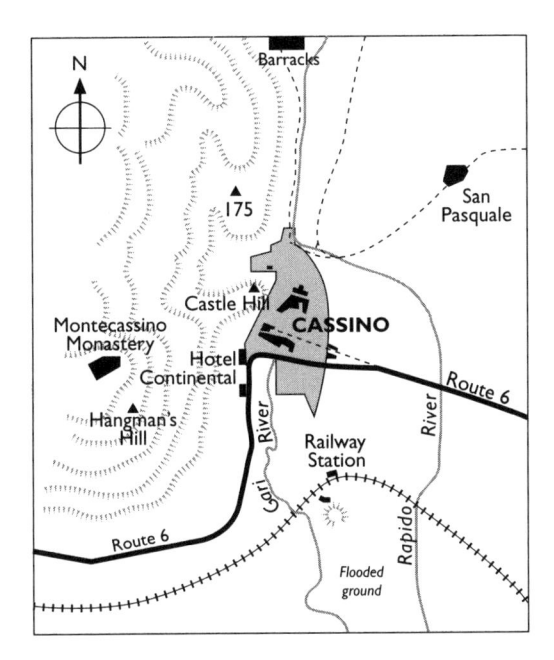

Map 11b The Cassino area, February–March 1944

Under Freyberg's plan, the 4th Indian Division would take the monastery hill from the north while the New Zealanders crossed the Rapido and isolated Cassino township from the south-east, allowing tanks to drive into the Liri Valley. Because of the flooded ground and demolitions, only a single battalion could be used in the New Zealand attack. Attacking about midnight on the 17th, 28th (Maori) Battalion managed to secure positions around the railway station south of the town. Close-quarter fighting followed as the Germans mounted an immediate counter-attack, which drove the New Zealanders out with 130 casualties. With the Indians proving no more successful in their attacks on the hill, a lull in the fighting developed. While the New Zealand Corps clung to its precarious positions in the mud, the high command dithered. When no new ideas emerged, the corps was ordered to proceed with its attacks. By this time the New Zealand division had lost its temporary commander, severely wounded by a mine, and his place had been taken by Brigadier G.B. *Parkinson. Because of delays imposed by wet weather, it was not until 15 March that 6th New Zealand Brigade attacked Cassino from the north, preceded by a massive aerial bombardment which reduced the town to a giant pile of rubble, but failed to smother German resistance. In *Western Front–like conditions, the New Zealand infantry and supporting tanks fought their way into the ruins, while one battalion seized Castle Hill above Cassino. By dusk the attack had lost its impetus, and for the next eight days 6th Brigade continued to feed men into the battered town, without being able to dislodge the enemy holding it. The wrecked Continental Hotel in particular proved to be impregnable. On 19 March 5th Brigade was ordered into the rubble. Although there were now six infantry battalions in the town with armoured support, little progress could be made amid the ruins in the face of the tenacious German paratroopers. By the 23rd Freyberg was forced to admit that the division had 'come to the end of its tether' and called a halt to the fruitless attacks. Isolated outposts were withdrawn and the division went on to the defence. The New Zealand Corps was dissolved on 26 March. Freyberg resumed command of the New Zealand division, which was withdrawn from Cassino in early April. The fighting had cost it 343 lives—a costly failure which ranked alongside Passchendaele as among New Zealand's worst military disasters.

In May 1944 the 8th Army and 5th Army finally broke through the Gustav Line by an outflanking thrust. Monte Cassino fell at last, occupied by Poles with the assistance of New Zealand artillery. A New Zealand armoured regiment attached to a British division and another to an Indian division took part in the pursuit of the retreating German forces, which was often delayed by demolitions, booby traps, and rearguards. On 4 June 1944 Allied troops entered Rome. However Clark, in his haste to occupy the city, had incompetently allowed the Germans to escape. In mid June 2nd New Zealand Division was pulled out of the line, and moved to the Acre area to rest and refit. Many of the troops took the opportunity to visit Rome, where a New Zealand Club was soon established.

Following the successful *D-Day landings in Normandy in June 1944, the Italian theatre's priority in Allied strategy was further reduced. This was underscored, soon afterwards, by the withdrawal of six divisions for the Allied invasion of southern France, which took place in August. As a result, the New Zealanders found themselves essentially participating in a sideshow, one which nevertheless had the effect of tying down German forces which could otherwise have been used in the vital North-west European theatre. In July the New Zealand division moved north to Lake Trasimene. It was given the task of taking the town of Arezzo before moving on Florence. German positions on Monte Lignano were taken and Arezzo fell on 16 July. On the 22nd the New Zealanders began their advance on Florence, with New Zealand tanks occasionally engaging more heavily armoured German Tiger tanks. Good progress was made until the 27th when the division came up against determined German resistance in the Pian dei Cerri hills just south of the city. It took seven days' fierce fighting before German resistance in the hills was broken. The next morning, 4 August, New Zealand troops entered

Italian campaign

New Zealand infantrymen cautiously approach a blown bridge across the Lamone River during the advance to Faenza in December 1944 (*War History Collection, Alexander Turnbull Library, F-7945-35mm-DA*)

the southern part of Florence. During the next two weeks German positions south of the Arno River were cleared before the division was withdrawn for a rest. The advance to Florence had demonstrated the New Zealanders' increasing professionalism, though German mortars and artillery had exacted a heavy toll. The division had suffered more than 1000 casualties in the advance. Question marks remained over its morale: in one action troops had again refused to advance, and there were problems with ★discipline, especially looting. The exhaustion of many of the 'old hands' worried Freyberg. Conscious of the decline of morale in his division, he advised the New Zealand government in June of his belief 'that the time may well be opportune for the complete withdrawal of the 2nd NZEF'. However, there was to be no change: men from the disbanded 3rd New Zealand Division were sent to Italy to reinforce the division. A long period of rest and reorganisation was clearly demanded, but this would have to wait until late October 1944.

With the liberation of Florence, the Allied armies moved north to the next German line of defence, the Gothic Line. The intention was to use the 8th Army in the east to break the line and thrust into the north Italian plain. Taken by surprise, the Germans could not prevent their line being breached. Sent north to reinforce the Canadian Corps on the Adriatic coast in September, the New Zealanders were not immediately committed when the offensive resumed on 13 September, but New Zealand artillery supported the advance of the Canadian Corps and New Zealand armour assisted a Greek brigade in taking Rimini. Having finally cleared the Apennines, the 8th Army had now reached the flat Romagna plain. Hopes were high that it would now be able to employ its mass of tanks and artillery to good effect. But the area was riven by numerous canals, rivers, and floodbanks. The New Zealanders entered the front line on 21 September, and pushed along the coast towards Ravenna. The operation turned into a hard slog among farms and vineyards against German paratroopers and Russians in German service. By the end of the month the New Zealanders also had to cope with driving rain and deep mud. The slow advance bogged down on the Fiumicino River.

A miserable period was spent in early October in sodden conditions, with both armies continuing to harass each other with artillery, mortars, and machine-guns. Not until 11 October did the division resume the attack, crossing the Fiumicino River and pushing on to the Pisciatello River. Anxious to increase the pace of the advance Freyberg tried to use 4th Armoured Brigade to break through to the Savio River, but without success. Although the Savio River was finally reached on 20 October, losses among the tanks had been heavy. Far from breaking out on to the Romagna plain, the New Zealanders had found themselves in a difficult contest in boggy and close country. In seven weeks they had advanced less than thirty kilometres at a cost of 1108 casualties.

While in reserve in the central Apennines, the New Zealand division underwent a major reorganisation.

The need for infantry had been amply demonstrated in the fighting so far, and it was clear that the division, with only two infantry brigades, was at a disadvantage. To remedy this situation the anti-aircraft regiment was disbanded and army service and anti-tank units were reduced to provide more infantry, while the Divisional Cavalry was reorganised as an infantry battalion. Long-service soldiers were sent home on furlough, and leave in Italy was arranged for those who remained behind. A further reorganisation in February 1945, which included forming the Machine Gun Battalion into an infantry battalion, would finally make possible the formation of a third infantry brigade (9th Brigade).

Returning to the front in late November 1944 near Faenza on the Lamone River as part of V Corps, the New Zealanders assisted in operations to cross the river while engineers toiled to build bridges and roads up to the front. At 11 p.m. on 14 December, preceded by the usual artillery barrage, 5th Brigade launched an assault on German positions west of Faenza with the aim of cutting off the town and pushing on to the Senio River. Although Faenza was taken, the brigade could not break the German line. Another attack on the night of the 19th, made by 6th Brigade and supported by more than 300 guns, brought the New Zealanders up to the Senio River. There the offensive was halted, and the division settled down for winter. The fighting was limited to occasional skirmishes and raids. By the time the New Zealand division was relieved two and a half months later, its fatal casualty list since entering the line in November had risen to 194.

When the New Zealanders returned to the Senio River at the end of March 1945, they did so against a foe whose weakening morale was reflected in an increasing number of deserters crossing the line. From 1 April patrols began to secure the southern stopbank of the river. Eight days later, a massive bombardment by about 1700 aircraft and 1300 artillery pieces heralded the opening of a new Allied offensive. That evening the infantry assault, with the support of specialist engineer vehicles and flamethrower tanks, overran the German defences on the Senio. By the next morning engineers had constructed bridges over the river, and the remainder of the New Zealand division moved forward to exploit the bridgehead gained by the infantry. That day the New Zealanders advanced nearly ten kilometres, with 28th (Maori) Battalion crossing the Santerno River to prevent the Germans from establishing another defence line. By 12 April tanks from 4th Armoured Brigade were also across the Santerno. As German resistance crumbled, the division pushed on to the Sillaro River, which was stormed on the night of the 15th, and beyond to the Gaiana River, where the advance was halted by German paratroopers. In the last set-piece assault of the war for the New Zealanders, the German defences on the Gaiana River were broken with an artillery barrage and flamethrowers preceding the infantry assault. Determined not to let the enemy recover, Freyberg drove his forces on, crossing the Idice River north-west of Bologna by the 20th. The New Zealand division thrust northwards, crossing the Po River on 25 April. The German Army had collapsed by this point, with only pockets of fanatical resistance remaining. Padua was entered on the 28th to the rejoicing of its inhabitants, and the numbers of prisoners of war increased to the thousands. The next day New Zealand troops entered Venice to a tumultuous welcome, before racing on towards Trieste, amid surrendering German units. On 1 May the Isonzo River was crossed, and the New Zealanders linked up with Josef Tito's Yugoslav partisans. German troops in Italy capitulated on 2 May. A tense situation now developed as the Yugoslav partisans sought to take over Trieste. New Zealand troops stood firm, and it was not until mid June that the communist partisans withdrew from the disputed territory. In late July the New Zealanders moved to the Lake Trasimene area, where they began to demobilise.

Launched as an opportunistic attempt to capitalise on the defeat of Italy and bring about a cheap victory in the Mediterranean, the Italian campaign eventually became a strategic backwater. No decisive victory was achieved over the German armies in Italy until the war had already been decided on the vastly more important Eastern and North-west European fronts. Yet the Allied campaign was not unsuccessful. Hitler was forced to commit a proportion of his army's strength to a secondary theatre. While tensions within the Allied coalition and the skill of the German defenders prevented a great victory in Italy until May 1945, the fighting in the peninsula contributed to the grinding-down of German military power. In this theatre 2nd New Zealand Division played a small but significant part in the ultimate defeat of Nazi Germany. The price was high: 2003 New Zealanders lost their lives in Italy, and another 6705 were wounded.

N.C. Phillips, *Italy*, Volume I: *The Sangro to Cassino* (War History Branch, Wellington, 1957); R. Kay, *Italy*, Volume II: *From Cassino to Trieste* (Historical Publications Branch, Wellington, 1967).

J

Jamieson, Air Marshal Sir David Ewan (19 April 1930–) was the government's chief military adviser during the crisis over ★ANZUS in the 1980s. His career in the RNZAF began in 1949. After serving in 75 Squadron at Ohakea from 1954 to 1957, he spent several years on attachment to the RAF in the United Kingdom and Germany. He was commander of the RNZAF in Malaysia during ★Confrontation, and Senior Staff Officer in RNZAF Operations Group from 1967 to 1969. He alternated between command positions, study in overseas staff colleges, and staff positions at Defence Headquarters until 1979, when he became Chief of Air Staff. In 1983 he began a three-year term as Chief of Defence Staff, in which capacity he found himself, after the formation of a Labour government in 1984, confronted with implementing policies which he strongly opposed. He was deeply involved in the negotiation of the projected visit in 1985 of USS *Buchanan*, the sudden rejection of which by the government led to the termination of New Zealand's active participation in the ANZUS alliance (see BUCHANAN AFFAIR). Although dismayed by the conduct of his political masters, he acted with complete professionalism throughout this period. Only after his retirement in 1986 did he become an outspoken critic of the government's approach. His *Friend or All: New Zealand at Odds with its Past*, published in 1990, is a powerful indictment of the Labour government's anti-nuclear stance and of the National Party's eventual adoption of it. He was made a CB in 1981, and a KBE five years later.

Japanese threat Japan loomed surprisingly large in the thinking of New Zealand governments in the years from the 1890s. White New Zealanders, most of them immigrants from the British Isles, carried with them a belief in Anglo-Saxon racial superiority, in the strength of the Empire, and in the ability of the British navy to defend it. From the 1890s the rise of Japan challenged these comfortable assumptions and from that time race and security became the pervasive themes of official statements and public comment about Japan.

Japan's victory in the Sino-Japanese War of 1894–95 drew attention to the vulnerability of the Empire's position in the Pacific. Japan had become a sea power and a potential challenger to the capacity of the Royal Navy to defend New Zealand. At the Colonial Conference in 1897 the New Zealand Premier, Richard ★Seddon, expressed his disquiet at the implications for New Zealand's security of the strength of the Japanese fleet. Japan's victory also raised the spectre of the ★'yellow peril'. Fears that workers accustomed to lower standards of living would undermine the European labouring population led politicians and trade unionists, from 1899 to the 1930s, to back laws designed to restrict all Asian immigration.

Although seen as 'beneficial' to Australasia, the ★Anglo-Japanese Alliance of 1902 sparked little reaction in New Zealand. It ensured that the growing Japanese navy would offset the weakness of British naval power. The Japanese victory over Russia in 1905 roused alarm, however, for it demonstrated the degree of Japan's new strength. Another Anglo-Japanese agreement in 1905 was given a cautiously favourable reception, and in New Zealand the hope was expressed that any Japanese interest in emigration would now be diverted to the Chinese mainland. At the same time it was clear that naval competition between Great Britain and Germany was undermining the capacity of the

British navy to defend New Zealand in the event of war in Europe. New Zealand's unease was fuelled by Japan's annexation of Korea in 1910 and Japanese activity in the Pacific Islands, notably New Caledonia, where Japanese labourers worked in the nickel mines. Nevertheless, Seddon's successor, Sir Joseph ★Ward, supported the signing of a third Anglo-Japanese agreement in 1911. The unpalatable truth was that the Pacific was 'almost bare of British ships' and at the 1911 Imperial Conference the Admiralty had argued that issues of strategy, naval expenditure, and stability made desirable a renewed alliance with Japan. As a long-term measure New Zealand looked to the creation of a British Pacific fleet, as outlined at the Imperial Defence Conference in 1909. With this objective in mind Colonel James ★Allen, the Minister of Defence in the Reform ministry which took office in 1912, favoured the development of a local naval capacity in New Zealand as a contribution to the imperial effort. The ★Naval Defence Act in 1913 was the first step in this process. As Japan became one of the greatest naval powers in the world, New Zealand, it was said, must do everything it could to provide for its own defence.

The ★First World War brought Japan and New Zealand into closer proximity. At the request of the British, New Zealand and Australian forces occupied the German territories in Samoa and New Guinea respectively. Japan, which entered the war on the side of the Allies on 23 August, meanwhile seized the German islands north of the equator—a development which caused Allen in particular much disquiet. On the other hand, the New Zealand government was grateful for the protection of the Japanese navy against the potential threat posed by the German East Asiatic Squadron based at Tsingtao, China, and in the central Pacific when the war began. When the Main Body of the ★New Zealand Expeditionary Force left Wellington for Europe in October 1914, its escort included the Japanese battlecruiser *Ibuki*. With German raiders threatening the vital Allied sea lanes, Japanese cruisers patrolled the South Pacific later in the war and occasionally visited New Zealand.

Japan's support for the Allied cause did not erase New Zealand's suspicion of its post-war intentions. If Japan retained control of the German islands north of the equator—an outcome made likely by a secret British agreement with Tokyo in 1917—New Zealand Prime Minister William ★Massey was determined that Samoa should be New Zealand's outpost of forward defence against further Japanese penetration. In the event Japan, Australia, and New Zealand retained the territories they had occupied as mandates of the new ★League of Nations. Under this regime the territories were to be administered according to the laws of the mandatory state (allowing New Zealand to restrict immigration to them) and could not be fortified. Hostility to Japan became overt when, during the drafting of the Covenant of the League of Nations, Japan sought to have inserted a clause recognising the principle of racial equality. Concerned by the implications for its exclusive immigration policy, New Zealand was among those countries which rejected this proposal, which was not adopted (despite having majority support).

At the Imperial Conference in 1921 the key issues were the future of the Anglo-Japanese Alliance and the maintenance, in the face of financial stringency, of a navy capable of defending the British Empire. New Zealand, like Australia, favoured renewal of the alliance, arguing that Britain had demonstrated a capacity to keep the Japanese loyal, but Canada strongly opposed such a course because of the likely impact on relations with the United States. The issue was deferred when the United States invited the great powers to a conference in Washington to discuss naval disarmament, the Pacific, and China. As a result of these deliberations, the Anglo-Japanese Alliance was superseded by a Four Power Treaty under which Britain, the United States, Japan, and France agreed to respect each other's rights in relation to their possessions in the Pacific. A naval treaty restricted the tonnage and armament of certain classes of battleships, established a naval ratio between the British Empire, the United States, and Japan respectively, and prohibited the construction of any fortifications in the Pacific outside Singapore and Hawaii (see DISARMAMENT). The treaties received a mixed reception in New Zealand. Although an atmosphere of cooperation between the three main Pacific powers had been fostered by the successful outcome of the conference, it was recognised that the Four Power Treaty was weak, as was the League of Nations, while the naval agreement left Japan supreme in the western Pacific and free to build aircraft and vessels other than battleships. The planned British naval base at Singapore had not yet been approved. Its completion, as a measure of insurance against future trouble, became a preoccupation of New Zealand governments in the 1920s (see SINGAPORE STRATEGY). Since the base made sense only if Japan was the potential enemy, it was clear that for the majority of New Zealanders Japan remained a threat.

Those who were chronically suspicious of Japan appeared vindicated by events in Manchuria and Shanghai in 1931–32. The New Zealand press became increasingly critical of Japan's actions there and elsewhere in China. New Zealand voted with the majority at the Assembly of the League of Nations in endorsing the Lytton Report, which found that Japan's actions in Manchuria had not been legitimate measures of self-defence. This precipitated Japan's departure from the League. When an undeclared war broke out between

Jayforce

Japan and China in 1937—the effective start of the ★Second World War in the Pacific—New Zealand was among those League members urging action in support of China. But events in Europe overshadowed crises in the Far East, and in late 1939 New Zealand, in agreeing to dispatch another expeditionary force to Europe, accepted assurances that Japan was unlikely to want to go to war on Germany's side (because of its abhorrence of the Nazi–Soviet Non-Aggression Pact) and that it would be constrained even if it did by the deterrent effect of the Singapore base.

The Japanese attack on Pearl Harbor in December 1941, the sweep of the Japanese through South-east Asia, and the fall of Singapore shocked New Zealanders. The 'Japanese threat' which for fifty years had been more imagined than real now appeared deadly serious. Although New Zealand never featured more than on the fringe of some of the various Japanese proposals for the Greater East Asian Co-Prosperity Sphere (and it was to be isolated rather than invaded in Japanese operational plans of early 1942), this was not evident to New Zealanders alarmed by Japan's rapid advance following Pearl Harbor and aware of the weakness of New Zealand's defences (see ANTI-INVASION DEFENCES). The collapse of British power in the western Pacific brought into question the proper focus of New Zealand's war effort between Europe and the Pacific—a debate not finally resolved until 1944 (see PACIFIC VERSUS MEDITERRANEAN; PACIFIC WAR; SOLOMONS CAMPAIGN). Once the Japanese advance had been halted by American victories and the perceived direct threat to New Zealand had receded, New Zealand policy-makers became preoccupied with seeing that checks were placed on any future tendency of the Japanese to militarism. Concern over Japan's military potential brought New Zealand, with Australia, to pursue a security treaty with the United States, especially after 1947 when it became clear that the Americans were determined, in the face of the developing ★Cold War, to sign a 'soft treaty' with Japan. The ★ANZUS treaty thus became part of the Japanese Peace Treaty arrangements signed in 1951. Meanwhile thousands of ordinary New Zealanders had had their first direct contact with Japanese people, as members of ★Jayforce and ★Kayforce, and the relationships had generally been positive. One outcome of New Zealanders' involvement in the ★Korean War was the arrival in New Zealand of a group of up to fifty Japanese ★war brides. Official perceptions of Japan were slower to mellow. In 1952 New Zealand established a legation in Tokyo in order to obtain intelligence about both Japan and also, more especially, North Asia, which was seen as an area of extreme sensitivity at the time. New Zealand objected to Japan's application to join GATT in 1952. It was not until the 1960s, when the threat of British entry into the European Economic Community galvanised New Zealand into looking for new markets, that serious efforts were made to overcome suspicion of Japan. The expansion of trade in the 1970s, the impact of tourism, confidence in the security relationship between Japan and the United States, increasing contacts in educational and other fields—all helped to remove any sense of Japan as a potential threat to New Zealand's security.

M.P. Lissington, *New Zealand and Japan 1900–1941* (Government Printer, Wellington, 1972); A. Trotter, 'Friend to Foe', in R. Peren (ed), *New Zealand and Japan, 150 Years* (Ministry of Foreign Affairs, Tokyo, 1999).

ANN TROTTER

Jayforce Just six days after Japan's capitulation on 15 August 1945, the New Zealand government agreed in principle to New Zealand's participation in the occupation of that country as part of a Commonwealth force. Its share was eventually settled as a brigade group and an air force squadron. But there was to be a long delay before these forces were committed. The United States, in control of the occupation arrangements, proved to be in no hurry to have a Commonwealth presence, not least because the situation in Japan had proved far easier than anticipated and the objectives of disarmament and demilitarisation had been largely achieved within a short period. Negotiations over the role of the proposed Commonwealth occupation force dragged on, with the result that the official announcement of the establishment of the ★British Commonwealth Occupation Force was not made until 1 February 1946. By this time many in New Zealand doubted the necessity for participation by their country in the occupation. New Zealand policy-makers meanwhile had been grappling with the awkward problem of where to find the necessary troops to fulfil such a commitment. The government's hopes that sufficient volunteers could be obtained from 2NZEF in Italy proved misplaced, and most of the just over 4000 troops needed to fill the ranks of the designated unit for the occupation, 9th Infantry Brigade Group, had to be drafted, mainly from the 13th to 15th Reinforcements. Under the command of Brigadier Keith ★Stewart, this force proceeded to Japan in February 1946. It was replaced in mid 1946 by men specially recruited in New Zealand for Japan on a year's engagement, who were in turn replaced by a further draft of volunteers in mid 1947. Brigadier Leslie Potter took command of the force in July 1946. Although officially 2NZEF (Japan Section), the troops in Japan were generally known as Jayforce. The provision of the air force squadron caused comparatively few problems, since all its personnel were volunteers. In March 1946 14 Squadron RNZAF, equipped with

Jayforce

Corsairs and numbering about 280 pilots and ground-crew, was dispatched from New Zealand under the command of Squadron-Leader J.J. Willimoff.

In the MacArthur–Northcott Agreement of December 1945, the Commonwealth forces had been allocated to Hiroshima prefecture, but the zone was later extended. As a result Jayforce was deployed in Yamaguchi prefecture on the southern tip of Honshu and on Eta Jima Island. Initially 14 Squadron was stationed at Iwakuni (but it was redeployed to Bofu in March 1948). Yamaguchi was a relatively poor rural area of about 3200 square kilometres with about 1.4 million inhabitants. In September 1947 Jayforce took over responsibility for neighbouring Shimane prefecture as well, following the departure of the Indian contingent from the BCOF.

The Commonwealth troops had two main tasks—demilitarisation and demobilisation. The New Zealanders accordingly spent much time, especially in the early months, searching for military equipment. However, Yamaguchi had not had a major military presence during the war, and little materiel was found. Repatriation

A Jayforce patrol passes through a Japanese village (War History Collection, Alexander Turnbull Library, F-261-1/2-J)

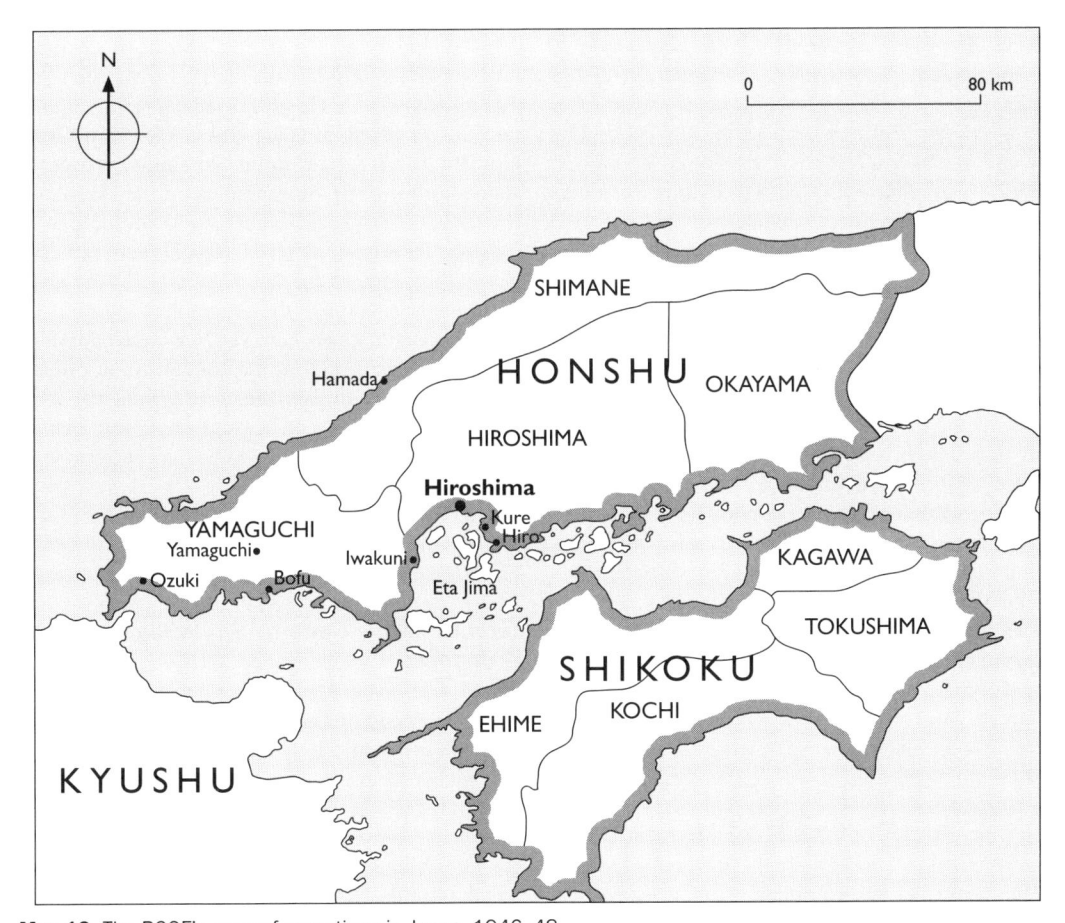

Map 12 The BCOF's zone of operations in Japan, 1946–48

centres, both of Japanese coming home and Koreans being returned to their country, were overseen. Operations designed to prevent illegal immigration of Koreans into Japan were also carried out. Later Jayforce personnel became involved in policing duties, especially anti-blackmarket operations. On six occasions a composite ceremonial guard battalion was sent to Tokyo in rotation with other BCOF units. Parliamentary elections were supervised in April 1946.

On arrival in 1946 the New Zealanders were confronted by unsatisfactory conditions, which further increased the resentment of the drafted troops. Much had to be done to improve billets. The replacement drafts found things better in this respect, but there was less to do. Boredom became the main enemy of the troops. There was increasing contact with the Japanese, as non-fraternisation rules were progressively relaxed. A high *venereal disease rate among the troops was soon causing alarm among senior officers.

Once Great Britain and India had withdrawn their forces from BCOF in 1947, New Zealand's enthusiasm for continued involvement in the occupation rapidly waned. The military necessity for the force had clearly diminished, but a reluctance to remain in an Australian-dominated environment was also evident in Wellington. On 21 April 1948 the Cabinet decided to withdraw New Zealand's forces from Japan. Most of the troops and airmen were back in New Zealand by the end of 1948, and they were followed by the last New Zealand officers in early 1949. During the course of the occupation fifteen members of Jayforce were killed in accidents or died of illness in Japan, and were buried in the Commonwealth cemetery at Yokohama.

In all, about 12,000 New Zealanders, mainly men but including several hundred women, served in the force. It was the first time a large number of New Zealanders had been involved with Asia and Asians. Many of the New Zealanders who served in Jayforce had their adverse preconceptions about the Japanese altered by their experience. They came home with a new appreciation of Japanese culture. Nevertheless the long-term impact of the deployment was limited in a country which remained firmly Eurocentric in outlook. Many of the veterans resented the lack of recognition they received for their service. In 1995 this received partial remedy with the institution of the NZ Service Medal 1946–49 for service in Japan.

L. Brocklebank, *Jayforce: New Zealand and the Military Occupation of Japan 1945–48* (Oxford University Press, Auckland, 1997).

Jellicoe, Admiral of the Fleet Sir John Rushworth, Earl (5 December 1859–20 November 1935) was influential in the determination of New Zealand's defence policy after the *First World War. Entering the Royal Navy as a boy in 1872, he took part in the Egyptian War of 1882 and the Boxer Rebellion in 1900 (where he was badly wounded) and reached flag rank in 1907, in which year he was also made a KCVO. He commanded the Grand Fleet from 1914 to 1916 before becoming First Sea Lord, a post he held until his dismissal in December 1917. In both roles his performance became a matter of controversy, because of his failure in the first to defeat the German High Seas Fleet at the Battle of Jutland and in the second to respond effectively to the German unrestricted submarine campaign of 1917. He was created Viscount Jellicoe of Scapa in early 1918, and later in the year departed aboard HMS *New Zealand on an Empire Mission to advise Dominion governments on naval defence. During the thirteen-month voyage he was promoted to the rank of admiral of the fleet. He reached New Zealand in October 1919, and presented a three-volume report on his departure which pointed to the need to make provision against the threat posed by the Empire's ally, Japan. Although his proposal for an Eastern Fleet of the Empire proved impractical, New Zealand followed his advice in establishing the *New Zealand Division of the Royal Navy. A popular Governor-General of New Zealand from 1920 to 1924, he formed a particularly good relationship with the Prime Minister, W.F. *Massey, and did not hesitate to advise him on imperial issues, even opposing the views of the British government he represented in the Dominion, as over the abandonment of the Singapore base in 1924. Following his return to Great Britain, he was advanced to an earldom. He was appointed by New Zealand as a delegate at the Geneva Naval Conference in 1927, at which he strongly supported the Admiralty's position on cruiser strength. When, however, New Zealand tried to repeat the arrangement at the London Naval Conference in 1930, the British Labour government ensured that he was not present because of its fear that he would undermine its policy of making concessions on the cruiser issue.

I. McGibbon, 'The Constitutional Implications of Lord Jellicoe's Influence on New Zealand's Naval Policy, 1919–1930', *New Zealand Journal of History*, vol 6, no 1 (1972).

Jervois, Major-General Sir William Francis Drummond (10 September 1821–17 August 1897) played a major role in the establishment of New Zealand's *coast defences in the 1880s. After graduating from the Royal Military Academy in 1839, he was commissioned in the Royal Engineers and spent two years at the School of Military Engineering at Chatham. An expert in harbour defences, he served at the War Office from 1856 to 1862 designing a scheme for the United Kingdom, which he proceeded to implement as Director of Works for Fortifications

Admiral of the Fleet Viscount Jellicoe and officers of HMS *New Zealand* with members of the New Zealand Cabinet and officers of the New Zealand Military Forces following a luncheon at Parliament House, Wellington, in 1919. Lord Jellicoe, Prime Minister William Massey, and Sir Joseph Ward are seated in the centre of the front row, and the Minister of Defence, Sir James Allen, is fourth from the left in the second row (*Imperial War Museum, Q107022*)

from 1862 to 1875. He was made a KCMG in 1874. During the American Civil War, he twice visited the United States, and surreptitiously sketched defences at Boston and Portland. His reputation was further enhanced by reports he prepared on British colonial defences in North America and elsewhere. His first association with New Zealand's defences came in 1871 when approached by the Colonial Treasurer, Julius Vogel, for advice; his recommendation of a scheme of heavy guns at the main ports was influential in the colonial government's decision to acquire the necessary ordnance later in the decade. While serving (from 1875) as Governor of the Straits Settlements, he was invited to inspect the defences of the Australian colonies, during the course of which he was transferred to the governorship of South Australia. When, in 1883, he became Governor of New Zealand the colonial government saw advantage in using his expertise to update harbour defence proposals. His views, which were expressed publicly in an address to the New Zealand Institute in October 1884, followed the lines of his earlier advice. New Zealand's security ultimately depended upon British seapower, but the colony must be prepared to deal with enemy raiders which might descend on New Zealand's ports seeking to capture booty or to divert imperial strength from other more important regions. The heavy gun, in his opinion, had not been supplanted by technological advances such as the mine and torpedo; he now recommended that New Zealand obtain the very latest, and expensive, eight-inch guns. The ★Pendjeh crisis of early 1885 induced the government to order these new guns while hastily mounting the less advanced ordnance already in the colony. Jervois informally presided over the emergency programme and later the installation of the more modern ordnance when it arrived. The naming of the fort on Ripapa Island in Lyttelton Harbour after him reflected his key role in the development of New Zealand's defences. Even after he returned to the United Kingdom in 1889, his advice on defence matters continued to be sought by the New Zealand government.

Johnston

Johnston, Brigadier-General Francis Earl (1 October 1871–7 August 1917). Born in Wellington, Johnston was educated in England, where he gained a commission in the Prince of Wales' (North Staffordshire) Regiment in 1891. He took part in the Dongola Expedition in northern Sudan in 1896 and the ★Boer War. In 1914, while on leave in New Zealand, he was seconded to the New Zealand Military Forces to command the Wellington Military District with the temporary rank of lieutenant-colonel. Following the outbreak of the ★First World War, he was appointed commander of the New Zealand Infantry Brigade in 1NZEF. Despite poor health, and, it seems, a drinking problem, he commanded most of the brigade's operations at ★Gallipoli. His lack of fear, impetuosity, and unswerving loyalty to superiors were demonstrated, but he must bear major responsibility for the failure of the attack on Chunuk Bair in August 1915. This is because he volunteered his brigade for the most difficult task of taking the heights, when its men were riven with dysentery and debilitated by months of inadequate food and the constant enemy fire, and because he exercised poor judgment and did not properly coordinate the efforts of his battalions to hold the summit, once it was taken. The use of alcohol as a palliative for his mental and physical condition severely affected his judgment. Despite this, he was made a CB in November 1915, and was also twice mentioned in dispatches. He commanded his brigade on the ★Western Front until December 1916, when he was directed to seek medical advice; diagnosed as a neurasthenic, he did not return to the front until July 1917, when he took command of the 3rd New Zealand (Rifle) Brigade. On 7 August, he was killed by a sniper while visiting exposed outposts. His brigade major at Gallipoli described him as 'a capable tactician with a good eye for country [who] if he erred at all … erred on the side of recklessness and inability to weigh the situation calmly'. He might have had an eye for country but, nonetheless, his record indicates that his ability to adapt tactically was limited. He was, however, one of the few senior regular officers available in 1NZEF's formative years. Because of his close family connections with the New Zealand political, business, and farming establishment, he was no doubt a political asset to 1NZEF's commander, Major-General Sir Alexander ★Godley.

RAY GROVER

Johnston, Brigadier-General George Napier (20 August 1868–3 April 1947). Born in Quebec, Canada, Johnston received a commission in the Royal Artillery in 1888 after spending four years as a cadet at the Royal Military Academy, Kingston. A variety of postings included four years in India as an artillery instructor, shortly after which he was selected, in 1904, for secondment as Artillery Staff Officer for New Zealand. He relinquished this post in 1907, but had performed so well that he returned in 1911 to become Director of Artillery. In July 1914, he became Inspector of Artillery. When 1NZEF was formed in August 1914, he was given command of the Field Artillery Brigade. He served as CRA of the ★New Zealand and Australian Division at ★Gallipoli, and from 1916 held the same position in the New Zealand Division on the ★Western Front. During the war, his services were recognised by his appointment as a DSO and CMG, and no less than eight mentions in dispatches. A most versatile artillery commander, he ensured that his gunners were well trained. Despite inadequate guns and ammunition and unrealistic demands, his artillery on Gallipoli was highly praised. It adapted quickly to the conditions on the Western Front in 1916, supporting raids at Armentières before serving continuously in the line for fifty-two days during the Battle of the Somme. At Messines in 1917, his insistence on frequent practice was justified by the close timing of lifts in the creeping barrages. Improvisation compensated for congestion, mud, and limited cover at Passchendaele in the attack on 4 October 1917. However, even worse conditions prevented adequate guns being brought up and sited prior to the disastrous attack on 12 October. Johnston had warned Major-General Sir Andrew ★Russell on 11 October that his artillery would be impotent during the attack, and so it proved. In response to the open warfare from August 1918 onwards, tactical control of the artillery supporting the infantry was grouped under a commander, who attached himself to infantry brigade headquarters with his batteries up with the leading infantry. By leapfrogging his batteries, Johnston was able to guarantee continuing artillery support for some time after the static fire of flanking British divisions had petered out. This gave the New Zealand Division tactical superiority among the British divisions on the front in the final months of the war. After a brief period as acting commander of the New Zealand Division in 1919, Johnston was discharged from 1NZEF and reverted to the British Army. He was CRA of the 52nd (Lowland) Division from 1920 until his retirement in 1924. He died at Dar es Salaam, Tanganyika.

RAY GROVER

Jones, Frederick (16 November 1884–25 May 1966), a former boot clicker, entered Parliament as a Labour Party member in 1931. His appointment as Minister of Defence in December 1935 reflected the relatively low importance accorded to defence by the first Labour ministry, for he carried little political weight. He retained the portfolio for fourteen years, making him easily New Zealand's longest-serving

Minister of Defence. Though a member of the Council of Defence from 1937, and later of the ★War Cabinet, he had nothing to offer in the debate over New Zealand's defence strategy, and confined himself to administration. After 1940, he tended to be bypassed by service heads, who dealt directly with the Prime Minister, Peter ★Fraser, on matters of importance. He had to contend with embarrassing mutinies by servicemen angered by their poor pay and conditions of service in 1946 and 1947. He was New Zealand's High Commissioner in Canberra from 1958 to 1961.

Jowett (née Berry), Lieutenant-Colonel Vida Eliza (8 February 1893–1 June 1982) was the first commander of the New Zealand Women's Auxiliary Army Corps. Born at Waimangaroa, she was the Dominion President of the Plunket Society for many years and was a member of the Dominion Central Executive of the Women's War Service Auxiliary. She became Chief Commander of the newly established WAAC in July 1942. In forming the corps, she had to fight hard against a reluctance among many male soldiers to accept women's involvement in the military. She was made an OBE in 1944. Although she retired in August 1947, she remained honorary commandant of the corps for another six years.

Judson, Major Reginald Stanley (29 September 1881–26 August 1972), who received three gallantry awards within the space of a few months in 1918, was one of New Zealand's most decorated soldiers of the ★First World War. An Auckland boilermaker, he enlisted in 1NZEF in October 1915. While serving as a corporal in the Auckland Regiment in September 1916, he was seriously wounded. It was not until June 1918, after convalescing in England, that he returned to the front. For his conduct in a series of actions against German positions and patrols near Hébuterne in late July, he was awarded a DCM. The capture of two machine-gun posts at Puisieux-au-Mont on 16 August won him an MM, and his leadership of a bombing party in an attack on German positions near Bapaume ten days later led to his being awarded a VC. In this latter action he had worked his way up a trench and bombed enemy machine-guns with a bravery that observers thought almost foolhardy. After being gassed in September, he was sent to England to an officer cadet training unit and later commissioned. Following his discharge from 1NZEF in 1919, he became a member of the ★New Zealand Staff Corps, with which he served until January 1938. He was recalled to duty for home service in November 1939, and finally retired in 1946.

K

Kain, Flying Officer Edgar James ('Cobber') (27 June 1918–7 June 1940) was the first Commonwealth air ace of the ★Second World War. Born in Hastings, he entered the RAF with a short-service commission in December 1936. When war broke out, he was serving with 73 Squadron, which was quickly deployed to France. He shot down his first German aircraft on 8 November 1939. Always flying with a Maori tiki as a talisman, he was fortunate to escape injury when his aircraft was badly damaged in a dogfight in March 1940. He was again shot down later in the month, though not before claiming two more victims. This brought his personal tally to five, and won him the coveted status of an ace. Tall, handsome, exuberant, and outgoing, he became the darling of an English public starved of heroes during the Phoney War. His popularity increased still further when he became engaged to a glamorous English actress, Joyce Phillips, in April. With the onset of heavy fighting in France in May, his tally steadily rose; by early June he claimed seventeen kills. He was killed accidentally while celebrating his departure on leave: during a low-level aerobatic manœuvre his aircraft struck the ground and went out of control.

M.G. Burns, *Cobber Kain* (Random Century, Auckland, 1992).

Kain (née Tyson), Wing Officer Frances Ida ('Kitty') (9 September 1908–16 August 1997) was the commander of the New Zealand Women's Auxiliary Air Force during the ★Second World War. Dunedin-born, she was a teacher in Malaya when war broke out. Returning to New Zealand, she found work as a dietitian at the University of Otago Medical School before being appointed superintendent of the newly established WAAF in March 1941. She selected, organised, and supervised the WAAF, which by 1943 numbered 3600 women. Impending motherhood led her to relinquish her command in December 1943.

Kawiti, Te Ruki (?–5 May 1854) was a notable warrior and war leader in the Far North. Of the Ngati Hine hapu of Nga Puhi, he took part in the ★Musket Wars and was with ★Hongi Hika at the defeat of Ngati Whatua at Te Ika-a-ranga-nui in 1825. He later intervened in the ★Girls' War. Kawiti reluctantly signed the Treaty of Waitangi in May 1840 but five years later joined Hone ★Heke in his challenge to British authority in the north. Kawiti fought the British at the Battle of Puketutu (8 May 1845), launching attacks against them as they formed up to attack Heke's pa. Kawiti was responsible for the construction of the particularly strong 'musket pa' at Ohaeawai. It incorporated several notable features: palisades to slow the enemy charge, firing trenches, pits to provide shelter from artillery fire. Kawiti was not content to sit still—in a daring sortie on 1 July his men seized a British flag and caused the infuriated British commander, Colonel Henry ★Despard, to launch an ill-conceived assault, which was repulsed with heavy losses. Kawiti built a second pa against the British at Ruapekapeka. After a two-week bombardment in January 1846, the British attacked, but he had withdrawn in the hope, it seems, of drawing them into an ambush behind the pa. Heke and Kawiti withdrew after a confused mêlée, and the fighting in the north thereafter petered out.

Kay, Air Vice-Marshal Cyril Eyton ('Cyrus') (25 June 1902–29 April 1993) was born in Auckland and entered the RAF on a short-service commission in

1926. After spending a period as a civil pilot and instructor, during which time he took part in a number of long-distance races, including the first England–New Zealand flight in 1934, he secured a commission in the RNZAF in 1935. When the ★Second World War began, he was in England preparing to ferry out to New Zealand the first six of thirty Wellington bombers which had been acquired for the RNZAF. When these aircraft were immediately made available to the RAF, Kay became a member of 75 Squadron, in which they were placed. He led the squadron's first operational sortie, a pamphlet drop over Germany, on the night of 27–28 March 1940. Later that year, he assumed command of the squadron and was awarded a DFC. Returning to New Zealand in October 1942, he commanded the New Plymouth, Ohakea, and Wigram air bases till the end of the war. After attending the ★Imperial Defence College, and commanding the RNZAF headquarters in London (1951–53), he became a member of the Air Board, with responsibility for personnel matters in 1953. He was Chief of the Air Staff from 1956 to 1958, during which he presided over the RNZAF's 21st birthday celebrations.

C. Kay, *The Restless Sky: The Autobiography of an Airman* (George C. Harrap, London, 1964).

Kayforce was the New Zealand ground force contribution to the United Nations effort in defence of the Republic of Korea from 1950 to 1953. (See KOREAN WAR)

King, Lieutenant-Colonel George Augustus (3 March 1885–12 October 1917) commanded the 'Maori battalion' in the ★First World War. Born in Christchurch, he began his military career in the ★Volunteer Force in 1904. Seven years later, after serving in the North Canterbury Mounted Rifles Volunteers, he became a regular soldier when he joined the ★New Zealand Staff Corps. As staff captain of 1NZEF's Mounted Rifles Brigade, he served at ★Gallipoli and was made a DSO for 'distinguished services in the field'. From March 1916 he commanded the newly formed New Zealand Pioneer Battalion (see PIONEERS), a 'menagerie' of Pakeha, Rarotongans, Niueans, and Maori, welding it into one of the most effective pioneer units on the ★Western Front and earning a bar to his DSO. In August 1917 he took command of 1st Battalion, Canterbury Regiment, but was killed by ★friendly fire two months later at Passchendaele.

Kippenberger, Major-General Sir Howard Karl (28 January 1897–5 May 1957). 'Kip', as he was universally known, was the archetypal New Zealand citizen soldier. A country lawyer from the quiet mid-Canterbury town of Rangiora, he became during the ★Second World War a composed, determined, and widely admired battlefield commander, and a key member of the 2nd New Zealand Division. Then the soldier put a further stamp on national life as a civilian, a studious, authoritative military historian, Editor-in-Chief of the Official War History series, still New Zealand's largest publishing project (see OFFICIAL WAR HISTORIES).

Quiet, intense, and seriously maimed, Kippenberger to many symbolised the triumphs and tragedies of New Zealand's wars. When he died in 1957 at the comparatively early age of sixty, worn down by the strain of his wounds, he was given a hero's funeral. Old soldiers saluted as the cortège passed. For he had earned their affection and respect as much by his leadership as by his evident compassion and regard for their lot. He had been there himself, as a private soldier with a searing, if short, battlefield experience in the previous war. More importantly, perhaps, he was home-grown, a New Zealanders' New Zealander. Never a member of the regular forces, devoid of specialised professional officer training at British staff colleges, he had transcended the exiguous training of a Territorial officer in Canterbury between the wars to become a skilled, forceful leader of New Zealanders in battle at some of the turning points of the Second World War. After it was all over, this part-time soldier wrote *Infantry Brigadier*, a spare, wry, elegant narrative of his war; not only a bestseller, it is also probably the only New Zealand military study ever to earn a place in staff college libraries around the world.

Kippenberger was born at Ladbrooks, south of Christchurch, where his father, Karl, was head teacher. His grandfather had come to New Zealand in 1863 with a small family group from the Rhineland village of Kinderbeuren on the Moselle. His mother, Annie Howard, was of English and Northern Irish stock, daughter of a radical Methodist clergyman and teacher. Howard grew up on a farm near Oxford. He attended Christchurch Boys' High School. His formal schooling was not a success, but he was always a deep and avid reader and discovered military history at an early age. (His personal library of campaign histories, military biography, and history is housed in the Kippenberger Wing of the Queen Elizabeth II Army Memorial Museum at Waiouru.) He worked for a time on his father's farm, but his mind was already captured by the passionate drama and tragedy of war.

At age eighteen, he volunteered for active service, and was dispatched to the ★Western Front in early 1916, not long after his nineteenth birthday. Drafted into the 1st Battalion, Canterbury Regiment, he went 'over the top' three times during the Third Battle of the Somme in September. For five quieter weeks near Armentières in Flanders, he was a battalion sniper

Kippenberger

Lieutenant-Colonel Howard Kippenberger (with pipe) holds a staff conference in Egypt in 1941 (War History Collection, Alexander Turnbull Library, F-687-1/4-DA)

before being wounded in the right elbow from New Zealand artillery fire, falling short. The radial nerve was severed and the bone chipped. Within ten weeks of first marching towards the guns at the Somme, he was invalided home to New Zealand, where he arrived before his twentieth birthday. He was lucky; with remedial surgery he regained almost full use of his arm.

Kippenberger attended Canterbury University College and qualified as a solicitor in 1920. Admitted as a barrister six years later, he became a partner in a Christchurch law firm, but was based in Rangiora. A borough councillor for eight years, he was also founder and later president of the local golf club and captain of the cricket club, boasting that he was the slowest spin bowler in Canterbury. He joined the ★Territorial Force in 1924 and was commissioned as a second lieutenant in the Canterbury Regiment. For years he spent his evenings in dreary drill halls and his holidays crawling about the Canterbury foothills learning basic infantry manœuvres at annual camp. He had steady promotion and in 1936 assumed command of the regiment in the rank of lieutenant-colonel. It was a lonely and unpopular commitment. He later wrote, 'The period 1930–38 was probably the most discouraging the New Zealand Army has ever faced. Those who soldiered on, Regular and Territorial, knew that they had no support from Government or the great majority of the public. It was good experience. No one, professional or amateur, who continued to serve throughout that period, could ever be completely discouraged by the disappointments and disasters we were soon to suffer.'

Kippenberger sailed for the Middle East as the commander of 20th Battalion in January 1940. He shaped them into a competent fighting unit through the long period of working up 2nd New Zealand Division in Egypt, then led them through the frustrations of the futile campaign in ★Greece; during the withdrawal he led a small demolition squad back to the New Zealand lines after being cut off by the rapid German advance. On ★Crete he was made a temporary brigadier; after his motley brigade of untrained Greeks and New Zealand units dematerialised he organised a determined New Zealand assault on a German salient at Galatas before rejoining the 20th in a disciplined retreat across the mountains. When the 8th Army moved to relieve Tobruk in November 1941 Kippenberger was wounded after the battalion's successful night attack on Belhamed ridge. Taken prisoner, he suffered the mortification of watching helplessly while his 'beloved Twentieth' was overrun by German panzers.

After Kippenberger made a cool escape from a German field hospital, divisional commander Major-General B.C. ★Freyberg promoted him to command 5th Infantry Brigade. He came into his own. Steadiness under pressure was amply demonstrated during the New Zealand division's famous breakout at Minqar Qaim when, with brigade transport found to be missing, he crammed his force into Bren gun carriers and any other available vehicles and crashed through the German encirclement. In the battles of El Mreir and Ruweisat during the 'long hot summer' of 1942, when the 8th Army fought General Rommel to a standstill at El Alamein, Kippenberger is widely considered to have excelled—despite the often tragic inadequacies of liaison between British armoured forces and deployed infantry. At the Battle of El Alamein itself 5th Brigade was the only formation in the 8th Army to achieve all its objectives in the initial assault and was again in the van in the subsequent breakout. Kippenberger's services were recognised by his appointment as a DSO. At Medenine, in Tunisia, he organised a classic defence against what was Rommel's last major assault on the 8th Army in North Africa. Confronting a formidable obstacle at Takrouna, 5th Brigade again distinguished itself, although at heavy cost—to the great distress of the Brigadier, whose own tactical plan for the attack has been faulted by historians. Twice during this period he temporarily commanded the 2nd New Zealand Division, while Freyberg was either wounded or elevated to corps command, and he was awarded a bar to his DSO.

After the Axis surrender in North Africa in 1943, Kippenberger went home on a far from restful furlough in New Zealand. Torn between sympathy for the many soldiers who rebelled against returning to the war zone, when there were so many who had not served, and his own stern notions of duty, he undertook several painful speaking engagements to rally the veterans (see FURLOUGH AFFAIR). Rejoining the division, now participating in the *Italian campaign, before the battle of the Sangro River in later 1943, he was engaged in the New Zealanders' less than successful attempts to break the German line at Orsogna. In February 1944 he again assumed command of the New Zealand division in the rank of major-general for an assault on the town of Cassino. In early March, descending from the adjacent Mount Troccio where he had been observing the battlefield, he trod on a mine; one foot was blown off, the other had to be amputated. 'A pity this had to happen, Jim,' he said to his staunch friend and successor as commanding officer of 20th Battalion, Brigadier James *Burrows. 'I was getting on quite well as a soldier.' Following convalescence in the United Kingdom, he oversaw the repatriation of New Zealand *prisoners of war from Germany.

Back home he became an influential President of the RSA (1948–55) and a protagonist of a doubtful cause, the post-war 'populate or perish' campaign. He was made a KBE in 1948. A keen rugby football enthusiast, he stood against national obsessions by repudiating the exclusion of Maori players from the 1949 All Black side to tour South Africa. 'I had the Maoris under my command for two years and in that time they had 1500 casualties and I am not going to acquiesce in any damned Afrikanders saying they cannot go. To hell with them.' So strong was the adverse public reaction that even he felt obliged to withdraw his 'objectionable' remarks some days later.

To Howard Kippenberger, New Zealand patriot, the ultimate test was the mettle of New Zealanders faced with the most testing of circumstances. 'Few were saints, but they were men whom one was proud to command and in whose midst their commander felt humble.'

H.K. Kippenberger, *Infantry Brigadier* (Oxford University Press, London, 1949); G. Harper, *Kippenberger: An Inspired New Zealand Commander* (HarperCollins, Auckland, 1997).

DENIS McLEAN

Kitchener, Field Marshal Horatio Herbert, Earl (24 June 1850–5 June 1916) was the Empire's most prestigious soldier at the outbreak of the *First World War. He had a New Zealand connection: his father had acquired a sheep station in the South Island during the 1860s, and resided on it at times. Kitchener himself did not come to New Zealand in this period, though an elder brother managed the property until late in the century. Commissioned in the Engineers in 1871, Kitchener served as a volunteer in the French Army during the Franco-Prussian War. He took part in the unsuccessful attempt to relieve Khartoum in 1885, and became commander-in-chief of the Egyptian Army in 1892. He led an invasion of the Sudan in 1896, and defeated the Mahdi's army at Omdurman two years later. He was Lord Roberts's Chief of Staff in South Africa in 1899, before succeeding him as commander-in-chief in the November the following year. He oversaw the frustrating but eventually successful operations which characterised the latter stages of the *Boer War. From 1902, as commander-in-chief in India, he instituted far-reaching reforms of the Indian Army. He visited Australia and New Zealand in 1910, and advised both governments on the new Territorial schemes they were introducing. Arriving in New Zealand on 17 February 1910, he received an enthusiastic welcome as a great imperial hero. He went out of his way to be agreeable during his stay of just over a fortnight. He did not prepare any specific report for the New Zealand government, but rather urged it to follow the advice he had given Australia. He placed great importance on the achievement of compatibility between the forces of the two Dominions and recommended the creation of a *New Zealand Staff Corps whose strength would be ensured by training officers at the military college planned by Australia. He also recommended an extension of the *compulsory military training scheme by raising the age limit to twenty-five and a substantial increase in the number of *Territorial Force areas. He endorsed the proposed replacement of the Council of Defence with a GOC. From 1911 to 1914 he was Viceroy of Egypt, and after the outbreak of war reluctantly accepted the appointment of Secretary of State for War in 1914. Foreseeing a long war, he set in motion a vast mobilisation, which saw the British Army grow from twenty to more than seventy divisions, a total of more than 1.5 million men. Kitchener was not enthusiastic about the ★Gallipoli campaign, and eventually agreed to the withdrawal of the troops from the peninsula after a visit to it in November 1915. In the following year, he was drowned when HMS *Hampshire* in which he was travelling to Russia sank after hitting a mine, just days before the hopes that 'Kitchener's Army' would break the impasse on the ★Western Front were dispelled by the disaster on the Somme in 1916.

The Kiwi Concert Party puts on a performance for New Zealand troops in the Volturno Valley, Italy, in May 1944 (*War History Collection, Alexander Turnbull Library, F-5773-35mm-DA*)

Kiwi Concert Party Traditionally soldiers relied for entertainment on their ★bands. However, the rise of popular entertainment in the late nineteenth century and the creation of vast citizen-based armies in the twentieth century led to the formation of units specifically charged with providing entertainment for the troops, reinforcing much impromptu and amateurish activity of a similar nature. During the ★First World War, New Zealand soldiers formed entertainment groups based on the popular vaudevilles, 'pierrots', and music halls of the period. A particular feature of military entertainment groups were men impersonating women for female roles in songs and plays. In 1916 a Divisional Concert Party, 'The Kiwis', was established. It staged nightly concerts and films to raise morale and provide an alternative attraction to French estaminets and brothels. In the ★Second World War 2NZEF commander Major-General B.C. ★Freyberg saw value for morale in establishing a New Zealand Entertainment Unit in January 1941. The 'Kiwi Concert Party', nicknamed 'Freyberg's Circus', had a strength of about thirty men, including a small orchestra, singers, and comedians. A dance band was occasionally provided to the New Zealand Clubs, and smaller concert groups performed at hospitals. Shortly after its first revue, the Concert Party was sent to ★Crete, where it suffered five casualties and the loss of its instruments during the brief campaign which ended with the loss of the island. The Kiwi Concert Party's programme of songs, comedy skits, and serious music proved extremely popular with New Zealand and Allied audiences in North Africa and Italy. Tours were made to Malta and New Zealand. Apart from these unit activities, soldiers were adept at producing their own entertainment. This was especially evident on ★troopships and in POW camps, where concerts and plays were a means of relieving boredom.

While no entertainment unit was established in Kayforce during the ★Korean War, New Zealand troops had plenty of entertainment available to them, especially after the front line became settled. They visited shows staged by various Allied units. In July–August 1952 a New Zealand concert party led by Oswald Cheeseman toured, followed at intervals by at least six more groups. A Kayforce Maori Concert Party, formed later in the war, proved popular with both troops and civilians. New Zealand troops in the ★Vietnam War were also entertained by New Zealand artists and groups such as the Maori Volcanics; as in Korea, they also attended Australian and American concerts. In Malaya a Maori Concert Party had earlier, in 1957, been formed by 1st Battalion, New Zealand Regiment, from Maori soldiers and their dependants. The party gave numerous performances while the battalion was stationed in Malaysia and Singapore during the ensuing twenty-two years, and provided a Maori dimension to ceremonial parades. Since then in New Zealand a NZDF Maori Culture Group, Te Hokowhitu a Tumatauenga, has been formed to highlight the importance of Maori culture in the New Zealand armed forces. It performed at the Royal Tournament in London in 1997.

T. Vaughan, *Whistle As You Go: The Story of the Kiwi Concert Party* (Random House New Zealand Ltd, Auckland, 1995).

Korean War, which began on 25 June 1950 when troops of the Democratic People's Republic of Korea (DPRK) invaded their southern neighbour, the Republic of Korea (ROK), essentially comprised two wars in one. The first, from June to September 1950, was a clash between the two Korean states, with the ROK supported by the United States and some Commonwealth and other states. The second, from Octo-

Korean War

ber 1950 to July 1953, was a contest between the United States and the People's Republic of China, each supported by their respective Korean allies and, in the case of the United States, fifteen other powers.

That two Korean states existed in 1950 was an outcome of arrangements for the surrender of Japan in August 1945 which had resulted in the entry of both Soviet and American forces to the peninsula. The ostensible purpose of this deployment was to take the surrender of Japanese troops, but both great powers were determined to maintain a foothold in this strategic area. The demarcation line on the 38th Parallel was rapidly transformed into a quasi-border as relations between the Soviet Union and its former wartime allies worsened with the onset of the ★Cold War, and both sides encouraged political factions sympathetic to themselves. Partition became inevitable when negotiations to provide a unified Korean administration fell down. In 1948 the ★United Nations oversaw the creation of the ROK with Syngman Rhee as President, to which the Russians responded by establishing the DPRK with Kim Il-sung at its head. Koreans were unreconciled to this outcome, and on both sides of the 38th Parallel there was determination to reunify the peninsula. Border incidents were common.

The June 1950 invasion was initiated by Kim Il-sung, but Josef Stalin's approval was crucial and Soviet assistance in the form of arms and advice was provided to the Korean People's Army (KPA). Catching the South Koreans by surprise, the KPA made rapid progress, capturing the southern capital Seoul within three days of its onslaught. However, with the United States to the fore, the United Nations Security Council had called for a withdrawal, and when this was ignored urged members to assist South Korea. Early in July it set up a UN Command, responsibility for which was delegated to the United States. General Douglas MacArthur, the Supreme Commander, Allied Powers in Japan, was appointed as Commander-in-Chief, UN Forces in Korea.

New Zealand was one of the first states to answer the Security Council's call with combat assistance (sixteen would eventually do so). On 29 June, the government offered two frigates, and HMNZS *Tutira* and *Pukaki* left Auckland on 3 July. They joined other Commonwealth forces at Sasebo, Japan, on 2 August and immediately began escorting supply ships between Japan and the Korean port of Pusan, by then the centre of a narrow pocket. While forming part of the UN Command, they operated within a Commonwealth framework, under the command of a British flag officer. They took part in Operation Chromite, the successful amphibious counterstroke launched by MacArthur at the port of Inch'on, near Seoul, on 15 September 1950. Their role was to escort the troopships carrying the attack force, and then to form part of a protective screen around Inch'on.

Caught between the UN forces at Seoul, which had been quickly liberated, and those advancing from Pusan, the KPA disintegrated, either being captured or fleeing through the hills to the north. The first Korean War had thus resulted in a decisive victory for the UN. The UN's initial purpose was fulfilled: the Republic of Korea had been preserved. Nevertheless, with the DPRK in disarray, the United States was tempted to press forward to achieve the UN's political aim of unifying Korea, despite warnings from Beijing that China would respond forcibly to any UN crossing of the 38th Parallel. When UN forces invaded North Korea on 9 October, they precipitated a new Korean conflict. Although some elements of the UN Command reached the northern border on the Yalu River, Chinese forces, ill-equipped but in large numbers, had secretly entered North Korea, and from late October they mounted a series of offensives, the second of which led to a 'big bug out' of UN forces, which rapidly fell back south of the 38th Parallel. The Chinese People's Volunteers, as the intervening Chinese troops were termed, then endeavoured to drive the UN forces into the sea. Seoul was abandoned to them on 3 January 1951, but stiffening resistance by the UN Command, under a new field commander, General Matthew Ridgway, led to their being held south of the capital.

At this point a further New Zealand contingent joined the UN Command—Kayforce. On 26 July 1950, in response to a further plea from the UN Secretary-General, Trygve Lie, the government in Wellington had agreed to the dispatch of a 1000-man ground force. Arrangements had quickly been made for this force to serve as part of a Commonwealth formation. Kayforce, comprising 16th Field Regiment and small ancillary units, had to be recruited, trained, and dispatched to Korea, and would have missed the war altogether but for the Chinese intervention. There was no shortage of volunteers, five men coming forward for each place within five days. The 1056-man force embarked from Wellington on 10 December 1950, and arrived at Pusan on New Year's Eve. It joined the 27th British Commonwealth Infantry Brigade on 21 January 1951, and was in action for the first time four days later. Thereafter it took part in the operations which led the UN forces back to and over the 38th Parallel, recapturing Seoul in the process.

When, in April 1951, the Chinese launched the opening step of their Fifth Phase Offensive, 27th British Commonwealth Brigade fought a successful defensive battle against a Chinese division at Kap'yong, after filling a gap in the UN line caused by the collapse of a South Korean division. The New Zealand gunners

267

Korean War

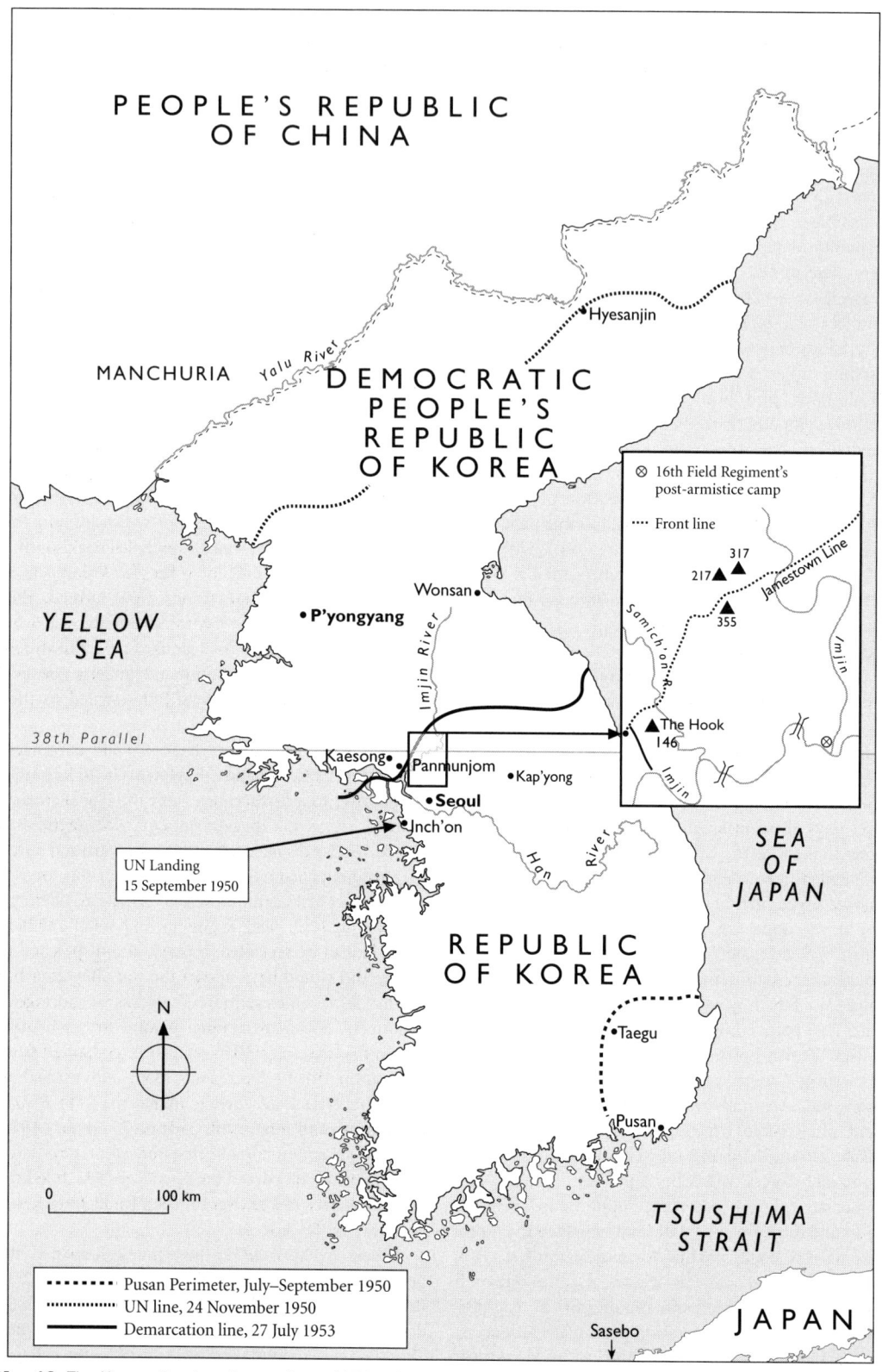

Map 13 The Korean theatre of operations, 1950–53

Kayforce's 16th Field Regiment in action up the Kap'yong Valley in April 1951 (*Bill Olson/National Archives of Canada, PA-151516*)

played a vital supporting role for 3rd Battalion, Royal Australian Regiment, and 2nd Battalion, Princess Patricia's Canadian Light Infantry, from 23 to 25 April. For this action, in which it suffered its first fatal battle casualty, the regiment was awarded a South Korean Presidential Citation, conferred at a parade in February 1952. The Chinese offensive in this sector had been effectively checked, though Kap'yong later had to be abandoned as the UN forces fell back to positions just north of Seoul in good order.

The failure of their Fifth Phase Offensive—its second step in May 1951 proved disastrous—helped convince the Chinese that outright military victory in Korea was beyond their capacity. Armistice talks opened at Kaesong in July 1951, but were soon broken off. Although they resumed at Panmunjom on the following 25 October, progress was very slow. During 1952 the fate of communist POWs would emerge as a seemingly irresolvable sticking point, with the communist negotiators firmly rejecting the UN contention that the POWs should have the right to elect not to be repatriated to their home countries. In the meantime the UN forces sought to keep up pressure on the enemy, and the New Zealand frigates were involved in operations up the Han River which were partly designed to influence the communist negotiators at the nearby talks. UN air forces maintained a strong bombing campaign over North Korea, though with increasing resistance from enemy fighters that were, in many cases, piloted by Russian airmen. In October 1951, now deployed on the Imjin River as part of ★28th British Commonwealth Infantry Brigade, the New Zealand gunners took part in Operation Commando, during which Commonwealth troops advanced from five to seven kilometres through rugged terrain to seize a better defensive line. This was the regiment's busiest month of the war—it fired 72,000 shells. During November 1951, Chinese counter-attacks sustained the intensity of operations, and the Commonwealth troops were pushed back some distance. In responding to a major Chinese attack on the 4th, the New Zealand regiment fired its highest daily total of the war (10,000 shells). During this phase of the war a great improvement in the Chinese forces' artillery capacity made itself felt.

These operations were carried out by the 1st Commonwealth Division, which had been formed on 28

Korean War

July 1951 by combining 29th British Brigade, 28th British Commonwealth Brigade, and 25th Canadian Brigade. New Zealand had welcomed this development—a unique experiment in Commonwealth relations. It agreed to provide a substantial proportion of the divisional signallers, as well as a transport company, as part of an expansion of Kayforce to a strength of 1500 men. The Expansion Draft left Wellington on the *Wahine* on 2 August 1951, but was shipwrecked at Masela Island north of Darwin. The men were eventually flown from Darwin to Japan, where Kayforce's base had been established at Hiro in June 1951. On 15 October 1951 10th Company RNZASC joined the Commonwealth Division, which was commanded by a British general. The non-operational control and general administration of Commonwealth forces in Korea was the responsibility of the Commander-in-Chief, ★British Commonwealth Forces, Korea, an Australian officer, initially Lieutenant-General Sir Horace Robertson, who was also Commander-in-Chief, ★British Commonwealth Occupation Force Japan.

Table 9 RNZN Involvement in the Korean War

Tutira	3 July 1950–3 December 1950
Pukaki	3 July 1950–30 May 1951
Rotoiti	7 October 1950–21 November 1951
Hawea	2 March 1951–8 March 1952
Taupo	29 August 1951–21 October 1952
Rotoiti	7 January 1952–19 March 1953
Hawea	4 August 1952–29 August 1953
Kaniere	2 March 1953–2 March 1954

Dates include transit to and from New Zealand.

At the end of 1951, a stalemate emerged as both sides improved their defensive positions. The front took on the character of a hilly ★Western Front. Much bitter fighting took place around the two bastions of the Commonwealth sector, Hill 355 and the Hook. The New Zealand gunners were kept busy during this phase of the war supporting infantry patrols, occasionally providing defensive fire to repel Chinese attacks, reducing enemy trenches and strongpoints, and providing routine harassing fire. In all, they would fire more than three-quarters of a million shells before the end of the fighting. They earned a reputation as an extremely proficient element of the Divisional Artillery. Other New Zealanders quietly performed their duties as signallers, drivers, infantrymen (nine regular officers and NCOs were attached for periods to the Australian battalions), and engineers. Seventeen Regular Force personnel, mainly NCOs, also gained combat experience while serving with British armoured units in Korea. Some relief from the conditions at the front was provided by leave schemes which allowed men to spend up to three weeks in Japan. At sea, New Zealand seamen took part in patrolling mainly on the west coast, and helped to protect South Korean–held islands. Successive reliefs ensured that all six New Zealand frigates saw service in the conflict. (See table 9.)

An armistice on 27 July 1953 finally brought the fighting to an end, though no peace settlement was subsequently achieved and the armistice arrangements continued in force for the next forty years. New Zealand's naval presence was reduced to one frigate, which from 1954 was attached to the British Far Eastern Fleet and made only periodic visits to Korea. The New Zealand gunners were based at a camp on the Imjin River till their withdrawal in November 1954, and 10 Company's role ended in May 1956 when the Commonwealth Division was disbanded. From this point New Zealand troops in Korea, an 80-strong transport platoon, served as part of the Commonwealth Contingent, Korea. Kayforce was finally withdrawn from Korea on 27 July 1957. Thereafter New Zealand was represented by a military liaison officer on the ★Commonwealth Liaison Mission, Korea, until 1971.

In all, about 4700 men served with Kayforce and a further 1300 in the frigates during the seven years of New Zealand's involvement in Korea. Forty-five men lost their lives in this period, thirty-three of them during the war (of whom two were RNZN personnel). One member of Kayforce was taken prisoner of war; held in northern North Korea for eighteen months, he was repatriated following the armistice, as was a New Zealander serving with the RAAF, who had been shot down near the North Korean capital, P'yongyang.

The Korean War had a dramatic indirect economic impact in New Zealand. The sense of crisis precipitated by the outbreak in 1950 encouraged the United States to seek to buy large quantities of wool not for uniform for use in Korea as many supposed at the time (and since), but to complete its strategic stockpiles. This demand led to the greatest wool boom in New Zealand's history, with prices tripling overnight. However, the inflationary effect of other commodity buying offset the advantages of the wool boom, with imported raw materials rapidly increasing in price.

Especially once it became obvious that the conflict would be confined to Korea, New Zealanders paid little attention to events in the peninsula, and there were occasional complaints that Kayforce was a 'Forgotten Force'. The outbreak intensified trends that had been apparent in New Zealand domestic politics in the late 1940s, and the National Party used anti-communism to good effect in the 1951 general election. In terms of foreign policy, the war also assisted New Zealand achieving its long-standing objective, a security commitment from the United States. Not only was New Zealand able to demonstrate its support as a small ally in the UN coalition but also events worked in its favour. The Chinese intervention introduced a sense of urgency in Washington which opened the way for the signature of the *ANZUS treaty on 1 September 1951.

I. McGibbon, *New Zealand and the Korean War*, 2 vols (Oxford University Press, Auckland, 1991, 1996).

Kupapa In the early 1860s, the Maori word 'kupapa' was a verb meaning (among other things) to 'be neutral in a quarrel'. After the outbreak of the Waikato War in 1863, the word also became a noun applied, often pejoratively, to Maori who fought alongside the Crown's forces. It is used here to refer to these 'friendly' Maori, whether or not they were actually called kupapa at the time. Nearly half of all Maori did not oppose the British in the *New Zealand Wars. This has had long-lasting consequences for Maori society, and Maori have had a continuing role in New Zealand's official armed forces.

The first Maori to ally themselves with the British were Nga Puhi led by the Hokianga chief Tamati Waka *Nene, who provided essential logistical and combat support in the Northern War of 1845–46. Nene was not 'pro-government'; like Hone *Heke, he had no illusions about British intentions, but unlike him he saw the protection of settlers and trade as taking precedence over forcible resistance to European encroachment on Maori freedom of action. Nene also used alliance with the British military to enhance his position in the Nga Puhi world. His forces in effect acted as one side in a three-sided conflict; they had the better of Heke's in their 'war within a war'.

In the Wellington campaign of 1846, the British were supported against *Te Rangihaeata's section of Ngati Toa by Te Ati Awa and (less enthusiastically) other Ngati Toa. The land-selling faction of Te Ati Awa played only an insignificant role in the Taranaki War of 1860–61, which for them was partly a continuation of an inter-hapu conflict. A few hundred Waikato and Te Arawa, known as 'Queenites', participated actively on the British side in the Waikato War of 1863–64. The former helped operate a supply line on the lower Waikato River, although some defected after this was successfully attacked by the Kingites. Most of the Arawa confederation based around Rotorua supported the British from March 1864, to prevent Ngati Porou crossing their territory to reinforce the Kingites.

Kupapa were vital to the colonists' operations after the withdrawal of the British troops in the later 1860s. Much of the fighting against *Te Kooti on the east coast was undertaken by kupapa of Rongowhakaata (his own iwi), Ngati Kahungunu, Ngati Porou, and Te Arawa. Like other kupapa, they were sometimes criticised by Pakeha for showing insufficient enthusiasm for or in battle, and it is true that their commitment was never total. The most wholehearted were Te Arawa, who were surrounded by enemies and needed this alliance to

Part of the Arawa Flying Column pictured after an action against Te Kooti at Kaiteriria pa, Lake Rotokakahi, in February 1870 (*Alexander Turnbull Library, F-20328-1/2*)

Kupapa

survive. Several 'de-tribalised' units subject to regular military discipline, notably the eighth division of the ★Armed Constabulary and later the 'Arawa Flying Column' (200 Arawa separated from their chiefs and operating under European officers), were formed. Other fighting groups coalesced around able leaders whose power within their tribe had grown because of their kupapa activities: Ropata ★Wahawaha of Ngati Porou and Te Keepa ★Te Rangihiwinui of Wanganui were the outstanding examples. On the other hand, some kupapa (like many European troops) joined up simply to collect pay. Levels of commitment often changed: Rongowhakaata and some Ngati Kahungunu were unenthusiastic opponents of Te Kooti until he killed their relatives, after which they pursued him relentlessly.

Several hundred Ngati Porou and an Arawa Armed Constabulary division took part in the capture of Ngatapa at the beginning of 1869, and executed most of the male prisoners who were taken. In May 1869, about 560 kupapa took part in the fruitless expedition into the Urewera in search of Te Kooti. That spring, a similar number of kupapa defeated Te Kooti in the Taupo campaign, which finished him as a serious military threat.

From February 1870, Maori controlled the expeditions against Te Kooti. Arawa, Kahunganu, and Te Keepa's and Ropata's men scoured the Urewera in operations which ended only after their prey found sanctuary in the King Country. But they acted on their own terms: Te Keepa made a separate treaty with a Tuhoe leader in March 1870; Ngati Kahungunu ceased actively pursuing Te Kooti later that year after negotiations with King Tawhiao's sister; and it seems that some of Ropata's men had previously fought for Te Kooti and continued covertly to assist him. Even the kupapa could appreciate his quest for autonomy.

The Field Force opposing ★Titokowaru on the west coast in 1868–69, while predominantly European, had also included several hundred kupapa, with a core of experienced Wanganui warriors led by Te Keepa. After the defeat at Te Ngutu-o-te-Manu in September 1868, the kupapa, 'strongly impressed by Titokowaru's mana', went home; they returned to participate in a second defeat, at Moturoa in November. After helping to garrison Wanganui town, about 400 kupapa took part in the advance to Tauranga-ika and the subsequent pursuit of Titokowaru and his allies in early 1869.

About 250 kupapa were killed in action during the New Zealand Wars. The colonists disliked relying on kupapa assistance; they did so because they had no choice. This debt did not prevent the kupapa subsequently losing much land through the Native Land Court. But fighting for the government, as much as fighting against it, had helped to reinforce tribal cohesion. And the kupapa chiefs who occupied the four Maori seats in the colonial Parliament that were granted in recognition of their efforts had at least gained a foothold in the Pakeha system.

The kupapa tradition also remained alive in a military sense. Maori were prominent in the ★commemorative contingents sent to London for Queen Victoria's jubilee and the coronations of Edward VII and George V. While non-white troops from overseas were formally barred from fighting in the ★Boer War by the British, some part-Maori with English names served in the New Zealand contingents; many already had experience in ★Volunteer Force corps such as the Ngati-Porou Rifles. The 500-strong 'Native Contingent' (under European leadership) which served in the ★First World War was divided into platoons recruited on a tribal basis; only a few volunteers were forthcoming from former Kingite territory, and ★conscription was eventually imposed, albeit without great success, in the Waikato–Maniapoto district. The composition of 28th (Maori) Battalion in the ★Second World War reflected the continued significance of the fissures between resistant and collaborationist Maori. Three of its four companies were centred on the tribal areas of Nga Puhi, Te Arawa, and Ngati Porou/Rongowhakaata. In the second half of the twentieth century many Maori have maintained the warrior tradition by building careers in the armed forces, in which some kupapa tribes, such as Ngati Porou, have continued to be over-represented. One, Major-General B.M. ★Poananga, rose to the ★New Zealand Army's highest position.

J. Belich, *The New Zealand Wars and the Victorian Interpretation of Racial Conflict* (Auckland University Press, Auckland, 1986); R.I.M. Burnett, 'Kupapas', *Journal of the Polynesian Society*, vol. 74, 1965.

DAVID GREEN

L

Land girls Like most of the war services for women during the ★Second World War, the impetus for the Women's Land Service came from women themselves. Keen to play their part in the war effort, women asked the government as early as September 1939 to establish an organisation modelled on the British Women's Land Army, but this initiative was dismissed by the Minister of Agriculture as unnecessary. For the next two years there was debate about women replacing men on farms, with those in favour pointing to the 60,000 British girls on the land. Opponents, including the Women's Division of the Farmers' Union, argued that a 'Kitchen Army' would be more use. Domestic help would, they reasoned, free farmers' wives for lighter farm duties, in the performance of which they would be more competent than untrained city women. But when the Women's War Service Auxiliary compiled a register of women volunteering for war work in 1940, few expressed a wish to do domestic work and many were keen on farm work. In Christchurch women grew beans for dehydration, while Hamilton's mayor claimed that up to 500 had volunteered for farm work. By November 1941, manpower shortages had undermined government opposition, and regulations for a Women's Land Corps were announced. Highly regimented, these required from farmers three references and the presence of a physically fit man on the property. Girls were not permitted to work for a relative, and the performance of household duties, except for cleaning their own quarters, was not expected of them.

The scheme got off to a slow start, with a mere 104 women placed on farms by March 1942. In the following September the corps was reorganised and renamed the Women's Land Service. A publicity campaign was launched by the ★National Service Department, with members of Parliament Mary Grigg and Mary Dreaver touring the country in Land Girl uniform. Pay was increased and the clothing issue improved. The latter comprised three overalls, an oilskin, sou'wester, straw hat, leather jacket, five pairs of socks, boots, and gumboots, with 'a coat and skirt of a rich nut brown ... and two kinds of hats—plain brown felt with upturned side, or a brown beret ... decorated with a sheaf of wheat'—for walking-out. Land girls were now permitted to work for relatives, and farmers' relatives always made up over half the numbers. In September 1944, the scheme's peak, there were 2088 land girls, of whom 1226 were on relatives' farms. In terms of numbers, and compared with women herd testers, the Women's Land Service was not significant. Isolation and unfamiliar physical work discouraged volunteers and many farmers thought farm work inappropriate for women. Most land girls worked on dairy farms, where there was a tradition of female labour. There was prejudice against Maori girls, with forty-six awaiting places on farms in March 1944. Nevertheless farmers and land girls who took part in the scheme considered it a success. Recruiting ceased in August 1945, and the service was disbanded in April 1946.

SUSAN UPTON

Land mines see MINES, LAND

Lange, David Russell (4 August 1942–). An Auckland lawyer, Lange entered Parliament for the Labour Party in 1977, and became Leader of the Opposition in 1983. After sweeping the Muldoon government from office in July 1984 with a platform that included an anti-nuclear policy, the fourth Labour government which he led introduced a series of radical economic reforms. Aggrieved party supporters were appeased, however, by the government's strong anti-nuclear stance. Although professing to support the continuation of New Zealand's participation in ★ANZUS, Lange irritated the American authorities by making no apparent effort to bring his party round to acceptance of the maintenance of naval visits by American warships. Following the USS ★*Buchanan* affair, which led to the severance of New Zealand's active participation in the alliance, he became the champion of ★anti-nuclearism, especially after participating in an Oxford Union debate on the subject. In denouncing nuclear deterrence, he rejected the Western strategy upon which New Zealand's defence policy had hitherto been based. His penchant for witty one-liners and off-the-cuff remarks did not sit well with the needs of diplomacy, but was effective politically, at least for a time. When retired senior service officers questioned the approach being adopted by his government, he savagely dismissed them as 'geriatric generals'. His relationship with the government's defence advisers was further soured by controversy over New Zealand's response to the coups in Fiji in 1987 (see CIVIL–MILITARY RELATIONS). Although the government was re-elected in 1987, his administration became increasingly beleaguered as the New Zealand economy foundered. When in April 1989 he declared the ANZUS Treaty a 'dead letter', even his own Cabinet baulked. This incident both reflected and contributed further to a waning of support for him among his party's caucus, and he relinquished office in August 1989. He subsequently published, in 1990, his own version of his government's anti-nuclear policy, *Nuclear Free—The New Zealand Way*. In that same year he went to Iraq in his private capacity to negotiate the release of New Zealanders taken hostage during the lead-up to the ★Gulf War.

Laurent, Lieutenant-Colonel Harry John (15 April 1895–9 December 1987) won a VC on the ★Western Front. Born and raised in Taranaki, he enlisted in 1NZEF shortly after his twentieth birthday, and was wounded while serving with the 3rd New Zealand (Rifle) Brigade on the Somme in 1916. His decoration stemmed from his actions on 12 September 1918, when the fighting patrol he was leading became lost behind enemy lines. In the process of extricating his men, he led a surprise attack upon a German trench which resulted in the capture of 112 prisoners. After attending an officer cadet training unit, he was commissioned in February 1919, shortly before his repatriation to New Zealand. In 1941–42 he was a ★Home Guard battalion commander in Taranaki, after which he commanded an air training corps.

League of Nations was a first attempt to create a world security organisation. Established in 1919 as part of the peace settlement with Germany, it owed much to the vision and promotion of US President Woodrow Wilson, though the United States in the end did not become a member. Apart from its security responsibilities, it had a range of subsidiary functions, including overseeing the administration of the enemy states' colonial possessions as mandated territories. Partly because its membership never included all the major powers, it proved ineffective as a security organisation. Although in its Covenant members agreed to preserve the territorial integrity and existing political independence of all members, a lack of confidence in these provisions was evident, and was increased when Italy and Japan in particular defied the League. New Zealand was a founding member of the League, and sat on its Council on several occasions between the world wars. It had regular dealings with its Permanent Mandates Commission in connection with its mandate, Western Samoa. During the late 1930s New Zealand governments became increasingly supportive of the League as the international situation deteriorated and the limitations of ★imperial defence became apparent. In 1936 New Zealand advanced suggestions to make it more effective which amounted in effect to a call for members to live up to their obligations. New Zealand

Prime Minister David Lange discusses a battlefield simulation exercise with New Zealand and American officers during ANZUS Exercise Triad 84 at Waiouru in October 1984 (*NZ Army*)

continued to champion the League after most countries in Europe, with a more immediate sense of danger, had long since given up on it. After expelling the Soviet Union for its invasion of Finland in December 1939, the League went into limbo. It was eventually replaced by the ★United Nations Organization.

Lee, John Alfred Alexander (31 October 1891–13 June 1982) challenged the basis of New Zealand's defence strategy in the late 1930s. He had served with the Wellington Regiment during the ★First World War, won a DCM for charging an enemy machine-gun post at Messines and later taking forty prisoners, and lost an arm as a result of a wound suffered in March 1918. From 1922 he was a Labour member of Parliament. When the Labour government was formed in 1935, his aspiration to be Minister of Defence went unfulfilled, but he proceeded virtually to usurp the minister's role by taking it upon himself to review the objectives of New Zealand's defence policy. He advocated the establishment of the RNZAF as a separate service and the formation of a Council of Defence (both later done). He was a member of the council when it came into being in May 1937. On strategy, he proclaimed New Zealand's isolation as its best defence, opposed the dispatch of another expeditionary force overseas (partly because of his belief that air power had made its safe transport impossible), and challenged the assumption that the preservation of sea communications with Great Britain was essential to New Zealand security. He favoured concentration on air force development, but the government eventually settled for a balanced programme involving all three services. Lee was expelled from the Labour Party in 1940, and lost his seat at the 1943 general election.

Lemon-squeezer, a wide-brimmed felt hat with its high crown pinched with four dents, is a distinctive emblem of the ★New Zealand Army. Among the first to wear a hat of this shape were members of the New Zealand contingents in the ★Boer War, some of whom pushed out their slouch hats to form a rough lemon-squeezer. In New Zealand, A Battery, New Zealand Field Artillery, modelled its headgear on the distinctive Royal Canadian Mounted Police hat. Members of the ★Territorial Force were issued with both a peaked cap and a felt hat, which they wore pinned on the left side and with a furrow in the crown, in the style that has become associated with the Australian Army's slouch hat. Responsibility for the introduction of the lemon-squeezer to the Territorial Force is attributed to Lieutenant-Colonel W.G. ★Malone, the commander of the 11th (Taranaki Rifles) Regiment, who, at a particularly wet annual camp at Takapau in 1911, seems to have encouraged his men to adapt their hats to this style.

Peter Fraser meets New Zealand troops in the Middle East in 1941 (*Alexander Turnbull Library, C-14457-1/2*)

This would not only overcome the practical problem of the hats' collecting rainwater but also provide a link with the regiment's provincial origins in the shadow of Mount Egmont/Taranaki, resembling the mountain motif of its badge. When he became aware of the change, the GOC, Major-General A.J. ★Godley, reluctantly gave his endorsement.

When the ★New Zealand Expeditionary Force was formed in 1914, the lemon-squeezer hat was adopted by Malone's Wellington Infantry Battalion. With the exception of the mounted rifles, other units followed suit in March 1916, probably in an attempt to distinguish themselves from Australians, and the lemon-squeezer became the distinctive hat of the New Zealanders. It was also worn by 2NZEF and ★Jayforce members, but was not issued to those who served in ★Kayforce, much to their irritation. Although the troops deployed in Malaya in 1957 also wore the lemon-squeezer at first, they were soon issued with ski caps, retaining the lemon-squeezer only for ceremonial occasions. In 1960 the ski cap replaced the lemon-squeezer completely in the New Zealand Army, and four years later it in turn was replaced by corps berets. The lemon-squeezer was reintroduced for ceremonial occasions in 1977. In 1999 the wide-brimmed furrowed-crown hat worn by the mounted rifles was introduced for all ranks of the Army, replacing the beret.

Lend-Lease was introduced, under the American Lend-Lease Act of March 1941, to provide a means by which the United States could facilitate the British war effort against Germany and Italy in the ★Second World War, but eventually was extended to thirty-eight countries, including the Soviet Union. Able to take advantage of its provisions from November 1941, New Zealand set up a supply mission in Washington for the purpose. The importance of the arrangements was enhanced by the entry of the United States into the war soon afterwards, and in June 1942 a US Joint Purchasing Board was established in New Zealand. Under Lend-Lease New Zealand received substantial quantities of American military equipment and munitions, as well as commodities like oil, petrol, tinplate, and wire. In the last two years of the war more than 7000 tractors were obtained to enhance production on New Zealand farms. Without Lend-Lease New Zealand would have confronted severe supply problems, and would have been hard pressed to sustain its war production. The cost of American assistance to New Zealand was offset by goods and services which New Zealand provided to American forces serving in the South Pacific. Roughly half of this Reverse Lend-Lease comprised foodstuffs, the provision of which exacerbated New Zealand's manpower problems and led eventually to the decision to withdraw the 3rd Division from the South Pacific. Camp facilities which were constructed by the New Zealand Public Works Department for ★United States troops in New Zealand were also charged to the Reverse Lend-Lease. The New Zealand authorities were dismayed, however, to realise belatedly that generous payments made by the Americans to New Zealanders for labour services were in fact being charged to Lend-Lease. The Lend-Lease arrangement was terminated in July 1946. For accounting purposes, the cost of the materiel supplied by the United States to New Zealand during the whole conflict was settled as £105 million, as opposed to New Zealand's more tightly controlled £81 million of goods and services provided to the United States. Despite the divergence in the two figures, no adjusting payment was made. The agreement provided for New Zealand to buy about £1.7 million worth of American equipment in the South Pacific, with the proceeds being used by the United States to purchase buildings in New Zealand and to further cultural relations between the two countries.

J.V.T. Baker, *War Economy* (Historical Publications Branch, Wellington, 1965).

Literature and war New Zealand's experience of war is unevenly reflected in literature. The ★Second World War produced, and continues to produce, a large quantity of fiction and autobiography and a lesser amount of verse. Other wars in which New Zealand has been involved have been less comprehensively covered; some have left next to no literary mark.

The ★New Zealand Wars of the nineteenth century were chronicled by several novelists, although little of this work can pretend to literary merit. H. Butler Stoney's *Taranaki* (1861), although subtitled 'a tale of the war', does little more than sketch the background to the war and recount its progress through military dispatches. It is avowedly a settler's view: the war was fomented by the King Movement and the Church of England, and the Maori are regarded as not fit 'to obtain a proper view of those principles of freedom or equality, being little more than savages'; they are 'a villainous and treacherous race' whose activities are impeding the progress of a potentially prosperous province.

'Comus' (John Featon), in *The Last of the Waikatos* (1873), uses a fictional framework to give an account of the Waikato War and to convey the message that the British victory opened the way for a prosperous future based on the European settlement of confiscated lands. In J.H. Kirby's *Henry Ancrum* (1872), the detailed descriptions of events in the Waikato War serve mainly to impede the progress of the hero's romance. A.A. Fraser, in *Daddy Crisp's Waifs* (1886) and *Ranoni, or the Maori Chief's Heir* (1888), was interested principally in using the Waikato War as a background to earnest moral instruction. Robert Scott, in *Ngamihi; or the Maori Chief's Daughter* (1895), uses romance as the basis of his story, which includes an account of the killing of the missionary Carl Volkner, 'one of the darkest spots on the record of the early history of New Zealand [which] gives a profound insight into the worst phases of the Maori character.' Written for a non-New Zealand audience, the novel lingers over detailed descriptions of tourist attractions such as Tongariro and Lake Tarawera.

The last of the nineteenth century novels, Rolf Boldrewood's *'War to the Knife' or Tangata Maori* (1899), has as its hero Roland Massinger, who emigrates to New Zealand in the 1840s. He is fascinated by the Northern War of 1845–46 and praises 'the valour of the Maori people, their chivalry, their eloquence, their dignity, their delight in war and skill in fortification'. His attitudes to the war in Taranaki are contradictory: as a settler, he thinks land should be purchased and not locked up, but he recognises that the government's purchase of land at Waitara was wrong. He eventually joins von ★Tempsky's ★Forest Rangers and sees action in the Waikato and the Bay of Plenty. Boldrewood's research is sketchy—a Nga Puhi contingent takes part in the fighting in the Waikato—and he had evidently never set foot in New Zealand: Hokianga is confidently located between the thermal region and Auckland.

William Satchell's *The Greenstone Door* (1914) was the first novel about the wars to treat the Maori as more than clichéd stereotypes. It opens some years before 1860 and deals with a European youth, Cedric Tregarthen, raised among Ngati Maniapoto. Although he takes no part in the fighting when war comes to the Waikato, he becomes an intimate of Governor George ★Grey and is well placed to sketch the background to the war. The Maori are portrayed as having learnt the attractions of civilisation without loss of self-confidence, while the conflict is precipitated by a too rapid influx of Europeans into the Waikato. Satchell is unable to resolve the conflict between his sympathy for the Maori and his attachment to Darwinian notions of the need for them to adapt to a stronger civilisation. He portrays Grey as drawn reluctantly into war and determined afterwards to build a united New Zealand and be fair to both races.

The Greenstone Door was to be the last novel about the New Zealand Wars for fifty years. Literary interest was not revived until the publication of the first novel in Errol Brathwaite's trilogy, *The Flying Fish* (1964). This deals with the first Taranaki War and gives a sympathetic view of Wiremu Kingi ★Te Rangitake and the King Movement. *The Needle's Eye* (1965) follows the course of the Waikato campaign while *The Evil Day* (1967) concerns the war with ★Titokowaru. All three novels follow closely the actual course of the fighting and introduce historical characters on both sides of the conflict. Brathwaite leans heavily on historical research, but his determination to be painstakingly accurate results in the trilogy having too much history and too little literary invention. Ray Grover followed a similar approach in dealing with the fighting in the 1840s: his *Cork of War: Ngati Toa and the British Mission, an historical narrative* (1982) is a semi-fictionalised account of the campaigns involving ★Te Rauparaha and Ngati Toa in the Wellington region.

Maurice Shadbolt also produced a New Zealand Wars trilogy, which was initiated with *Season of the Jew* (1986), a novel dealing with the campaign against ★Te Kooti. His hero's sympathy with Te Kooti is evident and the novel ends with an angry account of the trial and execution of Hamiora Pere, a young follower of Te Kooti. *Monday's Warriors* (1990) deals with the part played in Titokowaru's war by the military deserter Kimble Bent, and *The House of Strife* (1993) follows the events of the Northern War of 1845–46. All three novels, while closely researched, at times distort history to serve the needs of fiction and all are history seen from the vantage point of the late twentieth century.

Witi Ihimaera's *The Matriarch* (1986) also deals with Te Kooti but from a Maori point of view. The political and religious justifications for his actions are treated at length and the Matawhero massacre becomes the 'Matawhero retaliation'. Where Shadbolt had described the bloodshed in some detail, Ihimaera sees Te Kooti as a warrior rather than a rebel and the killings become a 'positive act of war'. He is less interested than either Brathwaite or Shadbolt in historical archaeology and more intent on presenting events as still-living history.

Little literature was produced from New Zealand's participation in the ★Boer War. H. Dobbie's story in the *New Zealand Graphic*'s Christmas number of 1900 is the only fictional work, while C. Marshall Nalder's *Battlesmoke Ballads* (1899) is a collection of Kiplingesque poems originally published in newspapers and periodicals. In part anti-Boer propaganda, some also reveal incipient nationalist pride at being able to fight alongside Great Britain: 'The Fernleaf and the Rata entwined in Empire's Wreath.' There were also a number of memoirs of the war, including Elizabeth Hawdon's *New Zealanders and the Boer War* (1902), Joseph Linklater's *On Active Service in South Africa with 'The Silent Sixth'* (1904), James G. Harle Moore's *With the Fourth New Zealand Rough Riders* (1906), F. Twistleton's *With the New Zealanders at the Front* (1902), and Frank Perham's *The Kimberley Flying Column* (1958?). In their fervent patriotism and their praise of New Zealand virtues over those of the British Army, these anticipate many of the narratives of the ★First World War. Maurice Shadbolt's 'The Birds of Grief Gully', one of the three stories in *Dove on the Waters* (1997), deals with the reverberations in the protagonists' later lives of an incident in the war.

The First World War produced a number of memoirs and writings by troops. Some New Zealanders contributed to *The Anzac Book*, compiled at Gallipoli in the closing weeks of 1915, while *New Zealand at the Front*, published in London in 1918, has as its most notable contribution K. L. Trent's poem 'Digger's Disillusion': he had dreams of martial glory when he enlisted but ends by becoming 'a tattered, weary digger/working knee-deep in a drain'. *Shell Shocks* (1916) also contains works by New Zealand troops. The official New Zealand war correspondent, Malcolm ★Ross, and his brother Noel published, in 1916, *Light and Shade in War*, which sees war as a curative for a 'disastrous decadence' caused by a 'great prosperity and a long peace'. The fighting is recorded as 'gallant deeds' and 'splendid heroism'. C.B. Brereton's *Tales of Three Campaigns* (1926) is an account of the 12th Nelson Company, while C.H. Weston's *Three Years with the New Zealanders* (1918) has New Zealand achieving separate nationhood as a result of the war.

Nothing else was published in the 1920s. Too little time had passed for men to reflect on their experience, and the gap between what people at home knew of the war and the reality of the soldiers' experiences at ★Gallipoli and on the ★Western Front was so great as to seem unbridgeable. In the 1930s, however, as war again seemed imminent, important books on the earlier conflict began to appear. Ormond ★Burton's *The Silent Division* (1935) is a tribute to the heroism and self-sacrifice of the ordinary soldier as well as a graphic account of what Burton had seen on the battlefield. In 'Rumour' (published in *Shell Shocks*), he had written an almost ecstatic glorification of the spiritually cleansing aspects of a war which promised to introduce 'a great era of noble idealism and of splendid self-sacrificing devotion'. After the war, shocked by the vindictiveness of the khaki election in Britain and disillusioned by the harsh terms of the Treaty of Versailles, he concluded that the sacrifices had been in vain and became a dedicated Christian pacifist. *The Silent Division*, apart from its preface, gives little indication of Burton's pacifism. He sees the war as producing the beginning of a sense of nationality; the willingness to die for a good cause is the supreme virtue and 'the finest manifestation of brotherhood'. The book is in some respects closer to Burton's feelings in 1914–18 than in 1935. Another pacifist, Archibald ★Baxter, in *We Will Not Cease* (1939), gave a searing account of the brutality of his treatment as a conscientious objector.

In 1936, Robin Hyde's fictionalised biography of Private John Douglas ★Stark, *Passport to Hell*, was published. It is an anti-heroic account of the war as an 'outrageous libel on the normality of the human mind'. Intriguingly, the novel does not mention anything of the causes or origins of the war; we never know what the armies are fighting for, only that men are killing each other in what seems an endless and senseless conflict. The only fictional accounts of the war by a combatant are John A. ★Lee's novels *Civilian into Soldier* (1937) and *Soldier* (1976). The first of these is as determinedly non-heroic as *Passport to Hell*. There is no invocation of either patriotism or idealism. 'The great tragedy of the war was … that ordinary men … were drawn into hideous conflicts in which their plain duty appeared to lie in the destruction of the lives of other men as kindly and decent as they.' One memoir of this period, C.A.L. Treadwell's *Recollections of an Amateur Soldier* (1936), regards the war as a 'holy war'. He is notably reticent about recording details of fighting. Of Passchendaele, where the New Zealand Division suffered almost 3000 casualties, he says only: 'We did all we were asked to do … It was a costly business.'

Two notable First World War memoirs were published in the 1960s. Cecil Malthus's *Anzac, A Retrospect* (1965) contains one of the clearest accounts of the fighting at Gallipoli and is notable for its criticism of command failures. Perhaps the best of the memoirs is Alexander Aitken's *From Gallipoli to the Somme* (1963). His account of the Battle of the Somme makes nonsense of 'all talk of the chevalieresque … or of the glory of war.' Of the final result he writes: 'the communiqué … was terse, suggesting a successful advance … This might pass for home consumption; I should rather have put it that unimaginative staff work at some level had extinguished three companies.'

The war plays a part in several works of fiction. The prevailing patriotism and anti-German sentiments are recalled in Robin Hyde's *The Godwits Fly* (1938) and James Courage's *The Young have Secrets* (1954). Maurice Shadbolt covers the Gallipoli campaign and the treatment of ★conscientious objectors in *The Lovelock Version* (1980), while his play, *Once on Chunuk Bair* (1982), takes Lieutenant-Colonel William ★Malone as its hero. In Maurice Gee's *Plumb*, the central character, a Presbyterian clergyman, is persecuted by his church for his pacifist and socialist objections to the war. Janet Frame's *Intensive Care* (1970) has as the principal character of its opening section a returned serviceman; the psychological effects of the war on Tom Livingstone are used as a metaphor for contemporary social ills: 'the War had gone away from the Western Front; it was at home, at home in our house in Eagle Street'. In Elizabeth Knox's *After Z-hour* (1987), six people trapped by a storm in a deserted house are visited by the ghost of a dead First World War soldier. His narrative is clearly based on the reading of contemporary diaries and letters and shows the influence of both Lee and Hyde.

The literature of the Second World War contains none of the invocation to heroism and patriotism found in much First World War material and none of the earlier illusions about the realities of warfare. John ★Mulgan's *Report on Experience* (1947) sketches the 2nd New Zealand Division in terms echoed in many memoirs and novels, both before and since: They were 'quiet and shrewd and sceptical … aloof and self-contained. … It seemed to me … that perhaps to have produced these men for this one time would be New Zealand's destiny.' Dan ★Davin's novel *For the Rest of our Lives* (1947) is part tribute to the mateship engendered among New Zealanders of widely differing backgrounds, part philosophical consideration of the place of war in human history. Its principal theme is the effect of war on the soldiers and the realisation that it would be forever with them. The theme is repeated in *The Sullen Bell* (1956), which treats a group of New Zealanders in London attempting to deal with the personal effects of the war. Davin's stories on the war, collected in *The Salamander and the Fire* (1986), progressively follow the 2nd New Zealand Division from ★Greece to Italy. John Reece Cole's collection *It Was So Late* (1949) contains stories dealing with the contrast between heroism and reality and, in 'Up at the Mammoth', a notable study of the delayed effects of ★shell-shock. Guthrie Wilson's *Brave Company* (1951) focuses on the fortitude of the ordinary soldier and gives very clear accounts of some infantry actions in Italy. Gordon Slatter's *A Gun in My Hand* (1959) deals with a returned soldier's difficulty in coming to terms with the war many years after its conclusion. In *I'll Soldier No More* (1958), M.K. Joseph considers, through a group of soldiers in Germany, the way in which a military unit brings varied people close together; his soldiers include a down-to-earth, nostalgic New Zealander and an intellectual more inclined to seek philosophical explanations for war. In *A Soldier's Tale* (1976), Joseph presents a soldier faced with an acute moral dilemma in Normandy. Natasha Templeton's *Firebird* (1994) is a fictionalised account of the ★North African and ★Italian campaigns and of Major-General C.E. ★Weir's part in the forced repatriation of Cossacks from Yugoslavia to the Soviet Union. C.K. Stead's *Talking About O'Dwyer* (1999) is centred on an incident during the Battle of ★Crete in which a Pakeha officer in the Maori Battalion shoots one of his own men, who has been badly wounded, during the withdrawal from the battalion's counter-attack at Maleme and later has a makutu (spell) placed on him by a member of the soldier's family. Fictional works set in the ★Pacific War include Errol Brathwaite's *Fear in the Night* (1959) and *An Affair of Men* (1961) and Phillip Wilson's *Pacific Star* (1976) and *Pacific Flight* (1964).

Notable among the verse of the Second World War is John Male's collection *Poems from a War* (1989): their philosophical and emotional calmness belie the fact that they were written on campaign in Italy. Other poets wrote little, although in 1943 Allen Curnow published 'Pantoum of War in the Pacific' and 'In Memoriam 2/Lieutenant T.C.F. Ronalds', his 'unsoldierlike acknowledgement' to a cousin killed in North Africa. James Bertram included several poems on his captivity in Hong Kong and Japan in *Occasional Verses* (1971), and M.K. Joseph's war poetry was published in *Imaginary Islands* (1951).

Among the memoirs of New Zealand combatants, the most notable is Howard ★Kippenberger's *Infantry Brigadier* (1949), a spare account by one of the 2nd New Zealand Division's leading commanders. Its detailed descriptions of preparation for battle and of the fighting made it a standard textbook on infantry tactics. Noel Gardiner's *Freyberg's Circus* (1981) is a lively and occasionally humorous account of the division, which includes a chapter of reflection on what it takes to make a man a soldier and the nature of heroism. James ★Burrows's autobiography *Pathway among Men* (1974) includes extensive material on his experiences as a divisional brigadier. Geoffrey ★Cox gave accounts of the fighting in Crete and North Africa in *A Tale of Two Battles* (1987) and told the story of the division's campaign in Italy and its part in the capture of Trieste and the tense stand-off with Tito's partisans in *The Race for Trieste* (1977). In *Countdown to War* (1988) and *Eyewitness* (1999), he recounted his experiences as a journalist observing the ★appeasement of Hitler in Czechoslovakia, of the Soviet Union's war with Finland, and the fall of France. Gordon Slatter revisited the Italian campaign in *One More River* (1995). In *D Day* (1944), Denis ★Glover memorialises the invasion of Normandy, while his autobiography *Hot Water Sailor* (1962) recalls his experiences on shipping convoys to Murmansk.

Of the several narratives by ★prisoners of war and escapees, Jim ★Henderson's *Gunner Inglorious* (1945) is a wryly humorous story of his capture by the Italians and experiences in a military hospital. James ★Hargest's *Farewell Campo 12* (1945) includes much detail on successful and unsuccessful attempts at escape; W.B. Thomas's *Dare to be Free* (1951) describes his escape from captivity in Greece; James Bertram, in *The Shadow of a War* (1947), tells of his experiences during the fall of Hong Kong and his captivity there and in Japan. Claude Thompson, also a prisoner of the Japanese, gave his account in *Into the Sun* (1996). Robin Hyde described her experience of the Japanese war in China in *Dragon Rampant* (1939).

There are several narratives of POW escapes, including Ernest Clark's *Over the Fence is Out* (1965), R.H. Thompson's *Captive Kiwi* (1964), George ★Clifton's *The Happy Hunted* (1952), and later accounts by Allan Yeoman, John Borrie, and Jack Hardie. Among those who were aided by partisans and guerrillas, there are accounts by Malcolm Mason in *The Way Out* (1946), John Broad in *Poor People—Poor Us* (1946), and Arch Scott in *Dark of the Moon* (1985), which deals with the escaped prisoners of the 'Hare Battalion'.

Several New Zealanders left accounts of time behind enemy lines, some as special agents. William Jordan's *Conquest Without Victory* (1969) is a strongly anti-communist account of his work with the Greek partisans and later the French Resistance. Lindsay Rogers, in *Guerrilla Surgeon* (1957), is more sympathetic to the political ideals of Tito's communist partisans in Yugoslavia. John Mulgan wrote in *Report on Experience* of the difficulties of working with resistance movements. The partisan war against the Germans is the subject of the Italian section of Maurice Shadbolt's *An Ear of the Dragon* (1971).

Conscientious objectors have contributed several memoirs to Second World War literature. The most detailed is Ian Hamilton's bitter account of life in prison camps and Mount Eden jail, *Till Human Voices Wake Us* (1953). Walter Lawry's *We Said No to War* (1994) covers life in the camps and the civilian reaction to conscientious objectors. Ormond Burton's *In Prison* (1945) is a brief account of prison stays following his arrests for preaching pacifism. In his novel *Live Bodies* (1998), Maurice Gee fictionalises the life of Odo Strewe, a refugee from Nazism who spent the war interned on Somes Island.

New Zealand military experiences since 1945 have been centred in Asia. The few literary mentions of the ★Korean War include R.A.K. Mason's anti-war poem 'Sonnet to MacArthur's eyes' (1950) and James

Llewellyn

K. Baxter's poem 'A Takapuna businessman considers his son's death in Korea'. Two novels by ★Kayforce veterans are set mainly in Japan, where the force had its base and the men enjoyed their leave. *The Score at Tea-time* (1957) by Peter ★Llewellyn, writing under the pseudonym Michael Ellis, is centred on a court martial in Tokyo. In E.E. Combe's *The Cold Moon of the Spring* (1965) a New Zealand signaller has a platonic relationship with a Japanese woman. Seemingly the only fictional trace of New Zealand's involvement in Malaya is Fiona Kidman's short story 'Circling to your left' (1993).

The fictional literature on the ★Vietnam War is largely anti-war in content. There are a significant number of poems of protest, beginning with those published in a special number of the periodical *Fern Fire* in 1966. They include poems by Charles Doyle, Hone Tuwhare, James K. Baxter, and others. Baxter wrote several other poems on the war, including 'A bucket of blood for a dollar', 'The gunner's lament', and 'a death song for mr mouldybroke'. Rewi Alley published two volumes of anti-war verse, *The Mistake* (1965) and *Twenty-five Poems of Protest* (1968). Allen Curnow's 'A framed photograph' (*Trees, Effigies, Moving Objects*, 1972) refers to the My Lai massacre and C.K. Stead's *Walking Westwards* (1979) sets the war in the context of a long history of wars and political crises. Janet Frame included 'Napalm' and 'Instructions for burning with napalm' in *The Pocket Mirror* (1967), and the war forms part of the background of her novel *Daughter Buffalo* (1973).

The war plays a part in several other works. Michael Henderson's *Log of a Superfluous Son* (1975) sets it among a catalogue of every conflict in which New Zealand has been involved (and several in which we played no part). Craig Harrison draws parallels for Maori political action in *Broken October* (1975). O.E. Middleton wrote of an anti-war protest in 'Demonstration' (*Mate* 15, 1967) and Fiona Kidman's short stories 'The last shot' (1971) and 'Border country' (1993) refer to the war. The few accounts of combat include Barry Mitcalfe's story 'The black cat' and Rod Elder's *Deep Jay* (1975). Colin Sissons's memoir *Wounded Warriors* (1993) deals with his combat experience in Vietnam and his prolonged attempt to come to terms with its meaning.

BRIAN O'BRIEN

Llewellyn, Captain Stephen Peter (18 July 1913–14 November 1960) was an official historian, public relations officer, and war novelist. Born at Hereford, England, he came to New Zealand shortly before the outbreak of the ★Second World War after working as a journalist. Enlisting in 2NZEF, he left New Zealand with the Divisional Ammunition Company in January 1940, took part in all the 2nd New Zealand Division's campaigns, and by August 1944 held the rank of sergeant. His historical activities began with his appointment as his unit's historian late in the war. From 1945 to 1947 he was employed in the Archives Section at Army Headquarters in Wellington, during which, making good use of his personal diary, he drafted the official history of the Divisional Ammunition Company, *Journey Towards Christmas* (1949), which stands out among the official history series for its literary qualities. He also prepared for the ★War History Branch a short account of the ships which carried 2NZEF, published as *Troopships* (1949). He was writing the official history of the 18th Battalion and Armoured Regiment when appointed as ★Kayforce's Public Relations Officer in 1950 (and the contract would eventually be terminated for lack of progress). His elegantly written reports from Korea provide good insights into the New Zealanders' involvement in the ★Korean War. He was made an MBE in 1953. During the last year of his four-year tour of duty in Korea, he commanded the Divisional Transport Platoon. In the six years between his return to New Zealand and his sudden death, he wrote several novels under the pseudonym Michael Ellis; the first of them, *The Score at Tea-time*, was based on his experiences with Kayforce.

Logan, Colonel Robert (2 April 1863–4 February 1935) commanded the force which captured German Samoa in August 1914. A Scot, he emigrated to New Zealand in 1881 and became a sheep farmer in the Maniototo district. A man of some local importance, he raised a mounted rifles corps in 1900, and from 1908 was a lieutenant-colonel in the ★Volunteer Force, commanding the Otago Mounted Rifles. After joining the ★New Zealand Staff Corps in 1912, he commanded the Auckland Military District until the outbreak of the ★First World War. Within days he was preparing the Samoa Expeditionary Force for departure. After taking the surrender of the German territory on 30 August, he remained in Apia until 1919 as head of the military government. Well meaning but unimaginative, he carried out this task effectively, but was severely criticised by a commission of inquiry for his mishandling of the response to the 1918 ★influenza pandemic, which ravaged Samoa.

Logistics is a military term first used by United States forces and adopted after the ★Second World War by NATO forces to define support systems. The ★New Zealand Defence Force has adopted the NATO definition: 'The science of planning and carrying out the movement and maintenance of forces.' In its comprehensive sense, it is those aspects of military operations which deal with the following: design and development, acquisition, storage, movement, distribution, maintenance, evacuation, and disposition of materiel; movement, evacuation, and hospitalisation of personnel; the acquisition or construction, maintenance, operation, and disposition of facilities; and finally the acquisition or furnishing of services. The aim of operational logistic support is to take care of as many administrative functions as possible so as to enable the field commander to concentrate on carrying out the operational plan.

While certain high-level logistic functions are carried out by the Ministry of Defence, for example the acquisition of capital items over the value of $5 million, the three services have responsibility for the acquisition of capital items below that figure and for their own functional logistic support at command level. These include peacetime and base logistic functions (such as the day-to-day running of the service and the introduction of new operational equipment, planning, and training). To perform these functions the Army has established a Logistics Executive as a branch of the General Staff. The RNZN's day-to-day functional support is coordinated and controlled from within the Fleet Support organisation under the command of the Maritime Commander, based at the Devonport naval base. The RNZAF splits its functional peacetime logistic support between the Air Staff in Defence Headquarters, Wellington, Air Command at Base Auckland, and individual support units. Policy and higher-level planning functions are conducted in the Air Staff, leaving the Air Command responsible for all logistic functions required for the day-to-day conduct of both base and operational logistic support to air units. Recently the RNZAF has contracted out catering, base repair, the provision of air frames for basic pilot training, and facilities management.

In the ★New Zealand Army the operational and base support logistic functions are performed by units of the ★Royal New Zealand Army Logistic Regiment (RNZALR), as well as elements of engineer units, medical and dental units, psychology and education elements, military police units, and the chaplains' department. RNZALR units carry out a range of logistic functions, including transport, movements, air supply, supply, warehousing, postal services, catering, waste management, and repair and maintenance. Increasingly the Army is contracting out base logistic functions in New Zealand; for example, warehousing, base repair, facilities management, and static facility catering. The Army's deployable operational formation, 7th Brigade, includes RNZALR and other units to perform its logistic functions.

In an operational environment, RNZAF elements would use agency support, usually the Army logistic system, for their supporting field operations. When deployed at sea, away from New Zealand, the RNZN would rely on support from other naval elements with which it was operating. The RNZN has some specialist logistic support units, including a fleet supply ship, HMNZS *Endeavour*, and a troop and equipment deployment and support ship, HMNZS *Charles Upham* (see SUPPLY SHIPS). These would contribute to the naval logistic support of deployments. While operating as a New Zealand contribution to a coalition force, units and sub-units of the Army and RNZAF would be supported by the logistic support system of one of New Zealand's allies, probably the coalition leader. In these circumstances a New Zealand national support element would usually be deployed to assist with New Zealand–sourced items for the contingent and to take care of national administrative matters, particularly those concerning personnel and New Zealand–sourced items of supply.

Because of the New Zealand Defence Force's limited resources in manpower and equipment, an independently deployed national force would require external assistance for any protracted operations. In times of tension or conflict, support might be provided by allies. In addition, the manpower resource provided by the RNZNVR and the Army's ★Territorial Force could be utilised. Other more extreme measures, some of which would require the enactment of legislation, could include ★conscription, commercial contracting, and the commandeering of commercial or state-owned enterprise resources.

GRANT CROWLEY

Long Range Desert Group Originally formed as the Long Range Patrols by Major R.A. Bagnold in June 1940 (and later renamed Long Range Desert Group or LRDG), the unit at first comprised mainly New Zealand volunteers from the Divisional Cavalry. Former Egyptian Army 30-cwt trucks, modified and armed with a miscellany of scrounged or captured weapons, were used for patrols. The unit's irregular nature belied careful attention to preparation and planning not often seen in other 'private armies'. Throughout late 1940 it undertook reconnaissance missions as far afield as Chad, attacking Italian outposts and cooperating with Free French forces. From November 1941 it began raiding enemy supply convoys and airfields, as well as carrying ★Special Air Service raiding parties. A daring attack on Barce [Al Marj] in Libya, one of a series of surprise raids, destroyed about thirty aircraft. Such operations invariably invited enemy air attacks which damaged or destroyed vehicles; escapes by LRDG personnel walking hundreds of kilometres from behind enemy lines became legendary. The most important role of the LRDG remained reconnaissance, in particular monitoring the main Axis supply route, the Tripoli–Benghazi road.

A Long Range Desert Group patrol pauses in the desert behind enemy lines in the Quattara Depression in 1942 (*War History Collection, Alexander Turnbull Library, C-6700-1/2*)

After the Battle of El Alamein the LRDG guided the 2nd New Zealand Division in a series of 'left hooks' designed to trap Rommel's retreating army. In early 1943 it reconnoitred possible routes to outflank the Axis Mareth line, and navigated the New Zealand division in the subsequent operation to effect this in March 1943.

In September 1943, after briefly training in mountain warfare in Lebanon, the LRDG was concentrated on the island of Calino, as part of British operations to capture the Dodecanese Islands. This deployment without its prior knowledge upset the New Zealand government. Allied incursions into the Aegean were met by a vigorous German response, which led in October to the LRDG's withdrawal to the island of Leros. From Leros it sent patrols to the outlying islands to observe German movements, as a result of which a convoy was destroyed. These reconnaissance patrols were greatly assisted by the Greek population, which warned them of German attempts to track them down. Following a disastrous attack on the island of Levita in October 1943, where forty men were lost, the decision was taken to withdraw the LRDG from the Aegean. Before the troops could leave Leros, however, the Germans launched a well-organised combined naval and air-borne attack on the island. The British garrison—a brigade—was defeated, but most of the LRDG escaped in caiques or rowboats. In December 1943 the New Zealanders were withdrawn from the LRDG and posted to the Divisional Cavalry.

R.L. Kay, *Long Range Desert Group in the Mediterranean* (War History Branch, Wellington, 1950).

Low, Sir David Alexander Cecil (7 April 1891–19 September 1963) is New Zealand's most influential war cartoonist. Dunedin-born, he began drawing at an early age. In 1911 he left New Zealand in search of better prospects in Australia, and by the 1920s was based in London as the *Evening Standard*'s political cartoonist. A strong opponent of *appeasement, he used his 'Colonel Blimp' character to comment on the British and French failure to respond firmly to Fascist aggression before the *Second World War. So savagely did he lampoon the Nazis, and their leader Adolf Hitler, that he was listed as one of those to be immediately liquidated once Germany had conquered Great Britain in 1940. His cartoons and radio broadcasts helped sustain morale throughout the war.

M

Macdonald, Lieutenant-Commander George James (30 September 1921–22 January 1982) was New Zealand's most decorated naval officer of the ★Second World War. Born in Wellington, and a keen swimmer and yachtsman, he joined the New Zealand RNVR in 1938. After serving in armed merchantmen in the early part of the war, he was sent to England, and in July 1941, after being commissioned, was posted to a motor torpedo boat. Operating from Felixstowe, the boat of which he was second-in-command was set on fire during a solo night attack on a German convoy early in March 1942 in which one enemy ship was sunk. For staying with the stricken boat and enabling it to be salvaged, he was awarded a DSC; he also received a Humane Society medal for rescuing a drowning sailor. Shortly afterwards, he assumed command of his own boat. His skilful and aggressive approach earned him a bar to his DSC in July 1943. A second bar was subsequently awarded for several operations undertaken by the 21st Motor Torpedo Boat Flotilla, which he commanded from late 1943. On 4–5 July 1944, his flotilla launched a number of attacks on enemy shipping, culminating in a daylight foray against a convoy which resulted in two enemy ships being sunk and two damaged. For these operations he was made a DSO. Demobilised in 1946, he became the Wellington city engineer and a notable inventor.

McDonnell, Lieutenant-Colonel Thomas (1831/33?–8 November 1899) was a prominent colonial soldier of the ★New Zealand Wars. After ventures on the Australian goldfields, as a Hawke's Bay sheep farmer, and as an interpreter at Thames, he obtained a commission in Lieutenant-Colonel M.G. ★Nixon's ★Colonial Defence Force cavalry on 14 August 1863. A dashing soldier, who made numerous reconnaissance sorties into enemy territory, he became a friend of Gustavus von ★Tempsky. In 1865, now holding the rank of captain, he was placed in command of Wanganui ★kupapa (raised and in effect led by Te Keepa ★Te Rangihiwinui), which, during the south Taranaki campaigns under Generals ★Cameron and ★Chute, drove opposing Maori inhabitants from their villages. In the course of one of these operations, McDonnell was wounded in the foot. Between September and November 1865 he led kupapa and colonial units in fighting in the Opotiki area. Following the close of Chute's Taranaki campaign in February 1866, he commanded the south Taranaki area, with the responsibility of surveying confiscated Maori land for ★military settlers. Opposition by local Ngati Ruanui to land confiscation continued, however, and on 1 August 1866 he attacked the village of Pokaikai, despite the fact it had made clear its desire for peace. Although a parliamentary inquiry subsequently found that his actions were 'improper and unjust', he retained his command. He later settled on confiscated land in south Taranaki. In March 1867 he briefly served against Hauhau in the Rotorua area. When war broke out in south Taranaki in June 1868 McDonnell, now an Inspector in the ★Armed Constabulary and the darling of the colonial press, was placed in command of the forces marshalled against ★Titokowaru. His first attack against Titokowaru's base at Te Ngutu-o-te-manu achieved only the burning of some whares. When he led a further expedition against the base, on 7 September 1868, his force was ambushed. His subordinates pleaded for orders to attack, but McDonnell's hesitation ensured the rout of his force. Bitter recriminations followed, and on 14 October he was dismissed. Anxious to redeem himself, McDonnell accepted a position under his rival G.S. ★Whitmore. But some of McDonnell's troops were ambushed while foraging near Waitotara on 18 February 1869, and he was forced to resign. Using his connections with the new Defence Minister, Donald ★McLean, McDonnell nevertheless secured reappointment to a field command, this time to lead a force of kupapa and Armed Constabulary against ★Te Kooti at Taupo. He claimed credit for defeating Te Kooti at Te Porere (3 October 1869), but failed to trap his quarry at Tapapa. With McLean no longer able to protect him, he was removed from command. He spent the rest of his life agitating for money, favour, and recognition, gaining some satisfaction in 1886 with the award of a ★New Zealand Cross.

Mace, Lieutenant-General Sir John Airth (29 June 1932–) was a leading infantry officer of the post-1945 Army. Born in Ashburton, he graduated from Duntroon in 1953 and was commissioned in the New Zealand Regiment. From 1955 to 1957 he was in Malaya with the New Zealand SAS Squadron, and took part in ★Malayan Emergency operations, gaining a mention in dispatches. After serving in the ★Defence Secretariat for two years, he commanded the squadron between 1960 and 1962 and again in 1965, following his return from attendance at the Staff College at Camberley in the United Kingdom. He was involved in ★Confrontation operations in 1966 as a company commander in 1RNZIR and the ★Vietnam War the following year as the first commander of V Company. He was later Director of Infantry and SAS (1969–70), and commander of 1RNZIR at Singapore (1971–73) and ★New Zealand Force South East Asia (1979–80). He studied at the Joint Services Staff College, Canberra, in 1974 and the Royal College of Defence Studies in London in 1981. After serving as Deputy Chief of Defence Staff for three years, he became Chief of General Staff in 1984, and was elevated to Chief of Defence Staff three years later. In these positions he was forced to cope with the impact of the ★ANZUS dispute on first the Army, then the forces as a whole, and to bring to an end 1RNZIR's long tour of duty in South-east Asia. He was made a CB in 1986 and a KBE in 1990.

McGavin, Major-General Sir Donald Johnstone (19 August 1876–8 May 1960) was 1NZEF's most prominent medical officer. An Englishman by birth, he served with the Royal Army Medical Corps in the ★Boer War before emigrating to New Zealand. He settled initially in Hawke's Bay, where he was involved in the ★Volunteer Force, and later practised in Wellington. From April 1915 he commanded 1NZEF's 1st New Zealand Stationary Hospital in Egypt, ★Salonika, and France. He was ADMS of the New Zealand Division from October 1916, and was made a DSO for directing the evacuation of wounded during the Battle of Messines. He was also appointed a CMG and later knighted for his wartime services. After the war he was, until 1924, Director-General of Medical Services in Wellington. During the ★Second World War he was medical adviser to the Manpower Board.

Machine-guns New Zealand's first automatic weapons were Maxim machine-guns, purchased in 1896. Utilising the recoil caused by a discharge to extract the empty cartridge, and feed a new one, these weapons were capable of firing about 500 rounds a minute. To prevent overheating, the barrel was surrounded with a water-filled sleeve. A tripod was used for firing. A copy of a Maxim machine-gun was made at the Petone railway workshops in 1915, but no further production of New Zealand–made weapons was attempted. In the ★First World War machine-guns came into their own, proving particularly deadly when coordinated to give interlocking fields of fire and to enfilade attacks. In 1NZEF New Zealand followed the British practice of allocating two machine-guns to each infantry battalion. At ★Gallipoli, however, the battalion machine-guns were grouped together to enhance their effect. By late 1915 the Maxim had been superseded by the Vickers medium machine-gun, an extremely reliable, water-cooled, belt-fed weapon, which had a maximum range of 4000 metres but was most effective at a range of between 700 and 1100 metres. It fired .303-inch projectiles in 250-round belts at a rate which, if it had been continuous, would have been up to 500 rounds a minute. Although the barrel was lighter than the Maxim—fifteen as opposed to twenty kilograms—a four-man crew was needed to carry it, along with its tripod, sights, cooling water, and ammunition.

In February 1916 the New Zealanders' machine-gun support was reorganised: the weapons were taken from their battalions to form separate machine-gun companies of 185 men in each infantry brigade. The next step in better coordinating these weapons, in March 1918, was to group the machine-gun companies into a 932-strong battalion of sixty-four guns. Machine-guns were also used to fire suppressive 'barrages' in support of attacks. In the attack at La Basseville on 31 July 1917, for example, the New Zealand machine-gunners swept the German positions ahead of the attacking New Zealand infantry with more than 600,000 rounds. To compensate for the loss of their Vickers guns, and to overcome the problem of providing infantry with mobile firepower, infantry battalions had been equipped with the highly effective, American-designed Lewis light machine-gun in early 1916. This gas-

A New Zealand Vickers machine-gun in action at Minqar Qaim in July 1942 (*War History Collection, Alexander Turnbull Library, F-6732-1/4-DA*)

operated and air-cooled weapon fired 47- or 97-round drum magazines of .303-inch bullets. Mounted on a tripod, and operated by one man, though another was needed to carry ammunition, it had an effective range of 550 metres. Although theoretically capable of firing 550 rounds a minute, its normal rate of fire was 120 rounds a minute because of the need for magazine changes. Initially, battalions received only four such weapons, but by 1918 each possessed thirty-two. Captured German machine-guns were also used to boost the infantry's firepower. Mounted rifles regiments had begun the war with a section of two Hotchkiss light machine-guns. In 1916 the sections were formed into a 228-strong machine-gun squadron of twelve machine-guns to provide support for the New Zealand Mounted Rifles Brigade. In August 1918 a second machine-gun squadron was raised from New Zealanders in the Imperial Camel Corps, to serve with the Australian 5th Light Horse Brigade.

No machine-gun battalions or squadrons were formed in New Zealand after the war, but in 1922 a company in each battalion was reorganised as a machine-gun company. Following the outbreak of the ★Second World War, the 27th (Machine Gun) Battalion, comprising 734 men with forty-eight Vickers guns, was raised for service with the 2nd New Zealand Division. The machine-guns were usually parcelled out to support infantry battalions, providing the infantry with defensive firepower and suppressive fire in attacks. In the ★Italian campaign massed machine-guns were used to supplement barrages and to harass German positions with long-range indirect fire. When in February 1945 the battalion was disbanded, its Vickers guns were distributed to machine-gun platoons in the infantry battalions. In the Pacific theatre, two machine-gun companies were raised in June 1943 for service with the 3rd New Zealand Division in the ★Solomons campaign.

In infantry battalions the Lewis gun had been superseded by the Bren light machine-gun from 1938, though it continued in use until late in the war. Each of a platoon's three sections had a Bren gun. Of Czechoslovak origin, the Bren had been developed by Czech and British companies (its name derived from Brno and Enfield where the two companies were located). Gas-operated and air-cooled, it was an accurate and reliable weapon with a distinctive curved top-mounted 30-round magazine of .303-inch cartridges. Using a bipod, it had an effective range of 550 metres; its theoretical rate of fire was about 500 rounds a minute, but in practice the rate was about 120 rounds fired in short bursts. Although they were placed at a disadvantage by equivalent belt-fed German machine-guns, which possessed a much higher rate of fire, New Zealand troops still favoured the Bren. The weapon was used by New Zealand troops in Malaya following the war. Converted to take 7.62 mm ammunition, it remained in service with the ★New Zealand Army until the late 1980s.

In 1965 the L7A1 general purpose machine-gun (popularly known as the 'Gimpy'), a belt-fed, 7.62 mm calibre, general purpose weapon, replaced both the venerable Vickers guns in battalion machine-gun platoons and the Bren as the principal weapon of infantry sections. In the latter, the Minimi C9 5.56 mm calibre light machine-came into use in 1986.

McIndoe, Sir Archibald Hector (4 May 1900–12 April 1960) was one of New Zealand's greatest war surgeons. Born in Dunedin, he graduated from the Otago Medical School in 1923 and, after spending a period at the Mayo Clinic in the United States, secured a position at St Bartholomew's Hospital in London. Contact with Harold ★Gillies, a New Zealander who had been a noted plastic surgeon in the ★First World War, encouraged him to specialise in plastic surgery. During the ★Second World War, he treated disfigured airmen at a plastic and jaw injury centre which he ran in Queen Victoria Hospital at East Grinstead, Sussex. Appalled by the damage caused to raw wounds by the standard method of coating them with tannic acid, he developed the practice of treating severe burns by saline baths, an idea which came to him after observing that airmen who came down in the sea were less scarred than others. In all, about 4500 mutilated men benefited from his skills during the war. Knighted after the war for his pioneering work, he established a successful medical practice, as well as serving as president of the 'Guinea Pig Club' of his wartime patients.

McIntyre, Major Peter David (4 July 1910–11 September 1995) is New Zealand's best-known war artist. Born in Dunedin, he was working as a freelance artist in London after studying art at the Slade School of Fine Art when the ★Second World War began. Enlisting in the British section of 2NZEF in London, he became a gunner in 34th Anti-Tank Battery, which joined the First Echelon in Egypt early in 1940. His talents were recognised to the extent that he was invited to paint a security poster, which later became a widely distributed postcard, and worked on the divisional Christmas card. These activities led to his transfer to the draughting office in Divisional HQ, where 2NZEF commander Major-General B.C. ★Freyberg, noticing some of his informal sketches and watercolours, appointed him official war artist in January 1941 with instructions to 'Paint all my brigadiers'. Always conscious of the tension between interpretative art and visual record, he developed a style of romantic realism in endeavouring during the next four years to capture what he perceived as the character of the ordinary New Zealand soldier. His depictions of ★Crete, Sidi Rezegh, and Cassino are especially evocative, though he later described his painting as 'at best a hasty record'. Exhibitions of his work were put on in Cairo, and later in the United Kingdom, Italy, and New Zealand. Following the war, he was disappointed not to be given the opportunity to weld together his war art as a whole before being demobilised. His collection of paintings and informal sketches, the value of which he only belatedly recognised (professing later to have 'thought little of them at the time'), are part of the war art collection lodged in the National Archives, Wellington. In preparation for an autobiographical account of his experience as war artist published in 1981, he took the opportunity to repaint most of the paintings, adding new details and simplifying some.

P. McIntyre, *Peter McIntyre: War Artist* (A.H. & A.W. Reed Ltd, Wellington, 1981).

McIver, Lieutenant-General Donald Stuart (22 January 1936–) is the highest-ranking New Zealand–born officer to command troops abroad. Born in Auckland, he joined the New Zealand Army in 1952 and, after graduating from the Royal Military College at Duntroon in 1957, was commissioned and posted to the New Zealand Regiment. He gained active service experience in Malaya/Malaysia in 1958–59 and 1963–65 and in South Vietnam, where he was second-in-command of 2nd (Anzac) Battalion, in 1971. During his later career, he commanded the Army's 1st Task Force Region in 1978–80, was Deputy Commander of

Major Peter McIntyre sketching at Cassino, Italy, in 1944 (*War History Collection, Alexander Turnbull Library, F-5510-35mm-DA*)

★New Zealand Force South East Asia in 1980–81, and attended the Royal College of Defence Studies in London in 1984. In 1987 he became Chief of General Staff, but his tenure was cut short by his appointment, in February 1989, to command the Multinational Force and Observers, which since 1982 had been monitoring compliance with the Israel–Egypt peace treaty in the Sinai. The first New Zealand officer to command a peace-keeping force, he held the post until 1991, with the rank of lieutenant-general. Retiring from the Army in 1991, he was for the next eight years the Director of the New Zealand Security Intelligence Service. He was made an OBE in 1981 and a CMG in 1995.

RICHARD TAYLOR

Mackenzie, Sir Clutha Nantes (11 February 1895–30 March 1966) played an important role in sustaining morale in 1NZEF. Born in Balclutha, he was the son of a prominent politician, Sir Thomas Mackenzie, who was New Zealand's Prime Minister briefly in 1912 and High Commissioner in London throughout the ★First World War. After attending Ruakura agricultural college, he worked on a farm until he enlisted in 1NZEF in August 1914. While serving as a trooper in the Wellington Mounted Rifles at ★Gallipoli, he was blinded on 12 August 1915. Sent to England to recover, he became the editor of the fortnightly news magazine *Chronicles of the N.Z.E.F.* In 1917 his lobbying of the Minister of Defence for the production of a history of the efforts of 1NZEF which would capture the spirit of the men who formed it helped ensure that a 'Popular History' of the war would be undertaken. After the war he published an account of his experiences, *The Tales of a Trooper* (1921). From 1923 he was Director of the Jubilee Institute for the Blind, and he was knighted in 1935 for his services to the blind.

Mackie, Wing Commander Evan Dall ('Rosie') (31 October 1917–28 April 1986) was one of the highest-scoring New Zealand fighter aces of the ★Second World War. An electrician from Waihi, he entered the RNZAF in January 1941 and, after reaching the United Kingdom, was posted to 485 (New Zealand) Squadron in the following November. He helped down his first enemy aircraft in March 1942. Serving with 243 Squadron in North Africa from January 1943, he earned a DFC for a string of victories. He was equally successful while commanding the squadron during the ★Italian campaign, and briefly commanded 92 Squadron. For most of 1944 he was involved in staff duties in England, and did not return to active operations until December. During the final phase of the war in Europe, he commanded the Tempest-equipped 80 Squadron as it ravaged enemy communications. For this service he was made a DSO. In all he destroyed twenty enemy aircraft and shared in the destruction of three others. Although briefly contemplating a career in the RAF, he opted to return to civilian life in New Zealand instead.

M. Avery and C. Shores, *Spitfire Leader* (Grub Street, London, 1997).

McKinnon, Major-General Walter Sneddon (8 July 1910–20 May 1998) was a leading protagonist of New Zealand's involvement in the ★Vietnam War. Born at Invercargill, he secured a commission in the army in 1935 after attending Otago University and graduating with a science degree. He attended artillery and radar courses in the United Kingdom between 1938 and 1940, and served with 2NZEF in the ★Solomons campaign. After graduating from the Staff College at Camberley in 1944, he took part in the latter stages of the ★Italian campaign before spending a brief period in Japan with ★Jayforce. By the time he had attended the Joint Staff College in the United Kingdom in 1948, headed New Zealand's Joint Services Staff in Washington (1954–57), and commanded both Southern and Northern Military Districts, he was well qualified to assume the position of Adjutant-General in 1958. He was made a CBE in 1961. After a two-year term as Quartermaster-General, he became Chief of the General Staff in 1965, just as New Zealand was being pressed by the United States to send forces to assist it in South Vietnam. His firm advocacy of the proposition that New Zealand must pay the fees required of its membership of the ★ANZUS 'club' helped persuade a reluctant government to contribute an artillery battery. By the time he retired in 1967, the government had also agreed to deploy the first of two rifle companies to South Vietnam. Made a CB in 1966, he later served as chairman of the New Zealand Broadcasting Commission.

McLean, Denis Bazeley Gordon (18 August 1930–) was the government's chief civilian defence adviser during the ★ANZUS dispute in the 1980s. Born at Napier, he was a Rhodes Scholar in 1954 and joined the Department of External Affairs three years later. Among a variety of postings, he was seconded to the Ministry of Defence to serve as Assistant Secretary (Policy) in the late 1960s. In 1971 he attended the Royal College of Defence Studies in London. After serving briefly as Deputy Secretary, he succeeded J.F. ★Robertson as Secretary of Defence in 1979. His task became difficult when the fourth Labour government took steps after 1984 which appeared to him to undermine the basis of New Zealand's defence policy. The government's perception that he was unenthusiastic about their policy on nuclear ship visits led to an increasingly strained relationship, culminating in his resignation in 1988. During the next two years, he spent periods as a visiting fellow or associate studying defence issues at the Strategic and Defence Studies Centre in Canberra and the Woodrow Wilson Center for International Scholars and Carnegie Endowment for International Peace in Washington. He was made a CMG in 1989. With his strong defence background, his appointment in 1991 as New Zealand's Ambassador in Washington was widely regarded as signalling a desire on the part of the National government to improve relations with the United States. By the time he retired in 1994, considerable progress had been made, though a resumption of ANZUS participation by New Zealand was precluded by its non-nuclear policy.

McLean, Sir Donald (25 October 1820–5 January 1877) was responsible for the defence portfolio in the final stages of the *New Zealand Wars. A Scot, he emigrated to New Zealand in 1840 and, after acquiring a knowledge of Maori, was appointed as government mediator with Maori in Taranaki. From 1853 he was the chief land purchase commissioner and from 1856 Native Secretary. He bears a substantial responsibility for the outbreak of the Taranaki War in 1860 because of his failure to counsel the Governor against the purchase of the Waitara block contrary to the wishes of Te Ati Awa chief, Wiremu Kingi *Te Matakatea. As the General Government Agent for Hawke's Bay from 1863, he used skilful diplomacy to discourage Hawke's Bay Maori from being influenced by the King Movement. When Hauhau made incursions into the province in 1865–66, he took a hard line, and the harsh treatment of prisoners, including *Te Kooti, was to lead ultimately to renewed fighting on the East Coast. This development led to his being given control of Maori affairs as Native Minister in 1869—he had been elected to Parliament three years earlier—and he also became Minister for Colonial Defence. Now more conciliatory, he managed to secure peace, not least by reducing the confrontation with Maori by turning away from land confiscation, treating with Kingite leaders, and concentrating on establishing effective garrisons on the frontier rather than pursuing Maori 'rebels' such as Te Kooti or *Titokowaru to the bitter end. By the time he was made a KCMG in 1874, the conflict had faded away. He resigned from office two years later.

MacLean, Matron Hester (25 February 1859–2 September 1932) was a key figure in the development of New Zealand military nursing. An Australian, she qualified as a nurse in 1893 and emigrated to New Zealand thirteen years later to take up the position of Assistant Inspector of Hospitals in the Department of Hospitals and Charitable Aid. In 1911 she was appointed matron-in-chief of a proposed military nursing reserve. When the New Zealand Army Nursing Service was established in 1915, she became its head. She took the first group of NZANS nurses overseas in April 1915, but returned soon afterwards to administer the service from New Zealand. She was kept busy throughout the war performing both her civilian and military tasks, and acted as a chief health officer during the 1918–19 *influenza pandemic. She retired in 1923. She contributed a chapter on nursing to *The War Effort of New Zealand* (1923) and wrote an autobiography, *Nursing in New Zealand* (1932).

Mair, Captain Gilbert ('Tawa') (10 January 1843–29 November 1923) was a prominent colonial soldier of the *New Zealand Wars. The son of an early trader, he was probably born in Whangarei. As a young man he trained as a surveyor and became fluent in Maori. When fighting broke out with the Hauhau in the Tauranga district in 1867, he enlisted in the 1st Regiment of the Waikato Militia. While serving with a force of Te Arawa *kupapa commanded by his brother William, he distinguished himself by his courage in several skirmishes. The rescue of a soldier under fire in his first action earned him a mention in dispatches. Scouting with a party of Te Arawa soon after being commissioned as an ensign in February 1867, he discovered a large party of Waikato raiders heading for Rotorua, and defeated them in a fierce fight in a disused pa. A few days later he participated in the attack on Puraku pa near Rotorua, which led to the Waikato being driven out of the district. In March 1869 he helped organise the local defences in the Bay of Plenty against *Te Kooti, and in June took part, as commander of the Te Arawa scouts, in Colonel G.S. *Whitmore's offensive against Te Kooti and his Tuhoe allies in the Urewera. Returning to Rotorua in February 1870, he intercepted Te Kooti and his followers as they were about to negotiate with Te Arawa elders under truce and, after throwing down the white flag, routed them, though Te Kooti escaped. This exploit won him the *New Zealand Cross. Commanding the 'Arawa Flying Column' (an irregular force of about 100 men) with Captain G.A. Preece, he unsuccessfully scoured the Urewera for Te Kooti until May 1872. These operations included a daring attack on Te Kooti's camp at Waipaoa. Mair's resourcefulness, courage, and sensitivity to his Maori charges combined to make him one of New Zealand's most effective bush fighters and commanders of kupapa. Two of his brothers, William and Henry, also commanded settler or kupapa units with distinction during the wars.

G. Mair, *Reminiscences and Maori Stories* (Brett Printing and Publishing Ltd, Auckland, 1923).

Malayan campaign

Malayan campaign, which was precipitated by Japan's desire to neutralise the major British naval base at Singapore, resulted in one of the worst defeats ever for British arms. In a well-planned and executed operation, a Japanese force which was numerically smaller than its opponent landed in northern Malaya, pushed rapidly down the peninsula against a poorly organised defence, and with seeming ease captured the base, which many in New Zealand had long believed to be impregnable. The speed with which Japan captured the British position in Singapore, which had underlain New Zealand's defence strategy for two decades, came as an immense shock to New Zealanders, and was to have a fundamental impact on their country's stance in the world.

Once New Zealand had accepted that a British battlefleet stationed permanently in the Pacific was beyond Great Britain's means in the 1920s, it had strongly endorsed the second-best *Singapore strategy. As the international situation deteriorated in the 1930s the base's security became a matter of increasing interest to defence planners in Wellington. Could it hold out long enough for the British battlefleet, coming from European and Mediterranean waters, to relieve it? While the prospect of early relief had existed in the 1920s, and the nearest Japanese forces remained at a considerable distance from Singapore, the greatest danger seemed to be seaward attack on the base, against the threat of which 15-inch guns were eventually installed. The danger of an attack being mounted overland was not entirely discounted—as would often be suggested by ill-informed critics after the campaign—but it was given little priority until the late 1930s, when the 'period before relief' stretched ominously. By 1939 the possibility of the base having to hold out for six months left those responsible for the protection of the base with a difficult problem, never satisfactorily resolved. Acceptance that the Malay peninsula would also have to be held raised questions about the availability of resources, especially after war began with Germany in 1939. Coordination of effort was hindered by inter-service rivalry.

The defence of the base was made more difficult by successful Japanese encroachment southwards, both directly in China and indirectly in Indo-China, where the Vichy authorities in 1941 were forced to accept Japanese forces. Aircraft operating from Phu Quoc Island west of the Mekong Delta provided support for Lieutenant-General Tomoyuki Yamashita's 25th Army, which landed on the coast of the north-eastern Malay state of Kelantan and at Singora and Patani in southern Thailand early on 8 December 1941—ninety-five minutes before Japanese naval aircraft launched their assault on the American fleet at Pearl Harbor. This formation, which comprised three divisions and 60,000 men in all, had been training for the operation for more than a year before embarking from Hainan Island on 4 December. As part of the Japanese high command's overall operational plan, Yamashita had been given 100 days to capture the Singapore base.

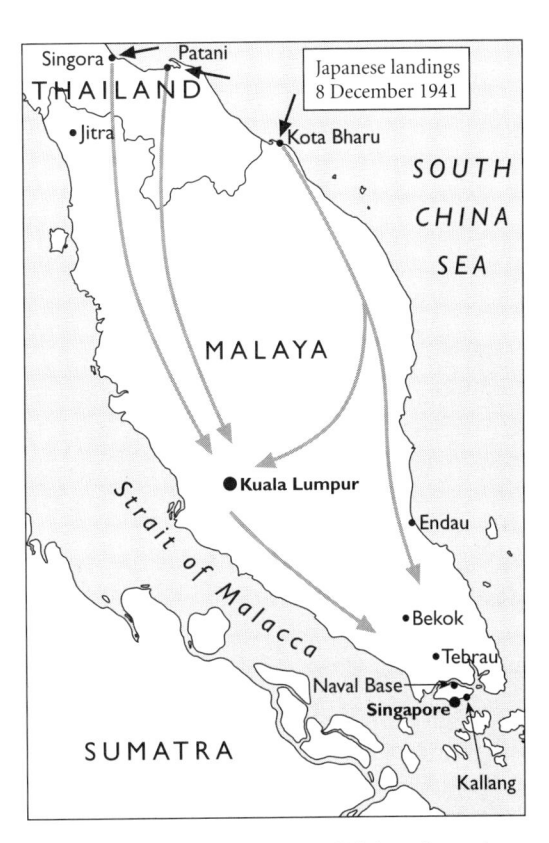

Map 14 The Japanese invasion of Malaya, December 1941–February 1942

To meet this thrust, British plans revolved around using aircraft to intercept the Japanese invasion fleet or to neutralise any landing—an approach which led to a fatal dispersal of British strength. Far from developing the mobile capacity to respond quickly to breakthroughs, the GOC Malaya, Lieutenant-General A.E. Percival, found his hands tied by the need to protect the vital airfields. Although having thirty-one battalions available, he was further hampered by the lack of tanks. The faulty British strategy was compounded by weak leadership, as the British Commander-in-Chief, Air Chief Marshal Sir Robert Brooke-Popham, failed to order Operation Matador, a British pre-emptive seizure of Singora, when the invasion became imminent. There were, moreover, never enough aircraft to make the British approach effective. Planners had estimated that from 336 to 566 aircraft were needed; but requirements elsewhere, particularly the need to bolster the Soviet Union after Germany's invasion in June

Malayan campaign

Pilots of 488 Squadron RNZAF return from a sortie in their Brewster Buffalo fighters during the Malayan campaign of 1941–42 (*RNZAF, 7116*)

1941, ensured that reinforcement on this scale was impossible. In December 1941, Brooke-Popham had a mere 158 mostly obsolete aircraft, with a further 88 in reserve, against which the Japanese disposed more than 450 army and 150 naval aircraft. Among the meagre air force resources gathered together for the defence of Malaya in 1941 was New Zealand's only direct contribution to the campaign—488 Squadron (an RNZAF unit) and 1 Aerodrome Construction Squadron RNZAF. Commanded by Squadron-Leader W.G. Clouston, the former was stationed at Kallang aerodrome just east of Singapore city, but was not yet operational when the Japanese attacked. Its plight was symptomatic of the Allied problem in Malaya: its twenty-one American-designed Brewster Buffalo fighters were simply outclassed by the main Japanese fighter, the Mitsubishi A6M2 Zero. The Buffaloes were received with neither radios nor armour (a deficiency soon remedied). The aerodrome construction squadron, which was manned by RNZAF personnel and recruits from the Public Works Department and private construction companies, had been engaged before the Japanese invasion on the construction of aerodromes at Tebrau and Bekok in southern Malaya.

The pilots of 243 Squadron RAF were also almost all RNZAF personnel, while others served in two further RAF squadrons (36 and 100) equipped with obsolete Vickers Vildebeeste torpedo-bombers. Altogether about 400 RNZAF personnel were engaged. New Zealanders also served in the theatre with the Royal Navy, including a contingent of specially recruited RNVR yachtsmen (see ROYAL NAVY IN THE SECOND WORLD WAR, NEW ZEALANDERS IN). Unlike Australia, which made available the two-brigade 8th Australian Division, New Zealand did not contribute any ground forces to the campaign, though a number of New Zealand civilians working in Malaya fought as members of local volunteer battalions.

The Japanese landings in Thailand and northern Malaya, the former unopposed, were all successful. An attempt to disrupt them by the Royal Navy's Force Z, consisting of the battleship HMS *Prince of Wales* and battlecruiser HMS *Repulse* (far short of the major fleet envisaged in the Singapore strategy, as originally conceived), ended with the sinking of both vessels on 10 December 1941. Yamashita's forces quickly seized the initiative. Breaking through the 11th Indian Division at Jitra on 12–13 December, they had soon established operational airfields in north-west Malaya and thrust southwards. On the eastern coast Japanese forces seized the key airfield at Kota Bahru. The III Indian Corps, entrusted with defending northern Malaya, was unable to restore the situation, and the Japanese effectively enveloped successive British blocking positions as they moved south along both coasts of the peninsula. The defending forces fell back to Johore, but attempts to form a line there collapsed after Yamashita, exploiting Japan's command of the sea, used amphibious landings to outflank the defenders, who by the end of January had all withdrawn to Singapore Island.

On 3 January 1941 488 Squadron took part in its first major operation, and had its first encounter with the Japanese nine days later. Kallang was heavily damaged by Japanese air attack on 9 January, and Japanese air superiority was such that a fortnight later 488 Squadron had been reduced to between one and four operational aircraft depending upon the efforts of the ground staff. From mid January, 488 and 243 Squadrons were virtually the only air defence available for Singapore Island. Although the New Zealanders received nine Hurricanes which had arrived by sea on 13 January, eight of them were destroyed or damaged on the ground by an air raid on 27 January which also virtually wiped out 243 Squadron's aircraft (a day after the Vildebeestes had suffered severe casualties in an attack on a Japanese landing force at Endau). The hardworking ground staff managed to get several of the Hurricanes operational in the next few days, but 488 Squadron's surviving aircraft were withdrawn to the Dutch East Indies on 2 February, leaving the ground staff to service a newly arrived RAF squadron for a few more days before following. The men of the Aerodrome Construction Squadron, before withdrawing to Singapore, had meanwhile been forced to blow up the airfields they had been working on. They, too, were evacuated to the Dutch East Indies, with some difficulty, in early February. In all, thirty-five New Zealand airmen lost their lives during the campaign. About forty New Zealanders were killed serving with the Royal Navy both in the Malayan campaign and in fighting at Hong Kong in December 1941, including fourteen of the RNVR yachtsmen.

Despite Churchill's rhetoric about Singapore being a fortress that would be defended to the death, the end came quickly after the Japanese launched their assault on the island on 8 February. Faulty British dispositions provided no capacity to respond effectively to breakthroughs, and the under-strength Australian units which bore the brunt of the initial offensive were pushed steadily back. Once it became apparent that the island could not be held, Percival was given permission to surrender when effective resistance was no longer possible. This he did at a meeting with Yamashita on 15 February 1942, the British forces laying down their arms at 8.30 p.m. that evening. About 130,000 troops went into captivity—the largest-ever surrender in British history. The fall of Singapore was a great shock to New Zealanders, long schooled in the impregnability of the base, but the relatively small numbers of New Zealanders involved in the Malayan campaign (and the fact that only a few of them fell into Japanese hands) ensured that it did not have the same impact as in Australia, where an undercurrent of bitterness against the British could be discerned even forty years later. But the brutal revelation of the limitations of British power in the region underlay New Zealand's post-war search for security which would culminate in the signature of the ★ANZUS pact in 1951.

H.R. Dean, *The Royal New Zealand Air Force in South-East Asia 1941–42* (War History Branch, Wellington, 1952).

Malayan Emergency was a twelve-year conflict in the Malayan peninsula which arose from an attempt by the Malayan Communist Party (MCP) to overthrow the British colonial administration of Malaya. Declared on 18 June 1948, the Emergency was the immediate response to the murder of three British planters in northern Malaya but had its roots deep in the post-war economic and political dislocation of Malaya and a sense of alienation among the Chinese community in particular. The guerrilla campaign mounted by the military arm of the MCP, which in 1949 became the 'Malayan Races Liberation Army' (MRLA), soon confronted the British authorities with a serious security problem. This was partly because of the MRLA's military effectiveness. Its origins lay in the Malayan People's Anti-Japanese Army, which had been formed during the ★Second World War. Although the Anti-Japanese Army's resistance activities were relatively limited, and it was ostensibly disbanded following the war, its structure and much of its weaponry remained available for reactivation. At its peak in 1951 the MRLA numbered about 8000 men. The support the guerrillas received from a segment of the Chinese community, and the acquiescence of much of the rest, was an important element in sustaining their campaign. This stemmed from discontent among Chinese over their status within the colony—the British withdrawal of proposed measures that would have offered eventual citizenship in 1946 had inflamed Chinese opinion—and from the failure of the administration to ensure law and order.

The British response to the guerrilla challenge was at first marked by uncertainty and ineptitude. Not until 1950 was a more coordinated programme developed, following the appointment of the retired British army officer, Lieutenant-General Sir Harold Briggs, as Director of Operations. He emphasised the

Malayan Emergency

A Canberra B2 of 75 Squadron, based at Singapore from 1958 to 1962, with one of 41 Squadron's Bristol Freighters. Hired from the RAF and retaining their British serials, the Canberras carried on their fins the squadron's distinctive markings consisting of an outline of New Zealand superimposed on a kiwi (*RNZAF*)

need to separate the guerrillas from their support, both by improving the position of the Chinese community generally and by physically concentrating civilians living near guerrilla areas in 'New Villages'. A coordinated and systematic approach, moving from south to north, was proposed. This programme was vigorously implemented by General Sir Gerald Templer, who was appointed High Commissioner with full powers over the military, police, and civil authorities in early 1952 (his predecessor, Sir Henry Gurney, had been ambushed and killed by guerrillas in October 1951). By 1954, when Templer departed, these measures had transformed the situation. The CTs (communist terrorists), as the guerrillas were now termed, had been forced back into the jungle, where they struggled to sustain themselves. From this time, the operations against them were in the nature of a mopping-up exercise.

New Zealand's first involvement in Emergency operations occurred in 1949 following the deployment to Singapore of a flight of 41 Squadron's Dakotas in response to the threatening situation in ★Hong Kong. Attached to the British Far East Air Force, these aircraft were used, as a secondary task to their flights to Hong Kong, to drop supplies to forces engaging the MRLA. One aircraft was stationed in Kuala Lumpur to carry out this role. By the time the flight was withdrawn in December 1951, it had carried out 211 sorties, dropping 284,000 kilograms of supplies. Several ★New Zealand Army officers served in Malaya while on secondment with British units from 1949. In January 1951 ten officers and fourteen NCOs also went there with the 1st Battalion, Fiji Infantry Regiment. Under the command of Lieutenant-Colonel R.A. ★Tinker initially, this unit gained a high reputation for effectiveness in operations against the guerrillas. By the time it was withdrawn in 1956 about forty New Zealanders had served with it, and two had been accidentally killed. In 1954 an RNZN frigate, HMNZS *Pukaki*, carried out a bombardment of a suspected

Malayan Emergency

Map 15 Malaya during the Emergency, 1948–60

guerrilla camp, while operating with the Royal Navy's Far East Fleet. This was the first of a number of bombardments by RNZN ships over the next five years.

New Zealand became more directly involved in Emergency operations in 1955, following its decision to contribute forces to the ★British Commonwealth Far East Strategic Reserve. The Reserve's primary role was to deter communist aggression against South-east Asia, and to provide a capacity for the immediate implementation of defence plans in the event that deterrence failed. As a secondary role, the forces committed to the Reserve were permitted to take part in actions against the guerrillas. The Army's initial contribution to the Reserve, a ★Special Air Service Squadron commanded by Major Frank ★Rennie which formed part of 22nd SAS Regiment, was particularly suited for such operations, which now consisted of seeking out the guerrillas in their jungle sanctuary. From April 1956 it deployed in the Fort Brooke area bordering the states of Perak and Kelantan and in a series of operations eliminated the local MRLA organisation, at a cost of one fatal casualty. During 1957 the squadron operated in Negri Sembilan in an area dubbed Mountainous by the guerrillas, between the towns of Seremban, Kuala Pilah, and Tampin. Again it was successful in destroying the local MRLA group.

Meanwhile RNZAF units in the Strategic Reserve were also operating against the guerrillas. On 1 May 1955 Vampires of 14 Squadron carried out the RNZAF's first operational strike mission since the Second World War and the first in jet aircraft. Between April 1955 and March 1958 the squadron, now equipped with Venoms, mounted 115 strike missions, which fell into two categories—'Firedogs' (preplanned bombing, strafing, and rocket attacks against suspected guerrilla targets) and 'Smash Hits' (immediate on-call strikes against opportunity targets in response to a guerrilla raid or 'hot' information). The Canberras of 75 Squadron, which replaced 14 Squadron in the Reserve in July 1958, were also used on bombing missions. While the effectiveness of the air strikes against targets in the jungle was inevitably limited, they provided much valuable training experience to the pilots. In July 1955 41 Squadron, half of which was deployed in the Strategic Reserve, had resumed supply dropping operations in support of anti-guerrilla forces using the highly effective Bristol Freighter.

From March 1958 1st Battalion, New Zealand Regiment, which had replaced the SAS Squadron in the Strategic Reserve, took part in operations designed to clear Perak of insurgents. Operating from Ipoh and later Grik, it mounted a series of deep jungle patrols. Its achievements in eliminating guerrillas were second to none among ★28th British Commonwealth Infantry Brigade's battalions. By the time that it was replaced by 2nd Battalion, NZR, in late 1959, most of the guerrillas had retreated across the border into southern Thailand. The greatly improved security situation was reflected in the official termination of the Emergency on 31 July 1960. For the next four years New Zealand infantrymen would periodically deploy in the border security area as part of counter-insurgency measures. The insurgents did not finally give up until the 1980s.

Fifteen New Zealand servicemen lost their lives in Malaya during the Emergency. Of these, three died as a result of enemy action. Among the casualties was the crew of a Bristol Freighter which flew into a mountain in 1956. For the New Zealand Army, with its experience of jungle warfare limited to the few small actions by 2NZEF's 3rd Division and its post-war preparations focused on the Middle East, the operations in Malaya marked a new departure. They were an important stage in the movement of the New Zealand military forces from a non-regular to a regular framework of organisation. They offered the opportunity to develop professional skills in a difficult but not too threatening operational environment, and laid the basis for effective service in the ★Vietnam War in the 1960s.

CHRISTOPHER PUGSLEY

Malone, Lieutenant-Colonel William George (24 January 1859–8 August 1915) was an inspirational battalion commander at ★Gallipoli. Born in Kent, England, he received part of his schooling in France. His first taste of soldiering came in the City of Westminster Rifle Volunteers (and later Royal Artillery Volunteers) while he was working in a London office in the late 1870s. After emigrating to New Zealand in 1880, he served briefly in the ★Armed Constabulary, farmed near Stratford, became a land agent and later (after studying at night) a lawyer in the 1890s, and was active in local affairs. He helped form and then commanded the Stratford Rifle Volunteers early in the new century and later commanded the 4th Battalion, Wellington (Taranaki) Rifle Volunteers, which following the establishment of the ★Territorial Force became the 11th (Taranaki Rifles) Regiment. He read widely on military history and current military practices. While on exercises in 1911, he unofficially introduced the ★lemon-squeezer to the Force when he had his troops push out the crown and indent the sides of their hats to give them a Mount Egmont–like appearance and a better moisture-draining quality. Given command of 1NZEF's Wellington Battalion in 1914, he proved a forceful officer who was determined to fashion a unit of the highest quality. He trained his men relentlessly in Egypt. After landing at Gallipoli, he played an important role in stabilising the Anzac position, and later commanded the critical positions at

Quinn's Post and Courtney's Post. He became increasingly critical, privately, of his superiors and the conduct of the campaign, and his demands on behalf of his men brought him into conflict with his superior, Colonel F.E. ★Johnston. During the offensive in August 1915 he led his battalion in the seizure of the Apex on Rhododendron Ridge, but baulked when ordered to attack the summit after an attempt by the Auckland Battalion had collapsed, insisting that he would not send his men 'over to commit suicide'. The attack was delayed until early the next morning, 8 August, when the Wellingtons had little difficulty in taking the summit. After daylight, they threw back fierce Turkish counter-attacks in fighting which would leave ninety per cent of the battalion dead or wounded. In this desperate situation Malone was a dynamic leader, personally leading his men forward to drive the Turks back from the crest until at about 5 p.m. he was killed by the explosion of a shell from his own side's artillery. Following the subsequent loss of Chunuk Bair and the failure of the offensive, senior officers sought to make Malone a scapegoat. Claims that he had failed to entrench his men to the best advantage on the summit have since been refuted in recent historical reassessments of New Zealand's role in the campaign, notably by Christopher Pugsley in his *Gallipoli: The New Zealand Story* (1984). Malone, the effective citizen soldier impatient with British regular incompetence, has become a symbol of New Zealand nationalism. Maurice Shadbolt depicted him as 'Colonel Connelly' in his play *Once on Chunuk Bair*. He is commemorated by a memorial gate at Stratford, and the annual class of Territorial officer cadets is named after him. Both of Malone's sons served at Gallipoli with the Wellington Mounted Rifles, and both were wounded; one, Lieutenant E.L. Malone MC, would later die of wounds received on the ★Western Front in March 1918.

Manahi, Sergeant Haane te Rauawa (25 September 1913–29 March 1986) was a gallant soldier whose failure to receive a ★Victoria Cross became a source of controversy following his death. Born at Ohinemutu, with a Te Arawa whakapapa, he joined 2NZEF's 28th (Maori) Battalion in 1939, served in ★Greece, ★Crete (where he was wounded), and the ★North African campaign, and by February 1942 was a lance-sergeant. In April 1943 he distinguished himself by his exemplary conduct in storming Takrouna, a Tunisian village perched atop a sheer escarpment which dominated the surrounding area, during the latter stages of the campaign in North Africa. Although 5th Brigade's night attack on the feature on 19–20 April failed to achieve its objectives because of artillery and mortar fire and landmines, two sections, one of which was commanded by Manahi, managed to clamber up its western precipice and seize the pinnacle at first light. They clung stubbornly to the position even when subjected to heavy shellfire. When part of the pinnacle was lost to a counter-attack during the afternoon, the enemy were driven out after vicious hand-to-hand fighting. The next morning the Italians retook the pinnacle, but once again Manahi led a counter-attack. Later that afternoon, working around the Takrouna feature, he and two men took several machine-gun and mortar posts, after which the encircled defenders surrendered. A recommendation for a VC was submitted by his commander, but Manahi was instead awarded an immediate DCM. In June 1943 he was repatriated to New Zealand and discharged. Since his death relatives and others have mounted a campaign to remedy the alleged injustice done to him over the VC recommendation (though he was by no means the only New Zealander whose recommendation failed). There have been claims that he was turned down in London because of a reluctance to see another Maori awarded the decoration so soon after that of Lieutenant Moana-nui-a-kiwa ★Ngarimu. It has not, however, been possible to ascertain what happened to Manahi's recommendation. Whatever the merits of his case, a virtually insuperable barrier to any retrospective action exists in instructions issued by King George VI that there should be no further awards of decorations for the ★Second World War after 1949.

J.F. Cody, *28 (Maori) Battalion* (War History Branch, Wellington, 1956).

Maniapoto, Rewi Manga (?–21 June 1894) belonged to Ngati Paretekawa hapu of Ngati Maniapoto. In 1831 he accompanied ★Te Wherowhero's expedition against Te Ati Awa, during which Pukerangiora pa was taken. By the 1850s he was the dominant chief of Ngati Maniapoto and one of the driving forces in the creation of the King Movement. In 1860, with the permission of Maori King Te Wherowhero, he led his tribesmen into Taranaki to support Maori fighting British forces there. They took part in the attack on the British redoubt at Huirangi on 23 January 1861. Back home, he expelled the government magistrate J.E. Gorst from the Waikato in March 1863, and led Ngati Maniapoto in the ensuing Waikato War. Along with Wiremu Tamihana ★Te Waharoa, he proved one of the most effective leaders of the Kingite forces and an able strategist. Although not present at Rangiriri—he considered the position unwise—he commanded the fortress line at Paterangi–Pikopiko. No battle took place, however, for the line was outflanked by the British commander, Lieutenant-General Duncan ★Cameron, in February 1864, and Rewi's home at Kihikihi was destroyed by British troops. Rewi fell back south of the Puniu River to cover the lands of his own tribe. When in March, and against his wishes, warriors from other tribes rashly determined to make a stand at Orakau, he was the unquestioned leader during the ensuing siege. To calls to surrender he is said to have defiantly responded 'Ka whawhai tonu matou, Ake! Ake! Ake!' ('We will fight on for ever and ever'). On 2 April he led the breakout of the defenders. Following this defeat, the Waikato tribe retreated into Ngati Maniapoto territory. In 1869 Rewi allowed ★Te Kooti to enter his lands, but the King Movement refrained from taking up arms again. Instead Rewi escorted Te Kooti back into the Taupo area, and returned to the King Country after the fugitive leader's defeat at Te Porere. Probably realising the impossibility of regaining the Waikato by military means, Rewi announced in November 1869 that he was ending hostilities. A peace settlement was eventually negotiated in 1878.

Maori and the Boer War Even before the outbreak of the ★Boer War, some Maori had revealed a willingness to contribute to the imperial cause in South Africa. The failure of the Jamieson raid, and the subsequent Anglo-German crisis in 1896, induced the Arawa tribe, for example, to offer to raise a guerrilla unit for service there. When three years later the New Zealand government offered a contingent of volunteers for service in South Africa, the Premier, Richard ★Seddon, implied that Maori men would be accepted for service, and that it was possible that a Maori contingent would be sent. Despite being personally sympathetic to the Boers' position, Wi Pere, the member of Parliament for Eastern Maori, offered to lead a contingent of 500 Maori to South Africa, as did Legislative Councillor Henare ★Tomoana. The three other Maori members of Parliament also voiced their support for the imperial cause, as did Maori leaders outside Parliament, including Ngati Porou rangatira Tuta Nihoniho, who proposed to send an ancestral mere named Porourangi to the imperial Commander-in-Chief, Lord Roberts. The small northern Kaipara Te Uri O Hau hapu of Ngati Whatua pledged funds owed to them by the government to the cause. Despite the manifestation of strong patriotic support for the imperial war effort in South Africa by some tribes, direct Maori participation was ruled out by the imperial authorities. The use of non-white troops in a 'white man's' war was deplored by some sectors of New Zealand society. Seddon continued to advocate Maori military participation. In March 1900 he claimed that Maori chiefs had offered 2000 troops for the war, 'men as good as any Boers who ever pulled a trigger'. Later that year, he proposed that the Sixth Contingent should be half manned by Maori drawn from the ★Volunteer Force. The Colonial Office in London rebuffed this suggestion, though the Colonial Secretary thought it a pity that New Zealand had not just sent Maori men as part of its contingents, on the grounds that 'no one would have known the difference'. In fact, this had happened on a small scale, with a number of part-Maori men gaining places in the contingents. The authorities turned a blind eye to such enlistments, especially if the person could speak good English. Among Maori participants in the Boer War were H.R. Vercoe, Arthur Te Wata Gannon, and William Pitt, who during the ★First World War all served with the Native Contingent and the Pioneer Battalion. Nothing came of a proposal that Maori volunteers be used as garrison troops in other parts of the Empire, thereby freeing up British troops for service in South Africa. During the conflict, Maori communities participated strongly in patriotic fund-raising events to support the fitting out of the Rough Rider volunteer contingents. A large carnival at Wellington in March 1900 to raise funds for the Transvaal War Fund was one of a number of similar events. At such gatherings, Maori participants delighted the audiences with haka such as 'Kiki to Poa' (Kick the Boer) and war dances to mark imperial successes.

ASHLEY GOULD

Maori and the First World War Te Hokowhitu a Tu, 'The Seventy Twice-told Warriors of the War God', so named by East Coast rangatira Wi Pere, embodied the active war effort of the Maori people during the Great War. Maori tribes responded in various ways to the outbreak of war in 1914. Not all wanted their young men to enlist; nor was the offer of those who wished to do so refused. Some offered men for home defence, while others expressed a willingness to underwrite some of the costs of war. The early declarations of support came mainly from traditionally 'loyal' tribes and 'Europeanised' Maori. To the early offers of help that flowed from various tribes in the first month of the war, the government responded that Maori could volunteer for the ★New Zealand Expeditionary Force (as some had done for the New Zealand contingents sent to the ★Boer War). However, it was soon moved to seek approval from London for a Maori contingent to form part of the Dominion's war effort. Permission was granted for a 200-man force for garrison duty in Egypt; a further New Zealand request soon led to the figure being raised to 500, the balance to be used for occupation duties in newly captured German Samoa. The recruitment of the contingent, overseen by a Maori Recruitment Committee (MRC) consisting of the four Maori members of Parliament and Sir James Carroll, was fraught with many difficulties. Delays in deciding where the unit would serve resulted in a number of desertions from the contingent's training camp at Avondale in Auckland. Tribal leaders had sent some men to act as elders for the young men and to safeguard the mana of individual tribes. In the European military environment the role of these men was not recognised with promotion and rank, leading to internal dissent. The contingent was organised into two companies with grouping at the platoon level based on the tribal and geographical origins of the men. Because of the realisation in Wellington that a Maori garrison force might be provocative to the Samoans, the whole 'Native Contingent', about 518 in number, was eventually sent to Egypt in February 1915. Despite being commended by New Zealand and British commanders for its professionalism and appearance, it was transferred to Malta for garrison duty. However, just days after the landing at ★Gallipoli, the imperial government requested that the Maori troops be committed to active service on the peninsula. Although the troops themselves were enthusiastic at the prospect, there were objections from Maori in New Zealand. Many of the men had been allowed to volunteer by their elders only on the understanding that they would serve as garrison troops. Active service would also demand ongoing reinforcement of the unit, which was viewed as problematical by the MRC.

Upon landing at Anzac Cove on 3 July 1915, the Maori went into the line at No. 1 Post, alongside the New Zealand Mounted Rifles Brigade. Foreshadowing their future role, they dug trenches and carried out other labour tasks, as well as directly engaging the Turks. During the August offensive, the trenches echoed with the sounds of haka as the Maori companies assisted in clearing the approaches to Chunuk Bair. Of the 477 officers and men who landed, 134 remained to be withdrawn to Egypt on 14 December 1915. Fifty men had been killed in action or had died of wounds or illness.

From their arrival at Gallipoli until after the August actions, the Maori contingent fought as a unit under the command of a Pakeha officer with Maori officers commanding from company level down. The most significant problems for the Maori contingent were the re-emergence of intertribal rivalries, first seen in the New Zealand training camp, and a clash between the commander and several officers. The small size of the contingent, the number of casualties it sustained in August 1915, and its lack of a reliable reinforcement stream, together with the sending home of four officers for incompetence (one of whom also had a medical problem), induced 1NZEF commander Major-General Sir Alexander ★Godley to divide the contingent's platoons up among the battalions of the New Zealand Infantry Brigade. So far as possible tribes and hapu were kept together. Nevertheless the MRC objected to this course because of the loss of identity involved, and the adverse effect of the resulting loss of mana on the contributing tribes in New Zealand. The issue of the returned officers also created an almost irreconcilable rift between the Maori politicians and the Minister of Defence, Colonel James ★Allen. The whole affair reflected a major difference of opinion between the contingent's Maori officers and its Pakeha commander. The three officers without medical problems were eventually returned to the front in France, where they served with distinction.

Following the establishment of the New Zealand Division for service on the ★Western Front, the Maori survivors from Gallipoli, a second Maori contingent, and the contingent's third reinforcement, which also contained men from Niue and the Cook Islands, were organised into a Pioneer Battalion. Commanded by Lieutenant-Colonel G.A. ★King, with Major Peter Buck as second-in-command, it was brought up to establishment by the inclusion of troopers of the Otago Mounted Rifles Regiment. This arrangement served the dual purpose of meeting the earlier concerns in New Zealand about identity by reconstituting the Maori as a single unit and relegating them to a less casualty-prone non-combat role. By emphasising the importance of pioneers within the divisional hierarchy, Godley appealed to Maori mana and sense of pride. The Pioneer Battalion, along with other New Zealand units, briefly went into the trenches guarding the eastern bank of the Suez Canal from Turkish attack. While awaiting departure for France in April 1916, it was given infantry training. This was important because the military authorities in New Zealand continued to send Maori and Pacific Island men overseas with minimal training.

From arrival with the New Zealand Division on the Western Front late in April 1916, the Maori Pioneers participated in a number of the major British offensives and were, for a period in 1917, seconded for service with the French 1st Army. In August and September 1916, during the Battle of the Somme, they gained a reputation for dogged and determined work. Two famous communication trenches, Turk Lane and Fish Alley, were dug towards the front-line trenches. While ostensibly a non-combat unit, the Pioneers suffered from the enemy's use of gas, artillery, and sniping. The remainder of their service on the Western Front followed a similar pattern of trench construction, and reconstruction, repairing damage caused to roads by shelling, positioning barbed wire, road and light rail construction, and other labouring tasks.

The Pioneers also ran the Divisional Trench Warfare School, and a number attended divisional and corps schools for instruction in the use of grenades and Lewis guns. The first Maori casualties on the Western Front were suffered on 21 May 1916. Early in their deployment the Pioneers prepared for special night-time trench raiding, including using meres. No success was had with the two raids actually staged. The second raid, on the evening of 11 July 1916, was led by a scouting group under the command of Lieutenant H.R. Vercoe, who subsequently transferred to the Canterbury Regiment. This was the only occasion on the Western Front where the Maori Pioneers operated officially in a directly offensive role.

The Niue men, unaccustomed to the cold of northwestern Europe, were returned to New Zealand at the end of May 1916. The pioneers were also reinforced at times with men from Samoa, the Cooks, Tonga, and Fiji. These men found the climatic conditions trying and most were eventually returned to their homes. The men from the Cooks, however, served with the New Zealand Mounted Rifles Brigade in the ★Sinai–Palestine campaign. The impact of continuous service on the Western Front increased the need for regular reinforcement for the Pioneer Battalion. The MRC sought to have the forty or so Maori serving with other units transferred to the Pioneers, but generally these men did not wish to leave their combat battalions.

★Conscription of Maori would, of course, have solved the Battalion's manpower problems. However, when compulsion was introduced in New Zealand in 1916, Maori were excluded from its application. Although Waikato refused to provide men, and Taranaki and Tuhoe did so only reluctantly, sufficient volunteers were forthcoming until the drain on manpower caused by the incessant casualties on the Western Front created a crisis. In June 1917 the conscription provisions were extended to Maori at the request of the MRC. While there were protests from several quarters that conscription breached the terms of the Treaty of Waitangi, the measure had the support of those tribes which had provided the bulk of Maori volunteers. It was, in reality, only intended to be enforced against Waikato, who, despite the strenuous efforts of Maui Pomare and Allen, remained unmoved by calls for them to serve, a stance reinforced by a sense of grievance over the loss of their land after the ★New Zealand Wars of the 1860s. After a minor confrontation, police moved in to arrest defaulters at Huntly's Waahi Pa. The government's punitive action was not restricted to just a few young relatives of the Maori King. About 100 of the 500 balloted Maori were arrested. A number were in camp at Narrow Neck at the end of the war, but no Maori conscript served overseas.

On the Western Front the Maori soldiers endured long periods of routine, intermingled with moments of intense action. On leave, they experienced the world of the French peasants as they assisted in bringing in crops of potatoes and grain. Far more revealing for them were the periods spent in the United Kingdom either on extended leave or recuperating from wounds or illness. As with other New Zealand units, the incidence of ★venereal disease was high. The Pioneers' depot was situated initially at Sling Camp on the Salisbury Plain, but early in 1918 it was moved to Bournemouth to be incorporated with the New Zealand Engineers Depot. Despite some early suspicion, the Maori quickly became accepted by local civilians, and were renowned for winning most of the swimming carnivals run by the Royal Engineers. They also travelled to hospitals and camps performing concerts of song and haka. Members of the battalion played for the divisional rugby team in France.

Following the failure of the great German offensive of 1918, the Pioneers continued their specialist role. When the Armistice finally came, they expected to take their place with other New Zealand units as part of the occupation force in Germany, but on 20 December 1918, following orders from the British high command, the battalion was turned back at the border. So commenced the long trip home to Aotearoa Te Wai Pounamu. In March 1919 a little more than a thousand of the Pioneers embarked for New Zealand on the troopship *Westmoreland*, leaving nearly 400 of their number hospitalised in France and England. They were one of only two units to return as a formed body.

After much debate within Maori circles as to the point of disembarkation for the troops, Auckland was preferred to Gisborne. Apart from logistical reasons, Nga Puhi had pointed out that their men provided a substantial proportion of the original contingent. Captain Vercoe, of Arawa descent, was given responsibility for organising a large public welcome for the soldiers at Auckland's Domain. Disembarking on 6 April 1919, the battalion was the first unit of returned soldiers to march through the streets of Auckland in wartime formation. When the East Coast men reached Gisborne, they were welcomed at the 'Hui Aroha', which included the dedication of a memorial to Wi Pere. The hui also provided the opportunity for fund-raising for the East Coast Maori Soldiers' Fund. Welcoming festivities for the men from the southern North Island and the South Island were held at Wanganui's Putiki Pa and extended over nine days, with prodigious quantities of food being consumed. The South Island contingent were welcomed in Christchurch, and again at Kaiapoi.

While still in camps in France and the United Kingdom, the Maori soldiers had been involved in educational lectures and briefings organised by 1NZEF. They were also given information about rehabilitation matters aboard ship on the way home. On the *Westmoreland* the men prepared for demobilisation by studying such subjects as 'general education', 'agricultural education', 'motor mechanics', and 'book-keeping'. For a number of reasons these efforts were not very successful, but they belie claims by some historians that the Maori troops received no *repatriation assistance on their return.

The Maori community sought to provide meaningful assistance for its returning men. A case in point was Apirana Ngata's initiative to establish the East Coast Maori Soldiers' Fund, an organisation modelled on the myriad patriotic and war relief societies which had emerged in the early days of the war and which were characterised by militant patriotism and jingoistic fervour. Unfortunately the money was squandered through injudicious investment in three farming properties which were subsequently managed poorly. Similar funds, although much smaller in respect of the resources they commanded, were established in the Northern, Western, and Southern Maori electoral districts, while Lady Pomare also established a soldiers' welfare fund. The Tuwharetoa tribe, along with a hapu from Taihape, made a spectacular, mana-driven, and agriculturally useless gift of land for Maori soldier settlement in the Kaimanawa Ranges.

Thirty-nine Maori pioneers, or 1.8 per cent, were assisted to acquire land under the centre-piece of the government's repatriation programme, the discharged soldiers legislation, compared with about 10 per cent of the nearly 90,000 Pakeha soldiers who returned from the war. The reasons for this disparity are more complex than merely asserting, as have a number of historians, that Maori were not included in the official scheme. More significant than their presumed exclusion was their inclusion on equal terms with Pakeha soldiers. For the government had decided on 28 March 1916 that, for the purposes of repatriation assistance, Maori soldiers were to be considered on identical terms to Europeans. In the context of the moment it was significant and gave meaning to the spirit of comradeship and equality that developed among all those who had served with the Pioneers during times of mutual sacrifice, be they Maori, Pakeha, or Pacific Islanders.

J. Cowan, *The Maoris in the Great War* (Whitcombe & Tombs Ltd, Auckland, 1926); P.S. O'Connor, 'The Recruitment of Maori Soldiers, 1914–18', *Political Science*, vol 19, no 2; C. Pugsley, *Te Hokowhitu a Tu: The Maori Battalion in the First World War* (Reed, Auckland, 1995).

ASHLEY GOULD

Maori and the Second World War see MAORI WAR EFFORT OVERSEAS IN THE SECOND WORLD WAR

Maori defence works Polynesian ancestors of the Maori brought with them a tradition of warfare when they first came to New Zealand—probably about the twelfth century AD according to current knowledge. It is, however, not clear if this included experience of fortifications employed at earlier island homes, or if defensive works developed in New Zealand independently, subsequent to Maori arrival. In the Pacific region, fortifications are also found in Fiji, Tonga, and Samoa, as well as in the Austral and Marquesas islands, where hilltop earthworks are similar to Maori pa.

A recent analysis of radiocarbon dates from archaeological excavations suggests that the earliest fortified pa in New Zealand were built around 1500. According to the evidence, pa made an appearance at this time in a number of regions in the northern part of the North Island, none having priority. Also, since a variety of pa forms were then in use, any suggestion that there was an historical development in pre-European fortification styles can be discounted.

In August 1998 the New Zealand Archaeological Association site record scheme held records of 6813 fortified pa, based on the field evidence. Of these, 6697 were in the North Island, and just 116 in the South Island. Most are near the coast, so that a pa distribution map clearly delineates the coastline of much of the North Island. Inland areas with numbers of pa include parts of Northland, Waikato, Hauraki, the Bay of Plenty, and Hawke's Bay.

Fortifications were not just fighting positions, but settlements in which whole communities lived, or gathered when an attack was threatened. Typically, pa were part of a pattern of settlement in the tribal landscape in which undefended hamlets and temporary camps also were occupied as part of a yearly round of economic activity. Sometimes only the very old and the young would remain at a pa; at other times it might serve as a central place for wider community activity (of iwi, hapu, or whanau). The large number of kumara storage pits on some pa suggests an important role in protecting food resources. When enemies threatened, the pa offered a safe haven with food supplies already in place.

Pre-European Maori fortifications had to contend with a limited range of offensive weapons, mainly hand clubs and wooden staffs for hand-to-hand combat. Long spears were thrust through stockades. Missiles were confined to rocks and stones, and the occasional use of fire-sticks to set alight the tinder-dry thatch of houses. An important strategy was the siege of a pa to deny its inhabitants food and water.

Fortified pa were located according to need, usually close to the economic resources that maintained a community. Behind the defences were areas which might be as small as 200 square metres, or alternatively of several hectares, as at the volcanic hill pa of the Auckland isthmus. Pa could stand alone, or

Maori defence works

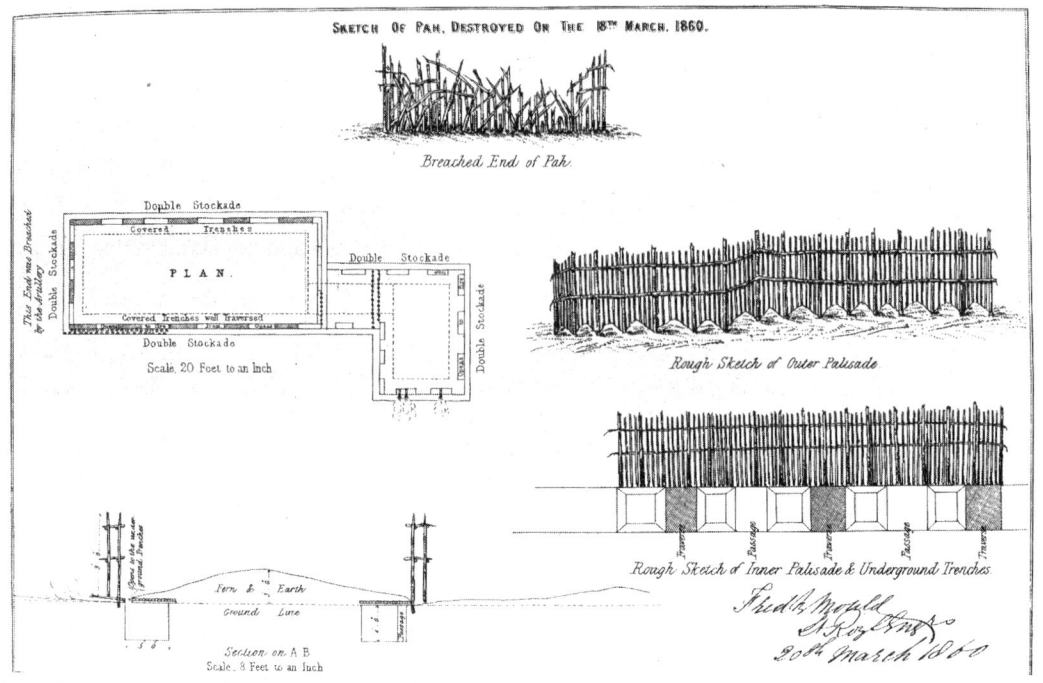

Plan of a pa destroyed by British forces on 18 March 1860 drawn by Lieutenant F.B. Mould RE

make up a network of supporting works scattered over iwi or hapu territory. They could be located aggressively at a contested boundary or in control of an important route, or might be placed well within tribal lands to serve as a retreat. Some pa were occupied only very briefly, others were important tribal citadels for many generations.

Where a position was naturally strong, well-developed artificial defences were not needed. For pa at the summit of small islands, as in the Bay of Islands, the sea and surrounding cliffs provided the necessary defences. Examples of these tiny retreats are given in the accounts of late eighteenth century European explorers. Swamp pa on natural or artificial mounds were protected by surrounding water or swamp—for example, beside Hauraki rivers or Waikato lakes. Precipitous hill country and steep-sided promontories above the sea also provided naturally strong positions, where short lengths of transverse defences (across the approaches) were all that was needed for security, the rest being left to nature.

Where naturally strong positions were lacking, an immense effort was put into constructing artificial defences, the greater part of a total pa area often being taken up by its defensive works. Ring-ditch pa, common in Taranaki, comprised a platform (or platforms) for accommodation, enclosed by an excavated trench, or trenches, and timber stockades. Where the landform suited, as at Auckland's volcanic cone pa, terrace and scarp defences confronted an enemy with successive steep scarps topped by stockades.

Massive stockades could include entire tree trunks, standing four or five metres high and set two metres into the ground to prevent them from being pulled out in an attack. Tiny entrances gave control over what were otherwise weak points, as did winding approaches through successive defensive lines which allowed defenders to use their long jabbing spears and stockpiled stones. Defenders occupied fighting platforms which were high above gateways and at other places where extra forces were needed.

Large pa were a maze of small enclosures occupied by different family groups. In each enclosure were dwelling houses, cooking sheds, and pits or elevated platforms for food storage. The summit platform (tihi) was usually occupied by a senior chief of the pa. Divisions within the pa reflect a segmented community, which nonetheless came together in the face of a threat to the whole. The maze of access ways and enclosures also assisted in defence by making up a succession of defensive positions.

In the early nineteenth century the availability of muskets meant that a garrison or community was no longer protected in the exposed hilltop positions preferred for hand-to-hand fighting. At Tataraimaka in Taranaki, in about 1818, an attacking force with a few muskets was able to pick off the leading chiefs who manned the fighting platforms, before storming the pa. Guns altered the balance of attack and defence. In response, Maori engineers developed a range of concealed firing positions—'rifle pits', transversed trenches, projecting angles for flanking fire, and covered ways—to return the advantage to the well-protected garrison. The so-called 'gun-fighter pa' used in intertribal fighting was sited on low-lying ground, with an all-round visibility for a field of fire which was not wanted in the days of hand-to-hand fighting.

A second major response to European technology arose in the 1840s, no longer in relation to intertribal fighting but with the enemy now the very Europeans who had brought with them the new technology. The new factor was artillery. Outstanding early examples of what historian James Belich has termed 'modern pa' are Ohaeawai and Ruapekapeka in the Bay of Islands district, where the engineer was the Nga Puhi war leader *Kawiti. Innovations focused on protecting the pa garrison against artillery fire and ensuring the destruction of the follow-up enemy assault force. Modern pa achieved their greatest success against European forces in 1845 at Ohaeawai, in 1860 at Puketakauere, Taranaki, and in 1864 at Gate Pa, Tauranga.

Illustrated on p. 300 is Te Kohia, near Waitara, where the cross-section shows a typical double stockade line and covered rifle pits. Defenders sat out a bombardment in covered pits within the pa. In the subsequent assault they took up positions in the trenches, pushing the barrels of their guns through the inner stockade and beneath the raised outer line. Not shown is the flax screen which was usually forward of the outer stockade to absorb artillery fire and hide any damage to the defences. At Puketakauere, Maori in concealed rifle pits forward of the pa escaped the bombardment and poured an unexpected fire on advancing troops.

At Gate Pa British artillery comprised two 24-pounder howitzers, two 8-inch and six Coehorn mortars, and Armstrong guns including two 6-pounders, two 40-pounders, and a huge 110-pounder. The pa and garrison of approximately 235 fighters was pounded for most of a day. When a breach was made in the defences and an assault force charged in, the defenders fought back from a maze of rifle trenches and underground bunkers to drive the enemy from the pa. It was a remarkable conclusion to the history of Maori skill and experience in fortification engineering. (See also MAORI TRADITIONAL WARFARE; MUSKET WARS; NEW ZEALAND WARS)

NIGEL PRICKETT

Maori in the armed forces Maori involvement in the armed forces has steadily increased in importance over the last 150 years. The first proposals for harnessing Maori martial capacities in the interests of the state were made in the 1850s, though only in the context of overseas service. Governor George *Grey in 1852 suggested that, in the event of war between the British Empire and France, a force of 4000 Maori recruits, officered by Europeans and stiffened with European regulars, should be raised to seize Tahiti, the first manifestation of *forward defence thinking in New Zealand. A similar suggestion was made by Colonel R.H. *Wynyard, the officer commanding the imperial troops in New Zealand, during the Indian Mutiny five years later. The supposed benefits for New Zealand's internal security, by the removal from the colony for a time of potential Maori warriors, were not unrecognised by both Grey and Wynyard. Neither suggestion found any favour in London.

Although there was no requirement for Maori men to enrol in the *Militia, which was designed to protect European settlements primarily against the threat of Maori attack, Maori participation in the *New Zealand Wars on the government side (see KUPAPA) helped undermine this exclusive approach. This was reflected in the *Volunteer Force, in which Maori corps were formed as a result of both the 1878 and 1885 *Russian scares. Maori sections were also formed in some corps. Although most Maori Volunteer corps soon disbanded, one at least, the Wairarapa Mounted Rifles, proved very successful, and was compared 'most favourably' with other mounted corps in New Zealand in the early 1900s. Colonel A.P. *Penton, the Commander of the Forces from 1896 to 1901, did not favour Maori units because of his doubts regarding their reliability, especially in handling weapons, and perceived language problems. As a result no Maori corps were accepted during the upsurge in the Volunteer Force which resulted from the *Boer War.

The fighting in South Africa again brought to the fore the question of possible Maori service overseas. For more than twenty years Maori offers of men for such service had come to nothing. A 'whole regiment' had been offered during the 1878 Russian war scare, and in 1885 the Ngati Haua chief Hote Tamehana, an old New Zealand Wars foe of the Europeans, had offered a 200-man party for service when the Mahdi led a successful uprising against British power in the Sudan. This probably underlay the government's willingness to contemplate Maori participation in a 1000-man force it considered offering for service in Afghanistan soon afterwards during the *Pendjeh crisis. Maori offers to serve in South Africa during the Boer War were rebuffed (see MAORI AND THE BOER WAR), as was a suggestion in 1902 that a 1000-strong Maori force be raised for service anywhere in the world, thereby releasing imperial troops for deployment in South Africa. Penton's successor, Major-General J.M. *Babington, was sympathetic to the idea of

Maori in the armed forces

Kayforce Padre R.H. Rangiihu leads a Maori concert party during the visit of Brigadier C.E. Weir to the 16th Field Regiment in South Korea in September 1954 (*Kayforce Collection, Alexander Turnbull Library, K3027*)

Maori participation in the forces. He thought that training Maori men would be the 'easiest thing possible', especially given their fondness for military life. His influence was probably responsible for the 'new departure' in defence policy which the Premier, Richard ★Seddon, announced in April 1902. Maori mounted corps were to be formed throughout the colony, with as many as 5000 Maori volunteers being enrolled and serving under a commander of Maori corps. Seddon also foresaw Maori involvement in his proposed ★Imperial Reserve. But Babington's efforts to turn this vision into reality over the next four years came to nothing, perhaps because Seddon had second thoughts about raising such a large Maori force.

When ★compulsory military training was introduced in 1911, no compulsion was applied to Maori men except in regard to the Senior Cadets. But many Maori volunteers served in the ★Territorial Force. In areas with large Maori populations they were formed into separate troops or sections, either within existing units or additional to them. Nevertheless Maori participation in the Territorial Force was not regarded with much favour by the mainly imperial officers who dominated the upper levels of the military hierarchy. A meeting of senior officers in 1914 noted, for example, that 'as a rule' Maori Territorials were 'dirty in their habits, and untrustworthy as regards care of arms, equipment, and clothing issued to them'. But their quickness to learn and enthusiasm were noted.

In the ★First World War it appeared at first that Maori involvement would again be prevented, despite Prime Minister William ★Massey's belief that as 'free citizens of the Empire' Maori men should have 'the privilege of fighting for the Empire'. Eventually, however, a contingent was sent (see MAORI AND THE FIRST WORLD WAR), and in 1918 a conspicuously unsuccessful attempt was even made to apply ★conscription to Maori males of military age in the Waikato, where feeling was still strongly influenced by the New Zealand Wars. Following the war, the Army authorities reverted to their unenthusiastic approach to Maori involvement in the Territorial Force. Some of the 'right type' were allowed to join, but it was believed that any substantial influx of the roughly 9000 Maori men of military age would be disruptive, because many Europeans were reluctant to serve in the same units as them. A suggestion in 1939 for the creation of a Maori pioneer battalion came to nothing.

During the ★Second World War Maori involvement was more conspicuous (see MAORI WAR EFFORT OVERSEAS IN THE SECOND WORLD

WAR), and greatly boosted Maori mana within society in general and the armed forces in particular. In May 1941 a drive began to enlist Maori in the Territorial Force, and Maori sub-units were formed in some northern regiments. By the end of October 1941, 559 Maori were serving overseas with 2NZEF, 741 in the Territorial Force, and 487 in the ★Home Guard. In January 1942 all Maori registered for 2NZEF and the Territorial Force were called up immediately and posted to units near their homes. It was decreed that they were to have equal opportunities for promotion. A second Maori Battalion was formed for home defence from men who had volunteered for overseas service, and a third, from men enlisted for home service only, was mooted. The latter forced attention to be given to increasing the number of Maori officers in the Territorial Force (there were only three in mid 1942). The tradition of having separate Maori units continued in ★Jayforce, with the 270-strong D Squadron, Divisional Cavalry Regiment, being organised on a tribal basis. There had, of course, never been separate Maori units in the RNZN or RNZAF.

Changing demographic and social patterns following the Second World War led to the increasing integration of Maori and European society, especially with a large Maori influx into cities and towns. These changes were reflected in the armed forces, with the proportion of Maori servicemen greatly increasing. Major-General K.L. ★Stewart, the CGS from 1949 to 1952, was firmly of the view that the Army should end the practice of highlighting a distinctive Maori involvement in the Territorial Force by raising separate Maori units. Formal integration was not necessary because there had never been any strict segregation. As a result, no separate Maori unit was included in ★Kayforce in 1950, though as the Korean conflict progressed informal arrangements did lead to some unofficial Maori sub-units, for example, Maori gun crews within 16th Field Regiment or a transport platoon within 10th Transport Company. The number of Maori volunteers for Kayforce steadily increased. As a percentage, they represented 7.5 per cent of the main body in December 1950 (at a time when the Maori were just under six per cent of the New Zealand population), 13.4 per cent of the Expansion Draft in August 1951, 20.6 per cent of the replacement drafts in 1952, and 28 per cent of the reinforcements in the final stages of the war. Overall, one in seven of those who served in Korea was Maori, a small proportion of them aboard RNZN frigates.

These figures were replicated in the New Zealand involvement in South-east Asia. Of 709 men in the infantry battalion dispatched to Malaya in January 1958, 22.9 per cent were of Maori descent. New Zealand troops overseas had always, in a relatively superficial way, incorporated a Maori dimension in their behaviour, partly as an identifying trait. The haka, for example, was often performed by troops of purely European extraction. With the greater Maori involvement in the Army, Maori cultural elements assumed an increasingly important place in Army activities, both in New Zealand and in South-east Asia. Apart from the haka, the karanga (sentry call) and the wero (challenge) were incorporated into the battalion's formal routines. A Maori concert party was formed. In 1962 a meeting house and marae was constructed in the battalion's lines in Terendak. Opened and consecrated as 'Tumatauenga' (Maori god of war), it was a place to hold important unit functions, and a setting for the Maori concert party's performances. When the battalion moved to Singapore, it was recreated at Neesoon, and later at Dieppe Barracks. The growing Maori component of the Army was highlighted in 1978, when Major-General B.M. ★Poananga became CGS, the first (and so far only) Maori to hold the Army's highest position.

During the 1990s official encouragement of Maoritanga has grown substantially with the incorporation of Maori language and ceremonial dress in the Army in particular. About 30 per cent of service personnel are Maori, a rate about twice their representation in the general population. Mostly in the Army, they are heavily represented in the 'combat' arms, though still disproportionately few in the officer corps. The New Zealand Army is the largest single employer of Maori.

Maori traditional warfare War was a major activity among Māori. As well as a strenuous and emotional activity, it was full of ritual and ceremony at every part of the process. Fighting could be provoked in a number of ways, the most common being curses, quarrels as to land boundaries, squabbles over resources and women, and the desire to take revenge for murders. Almost all of these pretexts involved a breach of personal or tribal mana (prestige), which was one of the major incentives for war. Disgrace inflicted by a perceived defeat or loss of mana, though sometimes aimed only at a high-ranking individual, affected the whole hapū who, as kin, also shared the ignominy. A simple intentional or unintentional insult (kanga) by word of mouth or slight on the mana of a tribe, hapū, or chief was never allowed to pass with impunity. A blood atonement was required to restore mana. Speaking of war and insult, one nineteenth century Ngāti Kahungunu chief, Te Hāpuku, remarked that 'a blow is soon forgotten but a kanga (cursing word) lives forever'. Defeat in battle or captivity by an enemy did not constitute a total loss of mana. This only occurred when captivity and defeat went unavenged. To fail to avenge a chief's death or respond to an insult left mana

Maori traditional warfare

A party of Maori armed with traditional weapons, including the mere, patu, and taiaha, after the affray at Moutoa Island in 1864 (*Alexander Turnbull Library, G-12420-1/2*)

unrestored—huka-kore (of no consequence or unavenged). And so utu (revenge) played a large part in the restoration of mana.

Whakapapa (genealogy) was integral to the negotiation of alliances in war. Relationships with other tribes and chiefs enabled political and tribal coalitions to be made for common warlike goals. Invitations to provide assistance in warfare could come in many varied traditional ways. Sometimes an important tribal heirloom or weapon, known as a rākau-whakaware, was sent to a neighbouring tribe as a gift to join a war party. The weapon may on occasions have been smeared in human excrement; washing it clean denoted agreement to join the fight. Food also played a large part in such invitations. This was take-kai-kinaki. After the death of Tī-waewae of the Lake Tūtira district, the Ngāti Tātara-moa, then also known as Ngāti Kura-mōkihi, asked Hunuhunu to seek support for a battle of revenge against the Urewera people. He took with him a calabash of preserved tui (a species of bird), a delicacy which he offered to chiefs like Te Apa-tū of Wai-hīrere, Tiaki-wai at Awa-tere, Ngārangi-mate-ao at Rua-taniwha river, Puhi-rua at Pā-kōwhai, and Tū-akiaki at Te Reinga. At first none of the chiefs accepted the delights. Only when Tū-akiaki partook of the kai (food) were the others persuaded to do so as well. They all went to the aid of Ngāti Kura-mōkihi. This conflict culminated in the death of the Mataatua paramount chief Te Maitaranui. A variation on this process of alliance formation was ngākau, where repulsive food was offered; accepting and eating indicated a willingness to ally with the applicant. Other forms of request included songs, such as Matangi Hauroa's famous tiwha 'Takoto rawa iho ki te pō', appealing for assistance in war.

Traditionally there was a season for war. This was when the star Rehua or Antares presided over the seasons—the time of gathering in and storing food crops for Takurua (winter). In this period Rehua's name becomes Rehua-kai-tangata (Rehua the consumer of men), which refers to the time of war, when people die. With stores of food and other resources available and no food preparations to be done, the men were free to engage in war and utu.

Many traditions and narratives liken the war party to environmental phenomena. He ō Kākā was an aphorism that spoke of warriors on the warpath travelling with a weapon in one hand and food in the other, thereby emulating the habits of the Kākā bird. Mata-kai-kutu (louse-destroying spirit) was the descriptive phrase for a warrior intent on destroying his enemy (lice). Kai-rākau was a generic term for a body of men skilled in arms; Rangamārō was a war party that would keep fighting until the enemy was defeated or they themselves were annihilated on the battlefield; Te uira waewae (footsteps of lightning) denoted a war party on the move. Sometimes the war party comprised not only men but also women and children. While on the road to war, scouting parties known as kiore (rat) were sent ahead of the main parties. The head scouts were also called Torokaha (a name for a leading rat). These men were dedicated to Tū-mata-uenga (god of war) since they were given over to death if captured.

Rank and command in battle were important. Often men of superior rank as commanders held titles such as kaingarahu. Kai-kawe-i-ngā-riri was the designation of one who carried the burden of the people on his shoulders and fought for their well-being. People would approach these warriors to seek utu on their behalf. Young warriors always tried to make their mark in battle, though without overstepping the mana of their superiors. The youngsters would try to bite the head of the greatest enemy chief on the battlefield. If accomplished, the mana of the opposing chief was destroyed and the warrior received acclaim and mana.

Etiquette prevailed even on the battlefield. Young warriors did not take over the right of greater chiefs for supremacy in the fight. In the battle at Hataitai between Tūāhu-riri and Hika-oro-roa, a youngster named Turuki ran in front of Hika-oro-roa, who belittled him for his insolence. Turuki went and told his uncle Tū-te-kawa, then an ally of Hika as well as a brother-in-law to Tūāhu-riri, what Hika had said. Feeling the shame of this insult, Tū-te-kawa chose to divulge Hika's battle plan to Tūāhu-riri, allowing him to escape. However, Tūāhu-riri's wives were killed by Tū-te-kawa, perhaps so as not to allow Hika the satisfaction of killing them and to disgrace Tūāhu-riri's hapū. When Hika and

Maori traditional warfare

Tū-te-kawa departed the killing scene by canoe, Tūāhu-riri recited a charm that conjured up a storm to overturn the canoes. He then yelled out to Tū-te-kawa to return his clothes and war belt, while at the same time advising him and his waka to hug the coast, lest he perish in the forthcoming storm. Hika and his people perished at sea.

Other quarrels and insults were resolved through feasts called Hau-kai-hau, where the best foods of two opposing chiefs would be laid before each other, the side with the best served delicacies having to concede land and women to the victor. When the Heretaunga chief Tama-i-waho made a belittling statement that Te Rehunga had a small house, Te Rehunga replied, 'Ahakoa iti taku whare, i ahu mai au i te kopua kana-panapa' (Although my house is small, it emanates from the centre of the pool). Tama-i-waho tested Te Rehunga's mana by applying the hau-kai-hau concept, which saw Te Rehunga collect food delicacies from his lands and lay them before the chiefs of Tama-i-waho, who could not reciprocate in the same manner. As a result Tama-i-waho was obliged to gift lands and resources to Te Rehunga. Many of these types of feasts took place in the East Coast regions.

Rākau Māori (Māori weapons) consisted of a number of war clubs and spears. Maori warfare involved purely hand-to-hand combat. The primary weapons of chiefs and warriors were the mere pounamu (a short greenstone club), patu onewa (stone club), patu parāoa (whale-bone club), koti-ate (a short club), waha-ika (a bone weapon), tewhatewha (a long-handled weapon with an axe-shaped head), and taiaha (quarter staff). The last named was a chief's weapon of authority, used in attack and defence, with the feather tufts around its neck being used to distract an opponent. Another weapon of authority was the whale-bone hoe-roa. Although it has sometimes been suggested that projectiles were seldom used in Māori warfare, there is evidence of many forms of spears: the huata (spear), hoto (spear made of stingray barbs), and koikoi (a double-edged spear). The slings for throwing spears and stones were known as kōtaha or kōpere. Karakia or charms known as hoa-rākau were recited over many of these weapons to render them effective in war. The most beautiful of Māori arms were the mere pounamu, possession of which was regarded as a sign of great mana. They were an heirloom proudly passed down through the generations. Pahikaure, the celebrated mere pounamu of the Tū-whare-toa chief Herea ★Te Heuheu Tukino, was regarded as a sacred weapon. Originally obtained from a battle at Ara-tipi at Wai-mārama, it was said to have the power to become invisible if not held by its rightful owner. It was also said this heirloom had been buried five times with ancestors. In times of desperation some warriors used their weapons as a ransom for their lives. When the D'Urville Island chief Tū-te-pōuri-rangi of Ngāti Kuia found himself in a defensive position, he threw his weapon Kauae-whiria (the jawbone twister) into a waterfall and bargained for his life to be spared if he revealed its whereabouts to his captors. In peaceful times the mere and the patu were strapped to the inner part of the forearm in case of surprise attacks. In addition, a warrior's weapon was also used as his pillow, hence the terms urunga parāoa (whalebone pillow) and urunga pounamu (greenstone pillow). In battle, some warriors had weapon carriers alongside them: even ★Te Rauparaha, as a youngster, had carried his uncle Hape's weapons.

The clothing worn by warriors was conspicuous by its absence, apart from a kilt or apron, or in some cases a dogskin war-cloak known as tapahu. Another cloak was the pauku or pukupuku used as a shield against spear thrusts. Before battle the pauku cloaks were placed in water, causing the fibres to swell and thereby forming a thick mass said to be impenetrable to spears. Other clothing used for protection were the tōpuni and puahi cloaks, and for long-distance journeys pāraerae or flax sandals were worn. Body decoration such as the moko (facial tattoo) and kokowai (red ochre) or tutu smeared over the face and other body parts gave a fierce countenance to a warrior.

There were many forms of battle strategies adopted by Māori, all with names poetically and metaphorically selected to mimic the habits of environmental phenomena. Kura-takai-puni (encircle the encampment), for example, was a solid company of warriors dedicated to making one charge and not becoming separated throughout the movement which, resembling a fern frond, encircled the enemy until they are destroyed; similar movements to this were named Porowhitawhita (encircle), Kawau-ruku-roa (the long diving cormorant), and Kawau-mārō (the cormorant of firm flight). In the last named a single wedge of warriors was formed to charge the enemy whether for victory or defeat.

Close hand-to-hand combat was the form of fighting preferred by Māori. Face-to-face battle conventions included Riri-tuku-tahi, a headlong charge; Tuku-tahi-pātata, a close hand-to-hand combat; Te āpiti-tū, a face-to-face fight when forces are locked together; Toka-tū-moana, a short-range fight where every man fought equally. Retreating during battle was very common in Māori strategy, not so much to depart the scene but more to rally for another attack; one term for this type of action was called Tai-whakaea (the avenging tide). Other forms of this were Manu-kāwhaki (a driving bird), which constituted a regular retreat and attack system drawing out the enemy by stratagem and forming a continual running battle and

Maori traditional warfare

which was also known as Pārera-nekeneke (ducks in movement); Rua-te-pupuke, a retirement of warriors to the right and left of the enemy, followed by a re-forming and attack on the enemy's flanks and rear; Riri-hunuhunu, a feigned retreat to lead the enemy to an ambush.

Treachery was a major instrument of revenge. Trickery or wit was a major ruse of the Maori and can be seen in many battle situations. Enticing your enemy out of their fortified village took a good trick. One way was to pretend you were stranded whales. In the battle against the people of Heipipi, Tāraia ordered his men to clothe themselves in black garments before swimming out to sea with their weapons concealed. They then came ashore as if they were a school of stranded blackfish. The inhabitants of Heipipi pā emerged from their palisades to take their share of food from the sea, and were set upon by Tāraia and his people once they were in close proximity. Another incident like this was recorded in the Hokianga, where a tribe bred many dogs. After the numbers grew, they slew their pets, and stitched the skins together around a framework of manuka poles to resemble a huge whale. A hundred men were concealed inside the 'whale', which was towed at sea in the night to a beach in front of their enemy's village. When the villagers came out to divide the stranded whale among them, the hidden men emerged from this virtual Māori Trojan horse to defeat them. At other times, the arrival of visitors would lead to anxious attempts to deduce whether they were friend or foe. One tribe sent their youngest children to wander through the approaching visitors and detect whether they had hostile intentions. Hatu-patu of Te Arawa fame tricked his enemies by dressing up the trees with red feather cloaks to give the illusion that he had double or treble the number of men in his actual force. Porou-mata of the East Coast used the same technique, called rama-pito-rua, under which double ended torches were lit at night to strike fear into the hearts of the owners of a kūmara patch he was raiding. Aroaro-tahurihuri was another battle where the aruhe (fern root) diggers of Ōtatara pā were ambushed while on the returning track, the enemy men replacing the diggers. Once all the supposed diggers were in the pā and an attack made, the Ōtatara people did not know where to turn, hence the name of the battle. This was the conquering battle of the Whatumamoa people.

Others used omens of death to discourage their enemy. Kahungunu possessed a pet kawekaweau (a large lizard). He placed the ipu (bowl) where this lizard lived, at the entrance of the pā, as the enemy were approaching and opened the lid. When the kawekaweau emerged, it was seen by the enemy as an omen of death, and they were deterred from attacking. Others used tribal atua (deities) to escape. At Awa-mārahi marae in the Tuakau district, the people of the pā were surrounded. The chief inside the pā made a pole with big pāua eyes during the night and built a fire at its base. The reflection of the glowing eyes glaring down at the waiting enemy led them to delay their attack until the morning, providing enough time for the people to escape.

Victory resulted in not only the acquisition of lands and spoil but also the restoration of mana. Conquest in battle was known as Te rau o ngā patu or raupatu, which figuratively speaking means a hundred flashing war clubs, while claims to land based on conquest were known as ringa-kaha (by the strong hand). Raupatu (conquest) from the defeated people's point of view often resulted in a permanent loss of mana and often control of their lands. Those unable to hold their lands and keep their own 'fires alight' on the land were considered to have suffered defeat with a consequent loss of mana. Defeat, or even a likely defeat, was not taken lightly by Māori. It was a source of great shame if a war party abandoned the fight or even returned home defeated. In the battle between Tāraia and Rākai-moari, at Ara-paoa-nui, Hine-pare castigated her husband Tāraia and his men for abandoning the fight, exclaiming how their actions would lead to her femininity being left for the enemy. Her people's courage was restored, and they turned and carried on the fight till victorious. At other times, a returning defeated party would be greeted at home by a tribe angry and ashamed at their lack of virility. To be taken prisoner and treated as a slave was considered an even greater shame.

Peace and the restoration of mana was sought after warfare. Being able to negotiate peace in wartime was considered a major trait of a warrior leader. It was part and parcel of being a soldier of rank. Peace treaties were made in a number of ways, including by negotiation, termed Kōrero-ā-whare (talk of the house), politically arranged marriages, and payment of ransoms. Rongo-ā-whare was a peace made by women. If an outside army won the day, any peace talks were usually followed by a marriage of convenience between the victors and the defeated land owners. This was to combine the two peoples together and place the mana of the victors on the land through marriage. Sometimes people became tired of constant warfare and sanctuaries of peace were created. One example was Te Marae-o-Hine, a sanctuary which belonged to Rongo-rito, a woman of Ngāti Raukawa. Another was the Wai-roa pā, which belonged to Rauhina, a wife of the warrior chief Tapu-wae. Refugees who reached these women's pā entered a place of sanctuary.

Another avenue for long-lasting peace was contained in the concept of a greenstone door. The tatau pounamu or the symbolic greenstone door was a peace treaty device meant for a more permanent peace contract between two warring factions. This usually saw two prominent mountains between tribal land boundaries chosen to represent that doorway of peace, which was also sealed with a political marriage. In such a peace agreement the door was closed to all those wanting to draw blood.

BRADFORD HAAMI

Maori War Effort Organisation (MWEO) was formed to meet New Zealand's special needs relating to Maori participation in the ★Second World War. In particular the sustenance of 28th (Maori) Battalion, which left New Zealand with the Second Echelon of 2NZEF in May 1940 (see MAORI WAR EFFORT OVERSEAS IN THE SECOND WORLD WAR), presented special problems. Although ★conscription for both military and civilian purposes was introduced a month after the battalion's departure, it was not applied to Maori at the request of Maori members of Parliament, so that the battalion was left dependent upon voluntary enlistment for its reinforcements. Even if compulsion had been introduced, identifying Maori eligible for war service and direction into essential industries would have been difficult because there were no Maori electoral rolls and registration for social security purposes covered only a quarter of the estimated Maori workforce. During 1941, the voluntary system of enlistment came under strain. Steered by a committee of five Maori members of Parliament chaired by Paraire Paikea, an intense publicity campaign was mounted from May, though with only partial success. Enlistments from some districts, especially those affected by confiscations following the ★New Zealand Wars, remained a cause for concern.

Paikea was convinced of the need for an organisation to handle recruitment and deal with all Maori war-related activities. Assisted by his Ratana–Labour parliamentary colleagues, he drafted a scheme and won support for it among the Maori community by stressing the organisation's political potential. It would provide Maori with a unique opportunity to demonstrate their capacity for leadership and planning. Commitment from tribal districts suspicious of the government ensured that others would not hold back. With Maori leaders giving their full support, the government approved the establishment of the Maori War Effort Organisation on 3 June 1942. Within six months the MWEO's structure was in place. The country was divided into twenty-one zones, and 315 tribal committees were formed. One or two members from each committee joined one of forty-one executive committees; twenty recruiting officers helped coordinate the committees' activities. Colonel H.C. Hemphill headed the MWEO as Chief Liaison Officer, operating in association with the Army authorities but directly responsible to Paikea. The Maori parliamentary committee insisted that the MWEO follow Maori custom and tradition in the selection of Maori recruiting officers, even if the practice was at odds with military and administrative procedures. In July 1942 the Cabinet agreed that the principle of tribal leadership should be extended to Maori involvement in ★Territorial Force units in New Zealand and in the ★Home Guard. Recruitment was given a boost when the government also accepted the parliamentary committee's proposal that restrictions on the enlistment of Maori with dependent children above a certain limit be dropped.

Although the MWEO's main function was assisting with recruiting for the forces, its work expanded in other directions. The committees had a good knowledge of local conditions and were often required to consider education, vocational training, and better land use. A crucial part of their war effort was encouraging local food production. Committee work was voluntary and received no government funding. The MWEO's role grew as manpower needs escalated. Committees were given responsibility for the registration of all Maori males between eighteen and fifty-nine years of age and females between twenty and thirty. They were able to enforce registration and, in the light of the capacity of local people, to recommend the kind and locality of employment. Their powers were extensive: manpower officers of the ★National Service Department were required to consult with tribal committees before issuing directions which affected Maori. Specific urgent needs required speedy action, and freezing works and dairy factories depended on local Maori assistance. The committees handled a range of issues: employer–employee relationships, absenteeism, tracing workers who used aliases to change jobs, and other irregularities. By 1943, in Auckland and Wellington several hundred young Maori women were living in the poorest city areas while working in hotels and restaurants; when this problem came to the MWEO's attention, a recommendation was put to the government that Maori women welfare officers be appointed to the Native Department.

When the MWEO was established, the government underestimated its significance, assuming that it would have a six-month life at a cost of £7000. The arrangement clearly proved its worth: in 1943 more than 27,000 Maori of an estimated population of 95,000 were either in the armed services or had been placed in essential industries. In that year Paikea asked that the time-frame be extended. He reasoned that the MWEO was not only essential in meeting the country's wartime demands and short-term Maori needs but also that it would have a key role in post-war

Maori War Effort Organisation

Maori development. It had given Maori a new confidence: the government had allowed the Maori people to organise in their own way, to move into the mainstream of economic and social life, and above all to assume positions of leadership. This last had probably been the decisive factor in overcoming Maori suspicion, although other aspects had been significant, such as promises that confiscation claims would be settled at war's end (particularly important to securing Te Puea's help) and that rehabilitation for Maori servicemen would be adequate.

Although the government agreed to extend the MWEO's existence to the end of April 1944, officials who had accepted the principle of Maori leadership in a war crisis were less than willing to tolerate the prospect of it in peacetime. The organisation's position was weakened, too, by Paikea's death in April 1943. Although the Prime Minister, Peter ★Fraser, had ultimate responsibility as minister in charge of the Maori War Effort, effective leadership of the MWEO passed to Eruera Tirikatene, who was committed to fight for its survival but did not command the political influence of his predecessor. In any case, war needs had become less pressing by the middle of 1943. With sufficient Maori recruits for its purposes, the Army could not justify maintaining its recruitment officers, and the Treasury recommended that the MWEO be terminated on 31 January 1944.

Within the Native Department there was no commitment to preserving the MWEO. Initial support for the organisation as a means of making the extensive contact with Maori communities demanded by wartime conditions had waned as the MWEO's activities steadily encroached upon its own. The jurisdiction of each authority was not always clear. The department's work had expanded in a somewhat ragged fashion just prior to the war, and its resources were strained by wartime requirements. Rehabilitation now became the key driver for change. Insisting on equality of opportunity and treatment for Maori in housing, land settlement, and training, the Rehabilitation Department forced the Native Department to review its processes and standards. It did so gradually, but Maori returned servicemen, able to apply for rehabilitation assistance under the auspices of either the Native Department or the Rehabilitation Department, found the former wanting. Hoping for a new deal in the post-war Maori world, they joined with the MWEO and the Maori members of Parliament in a political battle over the future of Maori policy and the role of the Native Department. Though the MWEO won a reprieve for the duration of the war, its operations were gradually scaled down.

By the middle of 1943 Rex Mason, a Minister of Native Affairs with little understanding of the MWEO, considered that it was undermining his department's credibility. In 1944, in an attempt to curb the MWEO's growing influence, he initiated the introduction to the department of a system of welfare officers. He also drafted a bill to revive Maori councils, most of which were defunct or had been incorporated into the MWEO. The MWEO's representatives and the Maori members of Parliament, struggling to secure a place for the MWEO in the structure of government Maori policy, rejected the bill. The members of Parliament recommended the establishment of a new Department of Maori Welfare (or Administration) which, like the MWEO, would incorporate Maori from the senior administrative level to grass-roots tribal committee structure. The aim was to retain a degree of autonomy, with government resources being used more effectively for accelerated Maori development.

The Native Department opposed the plan. Prime Minister Peter Fraser, though sympathetic to Maori aspirations, was anxious to avoid a rise of Maori nationalism. He preferred reforms which would allow the department to deal more adequately with Maori affairs. Mason was left to finalise the necessary legislation and was influenced by Sir Apirana Ngata (still influential after losing his Eastern Maori seat in 1943), who also feared the political potential of the MWEO.

The Maori Social and Economic Advancement Act 1945 left the structure of the Board and Department of Maori Affairs intact without specific provision for Maori leadership in either agency. The tribal and executive committees were incorporated into the department's structure and were enabled to engage in a range of activities which could be subsidised on a pound for pound basis. Essentially the legislation was a compromise that satisfied no one. Maori were generally doubtful about its prospects of successful implementation and Native Department staff viewed it as a means of absorbing the MWEO's personnel into their ranks. As Minister of Maori Affairs for the last three years of the first Labour government, Fraser pushed for the Act's speedy implementation, but it was not a compulsory measure and progress in implementing it was slow. By March 1948, 85 per cent of the Maori population was organised in the areas gazetted under the Act.

Fraser had high hopes for the new structure. Believing that Maori spirit and energies, revitalised by the war effort, could be harnessed for peacetime development, he recognised that if the MWEO was absorbed into the day-to-day activities of the department its vitality would be sapped. He wanted the tribal committees to take the initiative in generating plans and proposals for Maori advancement and to approach government agencies for assistance. But, given the terms of the Act, his expectation that Maori might consider the tribal committee structure a measure of self-government was unrealistic. Firmly under departmental control, the committees were to work only at local level. Tribal power was divorced from responsibility for development of any sound economic base for Maori advancement, and there was no provision for the committees to play a role at national level, as the MWEO had hoped. Established and accorded special powers because of war needs, the MWEO had fulfilled its role, and paternalistic patterns of government policy-making and decision-taking were reasserted.

C. Orange, 'A Kind of Equality: Labour and the Maori People 1935–1949' (MA thesis, University of Auckland, 1977).

CLAUDIA ORANGE

Maori war effort overseas in the Second World War Maori made a sustained and valuable contribution to the armed forces during the ★Second World War. Many volunteered immediately for 2NZEF, and left New Zealand with the First Echelon in January 1940. There would be men of Maori descent in most of the battalions throughout the war, while numerous Maori volunteers also served in the other services. They were to be found, for example, in aircrew serving with the RAF in both Europe and the Far East. Sergeant B.S. Wipiti shared the distinction of shooting down the first Japanese bomber over Singapore in 1941, while Sergeant P.P. ★Pohe was the first Maori pilot to arrive in England after passing through the ★Empire Air Training Scheme. He flew bombers over Germany until shot down; he was, in 1944, one of forty-seven Allied airmen executed after escaping from Stalag Luft III. A handful of Maori women went abroad with the New Zealand Army Nursing Service, while many younger men served in the RNZN and RNZAF. Some did so because their qualifications fitted them for a particular service, others joined out of interest, others again joined because they were under age but found they could be accepted into the service of their choice. Since enlistments for 2NZEF, particularly in areas of dense Maori population, were overseen by Maori registration officers who often knew the candidates' families, there was less chance of army service if under age.

Nonetheless, the Maori war effort is most directly associated with 28th (Maori) Battalion, the all-Maori unit which the government had agreed to establish in October 1939 following representations by the Maori members of Parliament on behalf of the tribes. A volunteer unit (apart from the officers appointed), it would be additional to the nine battalions and support units already forming for 2NZEF. Most Maori who had already volunteered for overseas service transferred to the Maori Battalion. Constructed out of a desire by Maori to represent themselves, the unit reflected, at the same time, an eagerness not only to prove that they were the equal of their Pakeha comrades in war but also to earn the full benefits and privileges of New Zealand citizenship, for even in 1939 the sense of equality and acceptance was marginal.

The battalion was organised on tribal lines under tribal leaders, though influential Maori were to be disappointed by the appointment of Pakeha officers to senior positions. Major G. ★Dittmer, a professional soldier, was its first commander. After preliminary training at Trentham for prospective officers and NCOs, the battalion went into camp at Palmerston North in late January 1940. Three months later, its main body, numbering 681 including thirty-nine officers, left Wellington for Egypt with 2NZEF's Second Echelon. Because of the diversion of the Echelon to the United Kingdom, the Maori troops found themselves training for the defence of southern England, occupying a variety of camps. The battalion's first casualty occurred in September 1940, when a dispatch rider was accidentally killed during a night manœuvre; he was buried with full military honours in Maidstone Cemetery.

The battalion departed for the Middle East in January 1941. Arriving at Helwan Camp, it was met by 300 reinforcements. With more than a year's training, and a series of route marches to improve fitness after the lengthy sea voyage, the troops were more than ready for their baptism of fire. This was to come in ★Greece, to which 2nd New Zealand Division was deployed in March 1941. In its first encounter with the enemy, at Petra Pass, the battalion suffered four killed and eighteen wounded. Following the exhausting retreat and evacuation, six officers and seventy-seven men, mostly from the reinforcement company, became ★prisoners of war after being cut off at Kalamata. In ★Crete, the Maori Battalion occupied positions in the Platanias area when the German airborne invasion began on 20 May. Two days later, it took part in the belated New Zealand night counter-attack on the key Maleme airfield. The Maori troops used the bayonet to good effect to eliminate numerous enemy machine-gun nests, but were unable to reach their objective before daylight exposed them to enemy air attack and forced a withdrawal. On 27 May they launched a famous bayonet charge, after enemy troops had quietly closed with them while they rested. The instant Maori reaction—a haka followed by a charge made more terrifying for the hapless enemy by the sound of war cries—typified the Maori style of fighting throughout the war. At the cost of four killed and ten wounded, the Maori eliminated about 100 Germans and put the rest to panic-stricken flight. In reference to this incident, the official historian of the campaign would later note the 'most conspicuous élan and valour shown that hard day', which, by checking the enemy advance, greatly assisted the retreat of the Commonwealth forces. The battalion was successfully evacuated to Egypt.

Maori war effort overseas

Members of 28th Maori Battalion prepare for action at Faenza in 1945 during the Italian campaign (*War History Collection, Alexander Turnbull Library, F-8057-1/2-DA*)

The Maori Battalion returned to action in the *North African campaign later in 1941. On 23 November it captured Sollum Barracks, taking 247 Italian prisoners. When Dittmer was wounded, Captain E.T.W. Love became the first Maori to command the battalion, albeit temporarily. An attack on a column of tanks and motorised infantry three days later and an ambush of another enemy column at Menastir on 3 December inflicted heavy casualties at minimal cost to the battalion. Further important actions occurred at Sidi Magreb (where more than a thousand Italian prisoners were taken) and at Gazala before the battalion, now commanded by Lieutenant-Colonel H.G. Dyer, was deployed to Syria. When it returned to Egypt in June 1942, it had a Maori commander, Love having taken over from Dyer the previous month. During the New Zealand division's dramatic breakout at Minqar Qaim, the Maori troops carried all before them in a ferocious bayonet attack. Their performance here and in later battles at El Alamein in July–August 1942 led German commander Erwin Rommel to complain that they were 'scalp hunters'. The battalion distinguished itself during the Munassib depression offensive in early September and during the action at Miteiriya Ridge during the Battle of El Alamein in October. On 2 November it played an important role in the final breakthrough, providing a firm base while other Allied units breached the enemy defence.

During the latter stages of the North African campaign the Maori Battalion was again well to the fore. At both Medenine and Point 209 (Tebaga Gap) during March 1943, it excelled in defensive and offensive operations respectively. At the latter, it virtually annihilated a German panzer grenadier battalion, though suffering heavily itself; C Company, which bore the brunt of the fighting, had gone into the battle with 128 men and returned with thirty-one. Among the many decorations awarded to members of the battalion for this operation was the *Victoria Cross, which went posthumously to Second Lieutenant Moana-nui-a-kina *Ngarimu, the first Maori to be so honoured. Many members of the battalion believed that a second such award should have been made to Lance-Sergeant Haane *Manahi for his part in action at Takrouna a fortnight later, in which the Te Arawa and Mataatua–based B Company performed outstandingly.

The battalion's hard fighting in 1942–43 was reflected in the casualty rate among its commanders: Love died of wounds in July, his successor, Lieutenant-Colonel Frederick *Baker, was wounded in November, and Major I.A. Hart, who then took over, was immediately mortally wounded as well. Lieutenant-Colonel

C.M. ★Bennett became commander as a result, but he, too, was wounded at Takrouna in April 1943 and was replaced by Lieutenant-Colonel K.A. Keiha. Among the troops the cost had also been high, one company alone having lost the services of 164 men by February 1943. Feeling the strain, senior officers of C Company, in that month, felt constrained to report to Sir Apirana Ngata on the disconsolate state of the battle-weary battalion, and especially their own company; they urged Ngata and their elders to reconsider the question of keeping the battalion in the field. By the time this letter was received by Ngata, the battalion had suffered further heavy casualties at Tebaga Gap. When the matter was brought to the attention of the Prime Minister, the need for a furlough scheme was accepted. As a result Keiha and 128 men of the main body returned to New Zealand on three months' furlough; the ★furlough affair ensured that few of them would return to the Middle East. Their places meanwhile had been taken by reinforcements drawn from the 2nd Maori Battalion, which had been raised in response to the threat of invasion by Japan (see MAORI IN THE ARMED FORCES).

After a period of rebuilding and retraining the battalion was committed to the ★Italian campaign. Among the troops there was a sour taste arising from the failure to award Manahi a VC and the reversion to a Pakeha commander, Lieutenant-Colonel M.C. ★Fairbrother, the official reason being that there was no sufficiently experienced Maori officer to take the position, though superior officers' unhappiness with the state of the battalion may have been influential. The battalion's introduction to the fighting on Italian soil was sobering: their first attack, at Orsogna in December 1943, failed with more than fifty casualties, while at Cassino A and B Companies sustained horrendous casualties during a failed attack on the railway station in February 1944. Of the 200 men who started out, 128 were killed, wounded, or captured. Under Major R.R.T. Young since December 1943, the battalion thereafter took part in the advance to Florence. From November 1944 it was once again under Maori command, namely that of Lieutenant-Colonel Arapeta ★Awatere. After being forced to withdraw from Faenza in December, the Maori troops settled down in billets at Forlì before taking part in the final advance to Trieste. When Awatere returned to New Zealand in June 1945, Major J.C. Henare became the battalion's last commander.

With the exception of 270 men who were deployed to Japan as part of the Divisional Cavalry Regiment (see JAYFORCE), the battalion returned to New Zealand in January 1946. Between 1939 and 1945, 15,744 Maori had volunteered for service both at home and abroad, a figure made all the more remarkable by the fact that the Maori population of New Zealand at the time was just under 100,000. Of the 3600 who saw action with 28th (Maori) Battalion, 649 were killed or died on active service, and 1712 were wounded. A further twenty-nine died after being discharged as a direct result of their service. Two men died while training as reinforcements in New Zealand. Lieutenant-General Sir Bernard ★Freyberg, 2NZEF's commander, could well write later that no infantry battalion in his force 'had a more distinguished record, or saw more fighting, or, alas, had such heavy casualties as the Maori Battalion'.

J.F. Cody, *28 (Maori) Battalion* (War History Branch, Wellington, 1956); W. Gardiner, *Te Mua o te Ahi: The Story of the Maori Battalion* (Reed, Auckland, 1992).

MONTY SOUTAR

Maritime reconnaissance aircraft, RNZAF

★Bomber aircraft patrolling the coast carried out the RNZAF's first maritime reconnaissance operations. New Zealand's first purely maritime reconnaissance aircraft were the Walrus biplane flying boats carried by the ★cruisers HMS *Achilles* and *Leander*. During the ★Second World War, Lockheed Hudson bombers, too slow and poorly armed for front-line bombing duties, were particularly valuable as maritime reconnaissance aircraft, undertaking long-range patrols about the South Pacific. For most of the war, however, maritime reconnaissance was carried out by Consolidated PBY Catalinas. These were replaced in the 1950s by Short Sunderland flying boats, which were in turn replaced by Lockheed P3 Orions in 1967.

The principal RNZAF maritime reconnaissance aircraft have been:

Catalina, Consolidated (8–9-crew flying boat). Wingspan 31.7 m; length 19.5 m; armament 4 x .303-inch machine-guns, 4 x 650 lb depth charges or 2 Mark 13 torpedoes; maximum speed [PB2B-1] 312 km/h; range 5000 km; power 2 x 1200 h.p. Pratt and Whitney Twin Wasp radial engines.

The first twenty-two Catalinas (PBY5s) entered service with the RNZAF in April 1943, equipping 6 Squadron and 3 Operational Training Unit. In 1944 thirty-four more (PB2B-1s) were delivered to 5 Squadron and the Operational Training Unit. Catalinas were active during the ★Solomons campaign, carrying out long-range patrols, escorting ferry flights, and undertaking search and rescue missions. In all about 150 men were picked up from the sea by New Zealand 'Dumbos', the nickname given to air–sea rescue Catalinas. After the war the aircraft in the best condition, fitted with a radar above the cockpit, were flown by 5 Squadron, which was based at Lauthala Bay, Fiji. The Catalinas were withdrawn from service during 1953, and all were sold for scrap.

An RNZAF P3 Orion attacks a submarine during an anti-submarine warfare exercise (RNZAF)

Orion, Lockheed P3K (10-crew). Wingspan 30.37 m; length 36 m; armament 4 x Mark 46 homing torpedoes or 4 x Mark 83 bombs; maximum speed 761 km/h; range 7100 km; power 4 x 4910 e.s.h.p. Allison turboprops.

New Zealand was the first customer outside the United States to acquire Orions. Five were delivered in 1967, and equipped 5 Squadron at Whenuapai. A sixth was purchased from the RAAF in 1985. The Orions have since operated from the Antarctic to the equator. Although first and foremost an anti-submarine weapon—the aircraft carry an array of sophisticated radar, sonar buoys, and homing torpedoes—they have also routinely carried out resource protection patrols and search and rescue missions. During the 1980s data systems, tactical displays, and navigation systems were modernised, and a further modernisation was carried out in the following decade.

Sunderland, Short (13-crew flying boat). [MR5] Wingspan 34.3 m; length 26 m; armament 12 x .303-inch machine-guns, 2000 lb depth charges, bombs; maximum speed 343 km/h; range 3300 km; power 4 x 1200 h.p. Pratt and Whitney Twin Wasp radial engines.

The Sunderland was a military derivative of the Empire class flying boats. Apart from four Mark III Sunderlands used as ★transport aircraft at the end of the Second World War, the RNZAF operated sixteen ex-RAF reconditioned MR5 Sunderlands between 1952 and 1967. They were flown by 5 Squadron from Lauthala Bay, Fiji, and briefly by 6 Squadron from Hobsonville. Apart from undertaking the conventional maritime reconnaissance role of searching for submarines, they ferried passengers to outlying islands and carried out mercy missions until replaced by Orions. The sole surviving New Zealand Sunderland is displayed at the Sir Keith ★Park Airfield at the Museum of Transport and Technology in Auckland.

Singapore III, Short (7-crew biplane flying boat). Wingspan 27.4 m; length 19.5 m; maximum speed 233 km/h; range 1600 km; power 4 x 730 h.p. Rolls-Royce Kestrel engines mounted in tandem pairs.

Four of these obsolete flying boats reached Fiji in late 1941. The only really long-range aircraft available to the RNZAF at the time, they undertook maritime reconnaissance and search and rescue missions (picking up more than fifty ditched aircrew and sailors) before being replaced by Catalinas in April 1943.

Marquette, sinking of On 23 October 1915 the troopship *Marquette* was heading for ★Salonika carrying an ammunition column, a New Zealand Army Medical Corps hospital, and about 600 horses. That morning the ship was torpedoed by the German submarine *U-35*. The ship took less than ten minutes to sink, during which several lifeboats were damaged while being launched. It was several hours before rescue craft arrived, by which time 167 had drowned, including twenty-two New Zealand medical orderlies and ten nurses. The New Zealand nurses displayed great courage throughout the ordeal. Those who were lost are commemorated in a nurses' chapel at Christchurch Hospital.

Marsden, Colonel Sir Ernest (19 February 1889–15 December 1970) oversaw New Zealand's defence science effort during the ★Second World War. English-born, he attended Victoria University, Manchester where he studied under Ernest Rutherford. In 1914 he became Professor of Physics at Victoria University College in Wellington. Enlisting in 1NZEF in January 1916, he was sent to the ★Western Front, where he was posted to the Divisional Signal Company. In 1917 he was seconded to the Royal Engineers and was involved in the location of enemy artillery by sound-ranging. He was awarded an MC and mentioned in dispatches. Shortly after returning to New Zealand after the war, he relinquished his chair to become Assistant Director of Education. From 1926 he was Director of the Department of Scientific and Industrial Research. In 1939 he went to Great Britain to be briefed on secret new defence technologies, of which radar was the most important. On his return he was appointed Scientific Adviser to the ★Army Department (and later Director of Scientific Developments). His most important achievement lay in the radar programme which he initiated in New Zealand. At some stage he became aware of Allied plans to build an ★atomic bomb, and he ensured that a handful of New Zealand scientists were involved in the programme. After resigning from his position in the DSIR in 1947, he was for six years scientific adviser in the New Zealand High Commission in London. In 1956 he became chairman of the Defence Science Advisory Council. For his services to science, he was made a CBE (1935) and CMG (1946), and was knighted in 1958.

Massey, William Ferguson (26 March 1856–10 May 1925) was New Zealand's prime minister during the ★First World War. An Ulsterman by birth, he came to New Zealand in 1870, and was a farmer before entering Parliament in 1894. He formed a Reform Party administration in 1912, and remained prime minister until his death. On the outbreak of war in 1914, he wasted no time in pledging New Zealand's full support for the imperial cause, and his government quickly raised expeditionary forces for both the occupation of German Samoa and dispatch to Europe. He came into conflict with the Governor, Lord Liverpool, over the provision of an adequate escort for the latter. Massey made three extended visits to Europe during and immediately after the conflict. With Sir Joseph ★Ward, with whose Liberal Party he had formed a National coalition administration in 1915, he attended the Imperial War Conferences in 1917 and 1918, sat in the Imperial War Cabinet, and visited New Zealand troops in France. In 1919 he attended the Paris Peace Conference and signed the Treaty of Versailles on behalf of New Zealand; he also obtained in London the loan of the cruiser HMS *Chatham* to recommence the development of the New Zealand Naval Forces. At Imperial Conferences in 1921 and 1923 Massey took part in important discussions on ★imperial defence strategy, especially the future of the ★Anglo-Japanese Alliance. His desire to see the relationship with Japan continued stemmed largely from a perception of the Empire's relative weakness in the Pacific; he firmly supported the inherently anti-Japanese development of the proposed Singapore naval base, towards which New Zealand offered £200,000 in 1923. Primed by the Governor-General, Lord ★Jellicoe, he strongly criticised the British Labour government's decision to halt work on it in 1924. A great imperialist—he once declared that 'if it were possible for the point of view of New Zealand and the point of view of the Empire as a whole to come into conflict, I would go for the Empire at once'—he believed that the British Empire provided a framework within which New Zealand could find both economic and military security, and that New Zealand must assist in ensuring the Empire's position.

Mead, Major-General Owen Herbert (24 January 1892–25 July 1942) is the highest-ranked officer of the New Zealand armed forces to have been killed on active service. A native of Blenheim, he began his military career when he was commissioned in the ★Territorial Force in 1911. Volunteering for 1NZEF in August 1914, he went to Egypt as a lieutenant in the Canterbury Battalion, and later served at ★Gallipoli and on the ★Western Front. His conduct during the fighting on the Somme in September 1916 earned him the first of two mentions in dispatches. From September 1917 he commanded the 2nd Battalion, Canterbury Regiment. He was made a DSO. After the war he secured a permanent commission in the ★New Zealand Staff Corps. After attending the Staff College, Camberley, in 1927–28, he occupied increasingly important positions. He was Adjutant-General from 1935 to 1938 before taking command of the Northern Military District. Perhaps unlucky not to secure a senior command in 2NZEF's 2nd New Zealand Division, he had to be content with the positions of Adjutant-General and Second Military Member on the Army Board. From October 1940 he commanded the Southern Military District and 3rd (Southern) Division. In February 1942 he was appointed to command the Pacific Section of 2NZEF, with particular responsibility for the defence of Fiji, a key outpost in New Zealand's defences against the Japanese. He was killed when the RNZAF Hudson in which he was travelling to Tonga was lost at sea.

Medical treatment By today's standards, military medical treatment in the nineteenth century was primitive and often deadly. Maori traditional medicine was unable to cope with gunshot wounds or introduced disease. The former were treated by bathing the affected area with the boiled juice of flax roots and plugging it with a dressing of clay. British medical practice was also rudimentary. Surgeons were attached to units and a few doctors accompanied the main forces, but there was no permanent medical organisation. Most injuries were simply treated on the field, and amputation was the safest method of dealing with severe wounds to the limbs. For more serious wounds the accepted treatment was to evacuate the patient to a hospital to the rear, and let nature take its course. In the later nineteenth century there were advances both in medical treatment, for example an awareness of the importance of sterile bandaging in preventing sepsis, and also in the status of medicine in the military (see RED CROSS). Even so, the overall standard of treatment remained low.

The shortcomings of existing medical arrangements were brutally exposed during the ★Boer War, in which 139 New Zealanders died of disease (mainly typhoid) caused mainly by poor sanitation and ineffective medical treatment. Among the lessons learnt during this conflict was a greater awareness of the need for sanitation, and the medical services in New Zealand were expanded and reorganised. The New

Medical treatment

Zealand Medical Corps was established in 1908, grouping together the assorted surgeons attached to ★Volunteer Force units and converting the bearer corps into field ambulances. A three-stage process for casualties was devised: casualties were to be stabilised at field ambulances near the front line before being evacuated to a casualty clearing station further back, and thence to more established hospitals.

This evacuation framework fell apart at ★Gallipoli in 1915, as incompetent planning and the sheer scale of casualties overwhelmed the available medical resources. In both the April landings and the August offensive, the casualty clearing stations on the beach and advanced dressing stations in the gullies became choked with an unexpectedly high number of casualties. The stations themselves were often under fire because of their exposed positions. From the field ambulances and casualty clearing stations on shore the wounded were evacuated to ★hospital ships and ambulance carriers (dubbed 'black ships'). Poor coordination and mismanagement ensured that the wounded were often left on the beach too long; once on board they found appalling conditions. From the ships casualties were taken on to hospitals in Egypt, or later Lemnos, Malta, or England. Such was the chaos of the operation that relatively lightly wounded men were sent to England, while casualties still convalescing found themselves being sent back to Gallipoli. After a few months in the crowded positions on the peninsula, soldiers began to come down with dysentery and typhoid, which thrived because of open latrines, unburied bodies, swarms of flies, and the heat. The men's resistance was reduced by poor food and their general exhaustion. There was a shortage of even the most basic medical supplies. In spite of the best efforts of the medical staff most of the force became severely debilitated. By the end of August 1915, 10 per cent of the New Zealanders at Gallipoli were being evacuated sick each week.

Medical arrangements were significantly better on the ★Western Front; the static and highly structured environment of trench warfare and the closeness of hospitals in England meant that the medical system, in the main, worked well. Wounded were first taken to a regimental aid post just behind the front line, usually in a dugout or captured pillbox and often under fire (medical personnel sometimes wore protective steel body shields). At these posts, which normally consisted of a medical officer and several stretcher bearers, wounds were examined, dressed, and tagged before the soldier was evacuated to an advanced dressing station (of which the New Zealand Division usually operated two) several kilometres further to the rear and then on to the main dressing station. At the latter relatively minor or urgent life-saving surgery (such as the amputation of shattered limbs) would be carried out if necessary. ★Shell-shock cases were sent to a rest centre attached to the main dressing station. Horsed or motor ambulances took the wounded man on to a casualty clearing station, effectively a surgical hospital with specialist surgeons, anaesthetists, and nursing sisters, where most of the important surgery was undertaken. From there the wounded soldier would be sent on to stationary hospitals in France. Further treatment and recovery were undertaken in England, where 1NZEF operated three general hospitals. After convalescence, recovered soldiers would eventually be returned to their units, while invalids were repatriated to New Zealand.

Wounded New Zealanders are prepared for evacuation at Bir el Chleta, Libya, in 1941 (*War History Collection, Alexander Turnbull Library, F-3733-1/2-DA*)

Medical provisions extended beyond the mere evacuation of wounded. Dental hospitals were established for the troops, and chiropodists attached to battalions treated foot ailments. At the front, divisional sanitary sections ensured the disposal of waste and the treatment of water, and rest stations allowed mildly sick soldiers to recover without being taken off the divisional strength. Divisional baths and laundries also reduced the incidence of disease. Disinfestation of lice was of particular importance in lessening the danger of typhus, and regular applications of whale oil and fresh socks reduced the incidence of 'trench foot'. Nevertheless, living in often muddy, exposed bivouacs, exhausted soldiers were susceptible to pneumonia, dysentery, and other illnesses. At the end of 1918 the ★influenza pandemic spread rapidly through the New Zealand Division.

Similar medical procedures were employed, albeit on a lesser scale, in the ★Sinai–Palestine campaign, though the wounded were carried by sand carts or endured a tortuous journey by cacolet camel over much greater distances than on the Western Front.

Another major difference from the campaign in France was the prevalence of malaria, which afflicted the New Zealanders while they were stationed in the Jordan Valley in late 1918. More than 700 cases were treated by the New Zealand field ambulance in the first two weeks of October alone.

During the *First World War there were major advances in medical techniques—for example, the death rate from abdominal wounds, which very few survived in the early part of the war, had declined to roughly 50 per cent by the end of the war. It was recognised that wounds recovered better if they were operated on as quickly as possible and left open to drain and were irrigated with antiseptics (the Carrel–Dakin method). Progress was made in the treatment of shock, and by 1918 blood transfusions were being performed near the front line. Great advances were also made in the field of plastic surgery, a New Zealand facial plastic surgery section being opened in England in 1918.

Evacuation procedures in the *Second World War were similar to those of the previous conflict. A wounded soldier would first be taken to a regimental aid post. This was usually located in a house near the front line, though in the desert it might be merely marked by a flag. The wounded soldier would receive essential first aid (and in extreme cases a blood transfusion) before being taken by truck, Bren gun carrier, or jeep to the advanced dressing station, which usually was staffed by three medical officers and sixty orderlies from a field ambulance unit. Essential surgery, such as amputations of shattered limbs or removal of foreign bodies, was undertaken, but the emphasis was on stabilising the casualty before moving him on as quickly as possible. The casualty was then taken to the main dressing station by ambulance. These ideally were beyond the reach of the enemy, but in the confused fighting of the Crusader offensive in the *North African campaign the New Zealand Main Dressing Station was overrun by the Germans and caught up in the fighting before being recaptured after several days. Those with major abdominal or chest injuries and those fit to travel were sent on to the casualty clearing station or specialist Allied surgical units. Until the 1st (New Zealand) Casualty Clearing Station was formed in 1942, New Zealand troops relied on British casualty clearing stations. At these stations, usually housed in either tents, caravans, or a large public building, more elaborate surgery and post-operative treatment was performed. From there the casualty was evacuated to a general hospital, sometimes by air, perhaps hundreds of kilometres to the rear. Invalids or long-term convalescents were repatriated to New Zealand, usually by the hospital ship *Maunganui*.

The wounded soldier of the Second World War stood a far greater chance of survival than did his counterpart in the earlier world war. By 1944 only one out of every twenty wounded soldiers was dying (as compared to one in ten in 1914–18). The basic methods of surgery remained the same—wounds were cleaned and sterilised and left open until the wound became healthy. However, a number of innovations and discoveries had combined to revolutionise medical treatment. Ambulances (particularly the jeep in the front line) and air transport of casualties made evacuation quicker and less traumatic. By the time of the *Italian campaign air evacuation had become standard. Mechanisation also allowed surgical theatres to be brought much closer to the front line. By 1942 mobile field surgical units and field transfusion units of surgical teams were being stationed well forward at the field ambulances to decrease the time taken for casualties to be operated on. Other specialist mobile surgical sections were moved forward to the casualty clearing stations, enabling even specialised and difficult surgery to be performed closer to the front line. Sulphonamide antibiotics, developed in the 1930s, were used liberally, and from 1943 the miracle drug penicillin considerably reduced the chances of infection (particularly 'gas gangrene' from muddy conditions). Surgical techniques were refined with experience. Fighting inside armoured vehicles, ships, or aircraft exposed personnel to appalling burns. Great strides were made in the treatment of burn injuries, with saline baths becoming standard treatment. The expatriate New Zealand surgeon, Sir Archibald *McIndoe, led the field in plastic surgery.

Since the Second World War medical treatment in war, like civilian medicine, has continued to make leaps forward. In the *Korean War helicopter evacuation became standard, further decreasing the time between wound and medical treatment. By the *Vietnam War this development, together with continually improving surgical techniques and drugs, had dramatically increased a wounded soldier's chances of survival.

A.D. Carberry, *The New Zealand Medical Services in the Great War 1914–1918* (Whitcombe & Tombs Ltd, Auckland, 1924); T.D.M. Stout, *New Zealand Medical Services in Middle East and Italy* (War History Branch, Wellington, 1956); T.D.M. Stout, *Medical Services in New Zealand and the Pacific* (War History Branch, Wellington, 1958).

Meldrum, Brigadier-General William (28 July 1865–13 February 1964) was an outstanding regimental and brigade commander of the *First World War. Born in Whangarei, he was practising as a lawyer in Hunterville when he joined the *Volunteer Force in 1900, forming and serving in the Hunterville Mounted Rifles Volunteers. By 1914 he was commanding the 6th (Manawatu) Mounted Rifles Regiment. Joining 1NZEF after the outbreak of war, he left with the Main Body in command of the Wellington Mounted Rifles.

Melvill

At ★Gallipoli, he proved an efficient and conscientious field officer. His regiment particularly distinguished itself during the August 1915 offensive when, after seizing the foothills below Chunuk Bair with careful reconnaissance and tactical finesse on the 6th, it relieved the Wellington Infantry Battalion and held the crest of this vital feature against ferocious Turkish attacks for twenty-four hours until relieved. In the ensuing ★Sinai–Palestine campaign, the regiment was again to the fore. At the Battle of Romani in August 1916, it held the tactically important Wellington Ridge against repeated Turkish attacks. Told to defend the Anzac camps, Meldrum replied with typical panache: 'If they get through my line here they can have the damned camps.' At Magdhaba and Rafa and during the First Battle of Gaza, he further enhanced his reputation as the outstanding regimental commander of the New Zealand Mounted Rifles Brigade. A daring and determined commander of the brigade itself from 23 April 1917, he was especially prominent during the encirclement of Beersheba and pursuit to Jaffa. Although never reckless with his men's lives, he earned the nickname 'Fix-Bayonets Bill' for his dashing approach. For his services during the war he was made a CB, CMG, and a DSO. After the war he became an unsuccessful businessman and West Coast magistrate. He served as a group director of the ★Home Guard during the ★Second World War and chaired the local Armed Forces Appeal Board from 1942 to 1944.

Melvill, Major-General Sir Charles William (5 September 1878–15 September 1925). Born in England, Melvill was the son of Teignmouth Melvill, who as a lieutenant in the 24th Regiment won the VC for saving the Colours at Isandlwana during the Zulu War of 1879. He served in India with the South Lancashire Regiment, in which he was commissioned in 1897, before emigrating to New Zealand in 1907 to take up the life of a gentleman farmer in Otago. He returned to the colours when he joined the ★New Zealand Staff Corps in March 1911. He was attending the Staff College at Camberley, England, when the ★First World War began. Returning to his old regiment, he served with it on the ★Western Front until November 1915, when he transferred to 1NZEF. From early 1916 he commanded the 4th Battalion, 3rd New Zealand (Rifle) Brigade. After leading his battalion in the fighting on the Somme in September 1916, he was given command of the 2nd Infantry Brigade; in June 1917, during the Battle of Messines, he took over 1st Infantry Brigade. A capable and aggressive commander, he temporarily commanded the New Zealand Division in June 1918. During the final stages of the war he achieved an important success at Crèvecoeur on the Hindenburg Line, capturing it with a bold flank attack.

From February 1919 he helped oversee the disbandment of 1NZEF as officer in charge of administration and commanding the troops in Great Britain. For his war services he was made a DSO, a CMG, and a CB, as well as being mentioned in dispatches four times. After returning to New Zealand, he commanded the Central Command until his appointment in April 1924 as Commandant of the New Zealand Military Forces, a post he held until his sudden death. During his brief tenure he tried to make some headway with senior officer training.

Merchant marine Alongside the plaques of honour for the armed services inside the ★National War Memorial visitors will see one for members of the Merchant Navy. They are the only civilians honoured there. As the slightly archaic term 'merchant navy' suggests, this is a holdover from earlier times when governments regarded their merchant fleets as a 'fourth service', when the fishing and merchant fleets provided recruits—willing or otherwise—for naval service, and when merchant ships and warships were more readily interchangeable.

New Zealand's infant colonial government drew on merchant shipping when warfare broke out between colonists and Maori in the mid 1840s and again in the 1860s. While Royal Navy vessels and a handful of purpose-built colonial gunboats carried out escort, invasion, and shore bombardment roles, the government took over a larger number of barges, steamers, and small coastal sailing craft for war purposes. These included the armed schooner *Caroline*, the armed cutter *Midnight*, the steamers *Luna*, *Auckland*, and *Sandfly*; they supported the Taranaki and Waikato campaigns or they served on the Hauraki Gulf patrol. Other ships, chartered rather than purchased, transported troops, supplies, and civilians. Maori seized three small sailing vessels, the *Eclipse* at Opotiki in March 1865 and the ketch *Florence* and the schooner *Rifleman* at the Chathams in June 1868, but in general the merchant fleet operated with impunity.

New Zealand's complete dependence on sea trade encouraged government interest in fostering the merchant marine after the wars, albeit fitfully. The state intervened in training and employment conditions. From 1866 the Marine Department enforced regulations and improved coastal navigation and safety. The department also acquired lighthouse tenders, which also transported personnel, undertook search and rescue work, and surveyed harbours, and would have been available for war purposes if required. The government also supported mail contracts (where the powerful mail steamers were seen as a wartime asset) and training through the Naval Training Schools Act 1874. The training school established at Kohimarama under this legislation trained merchant seamen until it closed in 1882. The Training Ships Act 1906 produced trainees for both the merchant and naval services (with the merchant marine taking 500 of the 527 trainees produced). To support the programme the Defence Department purchased the old gunboat HMS *Sparrow* (renamed *Amokura*), and transferred it to the Marine Department, which operated it until 1919.

The New Zealand merchant fleet had grown rapidly during colonial times. Local businessmen failed to establish more than a foothold in the long-distance trade between New Zealand and the United Kingdom (the New Zealand Shipping Company, established at Christchurch in 1873, soon passed into British ownership), but the Dunedin-based Union Steam Ship Company of New Zealand seized a near-monopoly of the coastal and trans-Tasman trades, and made a strong showing in several Australian coastal, Pacific Islands, and trans-Pacific routes. By Edwardian times, it was larger than the five largest Australian companies combined, and its ships would serve British and New Zealand authorities in both world wars.

The world wars proved costly in terms of lives and ships. New Zealand–owned ships were on the New Zealand section of the Register of British ships and were effectively at the disposal of the imperial war effort. In 1914 the Union Company transferred the registry of many of its larger ships from Dunedin to London when it took out war risk cover with the Liverpool Association, and even the fast ferry *Wahine* (for example), a short-sea vessel, was taken over by the British for use as a minelayer and dispatch vessel in the Mediterranean. Many of the so-called 'Home boats' running between the United Kingdom and Australasia became *troopships or auxiliary naval vessels, forcing both British and New Zealand companies to scratch together substitute services.

Ships left in commercial service came under the control of the British Ministry of War Transport. In New Zealand export loading and discharging were centralised at the larger ports, linked by feeder vessels, and from 1939 and for several years after the war coastal and intercolonial ships were allocated routes by the Shipping Controller. Shipping shortages during the *First World War forced some companies to re-rig old coal hulks for further trading. The rigours of wartime running meant that many ships handed back to owners after both conflicts required extensive refitting before they could be used again.

No New Zealand civilians were at greater risk from enemy action than seafarers. During the *Second World War there were 110 merchant marine deaths (compared with 573 navy) and a further 123 were captured or interned (compared with 57 navy). Many New Zealand merchant seamen lost their lives in distant waters, one of the worst incidents occurring in November 1917 when the Union Company's cadet steamer *Aparima* sank eight minutes after being torpedoed off the south coast of England; half the crew of 114 died, twenty-four of them New Zealanders. But seafarers did not have to voyage far to die. In 1914–18 and 1939–45 German warships made incursions into local waters, sinking several ships by mine or gunfire. On 20 August 1940 the New Zealand Shipping Company's freighter *Turakina* put up a celebrated fight in the Tasman when Captain James Laird found himself confronting the auxiliary cruiser *Orion*'s six 5.9-inch guns with his single 4.7-inch piece; thirty-five died. *Orion*, *Komet*, and support vessels also accounted for the *Niagara*, HMS *Puriri*, *Holmwood*, and *Rangitane*.

New Zealand still depends on sea trade for almost all its imports and exports, but policy-makers no longer place a high value on a domestically owned merchant marine as a strategic asset. Indeed, the state-owned Shipping Corporation of New Zealand, formed in 1974 after decades of intermittent advocacy from primary producers and trade unionists, was sold to overseas owners in 1989. In 1994 New Zealand sent its armoured personnel carriers and stores to the Balkans aboard a foreign-flag vessel, a situation which was replicated five years later when New Zealand deployed *peace-keeping forces to *East Timor. During the 1950s the New Zealand Naval Board's annual reports mentioned holding merchant navy defence courses. In 1998 formal navy interest was expressed through the 144-strong RNZNVR Naval Control of Shipping (NCS) Organisation Branch. This is the navy's liaison with the shipping industry and is responsible for coordinating the nation's trade (more than 95 per cent of which still moves by sea) in an emergency. Working with the National Shipping Authority, a voluntary body of shipowners, agents, and port authorities, the NCS Branch maintains databases and assesses ships for possible requisitioning, and will mobilise NCS personnel if required.

GAVIN McLEAN

Mesopotamia After war broke out with the Ottoman Empire in November 1914, British and Indian forces were committed to Mesopotamia (now Iraq) immediately to preserve and advance British interests in the area. An Australian aircraft unit sent to Basra in May 1915 included a New Zealand pilot, Lieutenant W.W.A. *Burn; in July he became the first New Zealand pilot to die in action. In response to a request by the government of India in December 1915 for wireless personnel for the campaign in Mesopotamia, the New Zealand government agreed to raise a wireless troop. The 63-strong unit left New Zealand in March 1916, and four months later amalgamated with

Middle East commitment

A horse-drawn wagon of 9th (New Zealand) Station of the Mesopotamian Expeditionary Force's 1st Wireless Signals Squadron arrives at the outskirts of Hamadan in Persia (Iran) on 29 June 1918. The station was responsible for much of the communication between the British headquarters and Dunsterforce (Australian War Memorial, P0562.126)

Australian wireless units to form the Anzac Wireless Squadron, which provided mobile wireless communications and intercepted Turkish communications. It took part in the advance up the Tigris River to Baghdad, which it entered in March 1917. Later that year it was deployed in Persia (Iran) before being sent to join the New Zealand Divisional Signal Company on the ★Western Front. Fever and dysentery made life unpleasant for the New Zealanders, five of whom lost their lives in Mesopotamia.

Middle East commitment was a response to the possibility of war with the Soviet Union as the ★Cold War intensified in the aftermath of the ★Second World War. At the Commonwealth Prime Ministers' Meetings in London in late 1948 Prime Minister Peter ★Fraser sought advice from the British Chiefs of Staff as to how best New Zealand might assist a new Commonwealth war effort. The chiefs advised that the maximum effort should be made to hold the Middle East, which was the site of airfields from which the Soviet Union could be bombed, a vital communications focus, and a major source of oil supplies. Australia and New Zealand, they suggested, could make a valuable contribution by sending as many forces as possible to the Middle East. This could be done without risk because of the lack of potentially hostile naval forces in the Pacific. To be effective, it was explained, New Zealand's forces would need to be in the theatre within ninety days of the outbreak of war to beat any Soviet advance into the Suez Canal area. This was a much faster timetable than in the Second World War, when the dispatch of the 2nd New Zealand Division had taken a full year. To meet it the reintroduction of ★compulsory military training would clearly be necessary, and the government secured a favourable response to such a course in a referendum held on 3 August 1949. In the following month it advised London that, in the event of war, it would provide an augmented infantry division, ten RNZAF squadrons, and any naval vessels not required in the Pacific. This commitment was predicated on there being 'no major change affecting New Zealand in the strategic situation now forecast'. After some hesitation, mainly on grounds of expense, the National government, which assumed office in December 1949, endorsed the commitment, which was the basis of New Zealand defence policy until 1955. In contrast, Australia did not make any formal commitment to send its forces to the Middle East, insisting that it would determine its policy in the light of the conditions at the time. In 1950–51 the Middle East commitment was advanced by the South Pacific Dominions as a reason why they needed a security commitment from the United States (see ANZUS). Several RNZN ★frigates served with the Royal Navy on exchange in the Mediterranean in the early 1950s, and 14 Squadron was stationed in ★Cyprus from October 1952 to April 1955. Army preparations in New Zealand were centred on creating the division, and some attention was given to logistics requirements in the Middle East. Overall, preparations were complicated by Egyptian nationalism, and strategic developments soon made a global war less likely and the protection of the Suez Canal a less compelling need. In 1955 the commitment was switched to South-east Asia.

W.D. McIntyre, *Background to the Anzus Pact: Policy-Making, Strategy and Diplomacy, 1945–55* (Canterbury University Press, Christchurch, 1995).

Miles, Brigadier Reginald (10 December 1892– 20 October 1943), who was born at Springston, Canterbury, entered the Royal Military College, Duntroon, as an officer cadet in 1911. After graduating, he joined 1NZEF as a junior officer in a howitzer battery. While serving as a forward observation officer, he was wounded at ★Gallipoli, and won an MC for gallantry on the Somme in 1916. From 1917 he was a battery commander. During the German offensive in 1918, his battery distinguished itself on 10 April by fighting on under serious threat from advancing German forces until its ammunition was almost exhausted. For his actions that day, which included rallying some nearby infantry and culminated in his being wounded while making a reconnaissance, he was recommended for a ★Victoria Cross, but was made a DSO instead. He ended the war as brigade major of the New Zealand Divisional Artillery. After spending the inter-war period in a variety of staff posts in New Zealand, interspersed with attendance at courses in England, he returned to active service with 2NZEF. From 1940 he was Commander Royal Artillery of the 2nd New Zealand Division, in which role he performed admirably during the ★Greece campaign before he was evacuated, exhausted and ill, to Egypt. Back in command of the Divisional Artillery during the Crusader offensive, he had the misfortune to have one of his regiments overrun by the Germans at Belhamed. Apparently unhappy with the way this situation had developed, Miles himself went forward to be with the gunners, looking 'for all the world as though he were going duck-shooting'. Taken prisoner, he was held in Italy until March 1943, when he and Brigadier James ★Hargest escaped through a tunnel with four other officers. Hargest and Miles succeeded in reaching Switzerland, and were both awarded bars to their DSOs for their exploit. Miles subsequently crossed Vichy France to Spain, but, overcome by depression, he took his own life near Barcelona.

Military districts were the basis of administration for the ★New Zealand Army from the 1850s until 1970. Provision was made for the establishment of military districts in the Militia Ordinance of 1845. These remained undefined until 1858, when the Auckland Militia and Volunteer District was established, to be followed in the next year by districts in Wellington, Taranaki, Napier, and Christchurch. By 1866 there were fifteen districts in the North Island and seven in the South Island. In 1895 the districts were reduced to Auckland, Wellington, Nelson, Canterbury, and Otago. Each district was commanded by an officer of field rank. He had a few drill instructors to assist him, but the defence system as a whole was hopelessly inefficient, and the district commanders had only limited authority over the units in their districts. It was not until 1911 that the military districts system was established as the organisational and administrative basis of the army. Four Military Districts—Auckland, Wellington, Canterbury, and Otago—were formed, with each district headquarters commanding all units inside its boundaries. In each district there was an established number of ★Territorial Force battalions, regiments, batteries, and supporting arms. When 1NZEF was raised in 1914, each Military District had the task of providing an infantry battalion, a mounted regiment, and a share of the supporting artillery, engineers, and ambulances. In practice the southern districts soon ran into problems in meeting their quotas, and the recruiting system effectively became centralised. After the war the Military Districts were reorganised in line with demography and to better reflect the divisional structure of a future expeditionary force. They were reduced to three—Northern, Central, and Southern— and renamed Commands, each of which raised an infantry brigade, a mounted rifles brigade, and supporting units. In 1937 the name Military District was reintroduced, with the Territorial Force reorganised and pared down; each district was to be responsible for a composite mounted rifles regiment and a composite infantry battalion. With the outbreak of the ★Second World War the Territorial Force was greatly expanded, and each Military District raised two or three brigades for home defence. The Military Districts were initially responsible for the raising of their quota of 2NZEF. After the war each district was responsible for the command of units within its boundaries. In 1964 the Army was reorganised into a Field Force and a Static Support Force, with the Military Districts being reduced to administrative divisions of the latter. They were abolished in 1970, but re-emerged eight years later with the establishment of three Task Force Regional Headquarters at Auckland, Palmerston North, and Christchurch. Each HQ was responsible for all Army units and activities within its region (with the exception of the Army Training Group at Waiouru). In 1983 the regional task forces were reduced to one in each island.

Military engineers New Zealand's military engineering tradition dates from the ★Maori defence works which came to dominate Maori warfare and which greatly impressed European observers. During the ★New Zealand Wars, Maori military engineers such as ★Kawiti, Pene Taka, and ★Titokowaru constructed immensely strong and sophisticated earthworks. On the European side, the role of military engineers was also vitally important. Officers and sappers of the British Corps of Royal Engineers oversaw the construction of roads, bridges, blockhouses, and

Military engineers

stockades (see FORTIFICATIONS). Perhaps the most impressive feat of military engineering was the military road cut through bush and swamp from Auckland to Waikato (the 'Great South Road'). The first New Zealand engineer units were raised in the 1860s, and a company of Auckland engineers served in the Tauranga Bush campaign of 1867. Engineering duties were also carried out by members of the *Armed Constabulary, who were engaged on road building in the 1870s and early 1880s.

During the *First World War, both a company and a troop of field engineers were raised in 1914 as part of 1NZEF. At *Gallipoli they were responsible for digging trenches, constructing dugouts, and making tracks, as well as some counter-mining against enemy tunnels. Three New Zealand Field Engineer companies served on the *Western Front from 1916, under the Commander Royal Engineers (CRE). Sappers dug trenches, built dugouts, erected barbed wire entanglements, built roads, milled timber, constructed light railways, built baths and laundries, and camouflaged batteries and supply dumps behind the lines. During the final advance in 1918, they constructed roads and bridges and dealt with booby traps left by the retreating Germans. The Field Engineer companies with the New Zealand Division were joined by two other specialist units, a Light Railway Operating Company (which constructed and operated railway lines in the Ypres sector) and the New Zealand Tunnelling Company (see MINING OPERATIONS IN THE FIRST WORLD WAR). An engineer field troop also served with the New Zealand Mounted Rifles Brigade in the *Sinai–Palestine campaign. It dug wells and built water troughs.

In the *Second World War New Zealand military engineers served in two main capacities: as field companies with the 2nd New Zealand Division and as rear echelon support units. Among the latter a forestry group cut and milled timber in England and Italy. Railway survey, construction, and operating companies served in the Middle East laying railway lines and operating locomotives until 1943. Army troop and mechanical equipment companies were responsible for heavy engineering jobs on the lines of communication in the Middle East, constructing roads, pipelines, aerodromes, and wharves. In the 2nd New Zealand Division there were four field engineer and field park companies. In *Greece, sappers rendered roads impassable, laid mines, and demolished bridges. The need to demolish roads and bridges quickly led to some ingenious solutions, including the use of *depth charges salvaged from warships. On *Crete field engineers of necessity fought as infantry. During the *North African campaign, they were particularly engaged in laying and removing minefields, a role that gained in importance as the sophistication and number of mines increased throughout the war. Although electromagnetic mine-detectors were available to find mines, it was found that gently probing the ground with a bayonet was the most reliable detection method. Sappers were vital in clearing and marking lanes through deep minefields during the crucial Battle of El Alamein, and were in the vanguard of the subsequent advance across North Africa, bulldozing roads and clearing the inevitable mines. The *Italian campaign placed even heavier demands upon the sappers. The weight and numbers of military vehicles far exceeded the capacity of Italian roads, a disadvantage magnified by the Germans' use of 'scorched earth' tactics in retreat. Winter mud and enemy artillery often made engineering tasks unpleasant or dangerous. Nevertheless, New Zealand sappers benefited from the increasing mechanisation of the Allied armies, in particular the availability of four-wheel-drive trucks, bulldozers, and box-girder Bailey bridges, which were notable for their strength and adaptability. A mechanical equipment company with additional bulldozers and trucks and an assault squadron with bulldozer tanks, bridging tanks, and other specialist armoured engineering vehicles were added to the strength of the New Zealand Engineers in early 1945. The success of the final advance in Italy owed much to the skill and ingenuity of New Zealand sappers in bulldozing stopbanks, bridging rivers, and clearing mines.

New Zealand engineers were involved from the earliest stages of the *Pacific War when 150 sappers were sent to Fiji to construct defences in 1941. Engineering tasks were particularly important in the amphibious and jungle warfare of the *Solomons campaign, and 3rd New Zealand Division, with four field engineer companies, had an unusually high proportion of engineers. Sappers milled timber, erected buildings, and constructed roads (often of coconut logs and mahogany planking), bridges, and aerodromes. Two works services companies based on New Caledonia erected buildings for base units and worked on wharves.

Since the Second World War military engineers have been among New Zealand's most frequently deployed personnel. A detachment sent to Korea with *Kayforce in 1950 built base facilities before being employed at the front as part of the field engineer component of the 1st Commonwealth Division. During the 1960s engineer detachments were sent to *Thailand to construct roads and an airfield, and to South Vietnam to build roads and public buildings. New Zealand engineers have regularly been deployed to the Pacific Islands to dig wells, build roads, and clear passages through coral reefs. Disaster relief operations within the Pacific and New Zealand are a frequent occurrence. Within New Zealand engineers assist the civilian community in constructing halls, school buildings, or bridges. More recently engineers have become involved in ★peace-keeping activities, including the provision of mine clearance training in Cambodia and Mozambique.

Military history and historians Military history has always been a minority interest among New Zealand historians, and remains a neglected subject in the country's universities. Notwithstanding this, after 1945 the government underwrote a massive official history of New Zealand's involvement in the ★Second World War which dwarfs those published in Australia, Canada, and South Africa, while the relatively small number of historians working on military history topics since the end of the war has nonetheless produced some distinctive work of great quality, and there are signs that interest in the field may even be spreading gradually to the universities.

The one area of New Zealand's military history which has attracted serious sustained and scholarly treatment is, not surprisingly, the ★New Zealand Wars of the nineteenth century between Maori and Pakeha, and here academic historians not otherwise associated with military history have made a distinct contribution. The subject is also one which has most clearly reflected some of the shifts in the writing and transmission of history which have occurred over the last thirty years, especially with the new emphasis on matters of race, gender, and class. Indeed James ★Cowan's two-volume *New Zealand Wars: A History of the Maori Campaigns and the Pioneering Period* (1922–23) may be said to have prefigured some of those changes. Unlike some subsequent work, Cowan rejected terms such as 'Maori Wars' or 'Land Wars' in favour of a title which was both descriptive and inclusive, and which finds favour today. Fluent in Maori, he demonstrated a concern for capturing and using the oral tradition and for emphasising the worthy qualities of the Maori which remains the main strength of his book. Although dated in other respects, Cowan's is still the most detailed and careful reconstruction of the operational dimensions of the conflict. Subsequent work such as Keith Sinclair's *Origins of the Maori Wars* (1962), Brian Dalton's *War and Politics in New Zealand 1855–1870* (1967), and Ian ★Wards's *Shadow of the Land* (1968) all built on the foundations laid by Cowan even as they extended and revised his interpretations. James Belich's prize-winning *New Zealand Wars and the Victorian Interpretation of Racial Conflict* (1986) has attracted criticism from those concerned with the accuracy of his depictions at the tactical and operational level, but there can be little doubt that it represents a substantial new interpretation of the subject, made more influential through Belich's major television documentary of the same name, screened in 1998.

Treatment of other aspects of New Zealand's military affairs in the nineteenth century and the lead-up to the ★First World War is sketchy. The period as a whole has been analysed by Ian McGibbon, *The Path to Gallipoli: Defending New Zealand 1840–1915* (1991), but this deals with New Zealand's military affairs mainly from a domestic perspective. Valuable though this is (and there is as yet no volume of comparable range and quality dealing with the Australian colonies), it can allow only limited discussion of the broader contexts of ★imperial defence in which New Zealand governments operated, while there is little scope for discussion of the wider social and economic impact of the British Army and Royal Navy upon New Zealand colonial society. New Zealand's involvement in the ★Boer War, proportionately larger than that of the Australian colonies, was described in D.O.W. Hall's *New Zealanders in South Africa 1899–1902*, which was recognised to be inadequate even when it was published in 1949. Another short history, John Crawford's *To Fight for the Empire: An Illustrated History of New Zealand and the South African War, 1899–1902*, published in 1999, is an improvement, but only serves to highlight the need for a full-scale history of New Zealand's participation in this conflict.

Much the same was true of the New Zealand historiography of the First World War until relatively recently, and there are still significant gaps in the literature. The four semi-official volumes published in the 1920s remain in some cases the only works available in their area (on the campaign in Sinai and Palestine, for example), and the stodgy prose, lack of analysis, and absence of scholarly references makes them an unsatisfactory substitute for serious studies of New Zealand's war effort of the kind produced in most of the other Commonwealth countries involved. Efforts to reclaim the history of 1NZEF have been made by Christopher Pugsley whose *Gallipoli: The New Zealand Story* (1984) was the first book-length treatment of the subject published in more than half a century. The New Zealand Broadcasting Corporation documentary of the same name, broadcast in 1985, further publicised a dimension of their history increasingly unfamiliar to large numbers of New Zealanders. Pugsley has also published a slim monograph on the (Maori) Pioneer Battalion (1995) and a study of ★discipline and the New Zealand soldier, *On the Fringe of Hell: New Zealanders and Military Discipline in the First World War* (1991), which is, *inter alia*, a history of the New Zealand Division, but much clearly remains to be done. The social and domestic dimensions of the war have received some fine scholarly treatment at the hands of Paul Baker and P.S. O'Connor, on conscription, and Jane Tolerton, on

Military history and historians

★venereal disease and Ettie ★Rout, and some oral history work has been published as well, notably by Maurice Shadbolt. It is difficult to account for the paucity of treatment of events which had such a devastating impact on a small settler society, especially when contrasted with the amount of material produced across the Tasman.

The inter-war period posed the same challenges for the armed forces and governments in New Zealand as in the rest of the empire, and while the literature on the period is not extensive, the coverage is rather more complete. This is largely the work of David McIntyre, whose *Rise and Fall of the Singapore Naval Base 1919–1942* (1979) makes a major contribution to the study of empire defence, and not only to the role in it played by New Zealand. His *New Zealand Prepares for War* (1988) ably analyses the domestic military policies of the period and their impact on the New Zealand armed forces, while Ian McGibbon's *Blue-water Rationale: The Naval Defence of New Zealand 1914–1942* (1981) combines both domestic and external dimensions in a study of the development of naval thinking. The glaring absence in the literature for this period is discussion of the longer-term consequences of the Great War on New Zealand society, although Maureen Sharpe has examined the development of ★Anzac Day and related ideas about war and peace before 1939.

The Second World War was the subject of a massive official history, running to forty-eight volumes and twenty-four episodes and studies. Unlike the other official histories of the war produced in the Commonwealth after 1945, it included not only treatments of the campaigns fought by 2NZEF and of the home front and the impact of the war there but also an extensive group of unit histories and three volumes of documents. There was even a volume devoted to the experiences of New Zealand's ★prisoners of war, a volume replicated in no other national official history. Accordingly the Second World War is easily the best documented of New Zealand's twentieth century wars, but even then there are inadequacies. In particular, the activities and experiences of the 3rd Division, which fought in the Pacific until it was disbanded in 1944, were covered in a separate and unofficial series which lack both the authority and the presentation of the other volumes. The campaign volumes are immensely detailed and reflect the historiographical conventions of their time. That more remains to be said is demonstrated by John McLeod, *Myth and Reality: The New Zealand Soldier in World War II* (1986), which claims to depict the New Zealanders on a 'more realistic' basis, and which concentrates on discipline both in and out of battle, crime, morale, and the furlough drafts among other topics. The result is certainly a more realistic portrayal than that developed in the public mind by wartime propaganda, but as always with such treatments there is a risk of sensationalising the subject matter.

The Second World War is also the only conflict which has attracted the activity of military biographers. Both ★Freyberg and ★Kippenberger have received monographic study, by John Tonkin-Covell and Glyn Harper respectively, but there is no composite study of the officer corps of any of the services, while significant figures like ★Russell and ★Godley from the First World War and ★Thornton in the post-1945 period are untouched. Nor has the 'war and society' approach, so productive elsewhere in the English-speaking world, made much of an inroad in New Zealand historiography. The official history treats domestic issues at great length (although it is significant that the third of the volumes dealing with 'the people at war' did not appear until 1986), and Deborah Montgomerie has argued for a more limited wartime impact on working women than is often assumed, but other work in this area remains unpublished. The academic interest in grief, memory, and the psychiatric consequences of war service which has flourished elsewhere in recent times is reflected in Alison Parr, *Silent Casualties: New Zealand's Unspoken Legacy of the Second World War* (1995).

The history of New Zealand's active military role in the region after 1945 is being written, gradually, with some work of outstanding quality and interest in print. The role of the ★British Commonwealth Occupation Force in the post-war occupation of Japan has long been a neglected subject generally, but New Zealand's part has been well documented by Ann Trotter, *New Zealand and Japan 1945–1952: The Occupation and the Peace Treaty* (1990), and by Laurie Brocklebank, *Jayforce: New Zealand and the Military Occupation of Japan 1945–48* (1997). The country's involvement in the ★Korean War in concert with its Commonwealth partners and under United Nations' auspices and American command has been the subject of a two-volume official history by Ian McGibbon. The first volume of *New Zealand and the Korean War* (1992) deals with domestic politics and foreign and defence policy and is an excellent analysis of New Zealand's place and role in the world at this time. The second volume (1996) deals with combat operations, and provides as well an analysis of Commonwealth military cooperation in the context of Korea which may be seen as a continuation of the pre-war system of imperial defence on whose history New Zealand historians have made some important contributions. Another feature of that system, British concern to involve Australia and New Zealand in the defence of the Suez Canal zone, is examined by Malcolm Templeton, *Ties of Blood and Empire: New Zealand's Involvement in Middle East Defence and the Suez Crisis 1947–57* (1994).

The involvement in the ★British Commonwealth Far East Strategic Reserve, the ★Malayan Emergency, and ★Confrontation with Indonesia is another facet again of this involvement in a Commonwealth military system and is the subject of another official history, as yet incomplete. The same applies to the history of involvement in the ★Vietnam War. On the latter, there are in addition early articles by David McCraw and Roberto Rabel which examine New Zealand's diplomatic and strategic policies governing its involvement in the war, a history of the artillery regiment which served there by S.D. Newman, *Vietnam Gunners: 161 Battery RNZA, South Vietnam, 1965–71* (1988), and an oral history by Deborah Challinor, *Grey Ghosts: New Zealand Vietnam Vets Talk about their War* (1998). Gary Brooker has written a short memoir of his service with one of the New Zealand infantry companies attached to an Australian battalion in Phuoc Tuy province, *Two Lanyards in Vietnam* (1995), but New Zealand historians have yet to subject their country's involvement in that war to any very widespread or searching scrutiny. The fact that conscripts were not sent to the war may help to explain why it has not attracted the attention devoted to it in Australia.

There are a number of historians, like Vincent Orange and Joel Hayward, who write in other fields of military history but in general it is clear that military history is marginalised in the country's universities and that there are few incentives for students and others to pursue work in the area. Massey University has forged a link with the Army's ★Military Studies Institute, and Waikato University has attempted to develop a military history programme, but with mixed results. In the 1950s and 1960s W.E. Murphy, who had worked on the official history under Kippenberger, offered some subjects at Victoria University of Wellington which had a military dimension, but this was in political science. In thirty years of publication the *New Zealand Journal of History* has published no more than half a dozen articles in the field of military history, broadly defined, almost all of them with a social history emphasis. One explanation for the lack of attention to the subject has been advanced by the Canadian historian, Ron Haycock, who notes that, unlike Australia and Canada, New Zealand has lacked a military college which would provide a focus for such work. The relocation of the Military Studies Institute to Trentham and a strengthening of its link with Massey may turn this situation around over time, but there is a great deal of ground to make up. (See also OFFICIAL WAR HISTORIES)

JEFFREY GREY

Military law The first military law to apply in New Zealand, indeed probably the first European law, was the Naval Discipline Act 1749, which governed the captain and ship's company of HMS *Endeavour* when they explored parts of the coast in 1769. Thereafter, the history of military law in New Zealand is essentially the history of the various formations which have, from time to time, comprised New Zealand's military and paramilitary forces. Between 1840 and 1870 the main part of the forces available to the government were British regiments posted to New Zealand. They were governed by the British Mutiny Acts and Articles of War; visiting ships likewise operated under the Naval Discipline Act, first of 1749 and then of 1866. Meanwhile numerous forces were authorised to be raised in or for service in New Zealand. These included the ★Militia, the Royal New Zealand Fencibles, a Native Force which was never raised, the ★Volunteer Force, the Naval Volunteers, and the Constabulary Force. There was an accompanying variety of legal and disciplinary arrangements. The Militia Ordinance 1845 incorporated the British Mutiny Acts and Articles of War as the disciplinary structure of the Militia. The Militia Act 1858 established the Naval Volunteers and brought them under the same disciplinary system, since they were essentially land-based forces providing coastal artillery and a coastguard. The ★Fencibles and the Native Force were to be subject also to the Mutiny Acts and Articles of War with the addition, in the case of the Fencibles, of a sentence of loss of the land which was part of their contractual remuneration. Since the Militia were limited to serving in their local area, the Constabulary Force and the ★Colonial Defence Force were raised to provide more permanent and flexible forces. The ★Colonial Defence Act 1862 placed the latter body under the Mutiny Acts. In 1867, once the ★New Zealand Wars were past their worst, the Defence Force, and the numerous special forces that had been raised under that Act, were disbanded and the ★Armed Constabulary created. Many members of the Defence Force transferred to the Armed Constabulary which was subjected to a police discipline system based on that of the Royal Irish Constabulary. At first, this force operated only under the police disciplinary code, but after the disastrous engagement at Te Ngutu-o-te-Manu the Colonial Forces Courts-Martial Act 1868 extended the provisions of the Mutiny Acts and the Articles of War to the Armed Constabulary while it was on ★active service.

In 1870 the Militia Act consolidated much of the legislation relating to the part-time forces, but eight years later the first of the major ★Russian scares precipitated new volunteer legislation and the raising of further naval artillery volunteers. The United Kingdom then enacted the Army Discipline and Regulations Act 1879, which was soon replaced by the Army Act 1881. These put the Articles of War on to a statutory rather than prerogative footing and created a code

Military law

of military law for use throughout the Empire. The British Act provided the basis for the reforms of 1886 when the Armed Constabulary was disbanded and separate Police and *Defence Acts passed, creating separate forces. Military personnel could, however, be deployed in support of the police and could even be placed under the police disciplinary system. This does not appear ever to have happened, and further separation of the police and military forces took place in 1909. The Volunteer Force, which numbered about 13,000 by 1906, was characterised by a poor state of discipline and morale; the corps had effectively become social clubs whose members cavilled at the occasional imposition of military duties. The replacement of the Volunteer Force with a *Territorial Force, the role of which was to support the Permanent Force, was intended to remedy this situation. Nevertheless, the defence forces were still largely part-time, and the new legislation showed a preoccupation with offences such as failing to attend parades and bringing alcohol into camp. The *Boer War had meanwhile provided the first opportunity for New Zealand servicemen to serve overseas. The successive contingents of volunteers sent to South Africa from 1899 simply operated under the Army Act 1881. This was also the case with 1NZEF during the *First World War, the colonial forces being effectively integrated into the British forces that they fought alongside. The execution of five New Zealand soldiers for military offences remains a matter of controversy (see DEATH PENALTY).

Until 1913 New Zealanders serving in the Royal Navy under the terms of the *Australasian naval agreements were subject to the British Naval Discipline Acts. The *Naval Defence Act of that year authorised the raising of naval forces in New Zealand. In peacetime they would be subject to the Naval Discipline Act 1866 and the King's Regulations for the Royal Navy, with specified modifications. In time of war, the naval forces were to be put under the control of the Admiralty, as occurred in August 1914. Likewise there was initially no separate New Zealand air force; New Zealanders simply joined or were attached to the various British military aviation forces. Created as part of the New Zealand Military Forces in June 1923, the New Zealand Permanent Air Force and its Territorial equivalent were subject to the Defence Act 1909. A semi-official *Manual of Air Force Law* had been produced by the RAF and this became the daily reference for the New Zealand Permanent Air Force, subject always to the higher authority of the Defence Act. The Air Force Act 1937 removed the *Royal New Zealand Air Force from the scope of the Defence Act and provided that it would be governed by the British Air Force Act, subject to the terms of the 1937 Act and any regulations made thereunder. This state of affairs continued until 1950,

when the Royal New Zealand Air Force Act was passed in almost identical terms to the New Zealand Army Act of the same year. The 1950 Acts created self-contained codes of military law for the *New Zealand Army and RNZAF for the first time. They no longer referred to British Acts. Nonetheless, British developments were followed closely, and in 1953 a Courts Martial Appeals Court was created shortly after the British court of the same name was set up. For various reasons, however, the New Zealand Courts Martial Appeals Court differs in status from its British counterpart, being the equivalent of the High Court rather than of the Court of Appeal, to which an appeal from the CMAC lies. At the same time New Zealand paralleled Great Britain in civilianising the office of Judge-Advocate General. In 1998 this post was held by a High Court judge, with a District Court judge as deputy, but it had previously been held by the Solicitor-General. The RNZN, meanwhile, from its creation in September 1941 until the coming into force of the Armed Forces Discipline Act 1971 was governed by the British Naval Discipline Acts. The British Naval Discipline Act 1957 automatically came into force so far as the RNZN was concerned by virtue of a provision of the Navy Act 1954. Increasing problems were caused, however, by local divergences, of which only one example is that the WRNZNS was brought under naval discipline in 1967, ten years ahead of its British counterpart. The 1957 Act substantially altered summary trial procedures in the RNZN. Summary proceedings in the RNZN were thenceforth adversarial in nature with the prosecution conducted usually by the Officer of the Day or the Master at Arms, while the accused's divisional officer was expected to defend and speak for the accused. This contrasts with the Army (and RNZAF) system, in which commanding officers conduct an investigation without taking a plea and the soldier's platoon commander takes a more neutral role as an adviser to the command. This difference in summary trial procedures proved, in both Britain and New Zealand, a major stumbling block to efforts to unify the disciplinary systems of the three services. A further problem in Britain, namely that naval legal officers were naval officers first and lawyers second, whereas Army and RAF lawyers were full-time lawyers, did not apply in New Zealand owing to the very small number of permanent legal officers and extensive reliance on civilian lawyers acting as Territorial Force or Reserve officers.

In 1967 a tri-service working party was set up to draft a code of law for all three armed services. This was chaired by Colonel G.B.M. Law, who was the only person available to work on the project full-time. The working party reported to a steering committee consisting of the member for personnel from each service board and the Judge-Advocate General, Solicitor-

General J.C. White. The outcome was the Armed Forces Discipline Act, which was passed in 1971 along with a new Defence Act which centralised the administration and command of the three services. This legislation created a single post of Judge-Advocate General of the Armed Forces, modernised offences and penalties so that they were more in keeping with the ordinary criminal law, aligned powers of punishment in the three services, reformed court-martial procedure, and made the rulings on questions of law by the Judge-Advocate at a court martial binding on the court instead of merely advisory. Implementation of the Act was delayed, however, by the summary trial problem. The RNZN would not abandon its procedure and the Army and RNZAF would not or could not adopt the RNZN's. Attempts to produce a single tri-service system of summary trial continued for several years, with various compromises being discussed and rejected. The situation became more and more inconvenient, especially for the RNZN. This was because it still relied on the British Naval Discipline Act. In the 1970s the British made a number of changes in naval discipline and it was not desired to implement these changes in New Zealand when the implementation of the Armed Forces Discipline Act was in prospect. From 1 June 1972, therefore, it was decided that further changes to the British Naval Discipline Act would not have effect in New Zealand. This meant that the RNZN disciplinary system was orphaned, being based on an out-of-date version of a British Act. Eventually, the ★Defence Council, determined to cut the Gordian knot, obtained passage of the Armed Forces Discipline Amendment Act 1981, which allowed each service to retain its previous pattern of summary trial. This enabled the Armed Forces Discipline Act finally to come into force on 1 December 1983.

The constant challenge for the military legal and disciplinary systems is to resolve the tension between the fact that commanders of formations are responsible for their discipline and effectiveness, on the one hand, and demands, usually from outside the armed forces, for a greater appearance of independence on the part of the quasi-judicial authorities, on the other. At the time of writing, cases in the Supreme Court of Canada and the European Court of Human Rights have forced the Canadian and British armed forces to re-examine their systems and arguably to sacrifice to some extent the ability of commanders to control the discipline of their formations. These overseas events doubtless indicate the next challenge to be met by the New Zealand system of military law.

E. Deane and G.B.M. Law, 'A Brief History of New Zealand Service Law', *Manual of Armed Forces Law* (Ministry of Defence, Wellington).

BERNARD ROBERTSON

Military settlers Military settlements in New Zealand were a response to uncertainties created by the ★New Zealand Wars. The first such scheme involved the settlement of ★Fencibles, British military pensioners, in four localities in south Auckland, where they formed a passive defensive barrier as well as an employment pool for the city. The outbreak of fighting in the Waikato in 1863 led to a more extensive scheme, by which men were rewarded for active military service by grants of land. The colonial government decided to raise a force of 20,000 soldier settlers to create a 'frontier line' of armed settlers to protect existing European settlements and secure control of confiscated Maori land. One hundred settlements were envisaged in a wide belt from Raglan to Tauranga; there were also to be forty settlements in Taranaki and ten in Hawke's Bay, with additional settlements about Wanganui and Manawatu. The settlements would be linked by 1600 kilometres of strategic roads crisscrossing the North Island. It was intended that the costs of the scheme would be met by the profitable sale of further confiscated Maori land. Offering confiscated land in return for military service appeared to be a cheap means of raising colonial troops to garrison outposts and serve the supply lines.

Recruiting for military settlers commenced on 5 August 1863. It was hoped to attract goldminers and bushmen—'men, hardy, self-reliant, accustomed to bush life, expert in the use of firearms'—and the principal areas of recruitment were Australia and the South Island. Most of those who enlisted were young single men born in Great Britain and from the lower stratum of Victorian society—labourers and semi-skilled workers attracted by the promise of a free farm (see NEW ZEALAND WARS, AUSTRALIAN INVOLVEMENT IN). Men enlisted for three years, during which they would be liable for ★militia service. For actual service they would be paid at militia rates of pay, beginning at two shillings and sixpence per day for a private. As soon as land had been laid out by the government, the military settlers would take possession of a town allotment and a farm section. The size of the grant varied according to rank, with field officers receiving 400 acres and a private fifty acres. The land grant would be confirmed on the completion of the three-year engagement. Promises of employment on public works for the settlements were also made, thereby guaranteeing an income for the soldier settlers as they established themselves. The terms appeared liberal, or at least preferable to the vicissitudes of gold mining, and nearly 4000 men had enlisted as military settlers by the end of 1863.

The majority of the military settlers were formed into four regiments of the Waikato Militia. By December 1863 there were 3617 men in the 1st, 2nd, and 3rd

Military settlers

Regiments, and the 4th Regiment was in the process of formation. Attached to the Waikato Militia were two companies of ★Forest Rangers, who were also offered land grants in the Waikato. In all, 5397 men were to serve in the Waikato Militia. After training at Onehunga and Otahuhu, the regiments were sent to man outposts in south Auckland, thereby relieving the local militia and regular British troops. About 300 military settlers were garrisoned at the redoubt at Raglan, and more than twice as many were employed with the British Army's Commissariat. Detachments of the Waikato Militia also fought at several actions, including Orakau (31 March–2 April 1864). The colonial government was anxious to begin the process of settlement as quickly as possible, since the military settlers were being paid while they waited for their land grants. In June 1864 it was decided that the military settlements would be established in a series of stockades across the Waikato from Raglan to Tauranga. Advance parties of military settlers began to move on to their sites, erecting camps and stockades. The 1st Waikato Regiment settled at Tauranga, the 2nd at Alexandra (Pirongia) and Kihikihi, the 3rd at Cambridge, and the 4th at Kirikiriroa (Hamilton). A siege mentality prevailed at the townships; all were close to areas still under Maori control, and redoubts were the first structures to be erected. The settlers and their families lived in temporary camps of tents, which were gradually replaced by wooden huts of weatherboard construction or raupo whares. By March 1865, when farm sections began to be allocated, there were more than 2600 military settlers in the Waikato. Settlement at Tauranga, where another 800 settlers waited to be allocated their farms, was delayed by continuing conflict. The outbreak of hostilities in the eastern Bay of Plenty in 1865 led to the deployment of military settler units (two companies of Taranaki Military Settlers and a company of the 1st Waikato Regiment) to Opotiki. After a brief campaign, the Opotiki area was also confiscated and opened up for military settlement by the 1st Waikato Regiment. However, settlement here and in the Tauranga districts was delayed by continued Maori resistance. At Tauranga opposition to surveys of the confiscated land resulted in a series of military expeditions in early 1867 with military settlers and ★kupapa laying waste to Maori villages and crops. There was skirmishing in the Opotiki district after two settlers were killed in May 1867. The military settlers formed their own volunteer corps, which conducted expeditions against Maori until 1868.

Recruiting of military settlers for Taranaki commenced in Dunedin and Melbourne in August 1863. Although just over a thousand came forward, the usual strength at any one time was under 800. Smaller corps of bushrangers and cavalry were also raised from March 1864 for service in Taranaki on the same terms as for the Taranaki Military Settlers. The latter, under the command of Lieutenant-Colonel Maxwell Lepper, garrisoned stockades about New Plymouth. Numerous skirmishes were fought, with the principal engagements occurring at Kaitake pa (25 March 1864) and Ahuahu (6 April 1864). In 1865, 20,000 hectares of confiscated land were set aside for eleven military settlements dotted from Pukearuhe in the north to Okato in the south, principally at Okato, Oakura, Huirangi, Tikorangi, Urenui, and Pukearuhe. Fighting in north Taranaki thereafter subsided, though in 1869 a family and three military settlers were killed in an attack on the redoubt at Pukearuhe. In early 1865 the war had shifted to south Taranaki, and in March 1865 a company of Taranaki Military Settlers was sent to Patea. Both Taranaki Military Settlers and Patea Rangers garrisoned redoubts up the Wanganui River, and were besieged at Pipiriki in July 1865. Twenty thousand hectares were set aside for military settlement in the Patea district between Ohawe and Wairoa (Waverley). However, there was continued resistance from Maori inhabitants whose land had been confiscated for the settlements, and desultory skirmishing and the destruction of Maori villages continued until late 1866. The determined minority of military settlers who stuck at their land allotments in the district were forced to seek refuge in Patea township when fighting resumed in June 1868. Their farms were burnt, and several settlers who remained on their sections were killed.

Military settlement in Hawke's Bay began in April 1864 with the raising of the Hawke's Bay Military Settlers. During the course of its existence, about 250 men enlisted in the corps. Under the command of Major James Fraser, they took part in a number of actions in the East Coast and northern Hawke's Bay region, including at Pa-kairomiromi (3 August 1865), Pukemaire (3 and 8 October 1865), Waerenga-a-Hika (15–22 November 1865), Omaru-hakeke (25 December 1865), and Petane (12 October 1866). Just over 100 Hawke's Bay military settlers were granted land at Wairoa, Te Kapu (Frasertown), and Ormond, near Gisborne.

The nature of the military settlers scheme militated against its success. Mainly young, single, and without sufficient capital, the settlers were unlikely to succeed as independent farmers. The relatively small blocks of land available to men in the ranks were uneconomic. The plight of the settlers was made more difficult by the isolation of the settlements, which ensured that goods and transport charges were prohibitively expensive. The military settlers' farms were vulnerable to harassment by the dispossessed former Maori owners of the confiscated land. Even in areas where there was no actual fighting, the fear of Maori attack was often present. As a result, the military settlers were dependent on the continued support of the government. This was never forthcoming, because even a greatly attenuated settlers' scheme was beyond the capacity of the colony's revenues. Because of the rush to place settlers on their land (and therefore off pay), little or no infrastructure had been provided. The situation was made worse when the government in April 1865 curtailed expenditure on public works, thereby denying the settlers employment opportunities off their farms. Even pay for periodic militia musters was cut by the government. Predictably the military settlements soon collapsed. About half the men either deserted or provided substitutes before their three-year term was up. Most of the remainder either sold up or walked off their land. Of 2056 military settlers who were granted farms in the Waikato, only 214 remained by 1880. A similar process was repeated in the Bay of Plenty, Hawke's Bay, and Taranaki. The majority of land grants were ultimately taken over by wealthier farmers and speculators with the skills and capital to consolidate and develop the settlements. The grandiose scheme of creating self-sufficient armed settlements was ultimately a failure. Nevertheless, the military settlements were instrumental in bringing large areas of land under direct European occupation and provided the framework of future settlement for Waikato, Taranaki, and the Bay of Plenty.

P.D.M. Allen, 'Military Settlement in the Middle Waikato Basin' (MA thesis, University of Waikato, 1969); H.C.M. Norris, *Armed Settlers: The Story of the Founding of Hamilton, 1864–1874* (Paul's Book Arcade, Hamilton, 1956).

Military signalling The effective conduct of military operations depends on effective and reliable communications. The first military signalling in New Zealand was carried out by warring Maori, who used the putara (shell war trumpet), pahu (wooden gong), and kotaha (message sling) to carry messages. The ★British Army in New Zealand at first relied on the bugle, drum, and mounted couriers. During the Taranaki War of 1860–61, Sergeant William Marjouram established a network of semaphore stations on the high points around New Plymouth. Morse telegraphy arrived with specialist signaller Corporal Alexander Brodie, who in 1863 built a telegraph line from Auckland to Te Awamutu in support of General Duncan ★Cameron's advance into the Waikato and who is regarded today as the father of the ★Royal New Zealand Corps of Signals. Telegraph lines connected Auckland barracks to most outlying redoubts during the Waikato War. By the 1870s most New Zealand towns were connected by telegraph, enabling the ★Armed Constabulary quickly to concentrate against Maori resistance. The telegraph was also enthusiastically embraced as a means of improving ★imperial defence with the connection of Australia and New Zealand to Great Britain in the 1870s. Captain Falconer of the Torpedo Corps included signalling and telegraphy in the training syllabus in 1889, and specialist signal sections, using semaphore flags and heliographs, were first attached to engineer units of the ★Volunteer Force two years later. Artillery signal sections were also raised. Many (eventually all) members of the Volunteer Cycle Corps formed in 1889 were trained in signalling, and they were used for carrying messages. The first designated signal unit was the Cycle and Signalling Company formed in Auckland. Following the reorganisation of the military forces in 1911, it became the New Zealand Signal Corps. At this time, all members of the Post and Telegraph Department became members of the Post and Telegraph Corps. Both corps were subsumed within the Engineer Signal Service in 1913. Meanwhile naval communications were being revolutionised by the introduction of wireless: warships were used as relay points in 1908 to inaugurate a wireless link between Australia and New Zealand, and four years later a government station was opened near Auckland.

During the ★First World War signallers played a key role as members of 1NZEF, laying thousands of kilometres of telephone and telegraph cable by hand or horse-drawn cable wagons, often under fire. At ★Gallipoli Corporal Cyril ★Bassett became the only signaller to win the ★Victoria Cross. A Divisional Signals unit was formed for the New Zealand Division on the ★Western Front, where signallers continuously laid cable and repaired damage to the system caused by enemy bombardments. Even so, the runner remained the most effective means of communication in the front line, though rocket flares, messenger dogs, pigeons, and white sheets laid out on the ground for aerial observers were also utilised. In the ★Sinai–Palestine campaign the New Zealand Mounted Rifles Brigade Signal Troop worked alongside Australian signallers to provide brigade communications, by line, dispatch rider, and carrier pigeon. New Zealand signallers also served in ★Mesopotamia as part of an Anzac wireless squadron.

Between the world wars, signalling made few advances because of financial stringency. However, the New Zealand Corps of Signals, formed in 1921, gave increasing attention to wireless technology, which would dominate signalling in the ★Second World War. During that conflict, it provided communications for both the Army in New Zealand and 2NZEF. This included five Divisional Signals units, three District Signals units, a Fortress Signals unit, and an Army Signal Company. There was also a Signals Experimental Establishment. Much of the 2nd New Zealand Division's wireless equipment and battery generators were lost in the withdrawal from ★Greece; the lack of equipment would contribute to the subsequent defeat

Military signalling

The signals section of the Canterbury Engineer Volunteers takes part in an exercise in Hagley Park, Christchurch, about 1904. Heliographs, begbie lamps, and semaphore flags are on display (*Alexander Turnbull Library, F-230008-1/2*)

on ★Crete, after wireless sets failed in the fighting for the vital Maleme airfield. In North Africa 2NZEF commander Lieutenant-General B.C. ★Freyberg established a mobile communications network to link his brigade and support arms with his ever-moving tactical headquarters. During the ★Italian campaign 'Sigint' (signals intelligence) and electronic warfare countermeasures were adopted, and 'ground to air' and 'air to ground' signalling was perfected. In the Pacific Islands ★coastwatchers used wireless to warn of Japanese air and naval movements, and 3rd New Zealand Division signallers learned to deal with the problems of electrical storm interference, foliage blanketing, and seeping moisture during the ★Solomons campaign. The Signals Experimental Establishment designed the renowned ZC1 wireless set to overcome some of these problems. At its Army station at Johnsonville, near Wellington, the Army Signal Company intercepted Japanese military communications. After the Japanese capitulation, signallers went to Japan with ★Jayforce to provide communications for New Zealand's occupation sector.

The Second World War also led to a huge expansion of the signals capacity of the other two services. The RNZN and RNZAF jointly established a wireless telegraphy station at Waiouru in 1943 (from 1951 to 1993 HMNZS *Irirangi*). A naval intercept station was also located at Rapaura, near Blenheim. Port War Signal Stations, using semaphore, visual signals, and telegraphy, were established throughout New Zealand. RNZAF stations were linked by high frequency (HF) radio and teletype, and very high frequency (VHF) became standard for airfield and some close air support operations.

During the ★Korean War ★Kayforce signallers laid and replaced telephone links between artillery batteries, mounted a courier service by motorcycle and then jeep, and were responsible for radio communications. They formed a large part of the signals component of 1st Commonwealth Division. During the ★Malayan Emergency Major John Shirley's 'Shirley antenna' was well used—an aerial effective until VHF radio was introduced during the ★Confrontation. VHF thereafter provided 24-hour voice communication, allowing for speedy control of ambushes and patrols by commanders. In the ★Vietnam War 161st Battery signallers utilised American AN/PR-77 sets with ranges of up to ten kilometres, and New Zealand infantry signallers were issued with American-made AN/PRC-25 radio sets.

Military slang

Signals personnel of all three services have been involved in many ★United Nations and other ★peace-keeping operations in the late twentieth century. In Cambodia, for example, a signals troop was provided for the Force Communications Unit in Phnom Penh. Retention of expertise in Morse alongside state-of-the-art signals procedures has proved advantageous in some primitive areas during peace-keeping operations. In Cambodia superior communications were made available by 'Raven', a high-power HF set for voice and data, and by the global links provided by the International Maritime Satellite System. Military communication is today concentrated on the high-speed transmission of data by electronic means.

L. Barber and C. Lord, *Swift and Sure: A History of the Royal New Zealand Corps of Signals and Army Signalling in New Zealand* (New Zealand Signals Inc., Auckland, 1996); C.A. Borman, *Divisional Signals* (War History Branch, Wellington, 1954).

LAURIE BARBER

Military slang Military usage is an example of the process of developing, among people thrown together for a common purpose, a working language which not only helps communication but serves to build up camaraderie and esprit de corps. It can range from the most particular technical or reference jargon (mainly 'international' British–American) to companionable, witty, imaginative, or obscene words, phrases, and nicknames of the highest informality, much of which can be localised in place and time.

Of the armed services, the Army has had the closest extended and the best recognised linguistic association with the European settlement and development of New Zealand. It has had the numbers and persistent contact to preserve its own linguistic identity. Its vocabulary can be well researched from a large written archive of fiction and non-fiction. Other military branches tend to follow the jargon of their larger and older British or American counterparts, though this matter needs further study. Nor have the ★Jayforce, ★Kayforce, or Vietnam experiences provided viable New Zealandisms.

Of New Zealand army usage, the technical is mainly international–traditional. Some of the informal will also be traditional ('Tommy'); some may be generated in a particular war, or theatre of operations—Egypt 'maleesh', ★Western Front 'digger', Italy 'Teds' (from 'Tedeschi': Germans)—and may be shared with other participants therein. Items may lose all but historical currency when the theatre closes (e.g. Turkish 'dere', a gully on ★Gallipoli). Some elements may survive as popular New Zealand uses, brought back into 'civilian' New Zealand English by returned service people and fairly generally used or understood for a few years (e.g. 'Dig'). Some few will be added to the permanent store of New Zealand English (e.g. '*possie*', and those others italicised below), or indeed of international English (e.g. *take a dim view* indicating disapproval).

The ★New Zealand Wars provided (originally from general English slang) 'Jack' or 'Jack Maori' for a Maori opponent (on the Maori side, 'Tiaki'), the field equivalent of the commentators' and reporters' 'hostile' or 'Kingite' (as opposed to 'friendly (Maori)' or 'Queenite'). (The use was carried over to the ★Boer War as 'Jacky', a Boer opponent, to Gallipoli as 'Jacko', or the more ironically polite 'Johnny Turk', for a Turkish opponent, competing there with 'Abdul', the rhyming slang 'Joe' ('Burke'), and various other nicknames.) '*Hauhau*' was the usual informal name for Pai Marire opponents, 'A.C.' for the ★Armed Constabulary, and 'Bush Rangers' for the settler volunteer unit more formally known as ★Forest Rangers.

Besides 'Jacky', the Boer War introduced only '*donga*' from the Zulu for a steep-sided gully, in later New Zealand English use a dip in a golf course, and as '*in the donga*', in trouble; and 'Rough Riders' (originally a name for irregular mounted riflemen) for the troops of the New Zealand 'contingents', the term used here and in the ★First World War for the 'echelon' of the ★Second World War.

First World War terms (now mainly in historical use) include: '*Anzac*' in some of its many compounds; 'blue boy', a convalescent serviceman (from the blue hospital uniform worn); 'buckshee' (from the sense something free or extra), a superficial wound meriting a return home (Second World War, a 'homer'); 'Daisy Patch', the infamous killing field on Gallipoli; 'dead meat ticket', identity disc; a 'Diehard' or 'Last Ditcher', one volunteering to be evacuated among the last from the Gallipoli operation; the 'Dinkums' or 'Dinks' for the Rifle Brigade (from 'fair dinkum soldiers' applied ironically, partly from its commendations from the Governor-General, partly from its pride in its special drills and style), also called 'Lord Liverpool's Own', 'Trents' from Trentham Brigade, and 'Keystone Brigade' after Mack Sennett's Keystone cops; 'disaster' rhyming slang for piastre; 'Ehoas' (from Maori e hoa, 'Friend!'), the (Maori) Pioneer Battalion; '*Enzed*', New Zealand, and '*Enzed(der)*', originally a New Zealand soldier, thence any New Zealander; 'Fernleaf', a New Zealand soldier; 'fireship', lighted paper sailed as a prank down the stream flushing a communal toilet to hasten evacuation; 'Glaxo Camp', 'Glaxo Babies', the Tauherenikau Military Camp near the Glaxo babyfood factory or its occupants ('Glaxo builds bonnie babies'); 'gooseberry', a ready-made tangle of barbed wire; 'hop one's frame', to hasten, and 'hop the bags', to go over the top of the trench on attack; 'kerbstone jockey', an Army Service Corps member; 'komate' (from Maori), dead; 'Main

Military slang

Body man', a long-serving, experienced soldier (compare Second World War 'four-figure man'), 'Masseys', Army issue boots (from the name of the Prime Minister); 'the Mounted(s)', the Mounted Rifles; 'North Sea rabbits', herrings; 'Pen and Ink', the (Gallipoli) Peninsula; 'plunge', to send on a sudden attack or 'stunt'; 'rabbit hole' (Gallipoli), a refuge dug in the ground; 'sandbag duff', a pudding made from ground biscuit; 'the Silent Army' (or 'Division'), the 'NZEF' (which reputedly did not sing on the march); 'smack', a wound; 'the trump of the dump', anyone in authority; 'woodbine bride', an English war bride; 'zambuk', a medical orderly (from the sporting use, first aid person, after the name of a popular ointment).

From the Second World War come 'American invasion'; ('base-) bludger', one with a 'safe' job at base; 'Bludgers' Hill', the rising ground in Maadi Camp where the New Zealand Divisional Headquarters was located; 'Blue Orchids' or 'Glamour Boys', an Army nickname for Air Force members; 'budgie cage', a military punishment centre; *the cactus*, the back of beyond; 'Caravan A', issue cigarettes (a play on 'Craven A', a popular brand), also 'Vs' or 'Veefers' (from 'Victory' on the packet); 'coconut bombers', a nickname for the 3rd Division from its Pacific service; 'ech', echelon; 'four-figure man', a (surviving) member of the first group of 2NZEF volunteers (hence given a low identification number), thus an experienced soldier (also called a 'Thirty-niner', 'Grim Dig', and in the First World War a 'Main Body man'); 'George', a common name for Egyptians (from its use on coins); 'Groppi mocker', full dress clothing (from 'Groppi's', a Cairo restaurant); *jack up* (verb and noun), (to) wangle, arrange(ment), etc; *jungle juice*, a Pacific service name for strong or crude liquor; *Maori PT*, lying quietly on one's back dozing; 'munga food' (from 'mungaree', British tramps' and services slang, from Italian 'mangiare', common among Australians in the First World War but not recorded in New Zealand use until the Second World War); 'onion water', Egyptian ('Stella') beer; 'outer', a minor wound (missing the bullseye), 'out the monk', (?rhyming on 'drunk'), out of action; 'Pongo', a British soldier, then as a general synonym for 'Pommie'; 'purple death', *rooster's blood*, names for cheap (Italian) red wine; 'slittie', a slit trench; 'tankie', a tankman; 'troppo', crazy (as from tropical sunstroke).

Shared First and Second World War usage mainly from the Middle Eastern theatre includes: *Anzac* in various informal compounds; 'base walloper', from 'base wallah', the general derogatory word for any of those attached to base; 'blue', the remote desert; 'Divvy', the New Zealand Division; 'George' (from the Royal Georges omnipresent on British and Empire coins), an Egyptian name for soldiers reversed to a soldiers' name for Egyptians (compare the general use of 'Hori'); 'Piccadilly', applied to spit-and-polish styles, parades, etc.; *possie*, originally a firing position, thence any safe 'hole', thence into general New Zealand use for any personal space, special place, or situation; 'shrapnel', for copper coins, and specifically for French banknotes (from their flimsy susceptibility to develop holes); 'stoush', from general New Zealand use for military fighting, bombardment, or shellfire; 'stunt', a raid or attack (on the enemy). Egyptian Arabic words were variously anglicised and used in both wars: for example, 'feloose', for money, 'magnoon', for crazy (compare 'troppo'), and 'maleesh', indicating indifference or dismissal.

Some shared words differed in use or meaning: 'Kiwi', a New Zealand soldier or a New Zealander, was rare in the First World War, but common in the Second and after; 'the Kiwis' in the First World War denoted a divisional pierrot troupe or concert party, but in the Second and after, the 2NZEF ★'Kiwi Concert Party' and the rugby team, both highly successful during and immediately after the war. The 'Tuis', in the First World War, denoted a services pierrot entertainment troupe; in the Second, the New Zealand Women's Auxiliary Army Corps. Second World War use of the central term *digger* also diverged from that of the First. A part of goldfields history and in active gumfields use in 1914, 'digger' was applied by New Zealanders in the First to a New Zealand soldier, usually a private, but in the Second usually to an Australian soldier (which was also the Australian preference), giving way to 'Dig' as the New Zealanders' preferred self-name or mode of address, perhaps to reinforce a separate identity from Australian 'diggers'. In the First World War 'returned soldiers' received 'repat' aid, in the Second 'rehab'. ★'*Lemon-squeezer*' as the common nickname of the straight-brimmed hat seems not recorded before the 1940s, though the headgear came into general use in 1916, replacing the wide-brimmed slouch hat, the so-called 'smasher'. From POW camps came 'Scotchman's feed' for sniffing the mere scent of another's ★Red Cross food parcels. Conscientious objection generated 'shirker' (First World War), and 'hoon' and 'religo' (Second World War) respectively for non-religious and religious objectors in detention camps.

An engaging set of nicknames was given to various sections of 1NZEF. In the First World War, sections of the Rifle Brigade, informally the 'Dinks' (or 'Dinkums'), were identified by the shape or position of their ★colour patches as 'Square Dinks"(a play on the old-fashioned asseveration 'Square dinkum, mate!'), 'Triangle Dinks', 'Arse-ups' (with triangle inverted), etc. '(Bill Massey's) Tourists' were those who volunteered for the Main Body in 1914, followed by the 'Dinkums' (the serious fighting men, not the Rifle Brigade mentioned above), the 'Super-Dinkums', the

'War Babies' (supposedly born in the far-off days of 1914), and finally the 'Hard Thinkers', volunteering late after long, hard thought. 'Nat Goulds' were also later reinforcements of mainly conscripts (recalling the title of Nat Gould's best-selling 1899 novel *Landed at Last*); 'Stokers' were those who did not enlist for overseas service, choosing, in the words of the First World War song, to 'keep the home fires burning'. In the Second World War, early volunteers for the First Echelon were variously 'debt-dodgers', 'debt-evaders', 'one-steppers' (one step ahead of conscription or the law), 'wife-beaters', 'wife-dodgers', becoming, if they survived, 'Thirty-niners', 'four-figure men', 'Old' or 'Grim Digs'; or if late reinforcements, 'Deep Thinkers', or the 'Rainbow Boys' (appearing after the storm). The Second Echelon who arrived in Egypt via Great Britain were nicknamed '(Cook's) Tourists'.

H.W. Orsman (ed), *The Dictionary of New Zealand English* (Oxford University Press, Auckland, 1997), in which entries with a 'military' label, mostly informal in origin, fill a not inconsiderable niche, roughly 340 of the 6000 main entries, and about 450 items in a total of 9000 subentries (e.g. 'Anzac button'); E. Partridge, *A Dictionary of Slang and Unconventional English* (8th edn) (Routledge, London, 1984); 'New Zealand Slang' (especially a First World War slang scene written by A.E. Strong), in E. Partridge, *Slang Today and Yesterday* (Routledge, London, 1935); 'Soldier Slanguage' [Second World War], in *Korero* (Army Education and Welfare Service magazine), 17 July 1944.

HARRY ORSMAN

Military Studies Institute, with its HQ located at Trentham Military Camp, was established in July 1993 with a view to improving educational opportunities available to Army personnel and providing courses with credibility in the wider field of tertiary education. A response to the increasingly complex nature of defence preparations, it evolved out of an earlier Military Studies Centre established at Waiouru in 1991 as a subsection of the Queen Elizabeth II Army Memorial Museum. Although an Army unit, the Institute has a wider, tri-service, focus, and is open to both civilian Defence employees and members of the ★Territorial Force. It is charged with implementing the Army's educational policy, and among its tasks is the production of the *New Zealand Army Journal*. Each year it organises a conference on some aspect of defence. To broaden the scope of its programmes, it has developed formal teaching relationships with a number of tertiary institutions in both Australia and New Zealand, most notably Massey University, which has the best-developed distance education facilities in the country. A conjoint master's degree programme in defence and strategic studies has been developed, and work is proceeding on a bachelor's degree programme in defence studies. While the Institute's primary objective is the lifting of educational standards within the ★New Zealand Defence Force, it has come to play a valuable role in promoting discussion of defence issues in the wider community.

GLYN HARPER

Militia was a compulsory 'home guard' of European settlers, which could be called out in emergency for local defence. It had little involvement in the ★New Zealand Wars, and should not be confused with the assortment of voluntary corps of ★military settlers raised by the colonial government in that period. Authorised under the provisions of the Militia Ordinance 1845—a response to the outbreak of hostilities in the north—it embodied all able-bodied European men between the ages of eighteen and sixty, who were liable to be called out by the Governor for training or actual service within forty kilometres of their town. In 1845–46 the Wellington Militia found themselves manning redoubts and stockades at Thorndon, Karori, and the Hutt Valley. Militia rolls were compiled in Auckland and Taranaki, and later in Hawke's Bay and Nelson.

The Militia Act 1858 made militiamen liable for service anywhere within their militia district, although this was later restricted to within twenty-four kilometres of the district post office. The Militia were divided into three classes according to age and marital status (with the first class consisting of single men between the ages of sixteen and forty years). In early 1860 the Militia at New Plymouth and Auckland were called out for actual service. They manned outposts and mounted patrols. The Taranaki Militia gained a battle honour when it fought a minor engagement, in which a militiaman was killed, at Waireka. By 1862 there were 1400 men serving with the Militia at Auckland, Wanganui, Wellington, and Taranaki. Such service was 'extremely unpopular', in no small part because of the economic dislocation communities suffered when the Militia were called out. The low pay of militiamen was a further disincentive. Even the government disliked calling out the Militia, because of the strain it placed on the colonial finances, and Militia training was always reduced as quickly as possible.

With the outbreak of the Waikato War in mid 1863, the Militia were called out at Auckland, Taranaki, Wairarapa, Wanganui, Napier, and Wellington. In all about 3800 men were affected. However, the poor quality and limited radius of service of the Militia ensured that the brunt of the fighting fell on British regulars, military settlers, and volunteers. At Auckland, Taranaki, Wanganui, and Napier, the Militia were limited to garrisoning strongpoints near town. Apart from a few minor skirmishes near Papakura in 1863, in

Mine countermeasures vessels

Taranaki in 1863 and 1864, and near Napier in 1866, they saw little combat. In more secure districts, such as Wellington, Militia service was limited to occasional drills. By 1869 only the Taranaki Militia were still on duty in guard posts in the province. Elsewhere the Militia had gradually decayed, with the most enthusiastic men joining ★Volunteer Force corps.

With the release of the Taranaki Militia from service in July 1872, the Militia disappeared as an embodied military force. It remained as a list to which officers not with a Volunteer Force unit (generally regular officers and veterans of the New Zealand Wars) were posted for the purposes of establishing seniority. Officers in the New Zealand contingents for the ★Boer War were also appointed to the New Zealand Militia list. In 1902 permanent artillery officers formed a separate corps, the Royal New Zealand Artillery, and were taken off the Militia list. The New Zealand Militia ceased to exist in 1911, with permanent staff officers forming the ★New Zealand Staff Corps. Although the Militia were not called out after 1872, there were occasional reminders of the obligations it involved. Militia rolls were compiled during the Russian scare of 1885, and similar action was contemplated during the Anglo-German naval scare of 1909. The Council of Defence in 1908–09 saw the militia provisions as a possible means of ensuring adequate manpower for the military forces, but the government's lack of enthusiasm for any form of compulsion prevented any progress in this direction. Provision for a Militia was not finally removed from the statute books until 1950.

Mine countermeasures vessels German mines claimed New Zealand ships and lives in both world wars. Two fields laid by the raider *Wolf* in 1917 sank the *Port Kembla* and the *Wimmera* in 1917–18, the latter with the loss of twenty-six lives (see ENEMY OPERATIONS IN NEW ZEALAND WATERS). These blasts jolted local complacency and forced the Admiralty to hire the local trawlers *Nora Niven*, *Simplon*, and *Hananui II* as minesweepers. In 1919 three Royal Navy minesweeping sloops completed the job.

Between the wars the trawler *Wakakura* served as a minesweeping and gunnery training ship. The ★Second World War brought the return of German auxiliary cruisers and German mines, which again claimed victims in local waters—among them the auxiliary minesweeper HMS *Puriri*, which sank in the Hauraki Gulf in 1941; another converted sweeper, HMNZS *South Sea*, was lost after a collision in Wellington Harbour in 1943. The New Zealand government had already ordered the Bird class ships (see CORVETTES) and acquired four modern Isles class anti-submarine minesweeping trawlers in 1941, but again depended on requisitioned ships, taking over more than twenty trawlers and coasters and using them as anti-submarine minesweepers, training vessels, and dan-layers. Some were elderly and unsuited to wartime work, but most served until 1943–45 when they were returned to their owners.

New Zealand also built 'new' anti-submarine minesweeping trawlers, the Castle class. Constrained by the limited shipbuilding resources of the Dominion, the Marine Department dusted off the plans for a ★First World War design and ordered three composite (wood over steel) and fourteen steel-hulled, coal-fired anti-submarine minesweepers from Auckland and Port Chalmers shipyards. Completed in 1943–44, the Castles displaced about 550 tons standard, mounted one 12-pounder gun, carried a couple of machine-guns, depth charges, and sweeping gear, and could make about ten knots, about two knots slower than their British contemporaries. Although the centrepiece of the New Zealand wartime shipbuilding programme, the old-fashioned-looking, coal-fired Castles were a questionable investment. HMNZS *Waikato* and *Tawhai* were never completed, and four others were cancelled. The composites lay in reserve until 1954, but the rest were sold in 1946.

During the 1950s and the early 1960s, while the major powers commissioned hundreds of new wooden mine countermeasures vessels to counter the threat posed by modern pressure and acoustic mines, New Zealand ran down its forces. After clearing wartime fields, the Flower and Bird class corvettes went on to perform other duties and the Isles languished in reserve until sold in 1957. In 1952 Australia donated four Bathurst class steel minesweepers to New Zealand. The Naval Board's 1953 report stated that the ships had been refitted and were awaiting modern minesweeping gear, but although styled as ocean minesweepers by the RNZN, they were anything but: HMNZS *Echuca*, her modernisation incomplete, never went to sea, HMNZS *Stawell*, partially modernised, served as a training ship, then spent most of her career in reserve; and HMNZS *Inverell* and *Kiama*, more extensively refitted, served as training and fisheries protection ships until 1976 and 1974 respectively. In truth, the more sophisticated mines had rendered the wartime steel ships obsolete.

New Zealand's only credible post-war mine countermeasures vessels were two borrowed British Ton class coastal minesweepers, HMNZS *Santon* and *Hickleton*, which the RNZN operated as patrol craft in Malaysian waters in 1965–66 (see CONFRONTATION). Since 1987, when two American 'Phantom HDX' remote-operated submersibles were commissioned for deployment from the survey ship HMNZS *Monowai*, the RNZN has displayed a renewed interest in mine countermeasures warfare. A small diving force was formed around the diving tender HMNZS *Manawanui*. In 1991–92 the four RNZNVR inshore patrol craft received side-scan sonars and enhanced navigation equipment to permit their use as 'Q-route' mine survey boats; influence mine countermeasures gear will be added in due course.

G. Howard/C.C. Wynn, *Portrait of the Royal New Zealand Navy: A Fiftieth Anniversary Celebration* (Grantham House, Wellington, 1991); R.J. McDougall, *New Zealand Naval Vessels* (GP Books, Wellington, 1989); T.D. Taylor, *New Zealand's Naval Story* (A.H. & A.W. Reed, Wellington, 1948).

GAVIN McLEAN

Mines, land During the trench warfare of the *First World War, land mines were an offensive weapon (see MINING OPERATIONS IN THE FIRST WORLD WAR). Their prolific use as a defensive weapon, mainly designed to deny the enemy access to particular areas or impede his advance, dates from the *Second World War. Minefields were typically laid in irregular belts, and by the rules of war were meant to be clearly delineated with perimeter wire and warning signs. However, by the end of the war the Germans were using mines indiscriminately in an attempt to harass and demoralise the advancing Allies. The *Italian campaign was notable for the widespread use of mines and booby traps. The Germans employed two basic types of mine—the *Tellermine*, an 8.6 kilogram circular anti-tank mine detonated by a tank or heavy vehicle driving over it, and the *S-Mine*, a vicious anti-personnel mine which if actuated by tripwire or sensitive prongs would spring out of the ground to chest height and then detonate. Although detecting mines was initially a matter of gently prodding the ground with a bayonet, field engineers were using electromagnetic mine detectors by 1942. This led the Germans to introduce wooden and plastic mines, such as the anti-personnel *Schu-mine*. Mines were also booby-trapped to make their clearance more difficult. On the Allied side, New Zealand sappers laid thousands of anti-tank mines on the Alamein line in North Africa in 1942, usually 3.6 kilogram Mark IV and Mark V mines. Although no anti-personnel mines were used, booby traps were laid.

Following the Second World War, plastic became the preferred material for mines. Not only were plastic mines more difficult to detect but also they were cheaper, allowing more to be used. More sophisticated mines were also developed, such as the Claymore mine, a rectangular slab of explosive and hundreds of steel balls which would detonate in a fan-shaped blast. Both sides used mines to good effect in both *Korean and *Vietnam Wars. Unless carefully protected, minefields could, however, become double-edged weapons, as, for example, a large field laid by Australians—known as 'the fence'—in Vietnam, which provided the Vietcong with an excellent source of mines to be turned against their opponents. Because of their cheapness, anti-personnel mines have been used extensively in many Third World conflicts since 1945, and generally indiscriminately. The human cost of the many abandoned minefields having become a major international issue, the *Red Cross and other humanitarian agencies began to agitate from 1991 for a complete ban on anti-personnel mines. The campaign, which was characterised by the propagation of often greatly exaggerated statistics to increase moral outrage, was concluded successfully with the signature of the Ottawa Landmines Treaty in 1997. Nevertheless, there must be doubt whether this proscription will hold firm in any future conflict, given that military imperatives rather than paper agreements will no doubt be the dominant influence on the behaviour of adversaries. In accordance with the Ottawa Treaty, New Zealand has destroyed its stocks of anti-personnel mines. No anti-tank mines are held.

In recent times, New Zealand's involvement with mines has been largely confined to assisting countries to deal with the problem of clearing them after years of indiscriminate use. A detachment of engineers was sent to Pakistan in 1989 to teach mine-clearance techniques to Afghans, while mine-clearance teams have also subsequently served in Cambodia, Angola, and Mozambique. New Zealand field engineers have earned a substantial reputation for their de-mining expertise.

Mines, sea are a relatively inexpensive method of conducting naval warfare. They can be laid by almost any kind of platform, need no maintenance, and present a long-term threat to all maritime traffic. Although developed initially as a weapon controlled from ashore, they were used during the twentieth century mainly in a form where the victim detonated them. Their type depended on the means by which the detonation was triggered—contact, magnetic, acoustic, or pressure. Spherical in shape and filled with about 200 kilograms of explosive, contact mines were detonated when their distinctive horns came in contact with a ship's hull. While they were sometimes floated against potential targets, they were usually moored by cables attached to a heavy weight anchored to the seabed. The other types of mines were designed to be activated by ships' magnetic field, sound, or changes in water pressure, and normally were laid on the seabed. Since the *Second World War mine technology has made major steps forward, and modern mines possess an array of sensors and targeting devices.

In New Zealand waters mines first made their appearance as part of the *coast defences developed in the late nineteenth century. These were controlled submarine mines moored to the sea bed by *mine-

Mine-tenders

tenders. They were designed to be detonated by electric signal as an enemy ship passed overhead (though some were also exploded on contact with a ship's hull). By 1893 there were 245 mines in the country, but there were delays in instituting the minefields. The system was dispensed with in 1907.

About sixty contact mines were laid by the German raider *Wolf* off Three King's Island and Cape Farewell in 1917. Minesweeping accounted for thirty-seven of the mines, and a further twenty-one washed ashore. One of the latter killed three drovers when they attempted to drag it ashore at Waikoria Beach in April 1919. Further contact mines were laid in the Hauraki Gulf by the German raider *Orion* in 1940, and in the following year ten magnetic mines were laid in each of the approaches to Wellington and Lyttelton harbours. They were never detected and never exploded, which suggests that they may have been laid too deeply. New Zealand was forced to devote considerable resources to counter-mine measures. Degaussing (to remove magnetic fields) was carried out at Wellington and Auckland, and paravanes were fitted to deflect contact mines away from ships' hulls. Minesweeping was a major activity of the RNZN until June 1946, and mines were still occasionally being washed ashore for years afterwards. Mines were also used by New Zealand for defensive purposes as ★anti-invasion measures. Ten minefields were laid at Whangaroa, the Hauraki Gulf, the Bay of Islands, Great Barrier Island, Wellington, and Akaroa in 1942. Both moored contact mines and seabed controlled mines were used, with a total of 1391 mines laid. By the time mine-laying was halted in 1943, the programme had cost £1.5 million. Most of the mines were removed before the end of the war, but some remained. The last known mine from these fields was recovered in 1992. About forty mines remain unrecovered.

Mine-tenders The question of harbour defence was first given serious attention in the late 1860s, though two decades elapsed before gun batteries were installed at Wellington, Auckland, Lyttelton, and Dunedin, and a defensive mine-laying capability was achieved (see COAST DEFENCES). In this 'submarine mining' scheme, which lasted until 1907, 'dormant' mines were moored to the seabed ready to be detonated electrically from the shore should an enemy warship pass over them. For its implementation the scheme required a Defence Department steamer in each defended port to lay the mines and cables, and raise them periodically for inspection and maintenance. The vessels also transported Submarine Mining Corps personnel and stores to the manned observation stations, which in some cases were well away from formed roads, and they performed the same service for the harbour forts manned by the Garrison Artillery.

The first mine-tender was the 21.3-metre *Ellen Ballance*, which was constructed at Dumbarton, Scotland, in 1882 but assembled in Wellington, about 1884. Found to be too small for safety in rough seas, she was replaced as the Wellington mine-tender in January 1902 by the 27.4-metre *Janie Seddon*, which, with her twin the *Lady Roberts*, had been built at Paisley, Scotland, in 1901. The *Ellen Ballance* saw further service in Lyttelton and in Otago Harbour before disposal in 1907. Based in Wellington, the *Janie Seddon* had a long life beyond the end of the submarine mining scheme. She was a port examination ship in both world wars, was used to tow targets for coastal artillery practice, at times earned her keep by being hired to other government departments, and eventually was sold in 1946 and broken up in Motueka in 1957. Despite being hindered by defective boilers, the *Lady Roberts* filled a similar role to the *Janie Seddon* in the Otago and Auckland harbours until the early 1920s, when she was sold to the Department of External Affairs for use in Samoa.

DENIS FAIRFAX

Mining operations in the First World War
With the ★Western Front stalemated in trench warfare from late 1914, both sides began driving tunnels under their opponents' trench systems, the aim being to deposit large quantities of high explosive which could be detonated just before an attack went in. Following a request from the War Office in London, New Zealand formed a tunnelling company in October 1915 from miners and tunnellers. Under the command of Major J.E. ★Duigan, the 446-strong New Zealand Tunnelling Company arrived in France in March 1916. Its first activity was counter-mining operations at the foot of Vimy Ridge near Arras. Enemy countermeasures made this nerve-racking work. Only once was a tunnel blown by the Germans, burying two New Zealanders. The company was subsequently engaged in digging a tunnel system from the old underground quarries and cellars under Arras. The caverns were made safe and extended, and by April 1917 the New Zealanders had completed an astonishing underground system of assembly galleries, subways, kitchens, headquarters, and hospitals. On 9 April mines under the German front line were blown as part of the successful attack by the Canadian Corps on Vimy Ridge. The company constructed dugouts in the front line until March 1918, then dug trenches and built roads. In September it erected the Havrincourt bridge across the Canal du Nord, one of the longest single-span military bridges ever built. By the time its demobilisation began in December 1918, the company had suffered 202 casualties.

Missiles, in the New Zealand context, are generally confined to rocket-propelled guided weapons. The first in New Zealand service were Seacat GWS-22 surface-to-air (SAM) missiles in the RNZN, a quadruple Seacat launcher being installed on each of the Leander class *frigates (two on HMNZS *Southland*). The Seacat was a short-range missile, guided on to the target by wire or radio control from the ship. Seacats were replaced in the 1990s by Vulcan Phalanx six-barrelled gun systems. Australian-made Ikara GWS-40 anti-submarine missiles were carried by *Southland*. After launch the Ikara was guided by radar or radio to the vicinity of the enemy submarine. On receipt of a command, it then released a Mark 44 homing torpedo, which descended by parachute into the water and homed on its target. The system left New Zealand service when *Southland* was paid off in 1995. The Anzac class frigates are equipped with Raytheon Sea Sparrow surface-to-air missiles. The Sea Sparrows have a range of fifteen kilometres, homing on their target by radar.

The use of missiles by the RNZAF dates from 1970 with the introduction of AIM-9 Sidewinder air-to-air missiles (AAM). The AIM-9, originally designed in the early 1950s, has been continually improved, and is the standard anti-aircraft missile of Western air forces today. It is a short-range (eight kilometres) missile that homes in on a designated heat source such as a jet engine. AGM-65 Maverick air-to-ground missiles have armed the A-4K Skyhawks since 1985. The Maverick is a precision-guided missile: the pilot designates the target and then launches the missile, which is automatically homed in on the target by a television or infra-red tracker. More modern versions of the Maverick (not in New Zealand service) use a laser target designator to home in on coded laser energy reflected from the target. AGM-84 Harpoon long-range radar-guided anti-ship missiles were considered for the P-3 Orions but never purchased.

The *New Zealand Army acquired its first missiles in 1997 in the form of the Mistral man-portable air defence missiles, which use an infra-red seeker to home in on their target at a range of up to six kilometres. Twelve Mistral launchers were acquired to equip G Troop, 43rd Air Defence Battery.

Montgomery, Field Marshal Sir Bernard Law, Viscount (17 November 1887–25 March 1976) commanded the Allied forces at the Battle of El Alamein, the decisive battle of the *North African campaign. Commissioned in the Royal Warwickshire Regiment in 1908, he served with distinction during the *First World War and in the early stages of the Second commanded the 3rd Division. He was one of the few British commanders to return from Dunkirk with his

General Sir Bernard Montgomery inspects troops of 5th New Zealand Brigade in 1942 (*War History Collection, Alexander Turnbull Library, F-2672-1/2-DA*)

reputation enhanced. In August 1942 he took command of the 8th Army (in which the 2nd New Zealand Division was serving), determined to end the string of British defeats which had characterised the North African campaign. His troops soon warmed to his strong, rather eccentric, personality—and his methodical and meticulously planned approach to operations, which contrasted sharply with perceived earlier mismanagement. Montgomery greatly admired the performance of the New Zealanders at El Alamein, during the pursuit across North Africa, and in the early stages of the ★Italian campaign. In December 1943 he left Italy to assume command of the Allied land forces for the ★D-Day landings in Normandy. After the successful conclusion of the North-west Europe campaign—he took the German surrender at Lüneburg Heath on 4 May 1945—he was raised to the peerage for his war services. From June 1946 to September 1948 he was Chief of Imperial General Staff, in which capacity he toured New Zealand to much public acclaim in July 1947. He reinforced the New Zealand military authorities in their advocacy of a ★Territorial Force division based on ★compulsory military training. From 1951 to 1958 Montgomery was Deputy Supreme Commander of Allied Forces Europe.

Moore-Jones, Sapper Horace Millichamp (1867/68?–3 April 1922) was born in Malvern Wells, England, and emigrated to New Zealand in the mid 1880s. When the ★First World War began, he was working as an artist for *Pearson's Magazine* in London. Despite being over age, he joined the British section of 1NZEF, and was posted to the New Zealand Engineers as a draughtsman. At ★Gallipoli in 1915, he produced sketches and terrain models for intelligence and planning purposes, and a striking series of watercolour landscapes. His most famous work, however, was *The Man with the Donkey*, a watercolour depicting Australian stretcher-bearer John Simpson Kirkpatrick and his donkey carrying a wounded soldier to safety. Nicknamed 'Aunty' on account of his age and nature, Moore-Jones found soldiering a particularly demanding experience. He was wounded in action in May 1915, and again more seriously in November. After his evacuation to England, where he continued to paint while convalescing, he was repatriated to New Zealand in July 1916. He offered to sell his watercolour landscapes to the New Zealand government but without success. They were purchased instead by the Australian government for its planned War Memorial. Moore-Jones died while trying to save lives during a hotel fire in Hamilton. His pictures, now in Canberra, remain as enduring images of the Anzac experience at Gallipoli.

RICHARD TAYLOR

Morrison, Air Vice-Marshal Ian Gordon (16 March 1914–5 September 1997) has been described as the 'Builder' of the modern RNZAF. Born in Hanmer Springs, he took up a short-service commission in the RAF in January 1936, but later transferred to the RNZAF. He flew Wellington bombers with 75 Squadron until he returned to New Zealand in 1940 to take up duties as an instructor and staff officer. Despite an aircraft accident (for which he was severely reprimanded), he earned a reputation as an excellent trainer. In 1943 he became involved in the ★Solomons campaign as 1 (Islands) Group's Senior Staff Officer, later commanding the Ventura-equipped 3 Squadron. After the war he held a number of staff positions, and in 1950 attended the Joint Services Staff College in the United Kingdom. Exchange duty with the RAF, command of Ohakea base, and further staff positions followed, and in 1958 he attended the ★Imperial Defence College. He became CAS in July 1962, at a time when the service was being adversely affected by a lack of clear direction and the obsolescence of its aircraft. Under his leadership morale markedly improved, not least because of his success in advancing the RNZAF's interests. His tenacity and determination was the driving force behind a comprehensive re-equipment programme which included the first post–Second World War acquisition of American aircraft—the P-3 Orions, C-130 Hercules, and Bell UH-1 Iroquois helicopters that would serve the RNZAF well for more than thirty years. Made a CBE in 1957 and a CB in 1965, he retired in 1966.

Mortars first made an appearance in New Zealand during the ★New Zealand Wars. Coehorn mortars, essentially a stubby bronze tube mounted on a heavy wooden base plate, were used by the British Army. However, it was only during the ★First World War that mortars came into their own. The one most used by New Zealand troops with 1NZEF was the 3.2-inch Stokes mortar. An astonishingly simple weapon, it could throw a 5-kilogram bomb up to 750 metres. A battery of eight mortars was attached to each infantry brigade to give infantry close support. Three other batteries were equipped with heavier 6-inch Stokes mortars, and a fourth with massive 9.45-inch trench mortars (nicknamed 'flying pigs'). Mortar crews were the 'cinderellas' of the New Zealand Division—because their mortar fire on enemy trenches invariably invited retaliation, which endangered their own infantrymen. In New Zealand between the world wars, each battalion in the ★Territorial Force had a support platoon equipped with Stokes mortars. The Stokes were replaced by 3-inch mortars in 2NZEF, with a platoon of six mortars being included in each infantry battalion. These mortars could throw a 4.5 kilogram bomb out to 2500 metres. Each infantry platoon also had a

Mounted rifles

A New Zealand mortar crew loads its weapon at Colincamps on the Western Front in April 1918 (*RSA Collection, Alexander Turnbull Library, G-13122-1/2*)

small 2-inch mortar useful for firing flares and smoke bombs. From April 1944 the 2nd New Zealand Division operated a battery of sixteen 4.2-inch heavy mortars. In 1965 the Army began acquiring 81 mm L16 mortars, capable of throwing a 4.3 kilogram bomb 5700 metres. They remain in use more than thirty years later, their effectiveness having been enhanced by computerised mortar location and targeting systems.

Mould, Major-General Thomas Rawlings (31 May 1807–13 June 1886) commanded the Royal Engineers during the ★New Zealand Wars. After securing a commission in the Royal Engineers in 1826, he served in England and Ireland until posted to New Zealand in 1855. He soon found his talents as an engineer in demand by the civil authorities in the colony. As Inspector of Public Works for Auckland from 1856 and for the whole colony from 1857, he was involved in various public works schemes. In 1856, with the officer commanding the Royal Artillery in New Zealand, Captain W.M. King, he prepared a report on harbour defence requirements at Auckland, and in the following year visited other New Zealand harbours and anchorages to consider their defence needs. From February 1860 he was the Governor's Deputy for Auckland Province and in April was appointed a colonel in the ★Militia. He was a key figure in Major-General T.S. ★Pratt's operations in the Taranaki War of 1860–61, in which saps were driven towards Maori fortifications. He oversaw the most extensive field engineering works ever undertaken in New Zealand, at Te Arei. He also built many redoubts and blockhouses both in Taranaki and later in the Waikato during the fighting there in 1863–64. He was made a CB in 1862. Returning to the United Kingdom in 1866, he served another six years before retiring on full pay.

Mounted rifles The first New Zealand mounted troops were volunteer cavalry corps raised in Taranaki and Auckland, and the 'Mounted Defence Force' formed by Lieutenant-Colonel M.G. ★Nixon in 1863. In the 1870s the various volunteer cavalry corps were organised as Light Horse Volunteers, at this time consisting of twenty-one volunteer corps, the individual corps retaining their rather splendid titles. In 1886 the first mounted corps with the title of Mounted Rifles was established, indicating a shift towards a role of mounted infantry rather than conventional cavalry. In 1897 it was decided that the future role of the mounted units would 'be that of a body of infantry soldiers capable of being transferred rapidly from one position to another, to act as infantry, and not as cavalry'. As a result carbines and swords were withdrawn, replaced by Martini-Enfield rifles.

The effectiveness of the ten contingents of mounted riflemen sent by New Zealand to the ★Boer War convinced many New Zealanders that they had a natural affinity for this style of warfare. Volunteers flocked to join or form mounted rifles corps. Nearly fifty came into being in 1900. This enthusiasm for mounted riflemen was encouraged by British officers. In 1903 the Commandant, Major-General J.M. ★Babington, noted the availability in New Zealand of 'large numbers of men who are good riders, and accustomed to work such as gives them an eye for country and inculcates independence'. In 1906 mounted rifles battalions were redesignated as regiments and companies as squadrons. Five years later, when the ★Volunteer Force corps which made up these units were reshaped into the ★Territorial Force, twelve mounted rifles regiments were established. With the outbreak of the ★First World War, each of these regiments provided a squadron for 1NZEF. Four mounted rifle regiments were thereby formed, each of 549 men and 608 horses. The Auckland, Wellington, and Canterbury Mounted Rifles formed the New Zealand Mounted Rifles Brigade under the command of Colonel A.H. ★Russell, while the Otago Mounted Rifles served as divisional cavalry. In May 1915 all four regiments were committed as infantry at ★Gallipoli, as part of the

★New Zealand and Australian Division. The NZMR Brigade suffered such heavy losses that by the end of August it was down to just 365 men.

Following the evacuation from the peninsula, the mounted riflemen were re-formed in Egypt, with many seasoned troopers joining infantry battalions and heading off to the ★Western Front with the New Zealand Division. The Otago Mounted Rifles went too; it would eventually be reduced to a single squadron. The NZMR's three mounted rifles regiments formed part of the Australian–New Zealand Mounted Division, which took a leading part in the ★Sinai–Palestine campaign. The New Zealanders' impressive record was marred only by several brutal incidents, including the massacre of Arab civilians at Surafend. The brigade returned to New Zealand without its horses in June 1919.

In the post-war reorganisation of the military forces in New Zealand, the mounted rifles were reduced to nine territorial regiments. Although remaining a prestigious arm, the mounted rifles were overtaken by technological change. Only belatedly, in 1939, did they begin to mechanise. With mounted troops not required for 2NZEF, volunteers from the mounted rifles regiments formed the New Zealand Divisional Cavalry Regiment, which was equipped with Bren gun carriers and armoured cars. Initially the troopers wore the mounted rifles' distinctive slouch hat, but eventually the ★lemon-squeezer was adopted. In New Zealand the Territorial mounted rifles regiments remained in existence until mechanised as light armoured fighting vehicle (LAFV) regiments of the New Zealand Armoured Corps in 1942. In 1940 nine independent mounted rifles squadrons were formed to patrol remote areas, and they operated for three years. In 1944 the nine LAFV regiments were amalgamated to form three armoured regiments. All disappeared in the 1950s. Currently the mounted rifles' traditions are maintained in the ★New Zealand Army's armoured unit, the Queen Alexandra's Mounted Rifles.

Mulgan, Lieutenant-Colonel John Alan Edward (31 December 1911–26 April 1945), an important literary figure, is chiefly known for his classic New Zealand novel *Man Alone*, published in 1939. During the ★Second World War, he was also a highly competent field officer. His *Report on Experience*, published posthumously in 1947, presents enduring insights into soldiering and the New Zealand in which he was born and brought up. After studying at Auckland and Oxford universities, he was working for the Clarendon Press when the Second World War began. He already held a commission in a Territorial battalion of the Oxford and Buckinghamshire Light Infantry, and served with British units initially, including the Royal West Kent Regiment in the ★North African campaign.

He doubted whether the British Army gave strong enough emphasis to battlefield capability—as compared to what he perceived in 2nd New Zealand Division—and, after criticising a superior officer, he was eventually transferred to Special Operations Executive's Force 133, which supported resistance forces in Greece. Although he was known for his self-control, pragmatism, and effectiveness—he was awarded an MC for his activities with partisans in Thessaly and the Pindos Mountains—he finished the war doubting that the results achieved were commensurate with the pain inflicted on civilians, many of whom were slaughtered by the Germans in retaliation. He was later involved in providing compensation to pro-Allied Greeks. Returning to Cairo in 1945 after a period of great strain and in a state of disillusionment, he soon afterwards took his own life.

RAY GROVER

Murupaenga (?–1826), a chief of the Ngati Rongo hapu of Ngati Whatua, was prominent in the wars between Ngati Whatua and Nga Puhi at the beginning of the nineteenth century. In 1806 he led attacks against the Bay of Islands and Hokianga. A year later he took Ngati Whatua to the assistance of Waikato, where at Hingakaka—possibly the largest battle ever fought on New Zealand soil—a great victory was won over a coalition of Ngati Toa, Ngati Raukawa, and allied tribes. Returning north he ambushed Nga Puhi invaders at Moremonui. Despite possessing some muskets, Nga Puhi were defeated. So great were Nga Puhi losses that the battle became known as Te Kai-a-te-karoro ('the seagulls' feast'). In or around 1818 Murupaenga invaded Taranaki with ★Te Rauparaha and ★Tuwhare. In 1819–20, along with Tuwhare, ★Patuone, ★Nene, and Te Rauparaha, he launched a great raiding expedition down to the southern part of the North Island, destroying pa and taking captives. On returning home he once again waged war on Nga Puhi, who were intent on avenging their defeat at Moremonui. He accompanied ★Hongi Hika and ★Te Wera Hauraki's expedition against Te Arawa in 1823. In 1825, war between Nga Puhi and Ngati Whatua resumed, the former being led by Hongi Hika and including ★Kawiti and other leaders. At Te Ika-a-ranga-nui Hongi Hika routed Ngati Whatua, and Murupaenga was forced to flee. He was killed in a Nga Puhi raid in the following year.

Museums, military New Zealanders have been ambivalent about commemorating their military past. Late in the nineteenth century displays of medals, tunics, side arms, and photographs quickly became standard items for local history museums. In 1917, Prime Minister William ★Massey succumbed to

Museums

wartime fervour and authorised a national war museum similar to those proposed by Great Britain, Australia, and Canada. The post-war recession and other complications cooled his ardour. The considerable quantities of material sent out to New Zealand between 1919 and 1925 had to be consigned to 'temporary' storage at the Dominion Museum, while the war museum project spluttered then died; even the *National War Memorial would take decades to build. After the *Second World War the Army transferred more *war trophies to museums, of which the Auckland War Memorial Museum (opened in 1929) mounted the country's most significant military history exhibits. The Auckland Museum's war collection, which includes a Spitfire and a Japanese Zero, was given new prominence in the 1990s with a major refurbishment. It is now presented as the 'Scars on the Heart' Exhibition. An impressive memorial hall contains the names of Auckland's war dead. A major database is being developed.

Open air museums and historic sites proliferated after 1945. The new National (later New Zealand) Historic Places Trust recorded, marked, and conserved sites associated with the *New Zealand Wars and in 1960–61 reopened the remains of the Paremata Redoubt (near Porirua Harbour) and Te Porere. In recent decades its work has been supplemented by local authorities, the Department of Conservation, enthusiasts' groups, and local historical societies. So far coast defence installations such as Wright's Hill (Wellington), Ripapa Island (Lyttelton), and Taiaroa Head (Otago) have proved especially popular.

For many years the *New Zealand Army maintained small specialist displays at Dunedin, Burnham, Linton, and Waiouru. In 1964 it set up an embryonic museum in the original Waiouru homestead. Thirteen years later Chief of General Staff Major-General R.D.P. *Hassett launched 'Operation Heritage' to develop a national army museum intended to function as a memorial, to acquire, preserve, and display aspects of military history, and to serve as a research and teaching facility. Events moved rapidly: the Army Memorial Museum Trust Board was incorporated in August 1977. Spearheaded by a well-publicised run across New Zealand by Major Albert Kiwi and his dog Freefall, fund-raising got underway. The builders soon followed. Army engineers and voluntary labour braved a tough winter to complete the Miles Warren–designed fortress-like structure in just 276 days. The Governor-General opened the 1300-square metre Queen Elizabeth II Army Memorial Museum on 15 October 1978.

Looming dramatically out of the tussock and 'guarded' by restored tanks and guns, the complex captures the attention of Desert Road travellers. Nevertheless, the exterior played second fiddle to interior designer Gary Couchman's display concepts, which set new standards for New Zealand museums. More than 100,000 people passed through the doors during the first twelve months. Since 1978 the museum has been developed extensively. Stage II, opened in July 1983, increased work, storage, and gallery space. Stage III was finished in 1995—the Kippenberger Pavilion and the memorial greenstone wall, Tears on Greenstone (Roimata Pounamu), which commemorates the more than 28,000 New Zealand war dead from the armed forces and the *merchant marine. Although casual visitors are more likely to be interested in the galleries, shop, and café, the extensive library and archival facilities make the museum an important research and teaching resource. At Linton Camp near Palmerston North the School of Military Engineering continues to administer the Royal New Zealand Engineers Corps Memorial Centre, which houses unit archives, rolls of honour, medals, and uniforms, and some military engineering equipment.

By 1976 the RNZAF had assembled a collection of artefacts at Wigram, then its principal training base. Storage conditions were poor and it was not until 1978 that part of a hangar could be set aside for museum purposes. In 1979 a trust board for the Royal New Zealand Air Force Museum was established. The museum moved into a new D.E. Donnithorne–designed building which opened in 1987 to commemorate the fiftieth anniversary of the establishment of the RNZAF. Like Waiouru, Air Force World is an award-winning, state-of-the-art museum. Videos, a history hall, and a Battle of Britain display back up its large collection of historic aircraft, most of them theatrically displayed. The museum had been intended to be the first stage of an RNZAF College modelled on the Air Power Studies Centre in Australia, but for various reasons the concept failed to eventuate, leaving the museum as a stand-alone facility. In 1997 the museum completed the refurbishment of a 1937 art deco store to house its research collections. In addition, there is the Ohakea Wing, RNZAF Museum at Ohakea, the RNZAF's principal strike base.

Like the other services, the RNZN's museum grew from a need to care for relics and trophies to embrace a more comprehensive set of objectives. A 1953 suggestion to establish a museum met with dismay from a naval officer worried about 'denuding the chapels and officers messes in both *Philomel* and *Tamaki* of all the valued treasures which have been long displayed with great pride', and in the 1960s many items were transferred to other museums. When the RNZN's first museum was established at HMNZS *Philomel* in 1974, it was a one-room affair, open just a couple of hours a week. In May 1982 the enthusiasm of the Chief of Naval Staff, Rear-Admiral K.M. Saull, enabled it to move into a converted wooden building on the base perimeter. This modest structure was extended in late 1989. The museum trust board met for the first time in 1987 and gained its first full-time director the following year. In 1992 the trust commissioned plans for a new building, which will form the centrepiece of a complex that will also include large relics such as a turret from HMNZS *Achilles* and a preserved HDML. Highlights included displays on seamanship, weapons, and medals, women in the navy, and the ★First World War Q-ship commander, Lieutenant-Commander W.E. ★Sanders.

GAVIN McLEAN

Musket Wars Ferocious Maori intertribal wars distinguished by their duration, geographical spread, and destructive effects, the Musket Wars during the first four decades of the nineteenth century were the most intense conflicts to occur in New Zealand. The first battle in which muskets were used took place in 1807, when a Nga Puhi war party which had a small number of the weapons was defeated by Ngati Whatua at Moremonui. The last was Kuititanga in 1839, wherein Te Ati Awa defeated Ngati Raukawa at Waikanae. The fiercest fighting took place between 1818 and 1836, with the level of violence peaking in the years 1832 and 1833. During the course of about 3000 raids, battles, and sieges, many tribes were slaughtered and eaten, while the remnants fled to distant regions to avoid annihilation. Only the remote King Country and lightly populated Fiordland region escaped the carnage. More New Zealanders probably died during the Musket Wars than in any subsequent conflict in which they took part, whether in New Zealand or overseas. Although exact casualty figures cannot be determined, between 20,000 and 30,000 may have died either in battle or of disease (with one estimate putting the mortality as high as 80,000).

The causes of the wars were closely interwoven with technological, economic, social, and political changes sweeping tribal New Zealand in the early nineteenth century. The fighting was representative of the distinctive type of indigenous Polynesian gun warfare which also destabilised nineteenth century Hawaii, Tonga, Tahiti, and Samoa. Its origins lay in the vast worldwide traffic in cheap trade guns of European manufacture. The scale of gun trading by commercial and Royal Navy vessels in New Zealand was impressive. Observers calculated that there were just 500 muskets among Nga Puhi in 1820; by 1826 many thousands of guns were being noted among the northern tribes. An intertribal arms race had developed as possession of flintlock guns became a condition of survival. Maori communal subsistence economies were transformed into semi-commercial musket economies. Whole tribes worked feverishly to produce flax, pigs, and potatoes for the musket trade. Musket raiding, slave taking, and the cultivation of introduced potatoes became inextricably linked. Large-scale potato production by slaves made possible larger accumulations of muskets, while providing a durable provision for expeditions seeking slaves.

Warfare arose from the tribal dynamics of the period, as the fiercely competitive Nga Puhi tribal confederation was forged and Ngati Toa people broke away from the powerful Waikato confederation. Clashes also arose from attempts by distant tribes to secure access to gun-trading ports at Whangaroa, Kororareka, Hauraki, Maketu, Kawhia, Poverty Bay, Hawke's Bay, and Kapiti. Raiding permitted tribes a temporary respite from the pressures and confusion arising from European contact, but the nature of Maori kinship ties and the desire for vengeance (utu) ensured that more and more tribes were drawn into conflict.

The fighting appeared chaotic to European observers, but musket warfare was never conducted randomly or indiscriminately. Ambitious chiefs went to war with the new technology in pursuit of traditional Maori goals. The seeking of revenge for insults or for the killing of relatives was an age-old motivation for warfare, which involved slave taking, plundering, and the desire to devour the flesh of enemies. While enhancing their personal and tribal standing (mana), chiefs of musket-armed tribes were also pre-empting possible attack by rivals who were also accumulating guns. Sometimes musket warfare was instigated by European actions. The kidnapping and sale of Nga Puhi women by convicts aboard the *Venus* in 1806, for example, led to Nga Puhi raids of 1818, while Captain Brind's sexual indiscretions prompted the bloody factional ★Girls' War at the Bay of Islands twelve years later.

Nga Puhi, who enjoyed the advantage of residing in the vicinity of the main provisioning port for European shipping in the Bay of Islands, launched the first musket raids. The Whangaroa chiefs Te Puhi and Tara descended on the East Cape tribes in 1815, and in the following year Taukawau led the first raid by Hokianga Nga Puhi to Taranaki. Fierce inter-hapu rivalry and increased gun trading in the period 1818–20 were reflected in the departure of numerous powerful marauding war parties (taua) from the Bay of Islands, bound for Tamaki, Thames, Hauraki, the Bay of Plenty, East Cape, and Hawke's Bay. Many rival chiefs led these raids, the most prominent being Te Morenga, ★Tuwhare, ★Hongi Hika, ★Pomare, and ★Te Wera Hauraki.

Long-distance, interseasonal musket raiding by Nga Puhi revolutionised Maori warfare and upset the established intertribal balance of power. Hitherto

Musket Wars

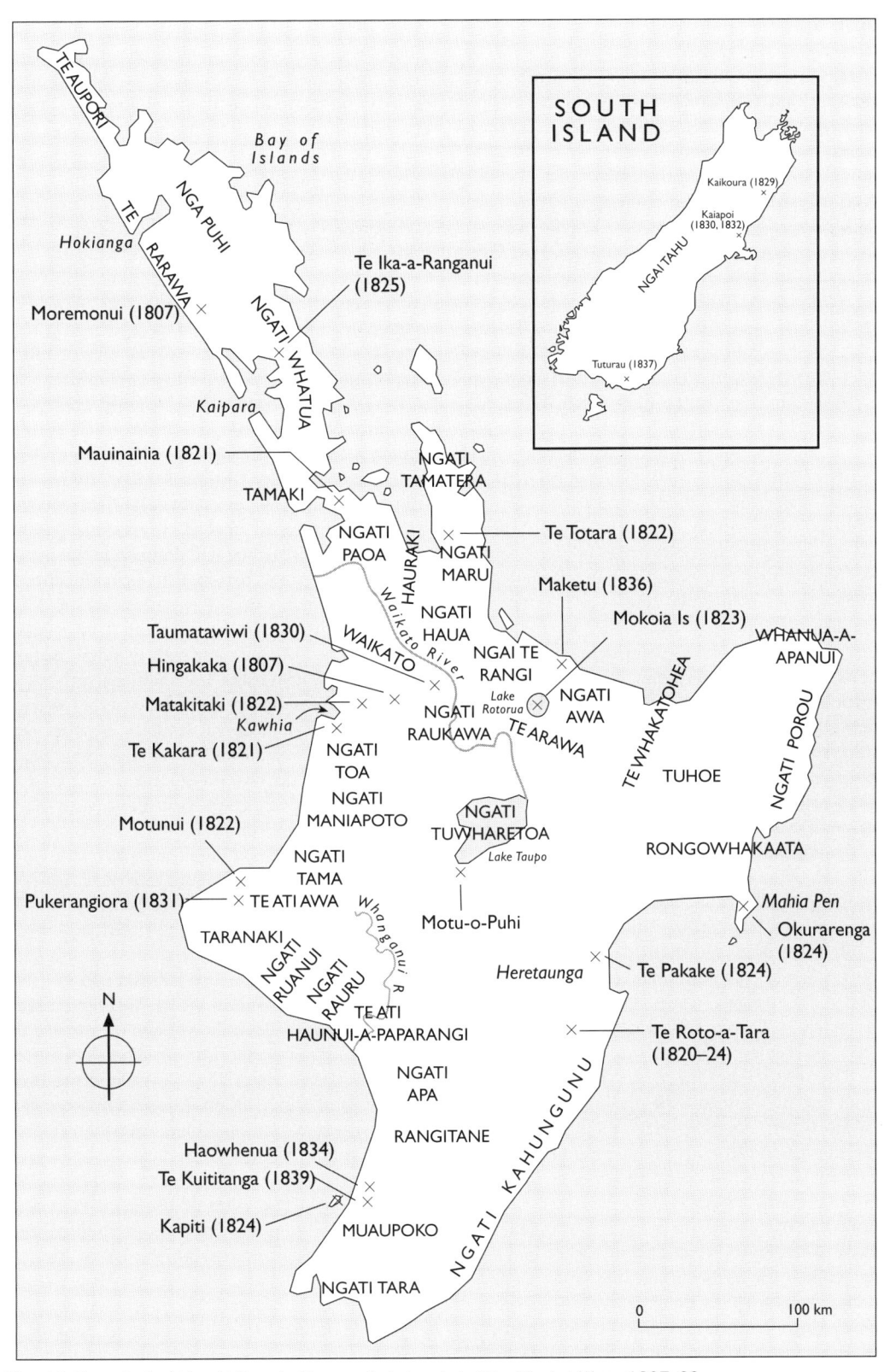

Map 16 The principal Maori tribes, battles, and sieges during the Musket Wars, 1807–39

Musket Wars

warfare had been conducted during summer, and was mainly confined to raids, ambushes, and sieges of vulnerable pa within or close to group territory (see MAORI TRADITIONAL WARFARE). Demarcated into recognised tribal and subtribal lands, Maori New Zealand was relatively stable by the end of the eighteenth century. This stability was shattered by the musket raids, which created a domino effect as tribes attacked by Nga Puhi invaded their neighbours' territories in a series of escalating wars. By 1820 Ngati Whatua, Ngati Paoa, and Ngati Maru had begun their own musket raids. Tribes allied to Nga Puhi sought to enhance their own mana through warfare. In 1819 Hokianga Nga Puhi under ★Patuone and Te Roroa under Tuwhare set off on an extraordinary eighteen-month overland raid to the Cook Strait region. Nga Puhi raids created a new and complex pattern of permanent and temporary intertribal alliances. Ngati Tuwharetoa, Tuhoe, and Ngati Raukawa launched the first of many joint attacks against the Hawke's Bay–based Ngati Kahungunu in 1820. Ngati Whatua, Waikato, and Ngati Maniapoto tribes provided contingents for their own raid to the Cook Strait region—the Amiowhenua (circling the land)—in the following year. The expeditions of this period ranged in size from 300 to 1200 warriors, who were usually drawn from several tribes or subtribes and armed with up to fifty prized muskets. Their victims, armed with traditional Maori weapons of stone, bone, or wood (rakau), either fled in panic from the sound and effects of gunfire or stood bewildered to be slain or enslaved. Nga Puhi in particular returned home with many prisoners and much booty in the form of canoes, cloaks, tattooed heads, and baskets of human flesh.

In 1821 Hongi Hika returned to the Bay of Islands from London and Sydney with a cargo of 300 muskets and munitions. Uniting Nga Puhi factions, he created an intertribal army spearheaded by 2000 Nga Puhi warriors armed with a thousand muskets. This force stormed the Ngati Paoa stronghold Mokoia–Mauinaina at Tamaki and that of Ngati Maru, Te Totara at Thames. At Matakitaki pa on the Waipa River in 1822, Hongi led a Nga Puhi army, 3000-strong and fully armed with muskets, to defeat the Waikato tribes. Dragging their canoe fleet overland from the Bay of Plenty in 1823, 1200 musket-armed Nga Puhi warriors led an intertribal army to victory over the Arawa tribes on Mokoia Island in Lake Rotorua. At the battle of Te Ika-a-ranga-nui near Kaiwaka in 1825, Ngati Whatua were crushed by Hongi Hika's forces and driven from their lands, suffering heavy casualties. The tactic of concentrating within a central fortress proved calamitous for defending tribes. Between 1000 and 2000 men, women, and children are reputed to have been slain in each of Hongi Hika's battles. Contrary to popular belief, these were bitterly contested conflicts, with Nga Puhi suffering heavy casualties as well. Hongi turned imminent defeat into victory by tactical innovation at Tamaki and Rotorua, launching a flying musket wedge (kawau maro) into the ranks of the musketless defenders before destroying them with gunfire.

Fortress pa rarely fell in pre-musket warfare, which was generally conducted by small raiding parties. Competition for territory was a principal cause of conflict, but the defeat and dispersal of a major tribal confederation was unusual. During the 1820s, however, a military manpower revolution occurred as groups hitherto excluded from warfare by the warrior elite—non-kinsmen, boys, slaves, Europeans—swelled the ranks of the musket armies as musketeers. These powerful intertribal groupings were more capable of overcoming the large fortress pa by siege or storm—and sometimes subterfuge. Although chiefs of musket-armed tribes always sought a just cause (take) for their campaigns, the greater force at their disposal ensured that the scale of slaughter and destruction was generally out of all proportion to the original offence to tribal honour. Hongi Hika, ★Te Wherowhero, and ★Te Rauparaha all launched attacks on their enemies which became virtually campaigns of extermination. For some defeated tribes no traditional process of peacemaking was offered; instead they were ruthlessly hunted from their ancestral lands by invaders who rarely settled there themselves. Hongi Hika might make peace with the Waikato and Arawa, but his forces showed no mercy to hapless Ngati Paoa, Ngati Maru, and Ngati Whatua survivors.

While the grand Nga Puhi campaigns were going on, intertribal warfare continued unabated elsewhere in New Zealand. Ngati Maru recovered from their 1821 defeat to raid Ngai Te Rangi at Tauranga a year later. The Waikato similarly recovered to continue raiding Taranaki in 1822. The Taranaki tribes in turn fell upon the communities on the Wellington coast, while in the Bay of Plenty Te Whakatohea attacked the Tuhoe. A series of inter-hapu feuds broke out among the South Island's Ngai Tahu. Throughout the 1820s contingents of Nga Puhi musketeers travelled extensively, assisting many tribes to conduct their own campaigns of conquest.

The musket armies did not always dominate the Maori battlefield. From the mid 1820s Nga Puhi expeditions suffered a series of reverses, beginning with a Waikato ambush of Pomare on the Waipa River in 1826. The Waikato did the same to Rangituke on Kawau Island in the following year. With the deaths of the leading northern chiefs Muriwai and Hongi Hika in 1827 and 1828 respectively, and inter-factional fighting among Nga Puhi, the number of Nga Puhi raids diminished. Military ascendancy shifted from Nga Puhi to the Waikato tribes under Te Wherowhero. The latter had acquired a limited number of flintlock guns through Kawhia Harbour after driving out Ngati Toa under Te Rauparaha in 1821. Combining with Ngati Maniapoto, they continued to raid the Taranaki tribes. In 1822 Waikato incursions were temporarily checked with defeats by Nga Puhi at both Matakitaki and by a combined Te Ati Awa and Ngati Toa force at Motunui. The intensity of Waikato raids increased after 1827 with the arrival in Waikato territories of shore-based gun-traders like Captain Kent, Captain Payne, John Cowell, and Charles Marshall, who played a critical role in arming specific subtribes. In 1830 the Waikato contingents combined with Ngai Te Rangi and Ngati Haua forces under Te Waharoa to defeat Ngati Maru at Taumatawiwi and drive them from the Hauraki Plains. Late the following year a 4000-strong Waikato and Ngati Maniapoto musket army assembled on the Mokau River before invading Taranaki. This force overwhelmed several major fortresses, including Pukerangiora pa, where starvation forced 4000 members of the Te Ati Awa tribe to submit after a three-month siege. The Waikato invasion initiated a series of migrations by Taranaki tribes. In 1832 the Waikato tribes themselves came under attack when Nga Puhi dispatched against them a last great war party, 3000-strong, under Tirarau and Pukerangi. The pursuit and defeat of Pukerangi's force at Tamaki left the Waikato tribes free to combine with Ngati Haua for a succession of attacks against not only Ngati Raukawa in the southern Waikato but also Te Arawa in the Bay of Plenty.

Parallel campaigns continued elsewhere in New Zealand, as remote central North Island tribes acquired guns and belatedly began their own wars. From the mid 1820s the Tuhoe attacked Ngati Pukeko and Ngati Awa in the Bay of Plenty; aided by six tribal groups, they raided Hawke's Bay for much of the 1830s. Several tribes, including Ngati Raukawa, combined with Ngati Tuwharetoa warriors under Mananui ★Te Heuheu Tukino. Throughout the 1830s these forces also raided Ngati Kahungunu, who managed nevertheless to hold their positions in Hawke's Bay and Wairoa. During 1822 Te Rauparaha led his musket-armed Ngati Toa people on a migration from Kawhia to Otaki on the Kapiti coast, decimating the tribes of the Manawatu and Horowhenua in the process. Te Ati Awa of Taranaki and Ngati Raukawa from south Waikato, also under pressure from Waikato attacks, joined him, creating a new confederation of tribes in the Cook Strait region. From their Kapiti Island base Te Rauparaha's forces relentlessly pursued Muaupoko in the Horowhenua and attacked both Ngati Ira at Wellington and Ngati Kahungunu in the Wairarapa. At the battle of Waiorua on Kapiti Island in 1824 Ngati Toa defeated a huge invading force of tribes which had allied against them. Trading with Cook Strait whaling vessels, Te Rauparaha armed his forces with 2000 muskets. Further weapons were obtained by the chief Te Pehi Kupe during a trip to London and Sydney. Following his return in 1828 Ngati Toa launched themselves against Ngai Tahu tribes of the South Island. With their Ngati Koata, Ngati Tama, and Ngati Rarua allies, they won victories at Kaikoura in 1828, established control over the West Coast Poutini Ngai Tahu and the greenstone trade, and attacked and slaughtered the people of the chief Tamaiharanui at Akaroa on Banks Peninsula in 1830. The northern invasions culminated in the storming of the great Ngai Tahu fortress Kaiapoi in 1831, and the fall of Onawe pa on Banks Peninsula.

Te Rauparaha's invasion in 1828 had induced Ngai Tahu to end their own internecine wars. Between 1832 and 1839 the southern Ngai Tahu chiefs Tuhawaiiki and Te Whakataupuka, heavily armed with muskets and ships' cannon, joined the Otago chief ★Taiaroa in a series of retaliatory raids by whaleboat, nearly capturing Te Rauparaha and forcing Ngati Toa and their allies back to Cloudy Bay. In 1837 Te Rauparaha, tiring of war, refused to accompany his kinsman Te Puoho on his epic overland raid against the southern Ngai Tahu. Te Puoho was defeated and killed near Mataura, Southland. Te Rauparaha's confederation continued to be weakened by conflicts between Ngati Raukawa and Te Ati Awa, who clashed at Haowhenua (1834) and Te Kuititanga (1839).

The Musket Wars were Maori in motive and style, but they were not exclusively Maori. European traders supplied the armaments and accoutrements necessary for military campaigns, while ships' armourers and settler blacksmiths repaired defective Maori guns before campaigns. Europeans purchased the spoils of Maori warfare, particularly tattooed heads, conquered lands, and the sexual services of female slaves. Opportunist sea captains transported Nga Puhi, Ngati Toa, and Te Ati Awa expeditions to distant battle zones at Tauranga, Banks Peninsula, and the Chatham Islands. European gunners crewed tribal artillery pieces during battles, and many Europeans (Pakeha–Maoris) accompanied musket war parties as tribal fighting men. Whereas early fighting Pakeha–Maoris were isolated individuals among the tribes, small contingents of them were deployed by Nga Puhi, Ngati Paoa, Te Ati Awa, and Waikato as the wars gathered momentum.

The weapons of Nga Puhi musket armies of the 1820s were collections of cast-off military muskets, blunderbusses, shotguns, volley guns, muskatoons, and cheap single- and double-barrelled trade muskets. Canoe fleets provisioned the warriors in the field, transporting up to 3000 baskets of potatoes. By the early 1830s musket armies of the raider tribes Waikato and Ngati Toa were accompanied by immense numbers of slaves carrying provisions and munitions. As the provisions were depleted, the slaves themselves were devoured. Warrior forces in this period were more uniformly equipped with two or more cartridge boxes, steel tomahawks (patiti), and expensive Brown Bess military muskets.

By the mid 1830s the proliferation of musket or gunfighter pa reflected an emphasis on defensive warfare. First observed among Nga Puhi at Okarutope and Waimate in 1815, such pa were constructed to resist and deliver musket, and later artillery, fire. Incorporating firing trenches, covered ways, protective banks of earth, and flanking angles for crossfire, they became too costly to attack. With the concentration of tribal populations in these dispersed positions the great musket armies could no longer rely on provisions gathered from centralised plantations or on large-scale cannibal feasts to sustain them during campaigns. Battles became more sporadic and inconclusive, with the prodigious expenditure of ammunition often inflicting only minimal casualties. The decline in musket warfare was the result of the changing nature of armaments and the prohibitive cost of financing predatory expeditions. Seeking advantage over rivals and enemies, thirty-seven tribal chiefs had between them acquired eighty ships' cannon by 1839. During the early 1830s Nga Puhi and Ngai Tahu had begun a series of audacious long-distance artillery campaigns by cutter and whaleboat, but most artillery was incorporated into the defences of musket pa. The trend towards artillery warfare received a setback with the collapse of the flax boom from 1831, but the acquisition of cannon by tribes and the replacement of shoddy trade guns with powerful military muskets contributed to the creation of a new intertribal balance of power or balance of terror.

Exhaustion and war-weariness were further reasons for the decline of musket warfare in the late 1830s. Physical and spiritual dislocation left many Maori dispirited and depressed. Years of living in unhealthy areas, toiling to produce commodities for the musket trade, had taken their toll, and would cause high mortality rates long after the fighting petered out. In these circumstances missionary peacemakers, to whom some chiefs looked to break the cycle of violence (venerated Maori peacemakers having proved too few to be effective), became more influential, and many warriors converted to Christianity. The desire for peace left some chiefs positively welcoming the Treaty of Waitangi in 1840. As the fighting died away, the tribes began to compete economically rather than on the battlefield, exchanging land for a wider range of trade goods than just muskets; several chiefs had purchased their own schooners by 1840.

The Musket Wars had a major effect on Maori demography. Apart from the decline in overall numbers—it would be 1960 before these again reached pre–Musket Wars levels—they caused a major redistribution of population. Forty major migrations (heke) were set in motion. Vast reaches of the country were left empty, with the Kaipara, Tamaki isthmus, lower Waihou, and Taranaki regions all being temporarily abandoned. The coastlines of the Bay of Plenty and East Coast, and the Kaikoura and Canterbury coasts, had been depopulated by the fighting. Some districts were mainly inhabited by women. Tribes occupying or reoccupying abandoned lands became embroiled in endless legal claims after 1840.

The Musket Wars assisted European penetration of New Zealand, by distracting Maori attention from its implications. Nevertheless Europeans settling permanently in the 1840s continued to do so on Maori terms and for another twenty years the dominant military force in New Zealand was Maori. Although the Musket Wars had severely disrupted tribal New Zealand, they had not destroyed it. Major intertribal battles had ceased before Great Britain imposed the Pax Britannica on tribal New Zealand in 1840, but skirmishing continued into the 1870s, flaring up during the ★New Zealand Wars as tribes sought to settle old scores.

R.D. Crosby, *The Musket Wars: A History of Inter-Iwi Conflict, 1806–45* (Reed Books, Auckland, 1999).

TREVOR BENTLEY

Mutinies, collective and deliberate acts of indiscipline, have traditionally been regarded as among the most serious of military crimes. Until 1989 mutiny was a capital offence in the New Zealand armed forces (see DEATH PENALTY). However, in practice, 'mutinies' have been treated as reflections of legitimate frustration in the ranks. The authorities' usual response has been quietly to conciliate the 'mutineers' or, in more serious incidents, immediately to discharge them from the service. Minor incidents have been dealt with as lesser disciplinary offences. Mutinous conduct by New Zealand troops has generally stemmed either from boredom or alcohol or from perceived grievances leading to civil-style strike action.

Collective insubordination was a regular feature of locally raised ★Militia units during the 1840s and 1860s; it usually took the form of desertion by militiamen who considered that they had given sufficient service in the field. The most serious mutiny by New Zealand troops in the nineteenth century involved the ★Armed Constabulary's No. 5 Division. In September 1868 its members refused to carry out the orders of Lieutenant-Colonel Thomas ★McDonnell, believing

Mutinies

that he had been responsible for their recent defeat at Te Ngutu-o-te-Manu and for the death of their commander, Major Gustavus von ★Tempsky. Two of the 'ringleaders' were court-martialled, and the company was disbanded, with some of its members being transferred to other Armed Constabulary companies. Men implicated in the mutiny were refused pensions and war medals. Several other mutinies followed: in 1869 Armed Constabulary men on the East Coast refused all except garrison duties as a protest against poor food and delays in receiving their pay, while in the following year constables at Runanga caused the disbandment of their unit by refusing duty.

During the ★First World War thirty-four members of 1NZEF were convicted by courts martial for mutiny, though only one, Private John Braithwaite, was sentenced to death (by a British not a New Zealand court). One of the best-known 'mutinies' involving New Zealanders took place at Étaples base camp on 9 September 1917. Simmering resentment over heavy-handed camp administration and discipline came to a head after a New Zealander was arrested. Demands for his release degenerated into a full-scale riot, directed against the hated British military police. Men in the camp refused duty and protest meetings were held, but the mutiny petered out after a few days. The majority of the rioters were British, and no New Zealanders were court-martialled for the Étaples mutiny. The largest First World War mutiny involving New Zealand troops occurred later in 1917. Fourteen members of the New Zealand Divisional Employment Company were court-martialled for striking against long hours of work in the divisional laundry. Following the Armistice in 1918, there were a number of disturbances as troops became discontented at the slowness of their ★repatriation. Serious disturbances broke out at Sling and Bulford camps in England in March 1919. Barracks and canteens were wrecked. Although military authorities feared that the unrest was a sign of Bolshevist influence, boredom and frustration, not ideology, lay at the heart of the trouble. There were similar outbreaks among mounted riflemen in Egypt in December 1918 and July 1919.

Between the world wars the most serious incident of mutinous conduct involved the ★New Zealand Division of the Royal Navy. Some of HMS *Leander*'s sailors staged a brief strike in protest at their low pay in June 1939. Although the incident was quickly resolved, an irate deputy Prime Minister Peter ★Fraser subsequently threatened to put the navy on 'rotten row'. In the early stages of the ★Second World War boredom and frustration over disorganisation caused a number of minor 'mutinies' on board 2NZEF ★troopships. The worst incident occurred at Bombay on 19 September 1940. For troops upset over the crowded and filthy conditions on their troopship *Ormonde*, being deprived of shore leave because of maladministration was the last straw. Just after midday a party from 25th Battalion and 6th Field Regiment rushed the bridge of the ship, preventing its departure. When it sailed next morning, armed sentries were posted to prevent any repetition of the incident. In camps in New Zealand there were occasional problems when soldiers asserted what they felt were their rights as citizens. In 1940 a 'No beer no drill' protest was held at Papakura camp, while in December 1941 some troops took unauthorised 'Christmas leave' simply by walking out of their camps. The most serious incident involving New Zealand troops was the ★furlough affair of 1944. Indisputably an act of collective indiscipline, it was, nevertheless, not treated as a mutiny by the government. The offenders were court-martialled for 'disobeying a lawful command given by a superior officer'.

After the Second World War, there were tensions in the armed forces, caused partly by the dislocation and uncertainty of demobilisation but exacerbated by discontent over levels of pay. On 17 September 1946 about 800 RNZAF airmen staged 'sit down' strikes at Whenuapai, Hobsonville, and Mechanics Bay in protest at arbitrary changes in their conditions of service and in support of a 40-hour week. Protest meetings were also held at Ohakea, Te Rapa, and other bases. After refusing an ultimatum to return to work or face immediate dismissal, 267 airmen were eventually discharged. The most serious naval mutiny in New Zealand took place at Devonport naval base on 1 April 1947. Frustration had been steadily building up among sailors over their relatively poor rate of pay. When new pay scales were finally announced, they were angered by the lack of mention of promised retrospective pay. Sailors from HMNZS *Philomel* and *Arbutus* held a stopwork meeting, before walking off the naval base. Although assurances that the pay would be retrospective to April 1946 were given that night, the sailors decided to remain on strike in support of further demands for a welfare committee and a promise that no disciplinary action would be taken against them. On 3 April they were given an ultimatum: return to work that morning or be discharged. Twenty-three ratings returned, but 180 chose immediate discharge. Convicted of mutiny without violence, the returnees received suspended sentences. The others lost leave entitlements and part of their deferred pay, and were barred from further employment with the government. Later that month eleven ratings walked off HMNZS *Hautapu* at Timaru in protest at the treatment of the discharged sailors. For their trouble they received twenty-four days' detention. There was similar unrest on the cruiser HMNZS *Bellona*; forty-nine ratings who walked off the ship were charged

Mutual Assistance Programme

with desertion. The loss of so many experienced ratings because of these incidents was a major blow for the RNZN.

Mutual Assistance Programme, established in 1973, provides a framework for a range of activities which the ★New Zealand Defence Force carries out bilaterally with the armed forces of some South-east Asian and Pacific Island states. New Zealand's earliest defence assistance activities were confined to Fiji and Tonga, apart from Papua New Guinea the only Pacific Islands entities with military forces. From 1949 a New Zealand officer was made available to command the Royal Fiji Military Forces (RFMF), and Fijian soldiers were able to spend periods in the ★New Zealand Army; in return New Zealand benefited from the use of Fijian facilities, including the use of jungle areas for exercises by New Zealand units. This relationship continued after Fiji attained independence in 1970. When a Fijian took command of the RFMF in 1974, a New Zealand officer served as chief of staff for another six years. New Zealand has helped support Fijian participation in UN ★peace-keeping. As a result of the ★Fijian coups, MAP assistance to Fiji was suspended from 1987 to 1992. New Zealand was also closely associated with the development of the Tonga Defence Force, providing administrative and training support and, from 1952 to 1977, an officer to command the force. More recently, assistance has focused on trade training and officer development. An active programme has been developed with Papua New Guinea covering a range of activities. New Zealand has also provided engineering construction assistance in Vanuatu, management training for police in the Solomons Islands, and support for the patrol craft operated by Samoa and the Cook Islands respectively.

New Zealand assistance to the Malaysian Armed Forces began in 1964, with the training of Malaysian personnel in New Zealand. From 1968 members of the Singapore Armed Forces also attended courses in New Zealand. New Zealand seconded personnel to the Malaysian Armed Forces and made gifts of surplus equipment, notably two Devon aircraft to Malaysia in 1968 and two Airtourer aircraft to Singapore in 1970. Since its institution in 1973, the programme has been extended to Brunei, Indonesia, the Philippines, and Thailand.

The establishment of the Mutual Assistance Programme represented no significant change of direction or scope of such activities, but it did emphasise their mutual benefits. The bilateral defence aid programmes help to sustain and improve New Zealand's general relationships with the various countries involved, and contribute, albeit on a small scale, to the effectiveness and self-reliance of those states' armed forces. In many cases, the assistance is of a humanitarian nature, assisting the general community of the state by, for example, improving capacity to build needed facilities. New Zealand also gains exercise and training opportunities from the programme.

N

N Force In September 1942 a 1500-strong force of New Zealand infantry and artillery was deployed in Norfolk Island, an Australian territory lying 800 kilometres to the north-west of New Zealand, which was strategically important because of its cable station linking New Zealand and Australia. An airfield was constructed. The 'New Zealand occupation' (as local inhabitants described the New Zealand presence) lasted until July 1946, when the last New Zealanders, RNZAF personnel, were withdrawn.

Napier earthquake occurred at 10.47 a.m. on 3 February 1931, causing severe damage to the towns of Napier and Hastings. The shock and resulting fires killed 256 people and injured hundreds more. The sloop HMS *Veronica*, which had docked at Napier port earlier that morning, quickly requested assistance by radio. Parties of sailors went ashore to render assistance, to be joined later in the day by crews from the merchant ships *Northumberland* and *Taranaki*. They fought fires, dug people out of the rubble, administered first aid, and cleared streets. Later they established food depots and restored the water supply, while patrols of marines deterred looters. Some of the earthquake victims were given refuge on *Veronica*. HMS *Dunedin* and *Diomede* arrived at Napier the next day, bringing much-needed medical supplies and doctors and nurses from Auckland Hospital. Within a few days local ★Territorial Force soldiers had been formed into a Special Police to assist the police. In nearby Hastings, also devastated, ex-soldiers and Territorials formed platoons of relief workers, while other officers organised food supplies, emergency tenting, a soup kitchen, and patrols to prevent looting and control spectators and refugees. Within forty-eight hours of the earthquake 500 army tents, 13,000 blankets, shovels, picks, field kitchens, and a field ambulance had arrived from Trentham. Soldiers from the Permanent Force took control of earthquake relief camps which were established in Hawke's Bay and Manawatu, while others dug graves and demolished buildings. Shortly after the earthquake air force personnel organised flights by Permanent Air Force and aero club aircraft to carry mail and medical supplies. The last military personnel were not withdrawn from earthquake relief duties until July 1931.

National identity and war Most nations have looked to the field of war to display their national character. They have their pantheon of war heroes, their list of famous battles, their memorials to fallen or conquering heroes. New Zealand is no exception; and for much of the twentieth century, war made a major contribution to New Zealanders' sense of themselves. Surprisingly, this was not the case during the previous century. Maori, of course, had long seen war as significant to their own identity, whether iwi or collective Maori identity. Battles were where many rangatira established their fame, and, in the case of figures like ★Te Rauparaha or Rewi ★Maniapoto, that fame extended to the European population. But, despite a quarter-century of armed conflict within New Zealand itself, most colonials did not regard war as an important arena for expressing their distinctiveness. This was partly because many of those who fought for the Queen in the ★New Zealand Wars were not colonials, but British regulars, Australian settlers, or Maori ★kupapa. It was partly that from the Pakeha perspective the wars were a succession of frustrating stalemates. Pakeha remembered Maori bravery and chivalry at

National identity and war

Seamen are transported through the damaged streets of Napier following the earthquake in February 1931 (P.W.T. Ashcroft Collection, Alexander Turnbull Library, F-139893-1/2).

Gate Pa and Orakau, but they forgot their own role. Memorials at the time were few; the battle sites were left unmarked and deserted.

The New Zealand Wars did, however, seed two ideas about New Zealand identity. The first was a respect for the military prowess of the Maori which, so the myth went, laid the basis for future good relations. The second was a view that the war had been hampered on the Crown's side by bumbling British officers and this was contrasted with the adaptability and guerrilla skills of the colonial forces, especially Harry Atkinson's Taranaki Bushrangers and von ★Tempsky's ★Forest Rangers. Neither of these ideas was widespread, but both would flower subsequently.

The outbreak of the ★Boer War in 1899 began to give war a new importance in New Zealand identity. The conflict was seen by New Zealanders as a place where a small colony could make a mark, and the qualities of their men could be displayed before the eyes of the Empire. Crowds cheered the troopers goodbye and newspapers followed the ten contingents' activities closely. Certain incidents, such as the capture of 'New Zealand Hill' at Slingersfontein in January 1900, became symbols of a people's achievement. A stereotype of the New Zealand soldier began to emerge. By comparison with the British 'Tommy', he was taller and stronger, better suited by his pioneering background to the rough war on the veldt, and his officers were modest chaps, able to lead their men by natural example

not class authority. On the backs of his soldiers' successes, Premier Richard ★Seddon took on pretensions as an important statesman of the Empire. It would be incorrect to describe the Boer War as contributing to a 'national' identity. In farewelling the troopers in 1899, a Wellington newspaper noted that 'while the empire is their nation New Zealand is their home'. So the identity that emerged remained very much a colonial identity within the Empire.

In the years following the war, an enlarged sense of New Zealand's distinctive role in the Empire emerged. The context was the growing concern in Great Britain about its ability to compete with Germany and Japan in the struggle for economic and military dominance. There was a fear that Britain's urban condition had weakened the physical and moral vigour of the race. In this crisis the lesson of the Boer War, reinforced by the success of the 1905 All Blacks, was that New Zealand could provide men, toughened and made adaptable on the frontier, who would successfully fight the Empire's wars. Her men's martial virtues gave New Zealand a special role in the Empire. ★Compulsory military training was introduced, and around the country ★war memorials were erected, first to those who had died in South Africa and then to the New Zealand Wars. Several of the memorials featured the figure of Zealandia, daughter of Britannia, for the first time showing her youthful face to the world. The memorials were consciously promoted as examples to the young men of New Zealand.

The ★First World War became the proving ground of this identity. New Zealand entered the war alongside Britain, and New Zealanders eagerly awaited the first test of battle to display the quality of her nationhood through her men. When news of the ★Gallipoli landings reached home, there were cheers and a half holiday. In the far north Mona Tracy recalled the question shouted across fields:

> 'Our boys?'
> You gave the answer proudly, thrilled to realise that you belonged to the country that had mothered them.
> 'They're doing fine!'

The reputation of our boys and the country had become one. Over the next three and a half years, certain moments became imprinted in the nation's consciousness—the terror of the Somme, the victory at Messines, the mud and slaughter of Passchendaele, the epic capture of the walled town of Le Quesnoy. The names were etched in stone on memorials which began to appear in every locality. The form of that national identity, spelt out in the tributes of British leaders and reporters and repeated by local politicians, was an elucidation of elements noted earlier. Once more New Zealanders felt a pride that they were 'good' at war—brave soldiers, dependable men who did not fluster or grumble and maintained self-control. They were bigger than the British ('a race of giants', in Ashmead Bartlett's much-quoted words from Gallipoli) and from their pioneering background they had initiative and ingenuity, not restricted by the 'red tape' which was supposed to bind their British cousins. They were also said to be modest and well behaved, 'natural gentlemen'. Two other components of the stereotype were frequently noted. One was that, again by comparison with the British, the New Zealanders were a classless lot. In the trenches, the *School Journal* wrote, 'all distinctions of class and creed were cast aside'. The second was that the participation of Maori in the conflict served to unify the races of New Zealand. Maui Pomare suggested in 1916 that misunderstandings between Maori and Pakeha were swept away as 'their blood commingled in the trenches of Gallipoli'.

In editorials and politicians' speeches the belief was established that in the Great War, and at Gallipoli in particular, New Zealand had come of age. A colonial people had found its national identity. This view found expression in the status accorded ★Anzac Day, and in the adoption of various symbols of nationhood—the ★lemon-squeezer hat, the emerging use of the term 'Kiwis', and the fernleaf on the 'Onward' badge and on soldiers' graves. Yet we need to qualify the extent to which the New Zealand identity produced by the Great War was a 'national' one. For a start Anzac Day commemorated a landing which occurred at the direction of Britain, at a time when the New Zealanders were under the command of a seconded British officer, Major-General Sir Alexander ★Godley, and in an action in which the New Zealanders played a subordinate role to the Australians. Nor did the terrible losses and the bunglings of the war lead to any public disaffection with Britain or her Empire. On the contrary, the years immediately following the war saw a strengthening of the imperial link. There were huge attendances when the Prince of Wales visited New Zealand in 1921; and when the ★Chanak crisis of 1922 promised the prospect of another imperial engagement in the Middle East men volunteered in droves. When politicians claimed that the war created nationhood, they were not asserting any degree of national independence from Britain or the Empire. The New Zealand soldier was seen, in the King's words, as 'a worthy son of the Empire'.

Among the soldiers themselves the experience of war did produce a more assertive nationalism. In the early stages of the war the New Zealanders liked to think of themselves as rather different from the Australians, more genteel, better disciplined, and in a sense more 'English'. But once they had landed at Gallipoli their views changed. Dismayed by the incompetence of British officers and impressed by the bravery of the Australians, they recorded in their letters and diaries a new admiration for their trans-Tasman cousins and a growing contempt for the English. On finally reaching England itself, they realised just how different they were from the people of the mother country. Peter Howden, a New Zealand officer from a respectable Anglophile background, was typical. He decided: 'The general opinion is that we should hand it over to the Germans and apologize to them for having nothing better to give them.' But even while asserting a more independent nationalism, few 'diggers' drew republican conclusions from their war experience.

The soldiers themselves developed other images of New Zealand identity. The most important was 'mateship'. This was more than the comradeship of the battlefield (which was often expressed in the official legend). It included also the informal mateship of the 'two-up' schools and the good times in the liquor dens of Egypt or the brothels of Armentières. At Gallipoli, one veteran recalled, the word 'bastard' passed into universal use. The hard-drinking, hard-swearing Kiwi, lacking spit-and-polish pretensions, but a good chap underneath—this was another stereotype which the soldiers carried home, even if it was not much talked about at Anzac Day services.

By the 1920s, then, war had moved to the heart of New Zealand identity. There were huge attendances at parades on Anzac Day, which had become, more than any other, the national day. When a new war broke out in 1939, soldiers were recruited with appeals to the Anzac spirit. Once more New Zealand made a massive contribution to the world war. Once more thousands died and New Zealand troops, having again been sent off at Winston Churchill's request to another poorly supplied diversionary front (★Greece this time instead of Gallipoli), ended the war fighting in Europe. Again after initial defeats, the New Zealanders won important victories in North Africa and Italy and once more the myths of national identity which emerged were familiar—the Kiwi soldier as a man of courage, a bit deficient when it came to saluting but full of initiative and ingenuity. Again the alleged classlessness of the New Zealand Army was praised and the success of the Maori Battalion was said to have encouraged a new respect between the races.

There were some slight modifications to the myth. This time it was not so much the height of the Kiwis which was noted, but rather their brawny strength. Rather more individuals emerged from the war as national heroes—the double VC winner ★Upham, the generals ★Freyberg and ★Kippenberger. For the first time New Zealanders acclaimed their successes in other services besides the Army—the role of HMS *Achilles* in the Battle of the ★River Plate and the participation of New Zealand airmen in the Battle of Britain became well known. There was, too, a gentle movement in identity towards a more independent stance. This time the New Zealand government insisted that Major-General B.C. Freyberg, a New Zealander by background, if not birth, should command the New Zealand troops and the government insisted upon being consulted on the use of their men. Yet the spirit remained 'Where Britain goes, we go', and this was strikingly expressed in 1943 when, unlike Australia, New Zealand decided not to bring a division back to defend the homeland from the ★Japanese threat but allowed them to continue to serve in the European theatre.

After two world wars in thirty years in which about 28,000 men had died and more than 250,000 had served overseas, New Zealanders had come to regard war as the finest demonstration to the world of their national character. For the twenty years after VJ day, the centrality of war to national identity was barely questioned. Though some pacifists in both wars had consistently resisted such a definition of New Zealandness, and in the First World War some iwi had refused to serve, such dissent had become minimal. The Waikato Maori had their Second World War heroes too, and the labour leaders who had resisted ★conscription in 1916 had implemented it in 1940. During this period the war mythology ruled supreme. From 1949 there was ★compulsory military training, attendances at Anzac Day parades were large, the RSA flourished, and when other conflicts called for New Zealand men—in Japan with ★Jayforce and in Korea with ★Kayforce—young New Zealand males were keen to serve.

From the mid 1960s the situation changed. In the context of a controversial war in Vietnam, a new generation began to question first that war and then the whole war mythology. Anzac Day services were disrupted and pacifist sentiments flourished. Following the settlement of war in South-east Asia, attention focused upon the presence of American nuclear-powered and nuclear-armed ships in New Zealand harbours. After a series of public protests, the Labour government elected in 1984 decided to enforce a nuclear-free policy which it subsequently enacted into law. This decision brought conflict with old allies, the United States, Australia, and Britain, and it attracted world attention to New Zealand's position. By 1990 the anti-nuclear stance had become such an important part of New Zealand identity that the newly elected National government dared not challenge that policy. This was a very different role for New Zealand in the eyes of the world. She was now the standard-bearer of the anti-nuclear message rather than the foot soldier of the British Empire.

At the end of the twentieth century war remained a part of New Zealand national identity. Prime ministers still claimed that New Zealand had found its identity at Gallipoli, attendances on Anzac Day were once more on the rise, and there was considerable interest in New Zealand's military history. But now there was a competing vision which suggested that New Zealand's character could be judged as much by anti-nuclear protesters as by diggers in the trenches of Gallipoli or Flanders.

JOCK PHILLIPS

National Military Reserve was established by the Labour government of M.J. ★Savage in May 1939 for home defence duties. It was open to volunteers between the ages of twenty and fifty-five, with previous military service. Five thousand of these men would become Territorial Reserves. While the ★Territorial Force had no difficulty reaching its recruiting targets—its establishment had been increased from 10,000 to 16,000 at the same time as the Reserve was formed—recruitment for the Reserve initially fell far short of expectations, fuelling demands by the opposition National Party for a return to compulsion as a means of providing the necessary manpower. The outbreak of war in September soon changed the picture: within four days 7000 men had volunteered for the Reserve. During 1940 the Reserve was restructured to include four regionally organised battalions, with headquarters in the four main cities. Companies, based around significant population centres, were established throughout each of the four regions, though some which soon outgrew company status were reorganised as small battalions. On 12 December 1941, five days after the onset of the ★Pacific War, 4600 men of the Territorial Force and the National Military Reserve were mobilised to man the ★coast defences, to be followed on 10 January 1942 by the remainder of both forces. Enlistment criteria for the Reserve were relaxed to allow in men without previous military experience and with up to three dependent children. On 6 February the Reserve was incorporated into the Territorial Force, which remained on active service until the end of July 1943, guarding vital points, coastwatching, and manning defences; it also acted as 'enemy forces' for 3rd Division units preparing for service in the ★Solomons campaign. The National Military Reserve, which has lived in the shadow of New Zealand's much larger Territorial Force and the ★Home Guard, made an important contribution to New Zealand's war effort on the home front. The reservists maintained New Zealand's record of volunteering in crisis, bolstered the pool of deployable personnel, and helped galvanise a sense of national resolve during the dark days of early 1942.

RICHARD TAYLOR

National Service Department was formed in July 1940, following the gazetting of the National Service Emergency Regulations of 18 June which introduced ★conscription. It was composed of the Registration Branch of the Social Security Department (which became the Manpower and later the Military Mobilisation Division) and the Employment Division of the Department of Labour (which became the Employment and Rehabilitation Division, from 1942 the Industrial Manpower Division), together with a Civil Defence Division. Prior to this a Manpower Committee had drawn up a schedule of 'reserved' occupations, while the Social Security Department had undertaken a national register of manpower. The department's first task was to organise the orderly transfer of men from industry to military service overseas and to build up the ★Territorial Force. The inadequacy of the Social Security register soon led to the creation of a new register. Around 400,000 registrations were made, first of single men between nineteen and forty-five years of age, followed by eighteen-year-old single males for the Territorials, and married males. The department conducted the first ballot, for compulsory Territorial service, in October 1940. A large number of ballots followed. By December 1941 all single men between the ages of twenty-one and forty years had been called up for overseas service and those between eighteen and forty-five for the Territorials. Those deemed to be in essential industries were held back from the forces. With the outbreak of the ★Pacific War, the department entered a new phase of balloting to increase the strength of the Territorials. The department's control over industry was also strengthened by regulations gazetted in January 1942 to direct industrial manpower. Further ballots of married men between eighteen and forty-five years took place during 1942, followed by additional ballots of those turning eighteen years old in 1943–45, making a total of twenty-four ballots during the war.

The Industrial Manpower Division, working through district Manpower Officers in twenty-two centres and seventeen district Manpower Committees (together with Armed Forces Appeal Boards), restricted flows out of essential industries, directed workers into those industries, and attempted to control absenteeism. In the latter half of 1942 the department argued for greater control over industry. The combined demands of war and the economy had exhausted the pool of labour; the home forces were below their defensive minimum and agricultural and industrial production was suffering. But with a diminished Japanese threat attention turned to supplying Allied forces in the Pacific and the 3rd New Zealand Division engaged in the ★Solomons campaign. Home defence was substantially wound down and men were released for overseas service and for industry, particularly farming and food processing. The department surveyed all home forces personnel as a result. By 1944 the production of foodstuffs had become ever more important and the department directed repatriated 3rd Division personnel into essential industries. In the latter part of the year veterans of 2nd Division also required repatriation from the Middle East and absorption into industry. By the end of the war about 176,000 directions had been made into essential industries, including nearly 40,000 women. With the end of the war in sight the department's attention moved even more to placing returned servicemen in employment. A Rehabilitation Section, which had been formed in the department in November 1943, became a separate department in April 1944 (see REPATRIATION). During 1945 demobilisation replaced mobilisation as the department's focus, and the promotion of full employment took over from direction into essential industries. With demobilisation rapidly completed, and servicemen absorbed into industries without difficulty, the department was wound up in 1946 and replaced by the peacetime National Employment Service.

JOHN E. MARTIN

National War Memorial Although Parliament approved a national war memorial in 1919, the country was halfway towards the next world war before the foundation stone was laid. In the meantime the

Wellington Citizens' War Memorial Committee grabbed a prominent site near Parliament for its monument. Finally, in 1928 the government approved an inner-city Mount Cook site for an art gallery, museum, and forty-nine-bell carillon, the last to house bells funded by a public subscription campaign led by Sir Harold Beauchamp.

Architects Gummer and Ford won the prize for their design. Their museum is in a heavy, stripped classical style, but their carillon is a thoroughly modern art deco 'erect phallic shape'. Work began in 1931 and was completed for an *Anzac Day 1932 dedication when Governor-General Lord Bledisloe switched on the Lamp of Remembrance atop the tower and the *Evening Post* reported hearing 'magic from the skies'. Just over 50 metres tall, New Zealand's only carillon is one of the largest in the world. Its art deco qualities have been recognised by a Category I Historic Places Trust registration. The Carillon's weekly recitals, often commemorating important battles, added a new feature to Wellington life.

Although the museum was opened in 1936, the planned Hall of Memories fell victim to first the Depression, then the *Second World War. The first plans were prepared in 1937, and Gummer and Ford forwarded a new set in 1949, but the project did not go to tender until 1960. Graham & Son, builder of the Carillon, won the job, which it completed in 1964, just two years before Gummer's death. Recesses commemorate the services and campaigns. Four Rolls of Honour bear the names and ranks of the 28,654 New Zealanders who have died in conflicts from the *Boer War to the *Vietnam War. Lyndon Smith's bronze statue of a family group forms the focal point for the complex, which is visited by approximately 20,000 people a year.

The Carillon's Putaruru stone had badly deteriorated by the late 1950s. Although repairs were approved as part of the Hall of Memories project, work did not finally begin until 1981–82. Among other things, a section of the campanile was replastered, Canaan marble replaced the Putaruru stone, and the metal louvres, window frames, and grilles were replaced. In 1985 the Carillon, increased to sixty-five bells, was restored, ready for rededication in the presence of Queen Elizabeth II in the following year. (In 1995 the original specification for bells would finally be achieved; four large bass bells were added to commemorate the fiftieth anniversary of the end of the Second World War.) The mid-1980s conservation work rectified the structural problems, but did nothing for the memorial's increasingly unfortunate location. Its link to the city, the planned tree-lined boulevard from Buckle Street to Courtenay Place, had never been built and during the 1980s planned motorway extensions (not proceeded with) posed a further threat. The Museum of New Zealand's departure for its new waterfront site in 1998 has left this important structure more isolated than ever. At century's end its setting was marred by an adjacent petrol station.

C. Maclean, *For Whom the Bell Tolls: A History of the National War Memorial* (Heritage Group, Department of Internal Affairs, Wellington, 1998).

GAVIN McLEAN

Naval bases New Zealand's first and most important naval base was established at Devonport, on the north shore of Auckland harbour, shortly before the *First World War. A naval presence had first been established there in 1841, when the Royal Navy erected a boat shed, stores building, and a house at Sandspit, now the location of the Windsor Reserve. A two-storey barracks was built in 1864. In 1892 the Royal Navy was granted land next to the Auckland Harbour Board's *Calliope Dock in exchange for the Windsor Reserve land for coal and other naval stores. Although the area was made available for a naval base in 1909, in the expectation that it would become the headquarters of a unit of the proposed Pacific Fleet, little was done to develop the site for the time being. In 1921 HMS *Philomel* was moored at Devonport to serve as a training ship and depot. Throughout the 1920s there was desultory construction of stores buildings and oil tanks, but it was not until after 1935 that rapid expansion took place. Some land and buildings surrounding Calliope Dock were acquired from the Auckland Harbour Board, and further barracks, stores buildings, and oil tanks were constructed. The development of HM Dockyard, Devonport, accelerated during the *Second World War to meet wartime demands, including servicing large warships of the US Navy. Tunnels were dug into the cliffs bordering the dockyard for fuel tanks, and there was extensive reclamation and dredging. A traffic tunnel was constructed to Shoal Bay, where land had been reclaimed for a Stores Depot. Nevertheless lack of space remained a problem, and in 1941 the quarantine station on Motuihe Island was commissioned as the training establishment HMS *Tamaki*. Two further naval bases were commissioned during the war: HMNZS *Tasman* at Lyttelton, for communications training and to provide a minesweeper base, and HMNZS *Cook* at Wellington's Shelly Bay, as an administrative and minesweeper base. Other smaller schools, stores, and signals, coastwatching, and radar stations were also established around the country, though their existence was purely temporary. New Zealand minesweepers in the *Solomons campaign were administered by HMNZS *Cook II* at Espiritu Santo. In September 1943 the base was relocated forward to Renard Sound in the Russell Islands and renamed *Kahu*. From January 1941 to late 1945 a naval

HMNZS *Achilles* undergoes a refit in Calliope Dock at Devonport naval base in 1943 (*RNZN*)

base, HMNZS *Venture*, was also maintained at Suva, Fiji. The RNZN's London office was named HMNZS *Cook* III (and from 1949 *Maori*).

After the war *Philomel* was towed from the Devonport naval base and eventually sunk, though its name was transferred to the depot facilities there. The facilities at Shelly Bay were transferred to the RNZAF in 1946, and those at Lyttelton were sold ten years later. In 1951 the naval radio station at Waiouru (which had been opened in 1942) was commissioned as HMNZS *Irirangi*. The four naval reserve divisions at Auckland, Wellington, Christchurch, and Dunedin were also commissioned as shore establishments in the 1950s, taking the names *Ngapona, Olphert, Pegasus,* and *Toroa* respectively. The naval headquarters at Wellington was also named HMNZS *Wakefield*. In the 1960s *Tamaki* moved to the Narrow Neck area, and in 1979 assumed responsibility for all naval training. A rationalisation of naval property in the 1990s led to *Irirangi* being decommissioned, with most communications facilities thereafter being controlled from Auckland. Most of *Tamaki* was relocated to the North Yard at Devonport. The base at Devonport continues to be the RNZN's principal base, with about 2200 persons employed there. Because it occupies such valuable real estate, there have been some calls in the local community for its transfer elsewhere during the 1990s. Whangarei and Wellington have both been advanced as possible alternative sites, but any change is inhibited by the likely cost and disruption to personnel.

Naval Defence Act 1913 provided the statutory basis for the establishment of the New Zealand Naval Forces. When Australia, following the 1909 Imperial Defence Conference, determined to establish the Royal Australian Navy, New Zealand did not follow suit, preferring to continue contributing to an imperial fleet.

Naval visits to New Zealand

Few wanted to set up a separate New Zealand navy. Reform Party Defence Minister Colonel James ★Allen would go no further than establishing a 'local unit' of the Royal Navy, beginning by training local men on a locally based ship. The Naval Defence Act, passed on 11 December 1913, drew on the equivalent Australian legislation, but had two significant differences: it did not authorise New Zealand to build its own warships and it provided for the automatic transfer of the New Zealand ships to Admiralty control whenever war broke out or even threatened. This latter provision, Allen thought, would 'make it perfectly clear to our Australian friends that we consider it essential to recognise the same control', though in practice there would prove to be little difference in the way control was handed over to the Admiralty after the outbreak of the ★First World War. (Far from the automatic provision operating in August 1914, the New Zealand government actually had to ask the Admiralty if it wanted *Philomel* transferred to its control.) The Act empowered New Zealand to raise and maintain permanent naval forces, to apply the naval discipline acts and Admiralty instructions to these forces, and to reconstitute the Naval Reserve. Under its provisions, New Zealand, on 15 July 1914, commissioned the old 'P' class cruiser HMS *Philomel* as its training ship, and Captain P.H. ★Hall-Thompson became Naval Adviser to the New Zealand government. An administrative division of the Royal Navy had been set up in 1913 to encompass the ships on the ★New Zealand Station. The Reform government, which increased the annual subsidy to the Royal Navy to £150,000, would have liked modern cruisers for its money but could not persuade the Admiralty to dilute its northern hemisphere resources. Instead it had to make do with two old ★'P' class cruisers, HMS *Psyche* and *Pyramus*, and the venerable gunboat HMS *Torch*. An amendment in 1936 gave statutory basis for the New Zealand Naval Board, which had been established by an Order-in-Council in 1921. The Naval Defence Act 1913 and its various amendments were repealed by the passage of the Navy Act 1954.

GAVIN McLEAN

Naval visits to New Zealand Nations send their warships to foreign ports for many reasons, the most frequent being training, rest and recreation, and 'showing the flag'. During the 1990s events in Southeast Asia and the Arabian Gulf demonstrated that the deployment of warships remains a powerful instrument of diplomacy. New Zealand was colonised under the protection of the Royal Navy, but in the twentieth century the United States has arguably made better use of its navy to influence New Zealanders. The 1908 visit of the 'Great White Fleet' and the 1925 cruise of most

Naval visits to New Zealand

of the US battlefleet created a stir akin to the combination of a world fair and a royal visit, the earlier call creating an air of 'Fleetitis' and the 1925 visit drawing a favourable public response while New Zealand politicians tried not to antagonise Japanese opinion. Since then the United States Navy has continued to make both its presence and its absence felt. The 1961 New Zealand Naval Board annual report noted that the first nuclear submarine to visit the country, USS *Halibut*, had 'aroused considerable interest when she paid goodwill visits to Auckland and Wellington'. Later American nuclear visitors were not so well received, a development culminating in the post-1984 ban on port visits by nuclear-armed, -capable, or -propelled warships. In November 1968 the Americans set another record when the 81,000-ton full-load aircraft-carrier USS *America* anchored in Wellington Harbour, the largest warship ever to visit the country.

Exploration and science had brought the first European warships into New Zealand waters towards the end of the eighteenth century. Cook's *Endeavour* was followed by others such as George Vancouver's sloop HMS *Discovery* in 1791. In 1835 Captain Robert FitzRoy, a later Governor of New Zealand, anchored HMS *Beagle* in the Bay of Islands, bringing with him Charles Darwin, who found neither the inhabitants (Maori and European) nor the country to his liking. The Bay of Islands also hosted Captain James Clark Ross's HMS *Erebus* and *Terror* in 1841. Other powers sent scientific expeditions to New Zealand. The French had been active from the beginning, and even the Austrian Navy put in an appearance, when its frigate SMS *Novara* brought Dr Ferdinand Hochstetter to New Zealand in 1858–59. In the twentieth century Antarctica has dominated scientific endeavour. Until long-range aircraft took over many of their functions, ships supporting the US Navy's Operation Deep Freeze used Lyttelton and, to a lesser extent, Dunedin and Wellington.

Warships supported the process of colonisation, transporting officials, troops, and all the paraphernalia of colonisation, right down to cannon and the very flags run up the settlers' flagpoles. New Zealand's first governors, William Hobson and Robert FitzRoy, were naval officers. HMS *Herald* brought Hobson to the Bay of Islands in January 1840, just days before the signing of the Treaty of Waitangi. The frigate then cruised south collecting further signatures of the treaty. At Akaroa HMS *Britomart* was used to impress the French. The declaration of British sovereignty prevented the development of an independent French colony, and historian Peter Tremewan observes that the French had already lost the race before the *Britomart* slipped into port ahead of *L'Aube*. Nevertheless, a French corvette, first *L'Aube* and then the *Rhin*, would remain on station at Akaroa from 1840 until early 1849. The French flag, by arrangement, was not replaced by the Union Jack until 1848.

New Zealand ports also hosted the warships of nations holding colonies in the Pacific. British warships were only to be expected (see ROYAL NAVY IN NEW ZEALAND), but numerous port calls were also made from the late 1870s by small white-painted cruisers and sloops from the German Pacific Squadron (based in Samoa) and units from the French colonial territories. Germany lost its territories in 1914 and Great Britain and the Netherlands no longer base ships in the Pacific, but French colonial warships continued to visit New Zealand ports during the 1990s.

Warships have carried out hostilities in New Zealand waters. The most notable was the action of HMS *Alligator* in 1834, when three Taranaki pa were bombarded to such effect that Hobson, showing the flag in HMS *Rattlesnake* three years later, believed that Maori were still wary of British warships. There have been three such occasions since 1840. The first was the ★New Zealand Wars, in which the Royal Navy took an active part, about twenty of its ships supporting the campaigns of the 1860s. The other times were the world wars of the twentieth century, during both of which German auxiliary cruisers claimed victims off the coasts. Japanese and German submarines also penetrated New Zealand waters during the ★Second World War, but caused no casualties. (See ENEMY OPERATIONS IN NEW ZEALAND WATERS)

The wartime threat also brought ships from Allied navies to New Zealand in considerable numbers. New Zealand troop convoys were escorted by Allied ships, 1NZEF's Main Body sailing in October 1914 under the protective guns of the British and Japanese armoured cruisers HMS *Minotaur* and HIJMS *Ibuki* and the smaller HMS *Psyche* and *Philomel*. During the Second World War, ships from the United States and the British Pacific Fleet called at New Zealand ports to escort merchant ships, to rest crews, and to repair damaged ships. Wellington's Jubilee floating dock and Auckland's ★Calliope Dock were kept busy servicing a variety of Allied warships, such as the Dutch submarine *O-21*, which entered Jubilee in early 1945.

Training cruises have brought many warships to New Zealand. Notable inter-war visitors were the German light cruiser *Emden* in 1929 and the French specialist training cruiser *Jeanne d'Arc* in 1938. In 1963 the Japanese Maritime Defence Force destroyers *Teruzuki*, *Harusame*, *Ariake*, and *Yugure* paid the first post-war visit to New Zealand by Japanese warships. Since then Japanese warships have returned many times. Other frequent visitors have been the ships of the RAN for courtesy visits or for major exercises and

Naval visits to New Zealand

The Japanese Naval Training Squadron in Wellington in 1932, one of five such visits by Japanese warships between the world wars. The New Zealand officer saluting is the GOC, Major-General W.L.H. Sinclair-Burgess (*W.H. Raine Collection, Alexander Turnbull Library C-24254-1/2*)

the much-admired sail training ships of several—mainly South American—nations.

Several of those sail training ships visited New Zealand after participating in Australian bicentennial celebrations. International events and ceremonies generate visits. In 1879 the Austro-Hungarian frigate *Heligoland* visited Auckland after conveying exhibits to the Sydney Exhibition. British warships put in an appearance during the 1906–07 international exhibition at Christchurch, and on 5 October 1991 ships from Australia, Canada, Malaysia, Singapore, Western Samoa, Vanuatu, Tonga, and the Cook Islands participated in an international review honouring the 50th anniversary of the RNZN.

Finally, naval visits were also made for purposes of trade, commonly held to follow the flag. Most of the early European explorers were assessing New Zealand's resources, and British naval vessels like HMS *Dromedary* harvested kauri in the Bay of Islands in the 1830s. In later times, naval visits could be used to promote trade opportunities. In 1923, for example, French Ministry of Trade staff accompanied the armoured cruiser *Jules Michelet* to New Zealand to promote French products. More recently, the British frigate HMS *Monmouth* visited Wellington to demonstrate the Westland Lynx helicopter to the RNZN, which was then seeking to purchase helicopters for its own frigates.

T.D. Taylor, *New Zealand's Naval Story* (A.H. & A.W. Reed, Wellington, 1948).

GAVIN McLEAN

Navy Department was formally constituted on 30 September 1954. Following the creation of the ★New Zealand Division of the Royal Navy in 1921, naval administrative matters had been handled by a small Navy Office in Wellington. With the First Naval Member of the Naval Board often absent at sea as commander of the New Zealand squadron, his secretary, a naval officer, was in charge of the office. The position of Naval Secretary was formally established on 31 October 1936, but it was not until 1950 that provision was made for a civilian to become Navy Secretary. The department's functions were taken over by the Ministry of Defence on 1 January 1964, at which time the Navy Secretary became Deputy Secretary of Defence (Navy).

Nene, Tamati Waka (1780s?–4 August 1871) distinguished himself in many battles as a young man during the ★Musket Wars. Of high-ranking Nga Puhi descent from the Hokianga area (his elder brother was ★Patuone), he took part in the great expedition led by ★Murupaenga, ★Tuwhare, and ★Te Rauparaha, which, possessing the advantage of muskets, devastated the lower North Island in 1819–20. He also fought in the campaigns of the 1820s against Ngati Whatua and Waikato. As one of the leading Nga Puhi chiefs from the late 1820s, he sought to control Pakeha–Maori relations, and was a supporter of the Treaty of Waitangi. Although soon disillusioned by the challenge to his authority posed by the new colonial government, he opposed the cutting down in March 1845, by Hone ★Heke, of the flagstaff he had erected at Kororareka. Siding with the government, he established a pa at Okaihau inside Heke's territory, and it was used to plunder Heke's crops. After some inconclusive skirmishing between Nene's and Heke's forces, the latter was badly wounded at Te Ahuahu on 12 June 1845—the only real defeat inflicted on the rebels during the war. Nene was also at the battles of Puketutu, Ohaeawai, and Ruapekapeka, though more as an observer than as a participant. His significance was enhanced by the inability of the British forces to inflict a decisive defeat on Heke and ★Kawiti on the battlefield, though they were ultimately subdued. Among the European settlers, his role in the conflict was seen as reassuring, and he became a trusted adviser of successive governors.

Nevill, Air Vice-Marshal Sir Arthur de Terrotte ('Trink') (29 April 1899–14 March 1985) was the second New Zealand officer to become Chief of the Air Staff. Born at Dunedin, he was educated at Victoria University College before entering the Royal Military College at Duntroon in 1916. After his graduation, he was commissioned in the RNZA and attached to the Indian Army. He gained some active service experience on the North-west Frontier of India. Back in New Zealand, he held a series of staff and regimental appointments from 1922 until 1930, when he was appointed to the New Zealand Permanent Air Force. He attended the RAF Staff College at Andover in the United Kingdom from 1934 until 1936 and was then New Zealand Liaison Officer in the British Air Ministry. He served on the Air Board as the Air Member for Supply (1937–42), as AOC RNZAF HQ in London (1942–44), and as Deputy Chief of Air Staff (1944–46). In 1946 he became CAS, in which capacity he oversaw the difficult task of adjusting the RNZAF to peacetime requirements. After retiring in 1951, he served as Deputy Director of Civil Aviation before becoming Director in 1956, a post he held for eight years. He was made a KBE in 1950.

New Caledonia The collapse of France and the creation of a collaborationist Vichy regime in June 1940 brought into question the status of France's territories in the Pacific: New Caledonia and French Polynesia. The possibility of a pro-Axis administration in either worried both Canberra and Wellington, but in September both territories declared their support for the

Free French. The Australian cruiser HMAS *Adelaide* delivered a Free French Governor to New Caledonia in September, about the same time that HMS *Achilles* went to Tahiti to support the new regime established there. During the ★Pacific War, New Caledonia's importance was enhanced by the Japanese advance into the South Pacific. It became the largest forward Allied base in the theatre. From July 1942 to March 1943 9 Squadron RNZAF flew Hudson bombers from it on anti-submarine patrols. A more substantial New Zealand presence was established in November 1942, when the 3rd New Zealand Division began arriving to form a garrison force while preparing for active participation in the ★Solomons campaign. By March 1943 nearly 20,000 New Zealanders were stationed on the island. Spread out on its western side in defence of aerodromes, radar sites, and beaches vulnerable to attack, the division had its headquarters and base at Bourail, 160 kilometres north of Noumea. As time passed, tents were replaced by thatched *bures*, and roads and base facilities were constructed. The troops were kept busy with jungle and amphibious warfare training until they moved forward to Guadalcanal in August 1943. With New Caledonia remaining as their rear base, the New Zealand presence did not finally end until October 1944.

New Zealand, HMS An Indefatigable class battle-cruiser, HMS *New Zealand* was laid down at the Fairfield Shipbuilding & Engineering Company's yard in Glasgow on 20 June 1910 and launched on 1 July 1911. Measuring 180 metres in length and 24 metres in breadth, she displaced 19,100 tonnes, and with her 44,000 horsepower coal-powered turbines was capable of a top speed of about 26 knots. She carried eight 12-inch guns in four twin turrets, with sixteen 4-inch guns as secondary armament. Her crew numbered about 800 prior to the war, but rose to over 900 during the ★First World War.

The genesis of *New Zealand* lay in a dramatic gesture by the New Zealand Prime Minister, Sir Joseph ★Ward, in March 1909. Worried by evidence that Great Britain was falling behind in the naval race with Germany, he induced his government to offer to meet the cost of a 'first-class battleship of the latest type', and another if necessary, to be added to the Royal Navy. Although Ward had not consulted Parliament before making his offer, his action caught the public imagination, and few challenged his action. With the British government's acceptance of the offer, New Zealand was committed to an expenditure which would ultimately total more than £1.7 million—the necessary loans demanding payments of £140,000 per annum for eighteen years. As a British ship, she was manned by Royal Navy personnel, a handful of whom were New Zealanders, including several officers. (So that the new ship could take the name of New Zealand, the pre-Dreadnought battleship HMS *New Zealand* already serving in the British fleet was renamed *Zealandia*.)

In view of Ward's offer, plans were drawn up for the new vessel to be stationed at Hong Kong as flagship of a unit of a proposed Pacific battlefleet. However, by the time she was commissioned, on 19 November 1912, this intention had been altered by the growing German threat to Britain's naval pre-eminence in Europe. Ward's successor, Thomas Mackenzie, had acceded to a British request that *New Zealand* be deployed with the British main fleet in the North Sea. Nevertheless, despite the supposed urgency of the situation, New Zealand was promised a visit by the vessel—and this took place during a nine-month world tour by the ship in 1913. This visit, from 12 April to 28 June, proved very popular with New Zealanders, more than 375,000 of whom visited the ship. Among many gifts made to the ship was a tiki which would later assume considerable symbolic importance for the ship's crew. Her commander, Captain Lionel Halsey, was also given a piu piu, probably by the Taupo chief Tureiti Te Heuheu Tukino, with a request that he wear it in action. A myth later developed that Te Heuheu had predicted that no damage would occur to the ship so long as he did so.

New Zealand returned to Britain in December 1913, and joined the 1st Battle Cruiser Squadron. She was present at all three major engagements with the German High Seas Fleet during the First World War. At the first, at Heligoland Bight on 28 August 1914, Halsey wore both the piu piu and the tiki. *New Zealand* fired 82 rounds from her 12-inch guns and two torpedoes, and was instrumental in sinking the German light-cruiser *Köln*. Despite several near-misses, *New Zealand* came through the action unscathed. At the time of the next clash, at Dogger Bank on 24 January 1915, *New Zealand* had just joined the 2nd Battle Cruiser Squadron. When action became imminent Halsey got many messages from all over the ship hoping that he was again going to wear the piu piu. The crew were further convinced of its talismanic effect when the ship again went undamaged. At 9.33 a.m. New Zealand opened fire at long range on the *Blücher*, and continued to do so until the German ship struck at 11.50 a.m., 139 rounds in all.

At the Battle of Jutland on 31 May 1916, *New Zealand* was again in the thick of the action. Opening fire at 3.57 p.m. when the Battle Cruiser Fleet engaged the German battlecruisers, she continued in action until darkness fell and the Germans made their escape. In all, she fired 430 shells, mainly at the German battle-cruisers *Moltke* and *Von der Tann*. Although three British battlecruisers blew up during the battle, probably as a result of shells penetrating their magazines

New Zealand

New Zealand's gift battlecruiser, HMS *New Zealand*, arrives in Lyttelton Harbour in 1919 (*The Press (Christchurch) Collection, Alexander Turnbull Library, G-2288-1/1*)

because of a design fault which *New Zealand* shared, she again escaped serious damage. One German 11-inch shell struck her stern turret; it blew a hole in the deck and sent splinters flying, but caused no casualties. Once again the crew attributed their good fortune to the piu piu and tiki. In fact Captain Green, who had succeeded Halsey, had worn the tiki, but, being somewhat rotund, had merely hung the piu piu in the conning tower. When Admiral Sir David Beatty, the commander of the Battle Cruiser Fleet, came on board *New Zealand* a few days after the battle, he is reputed to have said, in commenting on their unscathed state: 'I know you all think it was due to this tiki-wiki thing your captain wore, but next time you may not be so lucky, so make sure he puts the whole uniform on.' (The piu piu remains in the Halsey family's hands, while the tiki is now in the Canterbury Museum.)

Fittingly, *New Zealand* was present at the surrender of the German fleet on 23 November 1918. In the following February she was detached to carry Admiral of the Fleet Viscount ★Jellicoe on his year-long mission to advise Indian and Dominion governments on naval defence requirements. As a result she again visited New Zealand from 20 August to 3 October 1919. As in 1913, she was a source of great interest to the public, who visited her in droves. *New Zealand* returned to Britain early in 1920, but soon afterwards fell victim to efforts by the great powers to regulate naval power. During the Washington Naval Conference of 1921–22 she was among a great number of older British capital ships earmarked to be scrapped as part of a comprehensive naval limitation agreement. She was broken up at Rosyth in 1924. Several of her guns and fittings were sent to New Zealand. Some of the 4-inch guns were later used in port defences during the ★Second World War, while two of her 12-inch guns are mounted in front of the Auckland War Memorial Museum. But for the end of the Second World War the name *New Zealand* would have been perpetuated in another British warship, a Malta class fleet aircraft-carrier, which was ordered in 1943 and included in the 1945 building programme, but cancelled in January 1946.

I. McGibbon, *The Path to Gallipoli: Defending New Zealand 1840–1915* (GP Books, Wellington, 1991).

New Zealand Army

New Zealand and Australian Division was one of the two divisions which made up the Australian and New Zealand Army Corps at ★Gallipoli in 1915. Although the possibility of a joint, divisional-sized expeditionary force had been discussed by the New Zealand GOC, Major-General A.J. ★Godley, in Melbourne in 1912, practical considerations lay behind the establishment of the New Zealand and Australian Division in Egypt three years later. There were too few New Zealanders in 1NZEF's Main Body to form a division, while the Australian Imperial Force was more than a division strong. Two Australian brigades, 1st Light Horse and 4th Infantry, were therefore combined with the New Zealand Infantry Brigade and the New Zealand Mounted Rifles Brigade to form the division, the title of which reflected the fact that 1NZEF provided both its commander, Godley, and its HQ staff. The new formation, which Godley described as 'a very abnormal division', was seriously deficient in artillery. Only the New Zealand Artillery Brigade (equivalent to a field regiment) was available, whereas a division would normally have three such brigades. The engineer and service corps companies were makeshift. Elements of the division began landing at Gallipoli on 25 April 1915. With Godley's elevation to command the ★ANZAC, command of the division passed to Major-General Sir Andrew ★Russell on 25 November 1915, and he oversaw its evacuation from the peninsula during the following month. It went out of existence with the establishment of the New Zealand Division in early 1916.

New Zealand Army has existed as a formal entity only since the passage of the New Zealand Army Act 1950. This legislation formalised the situation which had existed since 1937, when the RNZAF had been separated from the New Zealand Military Forces and an Army Board established. The term New Zealand Army had come into general use during the ★Second World War. Structurally the Army comprised a small regular component supporting a much larger citizen-soldier element. The professional Regular Force carried out the staff and instructional role, while the ★Territorial Force provided the bulk of the manpower. Not only was the idea of a standing army an anathema to most New Zealanders, it was also judged to be beyond New Zealand's means. Nor was it considered necessary in the existing international conditions.

The New Zealand Army's role in 1950 was to prepare for New Zealand's traditional contribution to the collective effort—the provision of an expeditionary force. To fulfil the ★Middle East commitment, it was planned to raise a Territorial division of about 30,000 men, who were to receive ★compulsory military training to ensure that they would be ready to depart much sooner than had been the case in 1939–40. The responsibility for organising and training this potential 3NZEF lay with the Regular Force, which provided cadres for the units and instructional staff for the CMT scheme. Since no home defence role was envisaged for the Army, and '3NZEF' would be equipped from stockpiles established in the projected theatre of deployment, there was no need to acquire equipment and munitions for its use in New Zealand apart from that required for training purposes. Relatively inexpensive war surplus materiel was available. Even after New Zealand switched its commitment to South-east Asia in the mid 1950s, this pattern was sustained. To ensure that it was not disrupted, a largely volunteer ★Kayforce was raised for the ★Korean War in 1950.

The expeditionary force concept was undermined by developments in the 1950s which rendered increasingly unlikely large-scale warfare on the Second World War model. The emphasis shifted to the rapid deployment of small forces to deal with 'brush-fire' situations which, if left to smoulder, might flare up into something more serious. Such a response could not be provided by the cumbersome '3NZEF' structure. What was needed were mobile, trained, and fully equipped forces ready to go at the outset of an emergency. This problem was compounded by the decision, in 1957, to deploy an infantry battalion in the ★British Commonwealth Far East Strategic Reserve. During the late 1950s the emphasis of Army planning shifted from amateur to professional, and successively from division to brigade to battalion group, as the full implications of sustaining such forces became apparent. The cost of equipment, now that war surplus stocks were becoming exhausted, was a daunting consideration for governments, especially after it became apparent in the early 1960s that the former practice of slotting into British logistic arrangements in operational theatres would no longer be possible.

The Army's attention now became focused on the battalion in Malaya, which received new rifles, ★machine-guns, and ★anti-tank weapons. Lightweight ★artillery and light tanks were also obtained. Even the appearance of the Army changed with the purchase of American-style helmets. The battalion in Malaya, it was determined, would form the core of a 6000-strong mixed Regular/Territorial combat brigade; there would also be a weaker (mainly Territorial) reserve brigade of 3000, a static support force of 3000, and a logistic support group of 3000. Regiments with a century of traditions found themselves disbanded or amalgamated in the ensuing reorganisation, though the Army tried hard to retain vestiges of the old Territorial designations in the new unit titles. Even so, the plans reflected the Army's continuing adherence to the concept of deploying large-scale forces from New Zealand, an approach which was encouraged by

New Zealand Army Air Corps

★SEATO plans. It was, however, the experience of the battalion in Malaya which pointed the way to the future: it was deployed in ★Confrontation operations and later supplied companies for ★V-Force.

During the 1970s the Territorial Force, its relevance to New Zealand's defence preparations no longer clearly apparent, was downgraded in importance. Compulsory training ended late in December 1972, and a comprehensive review of the Army's role gave top priority to the development of a capacity to deal with counter-insurgency, respond to emergencies in the South Pacific, provide defence aid and cooperation, and participate in UN ★peace-keeping. A reorganisation in 1974 established a second regular infantry battalion. All units in the North Island were grouped into 1st Brigade Group, and those in the South Island in 3rd Brigade Group. By the end of the decade, however, a new concept had been introduced: a 'core force' of a regular infantry battalion (plus one in Singapore) would be supported by a 'framework force' of predominantly Territorial units. This was refined in 1983, with the regular infantry battalion group being supplemented by a mainly Territorial brigade.

The Army faced problems with its role and equipment in the 1980s. The end of New Zealand's active participation in ★ANZUS, and the fourth Labour government's desire for a more independent approach focused on the South Pacific, placed a premium on improving the Army's capacity even as it made such an approach more difficult, since previous training and equipment procurement arrangements were no longer suitable or available. Although new trucks, assault rifles, machine-guns, and light artillery were obtained, much of the Army's equipment remained outdated. Declining budgets forced attention to rationalisation of existing resources. Numerous Army bases were closed and sold. Logistic and support units (the 'tail') were pared, so that more resources could be devoted to combat arms (the 'teeth'). By this stage the Army was based around two regular infantry battalions and supporting troops, with the Territorial Force reduced to simply augmenting the regular battalions in the event of a major—and highly improbable—general war. The increased demands of peace-keeping during the 1990s brought the issue of Army equipment to the fore. The deployment of a company-sized force to Bosnia–Herzegovina in 1995 and a battalion-sized force to ★East Timor four years later highlighted deficiencies. The Army was able to secure recognition at a political level that the modernisation of its equipment was a top priority.

New Zealand Army Air Corps Army aviation began in 1912 when Lieutenant W.W.A. ★Burn, in England, was ordered to undergo pilot training, but no further action was taken before the outbreak of the ★First World War. Not until June 1923 was a military aviation unit established—the New Zealand Permanent Air Force. It was redesignated as the ★Royal New Zealand Air Force in 1934, but was established as a separate service three years later. In 1947 the ★New Zealand Army involvement with aviation resumed with personnel being trained for artillery-spotting from aircraft. J5 Auster aircraft were acquired for this purpose in 1948. By the late 1950s these were obsolete, and they were eventually replaced with light helicopters. The need for an army aviation unit had become apparent. Following similar developments in Allied armies, the Army established the New Zealand Army Air Corps on 9 August 1963. From 1966 Army personnel served with 3 Squadron RNZAF flying Iroquois and Sioux helicopters for reconnaissance and support duties for the Army. By the 1980s the corps had shrunk to a Territorial unit of air gunners and cargo handlers, and it was disbanded in 1995.

New Zealand Army Legal Service was formed as the New Zealand Army Legal Department on 3 February 1927. It comprised the Judge Advocate-General (a position that had been created in 1911), a deputy, and three legal officers. All were ★Territorial Force officers who were lawyers in civilian life. A small legal staff under a Deputy Judge Advocate-General served with 2NZEF in the ★Second World War. In 1955 the Legal Department was reorganised into the New Zealand Army Legal Service. At the same time the Judge Advocate-General became a civilian appointment responsible for the provision of judge-advocates at courts martial and the review of the courts' proceedings. Following the creation of the position of Director of Legal Services in 1970, the NZALS came to undertake a tri-service role. Today the members of the corps are primarily Regular Force officers.

New Zealand Army Pay Corps was responsible for the pay of soldiers. Initially founded as the New Zealand Army Pay Department in 1917, the corps was disbanded in 1931 as a cost-cutting measure but was briefly re-formed during the ★Second World War and again during the ★Korean War. Reactivated again in 1969, the New Zealand Army Pay Corps was disestablished on 30 June 1993 as administration of pay was devolved to a unit level.

New Zealand Army Physical Training Corps was established on 1 June 1987, about twenty-three years after a specialist physical training corps was first proposed. The approximately thirty NCOs who make up the corps are charged with providing instruction in physical training in the ★New Zealand Army, as well as coordinating service sporting activities. The corps is unique in that it has no commissioned officers.

New Zealand Cross

New Zealand Cross originated during the ★New Zealand Wars. From the time of its institution in 1869 it was treated and regarded as being equal in status to the ★Victoria Cross. Like the VC, its history and status, and that of its twenty-three recipients, are complex and have not been without controversy. Even when the VC became available to colonial military personnel in January 1867, they could only be considered if they were under the command of a British officer at the time of their exploit. With British forces in the process of being withdrawn from New Zealand after 1866, the New Zealand authorities remained conscious of a lack of an appropriate means of recognising exemplary service by colonial personnel. After Colonel G.S. ★Whitmore proposed, in 1868, the award of rosettes and chevrons, and monetary grants, to members of the ★Armed Constabulary who distinguished themselves in action, the idea of a decoration equivalent to the VC emerged. It came to fruition with the institution on 10 March 1869 of a 'Decorative Distinction', which was available to members of the ★Militia, ★Volunteer Force, and the Armed Constabulary who, 'when serving in the presence of the enemy, shall have performed some signal act of valour or devotion to duty, or who shall have performed any very intrepid action in the public service, and neither rank, nor long service, nor wounds, nor any other circumstances or condition whatsoever, save merit of conspicuous bravery shall be held to establish a sufficient claim to the honour'. By the time the instituting Order in Council was forwarded by the Governor to London in July 1869, five awards had been made. The response from London was predictably unfavourable: the Governor was censured for overstepping the authority of his office. Despite its unorthodox origins, the decoration received Queen Victoria's assent and became effective on 22 December 1869. No action appears to have been taken to sanction the awards made before the Queen gave her approval. The precise status of the NZC has always been a matter of debate. Although treated and regarded in New Zealand as being equivalent to the VC, it was not accorded any precedence in relation to the wearing of other decorations and medals from the Crown. Furthermore, the fact that all awards were sanctioned by the Governor rather than the Sovereign raises the question as to whether the NZC was a governmental rather than a Royal honour.

Table 10 Roll of the New Zealand Cross
Name, Rank and unit, Place and date of act, *New Zealand Gazette* (date of award)
TE AHURURU, Henare Kepa, Constable, 1st Division, Armed Constabulary, Moturoa, 7 November 1868 (25 March 1869)
BLACK, Solomon, Constable, 1st Division, Armed Constabulary, Ngatapa, 8 January 1869 (25 March 1869)
BIDDLE, Benjamin, Constable, 1st Division, Armed Constabulary, Ngatapa, 8 January 1869 (25 March 1869)
LINGARD, William, Trooper, Kai Iwi Cavalry Volunteers, Tauranga-ika, 28 December 1868 (3 June 1869)
HILL, George [Rowley], Sergeant, 1st Division, Armed Constabulary, Jerusalem Pa, 10 April 1869 (26 June 1869)
SMITH, Angus, Cornet, Bay of Plenty Cavalry Volunteers, Opepe, 7 June 1869 (6 November 1869)
CARKEEK, Arthur Wakefield, Sergeant, Armed Constabulary, Ohinemutu, 8 February 1870 (7 July 1870)
FEATHERSTON, Isaac Earl, CMG, Staff, Native Contingent, Otapawa Pa, 13 January 1866 (28 October 1875)
ROBERTS, John Mackintosh, Inspector, Armed Constabulary, Moturoa, 7 November 1868 (11 May 1876)
[TE] RANGIHIWINUI, Keepa, Major, NZ Militia (Native Contingent), Moturoa, 7 November 1868, Otauto, 13 March 1869 (11 May 1876)
WAHAWAHA, Rapata [Ropata], Major, Native Contingent, Ngatapa, 5 January 1869 (11 May 1876)
MACE, Francis Joseph, Captain, Taranaki Militia, Kaitikara River, 4 June 1863, Kaitake, 11 March 1864, Warea, 20 October 1865 (11 May 1876)
PREECE, George [Augustus], Sub-Inspector, Armed Constabulary, Ngatapa, 5 January 1869 (11 May 1876)
WALKER, Samuel, Assistant-Surgeon, Armed Constabulary, Otauto, 13 March 1869 (11 May 1876)
MALING, Christopher [Louis], Sergeant, Corps of Guides, Tauranga-ika, 26 February 1868 (11 May 1876)
SHEPHERD, Richard, Sergeant, Armed Constabulary, Otauto, 13 March 1869 (11 May 1876)
AUSTIN, Samuel, Sergeant, Wanganui Volunteer Contingent, Putahi Pa, 7 January 1866, Keteonetea, 17 October 1866 (11 May 1876)
RODRIQUEZ [DE SARDINHA], Antonio, Trooper, Taranaki Mounted Volunteers, Poutoko, 2 October 1863, Kaitake, 11 March 1864 (11 May 1876)
ADAMSON, Thomas, Private, Corps of Guides, Ahikereru, 7 May 1869 (11 May 1876)
McDONNELL, Thomas, Lieutenant-Colonel, NZ Militia, Paparatu, October 1863, Putahi Pa, 7 January 1866 (1 April 1886)
MAIR, Gilbert, Captain, NZ Militia, Rotorua, 7 February 1870 (1 April 1886)
WRIGG, Henry Charles William, Cornet, Bay of Plenty Cavalry Volunteers, Opotiki, 29 June 1867 (18 March 1898)
NORTHCROFT, Henry William, Ensign, Patea Rangers, Pungarehu, 2 October 1866, Tirotiro Moana, 5 November 1866 (7 July 1910)

New Zealand Defence Force

The NZC was a silver cross *paty* or *formy* with, on the obverse, the name of the colony within a wreath of laurel, and was suspended from a crimson ribbon. The name of the recipient was engraved on the reverse of the cross. Its design was settled by a five-man commission appointed in July 1870. The contract for producing it was given to a firm of London goldsmiths, which suggested a number of modifications to the proposed design, making it look more like the VC. In 1908 the dies for the NZC were returned to the New Zealand Agent-General in London and were held by that office until returned to New Zealand in 1953 and deposited in the Dominion Museum. Apart from the twenty-three awarded, ten specimens were authorised before the dies were returned to New Zealand. In 1956 a further three (plus one unauthorised) specimens were struck from the by then deteriorating dies. A small number of unauthorised crosses and replicas of the decoration have been produced.

In 1873 a commission was appointed to consider all nominations and claims for the NZC. The lobbying from officers on behalf of individual veterans and from veterans for themselves was often intense and occasionally acrimonious. Although the government closed nominations for the NZC in 1897, intense lobbying continued with the result that two further awards were made, in 1898 and 1910. (See table 10.) Among those whose claims for the NZC were unsuccessful were Armed Constabularymen Patrick Ready, Michael O'Connor (or Connors), James Shanagan, and Sergeant-Major David Scannell, Lieutenant Charles Arthur Melchior Hirtzell (New Zealand Militia), Major John Nixon (Wanganui Militia), and Major Te Pokiha ★Taranui (a ★kupapa officer). Sir George ★Grey and Sir Walter Buller were proposed for the NZC for their part in the attack on Weraroa pa. Successful recipients received an annual pension of £10.

In 1998 it was announced that the Queen had approved the institution of a new NZC to replace the British ★George Cross as the premier New Zealand royal honour for acts of bravery by civilians and military personnel in non-combatant situations. This development opened a new chapter in the history of this fascinating decoration, and the first awards were announced in October 1999. (See HONOURS AND AWARDS)

PHILLIP O'SHEA

New Zealand Defence Force was established in November 1989 when the Ministry of Defence was divided into two separate organisations. It comprises the RNZN, the ★New Zealand Army, and the RNZAF, and is under the command of the Chief of Defence Force. The new organisation, which was given statutory backing in the ★Defence Act 1990, arose from the government's determination to differentiate between funders and providers in government administration and to ensure contestable advice on defence matters. The changes coincided with a decline in funding: defence expenditure fell by 12 per cent between 1990 and 1993. The NZDF sought to overcome the problems arising from its straitened circumstances by rationalising its property holdings and transferring assets from the 'tail' to the 'teeth'. Personnel strength was reduced, with the Regular Force strength falling from 11,745 in 1990 to 9462 in 1997. The NZDF provided New Zealand's contribution to the coalition effort in the ★Gulf War and has been active in a ★peace-keeping role in various parts of the world. (See DEFENCE, HIGHER ORGANISATION OF)

New Zealand Division of the Royal Navy, formally constituted by an Order-in-Council on 20 June 1921, was for two decades the basis of New Zealand's naval defence activity. It was administered by the New Zealand Naval Board, which had been established three months earlier by another Order-in-Council. Captain Alan ★Hotham RN, the Commodore Commanding the New Zealand Squadron, became First Naval Member. The Chief Staff Officer, stationed ashore, was also a member, though at first on a temporary basis (the arrangement was not formalised until 1928 after it had become apparent that the Commodore would remain at sea for the foreseeable future). The Minister of Defence presided over the board.

The origins of the Division lie in steps taken by New Zealand just before the ★First World War to establish its own naval forces. The ★Naval Defence Act 1913 opened the way for the acquisition of the training ship HMS *Philomel* in July 1914. With the establishment of the Royal Australian Navy, the ★Australia Station (shorn of its eastern part) became an Australian responsibility; an 'administrative division' of the Royal Navy's China Station was established to cover New Zealand. The Senior Naval Officer, New Zealand Division, the commander of one of the old imperial cruisers stationed in New Zealand, oversaw naval activities in New Zealand waters until all the cruisers departed late in 1914 for operational service elsewhere.

The establishment of the New Zealand Division of the Royal Navy following the First World War owed much to the work of Admiral of the Fleet Lord ★Jellicoe, the former commander of the Grand Fleet, who toured the Dominions and India to advise on post-war naval policy in 1919. By the time he set out, aboard HMS ★*New Zealand*, almost all the Dominions had rejected the concept of the single navy under a peacetime centralised naval authority. Prime Minister William ★Massey and Defence Minister James ★Allen favoured some local forces, albeit ones that could contribute to

New Zealand Division of the Royal Navy

Seamen take part in gun drill on HMS *Philomel* (Auckland Weekly News Collection, Alexander Turnbull Library, C-24253-1/2)

★imperial defence in wartime, but they had given little serious thought to naval policy, apart from requesting Naval Adviser Captain P.H. ★Hall-Thompson's views. When the Admiralty offered a modern cruiser for training in March 1920, Massey was inclined to accept immediately, but was restrained by Allen and Hall-Thompson. Jellicoe's report to the New Zealand government, in October 1919, was similar to advice given by the now-departed Hall-Thompson. It cemented Massey's and Allen's thinking in favour of a small element of local defence supplementing ships that could make an integrated contribution to the Royal Navy in wartime. The specifics of the establishment—three light cruisers, six submarines, and a depot ship, followed later by six destroyers and supported by obsolete destroyers and trawler minesweepers for purely local protection—were less important than his recommendation for a New Zealand Division of the Royal Navy, overseen by a naval board set up in terms of the Naval Defence Act 1913.

New Zealand applied for but then declined war-surplus 'PC' class torpedo boats and submarines as crewing problems began to make themselves apparent. By 1920, when the Cabinet approved the New Zealand Division concept, the country was deep in economic recession. Caution became the watchword for the politicians, who cut their shopping list to acquiring the coal-burning cruiser HMS *Chatham* and patching up the ancient 'P' class cruiser *Philomel* as a non-seagoing training ship. The 1913 pattern of New Zealand naval development was thus re-established.

Hotham persuaded the government that Devonport, with its rudimentary naval facilities and the ★Calliope Dock, was a better base than Wellington, where *Philomel* had languished since 1917. The ancient cruiser limped north for hulking, and during the 1920s the navy expanded Devonport to support the oil-fired cruisers deemed necessary. Throughout most of its two decades the New Zealand Division consisted of a pair of ★cruisers, a Castle class minesweeper acquired in 1926, and a fleet oiler. Two sloops (initially Flower class vessels) maintained by the Admiralty in New Zealand waters were not strictly part of the Division, but were attached to it for administrative purposes. The first of two 'D' class cruisers, HMS *Dunedin*, replaced *Chatham* in 1924, and she was soon joined by HMS *Diomede*. The cruisers, which were borrowed from the Royal Navy, made regular cruises to the Pacific Islands and back to the United Kingdom for

363

refits (during which advantage was taken of British naval schools for training New Zealand personnel). At irregular intervals they carried out exercises with RAN warships. In 1928 both *Dunedin* and *Diomede* were briefly deployed to Western Samoa in support of the administration, which was beset by nationalist agitation (see SAMOA, NEW ZEALAND'S MILITARY ROLE IN). *Dunedin* returned to Samoa in January 1930, and five years later she was deployed to Aden as part of British precautionary measures following Italy's invasion of ★Abyssinia.

During the 1930s Leander class cruisers replaced the 'D' class cruisers, and Leith class sloops the Flowers, but with the exception of the three Bird class training vessels ordered in the late 1930s, the New Zealand Division underwent very little growth until the last months of peace. The Labour government resisted British pressure to acquire a third cruiser. Nevertheless, the ships and the infrastructure at Devonport were not New Zealand's only contribution to imperial naval power; from 1927 the Dominion also contributed £1 million towards the cost of the Singapore naval base (see SINGAPORE STRATEGY).

Inevitably, the New Zealand Division drew heavily not only on British tonnage but also on British manpower, especially in its early years. British officers formed a large part of the local establishment: even as late as 1939 there were only eight New Zealand officers in the Division. The gradual expansion of the recruiting and training programmes brought new opportunities to New Zealanders. There were other advantages besides. Locally based ships could render assistance to civilians in time of distress and emergency, as in the ★Napier earthquake, and they also helped to make the link between New Zealanders and the navy stronger and more visible.

Nevertheless, the creation of the Division should not be overemphasised as a symbol of nationalism. Massey and Allen had never intended the Division to threaten Admiralty control of resources in time of crisis, and the pattern of 1914 was repeated in 1939 when war again broke out between Great Britain and Germany. In September the sloops HMS *Leith* and *Wellington* and the survey ship HMS *Endeavour* departed New Zealand waters immediately, and the government, notwithstanding the automatic provisions of the Naval Defence Act, deliberately placed the cruisers HMS *Achilles* and *Leander* under the Admiralty's operational control (though it was exercised by the New Zealand Chief of Naval Staff while the ships were on the ★New Zealand Station). Within months *Achilles* had distinguished herself at the Battle of the ★River Plate. The authorities busied themselves with arranging for a steady stream of New Zealanders to be sent to the United Kingdom for service with the Royal Navy (see ROYAL NAVY IN THE SECOND WORLD WAR, NEW ZEALANDERS IN). Despite some reluctance on the part of the Prime Minister, Peter ★Fraser, who maintained that it was 'not the time to break away from the Old Country', the Division arrangement was brought to an end in 1941. An Order-in-Council on 1 October reconstituted New Zealand's naval forces as the ★Royal New Zealand Navy. New Zealand warships now became HMNZS rather than HMS, but there was no change to the structure or operation of the naval forces themselves.

I. McGibbon, *Blue-water Rationale: The Naval Defence of New Zealand 1914–1942* (Historical Publications Branch, Wellington, 1981).

GAVIN McLEAN

New Zealand Expeditionary Force During both world wars, New Zealand dispatched overseas a large proportion of its manpower of military age to participate in the imperial or British Commonwealth war efforts. The first such force, in 1914–18, was designated the 'New Zealand Expeditionary Force'. When New Zealand set about creating a new force in 1939, the term 2nd New Zealand Expeditionary Force (2NZEF) was used to differentiate it from its predecessor, which came to be styled 1st New Zealand Expeditionary Force (1NZEF). The acceptance by New Zealand of the ★Middle East commitment in 1949 led to plans being developed for yet another expeditionary force. Although never implemented, they led to the widespread use of the term 3NZEF within the military hierarchy.

The origins of 1NZEF lay in the recognition, following the ★Boer War, that provision should be made to send New Zealand troops for imperial service in the event of a major war. In 1909, at New Zealand's request, the Chief of the Imperial General Staff considered New Zealand's contribution to ★imperial defence. He advised New Zealand to form an expeditionary force of one infantry brigade and one mounted rifles brigade for imperial service in the event of war. Although provision had been made in the ★Defence Act 1909 for the creation of a voluntary 'special force' for overseas service, no publicity was given to this overseas component of the defence reforms, which were advanced in terms of home defence. As early as 1912 the GOC, Major-General A.J. ★Godley, sought 'provisional sanction' from the government for the proposal to send an expeditionary force overseas in the event of war, so that he could begin preparations. Assuming Germany as the likely enemy, he suggested three possible uses for such a force: to attack the enemy's colonial possessions, to reinforce Egypt in case Turkey sided with Germany, or to fight with the British Expeditionary Force in the main theatre in

New Zealand Expeditionary Force

New Zealand troops arrive in Suez in December 1914 (*NZDF*)

Europe. Godley favoured the last-named course, but suggested that a New Zealand force might best be sent initially to Egypt where its ultimate destination could be decided in light of the circumstances at the time. Without making any commitment regarding destination, Minister of Defence Colonel James ★Allen gave the go-ahead for planning such a force. Godley discussed the proposal in both Australia and the United Kingdom before the Cabinet, in June 1913, agreed to preparations proceeding on the basis of a force of 7500 men. It was envisaged that the pre-planned ranks of the force would be filled with volunteers from the ★Territorial Force at the time of the emergency.

When the ★First World War began in August 1914, therefore, New Zealand was relatively well prepared for rapid action. An offer to send an expeditionary force was rapidly accepted by the British authorities, and Prime Minister William ★Massey announced on 7 August that it would be sent to Great Britain as quickly as possible. As early as 30 July the ★military districts had begun preparing for mobilisation. The scheme provided for each regiment or battalion of the Territorial Force to provide a squadron or company respectively (i.e. about a quarter of its strength). This would produce an infantry brigade of four battalions, a mounted rifles brigade of four regiments, as well as supporting arms of artillery, engineers, and field ambulances. This force would be commanded by Godley. There was no shortage of volunteers. Indeed men had begun coming forward even before recruiting opened on 8 August. So effectively did the process work that London was informed that the force could leave on 27 August if necessary, though a delay of several weeks beyond that would be preferable. The speed with which New Zealand prepared the force was made even more remarkable by the fact that the military authorities were concurrently arranging a separate expedition to occupy German Samoa (see SAMOA, NEW ZEALAND'S MILITARY ROLE IN).

The New Zealand Expeditionary Force's first attempt to leave, on 25 September 1914, was aborted because of the threat posed by the German East Asiatic Squadron (see CIVIL–MILITARY RELATIONS). When it finally left, on 16 October, it was escorted by both British and Japanese warships. The 8454 men (ten per cent of whom were first reinforcements) who comprised the Main Body represented one in eighteen of Pakeha New Zealand males between the ages of twenty and forty. They remain the largest body of men to leave New Zealand at one time. The ten ★troopships

365

New Zealand Expeditionary Force

met up with the AIF's twenty-seven in King George Sound in Western Australia, and the convoy headed across the Indian Ocean to the Suez Canal.

Although it had been intended that the combined force would go to Britain, it was disembarked in Egypt because of the threat to the Suez Canal posed by the Ottomon Empire's entry to the war on the side of the Central Powers on 5 November. The New Zealanders established camp at Zeitoun, near Cairo, and began training in earnest. In December they were joined by compatriots who had volunteered for service in the United Kingdom. On 3 February 1915 Private William Ham became 1NZEF's first fatal casualty when several New Zealand units helped repel a half-hearted Turkish attack on the Suez Canal. The two New Zealand brigades and supporting services were combined with two Australian brigades to form the *New Zealand and Australian Division, which took part in the *Gallipoli campaign from April to December 1915. During the ensuing three years elements of 1NZEF also took part in the *Salonika, *Senussi, *Mesopotamia, and *Sinai–Palestine campaigns.

In the meantime the authorities in New Zealand arranged for the dispatch of regular reinforcement drafts. Recruits were sent to Trentham to begin their fourteen weeks of training. Further training was also undertaken at Featherston and at smaller bases at Narrow Neck in Auckland and Awapuni in Palmerston North. The Second Reinforcements of 1752 men left for Egypt on 14 December 1915, to be followed by further reinforcement drafts approximately every month. In all forty-two drafts, each of around 2000 men, had left New Zealand by the end of the war, *conscription ensuring a constant flow of reinforcements for 1NZEF after volunteering had fallen away by 1916.

During 1915 a rifle brigade had been raised and dispatched to Egypt. This opened the way to the establishment of a New Zealand Division in early 1916. To create an additional infantry brigade, an extra four infantry battalions and nine artillery batteries were created by splitting existing units, and filling the ranks of the new units with reinforcements. A Pioneer Battalion was formed by amalgamating surplus mounted riflemen with the 'Native Contingent'. Extra bakery, supply, and butchery units were formed as line of communications units. The expansion of 1NZEF to an infantry division and mounted brigade led to some friction as many battle-hardened NCOs were placed under the command of inexperienced officers from New Zealand. Increasingly, however, 1NZEF drew its officer corps from the ranks of its experienced NCOs, and nearly half its officers were to be commissioned from the ranks by the end of the war. Although Godley had been promoted to corps commander, he remained commander of 1NZEF; the divisional commander was Major-General Sir Andrew *Russell.

The main focus of 1NZEF after April 1916 was on the *Western Front, where the Division was deployed, initially in the Armentières sector. From France 1NZEF's 'tail' stretched back to England where the administration and base details of 1NZEF were commanded by Brigadier-General G.S. *Richardson. The main depot and camp for 1NZEF was at Sling on the Salisbury Plain, Wiltshire, where up to 5000 reinforcements from New Zealand or men rejoining their units were shaken down and trained in reserve battalions prior to departure for France. Training was based around the 'bull ring', where soldiers paraded before being assigned to training; most of the nine weeks' training in England that most reinforcements received was devoted to musketry and route marching. Overcrowding at Sling led, in 1917, to the establishment of subsidiary camps scattered throughout England: at Brocton, Staffordshire, for the Rifle Brigade, Ewshot (near Aldershot) for the artillery, Belton Park (near Grantham, Lincolnshire) for machine-gunners, and Boscombe (near Bournemouth) for engineers and pioneers. From France came the sick and wounded to be treated at the three New Zealand General Hospitals—at Brockenhurst (Hampshire), Walton-on-Thames (Surrey), and Codford on Salisbury Plain. The first two named were able to treat more than 1600 men each, while Codford was smaller. After treatment, sick and wounded soldiers were sent to the convalescent home at Hornchurch (Essex), and officers were sent to a convalescent home at Brighton. Recovered troops went to Codford convalescent depot before being sent to Sling and on to the base depot at Étaples in France. Permanently unfit soldiers were sent to the discharge depot at Torquay to await repatriation to New Zealand. In November 1918 there were 26,600 men in the United Kingdom, of whom 16,400 were in hospitals, convalescing, or at evacuation depots, another 9100 in training camps and depots, and 550 NCOs in British officer cadet battalions. In France there were a further 17,400 serving with the division and nearly 4000 with other 1NZEF units. There were a further 3700 1NZEF personnel in the Middle East, either serving in the New Zealand Mounted Rifles Brigade or in base units.

Following the Armistice on 11 November 1918, the process of demobilisation soon began to deplete 1NZEF's ranks. Troops were returned from the continent to England, and on to New Zealand as transports became available, those from the Main Body leaving first, and the rest following in the order of their reinforcement draft. Nationalist disturbances delayed the *repatriation of 1NZEF from Egypt until July 1919 (see EGYPT, NEW ZEALANDERS IN). When 1NZEF officially ceased to exist on 1 November 1919, its

New Zealand Expeditionary Force

remaining members were transferred to the New Zealand Military Forces. The last twenty-four returned to New Zealand in March 1920. It had cost New Zealand £80 million to establish, maintain, and demobilise 1NZEF. In all, 124,211 men were mobilised, with 100,444 being sent overseas; there were 59,483 ★casualties, 18,166 of them fatal.

The idea that New Zealand would again send an expeditionary force in the event of a new war was implicit in the military authorities' approach to defence planning between the world wars. Moreover, the ★Chanak crisis of 1922 indicated that, despite the huge sacrifice of lives in the Great War, men were still prepared to volunteer for such activity. The ★Territorial Force provided the means by which such a force could be raised relatively quickly in an emergency, on the 1914 model. But developments in the 1930s undermined the capacity for such action. First the onset of the Depression led to the abandonment of ★compulsory military training, which severely weakened the Territorial Force. Second, the election of the Labour government in 1935 made it difficult to reverse this trend even as the international situation became more threatening. With the Labour Party ideologically and temperamentally opposed to the concept of dispatching troops overseas, the government would make no public pronouncement to the effect that such a force might be necessary. In private, however, it did not reject the idea, and the military authorities continued to plan on the assumption that overseas service might be required.

New Zealand was less prepared than in 1914 to dispatch an expeditionary force when the ★Second World War began. On 6 September 1939, just three days after the declaration of war, the government announced the mobilisation of a brigade group–sized 'Special Force' for overseas service. Within a month the strength of the proposed force had been raised to a division. The Special Force in consequence became the first of three echelons, each of which roughly corresponded to a brigade of the division. Volunteers began enlisting on 12 September, and those selected entered camp in October at Ngaruawahia (later Papakura), Trentham, and Burnham for three months' training. When acting Prime Minister Peter ★Fraser discussed the deployment of the force in London in late 1939, it was agreed that it should follow in 1NZEF's path by going first to Egypt. He also took the opportunity to interview Major-General B.C. ★Freyberg, and recommended his appointment as GOC of both 2NZEF and the 2nd New Zealand Division. Freyberg visited New Zealand at the end of the year and left with the First Echelon on 5 January 1940. In contrast to the position in 1914, when the force had been regarded as completely under British military control, careful attention was given to

A recruiting poster for 2NZEF (*Alexander Turnbull Library, F-146805-1/2-CT*)

his role as the commander of a small national army within a British command framework (see FREYBERG'S CHARTER).

In Egypt, 2NZEF established itself at Maadi and Helwan (twelve and twenty-four kilometres south of Cairo respectively). The former became its base and training depot. The Second Echelon, which left New Zealand on 2 May 1940, was diverted to Britain because of the crisis precipitated by Germany's successful onslaught on France and the Low Countries. Titled 2NZEF(UK), and comprising mainly 5th Brigade, it formed part of GHQ reserve for the defence of England against German invasion and was based at Aldershot. In September it was deployed in Kent. Not until January 1941 did it begin leaving for Egypt, finally joining the rest of 2NZEF just before the 2nd New Zealand Division was deployed to ★Greece. Although its departure had been delayed because of concern in Wellington about Japan's intentions, the Third Echelon had in the meantime reached Egypt in October 1940. Apart from Greece, the division was involved successively in the battle for ★Crete, the ★North African campaign, and the ★Italian campaign.

There were four elements of 2NZEF: the 2nd New Zealand Division, non-divisional units, line of

New Zealand Expeditionary Force

communication units, and Base units. The principal formation of 2NZEF was 2nd New Zealand Division of approximately 15–20,000 men, organised into three infantry brigades with supporting artillery, reconnaissance, engineer, signals, medical, and service units. Most of the non-divisional units were specialist engineer units formed at the request of the British government in late 1939 from Public Works Department and Railways personnel and experienced forestry workers. A forestry group of about 500 men milled timber in England until 1943, then joined 2NZEF in Italy, before being repatriated to New Zealand in September 1944. A railway operating group, a railway construction group, two army troops companies, and a mechanical equipment company also served in the Middle East. These units were engaged in railway operation and construction, port construction, and pipe-laying until late 1943. New Zealand volunteers serving in the ★Long Range Desert Group in theory remained part of 2NZEF; in reality they were no longer under New Zealand control, and Freyberg, revealingly, was unaware that the LRDG had been sent to the Dodecanese in 1943. After the failure of this operation 2NZEF was quick to demand the return of the New Zealand personnel. After 1943 the only non-divisional units raised were POW interrogation, repatriation, and graves units; non-divisional units such as the tank transporter company or mobile bakery were effectively part of the division. The most important of the line of communication units were the three general hospitals and the convalescent depot, each of approximately 1000 beds. For most of the war the hospitals and convalescent depot were based in Egypt, though one hospital accompanied the division to Greece in April 1941, and another was stationed in Syria in 1942 and at Tripoli in 1943. By early 1944 all the hospitals and the convalescent depot had been relocated in Italy. Three rest homes were established in Cairo in 1941, which held another 200 patients. Also considered to be line of communication units were the ★Kiwi Concert Party, and the clubs for 2NZEF personnel established at Cairo, and later at Bari, Rome, Florence, and Venice.

At the end of 2NZEF's 'tail' were the Base supporting units. These were given combatant unit titles in May 1942 as part of an effort to confuse the Germans—Maadi Camp, for example, going under the name 6th New Zealand Division until November 1944. Commanding the miscellany of line of communication and Base units was the Officer in Charge of Administration of 2NZEF, Brigadier W.G. ★Stevens. HQ 2NZEF, containing postal, pay, ordnance, and other administrative sections, was established at Maadi in September 1940 until January 1944, when it was transferred to Italy. It operated from Bari until September, then at Senigallia. Reinforcements arriving at Maadi from New Zealand were assigned to training units before being sent on to the division. The training depots had an erratic existence according to the irregular supply of reinforcements from New Zealand and the needs of the division, but by the end of the war about 76,000 men had been trained at Maadi. Maadi also held a reception depot for men rejoining their units and a discharge depot for men awaiting repatriation to New Zealand. In March 1942 an Advanced Base was established in Palestine as a depot between the division stationed in Syria and Maadi Camp. The Advanced Base returned to Maadi in June 1942, but reformed at Tripoli in February 1943. When the division went to Italy the Advanced Base followed, setting up at Bari in October 1943, in effect becoming a miniature Maadi Camp.

In June 1943 the first of about 7000 men from the first three echelons returned to New Zealand on furlough (see FURLOUGH AFFAIR). In late 1944 provision was made for men with three years' service overseas to be repatriated, and this system was working effectively when the fighting in Europe ended. After the German capitulation the process of repatriation was completed under the supervision of Stevens, who took over from Freyberg as 2NZEF's commander on 22 November 1945. By the time the force was formally disbanded on 28 February 1946, it had suffered 29,584 casualties in the Mediterranean and European theatres, of whom 6068 died on active service.

A Pacific section of the force, 2NZEF(IP), was formed in February 1942 from two brigades garrisoning Fiji, which later became part of the 3rd New Zealand Division. After training and reinforcement in New Zealand, it was deployed to ★New Caledonia in January 1943 under the command of Major-General H.E. ★Barrowclough. Base and training units and the force HQ were located at Bourail, with Colonel W.W. Dove as Officer in Charge of Administration. A general hospital was also established at Bourail but was moved to the south of the island in late 1943. By mid 1943 2NZEF(IP)'s strength had risen to just over 17,000, of whom about 2500 were at base. In August 1943 the 3rd Division moved forward to Guadalcanal to take part in the ★Solomons campaign. To overcome the problems arising from its long lines of communication, stretching back 1600 kilometres to New Caledonia, a Field Maintenance Centre was established as a depot on Guadalcanal. However, the maintenance of two divisions in the field proved beyond New Zealand's resources. Early in 1944 the government decided to withdraw and disband 3rd Division in favour of sustaining 2nd Division in the Mediterranean theatre. The last of 2NZEF(IP)'s personnel returned to New Zealand in October 1944. Of the force's 442 casualties, 203 were fatal.

New Zealand Staff Corps

With the end of the fighting in Europe, plans were soon being prepared for the deployment of 2NZEF against Japan, but these ceased with the surrender of Japan in August 1945. Instead New Zealand provided a brigade group to participate in the ★British Commonwealth Occupation Force. This was replaced in 1946 by a force recruited in New Zealand. Although officially titled 2NZEF, Japan Section, New Zealand's contribution to the Commonwealth force was more commonly known as ★Jayforce.

In 1949 New Zealand accepted a commitment which might have resulted in yet another expeditionary force being deployed in Egypt (see MIDDLE EAST COMMITMENT). In order to provide an augmented infantry division in the Middle East theatre within ninety days of the outbreak of war with the Soviet Union, New Zealand introduced compulsory military training for eighteen-year-olds. Preparations were begun for the transport of 3NZEF to the Middle East and for the stockpiling of equipment in theatre, but in the event they were never implemented. The '3NZEF' concept faded away in the late 1950s as New Zealand focused on the problem of insurgency in South-east Asia, and was formally abandoned in 1964.

J. Studholme, *Record of Personal Services during the War of Officers, Nurses, and First-class Warrant Officers; and other Facts relating to the N.Z.E.F.* (Government Printer, Wellington, 1928); W.G. Stevens, *Problems of 2NZEF* (War History Branch, Wellington, 1958).

New Zealand Force South East Asia When in 1973 both Australia and Great Britain indicated their intention to withdraw their forces from Malaysia and Singapore, New Zealand did not follow their lead. With the disbandment of the ★ANZUK Force on 31 January 1974, New Zealand's forces in Singapore became part of New Zealand Force South East Asia. The naval contribution to the force soon became increasingly intermittent, and 41 Squadron RNZAF was disbanded in 1977 when its Bristol Freighter aircraft went out of service, leaving a small Iroquois-equipped RNZAF Support Unit to support 1RNZIR. Although publicly justified in terms of support for New Zealand's foreign policy objectives, the continued presence of New Zealand servicemen in the region owed more to the likely cost of relocating the infantry battalion to New Zealand, particularly for the provision of sufficient accommodation, and to the recruiting advantages which the prospect of overseas service were thought to provide. The force exercised with Malaysian and Singaporean troops, and promoted New Zealand's bilateral defence ties with their respective governments. The New Zealand presence did not finally come to an end until 1989, when the force was disbanded and the troops were withdrawn to New Zealand.

New Zealand Intelligence Corps Traditionally the role of intelligence gathering in the ★New Zealand Army has been carried out by personnel from other corps assigned to intelligence posts at unit and formation headquarters. During the ★Second World War intelligence officers wore an 'Intelligence Corps' badge, but it was not a formally established corps. Specialist intelligence platoons were formed in 1964, and were reorganised in 1975 to form the New Zealand Army Intelligence Centre. The need to become more self-reliant in intelligence gathering following the ★ANZUS rift of the mid 1980s led to the formation of the New Zealand Intelligence Corps in March 1987. Currently the corps consists of two units, the School of Military Intelligence and Security at Waiouru and the Force Intelligence Group, which comprises a number of sections responsible for operational intelligence, counter-intelligence, photographic interpretation, and interrogation.

New Zealand Permanent Staff was founded in 1911 as a corps of 200 NCOs for the instruction of the newly formed ★Territorial Force. The quartermaster-sergeants and sergeants-major were the professional backbone of Territorial units, serving as instructors, administrators, and assistants to Territorial officers and members of the ★New Zealand Staff Corps. During the ★First World War the NCOs of the Permanent Staff provided an important core of experience and professional expertise for 1NZEF. Twenty-eight members of the Permanent Staff were killed during the war. After the war a reorganisation and later financial constraints resulted in the strength of the Permanent Staff shrinking to 110. Those that remained in 1939 proved valuable in the formation of 2NZEF. Virtually all the regimental sergeants-major were Permanent Staff or Royal New Zealand Artillery NCOs. As the war progressed, many Permanent Staff NCOs were commissioned as officers to reflect their greater responsibility as instructors or quartermasters. The New Zealand Permanent Staff was disbanded in January 1947 with the integration of Regular and Territorial corps; most personnel were attached to the New Zealand Regiment as instructors.

New Zealand Staff Corps was founded in 1911, following the recommendation of Field Marshal Lord ★Kitchener for a corps of professional staff officers to administer the newly formed ★Territorial Force. It was envisaged that its establishment of 100 would be filled by graduates of the Royal Military College at Duntroon, Australia, to which New Zealand sent its first ten cadets in 1911. Most of the staff were assigned as adjutants in Territorial units, staff officers in area groups, or commanders of the ★military districts. In

New Zealand Station

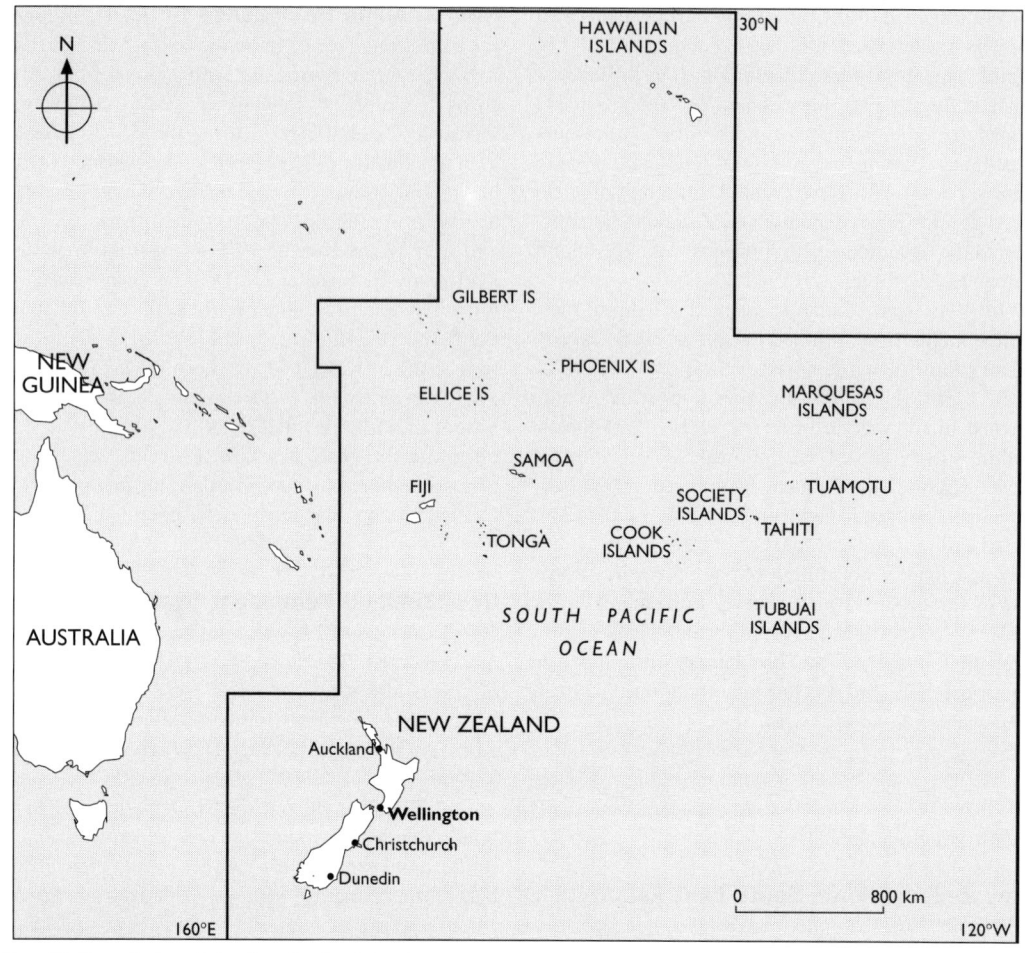

Map 17 Boundaries of the New Zealand Station

administering and instructing the Territorial Force, the NZSC was joined by a smaller body of professional officers in the Royal New Zealand Artillery. Eighty-five staff officers served with 1NZEF during the ★First World War; fourteen lost their lives. In 1919 the NZSC was reorganised, with promising officers with war experience being taken on to replace temporary appointments made during the war. It was dubbed by the GOC, Major-General E.W.C. ★Chaytor, the '*corps d'élite*' of the military forces, responsible for setting the professional standards. However, budgetary constraints led to the corps being severely cut back in 1922 to 75. This had serious long-term effects because many promising officers, demoralised by their uncertain prospects, left the service for civil employment. The Depression of the early 1930s further savaged the NZSC, with the corps shrinking to a low of fifty-five officers. During the ★Second World War, this small group provided a professional core for 2NZEF; more than a third of those who held brigade command from 1939 to 1945 were staff officers. When the corps was disbanded in 1947, its personnel were assigned directly to integrated Territorial and Regular Force corps.

New Zealand Station was the administrative term for the area of responsibility covered by the ★New Zealand Division of the Royal Navy, established in 1921, and later the ★Royal New Zealand Navy. The Station's boundaries encompassed New Zealand and the waters between it and Antarctica, as well as the sea area containing the various island groups to New Zealand's north and north-west, including the Hawaiian Islands. Initially commanded by a commodore, the Station was raised to rear-admiral status in 1934. The use of the term New Zealand Station began to decline from the mid 1950s.

New Zealand Wars The New Zealand Wars of 1843–72 were a series of clashes between various Maori tribes of the North Island and the British, imperial and

New Zealand Wars

colonial, and their Maori allies. Once known as 'the Maori Wars' or even 'the Maori Rebellion', their current alternative names are the 'Anglo-Maori Wars' and the 'Land Wars'—the last label tends to be restricted to the conflicts of 1860–72. The Wars are often said to have begun in 1845, with the Wairau affray of 1843 as a disconnected prologue. It is possible to identify about twenty separate 'wars', depending on definition and interpretation of linkages. They can usefully be divided into three groups: the limited and localised conflicts of the 1840s; the grand clash of 1860–64 between the British Empire and the Maori King Movement in Taranaki and Waikato; and the diverse and widespread fighting of 1864–72, whose main combatants were colonial troops and their Maori allies on the one side, and the followers of Maori prophetic leaders on the other. The scale of conflict varied enormously, from a few dozen to many thousands. The Wars were decisive in New Zealand history. It was they, rather than the Treaty of Waitangi signed in 1840, that ultimately turned the tide against Maori independence.

The underlying cause of most conflicts was a difference in perception of European government authority, arguably stemming from, or symbolised by, the difference between English and Maori versions of the Treaty of Waitangi. The British believed that they had, or should have, sovereign authority over Maori. Some Maori believed that their local autonomy persisted. Maori were well armed with muskets and, in the 1840s, experienced in their use, but in other respects their resources were usually greatly inferior to those of their British opponents, notably in numbers, artillery, and logistics. Maori attempted to compensate for their disadvantages through the adaptive innovation of their military techniques, notably the 'modern pa', an early type of trench-and-bunker earthwork.

The Warring Forties
The Northern War, 1845–46

The first full war between British and Maori was the Northern War, also known as the Flagstaff War or Heke's War, fought in and around the Bay of Islands. The resisters consisted of a group of Nga Puhi hapu led by Hone ★Heke Pokai and ★Kawiti. Other Nga Puhi hapu, led by Tamati Waka ★Nene among others, actively opposed Heke and Kawiti. Still others remained neutral. It has been suggested that the split within Nga Puhi followed factional lines dating from the ★Musket Wars of the 1820s. But the fit was not perfect, and differing perceptions of the degree of threat posed by government interference with chiefly authority were also a factor. The main British participants were elements of three imperial regiments (96th, 99th, and 58th), sometimes supported by naval sailors

A sketch, signed by Lance-Sergeant John Williams (58th Regiment), of the repulse of a Maori counter-attack at Ohaeawai on 1 July 1845 (*Alexander Turnbull Library, D-P320002-EF-CT*)

New Zealand Wars

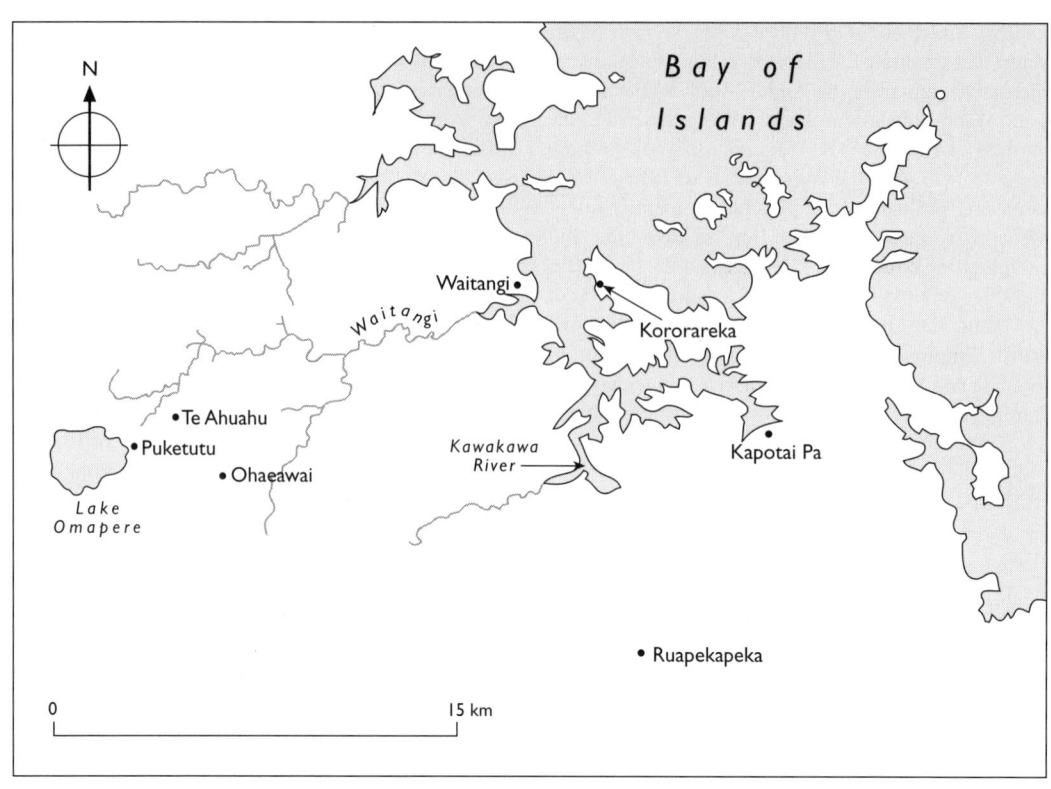

Map 18a Bay of Islands, 1845–46

and marines, civilian volunteers, and, in the last expedition of the war, by sailors and former artillerymen of the East India Company serving as ★Militia volunteers.

The war was triggered by Hone Heke's thrice-repeated cutting-down of the flagstaff at Kororareka in 1844 and early 1845, intended to symbolise his rejection of government control. In February, 1845, Governor Robert FitzRoy ordered troops and the warship *Hazard* to Kororareka and sent to Australia for reinforcements. On 11 March, Heke and Kawiti launched a well-planned attack on Kororareka with about 450 men. After some hard fighting they defeated the 300 or so British defenders, who evacuated the town, which was burned. Over the next nine months, the British mounted a succession of punitive expeditions from the Bay of Islands into the interior, and this constituted the basic pattern of operations.

The first expedition, in May 1845, consisted of 460 British under Lieutenant-Colonel William Hulme. Hulme began on 30 April by destroying Otuihu, the coastal pa of the neutral chief ★Pomare, who was suspected of sympathising with Heke. Hulme then moved inland against Heke's new pa of Te Mawhe, near Puketutu. Heke's garrison was supported by a taua under Kawiti, which remained hidden in the bush outside the pa. When Hulme attacked on 8 May, Kawiti's intervention, together with sallies from the pa, prevented him from pressing home his assault. Each side lost about 50 killed and wounded, and the British demonstrated a slight tactical edge over the Maori in open battle, but Hulme was thwarted and retreated to the coast. On 15 May a boat expedition under Major Cyprian ★Bridge, supported by pro-government Maori, destroyed a coastal pa belonging to Kawiti's allies, the Kapotai hapu. Like the taking of Otuihu, this demonstrated the vulnerability of traditional coastal pa to navy-assisted British attack.

Skirmishing between the forces of Heke and Tamati Waka Nene had occurred before the attack on Te Mawhe, but intensified after it, culminating in a substantial battle at Te Ahuahu on 12 June. Neither Kawiti nor the British were involved. Heke had about 500 men to Waka Nene's 300, but was defeated and severely wounded after heavy fighting. Realising that the Maori resisters were now vulnerable, the British mounted a second expedition inland with 615 men and five cannon under Colonel Henry ★Despard, this time against Kawiti's modern pa of Ohaeawai. Despard bombarded the pa for a week from 24 June, then launched a heavy assault on 1 July, expecting the garrison to have been decimated and demoralised by his cannon. Kawiti's garrison is said to have been only 100 strong, but the pa incorporated a new feature—anti-artillery bunkers—which had protected the occupants from cannon fire. They were able to repel the British storming party, inflicting 110 casualties while suffering little loss themselves. Kawiti abandoned Ohaeawai ten days later, and Despard destroyed the empty pa before returning to the coast, but few doubted that the Maori had secured a major victory.

As a consequence of Ohaeawai, FitzRoy attempted to negotiate peace, and there was a lull in operations. But before FitzRoy could conclude the negotiations, he received news of his dismissal and replacement by Governor George ★Grey. Grey arrived from South Australia on 14 November 1845, and mounted the last and largest of the British punitive expeditions. British forces totalled nearly 1300, with thirteen cannon and mortars. Maori allies may have brought the total close to 2000. The expedition assembled at Kawakawa in early December, and then marched inland against Kawiti's new pa of Ruapekapeka, which was not reached until Christmas. Heke, finally recovered from his wound, joined Kawiti inside Ruapekapeka on 9 January 1846. A day-long bombardment followed. The fact that he and his sixty reinforcements (which brought the garrison to perhaps 500) entered without difficulty proves that the siege was by no means tight. On 11 January, however, the pa was largely evacuated and the British and their allies occupied it with little resistance, though there was some fighting in the bush outside the pa. The British lost twelve killed and thirty wounded. Estimates of Maori dead vary between nine and twenty.

There is still some controversy over the confusing and anti-climactic events at Ruapekapeka on Sunday, 11 January 1846. One view is that the Maori were outside the pa at prayers when the irreligious British attacked. Another is that they had decided to abandon the pa, but wished to draw the pursuing British into an ambush outside it. The engagement of 11 January itself can be seen as a draw, or even a tactical British success. But Heke and Kawiti escaped with their forces intact, having absorbed the energies of 2000 enemies for over a month. Ruapekapeka had been purpose-built as a target for the British, and its loss was not damaging in itself. The case for a strategic Maori victory in this campaign is strong, and so—contrary to persistent European legend—is the case for a limited Maori success in the war as a whole. Heke and Kawiti were not penalised in any way, and appear to have remained as independent as ever.

A 'Southern War'? 1843–47

Apart from the Northern War, the 1840s saw three outbreaks of conflict in the Cook Strait region: at Wairau in 1843, at Wellington in 1846, and at Wanganui in 1847. Traditionally seen as separate, the three conflicts all involved elements of the Ngati Toa alliance which, under its great leader ★Te Rauparaha, had established a hegemony in the region in the 1820s. In each case, conflict was triggered by Pakeha attempting to assert sovereign authority over particular districts. In each case, conflict was muted by the fact that most of the Ngati Toa alliance, which included some Ngati Raukawa, Te Ati Awa, and Wanganui, believed Pakeha to be more valuable than they were dangerous. Some, including Te Rauparaha himself in 1846, remained neutral. Others actively supported the Pakeha, and only a minority of the alliance was ever in arms against them.

The Wairau clash took place on 17 June 1843 (see WAIRAU MASSACRE), when a party of settlers from Nelson under Magistrate Henry Thompson and Captain Arthur Wakefield attempted to arrest Te Rauparaha on land they believed he had sold. Instead, twenty-two of the Europeans were killed, some after surrendering, as against six or fewer Maori. Governor FitzRoy took no further action against Ngati Toa, to the rage of the settlers. But when land disputes between the Ngati Toa alliance and the settlers flared anew in Wellington in early 1846, Governor Grey took a different attitude.

At the end of the Northern War, Grey moved most of his forces south to Wellington where local Maori were disputing settler occupation of parts of the Hutt Valley. Hostilities broke out on 2 April 1846, and continued to August. Maori resisters were led by ★Te Rangihaeata, Te Rauparaha's lieutenant, and the Wanganui chief ★Te Mamaku. After minor skirmishing, an engagement took place at Boulcott's Farm, in the Hutt Valley, where Te Mamaku made a surprise attack on a British post on 16 May. The British lost ten killed and wounded; Maori casualties are unknown. In July the British forces, now amounting to more than 1000 imperial infantry, sailors, marines, and Maori allies, commenced operations against Te Rangihaeata's pa of Pauatahanui. Te Rangihaeata evacuated the pa on 1 August and retreated north. Apart from a sharp rearguard action on 6 August, there was little fighting. Te Rangihaeata may have been short of supplies, demoralised by the paucity of active support from his kin and allies, or wary of an encircling movement being carried out by pro-government Maori. He may also have been affected by Grey's seizure and imprisonment of Te Rauparaha on 23 July. Though low in military intensity, this 'Wellington War' went a considerable way towards establishing government authority in the immediate environs of the town.

Conflict in Wanganui the following year was again characterised as much by Maori cooperation with the British as by hostility. Te Mamaku and some upper-river Wanganui were alarmed by the arrival of troops at Wanganui town; lower-river hapu were not, and

New Zealand Wars

supported the British. A small group of Te Mamaku's adherents raided the farm of the Gilfillan family in the Mataraua Valley near Wanganui on 18 April 1847, killing Mary Gilfillan and three of her children. The killers were captured by their lower-river kin, and four were hanged in Wanganui town. In mid May, several hundred upper-river Wanganui Maori, led by Te Mamaku among other chiefs, marched to the outskirts of the town and blockaded it. Minor skirmishing over two months culminated in a clash on 20 July, sometimes known as the Battle of St John's Wood. About 400 troops emerged from the town under Lieutenant-Colonel W.A. McCleverty and skirmished with a similar number of Maori. Each side suffered a dozen casualties, and Te Mamaku and his allies returned home. The fighting in Wanganui had no discernible result, except to demonstrate that both Maori and Pakeha could and would defend their own spheres of control.

King and Empire
The collapse of cooperation

The fighting in Wellington and Wanganui in 1846–47 was limited and ambiguous, with some Maori as enthusiastic in supporting the British as others were in resisting them. This underlines the fact that Maori–Pakeha relations in 1840–60 were characterised more by cooperation than conflict. A periphery of European settlements, scattered around the coasts of the North Island, became economically interdependent with the Maori hinterland. The British controlled the territory around their settlements—an area which in 1860 comprised about 20 per cent of the North Island—while Maori controlled the rest. The two spheres interacted intensively, if sometimes uneasily, but the relationship was not one of dominance by either party. Many settlers and officials resented parity with Maori, which was in discord with racial and imperial preconceptions and with the illusion that the Treaty of Waitangi had made New Zealand British in 1840. Maori independence could be seen as temporary, however, while their sphere continued to shrink through the sale of land. During the 1850s, land-selling diminished, landholding sentiment grew, and in 1858 a proto-nationalist and landholding organisation, the King Movement, was formed, centred on Waikato but always extending to other tribes as well.

Maori independence now appeared to have some prospect of permanence. Settlers and the new Governor, Colonel Thomas Gore Browne, found this situation unacceptable, and felt that Maori needed a 'sharp lesson' about who should really be in charge. In 1859, an apparent opportunity to administer such a lesson emerged in Taranaki. A Te Ati Awa chief, Teira, offered a 243-hectare block of land at Waitara for sale to the government, over the objections of a senior chief, Wiremu Kingi ★Te Rangitake. Pakeha in general already had more land than they could use, but the settlers of New Plymouth, restricted to 24,300 hectares, were unusually land-hungry. Yet it was the sovereignty issue, not the land issue, which motivated Browne and London. Browne insisted on accepting Teira's offer, and when Wiremu Kingi's supporters passively resisted the surveying of the Waitara Block in March 1860, the Taranaki War broke out. The precedence of broader issues over a particular block of land was soon demonstrated by the growth of Maori support for Wiremu Kingi. Within weeks, Te Ati Awa had been joined by other Taranaki tribes and, within months, by the King Movement.

The Taranaki War, 1860–61

British forces in the Taranaki War grew to 3500 men, mainly comprising imperial troops (elements of the 12th, 14th, 40th, 57th, and 65th Regiments). They were commanded first by Colonel Charles ★Gold and then, from 3 August 1860, by Major-General Thomas ★Pratt. The Maori forces fluctuated from a few hundred to perhaps 1500. The main Te Ati Awa commander was not Wiremu Kingi but his 'general', Hapurona. The Waikato leaders Rewi ★Maniapoto and Tawhana Tikaokao are said to have been prominent in the latter stages of the war.

The first shots were fired on 17 March and the first significant action took place at Waireka on 28 March. It was a confused encounter, a series of skirmishes between various Maori and British parties. The climactic event, the storming of Kaipopo pa by a naval party which killed scores of Maori, appears to have been largely legendary. But up to 17 Maori, including the important Ngati Ruanui chief Te Rei Hanataua, were killed elsewhere in the skirmishing. The British lost fourteen killed and wounded. The basic pattern of the war evolved from April, and remained constant throughout 1860. It consisted of sporadic British forays from their base at New Plymouth and their camp at Waitara into the Maori-controlled interior. Maori absorbed these British thrusts with a loose cordon of cheap and expendable modern pa. The British took empty pa galore but could not pierce the cordon. On one occasion, on 27 June, a British force of 350 under Major Thomas Nelson attacked the pa of Puketakauere. It was severely defeated, with sixty-four casualties, by Maori under Hapurona and the Kingite chief Epiha Tokohihi. After Puketakauere, the Maori cordon around New Plymouth tightened to the point of siege. About 100 settlers died of disease in the overcrowded town. The pressure eased in September and October, when Maori warriors returned home to help plant their crops. On 6 November, General Pratt and 1000

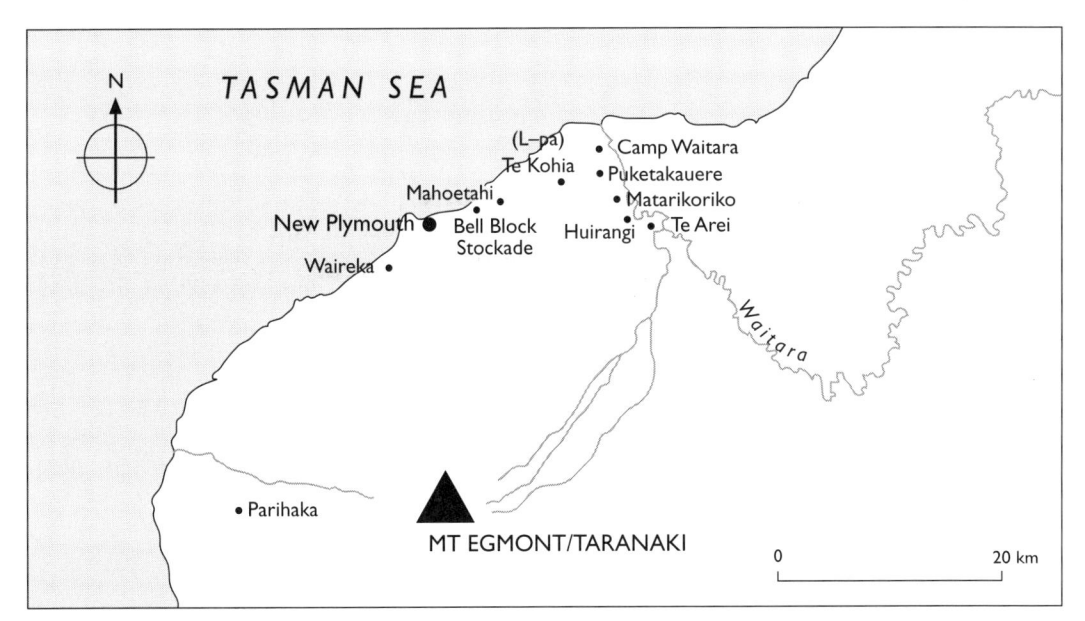

Map 18b Taranaki, 1860–61

men surprised a newly arrived Waikato force of 150 in a half-built pa at Mahoetahi. The Maori force was routed with about 50 killed. But this victory had little strategic effect and British frustration with this 'strangest kind of war' intensified.

By the end of the year, Pratt and his able advisers, Colonels T.R. ★Mould and Robert ★Carey, had developed a more promising strategy. Instead of sporadic forays, they began mounting continuous pressure on one point of the pa cordon, using the systematic siege warfare technique known as sapping, and holding the ground gained with a series of redoubts. These operations forced the Maori to abandon pa at Matorikoriko at the end of December 1860, and Huirangi at the end of January 1861. The sapping strategy may have frustrated Maori into mounting an exceptional frontal assault against Number Three Redoubt, Huirangi, on 23 January. It was repulsed with loss. But as February wore into March, and sapping operations against a series of pa at Te Arei continued week after week, it began to dawn on the British that at great cost in energy and considerable cost in blood they were eating away into defences that were in practice infinite. Governor Browne concluded that Maori independence could not be crushed in Taranaki after all, and negotiated a truce on 18 March 1861. He began preparing to invade the Waikato but was dismissed and replaced by Grey before he could do so.

The Waikato War, 1863–64
Renewed fighting broke out in Taranaki on 4 May 1863, when Maori ambushed a British detachment near Tataraimaka. The new British commander, Lieutenant-General Duncan ★Cameron, defeated a small Maori force at Katikara a month later. These two actions, together with a few other minor operations which took place in Taranaki over the next nine months, are sometimes known as the 'Second Taranaki War'. They are probably better seen as a prelude to the Waikato War, which broke out in July 1863, and were certainly intended as such by Governor Grey.

A key determinant of the course of the Waikato War was the systematic preparation undertaken by Grey from 1862. A road (the Great South Road), built by imperial troops, was pushed south from Auckland to the Kingite border on the Mangatawhiri River, and an advanced base (the Queen's Redoubt) was established there. A Commissariat Transport Corps and telegraph line were organised to ensure supply and communication. Steamers were acquired to enable the British to use the Waikato River for supply and transport. Grey manipulated the British government into leaving intact the army assembled for the Taranaki War, despite the strident demands of Australian governors for the return of their troops. Any decrease in the use of imperial troops against bushrangers or resisting Australian Aborigines dating from the 1860s can be credited to George Grey. Grey used the outbreak in Taranaki in May to prise further regiments out of London. In the end, ten imperial infantry battalions, plus support units, were massed in New Zealand—a total of about 12,000 men including sailors and marines serving on shore. Colonial troops included two small regular units, the ★Colonial

New Zealand Wars

Map 18c Waikato, 1863–64

Defence Force and the famous ★Forest Rangers, a fluctuating number of Auckland militia, and a new specially raised militia, the 'Waikato Militia' or ★'Military Settlers', who eventually numbered about 5000 (including a unit raised later for Taranaki). About half these men were recruited in Australia. They were to be rewarded with confiscated Maori land after they had served their term. A minority of Waikato hapu and a majority of the Arawa confederation supported the British in the war, bringing the total mobilisation close to 20,000 by early 1864.

Rough estimates suggest that, in response, the King Movement mobilised fewer than 5000 warriors, of whom no more than 2000 were ever in the field at the same time and the same place. The disparity in numbers can obscure the fact that this was a remarkable achievement for a traditionally disunited tribal people. The King Movement has sometimes been seen as a largely Tainui or Waikato organisation, but this was clearly not the case in 1863–64. Many—indeed, most—tribes outside the Waikato region and the Tainui kin-group contributed fighting men or other forms of support. As in southern Africa and North America, sustained conflict with Europe led to unprecedented pan-tribalism, even proto-nationalism. Known Kingite leaders include Wiremu Tamihana ★Te Waharoa, Rewi Maniapoto, and Tawhana Tikaokao.

The British invasion of Waikato began on 12 July 1863. It was preceded by the rounding-up of those Maori living between Auckland and the Kingite border who refused to take an oath of allegiance—a painful event permanently etched in the memory of the relevant hapu. The Kingites appear to have imposed a matching split on Pakeha–Maori families living in Kingite territory. Maori wives and some children stayed; Pakeha husbands and other children left for Auckland, a mass divorce whose trauma showed how intertwined the two peoples could become. Auckland was the main British base, and the town received a significant economic boost: imports quadrupled and the population doubled. But Maori raids reached as far north as Howick, there were alarms in Auckland itself, and outlying settlers to the south lost a few lives and much property.

The first fighting occurred on 17 July. Cameron and his advance guard of 550 men attacked and defeated a small Maori force entrenching at Koheroa. But it was not until three and a half months later that his army was able to advance further south. The delay appears to have been due to a two-pronged Maori strategy. A large pa at Meremere blocked advance south along the Waikato. With his steamers and superior numbers, Cameron could have overwhelmed Meremere in a pincer movement. But he was unable to concentrate sufficient troops against the pa because of a Maori raiding campaign behind his lines—the second prong of the Maori strategy. The raids forced Cameron to use most of his troops to protect his lines of supply. But British reinforcements kept flowing into Auckland, a threshold was reached, and on 31 October he finally mounted his pincer movement against Meremere with a striking force of 2400 men. The Maori garrison, numbering perhaps 1000, evacuated the pa without a fight and the British became the proud owners of a functionless pile of dirt.

In the Northern or Taranaki Wars, a British push similar to that against Meremere would normally have been followed by a return to base and a period of recuperation before a new expedition was mounted. In the Waikato, however, Grey's preparations meant that the British offensive could be quite close to continuous. Maori, on the other hand, still needed periods of recuperation to accumulate supplies and allow their part-time warriors to contribute to normal economic activity. The Kingites had built another pa at Rangiriri, designed like Meremere to block an advance along the Waikato. But when Cameron attacked it on 20 November they had been unable to reassemble a sufficient garrison. Their forces, under Wiremu Tamihana and Pene Pukewhau Te Wharepu, numbered no more than 500. More were on the way, and the garrison might well have doubled within a week, but Grey's preparations meant Maori did not have that week. For various reasons, the Battle of Rangiriri is not easy to reconstruct. Cameron intended a pincer movement similar to Meremere: a frontal attack by the main force, and an attack from the rear by a river-borne force intended to cut off the Maori escape. At Rangiriri, the river-borne prong was delayed by the current. The frontal attack bounced off the strong Maori right, but penetrated the thinly held Maori left and joined up with the river force once it had landed. Though surrounded on three sides, the Maori position remained strong: a cleverly designed earthwork redoubt supported the right front of the pa, and acted as a citadel, while an evacuation route remained to the east. A series of British assaults on the redoubt all failed. Most of the garrison evacuated during the night, but a rearguard of 180 were captured on the morning of 21 November after confusion over a flag of truce. Rangiriri was a substantial British victory, but it did not represent a tactical solution to the problem of the modern pa.

Cameron pushed on up the Waikato River and occupied the Kingite 'capital' of Ngaruawahia on 8 December. The King Movement was not a capital-centred state and this was not a major blow in itself. The next episode in the war, however, *was* a major blow to the Kingites. Early in 1864, they had constructed a formidable constellation of modern pa centred at Paterangi, protecting the important agricultural centre of Rangiaowhia. Taking a lesson from Rangiriri, Cameron decided not to attempt a direct assault on the Paterangi Line, but rather to outflank it in a night march through the bush, guided by a Maori turncoat. He raided Rangiaowhia, which mostly contained non-combatants, on 21 February, and so forced the Maori evacuation of the Paterangi Line on 22 February. A rearguard action at Hairini on that day enabled the Maori army to escape intact, but unlike Meremere, Rangiriri, and even Ngaruawahia, the Rangiaowhia district was itself an important loss.

In late March, a Maori force of about 300 began building a pa at Orakau near the British forces, as a challenge to battle. Rewi Maniapoto did not consider the strategic move to be wise, but nevertheless exercised the tactical command. A British force of 1100 men under Brigadier-General G.J. Carey attacked Orakau on 31 March. The defences were not complete, but three assaults were repulsed. Carey then belatedly took advantage of Orakau's great flaw: unlike most modern pa, it could be surrounded. Cameron arrived

New Zealand Wars

Earthworks at Paterangi in 1864 (*Hawke's Bay Museum, 5597-21*)

with reinforcements, and the British tightened their grip on 1 and 2 April. Then, late on 2 April, the garrison sortied and managed to cut its way out. The Maori suffered heavy casualties in the process, however—perhaps eighty killed and forty wounded, compared to seventeen British killed and fifty-one wounded. The disproportion between killed and wounded attests to the fact that many Maori wounded were bayoneted to death—not an uncommon practice on either side. At the time, the British rightly saw Orakau as a minor success which could have been major—a lost chance of decisive victory in the Waikato War rather than the thing itself. Subsequently, Orakau was reconstructed into a war-winning victory for the British and a heroic 'last stand' for the Maori.

The war in the Waikato basin now ground to a halt. Cameron's large army had conquered a sizeable chunk of the Waikato, but beyond his lines the King Movement remained independent, battered but intact. Cameron and Grey still hoped for a decisive 'last battle' which would demoralise Maori and induce them to submit. Soon after Orakau, a chance of just this appeared to present itself at Tauranga. Cameron had previously dispatched an expedition to Tauranga in January 1864, to cut off the flow of Maori reinforcements from the East Coast, who were reaching the Waikato through Tauranga. Local Maori assembled under their chief Rawiri ★Puhirake, and attempted to provoke this British force into attacking them. After raids and written challenges failed, they built a pa, Pukehinahina or the Gate Pa, within five kilometres of the British camp near Tauranga. Cameron could use Tauranga Harbour to quickly concentrate a large force against this small pa, and in late April he did so. On 28 April he moved against the Gate Pa, which was garrisoned by 230 Maori men and one woman, with 1700 troops and seventeen pieces of artillery. On 29 April, after a heavy bombardment, a strong storming party was sent against the pa. It succeeded in entering the main position over aboveground defences flattened by the bombardment, but was then ambushed inside the pa by an intact garrison, and forced to flee. Though the garrison evacuated the pa that night, it was a traumatic defeat for the British in general and Cameron in particular. Partial compensation was obtained on 21 June, when a British force under Colonel Greer, acting on Cameron's standing orders, caught Rawiri Puhirake in an unfinished pa at Te Ranga. Puhirake was defeated and killed. The peace subsequently made by Governor Grey in Tauranga, on 25 July, owed something to both battles.

Curiously enough, the last act of the Waikato War took place in Northland. The Kingite prisoners captured at Rangiriri had been incarcerated on the island of Kawau, north of Auckland. On 11 September 1864, they seized all the boats on the island and rowed themselves to the Northland coast 6.5 kilometres way. Soon, Auckland feared attack, and colonial and imperial forces made preparations to move against the prisoners in the pa they had built near Warkworth. The scene was set for a Northland rematch of the Battle of Rangiriri. But some Nga Puhi supplied the prisoners with food and guns, and promised them protection. The British could not risk adding Heke and Kawiti's people to their enemies, and the prisoners were allowed to make their way home to Waikato unmolested. Despite this last act going in their favour, the Kingites lost the Waikato War. But they did so only narrowly; the King Movement survived; and few British at the time were pleased with the result of their own immense military effort.

Prophets, Colonials, and Kupapa

From early 1864, a new kind of war emerged in the midst of the old. One of its dimensions was the involvement of a series of Maori prophetic movements, each with a differing balance of Christian, traditional, and innovative ideology. These movements were all pan-tribal, and some seem to have been more subversive of tribalism and some other traditions than the equally pan-tribal King Movement. As a result, they provoked hostility not only from Pakeha but also from many tribal chiefs. Maori fighting on the same side as the British, now known as ★kupapa (originally 'waverers') or kawanatanga (government), increased in numbers and importance. At the same time, with London growing tired of the costs of war and General Cameron growing tired of the modern pa, there was increasing pressure for the withdrawal of imperial troops and a corresponding increase in the prominence of colonial leaders and units.

Taranaki and Wanganui, 1864–66

During 1863, a Taranaki prophet named Te Ua Haumene developed the remarkable Pai Marire ('good and peaceful') religion, also known as Hauhau. Te Ua himself does not seem to have intended Pai Marire as a warlike creed, but the attitudes of his supporters and opponents ensured that it became so. On 6 April 1864, a group of Te Ua's followers attacked and defeated a mixed colonial and imperial patrol at Te Ahuahu in North Taranaki. On 30 April, a larger group under the subordinate prophet Epanaia Kapewhiti attacked a British redoubt at Sentry Hill, Te Morere. This rare Maori frontal attack on a British fort, apparently encouraged by a belief that Pai Marire incantations would yield protection from bullets, failed with heavy losses. Undeterred, another Pai Marire prophet, Matene Rangitauira, led a force down the Wanganui River. Believing their territory and their allied Pakeha town of Wanganui to be threatened, the lower-river hapu defeated Matene in a fierce but semi-ritualised battle on Moutoa Island. These defeats did not damage the appeal of Pai Marire, which helped energise subsequent Maori resistance on both west and east coasts.

Frustrated in the Waikato, Grey decided to use the imperial army, while he still had it, against a secondary bastion of Maori independence, south Taranaki. The main British striking force, 3700 men under a reluctant General Cameron, landed at Wanganui at the beginning of 1865. Cameron moved north in late January. He was opposed by 540 local Maori under the Ngati Ruanui chief Patohe, with some Waikato Kingite support. His first camp, at Nukumaru, was attacked fiercely but unsuccessfully on 24 and 25 January. Cameron declined to attack a formidable pa at Weraroa and, leaving it masked in his rear, pushed methodically north into south Taranaki. Weraroa lost its function, and colonial troops were able to take it without fighting four months later. Cameron heavily defeated a small Ngati Ruanui force which made the mistake of fighting in the open at Te Ngaio on 13 March. He reached the Waingongoro River on 31 March and halted his advance. Cameron left New Zealand in August 1865 and was replaced by Major-General Trevor ★Chute. Chute conducted the last imperial campaign in January and February 1866, a series of depredations against Maori villages and traditional pa, notably Otapawa (14 January). A similar but less successful campaign was conducted between August and November 1866 by colonial and kupapa forces under Thomas ★McDonnell. McDonnell began with a surprise attack on the peaceful village of Pokaikai on 2 August, but met heavier resistance at Pungarehu on 2 October. Conflict on the west coast then lapsed into uneasy peace.

East Coast wars, 1865–68

Conflict on the East Coast was sparked early in 1865 by the arrival of Pai Marire evangelists from Taranaki. It is not clear that Te Ua and some of his emissaries intended aggression but one, Kereopa ★Te Rau, was involved in the killing of the missionary Carl Volkner at Opotiki on 2 March 1865. Kereopa and other Pai Marire emissaries made hundreds of converts among local tribes; and colonists and kupapa undertook several campaigns against them between June 1865 and January 1866. One, June–October 1865, was in effect a civil war between Pai Marire and pro-government factions of the Ngati Porou tribe. Despite early successes, the Pai Marire faction was overcome by groups led by Ropata

New Zealand Wars

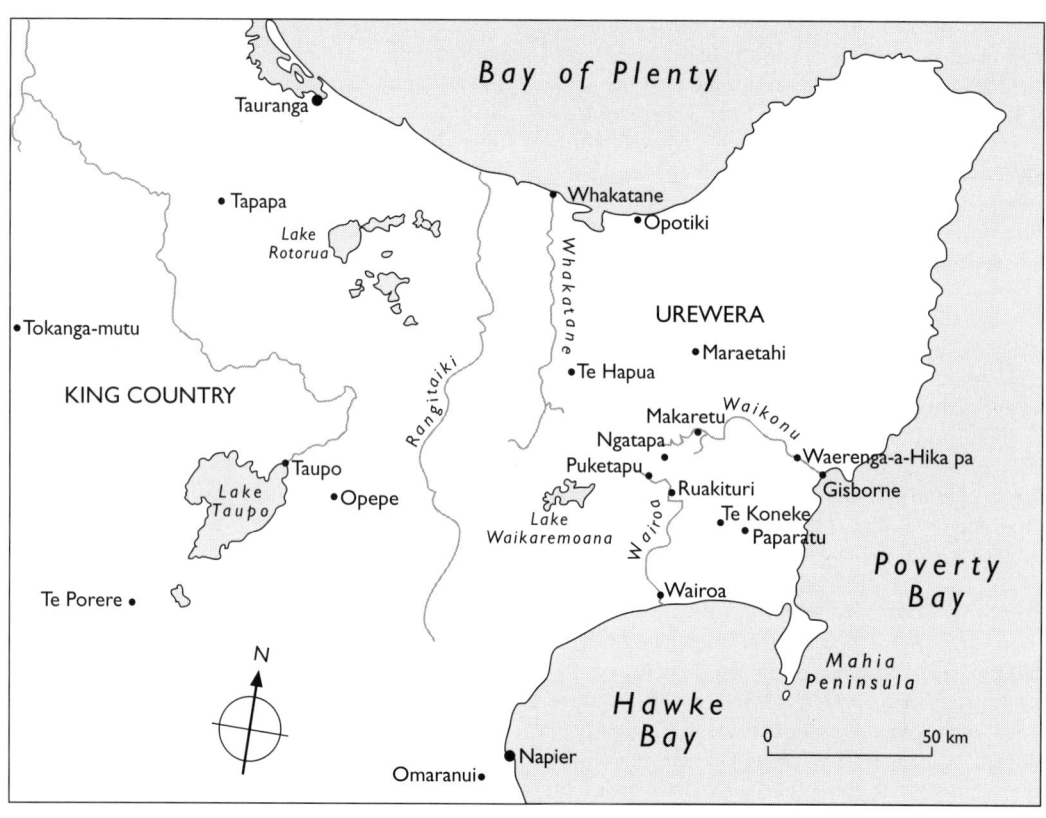

Map 18d East Coast region, 1866–72

★Wahawaha, Mokena Kohere, and Henare Potae, with government help. Thereafter Ngati Porou, who had provided substantial support to the King Movement in the Waikato War, were solidly pro-government. During the same period, the Arawa confederation conducted a series of expeditions against Pai Marire supporters. The latter phases of these two campaigns merged with a third—the operations of the 'East Coast Expedition' of colonial troops from Taranaki which landed at Opotiki in September 1865. Until October, these forces operated against Pai Marire adherents inland of Opotiki. In November, they moved against the tribes of Poverty Bay who were suspected of Pai Marire sympathies. The major engagement was the siege of Waerenga-a-Hika pa, which fell on 22 November 1865. Maori resistance seems to have been somewhat half-hearted, as though the garrison was not fully committed to war. About 400 were taken prisoner, some of whom were exiled to the Chatham Islands. In December 1865 and January 1866, northern hapu of Ngati Kahungunu engaged in their own civil war, pro-government against Pai Marire factions. Again, with the help of the government, the kawanatanga faction triumphed.

It is primarily this cluster of campaigns which is sometimes known as the 'East Coast War', but there were also four other, less directly linked, campaigns in the region. In October 1866, a party of Pai Marire adherents, mainly Ngati Hineuru, 'invaded' Hawke's Bay and camped at Omarunui. Their motives are not entirely clear. It is possible that that they were only eighty strong, and that their position was unfortified. In any case, they were attacked by Napier militia and Ngati Kahungunu kupapa under Lieutenant-Colonel George ★Whitmore on 12 October. Twenty-one were killed and fifty-eight captured. Some of the latter joined the Waerenga-a-hika exiles in the Chatham Islands. Premier Edward Stafford himself alleged that some of the sixteen government casualties 'resulted from the cross-fire of our own people'. The second campaign—in reality a long series of raids, punitive expeditions, and skirmishes which took place inland of Opotiki between early 1866 and early 1868—resulted from the reluctance of the Tuhoe and related groups to accept the confiscation of land in the north of their territory. There were few casualties on either side, but one chief, Eru Tamaikowha, showed himself to be a guerrilla leader of considerable resource. The third of these discrete campaigns also arose from resistance to confiscation, this time in the area inland of Tauranga. Small sections of Ngai Te Rangi and Ngati Ranginui, numbering about sixty, fought a low-intensity guerrilla war against 800 colonial troops and Arawa kupapa for the first three months of 1867. The fourth and last of this set of East Coast campaigns consisted of an incursion into the territory of the kupapa Arawa in March 1867, by a group apparently consisting mainly of Waikato, led by the prophet Hakaraia. Little has been published about these operations. Indeed, for the whole of the East Coast wars, good studies of politics have not been matched by close investigation of military aspects, and this conflict in particular requires further research.

Titokowaru's war, 1868–69

After November 1866, Taranaki remained in a state of uneasy peace until June 1868. Peace was undermined, however, by gradual government implementation of the confiscation of Maori land. South Taranaki Maori resisted these encroachments first passively, then actively but non-violently, then violently. On 9 June 1868 fighting again broke out between colonial troops and the followers of the Nga Ruahine prophet leader, Riwha ★Titokowaru. Titokowaru began his war with fewer than 100 warriors against a 'Patea Field Force' under McDonnell, now a lieutenant-colonel, which eventually totalled 1000 men. He attempted to rectify the disparity by provoking McDonnell into attacking him at a time and place of his own choosing. The provocation included propaganda and raids, notably an attack on the small colonial redoubt of Turuturu-mokai on 12 July. The time was as soon as possible before McDonnell could fully mobilise and train his troops, and the place was Titokowaru's home village of Te Ngutu-o-te-Manu. McDonnell's first two expeditions to Te Ngutu (12–13 and 21 August) proved abortive, but the third, on 7 September, resulted in a full-scale battle deep in the bush between 350 colonials and kupapa and sixty of Titokowaru's warriors. Despite the disparity in numbers, Titokowaru won a complete victory. McDonnell lost his second-in-command, Major Gustavus von ★Tempsky, and suffered fifty other casualties. An unusual feature of this Maori victory was that it not only repelled an enemy expedition, but also led to a considerable reconquest of territory.

McDonnell was replaced by Colonel Whitmore, who pulled together the demoralised Patea Field Force and secured reinforcements. Early in November he was outflanked by Titokowaru, who made a sudden march south to Moturoa, near Waverley, where he built a pa. With the out-districts of Wanganui exposed, Whitmore felt compelled to attack him there on 7 November. Again, despite superior numbers, the government forces were severely defeated. Apart from two outlying posts at Patea and Waverley, the whole of south Taranaki was abandoned to Titokowaru and the colonial army withdrew to the outskirts of Wanganui. Titokowaru, with mounting support from local and even distant tribes increasing his numbers to perhaps 400, followed them up, building a large modern pa at Tauranga Ika, near Nukumaru, as his base. There was then a lull in fighting while Titokowaru consolidated his position, and Whitmore took some of his troops to the East Coast to oppose ★Te Kooti. Whitmore returned in mid January and with forces now approaching 2000 men advanced on Tauranga Ika. Whether he would have had any better luck than at Te Ngutu or Moturoa will never be known, because Titokowaru abandoned his pa on 3 February and retreated north, his force breaking up as he went. The reasons for the abandonment of Tauranga Ika and the collapse of Titokowaru's support remain somewhat mysterious, but it was clearly a matter of some internal dispute rather than enemy action.

Titokowaru fought several successful rearguard actions on his retreat north. But, with an ever-diminishing band of followers and in the face of very vigorous pursuit, escape was ultimately all he could manage. He took refuge in inland north Taranaki, and government forces reoccupied the south. Some of his followers, notably the Pakakohe, were hunted down, captured, and sent to prison in Dunedin, where a number died. Just how serious a threat Titokowaru represented was underlined ten days after the abandonment of Tauranga Ika, when Kingite raiders struck the north Taranaki settlement of Pukearuhe, or the Whitecliffs, killing nine people. It is difficult to visualise the colonial government coping with an alliance

Bush fighting: volunteers ambushed at Te Ngutu-o-te-Manu in 1868, a wood engraving by Samuel Calvert (*Alexander Turnbull Library, D-PP0047-10-08*)

between Titokowaru, the King Movement, and Te Kooti. But the collapse of Titokowaru's support made the issue hypothetical.

Te Kooti's war, 1868–72

Te Kooti was a man of the Rongowhakaata tribe of Poverty Bay. He had fought on the government side at Waerenga-a-Hika in November 1865, but had then been arrested on suspicion of aiding the enemy. He was imprisoned without trial on the Chatham Islands, along with the Hauhau captured at Waerenga-a-Hika and Omarunui. On the Chathams, Te Kooti developed his remarkable Ringatu religion, and with it a strong hold over his fellow prisoners. On 4 July 1868 he led them in an extraordinary escape from the islands aboard the captured schooner *Rifleman*. Te Kooti and his 300 followers, about half of whom were adult males, were soon pursued by government forces, despite their request for peace. Though only a minority of Te Kooti's men had guns as yet, they checked their pursuers on three occasions (Paparatu, 20 July, Te Koneke, 24 July, and Ruakituri, 8 August) before escaping to Puketapu in the mountains fringing Lake Waikaremoana.

Three months later, on the night of 9–10 November 1868, Te Kooti and his best warriors made a well-planned surprise attack on the Maori and Pakeha settlements of Poverty Bay. About thirty Europeans and at least twenty Maori, men, women, and children, were killed, some Maori being executed in the days after the raid. Te Kooti remained at Poverty Bay for a week, then commenced a withdrawal inland in the face of vengeful colonial and kupapa forces. Te Kooti dug in at Makaretu (or Te Karetu) on 23 November to block pursuit. The force in front of Makaretu grew to 800 men, almost entirely kupapa of Ngati Kahungunu, Ngati Porou, and Rongowhakaata, Te Kooti's own tribe. On 2 December the kupapa stormed the position, only to find that Te Kooti had gone with most of his people, leaving only a gallant rearguard of about eighty men, who were overwhelmed. Te Kooti took refuge at the naturally strong traditional pa of Ngatapa. The kupapa, reduced to 450 men by a dispute between Ngati Kahungunu and Ngati Porou, pursued him there. Despite the determined leadership of Ropata Wahawaha, their 5 December attack on Ngatapa failed.

Te Kooti's attack on Poverty Bay, and his subsequent escape from vengeance, alarmed and enraged the colonists. The pick of the colonial forces were shifted from Wanganui to Napier under Colonel Whitmore, and a combined force of 700 constabulary and Ngati Porou had assembled before Ngatapa by 30 December 1868. There were at least 500 people inside the pa, including Maori prisoners from Poverty Bay, but only about 200 Ringatu warriors. Despite the natural strength of Ngatapa, the government forces gradually surrounded the pa, and Te Kooti seemed doomed. But, on the night of 4–5 January 1869, he and most of his people lowered themselves by ropes down a sheer cliff face and escaped into the bush. Many were captured in a vigorous pursuit, however, and 120 adult male prisoners were executed with the consent of government officials.

The government hoped that Te Kooti was crippled, even killed. In fact he was recuperating among his Tuhoe friends in the Urewera mountains. In March and April, he launched two sustained and successful raids on Whakatane and Mohaka. Whitmore again returned from Taranaki in an attempt to deal with him. In May, government forces mounted an ambitious three-pronged invasion of the Urewera with 1300 colonials and kupapa. The invasion did some damage to Tuhoe, but did not succeed in catching Te Kooti. In June 1869, Te Kooti left the Urewera in any case. He began an epic fighting journey that was to take him, his followers, and his opponents right around Lake Taupo, to Rotorua, and back to the Urewera over the next nine months, circling the heart of the North Island.

During the initial movement from the Urewera to south Taupo, Te Kooti's men surprised and destroyed a colonial cavalry patrol at Opepe on 7 June 1869, killing nine. Operations then halted over winter, as a new colonial government reoriented itself to Te Kooti's new location. Te Kooti was able to make a side trip to Tokanga-mutu, the King Movement capital, where he tried (and ultimately failed) to obtain Kingite support. He did obtain a certain amount of support from Ngati Tuwharetoa of Taupo, though the mix of commitment and coercion is unclear. Fighting recommenced in September 1869 when, in an attempt to divide and defeat his massing enemies, Te Kooti made two unsuccessful attacks on Ngati Kahungunu kupapa under Henare ★Tomoana. Te Kooti then built a pa at Te Porere, and was severely defeated there by 540 colonials and kupapa under McDonnell, Keepa ★Te Rangihiwinui, and Tomoana on 3 October. Te Kooti lost thirty-seven killed, but succeeded in making his escape with the rest—his numbers at this time are particularly difficult to estimate. Te Porere is now the best preserved modern pa site in the country, and it is important to note that it is not a good example of the art form. Mastery of the modern pa system was not among Te Kooti's numerous military skills.

Te Kooti marched around the western shore of Lake Taupo and reached the southern Waikato by January 1870, where he joined the prophet-leader Hakaraia at his village of Tapapa. About 1200 government troops, mostly kupapa, converged on Tapapa. One government official commented, 'If we do not get Te Kooti, we never deserve to'. Te Kooti fled Tapapa, then on 25 January doubled back on his pursuers and attacked them. His men had mixed success in the resulting skirmishes, but the confusion among his pursuers enabled him to complete his escape. After marching north towards Te Puke, Te Kooti then turned south to Rotorua, and began negotiation with Arawa elders. Younger Arawa warriors, along with Lieutenant Gilbert *Mair, arrived on 7 February, in the midst of these talks, and immediately attacked Te Kooti and his followers. Only an inspired rearguard action by Eru Peka McLean, Te Kooti's bilingual half-caste lieutenant, enabled Te Kooti and his people to escape into the Urewera mountains, their old refuge.

For the next two years, government forces—mainly kupapa of various tribes—hunted Te Kooti from pillar to post throughout the Urewera. Tough, well-armed, and well-led Arawa, Wanganui, Ngati Porou, and Ngati Kahungunu expeditions hunted almost competitively. The fugitives' camps were stormed at Maraetahi, on 23 March 1870, and Te Hapua, on 1 September 1871, but Te Kooti himself escaped these and other close shaves. Early in 1872, he fled the Urewera to the King Country, accompanied by only six followers. There he found safe sanctuary and the New Zealand Wars ended.

Conclusions
Technologies of war

The key to the relative effectiveness of Maori resistance was the modern pa. Modern pa and strategies associated with them featured most in campaigns in which Maori were most successful, and least in those in which they were least successful. The modern pa evolved from the traditional pa, through the intermediate stage of the 'gunfighter' or Musket Wars pa. But in its purest form it differed strikingly from its predecessors. It was made largely, in some cases almost entirely, of earth, not wood. Its profile was low, not high. It was located away from population centres rather than beside them, and its key components were anti-artillery bunkers and firing trenches, not fighting stages and ditches.

The assertion that, with the modern pa, the Maori invented modern trench warfare has proved a little controversial. The counter-claim that Maori somehow plagiarised their techniques from European precursors does not stand up to scrutiny, but the notion that there were European precursors is more legitimately contestable. Two obvious candidates for the birth of modern trench warfare are the *Crimean War of 1854–56 and the American Civil War of 1861–65. But these postdate the appearance of the modern pa in the Northern War by at least nine years. Earlier, even much earlier, European precedents for the use of earthworks and trenches, especially during sieges, are easy to find. But *trench warfare*—wars in which the principal type of battle was the attack and defence of earthwork trench-and-bunker systems—is not. The British showed some technical interest in Maori pa during the Wars, but it seems that their lessons were forgotten if they were ever learnt, and had to be reinvented the hard way on the *Western Front in the *First World War.

One such lesson was that modern pa were almost as effective against modern firearms as against earlier technology. The New Zealand Wars straddle the 'firearms revolution' of the mid nineteenth century, which is said to have facilitated European conquests worldwide. In the Taranaki War, the British used Enfield rifles and heavy Armstrong guns instead of muskets and smooth-bore cannon. Colonial troops subsequently added revolvers and breech-loading carbines. In May 1864, an Armstrong gun fired a hundred 50-kilogram shells into the Gate Pa, a small earthwork, at virtually point blank range. Some shots missed; most hit, yet the garrison survived. The modern pa was an effective antidote to European superiority in guns, even after the 'firearms revolution'.

Yet the modern pa could not compensate for other Maori disadvantages. One, about which few details are known, was the supply and support of their own weaponry. In the later 1860s, Maori quite often captured rifles, carbines, and revolvers from colonials or kupapa. Maori also used cannon on several occasions in the New Zealand Wars, though never with decisive effect. Muskets and shotguns, the latter preferably double-barrelled, remained their mainstay, possibly because of the greater difficulty of ammunition supply for cannon and modern firearms. Even muskets and shotguns, moreover, presented logistic difficulties. There is evidence to show that Maori sometimes made their own gunpowder, that they repaired guns, and recycled cartridges and percussion caps. But homemade ammunition was unreliable in quality and quantity, and Maori did not make guns. American whalers, illicit European gun-runners, and above all neutral and even kupapa Maori, were sporadically sources of guns and ammunition. But the problem of resisting Europe while relying on it for technology was never fully solved.

Another important European advantage was the possession of steamships, which were first used in the Wellington conflict of 1846 but became increasingly important from 1863. Steam allowed the British to penetrate up the Waikato River against the current into the heartland of the King Movement. Steamers and the barges they towed provided troop transport, artillery support, and, above all, supply transport for Cameron's invasion. Steamships were also important in allowing the colonial forces to switch rapidly between the war against Titokowaru and the war against Te Kooti in 1868–69 (see COLONIAL NAVAL ACTIVITIES).

In the end, however, the greatest European advantage and Maori disadvantage was in the depth and

New Zealand Wars, Australian involvement in

breadth of resources. Maori were outnumbered in most engagements, often massively. The resisting Maori were part-time soldiers; their enemies were normally full-timers. This was true of most colonial troops and of some kupapa, as well as of professional imperials. Even a militiaman in the field for six months was replaced in his domestic economy by his pay, and supplied with rations. Maori soldiers remained a vital part of their domestic labour force, and sometimes had to find their own food. Given these disparities, it seems reasonable to conclude that the eventual Maori defeat in the New Zealand Wars was less remarkable than the degree of their success along the way.

The New Zealand Wars in memory

It can be claimed that the New Zealand Wars fell victim to historical amnesia. This is not wholly true. There was quite a vigorous nineteenth century literature. One minority strand (including T.B. Collinson, *Remarks on the Military Operations in New Zealand*, 1853; Frederick Maning, *History of the War in the North ...*, 1862; Hugh Carleton, *The Life of Henry Williams ...*, 1874), subsequently shunted aside by the majority interpretation, doubted British victory in the Northern War. Another strand (e.g. various *Southern Monthly Magazine* articles, 1864), beginning in 1860 and emphasising the supposed superiority of colonial to imperial troops, was significant in the development of New Zealand proto-nationalism in that it discerned a difference between New Zealand Britons and metropolitan Britons. The contribution of colonial units to military operations in the Taranaki War of 1860–61 was respectable but not major. Yet a legend emerged which in some ways foreshadowed the Anzac legend of the First World War, namely that pragmatic amateur New Zealanders made better soldiers than hidebound British professionals. This view was developed most fully by the colonial politician William Fox (*The War in New Zealand*, 1866). In one of New Zealand history's earliest debates, British soldier Colonel James Alexander responded with a defence of the performance of imperial troops (*Bush Fighting ...*, 1873)—a defence revived virtually point for point by historian B.J. Dalton in 1966 ('A New Look at the Maori Wars of the Sixties', *Historical Studies*, vol. 12, no. 46). The Wars also featured in nineteenth century fiction, including that of G.A. Henty, an important disseminator of British imperial mythology to the young (*Maori and Settler. A Story of the New Zealand War*, n.d.). The best twentieth century fictional treatments of the Wars are those of novelists William Satchell (*The Greenstone Door*, 1914), Errol Brathwaite (New Zealand Wars trilogy, 1964–67), and Maurice Shadbolt (New Zealand Wars trilogy, 1986–93). There were cinematic treatments by Rudall Hayward (*Rewi's Last Stand*, 1925 and 1940, *The Te Kooti Trail*, 1927) and Geoff Murphy (*Utu*, 1983).

Twentieth century historians of the wars before the 1980s include British army historian J.W. Fortescue (*A History of the British Army*, 1899–1930) and popular historians Edgar Holt (*The Strangest War*, 1962), Tom Gibson (*The Maori Wars*, 1972), and Tony Simpson (*Te Riri Pakeha ...*, 1979). Academic historians, such as Keith Sinclair (*The Origins of the Maori Wars*, 1957), tended to concentrate on causes and consequences rather than course and combat. An important military study was *The New Zealand Wars ...* (1922–23) by James ★Cowan, which was based partly on Maori and Pakeha oral evidence. Revision took place in the 1980s, with the publication of James Belich's *New Zealand Wars and the Victorian Interpretation of Racial Conflict* in 1986. A recent series of articles by Christopher Pugsley (*New Zealand Defence Quarterly*, 1996–99) argued that Belich had swung back the pendulum too far in favour of Maori. Revisionist histories, most notably Judith Binney's study of Te Kooti (*Redemption Songs ...*, 1995), have used a considerable amount of Maori evidence. But modern Maori histories of the wars, by Maori and using Maori historical techniques as well as sources, have yet to emerge. When and if they do, they will face the challenge of using an essentially tribal art form to understand an essentially pan-tribal phenomenon.

Despite this substantial corpus, the claim that the Wars fell victim to amnesia, or at least to a strange process of downplaying and dilution, is partly true. In 1933, the respected historian Sir James Hight wrote: 'The Wars have no claim to great importance. ... They were small in scale, taught few ... lessons in the art of war, and are scarcely entitled to be classed in the category "war" as recognised by international law.' As late as 1983–84, fewer than five per cent of first-year New Zealand history students, let alone the general public, had ever heard of Titokowaru. Even in the present, a comparison of the historic sites and monuments of the New Zealand Wars and the American Civil War suggests a staggering disparity in remembrance. Reaction to a television documentary series on the Wars, screened in 1998, suggested that their drama, trauma, and significance was news to most New Zealanders.

J. Cowan, *The New Zealand Wars: A History of the Maori Campaigns and the Pioneering Period*, 2 vols (Government Printer, Wellington, 1922–23); J. Belich, *The New Zealand Wars and the Victorian Interpretation of Racial Conflict* (Auckland University Press, Auckland, 1986).

JAMES BELICH

New Zealand Wars, Australian involvement in

The ★New Zealand Wars were the first in which Australia was significantly involved. When conflict first

384

New Zealand Wars, Australian involvement in

erupted, in 1845–46, imperial troops based there were deployed to New Zealand, a pattern that was repeated during the more serious fighting of the 1860s. Until 1861, when a separate New Zealand command was established, the commander of the imperial forces in Australia was responsible for the military campaign. The first direct Australian involvement in New Zealand occurred as a result of the Taranaki War of 1860–61, and was naval in character. The Victorian Naval Service became the first distinctive Australian colonial unit to engage in hostilities, when the Victorian colonial government released the 880-ton naval war steamer *Victoria* for operations in New Zealand waters on 1 May 1860, after she had transported imperial troops from Hobart to New Zealand. During July 1860 some Victorian naval personnel joined the Royal Naval Brigade then defending New Plymouth, and took part in the local fighting in the following December. The *Victoria* remained on station in a logistic role until late in 1863.

During the Waikato campaign of 1863–64, Australian involvement was more extensive. The New Zealand government paid £9500 to the Sydney-based Australian Steamship Navigation Company to build a 304-ton river gunboat, *Pioneer*, which took seventeen weeks to complete. The first war vessel constructed in Australia for export, she was driven by a rear paddle wheel and was fitted with twin turrets for Armstrong cannon and cupolas for rifles. With a composite crew of New South Welshmen and New Zealanders, she began operations on the Waikato River in late October 1863. In March 1864 two further steam paddle gunboats, the *Koheroa* and *Rangiriri*, were constructed in Sydney by P.N. Russell & Company. Each was transported across the Tasman in three sections and assembled at Port Waikato. The government also purchased the *Gundagai* (98 tons) from the Adelaide Murray Navigation Company, and appointed as Superintendent of the River Transport Flotilla Francis Cadell, the pioneer river navigator of South Australia. The *Alexandra* (340 tons) and *Lady Barkly* were also acquired in Victoria and New South Wales respectively.

The Australians were also a source of war materiel. Rather than wait the eight to ten weeks required to ship artillery from the United Kingdom to New Zealand, the colonial government purchased from the Victorians six Armstrong 12-pounder guns complete with ammunition. Tenders were called in Sydney for twenty cavalry trumpets, forty bugles, and hundreds of greatcoats. Draught horses and mounts for the ★Colonial Defence Force cavalry, weapons, ammunition, uniforms, and machinery used by the River Transport Flotilla were also purchased. Five hundred Enfield rifles were shipped from the imperial barracks in Hobart, and a battery of mortar pieces, designed and cast in Sydney, were probably the first armaments to be manufactured and exported from Australia.

It was as a source of manpower, however, that the Australian colonies made their greatest mark in New Zealand. Determined to enlist 5000 ★military settlers to garrison the Waikato, the government looked across the Tasman to fill the ranks. With considerable public support, Lieutenant-Colonel G.D. Pitt of the New Zealand Militia began recruiting in Melbourne in August 1863, the first 400 recruits being described in the press as 'Pitt's Militia'. Before the Australian colonial governments lost enthusiasm for this drain on their manpower in early 1864, about 2450 Australians had been recruited in Victoria, New South Wales, Tasmania, Queensland, and South Australia—38 per cent of the eventual 6336 military settlers. Most of the Australian recruits originated in Great Britain—only 5.5 per cent were Australian-born—and were drawn from labouring or trade backgrounds. There were several groups from the numerous Australian militia regiments.

Transported to New Zealand with their families in more than eleven ships, the recruits were initially housed in cheap corrugated iron huts at Otahuhu Camp, fifteen kilometres south of Auckland, where basic training was undertaken. They were thereafter posted to five regiments: 1st to 4th Waikato Regiments and the Taranaki Military Settlers. The 1st and 4th Waikato Regiments and the Taranaki Military Settlers had a majority of Australians in their ranks: 55 per cent, 67 per cent, and 61 per cent respectively. Within the regiments, several distinctive Australian groups were retained. On 14 September 1863 twenty-six men of Pitt's Militia, serving in the 1st Waikato Regiment, relieved a garrison under siege in the Pukekohe East Presbyterian Church stockade. A company of Melbourne Volunteers (also known as the Melbourne Contingent) distinguished themselves during the battle of Kaitake near New Plymouth on 25 March 1864, General Duncan ★Cameron praising the 'spirited manner' in which they had assaulted one of the key enemy stockades. At least three companies of the Taranaki Military Settlers were Victorians.

The Waikato War generated great public interest in both Victoria, which contributed more men and materiel than any other colony, and New South Wales. In August 1863 Howard Willoughby was sent by the Melbourne *Argus* to report on the war—Australia's first war correspondent. His incisive and impartial reports outlined the incipient characteristics that would come to define Australia's soldiers in the following century. At Christmas time 1863 he wrote: 'They have to march without beer, they have to fight without beer.'

More than twenty Australians were killed in action during the New Zealand Wars. Among them was Major Walter Herford, a solicitor and volunteer militia officer from Adelaide, who was wounded at Orakau and died three months later. Lieutenant J.S. Perceval was killed with six other Victorians in the Titi Hill battle. J.S. Phelps, an assistant surgeon, is the only known Australian-born professional soldier to lose his life while serving with a British regiment in New Zealand. At least thirteen Australians also lost their lives to disease or accidents, mostly drownings. Able Seaman Henry Serjeant of the Victorian Naval Service, who died at New Plymouth in August 1861 after being accidentally shot in the foot, is probably the first member of a distinct Australian unit to become a casualty. More than 300 deserted, most likely to try their hand on the goldfields of Thames and Otago. With the disbandment of the regiments in 1867, the military settlement scheme was implemented, albeit inadequately. Only about half of the Australian recruits remained to take up their allotments, and a high proportion of them, tiring of the poor conditions, and many of them single men, soon abandoned their holdings. Probably most returned to Australia.

L.L. Barton, *Australians in the Waikato 1863–64* (Library of Australian History, Sydney, 1979); F. Glen, *For Glory and a Farm* (Whakatane Historical Society, Whakatane, 1983).

FRANK GLEN

New Zealand Women's Royal Army Corps see WOMEN IN THE ARMED FORCES

New Zealanders in the service of other nations

The great majority of New Zealanders who have served in other nations' forces have done so in the British armed forces. This is a reflection of New Zealand's status as part of the British Empire, and later Commonwealth, and of close ties of kinship that have existed between Great Britain and New Zealand. Until well after the ★Second World War New Zealanders identified with Britain, and regarded themselves as British. Inevitably some of them chose to make their careers in the British forces, where opportunities for advancement were greater than in New Zealand. This process was greatly enhanced by the two world wars, when many New Zealanders residing in Britain chose to enlist in the British forces. In 1916, for example, there were forty-nine New Zealanders in the King's Oversea Dominions Regiment (King Edward's Horse), a unit formed just after the ★Boer War and manned exclusively by personnel from the Dominions and colonies. Others were dispatched by New Zealand to serve in the Royal Navy and the RAF for the duration, and a significant number, particularly in the RAF, continued on to peacetime careers in these services, the most prominent being Air Chief Marshal Sir Keith ★Park. The highest-ranked New Zealander in the British forces has been Marshal of the Royal Air Force Sir Samuel ★Elworthy, who was Chief of the Defence Staff from 1967 to 1971. Admiral Sir Gordon ★Tait, Second Sea Lord from 1977 to 1979, and Lieutenant-General Lord ★Freyberg are the New Zealanders who have achieved the highest British naval and military ranks respectively. A smaller number of New Zealanders have served in other Commonwealth forces, especially Australian. There were several hundreds of New Zealanders in the Australian Imperial Force during the ★First World War—balanced by a considerable number of Australians serving in 1NZEF. The same situation occurred during the Second World War and, on a lesser scale, the ★Korean War. During the Second World War a handful of New Zealand civilians also joined local volunteer battalions in Malaya and Hong Kong when the Japanese threat became acute.

By comparison very few New Zealanders have served in non-Commonwealth forces. They were constrained by the provisions of the Foreign Enlistment Act 1870, a British statute which applied in New Zealand, as in other colonies. This prohibited enlistment in military service against a state that was at peace with the British Empire. No prosecutions have ever been brought against New Zealanders under this legislation. In December 1989 the UN General Assembly adopted the International Convention against the Recruitment, Use, Financing and Training of Mercenaries. Twenty-two ratifications are required for this measure to come into force, but there had only been seven by 1997.

Apart from the exigencies of war (see RESISTANCE IN EUROPE, NEW ZEALANDERS AND), there are a number of reasons why New Zealanders have joined foreign forces—personal circumstances, financial gain, a search for adventure, ideological motivation, evasion of uncongenial circumstances, or ethnic solidarity. A number of New Zealanders have served in the United States armed forces, including Lieutenant Patrick ★Shanahan, J.A. Tyrell-Baxter, who was granted a chaplain's commission during the Second World War, and Captain R.M. Reston, a ★Kayforce member who later joined the US Army. An unknown number of New Zealanders have also served in the French Foreign Legion, the most prominent being James ★Waddell. New Zealanders have occasionally served as mercenaries, the most notable example perhaps being Bernard Freyberg. At least one was killed while serving with Rhodesian forces during the 1970s.

The earliest known example of New Zealanders serving in foreign forces for ideological reasons occurred during the Spanish Civil War. On the Republican side, at least ten men served in the International Brigade, most in the British Battalion. They included Tom Spiller, who went to Spain in 1937 but subsequently returned to New Zealand on a propaganda tour. Captain E.N. Griffiths served as a fighter pilot in the Republican Air Force. Three of the New Zealanders were killed in action during the war. A New Zealand doctor, D.W. Jolly, served with a British medical unit, while three nurses were sent from New Zealand in 1937. Two other New Zealand women are known to have been involved as nurses as well. At least one New Zealander, Philip Cross, fought on the Nationalist side. He happened to be in Spain with a film company, and was motivated by a desire for adventure rather than ideology. During the Second World War only one New Zealander, R.N. ★Courlander, is known to have joined an enemy force.

During the First World War, some attempts were made by unnaturalised Dalmatians, whose classification as enemy aliens prevented them from being conscripted for 1NZEF, to form units for service with the Serbian Army, but the New Zealand government resisted requests for assistance in transporting them to the theatre of war, and eventually, much to their chagrin, interned many of them. More recently, members of the Jewish community may have served in the Israeli Army.

S.M. Skudder, ' "Bringing it Home", New Zealand responses to the Spanish Civil War, 1936–1939' (PhD thesis, University of Waikato, 1986).

Newall, Colonel Stuart (9 May 1843–3 August 1919) was a leading colonial soldier in the late nineteenth century. A Scot, he emigrated to New Zealand in 1863, and, after trying his hand on the goldfields, enlisted in the Waikato Militia. Transferring to the ★Armed Constabulary in 1868, he served in the campaigns against ★Titokowaru and ★Te Kooti. Commissioned in the field as a sub-inspector in 1869, he spent the next decade commanding Armed Constabulary posts in the Waikato. He was commissioned in the New Zealand Militia in 1874. In 1881 he helped arrest Te Whiti o Rongomai at ★Parihaka. Two years later he transferred to the ★Permanent Militia, and became Adjutant of the Canterbury Volunteer District. He proved an able administrator, and in 1891 was appointed to command the Wellington, Wairarapa, Taranaki, and Wanganui military districts. In 1898 he led a 120-man contingent to crush the ★Dog Tax rebellion in Northland. From March to December 1900 he commanded the Fifth Contingent sent by New Zealand to the ★Boer War, and was mentioned in dispatches. He then returned to New Zealand to resume command of the Wellington Military District. He was made CB in 1901, but was suddenly retired two years later, probably because of his age. He led a group of special constables ('Massey's Cossacks') in Wellington during the 1913 maritime strike, and was from 1915 to 1918 Commandant of King George V Hospital at Rotorua.

Ngarimu, Lieutenant Moana-nui-a-kiwa (7 April 1919–27 March 1943) is the only Maori to win the ★Victoria Cross while serving with New Zealand forces. Born at Whareponga north of Waipiro Bay, of Te Aitanga-a-Mate hapu of Ngati Porou, he was the son of a sheep station owner. After schooling at Te Aute College, he shepherded on his father's station. Volunteering for 28th (Maori) Battalion, he left New Zealand with 2NZEF's Second Echelon in May 1940. He was commissioned in April 1942, and served as an intelligence officer before being given command of a platoon in C Company. His decoration recognised his inspirational conduct during the breakthrough at Tebaga Gap in the latter stages of the ★North African campaign. On 26 March 1943 he led his platoon in an attack on one of the lower hills of Point 209. Two machine-gun posts were destroyed as the Maori troops swept on to the crest. They then repelled a fierce German counter-attack. Although wounded in the leg and shoulder, Ngarimu would not leave his men. Close-quarter fighting raged during the night as the Germans attempted to push his depleted platoon off the hill. At one point Ngarimu resorted to stones to supplement his submachine-gun in driving back an attack. He also led a counter-attack to reclaim some overrun positions. When the Germans next morning launched another attack he stood to meet them, firing his submachine-gun from the hip until killed. His posthumous VC was presented to his family in an official ceremony at Ruatoria on 6 October 1943. He is commemorated by a scholarship.

Nicholas, Sergeant Henry James (11 June 1891–23 October 1918) was a ★Victoria Cross winner in the ★First World War. A carpenter from Christchurch, he volunteered for 1NZEF in February 1916, and joined the 1st Battalion, Canterbury Regiment, on the ★Western Front in the following September. He had already won an MM by the time he took part in the New Zealand attack on Polderhoek Chateau on 3 December 1917—the action in which he earned the highest decoration. He distinguished himself by rushing forward ahead of his section to destroy a German strongpoint which was inflicting heavy casualties on the advancing troops. He used bomb and bayonet to overcome the sixteen-man enemy garrison. A sergeant from June 1918, he was killed in a skirmish with a German force at Beaudignies during the last month of the war.

Nixon, Colonel Marmaduke George (1814–27 May 1864) was the 'father of New Zealand Cavalry'. Born in Malta, he attended the Royal Military College, Sandhurst, before obtaining a commission in the 39th Regiment. He served in India and took part in the Gwalior campaign in 1843. After retiring in the rank of

North African campaign

major, he emigrated to New Zealand in 1852. When fighting broke out in Taranaki in 1860, he raised a volunteer corps, the Royal Cavalry Volunteers, to protect settlers south of Auckland. Although disbanded in 1862, this unit was in effect reconstituted in the following year, when Nixon, a member of Parliament since 1861, was invited to form a 'Mounted Defence Force'. Troops were stationed in Auckland, Howick, and Otahuhu before Nixon, who was appointed as a Commandant in the *Colonial Defence Force, led them in the invasion of the Waikato. On 21 February 1864, during the outflanking movement which finally defeated the Kingite forces, his cavalry corps launched a surprise attack on the largely unprotected settlement of Rangiaowhia, south of Te Awamutu. While he and his troops, dismounted, were helping mop up Maori resistance, he was shot in the chest from the doorway of a hut. When he succumbed to his wound some months later, he became one of the highest-ranked fatalities among the imperial and colonial forces in the *New Zealand Wars.

North African campaign Between February 1940 and May 1943 2NZEF fought Germans and Italians in Egypt, Libya, and Tunisia as part of an ultimately successful Commonwealth effort to clear North Africa of enemy forces. This campaign stemmed from North Africa's strategic importance to the Commonwealth. Not only was the Suez Canal a vital communication artery but also the Middle East oil fields were crucial to the sustenance of a mechanised war effort. Italy's entry to the war on Germany's side on 10 June 1940, therefore, presented a substantial danger, given the proximity of its forces in Libya and *Abyssinia (Italy's colonial possessions) to the Suez Canal. But it also represented an opportunity, for the North African theatre was the only place, after France fell, where the land war could be taken to the enemy with any hope of success. The defeat of Italy, the weaker member of the Axis, would give control of the North African coast and bring many advantages. The movement of Allied convoys through the Mediterranean would be facilitated, and the position of Malta rendered more secure.

The physical conditions in North Africa were daunting. Between the Nile Delta in the east and the rugged terrain of Tunisia 2200 kilometres to the west lay a wide, flat area of rocky desert, broken by escarpments and sunken depressions. Nights in the desert could be extremely cold and the winter was often rainy, but the usual conditions for the troops were heat and flies, made more unpleasant by occasional sandstorms. Sand also wreaked havoc with machines, while the transport of the vast quantities of fuel and water needed by any army to cross the desert presented huge logistical problems, not eased by the fact that there was only one good road, which ran along the coast. Allied supply lines extended around Africa; only in desperate circumstances would a convoy of merchant ships risk passing through the Mediterranean directly to Egypt. Although Axis supply lines from Italy to Libya (later Tunisia) were considerably shorter, they were exposed to British air and naval attack from Malta. The outcome of the campaign would ultimately be determined by the imbalance in the resources devoted to it by the two sides. Whereas the Allies were willing, and able, eventually to build up an overwhelmingly superior force, the Germans in particular regarded the theatre as a sideshow to the Eastern Front, and only belatedly poured resources into it.

At first, however, the advantage in material terms seemed to lie with the Axis. An Italian Army of 250,000 men was poised to strike at Egypt. When this mighty host crossed the frontier in September 1940, however, it moved with great caution. After advancing just 100 kilometres, it paused to rebuild its supplies. Three months later it was decisively defeated by the heavily outnumbered Western Desert Force, composed of British, Indian, and later Australian divisions. The daring British counter-offensive captured many of the Italians; by January 1941 the remainder had rapidly retreated to Tripoli, with the British in pursuit. There was limited New Zealand involvement in this successful operation: some signals, railways, engineer, and transport units, as well as New Zealand volunteers in the *Long Range Desert Group. However, most New Zealand units remained in Egypt to train. It was not until March 1941 that the 2nd New Zealand Division was concentrated as a single unit, just before it was dispatched to *Greece as part of the ill-fated Allied intervention. This diversion of British resources was to prove crucial in North Africa. The Italian disaster in Libya had induced Adolf Hitler to

A member of a German tank crew is taken prisoner by New Zealand troops (War History Collection, Alexander Turnbull Library, F-36341-1/2)

North African campaign

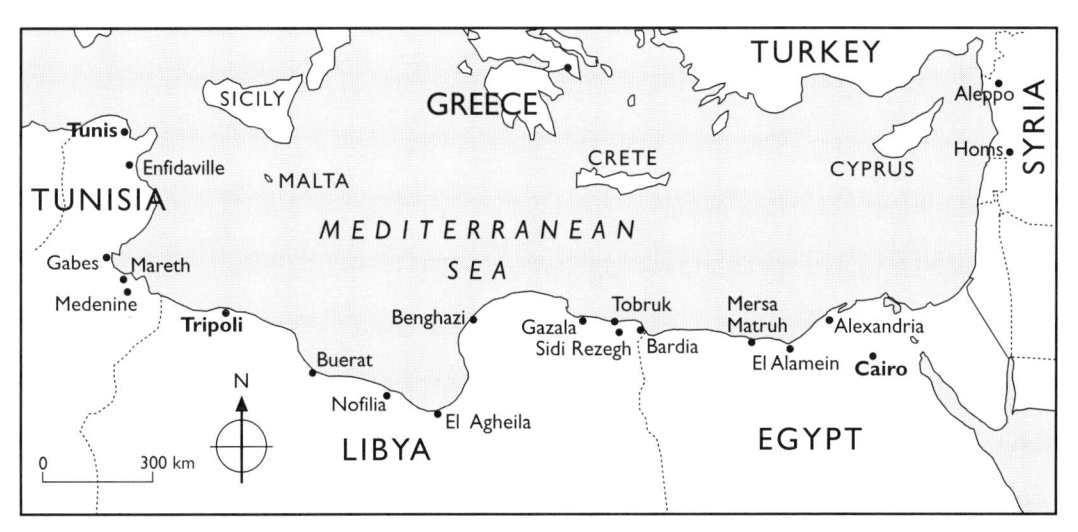

Map 19a The North African theatre of operations, 1940–43

send a force of German armoured units under General Erwin Rommel to bolster the Italian defence. The *Deutsches Afrika Korps* would provide the hard core of the larger German–Italian army, which was nominally under Italian command. Despite orders to remain on the defensive, Rommel wasted no time in making his presence felt. By April 1941 he had thrown the British forces back as far as Egypt, leaving an Australian division besieged in the Libyan port of Tobruk. After two attempts by the Western Desert Force to relieve Tobruk had ended in failure, a frustrated British Prime Minister, Winston Churchill, replaced the exhausted C-in-C, Middle East, General Archibald Wavell, with General Claude Auchinleck in late June 1941.

Meanwhile 2nd New Zealand Division had returned from its defeats in Greece and ★Crete and begun refitting and training for further operations. British reinforcements flowed into Egypt and by November Auchinleck, under pressure from Churchill for action, was ready to launch Operation Crusader, designed to destroy the *Afrika Korps* and lift the siege of Tobruk. The 8th Army (as the Western Desert Force had been redesignated in September) planned to envelop the German and Italian strongpoints near the frontier, using most of its infantry, including the New Zealand division. At the same time, its armour—about 530 tanks—would thrust inland and seek out and destroy the *Afrika Korps* in a giant tank battle, while the Tobruk garrison broke out. When the offensive opened on 18 November 1941, the New Zealanders swung behind the frontier forts. By the 22nd they had taken Fort Capuzzo, and were approaching the fortresses of Bardia and Sollum. That afternoon the 4th and 6th Brigades were ordered to move west towards Tobruk, leaving Brigadier James ★Hargest's 5th Brigade to mask Bardia and Sollum. At New Zealand Divisional HQ, it was assumed, incorrectly, that the operation was proceeding to plan, and that the New Zealand division would be used to support the victorious British armour in relieving Tobruk. In reality the British armour had been defeated by the *Afrika Korps*, though confusion and overconfidence among the British command ensured that the extent of the disaster went unrecognised. Thus the battle came to be shaped into two separate actions: 2nd New Zealand Division determinedly fighting its way west towards Tobruk across two strongly defended escarpments, Sidi Rezegh and Belhamed, while the *Afrika Korps* ranged across the desert attacking British formations behind it.

By the morning of the 23rd, 6th Brigade had reached Sidi Rezegh, an escarpment about forty kilometres south-east of Tobruk. An attack was made on Point 175 on the edge of the escarpment, but it met with tenacious German resistance. By nightfall only half the feature was in New Zealand hands. Casualties had been heavy, with one battalion alone losing more than a hundred men killed. Even as this fighting was taking place, however, the situation was being transformed about fifteen kilometres to the south: the *Afrika Korps* scattered two British armoured brigades and virtually annihilated a South African brigade. An elated Rommel ordered his armoured force to drive south-east to destroy what he believed to be the remnants of the British force in the vicinity of the frontier forts, an advance later described as the 'dash for the wire'.

While the *Afrika Korps* raced towards the frontier, the New Zealand division was still battling its way west towards Tobruk. At dawn on 25 November 6th Brigade launched another attack, advancing about six kilometres

North African campaign

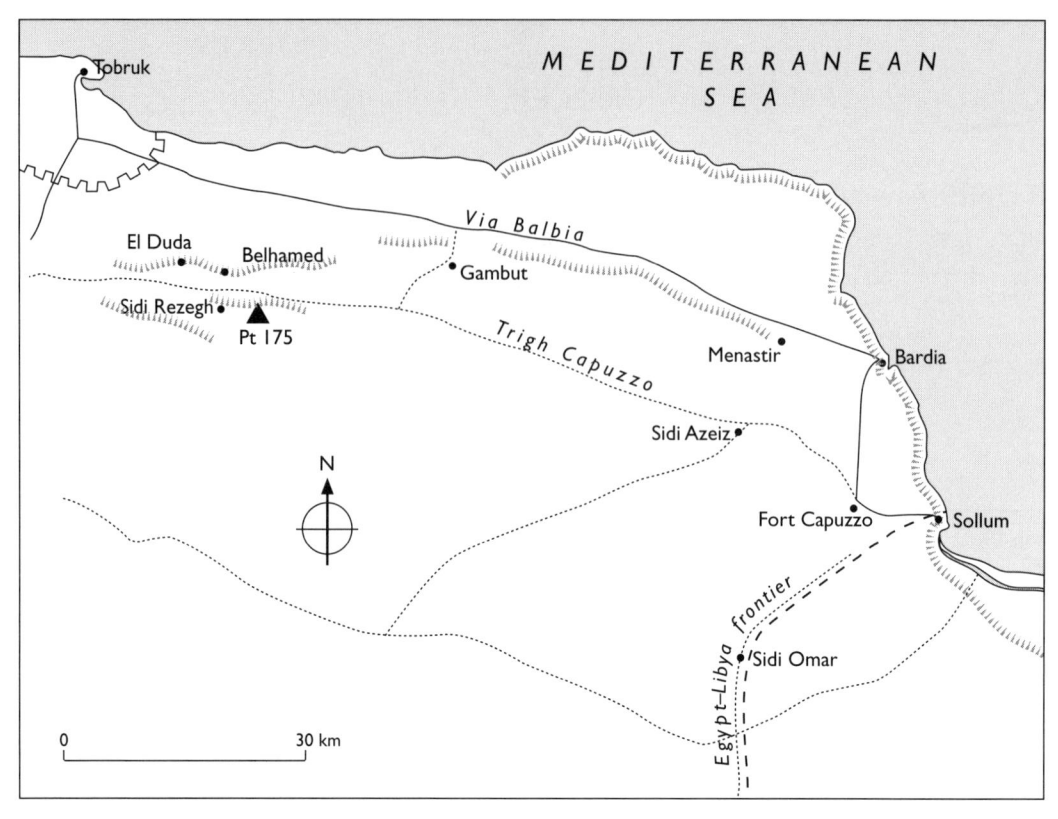

Map 19b The Crusader offensive, November 1941

along the Sidi Rezegh escarpment, while to the north 4th Brigade drew roughly level with it. That night both brigades made attacks, with 4th Brigade taking the Belhamed escarpment in a silent night attack. Six kilometres to the south 6th Brigade continued to meet fierce resistance on Sidi Rezegh. It took another costly night attack to clear the feature. Early on 27 November a battalion of 4th Brigade linked up with elements of the Tobruk garrison at Ed Duda. Even as it did so the New Zealand division's position was becoming increasingly precarious. It had sustained heavy losses in the previous few days without completely suppressing German resistance. More seriously Rommel, unable to relieve the frontier garrisons and running low on supplies and tanks, had on 27 November decided to return to the Tobruk front. In the path of the *Afrika Korps* was 5th Brigade HQ, along with a mass of transport and some artillery. After a desperate but one-sided fight the HQ was overrun, and about 700 men, including Hargest, were taken prisoner.

While the *Afrika Korps* swept towards the two New Zealand brigades from the south-east, the New Zealand GOC, Major-General B.C. ★Freyberg, was preoccupied with consolidating the 'corridor' to Tobruk. An attack by 4th Brigade wiped out an important German position just south of Belhamed, but on Sidi Rezegh the already depleted 6th Brigade lost three companies to a surprise attack. By 29 November the situation was perilous. Whereas Freyberg believed the main threat to lie in the east, the bulk of the Axis armour in fact was poised immediately to his south. The brunt of the Axis attack fell on 6th Brigade, which, being strung out along the escarpment in isolated pockets, was in a poor state to resist. On the afternoon of 29 November Point 175 was lost to the Italian Ariete Division, and next day the remainder of the brigade came under attack by the 15th Panzer Division. By evening two New Zealand battalions had been overrun, and only a few pockets remained on the escarpment. When the Germans attacked again at dawn on the 30th, this time north against the Belhamed position, a field regiment and a battalion were overrun. Some elements of 4th Brigade escaped into Tobruk, while remnants of both New Zealand brigades, about 3500 men, prepared to make a stand at the wadi at Zaafran. On the night of 1–2 December they withdrew to the South African brigade at Bir el Chleta.

Although Rommel had severely mauled the New Zealand division, his resources were exhausted. An attempt to relieve Bardia and Sollum was blocked after one of the Axis advance guards was ambushed by 5th Brigade on 3 December. Axis strength was further depleted in continued fighting, and its supply position was becoming desperate. On 7 December, therefore, the German–Italian army fell back to the Gazala position, west of Tobruk. After a series of clashes between Allied forces and Axis rearguards, during which the 5th Brigade took more than 2300 POWs for the loss of about 200 casualties, the German and Italian forces pulled back to El Agheila. The New Zealand division returned to Egypt to recover from its severe losses. That the operation had been a victory for the Allies was accentuated by the fall of the last of the enemy fortresses on 17 January 1942, bringing the total number of German and Italian prisoners to 30,000. However, the cost had been high: British losses amounted to 17,700, of whom 4620 were New Zealanders, making it the most costly battle of the war for New Zealand. Tragically a ship carrying wounded men from Tobruk, the *Chakdina*, was sunk on 5 December, with the loss of eighty New Zealanders.

After a brief sojourn in Egypt refitting and absorbing reinforcements, 2nd New Zealand Division moved to Syria in February 1942. This deployment was designed to cover the possibility of a German invasion of the Middle East through the Caucasus—a danger that never materialised. The Syrian interlude provided the New Zealanders with the opportunity for intensive training in light of the experience gained in the recent battles. It was particularly important in the development of artillery tactics for the division. The field guns were now to fight as a concentrated divisional unit rather than dispersed as previously. Prearranged fire patterns were also established. These innovations greatly enhanced the firepower of the division, and were later adopted by the British Army (see ARTILLERY). However, efforts by the Middle East Command to reorganise the division into 'battle groups' were ignored; Freyberg was adamant that in future the division would fight as a unified force. The course of the ★Pacific War had meanwhile brought into question the division's continued deployment in the Middle East. Although the government in Wellington in mid March agreed that it should remain where it was, Freyberg was warned that he would have to do without reinforcements for the time being.

While 2nd New Zealand Division rested and trained in Syria, the British position in Libya had collapsed. In late January 1942 Rommel had bundled the British forces back to the Gazala line before Tobruk, where they were soon outflanked. By mid June the 8th Army was in disorganised retreat, the disaster being magnified by the fall of Tobruk on 21 June. Hastily recalled to the Western Desert, the New Zealanders had begun occupying positions at Mersa Matruh just inside the Egyptian border on the 20th. A week later the division was moved to a position south of Mersa Matruh, at Minqar Qaim. The fighting that followed was marked by the chronic confusion which had characterised 8th Army's previous operations. As British forces retreated, the New Zealand division was left isolated, for the German 21st Panzer Division blocked any escape to the east. In this dire situation Freyberg was incapacitated by a shell splinter, and Brigadier L.M. ★Inglis took temporary command of the division. With a view to breaking out of the encirclement, a surprise night attack was launched just after midnight on 28 June. In the vanguard was 4th Brigade, with the rest of the division close behind. The onslaught caught 21st Panzer Division by surprise. Amid desperate fighting, the ferocity of which would lead to later German claims (never substantiated) that the New Zealanders had committed atrocities, most of the New Zealand division got through to the El Alamein position. The dramatic breakout at Minqar Qaim was one of the epic events of the North African campaign. It was also costly, the New Zealanders having suffered nearly 1000 casualties.

The last defensible position before the Nile Delta, the 60-kilometre Alamein line between the coast and the impassable Qattara Depression in the south was relatively secure. By the time the German–Italian forces reached the position in July 1942, both armies were exhausted. The Germans were down to fifty-five serviceable tanks, while the British forces, apart from the New Zealand division, had been broken up into largely ineffectual battle groups in an ill-conceived attempt to increase units' mobility. A series of confused engagements followed, during one of which, on 3 July, the 4th Brigade surprised the Italian Ariete Division, destroying much of its artillery.

In mid July 2nd New Zealand Division was given the task of seizing the Ruweisat Ridge, which dominated the middle of the Alamein position. However, the high command's planning was once again confused. It was based on faulty intelligence, and coordination between the various formations involved was virtually non-existent. The 4th and 5th Brigades began their attack an hour before midnight on 14 July. By daybreak both were on their objectives on the ridge, though in some disarray and unable to entrench themselves because of the hard rock. Support weapons were lacking, and there was no sign of the expected armoured support. This proved decisive when tanks of the German 15th Panzer Division struck 5th Brigade at dawn. After some gallant resistance from a few antitank guns, much of 22nd Battalion went 'into the bag'. At dusk it was 4th Brigade's turn, as two battalions were overwhelmed. The battle for Ruweisat Ridge was an unmitigated disaster. For an entire day infantry were

North African campaign

New Zealand transport south-east of Mersa Matruh in late June 1942 (*War History Collection, Alexander Turnbull Library, F-2551-1/4-DA*)

left on an open ridge without artillery or armoured support, while senior British commanders seemed almost paralysed with indecision. More than 1400 New Zealanders were killed, wounded, or captured.

Sporadic fighting continued between the two armies. Still believing it possible to defeat the *Afrika Korps*, Auchinleck determined to launch another attack, but as ever planning was hampered by overconfidence and confusion. The New Zealanders were given the task of seizing the El Mreir Depression, through which British armour would exploit. The attack by 6th Brigade began after dark on 21 July, and before first light it was digging in on its objectives. Despite repeated pleas by New Zealand commanders for armoured support, none was forthcoming. The only armour present at El Mreir at dawn on 22 July were 21st Panzer Division's tanks. While one battalion managed to escape, the other two were caught in the depression and effectively destroyed. As a result of this débâcle, 2nd New Zealand Division lost another 900 men, from its only complete brigade. After another abortive attempt by the 8th Army to destroy the *Afrika Korps* at the end of July, both armies went on to the defensive and began digging in and mining their positions. The New Zealanders occupied a fortified position, New Zealand Box, towards the southern end of the Alamein line.

Since its return to Egypt in June 1942, the division had suffered more than 4600 casualties (of whom 822 were killed) during the course of two bad defeats and a fortunate escape. One brigade, 4th Brigade, had had to be withdrawn because of its severe losses, reducing the division to just two brigades. These losses sapped the New Zealanders' morale and instilled in them an intense distrust of British armoured units and high command. Churchill, too, had had enough of the disasters. In August 1942 he sacked Auchinleck. General Harold Alexander became C-in-C Middle East. Command of the 8th Army also passed fortuitously (because of the death in a plane crash of Lieutenant-General W.H.E. Gott) to Lieutenant-General Sir Bernard ★Montgomery, who soon demonstrated incisive leadership; he demanded methodical planning and more careful direction of operations. He came to the fore at a time when Allied material superiority was beginning to tell. His determination to hold the Alamein line and his evident professionalism did much to dispel the prevailing despondent mood in the 8th Army. New Zealand morale was further improved by Freyberg's resumption of command of the division. The strength of many units remained low, however, and additional reinforcements were not promised until August.

Rommel's position was becoming precarious. With North Africa a sideshow to the more important Eastern Front in German eyes, he was starved of reinforcements; those that he did receive, and his supplies, had to run the gauntlet of Allied air and naval attacks, which were rendered increasingly effective by ★ULTRA intelligence. Conscious that the Allies were growing steadily stronger, he resolved to seize the initiative. Breaching the minefields on 30 August, the *Afrika Korps* swung south of the New Zealand Box in an attempt to outflank the Allied defences. Forewarned by ULTRA, the Allies pounded Rommel's columns without respite, both with artillery and from the air. An armoured clash took place at Alam Halfa, but Rommel's tanks were short of fuel and he was forced to withdraw. Up to this point, the situation in the New Zealand Box had remained relatively quiet. On 3 September, however, the New Zealanders took part in a limited counter-attack. The night assault overran some German and Italian positions, and the next day a German–Italian counter-attack was repelled. But that evening the New Zealand and British troops were withdrawn back to their original positions and the gaps in the minefields closed. Rommel was allowed to retreat back to his original positions.

Montgomery was determined to end the pattern of advances and retreats across the desert by defeating the German–Italian Army decisively at Alamein. His Army enjoyed a crushing superiority over Rommel in all respects, with the Axis forces being hampered by lack of fuel in particular. To ensure success in the looming battle Montgomery instituted an intense training regime. For their part the Germans and Italians concentrated on laying deep minefields. Italian units were dug in and 'corseted' with German formations. Rommel's armour was held in reserve to counter-attack. Montgomery's plan envisaged a setpiece battle of attrition, divided into three phases. A frontal assault by four infantry divisions (including the New Zealanders) in the north would 'break-in'. Its way opened, armour would follow through to form an armoured bridgehead upon which it was hoped Rommel would smash his reserves in the 'dogfight' phase. The remnants of the German–Italian Army would then be destroyed in the 'breakout'. For the battle the British 9th Armoured Brigade was attached to the New Zealand division.

For the participants, the Battle of El Alamein began memorably on 23 October when at exactly 9.40 p.m. about 900 guns opened fire on known Axis positions. Twenty minutes later the infantry assault began, in the New Zealand sector under the protective curtain of a First World War–style creeping barrage. By dawn the New Zealand infantry were digging in either on or just short of their objectives. The infantry assault had made significant gains, but the armour, slowed by congestion in the minefields, poor coordination, and cautious leadership, was unable to form in front of the infantry. Although tanks moved forward during the following night, the Axis defences remained unbroken. During the next few days the New Zealanders consolidated their positions on the original objectives, before being relieved during the night of 27 October. The New Zealand artillery went north to support the British forces in the battle raging there.

Disappointed with the lack of progress on 25 October, Montgomery had decided to 'crumble' the Axis defences in the north, using the 9th Australian Division covered by British armour. For the next week a salient was driven into the Axis line. This forced Rommel to make counter-attacks, which were contained in sometimes desperate fighting in which intense Allied artillery bombardments and air attacks by Air Marshal Arthur ★Coningham's Western Desert Air Force played crucial roles. While this battle of attrition proceeded, Montgomery was preparing the attack that would breach the Axis line further south. The task of leading this operation (dubbed Supercharge) was given to 2nd New Zealand Division, which was augmented by two British infantry brigades. The attack opened at 1.05 a.m. on 2 November, with the British infantry brigades forcing open a path for 9th Armoured Brigade. After clearing the prepared Axis positions, the latter ran into German armour. Both sides lost heavily in the ensuing clash, but by evening the *Afrika Korps* was in a desperate position. With his depleted tanks low in fuel, Rommel concluded that the battle was lost. His decision to withdraw brought immediate intervention from Berlin. Hitler ordered the German–Italian troops to 'stand fast', but it was too late. The Axis defences at El Alamein were already in a state of collapse. From 4 November the Axis forces went into headlong retreat, with the British armoured divisions and 2nd New Zealand Division in pursuit. Six days later New Zealand infantry brushed aside a rearguard at Halfaya Pass, taking 600 prisoners for the loss of just two casualties. The division was then pulled out for a rest near Bardia.

El Alamein determined the outcome of the campaign. The British forces' first decisive victory of the war over a German army, it was an important boost to morale both in the army and at home. The German–Italian Army had been shattered, losing more than 30,000 prisoners. The Allies had suffered 13,650 casualties, including 1700 New Zealanders. In spite of Montgomery's caution in pursuit, Rommel could not form a defensive line until he reached El Agheila, after a retreat of 1350 kilometres. The Axis position in North Africa was further undermined when on 8 November the Americans and British landed in French Morocco and Algeria. The Germans responded vigorously to this threat: forces hastily transported across the Mediterranean to the Vichy French territory of Tunisia by sea and air managed, in December, to halt the Allied advance barely twenty kilometres west of Tunis. Had these forces been available to Rommel six months previously, he might well have secured victory;

North African campaign

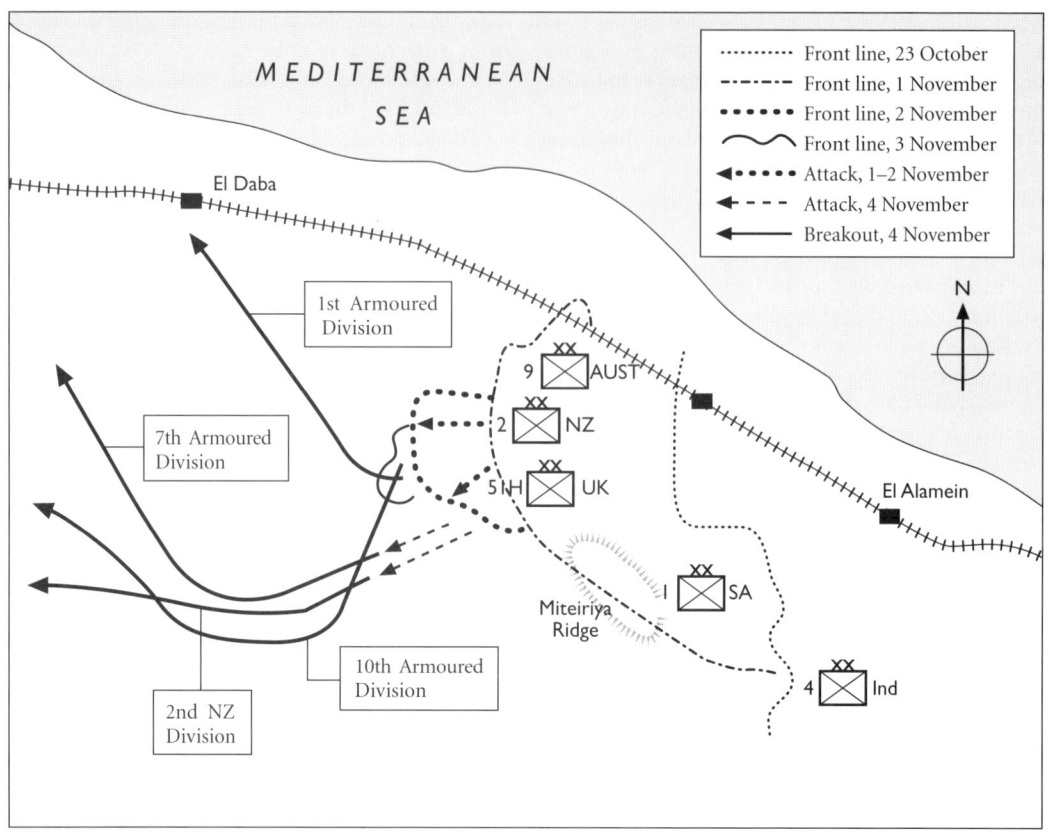

Map 19c The Battle of El Alamein, October–November 1942

their advent now merely served to magnify the scale of the eventual Axis defeat.

The victory at El Alamein had brought into question New Zealand's continued involvement in the Mediterranean theatre. In late November the New Zealand government pressed for the division's return to the South Pacific, but it was subsequently agreed that it would remain in North Africa until the end of the campaign. It was still with 8th Army, therefore, when it attacked Rommel's position at El Agheila on 12 December. Rommel had already begun to withdraw, with the result that a 'left hook' mounted by the New Zealanders failed to trap the *Afrika Korps*. A few days later the process was repeated at Nofilia, with the same result. On 23 January the New Zealand division entered Tripoli.

By this time Rommel had fallen back into Tunisia. Occupying the formidable Mareth Line on the border between Tunisia and Libya, he secured his flank in February with a successful surprise attack at Kasserine on the Allied armies pressing from the west. He then turned against the 8th Army east of the Mareth Line at Medenine on 6 March 1943. New Zealand troops saw little action, however, because concentrated British and New Zealand artillery fire drove off the Germans with heavy losses.

The 8th Army now prepared to storm the Mareth Line. While a frontal attack pinned the enemy, the New Zealand division, reinforced with British and French units to form the New Zealand Corps, swung around far to the south of the Mareth Line in another 'left hook' with a view to falling on the German–Italian Army's rear at Tebaga Gap. This position was reached on the night of 20 March. In a night attack on the 21st, 6th Brigade breached the Italian positions, but the supporting armour failed to exploit the success. By 22 March German reinforcements began arriving. Frustrated by Freyberg's slowness in breaking through, Montgomery sent an armoured division to reinforce the New Zealanders, and effectively replaced Freyberg as corps commander with Lieutenant-General Brian Horrocks.

Montgomery's new plan was to smash through the Tebaga Gap in a large-scale assault (Supercharge II). After an artillery barrage and a low-level air attack of unprecedented intensity, a combined infantry and armoured assault overran the Tebaga Gap on 26 March. Within two hours British armour was pushing through into the rear of the Axis position. However, after the breakthrough had been made, fierce fighting raged until the 27th on the southern flank at Point 209, the objective of 28th (Maori) Battalion. It was here that Lieutenant Moana-nui-a-kiwa ★Ngarimu won a posthumous VC. The New Zealanders followed up the retreating Axis forces, which, having extricated themselves from the Mareth position, fell back to the north. Turning the Mareth Line had cost 2nd New Zealand Division 646 casualties.

After they had been driven out of the 'Akarit line' at the beginning of April, the Axis forces retreated northwards. New Zealand artillery was fully engaged in this operation but the role of the rest of the division was to exploit a breakthrough made by other forces (in the end not required because the enemy chose to withdraw). No good defensive line existed in the 240 kilometres between Wadi Akarit and Enfidaville. With the enemy not attempting to make a stand on the relatively flat coastal plain, there were no longer any opportunities for an outflanking attack. By 13 April the New Zealanders had reached the outposts of the 'Enfidaville line'. The New Zealanders' role in the forthcoming attack was to clear the rugged coastal foothills, where the village of Enfidaville on the right and a steep hill called Takrouna on the left lay in the path of their advance. The infantry attack began shortly before midnight on 19 April. On the right 6th Brigade quickly reached its objectives. A patrol entered Enfidaville at first light to find it deserted. On the left the attack by 5th Brigade was disorganised by minefields. By dawn little progress had been made and much of the brigade was under intense enemy fire. But that morning a platoon of 28th (Maori) Battalion clambered up the Takrouna feature and seized the buildings on its top in fierce fighting. The pinnacle was later lost, but early on 21 April it was retaken by a group led by Sergeant Haane ★Manahi. The fight for Takrouna became part of the lore of 2nd New Zealand Division, the seizure of this dominating position having cost more than 500 casualties. It proved to be the New Zealanders' last major action of the campaign, though a series of minor operations were mounted in early May to pin down Axis forces. The main effort to destroy the Axis defences had switched to the north-west. Axis resistance collapsed on 13 May 1943. About 238,000 Axis troops surrendered (more than at Stalingrad three and a half months earlier). On the 15th the New Zealanders began their nearly 3000-kilometre drive back to their base in Egypt.

The successful conclusion of the North African campaign brought huge strategic advantages to the Allies. Not only was the threat to the Middle East removed but also the Allies were presented with many opportunities for taking the war to the European mainland. Italy was firmly in the Allied sights; its stomach for war greatly lessened, it would not long resist once the Allies landed on its shores. The campaign had taught hard-won lessons in tactics and equipment, and the experience gained would serve the Allies well when they confronted the enemy in other theatres. In the event New Zealand's decision to leave the 2nd New Zealand Division in the Middle East proved justified: no invader set foot on New Zealand soil and the division played a significant part in the final defeat of the *Afrika Korps*. But the contribution had come at a heavy cost: 2989 New Zealanders fell during the North African campaign; another 7000 were wounded and 4041 became POWs.

J.L. Scoullar, *Battle for Egypt* (War History Branch, Wellington, 1967); W.E. Murphy, *The Relief of Tobruk* (War History Branch, Wellington, 1961); R. Walker, *Alam Halfa and Alamein* (War History Branch, Wellington, 1967); W.G. Stevens, *From Bardia to Enfidaville* (War History Branch, Wellington, 1962).

GLYN HARPER

Northern War see NEW ZEALAND WARS

Nuclear weapons testing The involvement of the New Zealand armed forces in nuclear weapons testing has reflected changes in national policy on the testing of such weapons since the 1950s. In the first years of the nuclear age New Zealand supported the development of atomic and later thermonuclear weapons by its allies, the United States and the United Kingdom. It was willing to participate in testing programmes, though Prime Minister Sidney Holland firmly rejected a suggestion in 1955 that the Kermadec Islands might be used as a site. In 1952 RNZAF aircraft based at Whenuapai assisted with the monitoring of radioactive fallout from the first British ★atomic bomb test, which was conducted at the Monte Bello Islands off the north-west coast of Australia. As part of the fallout monitoring programme for the British tests in Australia, RNZAF personnel in Fiji collected rainwater samples. A small RAF detachment carried out the same task at RNZAF Base Ohakea. In 1956 five New Zealand officers joined the Indoctrinee Force, which participated in the first two atomic bomb tests conducted at Maralinga in Australia as part of the Buffalo series. The aim of the force was to give Commonwealth military personnel experience of the effects of atomic weapons. Two New Zealand officers observed one of the tests conducted at Maralinga in 1957. New Zealand officers also observed an American test in Nevada in September 1957 and another at Eniwetok in the Pacific the following year.

Early in 1956 HMNZS *Lachlan* surveyed the Northern and Southern Line Islands, the proposed site for the British thermonuclear weapon testing programme code-named Operation Grapple. Following

Nuclear weapons testing

the survey, Christmas Island and Malden Island were selected for use in the testing programme. Two New Zealand frigates, HMNZS *Pukaki* and *Rotoiti*, acted as weather ships during the four British tests conducted off the islands in May and November 1957. *Pukaki* fulfilled the same role at five further tests held off Christmas Island in August and September 1958. The RNZAF was heavily involved in establishing and supporting a fallout monitoring network in various Pacific Islands as part of Operation Grapple. Two New Zealand officers and a government scientist were official observers at the first British thermonuclear weapon test on 15 May 1957. In recent years the possibly adverse effects on the health of New Zealand personnel involved in Operation Grapple have become a matter of controversy in New Zealand. However, a 1999 inquiry led by Sir Paul Reeves found no evidence that any RNZN vessel or crew member received any significant exposure to radiation during the tests.

New Zealand's stance on nuclear testing began to change from the late 1950s, as public consciousness of the potential health hazards associated with atmospheric nuclear testing grew. In 1962 the government established an independent monitoring network to record fallout from the American atmospheric thermonuclear tests at Christmas Island. The RNZAF played a major role in this project. With the end of American testing in the Pacific, the only power conducting tests in the region was France, which had shifted its programme from Algeria to Moruroa Atoll in French Polynesia. In June 1973, as a protest against its continuing atmospheric testing, Norman Kirk's Labour government dispatched the frigate HMNZS *Otago*, with a Cabinet minister aboard, to the vicinity of Moruroa. *Otago* was in the French-declared exclusion zone off the atoll on 22 July when the first detonation took place. She was then relieved by HMNZS *Canterbury*, which returned to New Zealand in August after witnessing a second French test.

Although France ceased testing in the atmosphere following these tests, its underground testing at Moruroa had by the 1990s aroused similar opposition in New Zealand. When a new programme was instituted in 1995, a flotilla of unofficial protest boats made its way to the vicinity of the atoll. Jim Bolger's National administration sent the research ship HMNZS *Tui* to patrol off the atoll in August 1995, reflecting the now bipartisan opposition to nuclear weapons in New Zealand. *Tui*, which had two New Zealand members of Parliament and journalists aboard, spent more than a month off Moruroa and provided support for the protest flotilla.

J. Crawford, '"A Political H-Bomb": New Zealand and the British Thermonuclear Weapon Tests of 1957–58', *Journal of Imperial and Commonwealth History*, vol. 26, no. 1 (1998).

JOHN CRAWFORD

Officer training Formal officer training was almost non-existent in the New Zealand military forces in the nineteenth century. Attempts by successive ★Commandants to encourage training of officers foundered on apathy, parsimony, and the belief prevalent at the time that one merely had to be a gentleman to be an effective officer. Schools of Instruction for officers were poorly attended and actual training was limited to basic instruction as a junior officer (mostly in drill) and annual camps. A small number of officers from the ★Permanent Militia were sent to the United Kingdom for specialist artillery and engineering training. In 1909 volunteer officer training corps were established at New Zealand university colleges to encourage better-educated men to volunteer as officers in the ★Volunteer Force, but the four corps were disbanded on the establishment of the ★Territorial Force. The creation of the Territorial Force allowed a training regime to be implemented for officers, including annual courses of instruction. More importantly, to provide the Territorial Force with its cadre of trained professional officers, officer cadets were sent to the new Royal Military College established at Duntroon, near Canberra. From 1911, up to ten promising officer cadets attended annually, enough to provide the New Zealand forces with a continual stream of trained professional officers. By 1914 there were twenty-six cadets at Duntroon. Arrangements were also begun for six cadets annually to be sent to the Royal Military College at Sandhurst in the United Kingdom.

During the ★First World War, military education was an attenuated affair. Cadets continued to be sent to Duntroon, though their three-year courses were shortened so that they could join 1NZEF. Officer training in New Zealand itself was limited to short courses in tactics, weapons, and drill at Trentham or at officer cadet training units in England. After the war New Zealand's straitened circumstances led to the practice of sending cadets to Duntroon being halted; the course at Sandhurst, of one year's duration only, was preferred. Sandhurst graduates would spend the following year with a British regiment to gain practical command experience. Officer training was severely curtailed during the Depression of the early 1930s. Not until 1934 did New Zealand officer cadets again begin attending Duntroon.

The need to produce large numbers of officers quickly during the Second World War led to the establishment of an Officer Cadet Training Unit at Trentham in 1939, while courses at Duntroon were reduced. Officer training for 2NZEF was carried out at British schools throughout the Middle East, with OCTUs at Abbassia in Egypt and other sites in the Middle East providing a four-month officer training course for promising NCOs selected for commissioning. Junior officers also received specialist training at a variety of ★Army schools established during the war.

After the war Duntroon continued to be the principal source of training for professional officers. The Army School of Instruction was maintained at Trentham, with an OCTU to provide officers for ★Jayforce. By the 1950s officer training had expanded. Each year thirty cadets were sent overseas to attend one-year, two-year, or four-year courses at Portsea (Australia), Duntroon, or Sandhurst. An OCTU at Waiouru trained officer cadets for the Territorial Force and those commissioned from the ranks. In 1977 an Officer Cadet Training Company was established at Waiouru to provide a 12-month course for Army officers. A reorganisation of officer training in 1985 led to

Officer training

The passing out parade of the first all-New Zealand officer training unit is inspected by Brigadier W.G. Stevens at Taranto in 1945 (War History Collection, Alexander Turnbull Library, F-8972-35mm-DA)

officer cadets being trained in New Zealand. The training company was renamed the Officer Cadet School, and expanded to an annual intake of sixty officer cadets annually, including cadets from Australia, Papua New Guinea, Fiji, Malaysia, and other countries, who undergo a one-year course focused on field exercises, weapon training, battle craft, tactics, and physical training. Two New Zealand cadets annually are sent to the Australian Defence Force Academy at Canberra for a three- to four-year tertiary-level course. Increasingly aware of the importance of tertiary education in officer development, the Army has more recently made an arrangement with Massey University at Palmerston North under which a number of officer cadets in training at the OCS Waiouru undertake university studies during their vacations.

It was not until 1927 that air force officers began receiving formal training. For a short period before the Depression brought an end to the scheme, Permanent Air Force cadets were sent to the Royal Air Force College at Cranwell. Training in New Zealand was revived in 1938, and a flying training school was established at Wigram and another at Blenheim shortly afterwards (see EMPIRE AIR TRAINING SCHEME). More flying training schools were opened throughout the war, including two at Whenuapai and Harewood. An Initial Training School at Rongotai (later Levin) inducted aircrew, before they were sent on to elementary flying schools to learn the rudiments of flying, and, after qualifying, to the flying training schools. An Officer School of Instruction at Whenuapai instructed junior officers in staff duties and administration. Training was considerably expanded with the outbreak of the ★Pacific War. By 1943 a plethora of operational training units (OTUs) had been established to teach aircrew specialist subjects over several weeks before they were assigned to their squadrons. By the end of the war nearly 4000 aircrew had passed through OTUs.

Officer training went briefly into abeyance after the war, but resumed in April 1948. After initial training at Whenuapai cadet pilots and aircrew underwent an 82-week course at the Flying Training School at Wigram, after which more specialised training would be given at a variety of schools. Two officer cadets each were sent to the RAAF Cadet College at Point Cook (for a four-year course) and to Cranwell (for a 30-month course) annually from 1952. During the mid 1960s all officer training was centralised in the Flying Training Wing at Wigram, with officer cadets undergoing basic officer training of between two to six months. From there, aircrew went on to flying training, continued university studies at Canterbury University, or were directly commissioned if already from the ranks. From

1993 RNZAF officer cadets underwent an 11-week recruit course at Woodbourne, before attending an initial officer training course, after which they would be commissioned as pilot officers or to a rank equivalent to their previous status or occupation. Aircrew would then undergo up to eighteen months of flying training before going to their squadrons.

Officer training for naval personnel began during the ★Second World War through a variety of schemes, in which promising civilians and ordinary seamen were sent to the United Kingdom. From 1941 promising ratings attended 16-week courses in Australia before being commissioned as sub-lieutenants in the RNZNVR. After the war officer training continued at the Royal Australian Naval College at Flinders (from 1958 at HMAS *Creswell* at Jervis Bay) and the Royal Naval College at Dartmouth in the United Kingdom. Cadets underwent a comprehensive course of training lasting about two years. At the end of their first year, cadets were rated as midshipmen. After passing out of the college they were assigned to ships in the rank of acting sub-lieutenant. Specialists, such as engineers, would go on to further study at university. Until 1958 the first few years of sea service were spent with the Royal Navy or RAN. This meant that it was about four years before officers returned to New Zealand. The RNZN introduced a new scheme of officer training in 1965. Under it, entrants underwent a course of training at the Officer Training School at HMNZS *Tamaki* before going on to either 'on the job' training at sea or study at the University of Auckland. In a further overhaul of the officer training system in 1984, an initial training course for all junior officers—the junior officer common training course (JOCT)—was introduced. For the approximately fifty officers trained annually at the Officer Training School, there are three forms of entry. Midshipmen spend seven months on the JOCT before undergoing further training ashore, at university, technical institutions, or the RNZAF Flying Training Squadron at Ohakea. Direct entry officers join the RNZN with tertiary qualifications (such as law, software engineering, or medicine) before undergoing a six-month JOCT. Officers commissioned from below deck likewise train for a shorter period at the school. Initial training involves instruction in physical fitness, drill and ceremonial, fire fighting and damage control, sea survival, discipline, and communication skills. After initial training officers (now usually promoted to the rank of ensign) receive further specialist training according to which branch of the service they belong.

Official war histories The preparation of official histories has had three main functions in New Zealand—to record activities so that lessons might be drawn from them, to meet popular demand for an account of New Zealand's part in the world wars, and more recently to provide a memorial to those who lost their lives on active service. Contrary to common belief, they are not the government's view of the war, though the genre has been sullied somewhat by political interference in the preparation of the ★First World War British official histories. The term 'official' denotes the fact that their production has been funded by the state. Authors' independent judgment has been jealously prized, and has been facilitated since 1945 by the formal responsibility of the Department of Internal Affairs for the preparation of official war histories.

Initially official history was a military preserve. With the active encouragement of the Premier, Richard ★Seddon, the Defence Department took early action to produce an account of New Zealand's part in the ★Boer War. After several false starts, F.E. Beamish, a Post Office accountant and militia officer, completed a draft history in 1909, but it did not find favour with the military authorities. A narrow conception of the purpose and scope of official history was held by the Chief of the General Staff, Colonel A.W. ★Robin, who would play a key role in New Zealand's approach to official war history for more than a decade. He later suggested, in relation to Beamish's manuscript, that 'opinions, criticisms and copies of irresponsible [ie non-official] letters and news papers do not constitute a history worthy of issue by a Government'. The manuscript languished in the departmental files, and cannot now be located.

Another strand of official war history emerged in the Department of Internal Affairs late in the First World War when the government commissioned James ★Cowan to write what he described as 'the Official History of the Wars in New Zealand'. Behind the initiation of this project, in February 1918, was recognition of the need to record the experiences of the dwindling band of survivors of the conflict. Cowan made admirable use of oral history and visits to the sites of battles in producing his work, which appeared in two volumes in 1922 and 1923. He was determined to do justice to both sides in the conflict, an objective that was facilitated by his fluency in the Maori language. *The New Zealand Wars* was the standard text for more than seventy years, and was reprinted in 1955 and 1983.

The probability that New Zealand's part in the First World War would be recorded in an official history was recognised in 1915. The official war correspondent, Malcolm ★Ross, was charged with gathering historical material. When, at war's end, the question of an official history was taken up, 1NZEF commander Major-General Sir Alexander ★Godley considered him to be the most appropriate person to prepare it. Not

Official war histories

only did Ross have the necessary historical resources, he also had personal experience of the front, having been present at ★Gallipoli and on the ★Western Front. Although his appointment was also supported by the Prime Minister, William ★Massey, he fell victim to the military authorities in Wellington, who persuaded acting Prime Minister Sir James ★Allen that he did not have the technical knowledge needed for the task of producing the official history. This, Robin insisted, would not 'be more than an exact statistical and chronological record of all events connected with the War, both in the Dominion and Overseas'. He envisaged the strategic and tactical appreciations and lessons to be drawn from the war being worked out by the ★Imperial General Staff at the War Office. Meanwhile the government had agreed to the production of a 'soldier's history' of New Zealand's war effort. In the face of calls for a more soldier-oriented history than would be possible in an official history (as then conceived)—Clutha ★Mackenzie had urged in 1917 the need to capture 'as far as humanly possible in literature, the spirit, the manliness and the glory of it all'—a reluctant Robin bent to the wind in proposing a 'supplementary work of a popular nature'. Despite his evident qualifications, as a journalist and as an observer at the front, for the position of 'popular' historian, and the example of his wartime colleague C.E.W. Bean in Australia, Ross was passed over in favour of field officers. Major Fred ★Waite, a farmer before enlistment, prepared the Gallipoli volume, and also oversaw the production of the other volumes. Colonel H. ★Stewart, who had been a Canterbury University College professor before enlisting in 1NZEF, wrote the Western Front volume, which appeared in 1921 and is still, three-quarters of a century later, the standard source despite its inaccessible and turgid prose. Regular staff officer Colonel C.G. ★Powles was enlisted to prepare the volume on the ★Sinai–Palestine campaign, using a manuscript already prepared by Major A.H. Wilkie. Lieutenant H.T.B. Drew, a journalist in civilian life, who established a temporary New Zealand Historical War Records Office within the Defence Department late in 1918, edited a volume covering various aspects of the war effort. Powles's volume also remains the standard work on New Zealand's involvement in the Sinai–Palestine campaign nearly eighty years later. No further action was taken on the official history, as originally conceived, but these 'popular' histories were, confusingly, described as the official history on their title-pages. ★Unit histories were commissioned by the units themselves, but they were overseen by a committee of senior officers at GHQ, who had the power to revise or alter texts.

During the ★Second World War, the possibility of an official history being produced was recognised in Wellington as early as 1940. An Official Archivist was appointed at 2NZEF's base headquarters to ensure the preservation of historical records, and following his conscription in 1941 E.H. McCormick, a man of considerable literary and publishing standing, was appointed Assistant Archivist (later becoming Official Archivist). Early in 1943, prompted by developments in Australia, he suggested the need for an interdepartmental committee to consider the war history question, and an Inter-Services War History Committee eventually began meeting in October that year. In March 1944 Cabinet approval was secured for the appointment of an editor-in-chief and a chief war archivist. McCormick was brought back from the Middle East to take the latter post, stopping over in Australia to study the Australian war history scheme on the way. A special Ministerial War History Committee which considered his proposals agreed to the creation of the ★War History Branch within the Department of Internal Affairs (ensuring that the Second World War official history would be produced under very different conditions from those of the First World War history). Underlying New Zealand's approach to the official history was the feeling that the popular-cum-official histories produced in the early 1920s had not done justice to 1NZEF, and that the Australian First World War history project had been much better than New Zealand's.

Major-General H.K. ★Kippenberger, a lawyer by profession and a popular senior officer of 2NZEF, took up the position of Editor-in-Chief of the war history project on 1 June 1946. During the next eleven years, working largely on a plan prepared by McCormick, he oversaw the conception and advancement of a history which ultimately comprised three main series, covering the war effort generally (The New Zealand People at War), campaign histories, and unit histories of 2NZEF units in the Mediterranean theatre (those in the Pacific were covered by an unofficial series). There was also a series of short episodes and studies, and three volumes of documents. A solid basis for the histories was provided by narratives prepared in the War History Branch by a staff of young professional historians. The histories themselves were written under contract by a range of authors including academics, military personnel, and journalists, some of whom failed to complete their tasks, leaving their volumes to be completed by War History Branch staff members. As public interest fell off, and Kippenberger's untimely death in 1957 removed his inspirational leadership, the impetus of the project began to wane in the late 1950s. The final volume, one of the People at War series, did not appear until 1986. The quality of the volumes varies: some are among the very best histories produced in New Zealand, while a minority are marred by a rather pedestrian style. With forty-eight volumes, the Second World War official history remains the largest publishing project undertaken in New Zealand.

The War History Branch also filled a major gap in New Zealand's official war historiography when it published, in 1949, a short account of New Zealand's part in the Boer War. Another attempt to prepare such an history had been made in 1929, when former war correspondent J.A. Shand had been commissioned, with responsibility for the project being given to the Department of Internal Affairs. Although Shand completed a draft in 1931, it suffered the same fate as Beamish's earlier manuscript, though for commercial rather than editorial reasons. In 1947 Kippenberger reluctantly agreed to take on the task of producing the history, and David Hall used Shand's draft extensively to prepare a new manuscript. As even its author admitted, the slim volume published in 1949 has many shortcomings, and the subject awaits a more extensive treatment a century after the event.

Partly because of the commitment of resources to the Second World War history project, New Zealand's post-war campaigns did not receive early attention. It was not until 1979 that work got underway on the official history of New Zealand's involvement in the ★Korean War. A professional historian was employed within the Historical Publications Branch (the successor to the War History Branch) for the purpose. The two volumes of the history appeared in 1992 and 1996 respectively. Meanwhile, authors had also been contracted to work on histories of New Zealand's military involvement in Malaya/Malaysia and the political and diplomatic aspects of New Zealand's participation in the ★Vietnam War. Since 1969 the Department of Internal Affairs' efforts in the official history field have been supplemented by the work of an historian in the Ministry of Defence, later the ★New Zealand Defence Force. The present incumbent is working on a history of New Zealand's involvement in ★peace-keeping operations.

Olphert, Lieutenant-Commander Wybrants

(15 September 1879–7 January 1938) was the founding officer of the Wellington Division of the Royal Naval Volunteer Reserve, which is named after him. An Englishman, he joined the New Zealand Shipping Company as an apprentice officer in 1895. He held a commission in the Royal Naval Reserve from 1902. After war broke out in 1914, he was given command of the armed yacht HMS *Scadaun*. On 21 June 1915 the *Scadaun* sank a German U-boat, an exploit which earned Olphert a DSC. But it was as commander of the ★Q-ship HMS *Salvia* that he made his mark. He destroyed three U-boats before being made a POW in June 1917 after the *Salvia* was torpedoed. He was made a DSO and bar for this Q-ship service. He returned to New Zealand after the war, and was commander of the Wellington Division of the Royal Naval Volunteer Reserve from 1928 to 1938.

Organisation for National Security

was responsible for preparing New Zealand's government apparatus for the transition to war during the late 1930s. Machinery for the coordination of New Zealand's defence activities had been established within the Department of Defence in 1933. A New Zealand section of the ★Committee of Imperial Defence (CID) was formed to organise 'national activities'. A series of subcommittees was created covering all aspects of government administration likely to be affected by the onset of war. Unlike the CID, however, the New Zealand section was chaired by the Minister of Defence rather than the Prime Minister, which reduced its standing within the government structure.

In March 1937 the coordinating arrangements, known since the previous August as the Organisation for National Security (ONS), were placed on a different basis. A Council of Defence (see DEFENCE COUNCIL), with the Prime Minister as chairman, was created to oversee the work of the ONS, which would henceforth be located in the Prime Minister's Department. A staff officer, Major W.G. ★Stevens, was seconded from Defence Headquarters to that department to serve as Secretary of the ONS, which now expanded its activities considerably as the international situation deteriorated. The object was to prepare the War Book, the manual of actions to be taken upon the outbreak of war. The ONS provided the secretarial services for the various committees, including the ★Chiefs of Staff Committee.

The measure of its success was the smooth transition to war achieved in September 1939. A comprehensive body of legislation was introduced rapidly and effectively with minimum disruption to the country as a whole. The ONS settled down thereafter to facilitate the coordination of the war effort. When Stephens went overseas with 2NZEF in January 1940, Foss ★Shanahan, his deputy, took over as Secretary. In March 1943 the ONS was subsumed within the ★War Cabinet Secretariat, of which it formed the nucleus.

W.D. McIntyre, *New Zealand Prepares for War: Defence Policy 1919–39* (Canterbury University Press, Christchurch, 1988); F.L.W. Wood, *Political and External Affairs* (War History Branch, Wellington, 1958).

P

'P' class cruisers For twenty years the handsome little Pearl and Pelorus class cruisers were a common sight in New Zealand waters. Five Pearl class ships were ordered in 1887 under the Imperial Defence Act and four more in 1889 under the Naval Defence Act. Added to the ★Australia Station in accordance with the 1887 Australasian Naval Agreement, HMS *Katoomba, Mildura, Wallaroo, Ringarooma,* and *Tauranga* formed the ★Australian Auxiliary Squadron. The 1889 quartet, which had slightly more powerful engines, commissioned with the intended 'P' names. All entered service in 1891–92. In 1897–1901 the Royal Navy took delivery of a second class of eleven vessels, the Pelorus class. Reduced versions of the Medea second-class cruisers, the Pearls were redesignated third-class ships prior to completion. They displaced 2575 tons loaded, were 80.8 metres long, and could make nineteen knots under forced draft and 17–17.5 knots under normal conditions, but like many small ships of the period, they lost speed after a few years' service. Their armour—a light 51.25 mm covering on the deck—and their armament—eight 8.7-inch quick-firers, arranged to give a broadside of four guns, eight 3-pounder guns, four lighter pieces, and four 14-inch torpedo tubes— suited them for colonial policing and training duties. They had a crew of about 220. The Pelorus class vessels were lighter (2135 tons loaded), slightly longer (91.4 metres), substituted 4-inch guns for 4.7-inch weapons, and had two 18-inch torpedo tubes, but were otherwise very similar to the Pearls.

The Pearls had relatively uneventful careers, spending considerable time in reserve or in training roles. *Tauranga* and *Ringarooma* arrived in New Zealand in October 1891. Thereafter the Pearls and Peloruses made port visits, inspected subantarctic depots and occasionally rescued shipwrecked mariners. In 1900 *Wallaroo* was deployed to China during the Boxer Rebellion, and in the following year *Ringarooma, Wallaroo,* and *Mildura* formed part of the escort for the Duke and Duchess of Cornwall and York. In January 1910 HMS *Pioneer* rescued survivors from the liner *Waikare*, wrecked in Dusky Sound. The Pelorus class ships HMS *Pegasus, Pioneer, Pyramus,* and *Psyche* spent considerable time in New Zealand before the war, the latter pair landing crew members during the 1913 waterfront strike (see CIVIL POWER, AID TO).

Only two of the Pearls escaped 'Fisher's Axe', the controversial mass scrapping of obsolescent pre-dreadnought-era warships in 1906. *Wallaroo* survived as a harbour service vessel from 1906 until 1920. HMS *Philomel*, ironically not one of the colonial quintet, had the greatest local influence. She joined the New Zealand naval forces in 1914 as a seagoing training ship (see CRUISERS), served at sea until 1917, and was then a training and depot ship at Devonport until sold in 1946 and scuttled off Coromandel in 1949. All but two of the newer Pelorus class survived until the ★First World War.

R.J. McDougall, *New Zealand Naval Vessels* (GP Books, Wellington, 1989).

GAVIN McLEAN

Pacific Defence Conference, convened by the New Zealand government, was held in Wellington in April 1939. The origins of the conference lay in the Labour government's desire, expressed as early as 1936, for coordination of the Commonwealth defence effort in the Pacific, especially as doubts grew about the soundness of the ★Singapore strategy. There was disappointment in Wellington when both Australia and Great Britain sent military officers rather than politicians as their representatives. The conference began by examining the strategic situation in the Pacific, during which British assurances that the Mediterranean would take second priority to reinforcing Singapore in the event of trouble with Japan were reiterated. Practical measures to cover the situation during a lengthening 'period before relief' were then considered. These included the establishment by Australia and New Zealand of a line of reconnaissance between Fiji and New Guinea, to give notice of any Japanese penetration. The conference also called for greater coordination of Australian and New Zealand defence activities. While useful in bringing issues to the fore, the conference had little practical effect. Changes in the British strategic approach even as the meetings took place undercut the assumptions upon which the discussions were based, and war intervened before many of the practical recommendations were implemented.

Pacific Islands, dispute with the United States over Strategic and civil aviation requirements combined to focus American interest on a number of British- and New Zealand–owned islands in the South Pacific during the late 1930s. Initially the United States claimed sovereignty over several islands in the British-administered Phoenix group, but in August 1939 claims to the Tokelaus and certain islands in the Cook Islands, both of which were administered by New Zealand, were also asserted. There was firm resistance in Wellington to any American encroachment on either British or New Zealand territories—a stance that was recognised in London and underlay Anglo-American negotiations on the matter. As a British diplomat told the State Department in 1938, 'taking an atoll away from New Zealand was as difficult as taking butter out of a dog's mouth'. Apart from their desire to ensure a British trans-Pacific air route, the New Zealand authorities feared that American possession of the disputed islands would complicate Commonwealth defence plans in the South Pacific—an approach which in retrospect seems strategically unwise, given the state of the ★Singapore strategy in the late 1930s. Far from encouraging American involvement in the region, New Zealand sought to assert British sovereignty by sending naval vessels to survey various islands, locate suitable sites for airfields, and establish wireless stations. Although Britain and the United States—New Zealand was never in direct negotiation with Washington on the issue—agreed to joint control of Canton and Enderbury in 1939, the outbreak of war led them to defer consideration of other island sovereignty questions for the duration, a position which New Zealand reluctantly accepted in 1941.

Pacific versus Mediterranean was a strategic dilemma which confronted New Zealand in 1942 and 1943, following the onset of the ★Pacific War. Should New Zealand leave 2NZEF in the Mediterranean theatre to fight on against Germany and Italy in accordance with the overall Allied strategy to give priority to Europe? Or should it withdraw 2NZEF to take part in the defence of the South Pacific against Japan? Australia had immediately withdrawn two of its three divisions in the Mediterranean; the other would follow after the Battle of El Alamein in October–November 1942. Accepting that shipping problems made a withdrawal difficult, New Zealand made no early move to recall its division. The urgency was reduced, in any case, by the arrival of American troops in New Zealand in June 1942, sent by the United States to make it possible for 2NZEF to remain in the Mediterranean. From that time the argument in favour of withdrawal tended to relate more to political than military issues, such as asserting New Zealand's position as a Pacific state and maintaining good relations with Australia. The issue was addressed after El Alamein, again after the Axis capitulation in Tunisia, and yet again in 1944 when manpower problems became serious. It was recognised that there was a fine balance between the two sides of the argument. Largely at the instigation of Peter ★Fraser, the government resolved to allow 2NZEF to take part in the ★Italian campaign—a decision which strained Australia–New Zealand relations. For a time New Zealand attempted to sustain ground forces in both Mediterranean and Pacific theatres, but in 1944 the Pacific effort was eliminated in favour of sustaining the 2nd New Zealand Division in Italy.

Pacific War began on the night of 7–8 December 1941 when the Japanese struck simultaneously at widely scattered British and American territories in South-east Asia and the Pacific. It ended after the dropping of two atomic bombs on Japan on 6 and 9 August 1945, soon followed by a ceasefire on 15 August and formal surrender on 2 September.

Japan's resort to force to establish a 'New Order in East Asia' with the rationale of liberating the Asia–Pacific hemisphere from Western imperialism, preserving it from communism, and creating a self-sufficient 'Co-Prosperity Sphere', was made possible by the outbreak of the ★Second World War in 1939. This offered the prospect that the colonial powers would be so weakened by the war in Europe, the Atlantic, and the Mediterranean that they would be unable to resist in Asia and the Pacific. But Japan's use of force to establish the New Order had pre-dated 1939. Since the Marco Polo Bridge Incident, when Chinese and Japanese troops exchanged fire near Peking in 1937, there had been continuous fighting. In the so-called 'Undeclared

Pacific War

War' or 'China Incident' Japan occupied much of North China, the Yangtze Valley, and ports on the South China coast. This Sino-Japanese conflict, in turn, can only be understood against the background of tensions since the 'Manchuria Incident' of 1931, when troops guarding a Japanese-operated railway occupied the whole of Manchuria and erected the satellite state of Manchukuo in 1932. In the same year a major outbreak of fighting between Japanese and Chinese forces at Shanghai, the main port of entry into China, was only prevented from escalation by mediation by a British diplomat. Japanese expansionism was evident, then, from 1931–32, and the Pacific War of 1941–45 was only the most dramatic and tragic phase in this wider conflict.

New Zealand was involved in the conflict as a Dominion in the British Empire/Commonwealth. As Japan, the rising 'Workshop of the East' in the twentieth century, sought to supplant the Asian/Pacific empire which had been established by Great Britain, the pioneer 'Workshop of the World' in the nineteenth century, New Zealand, as a part of that empire, became a land to be incorporated in the New Order. The Pacific War was thus part of a twenty-year final contest of empires which was not ended until the peace treaty was signed in 1951.

On the eve of the European War in 1939, both the British and the Japanese Empires were confronted by the dilemma of having to fight on two fronts. The Chinese continued to resist the Japanese invaders in the vast interior with supplies from the United States, Britain, and the Soviet Union. The Japanese Army failed to win the China War and faced insecurity in both north and south. In the north, there had been a series of clashes on the borders with the Soviet Union culminating in severe losses inflicted by the Russians at Nomonhan in May–September 1939. The Soviet threat from the north would remain a constant concern. To the south lay China's supply routes through Indo-China, Burma, and Hong Kong. In the south also lay the oil of the Netherlands East Indies, desperately needed by the Navy, as well as the tin, rubber, and rice of the British and Dutch colonies. Two strategic points in this region were acquired when Hainan was occupied by Japanese forces in February 1939, followed by the Spratly Islands in March.

The British Empire's dilemma was an east–west dilemma which was evident at the ★Pacific Defence Conference in Wellington during April 1939, between British, Australian, and New Zealand military and (on New Zealand's part) political representatives. For twenty years New Zealand's defence policy had been based on the main-fleet-to-★Singapore strategy of ★imperial defence. When it had been conceived in the 1920s, Germany was prostrate and Japan an ally. In the 1930s, as Japan expanded into Asia, the Nazis were rearming Germany, and Italy was embarking upon conquest in Africa. Britain knew it could never face three enemies, so in 1937 declared its priorities. Britain itself and the Singapore base were the 'keystones' of imperial defence; no anxieties in the Mediterranean were to prevent the dispatch of the Fleet to the East. Even as this priority was reiterated by British officers in Wellington in 1939, it was under review in London. Britain eventually informed the South Pacific Dominions that it could not say how soon, or in what strength, the fleet could be sent to the East.

To New Zealand this was not unexpected, and thought had already been given to regional defence in the Pacific. A commitment had been accepted in 1930 to garrison ★Fanning Island, in the Line Islands halfway between Hawaii and Samoa (and the site of a Cable and Wireless relay station) in the event of war. The Dominion ★Chiefs of Staff had also realised that the arc of islands to the north—New Caledonia, New Hebrides, Fiji, and Tonga—would constitute a threat in the hands of a hostile power. It was, therefore, agreed at the Wellington conference that an air reconnaissance line would be operated by Australia and New Zealand stretching from New Guinea to the Cook Islands. In 1936–38, the ★New Zealand Division of the Royal Navy surveyed various atolls in the Ellice, Phoenix, and Line Islands (lying between Fiji and Hawaii) as possible sites for airfields and anchorages. When the war broke out in Europe in 1939, New Zealand duly sent a thirty-two-man platoon to Fanning, but the main military effort at this stage was directed towards the Middle East. When Italy entered the war in June 1940 the British had to resolve their east–west dilemma. Therefore, on the eve of the fall of France, Churchill informed his Australian and New Zealand opposite numbers that, if Japan took the opportunity of the European war to advance in the Pacific, Britain, now facing the German and the Italian navies without the support of the French navy, could not send the fleet to Singapore. It would have to rely on the United States (not yet at war) to protect its interests in the Pacific. This induced probably the greatest period of uncertainty for New Zealand and prompted the government to seek diplomatic representation in Washington. The main war effort remained supplying food and wool to Britain, maintaining a division in North Africa, supplying aircrew for the RAF, and maintaining two cruisers for trade protection. However, in November 1940 an infantry brigade was sent to Fiji.

Japan resolved its north–south dilemma in ways which dramatically ignited the Pacific War. Still unable to defeat China, Japan turned south. The 'New Order in East Asia', first announced in 1938, was expanded to become the 'Greater East Asian Co-Prosperity Sphere' in July 1940. The core would remain

Pacific War

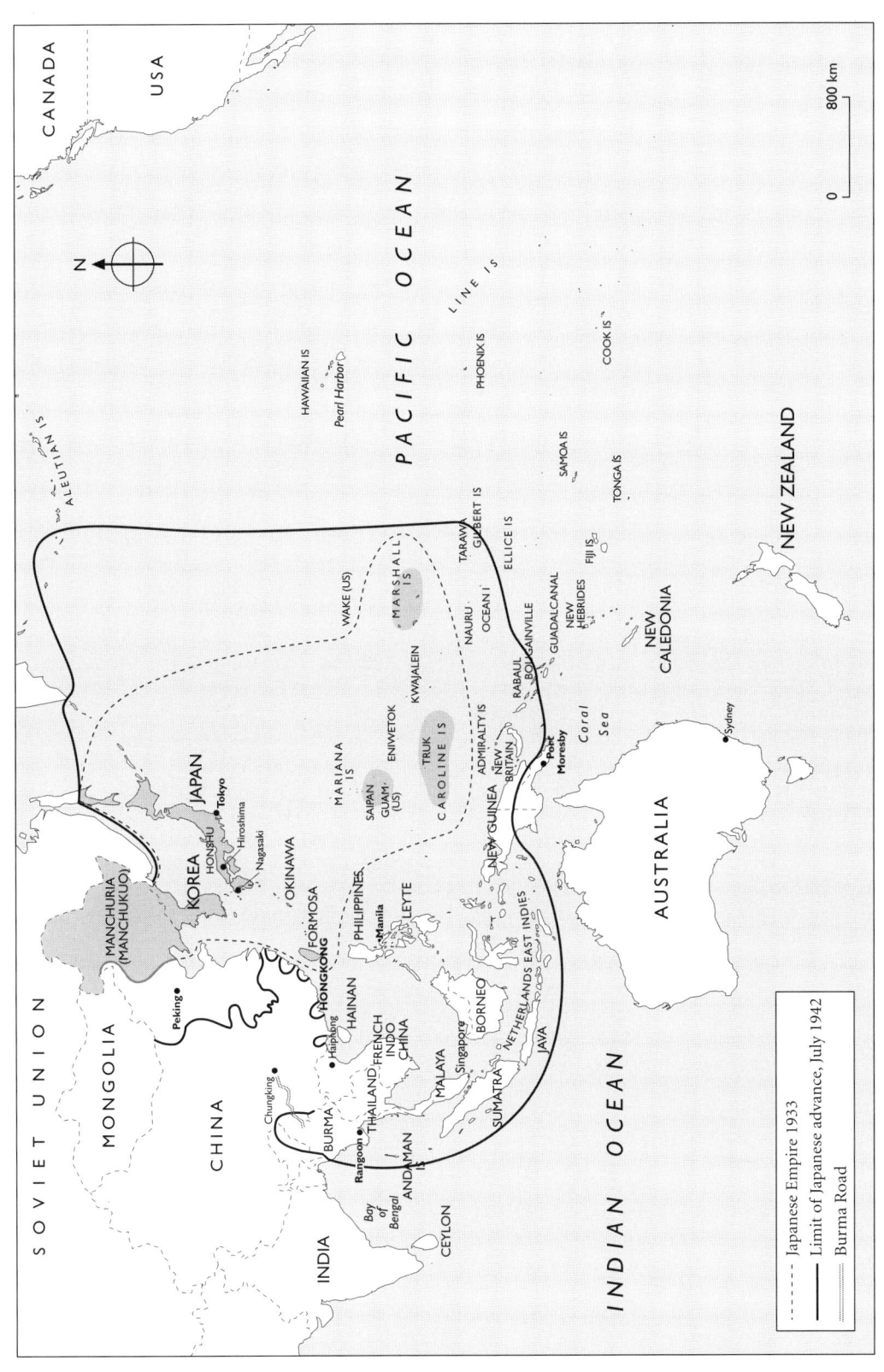

Map 20 The Pacific theatre, 1941–45

Pacific War

Japan–Korea–Manchukuo–Formosa–China, but, to ensure economic self-sufficiency, South-east Asia, Australia, and New Zealand were added. Once the China War was concluded, it was accepted that force might be necessary to achieve these ends. In September 1940, as Tokyo prepared to sign a Tripartite Pact with Germany and Italy, it was agreed that the Germans would be asked to recognise the Asian New Order and refrain from intervening in the colonies of their recent European conquests, namely French Indo-China and the Netherlands East Indies. Although it would not join the European War, Japan would embarrass the British war effort by supporting the nationalist movements in India and Burma and by neutralising Hong Kong and Singapore. The 'South Seas' was defined during these discussions as stretching from Burma to New Zealand.

In this way, the European War gave Japan its opportunity to strike south. During the Battle of Britain in August–September 1940, Japanese forces moved into northern Indo-China to cut the Haiphong route for supplies to China. When Germany invaded the Soviet Union in June 1941, Japan pressured the French Vichy government to allow occupation of harbours and airfields in southern Indo-China to provide the springboard for operations against the British, Dutch, and American colonies. This, in turn, led the United States to cut off supplies of oil and strategic materials and to freeze Japanese assets. Britain and the Netherlands East Indies did the same, and New Zealand followed a day later on 27 July 1941. Persisting with the southward move meant risking war with the United States, so Japan sought, by diplomatic negotiations in Washington, to find a way to reopen its vital American trade. But the American conditions were stringent—that Japan withdraw from not only Indo-China but also all China and Manchuria. The Japanese leaders felt humiliated and encircled. They needed the oil and other raw materials. The navy's planned peak of strength would be reached early in 1942. As the navy Chief of Staff said during the critical Liaison Conference before the Emperor on 1–2 November 1941: 'The time for war will not come later'. With no sure confidence in ultimate victory, but caught up in the impetus of their earlier planning, the Japanese moved on the night of 7–8 December 1941. In a startling twelve-hour detonation, they struck at the International Settlement in Shanghai, the north-east coast of Malaya, the US Fleet base at Pearl Harbor, south-eastern Thailand, Singapore, American airfields in the Philippines, and at Hong Kong, Guam, and Wake. At the moment when Japan struck, New Zealand was contributing to the Allied defences in three places. In Malaya and Burma there were about 400 airmen. In Fiji about five thousand army personnel were with 8th Brigade or with the Fiji Military Forces, and there was also an air reconnaissance squadron. There were about a thousand public works employees constructing three large runways for use in the American air ferry route to Australia. The cruiser HMNZS *Achilles* was convoying reinforcements to the island. Far away in the Central Pacific, there were fifteen radio operators and twenty-two soldiers as *coastwatchers in the Gilbert Islands and there was the platoon on Fanning Island.

The first direct impact of the Japanese advance on New Zealanders was at Butaritari Atoll on the northern Gilbert Islands. When it was occupied on 10 December 1941, three wireless operators and four soldiers were captured. Later, as the first of such prisoners of war to arrive in Tokyo, they were the object of some curiosity and were well treated. The rest of the coastwatchers were less fortunate. Butaritari was the eastern limit of the Japanese advance until the aftermath of an American marine raid on the atoll, on 16 August 1942, which wiped out the garrison. At this point, the Japanese moved south into Ocean Island and Nauru, followed by Tarawa and Abemama in September. Betio islet was turned into Japan's eastern fortress, with huge concrete bunkers, heavy artillery, hundreds of machine-gun posts, and a 2500-strong garrison. Probably in retaliation for an American air raid, during which a New Zealander was shot trying to escape, sixteen coastwatchers and five others were beheaded on 15 October 1942.

In Malaya, the pilots for 488 Squadron (an RNZAF squadron with an RAF designation) had started training on Buffaloes at Kallang, near Singapore, in October–November 1941, and had not been passed for operations when the war started. There were also twenty RNZAF pilots with 243 Squadron RAF, and a Maori sergeant-pilot, Sergeant B.S. Wipiti, was credited with the first Japanese plane shot down over Singapore. By January 1942, 488 Squadron was patrolling the skies over Malayan reinforcement convoys and was later equipped with Hurricanes, most of which were soon destroyed when Kallang was bombed. The last of their planes flew from Singapore on 8 February 1942 and, after a brief period of operations in Java, a remnant of the squadron reached Australia. A New Zealand aerodrome construction squadron had reached Malaya in October 1941 and started work on a bomber base in southern Johore. In December, some men moved north to start a new fighter strip, while others were posted to airfields in Singapore and one party went north to salvage heavy equipment. By January 1942, the recently completed works were demolished and on 1 February the squadron embarked with its equipment (see MALAYAN CAMPAIGN). Apart from New Zealanders serving in Royal Navy ships, the RNZN's presence at Singapore was confined to Commodore W.E. ★Parry (representing the Navy Board), who was present for consultations with Admiral Sir Tom Phillips, commander of the Royal Navy's Eastern Fleet. Parry immediately signalled for *Achilles* to join the fleet, but, although the cruiser sailed from Fiji, she was recalled after the sinking of HMS *Prince of Wales* and *Repulse* on 10 December. Between February and April 1942 *Achilles* and HMNZS *Leander* (back from the Indian Ocean) joined an American cruiser, an Australian cruiser, and two American destroyers in a short-lived Anzac Squadron. With the creation of the US ★South Pacific Area in April, the two RNZN cruisers came under this command. Meanwhile, Fiji's defences were reinforced by the arrival of 14th Brigade and a headquarters organisation, making a two-brigade division, referred to from May 1942 as the 3rd Division.

The big fear for New Zealand in the early days of 1942 was whether the country would be attacked. In a matter of only six months the Japanese established an extensive perimeter, stretching in the east from Wake Island, through the northern Gilbert Islands to Rabaul, New Britain, in the Australian-ruled New Guinea Territory, which was captured on 26 January 1942. In the north, Hong Kong and the British Borneo territories were soon overrun. Singapore surrendered on 15 February 1942. Allied naval forces were decimated in the Battle of the Java Sea on 24 February and the Netherlands East Indies surrendered on 8 March, while the Japanese landed at Lae and Salamua on the north-east coast of New Guinea. On the same day, in the west, Rangoon surrendered (see BURMA CAMPAIGN). The Americans held out on the Bataan Peninsula in the Philippines until 9 April and on Corregidor Island for another month until 6 May. The geographical basis for the Greater East Asian Co-Prosperity Sphere had been laid with astonishing dispatch. Where the Japanese would go next, and how the new empire was to be ruled, was less clear.

In the latter part of 1941 and early 1942 there was a spate of planning in Japan as to how the new empire in the 'South Seas Region' should be ruled. These papers indicate that only places of strategic significance were to be ruled directly through a series of governments-general. Most of the countries would be granted independence conditional on agreements granting Japanese bases and providing for diplomatic and economic cooperation. The New Order would be one of satellite states, somewhat on the Manchukuo model, set up on the basis of Asian nationalism in succession to Western colonialism, but with Japanese hegemony. Although no plans for the invasion of New Zealand have been revealed, this was probably due to the fact that such an operation never became possible. However, New Zealand certainly figured within the regions included in the new Co-Prosperity Sphere, and in some plans both Australia and New Zealand were cited as places for peasant colonisation.

Japan's intentions were, of course, not known in New Zealand and, in the aftermath of the devastating losses of Allied naval power with the bombing of Pearl Harbor and the sinking of the *Prince of Wales* and the *Repulse*, the situation was potentially very bleak. The authorities in Wellington, however, remained calm. On 10 January 1942 (more than a month before the fall of Singapore) the New Zealand Chiefs of Staff discounted the possibility of a Japanese invasion in a paper advising the government on civil defence precautions. Japanese plans, they suggested, would be guided strategically by the need to neutralise Allied naval power and to secure sea communications, and economically by the need to gain vital resources. These were oil, rubber, tin, nickel, coal, iron, and rice, which were all available in the lands of their southern conquests but not (except coal) from New Zealand. The COS expected that Japan's objectives would be cutting supplies to China via the Burma Road, occupying Singapore and Manila to neutralise British and American naval power, exploiting the resources of South-east Asia, and seizing strategically situated South Pacific islands to cut the Allied supply routes. Only the last of these would present a threat to New Zealand as Japan was likely to go for Fiji to cut the American reinforcement route to Australia. New Zealand might be subject also to raids. The conclusion reached was that the Dominion was not vulnerable because of its remoteness, the limits of Japan's naval and air strength, and the fact that New Zealand could not supply the raw materials Japan needed. The country was not, indeed, threatened with invasion, but Japanese submarines tasked with sea-lane destruction operated off the Australian and New Zealand coasts. On 8 March 1942, a submarine-launched reconnaissance plane flew over Wellington, and on 13 March over Auckland, followed by another on 24 May (see ENEMY OPERATIONS IN NEW ZEALAND WATERS). On 31 May two midget submarines penetrated Sydney Harbour.

The Japanese had started the war in the Pacific with resounding successes, but how to end it while the going was good eluded them. A negotiated peace in which the colonial powers—Australia, Britain, France, the Netherlands, and the United States—acquiesced in the Greater East Asian Co-Prosperity Sphere, because of their preoccupation with the European War, was the best prospect. But the manner in which they started the war precluded such a conclusion. On top of that, the United States had vastly superior industrial capacity and command of resources. Moreover, after their initial run of successes the Japanese strategists were disunited as to future objectives. The army wanted to

Pacific War

consolidate in South-east Asia while the China War was brought to a conclusion. The navy wanted to destroy the American fleet. As Australia was the most likely base for an Allied counter-attack, the navy staff wanted first to eliminate Australia from the war, but the army staff insisted the men and transport were not available. A compromise was reached that Australia would be isolated by the occupation of a line of islands from New Guinea to Fiji and Samoa—very much as the New Zealand COS had predicted. Limitations on Japanese action were imposed, first of all, by their finite resources. In 1942, as the army slogged on in China, still keeping a wary eye on the Soviet Union in the north, the navy sought to ensure the security of the western perimeter by a long-range fleet incursion into the Indian Ocean. Merchant ships were sunk in the Bay of Bengal. The Andaman Islands were occupied on 23 March. Harbours in Ceylon and southern India were bombed. A British aircraft-carrier and two cruisers were sunk and the Eastern Fleet scared off to the coast of Africa. However, American carrier-borne raids in the Central Pacific proved more than an irritation when the audacious 'Doolittle Raid' struck Tokyo on 18 April 1942. The navy became resolute that the most urgent need was the elimination of the US Fleet.

However, a second limitation became evident in that force was not concentrated. Two very different operations competed for Japan's resources in mid 1942. First, a landing at Port Moresby in Papua was planned as a prelude to a full-scale occupation of all New Guinea. Second, to lure the US Fleet to the long-dreamt-of great naval encounter in which it would be vanquished by Japanese battleships, Midway Island was to be occupied in June l942. It was a grand, if complex, plan. It collapsed after the Battle of the Coral Sea, 7–8 May 1942 (which caused the Moresby operation to be postponed), and the Battle of Midway, 4 June (which caused the Pacific Islands occupation to be postponed and then cancelled). The more limited aims of taking the eastern Solomons and driving overland to Port Moresby were foiled in punishing land battles at Guadalcanal, Milne Bay, and Kokoda, and a series of naval battles in the Solomons. The tide turned in 1942. There was no longer any fear among the people that New Zealand would be attacked.

In the long roll-back of the Japanese perimeter New Zealand had some minor roles, but only as part of wider strategic plans which were determined in the highest Allied councils. Even before Pearl Harbor, the basic priority had been accepted that the goal would be to defeat Germany first. Initially, if the United States went to war, it would go on the defensive in the Pacific, while Germany would be subjected to offensives in Europe. This priority was reaffirmed at the 'Arcadia' Conference in Washington in December 1941–January 1942. The first Allied offensives in the Pacific were directed at the Japanese base at Rabaul. It was agreed, early in July 1942, that marines under Admiral Ghormley's South Pacific Command would land first on Tulagi and Guadalcanal in the eastern Solomon Islands and drive westwards through the group towards Rabaul, and that General Douglas MacArthur's South West Pacific Command would clear the northern coasts of New Guinea and approach Rabaul from the south-west. The latter move was delayed by Japanese landings at Buna and Milne Bay on 22 and 25 July 1942. The US Marines landed at Guadalcanal and Tulagi on 7 August, and it took months of some of the worst fighting of the war before the roll-back could commence in earnest. But by 7 September the Australians had beaten the Japanese at Milne Bay, inflicting the first defeat on the Japanese army, and on 24 September at Kokoda, in the Owen Stanley Ranges, they stemmed the advance on Port Moresby. Japanese resistance continued on Guadalcanal until 9 February 1943. Thereafter the US Marines moved west to land on New Georgia on 30 June, Vella Lavella on 15 August, Bougainville on 1 November, and New Britain on 26 December. These advances were only achieved after costly naval engagements.

In this campaign all three New Zealand services had a role. The US South Pacific Command was headquartered in Auckland, and in June 1942 the US 1st Marine Division landed in New Zealand in fulfilment of President Roosevelt's promise that he would send an American division to New Zealand in return for 2nd Division staying in the Mediterranean (see UNITED STATES TROOPS IN NEW ZEALAND). The US Marines trained for amphibious warfare, as did New Zealand's 3rd Division after its return from Fiji, where the defences had also been taken over by the Americans. As the marines landed in the Solomons, New Zealand provided garrisons in ★New Caledonia, Norfolk Island, and ★Tonga, and the RNZAF operated from Fiji and the New Hebrides. By the end of 1942 the country's manpower was so overstretched that the Prime Minister, Peter ★Fraser, again pressed for the return of 2nd Division from the Mediterranean. Fraser stressed to Churchill that it was unwise to allow the whole offensive against Japan in the South Pacific to be entrusted to the Americans. He saw New Zealand providing a 'British' element.

In the event, New Zealand both stayed in the Mediterranean, and also played a role in the ★Solomons campaign from 1943 to 1945. Both cruisers and a flotilla of anti-submarine trawlers served with the US Fleet. On 5 January 1943, while covering relief convoys south of Guadalcanal, *Achilles* was dive-bombed and had a gun turret destroyed. At the end of the month, HMNZS *Kiwi* and *Moa* sank a Japanese submarine, *Kiwi* getting dented while ramming. *Moa* was herself sunk on 7 April 1943. Damage sustained by *Leander*, which was torpedoed in the Battle of Kolombangara on 12 July 1943, was so serious that she went to the United States for repair and left the New Zealand navy. In August–September 1943 the 3rd Division, reduced to two brigades, moved from New Caledonia to Guadalcanal, and was employed a brigade at a time in three island landings along extended lines of communication. The Fiji Military Forces (including New Zealand officers and NCOs) and the RNZAF also fought in the campaign. The 1st Fijian Commando (with a Tongan platoon) landed with the US Marines in New Georgia in July–August 1943; 14th Brigade and 1st Commando took over from the Americans the clearance of Vella Lavella in September–October 1943. On 27 October, 8th Brigade landed on Mono and Stirling in the Treasury Islands, and on 21 December 1943 the 1st Fiji Infantry Battalion joined the Americans on Bougainville. The RNZAF began in a small way in the Solomons with a bomber reconnaisance flight operating from Guadalcanal in November 1942. It moved forward with a fighter wing (of two squadrons) to Ondonga, in New Georgia, in October 1943 and to Torokina, on Bougainville, by January 1944, from which the bombing of Rabaul could intensify.

After the signing of the ★Australia–New Zealand Agreement in January 1944, in which Australia and New Zealand asserted their 'vital interest' in the Pacific peace settlement and their willingness to take their part in the policing of the region, there was some American reluctance to use Dominion forces. But New Zealand continued to contribute to the Allied effort in two sectors of the Pacific. First, in the northern Solomons, 3rd Division made one more landing on Nissan, in the Green Islands, on 15 February 1944. It was then recalled and later disbanded because of labour shortages at home caused by the growing food supply needs of the US forces in the South Pacific. In contrast, the RNZAF continued to expand its role in the Solomons. A seven-squadron Air Task Force was established in September 1944 now under MacArthur's South West Pacific Command. By 1945, when the Japanese base at Rabaul had been cut off by sea and air, it was ringed by RNZAF bases from which the beleaguered 100,000-strong garrison was bombed. These bases were at Nissan (Green Island), Emirau (St Matthias Group), Los Negros (Admiralty Islands), and Jacquinot Bay (New Britain).

The second theatre was off the coasts of Okinawa and Japan, where three New Zealand ships joined the British Pacific Fleet in the final months of the war. This eventuated only after the long, arduous advance across the Central Pacific by US forces. It had been decided at the Casablanca Conference, in January 1943, that the roll-back would be divided into three parts. While the drive towards Rabaul through the Solomons would continue, MacArthur would clear the northern coasts of New Guinea prior to returning to the Philippines. At the same time, the third thrust would be in the Central Pacific through the Gilbert Islands, Marshalls, Carolines, and Marianas to positions from which Japan's main islands could be bombed and eventually attacked.

This campaign began disastrously at Tarawa, in the Gilberts, on 20 November 1943 when over a thousand marines were mown down because the US commander refused to heed the advice of liaison officer Major F.G.L. ★Holland, a New Zealander who had spent twenty years in the islands, that there would not be sufficient tide the day of the assault. After Tarawa the advance was relentless. In February 1944, Majuro, Kwajalein, and Eniwetok in the Marshalls were taken. By June Saipan and Tinian and in July Guam, in the Marianas, had fallen. In October, MacArthur landed on Leyte with the Philippines President. Early in 1945 the Australians moved into Borneo.

New Zealand's role was with the British Pacific Fleet. First, several hundred New Zealand pilots made up a quarter of the ★Fleet Air Arm strength on the fleet's aircraft-carriers. They flew their early sorties against Japanese oil installations in Sumatra. After the fleet reached the Pacific in February 1945, first to Sydney, then to Manus in the Admiralty Islands, and on to the advance base at Ulithi, in the Carolines, the RNZN cruisers joined it. Totalling, by the end, more than a hundred warships (including four battleships, five fleet carriers, twelve auxiliary carriers, and ten cruisers), the Pacific Fleet was the most powerful ever assembled in the long history of British seapower. It had a cruiser, destroyer, and anti-aircraft ship from Canada and six Australian destroyers, as well as *Achilles* and HMNZS *Gambia*. It was serviced by a fleet train of over forty

Troops of New Zealand's 3rd Division landing on Nissan Island in 1944 (*War History Collection, Alexander Turnbull Library, F-44746-1/2*)

Paramilitary groups

vessels, including the New Zealand corvette HMNZS *Arbutus* as radar maintenance ship. Between 26 March and 25 May 1945 *Gambia* was part of Task Force 57, which had the role of bombing airfields in the Sakishima Group (between Formosa and Okinawa) to cover the American landings on Okinawa to the north—an operation which exceeded the size of the ★D-Day landings in Normandy. Towards the end of this operation, they were joined by *Achilles*. In the period when the fleet returned to bases in Australia for refit, *Achilles* joined a force which bombarded Truk in the Caroline Islands on 14–15 June 1945. Finally, both cruisers were part of Task Force 37, which bombarded the coasts of Honshu in July–August 1945. On the night of 29–30 July, HMS *King George V* bombarded railway workshops at Hamamatsu, about 250 kilometres south of Tokyo—the last time a British battleship fired its big guns in war. On 9 August—the day the Soviet Union joined the Pacific War and a second ★atomic bomb was dropped, this time on Nagasaki—*Gambia* took part in the bombardment of the Kaimashi steelworks in northern Honshu and it shot down a Japanese plane, probably the last aircraft engaged by the guns of the Pacific Fleet. After this action most of the fleet retired to Australia, but *Gambia* remained as part of the initial occupation force and on 30 August 1945 landed a platoon of seamen for the surrender of Yokosuka naval base.

Japan's formal and unconditional surrender was signed on the battleship USS *Missouri* in Tokyo Bay on 2 September 1945. New Zealand's signature was added by Air Vice-Marshal L.M. ★Isitt, and *Gambia* lay in the Allied fleet line. Air Commodore G.N. Roberts represented New Zealand at the surrender ceremonies at Rabaul on 6 September and Torokina on 8 September. Air Chief Marshal Keith ★Park, a New Zealander, who commanded the RAF in Southeast Asia, was present at the surrender in Singapore. Commander Peter ★Phipps was New Zealand's representative at the surrender of Nauru on 13 September and Ocean Island on 1 October.

There followed six years of occupation, which proved momentous for Japan's social, economic, political, and constitutional development. New Zealand participated in the ★British Commonwealth Occupation Force, which had responsibility for southern Honshu. ★Jayforce, made up of 9th Brigade, covered the Yamaguchi Prefecture. One unit was stationed with the Commonwealth HQ at the Imperial Japanese Navy's Academy on Etajima in the Inland Sea. A squadron of Corsair fighters was stationed at Iwakuni to the south. In the eleven-nation Far East Commission in Washington, which was formally charged with oversight of the supreme commander's policies, New Zealand's representative, Carl ★Berendsen, was an outspoken chairman of the Steering Committee. There was also a New Zealand judge on the eleven-nation International Military Tribunal for the Far East, which conducted the Tokyo ★War Crimes Trials.

After two years of occupation General MacArthur, the Supreme Allied Commander, was calling for a peace treaty to be signed. This was not done until 1951 because of procedural wrangles between the United States and the Soviet Union occasioned by the ★Cold War. The United States sought a peace of reconciliation with Japan, to secure Japan as an ally in the Cold War. New Zealand and Australia were less ready to accord a generous peace and sought a disarmed Japan subject to strict international controls. They were not prepared to sign a so-called 'soft peace' without an American guarantee of their security. Thus, the peace treaty signed in San Francisco on 8 September 1951, which ended the state of war, stripped Japan of its colonial empire, and restored full sovereignty to the main islands, was preceded, a week before, by the conclusion of the ★ANZUS alliance. The San Francisco Conference in September 1945 was for formal adherence by forty-eight nations to terms already negotiated, not for further discussions. New Zealand's delegate was given the task of moving the necessary procedural resolution and, to do this, Berendsen jostled in the aisle with Andrei Gromyko of the Soviet Union to get to the podium first. In this way, New Zealand had its hand in the concluding moments of the twenty-year final contest of empires.

O.A. Gillespie, *The Pacific* (War History Branch, Wellington, 1952); A.J. Levine, *The Pacific War: Japan versus the Allies* (Praeger, Westport, 1995).

W. DAVID McINTYRE

Paramilitary groups Leaving aside various groups formed during the ★New Zealand Wars, and the military police ★Armed Constabulary, the Boy Scouts were perhaps the earliest paramilitary group in New Zealand. Established by Major David Cossgrove in 1908, they were notable in their early years for the strong emphasis placed on teaching military skills and inculcating patriotic and militaristic values. Another product of Edwardian imperialistic fervour was the Legion of Frontiersmen, units of which were first formed in New Zealand in 1911. By 1914, 1200 men had joined this organisation out of a belief that individual self-reliance and marksmanship would contribute to imperial security. They wore a uniform similar in pattern to that of the Canadian Mounted Police. Denied permission to form their own unit in 1NZEF, Legionnaires enlisted as ordinary citizens. The Legion remained in existence at the end of the twentieth century. Since the ★First World War there have been few paramilitary groups. In contrast to Australia, where right-wing 'armies' such as the New Guard were formed, no militant extremist organisations were established in New Zealand during the Depression. Tiny cliques of right-wing extremists or survivalists claiming to be militant and armed have occasionally formed since the 1960s, but such groups have had a brief and insignificant existence.

Parihaka was the most significant incident involving the use of military force against Maori dissidents in the quarter of a century after the end of the ★New Zealand Wars. During that conflict the chief Te Whiti o Rongomai and his associate Tohu, adopting a passive stance, had withdrawn from contact with the belligerents. In the 1870s their village at the western foot of Mount Egmont/Taranaki swelled to more than 2000 inhabitants as it became a haven for the disillusioned. When grievances over European settlement of confiscated land in the Parihaka block led Te Whiti and Tohu to instigate a series of non-violent protests later in the decade, fears were aroused among the Europeans in the province, and elsewhere, that outright conflict was imminent. Although such fears were illusory, for Te Whiti and Tohu had no warlike intentions, the government responded to the public clamour for action by resolving on a display of force to effect the arrest of the two Maori chiefs. On 5 November 1881, a 644-strong ★Armed Constabulary force, supported by nearly a thousand settler volunteers and led by Native Minister John Bryce on a white charger, 'invaded' Parihaka, to be greeted on their arrival not by fanatical warriors but by singing children. No resistance was offered as Te Whiti and Tohu were arrested for sedition. Over the next three weeks the outsiders among the community were forcibly dispersed and their dwellings torn down.
H. Riseborough, *Days of Darkness: Taranaki 1878–1884* (Allen & Unwin/Historical Branch, Wellington, 1989).

Park, Air Chief Marshal Sir Keith Rodney (15 June 1892–6 February 1975), born in Thames, was the most prominent of a group of New Zealanders who made their careers in the RAF and held high rank in the ★Second World War. He enlisted in 1NZEF in December 1914, and fought at ★Gallipoli as a gunner in the New Zealand Field Artillery. Commissioned in July 1915, he transferred a few months later to the Royal Artillery, serving on the ★Western Front from March to October 1916. While recovering from a wound in England, he transferred to the Royal Flying Corps in December and underwent flying instruction before returning to France in July 1917. For the rest of the war he flew two-seater Bristol fighters with 48 Squadron, which he commanded from April 1918, being credited with eleven victories and in the process earning an MC and bar and a DFC.

After the war, Park sought unsuccessfully to obtain a regular commission in the New Zealand Military Forces before being one of the first intake of officers at the RAF's staff college at Andover in 1922. Various command and staff postings followed, including attendance at the ★Imperial Defence College in 1937, before he was appointed as deputy to Air Chief Marshal Sir Hugh Dowding, the commander of Fighter Command, in July 1938. Together they devised a comprehensive air defence system incorporating the recently introduced Spitfire and Hurricane fighter aircraft, radio control, and radar. In April 1940 Park assumed command of 11 Group, covering the crucial south-east England sector, including London. Within six weeks, he found himself having to improvise the air defence of the Allied forces being evacuated from Dunkirk, and used air patrols to deny the Luftwaffe complete air supremacy over the beaches. When in August 1940 the Germans began air attacks on British radar installations and airfields with a view to crushing British air power as a preliminary to an invasion of Great Britain, 11 Group bore the brunt of the onslaught. Park proved an inspiring leader for his hard-pressed pilots, often flying himself to embattled airfields in his trademark white flying suit. His skilful handling of his scarce resources was vital to British success in the Battle of Britain. The *Luftwaffe*'s switch to bombing London in September, a crucial tactical error, was in effect an admission of its inability to neutralise 11 Group. Even as the German air offensive wound down in October, Dowding and Park became embroiled in controversy over their handling of the battle, their cautious tactics being strongly criticised by Air Vice-Marshal Trafford Leigh-Mallory and others. Although Park's tactics have been vindicated in retrospect, he found himself effectively sidelined in December 1940 when posted to command a training group.

General Dwight D. Eisenhower meets Air Marshal Sir Keith Park (*RAF*)

Park

Not until January 1942 was Park again given another operational role. He commanded the air defence of Egypt, before becoming RAF commander on the strategically vital island of Malta in July. Apart from fighting off German and Italian air attacks, he mounted increasingly successful attacks against Axis shipping in the Mediterranean, which contributed significantly to the eventual Allied victory in North Africa. He was made a KBE in 1942. In January 1944 he became the commander-in-chief of British air forces in the Middle East, and a year later he took command of Allied air forces in South East Asia Command. This latter task involved directing a massive air supply operation in support of the advancing 14th Army in Burma (see BURMA CAMPAIGN). He was made a KCB in January 1945, and in the following year a GCB. When he retired from the RAF in 1946, he held the highest rank, air chief marshal, yet attained by a New Zealander. He took up residence in Auckland, where a reconstruction of a wartime airfield at that city's Museum of Transport and Technology is named after him. (See AIRMEN, NEW ZEALAND, IN THE RAF IN THE SECOND WORLD WAR)

V. Orange, *Sir Keith Park* (Methuen, London, 1984).

Park, Brigadier Ronald Stuart (18 February 1895–15 August 1980) commanded ★Kayforce during the ★Korean War. A native of Dunedin, he began his military career as a cadet in the Royal Military College at Duntroon in March 1914. With his course reduced by a third because of the needs of 1NZEF, he returned to New Zealand in mid 1916 and served on the instructional staff at Featherston Military Camp until November 1917. After serving in 1NZEF's HQ in London, he finally joined the 9th Battery, 2nd New Zealand Field Artillery Brigade, on the ★Western Front in July 1918. From October 1918, he was Staff Officer for Reconnaissance in the field artillery section of the New Zealand Divisional HQ. After the war, he underwent a specialist course in the United Kingdom before returning to New Zealand, where he held various posts in the coast artillery. From 1933 he combined the post of Staff Officer for Artillery at GHQ with responsibilities in the Central Military District. In August 1939 he went to London to become Military Liaison Officer, and soon found himself heavily involved in arrangements for the deployment in Great Britain of 2NZEF's Second Echelon in 1940. For more than five years from October 1941, he commanded 2NZEF's United Kingdom Section and also represented New Zealand on the British Chiefs of Staff Committee's Joint Planning Staff in London. He was military adviser to the New Zealand delegation to the Paris Peace Conference in 1946. From May 1947 to February 1950 he commanded the Northern Military District. Shortly after retiring from the Army in July 1950, he was appointed to command New Zealand's artillery-dominated ground force contribution to the UN Command in South Korea. Establishing his headquarters in Pusan, he oversaw the administration and control of Kayforce and liaised with the UN Command, a relatively straightforward task because no contentious issues arose. By the time he relinquished his command in November 1953, an armistice had brought the fighting to an end. For his military services he was made a CBE (1943) and a CB (1953).

Parkinson, Major-General Graham Beresford ('Ike') (5 November 1896–10 July 1979) was a senior 2NZEF commander. Wellington-born, he entered the Royal Military College at Duntroon in 1914, and was commissioned in the Royal New Zealand Artillery two years later. After serving as an instructor at Trentham, he joined 1NZEF on the ★Western Front in 1917, and rose to become brigade major of the New Zealand Field Artillery. Between the wars his career followed that of other permanent force officers, with attendance at courses in the United Kingdom alternating with staff and instructional duties in New Zealand. Seconded to 2NZEF in January 1940, he commanded the 2nd New Zealand Division's 4th Field Regiment. After performing well in the ill-fated ★Greece campaign, he returned to New Zealand in November 1941 to take command of the 1st New Zealand Army Tank Brigade, which was being prepared for service in the Middle East. However, with the onset of the ★Pacific War, he found himself instead commanding 7th Brigade, the ★New Zealand Army's reserve, at Waiouru. Returning to the Mediterranean in 1943, he commanded 6th Brigade in Tunisia and Italy. For most of March 1944 he temporarily commanded 2nd New Zealand Division during the difficult fighting at Cassino. His performance has been criticised for its tentativeness. Anxious to save lives and placing too much reliance upon a massive bombardment, he used his infantry in piecemeal attacks which made no headway in the town's rubble. After three months as CRA, he returned to command of 6th Brigade, but was aggrieved when passed over for further temporary command of the division in favour of the more junior Brigadier C.E. ★Weir. Parkinson led his brigade with drive and skill in the final river crossing campaigns in northern Italy. After the war, he served as Quartermaster-General at Army HQ in 1946, was Military Liaison Officer in London for the following three years, and completed his career, in 1952, as commander of the Southern Military District.

Parry, Admiral Sir (William) Edward (8 April 1893–21 August 1972) commanded the New Zealand cruiser HMS *Achilles* at the Battle of the ★River Plate.

Born in London, he entered the Royal Navy in 1905 and served at sea throughout the ★First World War. After commanding the Royal Navy's anti-submarine warfare establishment in 1936–37 and attending the ★Imperial Defence College in 1938, he was seconded to the ★New Zealand Division of the Royal Navy to command *Achilles* in January 1939. For his part in the defeat of the *Admiral Graf Spee*, the New Zealand naval forces' baptism of fire, he was made a CB. From May 1940 to June 1942 he was First Naval Member of the New Zealand Naval Board, Chief of Naval Staff, and Commodore Commanding the New Zealand Squadron. Because of the difficulties he soon experienced in combining responsibilities ashore with a seagoing appointment, he relinquished command of the Squadron and of *Achilles* on 15 October 1940. He proved a capable chief of staff, overseeing the development of an effective naval administration to deal with the much-expanded New Zealand naval effort, not only to train as many men as possible for the Royal Navy but also to deal with the threat posed by German mine-laying raiders. He was also heavily involved in New Zealand's preparations for dealing with possible Japanese entry to the war. So well regarded was he by the New Zealand government that it sought, unsuccessfully, to extend his term after the onset of the ★Pacific War. Reverting to the Royal Navy in June 1942, he commanded the battleship HMS *Renown* in 1943 and the naval component of Force L on ★D-Day. He served in the Allied Control Commission in Berlin in 1945–46 before becoming Director of Naval Intelligence at the Admiralty. His last major posting was as Commander-in-Chief of the Indian Navy from 1948 to 1951. He was made a KCB in 1950. His papers are lodged in the Imperial War Museum, London.

Patriotic funds first appeared during the ★Boer War, their object being to assist the New Zealand contingents dispatched to South Africa. More than £113,000 was raised. The distribution of moneys obtained for such purposes was regulated by the Patriotic Funds Act 1903. During the ★First World War patriotic funds multiplied. About 600 were formed to provide comforts and luxuries for the members of 1NZEF, alleviate distress among their dependants, and even to give relief to hapless Serbian and Belgian civilians. Throughout the war patriotic funds were controlled by local communities, and attempts by the

Cases of comforts for New Zealand forces being packed and stacked for shipment at a YMCA gymnasium in Wellington in January 1940 (*Evening Post Collection, Alexander Turnbull Library, F-58215-1/2*)

government to achieve uniformity in war relief and comforts to soldiers efforts were resisted. In 1915 the War Funds Act brought patriotic funds under greater scrutiny, but there remained a bewildering miscellany of uncoordinated local funds. An advisory board was established in 1916 to coordinate patriotic relief and eliminate duplication, but unwillingness to submit war relief to central authority persisted. Although a Dominion-wide scheme of patriotic war relief was never introduced during the First World War, £6.5 million had been raised by its end.

The *Second World War experience contrasted sharply with that of the First. Almost immediately, patriotic funds were brought under government control. The National Patriotic Fund Board was established in October 1939, along with eleven provincial Patriotic Councils. The provincial councils were responsible for providing comforts to troops within their own area and the dispatch of relief parcels, as well as for the collection of money from their areas. The National Patriotic Fund Board was the central agency, responsible for the provision of comforts to New Zealand soldiers and sailors, and for alleviating the distress of dependants, as well as coordinating and funding agencies such as the *YMCA, the Salvation Army, and the *Red Cross. In contrast to the First World War the public approach to the donation of money was subdued, perhaps because of the lack of community control. However, specific nationwide appeals, such as Red Cross appeals for refugee relief, were always well supported. By the end of the war about £9 million had been raised by the National Patriotic Fund Board. Within New Zealand recreational huts and equipment were provided for soldiers and sailors, and funds were donated to needy or sick servicemen or their dependants. Overseas, the ebullient Colonel Fred *Waite was appointed commissioner with the responsibility of coordinating comforts for soldiers. The National Patriotic Fund both directly and through various agencies (in particular the YMCA) provided important leisure facilities for New Zealand soldiers and sailors, such as films, games, writing materials, and newspapers, at the New Zealand Forces Club in Cairo (and later at Bari in Italy). Gift parcels of sweets and biscuits, especially at Christmas, and knitted woollen garments provided an important boost for troops.

The New Zealand Patriotic Fund Board was established in May 1948, taking over the functions of the National Patriotic Fund. It provided relief for sick, disabled, unemployed, or otherwise needy ex-servicemen and their dependants. Comforts were provided to New Zealand troops serving in the *Korean War and in Malaya. The main task of the New Zealand Patriotic Fund was to establish and manage residential homes for ex-servicemen and women. In 1987 the Patriotic Fund Board merged with the Armed Forces Canteen Council to form the Patriotic and Canteen Funds Board.

Patrol craft In both world wars New Zealand requisitioned small craft for patrol, training, and port examination purposes. The country acquired its first purpose-built patrol craft during the 1940s when the RNZN took delivery of two British types, the Fairmile 'B' and the Harbour Defence Motor Launch. The twelve Fairmiles (ML400–ML411) displaced 73 tons, made 18.5 knots, and shipped one 2-pounder, one 20 mm anti-aircraft gun, two machine-guns, a depth charge thrower, and twelve *depth charges. The sixteen smaller harbour defence motor launches (Q1183–Q1194 and Q1348–Q1351) displaced forty-six tons, made 11–12 knots, and carried a single 20 mm anti-aircraft gun, machine-guns, and eight depth charges.

The government ordered the more expensive Fairmiles in response to the submarine threat, but that problem had receded by the time they had emerged from Auckland boatyards in 1942–43. After being sorely tested in Cook Strait waters, the 80th and 81st Motor Launch Flotilla craft went north to take part in the *Solomons campaign. They conducted escort missions, but made no contact with enemy forces before returning to be laid up in 1945. Twelve HDMLs were allocated to New Zealand in February 1942, ten of which were supposed to be built in Britain. However, the loss of Q1090 with her transport en route to New Zealand in July 1942 and ongoing shipping problems ensured that no British craft were received. In the end, it was determined that the craft, augmented by a further allocation of ten in June 1942, should all be built in American yards. With six of the projected allocation later cancelled, the RNZN eventually took delivery of sixteen craft in 1943–44. Q1184 and Q1348 went to Suva, but plans to attach others to the British Pacific Fleet were cancelled, and most HDMLs stayed in home waters, replacing the requisitioned private launches.

Only two Fairmiles—renamed HMNZS *Kahu* and *Iris Moana*—served post-war as auxiliaries, leaving the burden to fall on the robust and economical little HDMLs. For many years the Army's *Bombardier* towed targets for its coastal batteries. Redesignated seaward defence motor launches (SDMLs) in 1949, many launches were re-engined and fitted with lattice masts and radar. Given names in lieu of numbers, they carried out fisheries protection, naval reserve training, inshore *hydrographic surveying, ceremonial, and conservation duties. HMNZS *Ngapona* got into the headlines after hitting rocks south of Coromandel Harbour in 1957 and was declared a total loss. Fisheries

A Fairmile launch with the cruiser HMNZS *Leander*, with two RNZAF Harvards about to mount a practice bombing attack on them (*RNZN*)

protection numbers built up steadily from the single Auckland-based launch in the late 1940s. Each Christmas–New Year during the 1960s several volunteer reserve launches gathered in the Marlborough Sounds during the RNZNVR 'Claymore' exercises. By 1970, though, the survivors were showing the signs of age. They left RNZN service, beginning with HMNZS *Maroro* and *Tamure* in 1972 and ending with HMNZS *Kuparu* in 1989.

The RNZN wanted six fast patrol boats for fisheries protection, but had to settle for four, the 25-knot, 107-ton Lake class HMNZS *Pukaki*, *Rotoiti*, *Taupo*, and *Hawea*. Ordered from Brooke Marine in the United Kingdom over the protests of local shipbuilders, the Lakes entered service in 1975, but proved less than ideal for enforcing New Zealand's vast new 370-kilometre exclusive economic zone. By 1991 all were for sale. The RNZN did better with its new volunteer reserve training craft, an unambitious revamp of a 1960s Australian torpedo recovery vessel design already used for the inshore survey craft HMNZS *Tarapunga* and *Takapu* and the diving tender HMNZS *Manawanui*. Constructed at Whangarei, the 92-ton, 12-knot HMNZS *Moa*, *Kiwi*, *Wakakura*, and *Hinau*, known as IPCs (inshore patrol craft), entered service between 1983 and 1985 and also gained a basic mine countermeasures role during the 1990s.

K.R. Cassells, *Fairmile Flotillas of the Royal New Zealand Navy* (New Zealand Ship & Marine Society, Wellington, 1993); R.J. McDougall, *New Zealand Naval Vessels* (GP Books, Wellington, 1989).

GAVIN McLEAN

Patuone, Eruera Maihi (?–19 September 1872) was an important chief of the ★Musket Wars era. Of Nga Puhi's Ngati Hao hapu, he took part in the wars which established Nga Puhi supremacy over the Bay of Islands in the early 1800s. At the battle of Waituna in 1806, he earned renown for killing the chief Tatakahuanui with a greenstone adze. In 1819–20 he took part in the great raiding expedition under ★Murupaenga, ★Te Rauparaha, and ★Tuwhare as far south as Whanganui-a-Tara (Wellington). After Tuwhare's death on the Wanganui River, Patuone assumed leadership of the expedition, returning to Hokianga with greenstone and fine cloaks. During the 1820s he took part in raids which devastated other tribes, fighting with ★Hongi Hika at the Battle of Te Ika-a-ranga-nui at which Ngati Whatua were defeated. In the 1830s he and his brother, ★Nene, took part in raids against Ngati Haua under ★Te Waharoa in the Thames area. He married a Ngati Paoa woman, thereby making an alliance with her tribe. He thereafter lived near Auckland, and was an important government ally.

Peace-keeping

Peace-keeping For almost fifty years New Zealand has been continuously involved in one or more international operations aimed at restoring or maintaining peace (see table 11). Since the founding of the ★United Nations it has been a consistent and strong supporter of the organisation. Under the collective security provisions set out in Chapter VII of the UN Charter, it has participated in four peace-enforcement operations: the ★Korean War, the ★Gulf War, and the international interventions in Somalia (1992) and in ★East Timor (1999). But most New Zealand involvement in such international action has been peace-keeping rather than peace-enforcement. Mainly because of the limitations on the operation of the UN Security Council arising from the great power veto, and the clamp imposed by the ★Cold War, resort to the Charter's collective security provisions was ruled out until the 1990s (apart from the special case of the Korean War). As early as the late 1940s the United Nations responded to this situation, when confronted by threats to peace, by undertaking peace-keeping activities outside the framework of Chapter VII. Designed to prevent and contain hostilities, these operations involved the deployment of military observers to supervise ceasefires or of larger military forces, armed for self-defence, to keep adversaries apart. In contrast to peace enforcement, the employment of such forces is dependent on the agreement of the parties to a dispute or conflict. With the end of the Cold War, opportunities for the United Nations to respond in a more active way to conflicts around the world have markedly increased. In recent years the United Nations has inserted more heavily armed forces into areas where conflict is continuing in order to deliver humanitarian aid or to pursue wider political aims. The term 'peace-support' operation is now widely used to encompass such non-traditional peace-keeping operations.

New Zealand's first offer to contribute to a peace-keeping operation was made as part of Commonwealth efforts to resolve conflict between India and Pakistan over the status of Kashmir. In January 1951 the Prime Ministers of both New Zealand and Australia offered to provide a joint military force to maintain order in the disputed province while a plebiscite on its future was held. Although this offer was not taken up, New Zealand agreed in November 1951 to provide three officers to serve with the United Nations Military Observer Group in India and Pakistan (UNMOGIP). In mid 1954 it somewhat reluctantly provided two officers (later increased to as many as seven) to serve with the United Nations Truce Supervision Organization (UNTSO) in the Middle East, an involvement which continues more than forty years later. New Zealand officers serving with UNTSO have, on several occasions, been seconded to other operations.

A New Zealand mine clearance training team in Cambodia in 1993 (NZDF)

When the United Nations Emergency Force (UNEF) was established in 1956 during the ★Suez crisis to supervise the withdrawal of foreign troops from Egypt, New Zealand offered to contribute a specially recruited 320-strong contingent to the force. Because of its strong political support for Great Britain during the crisis, however, this offer was unacceptable to Egypt. Between May 1964 and June 1967 New Zealand provided twenty policemen to serve with the United Nations Peace-Keeping Force in Cyprus (UNFICYP). The New Zealanders formed part of the United Nations Civilian Police and operated in the Limassol district. During 1964 and 1965 proposals for New Zealand to designate special standby military peace-keeping units made no headway, not least because Prime Minister Keith Holyoake regarded them as 'silly'. Concern about the level of defence spending and the scope of the armed forces' existing commitments further reduced enthusiasm for such a course.

From the beginning of New Zealand's involvement in peace-keeping, the armed forces were of the view that there was no particular value to them in the skills and experience acquired by officers serving as military observers. Because of this negative attitude and their heavy commitments in South-east Asia, they tended to use volunteer non-regular officers for peace-keeping assignments. This changed following the end of the ★Vietnam War. A greater appreciation within the Army of the professional benefits of such activities led to young regular officers being deployed as military observers. Nevertheless, the government in 1976, as part of efforts to reduce overseas expenditure, terminated the involvement in UNMOGIP and reduced the number of military observers it sent to UNTSO. These cuts mark the nadir of New Zealand's involvement in international peace-keeping.

At the end of 1979 the British government, the Rhodesian regime, and the African nationalist Patriotic Front reached agreement on a plan to settle the

Rhodesian dispute. Central to the settlement process was the establishment of a ceasefire in the war between the Rhodesian security forces and the Patriotic Front's guerrillas, a ceasefire which was to be supervised by the 1400-strong Commonwealth Monitoring Force (CMF). Initially, the Patriotic Front objected to New Zealand participation in the CMF, mainly because of New Zealand's sporting contacts with the white regime in South Africa. Once these objections were overcome, partly because of the Maori element in the proposed contingent, New Zealand's contingent arrived in Rhodesia (now Zimbabwe) a few days before the ceasefire came into effect at midnight on 28 December 1979. It quickly established an excellent reputation. The CMF as a whole played a key role in the successful settlement of the Rhodesian dispute and the establishment of an independent Zimbabwe, an outcome which encouraged a more positive view of peace-keeping within New Zealand government circles. (See RHODESIAN MONITORING FORCE)

In October 1981 New Zealand agreed to participate in the Multinational Force and Observers (MFO), which the United States was organising to monitor compliance with the peace treaty between Israel and Egypt. When the MFO began operations on ★Anzac Day 1982, the main New Zealand contribution was personnel for a joint Australia–New Zealand helicopter unit. Some personnel were also provided for staff positions in MFO headquarters, including the first New Zealand women to serve in a peace-keeping operation (two RNZAF NCOs posted in January 1985). The helicopter unit was disbanded in March 1986 following Australia's decision to withdraw from the MFO. New Zealand did not follow suit, probably because of the government's desire to contribute to wider Western alliance activities despite the dispute over ★ANZUS then raging. It continued to provide headquarters staff and also made available a twelve-strong training and advisory team. A New Zealand officer, Lieutenant-General Donald ★McIver, was MFO Force Commander between 1989 and 1991.

The 1987 defence review, produced by the fourth Labour government led by David ★Lange following the termination of New Zealand's involvement in ANZUS, contained a strong commitment to expand New Zealand's contribution to peace-keeping operations. Coincidentally, changes in the international environment, particularly as a result of the Soviet Union's less confrontational approach, increased the opportunities for United Nations peace-keeping initiatives. New Zealand participated in three significant operations during 1988–89. In August 1988 it agreed to take part in the UN Iran–Iraq Military Observer Group (UNIIMOG), which was being established to facilitate implementation of the agreement to end the Iran–Iraq War by monitoring the ceasefire between the opposing forces and their withdrawal to internationally recognised borders. New Zealand provided a group of military observers and an RNZAF transport aircraft and crew to the operation. Between April 1989 and December 1991 a New Zealand Army engineer team served in Pakistan with the United Nations Mine Clearance Training Team (UNMCTT), which formed part of UN efforts to relieve the humanitarian suffering caused by war in Afghanistan. The New Zealanders taught Afghan refugees mine awareness and clearance techniques and later travelled into Afghanistan to check that the training was being effective. During this period New Zealand also contributed thirty-two police officers to the United Nations Transition Assistance Group (UNTAG), which oversaw Namibia's move to independence. A small detachment of New Zealand Army engineers also served with UNTAG as part of a larger Australian unit.

A further defence review in 1991, setting out the policy of the National administration which had taken office the previous year, reaffirmed New Zealand's commitment to playing a significant role in international peace-keeping. This high-level commitment has been central to a substantial expansion in New Zealand's involvement in such operations. Between 1989 and 1999 New Zealand participated in more than twenty peace-support operations around the world. Of these, the most substantial have been in Cambodia, the former Yugoslavia, Somalia, and Bougainville. In Cambodia, a team of New Zealand Army engineers served with the United Nations Advance Mission in Cambodia (UNAMIC) between December 1991 and March 1992, when the United Nations Transitional Authority in Cambodia (UNTAC) took over its responsibilities. Under UNTAC New Zealand expanded its contribution to include signals personnel for the joint Australian–New Zealand force communications unit and RNZN personnel to patrol Cambodia's inland and coastal waters. The New Zealand engineers played a key role in developing the United Nations' de-mining programme in Cambodia. Since the end of UNTAC's mandate in September 1993, New Zealand has provided specialist staff for the Cambodian Mine Action Centre. So many calls were being made on New Zealand's limited resources by such peace-support operations that the government in 1993 adopted a set of criteria against which UN requests could be assessed.

★New Zealand Defence Force personnel have been serving in a variety of roles in the territory of the former Federal Republic of Yugoslavia since March 1992. Initially New Zealand committed military observers to serve with the United Nations Protection Force (UNPROFOR). In September 1994 New Zealand substantially expanded its contribution by deploying a

Peace-keeping

Table 11 New Zealand Participation in Peace-support Operations

Dates of NZ involvement	Name of operation; size of New Zealand contribution; main role of NZ personnel
1952–76	UN Military Observer Group in India and Pakistan (UNMOGIP); up to 7; military observers
1953–	UN Command Military Armistice Commission (UNCMAC) [Korea]; 1; monitoring ceasefire between North and South Korea
1954–	UN Truce Supervision Organization (UNTSO) [Israel and neighbours]; up to 7; military observers
1956–57	UN Emergency Force (UNEF) [Sinai]; 2–3; military observers detached from UNTSO
1958	UN Observation Group in Lebanon (UNOGIL); 1; chief military observer detached from UNTSO
1960–61	UN Operation in Congo (ONUC); 2; staff officers detached from UNTSO
1963	UN Yemen Observation Mission (UNYOM); 1; military observer detached from UNTSO
1964–67	UN Force in Cyprus (UNFICYP); 20; civilian police
1965–66	UN India–Pakistan Observation Mission (UNIPOM); c.2; military observers
1973	UN Emergency Force II (UNEF II) [Sinai]; c.2; military observers detached from UNTSO
1974–	UN Disengagement Observer Force (UNDOF) [Syria]; a few; military observers from UNTSO
1978–	UN Interim Force in Lebanon (UNIFIL); a few; military observers from UNTSO and personnel attached to the Fijian Forces
1979–80	Commonwealth Monitoring Force (CMF) [Zimbabwe]; 74; monitoring security forces and cantonment of guerrillas
1982–	Multinational Force and Observers (MFO) [Sinai]; up to 40; headquarters staff training personnel, helicopter crews, and support personnel
1988–91	UN Iran–Iraq Military Observer Group (UNIIMOG); up to 28; military observers, transport aircraft, support personnel
1989–90	UN Transition Assistance Group (UNTAG) [Namibia]; 47; 33 civil police and military engineers
1989–91	UN Mine Clearance Training Team (UNMCTT) [Afghanistan/Pakistan]; c.5; mine clearance training
1990	Bougainville Peace Talks; c.300; 3 RNZN ships provided venue
1991–	UN Special Commission (UNSCOM) [Iraq—destruction of weapons of mass destruction, etc.]; c.14; staff officers, medical and communications personnel
1991–92	UN Advanced Mission in Cambodia (UNAMIC); c.21; de-mining training and planning
1991–97	UN Angola Verification Mission II and III (UNAVEM II and III); up to c.15; staff officers, military observers, de-mining planning and training
1992–93	UN Transitional Authority in Cambodia (UNTAC); c.92; de-mining, communications personnel staff officers, naval monitors
1992–93	Unified Task Force (UNITAF) [Somalia]; c.66; transport aircraft, support and headquarters staff
1992–94	UN Operation in Somalia I and II (UNOSOM I and II); up to 50; supply personnel, headquarters staff
1992–96	UN Protection Force in Croatia, Bosnia–Herzegovina, and Macedonia (UNPROFOR); up to 260; reinforced infantry company, military observers, headquarters and support staff
1993–94	UN Military Liaison Team (UNMLT) [Cambodia]; 1; military observer
1994	South Pacific Peacekeeping Force (SPPKF) [Bougainville]; 13; headquarters staff, search teams
1994–95	UN Mission in Haiti (UNMIH); 4; military observers
1994–95	UN Operation in Mozambique (ONUMOZ); up to 9; de-mining training and planning
1994–	Cambodian Mine Action Centre (CMAC); 2; de-mining staff officers
1995–96	UN Confidence Restoration Operation (UNCRO) [former Yugoslavia]; 2; military observers
1995–96, 1998–99	Multinational Interception Force (MIF) [Persian Gulf—enforcement of sanctions against Iraq]; up to 250; RNZN frigates and personnel
1995–99	UN Preventive Deployment Force (UNPREDEP) [former Yugoslav republic of Macedonia]; 1; military observer
1995–	Mozambique Accelerated De-mining Programme (MADP); 2; de-mining planning

Peace-keeping

Table 11 New Zealand Participation in Peace-support Operations (continued)

Dates of NZ involvement	Name of operation; size of New Zealand contribution; main role of NZ personnel
1996	Implementation Force (IFOR) [Bosnia–Herzegovina—NATO-led force]; 15; staff and liaison officers
1996–98	UN Transitional Administration for Eastern Slavonia, Baranja, and Western Sirmium (UNTAES) [Croatia]; 4–5; chief military observer (1996–97), 4 military observers
1996–	Stabilization Force (SFOR) [Bosnia–Herzegovina—NATO-led force]; up to 27; staff officers, artillery and armoured corps personnel
1996–	UN Mission of Observers in Prevlaka (UNMOP); 1–2; chief military observer (1998–), military observer
1997–98	Truce Monitoring Group (TMG) [Bougainville]; 200+ and crews of 3 RNZN ships (c.300); commanders, headquarters and liaison staff, helicopters and support staff
1997–99	National Institute for the Removal of Explosive Devices (INAROE) [Angola]; c.3; de-mining planning and training
1997–99	UN Observer Mission in Angola (MONUA); up to 5; military observers
1997–	Unexploded Ordnance in Laos (UXOL); 2; staff officers
1998	Operation Griffin [Persian Gulf—coalition forces]; up to 100; SAS troop, 2 Orion maritime patrol aircraft
1998–99	UN Observer Mission in Sierra Leone (UNOMSIL); 2; military observers
1998–	Peace Monitoring Group (PMG) [Bougainville]; c.30; headquarters liaison and support staff
1999	UN Mission in East Timor (UNAMET); 5; military liaison officers
1999–	UN Mission in Kosovo (UNMIK); 1; military liaison officer
1999–2000	International Force East Timor (INTERFET); c.1200; frigate, tanker, transport aircraft, helicopters, infantry, SAS
2000–	UN Transition Administration in East Timor (UNTAET); c. 600; infantry

reinforced infantry company group to serve with the British UNPROFOR contingent in central Bosnia–Herzegovina. Unlike earlier peace-support initiatives, this step caused considerable public debate within New Zealand and differences of opinion between the government's defence and foreign policy advisers. The New Zealand company proved itself to be a very capable unit before its withdrawal following the end of the Bosnian war. New Zealand personnel continue to serve with the United Nations missions in the former Yugoslavia and have also served since 1996 with the NATO-led forces in Bosnia–Herzegovina.

Late in 1992 New Zealand deployed a supply detachment to serve with the United Nations Operation in Somalia (UNOSOM). Continuing fighting prevented UNOSOM from carrying out its mandate and in particular blocked the delivery of desperately required relief supplies. This situation led to the deployment at the end of 1992 of the Unified Task Force (UNITAF), a United States-led, but UN-authorised, peace-enforcement mission. New Zealand provided three Andover transport aircraft, support personnel, and staff officers to this operation. In July 1993, after UNITAF had been replaced by a larger United Nations force, UNOSOM II, the New Zealand supply detachment was expanded into a full supply platoon.

New Zealand has played a leading role in efforts to end the conflict on the island of Bougainville in Papua New Guinea. In mid 1990 New Zealand deployed three RNZN warships off the coast of Bougainville to act as the venue for peace talks between the Papua New Guinea government and secessionist leaders. In 1994 support and personnel were provided for the South Pacific Peacekeeping Force, which was deployed on the island as part of further unsuccessful peace efforts. Further talks hosted by New Zealand between Bougainville leaders loyal to Papua Guinea and secessionist leaders during 1997 resulted in an agreement for a ceasefire and the deployment of a Truce Monitoring Group (TMG) on the island. The TMG consisted of military and civilian personnel from New Zealand, Australia, Fiji, and Vanuatu. New Zealand provided the largest contingent and the group's first commander, Brigadier Roger Mortlock. In a major tri-service operation, three RNZN ships, RNZAF helicopters, and Army personnel were deployed to Bougainville. The TMG made a substantial contribution to improving the security and quality of life of the island's population and to the development of an environment in which a full political settlement of the conflict could be reached. Following the signing of the Canberra Agreement, a permanent ceasefire came into effect on Bougainville at the end of April 1998. The TMG was replaced by the Australian-led Peace Monitoring Group, to which New Zealand contributed a much smaller number of personnel.

Pendjeh crisis

In mid 1999 New Zealand provided military officers and civilian police for the United Nations Mission in East Timor (UNAMET), which supervised a referendum on the territory's future. The referendum, which resulted in a strong vote in favour of independence, was followed by a wave of violence by pro-Indonesian forces. International outrage at this violence led in September to the establishment of the International Force East Timor (INTERFET), a UN-authorised peace-enforcement mission. New Zealand played a significant role in the formation of INTERFET. Its naval and military contribution to it constitutes the largest New Zealand force deployed overseas in support of United Nations objectives since the Korean War. When control of INTERFET passed from Australia to the United Nations in February 2000, the intervention became a UN peace-keeping operation.

The NZDF has also been involved in two humanitarian relief operations which were closely related to peace-keeping missions. In 1994 an RNZAF C-130 Hercules played a valuable role in relief operations prompted by the civil war and genocide in Rwanda. In April 1999 a small medical team and a C-130 Hercules were deployed to the Balkans to assist with humanitarian relief operations for refugees from Kosovo.

In general military observers serve twelve-month tours of duty and other personnel involved in peace-keeping operations serve six months. Several New Zealand peacekeepers have been wounded and one accidentally killed. New Zealand's policy on involvement in both United Nations and non-United Nations peace-keeping or peace-support operations has reflected wider developments in its foreign policy and its long-standing commitment to the concept of collective security. Within the NZDF an appreciation has developed, particularly since the late 1980s, of the valuable operational experience which can be obtained from peace-support operations. A clear understanding has also developed of the way involvement in such operations, which enjoy wide public and political support, can raise the profile of the NZDF. New Zealand has a good reputation for providing well-trained and adaptable personnel who are capable of working effectively in multi-national operations. International peace-support operations have in recent years placed real pressure on the NZDF's limited resources. The NZDF has, nevertheless, rejected suggestions that its force structure should be tailored more specifically to participation in such operations. It remains convinced that to do so would damage its ability to fulfil its primary role of defending New Zealand's national security and would not improve its capacity to contribute effectively to peace-support operations. Similarly, the NZDF considers that general professional military training provides the best preparation for involvement in peace-support operations. Involvement in peace-keeping or more generally peace-support operations is a major part of the range of activities New Zealand undertakes as 'a good international citizen' and is likely to remain a significant part of the NZDF's activities in the foreseeable future.

J. Crawford, *In the Field of Peace: New Zealand's Contribution to International Peace-Support Operations: 1950–1995* (New Zealand Defence Force, Wellington, 1996).

JOHN CRAWFORD

Pendjeh crisis The occupation by Russian forces of the town of Pendjeh in northern Afghanistan in early 1885 precipitated a major Anglo-Russian crisis. It pre-empted bilateral negotiations over the boundary between Russia's newly acquired Transcaspian territories and Afghanistan, and aroused fears in London for the security of India. British demands that the Russians withdraw seemed likely to end in war between the two great powers. In New Zealand these events led to the greatest of the periodic ★Russian scares, and hasty action was taken to set the defences of the four main ports in order (see COAST DEFENCES). The government went further, proposing to offer a thousand-man force for service with imperial forces in Afghanistan 'or any other part of the globe where Her Majesty's Government might require them'. It was intended that a quarter of this force would be Maori—a reflection perhaps of a recent offer by Ngati Haua leader Hote Tamehana of a 200-man party from his tribe for service in the Sudan, where the Empire was beset by another crisis and New South Wales had actually sent a contingent. Before New Zealand transmitted its offer to London, news was received that the British and Russian governments had agreed to refer the Pendjeh dispute to arbitration. No further action was taken. Premier Robert Stout's claim in Parliament in June 1885 that New Zealand had been ready 'to stand together in aid of the Mother-country' foreshadowed the expeditionary forces which would be a feature of New Zealand's military experience in the twentieth century.

I. McGibbon, *The Path to Gallipoli: Defending New Zealand 1840–1915* (GP Books, Wellington, 1991).

Penton, Major-General Arthur Pole (6 October 1854–28 August 1920). Commissioned in the Royal Artillery in 1873 after being educated at the Royal Military Academy at Woolwich, Penton held a variety of military appointments over the next two decades. He was mentioned in dispatches during the Afghan War of 1879–80. In 1896, now a major, he was appointed as the Commander of the New Zealand Forces, with the local rank of colonel (see COMMANDANTS). After the fiasco of his predecessor

Colonel F.J. ★Fox's tenure, Penton's term was relatively tranquil. The product of a new more careful selection policy in London, he had greater *savoir-faire* than Fox, and was helped by relinquishment of the Defence portfolio by the autocratic Richard ★Seddon. However, he met with no more success in his attempts substantially to reform the ★Volunteer Force because of government opposition. Penton also continued to be denied powers enjoyed by commandants in other colonies, even after his title was changed to Commandant in 1900. He did make improvements in the forces, and oversaw the preparation of the colony's first ★defence scheme, which was completed in 1899. He was denied permission to go to the ★Boer War, but found his responsibilities greatly increased by the need to raise successive contingents as well as oversee a Volunteer Force which doubled in size during the war. Returning to the British Army in 1901, he rose to the rank of major-general before retiring in 1916. He was made a CB in 1910 and a CMG seven years later.

STEPHEN CLARKE

Permanent Militia (from 1902 Permanent Force) was the professional core of the New Zealand Military Forces from 1886 to 1911. During the 1885 Russian scare, 'special corps' of the ★Armed Constabulary's Field Force—a garrison artillery force of 120 men, a 20-man engineer corps, and a 50-man torpedo corps—had been formed to man the ★coast defences hastily thrown up. With an overall establishment of 350 men, the Permanent Militia, after being formally constituted by the ★Defence Act 1886, encompassed these corps, a 50-man field artillery corps, and the balance of the Field Force. The last-named were designated as Rifles, and divided into ten small companies. Apart from manning outposts in 'Native Districts', at Kawhia and Opunake, they provided labour for the fortifications at Wellington, where they were concentrated. In addition to its harbour defence duties, the Permanent Militia maintained the colony's munitions and war supplies, instructed artillery and engineer corps of the ★Volunteer Force, and, as a secondary duty, provided support for the Police and Prisons Department.

Financial constraints soon led to retrenchment. The Permanent Militia's commander, Lieutenant-Colonel J.M. ★Roberts, was retired in 1888, and by the following year its strength had shrunk to 196. The rifles had been disbanded, the field artillery had become part of the garrison artillery, and the engineers had been absorbed into the torpedo corps. There was a slow recovery in the 1890s—the Permanent Militia's establishment was raised to 270 in mid decade—and some officers (of whom there were only seven) and NCOs were sent to England for training. However, the government remained unsympathetic, and there was opposition in both Parliament and press to increases in the force, which were denounced as handing the colony over to 'militarism'.

In 1897 the artillerymen became No. 1 Company, and the torpedo-men No. 2 Company. Five years later the former was redesignated the Royal New Zealand Artillery, and the latter the Corps of ★Royal New Zealand Engineers. The abandonment of the submarine defences at the harbours in 1907 led to the absorption of the engineers within the RNZA. Although the term Permanent Force ceased to be used in 1911, with the reorganisation of the New Zealand Military Forces, the RNZA remained the permanent core of the new system, along with the newly established ★New Zealand Staff Corps.

Phipps, Vice-Admiral Sir Peter (7 December 1908?–18 September 1989) was New Zealand's most prominent naval officer in the two decades after the ★Second World War. Details of his birth are obscure, but he was probably born in Sydney. He became interested in the sea as a boy, and while working as a bank clerk in Christchurch joined the NZRNVR in 1928. His quiet disposition, common sense, and dedication would stand him in good stead throughout his naval career. Within two years he had secured a probationary commission. A member of the NZRNVR's Wellington Division, to which he had transferred in 1936, he was called up just before the Second World War began and employed as an assistant staff officer in the Navy Office, dealing with intelligence. In May 1940, he was one of a substantial group of officers seconded to Great Britain for service with the Royal Navy. He spent eighteen months from July 1940 escorting convoys in the English Channel as commander of HMS *Bay*, a 600-ton anti-submarine trawler, and was awarded a DSC in March 1941. In March 1942, he set out on a five-month journey home in command of HMNZS *Scarba*, an anti-submarine and minesweeping trawler which had been made available to the RNZN. He became involved in the ★Solomons campaign when appointed to command HMNZS *Moa*, part of the 25th Minesweeping Flotilla, in January 1943, and almost immediately helped destroy the Japanese submarine *I-1*, an exploit which won him a bar to his DSC and a US Navy Cross. After being wounded during a Japanese air raid on Tulagi soon afterwards, he was repatriated to New Zealand and did not return to sea until August 1944, when he assumed command of the 25th Flotilla, first in HMNZS *Mata*, then, from December 1944, HMNZS *Arabis*. Following Japan's capitulation, he represented New Zealand at the surrender of Japanese

Pioneers

forces in Nauru and Ocean Island. After securing a permanent commission in the RNZN in 1946, he performed well when confronted by mutinous personnel at HMNZS *Philomel* in 1947. Between 1948 and 1952 he was successively HMNZS *Bellona*'s Executive Officer, commander of the training establishment HMNZS *Tamaki*, and a staff officer at Devonport naval base. By the time he was promoted to captain in June 1952—one of two RNZN officers to have reached this rank at the time—he was seen as the navy's rising star. In 1953 he undertook courses in Britain before being seconded to the Admiralty, where he served in the Operations Division. After briefly commanding *Bellona*, he took command of the RNZN's last cruiser, HMNZS *Royalist*, and took her to New Zealand by way of the Mediterranean, where she almost became involved in operations during the ★Suez crisis. In 1957 he was appointed to New Zealand Naval Board as Second Naval Member. Three years later he became Chief of Naval Staff and First Naval Member. In 1963 he stepped up to become the first Chief of Defence Staff, a post he held until July 1965. The first RNZN officer to sit on the Naval Board and to attain the rank of admiral, he was noted for his low-key approach and administrative competence, qualities which proved useful during the difficult formative years of the Ministry of Defence. He was made a CBE in 1962 and elevated to KBE two years later.

Pioneers, in earlier times, cleared the way for an army and participated in the assaults on fortified positions. The term was resurrected by the British Army when confronted with trench warfare in 1915. Pioneer battalions were formed to provide labour for digging trenches and other duties in the front line. One was attached to each infantry division. Even before this, members of 1NZEF's 'Native Contingent' had been employed in this role at ★Gallipoli (see MAORI AND THE FIRST WORLD WAR). The Maori soldiers dug trenches and undertook 'navvy' work. During the August 1915 offensive, the contingent was broken up to augment the weakened infantry and mounted rifles units, with a platoon being attached to each of the assaulting regiments and battalions. Members of the contingent fought well in the battle for Chunuk Bair, though sustaining 108 casualties. When it became necessary in early 1916 to form a pioneer battalion for the New Zealand Division, the Maori contingent provided its core, along with 45 Niueans and 125 Rarotongans. Surplus men from the Otago Mounted Rifles Regiment (which had been reduced to a squadron) were drafted in to make up the numbers. This 'menagerie' of races was commanded by Lieutenant-Colonel G.A. ★King, with a Maori, Major Peter Buck, as his second-in-command. When the battalion was deployed on the ★Western Front in April 1916, the Niueans quickly

Men of the New Zealand (Maori) Pioneer Battalion perform a haka for the visiting Sir Joseph Ward and W.F. Massey in France in 1918 (*RSA Collection, Alexander Turnbull Library, G-13282-1/2*)

found the cold intolerable and had to be returned to Egypt. The pioneers were assigned to the Armentières sector, where they were employed in digging trenches and building roads. A trench raid on 9 July 1916 was their first taste of combat. In August they were sent to the Somme to prepare for the arrival of the rest of the New Zealand Division. Over the next month they worked an eight-kilometre communications trench leading to the front line ('Turk Lane'). After helping prepare for the Messines offensive in 1917, the battalion came to be composed entirely of Maori and Pacific Islanders with the replacement of its Pakeha companies by Maori reinforcements. Renamed the New Zealand (Maori) Pioneer Battalion on 15 September 1917, it laboured in cold and wet conditions at Passchendaele to construct 'corduroy' tracks of planks and light-railway lines behind the front line. Throughout 1918 the pioneers dug trenches, built roads and bridges, and erected barbed wire.

Although a Pioneer Corps, comprising men not suitable for infantry service, served in the British Army in the ★Second World War, no separate pioneer unit was formed by New Zealand, and most Maori members of 2NZEF served in a Maori infantry battalion. Since 1939 each infantry battalion in the New Zealand Army has had an assault pioneer platoon, providing it with combat engineering expertise.

Pitt, Major-General George Dean (1781– 8 January 1851) was the first general officer commanding in New Zealand. Irish-born, he assumed the surname Pitt in 1818. He was commissioned in the 42nd Regiment in 1805, but later transferred to the 96th. He took part in operations in the Caribbean in 1807–09 and in the Peninsular War from 1811 to 1814, his services being rewarded with appointment as a CB. He was Superintendent of Recruiting in the War Office before being dispatched to New Zealand, where he arrived in early 1848. In poor health, he would have been quite unfitted to oversee any active operations, but the situation in the colony was quiescent. He was appointed Lieutenant-Governor of New Ulster in February 1848, and in the following year became a member of the Legislative Council. As commander of the forces, he made substantial improvements to the Albert Barracks and built a fort on Point Britomart before dying at Auckland.

Poananga, Major-General Brian Matauru (2 December 1924–5 September 1995), of Ngati Porou descent, was the first (and so far only) Maori to attain New Zealand's highest military rank. His career in the Army's Regular Force began when he was sent to the Royal Military College at Duntroon in 1944. After graduating in December 1946, he served in ★Jayforce during the following two years, and then occupied various staff and training appointments in New Zealand. Between March 1952 and March 1953 Poananga was involved in the ★Korean War, first as a staff officer in the 1st Commonwealth Division's HQ and, for four months, on secondment to the 3rd Battalion, Royal Australian Regiment, with whom he soon made his mark as an aggressive patroller. His efforts earned him a mention in dispatches. In 1955 he went to London as a liaison officer, and subsequently attended the Staff College at Camberley. Between 1959 and 1961 he was in Malaya, serving as a company commander with 2nd Battalion, New Zealand Regiment (see MALAYAN EMERGENCY). After attending the Joint Services Staff College at Whenuapai, he took command of 1st Battalion, ★Royal New Zealand Infantry Regiment, in November 1965. The battalion was deployed in Borneo from May to October 1966, but the end of ★Confrontation left it with little to do, though Poananga was again mentioned in dispatches. In May 1967 he oversaw the dispatch of one of his companies to Vietnam to join ★V-Force. Returning to New Zealand at the end of 1967, he occupied various appointments, including commander of the Army Training Group at Waiouru, before attending the Royal College of Defence Studies in London in 1973. Shortly after assuming command of 1st Infantry Brigade in the following year, he was seconded to the Ministry of Foreign Affairs for two years to serve as New Zealand High Commissioner in Port Moresby. Following a further two years as Deputy Chief of General Staff, he became Chief of General Staff in November 1978. He was made a CBE in 1977 and a CB three years later. He retired to his family farm at Taupo in November 1981. Despite deteriorating health, he served as a member of the ★Defence Committee of Enquiry which in 1986 sought to ascertain public attitudes to defence.

Pohe, Flying Officer Porokoru Patapu ('Johnny') (10 December 1914–30 March 1944) was a leading Maori airman of the ★Second World War. Of Whanganui and Ngati Tuwharetoa descent, he was educated at Te Aute College and was farming at Taihape when war began. He immediately applied for pilot training, and was sent to England after gaining his wings in March 1941. From August 1941 to April 1942, he flew twenty-two bombing missions with 51 Squadron RAF before becoming a flying instructor at a training unit. He was commissioned in May 1942. On the night of 22 September 1943, two days after he rejoined 51 Squadron, his Halifax bomber was shot down over Germany. Held as a POW in Stalag Luft III at Sagan, he was one of seventy-six Allied aircrew who in March 1944 got away in what would later be called 'the Great Escape'. He was recaptured within a few days

Pomare I

but, with five other escapees, was murdered by the Gestapo while being transported back towards Sagan. Forty-four others, including two New Zealanders, suffered the same fate when retaken. This crime was ordered from Berlin as a deterrent to further escaping. Pohe was mentioned in dispatches for his war services.

Pomare I (?–1826), a Ngati Manu of Nga Puhi, was a leading chief during the *Musket Wars. Having established himself as chief over Matauwhi, south of Kororareka (Russell), he traded timber, crops, and shrunken heads for muskets with Europeans aboard visiting vessels. With these weapons his war parties wrought destruction over a wide area, and he became almost as feared as *Hongi Hika. In 1820 he raided the East Cape, and took Te Whetu-matarau pa at Te Araroa after an epic siege. Joining Hongi, he launched raids against the Auckland–Thames area in 1821. This was followed by attacks on tribes in the Bay of Plenty in the following year. In 1823, along with Hongi and *Te Wera Hauraki, he raided Te Arawa at Rotorua, during which the Arawa pa at Mokoia was stormed. After falling out with Hongi, he went with Te Wera to the East Coast, where he descended on Ngati Porou. He was back in the same area in 1924, taking part in intertribal warfare there. Some Ngati Kahungunu accompanied him back to the Bay of Islands in the hope of acquiring muskets themselves. In 1826 he raided south, but was defeated and killed by a Waikato and Ngati Maru combination.

Pomare II (?–1850), a nephew of *Pomare I, was prominent in the latter stages of the *Musket Wars. A member of Nga Puhi's Ngati Manu hapu, he was known as Whiria until 1826 when he took the names Whetoi and Pomare after his uncle's death. The chief of a village in the Waikare area, he gradually assumed ascendancy within Ngati Manu. In 1827 he led a war party to the south. His position within the tribe was enhanced by the outcome of the *Girls' War of 1830. Although Ngati Manu had the better of the main clash with the opposing forces led by one of *Hongi Hika's kinsmen, they were forced to withdraw from the Kororareka–Paihia area. He built a very strong pa, capable even of mounting cannon, at Otuihu, but long aspired to regaining his tribe's position at Kororareka. He fought the northern Nga Puhi in 1832–33 and the Waikato in 1836. Another conflict, with Titore in 1837, ended inconclusively when Otuihu successfully withstood a siege. The war seemed to confirm British fears of continuing anarchy in New Zealand—more than a hundred Europeans were involved in the fighting—and contributed to the British government's decision to annex New Zealand. Although Pomare signed the Treaty of Waitangi in February 1840, he soon became disillusioned by the impact of British sovereignty. Nevertheless he did not join Hone *Heke and *Kawiti in their war with the British in 1845. This did not prevent the British from arresting him in April 1845 and razing his pa. Eventually released, and presented with a boat as some compensation for the way he had been treated, he raised a war party to fight alongside the British, only to withdraw before the Battle of Ohaeawai in July 1845. He was later influential in the negotiations leading to peace.

Popular culture, war in Throughout the twentieth century war was influential in shaping New Zealand perceptions of *national identity and expressing some of the dominant beliefs and values of the era. Periods of patriotic excitement accompanied by the wartime mobilisation of national resources led to fervent expressions of emotion as well as a readiness to find collective solutions to political and economic crises.

New Zealand has never been invaded by a hostile military power and has not directly experienced the actualities of war since the land wars of the nineteenth century (see NEW ZEALAND WARS). For most of the population, war has been a distant melodrama rather than a battlefield reality. However, large numbers of troops were sent to the Middle East and Europe in two world conflicts. Substantial contingents also participated in the *Boer War, the *Korean War, the *Malayan Emergency, *Confrontation, and the *Vietnam War. The direct experiences of the veterans from all these campaigns and the casualties they suffered have had significant cultural consequences.

Popular culture is a way of describing the life of a people and what is generally accepted and approved by them. It incorporates most of the material artefacts and events of everyday life as well as its celebrations, its stereotypes, and its beliefs and values. In wartime, popular culture is energised by a flood of patriotic and morale-building exhortations and events that constitute an officially endorsed culture production intended to encourage people's participation in the war effort and their support for political and military leaders. What was to become a familiar pattern was established in the Boer War when troops assembled at camps in various parts of the country and, after a period of training, were sent overseas to the front. In the *First and *Second World Wars this process was accompanied by public parades, farewell ceremonies, and speechmaking along with emotional scenes on the waterfront as troopships departed for the battlefields. The individual soldier usually underwent a *rite de passage* in which he was granted a short period of final leave to farewell his family and settle his affairs. During this period he might be entertained at a round of special functions in his local community and presented with travel equipment or personal articles for use in the campaign. In some cases, the festivities might include a series of engagement parties and wartime marriage celebrations.

All this social activity was augmented by dances, concerts, and appeals for subscriptions for war loans as well as patriotic fundraising efforts. These latter were made necessary by the expectation that civilians would pay for any comforts the troops might want that were additional to the government's provision of bare rations, minimal clothing, spartan accommodation, and nominal rates of pay. Soldiers in the field depended largely on regimental canteens and welfare organisations like the Church Army, the Salvation Army, and the ★YMCA for cups of tea, cakes, tobacco, writing materials, and recreational facilities.

Social life in both world wars encouraged a sense of participation for a common purpose and was an important part of the mobilisation of resources in the war effort. Together with national programmes of expanded industrial and agricultural production, the civic activities of fundraising and patriotic celebration enabled non-combatants to enjoy the integrative gratification of community service in the common effort.

In the First World War a network of patriotic organisations made voluntary contributions of money and goods to soldiers, hospitals, the sick and wounded, the ★Red Cross, and a great variety of relief agencies. In 1916 the Women's Patriotic League originated a scheme to send 20,000 gifts a month to troops in 1NZEF. Each parcel cost 2s 6d and consisted of five items selected from condensed milk, sweets, jam, meat essence, concentrated soup, insect powder, soap, toothbrushes, shaving brushes, toilet paper, writing paper, socks, mufflers, balaclavas, and handkerchiefs. A Federation of Patriotic War Relief Societies contributed money to regimental funds for extra food, the upkeep of regimental bands, and the supply of sports gear. Poultry, eggs, and other farm products were bought in France with some of this money, and cocoa, beef tea, and other drinks were obtained so that men could have something hot to drink in the trenches at night.

In the Second World War funds for services' welfare were administered by a National Patriotic Fund Board, which had a network of provincial patriotic councils to organise fundraising and social events. The military authorities still could not supply the individual soldier with such necessities as shaving gear, toothbrushes, toothpaste, soap, haircuts, pyjamas, gloves, balaclavas, reading matter, and toilet paper, though sometimes in the field they distributed small issues of beer, tobacco, and chocolate free of charge. For their personal necessities troops had to depend mainly on what they could buy from canteens and on gifts mailed from the homeland. Food parcels sent under the auspices of the Red Cross helped keep many ★prisoners of war alive.

The government established the YMCA and the Church Army (an inter-denominational organisation that had been active in France in the First World War) as the principal officially endorsed outlets for the expenditure of National Patriotic Fund Board money in the Middle East and Italy. Consequently, much of the welfare work in 2NZEF was done by the YMCA secretaries with assistance from the Church Army and the Red Cross, as well as from a number of canteens and soldiers' clubs. Various religious denominations provided ★chaplains to work with units in the field. These activities were important for morale because they offered the individual soldier an informal channel for counselling and advice in dealing with the consequences of prolonged absence from the homeland as well as the moral problems associated with alcohol, sex, gambling, and crime that some men encountered.

Secretaries often faced danger and had to be resourceful. At Tripoli, one man salvaged a bombed-out hangar and made it into a YMCA hut with a hot water system and furniture from abandoned homes. When 6000 soldiers on a leave draft lined up at short notice for breakfast on the wharf at Tewfik, the secretary running the local canteen drew hot water from a steam locomotive and served tea with 6200 meat pies, 500 packets of biscuits, and 12,000 bananas. In north Italy YMCA quarters ranged from farmhouses, an orphanage, disused picture theatres, and an artillery barracks to luxury hotels in Venice and the Dolomites. One secretary toured a 16-piece Italian orchestra with singers and comedians around the 2nd New Zealand Division in 1944. At San Severino in 1945 the YMCA canteen also operated the dodgems from a stranded Italian circus. For four weeks in Trieste in 1945, the YMCA supplied welfare services for the occupation troops of several armies at a canteen and at the Café Dante, the largest restaurant and bakery in the city.

The wartime proceeds from sales of beer and goods in the chain of canteens operated in military camps throughout New Zealand went into a canteen fund that was available to help finance the system of welfare in the various armed services. After the Second World War the profits from canteen and patriotic funds were used to dispense grants to needy veterans and to run a chain of special homes for the incapacitated. They are administered by the Patriotic and Canteen Funds Board, which reports annually to Parliament. In the 1990s it still had substantial trust funds, assets, and income with which to finance its continuing operations.

Civilian armies tend to colonise the battlefield with export versions of the popular culture of their homelands. The troops in the Second World War were kept in touch with New Zealand by means of mail services,

Popular culture

broadcasts from the field, and reports from ★war correspondents. An official army newspaper carried a home news service, while a concert party offered light entertainment that closely reflected the values and tastes of the homeland popular culture. The troops themselves composed and sang satires and parodies of military life, and they staged informal entertainments which had a strong resemblance to the social gatherings and smoke concerts of peacetime. In 1959 a group styling itself the 'D-Day Dodgers' made a series of commercial recordings of some of these wartime soldiers' songs.

Sport was officially encouraged throughout 2NZEF, especially rugby, which was regarded as character-building because its combination of body contact and aggressive team conflict required dedication and the overcoming of fear of physical injury. In the Middle East campaigns, divisional fixtures against other 8th Army teams were a focus for the assertion of national identity as well as an opportunity for after-match sociable exchanges and the renewal of friendships.

The popular culture imprinted New Zealand soldiers in both world wars with a legacy of pioneering hardihood and adaptability. This contributed to the imagery of the 'hard man' implicit in comic stereotypes like the 'grim dig' of the Second World War and the illustrator Neville Colvin's 'Private Clueless' and 'Johnny Enzed', who featured in the 2NZEF newspaper *NZEF Times*.

As a culture production, the New Zealand style of war was presented as aggressive, innovatory, and dedicated to the offensive spirit. The elan of 2NZEF in the Middle East and Italy was implicit in its description by wartime journalists as 'a ball of fire'. Morale in the 2nd Division's infantry was remarkably high in spite of severe losses in the continuous operations in which they were involved. The egalitarian nature of the homeland culture expressed itself in a relaxed attitude towards the saluting of officers, while the social shortcomings of New Zealand life were demonstrated in a general tendency among the troops to overindulge in drink.

War has also been a means for the presentation of stereotypes of New Zealand national character on a global scale. New Zealand services personnel are seen as representatives of their country and its culture. This is dramatised by distinctive ★uniforms, insignia, and the symbolism of national identity. The ★lemon-squeezer peaked hat of New Zealand troops in the First World War gave them a unique appearance. Many of the territorial regimental cap badges that were worn in the First World War had distinctive New Zealand motifs that included fern leaves, native birds, and Maori emblems. Late in 1915, the New Zealand 'Onward' badge appeared with the fernleaf surrounds enclosing the letters 'NZ' above a scroll bearing the motto 'Onward' and surmounted by a crown. Though the wearing of regimental badges persisted among 2NZEF troops in the Second World War, the 'Onward' badge was officially selected as a single, authorised emblem that eventually became part of the distinctive appearance of the 2NZEF soldier. 'New Zealand' squadrons of the RAF in the Second World War maintained their distinct national identity by the use of Maori mottoes as well as native flora and fauna in the design of their squadron badges.

In 1947 the hat badge of the New Zealand Infantry Regiment became a kiwi within a circle inscribed 'New Zealand Regiment' enclosed by fern leaves and surmounted by a crown. In a 1964 reorganisation, the badge of the RNZIR incorporated a silver kiwi on a scarlet background within a blue circle. The whole was enclosed by fern fronds and surmounted by a crown. The scroll below bore the traditional inscription 'Onward'. The lemon-squeezer, though obsolescent, was retained for ceremonial occasions. The tradition of adopting indigenous images for distinguishing national identity has continued with the formation in the late 1990s of the ★Royal New Zealand Army Logistic Regiment, which adopted a badge incorporating the Southern Cross.

★Shoulder titles, or flashes, are another distinctive device worn by most regular military formations. In the Second World War, 2NZEF in the Middle East theatre adopted a white-on-black 'New Zealand' cloth title that was attached to each shoulder strap of the tunic. This arrangement is still used and serves to give New Zealand soldiers a unique identity wherever they might be, an important consideration in a multinational environment. For example, the New Zealand ★peace-keeping contingent in Bosnia–Herzegovina in 1996 wore New Zealand silver and black shoulder flashes and a black shoulder patch with a silver kiwi as well as the UN emblem. Such devices not only make the New Zealand national identity more prominent but also retain powerful traditional associations with the nation's past military achievements.

In the First World War, from 1917 onward, New Zealand and Australian soldiers described themselves as 'Diggers'. This designation was still current in the Second World War, but by then the term 'Kiwi' was also in use as a universal appellation for any New Zealander anywhere in the world. The First World War also generated a complex symbol that denoted the common interests and potentialities of Australia and New Zealand. This was the word ★'Anzac', which originated in Egypt as an acronym for the Australian and New Zealand Army Corps. The term took on deep emotional associations with the post-war institution of ★Anzac Day as the anniversary of the landing at ★Gallipoli on 25 April 1915. It subsequently became a day of national remembrance for the participants and casualties of all twentieth century wars. Anzac Day observances involve a ritual ceremonial in which the living reflect on the dead and the meaning of their sacrifice. Since 1939, veterans have paraded at dawn and marched to local war memorials where a short religious service is held and wreaths are placed in honour of the fallen.

After the First World War Anzac also had a symbolic meaning as an image of national identity. The sacrificial death of the Anzac warriors was held to signify the emergence of both Australia and New Zealand as mature nations with a distinctive military capability. Thus, in the Second World War, a jingoistic popular song entitled 'We Are the Boys from Way Down Under' concluded with the confident assertion: 'sons of the Anzacs are we'. But with the post-1945 decline of the British Empire, and the growth of stronger feelings of national autonomy by New Zealanders, Anzac as an image of identity lost some of its relevance. Anzac Day came under attack in the 1970s when there were disagreements about defence policy, objections to participation in the Vietnam War, and fear of involvement in the possible use of nuclear weapons. With the passage of time, attitudes towards the observance of the day have become less controversial, though its increasing secularisation and popularisation have drawn protests from veterans, for whom Anzac Day symbolises the relationship between the living and the dead. As popular rituals, its ceremonies and religious services link the ordinary lives of New Zealanders with a collective past that is endowed with sacred meaning and deeply embodied in the nation's history. Though the number of veterans has declined, recently the attendance of younger generations at Anzac Day ceremonies has increased, partly in an effort of discovery and partly out of a desire to identify with what has come to be seen as 'the spirit of Anzac'. Since the 1980s, peace-keeping operations by the New Zealand armed services have also contributed to more benign popular perceptions of the New Zealand military.

Military ★bands maintained by the various defence services are part of a long-standing popular culture tradition of brass band music evident on public ceremonial occasions and displays, and at open days in military establishments as well as recruiting drives and parades.

War has also become a popular peacetime amusement. It is a substantial component of television programming in the form of fictional war movies, documentaries, and global news reportage of actual conflicts. War gaming and Tag War are established recreations along with the collecting and reading of war comics, war fiction, military biographies, and historical works. A military style has at various times influenced the design of women's garments, while the wearing of surplus military clothing and equipment has been a fashionable diversion, as has the collection of miscellaneous items of militaria by enthusiasts. Tours of Gallipoli and the European battlefields are readily available as a nostalgic and sentimental travel experience.

Museums, in addition to their custodial responsibilities, are popular shrines and 'themed spaces' that celebrate and explain a historical past as well as the exploits of military leaders and heroes. The Queen Elizabeth II Army Memorial Museum was established in 1978 at Waiouru to house artefacts and records, in addition to a reference library and a research archive of material ranging from 1840 to the present day.

Popular culture continuously redefines the role of the warrior in response to changing currents of perception. In the 1990s, stereotypes of violently aggressive female warriors with names like 'Xena the Warrior Princess', 'Barbed Wire', and 'Tank Girl' emerged in movies and video films. Women also gained an increasing presence in the military services. They had served extensively in the New Zealand armed forces in the Second World War, but not in combat. This exclusion continued in peacetime, but a running debate ensued about the appropriate role of the female warrior. A government working party in 1990 recommended that women should be able to volunteer for combat jobs in the armed forces on the same basis as men. However, policy did not radically change, though women were subsequently included in the crews of naval vessels and were also selected for flying training. By the end of the 1990s women were serving in a variety of potential combat roles in the infantry, the artillery, and the engineers. For example, a female New Zealand officer led a battery of New Zealand gunners on a peace-keeping mission in Bosnia–Herzegovina. Measures to encourage a greater level of gender integration generally in the NZDF were introduced in 1998 as a result of an official inquiry.

Throughout the twentieth century popular attitudes to war have been crisis-driven. Jingoistic enthusiasm marked New Zealand's participation in the Boer War and patriotic fervour characterised its entry into the First World War. This was followed by the pacifism of the 1920s and 1930s and a reluctant acceptance during the Second World War of the collective necessity to resist Fascism and Nazism. But alarm at the lethal potentialities of modern military technology, and resistance to the use of nuclear weaponry, contributed to public dissension over participation in the Vietnam War. However, by the late 1990s there was growing agreement that the New Zealand troops who took part were professionals carrying out the government's wishes and had nothing to be ashamed of. In this spirit, a commemoration for veterans was held in 1998 'to help lay to rest the war that divided us'. But ideological controversy continued to characterise the public discussion of perennial problems concerning the role of the NZDF and the adequacy of its funding and equipment. During the 1990s the immediate prospect of hostilities involving New Zealand seemed to have been reduced by the end of the *Cold War. The NZDF was increasingly committed to peace-keeping in support of UN policies.

New Zealand popular culture received direct input from the Second World War when the country became a base and staging camp for American forces committed to the South Pacific front. The social life of cities like Auckland and Wellington was enlivened by contact with American troops stationed in training camps and hospitals, or on leave. In 1942–43 there were always about 25,000 US servicemen in the country. Some formed attachments with local families and there were many romantic liaisons and marriages. Jewish and Polish *refugees from Europe, as well as Dutch refugees from Indonesia, added another stream of diversity to the New Zealand population.

Visual evidence of the impact of war on New Zealand lingers in the form of *war memorials distributed widely throughout the country. Men and women who have served in the armed forces in wartime can be buried in one of the 170 services cemeteries around New Zealand. New Zealand also participates in the Commonwealth War Graves Commission, which commemorates members of the Commonwealth armed forces who were buried overseas in the course of operations. Street and place names in many New Zealand towns commemorate notable military commanders of both the nineteenth and twentieth centuries as well as a list of battles that range from engagements in the New Zealand Wars to the *Crimean War, the Indian Mutiny, and the two world wars. Children born during the Second World War were sometimes christened with the names of aircraft and battlefields, 'Alamein' and 'Bardia' being popular designations.

L. Cleveland, *Dark Laughter: War in Song and Popular Culture* (Praeger, Westport, Conn., 1994).

LES CLEVELAND

Pore, Heni (14 November 1840?–24 June 1933) was a member of Te Arawa tribe. Born in Northland, she was taken to Maketu as a child before attending missionary schools. She married Te Kiri Karamu but, after bearing five children, left him in 1861. Her family supported the King Movement in 1863, and Heni fought with Ngati Koheriki in the Hunua Range. The flag 'Aotearoa', which was captured by British troops and is now in the Auckland War Memorial Museum, was made by her. She escaped to Wiremu Tamihana *Te Waharoa's village near Matamata, where she translated captured documents for him. In April 1864 she went with Ngai Te Rangi warriors to Pukehinahina (Gate Pa). She refused to leave the pa, and stayed throughout the bombardment and the British assault. After the battle she gave water to wounded British soldiers, including the mortally wounded Colonel H.J.P. Booth—chivalrous behaviour which passed into the lore of the *New Zealand Wars. In 1865 she fought with Te Arawa *kupapa against Hauhau at Matata and Te Teko, and was adept in the use of a Minie rifle. She later worked as an interpreter at Rotorua.

Porter, Colonel Thomas William (2 August 1843–12 November 1920). The son of a Surrey agricultural labourer, Porter's surname was initially Potter. Details of his early life are obscure, not least because of his own later penchant for embellishment. At various times he claimed, for example, to have been the son of an officer of the Indian Army and of a midshipman in the Royal Navy. In 1863 he enlisted in the *Colonial Defence Force's cavalry (as Thomas Potter) in Hawke's Bay. Following his service, he took land on the East Coast, learned Maori, and later married a Maori woman. In 1868 he joined Ngati Porou *kupapa fighting *Te Kooti. During the first half of 1869 he was second in command of No. 8 (Arawa) Division of the *Armed Constabulary during the final campaign against *Titokowaru. In 1870 he was attached to Major Ropata *Wahawaha's kupapa, who were about to enter the Urewera in search of Te Kooti. Although Porter was involved in a few skirmishes, his role was probably less important than he later claimed. Back on the East Coast, he procured large amounts of Maori land for the Crown, transactions that later drew allegations of corruption. Commissioned in the New Zealand *Militia in 1870, he commanded the East Coast Militia and Volunteer District from 1877 to 1890, and later served in the same capacity in the Wellington District (1900–01). Porter commanded New Zealand's Seventh Contingent to the *Boer War—the most heavily engaged of all the contingents—and was made a CB for his services. He subsequently commanded the Ninth Contingent, before leading the New Zealand contingent to the coronation of King Edward VII in London. In February 1903, amid allegations of political bias, he assumed command of the Canterbury Volunteer District. Between October 1904 and June 1905 he was acting Under-Secretary of Defence. During the *First World War, he was commandant of the National Reserve, and from December 1917 he tracked down *conscription evaders as Inspector of Recruiting Services.

Powles, Colonel Charles Guy (15 December 1872–17 June 1951) prepared the official history of the New Zealanders in the *Sinai–Palestine campaign. Born in Wellington, he served in the *Boer War as a

Captain Thomas Porter (far right) with a party of Ngaitai kupapa at Opotiki in 1870 (*Cowan Collection, Alexander Turnbull Library, F-11006-1/2*)

member of New Zealand's Fourth Contingent in 1900–01, and was commissioned. He returned to farming, but in 1910 secured a regular commission. Posted to 1NZEF, he proceeded overseas with the Main Body in 1914. For his exemplary conduct at ★Gallipoli he was made a DSO. He subsequently served as brigade major of the New Zealand Mounted Rifles Brigade and assistant adjutant and quartermaster-general of the Australian and New Zealand Mounted Division. During 1918 he was seconded to the British 61st Division. Following his return to New Zealand in 1919, he was commandant of Trentham Camp, during which period he worked on the history, *The New Zealanders in Sinai and Palestine*, which was published in 1922. After commanding the Central Military District, he retired in 1927, and was later Principal of Flock House, Bulls, an agricultural training establishment. From 1941 to 1945 he was commandant of Waiouru Military Camp. His son Guy would become New Zealand's first Ombudsman in 1962.

Pratt, General Thomas Simson (1797–2 February 1879) commanded the imperial forces during the Taranaki War of 1860–61. His military service began when he joined his father's regiment, the 56th Regiment of Foot, in 1814. He commanded the 26th (Cameronian) Regiment in the Opium War of 1840–42. After service in India he was promoted to major-general in 1858 and two years later took command of the imperial forces in Australasia. Following the defeat of British troops at Puketakauere on 27 June 1860, he crossed the Tasman to take personal control of the forces involved in Taranaki. At New Plymouth, he found himself restricted to a small bridgehead by a cordon of hostile pa. The danger to the town led him to adopt the cautious strategy of digging his opponents out of their strongholds. Redoubts were built to cover the advance, and saps were dug towards pa before they were stormed. His first sap, begun on 11 October 1860 against Orongomaihangi pa, proved superfluous when the garrison withdrew. He inflicted a sharp defeat on a predominantly Ngati Haua force at Mahoetahi on 6 November, but the chain of pa across the Waitara River remained intact. He began the reduction of this defence system in December. Matarikoriko pa fell. An attack on the British redoubt covering Huirangi pa was beaten off with heavy losses, and the pa was taken on 1 February 1861 after much digging. Next to be dealt with was Te Arei pa; by the time it was abandoned on 17 March nearly one and a half kilometres of sap had been dug, excluding the construction of redoubts. Peace was made shortly afterwards. Pratt returned to Melbourne in April 1861. He was promoted to the rank of general in 1873 and retired in 1877. His strategy of redoubts and sapping was much derided by settlers at the time as slow and indecisive. Yet the systematic construction of redoubts enabled the British to establish control over enemy territory, while sapping proved an effective way of taking pa.

Prisoners of war

Prisoners of war New Zealand's experience of prisoners of war in overseas wars is largely confined to Western Europe and the Mediterranean, and to conflict with Germany. About 97 per cent of all New Zealand POWs were taken in fighting with German forces, and their Italian allies, mostly during the *Second World War. Their response to their predicament has been a significant subtheme of New Zealand military history, with emphasis being placed on escapes, the outwitting of their captors, and camp pastimes as much as their ability to endure difficult, often tedious, and sometimes dangerous conditions.

Of the 6500 men who served in the New Zealand contingents in the *Boer War, fewer than 100 were captured, including the first fatal casualty in overseas fighting, who died of wounds while in Boer hands in December 1899. Small groups of New Zealanders were taken prisoner in two battles during the first, conventional, phase of the war. Seventeen men of the First Contingent were captured (along with 200 other British troops) following a Boer ambush at Sanna's Post in March 1900. They spent ten weeks in captivity before being released when Pretoria fell to the British forces in June. Two died of disease while in the prison camp. In July 1900 twenty New Zealanders from the Third Contingent were captured while defending an isolated hill near Witport. One escaped, and the rest were soon released following a further British advance. In the second, guerrilla, phase of the war small groups or individuals were occasionally captured, usually while reconnoitring away from the British columns. By this stage the Boers, always on the move and short of supplies, rarely held their prisoners for long. Weapons, clothes, and horses were retained, but in general men were not. According to official historian D.O.W. Hall, 'the capture seemed to them [the Boers] a sort of practical joke, and, their sense of humour satisfied, it did not worry them that the released prisoners immediately returned to their units'. However, there was no humour for Africans captured with the British forces; they were likely to be summarily executed. This was the fate of a black servant serving alongside the Sixth Contingent.

During the *First World War 506 New Zealanders were captured by the enemy. Of these, 42 were taken by Turkish forces at *Gallipoli or during the *Sinai–Palestine campaign and 464 by the Germans on the *Western Front. Their experiences differed considerably according to their captor and the theatre. Although some attempt had been made, in the Hague Conventions of 1897 and 1907, to establish legal norms of warfare, the position of prisoners remained relatively poorly protected, and the agreements technically did not apply anyway because not all the belligerents were parties to them (though bilateral agreements between belligerents overcame this problem). Neither Turks nor Germans fully met the terms of the conventions in relation to their prisoners. Many of the problems that arose were addressed in the Geneva Conventions of 1929.

Most of the twenty-five New Zealanders taken at Gallipoli were casualties of the attack on Chunuk Bair in August 1915, and were wounded. The moment of capture was a chilling one: those wounded not killed by Turkish troops were taken to dressing stations and thence to hospitals, where the standards of medical treatment varied according to the attitude of the Turk (or German) in charge. In the Maltese hospital in Constantinople prisoners were forced to share mattresses and only rudimentary treatment was provided. Six of the men succumbed to their wounds or disease. Of the other seventeen in Turkish hands, the majority were taken in the August 1916 Battle of Romani during the Sinai–Palestine campaign when an Auckland Mounted Rifles patrol was surrounded. Roped together, they endured a miserable march north. Inadequate medical treatment was provided and at Smyrna they suffered Black Hole–like conditions when crowded into a single room with 100 other prisoners. Two New Zealand airmen serving with British and Australian units in the Middle East were also captured by the Turks.

Some POWs were eventually sent to work camps, where conditions varied widely. A fairly free and easy existence was enjoyed by those toiling on the Berlin to Baghdad railway, but at Afion camp others suffered extreme privations at the hands of a cruel camp commandant. Sick men were forced to work and whippings were constant. One private later attested that some of the prisoners were raped by enemy officers, and that one wounded New Zealander (who later died) was sodomised in hospital. Poorly fed, vulnerable to assault, and forced to endure insanitary conditions, the prisoners revised earlier, more favourable impressions of 'Johnny Turk' (though it must be noted that ordinary Turkish soldiers and civilians were often treated just as poorly by the Turkish authorities). It was only towards the end of the war that conditions improved.

On the Western Front most New Zealand POWs were taken during the more open fighting of the concluding eight months of the war. Until then, prisoner of war casualties generally arose from the incessant trench raids which characterised the stalemate warfare. While executing the New Zealand Division's biggest raid, for example, 500 men of the 2nd Battalion, Auckland Regiment, on 21 February 1917 captured a number of Germans but had thirty of their number taken by the enemy. During the German offensive of early 1918 the New Zealand Entrenching Battalion, without its officers, had the misfortune to be trapped by the enemy advance, and 185 men were forced to surrender on 16 April. Five months later fifty men of the 1st Canterbury and 2nd Auckland Battalions were surrounded and captured when they pushed forward too far at Cambrai.

In the various camps and hospitals, the New Zealand prisoners were generally well treated. Fit men were sent to work in sugar factories and coalmines and on farms. Food shortages were common, especially in the last year of the war, when Germans, too, were starving. Some prisoners later noted that their survival had depended upon the arrival of ★Red Cross parcels. The prison at Fort Macdonald in Lille, where many of the Entrenching Battalion men were held, was worse than the rest, with brutal guards and overcrowded and insanitary conditions. With hundreds of men forced to sleep in one room, and privies overflowing on to them, dysentery was soon a problem.

Although a high proportion of the New Zealand prisoners planned or attempted escapes, only a few were successful. Captain G.A. Avery's four attempts, including tunnelling out of Schweidnitz camp, were all unsuccessful. Private H. Wallis-Wells, who escaped in occupied France in 1918 and was assisted by a French family, managed to cross to Allied lines on 10 November 1918. Private J.R. Hanson also successfully escaped in the final days of the war, staying with a Belgian family in Brussels until the city was liberated.

On the basis of the experience of the previous two conflicts, the New Zealanders who joined 2NZEF or the other services had little expectation of becoming prisoners of war. Yet more than 9000 did so, 575 of them airmen (including one unfortunate RAF officer shot down and captured two days after the war began) and 194 sailors. The bulk (8348) were soldiers of 2nd New Zealand Division taken in the early débâcles in ★Greece and ★Crete and during the ★North African campaign. After July 1942 only small numbers fell into enemy hands following minor reverses in the division's advance across North Africa and in Italy. Those captured in Greece and Crete were placed in temporary or transit camps before being transferred by boat or train to permanent camps in Germany. Although generally captured by Germans, the New Zealanders in the Desert were placed in Italian-run transit camps before being moved to Italy. After the Italian armistice in September 1943, 3200 New Zealand prisoners were transferred from Italy to Germany. In all of the holding and transit camps, there was overcrowding, shortages of food and medical supplies, and poor sanitation. Sickness added to the shock of capture and the suffering of the many wounded. The train trips to Germany, in crowded cattle trucks, were bad, but not as dangerous as crossing the Mediterranean. When two vessels carrying prisoners (*Jantzen* and *Nino Bixio*) were torpedoed by British submarines, many prisoners were lost, 160 New Zealanders among them. These latter were a high proportion of the just over 400 New Zealanders who lost their lives, through incident or sickness, while being held as POWs.

Once in Italy and Germany, where they were mixed with POWs of the other Western Allies, prisoners settled into the routine of camp life. The common preoccupation was food, for rations in many camps were limited, especially as the war dragged on. Red Cross parcels were again a lifeline for prisoners. They provided not only nutrition, variety, and a boost to morale but also the wherewithal to trade for fresh fruit and vegetables with the acquiescence of venal guards. Boredom was the other big concern. Prison life promoted listlessness and depression: 'If ever there was a lazier, more useless, hungry and at times hopelessly boring life than that of a prisoner of war in a foreign country,' one inmate later recalled, 'I cannot imagine what or where it could be.' To counter this, camp committees organised a wide variety of recreational, sporting, and educational activities. At Stalag 383 in Bavaria, where 350 New Zealanders were held, a school was established with sixty different classes, along with two libraries, two theatres, and a number of orchestras, bands, and choirs. Many sports tournaments were also held. A problem in most camps, especially in winter, was a lack of fuel for cooking and heating. Ingenious 'blowers' were invented to burn every scrap of fuel. Any surplus wood in the huts and around the camps (including a sentry box stolen at Stalag 383) was consumed. All (except officers) were expected to work, which had some advantages. Farm work, although hard, provided extra food, while factory work offered opportunities to barter. The worst working conditions were in salt mines, coal mines, and quarries, where injuries were commonplace.

Relations with guards varied from camp to camp. Many behaved with strict fairness, but there were occasional instances of prisoners being punished or shot for trivial breaches of the rules. In general, however, the New Zealanders benefited from the German observance, with some exceptions, of the provisions of the 1929 Geneva Convention in relation to their prisoners of war from the forces of the Western Allies. This contrasted starkly with the German treatment of Russian and other prisoners taken on the Eastern Front. For them cruelty and starvation were the order of the day, with millions losing their lives.

As in the First World War, many New Zealanders sought to escape. In all 716 succeeded in doing so, the high proportion being attributable to two significant opportunities. The first occurred following the defeat in Crete, when many prisoners were held in poorly supervised camps, including one at Galatas. Large numbers were able to leave, whether temporarily to forage for food or permanently. Cretans risked their

Prisoners of war

Prisoners of war in Stalag 383, Germany, in 1945 (*War History Collection, Alexander Turnbull Library, F-3688-1/4-DA*)

lives to hide escapers, few of whom were ever betrayed despite sometimes severe reprisals by German patrols against villages. About 150 New Zealanders managed to evade recapture and eventually reach Egypt by submarine or fishing boat. A few joined Cretan guerrillas to fight the occupation forces. An even larger number (447) got away after the Italian armistice in 1943, many slipping through the wire or simply walking out of camp before the Germans took over (despite misconceived instructions from London that all prisoners were to remain in their camps until Allied troops arrived). Italian peasants sheltered and assisted them, again at enormous risk. Most of the escapers got through to neutral Switzerland or to Allied lines in southern Italy, although again some remained with local partisans. One New Zealander, Lance-Corporal David ★Russell, was retaken by the Germans while helping to run an escape route and, after severe interrogation, was executed.

Apart from these mass escapes, only a few New Zealanders successfully escaped from Italian or German territory. Many assisted in organising escapes and some even got past the wall or wire surrounding the camp, but successful escape required great luck, skill, and persistence. Sapper R. Natusch tried eight times before successfully fleeing Austria in September 1944, while in Greece Lieutenant W.B. Thomas reached Turkey only on his fifth attempt. New Zealanders played significant roles in two of the most famous escape attempts of the war. In March 1943 six senior officers tunnelled out of the 'General's camp' in northern Italy; two New Zealand brigadiers (★Hargest and ★Miles) reached Switzerland and later crossed Vichy France into Spain. In 1944 seventy-six men escaped through a tunnel from Stalag Luft III, the air force officers' camp in northern Germany. The German response was barbarous: after most of the escapers were retaken, fifty (including three New Zealanders) were executed. Habitual escapers were usually sent to punishment camps or, like Captain Charles ★Upham, to Colditz 'castle' in Saxony. However, as the war drew to a close, the Germans began incarcerating recaptured prisoners in concentration camps. Under this policy twenty-five New Zealanders were sent to Theresienstadt concentration camp in Czechoslovakia, and several others were held briefly in Buchenwald camp. One New Zealand prisoner, who joined the British Free Corps, an SS unit, in 1944, would be convicted after the war of voluntarily aiding the enemy (see COURLANDER).

Many New Zealand prisoners were badly wounded when captured, and 109 died. A number of wounded and sick prisoners, medical personnel, and civilian internees were repatriated through neutral countries during the course of the war: about 220 New Zealanders from Italy and 650 from Germany. In the last months of the war the Germans decided to move their POWs away from the advancing Allied armies. Thousands of men, including many New Zealanders, were forced to march across Europe in the middle of winter. With food in short supply, sickness, sullen and anxious guards, and the danger of being strafed by their own side's aircraft, this was the worst time of their imprisonment. At least one New Zealander was shot while seeking food, and others were killed or wounded by Allied bombs. When the camps and columns were finally liberated, the ex-prisoners were quickly transferred by plane to reception camps in the United Kingdom, where a New Zealand Reception Group under Major-General H.K. ★Kippenberger was waiting. For some the process took longer. Liberated by the Russians, 168 were repatriated by way of Odessa. One of their number was shot dead by a Russian soldier during the train journey south to the port. (Fifty years later a media flurry was caused in New Zealand when it was alleged that some New Zealand prisoners had disappeared into the Soviet Gulag at this time, but the only prisoner in German hands unaccounted for after the war almost certainly died of sickness and exhaustion during one of the forced marches.) In the United Kingdom, the fit men were given special leave before being shipped home.

Although deprived and sometimes ill treated, the New Zealand prisoners in Western Europe had a comfortable existence compared with that of the roughly 100 servicemen and merchant seamen who fell into Japanese hands during the ★Pacific War. Mainly survivors of warships sunk in what are now Indonesian waters or airmen serving in the RAF or the ★Fleet Air Arm, they were held in camps across South-east Asia or in Japan itself, along with more than 200 interned New Zealand civilians. Japan was not a party to the 1929 Geneva Convention, and both racial and cultural influences affected its treatment of prisoners. Regarding their own personnel who surrendered as the 'living dead', the Japanese had little sympathy for Allied personnel who did so. They ill-treated prisoners, especially captured aircrew, as a matter of course. Beatings, overwork, inadequate rations, and a shortage of basic medical supplies ensured a very high rate of mortality among Allied prisoners (for example, nearly 36 per cent of the 22,000 Australian POWs). Food was even more of an obsession in Japanese camps than it was in Western European camps, and most of the victims of the Japanese succumbed to malnutrition. A few Red Cross parcels got through to some prisoners, but most were plundered or retained by the guards. A number of New Zealand prisoners fell victim to war crimes, including seventeen ★coastwatchers beheaded in Tarawa after an American raid on the island. A New Zealand airman captured in Sumatra in 1945 was taken to Singapore and executed. When the *Lisbon Maru* was torpedoed while carrying POWs (including New Zealanders) from Hong Kong to Japan, survivors were machine-gunned in the water by the Japanese. Camps in Japan were often linked to and sited alongside industries essential to the war effort. Several New Zealanders were killed when these facilities were bombed by the Allies. If only because of their conspicuousness, European prisoners had little chance of successfully escaping, and the penalty for being caught was likely to be torture and execution. Nevertheless two New Zealanders, Pilot Officer E.D. Crossley and Lieutenant R.B. Goodwin, did manage to escape from camps in Hong Kong in 1942 and 1944 respectively, and after many adventures reached Allied lines in China.

The experience of being a prisoner of war of the Japanese had a profound influence on those who survived, leaving many after liberation and repatriation 'impatient with the pettiness, self-seeking and querulousness of people at home', which compared unfavourably, in their opinion, with the 'unselfishness and common sacrifice' they had observed as POWs. However, unlike in Australia, the public impact of the POW experience in New Zealand remained limited, if only because of the relatively small numbers involved. In more recent times former prisoners, bolstered by many hundreds of Dutch emigrants who had been held by the Japanese in the Dutch East Indies, have periodically come to notice as they pursue, so far unsuccessfully, compensation claims with the Japanese.

In the various campaigns in which New Zealand has been involved since 1945, New Zealand's prisoner of war experience has been almost non-existent. During the ★Korean War several members of ★Kayforce were captured by assaulting Chinese forces in November 1951, but all but one evaded their captors and returned to friendly lines. The exception, Gunner N.G. Garland, was held in a camp in northern North Korea until liberated after the armistice in July 1953, conceding later that conditions were 'not bad' even if harsh by Western standards. As with the other POWs, he had to endure attempts by his captor to indoctrinate him with communist ideology.

W.W. Mason, *Prisoners of War* (War History Branch, Wellington, 1954); D. McGill, *P.O.W.* (Mills Publications, Lower Hutt, 1987).

DAVID FILER

Prisoners of war in New Zealand

Prisoners of war in New Zealand While New Zealand's prisoners of war experience mostly occurred overseas (see PRISONERS OF WAR), POWs have also been held within New Zealand itself. Warriors captured during traditional Maori intertribal conflict, such as the *Musket Wars, could expect little other than enslavement—if they were not immediately slaughtered and devoured by their captors. A prominent prisoner might be held as a hostage. No substantial body of British and colonial troops became POWs during the *New Zealand Wars, though wounded soldiers sometimes fell into enemy hands; with few exceptions, for example at Gate Pa, they were dispatched by their captors. The government forces were by no means blameless, with surrendering Maori warriors being cut down by enraged troops on numerous occasions or sometimes with cold deliberation, as, for example, following the fall of Ngatapa in 1869, when 120 of *Te Kooti's followers were summarily executed. During the Waikato campaign several hundred Maori POWs, including 178 taken at Rangiriri, were gathered at Drury. Marched to Auckland with a large escort in November 1863, they were held on HMS *Curaçao* before being incarcerated in the prison hulk *Marion* in Auckland harbour. Never more than 214 in number, they were guarded by a 50-man detachment from the 3rd Waikato Militia, mainly Germans, under Captain Krippner. In August 1864 they were transported to Kawau Island, where they were unguarded. Ignoring their promise not to leave, they crossed to the mainland within six weeks and returned to the Waikato area. From 1866 Hauhau prisoners, including women and children, were held at a redoubt on the Chatham Islands. In July 1868, led by Te Kooti, nearly 300 of them escaped after overcoming their guards and seizing a schooner; they landed on the East Coast.

During the *Boer War the New Zealand government firmly rebuffed British suggestions that a number of Boer POWs be resettled on Stewart Island. New Zealand was too far from the scene of action to receive any German POWs during the *First World War. However, six of the crew of the German navy's armed merchant raider *Seeadler*, which ran aground on Mopelia Atoll in the Society Islands, were held in New Zealand in 1917–18 after their capture in the Fiji Islands. Escaping from Motuihe Island in December 1917, *Seeadler*'s captain, Commander Felix von Luckner, two members of her crew, and eight interned Germans made off in a captured scow which they seized in the Bay of Plenty. They were recaptured within a week in the Kermadec Islands.

New Zealand's only significant involvement with enemy POWs occurred during the *Pacific War. From September 1942 Japanese captured during fighting in the South Pacific were held at a camp near Featherston, where they were put to work. By early 1943 about 800 were being held, 60 per cent of them members of work units of the Imperial Army and the rest mostly naval personnel. To counter the prevailing mood of depression, and inclination towards mass suicide, among the prisoners (because of their sense of dishonour at being captured), the authorities bent over backwards to provide relatively congenial conditions—in stark contrast to the treatment of New Zealand POWs in Japanese hands. Even so, there were 67 deaths among the Japanese POWs held in New Zealand, including 48 killed by rifle fire during an affray in February 1943 (see FEATHERSTON INCIDENT). The remainder were repatriated to Japan in late December 1945.

Prize ships are captured enemy vessels taken over and put to use by a belligerent. The first and most significant prize ship in New Zealand service was the *Pamir*, a Finnish barque seized as a prize of war in Wellington harbour in December 1941 after New Zealand declared war on Finland. Operated by the Union Steam Ship Company on the government's behalf, she carried wool and tallow between New Zealand and North America until restored to Finnish ownership in 1948 as a token of friendship (made easier by the fact that she was losing money for the government). During the *Solomons campaign HMNZS *Matai* captured a Japanese barge, which was redesignated *Matai Junior*. The barge was taken over by American forces for intelligence-gathering purposes. After the *Second World War the RNZN was given a captured 13-metre German yacht by the Royal Navy. The yacht, named *Tangaika* ('spoils taken in war'), did training and recreational service at Auckland until it was sold in 1957.

Public Safety Conservation Act 1932 was passed in response to riotous behaviour during the Depression. It enabled the government in an emergency to issue a Proclamation of Emergency, under which wide regulatory powers were available. The Act provided the legislative basis for New Zealand's initial response to the outbreak of the *Second World War. An emergency was proclaimed on 1 September 1939, and the government issued a series of emergency regulations placing New Zealand on a war footing. On 14 September, however, the Act's role was superseded by specific legislative authority in the Emergency Regulations Act 1939. The Public Safety Conservation Act was again invoked in September 1950 and February 1951, when proclamations of emergency were issued in response to industrial strife (see INDUSTRIAL DISPUTES, USE OF ARMED FORCES IN). The Act was repealed in 1987, the government taking the view that its regulation-making provisions offered the executive

Hauhau prisoners on a prison hulk awaiting transport to the Chatham Islands in 1866. The Maori seated at front left is reputed to be Te Kooti (*Alexander Turnbull Library, F-4134-1/2*)

too much discretion. Instead of one broad-ranging measure, specific or sectoral legislative provisions have been made for dealing with emergencies.

Puhirake, Rawiri (?–21 June 1864) led Maori forces fighting the British at Tauranga during the ★New Zealand Wars. Of Ngai Tukairangi hapu of Ngai Te Rangi, he refused to become involved in the Waikato War against British forces in 1863, though many of his tribe went to fight with the King Movement. His attitude changed, however, when British troops arrived at Tauranga in January 1864. A strange kind of war ensued, with neither side wishing to take the initiative, even though Puhirake constructed a road to his pa so that the British would not be too weary to fight ('kei ngene te hoia'). In April 1864 he began constructing a pa at Pukehinahina (Gate Pa), closer to British positions at Tauranga. Designed by Pene Taka, this stronghold was a maze of bunkers, trenches, and concealed rifle pits. Perceiving an opportunity to gain a decisive victory, Lieutenant-General Duncan ★Cameron assembled a large artillery train to shatter the pa. But the garrison, sheltering in their bunkers, survived the bombardment to rout the ensuing British attack on 29 April 1864. As the shells ravaged the pa, Puhirake was inspirational, exhorting his tribesmen: 'Ko to manawa-rere, ko te manawa-rere, kia u, kia u!' ('Trembling hearts, be firm, be firm!'). In accordance with a code of conduct laid down by him, Henare Wiremu ★Taratoa, and other chiefs, the defenders behaved with great chivalry towards the British wounded. That night they vacated the pa. During May reinforcements arrived from other tribes. As part of an offensive strategy against the British at Tauranga, a new pa was built at Te Ranga, near Pukehinahina. However, Puhirake disliked the site of the pa, and its fortifications were incomplete when the British attacked on 21 June 1864. He was among those killed as British troops overwhelmed the defenders.

Puttick, Lieutenant-General Sir Edward (26 June 1890–25 July 1976) was, in April 1942, the first New Zealand–born officer to achieve the rank of lieutenant-general in the New Zealand Military Forces. Born in Timaru, he was a draughtsman when he began his military career in the ★Territorial Force. From May 1911 he was a junior officer in the 15th (North Auckland) Regiment. With the outbreak of the ★First World War, he immediately offered his services, and on 15 August 1914 departed from Wellington with the Samoa Expeditionary Force. After eight months in Samoa, he returned to New Zealand, but soon left to join 1NZEF as a company commander in the New Zealand Rifle Brigade. Soon after arriving in Egypt, he became staff captain of the 2nd Infantry Brigade, in which capacity he served until July 1916. He was then second-in-command of the 4th Battalion, 3rd New Zealand (Rifle) Brigade, until taking over as its commander in June 1917. He performed well at Passchendaele. From November 1917, he commanded the brigade's 3rd Battalion until wounded in March 1918. Evacuated to England, he later commanded the training depot at Brocton but, still unwell, was eventually repatriated to New Zealand in November 1918. His detailed personal diary of his First World War service, now in the National Archives, is a valuable source for historians of New Zealand's war effort. Opting to pursue a military career, he joined the ★New Zealand Staff Corps at the end of 1919. One of his first tasks was to lead an expedition to Fiji in 1920 to assist the administration there in dealing with a labour dispute (see FIJI EXPEDITIONARY FORCE). After filling a variety of staff positions, he was attached to the War Office in 1936, and subsequently attended the ★Imperial Defence College. His confidential reports indicated that his forte was administration rather than tactics, and in February 1938 he became Adjutant and Quartermaster-General and Second Military Member of the Army Board. He commanded the Central Military District in 1939. In this capacity, he played an important part in organising the Special Force (later 2NZEF) that was formed after the outbreak of war. He left New Zealand with the First Echelon in January 1940 as commander of 4th Infantry Brigade, which he led effectively in ★Greece. As the senior brigadier, he was given command of the 2nd New Zealand Division on ★Crete, after the divisional commander, Major-General B.C. ★Freyberg, was elevated to command Creforce. During the ensuing battle, however, Puttick's hesitance, still a matter of controversy, proved disastrous to the division's response to the German airborne invasion. As commander, he must take ultimate responsibility for the division's crucial failure to eliminate the threat presented by German paratroopers who landed in Prison Valley and at Maleme, which led to the loss of the island. Back in Egypt, Puttick was seen as the logical choice, because of his administrative capacity, to succeed Major-General J.E. ★Duigan as CGS. When Puttick arrived in New Zealand in early September 1941, he was confronted with the daunting task of sustaining 2NZEF in the Middle East while at the same time building up New Zealand's home defences and Fiji garrison in line with proposals made by the visiting General Sir Guy ★Williams. Puttick revitalised New Zealand's home defences. ★Territorial Force training was increased and the Fiji garrison built up, but he was hampered by equipment shortages. With the onset of the ★Pacific War, his immediate focus became the approaching ★Japanese threat. Although unconvinced that the Japanese would invade New Zealand, he saw the need for local defence measures to sustain morale, especially while the 2nd Division remained in the Middle East (a deployment he considered should be maintained until Germany was beaten). In 1942 he oversaw the mobilisation of the home defence forces and their rapid expansion as part of the ★anti-invasion defences. For the remainder of the war his considerable organisational skills were applied to the difficult task of juggling New Zealand's slender resources to meet commitments in both the Mediterranean and the Pacific, as well as production needs in New Zealand. With his enormous capacity for work, and his red hair, he earned the nickname 'the Red Hun'. He relinquished the position of CGS at the end of 1945, and in the following year his services were recognised by his appointment as a KCB. After leading the New Zealand contingent to the Victory Parade in London, he retired from the Army in September 1946. He was engaged by the ★War History Branch to write the official unit history *25 Battalion* (1960).

Q

Q-ships were disguised merchant ships used by the Royal Navy during the ★First World War as a decoy for German U-boats, which preferred to sink their prey by gunfire rather than depleting their limited torpedo stocks. Once on the surface the submarine was vulnerable to the hidden guns and torpedoes on the Q-ship. The effectiveness of the system depended on surprise. Once the enemy learned of the existence of such ships, as occurred when a Q-ship failed to dispatch its attacker to the deep, they tended to torpedo their victims without warning. About 200 Q-ships were deployed, and thirty-one were lost on operations. Eleven U-boats fell victim to them. A small number were used in the ★Second World War but they were almost completely ineffective and were withdrawn in 1941. A number of New Zealanders attached to the Royal Navy served with distinction in Q-ships, notably Lieutenant-Commanders Wybrants ★Olphert, Frank Worsley, and William ★Sanders.

Queree, Brigadier Raymond Candlish (28 June 1909–18 October 1975) was one of the architects of the post-1945 Army. He was born in Christchurch, and began his career as an officer cadet at the Royal Military College, Sandhurst, in the late 1920s. After serving with 5th Field Regiment and later the 7th Anti-Tank Regiment, he was brigade major of the Divisional Artillery from October 1940 to April 1941, when he became GSO2 of the 2nd New Zealand Division. He was wounded on ★Crete. He briefly commanded 4th Field Regiment in 1942 before, in September, becoming GSO1 of the division, a post in which he displayed ruthless efficiency during the next two years. He was made a CBE in 1944. Later described as highly professional, 'uncompromising, a strong disciplinarian and a master of detail', he was appointed CRA in August 1944. He oversaw the planning of the crushing artillery barrages behind which 2nd New Zealand Division advanced in the closing stages of the ★Italian campaign. For his skilful control of the artillery (often from forward posts or observation aircraft), he was made a DSO. As Quartermaster-General (1948–54) and Adjutant-General (1954–60), he displayed the same formidable administrative talents as the ★New Zealand Army prepared to fulfil the ★Middle East commitment. Nowhere were his skills more apparent than in the creation, in 1950, of ★Kayforce, the first New Zealand expeditionary force to take its heavy equipment with it when it departed from New Zealand. His sometimes sharp criticism earned him the nickname 'Sabre-tooth'. After heading the Army's liaison staff in London, he retired in 1964. He was the Director of Civil Defence from 1965 to 1970.

Brigadier R.C. Queree (left) with Captain John White, Lieutenant-General Sir Bernard Freyberg, and Brigadier W.G. Gentry in Egypt in October 1942 (*Sir John White Collection, Alexander Turnbull Library, F-2671-1/2-DA*)

R

Radford–Collins agreement, which concerns responsibilities for the protection and control of shipping in the Pacific in time of war, was negotiated by Vice-Admiral J.A. Collins, the Australian Chief of Naval Staff, and Admiral A.W. Radford, the Commander-in-Chief, Pacific, at a meeting at Pearl Harbor in February 1951, at which New Zealand's Chief of Naval Staff, Rear-Admiral F.A. Ballance, was also present. The meeting arose out of concern among the *ANZAM partners at their lack of knowledge of American intentions, which made ANZAM planning difficult. Radford, whose command encompassed the whole of the ANZAM area, refused to limit his freedom of action in any way. However, he did agree to ANZAM taking responsibility in a specified area, smaller than the existing ANZAM area, for a number of relatively minor tasks: convoy escort and routing, reconnaissance, local defence anti-submarine warfare, and search and rescue. The agreement also dealt with wartime liaison between the US command and ANZAM, and recommended examination of the possibility of a peacetime exchange of liaison officers. From New Zealand's point of view, the main effect of the agreement was to place Western Samoa, the Cook Islands, and Tokelau, over which it had jurisdiction, outside the purview of ANZAM planning, though New Zealand continued to be responsible for their local defence. Although the ANZAM machinery was later terminated, the agreement, still classified, remains relevant to Australian and New Zealand defence planning with the United States in the Pacific.

Rainbow Warrior incident On 10 July 1985 the visiting Greenpeace vessel *Rainbow Warrior* was sunk in Auckland Harbour by two bombs which had been laid by French secret service agents. One member of the crew, a Dutch citizen, was killed. The only known act of sabotage on New Zealand territory, this operation had been authorised by the French Minister of Defence, Charles Hernu, to prevent the *Rainbow Warrior* from proceeding to Moruroa Atoll as a protest against French nuclear testing there. Two of the French agents involved in the operation were apprehended and later pleaded guilty to manslaughter charges. They were sentenced to ten years' imprisonment, but a diplomatic settlement, negotiated by the UN Secretary-General, led to their being handed over to French custody (and the agreement that they were to be held on Hao Atoll for three years was later broken by the French government). New Zealand received an apology for the violation of its sovereignty and monetary compensation. The incident, which brought New Zealand–French relations to their nadir, was perhaps made possible by New Zealand's isolated position as a result of the *ANZUS rupture following the earlier *Buchanan* affair.

Ranks in the *New Zealand Defence Force are, as in most British Commonwealth countries, inherited from British military and naval tradition. They can be divided into three main groups: commissioned or officer ranks, non-commissioned ranks (NCOs), and those without rank, the sailors, soldiers, and airmen and airwomen of the services. The original relationship between rank and appointment or function is now blurred. For example, an RNZAF flying squadron is now more likely to be commanded by a wing commander than by a squadron leader; a brigade may be commanded by a colonel, and a naval ship is more likely to be commanded by a commander than a captain. How-

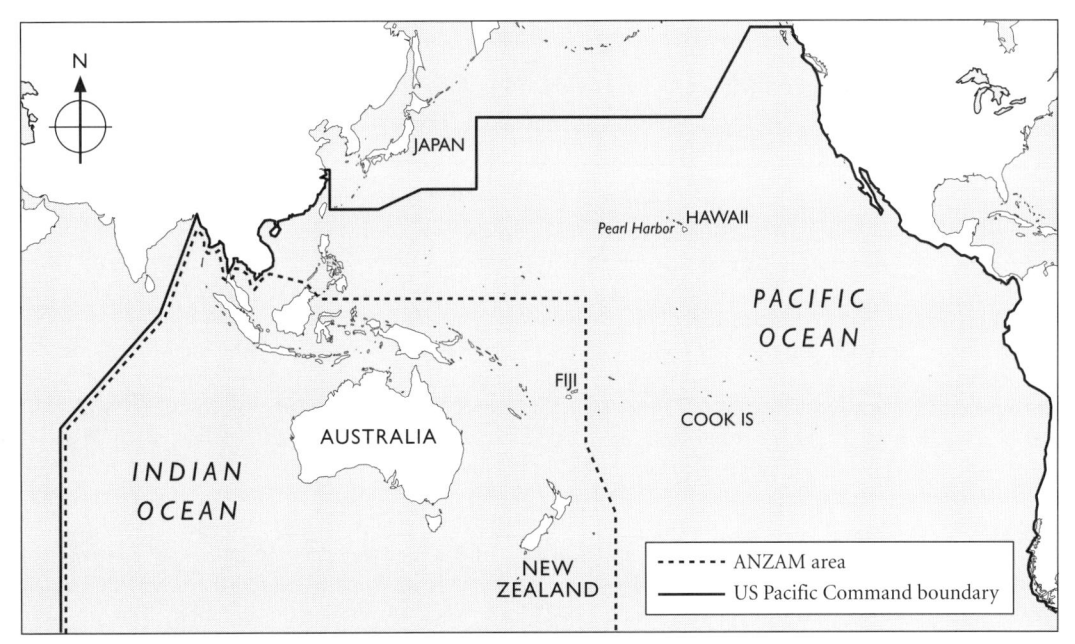

Map 21 The ANZAM region following the Radford–Collins agreement of 1951

ever, senior naval officers who have the right to fly flags are still referred to as flag officers; Army officers above the rank of brigadier are known as general officers and the equivalent in the RNZAF as air officers.

There are a number of traditional forms of address and other conventions which often confuse outsiders. Officers above the rank of an army lieutenant and equivalent are referred to verbally by their rank, and officers of this rank or below are referred to as 'mister'. Officers of general rank above brigadier are referred to as 'general', and lieutenant-colonels are called 'colonel' informally. Pronunciations are also different by tradition for the rank of a naval lieutenant or lieutenant-commander are known as 'l'tenant' or 'l'tenant commander', whereas an army lieutenant is referred to as a 'leftenant'. In written or formal form the full rank is used, for example 'major-general' or 'lieutenant-colonel'. In the NCO ranks staff and flight sergeants are informally referred to as 'staff' and 'flight' respectively. Lance-corporals are referred to as 'corporal' and warrant officers class two as 'sarn't major'. Warrant officers class one are called 'mister' or 'RSM' (for regimental sergeant major) in the case of a warrant officer class one holding the senior NCO position in a battalion or unit of similar size. They are usually called 'sir', or 'RSM' if appropriate, by their juniors, but they are never referred to by their rank. Senior NCOs are those of sergeant through to warrant officer rank. Private soldiers are called by their rank and name.

Officers in training are known as officer cadets, but this is a conventional form of address and is not a rank. Although there are divisions within the cadet structure, such as under officer and cadet sergeant, officer cadets technically have no ranks. They are referred to as cadet or mister in training. They wear white gorget patches on their collars to indicate this status.

Commissioned officers are entitled to compliments in the form of a salute from their juniors and all officers holding the Queen's Commission are saluted by all NCOs and other ranks. The term other ranks (ORs) was used for all ranks not commissioned but now refers only to those below NCO rank. NCOs are not saluted.

Leaving aside Prince Philip, who holds the highest rank in all three services (field marshal or equivalent), the most senior officer holding an appointment in the three services is major-general or equivalent. One officer holds the rank of lieutenant-general equivalent as the Chief of Defence Force. The Army has an appointment of Sergeant Major of the Army, which is the senior NCO appointment in the Army in the rank of warrant officer class one. The appointee also wears the distinguishing badge for the rank on the right arm below the shoulder, as opposed to wearing it on the wrist or lower arm position.

Officer ranks are generally worn on shoulder epaulettes and NCO ranks on the right arm, except for warrant officers, who wear a wrist band or, in service dress, a badge on the lower right arm. There is a move in informal orders of dress for all rank to be worn on epaulettes.

GRANT CROWLEY

Rations

Rations is the generic term for food in the New Zealand armed forces, particularly in the *New Zealand Army. The same description for military food items is used in most other Western countries' forces. Derived from the Latin term *ratio*, meaning a reckoning, it developed over the centuries as the term for a fixed daily allowance of food in the armed forces. The relative quantities of ration and subsistence items and other stores required for warlike operations have changed significantly over the years. In the seventeenth century subsistence food items accounted for around 98 per cent of resupply tonnages, with ammunition accounting for only 2 per cent. In the *First World War subsistence items accounted for less than 50 per cent of the total logistic tonnage required. In modern times, now that forage is no longer a consideration, rations account for only approximately 10 per cent of supply requirements.

Rations can be conveniently broken down into two main categories—hard and fresh. Hard rations are tinned, preserved, or dry items prepared for eating by the individual serviceman or woman. Early versions used in the *Boer War and in the First World War consisted of the infamous tins of bully beef and biscuits as the staple diet. These were supplemented by fresh food, tinned milk, jam, tea, and if available bread and fresh items. The range and type of tinned food had not much improved by the *Second World War. New Zealand forces overseas were fed on the British ration scale in both world wars. Modern versions of hard rations consist of a reasonably appetising range of tinned items, confectionery, food bars, dried products such as noodles, rice, milk, cocoa, tea, coffee, condiments, and dried fruit. They are typically packed into 24-hour plastic bag packs for one man, consisting of three meals. The pack provides for three hot or cold meals a day and snacks, though recent changes have reduced the tinned options in favour of more snack items to reflect soldier preferences. On operations a soldier would carry at least three packs. There is also a 10-person composite pack for use in more static locations which holds a greater variety of food items. The Army also uses a range of freeze-dried ration pack items, developed locally. These require significantly more water to be available to the soldier but are popular for their quality and light weight. They are favoured by forces engaged on special operations, for example the *Special Air Service, because of their lack of weight. At around twice the price of a standard individual 24-hour pack, the freeze-dried option is less popular with the authorities for normal use.

The individual ration pack provides around 2900 of the 4250 calories regarded as the ideal daily calorific intake for a soldier in the field. The composite pack provides slightly less calorific value, but this can be increased with supplementary items, such as bread and butter. Ration pack feeding for long periods without fresh food is not desirable for these reasons alone, regardless of the effect on morale of monotonous menu choices. A maximum of seven days on ration packs without fresh food supplementation is the accepted limit. Soldiers have tended to supplement the official ration packs with private supplies when in the field, particularly with favourite items or extra sweet items. The United States tray-pack system, known as MRE (Meals Ready to Eat), which uses high technology food preservation and stabilisation methods, has not been introduced in the New Zealand armed forces. Financial constraints have forced New Zealand to develop its own ration pack systems, albeit in an ad hoc and at times unscientific way. There have been recent efforts to draw on food technology expertise, with trials being conducted at Massey University.

The second category of rations is conventional fresh food, prepared in field kitchens, usually in bulk for hot-box distribution on operations. The Army has purchased the German Karcher mobile trailer kitchen for this purpose. In static camp and base locations, standing kitchens are used to prepare meals for consumption in standing mess facilities. When fresh food is ordered in the field and on operations, it is allocated on a system known as a frequency of issue. This is a list of items which changes periodically and is based on a weight allowance for each item per person being fed. In standing military locations in New Zealand and on RNZN ships, fresh rations are provided on a cost per man basis, around $9 a day in 1999, but this varies between services. Until recently Army supply depots purchased supplies in bulk and distributed them to camp kitchens on a scale basis similar to a frequency of issue. Today the kitchen manager or catering manager

A Wellington Regiment field cooker being used to prepare a meal just 900 metres from the front line at Colincamps on the Western Front (*RSA Collection, Alexander Turnbull Library, G-13209-1/2*)

orders the food direct from commercial suppliers. Messes often supplement the official ration from a mess allowance paid voluntarily by the mess members for special items. This is usually only the case in officer and senior NCO messes.

The trend in the armed forces in New Zealand is to contract out rationing functions in camps and bases. However, a core of enlisted service men and women is required to be recruited, trained, and held on unit establishments to ensure that the operational catering and ration supply posts are filled ready for deployment on operations or on field training exercises.

GRANT CROWLEY

Red Cross Founded by Henri Dunant, the Red Cross emerged as a strictly neutral, independent humanitarian agency to alleviate suffering in war. Dunant's agitation for the civilised treatment of wounded and sick in war bore fruit in the Geneva Convention of 1864, which recognised the neutrality of medical personnel, hospitals, and wounded soldiers. Since then the Geneva Convention has been extended to include ★hospital ships, ★prisoners of war, and, since 1949, civilians. The Red Cross symbol—a Swiss flag with the colours reversed—has become universally recognised as a sign of non-combatant (not necessarily medical) status, the bearers of which enjoy special rights.

Following the outbreak of the ★First World War, a great number of enthusiastic war relief and aid societies were created in New Zealand, foremost among them branches of the British Red Cross Society. To coordinate the enthusiastic contributions of volunteers, the New Zealand Branch of the British Red Cross Society was formally established in November 1915. Funds were raised for war relief of Allied soldiers and civilians. Bandages were produced and sent to British forces, as well as to France and Russia. A vast quantity of soldiers' comforts was also provided, including socks, gloves, cans of fruit, and cocoa, which were parcelled and sent overseas. The New Zealand Red Cross also raised money to equip two hospital ships, *Maheno* and *Marama*. Another important role for the Red Cross was to keep families of missing or captured soldiers informed of the soldiers' whereabouts and condition. Parcels for POWs were sent through the Red Cross Prisoners of War Bureau in Switzerland.

After the war the focus of the New Zealand Red Cross shifted to rehabilitation, with the establishment of convalescent homes and vocational training workshops for disabled ex-servicemen. In 1920 the activities of the Red Cross were formalised to include the alleviation of suffering in peace as well as in war, with funds being sent for the relief of starving children in postwar Europe. Another important change between the world wars was the establishment of ★Voluntary Aid Detachments of Red Cross, units of women with basic nursing training. The New Zealand Red Cross contributed to war relief in China in 1937–38: four doctors were sent to China to assist civilians displaced by the Japanese invasion.

The Red Cross greatly expanded its role in the ★Second World War. As in the previous conflict women sewed, folded, and knitted enormous quantities of bandages, pyjamas, and other comforts for wounded soldiers. In addition there were tinned foods, cakes, cigarettes, and chocolate for soldiers in hospital both in New Zealand and overseas. The New Zealand Red Cross kept lists of POWs, and from New Zealand an impressive voluntary effort aimed to send each prisoner a parcel containing tins of food, chocolate, tea, and cigarettes every week. These parcels were packed in Wellington and sent to prison camps in Germany and Italy by way of Switzerland. By the war's end the New Zealand Red Cross had sent more than 56,000 tons of relief parcels, which as the war wore on became increasingly important for the men's survival. In New Zealand enemy POWs and internees were overseen by a Swiss doctor assigned by the International Red Cross. War relief was also provided to Great Britain, with foodstuffs, fats, clothes, and footwear being sent there until 1955. Remittances were made to Allied Red Crosses during the war. Closer to home, Polish refugee children and American servicemen received Red Cross assistance.

The New Zealand Red Cross made a more direct contribution to the New Zealand war effort. Instruction in first aid, including precautions against air raids and gas attack, was given. The VADs flourished, their membership reaching 8000 by 1942. Men's VADs were created in 1939, and a women's Red Cross Transport Corps was created for the transport of sick and wounded. This uniformed wing of the Red Cross manned emergency first aid posts and casualty clearing stations in the main centres, transported wounded or convalescing soldiers, and assisted with nursing duties. Nearly 300 Red Cross VADs were sent overseas to perform basic nursing and clerical duties.

After 1945 the New Zealand Red Cross tended to focus upon community health care and disaster relief. Nevertheless, it continued to provide aid for the victims of war. In the 1950s woollen comforts and gift parcels were sent to Korea, while Hungarian ★refugees received assistance following the Soviet Union's military intervention there in 1956. New Zealand servicemen based in Malaya were given welfare assistance via the Australian Red Cross. The New Zealand Red Cross also sent a two-man medical team to the conflict in the Congo in 1960–61. A more important deployment of New Zealand Red Cross resources took place between

Refugees

1968 and 1975, when welfare teams assisted refugees in the Binh Dinh province during the ★Vietnam War. A major effort was made in 1979 to alleviate suffering among Cambodian refugees, with sixty-three medical personnel being sent to refugee camps on the Thai–Cambodian border. Other New Zealand personnel were sent to Pakistan in 1982 to assist Afghan war refugees, the beginning of a long-standing commitment by the New Zealand Red Cross to provide relief from the war in Afghanistan.

The end of the ★Cold War and the ensuing rise of brutal ethnic and religious conflicts has greatly increased the role of the Red Cross in providing humanitarian assistance in war. Within New Zealand refugees from armed conflict have been assisted by the New Zealand Red Cross, and a tracing service for refugees has allowed families to be kept in touch. More recently the Red Cross has initiated school-based education programmes on war and international humanitarian law. It has at times been outspoken in its advocacy on behalf of the victims of war and in support of international conventions banning inhumane weapons, especially anti-personnel landmines.

During the 1990s large numbers of Red Cross personnel have been sent to war-torn countries around the world. Since 1991 fifty-two New Zealand Red Cross delegates have served in twenty-two countries affected by war. Major commitments by the New Zealand Red Cross have been to Afghanistan (where a medical team has operated in Kabul since 1988) and Cambodia (where personnel have given relief to refugees). The Red Cross has been swift to respond to suffering caused by armed conflict; five nurses were sent to Zaire to help alleviate the plight of refugees from Rwanda within two weeks of the emergency there becoming apparent. In the Pacific New Zealand Red Cross delegates have provided aid to Bougainville. A New Zealand nurse with the Red Cross in the Russian republic of Chechnya was murdered in December 1996, the first New Zealand Red Cross worker to be killed in an armed conflict.

Refugees The first war refugees in New Zealand were victims of Maori intertribal fighting, especially during the ★Musket Wars in the first half of the nineteenth century. The fighting left many people homeless, and precipitated mass migrations by those seeking security from attack. The first sizeable group of refugees to enter New Zealand from overseas as a result of conflict did so during the ★Second World War: 202 British children evacuated as a temporary measure. New Zealand had offered to take 2500, but the practice of sending children out of Great Britain ended when a ship carrying child evacuees to Canada was torpedoed. Most of the children in New Zealand returned to Britain at the end of the war. In November 1944, 733 orphaned Polish children, accompanied by about 100 adult staff, arrived at Wellington, after a long journey via the Soviet Union and Iran. They were accommodated in a camp at Pahiatua jointly administered by the ★New Zealand Army and the ★Red Cross, with the assistance of a representative of the Polish government-in-exile. In 1946 about 122 Polish ex-servicemen were reunited with relatives in New Zealand, while about ninety staff and children returned to Poland. The last children left the camp in April 1949, most going to hostels in Wellington, where they integrated into society. After the war, approximately 4500 displaced persons emigrated to New Zealand, mostly from Eastern Europe. Since then, refugees have come to New Zealand periodically as a result of conflicts in various parts of the world, including 1100 Hungarians following the Hungarian uprising of 1956 and 700 Kosovo Albanians in 1999. The only sizeable group to arrive as a result of displacement in a war in which New Zealand was directly involved were roughly 4000 Vietnamese between 1978 and 1982. They had escaped from Vietnam mainly by boat following the end of the ★Vietnam War.

Regimental alliances From 1905 officers in the New Zealand Mounted Rifles enjoyed honorary membership of the King's Colonial Regiment of Imperial Yeomanry. More formal alliances between New Zealand and British military units began six years later. They were an attempt to foster regimental pride in units of the newly formed ★Territorial Force, as well as a gesture of comradeship. It was hoped that New Zealand units, through association with long-established British regiments, would gain a sense of tradition and pride. More recently alliances have been made with Australian and Canadian regiments for comradeship and to strengthen Commonwealth links. However, the importance of alliances has been mainly ceremonial. Presentations of musical instruments and mess silver are often made. Units and corps have frequently adopted the marches and items of uniform and corps badges of their alliance partner. The 2nd Battalion (Canterbury, Nelson, Marlborough, West Coast) RNZIR, for example, wears a dark green caubeen with a green 'hackle' in recognition of its partner, the Royal Irish Regiment.

Religion and war War affects religion and religious behaviour significantly. Religion for its part affects the conduct of war and the behaviour of its participants, civilian and military. Both these theses can be sustained from New Zealand evidence, and together can produce some explosive results. New Zealand has seen only limited confrontations but they have earned a significant place in historical analysis. Although New Zealand society has never been highly militarised in peacetime, and the religious and ethical issues of a war-torn society have rarely been critical, there have been some important confrontations.

Historically the best-known connection between the church and war has been the Augustinian notion of a just war. In secularised New Zealand society, this matter may be seen as technically irrelevant. Nevertheless churches were looked to by the state for a lead in the justification of war (not that the state waited for this, but the 'just war' has always been a post hoc seal of approval). Although New Zealand had no official state church, which could have been impelled to support the state in war, this was rendered less important by the fact that the mainstream churches were generally supportive at their annual conferences, at least until the ★Vietnam War. Thus the wars encouraged the major denominations to develop a sense of national commitment, if only to keep abreast with each other.

No modern war is ever fought just by the military. The mobilisation of society and the economy for 'total war' means that potential religious reactions become important, and must be controlled. Religious factors have frequently been invoked by some as an explanation for success or failure in war. If the army is unsuccessful and soldiers' lives are lost, then the gods of battle are displeased. Success must be celebrated with religious ceremony. Failure invokes a sense of national crisis. So the religious life of the community is under scrutiny in time of war. Whenever New Zealand has been at war, religious reflection about society has increased, and particularly during the world wars the religious jeremiad, expressing alarm about the condition of the state, has gained some recognition.

Meanwhile, within the armed services, religion has played a more regulated role. Church parades, preparation for battle, and the burial of the dead were part of the routine of army life. The military parade lends itself to religious ceremony. Military discipline finds religious sanctions convenient. On the other hand, religion for the armed services also reflects personal values and the desire for activity in leisure time. The inherent conservatism of the military slowed the secularisation of these functions, compared to civilian society. The contemporary identification of religion as one of the support services essential to good morale within the armed services has institutionalised its role in an age of secularisation.

There is also an ancient tradition in invoking religion in celebrating military success. The celebration of heroism, particularly heroic death, was given a high religious honour. Valour was constantly praised as self-denial and death as sacrifice for the nation or martyrdom for the cause of truth, and burials and commemorations confirmed this. ★Anzac Day parades and the laying up of ★colours invoke a rich brew of religious and military symbolism. ★War memorials also have a potential for religious symbolism, although compared to those of European countries, New Zealand war memorials have made little use of Christian symbolism.

War is in some respects an agent in the extension of nationalism, and nationalism has some of the features of a surrogate religion. Not surprisingly, then, some religious minorities dissented from the nationalist desire for victory at any price. The pressures of a more militarised society during the years of ★conscription produced a degree of tension for minorities, religious and political, within the state. While many of these silently dissented, others—particularly from the smaller Protestant denominations—refused to support war, and encouraged their members to become ★conscientious objectors. While the total number involved was small, they were deeply offensive to the majority.

The tensions of war always have ideological overtones. Everyone wants their cause to be seen as right, and neutrality or criticism can lead to passionate anger. Religious attitudes have, after all, been strands in many wars. The polemical aspect of warfare is always tinged with religion. From the early wars of the 1840s, when the British troops did not observe the Sabbath, such issues have divided opinion. In the 1860s settler opinion was incensed by leading missionaries, notably Octavius Hadfield, who had defended the Te Ati Awa stance in the Taranaki War and expressed concern at settler seizures of Maori land. There was an outcry against Hadfield, Selwyn, and 'the missionaries' because the settlers held that their church was failing them.

During the ★Boer War the provision of ★chaplains was only slowly put in place, and there was little interest in the issue among the churches. As the ★First World War approached, however, the need to defend the righteousness of the Allied cause led to strong pressure for church involvement. This took various forms. Churches typically prayed anxiously for the boys sent off to the front, in a mood of concern and excitement. They also prayed, seemingly with little embarrassment, for victory, and then with deeper concern as the casualties from ★Gallipoli mounted. When the church conferences of the major Protestant denominations met, they were swift to commend the war. Some clergy went further, and the Reverend James Gibb, a leading Presbyterian minister in Wellington, took part in recruitment campaigns. Those who volunteered were predominantly Anglicans. The smaller churches therefore featured strongly in the later conscription ballots. Up to the 25th Reinforcements 45.5 per cent of the recruits were Anglican, 23.3 per cent Presbyterian, and

Religion and war

only 12.4 per cent Roman Catholic, but in the ballots of 1917, the figures were 39.2 per cent, 26.1 per cent, and 17 per cent respectively. Military chaplains were provided according to a formula based on the religious affiliation of soldiers. This first state-paid clergy team in New Zealand reawakened the same denominational rivalries which had been expressed ever since the Church of England had rejected a scheme of proportional denominational assistance in 1842. Evidently unreconciled to its loss of establishment status, the Anglican hierarchy was insistent that it would not work under a Methodist Senior Chaplain, so a general became nominal chaplain-general.

An anti-militarist conference had been held in Wellington late in 1911, attended by both religious and socialist objectors. There should then have been no surprise that the introduction of conscription in 1916 caused deep concern in some denominations. The issue was particularly serious because this was New Zealand's first experience of an extensive mobilisation for war, and little thought had been given to the place of dissent. Quaker opposition was on strictly pacifist grounds, but some Baptists and many of the smaller religious groups, Brethren, Seventh-day Adventists, and Christadelphians, also had concerns about the encroachment of the world on the lives of their members. Yet the legislation made only the smallest recognition of conscientious dissent, allowing only for members of denominations formally committed to pacifism, in effect Quakers. In the First World War there were 440 defaulters.

Roman Catholics were slow to volunteer, and, although Catholic Irish numbers were not sufficient to prevent the introduction of conscription, as they were in Australia, there were very mixed feelings in the Catholic community. The insurrection in Dublin in 1916, and the Catholic colouring of some of the enemy powers increased suspicion of Catholics in the general society, and played into the hands of the Reform Party, given that the leader of the Liberals, Sir Joseph *Ward, was a Catholic. Meanwhile the conscription ballots exposed rivalries between denominations. Ministers were exempt from the ballot, but what of students for the ministry and members of religious orders? There were sharp debates about the status of Catholic candidates for their long ordination training and Catholic teachers, many of whom were lay brothers in the Marist Brothers order. And intense sectarian feeling was invoked in the community by the allegations of the Protestant Political Association of bias in public appointments.

The observance of Anzac Day commenced in April 1916, and for its first fifteen years was a commemoration in churches of the war dead. Roman Catholics were required to meet separately, but the other churches generally combined for a civic ceremony. These religious ceremonies were probably the most universal religious experiences of the inter-war years. Meanwhile the willingness of Christians to collaborate in state warfare was challenged in the churches. Throughout the Western world, including New Zealand, there was an extensive debate about the justification of war and the morality of killing while in uniform. In 1926 the Reverend James Gibb convened a United Committee for the Propagation of the Principles of Peace, which produced a report for the contributing denominations favouring a semi-pacifist position. In 1927 A.M. Richards, a Presbyterian ordinand, declined to undertake military training, and was arrested and imprisoned as a defaulter. Religious debates continued as war loomed. The circumstances of Hitler's values made the just war argument more tenable, although the involvement of Mussolini, who had reached a concordat with the Pope, led to doubts about Catholic loyalty. However, the forthright defence of the Allies made by Cardinal Hinsley of Westminster was welcomed by New Zealand Catholics.

During the early years of the *Second World War, the rapid increase in the scope of the war and its extension to the Pacific provoked serious fears among New Zealand people. As a result, there were significant signs of a rise in religious involvement, with an increase in church attendance, and a number of religious symbols, including weekly radio prayer for the war. However, many religious institutions were disrupted by war, and most theological colleges closed down as their intake was conscripted. The large missionary contingent from New Zealand were mostly called home, although some were interned, particularly in Japanese POW camps. New Zealand was spared physical attack, but a deep identification of churches with members who were suffering abroad prepared the way for aid projects which emerged after the war.

There were significant changes in denominational responses to war, as compared with those of the 1914–18 conflict. There had been a significant decline in religious tensions in New Zealand society, and it became possible for church people to pray together for national concerns. Most Protestant denominations combined in the National Council of Churches, formed in 1941, and even the Roman Catholic Church was represented in other inter-church bodies. Consequently it became possible to assign chaplains to each unit rather than have teams of denominational chaplains (except for Catholic chaplains). There was also a wide degree of cooperation in the provision of voluntary activities for those in the services through the *YMCA, although some denominations and sectors of the church, including the Anglicans and the Open Brethren, made separate contributions. The churches mostly held back from their own fundraising in order to support the

National Patriotic Fund. Some denominations such as the Open Brethren and the Seventh-day Adventists came more to terms with the wider society during the war. They encouraged their members to enlist as non-combatants, although the armed services insisted that one must volunteer for the Army, and non-combatant status could not be protected completely. Others such as the Jehovah's Witnesses and Quakers remained obdurately opposed to war. The military tribunals' failure to understand the role of individual conscience, Christian or ethical, was more surprising in this second round of conscription. This was of new importance because of the rise of individual pacifism among some younger members of the mainline denominations, often inspired by the Bible Class Movement and the Student Christian Movement. Since the largest group of religious pacifists was Methodist, there was a tendency for Christian pacifists to be drawn towards the Methodist Church, where they found some sympathy from ministers such as Ormond ★Burton. The church had shown strong sympathy to the pacifist cause in a 1929 report, but in the face of the war the majority suddenly pulled back. By the time of the 1940 Methodist Conference, wartime fever had gripped the nation, and the church imposed a Manifesto on Peace and War, which forbade 'political statements' by ministers that would have the effect of dividing congregations. Pacifist ministers felt that this was invoked against them rather than against the militarists of the church, and continuing political agitation by Burton led to his expulsion from the ministry in 1942.

The churches' approach to war might therefore be dismissed as time-serving. Yet they generally expressed serious concern about the state of New Zealand society. Although national conferences largely mirrored secular opinion with their concerns and alarms, the churches found many pastoral responsibilities among the bereaved, the fearful, and those whose lives and families had been disrupted. General Christian opinion was enthusiastically nationalistic, although there were greater cautions than in the previous war. As a result church people turned relatively quickly to a consideration of post-war society. A significant impact was made by the National Council of Churches in the discussions, partly through the Campaign for Christian Order initiated in 1941, and also the Conference on Christian Order held in 1945. The discussions within the Maori section of the conference were particularly significant.

After the Second World War, the ★Korean War and the ★Malayan Emergency hardly figured in the religious consciousness of the nation, although the ★Cold War atmosphere certainly did, leading to something of a religious revival, manifested in the response to the 1959 Billy Graham Crusade. But the ★Vietnam War was very different. Debates about the war surfaced in almost all the churches, and the Methodist Church in particular was associated with intense opposition to the war. Such attitudes placed great tensions on the relationship between the Army and the church, particularly in the chaplaincy services. Anzac Day services in this period lost their link with churches, other than invited individual clergy. A renewed debate on nuclear weaponry was strongly supported by liberal church leaders. A flotilla of boats opposing an American naval visit was led by the Dean of St John's Anglican Theological College, the Reverend George Armstrong, and other clergy made their own protests against war. Irritated National government leaders were eager to find more compliant clergy (for example, within the Salvation Army) or to threaten religious privileges. On the other side David ★Lange's ★anti-nuclearism was deeply influenced by his Methodist background. Increasingly chaplaincies lost their denominational ties and became a form of religious counselling service to the military. Today's secular society may seem to have little place for a religious contribution to war. Yet all the evidence suggests that, bearing in mind the changing balance of religious forces in the nation, there has been little change to the mixture of tensions and opportunities.

PETER LINEHAM

Rennie, Colonel Frank (9 August 1918–17 November 1992) was one of a group of officers that oversaw the transition of the ★New Zealand Army from a citizen to a regular basis. His career began in the ★New Zealand Permanent Staff in 1937. In the early part of the ★Second World War he instructed officer cadets at Trentham, before serving with 37th Battalion in Fiji from January 1942. Commissioned in May 1942, he took part in the ★Solomons campaign with 30th Battalion. After serving with the 2nd New Zealand Division in the final stages of the ★Italian campaign, he went to Japan with ★Jayforce. He was subsequently involved in various aspects of training in New Zealand until selected, in 1955, to form, train, and command the New Zealand ★Special Air Service Squadron which was to form part of New Zealand's commitment to the new ★British Commonwealth Far East Strategic Reserve. Within seven months, the squadron was engaged in ★Malayan Emergency operations. Returning to New Zealand in 1958, Rennie occupied training posts in New Zealand and later spent several years in London as the Army's liaison officer. From 1966 to 1969 he commanded the Fiji Military Forces during the difficult pre-independence period. He retired from the Army in 1970. His autobiography, published in 1986, provides valuable insights into the New Zealand Army of the 1950s and 1960s.

F. Rennie, *Regular Soldier: A Life in the New Zealand Army* (Endeavour Press, Auckland, 1986).

Repatriation

Repatriation involves three main aspects: the physical transport home of the troops, their reintegration into the economy, and the making of provision for those unable to work because of their injuries or state of health. It was a problem that arose in acute form in two periods, during and after the two world wars, when large bodies of men returned to New Zealand over a short period. The issue was also brought to the fore to a lesser degree by the *Boer and *Korean Wars. The state's efforts focused on three main areas—*soldier settlement on farms, *war pensions, and rehabilitation assistance ranging from vocational training to provision of housing loans.

Apart from soldier settlement, little was done by the state for soldiers returning from the Boer War. Although wounded veterans were entitled to some pension assistance from the state, no dedicated system of medical assistance or vocational training was provided. Charity, in the form of public subscription to *patriotic funds, was the primary source of assistance. Veterans were, however, given preference in appointments to some government departments. It became clear early in the *First World War that a more systematic approach would be necessary to deal with the much larger numbers involved in 1NZEF. In 1915 responsibility for dealing with returned soldiers was given to the newly formed Discharged Soldiers' Information Department, which assisted returned soldiers with travel arrangements following discharge, oversaw soldier settlement schemes, and made plans for the provision of vocational training to the returning soldiers. A comprehensive war pensions scheme was also introduced in 1915 to deal with those maimed by their service. This wartime system was superseded by the Repatriation Act 1918, which established a Repatriation Department. Under the control of four ministers, this new body was assisted by regional boards and local committees made up of leading local citizens, many of whom had been active in voluntary patriotic and war relief organisations. The Repatriation Department was criticised as being too late and unwieldy. By 1922, at a cost of £2.2 million, 17,000 men had been assisted to find employment, more than 7000 had received subsidised 'on the job' vocational training, and more than 6000 had been given loans to establish businesses or acquire tools of trade. Under the Discharged Soldiers Settlement Act 1915, about 12,000 returned men were assisted to buy or build urban houses. A few were also helped to acquire business premises.

Despite these measures, by the outbreak of the *Second World War, there existed in the community a sense that it had failed its defenders from the earlier conflict. In part this was a result of the pressure group tactics of the NZRSA in the period between the wars, but the community could hardly fail to observe the physical and psychological decline of veterans during the inter-war period. There was popular support, therefore, for government measures for rehabilitation. Legislation in 1941 created a Rehabilitation Council and a Rehabilitation Board, though it was to be November 1943 before a Rehabilitation Department was belatedly established. The Rehabilitation Board was charged with ensuring that returned servicemen were placed in employment, or given the means to earn a living, and were suitably housed. Fifty per cent of the state's new housing stock was directed towards returned soldiers. The Rehabilitation Department was responsible for policy development and its application, either directly, or in cooperation with other agencies of government. Substantial investment was made in vocational training, while tertiary education, including scholarships for overseas study, was heavily subsidised.

Almost 11,500 business loans valued at £7.5 million were made to returned servicemen, while 64,000 housing loans, valued at £98 million, were made, together with 18,000 preferential state house allocations. Rehabilitation cost the country approximately £264 million, most of which was in loans, and £72 million was non-recoverable. The latter figure included £1.8 million for educational assistance, £8.5 million for trade training, and £41 million for farm training and settlement.

Some of those who volunteered for *Kayforce in 1950 did so in the hope of obtaining rehabilitation assistance following their return. Although the Rehabilitation Board gave only a vague indication of possible benefits, in a major departure from the approach taken to Second World War veterans, it quickly resolved that Kayforce veterans should be rehabilitated into civilian life 'to the extent that they would not suffer through their service'. With reinstatement the main objective, they would not receive special concessions unless they had been disabled. With respect to housing assistance, unless special conditions existed, Kayforce applications were deferred until Second World War men had finally been dealt with. Cheap home loans, concessionary farm loans, assistance with education, and some preferential treatment for those returning to government departments were the chief rehabilitation benefits enjoyed by returning Kayforce personnel. The issue of benefits for naval personnel was contentious, since normal conditions of service on a 'world wide' basis were not considered to be as hazardous as the those experienced by army personnel. With the military authorities also supporting the notion of determining rehabilitation benefits on the basis of the 'hazards of service', the First World War model of defining merit on the basis of 'grappling with the enemy' had been revived.

Unlike most of the Kayforce veterans, New Zealand soldiers who took part in hostilities during the ★Malayan Emergency, ★Confrontation, and the ★Vietnam War were regular naval or air force personnel or, in the case of the Army, short-term regulars rather than civilian volunteers. Quite apart from the relatively small numbers involved, there was no perceived state obligation to assist them to return to civilian occupations on the completion of their service, other than some in-service preparations. The Army authorities, indeed, regarded any prospect of rehabilitation assistance as hindering their objective of ensuring that short-term regulars made the Army a lifelong career.

ASHLEY GOULD

Resistance in Europe, New Zealanders and

During the ★Second World War, resistance forces in Europe and the Balkans waged increasingly relentless campaigns against German or Italian occupation forces. This was at first war in the shadows, though later the scale of resistance increased markedly, as hit-and-run operations gave way to more orthodox conflict, in the Balkans in particular. Such resistance was encouraged by the Allies through the Special Operations Executive, an organisation established in Great Britain in July 1940 for this purpose and to carry out sabotage behind the lines. SOE's Force 133 was responsible for the Balkans.

New Zealanders became directly involved with resistance forces in a variety of ways. First, some were living in the occupied areas as civilians. Perhaps the best-known example was Wellington-born but Australian-raised Nancy Wake; married to a Frenchman, she participated in the French Resistance from 1940. Another New Zealand woman, Sidney ★Duigan, was in France when the war began. She joined the French Red Cross Nursing Corps, which was attached to the French Army. After escaping from captivity, she, too, was involved in the Resistance. Second, and most commonly, New Zealand troops evading capture, especially in ★Greece and ★Crete, or after escaping from prisoner of war camps might be assisted by, or even join, resistance groups. Third, New Zealanders were among those who were sent behind enemy lines with the specific purpose of cooperating with resistance groups in operations against the enemy.

Escaped New Zealand POWs served with Italian, Yugoslav, Czech, and Slovak partisans. The best-known, and earliest, was John ★Denvir, who was to earn the DCM fighting with Yugoslav partisans. A number of other New Zealand escaped POWs joined the Yugoslav partisans following the collapse of Italy in 1943, often obliged to do so to avoid German and Fascist Italian round-ups. Many of these men were motivated by the belief that some participation in operations seemed to be demanded in return for the succour provided by the partisans. For most, this was a relatively brief interlude: twenty-six New Zealanders were among a sixty-two-strong party evacuated in November–December 1943. An effective escape organisation was thereafter established which precluded the need for ex-prisoners to linger with Yugoslav partisan bands. However, some men found it difficult to make contact with the Allied liaison officers who ran the organisation. Private W.M. Horne, for example, served with a partisan battalion operating north of Trieste from January to September 1944 before managing to do so, and being evacuated.

Numerous New Zealand escaped prisoners also came in contact with Italian partisans. Again, some took part in active operations with these bands, but for most the primary objective remained to reach Allied-held or neutral territory. One who operated with the Italians for an extended period was Private F.M. Gardner. While serving with 19th Battalion, he had been captured in North Africa in July 1942 and held in a prisoner of war camp in Italy. He escaped from the train taking him north to Germany in September 1943, and found refuge with an Italian family near Germona, in the Udine province of North-east Italy. After joining a Yugoslav partisan band, he was captured by the Germans but escaped and returned to the Germona area. Gathering a group of Italians, he successfully blew up a train. His ability with explosives had brought him to the notice of the SOE, which used him to carry out more than a score of acts of sabotage, including the blowing of the main railway bridge over the Orvenco River near Germona. 'Franco', as he was known throughout the district, continued to serve in this capacity until the end of the war in Italy, at which time his band liberated Germona. For his exploits, which went unnoticed in the official history of New Zealand POWs, Gardner was awarded a DCM.

A number of New Zealanders were among agents dispatched by SOE behind the lines in the Balkans. In northern Italy, they helped organise escape routes for prisoners. A New Zealander serving with a British medical unit, Major L.S. Rogers, spent from 1943 to 1945 with the Yugoslav partisans, initially on the island of Vis, later on the mainland in Bosnia–Herzegovina, Croatia, and Slovenia. The most notable example of New Zealand involvement in SOE sabotage operations occurred in Greece. In September 1942 two sapper officers, Captain Arthur Edmonds and Captain C.E. Barnes, were parachuted into Greece with a sabotage party to destroy a viaduct on the railway line through Greece, the object being to interrupt an important supply conduit to the *Afrika Korps*. With a substantial force drawn from the two main Greek guerrilla groups—the

447

Resource protection

only time these rivals cooperated in such fashion—the saboteurs blew up the Gorgopotamos viaduct on 25 November 1942. They stayed on in Greece to form the British (later Allied) military mission, which set about developing a secret organisation. Other New Zealanders joined the mission: Captain W.S. Jordan, Lieutenant D.J. *Stott, and Sergeant R.M. Morton, and three New Zealand evaders who had been hiding in Greece since the departure of the 2nd New Zealand Division in 1941. Six other New Zealanders, including Lieutenant-Colonel John *Mulgan, also served with the mission in Greece; one of them was murdered by communist guerrillas in 1943. Perhaps the most spectacular success achieved by SOE in Greece was the destruction of the Asopos viaduct on 20 June 1943, an operation which involved an approach through a supposedly impassable gorge. For this exploit, which resulted in the railway line being cut for ten weeks, Stott was made a DSO. He and Morton were later involved in setting up a sabotage network in the Athens area, while Jordan operated with the Resistance in occupied France.

Two New Zealanders were among agents sent in to Crete by SOE—Staff-Sergeant Tom Moir and Sergeant D.C. Perkins. Captured by the Germans at the end of the Battle of Crete, both had escaped and, after spending an extended period hidden by Cretans, succeeded in making their way to Egypt. Moir was active as an SOE agent in Crete for several months before being captured in May 1943. Landed in Crete two months later, Perkins successfully organised resistance in the Selino area. So outstanding was his leadership that the Cretans christened him 'Vasili'. He was killed in action in February 1944.

Numerous New Zealand airmen also made a contribution to operations in support of resistance groups, making often hazardous flights at night and over mountainous terrain to carry supplies or to transport personnel. During the last eighteen months of the war about sixty New Zealanders were serving with RAF transport squadrons engaged in this type of work, especially in 148 Squadron. Yugoslavia was a major focus of such effort, with more than 11,600 sorties dropping or landing supplies and personnel and evacuating about 19,000 wounded partisans. Flights were made all over Western Europe and the Balkans, with some from Italy as far afield as Poland. In July 1944 Flight Lieutenant S.G. Culliford, flying a Dakota, succeeded in bringing out a Polish resistance leader with detailed information about the new German V-2 weapon. Subsequently very dangerous flights were made to Warsaw with supplies for the Polish Home Army during its ultimately unsuccessful uprising in August–September 1944.

J. Caffin, *Partisan* (Collins, Auckland, 1945); M. Elliott, *Vasili, The Lion of Crete* (Century Hutchinson, Auckland, 1987); W. Jordan, *Conquest without Victory* (Hodder & Stoughton, London, 1969); W.W. Mason, *Prisoners of War* (War History Branch, Wellington, 1954); M.B. McGlynn, *Special Service in Greece* (War History Branch, Wellington, 1953); F.N. Millar, *The 'Signor Kiwi' Saga* (Privately published, Manurewa, 1993); L. Rogers, *Guerrilla Surgeon* (Collins, London, 1957).

Resource protection is an important function of the armed forces. After the *Second World War a RNZN patrol boat began a fisheries patrol in conjunction with the Marine Department to deter poachers. This patrol continued into the 1950s, with the patrol craft HMNZS *Mako* and *Paea* monitoring waters around the New Zealand coast, being later joined on fishery patrols by HMNZS *Kuparu*, *Koura*, and *Manga*. On 1 January 1966 a 12 nautical mile (21 kilometre) fishing zone was established around New Zealand, with more distant patrolling of New Zealand's waters by HMNZS *Inverell*. In 1970 RNZAF Orion aircraft began fishery patrols. The introduction of the new fisheries protection launches (HMNZS *Rotoiti*, *Pukaki*, *Taupo*, and *Hawea*) coincided with increasing numbers of foreign (especially Japanese) fishing vessels coming into New Zealand waters—399 were identified in 1976–77. The importance of monitoring New Zealand's fish resources was magnified with the establishment on 1 April 1978 of its exclusive economic zone, which extends 370 kilometres from land. Its numerous island dependencies ensured that its zone would be the fourth largest in the world. Frigates were now used to patrol the zone, and the RNZAF gave greater emphasis to resource protection. In 1981 the RNZN boarded 551 fishing vessels. In that same year resource protection duties were extended when Orion aircraft began fisheries patrols for the Fijian government. During the 1980s Orion resource protection patrols were further extended to Tonga, the Cook Islands, Western Samoa, the Solomons, Kiribati, and Vanuatu. In view of the depletion of fishing stocks globally and increasing pressure upon fisheries in New Zealand and Pacific Forum EEZs, it is clear that resource protection will remain an increasingly important role for the armed forces.

Revolution in military affairs (RMA) is a term used since the early 1990s to describe the profound changes in the nature of warfare being brought about by rapid changing technology, particularly the exponential advances made in electronic and information technology. It is believed by many military observers that the increasing computerisation of the battlefield (or 'battlespace') represents a fundamental shift in the way that wars will be fought, and that existing organisation and doctrine must be re-examined. This belief was given credibility by the apparent effectiveness of new weapons technology in the ★Gulf War. Under the RMA future wars, its proponents contend, will be characterised by information warfare (in which enemy information networks are targeted both physically and by 'non-lethal' computer viruses, electronic jamming, or even psychological warfare), precision strikes with computer-guided munitions (such as 'smart bombs' and cruise missiles), and radically improved command, control, communication, and information systems (C3I). Some, perhaps optimistically, see the RMA as rendering war less lethal—and less risky for those initiating it. The impact of the RMA on thinking within the ★New Zealand Defence Force has been significant. The organisation, it is accepted, must be made more flexible and responsive to a swiftly changing technological environment.

Rhodes-Moorhouse, Second Lieutenant William Barnard (26 September 1887–27 April 1915), the first airman to win a ★Victoria Cross, had a New Zealand connection. His father had resided in New Zealand for a time and his mother was New Zealand–born (and the daughter of a Maori). He himself was born in London and never set foot in New Zealand. He became well known as an aviator before the ★First World War, taking part in a number of cross-country races in the United States. Soon after the outbreak of war in 1914, he enlisted in the Royal Flying Corps and was posted to 2 Squadron in France. During a bombing attack on the German rail junction at Courtrai [Kortrijk] in Belgium on 26 April 1915—an operation he foresaw would be particularly dangerous—his biplane was repeatedly hit by anti-aircraft fire. Though badly wounded, he pressed home his attack and managed to return to base, but died of wounds on the following day. His poignant final letter to his infant son (who was to be killed in action as a fighter pilot during the Battle of Britain) is on display at the RNZAF Museum, Wigram.

Rhodesian Monitoring Force In 1980 New Zealand deployed troops to southern Africa for the first time since the ★Boer War as part of the Commonwealth Monitoring Force, which had been established as a result of the Lancaster House agreement signed in London on 21 December 1979, ending the conflict in Rhodesia (Zimbabwe). The CMF's task was twofold: first, to supervise the ceasefire between the government led by Bishop Abel Muzorewa and the Zimbabwe Patriotic Front, comprising two Marxist guerrilla organisations, the Zimbabwe African National Liberation Army (ZANLA) and the Zimbabwe People's Revolutionary Army (ZIPRA); second, to oversee the concentration of the latter's guerrillas in designated areas pending the holding of elections. New Zealand

Ceasefire Assembly Place Mike at St Paul's Mission, Rhodesia, one of two such places run by the New Zealand contingent in the Commonwealth Monitoring Force in 1979–80 (*NZDF*)

was one of four countries—the others were Australia, Fiji, and Kenya—invited to join with Great Britain in forming the monitoring force. Its contacts with apartheid-dominated South Africa, especially in the sporting arena, left the Patriotic Front unenthusiastic about a New Zealand presence, but these objections faded when it was made clear that a significant proportion of New Zealand's contingent would be Maori.

The CMF had a strength of 1397, of whom Britain provided 1100, Australia 152, New Zealand 74, Kenya 50, and Fiji 23. Commanded by Colonel D.W. Moloney, the New Zealand Army Truce Monitoring Contingent Southern Rhodesia left for Rhodesia by air on 20 December 1979. Apart from a small headquarters element within the CMF Headquarters in Salisbury, the New Zealand contingent was directly involved in monitoring compliance with the ceasefire. In addition to providing eleven teams for attachment to units of the Rhodesian Army, it manned two of the sixteen assembly places—Mike and Lima in western Rhodesia—where the Patriotic Front guerrillas were concentrated. More than 1800 ZIPRA personnel came into Mike and 800 into Lima. Despite some initial problems, especially with supplies, the operation ran smoothly, and the New Zealand troops established a particularly good relationship with the guerrillas in their assembly places. Following the elections at the end of February, the New Zealanders were withdrawn to Salisbury, and left for home on 5 March 1980.

J. Crawford, 'Truce supervision: the Zimbabwe model', *New Zealand International Review*, vol 14, no 5 (1989).

Richardson, Lieutenant-Commander Archibald ('Ron') (20 March 1917–24 August 1944) was a distinguished ★Fleet Air Arm pilot during the ★Second

World War. Born at Gisborne, he was an electrical engineer when he was mobilised in September 1940. He was sent to the United Kingdom for service with the Royal Navy, and learned to fly at HMS *St Vincent*. While serving with 1840 Squadron aboard the aircraft-carrier HMS *Indefatigable*, he took part in a series of raids on the German battleship *Tirpitz*, which was ensconced in a Norwegian fiord. During the raid of 24 August 1944, he demonstrated great courage in pressing home his attack amid intense flak until his Hellcat dive-bomber was shot down and he was killed. Although the Commander-in-Chief Home Fleet strongly recommended him for the 'highest posthumous award', the ★Victoria Cross, he was awarded a posthumous mention in dispatches.

Richardson, Major-General Sir George Spafford (14 November 1868–11 June 1938) rose from the ranks to become perhaps New Zealand's greatest military administrator. Born out of wedlock in Ashton, Northamptonshire, he had few prospects when he enlisted in the Royal Artillery in 1886. His intelligence and conscientious performance soon gained him advancement, and he was a staff sergeant instructor in gunnery by 1891, when he was seconded to the New Zealand Military Forces as a gunnery instructor. He quickly made his mark, not least by making several inventions to facilitate artillery training; the Commandant called him 'as smart as it is possible for a man to be'. Married to a New Zealand woman in 1892, he found New Zealand so congenial that he was happy to extend his contract with the New Zealand government, with the result that he was still in New Zealand when his twenty-one year term of engagement in the Royal Artillery expired in 1907. By this time, he had been commissioned as a captain in the New Zealand ★Militia, and he threw himself into his work as Chief Instructor of Artillery Services. With the reorganisation of the New Zealand forces in 1911, he became a member of the ★New Zealand Staff Corps. After attending the Staff College at Camberley in the United Kingdom, where he again impressed by his determination and willingness to accept responsibility, he served as New Zealand's representative on the ★Imperial General Staff from December 1913. His administrative skills were very much in evidence when, following the outbreak of the ★First World War, he was involved in the formation of the Royal Naval Division; he helped B.C. ★Freyberg obtain a commission in it. He spent three months on the continent, initially as part of the division's improvised headquarters and later in the BEF's HQ. Back in England in November 1914, he was confirmed as assistant adjutant and quartermaster-general of the Royal Naval Division, with which he served at ★Gallipoli in 1915.

With his appointment in December 1915 as Deputy Adjutant and Quartermaster of XIIth Corps at ★Salonika, he had good prospects of further advancement, but in February 1916 he had no hesitation in acceding to a New Zealand request for his services. With characteristic zeal, he applied himself to the problems of administering 1NZEF and commanding the many New Zealand troops in the United Kingdom for training, medical treatment, or repatriation purposes. He was soon being lauded by both his political and military masters: the Prime Minister, W.F. ★Massey, thought him impossible to replace, while 1NZEF commander, Lieutenant-General Sir Alexander ★Godley, considered him 'head and shoulders' above his contemporaries of equal rank. As throughout his career, he at the same time won great loyalty from his subordinates, his own humble beginnings giving him an empathy with the men of the lower ranks. He was especially interested in soldier education, and would later write a chapter on the subject for the official history of New Zealand's war effort. He was made a CB in 1917 and a CBE two years later. After returning to New Zealand in 1919, he oversaw administration in the GHQ in Wellington and played a key role, as chairman of the Reconstruction Committee, in adjusting the military forces to a peacetime role. This rather mundane service held little appeal to him, and it was with some relief no doubt that he went as Administrator to New Zealand's mandate territory, Western Samoa, early in 1923, an appointment which effectively ended his military career. He was promoted to the rank of major-general. He approached his task in Western Samoa with the same progressive approach and well-meaning determination that had marked his previous military service, and his efforts seemed on the surface to be rewarded with success; he was made a KBE in 1925 and agreed, reluctantly, to a two-year extension of his term. During this extended period Richardson, for the first time in his career, found himself confronting a situation which was not amenable to his usual blend of hard work and administrative skill, requiring indeed the negotiating and temporising skills of a politician. A reaction to his policies had developed in the form of a nationalist agitation. So difficult did his position become that, just before his retirement in March 1928, he sought a show of force by New Zealand's cruisers, which proved futile (see SAMOA, NEW ZEALAND'S MILITARY ROLE IN). In retirement in Auckland, he worked hard on behalf of returned servicemen, especially those who had been disabled.

Rifle clubs Military support for rifle clubs in the nineteenth century stemmed from the government's belief that enthusiastic amateurs with occasional shooting practice could become effective soldiers. Free ammunition, subsidised rifles, and rail travel for members were provided. However, professional soldiers were less inclined to support such assistance. The Commandant, Lieutenant-Colonel F.J. ★Fox, complained in 1893 that they gave no practical assistance to volunteering, and were 'subversive of discipline'. Although official support ceased in 1895, it was resumed five years later after the ★Boer War experience had convinced the government that efficient soldiers could be produced from undisciplined rifle enthusiasts. The military authorities continued to point to the disadvantages of the clubs. Apart from draining recruits away from the ★Volunteer Force, they reinforced the prevailing idea that encouragement of rifle shooting was sufficient to make New Zealand secure. Nevertheless rifle clubs were seen in a more favourable light after the introduction of ★compulsory military training in 1911. They proved useful in giving Territorial recruits rifle training, as well as serving as a reserve for those unfit for Territorial service. By 1915 there were 8770 members in 240 clubs. After the ★First World War, the clubs declined in numbers and importance. In the ★Second World War, they again proved useful in encouraging rifle practice.

River Plate, Battle of, was the first major naval battle of the ★Second World War and the first involving the ★New Zealand Division of the Royal Navy. It was the culmination of a ten-week search for the German commerce raider *Admiral Graf Spee*, which had captured and sunk nine British merchant ships. These operations had included New Zealand's light cruiser HMS *Achilles*, which left New Zealand on 29 August 1939 under the command of Captain W.E. ★Parry. Joining the Royal Navy's America and West Indies Squadron, she operated on the west coast of South America until October, when she rounded Cape Horn and was attached to the South Atlantic Squadron's South America Division, commanded by Commodore Henry Harwood. She was with the heavy cruiser HMS *Exeter* and light cruiser HMS *Ajax* when they intercepted the German warship in the south Atlantic shortly after dawn on 13 December 1939. A Deutschland class armoured cruiser (dubbed 'pocket battleships' by the British), the *Admiral Graf Spee* was qualitatively superior to the three British ships. Her six 11-inch guns greatly outranged *Exeter*'s six 8-inch guns, let alone the 6-inch guns mounted on the other two British cruisers. In theory, she should have been able to dispose of the three British vessels before they could close to a range at which their own weapons could be effectively brought to bear. Undaunted by these possibilities, Harwood divided his force, attacking the German raider from two sides. *Exeter*, closing

The crew of HMS *Achilles* march through Auckland after their return in early 1940 from taking part in the Battle of the River Plate (*NZDF*)

on one side, was heavily damaged after the effectiveness of her 8-inch salvoes forced the *Admiral Graf Spee* to concentrate fire upon her. Meanwhile, the other British vessels managed to get close enough to strike some telling blows, though suffering damage as well. Four men were killed on *Achilles* and nine wounded, some seriously. Although not seriously damaged, the *Admiral Graf Spee* headed into the neutral port of Montevideo. During the next four days, while British reinforcements hastened to the scene, there was much diplomatic manoeuvring by both sides. Concluding that escape was impossible, and possibly reluctant to spill more blood in a hopeless fight, the German commander, Captain Hans Langsdorff, took his ship out of the harbour and scuttled it, before committing suicide. The outcome of the battle was a great fillip to morale throughout the British Commonwealth. When *Achilles* returned to New Zealand in early 1940, her crew were given a heroes' welcome. At the time of the battle, five officers and 316 ratings of her 567-strong complement were New Zealanders.

S.D. Waters, *The Royal New Zealand Navy* (War History Branch, Wellington, 1956).

PETER DENNERLY

Roberts, Lieutenant-Colonel John Mackintosh (21 December 1840–12 October 1928). After goldmining and farming, Roberts enlisted in William Jackson's ★Forest Rangers in August 1863. In November he was promoted to second-in-command of Gustavus von ★Tempsky's company. In 1864 he took land at Harapepe. When the Forest Rangers were re-formed as No. 5 Division, ★Armed Constabulary, Roberts again served as von Tempsky's second-in-command.

He fought against *Titokowaru at Te Ngutu-o-te-manu, but his division of the Armed Constabulary mutinied and were disbanded (see MUTINIES). He fought Titokowaru again at Moturoa (7 November 1868) and *Te Kooti at Ngatapa (1–5 January 1869). From 1870 he commanded Armed Constabulary garrisons engaged in road and telegraph line construction in the central North Island. After serving as a resident magistrate at Tauranga and commander of the local Militia and Volunteer District, he was transferred to Taranaki in 1879. Two years later he led the troops who carried out the police action at *Parihaka. He commanded the New Zealand *Permanent Militia in 1887–88 before having his services terminated as a cost-cutting measure.

Robertson, Sir John Fraser (3 August 1925–) was a key figure in the reorganisation of New Zealand's defence administrative structure in the 1960s. Born in Takaka, he joined the public service in 1942. His career was interrupted by service with the RNZAF, during which he took part in the *Solomons campaign as a pilot. Between 1945 and 1964 he occupied a variety of posts before becoming Secretary of the State Services Commission. A Harkness Fellowship had allowed him to study organisational restructuring processes in the United States, and after serving briefly as an Assistant Commissioner at the Commission he became Chief Deputy Secretary of Defence in June 1967. His appointment was designed to assist the process of reorganisation of the Ministry of Defence, which had stalled in the face of service resistance. After attending the *Imperial Defence College in London in 1968 and making a close study of many overseas defence organisations, he became Secretary of Defence in 1969, a position he would hold for ten years. Working effectively with the CDS, Lieutenant-General L.W. *Thornton, he developed a strategy for change which emphasised the involvement of those affected by it as a means of breaking down resistance, a process which when brought successfully to completion in 1971 established a diarchic system that endured for nearly two decades (see DEFENCE, MINISTRY OF). A later Secretary of Justice and Chief Ombudsman, he was made a CBE in 1981 and a KCMG in 1994.

Robin, Major-General Sir Alfred William (12 August 1860–2 June 1935) commanded the first combat force sent overseas by New Zealand. An Australian by birth, he emigrated to New Zealand as a boy. A keen member of the *Volunteer Force, he served from 1878 successively in the New Zealand Field Artillery Volunteers, the Southland Hussars, and the Dunedin Cavalry Volunteers (renamed the Otago Hussars in 1886); commissioned in the last-named in 1889, he commanded it from 1891 to 1898. Described by the Commandant, Colonel A.P. *Penton, as the 'smartest commanding officer in the Colony', he commanded the mounted element of the New Zealand contingent which was dispatched to Queen Victoria's Diamond Jubilee celebrations in 1897—the first colonial force to leave New Zealand. He became a regular soldier in September 1899 when he joined the Defence Department as instructor to the mounted rifles in the South Island. He established a tactical school for officers. His background and competence made him the obvious choice for the command of the first mounted rifles contingent sent by New Zealand to the *Boer War later that year. From May 1900 to April 1901 he commanded the 1st New Zealand Regiment in South Africa, an amalgam of the first three contingents. Highly rated by his British superiors, he was mentioned in dispatches three times and appointed a CB. He was given a hero's welcome when he arrived back in New Zealand in May 1901. After commanding the Otago Military District for five years, he was appointed Chief of the General Staff and First Military Member of the new Council of Defence in 1906. Some form of compulsion seemed to him to be necessary to improve New Zealand's defence capacity, but he could not budge a government wedded to the voluntary system until Sir Joseph *Ward accepted British advice to this effect in 1909 (see COMPULSORY MILITARY TRAINING). With the abolition of the Council of Defence in 1910 Robin became Adjutant and Quartermaster-General. He was New Zealand representative on the *Imperial General Staff from February 1912 until late in 1913. He was made a CMG in 1912. Back as Quartermaster-General, he was heavily involved in the preparation of the expeditionary forces which New Zealand dispatched to Samoa and Egypt following the outbreak of the *First World War. With the departure of Major-General Sir Alexander *Godley as commander of 1NZEF in October 1914, Robin became Commandant—a position he held until the end of 1919 (while also Quartermaster-General). His immense, albeit behind-the-scenes, contribution to the successful sustenance of 1NZEF in the field for four years was later acknowledged by Godley. He was made a KCMG and promoted to the rank of major-general in 1916.

Ropata, see WAHAWAHA

Ross, Malcolm (13 July 1862–15 April 1930) was New Zealand's first official war correspondent. Born at Saddle Hill, Otago, he attended Otago University before beginning a career in journalism. From 1897 he was a parliamentary reporter. In 1914 he accompanied the New Zealand force to Samoa as the representative of a group of newspapers. A friend of Prime Minister

William ★Massey, he secured appointment as New Zealand's official war correspondent in 1915. He was also charged with gathering material for a later official history. After reaching ★Gallipoli in June 1915, he worked closely with the Australian correspondent, C.E.W. Bean. He was made an honorary captain in April 1916. From June 1916 until the end of the war he covered the activities of the New Zealand Division on the ★Western Front. During 1916 he published *Light and Shade in War*, a collection of his writings, and those of his son Noel. At the end of the war, he was favoured by both Massey and 1NZEF commander, Lieutenant-General Sir Alexander ★Godley, to prepare the official history, but was excluded by the authorities in Wellington. Returning to New Zealand in September 1919, he resumed his parliamentary reporting. (See OFFICIAL WAR HISTORIES; WAR CORRESPONDENTS)

Ross, Rear-Admiral John O'Connell (9 December 1916–13 February 1983) was a leading naval officer and naval historian. Born at Port Chalmers, he was a civil servant when he enlisted in the Canterbury Division of the RNVR in 1936. He was mobilised in August 1939. After brief service in HMS *Achilles*, he was transferred to HMS *Philomel* for officer and anti-submarine training in 1940. In 1941 he was executive officer in HMS *Wakakura*, and in the following year took part in the ★Solomons campaign as a lieutenant in HMNZS *Matai*, part of the 25th Minesweeping Flotilla. In 1944 he was sent to England for further training. He returned to New Zealand two years later as a gunnery specialist. Securing a permanent commission in the RNZN, he served in HMNZS *Bellona* before taking part in the ★Korean War aboard HMNZS *Tutira* in 1950–51. After a posting at Naval HQ in Wellington, he was executive officer successively in the cruisers HMNZS *Black Prince*, *Bellona*, and *Royalist*. After three years in London as Navy Liaison Officer, he became Commodore, Auckland, in 1960 and subsequently commanded *Royalist*. He attended the ★Imperial Defence College and was with the Royal Navy on exchange for a period. From 1965 to 1969 he was CNS and First Naval Member of the Naval Board. He published *The White Ensign in New Zealand* in 1967. This was followed two years later by an account of ★hydrographic surveying in New Zealand, *This Stern Coast*.

Rout, Ettie Annie (24 February 1877–17 September 1936) ran an anti-★venereal disease campaign among 1NZEF troops during the ★First World War. Tasmanian-born, she emigrated to New Zealand as a child and was a Christchurch shorthand typist and labour activist when the war began. She formed the New Zealand Volunteer Sisterhood in 1915 and, in spite of government opposition, sent the first group of volunteers to Egypt later in the year to care for New Zealand soldiers. Realising that venereal disease was a major problem after arriving in Cairo early in 1916, she sought, without success, to convince the military authorities to use prophylactic methods, arguing that it should be treated on a medical rather than a moral basis. During 1916 she ran a soldiers' club at Tel El Kebir, and later a canteen at El Qantara, for New Zealanders fighting in the ★Sinai–Palestine campaign, the value of which was acknowledged by a mention in dispatches. Proceeding to London in 1917, she researched venereal disease prophylaxis methods among the foremost experts and put together a prophylactic kit which she distributed from the New Zealand Medical Soldiers Club, which she established near the New Zealand convalescent hospital in Hornchurch. She was instrumental in 1NZEF eventually deciding to dispense the kits, for a letter she published in the *New Zealand Times* so convinced the Minister of Defence, Colonel Sir James ★Allen, that the problem was serious that he endorsed her new methods. This caused such a furore, however, that newspapers in New Zealand were forbidden to mention her name in print. From April 1918, in Paris, she provided a sexual and social welfare service for troops on leave in the city, organising accommodation for them, giving advice, nursing the sick, and handing out cards to a brothel run on sexually hygienic lines which she supervised. In 1919 and 1920 she ran a ★Red Cross depot in the town of Villers-Bretonneux on the Somme. For this work she was awarded a French decoration. Her contribution to soldiers' well-being received little recognition in New Zealand—there is no mention of it in the official history—though the RSA did make a small financial tribute, albeit unpublicised. She remained in London after 1920, and only returned to New Zealand briefly, in 1936, shortly before she died, in Rarotonga, of a self-administered overdose of quinine.

JANE TOLERTON

Royal Navy in New Zealand The White Ensign flew in the Land of the Long White Cloud for the first time during the summer of 1769–70. Its bearer was not a sleek warship, but a lightly armed converted collier, HMS *Endeavour*, which charted a large part of the coastline under the command of Lieutenant James Cook. Cook returned in 1772 and in 1776–77, but New Zealand was too remote from Great Britain to assume any real strategic importance. New Zealand was included in the vast East Indies and China Station in 1819, but in the years leading up to 1840 British warships made only occasional visits to it. Ships occasionally transported missionaries, explored the coastline, or loaded kauri spars. In 1820 HMS *Dromedary* harvested kauri in the Bay of Islands and sent the sloop *Coromandel* south to the

Royal Navy in New Zealand

The Royal Navy's Flying Squadron in Auckland Harbour in 1870 (*Alexander Turnbull Library, G-4726-1/2*)

Firth of Thames for the same purpose. In 1834 HMS *Alligator* led reprisals for a Maori attack on the survivors of the shipwrecked *Harriet*. A year earlier, HMS *Imogene* had brought British Resident James Busby to the Bay of Islands. Between 1834 and 1837 Busby's concerns would send HMS *Hyacinth*, *Alligator*, *Zebra*, and *Rattlesnake* racing across the Tasman from the Australian colonies.

By the time that formal colonisation had been decided upon, however, the naval role had become critical. New Zealand's first Governors, William Hobson and Robert FitzRoy, were both naval officers. Hobson arrived in the Bay of Islands aboard HMS *Herald* on 29 January 1840. He hoisted the Union Jack and in August 1840 the commander of another warship, Captain Owen Stanley of HMS *Britomart*, asserted British ownership of Akaroa in the face of claims by the French. HMS *Herald* had earlier passed through collecting signatures to the Treaty of Waitangi. In 1841 the first signs of a naval base appeared at Sandspit, near the site of the present Devonport ferry wharf at Auckland. Over time it would spread westward along the Devonport foreshore.

New Zealand's cemeteries bear testimony to the price paid by the Royal Navy during the first decades of colonisation. Three ships left their bones on New Zealand's coastline—the naval transport HMS *Buffalo* at Mercury Bay in 1840, the armed brig HMS *Osprey* north of Hokianga in 1846, and the steam corvette HMS *Orpheus* on the Manukau Bar on 7 February 1863. The 1700-ton *Orpheus* remains New Zealand's costliest shipwreck by a wide margin. Sent across the Tasman in response to the deteriorating racial situation, Commodore W.F. Burnett's powerful, modern screw-propelled ship struck the treacherous bar in fine weather. Unfortunately, heavy swells hindered attempts to rescue the crew, 189 of whom lost their lives. This British death toll exceeded that of any action during the ★New Zealand Wars.

Elsewhere the Royal Navy supported imperial and colonial forces in the wars. Maori inhabitants posed no threat to the navy, whose ships transported soldiers and supplies with impunity and occasionally bombarded enemy shore positions; for example, during March 1845 when HMS *Hazard* and *North Star* bombarded sites in the Bay of Islands. In 1846–47 a longboat mounting a 12-pounder gun served first at Porirua and then on the Wanganui River. When sailors and marines fought ashore, however, forces were more evenly matched. Members of the Naval Brigade, Marines, and ordinary ships' personnel fought in many actions, sustaining casualties on several occasions. Victoria Crosses went to Samuel Mitchell from HMS *Harrier* for his attack on Gate Pa and to William Odgers from HMS *Niger* for storming Kaipopo Pa at Waireka. When the Royal Navy formalised its ★battle honours in 1954, the list included 'New Zealand 1845–7' and 'New Zealand 1860–6'.

When the wars finished, the number of warships on the coast declined. New Zealand had been included in the new ★Australia Station in 1859, but naval visits fell in number and were principally restricted to units of the Sydney-based squadron, though a notable exception was the Flying Squadron which arrived in 1870. The Admiralty maintained a small base on the north shore of the Waitemata, which had been increased in size in 1864. Under political pressure instigated by Devonport residents openly covetous of the site of the naval base, however, the Admiralty shifted the short distance to Calliope Point in 1891. The facilities were used to support the two Royal Navy warships which were based in New Zealand waters under the *Australasian Naval Agreement. In 1899 the Admiralty negotiated a new agreement with the Auckland Harbour Board, giving it priority access to the *Calliope Dock alongside its new boundary. Although a few buildings were constructed from 1893 onwards, Devonport's real growth would not commence until 1921 when the cruiser HMS *Chatham* arrived on the *New Zealand Station and the old cruiser HMS *Philomel* took up a permanent berth alongside the training jetty.

The *Russian scares of the 1880s had increased interest in defence issues. The New Zealand government paid for *coastal defence, small *torpedo boats, and mine warfare vessels, but the late Victorian and Edwardian eras saw a debate about the cost and location of naval forces, the Admiralty always preferring to maximise the mobility of its fleet by not tying it down in penny packets at too many colonial stations. In 1913 the *Naval Defence Act provided for the establishment of the New Zealand Naval Forces and a New Zealand branch of the Royal Naval Reserve, but permitted Admiralty resumption of control over New Zealand Station ships in times of emergency.

During the ensuing two decades, other British warships continued to visit the Dominion's ports. Although overshadowed by the 1908 and 1925 visits of the American fleet, the most prestigious British calls were the 1913 and 1919 visits of the battlecruiser HMS *New Zealand, the visit of the battlecruiser HMS *Renown* in 1920 carrying the Prince of Wales, and the 1924 visit of the Special Service Squadron, comprising the battlecruisers HMS *Hood* (the world's largest warship) and *Repulse*, light cruisers HMS *Delhi*, *Dragon*, *Dauntless*, *Danae*, and *Dunedin*, and HMAS *Adelaide*. All drew large crowds.

Many British warships, including the battleships HMS *Ramillies* and *Howe*, visited New Zealand waters during the *Second World War, but the United States Navy completely overshadowed the British Pacific Fleet by the end of the conflict. After the war the Royal Navy maintained a close relationship with the newly formed *Royal New Zealand Navy, which would rely on British warship designs for another four decades. In 1949, for example, New Zealand offered three frigates for the defence of *Hong Kong if required, and two RNZN frigates served in the Mediterranean while two RN Bay class served with the RNZN. In 1957 two more British Bays served in New Zealand, while HMNZS *Pukaki* and *Rotoiti* acted as weather ships for Britain's Christmas Island H-bomb tests. During the same decade RN and RNZN warships worked alongside each other in Korean and Malayan waters.

Royal Navy ships became a rare sight in New Zealand ports from the late 1960s as the British pulled back from 'East of Suez' and ran down their surface fleet. The aircraft-carrier HMS *Eagle* and the guided missile destroyer HMS *Glamorgan* led the last large squadron into New Zealand ports in August 1970, and the light carrier HMS *Invincible* visited Wellington in 1983. Just a year earlier the New Zealand government had sent a frigate to the Indian Ocean to free a Royal Navy vessel for *Falklands War duties, but *Invincible* attracted anti-war and anti-nuclear protests, a harbinger of the national anti-nuclear sentiment that would be enshrined in legislation in 1987 after the Labour government had banned the visits of nuclear-armed or nuclear-propelled warships. Britain's refusal to confirm or deny the presence of nuclear weapons aboard its ships effectively severed the 200-year connection between the White Ensign and New Zealand. The National Party regained office in 1990, but anti-nuclear sentiment remained strong and only a British post–Cold War decision to remove nuclear weapons from its surface ships ended the impasse. A sign that relations had returned to normal came at Wellington on 10 June 1995 when the Type 23 frigate HMS *Monmouth*, accompanied by RFA *Brambleleaf*, made the first RN entrance into a New Zealand port since 1983.

J.O'C. Ross, *The White Ensign in New Zealand* (A.H. & A.W. Reed, Wellington, 1967); T.D. Taylor, *New Zealand's Naval Story* (A.H. & A.W. Reed, Wellington, 1948).

GAVIN McLEAN

Royal Navy in the First World War, New Zealanders in New Zealanders were involved in virtually every aspect of the naval war during the *First World War. They were to be found at sea with the Grand Fleet, in the air with the Royal Naval Air Service, beneath the waves in submarines, in base appointments, and even in ad hoc land units serving in theatres as remote as the Caucasus. Although the exact number of New Zealanders who served in the Royal Navy cannot be determined, there were at least 500. The number would have been greater had not the New Zealand government, after the introduction of *conscription in 1916, prohibited men from leaving the country in order to join the Royal Navy. The New Zealanders in the Royal Navy, most of whom had joined before 1914, were scattered among the various ships, and only in rare cases were there more than one or two in any particular

Royal Navy in the Second World War

The RNVR contingent for service in the Royal Navy at the official farewell in Wellington for 2NZEF's Second Echelon, which it accompanied in May 1940 (*Evening Post Collection, Alexander Turnbull Library, G-49242-1/4*)

complement. The exception was HMS *Pyramus*, one of the ★Australia Station's ★'P' class cruisers, which had more than sixty New Zealanders among her crew when she went to war in 1914. After helping escort the Samoa Expeditionary Force, she was deployed in the Indian Ocean and later the Persian Gulf. In mid 1915, she was involved in operations leading to the destruction of the *Königsberg* in the Rufiji River in German East Africa. HMS *Philomel*, New Zealand's newly acquired training cruiser, also had about sixty New Zealanders on board when she departed New Zealand waters in 1914. During 1916 a deliberate effort was made to recruit New Zealanders to help crew 550 anti-submarine motor launches being built for the Royal Navy to assist in commerce protection. A British team which visited New Zealand in mid 1916 enlisted ninety-two officers and 101 motor mechanics in the Royal Naval Motor Boat Reserve. A number of these men later distinguished themselves in action, particularly during raids on Zeebrugge and Ostend, and were decorated. For the most part, however, this motor boat service consisted of monotonous and uneventful patrolling in British waters. Among the New Zealanders serving elsewhere in the Royal Navy, the most prominent was Q-ship commander Lieutenant-Commander W.E. ★Sanders, who won the only ★Victoria Cross awarded to a New Zealander for naval operations. Lieutenant A.B. Boyle was one of several New Zealanders to serve as officers on the battlecruiser HMS ★*New Zealand*. New Zealand's champion tennis player, Anthony Wilding, joined the Royal Marines at the outset of the war, but later transferred to the Royal Naval Air Service; he was killed in action serving as a captain with an RNAS armoured car squadron on the ★Western Front in May 1915. In 1917 Enid Bell became one of the first women to join the Women's Royal Naval Service. There were at least three New Zealanders, including Lieutenants S.J. Hanna and C.B. Hull, in the Royal Naval Air Service Armoured Car Unit, which served on the Russian front from 1915 to 1917, while others were in warships involved in the ★Russian intervention in 1918–19.

PETER DENNERLY

Royal Navy in the Second World War, New Zealanders in

The wartime ★Royal New Zealand Navy at its peak strength in September 1944 totalled 10,635 persons. Of these, 1242 officers and 3659 ratings, nearly one half of the navy, enlisted for 'Hostilities Only', were serving in the fleets of the Royal Navy in every theatre of the war. Somewhat surprisingly, at the outbreak of war the Naval Board had not anticipated a situation in which about 7000 New Zealanders would eventually serve with the Royal Navy, and in the early hectic months inexperienced volunteers for naval service were actively discouraged.

From 1921 onwards, naval personnel policy had focused on the recruitment of men for long-service engagements so that the two ★cruisers and ancillary vessels of the ★New Zealand Division of the Royal Navy would in time be manned exclusively by a body of local career ratings, replacing the Royal Navy sailors on which the Division then depended. The New Zealand section of the Royal Naval Reserve and Royal Naval Volunteer Reserve was expected to provide all the supplementary officers and ratings that might be required in an emergency. In the first few days of the war the Naval Board accelerated the replacement of RN ratings by local men, principally by retaining the 'time-expired', calling up reservists, and recruiting a few 'Hostilities Only' technical personnel.

This initial period was one of extraordinary confusion in recruiting. While the Admiralty had early requested surplus reservists, trained pilots, and some yachtsmen and mariners for the RNVR, along with telegraphists and electrical specialists, the local naval authorities were informing the public that aside from reservists and yachtsmen/mariners, former Royal Navy men resident in New Zealand and untrained volunteers were not wanted and should not bother a busy Navy Office with their applications. The effect of this was to drive would-be naval recruits to enlist in the other services or, if really keen, to arrange to go to Great Britain at their own expense to join the Royal Navy there. More or less simultaneously, a separate government announcement repeated the Admiralty request and offered free passages to Britain for successful applicants. The Navy Office then promptly fell into line by beginning to recruit technical ratings and offering thirty RNVR officers and 187 ratings to the Admiralty. By early 1940, a dilatory British response had accepted the RNVR contingent, a small number of yachtsmen who were destined for service in Malaya, and surplus trained ratings. Ten yachtsmen (selected from the 500 who volunteered) left in April 1940. In May a contingent of twenty-eight officers and 357 ratings left for Britain—RNVR personnel, signallers and technical specialists, and Royal Navy ratings from *Achilles*. In the same month two schemes for recruiting New Zealanders for the Royal Navy ('A' and 'B') were being advertised. In October 1940, the Naval Board accepted that training of 'Hostilities Only' ratings for the Royal Navy could be integrated with the training of the much smaller number of young men needed for the New Zealand Division and a new establishment, HMS *Tamaki*, on Motuihe Island, was set up for this purpose in January 1941. By the end of the war about 60 per cent of New Zealand naval personnel had received their initial training in *Tamaki*.

In mid July 1941, the principal recruiting schemes and categories (with numbers at that date) were:

'A' (ended 1940) was for the thirty to forty age group. Fifty yachtsmen or men with other relevant experience were sought for RNVR commissions. Promotion to lieutenant followed after three months training in HMS *King Alfred* at Hove, East Sussex. (33)

'B' (ended August 1945) was for ordinary seamen (twenty to thirty years) with potential for selection as officers. Sea experience was not essential. If not commissioned, these men were to continue to serve as ratings. (219)

'F' (or 'C') (June 1940 to June 1945) was for candidates for the ★Fleet Air Arm as commissioned RNVR pilots or observers. They were entered as Air Branch ratings and trained at HMS *St Vincent*, Gosport, Hampshire. (441)

'T' was for telegraphists and other technical ratings including engine-room artificers and shipwrights. (80)

'Y' (April 1940–December 1941) was for yachtsmen for RNVR service in Malaya. (32)

All the above were entered as members of the Royal Navy. At the same date, provided by the New Zealand Naval Forces, there were 308 New Zealand RNVR, thirty-five long-service ratings, 117 'Hostilities Only' ratings from *Tamaki*, and ten wireless mechanics serving in the Royal Navy. A further scheme, 'R' (September 1940), provided specialist radar ratings, initially for the New Zealand Division, but by late 1941 for the Royal Navy as well.

The affiliation of New Zealanders serving in the Royal Navy and their conditions of service were questions that needed resolution. The Admiralty, probably with the intention of keeping the drafting of ratings as uncomplicated as possible, had in early 1940 rejected a New Zealand proposal that an attempt should be made to have some ships manned solely by New Zealanders. Thus even though a significant proportion of the crews of some flotillas of small ships (and later the ill-fated cruiser HMS *Neptune*) and the personnel of some FAA squadrons were New Zealanders, there was no naval equivalent of the New Zealand squadrons in the RAF. The disparate streams of New Zealanders in the Royal Navy—those entered directly into the Royal Navy but sent from New Zealand (e.g. schemes 'A', 'F', and 'Y'); those who had gone to Britain and been entered there; New Zealand Division long-service ratings on loan; scheme 'B' ratings; and some technical specialists—highlighted the differences in conditions of service between those who were identified as 'New Zealand Division', and who were receiving a generally higher rate of pay, and the rest. (The differentials between New Zealand and Royal Navy rates of pay were quite substantial for ratings, less so for officers.)

By early 1941 it had been agreed with the Admiralty that, except for the small number of those who had joined the Royal Navy for a career, the New Zealand government would supplement the pay of New Zealanders who were in the Royal Navy for 'Hostilities Only' to bring it up to the New Zealand Division rates and that the cost of pay and allowances for all New Zealanders would be borne by the New Zealand government. By July 1942 all New Zealanders in the Royal Navy had been transferred to the RNZN; they were henceforth considered as 'on loan', with the Admiralty paying a lump sum per year for each, equivalent to their Royal Navy pay and allowances. Earlier, the New Zealand government had refunded the cost of the passage to Britain for those who had originally gone at their own expense. However, with the exception of career RNZN personnel, the management of these New Zealanders in the Royal Navy, especially

Royal Navy in the Second World War

with regard to postings and promotions, remained an Admiralty responsibility.

Many New Zealanders were content to fit into the close-knit, complex, and hierarchical worlds of the battleship, cruiser, or destroyer with their large complements of ratings divided among many branches and their junior officers filling watch-keeping slots and assisting the specialist officers. By contrast, there were several roles which were pre-eminently suited to young officers with minimal training but who were keen and quick to learn, in which youthful stamina was at a premium, and which, above all, allowed an independence of judgment and action generally denied to those in 'big ships'. The most notable of these were the flotillas of motorboats, the minesweeper/anti-submarine vessels, small convoy escorts, and the squadrons of the Fleet Air Arm, in all of which New Zealanders were well represented.

Minesweeping, almost a monopoly of the RNVR, was a particularly arduous task. The New Zealand reservists who arrived in Britain in July 1940 were assigned to ten minesweeper/anti-submarine vessels of the Tree class in two groups (24th and 25th MS/AS Groups), each of which was commanded by a New Zealander. These groups swept mines and escorted convoys in the English Channel, often coming under attack from German aircraft and enemy batteries on the French coast. The New Zealanders in minesweepers continued to see action in areas as diverse as Madagascar, the Mediterranean (including the ★North African campaign), and off the German coast in 1945. The largest single loss of New Zealand naval men in the whole war occurred in the Mediterranean theatre in December 1941, when 151 drowned in the cruiser *Neptune*, which was mined off Tripoli while seeking to intercept an Italian convoy.

About forty New Zealand naval men were killed and a similar number became ★prisoners of war during the Japanese attacks on Hong Kong, Malaya, and Singapore. Of the six New Zealanders in the capital ships of the ill-fated Force Z, two (a chaplain and a rating) were drowned in HMS *Prince of Wales* on 10 December 1941. Fourteen of the dead were scheme 'Y' yachtsmen, whose launches and other small craft were destroyed by the Japanese as they attempted to flee from Singapore with survivors of that disaster. Some boats, crammed with refugees, were sunk after a gallant but hopeless resistance; other groups made it safely to an island or a haven in Sumatra only to be killed or captured soon after landing. Several New Zealanders were killed and others taken prisoner when their ships were sunk in the Battle of the Java Sea in March 1942.

In the same month, but far away in the North Atlantic, scheme 'B' men, fresh to their sea service, were in cruisers escorting convoys to the Russian port of Murmansk. Many others served in the escort vessels for these convoys during 1942 and 1943, running the gauntlet of enemy U-boats, bombers, cruisers, destroyers, and powerful pocket battleships. New Zealanders were also in the crews of the Home Fleet ships under Admiral Fraser which sank the *Scharnhorst* in December 1943. Others again, further south, in the various types of escort vessels, were engaged in protecting trans-Atlantic convoys during the most intensive phases of the Battle of the Atlantic. John Holm's memoir *No Place to Linger: Saga of a Wartime Atlantic Kiwi* (1985) records the experiences of a RNZNR corvette captain at this time. About 1000 New Zealanders served in the Fleet Air Arm, forming more than 10 per cent of the officer strength. Flying training in Britain, Canada, or the United States was a rigorous endurance course. Those who failed as pilots became observers or air branch ratings while the fledgling qualified pilots were quickly sent to sea in operational squadrons. Many flew from HMS *Victorious* against the *Bismarck* in May 1941 and New Zealanders were in the ships of the shadowing force—one was killed in HMS *Hood*. *Victorious* spent six months with the US Pacific Fleet in 1943 before returning to the North Atlantic to escort convoys to Russia. New Zealanders were prominent in the attacks on the *Tirpitz* in a Norwegian fiord from early 1942 onwards; most conspicuously so Lieutenant-Commander Archibald ★Richardson of 1840 Squadron, HMS *Indefatigable*, killed in his third attack on the *Tirpitz* in August 1944 and recommended for a posthumous VC (a mention in dispatches was awarded). In 1942 pilots in HMS *Eagle* and *Argus* in the Mediterranean were protecting convoys to Malta while others again, based in Malta with the RAF, or flying from Alexandria, were decorated for successful strikes against enemy ships attempting to replenish the Axis armies in North Africa. New Zealand aircrew survived the sinking of the *Eagle* and the disabling of HMS *Indomitable* in an August Malta convoy. In early 1943 the hard-pressed Atlantic convoys were strengthened by the incorporation of small escort carriers and merchant aircraft-carriers (modified bulk carriers and tankers) which operated a few Swordfish aircraft. Many New Zealanders flew from these vessels while others provided the maintenance crews.

The light coastal forces of the Royal Navy were almost exclusively manned by the Volunteer Reserve, and New Zealanders were well represented in the motor torpedo boat flotillas which were formed to attack enemy coastal shipping in the Channel. Actions with the equivalent German E-boats, often at very short range, were brief and furious, and frequently left the vessels of both sides sinking or otherwise seriously damaged. In this sphere Lieutenant-Commander G.J. ★Macdonald, a Wellington civil engineer commanding the 21st MTB Flotilla, became the acknowledged 'ace' by earning a DSO, three DSCs, and two mentions in dispatches—all before he turned twenty-three years of age. A different type of ship, the landing craft (infantry), was to the fore in the invasions of Sicily in 1943 and Normandy in 1944, and later in the Burma campaign. New Zealanders served with distinction as officers in many of these. About 200 New Zealanders volunteered for submarines and a few undertook especially hazardous 'special operations' in midget submarines. Radar officers and ratings were spread throughout British fleets in the Atlantic, Mediterranean, and Pacific, and one specialist officer was in the meteorological team which advised on the ★D-Day landings.

On the whole, those New Zealanders who served with the Royal Navy tolerated the institutional peculiarities of the Service with good humour and, while bemused by English class feelings, were not intimidated by them, using their 'colonial brashness' to good effect in the naval environment and in their social relations with the British ashore. During the course of the conflict, 183 officers and 266 ratings (including some Royal Navy personnel on loan to the RNZN) lost their lives while serving with the Royal Navy, and sixty-three were taken prisoner of war (of whom nine died).

S.D. Waters, *The Royal New Zealand Navy* (War History Branch, Wellington, 1956).

DENIS FAIRFAX

Royal New Zealand Air Force Although the RNZAF was only established as a separate service in 1937, its beginnings can be traced back to 1913. In that year an officer then in the United Kingdom was ordered to attend the Royal Flying School to learn how to fly. In the following year the Imperial Air Fleet Committee in London presented a Blériot aircraft named 'Britannia' to New Zealand as the nucleus of a flying corps, but it was only flown briefly in New Zealand, in 1914. The pilot created a controversy when he took a female passenger aloft, whereupon the authorities placed the aeroplane in storage; later in the year it was sent back to England (see AIRCRAFT, RNZAF). During the ★First World War, two commercial New Zealand flying schools, which were partly funded by the British government, trained 250 pilots for service with the Royal Naval Air Service, the Royal Flying Corps, and the RAF.

In 1919 Colonel A.V. ★Bettington, an RAF officer serving as the government's air adviser, proposed the establishment of a permanent air force of seventy-nine officers and 299 airmen, supported by a territorial air force of 174 officers and 1060 airmen. Although no action was taken, a number of war surplus military aircraft were received from Great Britain as gifts and most were passed to commercial companies. An Air Board was established in 1920 to administer aviation in New Zealand, and three years later the government finally made provision for military aviation, though on a much less lavish scale than suggested by Bettington. The New Zealand Permanent Air Force (NZPAF) established on 23 June 1923 as part of the Military Forces had a strength of four officers and two other ranks; its Territorial adjunct, the New Zealand Air Force, comprised seventy-two officers. The only equipment available were leftover gift aircraft. Throughout the late 1920s the fledgling air force continued refresher training at Wigram (see AIR BASES). Construction of a new Air Station at Hobsonville began in 1928, and seaplanes were ordered for it. The first warlike operation by the New Zealand Permanent Air Force took place in Western Samoa in 1930. A Moth seaplane, with a pilot and two ground crew, which had been carried there on HMS *Dunedin*, took part in efforts to round up the nationalist Mau (see SAMOA, NEW ZEALAND'S MILITARY ROLE IN).

In August 1930 the declining New Zealand Air Force became the Territorial Air Force (TAF). Formed around four regionally based squadrons, it had a strength of sixty-six officers. However, the depression of the early 1930s prevented the purchase of any equipment for the squadrons. The NZPAF was also operating with minimum funding, but changes in the international situation, and the improving economic position, led to an increase in defence spending in mid decade. For the Royal New Zealand Air Force, as the NZPAF had been renamed in 1934, this meant the expansion of the establishment at Wigram, the ordering of modern Vildebeeste torpedo bombers, and an increase in personnel by March 1936 to twenty officers and 107 airmen. The TAF strength increased to seventy-four officers.

The Labour government which took office at the end of 1935 favoured concentration of New Zealand defence resources on developing the air force. Wing Commander Ralph ★Cochrane was seconded from the RAF to carry out a review of air defence requirements in 1936. He recommended that the RNZAF become a separate service, and that two medium bomber squadrons capable of seeking out enemy raiders and one army cooperation squadron be maintained for local defence, the defence of shipping routes, and the provision of assistance in ★imperial defence. As a result, the Air Force Act of 1 April 1937 separated the RNZAF from the Military Forces, and further legislation created an ★Air Department to oversee military and civil aviation interests in New Zealand. Cochrane agreed to remain in New Zealand to become the first Chief of the Air Staff. With the threat of a European war looming, three successive expansion programmes

Royal New Zealand Air Force

The Duke of York (in felt hat), later King George VI, inspects the New Zealand Permanent Air Force at Wigram during his visit to New Zealand in 1927 (*RNZAF, F153*)

were undertaken. Second-hand Baffin aircraft were received for the TAF from March 1938. Thirty new Wellington bombers were ordered from Britain, and land at Whenuapai and Ohakea was purchased for the establishment of new bases for them.

At the ★Pacific Defence Conference, held in Wellington in April 1939, agreement was reached that the RNZAF should build landing strips in Fiji, and undertake reconnaissance between the New Hebrides and Tonga. During the previous year New Zealand had offered to train a thousand pilots a year for the RAF in the event of war. This scheme was now modified—650 pilots, 300 observers, and 350 gunners would be trained. On 3 September 1939 the RNZAF comprised 91 officers and 665 airmen, while there were 79 officers and 325 airmen in the TAF. A total of 102 aircraft, mostly second-hand Baffins and Gordons, were available. The only new aircraft were five Oxfords and nine Vildebeestes.

With the outbreak of the ★Second World War the Wellington bombers, the first six of which were awaiting delivery, were made available to the RAF, together with the twenty airmen who were to have ferried them to New Zealand. They became the nucleus of 75 (New Zealand) Squadron. On 17 December 1939 the New Zealand government accepted proposals for the training of New Zealand personnel for the RAF both in New Zealand and as part of the ★Empire Air Training Scheme in Canada. In addition to providing 880 fully trained pilots per annum, it would send partially trained personnel (520 pilots, 546 observers, and 936 air gunners) to Canada. The United Kingdom provided training aircraft.

To meet these training commitments, the RNZAF was considerably expanded during the first year of the war. New flying training schools were established at Taieri, Harewood, New Plymouth, and Whenuapai, and an air gunners and observers school at Ohakea. An initial training school was set up at Rongotai, then moved to Levin. An aircraft factory to assemble Tiger Moth trainers was completed at Wellington by early 1940. Three territorial squadrons were mobilised to patrol the approaches to Auckland, Wellington, and Lyttelton harbours, flying obsolete Vildebeestes, Vincents, and Baffins. In mid 1940, German successes led to the expansion of the EATS, which would continue to operate at full pace until mid 1944. Of the 131,553 aircrew graduates before it terminated in March 1945, 7002 were New Zealanders. They, and the pilots trained in New Zealand, served with distinction in all theatres of the war. Many were members of the seven RAF 'New Zealand' squadrons (75 and 485–490) established under the EATS to ensure a continued linkage with the Dominion (see AIRMEN, NEW ZEALAND, IN THE RAF IN THE SECOND WORLD WAR).

The threat posed by German surface raiders and more generally by Japan induced the New Zealand government in 1941 to make strong pleas to London for modern aircraft for local defence. As a result the first of thirty-six Hudson bombers began arriving in mid 1941. To provide protection of the Fijian Islands, a New Zealand responsibility, four worn-out Singapore flying boats were gifted to the RNZAF shortly before the onset of the ★Pacific War. On 7 December 1941 the RNZAF had 641 aircraft, the majority of which were for training. Only the Hudsons were anywhere near modern. During the disastrous ★Malayan campaign the RNZAF was represented by 488 Squadron and an aerodrome construction unit, and RNZAF pilots also took part in the ★Burma campaign. By early 1942 the threat of Japanese invasion of New Zealand led to all available

Royal New Zealand Air Force

aircraft being allotted to shadow defence squadrons under the Forces Available For Anti-Invasion (FAFAI) scheme. Plans for arming Tiger Moths and other second-line aircraft were put into action. To overcome a shortage of men, women were recruited from early 1941 as members of the New Zealand Women's Auxiliary Air Force. During the following four years, more than 4700 WAAFs would serve (see WOMEN IN THE ARMED FORCES).

Following further strenuous pleas to the British and United States governments, Kittyhawk fighters began arriving in March 1942, and New Zealand–based fighter squadrons were formed. They subsequently took part in the ★Solomons campaign, the first engagement of the Japanese in direct combat in the South Pacific being by 3 Squadron (Hudsons), which had moved to Henderson Field at Guadalcanal in November 1942. They were followed in June 1943 by 15 Squadron (Warhawks). Until 1945 the RNZAF did not act in the Pacific as a strategic or tactical force with a specific task to perform. Its task was to provide combat squadrons to support US operations in removing Japanese forces from the Solomon Islands. Following lobbying by the New Zealand government, the US Navy, under which the New Zealand squadrons operated, provided the RNZAF with new combat aircraft. Operational squadrons were progressively equipped with Corsairs, Venturas, Avengers, Dauntless dive-bombers, and Catalina flying boats. Support for the operations in the South West Pacific Area was provided by Dakota and Lodestar transport aircraft, obtained under ★Lend-Lease, augmented from late 1944 by four Sunderland flying boats.

In 1943 Air Vice-Marshal L.M. ★Isitt became the first New Zealander to serve as CAS. He oversaw a steady build-up of RNZAF squadrons in the operational area. By the end of 1943, a New Zealand Fighter Wing with supporting servicing units had been established at Ondonga (New Georgia) and a Group HQ at Guadalcanal. Pilots of the fighter wing had ninety-nine confirmed destroyed and twenty-four probably destroyed Japanese aircraft to their credit, the highest score reached by the fighters in the theatre. Four other Japanese aircraft fell to the guns of Hudsons and Venturas, bringing the total enemy aircraft destroyed by the RNZAF in the Pacific to 103. During 1944, the RNZAF's operations in the South-west Pacific were based primarily on Bougainville, with strikes against Japanese forces on that island and at Rabaul. In early 1944 the absence of air opposition led to the Warhawk squadrons, followed by those flying Corsairs, switching from the fighter escort to the fighter-bomber role. A Dauntless squadron and two Avenger squadrons did single tours on Bougainville, while 6 Squadron (Catalinas) carried out reconnaissance and rescue missions in the area. As the focus of US operations moved north of the Solomon Islands, the RNZAF continued to harass the Japanese ground forces still in the area. Support facilities, including repair depots and aircraft assembly units, were expanded. In early 1945, agreement was reached with Australia and the United States for the RNZAF to take part in operations in Borneo with the Australians or in the Philippines with the United States. Mustang fighters were ordered to form new fighter squadrons, but the war ended before they could be brought into service. On VJ Day (15 August 1945) the RNZAF had more than 7000 personnel stationed throughout the Solomon Islands area from Espiritu Santo to Los Negros. Repatriating these personnel and the equipment to New Zealand was thereafter the priority task, which was finally achieved in early 1946. The RNZAF, which reached a peak of 42,000 in June 1944, had by March 1946 shrunk to a strength of 7154. The aircraft fleet had peaked at 1336 at the end of 1944. In all, twenty-four RNZAF squadrons had operated in the South-west Pacific theatre. From 3 September 1939 to 15 August 1945, 4149 RNZAF personnel had died on active service, the majority of them members of RAF Bomber Command squadrons.

The RNZAF's immediate post-war problems were to maintain 14 Squadron (Corsairs) in Japan as part of the ★British Commonwealth Occupation Force while deciding on future policy. A move back to British aircraft began in 1946 with the delivery of second-hand Mosquitoes. Throughout the late 1940s the RNZAF struggled with its direction and resources; uncertainties about the future led to an embarrassing strike by airmen in September 1946 (see MUTINIES), and there were tensions between those who had served in Europe and those who had served in the Pacific. Complicating its role was the need to provide internal and some external commercial operations using 40 Squadron's Dakotas and Lodestars. In 1947, these operations were absorbed by the newly established New Zealand National Airways Corporation, which was formed in the main from the squadron's personnel and aircraft. The onset of the ★Cold War led to new responsibilities. Aircrews were provided for the ★Berlin airlift in 1948–49, and New Zealand's acceptance of the ★Middle East commitment in 1949, as part of Commonwealth defence plans for a war with the Soviet Union, led to the recreation of the Territorial Air Force, the introduction of ★compulsory military training, and a wide-ranging re-equipment programme in the early 1950s. New aircraft included Vampire jet fighters, Hastings and Freighter transport aircraft, Sunderland flying boats, and Devon trainers. The RNZAF dispatched a Dakota detachment from 41 Squadron to Malaya in 1949 to support British forces in threatened ★Hong Kong; it took part in ★Malayan Emergency

Royal New Zealand Air Force

supply dropping operations until its withdrawal in 1951. Although not directly involved in the ★Korean War, the RNZAF flew transport missions in support of ★Kayforce. In 1952, 14 Squadron moved from Ohakea to ★Cyprus in accordance with the Middle East strategy. When New Zealand's commitment was switched to South-east Asia in 1955, the squadron moved to Tengah (Singapore) and its borrowed Vampires were replaced by Venom fighter bombers. It was replaced by 75 squadron, flying Canberras, in 1958. In 1955 41 Squadron with Freighters had also re-established itself at Changi. All three squadrons took part in Operation Firedog, the RAF's Malayan Emergency campaign. In New Zealand, the four Territorial squadrons were equipped with Tiger Moths, Harvards, and thirty Mustangs which had been held in storage since the end of the war. Always short of air and ground crews, the TAF was finally disbanded in 1957 following a review of New Zealand's defence preparations.

In 1956 the RNZAF's newly formed Antarctic Flight had taken a Beaver and an Auster to Antarctica to support the New Zealand Trans-Antarctic Expedition. These annual summer operations continued until 1960. This association with the Antarctic was re-established in 1965 when a Hercules made the first of what have become annual flights to the continent during the summer months. From 1945 to 1966 maritime operations for the RNZAF were based at Fiji. With Catalinas, later Sunderlands, 5 Squadron provided surveillance of a wide span of the South Pacific ocean, and flew medical evacuations and community assistance tasks. From 1952 to 1957, 6 Squadron operated as a Territorial unit, with Catalina and Sunderland flying boats.

During the 1960s the CAS, Air Vice-Marshal I.G. ★Morrison, successfully lobbied for the replacement of the RNZAF's ageing operational aircraft. In a major shift away from the traditional British orientation, American Hercules and Orion aircraft were obtained, along with the RNZAF's first helicopters (Iroquois and Sioux). The new fleet began arriving during 1965 as new commitments in South-east Asia affected the RNZAF. In 1964 14 Squadron (Canberras), on a regular short-term training deployment in Singapore, had been retained in the theatre as part of the Commonwealth build-up in the face of Indonesia's ★Confrontation of Malaysia; it did not finally return to New Zealand until November 1966. Following the commitment of combat forces to the ★Vietnam War in 1965, New Zealand's troops were airlifted to South Vietnam by 40 Squadron, and 41 Squadron's Freighters began regular resupply missions to ★V-Force from Singapore. From 1967 RNZAF helicopter pilots served in Vietnam with 9 RAAF Squadron, while other pilots did tours of duty with US squadrons as forward air controllers. In all, thirty pilots served in Vietnam

between 1967 and 1971. The RNZAF suffered one fatal casualty during the conflict—a member of the New Zealand Services Medical Team, who was killed by a land mine. The RNZAF presence in South-east Asia continued in Singapore until 1989, when the last remaining unit, 141 Flight (Iroquois), was withdrawn.

In 1970 the RNZAF took delivery of A4 Skyhawk attack aircraft, which remain in service thirty years later. The ageing Vampires were replaced by Strikemaster jet trainers in 1972. Aircraft fleet changes continued with the wartime Harvard trainers being superseded by New Zealand–built Airtrainers, the Freighters and Dakotas by second-hand Andovers in 1977, and Devons by second-hand Friendships in 1980. During the 1980s the Orions were upgraded, and a sixth was purchased, while ten second-hand Skyhawks were obtained from the RAN. To support the RNZAF's growing worldwide transport commitments, two Boeing 727 jet transports were purchased. The maintenance of the RNZAF's capacity was hindered during the late 1980s by the government's adoption of an anti-nuclear policy, which brought it into dispute with the United States (see ANZUS). The resulting cessation of the RNZAF's participation in United States and British–sponsored exercises had a dramatic effect on the efficiency of its combat squadrons. At the same time there was a move to increased involvement in ★peace-keeping duties, with the RNZAF taking part in deployments in the Sinai and Iran.

During the 1990s there have been dramatic changes in the RNZAF. As a result of the government's drive to reduce public spending and a further review of defence strategy in 1991, it underwent radical surgery. Bases at Te Rapa, Wigram, and Shelly Bay were closed, and flying training was shifted from Wigram to Ohakea in 1993. The personnel strength of the service fell by about 700 to around 3500. Commercialisation of non-core activities commenced in 1992, and after five years included most of the functions of the Repair Depot at Woodbourne. In 1998 commercial lease arrangements covered primary training aircraft (Airtrainers) and multi-engine conversion trainers (King Airs). Increasing numbers of jobs within the service were civilianised. At the same time the RNZAF's external operations expanded. Shortly before the ★Gulf War in 1991, two Hercules joined the Allied coalition forces in the Persian Gulf region. In the same year 2 Squadron (Skyhawks) moved to Nowra in New South Wales, where it continues to provide training for the RAN and conversion of RNZAF Skyhawk pilots. In 1993, an Andover Detachment spent five months in Somalia. Humanitarian airlifts were conducted to the Middle East and Rwanda. Transport support was supplied to the ★New Zealand Army contingent in Bosnia–Herzegovina from 1994 to 1996. In February 1998, the RNZAF contributed two Orions and seventy personnel to another US-led coalition force in the Persian Gulf. A Hercules and a Boeing provided logistical support for the contingent. During the Kosovo crisis in April–May 1999 a Hercules and twenty-seven RNZAF personnel took part in humanitarian airlift tasks. In December 1998 the government announced that F-16 multi-role fighters would be leased from the United States to replace the Skyhawks in 2002. The Labour-led government which took office in December 1999 not only cancelled the deal but also raised doubts about whether the RNZAF would continue to maintain an air combat capability.

As the RNZAF has matured, it has developed distinctive symbols of national identity. Initially standard British forms of identification, both of personnel and aircraft, were used. The development of the Empire Air Training Scheme during the Second World War provided the first impetus to change: there was a desire to highlight the national identity of the various Commonwealth personnel passing through the schools in Canada. Consequently New Zealand airmen destined for service in the European theatre carried white or silver-blue-on-black shoulder patches with the words or letters 'New Zealand' or 'R.N.Z.A.F.' superimposed above the eagle. Similar red-on-khaki patches were worn by airmen in the South Pacific theatre. Officers had just the words 'New Zealand' on their shoulders. After the war, these forms of identification were retained. From the 1960s epaulette slides with the words 'New Zealand' and the rank of the bearer have been standard. More recently airmen and women serving with UN or coalition forces have worn a small New Zealand flag and a white-on-black kiwi patch on their left sleeves. A similar process has occurred with aircraft identification. The standard blue-white-red RAF roundel was used on RNZAF aircraft until 1942, when the needs of operating in an American-dominated environment in the South Pacific led to the development of a variety of distinctive blue-white-blue RNZAF roundels, including several with American-style white bars at their sides. After the war, however, the RNZAF reverted to the RAF pattern roundel. It was not until the late 1950s that distinctive New Zealand forms were again introduced. A white fern was painted on the red centre of the roundel in 1957 but proved unpopular because of its 'white feather' appearance. In 1959 this problem was overcome with the introduction of a silver transfer, applied to the red disc, but this was still not considered satisfactory because of its closeness to the RAF marking. Since 1970 RNZAF aircraft have borne a roundel with a red kiwi in its centre. More recently, combat aircraft have worn a blue circle with red kiwi and, from the mid 1990s, a grey outer circle and grey kiwi. With the RAF roundel still in use in the 1950s, squadrons using leased British aircraft in Malaya also took the initiative in introducing markings on the tail-fins of their aircraft that were based on national symbols as a form of distinction. These included a kiwi (14 Squadron) and a map of New Zealand superimposed on a kiwi (75 Squadron). (See also AIRCRAFT, RNZAF and SQUADRONS, RNZAF)

J.M.S. Ross, *Royal New Zealand Air Force* (War History Branch, Wellington, 1955).

PAUL A. HARRISON

Royal New Zealand Armoured Corps, formed on 1 January 1942, encompassed the 1st Army Tank Brigade and mounted rifles regiments (which were redesignated light armoured fighting vehicle regiments). In October 1942 the three armoured regiments and Divisional Cavalry of the 2nd New Zealand Division in the Middle East were included in the corps. The prefix 'Royal' was granted on 12 July 1947. Currently the corps consists of the Queen Alexandra's Mounted Rifles (QAMR), which has two Regular Force squadrons based at Waiouru and two Territorial squadrons. (See MOUNTED RIFLES, ARMOUR)

Royal New Zealand Army Education Corps was founded in 1942 as the Army Education and Welfare Service, meeting the educational needs of soldiers, as well as providing welfare, propaganda, and entertainment services. It took a particular responsibility in the provision of rehabilitation services. In 1954 the New Zealand Army Education Corps was established. It was granted the prefix 'Royal' in 1963. Members of the Defence Psychological Unit, a tri-service unit established in 1976, are posted to the corps, but the primary responsibility of the corps remains the education of soldiers through such instruments as the ★Military Studies Institute.

Royal New Zealand Army Logistic Regiment was formed on 6 December 1996 from the ★New Zealand Army's three logistic corps—the Royal New Zealand Army Service Corps, the Royal New Zealand Army Ordnance Corps, and the Royal New Zealand Electrical and Mechanical Engineers. It was granted the additional title 'The Duke of York's Own' in June 1999. Founded on 6 May 1910, the New Zealand Army Service Corps (like all three logistic corps it received its 'Royal' prefix in 1947) was responsible for military supply and transport. It was only in 1913 that the corps was made effective under British officers and NCOs. A New Zealand Permanent Army Service Corps was formed in 1924, but remained very small. It was amalgamated with the New Zealand Army Service Corps in 1947. In 1979 the corps was redesignated the Royal New Zealand Corps of Transport, with its supply and clerical roles going to the Royal New Zealand Army Ordnance Corps. This latter had its origins in the ★First World War: both

Royal New Zealand Army Medical Corps

a corps and a department had been established on 1 February 1917 to run supply depots. Both elements had been brought together in the New Zealand Army Ordnance Corps in 1924. The RNZEME came into existence as the Corps of New Zealand Electrical and Mechanical Engineers in December 1942. It was responsible for the repair of mechanical and electrical equipment. (See LOGISTICS)

P. Cape, *Craftsmen in Uniform: The Corps of Royal New Zealand Electrical and Mechanical Engineers, An Account* (Corps of RNZEME, Wellington, 1976); J. Millen, *Salute to Service: A History of the Royal New Zealand Corps of Transport and its Predecessors 1860–1996* (Victoria University Press, Wellington, 1997).

Royal New Zealand Army Medical Corps
The first New Zealand medical units were volunteer bearer corps (later renamed field ambulances) established in 1898. No medical organisation existed for medical staff outside bearer corps or attachment as surgeons to ★Volunteer Force corps until 7 May 1908, when the New Zealand Medical Corps (NZMC) was formally established. An Otago University Medical Company was established in 1909 and provided a valuable recruiting ground for medical personnel. During the ★First World War, more than 3600 members of the corps served with 1NZEF. In 1919 the New Zealand Army Medical Corps was formed in the permanent force to maintain medical stores. The NZMC, which remained as a separate ★Territorial Force corps, was greatly affected by defence cuts during the Depression, but revived during the ★Second World War. After 1945 it was subsumed within the New Zealand Army Medical Corps, which in 1947 was granted the prefix 'Royal'. Currently the Royal New Zealand Army Medical Corps is responsible for the evacuation and treatment of casualties, as well as for promoting health, preventing disease, and providing assessment of armed forces personnel. (See MEDICAL TREATMENT)

Royal New Zealand Corps of Signals The New Zealand Corps of Signals was raised on 1 June 1921 from the New Zealand Post and Telegraph Corps, New Zealand Engineers. It was granted the prefix 'Royal' in 1947. The Corps device is the figure of Mercury, and its motto is 'Certa Cito', which is loosely translated as 'Swift and Sure'. Its domestic colours are light blue, dark blue, and green; tactical colours are white over royal blue. The Corps Day is 24 March and the Archangel Gabriel is the Corps patron. Within the Commonwealth the Royal New Zealand Corps of Signals is unique in having a Corps Patron—the Archangel Gabriel—and a ★Victoria Cross winner. (See MILITARY SIGNALLING)

L. Barber and C. Lord, *Swift and Sure: A History of the Royal New Zealand Corps of Signals and Army Signalling in New Zealand* (New Zealand Signals Inc., Auckland, 1996).

Royal New Zealand Dental Corps was formed as the New Zealand Army Dental Corps on 7 November 1915, ten dental officers having accompanied 1NZEF's main body in 1914. By 1918 the corps numbered 112 men, who were performing more than 200,000 operations annually. Although reduced to a Territorial basis between the wars, it expanded to more than 200 dental surgeons during the ★Second World War. Its services were extended to the RNZAF and the RNZN. In 1947 the corps, now including a regular component, was granted the prefix 'Royal'; in 1949 it was retitled the Royal New Zealand Dental Corps to reflect its tri-service nature. While its main role is the provision of dental services to all armed services personnel, it has also provided dental treatment to isolated communities.

Royal New Zealand Engineers, Corps of Volunteer field engineers took part in the Tauranga campaign in 1867, only a year after the first engineer corps was formed. During the next thirty years various volunteer corps were responsible for field engineering and signalling. A small permanent corps of engineers established following the 1885 war scare worked on the ★coast defences. Merged with the torpedo corps, it became No. 2 Company, ★Permanent Militia, in 1897; it was responsible for laying the minefields at the four main ports in the event of an emergency. On 15 October 1902 it was redesignated the Royal New Zealand Engineers. Following the decision in 1907 to remove the minefields from the defence scheme, the corps was absorbed into the Royal New Zealand Artillery. By 1914 there were four ★Territorial Force field engineer companies, four signals companies, and a railway corps. During the ★First World War the corps was involved in tunnelling, demolition, signalling, construction, and fortification. Between the wars the Corps of New Zealand Engineers consisted of three engineer depots, the signallers having formed their own corps in 1921. The Corps underwent an enormous expansion during the ★Second World War. Small detachments of field engineers served during both the ★Korean and ★Vietnam Wars. The prefix 'Royal' was granted to the New Zealand Engineers in 1947, and in 1953 the Corps of Royal New Zealand Engineers was formed, incorporating both Regular and Territorial components. (See MILITARY ENGINEERS)

Royal New Zealand Infantry Regiment In January 1947 the ★New Zealand Army's infantry units were brought together to form the New Zealand

Infantry Corps. The fourteen Territorial infantry regiments retained their identities, while Regular infantry instructors and specialist staff were posted to the newly formed New Zealand Regiment. In 1947 the corps was granted the title 'Royal'. Amalgamations in 1948 reduced the number of Territorial regiments to eleven, and in 1949–50 another two regiments became part of the ★Royal New Zealand Armoured Corps. In July 1957 a regular battalion, 1st Battalion, NZR, was raised for service in Malaya, and it was replaced by a second battalion in 1959. In 1963 the latter, 2nd Battalion, NZR, was reorganised as a depot unit for the 1st Battalion. On 1 April 1964 the corps was renamed the Royal New Zealand Infantry Regiment (RNZIR), with 1st Battalion, NZR, becoming the 1st Battalion, RNZIR. The nine Territorial infantry regiments were amalgamated to form six battalions, numbered 2nd to 7th, which retained their provincial distinctions. Thus, for example, the Wellington Regiment and Hawke's Bay Regiment were amalgamated to form the 7th Battalion (Hawke's Bay–City of Wellington's Own), RNZIR. In 1974 it was decided to re-form the depot battalion at Burnham as a regular infantry battalion, which was designated 2nd/1st Battalion, RNZIR. Each RNZIR battalion retains its own insignia and has its own honorary colonel. Queen Elizabeth II has been honorary colonel-in-chief of the regiment since 1964. (See INFANTRY)

Royal New Zealand Military Police is responsible for the enforcement of law and ★discipline in the ★New Zealand Army. Its tasks include security duties, traffic control, and general policing. The first New Zealand military police were members of the New Zealand Military Police Unit (NZMPU), which was formed in 1NZEF in 1915. They were mounted rather than foot policemen. Re-established in 2NZEF in 1939, the NZMPU provided provost services wherever the force was deployed. In 1946 it was replaced by three provost companies (later amalgamated as the 1st Divisional Provost Company). The New Zealand Provost Corps was established on 18 February 1949 but was not activated until March 1951. It was granted the prefix 'Royal' in July 1952. In December 1981 it was re-titled the Royal New Zealand Military Police.

Royal New Zealand Navy The New Zealand Naval Forces were known as the ★New Zealand Division of the Royal Navy from 1921 until September 1941, a title which accurately reflected the reality that the New Zealand Squadron, while maintained by the Dominion and administered in peacetime by a local Naval Board, was nevertheless widely considered to be merely a distant flotilla of an imperial navy with worldwide responsibilities. Aside from some disagreements with Great Britain over naval strategy in the Pacific, this situation, which accorded with New Zealand's foreign policy stance, was fully accepted by the government and was endorsed by influential public opinion.

When the ★Second World War began in September 1939, under arrangements confirmed the previous year the ships of the New Zealand Division came under Admiralty operational control, with orders for ships on the ★New Zealand Station being transmitted via the Chief of Naval Staff in Wellington. Thus the cruiser HMS *Achilles* was sent to the America and West Indies Station and, after rounding the Horn and joining the South Atlantic Squadron's South America Division, participated in the destruction of the pocket battleship *Admiral Graf Spee* at the Battle of the ★River Plate in December 1939. The other cruiser, HMS *Leander,* remained patrolling home waters and escorting Tasman convoys before going to the Indian Ocean in May 1940 as a unit of the East Indies Station's 4th Cruiser Squadron. The approval of the title 'Royal New Zealand Navy' by the King, with effect from 1 October 1941, while it gave the New Zealand Naval Forces the same status as other Dominion navies, did not alter the administrative and operational system, which continued until the end of the war. The RNZN (its ships now 'HMNZS') expanded considerably in numbers from early 1942 onwards, but while the two cruisers and some minesweepers operated in the Pacific with the US Navy, the greater proportion of officers and ratings engaged for 'Hostilities Only' served with the Royal Navy (ROYAL NAVY IN THE SECOND WORLD WAR, NEW ZEALANDERS IN THE). The cruiser HMNZS *Gambia* replaced the battle-damaged *Leander* in September 1943 and, with *Achilles*, took part in the final strikes against Japan as part of the British Pacific Fleet, as did HMNZS *Arbutus*.

Even amid the pressing demands of waging war, the outlines of an immediate post-war naval policy were being delineated in the terms of the 1944 ★Australia–New Zealand Agreement, which emphasised a regional defence zone in the South Pacific and recognition of the fundamental importance of a friendly United States. The naval requirement for continuing training opportunities with the Royal Navy was recognised. Although this higher strategic direction had been laid down, the early post-war years were difficult ones for the RNZN, as the Naval Board struggled with the demands of defining the shape of the post-war navy and the difficulties of manning it. The war had delayed consideration of the exact form a national navy should take and as it turned out the pre-war composition of two cruisers with auxiliary warships was to continue for too long.

Achilles and *Gambia* reverted to the Royal Navy, being replaced in 1946 by the Dido class loaned

Royal New Zealand Navy

★cruisers HMNZS *Black Prince* and *Bellona*. The RNZN's maximum wartime strength of about 10,500 had to be reduced to just over 2500 men, with the WRNZNS being disbanded. While some wartime personnel and reservists chose to stay on in the RNZN, there were too few, and manning shortages meant that only *Bellona* and the corvette *Arbutus* could be kept in commission, and the other ships were put into reserve. In February 1947 dissatisfaction over new pay rates (markedly lower than civilian levels ashore), ineptly handled by the Cabinet and Naval Board, led to ★mutinies (euphemistically described as 'strikes' or 'pay disputes') in *Bellona*, the minesweeper HMNZS *Hautapu*, and the base establishment HMNZS *Philomel*, and 200 ratings walked out. The resulting grave shortage of ratings led to the WRNZNS being re-established in May of the same year. After the heady days of the war, the Naval Board in its dealings with an unsympathetic and parsimonious Cabinet had come up against the reality that New Zealand, while patently a sea-girt nation, is not in peacetime especially conscious of its maritime interests and certainly does not take the continuing need for a navy to be a self-evident truth.

By early 1948, the core fleet composition had been determined. The two cruisers were to be supplemented by six ★frigates, HMNZS *Taupo, Kaniere, Hawea, Pukaki, Tutira,* and *Rotoiti*, which arrived in 1949. These wartime-built Loch class frigates were cheap at £1.5 million for the six and, being capable of anti-submarine and convoy escort duties and having a good cruising range, were well suited to the protection of sea communications. When *Bellona* and five of the frigates engaged in exercises with the RAN in 1949, they represented the largest RNZN post-war squadron of major warships ever assembled. In 1947, the RNZNVR was reconstituted with divisions in Auckland, Wellington, Christchurch, and Dunedin.

The RNZN's strategic direction soon changed with the beginnings of the ★Cold War. New Zealand had agreed to send frigates to defend ★Hong Kong and Malaya from Chinese attack, and in the event of war with the Soviet Union was committed to reinforcing Commonwealth forces in the Middle East to prevent a Russian drive from the Caucasus to the Suez Canal and Persian Gulf oilfields (see MIDDLE EAST COMMITMENT). As an expression of this, *Taupo* and *Hawea* were sent on exchange to the Royal Navy's Mediterranean Fleet in April 1950. When the government resolved to contribute naval forces to the ★United Nations effort in the ★Korean War, *Pukaki* and *Tutira* were the only frigates available for deployment at short notice. They sailed from Auckland on 3 July 1950, five days after the UN request. Based at the Japanese port of Sasebo, and serving within a Royal Navy framework, the frigates escorted supply convoys from Japan to Pusan, took part in the Inch'on landings, and patrolled the Korean coast. Through to September 1954, all the frigates did a tour in Korea (*Hawea* and *Rotoiti* did two), but keeping two frigates there together proved to be a strain both on naval manpower and on the maintenance programme. At times raiding parties were put ashore behind enemy positions on the west coast and the only RNZN battle casualty of the Korean War, an able seaman from *Rotoiti*, was killed in one of these forays in August 1951. In February 1952, *Taupo* joined an American destroyer in destroying a number of enemy sampans off the island of Yang-do. The New Zealand frigates which spent short periods under UN command in Korean waters from September 1954 to May 1959 were detached from the Royal Navy's Far East Fleet; from 1955 they were part of the ★British Commonwealth Far East Strategic Reserve. While the operational commitment was in Korea, the RNZN was involved in distasteful work at home during the 1951 state of emergency, when naval personnel replaced striking watersiders in the main ports, provided crews for coastal ships, and laboured in coal mines (see INDUSTRIAL DISPUTES, USE OF ARMED FORCES IN).

The numbers of the RNZN's minor war vessels were significantly increased in early 1952 by the receipt, as a gift, of four of the RAN's Bathurst class minesweepers, which were promptly placed in reserve owing to a manning shortage but later became training ships. In 1956, the modernised Dido class cruiser HMNZS *Royalist* replaced *Bellona*, and the first two modern anti-submarine frigates to replace the obsolescent Loch types were ordered—the Otago class HMNZS *Otago* and *Taranaki*, armed with twin 4.5-inch guns and (from 1963) Seacat surface-to-air ★missiles.

The 1957 defence review came at a time when strategic thinking had shifted away from potential Middle East commitments to a renewed Pacific and Asian emphasis. The role of the RNZN in the new era of ★ANZUS, ★ANZAM, and ★SEATO was to cooperate with Allied forces in the protection of trade routes, the denial of the seas to an enemy, and the support of land forces with a fleet composed of one cruiser, four frigates, and eight seaward defence motor launches. A cruiser and two frigates were in reserve. This was an ambitious concept considering that at this date the RNZN with 2500 ratings was well below its authorised ceiling of 3500. A cruiser was to alternate with one or two frigates as a contribution to the Singapore-based Commonwealth Strategic Reserve, an operational pattern centred on a South-east Asian presence which persisted until 1989 when ★New Zealand Force South East Asia was withdrawn. *Royalist* participated in SEATO exercises and with *Pukaki* had a minor role in the ★Malayan Emergency of the late 1950s, bombarding suspected communist terrorist positions. During ★Confrontation with Indonesia in 1963–66 the frigates on station as well as two minesweepers HMNZS *Hickleton* and *Santon*, especially commissioned to serve with a British squadron, carried out anti-infiltration patrols around Borneo and in the Malacca and Singapore Straits.

A major reorganisation of defence administration in the 1960s led to the effective abolition of the Naval Board, though the process was not formally complete until 1971. The RNZN, in common with the Army and RNZAF, came under the new ★Defence Council. It was some compensation for this loss of autonomy that the Chief of Naval Staff, Rear-Admiral Peter ★Phipps, became the first Chief of Defence Staff as a vice-admiral. In early 1966, the 'cruiser era' came to an end with the scrapping of *Royalist*, which had been confined to harbour following an embarrassing machinery breakdown during a voyage home from Singapore. The new frigate HMNZS *Waikato* was still being built, so HMNZS *Blackpool* was temporarily hired from the Royal Navy to supplement *Otago* and *Taranaki*. A naval air capacity, which had lapsed after the removal of the Walrus amphibians from the cruisers in 1942, reappeared with the ordering of two Westland Wasp torpedo-carrying ★helicopters for the *Waikato*. Kaman Seasprites, armed with ★torpedoes and air-to-surface missiles, have been ordered to replace the Wasps as aircraft for the Anzac frigates. RNZN helicopters are piloted by naval officers but maintained by seagoing RNZAF technical crews. A new Leander class frigate, HMNZS *Canterbury*, was commissioned in October 1971, replacing *Blackpool*, which was returned to the Royal Navy.

With only two 4.5-inch guns, the RNZN frigates of the time were not considered suitable for extended naval gunfire support operations in the ★Vietnam War. They would not, as British vessels, have fitted in easily in an American-dominated naval theatre (though the RAN did operate one such vessel in Vietnamese waters for a period). In consequence, the RNZN contribution in Vietnam was a small one, with twenty-seven members serving in a tri-service medical team from 1967 to 1971. New Zealand supported Britain in the ★Falklands War by sending a frigate to replace a British ship in the Indian Ocean, *Canterbury* and *Waikato* each being deployed twice to the area in 1982–83. A thirty-strong contingent was sent to Cambodia in 1993 as part of UN-sponsored ★peace-keeping operations, patrolling rivers and coastal waters. Naval medical personnel again served as part of the New Zealand contribution to the ★Gulf War in 1991. In 1995 and 1996, HMNZS *Wellington* and *Canterbury* were assigned for some months to the Multinational Interception Force in the Arabian and Persian Gulfs, an international task group enforcing United Nations economic sanctions against Iraq. Naval personnel have also served as members of peace-keeping units in Kashmir, Angola, Bosnia–Herzegovina, and the Sinai.

The RNZN diving branch, which was prominent in salvage operations on the sabotaged *Rainbow Warrior* in 1985, has its own modern tender HMNZS *Manawanui*, while the four Naval Reserve divisions were given an operational role from 1979 in naval control of shipping and mine countermeasures. Each has a Whangarei-built inshore patrol craft—HMNZS *Hinau*, *Kiwi*, *Moa*, and *Wakakura*.

The scrapping of the last cruiser in 1966 also signalled the end of the six-frigate navy; a nominal four-frigate standard was proclaimed in the 1966 defence review but was never consistently achieved, and in 1978 the drop to a three-frigate standard was endorsed. At present even a three-frigate standard (reaffirmed in 1998) with ships all of the same class appears to have become an unattainable ideal. The 1978 defence review resolved a question which had been debated for some time—would the RNZN be degraded to coastguard status or remain a 'blue-water navy'? The answer was that the maritime security of New Zealand demanded that the RNZN continue to be a combat force, albeit one impaired by the reduction in the number of its major warships to three only. While the options for a replacement frigate type were being examined, two second-hand Leanders were purchased from the Royal Navy. *Wellington* arrived in October 1982, immediately going into an extended refit which lasted more than three years. *Southland*, fitted with Ikara missiles, was delayed by a refit in Britain, and came out to New Zealand in July 1984. In between, a proposal for submarines to replace the frigates made an appearance in the 1983 defence white paper, but was recognised for the costly aberration it was and quickly abandoned.

Modifications of the Leanders did not alter the reality that this class in both the RNZN and the RAN was obsolescent. New Zealand cooperated with Australia in the Anzac frigate project, in which the ships, based on the German MEKO design, were to be constructed in Williamstown, Victoria, in a scheme which gave many opportunities for New Zealand industry to be involved. New Zealand agreed to buy two frigates with an option to buy two more. By 1999 HMNZS *Te Kaha*, the second of the class, was in service, HMNZS *Te Mana* was undergoing sea trials, and the option to buy the third frigate had been declined. These new frigates have a crew of 164, a significant reduction on the number required for a Leander type. Unlike the Australian versions, they do not have the full fit of weapons and have been criticised by a parliamentary inquiry for that reason.

Royal New Zealand Navy

The issue of nuclear weapon tests was viewed relatively benignly by the government in 1957, when *Pukaki* and *Rotoiti* supported the British programme of tests at Christmas Island, but attitudes had strikingly changed by 1973 when New Zealand's determined opposition to French nuclear tests in the Pacific was signified by the stationing of a frigate (provisioned and fuelled by the Australian tanker HMAS *Supply*) near the French test zone at Moruroa Atoll. This was a deliberate and well-publicised political ploy, designed to bring New Zealand indignation to the attention of the world while avoiding a naval confrontation with the French. The Moruroa protests were the action of a Labour government, so it was not surprising that a later Labour government took an even stronger anti-nuclear stance in 1984–85 by banning nuclear-armed vessels from New Zealand ports. Long-established arrangements with the United States, an ANZUS partner, and with Britain for joint exercises and specialist naval training collapsed, while cooperation with the RAN, a very US Navy–oriented service, was seriously strained.

Nuclear testing was the principal South Pacific issue involving the RNZN in the 1960s, but the emphasis changed when New Zealand became involved in various regional political episodes. *Wellington*, heading for Suva in 1987 at the time of the first of the ★Fiji coups, stayed offshore to evacuate New Zealanders if necessary and later docked in the port, while in 1990 in Bougainville HMNZS *Endeavour* was the venue for peace negotiations between the Papua New Guinea government and the Bougainville insurgents. *Canterbury*, *Endeavour*, and *Manawanui* supported the New Zealand Truce Monitoring Team in 1997–98. The lack of a ship to land a sizeable military force should this be required in the South Pacific spurred the acquisition of a Danish roll-on roll-off merchant ship in 1995 (see SUPPLY SHIPS). Named the *Charles Upham* after New Zealand's foremost Army hero, she was to be converted to a military sea-lift ship in a two-stage process. However, the final stage was left in abeyance in mid 1998 and the ship let to charter for two years.

Fisheries protection had been a naval responsibility since 1946, but with the promulgation of a 200 nautical mile (370 kilometre) exclusive economic zone in 1978 the protection of marine resources became more prominent in statements of naval policy. For much of the post-war era, fisheries protection had been the task of a few wooden motor launches. These were replaced by four new Lake class ★patrol craft in 1975, which were phased out in the early 1980s when official observers were routinely placed in foreign fishing vessels. Routine monitoring of the EEZ is carried out by the Ministry of Fisheries, using a combination of satellite surveillance and patrols by RNZAF Orion aircraft. RNZN involvement is now minimal, even though warships on passage through the zone will occasionally send a boarding party to fishing vessels to check on compliance with fishery regulations.

★Hydrographic surveying, which had been in abeyance since 1937, was resumed in October 1948 when an Australian ship was hired to initiate the post-war surveying programme. HMNZS *Lachlan* continued in service as a hydrographic vessel until the 1970s, when she was replaced by a converted trading ship renamed HMNZS *Monowai* after the earlier armed merchant cruiser. The wooden harbour defence motor launches used for inshore surveying were replaced in 1980 by larger purpose-built steel vessels—HMNZS *Takapu* and *Tarapunga*. A hydrographic office was set up in 1950 to produce charts, a task previously carried out by the Royal Navy. Research into scientific questions concerned with the military use of the sea is a function of a Defence laboratory in Auckland. Such investigations were supported for many years by a small oceanographic ship, HMNZS *Tui* (leased from the US Navy in 1970, and replacing a converted minesweeper of the same name), but from 1998 HMNZS *Resolution*, a former USN oceanographic ship, superseded both *Monowai* and *Tui*.

The Ross Sea Dependency has been administered by New Zealand since 1923, and while naval vessels had made voyages to the subantarctic islands, it was the requirement to transport and maintain the New Zealand Trans-Antarctic Expedition of 1957 which led to the acquisition of the first HMNZS *Endeavour* (formerly the *John Biscoe*, a veteran ice-strengthened support ship). The second *Endeavour*, an ex-US Navy Patapsco class tanker, replenished Scott Base every summer from 1962 to 1970, when the naval commitment ended. The third *Endeavour*, a Korean-built tanker, arrived in Auckland in 1988.

In the early post-war years the RNZN still relied heavily on British officers and technical ratings. Simultaneously with the acquisition of the Loch class frigates, the Cabinet approved the recruitment of additional Royal Navy men. The Naval Board set an upper limit of 25 per cent for Royal Navy personnel in the RNZN, though this figure was slightly exceeded in the early 1950s. The preponderance of former Royal Navy officers continued for many years, not an unexpected circumstance given that the first RNZN midshipmen had only been appointed in 1940. It was not until 1960 that the first New Zealand-born officer, Phipps, became CNS. The symbols of national identity were also slow in coming. In common with other Commonwealth navies, uniform and insignia have essentially remained identical to those of the Royal Navy; 'New Zealand' shoulder flashes worn by ratings during the

1939–45 war were for a long time optional for officers. About 1973 a stylised kiwi appeared on warship funnels, but when a distinctive New Zealand naval ensign replaced the White Ensign in 1968, the demeaning British practice of allowing the national naval flag to be used by a favoured yacht club was repeated.

The WRNZNS was disbanded in 1977, with its members being fully integrated with the RNZN proper. The first female captain was appointed in 1994. In 1989 female crew members were authorised for service in certain vessels and inevitably, as an institution with a strongly masculine ethos struggles with gender integration, the RNZN has had to live with some well-publicised sexual harassment cases.

The RNZN as a separate service contemplates an uncertain future. The theme of a naval struggle for adequate resources versus governmental scepticism noted in the early post-war years continues to resonate to the present day with the cancellation of the third Anzac frigate option. Public opinion is fickle; those who live surrounded by the sea do not necessarily value maritime defence. The process of whittling down the RNZN continues. In 1999 a replacement frigate for the Leanders had yet to be announced, while final conversion of the *Charles Upham* to a functional military sea-lift ship was not assured. Plans were in train to reduce the number of naval personnel from 2075 to 1861. The Naval Dockyard at Devonport was privatised in August 1994, and the RNZN lost prime responsibility for hydrographic services to Land Information New Zealand in 1997, leaving the Hydrographic Office as merely a contractor for chart-making. A vocal section of the National-led coalition Cabinet urged that the whole naval base be shifted from Auckland to a provincial port in order that Defence facilities could be made available for property development. Such a move would wrench the New Zealand fleet from its long-standing operational base and sever 150 years of historic association between the navy and the Auckland community. The advent of a Labour-led coalition government in December 1999 introduced new uncertainties about naval defence arrangements.

G. Howard, *The Navy in New Zealand: An Illustrated History* (A.H. & A.W. Reed, Wellington, 1982); G. Howard, *Portrait of the Royal New Zealand Navy: A Fiftieth Anniversary Celebration* (Grantham House, Wellington, 1991).

DENIS FAIRFAX

Royal New Zealand Nursing Corps New Zealand's first military nurses were usually the wives of volunteers, attached to ★Volunteer Force corps in an honorary capacity. At least thirty-one nurses were funded by public subscription to go to the ★Boer War, the first four departing in January 1900. However, the

A group of New Zealand nurses with the Minister of Defence, Frederick Jones, in Tunisia in 1943 (*War History Collection, Alexander Turnbull Library, F-3049-1/4-DA*)

Royal Regiment of New Zealand Artillery

military authorities showed little interest in establishing a nursing service in New Zealand. Although a New Zealand Medical Corps Nursing Reserve was authorised in 1908, no action was taken to bring it into being. Even after Hester ★MacLean was appointed matron-in-chief in 1911, bureaucratic inertia ensured that it would be another two years before the first nurses volunteered for service. Six nurses were sent to Samoa in August 1914 (see SAMOA, NEW ZEALAND'S MILITARY ROLE IN), but it was not until 1915 that the New Zealand Army Nursing Service was formed. On 8 April the first contingent of fifty nurses left to join 1NZEF. In all 550 nurses served with the NZANS during the ★First World War, either on board hospital ships or in hospitals in Egypt, ★Salonika, France, and Great Britain. Ten nurses lost their lives when their ship, HMT *Marquette*, was torpedoed (see *MARQUETTE*, SINKING OF). Approximately another hundred New Zealand nurses served with British or French forces, getting as far afield as ★Mesopotamia, Russia, and Serbia. In spite of the NZANS's valuable role in the First World War, it was not reconstituted until 1936. Nurses accompanied the first echelon of 2NZEF when it left New Zealand in January 1940, and took part in all the subsequent campaigns. Other nurses served in the Pacific with 2NZEF and with the RNZAF, on board hospital ships, on ambulance trains, and in all military hospitals in New Zealand. Altogether 602 nurses served overseas. The medical section of the Women's Auxiliary Army Corps also performed basic nursing duties, about 211 of its members going to Egypt and Italy. New Zealand nurses also served with ★Jayforce. In 1947 members of the WAAC medical section became other ranks in the NZANS. The service was renamed the Royal New Zealand Nursing Corps in 1953, the better to reflect its inter-service nature. During the ★Vietnam War, a handful of nurses served with the civilian surgical team in Vietnam from 1965 and with the New Zealand Services Medical Unit from 1967. In 1976 the system of ranks (matron, sister, etc.) peculiar to the corps was abandoned in favour of army rank titles. A year later men were allowed to join the corps, while other ranks from the nursing corps were reassigned to the Royal New Zealand Medical Corps. Since that time nurses have served in the ★Gulf War, Bosnia–Herzegovina, and Bougainville. (See WOMEN IN THE ARMED FORCES)

S. Kendall and D. Corbett, *New Zealand Military Nursing: A History of the Royal New Zealand Nursing Corps Boer War to Present Day* (Privately published, Auckland, 1990).

Royal Regiment of New Zealand Artillery is the senior corps of the ★New Zealand Army. Its ★Volunteer Force antecedents date from February 1866, when the first field artillery battery and naval artillery corps were formed. For administrative purposes the various field artillery batteries were grouped as the New Zealand Regiment of Artillery Volunteers and given alphabetical designations in 1878. Naval artillery batteries were formed into the New Zealand Garrison Artillery Volunteers in 1902. The development of the ★coast defences in the mid 1880s led to the establishment of a small corps of permanent artillerymen within the ★Permanent Militia. These were designated the Royal New Zealand Artillery on 15 October 1902. With the formation of the ★Territorial Force in 1911, the Regiment of New Zealand Field Artillery Volunteers (as it had been retitled in 1903) and the New Zealand Garrison Artillery Volunteers were subsumed within the New Zealand Artillery, forming the New Zealand Garrison Artillery and the New Zealand Field Artillery respectively. The permanent RNZA continued in its instructional and cadre role. After the ★First World War the New Zealand Artillery was titled the Regiment of New Zealand Artillery. In January 1947 it was amalgamated with the RNZA. In 1958 the regiment was redesignated as the Royal Regiment of New Zealand Artillery. (See ARTILLERY)

Rules of war are the product of three traditions: a chivalric sense of honour among warriors, Christian ideals of pacifism and mercy, and a legalistic conception of barbaric behaviour as neither rational nor just. Fundamental benchmarks of the rules of war included the acceptance of surrender from a defeated enemy, the humane treatment of ★prisoners of war, and the recognition of a white flag as a sign of willingness to parley. These rules were codified in 1864 in the Geneva Convention, which was signed by all major European powers. These conventions have been periodically revised, notably in 1929 and 1949, in these instances taking account of the experiences of the ★First and ★Second World Wars respectively.

During the ★New Zealand Wars both Maori and British generally fought according to the accepted rules of war—indeed, rules of conduct were established unilaterally by Maori combatants prior to the Battle of Gate Pa/Pukehinahina, and British wounded were treated mercifully. On the other hand, a possible attempt by the Maori defenders of the redoubt at Rangiriri to parley under a white flag was taken as surrender, while British forces sacked Ngaruawahia. Maori attacked settler homesteads, and settler forces burnt Maori villages. As the conflict dragged on (with Maori resistance becoming religiously based and settlers regarding Maori resistance as rebellion), the rules of war were increasingly ignored. Notable incidents included ★Te Kooti's massacre of settlers and pro-government Maori at Turangi (the 'Poverty Bay Massacre'), and the mass execution of Hauhau prisoners by Ropata ★Wahawaha after the siege of Ngatapa.

In the wars in which New Zealand has been involved overseas, the rules of war, as applying at the time, have generally been observed, though with some notable exceptions. For example, during the ★Boer War, as the conflict shifted to its less conventional phase, British (including New Zealand) troops began systematically burning Boer farms and executing Boer guerrillas found with British uniforms or rifles. In the heat of combat, observance of the rules of war in relation to the taking of POWs has often been ignored by both sides. Only occasionally have New Zealand personnel been accused of more deliberate breaches, such as the summary execution of enemy POWs. Although generally adhering to the rules of war in the Middle East and Western Europe in the Second World War, the Germans adopted a very different approach against the Russians on the Eastern Front. Existing conventions were routinely and deliberately ignored in this conflict, which was rendered more bitter by the racial conceptions underlying the German approach. Racial factors also increased the brutality of the ★Pacific War, in which Japanese forces committed many breaches of the conventions of war. However, the impact on New Zealand servicemen was reduced by the relatively small ground force involvement in this conflict.

Both world wars indicated gaps in the rules of war. The First had raised questions as to the status of POWs, and an attempt was made to address these in the 1929 Geneva Convention. A similar reconsideration was prompted by the experience of 1939–45, especially in relation to the treatment of civilians, who had died in unprecedented numbers as a result of military operations, especially bombing raids. A new agreement, in 1949, included four conventions, covering the treatment of wounded and sick in the field, the treatment of wounded, sick, or shipwrecked at sea, the treatment of POWs, and the protection of civilians. Additional protocols were added in 1977 relating to the protection of victims of international and internal conflicts. Other agreements setting out the rules of war include the 1954 Hague Convention for the Protection of Cultural Property in the Event of Armed Conflict, the 1977 Convention on the Prohibition of Military or Any Other Hostile Use of Environment Modification Techniques, and the 1980 UN Convention on Certain Conventional Weapons. The Geneva Conventions are embodied in New Zealand law. (See WAR CRIMES TRIALS)

Russell, Lance-Corporal David (30 March 1911–28 February 1945). A hospital orderly from Napier, Scottish-born Russell joined 2NZEF in September 1939, and served with 22nd Battalion in ★Greece and ★Crete. In July 1942, during the ★North African campaign, he was captured at Ruweisat Ridge. After escaping from his Italian POW camp late in 1943, he made contact with an Allied mission and assisted several other escaped POWs to reach Allied lines before being recaptured in early 1945. Escaping again, he found refuge with an Italian peasant, but was recaptured by Italian Fascists on or about 22 February. With the Italian peasant, he was subjected to an intense interrogation, but, despite being tortured, he did not incriminate the peasant, who was eventually released. For three days Russell steadfastly refused to disclose the whereabouts of other POWs or partisans, before being shot by a firing squad at Ponte de Piave on 28 February 1945. When his fortitude was subsequently recognised by the posthumous award of a ★George Cross, he became the first New Zealand recipient of this decoration.

Russell, Major-General Sir Andrew Hamilton ('Guy') (23 February 1868–29 November 1960) was New Zealand's pre-eminent citizen soldier. Born at Napier, he was the fourth in line to be named Andrew Hamilton, but was given the nickname 'Guy' as an infant. His great-grandfather had died while serving in the Peninsular War in 1811, and both his father and grandfather had come to New Zealand as officers in the 58th Regiment. He was educated in the United Kingdom, and won entry to the Royal Military College, Sandhurst, in 1886. After graduating with the sword for general proficiency, he served as a junior officer in the 1st Battalion, the Border Regiment, from 1887 to 1892, most of the time in India, and took part in active operations in Burma. Finding the prospect of garrison service in England unappealing, however, he resigned his commission to return to Hawke's Bay, where he took up sheepfarming at Tunanui. In 1900 he resumed his military career, when he formed and commanded the Hawke's Bay Mounted Rifles Volunteers. By the time the ★Territorial Force was created in 1911, he held the rank of major in the New Zealand Militia, and was commanding the 4th Regiment, Wellington (East Coast) Mounted Rifles Volunteers. He became commander of the 2nd (Wellington) Mounted Rifles Brigade, but declined an invitation to join the ★New Zealand Staff Corps in 1912. During the waterfront strike in the following year he was heavily involved in organising 'Massey's Cossacks', the Territorial-based special constables deployed in Wellington to help maintain order (see CIVIL POWER, AID TO).

With the formation of 1NZEF in 1914, Russell was given command of the New Zealand Mounted Rifles Brigade. He left New Zealand with the Main Body on 16 October 1914 as the highest ranked Territorial officer in the force. At ★Gallipoli, where his brigade was committed as infantry on 13 May 1915, he was responsible for the northern section of the Anzac defences, establishing his headquarters less than thirty metres behind the support trenches on what later became known as Russell's Top. After his brigade had successfully repelled an all-out Turkish onslaught on 19 May, he consolidated the position. During the August offensive, his brigade seized the foothills below Chunuk Bair to open a way for the infantry assault on the summit. In later attempts to seize Hill 60, it suffered heavy casualties and was subsequently withdrawn temporarily to Lemnos. On 27 November 1915 Russell, who had recently been made a KCMG, assumed command of the *New Zealand and Australian Division, which was successfully evacuated from the peninsula twenty-two days later. He would later be described by Mediterranean Expeditionary Force commander Sir Ian *Hamilton as 'beyond doubt the outstanding personality on the Peninsula' of those who survived.

Russell commanded the New Zealand Division on the *Western Front from May 1916 until the end of the war. He brought to his task the practical commonsense of a successful sheepfarmer, an atypical (among his compatriots) familiarity with the continent (gained on visits to his family, which had resided in Switzerland since the early 1880s), a useful ability to speak both French and German, and some background in the British Army. As ever, he emphasised intensive training and strict discipline. He made regular inspections of his units in the front line, often taking considerable risks (in 1917 a sniper's bullet creased his scalp), and insisted that they adopt an aggressive stance towards the enemy with a view to dominating no man's land. His skill as a commander was evident both on the Somme in September–October 1916 and at Messines in June 1917. For the latter operation, he developed a bold plan, and persisted with it even after doubts had been expressed at the highest levels. Although the plan worked perfectly, and the village was taken with minimal casualties, he was aggrieved when ordered to sustain a much larger force than he intended in the forward positions, with the result that many casualties were suffered during ensuing German artillery bombardments. At Passchendaele in October 1917, his usual attention to detail was lacking, and his division suffered its most serious set-back of the war when confronted by uncut barbed wire and inadequately supported by artillery. Afterwards he blamed himself for the disaster. He worked hard during the winter to restore the morale of his division, which had been further depressed by heavy losses at Polderhoek in December, and to maintain its high standard of training. Despite poor health, he came into his own as a tactical commander during the crisis precipitated by the German offensive in early 1918 and the

The commander of the New Zealand Division, Major-General Sir Andrew Russell, inspects one of the Otago Regiment's battalions on the Western Front (*RSA Collection, Alexander Turnbull Library, PA1-f-091-0439*)

subsequent counter-offensive, which eventually forced an armistice. His qualities were recognised by the Commander-in-Chief, Sir Douglas Haig, who offered him a corps in June 1918; before Russell was in a position to accept such an appointment, however, the opportunity had passed. By war's end he had been mentioned in dispatches nine times, and had been made a CB (1916) and a KCB (1917). Upon his return to New Zealand he was hailed as 'Ariki Toa' ('The fighting chief sent forward to lead').

Back at Tunanui in 1919, he resumed sheepfarming, but retained a keen interest in his former charges, serving as President of the New Zealand Returned Soldiers' Association from 1921 to 1924 and again from 1926 to 1935. An attempt in 1922 to enter Parliament as a Reform Party candidate failed, but he was prominent in a number of conservative causes between the wars. As President of the National Defence League, he was a persistent advocate of maintaining effective military forces. He also served as honorary colonel of the Wellington Regiment and the Wellington (East Coast) Mounted Rifles. At the outset of the ★Second World War, he gave advice and support on the formation of 2NZEF. He became a member of the ★War Council in June 1940. From 23 September he was Inspector-General of the Forces, in which capacity he energetically inspected units and facilities throughout New Zealand. For nearly three months from October to December 1940 he was acting CGS in the absence overseas of Major-General J.E. ★Duigan. After resigning from his position on 31 July 1941, Russell resumed his seat on the War Council and served until its disbandment in August 1942.

Russian intervention With the disintegration of the Russian war effort amid revolutionary turmoil in 1917, the British sought both to protect large amounts of supplies shipped to the northern Russian ports of Murmansk and Archangel in support of the Tsarist armies and to re-create an Eastern Front. A military mission was dispatched to the ports, with a view to training a 'White' Russian force. In the North Russian Expeditionary Force (NREF) there were four New Zealand volunteers, who were employed as instructors at Archangel. As the civil war in Russia became more intense, the security of the force deteriorated, and the decision was taken in March 1919 to withdraw it. So bad had the situation become, however, that a covering force was deemed necessary to extricate it. In the voluntary North Russian Relief Force (NRRF), which was quickly raised and deployed at Archangel in June 1919, there were a number of 1NZEF personnel. Other New Zealanders serving in Royal Navy and RAF units also took part in the NRRF's offensive in August, which drove the Bolsheviks back with heavy casualties; at least one New Zealander in the RAF lost his life.

Behind this shield the withdrawal of the NREF was unimpeded, and the last members of the NRRF left Murmansk on 12 October.

During 1918 an Allied presence had also been established in southern Russia. A small force, designated Dunsterforce after its commander, Major-General Lionel Dunsterville, was deployed to prevent the Turks and Germans from taking over the Caucasus region, with its valuable oil resources. It included thirty-seven 1NZEF officers and NCOs, who volunteered to take part in January 1918. In addition, there were several New Zealand naval personnel in an RNAS armoured car unit which formed part of the force (see ROYAL NAVY IN THE FIRST WORLD WAR, NEW ZEALANDERS IN). In April 1918 most of the 1NZEF personnel under the command of Major Frederick ★Starnes set off from Baghdad for Bijar in north-west Iran, where they trained local Kurdish levies. Some went further north to support Armenians, during which a New Zealand officer was killed and a sergeant earned a DCM while protecting a column of Armenian refugees from Turks and Kurds. A handful of New Zealanders under Lieutenant Edwin Wills went on to Baku, Wills acting as one of Dunsterville's intelligence officers. By late 1918 Dunsterforce had become embroiled in the ethnic and political turmoil of the area, but the collapse of the Central Powers had removed its raison d'être, and it was withdrawn early in 1919.

Russian scares were the most prominent of a series of panics which beset the public in the late nineteenth century whenever the British Empire came into confrontation with other powers. A sense of vulnerability arising from New Zealand's isolation was often exacerbated by a lack of up-to-date information about the international situation. Until 1876, when New Zealand was linked by cable to London, news took months to reach New Zealand; the ★Crimean War had, for example, been in progress for ninety-six days before word of its outbreak reached Wellington. Paradoxically, more up-to-date information after 1876 only served to heighten apprehension. Tension arising from international crises had immediate impact on New Zealanders, who were impelled to look to their defences against the possibility of a sudden raid. Numerous breaks in the cable link in its early days also caused anxiety. The first Russian scare arose over the Crimean War, leading to minor defence measures being instituted at Point Britomart in Auckland. There were periodic scares involving other powers—France in 1859 or the United States in 1862, for example—but Russia remained the bogey for most New Zealanders for the next half-century. The possibility of Russian raids in the South Pacific arose in 1863 and 1871, and in 1873 a public panic was instigated in Auckland by a newspaper hoax (see HOAXES);

Russian scares

A 64-pounder gun mounted *en barbette* at Kaiwharawhara, Wellington, as a result of the 1885 Russian scare (*NZ Police Centennial Museum*)

such concerns were not entirely unfounded, for there is some evidence of Russian plans to mount raiding operations in 1878 and 1884. In 1878 public anxiety reached unprecedented proportions when cables from London indicated that war between the British and Russian Empires was imminent. There was a near-panic in Wellington on 9 February 1878 when an unidentified ship, assumed to be a Russian raider but subsequently found to be an innocent British merchantman, steamed into the harbour. Urgent steps were taken to put the defences in order, but once the crisis subsided procrastination again became the order of the day. New Zealand's lack of protection against raids ensured renewed panic when an Anglo-Russian war again became a possibility as a result of the *Pendjeh crisis in 1885. The situation was not helped by another hoax: a Wanganui newspaper caused 'great excitement' by printing a detailed report of a Russian raid on Wellington. Public meetings throughout the country demanded immediate defensive preparations at the ports, and finally precipitated action on *coast defences. Although the crisis subsided, Russia remained a focus of New Zealand concern for another two decades. New Zealanders were strongly anti-Russian when war broke out between the Russian Empire and Japan, a British ally, in 1904. However, the Japanese navy's annihilation of the Russian Baltic Fleet at Tsushima in 1905 finally ended Russophobia in New Zealand—assisted by improving relations between London and St Petersburg in the face of rising German power in Europe. After 1905 it was Japanese, not Russian, power in the Pacific that aroused concern among New Zealanders.

G. Barratt, *Russophobia in New Zealand 1838–1908* (Dunmore Press, Palmerston North, 1981); I. McGibbon, *The Path to Gallipoli: Defending New Zealand 1840–1915* (GP Books, Wellington, 1991).

S

Salonika A strategically important port in northeastern Greece, Salonika (Thessaloniki) was occupied by the Allies in September 1915 (even though Greece was neutral) to support the Serbian Army, which had been driven out of its own country by the Austro-Hungarians. Contained in a narrow pocket, the Allies clung on to the city for the next three years, the stalemate mirroring that on the ★Western Front. A New Zealand presence was established at Salonika in October 1915 when the 1st New Zealand Stationary Hospital was dispatched there from Egypt. The transfer was marked by tragedy, when the troopship carrying the New Zealanders was torpedoed; thirty-two lost their lives (see MARQUETTE, SINKING OF). After reaching Salonika, the survivors established a tent hospital. Although fighting was limited, they were kept busy treating cases of frostbite, typhoid, and dysentery until March 1916, when they were withdrawn for service in France. In 1941 New Zealand troops would return to the area in an ill-fated attempt to prevent German forces overrunning ★Greece.

Samoa, New Zealand's military role in On 29 August 1914 New Zealand troops landed at Apia and took possession of Germany's Samoan colony—the second Germany territory, after Togoland, to fall to the Allies in the ★First World War. This action had been precipitated by a British request to the New Zealand government on 6 August to capture the wireless station in Samoa 'as a great and urgent Imperial service'. So rapid was the response that a 1374-strong composite force, mainly comprising Territorials, was ready to leave on 11 August. It included three companies of infantry, drawn from the 5th Wellington and 3rd Auckland Regiments, a field artillery battery, and elements from other corps, under the command of Colonel Robert ★Logan. When approached, Australian intelligence authorities indicated that the New Zealanders would face a German-officered constabulary of about eighty men and a gunboat, with the possible addition of reservists. The oft-heard story that New Zealand, when it enquired about the defences at Samoa, was told by London to look up *Whitaker's Almanac* is undoubtedly apocryphal.

Worries about the adequacy of the force's escort—the old ★cruisers HMS *Philomel* and *Psyche*—delayed its departure until 15 August, at which time the location of the German East Asiatic Squadron, which included two armoured cruisers, the *Scharnhorst* and *Gneisenau*, had not definitely been established. The initial destination of Suva was changed en route to Noumea to allow for an earlier junction with the battlecruiser HMAS *Australia* and the French cruiser *Montcalm*. This change promoted the myth that the New Zealand ships had narrowly missed being intercepted by the German squadron, which was in fact well to the north in the Marshall Islands at the time. The landing was effected without resistance, and an armed party was immediately dispatched to take possession of the wireless station. Next day, 30 August, the occupation was formally proclaimed, and the troops set about preparing camps and defences. On 14 September some excitement was caused by the appearance of the *Scharnhorst* and *Gneisenau* at Apia, but they made off without firing any shots; heading east, they bombarded Papeete and destroyed a British force at Coronel, off the west coast of South America, before being in turn annihilated by a British squadron at the Falkland Islands.

In April 1915 the New Zealand force in Samoa was reduced to 250 men. Most of the original members of

Samoa

Seamen and marines from HMS *Dunedin* with Mau prisoners in January 1930 (*Penrice Collection*)

the expeditionary force were withdrawn to New Zealand, and men over the age for active military service were dispatched to fill the ranks of the smaller residual force. Although Logan at first, in accordance with international law, sought to administer the territory through the existing German administration, he was soon forced to establish a new administration using local British residents and members of his force. German currency was replaced by British, and German concerns and assets were closed or liquidated. Germans without family ties were later deported. Logan's policy of minimum interference with Samoan life was well received by Samoans, whose support for remaining under British rule increased accordingly. But such feelings were undercut by the *influenza pandemic which struck late in 1918 and carried off one in five Samoans. Logan remained as Administrator until January 1919, when he was temporarily (and later substantively) replaced by Colonel R.W. Tate. At the Peace Conference, New Zealand secured agreement to its administering the territory as a mandate of the *League of Nations (a status officially conferred on 17 December 1920). The garrison was withdrawn early in 1920, and the military occupation was replaced by a civil administration on 1 May 1920.

New Zealand did not find its new charge easy to administer. During the 1920s, partly as a response to paternalistic measures introduced by Major-General G.S. *Richardson, the Administrator from 1923 to 1928, but fundamentally as a reassertion of traditional Samoan politics, an anti-administration movement, the Mau, emerged. The Administration found itself increasingly hard-pressed to maintain its authority. A serious upsurge in unrest followed the deportation of Mau leaders in December 1927. At Richardson's request, the New Zealand cruisers HMS *Dunedin* and *Diomede* were dispatched to Apia in February 1928 in a largely futile bid to overawe the Mau. They arrived off Apia on 21 February under the command of Commodore G.T.C.P. Swabey, the Commodore Commanding the New Zealand Squadron. On the morning of the 23rd, about 200 marines and armed seamen landed in two groups from boats mounted with Maxim guns. As they converged, they arrested four hundred Mau without resistance. Thereafter a search for arms in Apia and nearby villages was carried out, after which the seamen returned to their ships and the marines were stationed at the Central Offices and Vaimea Prison. Further arrests were made on 24 February. The prisoners were eventually held at Mulinu'u, where a double barbed wire fence built across the peninsula provided an ineffectual restraint on them. Patrols were mounted by the marines, but an attempt to arrest the Mau leader Tamasese Leolofi III on 8 March failed when they declined to use force, and henceforth they remained largely in the background. With the government anxious to avoid bloodshed, the limitations of using armed forces to support coercive efforts were demonstrated. Although the cruisers departed from Apia in March 1928, with *Diomede* cruising within two days' steaming distance of the town, the marines remained on shore until the beginning of May. There were no significant incidents.

A force of military policemen—three officers and seventy-one men—was raised in New Zealand to replace the marines. Sworn in under the ★Defence Act 1909, and subject to Army disciplinary regulations, they were gathered at Trentham Camp on 11 April 1928 for a period of intensive training in both police and military duties, before leaving from Auckland aboard the *Tutanekai* ten days later. The force, commanded by Major P.H. Bell, was regarded primarily as a police force, though equipped as a military force and wearing khaki uniforms. After disembarking at Apia on 28 April, the men were quartered in the British Club Barracks. Under the direction of the Administrator, they carried out a variety of tasks, patrolling, collecting dog taxes, and assisting in the arrest of criminals. Occasionally there were violent confrontations, as for example when further attempts, ultimately successful, were made to arrest Tamasese in November 1928. On 11 February 1929 the New Zealand Cabinet agreed to the replacement of the military police by a forty-five-strong civil police force. Twenty-eight of the military policemen volunteered to join this new force, which took over the military police arms and equipment. The rest of the military policemen arrived back in New Zealand on 3 May 1929.

Incidents continued, however. These culminated in an affray on 28 December 1929 (Black Saturday). An attempt to arrest several wanted men in a Mau procession led to a riot in which at least eight Samoans, including Tamasese, were killed by police gunfire. This led to the last phase of New Zealand's military involvement in Samoa. Once again *Dunedin*, now under the command of Commodore Geoffrey ★Blake, was dispatched to Apia, arriving on 12 January 1930. After the Mau had been proclaimed a seditious organisation the following day, about 1200 took to the bush. Two platoons of seamen and marines landed on the 13th, and were later followed by another platoon—about 150 men in all. After settling in, they set off into the bush in pursuit of the Mau. A De Havilland Moth seaplane, flown by Flight-Lieutenant Sidney ★Wallingford, provided a reconnaissance and pamphlet-dropping capability—the first active flying duties by the New Zealand Permanent Air Force. The 'war in the bush' took place in unpleasant climatic conditions for which the men were not well equipped. Their efforts were largely futile, moreover, as the Mau easily evaded them. Several Samoans were killed during these operations; Mau supporters alleged that there were more casualties. During February Mau determination began to falter, especially when the administration moved towards using non-Mau Samoans to assist in the operation. After talks with the Administrator, Colonel S.S. ★Allen, the Mau came out of the bush and dispersed. *Dunedin* left for New Zealand on 13 March, leaving twenty-five marines, who were eventually withdrawn on 4 April 1930. The improvement in the situation prompted the government in Wellington to drop plans to dispatch another force of military policemen, which had been hastily enlisted.

S.J. Smith, *The Samoa (N.Z.) Expeditionary Force 1914–1915* (Ferguson & Osborn Ltd, Wellington, 1924); M. Boyd, 'The Record in Western Samoa to 1945', in A. Ross (ed), *New Zealand's Record in the Pacific Islands in the 20th Century* (Longman Paul, Wellington, 1969).

Sanders, Lieutenant-Commander William Edward (7 February 1883–14 August 1917) was the only New Zealand seaman to win the ★Victoria Cross. An Aucklander by birth, he went to sea as a sixteen-year-old, and was a ship's mate when the ★First World War began. He served as third officer of two ★troopships before being called up as a member of the Royal Naval Reserve in November 1915. Joining the Royal Navy in January 1916, he was commissioned a sub-lieutenant in the following April and, after attending a gunnery course, served at first in minesweepers in the English Channel. He volunteered to serve on ★Q-ships—innocuous-looking merchant ships intended to lure German submarines into range of their disguised guns. After a few actions he was, in February 1917, given command of HMS *Prize*, a 200-ton schooner captured from the Germans and converted into a Q-ship, which operated out of the British port of Milford Haven. On 30 April 1917, Sanders's ship engaged *U-93*. After quickly debarking her 'panic party' and enduring twenty-five minutes of shelling, she opened fire herself when the submarine had moved in close for the kill. The submarine was heavily damaged by this close-range fire, and appeared to sink, with three of its crew, including its commander, being rescued from the sea. The badly damaged *Prize* struggled back to port (as did in fact *U-93*, which ensured that the role and tactics of the *Prize* were henceforth well known to German submariners). Sanders's VC was awarded for his coolness under fire in this action. Another attack on a submarine in June led to his appointment as a DSO. On 13 August 1917 *Prize* was attacked by *U-48*, which quickly withdrew when shelled. After stalking the Q-ship, the German submarine torpedoed her at 1.30 a.m. on 14 August. The ship blew up and sank with all hands. Sanders is commemorated by the Sanders Memorial Scholarship at the

University of Auckland (available to the sons and daughters of members of the Royal Navy or Merchant Marine) and the Sanders Cup for yachting.

Saunders, Air Chief Marshal Sir Hugh William Lumsden

(24 August 1894–8 May 1987) was responsible for initiating New Zealand's air war effort during the *Second World War. Born in Johannesburg, he served in the *First World War with the South African forces, before transferring to the RFC in 1917. An MM, a DFC, and an MC testified to his bravery in action. Following the war, he secured a permanent commission in the RAF and by 1939, when he was seconded to the RNZAF to serve as Chief of the Air Staff, he held the rank of group captain. Among his first duties in Wellington was to attend the *Pacific Defence Conference. Subsequently, he wasted no time in recommending an expansion of New Zealand's pilot training scheme, which was implemented in June 1939. This programme was further augmented following the outbreak of war in September and yet again as a result of the introduction of the *Empire Air Training Scheme. Saunders was a member of the New Zealand delegation to the conference in Ottawa which settled the details of the latter arrangement. With the perceived danger from Japan increasing in 1940, he oversaw the development of air defences in Fiji and began expanding the RNZAF's operational squadrons. These resources proved useful when Japan struck in December 1941, just before Saunders's secondment ended. After returning to the United Kingdom, he commanded Fighter Command's 11 Group before taking up a position in the Air Ministry in 1944. In 1945–46 he commanded the RAF in the Burma theatre. For his war services, he was made a CBE (1941), a CB (1943), and KBE (1945). After commanding Bomber Command in 1947, he served on the Air Council and was Inspector-General of the RAF (1949–50), before assuming command of Air Forces in Western Europe in 1951. He was Air Deputy to the Supreme Allied Commander Europe from 1951 to 1953. He was made a KCB in 1950 and a GCB three years later.

Savage, Michael Joseph

(23 March 1872–27 March 1940) was New Zealand's Prime Minister at the outset of the *Second World War. Australian-born, he emigrated to New Zealand in 1907 and became deeply involved in Labour politics. He was a strong opponent of *conscription during the *First World War. Elected to Parliament for the New Zealand Labour Party in 1919, he rose to lead the party from 1933 and, following the party's sweeping victory in the 1935 general election, became Prime Minister. At the Imperial Conference in London in 1937, he castigated *appeasement of the Fascist dictatorships, and discussed strategic issues with the British authorities, focusing in particular on the plans regarding the *Singapore strategy. His government improved New Zealand's air defences, but efforts to encourage voluntary enlistment in the Army did not produce the required manpower. Ill health—he was afflicted by cancer—forced Savage to leave most of the responsibility for developing New Zealand's response to the outbreak of war in 1939 to his deputy, Peter *Fraser. Nevertheless, on 5 September he made an important broadcast to the nation, during which he eloquently stated New Zealand's stance in the war with Germany: 'Both with gratitude for the past, and with confidence in the future, we range ourselves without fear beside Britain. Where she goes, we go, where she stands, we stand.'

B. Gustafson, *From the Cradle to the Grave: A Biography of Michael Joseph Savage* (Reed Methuen, Auckland, 1986).

Science and technology

have been devoted to war purposes since time immemorial. They underlay, for example, the constant advances in weapons technology in the nineteenth century, many of which had indirect impact on New Zealand's security. Their impact on the *First World War, in which they were applied in a systematic way by both the Allies and the Central Powers, was huge. At that time, however, New Zealand's very limited scientific and industrial base and isolation precluded it from taking any significant direct role in scientific research or technological development, though some inventions and ideas by private New Zealanders were forwarded to the British War Office. Some New Zealand scientists offered their services, but could find a role only in British agencies or services. One of New Zealand's leading scientists, Ernest *Marsden, the Professor of Physics at Victoria University College in Wellington, volunteered for 1NZEF and, while serving on the *Western Front, was seconded to the Royal Engineers, where he was involved in the location of enemy artillery by means of the newly developed sound ranging method.

In Great Britain, the deficiencies in the application of science to industry revealed by the First World War prompted the establishment of a Department of Scientific and Industrial Research (DSIR). The Dominions were urged to take similar steps. New Zealand was slowest to respond, not establishing its own DSIR until 1926. Focused on assisting primary industries, the new body's work initially had little or no application to defence. Indeed, the first specifically defence science research in New Zealand may have been the farcical Penny affair of 1935. Victor Penny of Auckland claimed that he had invented a 'Death Ray' using a radio beam to blow up objects and stop engines, and that he was the target of attention by foreign agents. He was sufficiently convincing for the authorities to install him on Somes Island and later at Fort Dorset to conduct his top secret research, but the project was abandoned in 1936 after having cost the government £1685.

Science for defence purposes in New Zealand really began in 1939, when the resources of the DSIR and its associated research institutes, the science departments of the universities, and the Post and Telegraph Department and other government departments were directed to the war effort. Marsden, now the Secretary of DSIR, was designated Scientific Adviser to the Defence Department (from June 1940 upgraded to Director of Scientific Developments with the rank of lieutenant-colonel). On his advice, a Defence Scientific Advisory Committee (DSAC) of senior New Zealand scientists was created to advise the ★Chiefs of Staff, assist in the formulation of policy, and liaise with scientific organisations overseas. Subcommittees of the DSAC coordinated the work, applying the available scientific and technical knowledge and expertise to immediate defence needs.

One of the first and most extensive projects was in radio direction finding, or radar, as it came to be known. This was a practical variation of the radio 'death-ray' idea dreamed of by many inventors, and had been developed rapidly in Britain in response to the urgent need to provide warning of approaching aircraft. In February 1939 the British ★Committee of Imperial Defence invited the Dominions to send technical representatives to learn about the secret new development. Marsden, who was sent from New Zealand, quickly appreciated not only the value of the new technology but also the fact that it would be some time before any British radar could be spared for New Zealand. He urged the New Zealand government to develop and build its own. A programme began immediately, initially with ad hoc groups of DSIR and university scientists, and Post and Telegraph radio engineers, which were later formalised as the Radio Development Laboratory (RDL).

The New Zealand radar programme was based throughout on improvisation and innovation with very limited resources. Beginning with information, plans, and some parts brought by Marsden from Britain, sets were developed especially for naval range-finding—the first operational New Zealand radar was installed in HMS *Achilles* in July 1940—and for coast warning. Later, attention turned more to the Pacific, and the RDL developed mobile, truck-mounted radar for the particular conditions of that theatre. Since the European theatre took priority for British and American radar production, New Zealand radar filled a real need for a short time in 1943–44 during the closing stages of the ★Solomons campaign. Some was operated by RNZN radar units, but with air-warning sets supplied to American units RDL scientists were put into uniform to operate them. They saw action from the Solomons to Peleliu in the central Pacific. A few RDL scientists also joined radar countermeasures operations with the Allied air forces in the South-west Pacific, using their radar search equipment on missions to detect and destroy Japanese radar. However, by 1945, as British and American radar became widely available in the theatre, the New Zealand radar programme became redundant and was wound down.

Another large project arose after it was decided that some munitions should be manufactured in New Zealand. This demanded engineering work carried out to a higher standard of precision than previously achieved in New Zealand, and the Physical Testing Laboratory established by the DSIR at the outbreak of war was extended to provide the necessary metrology services and to produce the high precision gauges needed for the manufacture of artillery fuses, trench mortars and bombs, grenades, and small-arms ammunition. Renamed the Dominion Physical Laboratory, it grew to become by the end of the war the largest division of the DSIR.

There were many other smaller projects in the physical sciences. DSIR physicists worked on 'degaussing' ships to protect them against magnetic mines. Their university counterparts organised the production of optical components for mortar sights and prismatic compasses, worked on hydrophones and infra-red barrage beams for harbour defence, and developed radio equipment for use in bush country. Chemists worked on anti-gas measures and methods of smoke production for smokescreens.

Existing programmes with special defence significance were extended and their results removed from scientific publication to military secrecy: ionospheric recording for predicting conditions for radio transmission, and magnetic survey for accurate magnetic bearings in navigation. Similarly, the Meteorological Service was transferred from DSIR to ★Air Department control and later to the RNZAF.

Most scientific research in New Zealand up to 1939 had been for primary industries in the biological and geological sciences, which were now also applied to defence needs. There was much work on finding local sources of strategic minerals such as mica and asbestos, or establishing the local production of materials such as linen flax and agar, or extending resources in limited supply such as superphosphate fertiliser. Grasslands scientists advised on how to produce hard-wearing turf for grass runways. Other work aimed to maximise food exports to Britain and to United States forces in the Pacific. Chemists developed processes for the dehydration of butter, fruit, vegetables, and—less successfully—meat. They also worked on providing enough vitamins in ration packs for troops in the Pacific.

Much of the wartime scientific effort was in small-scale, fragmented projects. There was no unified defence science organisation. The Defence Science Advisory Committee and its subcommittees worked to coordinate the effort and to liaise with service authorities, but not always successfully. Some of the work undertaken by the scientists went unused by the services, which tended to distrust local production and preferred to obtain technical equipment from the customary British sources. For instance, when a German refugee scientist working in New Zealand developed FM radio for Army use it went unheeded until it was reinvented overseas.

Under these circumstances there were often more scientists available than could be directly employed in the local war effort. New Zealand was able to supply scientists to Britain and other allies, just as it provided men for the British services. Even in the area of radar development, for which a special university training course was set up to supply local needs, three new graduates were sent overseas in response to an appeal from Britain (unfortunately their ship, the *Rangitane*, was intercepted and sunk by a German raider and they spent the rest of the war in a German POW camp). A contingent of thirty chemists was sent to work in Australia's munitions industry, which was much larger than New Zealand's. Other smaller groups of scientists, engineers, and technicians went to Britain to assist in developments in radio, underwater acoustics, and jet propulsion. In 1944–45 a picked group went to the United States and Canada to work on the Manhattan and Montreal ★atomic bomb projects.

Most of the defence science projects were wound up after the war or redirected to other scientific or industrial purposes. By 1947 only a few projects continued within the DSIR. However, in the following year the New Zealand government approved a plan to undertake scientific research as part of a wider cooperative Commonwealth scientific effort in researching underwater acoustics, sea temperatures, and magnetic conditions for ★anti-submarine warfare. Nevertheless, despite visits from British scientists to advise on underwater research, New Zealand defence science remained a low priority for the government and suffered from a lack of funding and direction. By the early 1950s DSIR heads were becoming uncomfortable with the secrecy and security restrictions associated with defence projects. After pressure from scientists and the armed forces, the government agreed in 1955 to transfer remaining naval defence science work from the DSIR to the Naval Research Laboratory (NRL) to establish a programme of underwater research. The NRL undertook acoustic and magnetic surveys of the seabed, and from 1960 also carried out metallurgical testing for the RNZN. Reflecting its widening role with the other services, the NRL was renamed the Defence Scientific Establishment (DSE) in 1970, but its primary task remained underwater acoustic surveying with the RNZN. In contrast to Australia, where the Defence Science and Technology Organization employed about 5300 people, New Zealand defence science remained small in scale, with less than sixty staff. During the 1970s the role of the DSE expanded somewhat, with testing of radios, development of command and control systems, advice and feasibility studies on electronic warfare equipment, degaussing of ships, ranging of ships, calibration of sensors, and the analysis of structural fatigue in airframes. The bulk of the work remained, however, on underwater acoustics and from the early 1980s detection of sea mines.

The defence forces themselves have given important assistance to scientific research. Most notable has been the transport of scientists by naval vessels to outlying islands and oceanographic research by naval survey ships. The RNZAF conducted experiments in aerial top dressing in the late 1940s, and regularly flies scientific personnel and supplies to Antarctica, in which they are assisted by an Army loading team. (See CIVIL COMMUNITY, AID TO THE)

War History Narrative, 'Department of Scientific and Industrial Research' (War History Records, National Archives, Wellington); J.D. Atkinson, *DSIR's First Fifty Years* (DSIR, Wellington, 1976); R.A. Galbreath, *DSIR—Making Science Work for New Zealand* (Victoria University Press, Wellington, 1998).

Scratchley, Major-General Sir Peter Henry

(24 August 1835–1 December 1885) was prominent in the development of external defences in the Australian colonies in the late nineteenth century. Commissioned in the Royal Engineers in 1854, he served in the ★Crimean War and in the Indian Mutiny before proceeding to Australia, where he spent from 1860 to 1863 assisting in the organisation of colonial forces and advising on defence plans. Back in England, he eventually become Director of Works in the War Office's Manufacturing Department. In 1877 he was appointed to assist Major-General W.F.D. ★Jervois in preparing reports on the defences of the Australian colonies and New Zealand. Scratchley visited New Zealand in early 1880, and prepared a major report on defence requirements, basing his proposals on the orthodox means of heavy guns (of which New Zealand already had twenty-two), supported by spar ★torpedo boats, to deal with the threat of raiding cruisers. The government accepted his advice, and Scratchley, back in Australia, prepared detailed plans for the proposed gun emplacements. Procrastination soon set in, however, as New Zealand's financial position deteriorated, though four spar torpedo boats were acquired. Scratchley's

report was eventually superseded by recommendations made by Jervois, who from 1883 was Governor of New Zealand. Scratchley retired from the Army in 1882, and two years later was appointed Special Commissioner for the New Guinea protectorate. He earned appointment as a KCMG for his services there, but soon afterwards died of illness contracted on one of his inspections.

Scrounging is a slang term for 'commandeering', pilfering, souveniring, or 'acquiring' items. As looting it is a crime under *military law. It is a habit that has been regarded with unofficial pride within the New Zealand armed forces, being representative of ingenuity and resourcefulness, the supposed traits of New Zealand soldiers. It has perhaps more to do with the fact that New Zealanders have often found themselves badly equipped and needing to augment their equipment or in the situation of tourists and anxious to acquire trophies or souvenirs.

In the *First World War, desperate necessity forced soldiers to steal, bludge, or borrow items ranging from binoculars to shaving mirrors. Greed was another factor—German POWs were searched by their captors for money, watches, and jewellery, it being regarded as an informal right of captors to relieve prisoners of their possessions. New Zealand soldiers were also zealous souvenir hunters, determined to acquire trophies to remind them of their experience. Foremost among such items was the German spiked 'pickelhaube' helmet, which was traded among the troops on the *black market.

New Zealand troops in the *Second World War continued the tradition of their forebears. Military necessity was one motivating factor; German 'Spandau' machine-guns, in particular, were highly prized for their rate of fire. Captured weapons were meant to be sent to the rear for assessment and conversion, but New Zealand units in the front line habitually augmented their firepower with such booty. Better-quality boots were obviously prized, as were warmer greatcoats. This acquisition of enemy clothes also appealed to the sense of sartorial elegance and eccentricity of 8th Army members, and many New Zealand soldiers took on a decidedly non-military and bizarre appearance by wearing civilian clothes, including top hats. Treasure hunting was one of the favourite pursuits of New Zealand soldiers, one report noting: 'A Kiwi is a long nosed sandy looking bird, which mooches about the desert, with hunched back and nose very close to the ground, chirping "Loot! Loot! Loot!"' During the *Italian campaign scrounging reached epidemic proportions, and chickens, wine, pigs, and musical instruments were widely considered by soldiers as legitimately 'liberated' from Italian civilians or their deserted homes. The failure of 2NZEF officers to put a stop to looting inevitably led to outright criminal activity by a minority, with some officers implicated in jewellery and art trafficking. Not until August 1944 were steps taken to tighten up *discipline in 2NZEF.

New Zealand soldiers in the *Korean War were no less adept at scrounging. Members of the main body of Kayforce complained bitterly that they were forced to resort to scrounging to make up for deficiencies in their equipment. According to one gunner they had become known as 'Ali Moody and his 1200 thieves'; others claimed that they had been 'reduced … to the beggar stage'.

Sea mines see MINES, SEA

SEATO The South-East Asia Treaty Organization was the institutional expression of the South-East Asia Collective Defence Treaty signed at Manila on 8 September 1954 by Australia, France, New Zealand, Pakistan, the Philippines, Thailand, the United Kingdom, and the United States. Article IV of the treaty covered each of the parties from armed attack, whether direct or insurgent. A protocol extended application of the treaty to Cambodia, Laos, and the 'free territory under the jurisdiction of the State of Vietnam' (South Vietnam). From a New Zealand perspective the conclusion of the South-East Asia Collective Defence Treaty brought together the United States and Great Britain and appeared to provide a flexible back-up against communist conventional attacks and insurgency in South-east Asia. The treaty was a response to the French defeat in Indo-China and was directed against the People's Republic of China and the Democratic Republic of Vietnam (North Vietnam). It was inspired by the United States, and was part of the broader Western effort designed to contain communism. Most signatories shared the concerns of the United States. New Zealand joined the treaty because of its apprehension about communist insurgency in South-east Asia. From Wellington's perspective, the treaty also deepened defence links with the United States and complemented the *ANZUS Treaty.

The Manila Treaty was institutionalised in 1955 with the establishment of SEATO's headquarters in Bangkok. The formation of a Military Planning Office, and the appointment of a Secretary-General, was approved in 1957. SEATO meetings provided New Zealand with the opportunity for security dialogue and cooperation with non-communist states in the region, especially the United States, Australia, and Britain. After Council meetings in Manila in 1958 and Wellington in 1959, some members designated specific military units for SEATO contingency planning purposes. This applied to the Commonwealth Far East Strategic

Second World War

Reserve based in Malaya, in which New Zealand was involved, though in the event it was never used in active operations under SEATO auspices. Military exercises were arranged, and detailed military plans to counter communist aggression in South-east Asia were prepared. SEATO provided an important focus for New Zealand military planning for nearly two decades. New Zealand provided senior military advisers to SEATO in the late 1950s and 1960s. Brigadier L.W. ★Thornton headed the Military Planning Office from 1958 to 1960. SEATO joined ANZUS guarantees with the standing Commonwealth defence arrangements in a strategy of ★forward defence for New Zealand in South-east Asia, but it never fulfilled a direct military role.

Complex military plans were developed for contingencies in South-east Asia. MPO Plan 2 dealt with a possible North Vietnamese attack on either South Vietnam or Thailand followed by a Chinese intervention. Under this plan 'massive retaliation' was designed to deter aggression and, if this failed, directly to destroy invading forces. Other plans covered large-scale North Vietnamese and Chinese aggression in the treaty area, North Vietnamese aggression in Indo-China, and possible insurgencies in the north of Thailand.

The alliance, which needed unanimous agreement from all parties to meet a common danger within the treaty area, was never politically effective. Beset with internal differences, SEATO failed to act collectively during the Laos crisis of 1961–62. Frustrated United States Secretary of State Dean Rusk and Thai Foreign Minister Thanat Khoman declared (without consulting other member states) that the obligations of the United States did not depend on the prior agreement of all parties to the treaty since treaty obligations were individual as well as collective. Although SEATO did not act collectively in the ★Vietnam War, the argument that treaty obligations were individual as well as collective was used by the New Zealand, Australian, and American governments to justify their deployments in Vietnam.

By the mid 1960s both France and Pakistan were disenchanted with SEATO, and reduced the scale of their participation. The latter, unable to interest SEATO members in containing India, finally withdrew in frustration in 1968, while France lingered on until 1975. Britain's withdrawal of its military forces from the South-east Asian region, completed in the early 1970s, also led to the termination of its commitments to SEATO. The organisation's purpose had, however, already been made largely redundant by the scale of American involvement in the Vietnam War after 1965. The Sino-United States rapprochement in the early 1970s further undermined its purpose. The peace agreement concluded by the Vietnamese parties to the Vietnam War and the United States in early 1973 confirmed

The New Zealand Prime Minister, Walter Nash, addresses the SEATO meeting held in Wellington in March 1959 (*Evening Post Collection, Alexander Turnbull Library, F-51964-1/2*)

SEATO's strategic irrelevance. At a Council meeting in New York in September 1975, it was agreed to disband SEATO. The last SEATO military exercise was held in 1976, and the organisation went out of existence on 30 June 1977. The Manila Treaty has not been revoked.

M. Pearson, *Paper Tiger: New Zealand's Part in SEATO 1954–1977* (New Zealand Institute of International Affairs, Wellington, 1989).

DAVID DICKENS

Second World War New Zealand was one of the first countries to become involved in the global conflict precipitated by Germany's invasion of Poland on 1 September 1939. Its 2176-day involvement, encompassing all but three days of the period now accepted as the Second World War, was matched only by Great Britain, Australia, and British colonial possessions. In contrast to its entry to the ★First World War, New Zealand acted in its own right by formally declaring war on Germany on 3 September (unlike Australia, which held that the King's declaration, as in 1914, extended to all his Dominions). From time to time it is suggested, somewhat disingenuously, that New Zealand entered the war even before Britain because its time zone in September 1939 was ten and a half hours ahead of Greenwich Mean Time. In fact, New Zealand acted only after formal advice was received of the expiry of the British government's ultimatum to Germany to withdraw from Poland, shortly before midnight on 3 September (New Zealand time). The state of war between New Zealand and Germany was held to have existed from the expiry of the ultimatum—in short, the same moment that war began between Britain and Germany (9.30 p.m., 3 September, New Zealand time).

For most New Zealanders, association with Britain in its time of crisis was both natural and necessary. As

Second World War

a firm opponent of ★appeasement, New Zealand had long advocated a strong stance against the Fascist dictatorships. Economic considerations alone ensured that a threat to Britain was seen as a threat to New Zealand—as in 1914. Given New Zealand's reliance on British power for security, and the lack of alternatives, defensive self-interest was another strong motivator towards involvement. Underlying both economic and defence aspects was a sentimental link that made support for the 'kith and kin' in Britain as natural as it was inevitable. Only one political party opposed New Zealand's participation in the war—the small Communist Party, faithful to the false promise of the Nazi–Soviet Non-Aggression Pact of 23 August 1939. In the fifty years after the war no significant academic critique of New Zealand's stance appeared, though an undercurrent of criticism can be discerned in suggestions, sometimes advanced in newspaper editorials, that New Zealand sent troops to fight in Britain's war. A failure to recognise either strategic imperatives or the close ties of self-interest as well as sentimental loyalty that bound New Zealand with Britain usually lies behind such pronouncements.

Strategy determined that New Zealanders involved in combat with Germans would mostly do so at a distance from New Zealand. New Zealand's security, it was accepted, depended on the success of British arms, which would inevitably be concentrated in Europe. Only there could the British Commonwealth be defeated; and New Zealand's contribution, necessarily relatively small, could help prevent such an outcome. As in 1914, the government immediately pledged to send an expeditionary force to assist the Commonwealth war effort in Europe, and the first of three echelons departed for Egypt in January 1940 (see NEW ZEALAND EXPEDITIONARY FORCE). Other New Zealanders were provided for the Royal Navy and Royal Air Force. New Zealand's naval vessels were placed under Admiralty orders, and its new medium bombers, which were about to be ferried to New Zealand, were made available to the RAF (see AIRMEN, NEW ZEALAND, IN THE RAF IN THE SECOND WORLD WAR; ROYAL NAVY IN THE SECOND WORLD WAR, NEW ZEALANDERS IN).

New Zealand's reaction to the outbreak of war was curiously muted. Even the departure of the First Echelon on 5 January 1940 excited little of the enthusiasm of the previous war. The 'phoney war' was shattered by the German onslaught in the west in May 1940. Denmark, Norway, the Netherlands, Belgium, and France all succumbed to the blitzkrieg tactics of the German forces, and most of the British Expeditionary Force was dramatically evacuated from Dunkirk. On 10 June 1940 Italy entered the war on Germany's side. This sudden reversal of fortunes had an immediate impact in New Zealand. Sweeping new powers, including ★conscription, were introduced, and a ★War Cabinet of both government and opposition members was established. Following Germany's invasion of the Soviet Union in June 1941, New Zealand declared war on Germany's Eastern European allies—Finland, Hungary, and Romania on 7 December 1941, and Bulgaria on 13 December 1941.

New Zealand's security in the Pacific was based on the illusion of the ★Singapore strategy. Before dispatching 2NZEF, New Zealand had received assurances from the British authorities that not only was Japan unlikely to enter the war but also that the Singapore plans would ensure Australia's and New Zealand's security even if it did. By 1941, however, the possibility of Japan entering the war had become increasingly worrying, more especially because of the uncertainty regarding the likely position of the United States, still in the grip of isolationist feeling, and the huge demands being made on British naval resources in other theatres. Japan's onslaught in December 1941 at once resolved many doubts, even as it created new ones. The United States was in the war, both in the Pacific and in Europe (following Hitler's strategic blunder in declaring war on it). If this promised ultimate Allied success, in light of the United States' immense productive capacity, it was little immediate comfort to New Zealanders as Japanese forces swept southwards. The ★Malayan campaign culminated in the fall of the much-vaunted Singapore naval base on 15 February 1942. With the United States battlefleet reeling from the losses inflicted by Japanese carrier-borne aircraft at Pearl Harbor on 7 December 1941, Japanese forces seemed poised to invade Australia and New Zealand, a danger underlined by Japanese bombing of northern Australian towns. The onset of the ★Pacific War brought the question of New Zealand strategy to the fore. With the enemy at the gates—albeit several thousand kilometres away—the question of bringing back New Zealand's troops from the Middle East for home defence became a matter of debate. (See PACIFIC VERSUS MEDITERRANEAN)

As with the First World War, the Second World War had important consequences for New Zealand's stance in the world, as it sought to bolster its interests in unfamiliar areas. For the first time it opened diplomatic relations with a non-Commonwealth power, establishing a legation in Washington in 1942. A similar step was taken in Moscow in 1944. Together with new high commissions in Canberra and Ottawa, they provided the basis for an independent approach to international issues. Later in the war New Zealand took an active role in efforts to establish an effective international security regime, which bore fruit in the ★United Nations Organization created at the San Francisco Conference in April–May 1945.

The Second World War was New Zealand's greatest national effort to date. About 140,000 men and women were dispatched overseas to serve in fighting formations, 104,000 in 2NZEF, the rest in the British or New Zealand naval or air forces. In March 1944 there were just under 70,000 New Zealand personnel serving overseas. Fatal casualties during the conflict numbered 11,625. Post-war calculations indicated that New Zealand's ratio of killed per million of population (at 6684) was the highest in the Commonwealth (with Britain at 5123 and Australia, 3232). At home, New Zealand mobilised for war. At first the emphasis was on production for the war effort, New Zealand's primary produce supplying vital foodstuffs for the United Kingdom. Conscription of men for the armed forces, from 1940, was matched by direction of labour for those not sent overseas. The development of a direct threat greatly intensified the process. In July 1942 New Zealand's military mobilisation—the largest in its history—peaked with 154,549 men and women under arms (including those overseas) and a further 100,000 in the ★Home Guard. In all, 194,000 men—67 per cent of those between ages eighteen and forty-five—and 10,000 women served in the armed forces. New Zealand devoted a very high proportion of its resources to the war effort: about 30 per cent of national income overall, with the figure rising to 50 per cent during the critical years 1942–44 (see WAR ECONOMY).

New Zealand's strategy in the Second World War was successful. Pre-war assumptions that seapower would be crucial to its physical and economic security proved justified, even if not in the way anticipated. It was American rather than British seapower that defeated Japan, and aircraft-carriers rather than battleships which were the decisive elements in the Pacific naval conflict. Ultimately New Zealand depended on the overall Allied victory, and this was achieved in 1945 with the capitulation of Germany (on 8 May) and Japan (on 15 August), Italy having been defeated two years earlier. In this respect the war's outcome resembled that of its predecessor in 1918. While the British Empire/Commonwealth, with its allies, had prevailed in both, the second conflict had demonstrated even more forcefully the limitations of British power. Its default in the Pacific in 1941–42 was to have profound consequences for the future of the British Empire and in due course for Britain's status as a world power. This could not but fundamentally affect the position of New Zealand, though the implications were resisted at first by the New Zealand public. In the meantime the government sought to buttress British power in the Pacific by obtaining a security commitment from the United States, now clearly the dominant power in the Pacific, an objective which was achieved with the conclusion of the ★ANZUS alliance in 1951.

J.V.T. Baker, *War Economy* (Historical Publications Branch, Wellington, 1965); N.M Taylor, *The Home Front*, 2 vols (Historical Publications Branch, Wellington, 1986); F.L.W. Wood, *Political and External Affairs* (War History Branch, Wellington, 1958).

Seddon, Richard John (22 June 1845–10 June 1906) was the dominant figure in the development of New Zealand's defence policy for a decade and a half. English by birth, he emigrated to New Zealand in 1866 and entered Parliament thirteen years later. He was Minister of Defence in the ministry formed by John Ballance in 1891, and when Ballance died two years later succeeded him as Premier. Although he relinquished his Defence portfolio in 1896, he resumed it again in 1900 after the outbreak of the ★Boer War. Seddon's first tenure of the portfolio was marked by controversy with the Commandant, Lieutenant-Colonel F.J. ★Fox, and later the Governor, Lord Glasgow, over reform of the ★Volunteer Force. Seddon inevitably prevailed in these squabbles. His relationship with Fox's successors was also strained; he was exasperated by their changing advice, which in some cases led to wasted expenditure. Sympathetic to the idea of the colonies assisting in ★imperial defence, Seddon was willing to offer New Zealand troops for service overseas during successive crises, though in the event only the war in South Africa, in 1899, led to a deployment. He advanced the idea of an ★Imperial Reserve as a means of formalising the process of colonial contributions to the imperial effort. Resuming control of the Defence portfolio, he championed the idea of a citizen army, which he believed had been demonstrated by the Boer resistance in South Africa, and opposed any substantial change to the structure of the Volunteer Force. Seddon accepted the strategic principles underlying imperial defence, especially its dependence upon seapower. He fought hard for an improvement in British naval strength in the South Pacific and endorsed the subsidy arrangements instituted under the ★Australasian Naval Agreement. To strengthen the strategic isolation of the South Pacific colonies, he also persistently urged the acquisition by the British Empire of territories in the Pacific that might be used by foreign powers as bases, including Samoa. He died suddenly in office while returning from a visit to Australia.

Self-reliance in partnership was the name given to the defence strategy set out in the 1991 Defence white paper *The Defence of New Zealand*. There it was defined as 'to protect the sovereignty and advance the well-being of New Zealand by maintaining a level of armed forces sufficient to deal with small contingencies affecting New Zealand and its region, and capable of

Self-reliant policy

The Premier, Richard Seddon (in top hat), at a review of the Canterbury Volunteers (*Canterbury Regiment Association Collection, Canterbury Museum, 12578*)

contributing to collective efforts where our wider interests are involved'. Although defined and made explicit in 1991 as the basis of New Zealand's strategy and force structure, the concept under a variety of names (★imperial defence, collective security, alliance membership) has permeated New Zealand defence thinking for more than a century. It has endured because it reflects New Zealand's unusual situation. Its geography means that, to borrow again from the 1991 white paper, its security *needs* (defence of its territory) are low, while its history and spread of trade mean that its security *interests* (defence of its well-being) are wide. This strategy requires New Zealand to be self-reliant in its ability to handle immediate national tasks, maintaining force elements able to deal with low-level threats to its territorial integrity, such as resource-poaching, terrorism, and illegal immigration. Higher-level threats, such as attacks on shipping, lodgment of forces, or direct invasion are not seen as credible except as part of a wider crisis in which the interests of other friendly countries would be involved; hence the partnership part of the strategy, which sees New Zealand protecting those broader security concerns which it shares with other countries, concerns which may 'stem from a shared political outlook, an interest in maintaining a favourable strategic environment, common economic interests and obligations of international citizenship'. These concerns can only be pursued by collective effort. The requirements of partnership are the principal driver of New Zealand's force structure. The self-reliant tasks can in most cases be carried out with the force elements which serve New Zealand's wider interests. New Zealand aims to maintain highly professional general-purpose forces which provide a range of capabilities from which the government can choose to respond to any contingency. The range need not be extensive, but the strategy requires that the force structure be flexible to cover the unforeseeable; deployable and sustainable over long distances; and inter-operable to be able to work quickly and effectively with likely partners, especially Australia, with which New Zealand is linked in ★Closer Defence Relations.

GERALD HENSLEY

Self-reliant policy was a policy attempted by the Weld ministry, November 1864 to October 1865, in relation to the ★New Zealand Wars. This was partly in response to the British government's decision to withdraw imperial garrisons from the self-governing colonies unless they were paid for by colonial

Senussi campaign

governments, and partly to end the imperial 'reservation' of control over Maori affairs that had been retained when responsible government was granted in New Zealand in 1856. In order to end this 'double government', Weld stipulated certain 'propositions' when called by the Governor to become Premier. The imperial troops were to leave; internal security would be handled by colonial forces (including the *Forest Rangers and *Military Settlers); and full control over Maori affairs would be handed over to the ministry. The policy was short-lived. In 1865, the Stafford ministry tried to retain the imperial troops, but to avoid paying for them. By 1868, as serious Maori resistance flared up again, there was only one imperial battalion left. Stafford's ingenious financial haggling failed to keep it and the imperial withdrawal was completed in 1870. This led to the worst crisis of relations between New Zealand and Great Britain. There were accusations that the mother-country was 'cutting the painter' and setting the colony adrift in a moment of need. There was also loose talk of independence from Britain, joining the United States, or securing defence from external attack by a treaty relationship. In spite of the rhetoric, the assumption of full control over Maori affairs was a major landmark in the evolution of self-government.

G. Hensley, 'The Withdrawal of British Troops from New Zealand, 1864–1870' (MA thesis, University of Canterbury, 1957).

W. DAVID McINTYRE

Senussi campaign A puritanical Islamic sect of Cyrenaica, Libya, the Senussi invaded western Egypt in November 1915. German and Turkish agitation, and military assistance, lay behind this incursion, which led to a rapid British response. A force quickly assembled in Egypt included the newly arrived 2nd Battalion, 3rd New Zealand (Rifle) Brigade. The New Zealanders garrisoned posts along the western desert railroad until it was relieved after a month. In December 1st Battalion, 3NZRB, was sent to garrison the coastal village of Mersa Matruh. This unit was involved in two actions against the Senussi tribesmen—one on Christmas Day, when it participated in an attack on nearby Senussi positions and suffered twenty casualties, and another on 23 January, which resulted in thirty-three casualties and the dispersal of the Senussi forces. In February 1916 the battalion returned to Ismailia. It was in this small campaign, which cost the lives of eight New Zealanders, that Edward *Puttick, who headed the *New Zealand Army during the *Second World War, first saw action.

Service journals Two main approaches have underlain the production of service journals. The first is educative, designed to create a forum for the discussion of military topics within the military forces. This was the basis of the establishment of the first service journal, the *New Zealand Military Journal*, in 1912. Produced at Defence HQ and published quarterly, it was distributed free to all serving officers of the New Zealand Military Forces. In accordance with its stated aim of providing 'articles of an interesting and instructive nature', it included a range of historical and contemporary material. The journal fell victim to the outbreak of the *First World War, its final issue appearing in October 1914. A quarterly *New Zealand Army Journal*, aiming to provide 'a medium for free expression of Military thought', appeared in July 1954, but only managed to survive for six issues, folding in August 1955. Although produced with the approval of the Army Board, this was a private business venture initiated by a serving *Territorial Force officer. A new biannual journal of the same name, produced by the Army Training Group at Waiouru, came into existence in 1985, and has since become the responsibility of the *Military Studies Institute. The second approach to service journals, focused more on raising public consciousness of defence issues and the armed forces than on enhancing professionalism, is represented by *New Zealand Defence Quarterly*, the first issue of which appeared in 1993. Published by the Ministry of Defence, it is notable for a lavish format designed to ensure a wide circulation. Although its contents range over historical and contemporary issues, it does not provide a forum for debate on military matters, since the contribution of unsolicited material from writers, military or otherwise, is not encouraged.

Service newspapers The first newspapers written by and for New Zealand soldiers appeared on the *troopships carrying the contingents to the *Boer War, and they were to be a feature of New Zealand involvement in subsequent conflicts. Varying widely in quality and presentation, such publications were designed to sustain the morale of troops by providing them with news from home and of the activities of their force or unit. They helped counter the boredom of life at sea or in the trenches, and by allowing jocular expression of grievances provided a safety valve. Some were prepared as souvenirs. Although the efforts at first were largely amateurish, ad hoc, and unit-focused, more professional arrangements were made in the *Second World War.

Boer War examples of service newspapers include the *Gymeric Times*, produced on the troopship *Gymeric* in 1900, and the Second Contingent's *The Veldt Lyre*, which appeared on Christmas Day that year. The troops who occupied German Samoa in 1914 were soon producing *Pull Thro'*, while the troopships of the Main Body of 1NZEF were hardly at sea before soldiers were busy preparing news-sheets such as the four-page *Tahiti Mail* and *The Lyre*, which provided a mixture of gossip, news, and nostalgic musings. Their nature varied greatly depending on the enthusiasm of the editor, the material provided by the troops, and the production facilities available. Many were produced on cranky old ship's presses, or hastily printed ashore during brief stopovers. Each troopship carrying later reinforcement drafts had its journal, bearing exotic names like *Stragglers' Echo*, *Oil Sheet*, and *Ye Ancient Athenian*. Although no New Zealand newspaper was produced at ★Gallipoli, scanty and often unreliable news was disseminated in a sheet posted almost daily on the piles of stores at Anzac Cove. In Egypt and the United Kingdom, and on the ★Western Front, the troops themselves produced a variety of rough 'trench' news-sheets, but there was initially no NZEF paper. The void was to a limited extent filled at first by W.H. Atack's *Letters to Lonely Soldiers* (later *Letters for Soldiers*), up to twenty copies of which were circulated. From December 1916, the troops were supplied with the fortnightly *The New Zealander*, which carried summaries of New Zealand news. Organised by G.H. Scholefield, this paper was funded by private New Zealanders but later received assistance from the government, the ★YMCA, and the New Zealand War Contingent Association (NZWCA). About 8000 copies were circulated. In 1918 the YMCA fortnightly newspaper *The Triangle Trail* was also available. The troops were also able to purchase the fortnightly news magazine *Chronicles of the N.Z.E.F.*, which was edited by the blinded 1NZEF soldier Trooper Clutha ★Mackenzie. Although not strictly a service newspaper, being published by the NZWCA in London, it solicited material from the troops, who were able to purchase it at half-price. Among unit newspapers, the *Macedonian Stretcher*, first produced by the 1st Stationary Hospital at ★Salonika, was still appearing in France in 1918. Another hospital journal, *Te Korero*, was circulated in Egypt in the latter part of the war, while members of the Anzac Mounted Corps in the ★Sinai–Palestine campaign had the *Palestine News*, and the monthly *Kia Ora Coo-ee* in 1918. In New Zealand a weekly sheet *Camp Courier* was privately produced for distribution to troops at Trentham Camp, who also had available to them the *Featherston Camp Weekly*.

In the Second World War camp, troopship, and 'trench' newspapers again appeared in considerable numbers. In New Zealand, a private entrepreneur produced an eight-page weekly newspaper, *Camp News*, which was distributed free to the troops; although initially intended for Army personnel in Wellington, it later catered for camps elsewhere and for men in the other services as well. It contained items of news, as well as contributed articles. Among the 'trench' newspapers 28th (Maori) Battalion's cyclostyled *News Flash* stood out. Written in a 'racy, conversational style' by a member of the battalion's headquarters, and including contributed items, it appeared once a fortnight and was circulated to where Maori soldiers might be, though there was much demand for it from Maori and Pakeha alike. In contrast to its predecessor, 2NZEF itself produced a newspaper, utilising the skills of troops with experience in journalism. In Egypt during 1940 the public relations section published a cyclostyled newssheet. In the following year a weekly *NZEF Mail* began appearing weekly, but was soon superseded by a more substantial publication, *2NZEF Times*, edited by E.G. Webber. For more than four years—its final number appeared in December 1945—it was published weekly and was free to the troops. A variety of contributions—news from home, material supplied by the official ★war correspondents, and literary contributions from the troops—filled its pages. By excluding correspondence from the troops, the authorities ensured that the paper did not become a vehicle for expressing grievances and thereby a cause of possible disciplinary problems. In the South Pacific a similar 3rd Division newspaper, *Kiwi News*, was edited by Garth Roydhouse, while New Zealand personnel in Great Britain were served by *Southern Cross*.

Perhaps the most notable New Zealand service newspaper production effort took place in ★Crete in 1941. With the help of several 2NZEF members with journalistic and printing experience and of some local Cretans, Geoffrey ★Cox, a New Zealander with Fleet Street experience, oversaw the publication of *Crete News*, the first issue of which appeared just before the German invasion. It comprised news gleaned from BBC radio bulletins. Despite many obstacles, including the kidnapping of the Cretan linotypist, three more issues were produced, the last as Canea was under bombardment before being overrun.

Members of ★Jayforce were initially provided with a cyclostyled *2NZEF Japan NewsSheet*, but the government was keen to see a newspaper similar to *2NZEF Times* set up (and resisted Australian attempts to discourage such a development). From August 1946, *Jayforce Times* was printed weekly in Wellington and flown up to Japan. Although not especially popular with the troops, it survived until May 1948 (with several souvenir issues being published later). During the ★Korean War a cyclostyled *Kayforce Times* was produced by the Public Relations Section on the troopship *Ormonde* in 1950, but its last, souvenir, issue appeared just before the main body arrived in Korea. A newssheet of news items from New Zealand, *Kiwi Kables* (later *Kahiti*), was subsequently produced, and a more substantial, though still cyclostyled, publication *Iddiwah* appeared at several months' intervals in the first half of 1953. Similar news-sheets were published by

Service newspapers

VIVE LA FRANCE.

A New Zealand gunner's cartoon which appeared in *Chronicles of the N.Z.E.F.* on 14 March 1917

New Zealand forces in Malaya. Currently, the Army produces a newspaper-format fortnightly publication *Army News*, while the RNZAF uses a magazine format for its *Air Force News* (until 2000 *RNZAF News*), also fortnightly. The RNZN publishes a monthly magazine, initially *Navy News* and from 1996 *Navy Today*.

Shanahan, Foss (10 June 1910–13 September 1964) was a key civilian adviser of the government on defence matters following the ★Second World War. Born at Alexandra, he was a nephew of Patrick ★Shanahan. Seconded from the Customs Department to the Prime Minister's Department in September 1939, he became Secretary of the ★Organisation for National Security in January 1940 and was Secretary of the ★War Council. From 1943, as the second most senior officer in both the Prime Minister's and External Affairs Departments, he assumed an increasingly important role in the coordination of political and military elements of New Zealand's defence policy. In addition to being Assistant Secretary to the ★War Cabinet and later Secretary of the Cabinet, he was Secretary of the ★Chiefs of Staff Committee from 1943 to 1955. In 1949 he secured agreement to the establishment of the ★Defence Secretariat and in the following year was instrumental in the re-establishment of the Council of Defence. Strongly anti-communist, he was an influential adviser to the government in determining New Zealand's contribution to the UN Command during the ★Korean War, in the diplomatic negotiations leading to the ★ANZUS alliance, and in New Zealand's adherence to ★SEATO. He later served as New Zealand's representative on the SEATO Council. As Commissioner in South East Asia, and later High Commissioner to Malaya, he was heavily involved in the negotiations over the stationing of New Zealand military personnel in Malaya as part of the ★British Commonwealth Far East Strategic Reserve from 1955. He was made a CMG in 1962, but succumbed to a brain tumour two years later.

Shanahan, Lieutenant Patrick (6 November 1867–7 December 1937). Born in Limerick, Ireland, Shanahan emigrated to New Zealand with his parents as a child. After attending school in Arrowtown, and a brief employment as a miner, he went to sea. Joining the British Army, he was stationed for a period in Egypt before returning to Arrowtown. He soon departed for the United States, where he enlisted in the US Navy in New York in 1890. He took part in the Spanish–American War of 1898. While serving as a chief boatswain's mate on the training ship USS *Alliance* in May 1899, off Annapolis, Maryland, he risked his life in rescuing one of the ship's crew from drowning. His heroism was recognised by the award of the US Congressional Medal of Honour—the only New Zealander to have been so honoured. In 1908 he visited New Zealand with the Great White Fleet. During the ★First World War, Shanahan took part in mine-laying operations in the North Sea. An uncle of Foss ★Shanahan, he retired as a lieutenant in 1922 and died in New York.

Shell-shock, variously referred to as war neurosis, battle fatigue, or neurasthenia, emerged as a term to describe psychologically damaged soldiers during the ★First World War. Currently it is recognised that there are two closely related reactions to traumatic events such as combat. The first is an immediate stress response, brought on by fear, shock, and exhaustion. Low morale, poor training, and inflexible tactics have all been demonstrated as contributing to combat stress response. The second is the long-term psychological scarring caused by the experience of traumatic events. Post-traumatic stress disorder (PTSD), as it is now termed, is a response to an overwhelming traumatic event outside normal human experience, usually marked by intense fear, terror, or helplessness. It may occur months or even years after the actual event. Symptoms include recurrent and distressing recollections of the event, avoidance of thoughts or feelings associated with the trauma, emotional detachment, feelings of hopelessness, irritability, difficulty sleeping, or hyper-vigilance.

Prior to the First World War there was little understanding of the long-term psychological effect of warfare on an individual. Psychological breakdown in a soldier was regarded as a sign of cowardice and therefore a moral failing. As a result, doctors were reduced to explaining psychological casualties as the concussive effects of exploding shells on a soldier's nerves (hence 'shell-shock') or debility. This physical explanation for a psychological condition was accepted by the Army authorities; it allowed soldiers to avoid the stigma of alleged cowardice. A doctor at ★Gallipoli wrote of one soldier who had psychologically broken down:

> He could not walk in a straight line, he had violent trembling of the whole body with twitching. He was holding both hands tightly clenched together and on making him loosen them they both shook violently. He cannot sleep, every shot makes him jump or twitch; he says he can never face fire again. This boy may be called a coward, but it is to be noted that he advanced under heavy machine gun fire and did not retire until ordered. I believe his nervous system, like his body, weak in the first place, has been permanently shattered.

This problem of psychological casualties caused by no apparent physical injury became noticeable again in the prolonged and deadly fighting on the ★Western Front in September–October 1916. Advanced dressing stations received a threefold increase in cases of shell-shock, 'hysteria', 'delirium', or 'morale shaken by shellfire'. These men were sent to hospital, with a view to their being returned to duty as soon as possible. By 1917 medical opinion had undergone an important change: it was accepted that concussion from shellfire was different from 'traumatic neurasthenia'. Sections were established at base hospitals for the treatment of the latter condition. In all 1370 New Zealanders, 10 per cent of all casualties sent home, were repatriated for acute neurasthenia. Particularly severe cases were sent to mental hospitals in New Zealand. However, a public outcry at the stigma this involved led to shell-shock cases being sent to Queen Mary's Military Hospital at Hanmer. Most veterans who were psychologically disturbed by their traumatic war experiences had no professional help, relying instead on the support of family and friends or coping by themselves.

In the ★Second World War recognition that fighting produced psychological as well as physical casualties led to rest centres being established at field ambulances. Here men suffering from battle exhaustion could recover their senses. After four or five days' rest most were returned to their unit. More severe cases were sent to base hospitals. Extensive welfare measures, such as entertainment, sport, and leave, were seen as a means of reducing the incidence of nervous disorders and improving morale. It was found in the early part of the war that low-level air attacks, especially dive-bombing, eroded morale and often led to psychological breakdowns. Prolonged periods of combat, with loss of rest and proper food, also created psychiatric casualties. For example, nervous disorders accounted for 40 per cent of the battle casualties during the arduous fighting in Tunisia in 1943. By then it was apparent that most of the cases were men with more than two years' active service; it was recognised that even good soldiers eventually 'burnt out'. By 1943 many of the long-service troops in the 2nd New Zealand Division had reached that point. In all more than 7000 people, most after service overseas with 2NZEF, were discharged from the forces during and after the war following a diagnosis of anxiety neurosis. This condition accounted for 18 per cent of all disabilities to New Zealand servicemen resulting from the Second World War.

New Zealand psychological casualties were significantly lower during the ★Korean War, reflecting the less intense exposure to combat of the soldiers sent there and the relatively short periods of service. More New Zealanders were involved in infantry combat in the ★Vietnam War, with a commensurate increase in psychological casualties. Greater professional understanding arising from the latter conflict led to the recognition of PTSD as a clinical condition in 1980.

One New Zealand study has estimated that 12 per cent of New Zealand Vietnam veterans have been afflicted by the condition. More recently, increasing numbers of service personnel have been sent on ★peace-keeping missions. Such duties vary widely in their nature, and do not necessarily expose soldiers to combat situations. Nevertheless, peace-keepers are often faced with traumatic and frustrating events, and tend to suffer from high levels of anxiety, depression, and psychological distress.

R. Clarke, 'Not Mad, But Very Ill: The Treatment of New Zealand's Shellshocked Soldiers 1914–1939' (MA thesis, University of Auckland, 1991).

Shoulder titles were first used on New Zealand ★uniforms during the ★Volunteer Force era, when most units had an abbreviated unit designation embroidered directly on uniform epaulettes. This sometimes included the company number or battery letter. During the ★Boer War some members of the New Zealand contingents had brass shoulder titles locally manufactured. These featured the contingent number and NEW ZEALAND, and sometimes included a fern leaf or kiwi. At home, with the introduction of khaki uniforms in 1900, brass or silver wire shoulder titles consisting of the letters NZ were provided. When members of the new ★Territorial Force were issued with khaki service dress in 1912, brass titles were used for each arm of service, for example NZMR for New Zealand Mounted Rifles. Brass titles were worn until the battledress uniform was adopted during 1940. In that year all 2NZEF troops in the Middle East and United Kingdom were ordered to use a slip-on cloth title with the words NEW ZEALAND in white-on-black on both shoulder straps as a national identification. From 1943 2NZEF in the Pacific used printed red-on-khaki slip-on titles and 3rd New Zealand Division identical ones in black-on-khaki. In the late 1950s coloured cloth shoulder titles were adopted to identify each ★New Zealand Army corps and regiment. These curved embroidered titles had the unit title spelt out in full in corps colours. When in 1997 a new service dress uniform was introduced, all existing shoulder titles were replaced with a curved white-on-black NEW ZEALAND title. The NEW ZEALAND slip-on title used by New Zealand Army personnel when deployed overseas was abolished, since new rank epaulettes incorporated this designation. While serving overseas during the Second World War, New Zealand airmen and sailors also wore the identification shoulder flash NEW ZEALAND, and the practice was later formalised in the RNZAF and RNZN (see ROYAL NEW ZEALAND AIR FORCE and ROYAL NEW ZEALAND NAVY).

M. Thomas and C. Lord, *New Zealand Army Distinguishing Patches 1911–1991* (Privately published, Wellington, 1995).

MALCOLM THOMAS

Sinai–Palestine The first priority for the British upon the outbreak of war between the British and Ottoman Empires on 30 October 1914 was the defence of Egypt and the Suez Canal. British defences were based around the canal itself, with the arid wilderness of the Sinai desert forming a kind of no man's land between Ottoman Palestine and Egypt. In early 1915 a half-hearted attack on the Suez Canal by the Turks was beaten off by British forces. (See EGYPT, NEW ZEALANDERS IN) For most of 1915 Turkish and British resources were diverted to the struggle at ★Gallipoli, and the Sinai desert lapsed into inactivity. The failure of the Gallipoli expedition and the completion of the Turkish rail line south to Beersheba caused renewed attention to be given to the defence of the Suez Canal. Canal defences were improved and in January 1916 Lieutenant-General Sir Archibald Murray assumed command of the newly created Egyptian Expeditionary Force (EEF). This initially contained units recuperating after Gallipoli, but there was a continual drain of divisions to France. By mid 1916 Murray was left with four under-strength British divisions and the Australia and New Zealand (or Anzac) Mounted Division commanded by Major-General Harry Chauvel. Forming part of the Anzac Mounted Division was the 2500-strong New Zealand Mounted Rifles Brigade under the command of Brigadier-General Edward ★Chaytor (see MOUNTED RIFLES).

In April 1916 the New Zealanders were deployed in the vicinity of Romani, thirty kilometres east of the Suez Canal. They patrolled the desert and dug wells while the railroad and water pipeline were moved forward from the canal. From July they were active in harassing and reporting on Turkish movements towards Romani. The Turks finally attacked on 4 August 1916, seeking to outflank the Romani positions. This move was anticipated and checked by the Anzac Mounted Division. Outflanked themselves and without water, the Turks withdrew, with the NZMR Brigade in pursuit. Only faulty British staff work prevented the encirclement of the Turkish force. Despite this failure, the battle was still a significant victory for the British forces. The fighting had cost the Turks about 9000 men. New Zealand casualties numbered 228. Despite the Turkish disarray, it was impossible for the British forces to advance quickly across the Sinai desert. Not until November had enough water been brought up to Romani for a further advance to be contemplated.

In December 1916 the Anzac Mounted Division was grouped with British yeomanry units and the Imperial Camel Corps (in which there were two New

New Zealand mounted riflemen watering their horses before the action at Richon le Zion, near Jaffa, in November 1917 (*Waiouru Army Museum, 1986.2089*)

Sinai–Palestine

The Imperial Camel Corps during a halt in their advance in the Sinai Desert (*Powles Family Collection, Alexander Turnbull Library, PA1-q-605-22*)

Zealand companies) to form the Desert Column under Lieutenant-General Sir Philip Chetwode. This force occupied El Arish on 21 December, after the Turks had evacuated it, and went on to capture Magdhaba on the 23rd. About 1300 prisoners were taken after a brisk fight at the latter. On 9 January 1917 Rafa on the Egypt–Palestine border was attacked. During this operation, the NZMR Brigade, after swinging out to the east, descended on the Turkish rear. Nearly 1500 prisoners were taken, at a cost of 467 casualties to the Desert Column, including 124 New Zealanders. As ever, water and supplies provided the key to action: the advance halted while a water pipeline and the rail line to Rafa were completed. By March 1917 preparations were ready for an attack on the next objective, Gaza, the principal town of southern Palestine. On 26 March the Anzac Mounted Division moved to envelop the defending Turks from the east while infantry assaulted them from the west. By afternoon, with the NZMR Brigade pushing into the northern outskirts of the town, Turkish resistance was on the point of collapse. However, Chetwode was unaware of the gains made and, fearful at the approach of a Turkish relief force, ordered a withdrawal.

In the meantime the war had been going badly for the Allies. With the German submarine campaign reaching crisis proportions, and the ★Western Front offering gains only at huge cost, the possibility of a victory at Gaza assumed increased importance in London. The invasion of Palestine provided an opportunity to inflict a decisive defeat on the Ottoman Empire. On 2 April 1917, therefore, the strategic objective of the operations was broadened. Murray was promised reinforcements and instructed to advance and take Jerusalem as soon as possible. The first step would be a renewed assault on Gaza. By the time this took place, between 17 and 19 April, the Turks had considerably strengthened their position. In spite of using gas and tanks and employing a more methodical assault, the British suffered a costly defeat. The EEF lost more than 6400 men, killed, wounded, or captured. There were 116 New Zealand casualties.

Following this reverse, further reinforcements were sent to the EEF. A series of command changes altered the British line-up: Murray was replaced by a more aggressive general from the Western Front, General Sir Edmund Allenby; Chetwode was promoted to command of the Eastern Force; Chauvel took over the Desert Column (later reorganised as the Desert Mounted Corps), and Chaytor replaced him in command of the Anzac Mounted Division. Allenby determined to turn the Gaza–Beersheba Line at its eastern

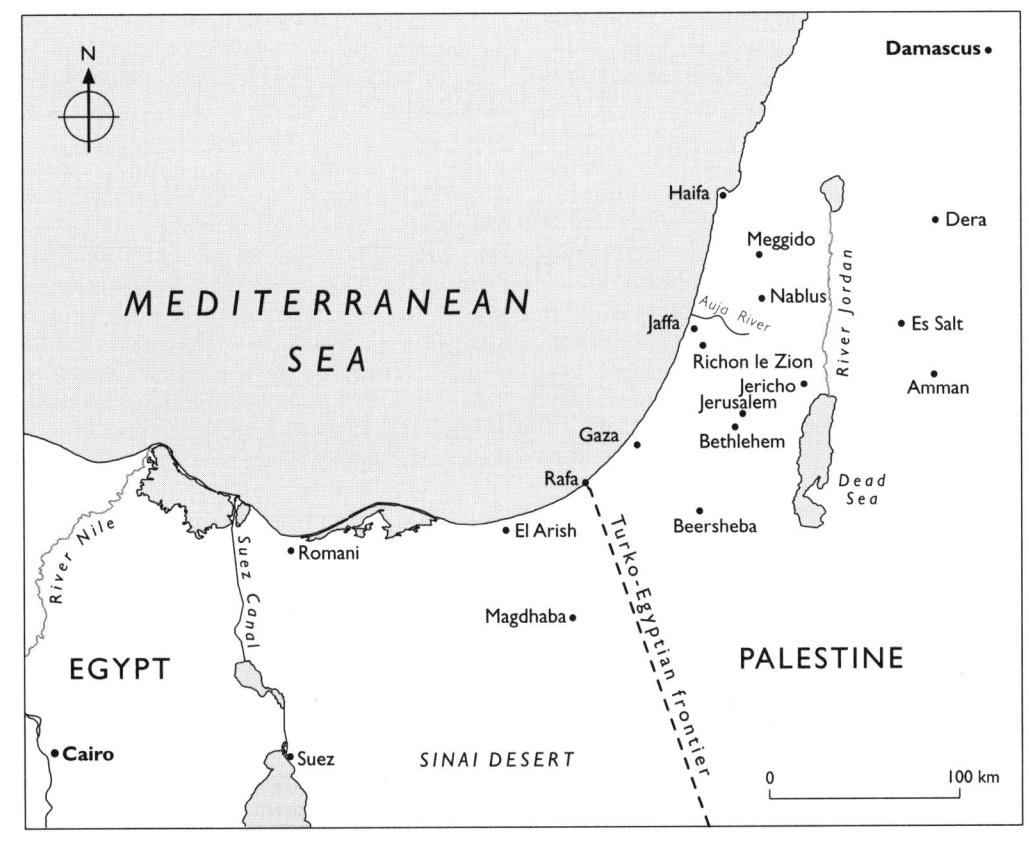

Map 22 Sinai–Palestine campaign, 1916–18: area of operations

end by capturing Beersheba, while pinning the Turkish forces elsewhere with a feint. All depended on the speedy capture of Beersheba and its water supply. When the attack opened on 31 October 1917, the town was encircled by the Anzac Mounted Division, which wheeled around on the extreme right with the intention of attacking Beersheba from the north. However, the town fell to a spectacular charge by the 4th Australian Light Horse Brigade. Further fighting ensued in hills north of Beersheba and it was not until 7 November that the Turkish defences were finally broken. The pursuit was delayed by Turkish rearguards and the exhaustion of the British troops and horses. The NZMR Brigade at one stage was in action for seventy-two hours without water. Allenby identified the main obstacle to an advance as 'one of supply rather than manoeuvre'. While much of the Ottoman Army had disintegrated, there was, nevertheless, continued heavy fighting with its rearguards. On 14 November the NZMR Brigade took a position at Richon le Zion (Ayun Qara) and held it against a fierce Turkish counter-attack (albeit at the cost of 174 casualties.) Two days later the New Zealanders entered Jaffa. The Desert Mounted Corps held the coastal plain while the remainder of the EEF pushed through the Judean hills towards Jerusalem. An attempt by the NZMR Brigade in late November to establish a bridgehead across the Auja river north of Jaffa was defeated. It was then pulled out of the line, and spent the next two months resting at Richon le Zion. Jerusalem was formally taken by Allenby on 11 December 1917, a 'Christmas present to the British nation' which boosted British morale after a year of disappointments on the Western Front and revolution in Russia.

After more fighting in late December, the front settled on a line running from north of Jaffa to north of Jerusalem. Supply lines were reorganised and the rail line brought forward. As the next step Allenby decided to occupy Jericho and push the strong Turkish forces still west of the River Jordan back across the river. The NZMR Brigade began operations on 19 February 1918, by using a goat track to skirt past Turkish positions on El Muntar hill. Within twenty-four hours the main Turkish defence line had been breached, and British forces entered Jericho on the 21st. Towards the end of March, a large raid was conducted against Es Salt and Amman. Although the operation was initially successful, cold, driving rain and strong Turkish resistance at Amman eventually forced a withdrawal. A month later another raid was launched against Es Salt by the Desert Mounted Corps, again without much immediate success. Nevertheless, the two raids had considerable strategic importance. They drew Turkish attention towards the right flank, and away from the coastal plain where Allenby was planning to attack.

Allenby's plans for a renewal of the offensive in Palestine were affected by the situation on the Western Front, where a massive German offensive threatened to break through the Allied line. Most of the EEF's British troops were rapidly dispatched to France to help bolster the front. This forced a reorganisation of the EEF's remaining resources. The Imperial Camel Corps was reconstituted as the 5th Australian Light Horse Brigade; its two New Zealand companies re-formed as the 2nd New Zealand Machine Gun Squadron, which was attached to that brigade. The Anzac Mounted Division meanwhile was stationed in the Jordan Valley screening the right flank of the EEF. The New Zealanders suffered the discomfort of searing heat (up to 46° in the shade) and the depredations of malaria while they awaited the opening of the offensive. When it finally began, on 19 September 1918, their task was to divert the Turks as part of Chaytor's Force, which comprised the Anzac Mounted Division and attached British, Jewish, Indian, and West Indian troops. The decisive attack was directed at Megiddo on the coastal plain. Turkish resistance quickly collapsed. British forces, including the New Zealand machine-gunners, were soon pushing north. Crossing the Jordan River on 22 September, the Anzac Mounted Division took Es Salt next day and Amman on the 25th. The operation was an astounding success—in five days the NZMR Brigade covered more than seventy kilometres and took about 3000 prisoners. By this stage the Turkish Army was in headlong retreat. The 2nd New Zealand Machine Gun Squadron mowed down a column of fleeing Turks in the Barada Gorge, north-west of Damascus. On 1 October Australian light horsemen entered Damascus as other mounted troops and Arab forces pushed northwards to Homs and Aleppo. With her armies defeated, Germany on the verge of collapse, and Bulgaria already having surrendered to the Allies, the Ottoman Empire's situation was hopeless. It sued for an armistice, which came into effect on 31 October 1918.

The NZMR Brigade had already, in mid October, returned to its old camp at Richon le Zion. While a regiment was sent to Gallipoli to monitor the armistice, the remainder settled into an uncongenial existence, pending their ★repatriation. In December antipathy towards the local Arab population boiled over following the murder of a New Zealand soldier, and Arabs were massacred at the nearby village of Surafend. At the end of December, the brigade was returned to Egypt, where it helped quell nationalist disturbances in March 1919. The last New Zealand troops left Egypt four months later.

The Sinai–Palestine campaign ended in a decisive defeat for the Ottoman Empire. New Zealand troops had played a central role, and had been recognised as the most effective of the mounted formations. Although conditions could hardly be compared with those on the Western Front, the men had to endure heat, thirst, and malaria. More than 150 died of disease. Battle casualties were relatively low because of the fluid nature of the fighting (unlike the trench warfare in France). In all the Allies suffered 51,000 casualties during the campaign. There were 1470 New Zealand casualties, of which 543 were fatal. The Sinai–Palestine campaign was never more than a sideshow to the main battle raging on the Western Front. Hopes of achieving a quick and easy victory over the Ottoman Empire proved illusory. Nevertheless, the collapse of Ottoman power in the Middle East was to have immense long-term consequences.

C.G. Powles, *The New Zealanders in Sinai and Palestine* (Whitcombe & Tombs, Auckland, 1922).

Sinclair-Burgess, Major-General Sir William Livingstone Hatchwell (18 February 1880–3 April 1964) was the pre-eminent New Zealand soldier of the inter-war period. Born near Manchester, England, he adopted the surname of his mother's second husband, Burgess; after the ★First World War he added Sinclair, the surname of his father. After emigrating to New Zealand with his family, he found employment as a carpenter and engineer and began his military career as a member of the ★Volunteer Force in 1900. By 1909 he was a captain in the New Zealand Regiment of Field Artillery Volunteers. He became a regular soldier in 1911, when he joined the ★New Zealand Staff Corps. After commanding an area group in Hamilton and serving as adjutant of the 16th (Waikato) Regiment, he went to Australia as an exchange officer. As a result, he served with the Australian Imperial Force during the First World War. For his command of the 9th (Tasmania) Battery at ★Gallipoli, he was made a DSO. He was wounded in May 1915, and ill health eventually led to his evacuation from the peninsula in October 1915. On the ★Western Front, he commanded the 3rd Field Artillery Brigade until 1917, when he became CRA of the 4th Australian Division. His service was recognised by his appointment as a CMG and a CB, and he was mentioned in dispatches six times. When he resumed his career in the New Zealand Military Forces in 1919, he quickly became a key staff officer at GHQ. In 1924 he became Director of Military Intelligence and Training, and three months later CGS. From 1931 to 1937, when he was ousted by the Labour government, he was also GOC. His first task was to adjust the military forces to straitened circumstances, which had led to the abolition of ★compulsory military training in 1930. Despite the continuing financial depression, he persuaded the government, in 1933, to begin a modest programme of rearmament because of the worsening international outlook. A six-year plan included the acquisition of Vildebeeste aircraft, new guns for port and anti-aircraft defences at Wellington and Auckland, and the formation of the RNZAF. He was also instrumental in establishing the New Zealand section of the ★Committee of Imperial Defence to coordinate defence preparations. His proposal that New Zealand establish a permanent infantry battalion and an artillery battery, which might gain experience in India, never made any headway. He was a champion of the mechanisation of the New Zealand forces. 'Sinky-Boo', as he was nicknamed, was a man of considerable presence, who particularly liked to wear full-dress uniform; he was an effective soldier, who presided over the military forces at a time of great difficulty but made some progress in preparing the New Zealand forces to meet a possible emergency. He was made a KB in 1934 and a KBE in the following year.

Singapore strategy In the period between the two world wars New Zealand's defence policy was based on a strategy of ★imperial defence usually dubbed the 'main fleet to Singapore' strategy. It was conceived in the years 1919–21 after Admiral of the Fleet Lord ★Jellicoe had visited India, Australia, New Zealand, and Canada to report to their governments on naval policy. Jellicoe had, however, in common secret sections of his reports identified Japan (then an ally under the Anglo-Japanese agreements of 1902, 1905, and 1911) as the potential enemy in the Pacific.

To counter Japan's projected 'eight–eight fleet' (comprising eight battleships and eight battlecruisers to match the similar fleet being built by the United States), Jellicoe proposed a new British Empire eight–eight fleet for the Pacific. With the addition of four aircraft-carriers, it would consist of twenty capital ships, and Jellicoe suggested that the £20 million annual cost should be shared, 75 per cent paid by Great Britain, 20 per cent by Australia and 5 per cent by New Zealand. Both the British and Australian governments balked at this cost, but agreed in 1921 to go ahead with part of the scheme, namely Jellicoe's proposed naval headquarters, dockyard, and base to be sited at Singapore. As there was no dockyard east of Malta to service a battleship fitted with an anti-submarine bulge, a new base was essential if ever the main fleet left the Atlantic and Mediterranean to engage the Japanese fleet. The basic strategic idea was that, in the event of a threat to the British Empire/Commonwealth in the East, the fleet would sail through the Suez Canal to Singapore, and thence operate from some advance base such as Hong Kong or another Chinese port to deter or destroy the Japanese fleet.

The decision to build the base was made in 1921. Preparations started on the site in 1923. They were suspended by the first British Labour government in 1924, though work, in fact, continued. A 'truncated scheme' was resumed by the Conservatives in 1926, only to be 'slowed down' by the second Labour government in 1929. Work resumed under the British rearmament programme in 1934 and the graving dock was formally opened in 1938. At that point, the dry dock had no caisson gate or workshops. The base was only completed in 1941 on the eve of the ★Pacific War. It was protected by ★First World War vintage 15-inch naval guns. It has often been claimed that these 'pointed out to sea', but in fact most were on all-round swivels.

From the outset, the Singapore base was an imperial project. The site was paid for by the Crown Colony government of the Straits Settlements (costing £123,000). The colony of Hong Kong contributed £225,000. The New Zealand government offered £100,000 in 1923. This lapsed with the cancellation, but, after resumption, the Dominion government contributed £1 million between 1928 and 1936. The Australian government contemplated a contribution, but put the money into building cruisers instead. The Federated Malay States contributed £2 million and the Sultan of Johore another half million.

When the Singapore strategy was adopted in the 1920s, Germany was recovering from the First World War and had no battlefleet. Japan resented the ending of the British alliance in 1921, but its armament programme was delayed by the devastating Tokyo earthquake of 1923. However, by the early 1930s, the Singapore strategy began to be compromised by dramatic changes in the balance of power. Germany began building 'pocket battleships' in 1929 which were only technically within the peace treaty restrictions. Japan occupied Manchuria in 1931 and landed a large force which briefly fought the Chinese at Shanghai in 1932. At this point there was only a floating dock and some earthworks at Singapore. The British Chiefs of Staff regarded these Japanese moves as the 'Writing on the Wall'. Soon rearmament commenced and in 1933 the New Zealand ★Chiefs of Staff also recommended a modest programme of rearmament after expressing their first doubts as to whether the British fleet would ever get to Singapore. In the same year, the Nazis came to power in Germany and accelerated the naval programme. In 1935, Italy began its conquest of ★Abyssinia. Three potential enemies had appeared at a

Sloops

time when the British navy could hardly match one of them. Thus, at the time of the 1937 Imperial Conference, when Dominion leaders sought assurances about the 'main fleet to Singapore' strategy, the British had to declare their priorities. They said that the defence of the British Isles and of Singapore were the 'keystones' of imperial defence; no anxieties in the Mediterranean were to delay the dispatch of the fleet to the East. However, by 1939 and as war loomed in Europe, this promise was reviewed. When New Zealand hosted the ★Pacific Defence Conference in April 1939 in Wellington, where British, Australian, and New Zealand defence representatives consulted, the tenuous state of the British promises was laid bare by Carl ★Berendsen. At the same time, staff conferences with the French in London induced the British Strategical Appreciation Sub-Committee of the CID to point out that there were 'so many variable factors' that they could not say in advance when and in what strength the fleet might be dispatched to Singapore.

Soon after the outbreak of the German War in September 1939, a conference of Dominion representatives was held in London, where Winston Churchill, back at the Admiralty, reiterated the general promise about the dispatch of the fleet to Singapore. After this assurance, New Zealand committed its expeditionary force of one division to the Middle East. However, in June 1940, with Italy's entry into the war and France on the verge of surrender, the British promise was rescinded except for the dire emergency of an invasion of Australia or New Zealand. Faced, now, with the German navy and the Italian navy (and without the French fleet), Churchill declared that if Japan took the opportunity offered by the European war to advance in the Pacific, the Commonwealth would have to rely on the United States. It was a major watershed, but the New Zealand government indicated that the decision was not unexpected and began the process of appointing a diplomatic representative in Washington.

On the eve of the Pacific War in 1941, Churchill tried to fulfil the old promise. He insisted, against reluctant Chiefs of Staff, that a 'formidable, fast, high-class squadron' in the Aden–Singapore–Simonstown triangle would have an effect similar to that of the German battleship *Bismarck* in the Atlantic. It would, he claimed, have a 'paralysing effect' on Japanese action. HMS *Prince of Wales* and *Repulse* and an aircraft-carrier were to go to Cape Town and thence to Singapore. The aircraft-carrier ran aground in the Caribbean, but the two capital ships, known as Force Z, reached Singapore on 2 December 1941. Admiral Sir Tom Phillips, the new Commander-in-Chief of the Eastern Fleet, immediately went to Manila to confer with Admiral Hart, commander of the US Asiatic Squadron. The New Zealand Navy Board was represented at these discussions. As soon as war broke out on 8 December, Phillips took his force to intercept the Japanese landings in north-east Malaya. It has often been argued that he should have retired to Australia or Ceylon to conserve his force, but, with the army and air force hard-pressed in northern Malaya, no naval commander would desert the scene of action. A famous landmark in maritime history ensued. The *Prince of Wales* and *Repulse* were dispatched by shore-based bombers on 10 December; their sinking spelt the end of the battleship as the main instrument of naval warfare. Singapore capitulated on 15 February 1942, the largest surrender in British military history and the greatest defeat since the Battle of Yorktown had signalled the loss of the thirteen American colonies (see MALAYAN CAMPAIGN).

The British Fleet did, finally, come to the Pacific to fight the Japanese in 1945. The main base was Sydney (which had been rejected in 1919) with advance bases at Manus and Ulithi. Twenty-five per cent of the ★Fleet Air Arm pilots on the carriers were New Zealanders, and three ships of the RNZN took part in operations off the coasts of Japan. At the end of the war, the British Pacific Fleet numbered four battleships, five fleet carriers, twelve auxiliary carriers, and ten cruisers and included Australian, Canadian, and New Zealand vessels, but all this paled beside the might of the US fleet. After the war, up until 1968, the Singapore naval base and the attendant army and air force bases housed considerable British and Commonwealth forces, which cooperated in the ★Malayan Emergency, in a deployment in ★Thailand, and in opposing ★Confrontation. The naval base became a commercial dockyard in 1968. After the agonised British withdrawal from 'East of Suez', spread over the years 1967–76, Australia and New Zealand left some forces in the region until 1988–89.

A.J. Marder, *Old Friends New Enemies: The Royal Navy and the Imperial Japanese Navy*, Volume I, *Strategic Illusions 1936–1941* (Clarendon Press, Oxford, 1981); W.D. McIntyre, *The Rise and Fall of the Singapore Naval Base, 1919–1941* (Macmillan, London, 1979).

W. DAVID McINTYRE

Sloops were small escort vessels similar to ★corvettes, lightly armed but with a long range. Two Royal Navy sloops were deployed on the ★New Zealand Station between the world wars. The Flower class escorts HMS *Veronica* and *Laburnum* arrived in New Zealand waters in 1920 and 1922 respectively. Launched in 1915, they displaced 1200 tons, mounted two 4-inch guns, four 3-pounders, and two 'pom-poms', and had a complement of 104. *Veronica* is chiefly remembered for the assistance rendered by her crew during the 1931 ★Napier earthquake. Both were replaced in 1934–35 by the Grimsby class sloops HMS *Leith* and *Wellington*, which mounted two 4.7-inch guns, a 3-inch anti-aircraft gun, and four 3-pounders. Shortly after the outbreak of the ★Second World War both reverted to Admiralty control and were withdrawn from New Zealand waters. Both later took part in the Battle of the Atlantic. An Egret class sloop, HMS *Auckland*, intended to replace them, never made it to New Zealand waters because of war requirements.

Small arms Personal firearms such as rifles, pistols, carbines, and submachine-guns are the basic weapon of infantrymen. The first small arms used in New Zealand were muzzle-loading muskets fired by a simple flintlock mechanism. Although inaccurate and unreliable, these weapons gave their possessors an overwhelming advantage over an enemy armed only with traditional weapons (rakau)—as was brutally demonstrated during the ★Musket Wars of the 1820s and 1830s. Many of the muskets used in this fighting were shoddy 'Brummagems' (a corruption of Birmingham, the arms manufacturing centre which turned out these weapons for sale on the fringes of the Empire). Civilian fowling pieces and shotguns (tupara) were also popular. Increasing numbers of the British Tower-pattern flintlock musket (the famous 'Brown Bess') also reached New Zealand. British troops deployed to New Zealand in 1844 were equipped with flintlock muskets, though some new percussion cap–fired weapons may also have arrived in the colony by this time. From the late 1850s British forces were equipped with the excellent Enfield rifled musket. The .577-inch calibre Minie bullet and rifled barrel gave this weapon unparalleled accuracy and hitting power, and provided a marked advantage to British troops in the ★New Zealand Wars. From the early 1860s officers armed themselves with a mixture of Colt, Tranter, and Adams revolvers, and some colonial units, notably the ★Forest Rangers, were equipped with Callisher and Terry breech-loading carbines. Early breech-loaders were chronically unreliable, but possessed a high rate of fire, important in close quarters fighting. From 1866 units were equipped with the Snider breech-loading rifle, a reliable weapon combining a breech-loading mechanism with an Enfield rifle barrel. It was the first British service weapon to use brass cartridges.

By the 1890s the Sniders were well past their usefulness, the Commandant, Lieutenant-Colonel F.J. ★Fox, noting that they were 'worn out and generally unserviceable, and in many cases unsafe'. With a new rifle clearly needed, Fox successfully urged the government to obtain breech-loading Martini-Henry rifles, although they were already being replaced in the British Army by more modern advanced magazine rifles. He reasoned that the Martini–Henry was more suitable for untrained

Two New Zealand Bren gunners of 23rd Battalion fire on targets from a strongpoint in a heavily shelled house in the Faenza sector in January 1945 during the Italian campaign (*War History Collection, Alexander Turnbull Library, F-8082-35mm-DA*)

volunteers and less costly in ammunition. However, much to Premier Richard ★Seddon's exasperation, Fox's successor, Colonel A.P. ★Penton, criticised the purchase of obsolete weapons. Seddon eventually agreed to obtain the smaller-calibre (.303-inch) Martini–Enfield, and the first contingents dispatched by New Zealand to the ★Boer War took this weapon with them. Because of their slow rate of fire and inadequate range, however, the Martini–Enfields were quickly replaced in South Africa by more modern Lee–Metford magazine rifles. Although Lee–Metfords were ordered for the New Zealand Military Forces in 1900, they were in turn soon replaced by a newer bolt action magazine rifle—the Magazine Lee Enfield (MLE) rifle. From 1907 the MLEs were gradually replaced by the Short Magazine Lee Enfield (SMLE). Weighing 4.1 kilograms, accurate, extremely reliable, and capable of a high rate of fire for a bolt action rifle, the latter was the principal weapon of the ★New Zealand Army until 1959. It fired a .303-inch calibre bullet and could be fixed with a 42-centimetre sword bayonet. Officers were armed with .455-inch calibre Webley revolvers. In the trench fighting at ★Gallipoli troops made their own 'jam-tin' grenades, but on the ★Western Front the New Zealanders were issued with M36 Mills Bombs, the predecessor of the various hand grenades which equip the New Zealand Army today. From 1916 each New Zealand infantry platoon was equipped with a Lewis light machine-gun to supplement the firepower of the riflemen (see MACHINE-GUNS).

Although New Zealand troops were equipped with the SMLE throughout the ★Second World War, the ★Home Guard also used surplus American rifles as a stopgap measure. The Lewis gun was replaced by the Bren light machine-gun, and officers and NCOs were

497

issued with Thompson or Sten submachine-guns. However, during combat New Zealand soldiers were always keen to acquire high quality German weapons, because of their higher rate of fire. The heavy .455 Webley revolver was replaced by a lighter .38-inch calibre weapon. Like Australia, New Zealand developed its own small arms in response to the shortage of such weapons reaching New Zealand, and some old SMLE rifles were converted into automatic rifles in an attempt to overcome the shortage of automatic weapons in New Zealand (see IMPROVISED WEAPONS).

During the early 1960s the New Zealand Army was equipped with a new generation of weapons utilising the 7.62 mm ammunition common to Western armies. The Belgian-designed FN L1A1 self-loading rifle (SLR) replaced the SMLE from 1959. Weighing five kilograms, it was a reliable weapon, favoured by well-trained troops for its accuracy and hitting power. A few years later the venerable Vickers medium machine-guns and Bren light machine-guns were replaced by L7 General Purpose Machine-Guns (GPMG or 'Gimpy'). Sterling 9 mm submachine-guns were also acquired to replace older submachine-guns in signals and armoured units. New Zealand troops in Vietnam were equipped with American M60 GPMGs, and scouts in infantry sections received lightweight American Armalite M-16A1 assault rifles, which fired a smaller 5.56 mm calibre bullet. Browning 9 mm automatic pistols were also acquired at this time.

The trend towards increasingly lightweight weapons possessing higher rates of fire, together with the perceived need to standardise with other Western armies using NATO 5.56 mm ammunition, led to the re-equipment of the New Zealand armed forces during the mid 1980s. In 1986 the C9 Minimi, another Belgian-designed weapon, was acquired as the standard light machine-gun. The Australian-manufactured Steyr AUG assault rifle was chosen as the replacement for the FN SLRs and Sterling submachine-guns. With its plastic parts and 'Bullpup' configuration (where the magazine and breech are placed in the shoulder stock so as to decrease the weapon length), the Steyr possesses a distinctly futuristic appearance. In 1992 the Browning 9 mm pistols were replaced with Swiss SIG-Sauer P226 pistols. In common with most Western special forces, the New Zealand ★Special Air Service are equipped with Heckler & Koch MP5 submachine-guns.

Smith, Commander William James Lanyon ('Kiwi') (1 December 1922–) was a noted midget submariner of the ★Second World War. Born at Gore, he was a schoolteacher when called up for service in the Army in February 1942. Transferring to the RNZN in May 1943, he was sent to England for training, and was commissioned in April 1944. He was part of the four-man crew of the midget submarine HMS *XE3*, which attacked a Japanese heavy cruiser in Singapore harbour on 31 July 1945. Mines were attached to the cruiser's hull. The submarine, which had been manœuvred under the enemy vessel, became trapped by it. After a nerve-racking fifteen minutes, it managed to wriggle free. Two of *XE3*'s crew were awarded the ★Victoria Cross, while Smith was appointed a DSO. He secured a permanent commission in the RNZN after the war and served in hydrographic survey ships. He was also a member of the 1956 Commonwealth Trans-Antarctic Expedition. He was Hydrographer of the Navy from 1961 to 1972.

Soldier settlement New Zealand possessed a tradition of organised land settlement to call upon when anticipating the return of its soldiers from twentieth century wars. Its systematic settlement in the latter half of the nineteenth century had included a soldier settlement component. The ★Fencibles scheme of the 1840s, which had included a settlement at Mangere for a Waikato contingent keen to protect their adopted economic entrepôt, and the ★military settlers of the 1860s in the Waikato were the most notable examples. However, some veterans of the ★New Zealand Wars also obtained free land grants on confiscated land on their discharge from imperial regiments, from locally raised ★militia units, and from ★kupapa contingents. Many did not take up their sections, preferring instead to sell their land scrip.

A small minority of veterans of the ★Boer War were settled on farm land on their return from South Africa. The scheme had developed largely as a response to blandishments held out to New Zealand troopers by the imperial government to remain as farmers in South Africa. Free grants of land were offered in the Orange Free State and Transvaal with a view to foiling any rural resurgence of Boer nationalism in these newly annexed territories. In New Zealand, political debate about assistance for troopers became entangled in the general clamour for opening up private land, much of it Maori-owned, for settlement. The single government initiative was the Otanake 'special settlement' of about 3200 hectares in thirty-six sections, located in the Mokau district sixteen kilometres from Te Kuiti. More than 500 returned troopers applied for this land when the settlement was opened for selection in 1902, but within five years the scheme was deemed a failure, with more than half the sections either unselected, forfeited, or abandoned. According to the Department of Lands and Survey, there was a great demand from civilians for this land, the implication being that inexperienced soldiers did not necessarily make good farmers. It was a lesson forgotten by the public within ten years.

Soldier settlement

The arrival of the first wounded men from ★Gallipoli in July 1915 focused the public's concern for soldiers, and produced a strong desire to reward the nation's defenders with land. Such sentiments were reinforced by a more recent New Zealand tradition of looking to land settlement, with its connotations of self-sufficient independence, as a cure-all for 'modern' society's ills. T.N. Brodrick, the Under-Secretary of Lands and architect of the soldier settlement scheme, extolled the advantages of such action for both soldiers and state: it matched, in his opinion, the desire for an outdoor life felt by soldiers, who were 'enamoured with the open-air life that a military campaign entails', while at the same time securing for the state resettlement of soldiers in the country rather than towns. There is little evidence that the community was responding directly to demands from returned soldiers for settlement schemes; rather it was guided by the desire to focus the attention of these men on a vocational outlet perceived to be morally superior to an urban existence. Rural land was regarded as a suitable reward for military service. Despite the contrary advice of some of its advisers, the government followed this approach for political reasons, passing the Discharged Soldiers' Settlement Act in 1915. A period of inactivity ensued, however. At first it was intended that only returned soldiers recuperating from wounds and illness would be given the opportunity to settle on small sections, situated near the major centres, and more suited to lighter rural activities, such as market gardening, orcharding, and poultry raising, which might supplement ★war pensions. A ten-year embargo on the transfer of soldiers' farms ensured that the post–New Zealand Wars experience of speculation in soldiers' land scrip was not repeated. Able-bodied discharged soldiers were expected to receive some preference in the existing land settlement programme.

Early in 1916 the Prime Minister, W.F. ★Massey, decided, primarily for political reasons associated with calls for ★conscription, to restrict all land settlement to discharged soldiers. Public support for such a measure was strong, particularly in underdeveloped rural regions. It was thought that about 5000 men would be settled under a programme which Massey described overseas as an experiment. The first soldier settlers obtained farms in the Wellington area, followed closely by the Takapau area of central Hawke's Bay in May 1916. Nine hundred men had been assisted on to the land by November 1918. Amendments made to the land settlement legislation in 1917 allowed interested community patriotic organisations to assist soldiers to acquire land. With the return of the troops from Europe in 1919, demand for farms greatly increased, stimulated by publicity about the programme. A lack of existing viable Crown land reserves forced the government to repurchase private freehold land under the Land for Settlements Act of 1908. Approximately 208 estates were purchased for subdivision, while about 5833 soldiers were assisted with state-funded mortgages to acquire private freehold or leasehold land, or to repay existing mortgages. In response to a booming free market in land, driven by high wartime prices for agricultural commodities, the government operated a conservative repurchase policy, much to the irritation of the returning soldiers, their supporters, and the real estate fraternity. Contemporaries also questioned the existing capacity of the Department of Lands and Survey adequately to meet the challenge. The RSA variously claimed for itself, or other non-governmental bodies, the task of settling soldiers. Its demands that land be compulsorily purchased at pre-war prices made no headway with Massey's Reform ministry, which was unwilling to interfere with the free market in land.

Approximately 10,500 settlers had been established by 1924. Included in the total were thirty-nine Maori soldiers settled on land throughout the North Island. In what was intended initially as an exclusively Maori venture, three were settled at Matata in the Otamarakau settlement. Several Maori patriotic initiatives produced doubtful results. At first the scheme was intended to benefit only those troops who had been in combat, but by 1919 progressive lobbying had secured the inclusion of all servicemen and women, including those serving in New Zealand or still in training camp, nurses, and VADs. Eight nurses obtained rural land for farming and orcharding.

Apart from having to overcome problems of inexperience, and wartime-induced shortages of livestock and materials, soldier settlers established on heavily indebted land were set back by the short economic depression in 1921. Approximately 1850 soldier settlers had, for various reasons, left their properties in the period up to 1924. The remainder received measured financial and other assistance from the state. Rent and mortgage payments were postponed, or sometimes remitted entirely. A process of revaluation of soldiers' farms was instituted after a national inquiry in 1923 revealed that 50 per cent of the 4332 properties investigated were struggling. The 1920s remained uncertain times for farmers and more particularly the soldier settlers, whose experience was being gained in the face of fluctuating prices for agricultural commodities and rising prices for most other goods. The slide of the world economy into depression in the late 1920s forced the Department of Lands and Survey to respond with a budgeting programme for individual soldier farmers. By 1934 about 1200 soldier settlers were receiving budgetary and other assistance, but their existence remained bleak.

Soldier settlement

Regional variation in the soldier settlers' experience was particularly significant. Although the problems associated with the central North Island bush districts have dominated more recent public perception of the scheme, soldier settlement was instituted throughout the country, but there was a North Island bias, with the North Auckland and Auckland land districts containing the largest number of settlers. Substantial lobbying activities from organisations such as local patriotic societies, Farmers' Union committees, county councils, and the National Efficiency Board's local committees resulted in the opening-up of all available Crown and settlement land in each of the eleven land districts. The view of the responsible authorities was that the soldiers were to decide for themselves if the land suited their individual needs. One result of this was the apparently injudicious, at least in retrospect, settlement of marginal land, such as that on the upper reaches of the Wanganui river, in inland Taranaki, in the northern reaches of the Hokianga harbour, and in the Catlins district of south-eastern Otago. The rate of failure in these areas was high. Measuring the 'success' of the scheme as a whole is difficult, but it is significant that in 1936 more than 50 per cent of the original settlers were still in occupation of their properties. The non-recoverable cost to the country was probably between £8 million and £12 million.

The success of these soldier farmers was dependent on a number of factors. In the face of incessant public demand, many of the district land boards had allowed underqualified men access to land. Although an agricultural training component was included in the plans for soldier settlement, what was attempted was overly bureaucratic, poorly coordinated, underresourced, and undermined by the attitudes of the prospective soldier students. With the booming land market making farm acquisition more difficult, soldiers were not prepared to waste time with training programmes which might not guarantee them acquisition of a farm. Introductory agricultural training was provided by the Army at various camps and hospitals, both in the United Kingdom and in New Zealand. Initially, this was part of rehabilitation programmes for wounded and ill soldiers. From 1918 agricultural training was part of a concerted, and now almost forgotten, educational programme to prepare the soldiers for civilian life. For discharged soldiers, training was provided by a combined programme run by the Repatriation Department and the Department of Agriculture. Central to the training schemes were the State farms, established in the 1890s to train the unemployed for rural occupations. Ruakura and Weraroa were the main training farms, but others were established at Motuihe Island near Auckland and Avonhead near Christchurch, and a specialist seed farm was established near Dumbarton in the Clutha valley. A cooperative venture, called Penrose training farm, was undertaken between the Wairarapa Patriotic Society and the government, with mixed success. It would be used again for the same purpose during the ★Second World War. The Repatriation Department also undertook administration of a special farm, established initially by the Army at Featherston Hospital, for the benefit of tubercular soldiers who had been refused admission to Ruakura State Farm. By March 1922 only 962 men had received formal agricultural or farm training, although about 21,000 soldiers had received some form of educational assistance from the Army while overseas.

Dissatisfaction with the treatment of soldier settlers in the inter-war period prompted a revolutionary approach to the rehabilitation of New Zealand's Second World War veterans. Early in the war it was anticipated that the land would provide some means of assisting the returned soldiers to rehabilitate themselves, both economically and psychologically, although the number of men to be assisted was thought to be limited. The emphasis of repatriation policy was placed instead upon the development of secondary industries as a means of employing the returning men. While the intention of the land settlement scheme remained essentially the same as earlier schemes, the extension of the welfare state by the first Labour government in 1938 had significantly altered the vision and perspective of the politicians and bureaucrats—many were veterans of the earlier conflict—whose task it was to craft a successful settlement scheme. State responsibility for individual welfare was, by 1940, perceived as a given.

The approach to the provision of land for veterans of the Second World War was also significantly different from that of the preceding conflict. Government agencies such as Lands and Survey possessed knowledge accumulated during the inter-war period and were able to call on the experience of administering the Land Laws Amendment Act 1929 by the Land Development Board. This had been a significant shift in policy from the former 'pioneer model' of land development. The government assumed responsibility for land development prior to letting or selling land to settlers. As opposed to the First World War scheme, which had expected some at least of the participating soldiers to exhibit true pioneering virtues as well as modern 'scientific' farming capabilities, Second World War farm settlement was based on the provision of developed operating farms, whose operation by experienced and trained men was to be subject to inspection and scrutiny by departmental experts. Because the shortcoming of the First World War approach was judged to have been the lack of practical farming experience possessed by many soldier settlers, a determined effort was made to establish a grading policy and an educational scheme that would provide a supply of capable and experienced settlers on to settlement land. The grading system was operating by April 1944, and training courses were established at two dedicated properties, one of which had been used during the First World War. The institutional experiment was soon abandoned for Pakeha soldiers, although it was continued with some success for Maori soldiers under the control of the Department of Maori Affairs. Subsidised practical training with established farmers was pursued in preference. Weaknesses were apparent with this scheme as well, but by 1954 3295 men had trained under it. A further 2000 had attended training courses at Massey and Lincoln agricultural colleges. Despite the scheme being intended in part as a recognition for service, the returning men were to be subject to an objective evaluation of their capacity to be farmers. There was no place for a repeat of the Massey government's First World War capitulation to public sentiment.

Concern was expressed that the new scheme might have an adverse effect on the economy through inflation of real estate prices, while officials advised that, as was the case after the First World War, the post-war economy would be affected by a declining market for New Zealand's primary produce. This pessimism gave added impetus to establishing a fully controlled and regulated economy, including regulation of the real estate market. Experience gained from the rural crisis caused by the 1930s Depression revealed the necessity to acquire land at values which reflected its actual productive capacity. Land was to be for production as a contribution to the national good, not for speculation by individuals. Two pieces of legislation established stability and control in the real estate market via local Land Sales Committees, a Land Sales Court, and benchmarking of farm land values at 1942 levels. Compulsory Crown purchase was established when existing farms were considered capable of economically viable subdivision. Farms being sold on the open market were evaluated for use as soldier settlement properties; the primary criterion was that returns from production would be sufficient to meet fixed financial outgoings, and provide for a reasonable standard of living.

The wartime government had recourse to three sources of land: existing single unit farms, larger farms or estates capable of subdivision into smaller economic units, and existing Crown land. The latter category, constituting very marginal areas, was not approached with the same enthusiasm as during earlier wars. Nor was it possible to consider the Maori land estate as available for European land settlement, although, as in the case of the First World War scheme, it was hoped that those Maori tribes possessing substantial estates would make these available for Maori soldier settlement. By 1954 567,000 hectares of European land had been acquired by the government for soldier settlement—445,000 hectares by voluntary agreement and 134,000 hectares by compulsory purchase. It transpired, however, that up to 1954, 72 per cent of soldier settlers were assisted to acquire single existing properties.

In a bid to ensure equality of sacrifice the Labour government placed great demands on those farmers wishing to retire. For one particular group, First World War soldier settlers reaching the end of their farming lives, land controls were the ultimate and final betrayal, denying them a capital gain. Balanced against this was the success of the legislation in preventing inflation of farm prices, which was the ultimate assistance rendered to Second World War soldiers. It was observed by the Minister of Rehabilitation that the scheme was to assist farmers, and those settling the land, not those leaving the land. As the prosperity of the post-war peace emerged, support for land sales controls declined. The Act was repealed in 1950 by the new National government. Its replacement was more benign and, combined with the Valuation of Land Act 1951, introduced market values, but retained mechanisms to protect incoming soldier settlers from overvalued land. By 1964 approximately 13,704 returned servicemen, or 5.3 per cent of all those enlisted, had been assisted to acquire farms with loans amounting to £76 million. More than 1000 graded men had acquired farms without assistance from the government, and about 1783 men had taken over family farms. The scheme was too successful in that delays occurred and the number of men waiting for properties increased as they passed through various training schemes and received the prized 'A' grading. By 1954 about 86 per cent of the total servicemen settled had acquired farms. The settlers benefited from a combination of buoyant overseas agricultural commodity prices and the guarantee provided by a continuation of wartime bulk purchase agreements with the United Kingdom. Government agriculture sector stabilisation measures ensured that soldier farmers of the Second World War did not face the same economic hardships as had their First World War predecessors.

By 1963, 268 Maori returned servicemen had been assisted either to acquire farms through cooperation between the Maori Rehabilitation Finance Committee and the State Advances Department or to take up Maori development land by the Department of Maori Affairs. While nurses were included in the First World War land settlement scheme, their position and that of other servicewomen in the Second World War was less assured. The official policy was that those women

Solomons campaign

who had served in the forces were equally entitled to assistance, although no specific policies were put in place for them. The accepted domestic role of women influenced the view of officials. Marriage was expected to negate the need for specific and ongoing assistance. The focus of official concern was in the arenas of training and education. The Rehabilitation Board saw its first priority as settling the returned men.

While the servicemen and women who served with ★Jayforce in the occupation of Japan were eligible, as part of 2NZEF, for the settlement scheme, those who took part in the ★Korean War shortly afterwards were not. Because of the large number of Second World War veterans awaiting land settlement in the 1950s, and the limited amount of land available, it was made clear to members of ★Kayforce at an early stage that they would not be able to participate in ballots for 'rehab farms', as they were popularly known; they could only look to concessionary loan finance for farm purchase, as provided for all ex-servicemen in the 1948 land legislation. The same applied to regular servicemen who took part in later conflicts in South-east Asia. (See REPATRIATION)

ASHLEY GOULD

Solomons campaign Following the onset of the ★Pacific War, Japanese forces rapidly occupied British and Dutch possessions in South-east Asia and by March 1942 were poised to move into the South Pacific. Japanese forces occupied the Solomon Islands, but an attempt to seize Port Moresby was foiled by American forces at the Battle of the Coral Sea in May 1942. After the decisive American victory at Midway in the following month, the Solomons became the scene of the first American counter-offensive against the Japanese on the ground. American forces (including troops which had been briefly stationed in New Zealand) landed on the southern island of Guadalcanal in August 1942 as the first step in a plan to take the major Japanese base at Rabaul. Aware of the potential danger to their whole position in the area, the Japanese responded vigorously. Guadalcanal became the scene of intense fighting.

New Zealand's initial participation in this struggle was limited to RNZN warships. The ★cruisers HMNZS *Leander* and *Achilles* escorted convoys to and from the island, while the 25th Minesweeping Flotilla (see CORVETTES) was involved in escorting convoys or searching for submarines from December 1942. On 5 January 1943 *Achilles* was struck by a bomb in an air attack; thirteen of her crew were killed. At the end of that month HMNZS *Kiwi* and *Moa* forced a Japanese submarine, *I-1*, to the surface, where it was engaged and rammed by *Kiwi*. Pursued by *Moa*, the Japanese submarine ran aground and was wrecked.

RNZAF Warhawks being serviced at an airfield in the islands (*NZ National Archives, AIR118, 72b*)

The RNZAF was involved in the Solomons from November 1942. Hudson bombers of 3 Squadron were deployed from Espiritu Santo to Guadalcanal's Henderson airfield to carry out reconnaissance tasks throughout the Solomons. New Zealand radar units followed in March 1943. RNZAF strength on Guadalcanal was augmented by the arrival of a number of fighter squadrons on six-week tours, beginning with 15 Squadron (equipped with P-40 Warhawk fighters) in April 1943. Apart from intercepting raiding Japanese aircraft, the New Zealand fighters were used to escort American bombers. They played an important part in the Allies' eventual achievement of air superiority in the region, and hence to the outcome of the campaign. For the time being, however, the Japanese continued to bomb Allied forces in the area, one of their raids accounting for the *Moa* on 7 April 1943.

With Guadalcanal finally taken in early 1943, the Americans began the move up the Solomons chain towards Rabaul. Landings were made on the island of New Georgia on 30 June 1943. A few days later the 1st Fijian Commando, with New Zealand officers and NCOs, began operations there. Losses among American naval units in battles for control of the sea around New Georgia were severe, and *Leander*, which had been refitting at Auckland, was urgently summoned to join an American task force charged with intercepting vessels carrying Japanese reinforcements to New Georgia ('the Tokyo Express'). On 13 July, while in action against Japanese ships at the Battle of Kolombangara, she was struck by a torpedo which killed or swept overboard twenty-eight men and blew a huge hole in her side. She limped back to Auckland, and later went to the United States for repairs. Heavy losses at sea did not prevent the Allied forces securing New Georgia in August.

Solomons campaign

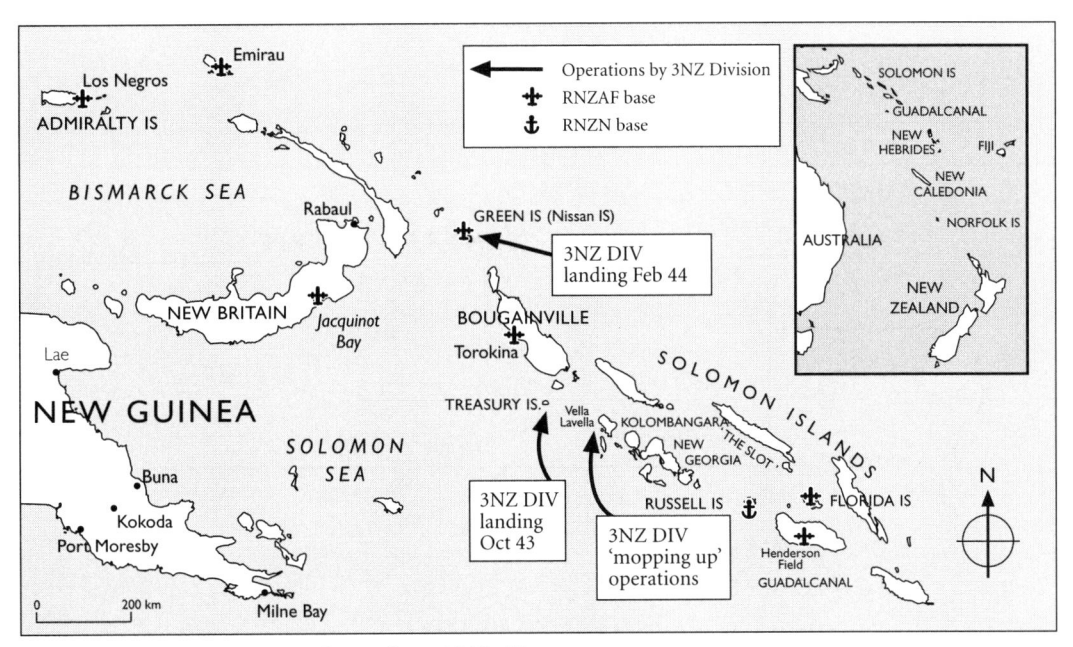

Map 23 The Solomons theatre of operations, 1942–45

Bypassing the next island in the chain, Kolombangara, the Americans then landed on Vella Lavella. To relieve American units in the 'mopping up' phase of this operation, the 3rd New Zealand Division, which had been garrisoning *New Caledonia, was brought forward via Guadalcanal. Its commander, Major-General H.E. *Barrowclough, faced difficult problems: his force had to fit into an American command framework, with its awkwardly different equipment, organisation, and tactics, and it was well below divisional strength, having only two brigades. However, 14th Brigade, which was assigned the task of clearing Vella Lavella, went about the task with vigour. After twelve days of fighting in dense jungle, which cost the lives of thirty-two New Zealanders, those elements of the Japanese garrison not evacuated had been wiped out. The division's air support, which in the final analysis determined the outcome, included New Zealand fighters based at Guadalcanal.

During the fighting on Vella Lavella, Allied strategy in the Pacific was modified by Anglo-American agreement at the Quadrant Conference. Heavily defended Rabaul, the principal Japanese base in the South Pacific, was to be neutralised and bypassed. Advances from Papua New Guinea and from the south would isolate it. As part of this strategy, two New Zealand fighter squadrons and servicing units were moved forward to Ondonga airstrip on New Georgia in October 1943. From there, they were within striking distance of Bougainville, which was invaded by American forces in early November. In preparation for this operation, 8th Brigade landed on the Treasury Islands (a small group immediately south of Bougainville) on 27 October. Only light opposition was encountered, and organised Japanese resistance had ceased within a week. By the time the Treasuries had been finally cleared of Japanese on 12 November, forty more New Zealand lives had been lost.

Airfields established on Bougainville brought Rabaul within range of Allied land-based aircraft, and on 17 December 1943 the RNZAF took part for the first time in air operations against the Japanese base. Some of the heaviest air fighting of the campaign resulted, with the New Zealand squadrons losing eight aircraft during the following week; Japanese losses were substantially higher. To continue the air offensive, the RNZAF fighter wing was moved up to Torokina airstrip on Bougainville. RNZAF Ventura bombers operating from Munda attacked Japanese shipping and conducted searches for survivors of the Rabaul raids. By early 1944 the Japanese air forces in the South Pacific had been destroyed, the New Zealand fighters shooting down their last aircraft of the war on 13 February. This brought the total number of Japanese planes destroyed by the RNZAF fighter squadrons to ninety-nine. RNZAF fighters also provided cover for 14th Brigade's 15 February 1944 landing on the Green Islands, north of Bougainville, as part of the encirclement of Rabaul. By the end of the month the small Japanese garrison had been wiped out; as in other operations, very few of the defenders surrendered. As soon as the islands had been cleared, the construction of airfields began.

503

Solomons campaign

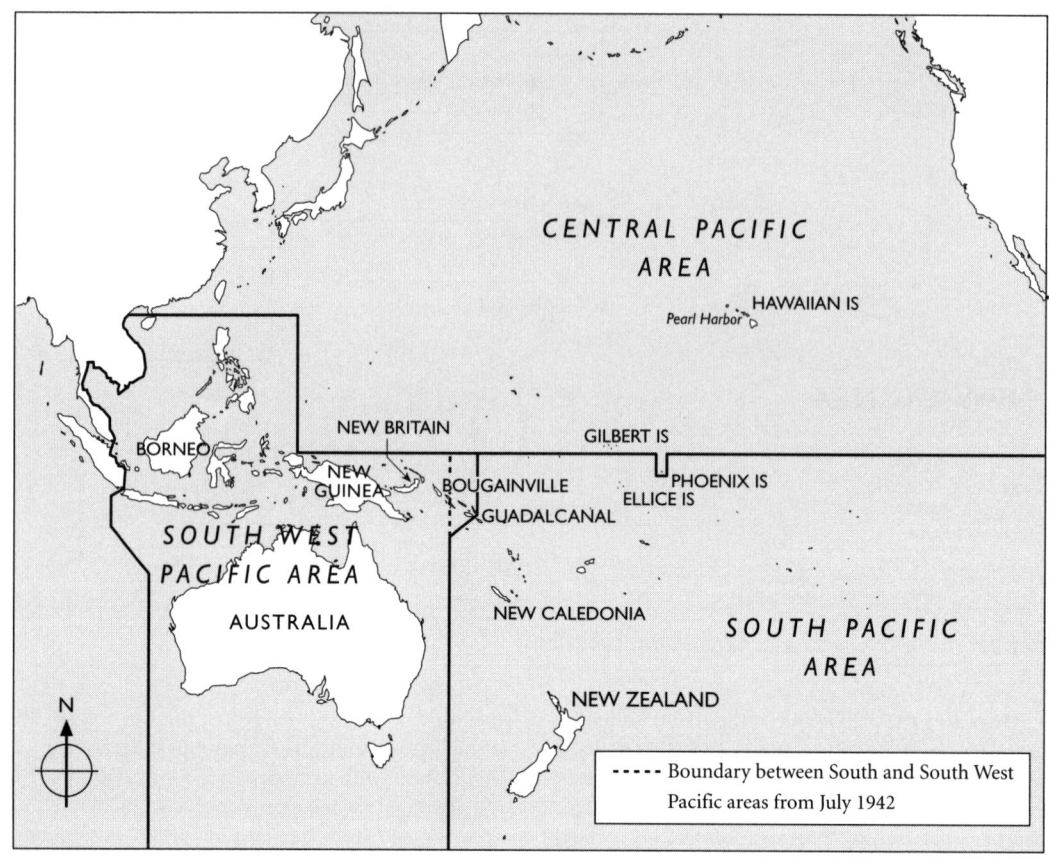

Map 24 Operational commands in the South and South-west Pacific, 1942–45

The Green Islands operation proved to be 3rd Division's last. Manpower shortages in New Zealand had left the government with no choice, once it determined to sustain the 2nd Division in Italy, but to disband 3rd Division, which had been pulled back to New Caledonia in April 1944. The divisional HQ, which had been established in Auckland in August 1944, finally closed on 20 October. Despite American unwillingness to share direction of the Pacific War with either Australia or New Zealand, the New Zealand government remained anxious that New Zealand should continue to play an active part in the war against Japan. The RNZN and RNZAF provided the means. Twelve Fairmile motor launches were sent to the Solomons for escort duties. RNZAF strength in the Solomons was also increased. Two dive-bomber squadrons (25 and 30) arrived at Piva, Bougainville, in March 1944 to carry out air strikes against Rabaul. By June 1944 there were eight RNZAF squadrons (four fighter, two bomber-reconnaissance, one dive-bomber, and one flying boat) in the Solomons, supported by seven servicing units, and in all numbering 5981 men. To coordinate this accumulation of units the New Zealand Air Task Force (ZEAIRTAF) was established in September 1944.

For the remainder of the war the RNZAF squadrons harassed the sizeable but ineffectual Japanese garrisons now cut off in the South Pacific. From November 1944 RNZAF Corsair fighter-bombers supported Australian troops fighting on Bougainville. Other squadrons bombed targets on New Britain and New Ireland. By 1945 the Japanese Army in the area had been reduced almost to a subsistence level, with troops in many cases living in caves to escape the Allied bombing. Their tribulations were finally brought to an end by Japan's capitulation in August 1945. Japanese forces in the South Pacific formally laid down their arms on 6 September 1945. Shortly afterwards New Zealand units began returning home.

The Solomons campaign was the first in which New Zealand forces served under American operational command. It was marked by effective cooperation between New Zealand and American fighting units, and New Zealand officers at times commanded American forces in action without major problems. All three New Zealand services played a role in the establishment of Allied ascendancy in the South Pacific area. However, after August 1943 the theatre had become of secondary importance to the American thrust through the central Pacific, and the New Zealand forces were essentially engaged in a 'mopping up' role as the main Allied forces elsewhere pushed towards Japan itself. Although the military utility of offensive operations in 1945 against the surviving Japanese garrisons in the Solomons—they had become in effect POWs on their now cut-off islands—is perhaps debatable, there were political advantages, in terms of ensuring a New Zealand voice in the post-war settlement with Japan, in maintaining an active role. In all, nearly 600 New Zealanders lost their lives during the campaign, including 345 RNZAF personnel.

O.A. Gillespie, *The Pacific* (War History Branch, Wellington, 1952); J.M.S. Ross, *Royal New Zealand Air Force* (War History Branch, Wellington, 1955).

South Pacific Area, consisting of New Zealand and the ocean area to its north as far as the equator, was established in March 1942. The Pacific theatre, which the British and American Chiefs of Staff had agreed would be a United States responsibility, was at that time divided into four areas—North, Central, South, and South-west Pacific. The latter, encompassing Australia and the area northwards to the Philippines, was the responsibility of the US Army, while the US Navy controlled the other three areas. This arrangement did not please New Zealand, which had been looking to the establishment of an Anzac Area and which regarded Australia and New Zealand as 'inevitably one strategical whole'. However, its protests at the separation were unavailing, and the arrangement persisted until the end of the war. The headquarters of the South Pacific Command was at Auckland from May to July 1942, when it was re-located to ★New Caledonia. The successive commanders of the area, all vice-admirals, were R.L. Ghormley (May–October 1942), W.F. Halsey (October 1942–March 1944), J.H. Newton (March 1944–March 1945), and W.L. Calhoun (March–October 1945).

Special Air Service (SAS) is the elite element of the ★New Zealand Army. Based on the British 22nd SAS Regiment, which was formed during the ★Second World War and included a number of New Zealanders, it shares the same badge with its motto 'Who Dares Wins'. Until 1986 it also wore the original SAS maroon beret. The secrecy surrounding its activities often leads to public misunderstanding of its function and role. The New Zealand Special Air Service was formed on 1 May 1955, and its main component, the SAS Squadron, was specially raised as part of New Zealand's contribution to the newly formed ★British Commonwealth Far East Strategic Reserve in Malaya. More than 600 men responded to the call for volunteers, and 182 entered camp in June 1955. From these were selected the contingent, 133-strong with reinforcements, which left New Zealand in November 1955 under the command of Major Frank ★Rennie. The squadron came under the command of 22nd SAS Regiment, and, after parachute training in Singapore, mounted its first operation, in northern Malaya, in January 1956. During the next two years its four (later five) troops took an active part in ★Malayan Emergency operations, seeking to eliminate communist guerrillas and to locate and regroup aboriginals who were vulnerable to being forced to assist the enemy. Operations averaged thirteen weeks in duration, with supplies being flown in by air. The squadron suffered two fatal casualties, one of whom was killed in action. It returned to New Zealand at the end of 1957 and was disbanded.

Following a reorganisation of the Army, the squadron was re-formed in 1959 with smaller numbers, who included some members of the ★Territorial Force. In 1963 it was renamed 1st Ranger Squadron, NZ SAS, a title which linked it to the nineteenth-century ★Forest Rangers, and its training wing was established at Papakura Camp. From June to September of the previous year, during a crisis over Laos, a 30-man detachment had been deployed at Korat, ★Thailand, as part of a build-up by ★SEATO members which included 6000 US personnel. Valuable contact was made with American Special Forces. In 1965, during the ★Confrontation, a 40-man SAS detachment was made available for operations in Borneo to reinforce 22nd SAS Regiment, under whose command it came, as did an Australian SAS squadron. The New Zealanders were deployed at Kuching in April 1965, where they operated under the British regiment's D (later A) Squadron. They took part in cross-border operations, with four-man patrols using long approach marches to reach their operational areas. There were several brief clashes with Indonesian forces. In meeting this commitment, the Army experienced some manpower problems, but a six-monthly rotation was ensured by expanding the SAS in New Zealand. The second detachment, which relieved the first towards the end of October 1965, was later stationed at Labuan, and two more detachments followed it. Patrolling continued until the end of the Confrontation in August 1966.

During the ★Vietnam War, a 26-man SAS troop served under the operational control of 1st Australian Task Force from December 1968 to February 1971. Five-man patrols had the primary role of gathering intelligence by searching out enemy locations or manning observation posts; as a secondary role, offensive operations were also conducted in one or two patrol strength. Operations normally lasted seven days, and 155 were mounted during the troop's twenty-six

Sport and the armed forces

months' active service. In contrast to the practice in Borneo, the New Zealanders were usually inserted in their operational area by helicopter. Although they gathered much useful information, it was not always used to good effect. The troop had one fatal casualty and nine wounded in Vietnam.

Based at Hobsonville Air Base, the SAS in the late 1990s (now designated 1st New Zealand Special Air Service Group) comprises about 140 personnel in five troops. Although most are members of the Army, the other two services are also represented. Apart from its traditional roles, the SAS is also involved in anti-terrorist preparations. Its training includes exchanges with other countries' forces, and it is probable that, under such arrangements, some members have taken part in combat operations, for example with the British SAS in the ★Gulf War. Such activities are not publicised. In February 1998 a 23-man detachment was contributed to a United States–led coalition as part of measures designed to persuade, or if necessary to force, Iraq to comply with 1991 ★United Nations resolutions regarding the destruction of its weapons of mass destruction (Operation Desert Thunder). Attached to an Australian SAS squadron, the New Zealanders took part in intensive training operations with both Australian and American special forces. The detachment was reduced to eleven in May 1998, and soon after all but one were withdrawn.

W.D. Baker, *Dare to Win: The Story of the New Zealand Special Air Service* (Lothian Publishing Company, Melbourne, 1987).

Sport and the armed forces Wherever they have served, New Zealand servicemen have been quick to look for opportunities to engage in sport. Among New Zealand forces serving overseas such activities have generally been promoted by the authorities in the interests of sustaining morale, keeping troops occupied and out of mischief, and encouraging fitness and skills. In peacetime, sports have been seen as a way of enhancing service and unit pride. During the nineteenth century there was an emphasis on sports with military connotations such as rifle shooting or boxing rather than games, especially because of the difficulty of providing facilities for the latter (though there were occasional rugby games between crew members of visiting British warships or ★Armed Constabulary men and local teams). New Zealanders serving overseas in the successive expeditionary forces or with naval or air forces have, however, indulged their passion for rugby at every opportunity, played cricket depending on the season, and taken part in athletics or swimming contests. Whether on the South African veldt, on the beach at Anzac Cove, on the sands of Egypt, or among the hills of Korea, impromptu games have helped pass the time for both players and spectators. While 'British' games tended to be the most popular, especially when New Zealand troops have formed part of Commonwealth contingents, New Zealand servicemen have demonstrated a willingness to try unfamiliar sports as well. Troops in Korea, for example, tried American sports such as baseball and basketball, and induced much hilarity among their Canadian and American counterparts by their floundering efforts on the ice hockey rink.

As befits a nation with a proud rugby tradition, rugby has been the most prominent service sport. Games were played by the contingents in South Africa, but it was during the two world wars, with the large numbers involved, that service rugby flowered. During the ★First World War, games were organised between units. Lieutenant-Colonel A. Plugge was appointed Divisional Sports Coordinator, and a divisional rugby team was formed, with players serving as physical instructors at the Divisional Training School when not playing. In 1917 the New Zealand Division's XV won the Somme Cup contested among British divisional teams, a French XV, and the New Zealand Hospital XV. Following the Armistice, representative teams were selected from 1NZEF personnel in both France and Great Britain, and from them was selected the New Zealand Services Team. This team played a series of matches in Britain, and won the King George V Cup in a tournament with other expeditionary forces' teams and a team representing the British forces. It subsequently played games in France before embarking upon a tour of South Africa, and played an Auckland team following its return to New Zealand. In May–June 1919 a team representing the New Zealand (Maori) Pioneer Battalion played nine matches in New Zealand. Inter-unit contests in other sports also took place. In 1918 there was a New Zealand services team in the 'British Empire and American Services Games' at Stamford Bridge in London—a kind of mini-Olympics.

Members of 2NZEF were not slow to institute sports competitions when they arrived in Egypt in 1940, a development strongly encouraged by the force commander, Major-General B.C. ★Freyberg, who presented the Freyberg Cup for rugby competition between units. Every Wednesday and Saturday five games were played on three grounds. As early as March 1940 an NZEF selection played an 'international' against a team drawn from the British Army and RAF. The Second Echelon in Britain also organised a competition among ten unit teams during the winter of 1940–41; games were played on grounds protected by light anti-aircraft guns against the danger of low-flying attack. A representative team also played a series of fixtures, wearing all black strip without the silver fern. Following the war a New Zealand Services team played a number of fixtures in Britain, Ireland, and France. It was soon overshadowed, however, by the 2NZEF team,

Squadrons

Members of 2NZEF take part in an impromptu game of rugby in Egypt in 1940 (*War History Collection, Alexander Turnbull Library, F-791-1/4-DA*)

which played thirty-three matches in Britain, Ireland, Germany, and France, including five against international teams. 'The Kiwis' (or 'Freyberg's All Blacks'), as the team became known, were renowned for their attacking style of play. A feature of the tour was the broadcasting of Lieutenant Winston McCarthy of the New Zealand Broadcasting Service.

In the Pacific theatre rugby was also to the fore as a form of recreation. The commander of 2NZEF (Pacific section), Major-General H.E. ★Barrowclough, emulated Freyberg by presenting the Barrowclough Cup for competition among the units of his force. During the ★Korean War inter-unit tournaments and games with teams from other contingents were common, and a ★Kayforce team toured Japan, playing university sides and an all-Japan XV. Similarly successive New Zealand battalions stationed in Malaya from 1957 competed in Far East Land Forces competitions against teams from British and Australian battalions and regiments.

In New Zealand service sport is now well organised, with keenly contested competitions in a range of sports. The King George V Cup is contested by rugby teams representing the three services and the Police. A Combined Services team, including Police, gained considerable prominence in the two decades after the Second World War, playing matches against touring international sides. It has toured overseas at irregular intervals, most recently in 1992. In 1995 a New Zealand Army XV toured Great Britain and Germany (taking along some of the 1946 Kiwis as supporters).

Squadrons, RNZAF Thirty operational squadrons have served with the RNZAF, while another seven have carried the 'New Zealand' title in the RAF. The numbered squadron system was introduced in New Zealand in 1930 with the creation of four TAF squadrons, 1 (army cooperation) Squadron in Auckland, 2 (bomber) Squadron at Rongotai, 3 (bomber) Squadron at Wigram, and 4 (army cooperation) Squadron based at Taieri. Because of budgetary problems and equipment shortages, these were largely paper units until 1938. In 1940 they were merged into the New Zealand General Reconnaissance Squadron at Whenuapai before being divided into separate squadrons and redesignated bomber reconnaissance squadrons as the war progressed. Rapid wartime expansion led to twenty-four further squadrons being formed for Pacific and home service. After 1945 these were reduced to the current level of seven, except during the life of the TAF between 1948 and 1957, when five additional squadrons (four fighter and one flying boat) were raised.

During the ★Second World War, seven squadrons carried the 'New Zealand' name as part of the RAF. Six were formed under Article XV of the ★Empire Air Training Scheme, drawn up in 1939. The seventh, and first to be raised, was 75 Squadron, formed in April 1940 from members of the New Zealand Flight sent to Great Britain to collect Vickers Wellington bombers ordered for the RNZAF. Because of operational exigencies, most squadrons had a mix of Commonwealth and Allied nationalities in their ranks. As a tribute to

Squadrons

A pre-war review of the RNZAF at Rongotai, Wellington. In the front rank, from right to left, are two Gloster Grebe fighters, three Avro 626 trainers, and a Fairey III. Behind are Blackburn Baffins, which flew the RNZAF's first operational sorties after the outbreak of war in 1939 (*RNZAF*)

75 Squadron's record, the RAF agreed in 1946 to transfer the number to the RNZAF. The remaining units were rapidly disbanded at the end of the war.

This summary does not include the myriad of non-operational squadrons, conversion units, flights, schools, and the important servicing units, which maintained aircraft under pool systems, created during the ★Pacific War. Nor does it cover the important ground units, the radar squadrons, the aerodrome construction squadron, base depot, test and assembly flights, and other supporting formations, all of which played an important role in the prosecution of the war. (See table 12.)

J.M.S. Ross, *Royal New Zealand Air Force* (War History Branch, Wellington, 1955); H.L. Thompson, *New Zealanders with the Royal Air Force*, 3 vols (War History Branch, 1953–59).

BRIAN LOCKSTONE

Table 12 New Zealand Operational Squadrons

RNZAF Squadrons

New Zealand General Reconnaissance Squadron
Formed from the four pre-war TAF squadrons at Whenuapai, 1940. Renumbered 1 Squadron, March 1940.

1 Squadron
Formed from the New Zealand General Reconnaissance Squadron, March 1940, at Whenuapai. Served New Zealand, Guadalcanal, New Georgia, Emirau. Disbanded September 1945. Number later transferred to 1 TAF Squadron based Auckland, 1948–57. Reformed in 1972 and disbanded in 1984.

2 Squadron*
Formed 1930 as Wellington TAF squadron, merged into NZ General Reconnaissance Squadron, 1940. 2 (GR) Squadron formed, Nelson, December 1940. Served New Zealand, Espiritu Santo, Guadalcanal, New Georgia, Bougainville, Green Island, Jacquinot Bay. Renumbered 75 Squadron in 1946. Number revived for Wellington TAF squadron based at Ohakea, 1948–57. Again revived 1984. From 1991 stationed at Nowra, New South Wales.

3 Squadron*
Formed 1938 as Christchurch TAF squadron, merged into the NZ GR Squadron, 1940. Re-emerged as 3 (GR) Squadron 1941. First RNZAF squadron on active operations, at Guadalcanal, November 1942. Served also New Zealand, Espiritu Santo, Bougainville, Emirau, Green Island. Disbanded 1945. Number issued to Wigram-based Christchurch TAF squadron, 1948–57. Reformed 1965 as 3 Squadron at Auckland as only RNZAF squadron to operate helicopters.

4 Squadron
One of the pre-war TAF 'paper' squadrons. Re-formed, Fiji, 1940. Served also Los Negros, Guadalcanal, Emirau. Disbanded 1945. Number allocated to Otago TAF squadron, Taieri, 1948–57.

5 Squadron*
Formed at Fiji in November 1941 as a maritime reconnaissance squadron. Served also Espiritu Santo, New Zealand. Disbanded November 1942. Reformed July 1944. It was the last squadron to operate flying boats.

*Operational in 1999.

Squadrons

6 Squadron
Number used by army co-operation squadron in New Zealand, 1942–43. Formed in Fiji in May 1943 as a flying boat squadron. Served Fiji, Espiritu Santo, Florida Islands, New Zealand. Disbanded 1945. Reformed as TAF squadron, 1952–57.

7 Squadron
Formed as a general reconnaissance squadron, Waipapakauri, February 1942. Disbanded May 1943.

8 Squadron
Formed at Auckland as a GR squadron and disbanded in May 1943. Reformed as a bomber reconnaissance squadron in October 1944 and disbanded again March 1945. Served New Zealand, Fiji, Guadalcanal, Emirau.

9 Squadron
Formed as a GR squadron in New Caledonia in July 1942. Renamed a BR Squadron. Disbanded June 1945. Served New Caledonia, Espiritu Santo, New Zealand, Bougainville, Fiji, Emirau.

14 Squadron*
Re-numbered in April 1942 from 488 Squadron survivors from Singapore. Served New Zealand, Espiritu Santo, Guadalcanal, New Georgia, Bougainville, Green Island, Emirau. Post-war service in Japan (BCOF), Cyprus, Singapore, New Zealand. RNZAF's first jet fighter squadron.

15 Squadron
Formed at Whenuapai as fighter squadron, June 1942. Served New Zealand, Tonga, Guadalcanal, New Georgia, Espiritu Santo, Bougainville, Green Island. Disbanded 1945.

16 Squadron
Formed at Woodbourne as fighter squadron, 1942. Served New Zealand, Espiritu Santo, Guadalcanal, New Georgia, Bougainville, Green Island, Jacquinot Bay. Disbanded October 1945.

17 Squadron
Formed as a fighter squadron at Ohakea in 1942. Served New Zealand, Espiritu Santo, Guadalcanal, New Georgia, Bougainville, Green Islands, Los Negros. Disbanded 1945.

18 Squadron
Formed at Ohakea, June 1943. Served New Zealand, Espiritu Santo, Guadalcanal, Bougainville, Green Island. Disbanded October 1945.

19 Squadron
Raised at Ohakea, December 1943. Served New Zealand, Bougainville, Emirau, Espiritu Santo, Los Negros, Jacquinot Bay. Disbanded October 1945.

20 Squadron
Number used by army co-operation squadron in New Zealand, 1942–43. Formed Ardmore, January 1944. Served New Zealand, Guadalcanal, Bougainville, Espiritu Santo, Green Island, Jacquinot Bay. Disbanded 1945.

21 Squadron
Number used by army co-operation squadron in New Zealand, 1942–43. Formed at Ardmore, May 1944. Served Guadalcanal, Bougainville, Green Island, Jacquinot Bay. Disbanded 1945.

22 Squadron
Number used by army co-operation squadron in New Zealand, 1942–43. Formed Ardmore, June 1944. Served New Zealand, Espiritu Santo, Guadalcanal, Bougainville, Emirau. Disbanded September 1945.

23 Squadron
Formed Ardmore, August 1944. Served New Zealand, Espiritu Santo, Los Negros, Guadalcanal, Emirau, Bougainville. Disbanded October 1945.

24 Squadron
Formed Ardmore, September 1944. Served New Zealand, Espiritu Santo, Bougainville, Green Island. Disbanded 1945.

25 Squadron
Formed Seagrove, Auckland, July 1943. Served New Zealand, Guadalcanal, Bougainville. Disbanded May 1944.

26 Squadron
Formed Ardmore, March 1945. Served Guadalcanal, Bougainville. Disbanded July 1945.

30 Squadron
Formed Gisborne, September 1943. Served New Zealand, Espiritu Santo, Bougainville. Disbanded May 1944.

31 Squadron
Formed Gisborne, December 1943. Served New Zealand, Bougainville. Disbanded August 1944.

*Operational in 1999.

Staff colleges

40 Squadron*
Formed at Whenuapai, June 1943. Served New Zealand. Disbanded 1947. Reformed in 1954.
41 Squadron
Formed at Whenuapai, August 1944. Served New Zealand, Singapore. Disbanded 1977.
42 Squadron*
Formed Rongotai, December 1943, from the Communications Flight. Disbanded 1946, becoming General Purposes Flight, Ohakea. Reformed in March 1950.
75 Squadron*
Former 2 Squadron renumbered in 1946. Served New Zealand, Singapore.
488 Squadron
Formed Rongotai, September 1941. Presumably intended to be an Article XV squadron in the RAF. Served Singapore. Following return of survivors to New Zealand, re-designated 14 Squadron.

*Operational in 2000.

Royal Air Force ('New Zealand') Squadrons
75 Squadron
RFC/RAF squadron 1916–19. Reformed March 1937 as a bomber squadron. Became 75 (NZ) Squadron, Feltwell, April 1940. Flew Wellington, Stirling, Lancaster, Lincoln bombers from bases in UK. Disbanded in October 1945. Number transferred to RNZAF in 1946.
485 Squadron
Formed Driffield, March 1941. Flew Spitfires from bases in UK and NW Europe. Disbanded 1945.
486 Squadron
Formed Kirton-on-Lindsey, March 1942. Flew Typhoon, Tempest, Spitfire fighters/fighter-bombers from bases in UK and NW Europe. Disbanded October 1945.
487 Squadron
Formed Feltwell, August 1942. Flew Ventura, Mosquito aircraft from bases in UK and NW Europe. Disbanded 1945.
488 Squadron
Formed Church Fenton, June 1942. Flew Hurricane, Beaufighter, Mosquito aircraft from bases in UK and NW Europe. Disbanded 1945.
489 Squadron
Formed Leuchars, August 1941. Flew Beaufort, Blenheim, Hampden, Beaufighter, Mosquito light bombers from bases in UK. Disbanded 1945.
490 Squadron
Formed Jui, Sierra Leone, March 1943. Flew Catalina, Sunderland flying boats. Disbanded, August 1945.

Staff colleges give specialist instruction in staff duties and higher-level command to officers of the three services. In 1907 Lieutenant-Colonel E.W.C. ★Chaytor became the first New Zealand officer to attend the Staff College at Camberley, England. Within a few years most senior officers in the ★New Zealand Staff Corps were being sent to either Camberley or the Staff College at Quetta, India. This practice continued after the ★First World War, and from 1927 senior New Zealand officers were also sent to the ★Imperial Defence College (IDC) at London. Air force officers attended the RAF Staff College at Andover. During the ★Second World War, the need for trained staff officers for 2NZEF led to New Zealand officers being attached to British staff colleges and schools, particularly the Middle East Staff College at Haifa. To meet requirements in New Zealand, a New Zealand Staff College was established at Palmerston North in October 1941; a British officer was seconded to New Zealand to command it. Four hundred officers graduated during its three years of existence.

After the war, Army and RNZAF officers continued to be sent to the United Kingdom for staff training at Camberley and Andover, with RNZN officers now attending the Royal Navy Staff College at Greenwich as well. From 1947 senior officers attended the Joint Services Staff College in addition to the IDC. During the 1950s New Zealand began making use of Australian staff colleges, with officers attending the Australian Army Staff College at Fort Queenscliff and the RAAF Staff College at Point Cook, both in Victoria. From 1972 New Zealanders attended 22-week courses at the Joint Services Staff College, which opened in Canberra that year. By the 1970s there were seventeen officers enrolled at overseas staff colleges annually. About 300 other officers and NCOs attended short staff and specialist courses in the United States, United Kingdom, Australia, and Malaysia each year.

A RNZAF Officers' School had been established at Whenuapai in 1950 to instruct officers in law and administration. Gradually enlarged during the 1950s to include staff duties, the school was renamed the RNZAF Command and Staff School in August 1960, and six years later the RNZAF Command and Staff College. Nineteen officers from the RNZAF, RNZN, and the New Zealand Police underwent 8-week to 16-week courses covering strategy, public relations, politics, intelligence, law, industry, and specialist service papers. In the 1990s about fifty students annually from New Zealand, Southeast Asia, and the South Pacific were being taught in a programme which included annual orientation trips to countries in the Asia–Pacific region.

Stark, Private John Douglas (17 July 1894–22 February 1942), one of 1NZEF's outstanding personalities, was born in Invercargill. He later claimed that his father was a Delaware Indian. When he volunteered for 1NZEF in February 1915, it was probably to escape trouble with the law. He served with the Otago Battalion at ★Gallipoli, where he was wounded. On the ★Western Front Stark (variously known as 'Darkie', 'Starkie', and 'Killer') became renowned among New Zealand troops for reckless courage as well as a disdain for authority. On the night of 11–12 July 1916 he particularly distinguished himself by rescuing wounded men from no man's land and destroying two German machine-gun posts after a failed trench raid. Although recommended for a ★Victoria Cross, he had to be content with the commutation of a prison sentence he had earned for an earlier offence. In September 1916, during the Battle of the Somme, the death of his brother reduced him to a state of berserk fury, his ensuing slaughter of the enemy extending to the cold-blooded killing of prisoners. Further offences against military discipline brought him a lengthy prison sentence in 1917, but he escaped from the military prison at Le Havre. After roaming behind the lines, he reattached himself unofficially to his old battalion. In June 1918 he was wounded while stalking an enemy sniper. The remainder of his sentence was remitted, and he returned to the front in October, where he was wounded again while leading a bombing party. A violent, ill-disciplined man, he was tolerated in the front line for his courage and ruthlessness. Among those who felt indebted to him was company commander Captain J.G. Coates, a later prime minister of New Zealand, who always maintained that Stark had saved his life by rescuing him from the battlefield. After the war Stark continued to lead a chequered life while working mainly as a labourer on relief projects. An account of his wartime exploits was published in 1938.

R. Hyde, *Passport to Hell: The Story of James Douglas Stark, Bomber, First Regiment, New Zealand Expeditionary Forces* (Hurst & Blackett Ltd, London, 1938).

Starnes, Major Frederick (11 October 1888–12 October 1973) was an outstanding New Zealand officer in the ★First World War. Born in Nelson, he was a farmer before he joined 1NZEF's Canterbury Battalion in August 1914 as a second lieutenant. He was badly wounded at ★Gallipoli during the August 1915 Chunuk Bair offensive. After convalescence in England, he returned to Egypt before proceeding to the ★Western Front with 2nd Battalion, Canterbury Regiment. On the night of 20–21 September 1916 during the Battle of the Somme, his battalion seized a tangle of trenches to cover the exposed left flank of the New Zealand Division. However, it came under immediate counter-attack. With the Canterbury positions almost encircled, Starnes rallied his tired men and led a series of bold attacks with grenades. After six hours of close quarters fighting the Germans finally withdrew at dawn. When they renewed the counter-attack that afternoon, Starnes eventually led a bayonet charge which routed them. He was fortunate to survive unscathed, for thirty-three fellow officers in his battalion had been killed or wounded during the battle. Although his battalion commander recommended him for a ★Victoria Cross for his exploits in this action, the divisional commander, Major-General Sir Andrew ★Russell, had a policy of not forwarding such recommendations for officers. Starnes had to be content with being made an immediate DSO. After volunteering for special service with the British Army in January 1918, he commanded a party of more than thirty New Zealanders in Dunsterforce, which operated in northern Persia and south Russia (see RUSSIAN INTERVENTION). His service earned him a mention in dispatches and appointment as an OBE. After being discharged in 1919, he farmed in Kenya.

Stevens, Major-General William George (11 December 1893–7 August 1975), a prominent staff officer in the ★Second World War, was chief administrator of 2NZEF in Egypt. A Londoner by birth, he emigrated to New Zealand with his family in 1895. He performed well at school, and was inclined to a career in civil engineering until his mother pushed him into seeking admission to the new Royal Military College, Duntroon, which he entered belatedly in 1912 after failing his initial medical examination. With the outbreak of the ★First World War, his class graduated early, and he was seconded to 1NZEF as a junior officer in the New Zealand Artillery in April 1915. He served at ★Gallipoli from August 1915 until the evacuation, apart from a period of illness in October, and on the ★Western Front. During 1918 he was on the staff of the New Zealand Divisional Artillery. His ambivalence about his career as a regular soldier was dispelled when he gained the opportunity to undertake a two-year course at the Staff College at Camberley in England. By the time he returned to New Zealand in early 1929, after attending the ★Imperial Defence College as well, he was convinced of the need for the coordination of defence preparations, encompassing both military and civil resources of the state. He commanded the General HQ Training Depot at Trentham, and from 1931 was also a staff officer in GHQ's Operations and Intelligence Branch (which he later described as 'a phantom branch'). He was New Zealand's exchange officer at annual exercises in Australia in 1937. On his return he was seconded to the Prime Minister's Department as Secretary of the newly formed Council of Defence. He was also Secretary of the ★Chiefs of Staff Committee, and during the next three years built up a web of coordinating committees as part of the ★Organisation for National Security, all designed to prepare New Zealand for a transition to a war footing. The success of the scheme owed much to his organisational ability. After going to Great Britain as military adviser to the acting Prime Minister, Peter ★Fraser, in late 1939, he was seconded to 2NZEF. He left with the First Echelon as assistant adjutant and quartermaster-general in 2nd New Zealand Division's HQ. From 1 October 1940 he was officer in charge of administration in 2NZEF HQ. He also commanded Maadi Camp in Egypt between August 1942 and early 1944, when 2NZEF HQ shifted to Italy. He was made a CBE in 1941, and a CB three years later. With 2NZEF in the process of being wound up, he was the obvious person to succeed Freyberg as its commander, which he did on 22 November 1945. When this task was completed in February 1946, he returned to New Zealand, visiting ★Jayforce en route. His lack of enthusiasm for resuming his career as a regular soldier was confirmed when he was passed over for command of the post-war Army. From 1946 to 1953 he was official secretary in the New Zealand High Commission in London. In retirement he authored two volumes in the official war history series—*Problems of 2NZEF* (1958), which he regarded as 'largely a personal report', and *Bardia to Enfidaville* (1962)—and later published a useful insider's perspective of 2NZEF's wartime commander, *Freyberg V.C., The Man 1939–1945* (1965). An unpublished autobiography, 'Recall without Repining' (1969), now lodged in the Alexander Turnbull Library in Wellington, provides an unparalleled insight into the life of a regular officer in the first half of the twentieth century, one who rose to high rank despite being sometimes ambivalent about his choice of career.

Stewart, Lieutenant-Colonel Hugh (1 September 1884–28 September 1934) wrote the official history of the New Zealand Division in the ★First World War. A Scot by birth, he had come to New Zealand in 1912 to take up the professorship of classics at Canterbury University College and had enlisted in 1NZEF in August 1914. He fought as a subaltern at ★Gallipoli, and earned an MC and the respect of his men for his courageous conduct. In March 1916 his leadership qualities were recognised in his promotion to command the 2nd Battalion, Canterbury Infantry Regiment, which he led with distinction on the ★Western Front. For his services there he was made a CMG and a DSO and bar. In all, he was mentioned in dispatches five times during the war. In November 1918 he became 1NZEF's Director of Education. Reluctantly accepting the commission to write the 'popular history' of the division, he relinquished his position and began working on his manuscript in late January 1919. By the following August he had completed a draft of the history, which was published in 1921. Stewart meanwhile had returned to his university position at Christchurch. He commanded a ★Territorial Force battalion and was elected president of the New Zealand Returned Soldiers' Association in 1924. However, in 1926 he left New Zealand to become Principal of University College in Nottingham, England, where he is commemorated in Hugh Stewart Hall. His sudden death occurred at sea while he was returning from a holiday in New Zealand.

Stewart, Major-General Sir Keith Lindsay (30 December 1896–13 November 1972). Born at Timaru, and afflicted with a pronounced stutter, Stewart began his military career at the Royal Military College, Duntroon, in 1914. Two years later, he graduated early to join 1NZEF, but did not leave New Zealand until mid 1917. From September 1917 he was adjutant of the New Zealand Training Units and Depots in Egypt. In 1919 he served in the headquarters of the Anzac Mounted Division. He was made an MBE for his war services. Resuming his career in the ★New Zealand Staff Corps in December 1919, he served in staff positions in Wellington and Palmerston North before attending the Staff College at Camberley in 1928–29. From 1931 to 1934 he was seconded to the Ceylon Defence Force, a successful posting for which he was made an OBE. After his return, he served in Dunedin and Christchurch before, in 1939, being seconded to 2NZEF. He left New Zealand with the First Echelon in January 1940 as GSO1 of the 2nd New Zealand Division. During the ★Crete campaign he was Brigadier General Staff in Major-General B.C. ★Freyberg's Creforce HQ. His health having deteriorated, Stewart returned to New Zealand at the end of

1941 to become Deputy Chief of the General Staff, in which capacity he was heavily involved in army preparations to meet possible invasion by Japan. Back in the Middle East, he commanded 5th Infantry Brigade from August 1943, with an interlude as commander of 4th Armoured Brigade between November 1943 and March 1944. He was captured by the enemy while making a reconnaissance of forward positions south of Florence on 1 August 1944 and held as a POW in Germany until liberated in the following March. Back in New Zealand, he was made a CBE. In preparation for New Zealand's contribution to the occupation of Japan, he returned to Italy to take command of 9th Infantry Brigade in November 1945 and took it to Japan in early 1946. He commanded ★Jayforce until July 1946. As Adjutant-General and Second Military Member of the New Zealand Army Board, he was deeply involved in the post-war reorganisation of the Army. From April 1949, as Chief of the General Staff, he oversaw the Army's preparations to fulfil the ★Middle East commitment, particularly by the introduction of ★compulsory military training, and to make a ground contribution to the UN effort in the ★Korean War. Stewart's undoubted administrative skills were complemented by a progressive and determined approach to issues. His insistence that there should be no specific Maori units in either 3NZEF or ★Kayforce set the pattern for the post-war Army. During 1950 he clashed violently with the Prime Minister, Sidney Holland, over the Army's state of readiness, which probably explains the government's failure to follow precedent by knighting him on his retirement in March 1952. Stewart had to await a Labour administration before being appointed a KBE in 1958.

Stott, Major Donald John (23 October 1915–20/21 March 1945). An Auckland machinist, Stott enlisted in 2NZEF in December 1939. Wounded and captured during the battle for ★Crete, he was taken to a POW camp in Greece, from which, on 6 August 1941, he made a spectacular escape with another New Zealander, Robert Morton. After several months in hiding, they reached Egypt in a Greek sailing boat. Stott subsequently entered an officer training school before being seconded in June 1942 to the Special Operations Executive. After being parachuted into Greece, he led a party that blew up the Asopos viaduct on 20 June 1943. For this exploit he was recommended for a ★Victoria Cross, but was instead appointed a DSO. Stott remained in Greece working alongside the resistance. As the German situation in the Balkans deteriorated, he became involved in clandestine talks with senior German officers in Athens; the discussions came to nothing, but Stott received a bar to his DSO. He returned to New Zealand in May 1944. In July he was attached to the Services Reconnaissance Department in Australia for special duties, and was promoted to major later in the year. As a member of ★Z Special Unit, he led a dozen commandos on a mission to Japanese-occupied Borneo in March 1945. Dropped by submarine off Balikpapan in rubber boats, the commandos encountered rough weather. Stott and a companion were lost, and were presumed to have drowned. (See RESISTANCE IN EUROPE, NEW ZEALANDERS AND)

G. McDonald, *New Zealand's Secret Heroes: Don Stott and the 'Z' Special Unit* (Reed Books, Auckland, 1991).

Stout, Colonel Sir Thomas Duncan Macgregor (25 July 1885–27 February 1979) was a leading New Zealand war surgeon. The son of the politician Sir Robert Stout, he was a surgeon at Wellington Hospital when he volunteered for overseas service in August 1914. He left New Zealand with the Samoan Expeditionary Force, with which he served until April 1915. Proceeding to Egypt, he joined 1NZEF's 1st New Zealand Stationary Hospital, which in October 1915 was sent to ★Salonika. He was fortunate to survive the sinking of the ★*Marquette*. After the hospital was redeployed to the ★Western Front in 1916, he was briefly attached to British casualty clearing stations during the Battle of the Somme. In June 1917 he was made a DSO and joined 1st New Zealand General Hospital at Brockenhurst in England. He embarked for New Zealand in 1919. In March 1940 he returned to the colours when he was appointed Officer Commanding (Surgical) of the 1st New Zealand General Hospital in Egypt. From 1941 until 1945 he was Consultant Surgeon to 2NZEF. He was made a CBE for his contribution to wartime surgical treatment. After the war he was employed by the ★War History Branch to prepare the medical volumes of the official history. His three works—*War Surgery and Medicine* (1954), *New Zealand Medical Services in Middle East and Italy* (1956), and *Medical Services in New Zealand and the Pacific* (1958)—provide a valuable reference tool for the treatment of war casualties. He was knighted in 1962.

Suez crisis The crisis which erupted in the Middle East in late 1956, following Egypt's nationalisation of the Suez Canal, confronted New Zealand with difficult diplomatic problems. It culminated in military action by Great Britain and France in collusion with Israel, which attacked Egypt on 29 October. Two days later British and French aircraft began bombing Egyptian airfields, and on 5 November an Anglo-French invasion began amid an international outcry. In New Zealand, where both government and public opinion were still avidly pro-British, there was broad support for the British approach. Only Australia and Israel

Supply ships

joined it in supporting the intervening powers in the ★United Nations. However, with the United States opposed to their action, Britain and France quickly bowed to international pressure, halting the operation on 7 November, and eventually making a humiliating withdrawal. A United Nations ★peace-keeping force was deployed to keep the Israelis and Egyptians apart.

New Zealand's response to the crisis was complicated by the presence in the Royal Navy's Mediterranean Fleet of its newly acquired cruiser, HMNZS *Royalist*, which was working up before proceeding to New Zealand. Because of her potential value to the invading force as an anti-aircraft and radar picket ship, there were hopes in London that she might be made available for the planned amphibious operation against Egypt. New Zealand agreed that, while she should remain in the Mediterranean, she should not become actively involved. For political reasons the government was reluctant to order her withdrawal, and there was some relief in Wellington when on 5 November, the day the British and French forces began their invasion of Egypt, the British authorities ordered her to Malta prior to sailing for New Zealand.

New Zealand offered subsequently to participate in the proposed United Nations peace-keeping force, and recruiting for a two-company infantry unit began on 15 November, but in the event no contribution was required. In demonstrating the limitations of New Zealand's 'where Britain goes, we go' approach, the crisis encouraged reassessment of New Zealand's approach to international affairs. The decline of Britain's power was brutally demonstrated, while the American stance during the crisis had been, in New Zealand eyes, less than satisfactory.

M. Templeton, *Ties of Blood and Empire: New Zealand's Involvement in Middle East Defence and the Suez Crisis 1947–57* (Auckland University Press, Auckland, 1994).

Supply ships New Zealand's early coal-burning warships could bunker in most ports. That flexibility disappeared in 1924 when HMS *Dunedin*, the first of the oil-burning 'D' class ★cruisers, joined the ★New Zealand Division of the Royal Navy. The ★merchant marine had barely begun the lengthy switch from coal to oil, so in the absence of reliable commercial supplies the government moved to make the Devonport naval base self-reliant. In 1924 it hired a tanker from the Admiralty and built the first of two 4600-ton capacity oil tanks. The Royal Fleet Auxiliary *Nucula*, the 4614-ton former mercantile tanker *Hermione*, had taken to the water at Newcastle as early as 1906. She had a loaded speed of about ten knots, so each year took about seven weeks to make each of her one to three voyages between California and Auckland. *Nucula* made three trips to Abadan in the Persian Gulf in 1934 when temporarily high US oil prices dictated a diversion, and occasionally refuelled the cruisers in the Pacific Islands, but the old ship spent most of her time moored off the base in care and maintenance with a reduced crew. The arrival of the longer-range Leander class cruisers and the construction of a 12,000-ton capacity tank at Stanley Bay brought an end to the seagoing career of the *Nucula*, which served as a stationary storage hulk off Shoal Bay until scuttled at sea in 1947.

During the ★Second World War the RNZN's supply fleet amounted to no more than harbour craft, fuel lighters, and small requisitioned coasters. It operated the 207-ton munitions carrier *Isa Lei* between 1952 and 1963, and built some new dumb lighters, but did not gain its first large supply ship until 1956, when the government bought the *Pretext* to transport the New Zealand section of the Commonwealth Trans-Antarctic Expedition to McMurdo Sound. Built at Wilmington, Delaware, in 1944, the wooden-hulled netlayer had served in the Royal Navy before being ice-strengthened after the war for use as a survey and Antarctic supply vessel. The 1275-ton ship took the name HMNZS *Endeavour*, then carried by a requisitioned munitions lighter. During her first Antarctic summer, *Endeavour* transported Sir Edmund Hillary and his team south, along with the materials needed for the construction of Scott Base. By 1959–60 the old ship's caulking and sheathing were causing concern, and so after she returned from her last Antarctic season in February 1961, she was laid up at Devonport and was sold the following year. By October 1962 another *Endeavour* had entered the fleet, the former USS *Namakagon*. One of twenty-three Patapsco class gasoline tankers, the 1944-vintage *Endeavour* displaced 1850 tons standard, 4335 tons fully loaded, was 94.7 metres long, and had a speed of fourteen knots. The steel-hulled ship was strengthened for navigation in the ice and refitted to provide accommodation for sixty-eight crew and fourteen scientists. For the next eight summer seasons she would become a familiar sight at McMurdo Sound supporting Scott Base. When not engaged in Antarctic work, *Endeavour* carried out scientific work, resupplied weather stations, and transported and dumped munitions. The RNZN extended the original five-year lease, but decommissioned the ship a year early in 1971 because of defence economies. She served the Taiwanese Navy until the late 1990s.

The RNZN went without supply vessels for the next seventeen years. It would feel the absence of a tanker as soon as 1973, when it had to rely on HMAS *Supply* to support its frigate protests against French atmospheric testing at Moruroa Atoll. During the 1980s first the country's strained relations with its

The frigates HMNZS *Waikato* and *Wellington* refuelling from the fleet supply tanker HMNZS *Endeavour* during exercises off the Australian coast in 1988 (*NZDF*)

★ANZUS partners and then the ★Fiji coups encouraged the RNZN to examine ways of making the fleet more self-reliant. In July 1986 it ordered a small fleet replenishment vessel from a Korean shipyard. A variant of Hyundai's HDA-12000 standard mercantile design, the 12,390-ton full-load vessel became the fourth HMNZS *Endeavour*. The 14-knot ship can carry 7500 tons of fuel, 100 tons of aviation fuel, 100 tons of water, and a limited amount of dry stores. Delayed by shipyard labour disputes and an engine breakdown while on trials, she was commissioned on 7 April 1988. The ship embarks a helicopter and is defensively armed with decoy launchers and two 20 mm anti-aircraft guns. She also has secondary civil emergency and training roles.

In 1985–86 the RNZN began planning the acquisition of a 12,000-ton, 18-knot logistics support vessel capable of operating two helicopters to perform supply, troopship, ★peace-keeping, and disaster relief duties. That work halted in 1990, then revived to culminate in the December 1995 announcement of the purchase of the eleven-year-old Danish roll-on roll-off cargo ship *Mercandian Queen II*. After a short refit this 7995-ton, 14.5-knot ship was commissioned as HMNZS *Charles Upham*. The RNZN planned to operate her as an austere freighter before thoroughly reconstructing her to take a company of troops and to operate two medium helicopters. The ship participated in a number of exercises and even operated a Wasp helicopter while replenishing fuel dumps in the Kermadecs, but the RNZN's plans foundered when serious engine and embarrassing stability problems put 'the chunder-barge' *Charles Upham* on newspaper front pages and then into reserve in August 1996. Because funds were not immediately available for the planned reconstruction, she was leased to a private firm in 1998, and soon caused controversy in New Zealand when it was reported that she was carrying oranges in the Mediterranean.

R. Gillett, *Australian and New Zealand Warships Since 1946* (Pacific Publishers, Auckland, 1988); R.J. McDougall, *New Zealand Naval Vessels* (GP Books, Wellington, 1989).

GAVIN McLEAN

Surafend massacre, the worst atrocity known to have been committed by New Zealand troops in the twentieth century, occurred shortly after the conclusion of the ★Sinai–Palestine campaign. Its roots lay in simmering antagonism between the members of the New Zealand Mounted Rifles Brigade, camped at Richon le Zion in Palestine, and the local Arab population. Many of the New Zealanders were convinced that Arabs had been guilty of looting and spying and even of shooting at them. On 9 December 1918 a New Zealand soldier was murdered after disturbing an intruder, whose tracks led to the nearby village of Surafend. When confronted, the head men of the village pleaded ignorance, and the matter was taken up by the divisional staff. In the meantime, some of the New Zealand mounted riflemen decided to take the law into their own hands. On the evening of 10 December a mob of them herded the women and children out of the village and beat to death any men they could find. The village and a nearby Bedouin camp were then burnt. Between twenty and thirty Arabs were killed.

In an address to the assembled Anzac Mounted Division, the furious Commander-in-Chief of the Egyptian Expeditionary Force, General Sir Edmund Allenby, later accused the troops of being 'murderers'. The story that he was then 'counted out' from the parade by angry Australian and New Zealand troops is probably apocryphal. Allenby refused, at first, to recognise the division with honours. No New Zealand soldier was ever court-martialled for participation in the massacre.

T

Taiaroa, Te Matenga (?–2 February 1863), a member of the Ngai Te Ruahikihiki and Ngati Moki hapu of Ngai Tahu, was a prominent South Island warrior chief during the ★Musket Wars. Although probably born near Lake Ellesmere, he established himself on the Otago Peninsula. He may have taken part in the attack on the crew of the *Sophia* in 1817. During the 1820s he was involved in fighting within Ngai Tahu. Having obtained muskets somewhat before their northern adversaries, his forces held an advantage, which they exploited to win several victories, including a significant battle at Wairewa. Among his feats was the capture of a pa on Ripapa Island in Lyttelton Harbour. From 1829 Ngai Tahu were confronted with a threat from without, in the form of the Ngati Toa chief ★Te Rauparaha, raiding south from his stronghold at Kapiti. Taiaroa joined the defenders of Kaiapoi pa when it was besieged by Te Rauparaha in 1831, but he was no longer there when it fell, possibly having been allowed to escape by Ngati Toa. Subsequently he took part in Ngai Tahu efforts to resist further Ngati Toa incursions in the South Island, and may have been present at Lake Grassmere when Te Rauparaha was almost captured. During the mid 1830s he campaigned against Ngati Toa in the northern South Island, eventually succeeding in expelling them from Ngai Tahu territory. During the summer of 1836–37 he took part in the force which defeated the raiding Ngati Tama chief ★Te Puoho-o-te-rangi at Tuturau. During the 1840s, following the ★Wairau massacre, he encouraged a rapprochement between Ngai Tahu and Ngati Toa which may have been anti-Pakeha in design. Although unenthusiastic about European settlement—he had not signed the Treaty of Waitangi in 1840 (despite the fact that his name appears on it)—he was later instrumental in the sale of substantial tracts of South Island land. His attitude was influenced by his conversion to Christianity in 1859, at which time he took the name Te Matenga (Marsden), and he tried to mediate in the Taranaki War of 1860–61.

Tait, Admiral Sir (Allan) Gordon (30 October 1921–), who made his career in the Royal Navy, reached the highest naval rank yet achieved by a New Zealander. Born at Timaru, he entered the Royal Naval College at Dartmouth shortly before the ★Second World War. He was involved in the Atlantic campaign and convoy protection on the route to north Russia in the first three years of the war before serving in submarines in the Mediterranean and the Far East. He was awarded a DSC in 1943 and was mentioned in dispatches. Between 1947 and 1956 he commanded a series of British submarines, with the exception of a three-year period spent in Wellington as aide-de-camp to the Governor-General of New Zealand, Lieutenant-General Sir Bernard ★Freyberg. After an attachment to the British High Commission in Canada and further ship commands, he commanded successively the 2nd Destroyer Squadron on the Far East Station and the 3rd Submarine Squadron. He was Chief of Staff, Submarine Command, in 1969–70 before commanding the Royal Naval College. After serving as Naval Secretary at the Ministry of Defence, London, from 1972 to 1974, he was Flag Officer, Plymouth, as well as commander of the NATO forces in the Eastern Atlantic's Central Sub Area. He was made a KCB in 1977, the year in which he became Chief of Naval Personnel and Second Sea Lord at the Admiralty. Following his retirement from the Royal Navy in 1979, he returned to New Zealand and embarked on a business career.

Takamoana, Karaitiana (?–24 February 1879) was one of the senior chiefs of Ngati Te Whatu-i-apiti and Ngati Kahungunu at Heretaunga, Hawke's Bay. As a young man he was among those who resisted the incursions of Mananui ★Te Heuheu Tukino. Captured at Te Pakake pa, Napier, in 1824 but released by ★Te Wherowhero, he returned to Heretaunga and continued to fight against opposing tribes. In the 1840s and 1850s he welcomed European settlement. However, a dispute with Te Hapuku over land sales led to conflict in 1857, from which Takamoana emerged victorious. From 1861 he was the paramount chief of the Hawke's Bay area. In 1865 he opposed the spread of Pai Marire into Hawke's Bay, possibly because his foe, Te Hapuku, had sided with the Hauhau. In September 1866 Takamoana's men and colonial troops under Lieutenant-Colonel G.S. ★Whitmore drove the Hauhau from their pa at Omarunui. From 1871 he held one of the Maori seats in Parliament.

Taraia Ngakuti Te Tumuhuia (?–March 1872), a prominent tribal leader during the ★Musket Wars, was a member of the Coromandel-based Ngati Tamatera, which, with Ngati Maru, were forced by Nga Puhi raids from 1818 to seek sanctuary to the south with the Waikato. Even so, he made common cause with ★Pomare I of Nga Puhi in an expedition through the Urewera in 1824. However, when Nga Puhi again invaded two years later, he resisted them, and reputedly killed Pomare. By the late 1820s his tribe had regained their lands in the Hauraki area. Now armed with muskets acquired from European traders, his war parties raided the East Coast and Bay of Plenty, fighting Te Whakatohea, Ngati Porou, and Ngai Tai. In the late 1820s he may have accompanied Ngati Raukawa to Kapiti. He fought with ★Te Rauparaha against Te Ati Awa at Haowhenua near Otaki in 1834. Having refused to sign the Treaty of Waitangi in 1840, Taraia claimed the right to settle disputes with other Maori in the age-old fashion, by force, and in 1842 raided Ngai Te Rangi of Tauranga. As late as 1850, by which time he was acknowledged as paramount chief of Ngati Tamatera and Ngati Maru, he was still leading war parties to avenge perceived wrongs. Although supporting the King Movement in the 1860s, he was too old to take part in the fighting, though a Ngati Maru contingent joined the Kingite forces.

Taranaki Wars see NEW ZEALAND WARS

Taranui, Major Te Pokiha (?–11 July 1901) was an important ★kupapa chief during the ★New Zealand Wars. Of Ngati Pikiao of Te Arawa, he took the name Te Pokiha (Fox) as a young man, probably when he was baptised. He was often called Major Fox by Pakeha. In early April 1864, near Lake Rotoiti, he took part in Te Arawa's defeat of a war party from the East Coast seeking to cross its territory to join the King Movement's struggle in the Waikato. The East Coast warriors were harried as they retreated to the coast, where they were shelled by British warships. In a battle at Maketu Te Pokiha distinguished himself by his bravery. He was determined to complete the destruction of the war party, which was achieved at Te Kaokaoroa on 28 April. In 1865 he led Ngati Pikiao kupapa against Hauhau who had committed several murders, including that of the missionary C.S. Volkner. He secured the surrender of Te Teko pa on the Rangitaiki River. He was again in action against the Hauhau in 1867, and took part in the battle of Puraku west of Rotorua in March. Following ★Te Kooti's incursion into the Bay of Plenty in March 1869, Te Pokiha's warriors, along with 150 ★military settlers, moved on Te Kooti's pa at Tauaroa in the Rangitaiki Valley near Murupara. However, they were unable to prevent Te Kooti from escaping into the Urewera. Te Pokiha, who was commissioned in the New Zealand Militia in May 1869, took part in a subsequent drive into this fastness by a column led by Colonel G.S. ★Whitmore. The Arawa kupapa seized a number of Tuhoe pa and destroyed crops. Te Pokiha led a charge against Te Kooti's rearguard at Orona, north of Lake Waikaremoana, but he proved sensibly cautious about continuing the drive because of the approaching winter and supply problems. In early 1870 he was among the defenders when Rotorua was threatened by Te Kooti. In March 1870 the Arawa kupapa were reorganised into the Arawa Flying Column, with whom Te Pokiha served until the fighting petered out.

Taratoa, Henare Wiremu (?–21 June 1864) was notable for his efforts to alleviate the effects of warfare during the ★New Zealand Wars. A leader of Ngai Te Rangi from the Tauranga area, he was educated by missionaries and at St John's College, Auckland. After working as a missionary in the Pacific Islands for several months, he became a lay reader and teacher in the Otaki area in 1858. Back in Tauranga, where he established a school in 1861, he was instrumental in drawing up a code of conduct when fighting spread to the area in 1864. It called for captured soldiers and women and children to be spared. Taratoa was present at the Battle of Pukehinahina (Gate Pa) on 29 April 1864, and is said to have treated wounded British soldiers with kindness. He was killed when British troops stormed the unfinished pa at Te Ranga.

Te Heuheu Tukino, Herea (?–1820) was a great leader of Ngati Tuwharetoa in the early nineteenth century. A distinguished warrior, he seized the leadership

Te Heuheu Tukino

of the tribe by defeating his chief rival, Te Wakaiti, in hand-to-hand combat. His son, Mananui ★Te Heuheu Tukino, was a leading figure of the ★Musket Wars.

Te Heuheu Tukino, Mananui (?–7 May 1846), who became paramount chief of Ngati Tuwharetoa, was renowned for his forceful leadership, military skill, sense of honour, and hospitality. During the early 1820s he led war parties into Hawke's Bay against Ngati Kahungunu, storming their stronghold on Lake Roto-a-Tara by building a causeway in 1822. A few years later he led a great war party (taua) of the Waikato, Hauraki, Te Arawa, Wanganui, Horowhenua, and Ngati Tuwharetoa against Hawke's Bay. Te Pakake pa (Napier) was stormed. Okurarenga pa was then besieged, and its desperate defenders were reduced to eating clay, whereupon Te Heuheu, considering that honour had been met, withdrew. Afterwards a Ngati Kahungunu war party invaded the Taupo area, but its leader, ★Te Pareihe, and Te Heuheu subsequently made peace. Te Heuheu accompanied a Ngati Raukawa invasion of Horowhenua in 1825 but declined to join ★Te Rauparaha. Attacks by Ngati Maru against the Taupo area brought home to Te Heuheu the importance of muskets, and he led parties to Maketu to acquire them from the trader Peter Tapsell. When Ngati Maru invaded again, they were defeated near Turangi. In 1832 Te Heuheu fought with Te Peehi ★Turoa at Wanganui against southern Taranaki tribes. Two years later he supported Te Rauparaha in fighting against Te Ati Awa at Horowhenua. Te Heuheu's brother, Papaka, was killed at Haowhenua. Te Heuheu conducted the subsequent peace negotiations. He refused to sign the Treaty of Waitangi in 1840, and opposed European settlement. In 1841, and again three years later, he led war parties down the Wanganui River to south Taranaki. He was killed in a landslide.

Te Kirikumara, Ihaia (?–9 July 1873), a chief of the Otaraua hapu of Te Ati Awa, was a leading ★kupapa leader during the Taranaki War of 1860–61. As a young man he was involved in his hapu's struggles during the ★Musket Wars. It took part in the defeat of the Waikato at Motunui in the early 1820s, but suffered retaliation in the following decade. Te Kirikumara managed to escape when the Waikato seized Pukerangiora pa in 1831; he subsequently joined a war party which mounted a revenge attack on Ngati Maniapoto at Mokau. In 1833, when the Waikato again invaded Taranaki, he was taken prisoner following a siege of Miko-tahi pa. While a captive, he was probably baptised; he took the name Ihaia (Isaiah). He was allowed to return to Taranaki during the 1840s, and later became involved in disputes, and sometimes fighting, over land disputes and other issues. In 1854 his pa at Manaku was stormed by Ngati Ruanui in revenge for his killing of a Ngati Ruanui man for committing adultery with his wife. In the following year he sided with a Te Ati Awa faction against Ngati Ruanui and other Te Ati Awa under ★Te Rangitake. There was brief peace, but fighting among Te Ati Awa resumed in 1858 following the assassination of a rival chief on Ihaia's instructions. In March Te Rangitake besieged him at Te Karaka on the Waitara River. After another peace settlement, Ihaia moved east to the Mimi River. When fighting broke out between the government and Te Rangitake in 1860, Ihaia sided with the government, and even guided British troops into position before their unsuccessful attack on Puketakauere pa. In 1869, he helped raise a kupapa force for operations against ★Titokowaru.

Te Kooti Arikirangi Te Turuki (?–17 April 1893), a member of Ngati Maru hapu of the Poverty Bay–based Rongowhakaata, was a prominent Maori guerrilla leader during the latter stages of the ★New Zealand Wars. As a young man he earned a reputation as a troublemaker among local European settlers. Although he fought with government forces at the siege of Waerenga-a-Hika near Gisborne in November 1865, he probably did so with little enthusiasm, for many of his relatives were among the Hauhau. Indeed he was soon afterwards arrested 'on suspicion of being a spy', but was released. Arrested again in March 1866, he was sent without trial to the Chatham Islands with a party of Hauhau prisoners, all the while protesting his innocence. After experiencing divine revelations based on his reading of the Old Testament, he led the prisoners in organising an escape. The schooner *Rifleman* was seized on 4 July 1868, and the escapees made for the East Coast. Te Kooti and his band would probably have headed straight into the King Country had the local magistrate, Major R.C. Biggs (who had ordered Te Kooti's 1865 arrest), not raised a force of volunteers to stop them. In three skirmishes, Te Kooti defeated his pursuers, and gained more adherents as a result. However, the killing of some Maori supporters of the government also made him enemies, and approaches to the Maori King, Tawhiao, to enter the King Country were rebuffed. From his base at Puketapu on the edge of the Urewera, Te Kooti decided to strike at the settlement at Matawhero (just west of present day Gisborne), where lay the lands of which he had been dispossessed and many of those who were responsible for his captivity resided. In the early hours of 10 November 1868, his forces descended upon homes in the Matawhero area in a calculated act of utu which resulted in the deaths of fifty-four people, both Pakeha and Maori. Many of the killings were also inspired by prophecy. The raid, dubbed the 'Poverty Bay Massacre'

Major William Mair reads a proclamation to his Arawa kupapa contingent at Kaiteriria, Lake Rotokakahi, Rotorua, during the pursuit of Te Kooti in February 1870. His brother, Captain Gilbert Mair, is leaning against the hut at left with shovels to his right. A flag captured from Te Kooti is on display at the back (*Alexander Turnbull Library F-20327-1/2*)

by Europeans, created much alarm among the European settlers and their Maori supporters.

A large ★kupapa force of mainly Ngati Kahungunu was soon hunting Te Kooti. A Ngati Kahungunu and Ngati Porou force under Ropata ★Wahawaha drove him out of Te Karetu, after wounding him in the foot. Retreating to the ancient fortress of Ngatapa, Te Kooti repelled an attack by Ropata on 5 December. On 1 January 1869 an ★Armed Constabulary force, supported by Ngati Porou and Te Arawa kupapa, besieged Ngatapa. After five days Te Kooti and his followers, about 300 strong, were forced to flee over a cliff. With about 120 of his followers (and some prisoners) caught and executed, he had suffered a crushing defeat, but he escaped deeper into the Urewera. With Tuhoe support he launched two raids, the first against the Whakatane area in March 1869 and the second at Mohaka south of Wairoa on 10 April. The latter began with a savage attack which killed nearly sixty Pakeha and Ngati Kahungunu inhabitants. A pa sheltering survivors of the raid held out until relieved a few days later.

Stung by the raids, government forces began a drive into the Urewera with a view to destroying Te Kooti's Tuhoe support and bringing him to battle. But Te Kooti was again able to escape the net, in the process destroying a volunteer cavalry outpost at Opepe, east of Taupo, on 7 June 1869. Going to the King Country via Tokaanu, he again unsuccessfully sought support from the King Movement. Back at Lake Taupo, he was repelled by a Ngati Kahungunu party which he attacked at Tauranga-Taupo on 10 September 1869. Fifteen days later, at Te Ponanga, Ngati Kahungunu, Te Arawa, and Tuwharetoa kupapa inflicted a defeat on his 250–300-strong force. His hopes of establishing himself in the Taupo area were finally dashed in October, when a kupapa and Armed Constabulary force stormed his pa at Te Porere, an action in which he was wounded in the hand. After being forced out of the upper Wanganui area, to which he retreated, by the advance of a 600-strong kupapa force under Topia Turoa and Te Keepa ★Te Rangihiwinui, he moved north to Tapapa in the Kaimai Range. His hopes of coming to terms with his adversaries were dashed when a tentative approach to the government through a Pakeha intermediary was rejected. On 25 January 1870 he was driven from Tapapa by a mainly Wanganui kupapa force. While attempting to pass through Te Arawa territory, he entered negotiations with Te Arawa elders at Ohinemutu, but was attacked by Gilbert ★Mair's kupapa force. A running fight ensued, from which Te Kooti managed to escape into the Urewera. Ngati Kahungunu, Ngati Porou, and Te Arawa parties thereafter scoured the rugged terrain for him.

Te Mamaku

From his mountain fastness north of Lake Waikaremoana Te Kooti, who by now had a £5000 reward on his head, struck at the eastern Bay of Plenty. About 200 Whakatohea men, women, and children were taken hostage to force the tribe's younger men to fight with Te Kooti's band. When Te Keepa, Topia, and Ropata caught up with him at Maraetahi on 25 March, Te Kooti managed to escape once more, fleeing with four wives and twenty followers into the Urewera. In June 1870 he launched yet another raid to gain recruits and weapons, this time against Tolaga Bay on the East Coast. However, local support was not forthcoming, and the small party managed to return to the Urewera, despite being ambushed by a Pakeha force at Waihapu. For nearly two years Te Kooti evaded capture, sometimes narrowly, before he again entered the King Country, in May 1872, and was eventually offered sanctuary there. His renunciation of war in the following year effectively brought the New Zealand Wars to an end. After being formally pardoned by the government, he devoted himself quietly to developing his Ringatu religion.

As a guerrilla leader Te Kooti carefully planned his raids and executed them with ruthless efficiency; he understood the value of deception, and was adept at spreading misinformation; and he benefited from an extensive knowledge of the terrain, which usually allowed him to evade the doggedly pursuing government forces. If attacked, he invariably slipped away to fight another day. Religious teachings, charisma, and intimidation ensured a remarkable degree of obedience and loyalty among his followers. However, he was never able to gain a major tribal following apart from the Tuhoe, for his terror tactics, in discouraging Maori support, were counter-productive. Few important chiefs sided with him for any length of time. When Te Kooti attempted to make a stand, he chose poor sites, as at Ngatapa and Te Porere, and was overwhelmed by the vastly superior government and kupapa forces arrayed against him.

J. Binney, *Redemption Songs: A Life of Te Kooti Arikirangi Te Turuki* (Auckland University Press, Auckland, 1995).

Te Mamaku, Hemi Topine (?–June 1887). A chief of Ngati Haua-te-rangi from the upper Wanganui area, Te Mamaku fought against ★Te Rauparaha in 1829. With Te Peehi ★Turoa, he escaped the fall of Putiki Wharanui pa by fleeing upriver. In 1846 Te Mamaku supported ★Te Rangihaeata against Pakeha encroachment in the Hutt Valley. He led the attack on Boulcott's farm near Naenae on 16 May 1846. Returning to the Wanganui area, he placed European settlement at Wanganui under his protection on condition that no soldiers were stationed there. After British troops arrived in December 1846, and Maori sentiment had been outraged by the execution of a young Maori for murder, fighting broke out. There were desultory raids and skirmishes as the settlement at Wanganui was blockaded by a large Maori war party. After an indecisive clash with British forces at St John's Hill in July 1847, a truce was arranged. When Te Mamuka was baptised in 1853, he took the name Hemi Topine (James Stovin). He later fought a brief war with Ngati Tu, and in 1858 joined the King Movement. He supported the Hauhau at the Battle of Ohoutahi, near Pipiriki, in February 1865, but was generally respected by the European settlers in the area.

Te Matakatea, Wiremu Kingi Moki (?–14 February 1893), a chief of the Taranaki tribe, was at first called Moki. Only after distinguishing himself with his marksmanship at the siege of his pa by Waikato in 1833 was he called Te Matakatea (the clear-eyed). A year later he protected the lives of a shipwrecked Englishwoman and her two children. After the shipwrecked sailors were killed by another tribe, the crew of HMS *Alligator* mistakenly sacked his pa at Te Namu in revenge. When the Waikato under ★Te Wherowhero returned to Taranaki in 1836, Te Matakatea held out when besieged at Waimate pa and eventually negotiated a peace. In 1840 he led Taranaki warriors in resisting an incursion by Mananui ★Te Heuheu Tukino. He was baptised in 1841. Drawn into the war in northern Taranaki in 1860, he joined Wiremu Kingi ★Te Rangitake in the initial fighting. After renouncing his adherence to the King Movement in 1862, he did not take up arms when fighting resumed in northern Taranaki in the following year. Following the wreck of a British ship on his coast, he escorted the survivors to New Plymouth, and was assured by Governor George ★Grey that his lands were secure. Nevertheless, much of his land was subsequently confiscated, and it would not be restored to him until the 1880s. During the 1870s he was a supporter of Te Whiti o Rongomai and was briefly imprisoned for his non-violent resistance.

Te Pareihe (?–1844) was a war chief of Ngati Te Whatu-i-apiti, one of the most important hapu of Ngati Kahungunu of Heretaunga, in Hawke's Bay. In the late eighteenth century he fought a number of campaigns against Ngai Te Upokoiri of the Ruahines. During a battle at Mangatoetoe, he was wounded and carried from the field but took revenge for this indignity at a later battle at Waipukurau. The conflict between Ngai Te Upokoiri and Ngati Te Whatu-i-apiti escalated as each side recruited large numbers of external allies, including Ngati Raukawa under ★Te Whatanui and Ngai Tuwharetoa under Mananui ★Te Heuheu Tukino. An invading force led by Te Heuheu besieged Te Pareihe at Lake Roto-a-Tara. Although the invaders eventually withdrew, Te Pareihe was forced to flee from his stronghold when it was invested by another Te Heuheu–led force in about 1822. After this he made a vital alliance with the leader of a Nga Puhi war party, ★Te Wera Hauraki. A party of Ngai Te Upokoiri and Ngati Tuwharetoa were subsequently defeated at a battle called Te Whitiotu near Waipukurau, but the threat from Te Heuheu remained, and in about 1824 Te Pareihe and most of his people moved to the security of the Mahia peninsula, at that time under the mana of Te Wera. Soon after, a great expedition of Ngati Tuwharetoa and Waikato invaded Heretaunga. Te Pareihe was besieged at Okurarenga pa, but managed to hold out, barely; the defenders were reduced to eating clay. Te Pareihe then sided with Ngati Porou and Rongowhakaata in various intertribal conflicts. In about 1827 he and Te Wera led a great war party against Ngati Raukawa ensconced at Heretaunga, after which it proceeded to the Taupo area. Although Te Heuheu and Te Pareihe eventually made peace, the latter's people were still threatened by other enemies. Battles were fought against both the Rangitane near present-day Dannevirke and the Waikato at Kihitu. It was only in the 1840s that Te Pareihe's hapu returned to the Heretaunga area.

Te Pehi Kupe (?–1828), of Ngati Toa from the Kawhia area, was a prominent Maori warrior during the ★Musket Wars. A senior chief of his tribe, he went with other Ngati Toa warriors such as ★Te Rauparaha and ★Te Rangihaeata on the great Nga Puhi raiding expedition of 1819. He fought the Waikato and Ngati Maniapoto during the early 1820s, and along with Te Rauparaha led Ngati Toa to safety in Taranaki and then Horowhenua. He fought the tribes of the Manawatu–Horowhenua area, during which four of his children were killed in a revenge raid by Ngati Apa. In 1824 he boarded the European ship *Urania*, and insisted on being taken to Great Britain. There he was introduced to King George IV and given numerous gifts. En route back to New Zealand in 1825, he traded these gifts for muskets. Back at Kapiti, he resumed fighting Ngati Apa. In 1828 with Te Rauparaha he raided Ngai Tahu in the South Island. Two settlements were sacked, but at Kaiapoi, after being admitted into the pa to trade, he was killed and eaten; his bones were made into fish hooks. Te Rauparaha's subsequent campaigns against Ngai Tahu were ostensibly to seek revenge for this treachery.

Te Puoho-o-te-rangi (?–1836/1837?) was the leader of the northern Taranaki hapu Ngati Tama during the ★Musket Wars. His tribe was under considerable pressure from the more powerful Ngati Maniapoto from across the Mokau river, sustaining a number of defeats. Te Puoho was an ally of Ngati Toa, assisting them in their campaigns, but Ngati Toa migration to the south in the early 1820s left Ngati Tama in an invidious position, and they eventually joined ★Te Rauparaha in occupying the Kapiti area. Te Puoho accompanied Te Rauparaha in many of his raids. The last Ngati Tama migration from Taranaki led to land disputes and fighting, and Te Puoho moved on to the north of the South Island. In 1836 he led a raid down the West Coast against Ngai Tahu, but was killed when they stormed his camp in the Mataura Valley.

Te Purewa (?–1842?) was, with two of his brothers, known among his Tuhoe tribe as Te Tokotoru-a-Kokamutu (the triad of Kokamutu). The trio were present at numerous battles throughout the early 1800s, fighting against Ngati Pukeko and Te Arawa. In the battle at Pukekaikahu, near Lake Rerewhakaaitu, one of them, Tamahore, was prevented by Te Purewa from accepting a duel because of his seniority as a chieftain; instead Te Purewa took up the challenge, killing his opponent and his opponent's second. After the battle peace was established by Te Purewa between Tuhoe and Te Arawa. Later a Ngati Maniapoto war party under Peehi Tukorehu wished to cross Tuhoe lands. It was agreed that Te Purewa and Tukorehu should fight a duel, with Tukorehu allowed to cross if successful. After the duel was drawn, peace and oaths of undying friendship were made on behalf of Ngati Maniapoto and Tuhoe. Te Tokotoru-a-Kokamutu also waged war against Ngati Tuwharetoa of Taupo, before peace was made between Te Purewa and Herea ★Te Heuheu Tukino. Later, when one of the triad, Tamahore, was killed by Te Whakatohea, Te Purewa sought revenge by making war on Ngati Pukeko and Te Whakatohea and from 1823 to 1827 on Ngati Ruapani and Ngati Kahungunu. There was also conflict with Ngati Awa, in which Te Purewa was again a prominent peacemaker as well as warrior. In 1836 he assisted Te Arawa against Ngati Raukawa, who were defeated at Te Matai Puku.

Te Rangi Paetahi, Mete Kingi (?–22 September 1883) was a prominent ★kupapa leader of the ★New Zealand Wars. Of Te Ati Haunui-a-Paparangi, he was the dominant chief of the lower Wanganui by the 1850s. In 1860 he pledged his loyalty to the Crown, and in 1864 opposed the spread of the Pai Marire faith. Mete Kingi, along with Haimona Hiroti and Tamehana Te Aewa, was one of the leaders of the pro-government Wanganui Maori grouping which defeated a Hauhau invasion at Moutoa, an island in the Wanganui River, on 14 May 1864. He fought in subsequent skirmishes, including that at Ohoutahi pa in February 1865. Leading a force of Wanganui kupapa, including Te Keepa ★Te Rangihiwinui, he brought about the fall of

Te Rangihaeata

Weraroa pa on the Waitotara river. Now often referred to as 'General' Mete Kingi, he took part in the expedition to Opotiki to avenge the murder of C.S. Volkner in late 1865. In early 1866 he led Wanganui kupapa in Major-General Trevor ★Chute's Taranaki campaign. In 1868 he entered Parliament representing Western Maori.

Te Rangihaeata (?–18 November 1855) was a leading rangatira of Ngati Toa. In 1819 he accompanied his uncle ★Te Rauparaha on an expedition through Taranaki and down the west coast of the lower North Island to the Wairarapa. As part of the settlement which brought the fighting with Ngati Apa of the Rangitikei area to an end, Te Rangihaeata took a Ngati Apa women of high status as his wife, thereby creating the basis of a future alliance. On returning to Kawhia he resisted a Waikato invasion, but Ngati Toa were defeated at Te Karaka and thereafter determined to migrate southwards. Te Rangihaeata was with the first Ngati Toa migration to the Kapiti area in 1821. A year later he was with Taranaki Maori who defeated the Waikato at Motunui. With Te Rauparaha, he fought lower North Island Maori to establish Ngati Toa in the area. During the early 1830s he lived on Mana Island; with land at Porirua, he benefited from trade with European whalers. He also took part in campaigns against Ngai Tahu in the South Island. In 1834 war broke out between the various migrant tribes of the lower North Island. Te Rangihaeata took part in this conflict, supporting Ngati Raukawa against Te Ati Awa. He repelled an attack by Ngati Tama upon Mana Island, driving them back to Ohariu. In 1839 he allowed the New Zealand Company to settle at Wellington and Nelson, and in the following year signed the Treaty of Waitangi. However, conscious of the erosion of his lands and authority by the settlers, he joined Te Rauparaha in resisting the encroachments of the New Zealand Company. Matters came to a head on 17 June 1843 when an armed party of settlers and officials tried to arrest both chiefs. During a brief clash in the Wairau valley Te Rangihaeata's wife was shot; in revenge he executed a number of the captured settlers. He never suffered any retribution for this action, not least because the impropriety of the Pakeha actions which led to the affray was recognised by the authorities in Auckland and London (see WAIRAU MASSACRE). He also opposed British settlement of the Hutt Valley, and made his presence felt by constructing a pa at Pauatahanui. He was believed to be behind the attack on Boulcott's farm on 16 May 1846, and fighting between British troops and his men soon erupted. On 12 July he led a charge across shallow water against a navy longboat. On 1 August 1846 his pa was seized by British troops. A further attack by a British and allied Maori force against his pa at Horokiwi (Battle Hill) was repelled. But with his lands about Porirua lost to the British, Te Rangihaeata retreated to the Horowhenua area.

R. Grover, *Cork of War: Ngati Toa and the British Mission; an Historical Narrative* (McIndoe, Dunedin, 1982).

Te Rangihiwinui, Major Te Keepa (?–15 April 1898), of the Muaupoko from the Horowhenua area, was one of the foremost ★kupapa leaders of the ★New Zealand Wars. Also known as Taitoko, and later as Meiha Keepa (Major Kemp), he went as a child with his tribe to the Wanganui area to seek asylum from ★Te Rauparaha. By the 1860s he was regarded as one of the most important pro-government Maori chiefs in that region. On 14 May 1864 he took part in the Battle of Moutoa, an island in the Wanganui River, in which Hauhau Wanganui were routed by pro-government Wanganui Maori. He was also involved in the fighting at Ohoutahi in February 1865. Raising a force of Wanganui kupapa, he helped construct redoubts at Pipiriki on the upper Wanganui River. Ostensibly under the command of Captain Thomas ★McDonnell, the Wanganui Native Contingent seized the principal Hauhau pa in south Taranaki at Weraroa on 21 July. Te Keepa was then recalled to take part in the relief of Pipiriki, which was besieged by Hauhau. Between September and November 1865 the Native Contingent was deployed at Opotiki with a view to punishing Te Whakatohea for their part in the murder of C.S. Volkner. During 1866 Te Keepa was one of the leaders of about 300 Wanganui and Horowhenua kupapa in the south Taranaki campaign which 'pacified' Nga Ruahine and Ngati Ruanui villages. When fighting broke out again in 1868, the Hauhau chief ★Titokowaru inflicted a number of defeats on government forces. Te Keepa was the only commander whose reputation survived these débâcles, his troops acting as rearguards for retreating government forces at Pungarehu and Te Ngutu-o-te-manu in September and November 1868 respectively. His actions earned him promotion to the rank of major in the New Zealand Militia. For the first time Pakeha volunteers chose to fight under a Maori officer. Commanding the 'flying column' in the pursuit of Titokowaru in early 1869, Te Keepa ruthlessly decapitated any captured rebels. Shifting to the pursuit of ★Te Kooti, he took part in the storming of Te Porere pa. With the upper Wanganui leader Topia Turoa, he hunted for Te Kooti in the Urewera. In March 1870 Te Keepa made peace with Tamaikowha of Tuhoe, and with Ropata ★Wahawaha drove Te Kooti from Maraetahi. After the wars he was a land purchase officer at Wanganui. He used his government position, mana, and heavily armed following to secure an extension of Muaupoko territory in Horowhenua.

Te Rangitake, Wiremu Kingi (?–13 January 1882). Of Te Ati Awa from north Taranaki, Te Rangitake accompanied his father, Te Rere-ta-whanga-whanga, in an exodus by Te Ati Awa to the Kapiti region in the 1820s. He fought alongside Ngati Toa and Ngati Raukawa in numerous raids, as well as against them over land in the Kapiti–Horowhenua region. By the 1840s he was regarded as the principal chief at Waikanae. Nevertheless, lands at Waitara in Taranaki remained unoccupied, and nearly 600 Te Ati Awa returned there in 1848. Te Rangitake was determined to resist the purchase of land by the British, but lesser chiefs succumbed to the government's offers. Despite Te Rangitake's desire for peace, the British were determined to gain the land at Waitara, and the dispute was increasingly regarded as a test of sovereignty. Open hostilities finally broke out on 17 March 1860, with British troops attacking the L-pa at Te Kohia on the boundary of the disputed land. Te Rangitake left command of his forces in the field to another Te Ati Awa chief, Hapurona. A series of raids against British farms surrounding New Plymouth, assistance from the King Movement, and the digging of lines of particularly strong pa helped blunt the British offensive, and a truce was secured in April 1861, though Te Rangitake never formally adhered to it. In 1865 the Waitara area was among lands confiscated by the government.

Te Rau, Kereopa (?–5 January 1872), of Ngati Rangiwewehi of Te Arawa, was a prominent Hauhau leader during the ★New Zealand Wars. When he was baptised during the 1840s, he took the name Kereopa (Cleophas). He fought with the Kingite forces in the Waikato campaign, during which his wife, two daughters, and sister may have been killed by British forces. At the Battle of Hairini on 22 February 1864, he challenged the British from in front of his trenches. Following the defeat Kereopa converted to the Pai Marire religion of Te Ua Haumene, and was sent to the East Coast to preach the new faith. At Opotiki he agreed to, but did not actually take part in, the murder of the missionary C.S. Volkner, regarded as a spy for the government; Kereopa later swallowed Volkner's eyes, an act which conferred mana on him among his followers. It led inevitably to fighting in the area later that year as the government sought to punish the offenders. Meanwhile Kereopa went on to the East Coast, where he converted many Tuhoe to the Pai Marire faith. An attempt to proceed to the Waikato in June 1865 was blocked by Ngati Manawa and Ngati Rangitihi of Te Arawa. After one of the ensuing skirmishes Kereopa swallowed the eyes of three decapitated Ngati Manawa warriors, thereby earning the name Kaiwhatu (the eye-eater). With government forces on his heels, he sought refuge with the Tuhoe. Despite a £1000 bounty on his head, he remained secure in the fastness of the Urewera for five years before the Tuhoe finally decided to withdraw their protection. An attempt to arrange his surrender failed. When he attempted to flee, the Tuhoe captured him and handed him over to the colonial forces in September 1871. He was taken to Napier, convicted of the murder of Volkner, and executed.

Te Rauparaha (?–27 November 1849) was one of the greatest Maori war leaders. Of Ngati Toa descent, he achieved paramountcy within his tribe through his immense skill as a politician and strategist, which he displayed initially in leading Ngati Toa war parties against the neighbouring Waikato in the struggle for control of the Kawhia area which began in the late eighteenth century. He travelled widely, not only in search of alliances but also to acquire muskets. In 1818 he attacked Taranaki, and in the following year accompanied a large Nga Puhi war party led by ★Patuone, ★Tuwhare, and Tamati Waka ★Nene. During this raid, which went as far south as Whanganui-a-Tara (Wellington), Te Rauparaha noted the powerlessness of the southern tribes against muskets, an observation which events following his return to Kawhia soon rendered more significant. When he killed a Waikato chief as utu for the murder of his wife at Waikato hands, Te Rauparaha brought down on his tribe an avenging Waikato and Ngati Maniapoto war party. While besieged at Te Arawi pa on Kawhia harbour, he was offered the opportunity to escape by Ngati Maniapoto leaders. By brilliant subterfuge he succeeded in evacuating his people to Taranaki, where they took refuge with the Te Ati Awa. Ngati Toa migration from Kawhia was called Te Heke Tahu-tahu-ahi. A Waikato invasion of Taranaki under ★Te Wherowhero in 1821–22 was defeated by Te Ati Awa and Ngati Toa forces at Motunui. In 1822 Te Rauparaha travelled north, seeking warriors from his Ngati Raukawa allies and encouraging other tribes to take revenge on his behalf. When he subsequently began the second migration of Ngati Toa to the south, resistance by Manawatu and Horowhenua tribes led to much slaughter. The Rangitane were massacred despite promises of peace by Te Rauparaha. An attack by forces of lower North Island and South Island tribes on Kapiti, which he had seized as a stronghold, was repelled. His position was strengthened by the arrival of more tribes from Taranaki as well as Ngati Raukawa. In 1827–28 Te Rauparaha launched raids against the South Island, his war party devastating tribes in the Marlborough Sounds and taking the Ngai Tahu pa at Kaikoura. But the Ngai Tahu stronghold of Kaiapoi withstood his assault. In 1830, with the help of Captain Stewart of the brig *Elizabeth*, Te Rauparaha abducted and killed Ngai Tahu chief Tama-i-hara-nui and, after visiting Sydney,

Te Waharoa

raided D'Urville Island and captured refugees from his previous raids. In 1831 he defeated Ngai Tahu and captured Kaiapoi and Onawe pa at Akaroa. When in 1833 he launched another expedition against the South Island, he found the going less easy, for Ngai Tahu had armed themselves with muskets. He was nearly captured at Kapara-te-hau (Lake Grassmere) in 1833. Thereafter he became more wary of venturing south, and refused to take part in his kinsman *Te Puoho's ill-fated expedition in 1837. By this time his home base was being undermined by conflict between his Ngati Raukawa and Te Ati Awa allies. During renewed fighting in 1839, he was defeated at Te Kuititanga, Waikanae, after siding with Ngati Raukawa. Part of his motivation in signing the Treaty of Waitangi soon afterwards may have been to consolidate and legitimise his conquests, now under increasing challenge from Maori adversaries. But the Pakeha were soon also encroaching on his holdings both in the Hutt Valley and in the northern South Island. When he and his nephew *Te Rangihaeata hindered the survey of disputed land at Wairau in 1843, a misguided attempt was made to arrest them by a party of officials and settlers from Nelson. Twenty-two of the arresting party lost their lives in the fight or its aftermath, many despatched by Te Rangihaeata as utu for the death of his wife (see WAIRAU MASSACRE). Fears that Te Rauparaha would attack Nelson or Wellington in the aftermath of this incident proved unfounded, and no action was taken against him, for the authorities in Auckland and London recognised that the Pakeha actions had been provocative and ill-founded. The continuing disputes over Pakeha settlement of the Hutt Valley culminated in an attack on soldiers stationed at Boulcott's farm by the Wanganui chief *Te Mamaku. Although not involved in this attack, Te Rauparaha was not trusted by the new Governor, George *Grey, who had him arrested in a dawn raid by a mixed group of soldiers and sailors on his village at Plimmerton. Te Rauparaha was detained on a warship and then at Auckland while Grey tried in vain to find cause for his trial, and was only allowed to return to his people at Otaki in 1848.

P. Burns, *Te Rauparaha: A New Perspective* (Reed, Wellington, 1980).

Te Waharoa (?–September 1838) was the most respected and feared chief of the Hauraki area during the *Musket Wars. Of Ngati Haua, he was taken captive as a child by Te Arawa and grew up in the Rotorua area. As a young man he returned to Ngati Haua, and later took part in battles against Ngati Toa under *Te Rauparaha. He may have joined *Te Wherowhero's invasion of Taranaki in 1822. In the early 1820s Ngati Maru moved south to escape the depredations of musket-armed Nga Puhi taua, putting pressure upon Ngati Haua. In 1827 Ngati Haua attacked Ngati Maru, and Te Waharoa established himself at Matamata. Three years later he defeated Ngati Maru in a battle at Taumatawiwi (though he was himself wounded). In 1831 he supported his allies at Tauranga against a Nga Puhi raid. During 1836 he led his tribe in wars against Te Arawa, sacking Maketu and slaughtering the inhabitants. At Ohinemutu he inflicted a sharp defeat on his foes after misleading them by feigning a retreat.

Te Waharoa, Wiremu Tamihana Tarapipipi (?–27 December 1866) was a reluctant adversary of the British during the *New Zealand Wars. As a young man he participated in fighting against tribes in the Waikato, Taranaki, and the Bay of Plenty. He came under missionary influence and learned to read and write in Maori. Following the death of his father, the great war chief *Te Waharoa, in 1838, he found himself in a leadership role in his hapu, Ngati Haua, having inherited his father's mana. Temperamentally disposed towards diplomacy rather than war, he opposed continuing Ngati Haua's hostilities with Te Arawa. When he was baptised in 1839, he took the name Wiremu Tamihana (William Thompson). During the next two decades, he immersed himself in tribal affairs, seeking to establish a community which embraced Christian principles. For his part in the creation of the Maori King in the late 1850s, he was dubbed the 'Kingmaker' by Europeans. During the Taranaki War he endeavoured to play the role of mediator and managed to arrange a truce in 1861. During the lead-up to the Waikato War, he adopted a conciliatory approach, but was distrusted by the colonial authorities and found himself at odds with the bellicose Rewi *Maniapoto. Even after the British invaded the Waikato, he tried to negotiate an end to hostilities. Only after the sacking of Rangiaowhia, in which many women, children, and elderly men were ensconced, did he finally take up arms. His participation in the fighting at Hairini on 22 February 1864 was his only belligerent action against British forces. As a 'covenant of peace' (te maungarongo), he laid his taiaha before Brigadier-General G.J. Carey on 27 May 1865; colonists interpreted it as a surrender. In the short period before his death, he petitioned Parliament for an inquiry into the origins of the war and for a return of lands confiscated from rebel Maori.

Te Wera Hauraki (?–1839), a Nga Puhi from the Bay of Islands, is known to have fought against Ngati Pou as a young man. In 1818 he accompanied an expedition to the Bay of Plenty, where he probably captured the woman who would later become his wife. Further expeditions followed, including one to the Mahia–Wairoa area in 1821. He was one of the leaders,

An artist's depiction of the 'surrender' of Wiremu Tamihana Te Waharoa to Brigadier-General G.J. Carey on 27 May 1865, published in the *Illustrated London News* (*Alexander Turnbull Library, D-PP0033-1865-2*)

along with ★Hongi Hika and ★Pomare I, of the expedition which defeated Te Arawa at Mokoia Island in 1823. After the battle he and Pomare headed east, where Te Wera and his party of musket-armed Nga Puhi settled at Mahia as protectors of the local people. From there they intervened in intertribal conflicts, during one of which Te Wera became the close ally and friend of ★Te Pareihe, the war chief of the Heretaunga area. Together they defeated Ngati Tuwharetoa at Te Whitiotu in about 1824, but had to withdraw from Heretaunga when Mananui ★Te Heuheu Tukino returned with a great war party, including Waikato. Te Wera and Te Pareihe were besieged at Okurarenga pa, where the defenders were forced to eat clay, so dire became their condition. In the mid 1820s the two chiefs stormed Ngati Raukawa-held Te Roto-a-Tara pa. Te Wera continued to fight in various conflicts until as late as 1836.

Te Whatanui (?–1846) was the leading chief of Ngati Raukawa at a time when that tribe was under increasing pressure from the Waikato. In 1821 he refused an invitation to join ★Te Rauparaha's migration to Kapiti, instead preferring the Heretaunga plains of Hawke's Bay. He joined forces with Mananui ★Te Heuheu Tukino at Taupo and took Te Roto-a-Tara pa. Te Whatanui then campaigned in the upper Wanganui area, fighting a number of battles. Ngati Raukawa settlement of the Heretaunga plain began, but the local people attacked Te Whatanui's pa at Puketapu, Te Whatanui barely escaping with his life.

He joined Te Heuheu in another attack against Ngati Kahungunu at Mahia, but was ultimately forced to abandon his hopes of settling in Hawke's Bay. Ngati Raukawa now headed across Rangitikei and Manawatu, fighting along the way, until they reached Kapiti, where they joined Te Rauparaha. Ngati Raukawa settled in the Manawatu–Horowhenua area, Te Whatanui making peace with the local Ngati Apa and Rangitane inhabitants. Later he raided through the Manawatu gorge to avenge his previous defeats in Hawke's Bay, which led to a counter-attack led by ★Te Pareihe and ★Te Wera Hauraki. Tensions between Ngati Raukawa and Te Ati Awa migrants culminated in fighting at Horowhenua in 1834 and 1839, in which Te Whatanui was heavily engaged.

Te Wherowhero, Potatau (?-1860), of the Waikato, fought as a youth in his tribe's wars against Ngati Toa. In 1820 conflict which might have arisen from his instigation of the murder of ★Te Rauparaha's wife led to a Waikato and Ngati Maniapoto war party invading Ngati Toa territory at Kawhia. The Ngati Toa were defeated at Te Kakara. Te Rauparaha was besieged at Te Arawi pa but managed to extricate himself and migrate with his people to Taranaki. In subsequent fighting in that region the Waikato were defeated at Motunui, after warriors, against Te Wherowhero's orders, impetuously charged the Ngati Toa and Te Ati Awa. As his force retreated, Te Wherowhero fought numerous duels, using a ko (digging instrument) as a weapon. That night he was allowed to escape by Te Rauparaha. Returning to the Waikato, Te Wherowhero had to contend with a Nga Puhi invasion led by ★Hongi Hika. Armed with muskets, the invaders stormed Matakitaki pa, and many of the defenders were slaughtered in the panic to escape. With Te Wherowhero providing the rearguard for the survivors, the Waikato retreated further south to escape later Nga Puhi forays until peace was made in 1823. During renewed fighting between Waikato and Nga Puhi in 1826 and 1827, Te Wherowhero led an attack on Nga Puhi at Whangarei. After a victory at Oparakau, the Waikato made peace and returned home. In 1831 Te Wherowhero invaded Taranaki. After holding out for three months, Pukerangiora pa finally succumbed. In the ensuing massacre of the hapless defenders, Te Wherowhero is reputed to have slain 150 prisoners himself. Now armed with muskets obtained from his son-in-law, the trader J.R. Kent, the Waikato defeated another Nga Puhi invasion in 1832. During further attacks against Taranaki tribes from 1833 to 1836, Te Wherowhero besieged a number of pa, with mixed results, before making peace and returning home to the Waikato. Although he did not sign the Treaty of Waitangi in 1840, he was on friendly terms with the British and, following the Northern War of 1845–46, pledged to defend the colonial settlement at Auckland. However, the continuing acquisition of land by the British in due course convinced him of the need for Maori unity to meet the challenge. For those promoting the King Movement, he was, as the greatest Maori warrior alive, the obvious choice as King. Te Wherowhero reluctantly accepted the title in 1858 but died two years later.

P. Te Hurunui, *King Potatau: an Account of the Life of Potatau Te Wherowhero, the First Maori King* (Polynesian Society, Wellington, 1960).

Teagle, Vice-Admiral Sir Somerford Francis

(9 June 1938–) commanded the ★New Zealand Defence Force in the early 1990s. From Lower Hutt, he entered the RNZN in 1956. After attending the Britannia Royal Naval College, Dartmouth, he gained his first command, the fisheries protection vessel HMNZS *Manga*, in 1962. Two years later he was back in England on an exchange posting in the Royal Navy. From 1967, he held various posts, including Executive Officer of HMNZS *Taranaki*. After attending the Joint Services Staff College in Canberra, he commanded *Taranaki*, then HMNZS *Canterbury* (1978–79). This was followed by shore appointments in Wellington and Auckland and attendance at the Canadian National Defence College. From 1986 to 1988 he was Commodore Auckland, before becoming Deputy Chief of Naval Staff and then, in May 1989, CNS. As CDF from 1991 to 1995, he was responsible for sweeping reforms in structure and management of the NZDF in a period of financial stringency. Defence property assets were rationalised with a view to shifting resources from the 'tail' to the 'teeth'. He later described as a 'small miracle' the fact that the much leaner NZDF retained its basic capabilities. He was made a KBE in 1994. After his retirement, he became an articulate advocate of the need to sustain adequate defence forces.

Tempsky, Major Gustavus Ferdinand von

(15 February 1828–7 September 1868) was born at Königsberg, Prussia. After brief service in the Prussian Army, he left for Central America in 1846. He lived for periods in both North and Central America, Scotland, and Australia, before the lure of gold in the Coromandel brought him to New Zealand in 1862. Following the outbreak of hostilities in Waikato in 1863, he served as a war correspondent for the Auckland-based *Daily Southern Cross*, and in this capacity was invited by Lieutenant William Jackson, the commander of a company of ★Forest Rangers, to accompany an expedition into the Hunua Ranges. Adept with the revolver and knife at close quarters, he soon made his mark as a fighter, and was offered a commission as ensign with the unit. When the Forest Rangers were re-formed in November 1863, he was promoted to the rank of captain. Present at the battles of Waiari, Rangiaowhia, Hairini, and Orakau, he was further promoted to major in April 1864 for his able—sometimes impetuous—leadership during the Waikato campaign.

Von Tempsky commanded the Forest Rangers during the action near Kakaramea, Wanganui, on 13 May 1865, for which he was praised as 'the lion of the hour' by the Premier, F.A. Weld. However, in September he was arrested for refusing to serve under Major James Fraser, and later court-martialled. Reinstated when a new Defence Minister was appointed, he took part in Major-General Trevor ★Chute's Taranaki expedition early in 1866. In January 1868 von Tempsky assumed command of the ★Armed Constabulary's No. 5 Division, with the rank of inspector. He was involved in the controversial relief of Turuturu-mokai on 12 July 1868, and the first engagement at Te Ngutu-o-te-Manu on 21 August 1868, but was killed at Te Ngutu-o-te-Manu in the following month. One of the most flamboyant figures in New Zealand's military history, he was widely admired for his courage and military ability, but deprecated by many for his arrogance, jealousy, and vainglory. To Maori contemporaries he was Manu rau ('many birds', from which 'the bird that flits everywhere'). His many watercolours present a romantic and detailed view of military and Maori life during the 1860s.

W.T. Parham, *Von Tempsky—Adventurer* (Hodder & Stoughton, Auckland, 1969); R. Young, *G.F. von Tempsky, Artist and Adventurer* (Alister Taylor, Martinborough, 1981).

RICHARD STOWERS

Territorial Force

An artist's depiction of the death of Major Gustavus von Tempsky at Te Ngutu-o-te-Manu on 7 September 1868, a lithograph from a painting by K. Watkins (*Alexander Turnbull Library, D-P033006-C-CT*)

Territorial Force For half a century New Zealand's army organisation was based on the Territorial Force, which was established in 1911 to replace the ★Volunteer Force. The inability of the latter to meet New Zealand's defence requirements had become patently obvious during the first decade of the twentieth century, and had led to advice being sought from the British authorities as to the most appropriate form of military organisation. New Zealand had been urged to create a 30,000-strong force, which would be capable of providing both home defence and assistance in ★imperial defence. A territorial system of organisation (that is, with units closely related to particular localities) was recommended, along the lines of the British Territorial Army. The authorities in Wellington accepted this advice, and provision was made in the ★Defence Act 1909 not only for a Territorial Force broadly along the lines proposed but also for ★compulsory military training. These arrangements were endorsed a few months later by the visiting Field Marshal Lord ★Kitchener, the Empire's leading military personality, though he suggested an extension of the period of compulsory training and an increase in the number of proposed territorial areas. Major-General A.J. ★Godley, with a staff of imperial officers, had the task of creating the Territorial Force out of the 'heterogeneous mass of scattered squadrons, batteries, and companies' of the existing Volunteer corps. He noted later that 'as far as possible the whole fabric was built up on the basis of the old Volunteer Force', but the thrust of the reforms was to create a standardised national army. Fifty-six areas promulgated in January 1911 were divided into sixteen area groups, which provided the sixteen (from 1912 seventeen) provincially based battalions of the force. These units were numbered nationally and named after their locality. The old system of elective officers was replaced; henceforth candidates for commissions would be drawn from 'the most suitable and most deserving from the ranks' and were required to pass a prescribed examination. Some former Volunteer officers were forced to resign, but most stayed on, as did a high proportion of the existing Volunteers. The CMT scheme, registration for which began in April 1911, provided the balance of the numbers needed to bring the force up to its establishment of 30,000. With a Permanent Staff of only 300, the success of the scheme was heavily dependent on the enthusiasm for their task of Territorial officers and NCOs, supported by the regulars who filled key positions in each unit. By April 1914 the Territorials numbered 25,684, of whom 73 per cent had attended camp in that year. From early 1912 seven-day camps were held annually. That in 1914 was visited by the Inspector-General of the Oversea Forces, General Sir Ian ★Hamilton, who praised the force: 'it is well equipped; well armed; the human material is second to none in

Territorial Force

the world; and it suffers as a fighting machine only from want of field work and want of an ingrained habit of discipline'.

The home defence aspect of the new scheme was stressed to win popular support. Although Territorials could not be obliged to serve outside New Zealand, the Territorial Force was seen as the basis of a future expeditionary force. Planning for such a contribution began as early as October 1912, and within two years was being implemented with the outbreak of the *First World War. The *New Zealand Expeditionary Force was raised on a Territorial basis, and there were 3602 Territorials (43 per cent) in 1NZEF's Main Body which left New Zealand in October 1914. At the outset of the war, harbour defence units of the Territorial Force were called out to man their defences because of the threat posed by the German East Asiatic Squadron, but the Territorial Force as such was never mobilised. The scheme remained in operation, and despite the drain of men for 1NZEF annual camps continued to be held until 1917.

Between the wars the Territorial Force experienced mixed fortunes. On the one hand, it benefited from the numerous men who had served in 1NZEF. A sense of esprit de corps developed in many units, and social activities were fostered by messes and clubs. At times it operated with considerable efficiency, particularly in the late 1920s. In these years, Territorial camps and manœuvres were regularly covered in the newspapers. On the other hand, economic and political developments tended to undermine the system. Spending cuts in the early 1920s led to a curtailment of training, with annual camps postponed and unit strengths reduced. These problems paled in comparison with those caused by the crisis which beset New Zealand in the early 1930s. CMT was abandoned in 1930, and training and equipment programmes were slashed. By April 1931 there were only 3655 Territorials, down from nearly 17,000 a year earlier. Attendance at camps fell drastically. There was little support for Territorial service among a general public preoccupied with economic survival and influenced by pacifist thinking. Even when the international situation became more threatening, there were obstacles to revival of the Territorial Force, not least the attitude of the Labour government which assumed power in December 1935. Many of its members had opposed *conscription in the First World War, and were imbued with anti-militarist ideas. In particular, they were reluctant to accept the concept, implicit in New Zealand's military preparations, of providing another expeditionary force in the event of war. The need for home defence preparations, however, provided an acceptable basis for reinvigorating the Territorial Force, though the Army authorities found it difficult to secure government approval for the measures they deemed necessary. In particular any form of compulsory training was ruled out, and establishments were set on the basis of voluntary enlistment. By May 1939 the force was only a little over 10,000 strong, but a further 6000 had been added by the outbreak of the *Second World War as the crisis deepened and the Prime Minister, M.J. *Savage, appealed for volunteers.

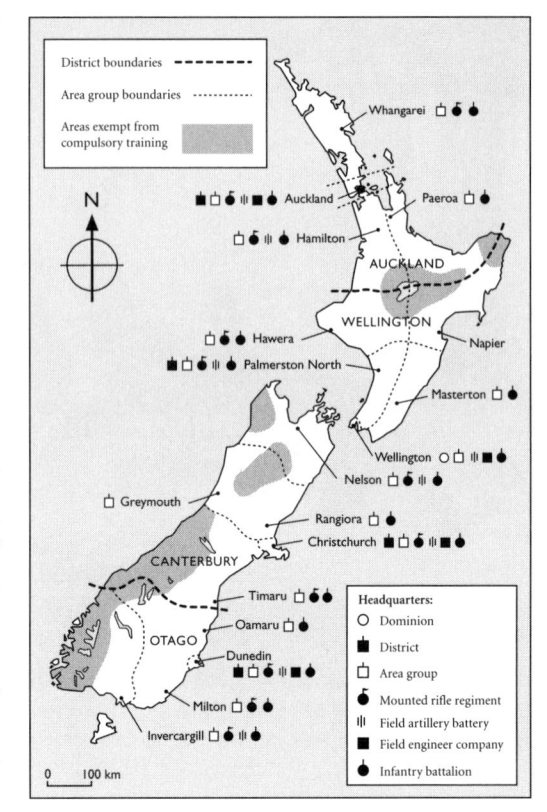

Map 25 New Zealand's military organisation in 1912

The formation of a New Zealand Scottish Regiment during 1939 was an important break in the Territorial tradition; it went against the locality-based unit approach by including men of Scottish descent from throughout the country.

There were considerable similarities between the 1914 and 1939 experiences of the Territorial Force. As in 1914, the coastal artillery and anti-aircraft units were immediately called out, and many Territorials volunteered for 2NZEF. However, in contrast to its predecessor, 2NZEF was not made up from the existing Territorial Force structure, though its infantry battalions did have a locality orientation. It never possessed the strong Territorial allegiances of its predecessor. During the war the Territorial Force assumed an increasingly important place in home defence preparations. Late in 1940 units of an expanded force—its

528

establishment was raised to 35,000—began to be filled by conscription, and units were called out for three months' intensive training. Fully mobilised cadres were established for Territorial units from February 1941. Further expansion occurred later in 1941, as the threat from Japan increased. By December the Territorials had reached a strength of 30,000 men, with another 9000 in the ★National Military Reserve. With the outbreak of the ★Pacific War, the Territorial Force was fully mobilised. To meet the new Territorial establishment of 66,366, men called up for overseas service were placed in the Territorials, and eighteen-year-old men were mobilised. Many officers were brought out of retirement to command Territorial units, and from 1942 numbers of 2NZEF veterans returned, which led to some resentment as veteran NCOs were placed under inexperienced or elderly officers. No longer suffering the drain of reinforcements for 2NZEF and now on active service, the Territorial units greatly improved their efficiency. In July 1942 the Territorial Force reached its peak strength of 66,191 men, with forty-one infantry battalions. In each of the three ★military districts there was a mobile field force of one division, comprising one to three brigades, whose task was to attack any enemy landings. They were supplemented by Fortress Area infantry battalions, coastal artillery regiments, and anti-aircraft batteries in the main centres and the Bay of Islands. More units guarded secondary coastal towns, and squadrons of mounted rifles patrolled the coastlines. From June 1942 the deployment of Territorial units overseas was permitted, with the 1st Battalion, New Zealand Scottish, and the 1st Battalion, Ruahine Regiment, being sent to garrison ★New Caledonia until they were disbanded to provide reinforcements for the 3rd Division in June 1943. Other Territorial battalions were sent to garrison Norfolk Island and Tonga. New Zealand could not sustain this level of defence preparedness for long because of the impact which the withdrawal of labour had on the economy, and the Territorial Force was substantially reduced in 1943. Coastal artillery and anti-aircraft batteries were reduced to cadres, and the Field Force shrank to eighteen infantry battalions and nine armoured or reconnaissance regiments. Conscription for Territorial service was abandoned. No recruit training took place after June 1943. With more than 8000 of their number called up to assist with the 1943–44 harvest, the Territorial Force had become essentially a labour pool under Army direction. By June 1944 it numbered only 3277 men, and thereafter it went into abeyance.

The Territorial Force was revived after the war to meet the requirements of New Zealand's involvement in Commonwealth defence plans (see MIDDLE EAST COMMITMENT). In contrast to the position previously pertaining in peacetime, it was explicitly based on the provision of a divisional-sized expeditionary force within a much shorter time-frame than had been the case in either world war. The administration and training of '3NZEF', as it was often described in official circles, was in the hands of the 4000-strong Regular Force, which also provided cadre personnel for most units. Symbolising the 'one army' concept, Territorial corps had been amalgamated with their Regular counterparts in 1948. To ensure that units were up to strength, CMT was reintroduced in 1949, and the first CMT recruits began joining their Territorial units in 1950 after their ten and a half weeks of basic and corps training at Waiouru or Burnham. Even as the force was brought to a hitherto unparalleled state of peacetime efficiency—attendance at annual camps was as high as 98 per cent—the changing nature of warfare and of international politics was undermining the basis of its existence. The declining likelihood of outright war between the great powers—a product of the development of nuclear weapons—reduced the significance of civilian-based military forces. Increasingly the focus was on the preparation of fully equipped forces capable of rapid deployment to deal with lesser conflicts. A Regular Force battalion was raised to serve in Malaya in 1957, and the concept of deploying a division in war gradually faded out of the picture.

Since the late 1950s the role of the Territorial Force has become increasingly problematical. Initially Army planning still envisaged a role for it in the preparation of a brigade group, but there were difficulties in sustaining the necessary strength once CMT ended in 1959. Under the National government from 1960 to 1972 the force was sustained at a strength of 10,000 by means of a limited form of compulsion. In 1963 the Army adopted a two-brigade structure: 1st Infantry Brigade Group, based at Auckland, was to be manned at full establishment with a strong Regular Force component, while 3rd Infantry Brigade Group, at Christchurch, would be maintained on a reduced establishment. Conferences of serving and retired officers oversaw the amalgamation of units to ensure continuation of regimental traditions, the process finishing in 1964 with the creation of the seven battalion–strong Royal New Zealand Infantry Regiment out of the nine Territorial regiments and the regular battalion. Under these provisions, Territorial units reached a reasonable level of efficiency, but retention of personnel, especially officers and NCOs, proved difficult. By the time that the Territorial Force reverted to voluntary enlistment in 1973, the rationale for its existence had been further weakened. Efforts were made to give the Territorial Force a defence role during the 1990s: each Territorial infantry 'battalion' was charged with providing a company for a composite battalion which would round out the two-battalion Regular

Thailand

A squad of Territorials of 7th Battalion (Hawke's Bay–City of Wellington's Own), RNZIR, in 1976 (*Evening Post Collection, Alexander Turnbull Library, F-23759-1/4*)

Force to a full brigade in the event of a full mobilisation. However, the unlikelihood of such a mobilisation gave the planning a sense of unreality. Increasingly Territorial service was seen in terms of meeting social goals rather than defence needs. In providing an opportunity for young men and (since 1974) women to obtain some military experience, the Territorial Force was a useful link between the Army and the wider community. By 1999 its strength had fallen to about 1500, a decline which was accelerated by employers' increasing reluctance to grant employees leave for military service. In an attempt to provide a more effective role for Territorials, the Army introduced a 'one-Army' concept in that year. Territorials are now attached to Regular Force units for training.

Thailand New Zealand troops began occasional deployments to Thailand in the 1960s as part of ★SEATO exercises, and a 30-strong ★Special Air Service detachment was based there in June–September 1962. Two of the RNZAF's Bristol Freighter transport aircraft were engaged in support of the SEATO logistic aid programme to Thailand between 1963 and 1965, and continued to support the Army deployment there until 1971. In 1964 thirty-three Army engineers assisted in the construction of an airfield at Mukdahan. They were replaced in 1966 by another team of engineers to construct a road in north-east Thailand as part of the Colombo Plan. The 144-kilometre sealed road was completed in 1971 and the engineers returned to New Zealand. New Zealand armed forces exercise on an irregular basis with the Thai armed forces under the ★Mutual Assistance Programme.

Thode, Lieutenant-Commander Connell Percy ('Con') (11 March 1911–) is the only RNZNVR officer to command a submarine. An Auckland businessman, he was seconded to the Royal Navy in February 1940. In October 1941 he became Navigation Officer in the submarine HMS *Proteus*, which made patrols in the Mediterranean. For his conduct after the *Proteus* was rammed by an Italian destroyer, he was mentioned in dispatches. After serving in training submarines and taking part in patrols covering Russian convoys, he took command of HMS *Scythian*, which patrolled the Strait of Malacca in 1945. He was awarded a second mention in dispatches for sinking twelve enemy vessels before the Japanese capitulation in August 1945. He was demobilised in New Zealand in 1946.

Thomas, Major-General Walter Babington ('Sandy') (29 June 1918–) was the youngest battalion commander in 2NZEF. Born at Motueka, he enlisted in 2NZEF in November 1939. As a junior officer in 23rd Battalion, his conduct was especially conspicuous during the battle for ★Crete, for which he would later be awarded an MC. Wounded and captured, he was taken to Greece, where, after numerous attempts, he succeeded in escaping. Making his way to Syria, he rejoined the 2nd New Zealand Division in

May 1942; this exploit would earn him a bar to his MC. A company commander in 23rd Battalion, he temporarily took over command of the battalion at Takrouna; for his bold leadership on this occasion he would later be made a DSO. After furlough in New Zealand, he was appointed to command 23rd Battalion in June 1944. Despite being wounded in fighting south of Florence two months later, he continued to lead the battalion with boldness and drive until the end of the *Italian campaign. After the war he commanded 22nd Battalion in *Jayforce before, in 1947, securing a regular commission in the British Army. He commanded 1st Battalion, The Royal Hampshire Regiment, in the *Malayan Emergency operations and was mentioned in dispatches for his service while brigade major of 39th Infantry Brigade Group from 1953 to 1955. After serving in the British Joint Services Liaison Staff in Canberra and in the British Army of the Rhine as commander of the 12th Infantry Brigade Group (1964–66), he was GOC of 5th Division from 1968 to 1970. His last posting was as Commander, HQ Far East Land Forces, in 1970–71. He was made a CB in 1971. After retiring, he returned to New Zealand. He had earlier published two accounts of his wartime experiences: *Dare to be Free* (1951) and *Touch of Pitch* (1956).

Thornton, Lieutenant-General Sir Leonard Whitmore ('Bill') (15 October 1916–10 June 1999) was New Zealand's most prominent soldier of the half-century following the *Second World War. Christchurch-born, he was one of four New Zealand students sent to Duntroon in 1934 after a hiatus of thirteen years. An outstanding student, he won the King's Medal in 1937 as the leading graduate of the senior class. Following his graduation, he was commissioned in the Royal New Zealand Artillery. During the Second World War, he was posted to 2NZEF, and served with 2nd New Zealand Division's Divisional Artillery in *Greece and in the *North African and *Italian campaigns. He commanded 5th Field Regiment in 1943 and 1944 and held a number of important staff appointments at Divisional HQ. When at the age of twenty-eight he became Commander, Royal Artillery in June 1945, he was the youngest brigadier in 2NZEF. For his wartime services he was made an OBE, as well as being mentioned in dispatches twice. After brief service with *Jayforce, he returned to New Zealand. As a staff officer he was heavily involved in establishing the *compulsory military training scheme in 1950. He attended the *Imperial Defence College in London in 1952, after which he headed the New Zealand Joint Services Liaison Staff there for two years. Highly intelligent, forthright in manner, and a skilful administrator, he moved rapidly up the Army's hierarchy. After serving successively as Quartermaster-General (1955), Adjutant-General (1956–58), and head of the *SEATO Planning Office in Bangkok (1958–59), he became CGS in 1960. During the next five years, he oversaw the shift of focus in Army preparations from an infantry division based on the *Territorial Force to a self-sufficient infantry brigade group based on both the Regular Force and a Territorial Force augmented by the compulsory training of a proportion of eighteen-year-olds under the National Service scheme. In 1965 he began a six-year term as CDS, in which capacity he helped complete the reform of the New Zealand higher defence structure, a process which he had resisted while CGS (see DEFENCE, MINISTRY OF). He was made a KBE in 1967. From 1972 to 1974 he was New Zealand's Ambassador to South Vietnam and Cambodia. In retirement he continued to have a considerable public profile as a commentator on defence issues. He was an effective frontman for several television documentaries on aspects of New Zealand's military history.

Thurston, Matron Mabel (22 July 1869–23 July 1960) was New Zealand's leading military nurse of the *First World War. Born in Cambridgeshire, England, she emigrated to New Zealand in 1901 and trained as a nurse. She was matron of Grey River Hospital for two years before becoming matron of Christchurch Hospital in 1908. She was also prominent in the New Zealand Nurses' Association. When war broke out in 1914, she immediately joined the New Zealand Army Nursing Service. She embarked for overseas service with 1NZEF in May 1916, having been appointed matron of the New Zealand Military Hospital at Walton-on-Thames in England. In August 1916 her role expanded when she became matron-in-chief of the NZANS overseas, her duties involving supervising the more than 400 New Zealand nurses serving in Britain, France, and Egypt. From January 1917 she was based in 1NZEF HQ in London. She proved an excellent administrator, earning the admiration of Brigadier-General G.S. *Richardson, the officer in charge of 1NZEF's administration, who described her as a 'splendid woman, and just the person for the position'. She was awarded the Royal Red Cross, first class, in 1917, and was made a CBE two years later. Despite her important war services, the Christchurch Hospital Board had become impatient with her continuing leave of absence by 1918, and she eventually resigned. She was matron of the King George V Military Hospital at Rotorua from 1920 to 1923, and later of the Queen Mary Hospital at Hanmer Springs and the Pukeora Sanatorium at Waipukurau. She returned to Britain permanently in 1927. During the *Second World War, she visited New Zealand troops in British hospitals under the auspices of the New Zealand War Services Association. She died in London.

Tinker

Tinker, Lieutenant-Colonel Ronald Arthur (13 April 1913–16 February 1982) was born at Christchurch, and was working as a taxi driver when he enlisted in 2NZEF in 1939. In Egypt as a member of 27th (Machine Gun) Battalion, he volunteered in July 1940 to join the Long Range Patrols (later the ★Long Range Desert Group), which penetrated deep behind enemy lines to raid enemy positions or gather ★intelligence during the ★North African campaign. An able navigator, he was rewarded for his efforts by a mention in dispatches in 1941 and an MM in the following year. He was commissioned in October 1942. When a reconnaissance patrol he took behind enemy lines in Tunisia in January 1943 was detected by the Germans, he led his men on an epic journey across the Chott El Jerid salt desert, an exploit which earned him an immediate MC. A few months later he guided the 2nd New Zealand Division in its 'left hook' at Tebaga Gap. In late 1943, he took part in an attempt by the LRDG, operating from a base on Leros, to wrest the Dodecanese Islands from the Germans. The operation collapsed when the Germans seized Leros, but Tinker managed to escape to Turkey, and thence to Palestine. After briefly returning to the New Zealand division, he was again seconded to the LRDG in June 1944. He took part in operations against the Axis forces in Yugoslavia and Albania, and parachuted into the latter to make contact with partisans. Following his demobilisation in 1945, he soon tired of civilian life and secured a commission in the ★New Zealand Army in 1947. In 1949 he was seconded to the Fiji Military Forces. He commanded the 1st Battalion, Fiji Infantry Regiment, in ★Malayan Emergency operations from January 1952 to May 1953. He was made an OBE for this service. He retired from the New Zealand Army in 1962.

Titokowaru, Riwha (c. 1823–18 August 1888) was one of the ablest of the military leaders who opposed British hegemony in New Zealand in the nineteenth century. Baptised a Methodist and literate in Maori, he was of Nga Ruahine hapu of Ngati Ruanui, of which his father was a prominent chief in the 1830s and 1840s. In 1854 Riwha, now the principal leader of Nga Ruahine, was one of the chiefs who agreed in 1854 to establish a Maori kingship and not to sell land. Having abandoned his youthful pacifism, he led a raiding party in the Taranaki War of 1860–61, and lost his sight in one eye in the assault on Sentry Hill on 30 April 1864. After the death in 1866 of Te Ua Haumene, the founder of the Pai Marire religion, he became the leader of a faith which incorporated Pai Marire, Christianity, and traditional Maori religion. During 1867 he energetically pursued peace with settlers and ★kupapa Maori, despite a government policy of 'creeping confiscation', to which he offered only non-violent resistance.

In June 1868, with further land confiscations effectively forcing Nga Ruahine to choose between war and starvation, Titokowaru and his people went to war. Within six months, in the face of initially overwhelming odds, they had thoroughly defeated one colonist force at his base of Te Ngutu-o-te-manu on 7 September and another at Moturoa on 7 November, and reconquered 130 kilometres of territory between the Waingongoro and Wanganui rivers. After these 'frightful disasters' the citizens of Wanganui feared imminent attack and a panicky colonial government contemplated making a separate peace with ★Te Kooti on the East Coast, abandoning responsible government (the price of regaining the services of imperial troops), and returning all confiscated land. The key to these successes, which saw Titokowaru's following grow from 150 to perhaps 1000 (including most of Ngati Ruanui and Nga Rauru), was his use of a 'strategy of controlled provocation', deception, and counter-attack. Raids and threats of raids on outlying settlers and positions were backed up by well-publicised instances of ritual cannibalism and written insults in order to encourage hasty government attacks on well-prepared positions. Titokowaru's fortifications were never what they seemed—all incorporated illusions such as false targets and apparent weaknesses. His defensive aptitude was complemented by offensive skill: in pursuit of his foes he took full advantage of rugged terrain and thick forest cover.

In February 1869, King movement forces intervened in support of Titokowaru, and a North Island–wide conflict seemed to have broken out. But Titokowaru was forced to abandon his stronghold of Tauranga-ika, where he had sought a decisive battle with the colonial troops led by Colonel G.S. ★Whitmore. The most likely explanation is that his mana tapu had been lost with the discovery that he was having a relationship with the wife of one of his commanders. After a hazardous retreat northwards, Titokowaru found shelter in Ngati Maru territory in inland Taranaki before returning to his own lands in 1871. He reached a modus vivendi with the government and established a profitable business selling grass seed to settlers. By 1879 he was coordinating active but non-violent opposition to the renewed confiscation of Maori land in south Taranaki. When the resistance centre of ★Parihaka was occupied by a massive government force in November 1881, he was among the leaders arrested and imprisoned. After his release in July 1882, Titokowaru continued despite increasing frailty to both preach peace and practise non-violent resistance until his death at Okaiawa.

J. Belich, *'I Shall Not Die': Titokowaru's War, New Zealand, 1868–9* (Allen & Unwin/Port Nicholson Press, Wellington, 1989).

DAVID GREEN

Tomoana, Captain Henare (?–20 February 1904), a Ngati Kahungunu from the Heretaunga plain in Hawke's Bay, was an important ★kupapa leader. In the late 1850s he and Karaitiana ★Takamoana fought another Ngati Kahungunu chief, Te Hapuku, to check that chief's land selling. Tomoana supported the government against ★Te Kooti, raising a Ngati Kahungunu contingent in 1868. He fought at Makaretu in December 1868, and in the next year led his men to the Taupo area in pursuit of him. Tomoana's kupapa clashed with Te Kooti at Tauranga-Taupo on 9 September, and in the following month drove him successively from his strongholds at Te Ponanga and Te Porere, but without capturing him. With his supplies running out, Tomoana was forced to return to Hawke's Bay, where he became embroiled in land issues. From 1879 he occupied one of the four Maori seats in Parliament.

Tonga New Zealand first considered measures for the defence of the Kingdom of Tonga, a British protectorate, in 1938. In June of the following year, it agreed to supply material for the tiny Tonga Defence Force (TDF). Late in 1940 a small group of officers and NCOs were sent to take control of the TDF, which was to be expanded to 480 men. Shortly after New Zealand had assumed formal responsibility for Tonga's defence on 18 November 1941, thirty-nine New Zealand gunners arrived to man a coastal artillery battery. Once the ★Pacific War had begun, Tonga assumed greater importance, and the United States took over responsibility for its defence in May 1942. Although Tonga was soon garrisoned by a large American force, the TDF remained under New Zealand officers. With a view to replacing American forces, which were moving forward, New Zealand resumed responsibility for Tonga's defence in October 1942. The New Zealand 34th Battalion joined the Tongan garrison, followed later by anti-aircraft and coastal artillery units. In February 1943 two Tongan battalions were formed with New Zealand officers and NCOs; they were integrated with the New Zealand units to create the 16th Brigade Group. Two months later a twenty-eight-strong Tongan platoon joined a Fijian commando unit operating against the Japanese in New Georgia during the ★Solomons campaign, the only action by a Tongan unit in the Pacific War. By August 1943 there were 1730 New Zealanders and 1535 Tongans in 16th Brigade, but with the improving war situation the garrison was thereafter quickly reduced to 211 troops whose main task was to service defence installations. In February 1944 16th Brigade Group was disbanded, and demobilisation of the TDF was completed in September 1945. Since the ★Second World War New Zealand has provided a range of military assistance to Tonga (see MUTUAL ASSISTANCE PROGRAMME).

Torpedo boats, spar Developed in the 1870s, the spar torpedo boat was designed to attack its prey by means of a mine delivered to its target—the ship's hull—on a spar projecting from the side of the boat. While it might be described as a 'most formidable' weapon in the hands of 'daring and determined men', it would also have been a very dangerous one for its crew. They would inevitably have had to endure heavy enemy fire from a close range as they manœuvred their craft into position to explode the mine.

In 1880 Colonel P.H. ★Scratchley recommended that New Zealand acquire twelve of these craft, three for each of its main ports. They would supplement the guns and mines that, under his proposed scheme, would form the basis of the port defences. In a defence procurement that left much to be desired, the government ordered four in 1882, only to learn more than a year later that the system had never been test-fired and that the explosion of a mine would probably be fatal to the boat. Constructed by John I. Thornycroft Ltd at Chiswick, London, the boats were 19.2 metres in length, displaced twelve tons, and had a one metre draught. They were powered by a 173 h.p. steam engine and had a speed of 17 knots. Each boat had a 1-inch Nordenfelt gun mounted on the top of its conning tower. A 16-kilogram explosive charge could be carried at the end of their 11-metre spar.

Shipped out to New Zealand at the beginning of 1884, the boats were distributed at the four main ports: *Defender* (Lyttelton), *Taiaroa* (Port Chalmers), *Waitemata* (Auckland), and *Poneke* (Wellington). They were operated, after 1886, by the Torpedo Corps of the ★Permanent Militia. *Waitemata* and *Poneke* were fitted with dropping gear for the modern fish-type (Whitehead) torpedo. But the boats' poor sea-keeping qualities made them unsuitable for launching such weapons; in all but calm seas it was predicted that they would capsize on doing so. The government was warned in 1893 that it would be 'perfectly hopeless to attempt to use these boats in daylight against a vessel carrying quickfiring guns'. Considered obsolete, they were stripped of fittings in the early 1900s and left to rust away.

Torpedoes Robert Whitehead developed the modern self-propelled torpedo during the late 1860s for the Austrian Navy, which was slow to recognise the potential of the weapon. At various times during the late nineteenth century the torpedo would be touted as a substitute for either fixed coastal defences or large warships. In accordance with the recommendations of Colonel P.H. ★Scratchley, New Zealand ordered four Thornycroft second-class spar ★torpedo boats in 1883. Although these boats were designed for the spar-mounted torpedo, two were fitted with Whitehead dropping gear. They proved to be unsuitable platforms for this weapon,

Training aircraft

Auckland's spar torpedo boat without its spar but fitted with Whitehead torpedo dropping gear (Wellington Museum)

however, and the first effective torpedoes were those mounted aboard the ★'P' class cruisers. With the exception of the reconstructed HMNZS *Royalist*, every cruiser forming part of the New Zealand naval forces carried torpedoes. HMS *Philomel* had a couple of submerged tubes for launching 14-inch torpedoes, but the rest carried the familiar 21-inch weapon. HMS *Chatham*'s two tubes were submerged, beam-mounted; the rest carried theirs above-deck in trainable mounts. The 'D' class introduced the TRI (Triple Revolving Mark I) mount to British ★cruisers and carried the very heavy armament of four triple tubes. The Leanders mounted two quadruple QR IVs, HMNZS *Gambia* and the Didos two triples. British torpedoes developed a good reputation for reliability. The inter-war Mark VII torpedo had a range of 14,600 metres at thirty-three knots, while the wartime Mark IX could reach 10,050 metres at forty-one knots or 13,700 at thirty-five knots, and carried a 367-kilogram explosive charge.

Ever since HMNZS *Black Prince* went into reserve in 1955 New Zealand ships have carried torpedoes for ★anti-submarine warfare purposes only. During the 1950s new faster and deeper-diving submarines forced navies to develop more sophisticated ahead-throwing mortars and homing torpedoes. The RNZN transferred its torpedo spares shop to Kauri Point in 1956, and during the early 1960s progressively upgraded the naval armament depot to handle the new anti-submarine torpedoes.

Unlike most of their Royal Navy sisters, the Type 12 frigates HMNZS *Otago* and *Taranaki* were commissioned with twelve fixed tubes for Mark 20(E) 'Bidder' 21-inch acoustic anti-submarine torpedoes. Because of their sluggish maximum speed of just twenty-four knots, these heavy torpedoes were complete failures and were later replaced by the American Mark 44 anti-submarine torpedo. So superior has the light torpedo proved to mortars that the frigate HMNZS *Canterbury* was commissioned in 1971 with two triple Mark 32 mounts in lieu of the Mark 10 anti-submarine mortar. The mortars were removed from the other New Zealand Leanders during refits. The lightweight Mark 44 torpedo could be delivered from deck-mounted tubes, from the Westland Wasp helicopter (and the new Kaman Super Seasprite SH-2F and G medium helicopters), from the Anglo-Australian Ikara, or from RNZAF Orions, greatly simplifying supply and maintenance requirements. Ikara, which had replaced the medium-calibre gun turret aboard HMNZS *Southland*, had a range of about twenty-two kilometres and the ship could carry sixteen rounds. In recent years New Zealand frigates and their shipboard helicopters have replaced the Mark 44 with the Alliant Techsystems Mark 46, a similar-sized but faster, deeper-diving, and more sophisticated weapon.

GAVIN McLEAN

Training aircraft, RNZAF The RNZAF and its predecessor, the Permanent Air Force, have used a range of aircraft for training purposes. In the early stages of the ★Second World War, around eighty aircraft belonging to airlines, aero clubs, and private owners were

Training aircraft

impressed into RNZAF service. Many of the single-engine machines, including Moths, Tiger Moths, Miles Hawks, and Miles Magisters, served as pilot trainers before the RNZAF's own Tiger Moths were generally available. The other single-engine types, unsuited to training, were allocated to second-line units. Airliners pressed into service—De Havilland Dragons, Rapides, Dominies, and Expresses—served in transport, support, and training roles.

Three of the world's best known trainers—the Avro 504, the Tiger Moth, and the Harvard—have been operated in New Zealand. Until the 1950s, the RNZAF generally used an ab initio or elementary trainer, followed by an advanced machine. Twin-engined training began during the Second World War. Since then, the pattern has been for one type of single-engine trainer to be employed on 'all through' instruction, prior to specialisation in multi-engine, helicopter, or fast jet flying.

The principal RNZAF training aircraft have been the following:

Airtrainer, Aerospace Wingspan 7.9 m; length 7 m; maximum speed 389 km/h; range 762 km; power 1 x 210 h.p. continental flat 6-piston engine.

Nineteen CT/4B Airtrainers were used by the RNZAF between 1976 and 1999. Thirteen improved models (CT/4Es) were obtained in 1998.

Anson, Avro Wingspan 17.1 m; length 12.9 m; maximum speed 188 km/h; range 1264 km; power 2 x 350 h.p. Armstrong Siddeley Cheetah engines.

Twenty-three Anson general reconnaissance trainers were acquired by the RNZAF in 1942–43, and used by the School of General Reconnaissance at Omaka, and later at New Plymouth. Following the war they served with the Air Navigation School at Wigram until replaced by Devons in 1952–53.

Avro 504K Wingspan 11 m; length 8.1 m; maximum speed 152 km/h; range c. 400 km; power 1 x 100 h.p. Monosoupape or 110 h.p. le Rhône engine.

The standard trainer for the British services from 1915, the Avro biplane first made an appearance in New Zealand in 1920, when twenty arrived under the ★imperial gift aircraft scheme. Eighteen were released to civilian use, and two were sent to Sockburn where, in 1924, they were used for the first refresher training offered to pilots of the newly formed air force reserve. The fleet was supplemented by six new Avros ordered in 1925. They only remained in service for three years, however, before being replaced by the first of the Moths, which were regarded as better ab initio trainers than the Avro 504Ks, whose whirling rotary engines (i.e., the crankcase and propeller rotated about the fixed crankshaft) were always difficult for new pilots because of the gyroscopic effects. The 504Ks were sold by tender in 1931.

Avro 626 Wingspan 10.4 m; length 8.1 m; maximum speed c. 140 km/h; range c. 480 km; power 1 x 277 h.p. Armstrong Siddeley Cheetah engine.

Four Avro 626s entered service at Wigram in 1935. They were used as multi-crew trainers until replaced

Aerospace CT4-B Airtrainers at the RNZAF's Central Flying School, Wigram (*RNZAF*)

Training aircraft

by Fairey Gordons in 1940, and thereafter for instrument flying training until the last was withdrawn in 1943. One was sold after the war into private ownership, but returned to the RNZAF Museum in 1987, where it is preserved.

Devon, De Havilland Wingspan 17.4 m; length 12 m; maximum speed 338 km/h; range 805 km; power 2 x 345 h.p. DH Gipsy Queen engines.

Between 1948 and 1981 the RNZAF operated thirty Devons (the RAF's name for the civil Dove) as trainers and transports. They brought about significant cost savings by replacing Oxfords as twin-engine pilot trainers, Ansons as navigation and signals trainers, and Consuls in the transport role. The Dove was De Havilland's replacement for the pre-war Rapide (built during the war as the Dominie). The Dove/Devon employed revolutionary manufacturing techniques, including the first metal bonding. The first two RNZAF Devons, acquired in 1948, were in fact built as Doves.

Friendship, Fokker Wingspan 28.9 m; length 23.5 m; maximum speed 470 km/h; range 3104 km; power 2 x Rolls Royce Dart turboprops.

Three ex-NAC/Air New Zealand Friendships were acquired in 1980 as replacements for the Devons and converted by Air New Zealand to provide navigation and air electronics training. A secondary role was maritime surveillance and search and rescue. Underwing fuel tanks were fitted, along with observation blisters. They were also given an extensive electronics refit. Accommodation was provided for an instructor, two student navigators, one air electronics operator, and up to eighteen passengers. The Navigation and Air Electronics Squadron at Wigram operated them until navigation training was transferred to the RAAF in 1993.

Gordon, Fairey Wingspan 13.9 m; length 11.2 m; maximum speed 168 km/h; range 700 km; power 1 x 609 h.p. Armstrong Siddeley Panther radial engine.

As the new monoplane bombers and fighters entered service with the RAF in the year immediately before the war, quantities of the elderly biplanes were offered to Commonwealth air forces. The RNZAF acquired forty-one obsolete Gordons. Although built as light bombers, they were taken up as 'service training' aircraft at the RNZAF's flying training schools until sufficient Harvards were available. Only a handful had dual controls on arrival. Spares were few and their old radial engines were a constant source of trouble for the engine fitters. Some were converted to tow drogues for gunnery students. They lasted in service until 1941–42.

Harvard, North American Wingspan 12.9 m; length 8.8 m; maximum speed 341 km/h; range 1400 km; power 1 x 550 h.p. Pratt & Whitney Wasp radial engine.

More than 20,000 Harvards (Texans in US service, Wirraways licence-built in Australia) were built around the world. The RNZAF operated 202 in four models. The Harvard's most distinctive recognition feature was a rasping sound on take-off, caused by the propeller tips reaching supersonic speed. The first twelve Harvards allocated to New Zealand under the EATS arrived in March 1941 and were posted to 1 Flying Training School at Wigram. As deliveries built up, Harvards rapidly took over as the main advanced pilot trainer. They were attached to a range of smaller units, as well as operational squadrons, while in New Zealand. At the end of the war, the early models were stored. Others were issued to the TAF squadrons and took over 'all through' training after the retirement of the Tiger Moth. Two served as forward air control aircraft during the 1970s and the last pilot trainers retired at Wigram in 1977.

Hind, Hawker Wingspan 11.4 m; length 9 m; maximum speed 300 km/h; power 1 x 640 h.p. Rolls Royce Kestrel engine.

The RNZAF acquired sixty-three Hinds from surplus British stocks to equip a flying training school at Ohakea. Many Hinds were fitted with dual controls, having been used by British schools. In 1942, they were issued to three army cooperation squadrons. They were withdrawn following the arrival of Harvards and most were broken up around 1943.

Macchi MB339CB Wingspan 11.2 m; length 11.3 m; maximum speed 960 km/h; range 1770 km; armament 2 x 12.7 mm machine-guns, practice bombs and 60 mm rockets; power 1 x 4400-pound thrust Rolls Royce Viper turbojet.

The two-seat Macchi 339CB was chosen in the mid 1980s to replace the Strikemasters. Eighteen aircraft were built in Italy, then broken down, and air-freighted to Ohakea. The 339 model was developed from the 326 operated by the RAAF. The RNZAF's first tandem-seat jet trainer (other than the two-seat versions of the A-4K Skyhawk) is operated by 14 Squadron at Ohakea.

Moth, De Havilland Wingspan 9.1 m; length 7.3 m; maximum speed 168 km/h; power 1 x de Havilland Gipsy engine.

A simple, robust, single-bay biplane of wooden construction (later models had metal fuselages), the Moth revolutionised general aviation around the world. Relatively cheap and easily maintained, it laid the foundations of the aero club movement in New Zealand. Four entered service with the air force at Wigram in February 1929, replacing the Avro 504K. A fifth aircraft, fitted with floats, was used in Western Samoa in early 1930 after being embarked in HMS *Dunedin*. Two 'Metal Moths' arrived in November 1930. Moths served as trainers until 1936, when elementary training was handed over to the aero clubs and four aircraft were put up for sale. With the outbreak of the Second World War, however, twenty-two civilian (mainly aero club) Moths were impressed. They were eventually replaced by the Tiger Moth. Two Moths served with the RNZAF in Fiji until around 1943. None survived the war.

Oxford, Airspeed Wingspan 16.2 m; length 10.5 m; maximum speed 300 km/h; power 2 x 370 h.p. Armstrong Siddeley Cheetah radial engines.

Universally known as the 'Oxbox', the Oxford was the RAF's standard advanced multi-engine trainer. The RNZAF acquired five in 1937 to train crews for the Wellington bombers on order from Great Britain, and additional machines were obtained after the outbreak of the Second World War. With most multi-engine pilot training carried out at Wigram, the Oxford became a familiar sight in Canterbury skies. Its use peaked in 1943–44, after which most were stored at Woodbourne until offered for sale. The survivors soldiered on as trainers and transports until replaced by Devons in 1952. Six were converted as Consul transports.

Strikemaster, British Aircraft Corporation Wingspan 11.2 m; length 10.3 m; maximum speed 835 km/h; range 1539 km; power 1 x 3410-pound thrust Rolls Royce/Bristol Viper turbojet.

Strikemasters were ordered in 1970 to replace the Vampire trainers, which were nearing the end of their airframe lives. Ten arrived by sea in 1972–73, and six more were delivered in 1975. They were used initially as advanced trainers and to convert pilots to the strike role, before playing a larger role in general pilot training. Until their replacement in 1991, the Strikemasters were operated by 14 Squadron at Ohakea.

Tiger Moth, De Havilland Wingspan 8.3 m; length 7.3 m; maximum speed 175 km/h; range 460 km; power 1 x 130 h.p. DH Gipsy Major engine.

Developed as a military trainer to succeed the Moth, the Tiger Moth had a metal and wood fuselage covered with fabric. It first appeared in New Zealand in early 1938 in the service of the Auckland and Wellington aero clubs. These privately owned aircraft were requisitioned by the RNZAF after the outbreak of war in 1939. In 1940 they were joined by the first of 100 ordered from the De Havilland Company of New Zealand and built at its Rongotai factory. As New Zealand's training effort expanded, many more were added. Many were placed in storage at Taieri in 1944. After the war, around 190 were sold or given away, mainly to aero clubs which had offered up aircraft for service in 1939. Tiger Moth strength steadily diminished after 1945. Other than those at Wigram, the four TAF fighter squadrons had two Tigers each for continuation training and 'hack' purposes. The final twenty-eight were sold in 1955–56, mainly to aero clubs.

Vampire, de Havilland Wingspan 11.6 m; length 10.5 m; maximum speed 855 km/h; range 1840 km; power 1 x 3500 lb dH Goblin turbojet.

Two-seater Vampire trainers (T55s and T11s) were used by the RNZAF to train pilots on the new techniques required by jet aircraft from 1952. They remained in service until 1972.

BRIAN LOCKSTONE

Training ships have generally been obsolescent ships or small vessels, such as patrol craft or yachts, suitable for training reservists or providing initial sea training. The first training ship in New Zealand was the *Amokura*, the former gunboat HMS *Sparrow* taken over in 1906 by the Marine Department to train boys in preparation for a marine or naval career. Based at Wellington, she trained groups of sixty boys aged thirteen and a half to fifteen in two-year courses until 1919. Hopes at first that this would assist in naval recruiting proved false, for only a few of the boys opted to join the navy; the ★merchant marine, into which most headed, was nevertheless an important element in New Zealand's security. When the New Zealand Naval Forces were formed in 1914, it was intended that forty boys would be entered in *Amokura* for naval purposes and another forty in the training cruiser HMS *Philomel*, but the outbreak of the ★First World War intervened. *Philomel* had to break off her initial training voyage to prepare for active service. In her absence, the antiquated escort sloop HMS *Torch* was used as a depot ship for the training of reservists until 1917. After the war the cruiser HMS *Chatham* assumed the training role for the ★New Zealand Division of the Royal Navy. In 1925 the Castle class minesweeping trawler HMS *Wakakura* was acquired as a training ship for the volunteer reserve divisions. To allow training in seamanship, gunnery, minesweeping, and torpedo work, three Bird class minesweepers, HMNZS *Moa*, *Kiwi*, and *Tui* were ordered in 1939, but by the time they arrived they were needed for active operations in the ★Solomons campaign. With New Zealand's commitment of Loch class ★frigates in the ★Korean War, *Kiwi* and *Tui* were recommissioned as training ships in order to maintain the training programme for the RNZNVR, a role they filled until 1955. They were replaced by the Bathurst class ocean minesweeper HMNZS *Stawell*, which trained naval reservists during the next four years. The frigates also served as sea-training ships—successively HMNZS *Hawea* and *Kaniere*. In 1960 the latter replaced HMNZS *Taupo* as an engineering training ship berthed at *Philomel*. HMNZS *Rotoiti* was the sea training ship until 1965, followed by the Bathurst class ocean minesweepers HMNZS *Inverell* and *Kiama* for the next eleven years. Second World War-era SDMLs (seaward defence motor launches) were used for training purposes by the RNZNVR from the late 1940s until the 1980s. They were replaced by four inshore patrol craft at each of

537

Transport aircraft

the reserve divisions. Sea training for junior ratings and midshipmen has been undertaken by one of the older frigates since the late 1970s.

Transport aircraft, RNZAF Military air transport in New Zealand developed rapidly during the ★Second World War. Two transport squadrons and a flying-boat flight operated services within New Zealand, through the South Pacific, and as far north as Japan in support of New Zealand units serving in the ★British Commonwealth Occupation Force. The professionalism and scope of the RNZAF's air transport services, which at the end of the war were being run on airline principles, with meticulous planning, accounting, and costing, were such that they were seen as a springboard for the development of post-war air services in the region.

Before the war, the RNZAF operated only a handful of communications aircraft. Many aircraft performed transport duties carrying one or two passengers on service business. A five-seat De Havilland 50A, used by the air force mainly on photographic surveys between 1927 and 1930, was leased to Air Travel Ltd to operate return flights between Christchurch and Dunedin three times a week, but the venture proved unsuccessful and the aircraft was sold in 1931. Five years later Wing Commander R.A. ★Cochrane recommended that air transport be encouraged with the backing of the regular air force. The development of air services by Pan American, then the protracted debate over the establishment of Tasman air services, awakened the government to the strategic implications of long-range air transport.

The ★Pacific War exposed New Zealand's air transport shortcomings. Five De Havilland 89 Dragon Rapides belonging to Cook Strait Airways were impressed by the RNZAF and began duties as observer trainers. They were dispatched to Fiji where, equipped with light bomb racks, they made maritime reconnaissance flights. The need for heavy-type civil aircraft was recognised by the government, which in January 1943 decided to obtain four Douglas C-47s under ★Lend-Lease. The first of them arrived in March 1943 to form the nucleus of 40 Squadron. Converted Hudson bombers and Lockheed Lodestars were later used as well. In 1944, four Short Sunderland IIIs, which had been converted to carry up to twenty-six passengers and freight, were obtained, providing the RNZAF with its first strategic transport capability. By the end of the war the RNZAF was running, in effect, scheduled airline services across the South Pacific and within New Zealand, supplementing Union Airways' modest efforts: 41 Squadron was operating daily C-47 internal services between Auckland (Whenuapai), Wellington (Paraparaumu), and Christchurch; 42 Squadron flew daily Rapide/Dominie services between Auckland, New Plymouth, and Wellington; and 40 Squadron flew

An RNZAF C-130 Hercules landing at McMurdo air strip in Antarctica (RNZAF)

as far west as Bougainville via Norfolk, the New Hebrides (now Vanuatu), and Guadalcanal, and as far east as Rarotonga. After the war, the RNZAF ran a weekly 11,000-kilometre air service between Whenuapai and Iwakuni in Japan, using C-47s. Meanwhile 41 Squadron had been pressed into domestic services to help shift the tens of thousands of repatriated New Zealand servicemen after Union Airways and NZ Railways had been overwhelmed. The RNZAF also continued to run scheduled domestic passenger services to supplement those of Union Airways. Other Dakotas (as the C-47 was then called) helped Railways shift cargo across Cook Strait.

After 1945, the C-47 fleet dwindled, with transfers to the new NAC fleet. NAC took over the RNZAF quasi-airline services in 1946–47. The RNZAF's first post-war transport acquisitions were new Bristol Freighters and Handley Page Hastings obtained in 1951–52. During the 1960s, the Lockheed Hercules succeeded the Hastings, while in the following decade the Dakotas and Freighters were replaced by second-hand Andovers, which operated until the 1990s. Three Boeing 727s were purchased from United Airlines in 1981 to augment 40 Squadron's Hercules capability. In the same year three Cessna 421C Golden Eagle light transports were acquired for VIP transports. Three Beech King Air B200s were leased in 1998.

The principal RNZAF transport aircraft have been:

Andover, Hawker Siddeley C1 Wingspan 29.8 m; length 23.7 m; maximum speed 460 km/h; range 3148 km; power 2 x 3245 effective shaft (e.s.) h.p. Rolls-Royce Dart engines.

Ten Andover turboprop tactical transports were bought from the RAF in 1976. They replaced both the Dakotas and Bristol Freighters, initially with 1 and 42 Squadrons. A military version of the HS 748 airliner, they had a swept-up rear fuselage. A rear ramp and cargo door were installed, giving them an air drop capability. They were worked hard during their service

Transport aircraft

lives, both in New Zealand and overseas, and were progressively retired between 1996 and 1998.

Boeing 727-22QC (8-crew long-range transport aircraft) Wingspan 32.9 m; length 40.5 m; maximum speed 950 km/h; range 4800 km; capacity 122 passengers; power 3 x 14,500-pound Pratt & Whitney turbofans.

During the mid 1970s, it became clear that 40 Squadron's Lockheed C-130H Hercules faced a heavy commitment, much of it pure passenger flying, in support of New Zealand forces stationed in Singapore. Three 'Quick Change' variants of the standard Boeing 727–100 commercial airliner were bought in 1981, two for service and one for spares. A VIP kit is available, while cargo can be carried on pallets.

'Dakota', Douglas C-47 (3-crew long-range transport aircraft) Wingspan 28.9 m; length 19.6 m; maximum speed 368 km/h; range 3400 km; capacity 21 passengers; power 2 x 1200 h.p. Pratt & Whitney Twin Wasp radial engines.

The military version of the DC-3, one of the best-known airliners, the C-47 served with the RNZAF from 1943 to 1977. Forty-nine aircraft were operated in all, in three versions. After first entering service with 40 Squadron, the C-47 quickly built up a reputation for reliable operations in the South and South-west Pacific in support of New Zealand forces. A second squadron, 41, was formed, and a third, 43, would have been established but for the sudden end of the war in 1945. After the war, several were transferred to NAC. One was released for conversion as the first aerial top-dressing DC-3. The remainder were used on internal flying, in support of New Zealand forces with BCOF in Japan, and in flights to the United Kingdom. One was converted to VIP configuration for the 1953–54 royal tour. With its highly polished finish, this immaculate aircraft carried many distinguished passengers, ranging from royalty to foreign heads of state and government, governors-general, and prime ministers, before its retirement in 1977. It now resides in the RNZAF Museum. Several were returned from NAC service in the 1960s and served as paratroop trainers and general transports. One served out its days towing targets mainly for RNZN gunnery training. After the war, the aircraft became generally, though incorrectly, known as Dakotas, a term that properly applied only to those ordered for the RAF.

Douglas DC-6 (4-crew transport aircraft) Wingspan 35.8 m; length 30.6 m; maximum speed 534 km/h; range 4345 km; capacity 64 passengers; power 4 x 2400 h.p. Pratt & Whitney Double Wasp jet engines.

Three DC-6 airliners served with the RNZAF between 1961 and 1968, when they were sold. They were the RNZAF's first pressurised transport aircraft, and were used on long-haul services to Singapore, the United States, the United Kingdom, and Europe. A principal role was supporting the New Zealand infantry battalion in Singapore.

Freighter, Bristol (3-crew) Wingspan 32.9 m; length 20.8 m; maximum speed 360 km/h; range 2300 km; capacity 32 passengers; power 2 x 1980 h.p. Bristol Hercules sleeve-valve radial engines.

For twenty-six years from 1951, the RNZAF operated twelve sturdy Bristol Freighters in the tactical transport role. They were used to support New Zealand forces in South-east Asia, including South Vietnam, and in a range of non-military programmes, such as those instituted by Sir Edmund Hillary in Nepal. With its fixed undercarriage and blunt nose, the Freighter gave few concessions to streamlining. The wartime unit, 41 Squadron, was revived to operate the Freighters, initially in New Zealand, then from 1955 to 1977 in Singapore. At home, the Transport Support Unit provided conversion training and local flying. Two were lost in accidents, one near Woodbourne in 1953 and the other in the Cameron Highlands in Malaya in December 1956. Two were loaned to Safe Air Ltd at various times to supplement its own Freighter fleet used on Cook Strait cargo services. Another was used in aerial top-dressing trials in 1954.

Hastings, Handley Page (5-crew) Wingspan 34.4 m; length 24.9 m; maximum speed 569 km/h; range 4640 km; capacity 50 passengers; power 4 x 2040 h.p. Bristol Hercules sleeve valve radial engines.

Four Hastings four-engine transports were used by the RNZAF between 1952 and 1965 as its first long-range transport. In 1952, the Hastings set up one of the world's longest (at the time) air services, between Auckland and Lyneham in Great Britain. They shifted the personnel of 14 Squadron from Ohakea to ★Cyprus in 1952, and from there to Singapore in 1955.

Hercules, Lockheed C-130H (5-crew long-range transport aircraft) Wingspan 40.4 m; length 29.8 m; capacity 92 troops, 74 stretchers, or 19,500 kg cargo; maximum speed 602 km/h; range 7876 km; power 4 x Allison 4508 e.s. h.p. turboprop engines.

Three Hercules were obtained in 1965, and two more two years later. They remain in service with 40 Squadron more than three decades later. They are some of the hardest-worked Hercules in any air force, their high serviceability rate attributable to the quality of RNZAF and civilian contract maintenance. They have carried royalty and prime ministers, soldiers, cars across Cook Strait during shipping disputes, police around New Zealand trouble spots, relief workers and aid, and standard military cargoes to many points of the globe. Two Hercules took part in coalition operations during the ★Gulf War in 1991. The RNZAF holds an option to replace the H models with C-130Js around 2005.

Lodestar, Lockheed (3-crew) Wingspan 20 m; length 15.2 m; maximum speed 435 km/h; range 2660 km; capacity 14 passengers; power 2 x 1200 h.p. Wright Cyclone radial engines.

Nine Lodestars served with the RNZAF between 1943 and 1949, supplementing the C-47s of 40 Squadron. The Lodestar had its origins in the smaller Lockheed 10A Electra operated prior to 1939 by Union Airways in New Zealand. Built purely as an airliner, without cargo doors, the Lodestars were used on express mail and passenger services to Fiji, Norfolk Island, Guadalcanal, and the New Hebrides. Most went to Union Airways, which became New Zealand National Airways Corporation after the war.

Rapide & Dominie, De Havilland Wingspan 14.6 m; length 10.5 m; maximum speed 253 km/h; range 895 km; capacity 8 passengers; power 2 x 200 h.p. DH Gipsy Queen engines.

The RNZAF operated fourteen of these elegant pre-war biplane airliners, in two versions, between 1939 and 1953. The first five were Rapide airliners taken into RNZAF service from Cook Strait Airways Ltd as trainers, light bombers, and coastal reconnaissance machines. The remainder were DH89B Dominies, built to RAF requirements. They arrived by sea in 1943–44, and were pressed into communications and anti-aircraft artillery cooperation service. From 1944, 42 Squadron Dominies operated scheduled passenger services between Auckland, New Plymouth, and Wellington. The last machines were sold in 1953, after being replaced by Devons.

BRIAN LOCKSTONE

Travis, Sergeant Richard Charles (6 April 1884–25 July 1918) became renowned for his daring exploits as a scout and sniper with 1NZEF on the ★Western Front. Born at Opotiki, he went under the name Dickson Cornelius Savage in early life and worked as a horse-breaker at Gisborne and in Southland before enlisting in August 1914. When the Otago Mounted Rifles, in which he was serving, was deployed to ★Gallipoli in May 1915, he was, to his dismay, ordered to stay behind in Egypt to tend the horses. Nevertheless he contrived to join the regiment on the peninsula unofficially; by the time he was discovered and returned to Egypt, he had already demonstrated a penchant for operating in no man's land. Transferring to the 2nd Battalion, Otago Regiment, in France, he again began prowling no man's land and the German positions, first at Armentières, later on the Somme, earning a reputation as a ruthless killer of Germans. Affectionately known as 'Dick, the Rough-house Merchant', he was awarded a DCM for eliminating snipers on the Somme. Travis's Gang, as the hand-picked battalion sniper and observation section he led was known, were conspicuous by their casual attire and informal attitude. Travis was awarded a Belgian Croix de Guerre and an MM in early 1918, the latter for a daylight reconnaissance which resulted in the elimination of a German machine-gun post and which, in the words of the official war correspondent, was 'conducted with the utmost audacity and coolness'. When the New Zealand Division took up position before Rossignol Wood in July 1918 he was again in his element, locating all the posts and wire on the objective of the New Zealanders' impending attack. Just before the covering barrage came down, he courageously blew up the wire in a key position with bombs to ensure that there would be no hold-up. Later, when two German machine-guns held up the advance, he charged the position and killed their crews, as well as a party of Germans who later attempted to recover the guns. He was killed by a stray shell the next day. For his actions at Rossignol Wood, he was posthumously awarded the ★Victoria Cross. New Zealand Division commander Major-General Sir Andrew ★Russell lamented the loss of 'the best all round scout the division has produced'.

G. Gasson, *Travis, V.C.: Man in No Man's Land* (A.H. & A.W. Reed, Wellington, 1966).

Trent, Group-Captain Leonard Henry (14 April 1915–20 May 1986) was one of three airmen to win a ★Victoria Cross during the ★Second World War. Originally from Nelson, he joined the RNZAF in November 1937, and gained a short-service commission in the RAF the following year. While flying Blenheim bombers with 15 Squadron, he earned a DFC for attacks on targets at Maastricht in May 1940. After various staff and instructional duties, he was appointed to 487 (New Zealand) Squadron in August 1942. The incident for which he was awarded a VC took place on 3 May 1943, when he led a daylight raid of eleven Ventura bombers on a power station at Amsterdam. The operation proved costly as German fighters took a heavy toll, but Trent pressed home his attack. After completing its bombing run, his aircraft was shot down. Trent parachuted to safety, and was taken prisoner. In 1944 he made an unsuccessful attempt to escape from Stalag Luft III. By the time he was liberated he had transferred back to the RNZAF, but in 1947 he secured a permanent commission in the RAF. He held various training posts, before becoming in 1956 commander of 214 Squadron, which was equipped with Valiant jet bombers. He participated in bombing operations on Egypt during the ★Suez crisis. In 1958, he flew a Valiant to New Zealand for the RNZAF's 21st anniversary celebrations. His final postings were as commander of RAF Wittering (1959–62) and Assistant Air Attaché in the British Embassy in Washington (1962–65).

J. Sanders, *Venturer Courageous: Group Captain Leonard Trent V.C., D.F.C.* (Hutchinson, Auckland, 1983).

Trigg, Flying Officer Lloyd Allan (5 June 1914–11 August 1943) was a ★Victoria Cross winner in the ★Second World War. A salesman from Whangarei, he joined the RNZAF in June 1941. In January 1943, after training as a pilot under the ★Empire Air Training Scheme in Canada and being seconded to the RAF, he was posted to Coastal Command's 200 Squadron, which flew anti-submarine patrols from its base in West Africa. He had already earned a DFC for attacks on German submarines when on 11 August 1943, during his forty-seventh operational sortie, he sighted *U-468* on the surface. Undeterred by heavy anti-aircraft fire, he closed with the German vessel and fatally damaged it with depth charges. His crippled Liberator then crashed into the sea. Its whole crew were killed. German survivors from the U-boat praised Trigg's courage in pressing home the attack. Their evidence was instrumental in his being awarded a posthumous VC, the only time this award has been made on the 'recommendation' of an enemy.

Troopships Most troopships started life as passenger liners, but they seldom resembled floating hotels by the time that soldiers tramped aboard to go to war. In September 1914 Colonel W.G. ★Malone condemned HMNZT 10, the former Shaw Savill & Albion Company liner *Arawa*, as 'filthy' and complained about a 'Government absolutely parsimonious in such small things as deck scrapers, sandsoap and tea towels!' In both world wars, soldiers' diaries complained of overcrowding, over-regimentation, and the boredom of sometimes being confined to ship while anchored off inviting-looking foreign ports en route to their destinations.

A century earlier, troopships had been bringing troops to New Zealand. In the early colonial period, Royal Navy ships transported the small numbers of soldiers required for garrison duties in New Zealand. The ★New Zealand Wars of the 1840s and the 1860s, however, greatly increased the size of the task. In April 1860, for example, the steam corvettes HMS *Cordelia* and *Pelorus* escorted the merchant ships *City of Sydney*, *City of Hobart*, and *Wongawonga* from Australia to New Plymouth. Aboard were several hundred men from the 13th and 40th Regiments and Royal Artillery personnel. Shortly afterwards, Australia's first warship, the *Victoria*, brought sixty men to help garrison Fort Niger, established earlier by men from HMS *Niger*. In November 1863 the large 3000-ton troopship *Himalaya* brought the 50th Regiment to Auckland from Colombo.

Troops departed New Zealand's shores en masse for the first time on 21 October 1899. That day an estimated 40,000–60,000 Wellingtonians farewelled 215 New Zealand mounted riflemen, with 249 horses, aboard Shaw Savill's hastily fitted-out *Waiwera*, off to support Great Britain in the ★Boer War. In a curious piece of colonial one-upmanship, the *Waiwera* raced the Australian contingents to South Africa, winning narrowly. Other contingents followed aboard ships which still bore their peacetime colours. Although the Boers had no navy, the voyages were not without risk: when an outbreak of measles accompanied by pulmonary complications swept through the *Britannic* on the way back to New Zealand, there were twenty fatalities among the returning troops.

Troopships played a vital role in both world wars. In August 1914, the rapidly converted Union Company liners *Moeraki* and *Monowai* transported the 1374-strong Samoa Expeditionary Force to Apia under Australian, British, and French naval protection. In October, with the whereabouts of the German East Asiatic Squadron still unknown, 1NZEF's 8400-strong Main Body sailed from Wellington aboard ten heavily escorted transports, three of them being Union Company ships, the *Maunganui*, *Tahiti*, and *Limerick*. Other Union vessels used as troopships during the war were *Willochra*, *Manuka*, *Warrimoo*, *Navua*, *Tofua*, *Mokoia*, *Aparima*, *Waitemata*, *Waitomo*, and *Waihora*. The company's ships carried 61,813, or 61 per cent, of the 100,444 New Zealand servicemen who went overseas.

The Union Company's passenger fleet had shrunk by 1939. The inter-island ferries *Rangatira* and *Wahine* and the *Taroona* and *Matua* carried troops to Pacific Island destinations. The *Awatea*, one of the fastest passenger liners afloat, transported troops for first the New Zealand and then the British government from 1939 until sunk off North Africa in November 1942. Most of the transports that took New Zealand troops overseas, however, were overseas-owned. The biggest gathering took place in Wellington in January 1940 when the *Rangitata*, *Empress of Canada*, *Orion*, and *Strathaird* sailed to join the *Dunera* and *Sobieski* with 2NZEF's First Echelon under the escort of the battleship HMS *Ramillies* and other warships. In May the *Empress of Britain*, *Aquitania*, and *Empress of Scotland* left the same port with the Second Echelon, joining the *Andes* in the strait. Throughout the war other ships, including several famous North Atlantic liners, took servicemen and women to and from New Zealand, but the most distinctive feature of the second conflict was the American use of the country as a staging post. American troopships such as the *President Adams*, *President Hayes*, and *President Jackson* became frequent visitors.

New Zealand used troopships for repatriation duties and to transport its Army and RNZAF personnel to Japan for occupation duties with ★Jayforce between 1947 and 1949. During the ★Korean War, New Zealand troops also left New Zealand by sea, the first contingent doing so in December 1950 aboard the

Tuis

hastily converted *Ormonde*, which enjoyed a more successful voyage than the elderly Union Company ferry *Wahine*, which struck a reef off the Indonesian island of Masela on 15 August 1951, fortunately without loss of life. Although air transport was used for the reinforcement of ★Kayforce from 1952, most of the New Zealanders were repatriated from Korea in the *New Australia* in November 1954. The last New Zealand troops in Korea left aboard the *Asturias* in 1957, but completed their journey from Hong Kong by air.

Britain continued to subsidise the construction of new troopships until the 1950s, when it would also charter both of the New Zealand government's immigrant ships, *Captain Cook* and *Captain Hobson*, for troop transport duties. By the end of that decade, however, long-range jet aircraft had displaced the classic troopship. Modern navies now operate amphibious warfare vessels such as assault ships, which can debark troops, vehicles, and supplies direct on to hostile beachheads. In 1995 New Zealand acquired an austere logistics support vessel, HMNZS *Charles Upham*. A planned reconstruction to permit her to carry a company of troops and to operate two helicopters had to be deferred for financial reasons, and she was leased to a private company in 1998. (*See* SUPPLY SHIPS)

T.D. Taylor, *New Zealand's Naval Story* (A.H. & A.W. Reed, Wellington, 1948).

GAVIN McLEAN

The departure of the troopship *Aquitania* from Wellington carrying part of 2NZEF's Second Echelon in May 1940 (*Alexander Turnbull Library, F-21894-1/2*)

Tuis were the first New Zealand women to serve overseas in the ★Second World War. Members of the Women's War Service Auxiliary, they carried out canteen duties in New Zealand Forces Clubs in Egypt. Their presence in the Middle East was the result of a request by the commander of 2NZEF, Major-General B.C. ★Freyberg, who had visited the New Zealand Club in Cairo in 1941 and found it 'dreadfully drab'. Convinced that comfortable all ranks clubs were essential to the morale of his force, he asked Prime Minister Peter ★Fraser for New Zealand women to staff the club lounge and provide 'a touch of home'. The WWSA having already compiled a register of volunteers, there was no difficulty in speedily meeting this request. Thirty recruits who reported to the Buckle Street barracks had two weeks to procure uniforms, have inoculations, and learn drill, rank recognition, hygiene, and security before they embarked in mid September 1941. When they arrived in Egypt, their leader, Freyberg's wife Barbara, suggested that they be called Tuis, a name which was quickly taken up by 2NZEF. Later additions brought the numbers to about forty. As well as staffing clubs, Tuis visited hospitals, wrote letters for blinded soldiers, packed prisoner of war parcels, and helped the troops shop for presents to send home. In November 1943 fifteen Tuis went to Bari to establish a club there. For the rest of the war they served in both Italy and London. When the Women's Auxiliary Army Corps had been constituted in July 1942, the Tuis had become part of the WAAC Welfare Division, and the WAAC chose the tui as the corps emblem. Lady Freyberg remained the head of the Tuis throughout the war. She was delighted to meet 'her girls' again while residing in New Zealand from 1946 to 1952 with her husband, now Governor-General.

SUSAN UPTON

Turoa, Te Peehi (?–8 September 1845), of Te Ati Haunui-a-Paparangi, was one of the major chiefs of the Wanganui tribes during the ★Musket Wars era. In the early nineteenth century he waged war against other tribes, taking war parties into southern Hawke's Bay as far as Porangahau. When in 1820 a war party of northern tribesmen under ★Tuwhare and ★Patuone entered the Wanganui area and advanced up the Wanganui River, Turoa was at the forefront of the local resistance. He gathered a large force of Wanganui Maori, and with the assistance of Taupo warriors, defeated the invaders at Kaiwhakauka. Tuwhare was mortally wounded in the battle. A few years later he repeated this success by defeating part of the Amiowhenua raid at Mangatoa. During the early 1820s he fought against the southwards migration of tribes under ★Te Rauparaha, whom he attempted to have treacherously killed at Papa-i-tonga. In 1824 he took part in the unsuccessful attack by southern tribes on Te Rauparaha's stronghold of Kapiti Island. In 1829 Turoa was at Putiki Wharanui pa when it was besieged by Te Rauparaha and Ngati Raukawa allies; when it fell, he was allowed to escape because of his merciful attitude to Ngati Raukawa when he had earlier besieged them at Makakote pa. He later took 300 Wanganui fighting men to join an expedition led by Mananui ★Te Heuheu Tukino against Ngati Kahungunu of Hawke's Bay, and in the 1830s continued to resist the migration of tribes to the lower North Island. He was a signatory of the Treaty of Waitangi, and was alleged to have sold the land for the settlement at Wanganui, though he denied having ever being paid for it.

Tuwhare (?–1820), a Ngati Whatua chief, was a leading warrior of the ★Musket Wars. After helping ★Murupaenga to defeat Nga Puhi at Moremonui in 1807, he greatly increased his power by acquiring muskets for his warriors. He accompanied Murupaenga and ★Te Rauparaha in a raid against Taranaki tribes in 1818. In November 1819 a great war party, led by Tuwhare, Murupaenga, ★Patuone, and Tamati Waka ★Nene, set out on an expedition to southern parts of the North Island. It began by skirmishing with Waikato Maori at Waitemata. ★Te Rauparaha joined at Kawhia, and his Ngati Toa connections enabled the war party to pass through Taranaki without fighting. However, it had to fight its way across the Wanganui River. Fighting continued as the raiders proceeded to Whanganui-a-Tara (Wellington), with a diversion to Wairarapa. Their muskets gave them a decisive advantage in the fighting with the local tribes. On the return journey Tuwhare decided to raid up the Wanganui River, while most of the expedition waited for him and his Ngati Roroa warriors at the river mouth. However, Wanganui Maori led by Te Peehi ★Turoa gathered against his party, and he was forced to retreat down river. Tuwhare's skull was split while storming Kaiwhakauka pa. He survived long enough to negotiate a peace with the Wanganui Maori, but died in Taranaki on his way home.

28th British Commonwealth Infantry Brigade

New Zealand military forces' association with 28th Commonwealth Brigade lasted nearly a quarter of a century. It began in April 1951, when the brigade's headquarters relieved that of 27th British Commonwealth Brigade at Kap'yong in South Korea. The artillery regiment and small ancillary units contributed by New Zealand to the ★United Nations effort in the ★Korean War formed part of the brigade, along with British, Canadian (later removed), and Australian infantry battalions, and an Indian field ambulance. As part of the 1st Commonwealth Division formed in July 1951, the brigade operated successfully under the command of initially British but later Australian officers until the ceasefire in July 1953. It remained in Korea until the United Nations forces were substantially reduced a year later, and was disbanded on 28 August 1954.

The brigade was re-formed in September 1955 as a result of the creation of the ★British Commonwealth Far East Strategic Reserve. Australia, Great Britain, and New Zealand (from March 1958) all contributed infantry battalions to the brigade, which from 1961 was located at Terendak Cantonment in Malacca, on the west coast of Malaya. The brigade's primary tasks were to prepare for operations in the defence of Malaya (later Malaysia) under ★ANZAM and, more importantly, ★SEATO. As a force on the spot, however, it was inevitably drawn into ★Malayan Emergency operations, and it continued to patrol the border with Thailand even after 1960. From 1964 to 1966 its units were also involved in ★Confrontation operations against Indonesian infiltrators in both southern Malaya and Borneo. In 1962, Brigadier R.B. Dawson became the first of three New Zealanders to command the brigade.

With the withdrawal of British units from the brigade in 1969 as part of the long-drawn-out withdrawal of the British military presence east of Suez, its Australian and New Zealand units were relocated to bases on Singapore island by March 1970. Following a change of government in Britain, British units returned to the brigade from late 1970. Under the ★Five Power Defence Arrangements concluded to replace the Anglo-Malaysian Defence Agreement, the brigade became part of the ★ANZUK Force on 1 November 1971. Now designated 28th (ANZUK) Brigade, it was stationed in Singapore until it was disbanded on 31 January 1974, following the withdrawal of Australia's battalion and the termination of the ANZUK arrangements. A purely British 28th Brigade lingered on until November 1975, by which time all British units had been finally withdrawn from Singapore. New Zealand's battalion stayed put until 1989 as part of ★New Zealand Force South East Asia.

H.B. Eaton, *Something Extra: 28 Commonwealth Brigade 1951 to 1974* (Pentland Press Ltd, Durham, 1993).

U

ULTRA is the generic name for highly secret communications intelligence obtained by deciphering intercepted German and Japanese military radio signals during the ★Second World War. In the war against Germany, it was derived from the decoding at Bletchley Park in England of many operational messages sent with Enigma enciphering machines which the Germans believed were completely secure. Although there were often breaks when codes changed, and some codes were never broken, the Allies gained a huge advantage from this capacity to read a proportion of German operational signals traffic, and it was instrumental in Allied success in the Battle of the Atlantic in particular. ULTRA intelligence gave a very clear picture of German intentions prior to the invasion of ★Crete, though there is still controversy over whether the Creforce commander, Major-General B.C. ★Freyberg, was fully aware of its provenance. During the ★North African campaign, ULTRA intercepts provided detailed information of German and Italian ship and aircraft movements, and facilitated the interruption of Axis petrol supply, an important reason for Rommel's ultimate defeat. Its value was such that extraordinary measures were taken to ensure that the enemy did not realise that their codes were being broken. Special liaison officers conveyed the intelligence to commanders in the field. The 'ULTRA secret' was not let out of the bag until long after the war. Similarly in the ★Pacific War United States cryptanalysts breached Japanese naval codes, just as they had earlier broken the Japanese diplomatic codes (providing intelligence known as MAGIC). Decoding of Japanese operational signals played a significant part in American successes in the battles of the Coral Sea and Midway in 1942. They were also instrumental in the interception and destruction by American long-range fighters of the aircraft conveying the Commander-in-Chief of the Japanese Combined Fleet, Admiral Yamamoto Isoroku, on a visit to forward bases in the northern Solomons in April 1943. A US–Australian cryptography unit at Brisbane also worked on decoding Japanese signals intercepted at various points in the South-west Pacific, including New Zealand (see INTELLIGENCE, MILITARY).

Uniforms Military uniforms are worn as a means of ordering the appearance of troops so as to distinguish friend from enemy or regiment from regiment. As a marker of rank, they also help establish and reinforce military hierarchies, and hence contribute to the effective command and discipline of troops. They have the important practical purpose of ensuring that servicemen and women are able to carry out their active service duties effectively in varying situations. But they also have a display function, especially on ceremonial occasions. Instilling pride in their wearers and impressing the civilian community, they serve as a drawcard, as the Commandant, Major-General J.M. ★Babington, noted in 1903: 'history indicates that dress, next to war, has been the best recruiting sergeant'.

Today's utilitarian military clothing, characterised by drab camouflage gear, bears little resemblance to the ornate, colourful British uniforms or hand-woven Maori war dress of the nineteenth century. While two distinct styles of war dress were once in evidence in New Zealand, neither has been retained in its mid nineteenth-century guise. Nowadays, when Maori servicemen and women form a significant part of the ★New Zealand Defence Force, a fluidity between Maori and European dress styles is apparent when soldiers divest themselves of uniforms to perform haka. However, this

Uniforms

The British Army's 65th Regiment on parade at New Plymouth in 1861 (*Alexander Turnbull Library, F-4631-1/2*)

does not extend beyond ceremonial occasions, for since the nineteenth century British modes of military dress have predominated in New Zealand.

Prior to the availability of European textiles and apparel, Maori war dress was woven from flax fibre (muka). It usually consisted of a waist mat (rapaki) secured with a weapon belt (tatua). Missionary Henry Williams described Maori warriors 'engaged in preparation, rubbing their muskets, decorating their heads with feathers and tying around their waists shawls and handkerchiefs of various colours … some of the leading men had a mantle of scarlet cloth trimmed with dogs' hair, others had splendid native mats'.

Each of the fourteen British regiments which served in New Zealand between 1840 and 1870 tried to preserve its characteristic uniform, in spite of problems of supply. Initially imperial troops in New Zealand, as elsewhere, wore close-fitting red tailored jackets of woollen cloth or serge. These were teamed with long pants of contrasting colour, usually navy or black serge in winter and white duck in summer. Headwear consisted of a forage cap or a tall cylindrical hat known as a shako. Accoutrements, including musket, bayonet, ammunition pouch, water bottle, and haversack, were carried suspended from shoulder and waist belts. Extant uniforms not only reveal the small physical size of their wearers by present-day standards but also provide an appreciation of the considerable weight, stiffness, and restriction of movement they experienced. Dress jackets were richly decorated with scrolls of gold braid, brass buttons, and insignia of rank. Service uniforms were of a slightly looser cut and less elaborately embellished. Both were designed to evoke impressions of military vigour. On campaign, uniforms were invariably stripped of their intended glamour. Describing fellow soldiers encamped before Kawiti's Ohaeawai pa in 1845, a 58th Regiment private noted: 'They had no change of garments, were ragged, tattered and torn, many without boots or tied on their feet with flax, their pants of many colours; blankets and greatcoats reduced in size to repair their continuations.' In 1860 a dark blue campaign uniform was adopted, mainly owing to supply problems with red serge cloth. This consisted of a smock or jumper, over which 'the great coat was worn, neatly rolled horse-collar fashion, and ready for the evening's bivouac'. Greatcoats, which were needed for warmth at night, were carried this way so as not to get torn or impede soldiers' movement in the bush.

At first, locally formed corps were less elaborately attired than the British regulars. In 1845 the 'corps of Pioneers' in the Bay of Islands were simply issued blue cloth shirts and caps. ★Militia units formed in the following decade were issued more extensive kit. The Auckland Militia Regiment, for instance, dressed entirely in dark blue—greatcoat, patrol jacket, shirt,

545

Uniforms

trousers, and forage cap or Balmoral hat. For the ★Armed Constabulary, regulation dress consisted of blue tweed or serge patrol jacket and trousers, worn with undershirt, woollen shirt, drawers, boots, brown leather leggings, and greatcoat. Yet, on campaign, the Armed Constabulary men usually modified their uniforms to include 'shawl dress', based on the Maori waist mat, because of the ease of movement it allowed in the bush and for crossing rivers.

Like their Maori opponents, each of the imperial, colonial, and ★kupapa (pro-government Maori) forces involved in the ★New Zealand Wars was identifiable by its dress. Complex interactions and alliances were delineated through clothing, most evident in the distinct blend of European and Maori garments worn by kupapa. Prominent kupapa leaders, such as Ropata ★Wahawaha and Te Keepa ★Te Rangihiwinui, used forms of Maori and European dress astutely and interchangeably. The Arawa Flying Column, which under Captain Gilbert ★Mair pursued both Hauhau and Te Kooti's forces, wore waist mats, made either from flax fibre or fringed tartan blankets. These were put on kilt-like, yet well short of the knees, and were combined with peaked caps, shirts, waistcoats, jackets, cartridge belts (percussion caps were kept in pockets), and boots. Anti-government Maori war parties (taua) wore a mixture of European clothes, flax cloaks, and waist mats, with either bare feet, flax sandals, or boots. Some are known to have adopted the dress of their opponents to move undetected within enemy territory. The Hauhau warrior Hakopa Te Matauawa wore a constabulary cap, tunic, and trousers with notable success during the conflict in south Taranaki in 1868–69.

★Volunteer Force corps were distinguishable from the Militia by the splendour of their clothing. Men of these corps, which were largely social in character, mostly wore waist-length scarlet or blue serge 'Garibaldi' jackets, blue serge pants for infantry or artillery or Bedford cord pants for cavalry, forage caps, swords with steel scabbards, and leather pouches and pouch belts. The style of Volunteer uniforms emulated that of the elaborate British Army uniforms. Like those of the imperial forces, the jackets were stiff and heavy, capable of fostering a military bearing even in the most stooped and soft-muscled men. 'Soldierly whiskers' appeared to have followed a civilian fashion, from the luxuriant beard preferred in the mid nineteenth century to the full moustaches and sideburns of later decades. Volunteer regulations specified that each corps select its own uniform with 'the approval of the Governor' and 'furnished at their own expense'. As the New Zealand textile and garment manufacturing industry became established, uniforms were increasingly manufactured locally. In 1881 the Wellington battery of the New Zealand Artillery Volunteers was fitted out with uniforms of Mosgiel blue tweed, constructed in their home town. From the 1880s the government increased its attempts to control the appearance of Volunteer corps. Detailed dress regulations were promulgated for different occasions, specifically ceremonial and working dress, and in the somewhat vain hope that distinctions of rank would be 'strictly observed'. Some Volunteer corps wore styles of military dress which reflected national origins. For example, in Dunedin the Irish Rifles trimmed their scarlet jackets with green facings, while the Highland Rifles wore Highland dress and 'feather bonnet'. Most Volunteer corps maintained the formality of British military style. Officers who cut a dash at society balls were noted favourably in the press and provided subjects for many late nineteenth century colonial illustrators and writers of romance novels.

Towards the end of the nineteenth century elaborate dress uniforms began to decline, as a more practical style was favoured. The most significant development was the introduction of khaki in 1891, initially for selected Volunteer corps. Locally made, this uniform was greeted with distaste. It was regarded as 'ludicrous in its shape … having the appearance of loose smocks', not lasting wear, and lacking any consistency of construction. A soft khaki felt hat, based on that of the Victorian Mounted Infantry, was also introduced. Worn with the right side of the brim looped up with a gilt hook, it was known as a 'slouch hat', and was practical and popular. This was the basis for the uniform worn by the first New Zealanders to proceed overseas on active service following the outbreak of the ★Boer War. The uniforms of New Zealand mounted riflemen in South Africa were not standardised in design and manufacture. They consisted of a khaki tunic, or light jacket, of either cotton or wool, worn with riding breeches. Soldiers were also issued with two woollen singlets, two shirts, two cholera belts, two pairs of socks and boots, a tweed overcoat, a leather belt, a pair of puttees, a slouch hat, and a forage cap. They wore badges with elements of New Zealand flora and fauna, most commonly the fern leaf and kiwi, among other national symbols such as the huia. Conditions on the veldt were hard, and uniforms, worn day and night, week after week, usually deteriorated rapidly. Supplies of replacement uniforms were unreliable, and the New Zealanders were known to have resorted to raiding British consignments and looting farmhouses for civilian clothes, especially overcoats.

Although khaki gained popularity with the outbreak of the Boer War, most Volunteer units persisted with their traditional scarlet, dark blue, or dark green full-dress uniforms. In 1900 the Commandant, Colonel A.P. ★Penton, lamented the absence of a 'typical dress': 'each corps is allowed to dress as it pleases.' A national service uniform in khaki was introduced in 1901. However, with each corps given the responsibility of outfitting itself and with the lack of availability of suitable materials, the appearance of servicemen remained uneven until the Volunteer Force was replaced by the *Territorial Force. New dress regulations issued in 1912 adhered closely to their British counterparts, and included the introduction of khaki service dress for the whole army. This consisted of a khaki jacket, trousers, and puttees, webbing belts for ammunition, and a variety of coloured piping around the cuffs, collar, and shoulder straps to denote each battalion. There was some latitude for the expression of national distinctions; for instance, for full dress the slouch hat could be worn with an imitation huia feather. This uniform was used by 1NZEF during the *First World War. Contrary to formal dress regulations, there was a degree of 'making do', of inconsistency of style, and unwarranted use of symbols of rank. A tattered look was not unusual in Egypt, where under hot, dry desert conditions full uniform was discarded in favour of singlets, shirts with their sleeves cut off, neck scarves, and crumpled hats. Mud, a constant feature of trench life on the *Western Front, and the lack of clean water made it impossible to maintain personal cleanliness. Lice thrived in these conditions, and when not fighting the men went to considerable lengths to delouse their clothing. Communal baths and a change of underclothing were available, but so intermittently that they gave only short-term relief. Steel helmets became standard wear on the battlefield; gas masks were issued where necessary. Cold metal and drab khaki marked their wearers as part of a complex military machine dedicated to the ruthless intent and brutality of armed combat—a far cry from the colourful glamour of the Volunteers. Distinctions between different regiments and battalions, and between officers and men, were indicated through dress. Metal numbers and letters were attached to the shoulder straps or collars, and in 1916 cloth *colour patches were introduced. Officers wore their badges of rank on their sleeves. Wounded officers were permitted to wear a two-inch strip of gold Russia braid on their left sleeve. Like their male comrades, New Zealand women serving with the New Zealand Army Nursing Service wore British-style uniforms. Consisting of a grey coat and red cape, with a fernleaf badge to represent New Zealand, the uniform was described by one nurse as 'early Victorian'. The *lemon-squeezer was integrally associated with New Zealand troops from the time of its formal adoption in March 1916, and served to distinguish them from Australians. The fernleaf badge, worn on the collar and hat, also indicated that the wearer was a New Zealander. Elements of traditional Maori warfare were incorporated into uniform design when the New Zealand Native Contingent adopted a badge consisting of a crossed tewhatewha (axe-like club) and taiaha (long wooden club).

The next significant changes occurred shortly before the *Second World War, with the introduction of battledress. This consisted of a waist-length khaki 'blouse' or jacket in wool drill, equipped with numerous pockets, and baggy trousers secured at the ankle with leather webbing gaiters. Designed by a committee, the 1937 pattern battledress was intended to accommodate new forms of weaponry and ammunition, and to give servicemen a more up-to-date appearance. It was regarded by many servicemen as ugly and uncomfortable; when bending forward the jacket rode up. The plainness of New Zealand servicemen's uniforms was highlighted when New Zealand was 'invaded' by smartly turned out American troops between 1942 and 1944. When on active service New Zealand uniforms were typically irregular in appearance. Because supply lines were often poor, servicemen were forced to wear whatever they could cadge or find. Members of the RNZAF wore a dark blue version of battledress. Air crew wore specially designed flying gear, including sheepskin-lined leather flying helmets, jumpsuits, and white padded life-jackets known as 'Mae Wests'. The *New Zealand Division of the Royal Navy and later the RNZN were closely modelled on the Royal Navy, and naval personnel wore identical clothing to their British counterparts. Women's services were established during the Second World War. Members of the Women's Auxiliary Air Force wore military-style jacket and beret, with plain shirt, tie, and skirt, while the Women's Royal New Zealand Naval Service uniform consisted of a navy serge costume, double-breasted coat, navy felt hat, white shirt, black tie, gun-metal lisle stockings, and black shoes. These stockings, despised by servicewomen forced to wear them in hot weather, became the subject of many official memoranda, for the Navy Office insisted that shedding these stockings would lead to slovenliness and sunburn.

In anticipation of extreme cold during the *Korean War, members of *Kayforce were provided with special-issue winter clothing, greatcoats, windproof trousers and jackets, heavy woollen jumpers, mittens with leather covers, string vests, and boots. This war surplus clothing had many shortcomings; the stitching in the boots quickly split and greatcoats were found to be too small to fit over numerous layers of clothing. Like earlier generations of New Zealand soldiers, the troops soon overcame these problems by their own resources; they begged, borrowed, and often stole what they needed, especially from the well-equipped Americans. During the summer, extreme heat led them to shed all but their underpants, boots, and socks whenever possible. Jungle greens were first worn by New

Unit diaries

Zealanders serving in Malaya in the late 1950s. Designed to tone in with the leaves of the tropical rainforest, these baggy cotton shirts and trousers did not appeal to the troops, who thought them lacking in shape and style. However, the centuries-old problem of supply had by now been solved with the development of the helicopter, which made it easier than ever to equip soldiers with clean uniforms and other supplies. During the *Vietnam War working dress consisted of 'denims': shorts, no shirts, socks over boots, and a hat. No underwear was worn, for freedom of movement and because of the heat. Protective clothing, such as flak jackets, was provided as protection against anti-personnel mines. These jackets proved too noisy, heavy, and restrictive to move in easily, and were not widely used. Similarly steel helmets were considered dangerous because they caused loss of mobility. Instead, soft jungle hats with a brim were worn as protection from the sun's glare.

An increasingly scientific approach was taken to the design and construction of military uniforms during the 1960s, when the Army Research and Development Section was established. It had sole responsibility for the development of textiles, clothing, and footwear to suit New Zealand armed forces personnel. Camouflage gear, first improvised by New Zealanders in the South Pacific during the Second World War, was officially introduced in 1977. The long-despised battledress was phased out, as were jungle greens. For the *Gulf War the camouflage colours were lightened to blend with the desert, and safari instead of standard black boots were issued. At the same time a walking-out dress of olive green Dacron was introduced. These have since been phased out because service personnel found that natural fibres, like cotton, allowed better sweat absorption and were not as flammable. In the 1990s the priority has been for 'smart, multi-functional uniforms, that reflect a distinctly New Zealand character'. The RNZN has recently developed a maternity uniform for expectant officers, but men's and women's uniforms are otherwise now identical in all aspects except cut.

During the nineteenth and twentieth centuries new clothing traditions have been invented, shaping the appearance of the New Zealand armed forces. This slow yet continuous shift in colour and style has occurred for a variety of reasons. Adjustments to soldiers' clothing have been made in response to developments in military tactics and weapons and to changing theatres of war. New approaches to textile technology, garment construction, and civilian fashion have also had an impact on uniform design. Not least important have been the desires to express national characteristics and uphold military traditions and alliances. Military clothing provides a visible and direct indication of how the New Zealand military has seen itself over time, and how it has wished to be perceived by others. The pursuit of exemplary standards of dress is a consistent theme in the history of New Zealand military clothing. Maintaining these standards and uniformity of dress was for a long time a difficult problem.

FIONA McKERGOW

Unit diaries Unit diaries, also referred to as war diaries, are the basic day-to-day record of an Army unit's activity while on active service. Under the Field Service Regulations of 1909, all military units and formations were required to keep such records throughout their existence. The RNZN has a system of reports of proceedings on the operations of its warships, while the RNZAF also instituted a unit diary system. During the 1970s recording of the activities of non-active service units was introduced. As a narrative summary of events, unit diaries are the basic 'bread and butter' source material for military historians, but they have their limitations. In the first place, they vary widely in quality. Some may provide no more than a scant summary, or even more frustratingly include repeated statements to the effect that routine operations continued or there was nothing to report. The best unit diaries contain not only extensive coverage of activities but also attachments that may include operational orders issued to the unit, strength returns, after action reports, and relevant maps. The quality of the diaries is a reflection of the character and ability of those who compile them—usually a junior officer serving as the unit adjutant or intelligence officer. The urgency of operations may lead to the diary assuming very low priority, and being written up some time after the event. Those of the *First World War, for example, were compiled on average about ten days after the action described. Unsurprisingly there are numerous inaccuracies, with activities sometimes being attributed to the wrong day. There is a tendency also to focus on positive events. Unit loyalty, and the scrutiny of commanding officers, may induce diary compilers to gloss over unit failures. The unit diary of 2nd Battalion, 3rd New Zealand (Rifle) Brigade, records the catastrophe at Passchendaele on 12 October 1917 simply as 'Battn attacked in front of PASSCHENDAELE RIDGE'. Censorship by higher authority is not unknown, with sections of unit diaries blacked out or removed altogether. Despite these drawbacks, unit diaries are an indispensable source. All surviving New Zealand war diaries are held in the war history records at the National Archives in Wellington.

GLYN HARPER

Unit histories, detailed records of the activities of and personalities involved in particular units, have been produced in considerable numbers in New

Zealand, mainly to meet the desire of many unit members for a souvenir of their service. The first unit histories to appear in New Zealand were short, usually pictorial, accounts of the contingents which took part in the ★Boer War. Following the ★First World War, many 1NZEF unit associations set about producing more substantial histories under the supervision of a committee of senior officers at GHQ. Of the twenty-one published, more than half were written by officers who had served in the unit concerned. The production of unit histories for those elements of 2NZEF which served in the Mediterranean theatre during the ★Second World War was entrusted to the ★War History Branch, after the Prime Minister, Peter ★Fraser, had determined that unit regimental funds, most of which were in a very healthy state, should be devoted to this purpose. Authors were chosen by a committee of senior officers of the respective units, and the volumes formed part of the Official History of New Zealand in the Second World War. Each surviving member was entitled to a free copy of his or her unit's history. The unit histories added to the workload of the War History Branch staff, who regarded them as a difficult chore and a distraction from the production of the campaign histories. The first of the twenty-one official unit histories was published in 1949; the journalist S.P. ★Llewellyn's account of the 1st Divisional Ammunition Company, *Journey towards Christmas*, written in an impressionistic style in the second person, received much acclaim for its literary qualities. It is widely regarded as the best written of all the unit histories. The history of the 28th (Maori) Battalion, by Great War veteran and public service clerk J.F. Cody, is the only unit history to run into a second edition. Units of 2NZEF's 3rd Division and its base organisation which served in the South Pacific fell outside these arrangements; thirteen 'unofficial narratives', written by members of the units, were produced under the auspices of the Third Division Histories Committee. Some privately prepared histories of wartime air force and naval units, such as 75 Squadron RAF and HMNZS *Achilles*, have also since appeared. No substantial unit histories were commissioned after the ★Korean War, the ★Malayan Emergency, or ★Confrontation. A history of 161st Battery in the ★Vietnam War appeared in 1988, and the activities of New Zealand infantry companies have been covered in several histories of the Anzac battalions produced in Australia. In New Zealand, histories of Army corps, such as Chaplains, Signals, Transport, and most recently Artillery, have been commissioned, and a number of ★Territorial Force units have had their activities recorded. Some 2NZEF units have produced new accounts of their activities, usually as the result of the personal enthusiasm of one or several of their members. Overall, unit histories vary greatly in quality. A very few make riveting reading, but most are a good, faithful record of the units' activities, full of detail about their members.

GLYN HARPER

United Nations New Zealand was one of the founding members of the United Nations in 1945. At the San Francisco Conference, its Prime Minister, Peter ★Fraser, had advocated a potent universal collective security organisation, which would draw forces from all nations and react collectively to international threats to the peace. He was unhappy with the machinery which finally emerged, stating later that the UN Charter was not security, but the way to security. In particular he objected strongly to the veto power accorded to the 'big five' permanent members—China, France, the Soviet Union, the United Kingdom, and the United States—in the body charged with maintaining international peace, the eleven-member Security Council; he believed this provision introduced a fatal element of uncertainty. The Security Council was to be given the means of dealing forcibly with powers that threatened international peace; a Military Staff Committee was established to draw up the blueprint for an international force, but the onset of the ★Cold War soon dashed any hopes of its early implementation. In the meantime New Zealand maintained its traditional security arrangements through association with the United Kingdom (see MIDDLE EAST COMMITMENT). Unexpectedly the Security Council was able to respond as envisaged in the Charter when North Korea invaded South Korea in June 1950. The Soviet Union, at the time, was boycotting the council over the question of China's seat. New Zealand was one of sixteen nations which contributed forces to the UN Command in the ★Korean War. Buoyed by the United Nations' initial success in Korea, and anxious to find a means of offsetting the Soviet veto in the Security Council (the Soviet delegate had resumed attending in August 1950), the General Assembly—in which all members were represented and none had a veto—adopted the 'Uniting for Peace' resolution. This provided that should the Security Council fail to react to a threat to international peace the General Assembly could meet in emergency session (or Little Assembly) and recommend action—a constitutional change which was bitterly opposed by the Soviet Union. Additionally, two new bodies were created: the Collective Measures Committee designed to investigate means by which international peace could be enhanced, and the Peace Observation Commission, of which New Zealand was a member, able to recommend the deployment of UN observers.

New Zealand took a seat on the Security Council for the first time in 1954–55. During this time it actively promoted UN initiatives in relation to the French position in Indo-China and the looming confrontation between the United States and China during the offshore islands crisis. It did its best to prevent direct US intervention in these crises, which might have led to outright war. The importance of the United Nations to New Zealand gradually declined after 1956 with the end of the Cold War impasse over the admission of new members, which had prevailed for almost a decade. Ironically, it was New Zealand which played a key role in overcoming the tit-for-tat vetoing by the Soviet Union and the Western powers of various states' applications to join. A significant expansion of the United Nations occurred with the admission of many newly independent Third World nations, whose presence had profound effects on the nature of the organisation. New Zealand found itself an even smaller voice in a much less familiar environment, and the United Nations' importance to New Zealand dwindled. Although the Security Council agreed to intervene in the Congo, then racked with civil war, this action, far from reinvigorating the organisation, almost crippled its ability to act. After approving the initial deployment of UN troops in the Congo, the Soviet Union refused to pay its share of operational costs and annual UN subscriptions. As the United Nations careered towards bankruptcy, there was talk of suspending Soviet voting rights. Following the Congo operation, the United Nations became less willing to intervene in such conflicts. In 1966 New Zealand was elected to a one-year term on the Security Council, a consequence of the enlargement of the council to fifteen members. Nonetheless, its scepticism about the United Nations as a security framework remained strong, a diplomat observing in 1968 that the Security Council was 'unlikely to be of any real protective value' to New Zealand. It would be another twenty years before the United Nations gained an opportunity to reassert itself, following the end of the Cold War. A more cooperative atmosphere among the great powers raised hopes that the long-stymied institutional machinery could now be utilised as envisaged in 1945. This was reinforced when the Security Council, for only the second time, was able to act under the peace enforcement provisions of the Charter in response to Iraq's invasion of Kuwait in August 1990. Although a UN Command was not established, as in Korea, a United States–led coalition implemented the Council's resolutions. New Zealand servicemen and women were among the forces involved in the ensuing ★Gulf War in early 1991 in a support capacity. For the first time in a major war involving Great Britain or the United States, New Zealand did not send combat troops. ★Special Air Service troops were also dispatched to the region in 1998, when Iraq's resistance to UN resolutions regarding weapons inspections precipitated a new crisis. The Security Council in 1992 initiated yet another peace enforcement measure to deal with a chaotic situation that had developed in Somalia. During the early 1990s there was also a proliferation of ★peace-keeping actions, in which New Zealand service personnel were heavily involved. New Zealand's more enthusiastic support for the United Nations was reflected in its determined and successful bid to secure another term on the Security Council, with the result that in 1993–94 New Zealand was involved in high-level decision-making in relation to crises in Bosnia–Herzegovina and elsewhere. Although UN peace-keeping has decreased since 1995, largely because of a more realistic assessment internationally of what it can be expected to accomplish, it remains a key role for the ★New Zealand Defence Force.

JOHN BATTERSBY

United States troops in New Zealand Between 1942 and 1944 New Zealand underwent a 'friendly invasion' of American troops. This was the first (and only) time that significant numbers of foreign troops had been based on New Zealand soil, and there was a substantial impact on society. Their presence was an outcome of New Zealand's concern for its security in the early stages of the ★Pacific War, and a desire on the part of its great power allies to ensure the retention of 2NZEF in the Mediterranean theatre of war. To this latter end, the British Prime Minister Winston Churchill successfully lobbied President Roosevelt in March 1942 to send an American force to New Zealand to allay local fears and undercut demands for the return of the New Zealand troops (see PACIFIC VERSUS MEDITERRANEAN). It was not until mid June 1942, however, that the Americans arrived in strength. A regiment of the US Army's 37th Division began landing at Auckland on 13 June, while most of the 1st Marine Division did so at Wellington the following day, moving into hastily constructed camp facilities. Vice-Admiral R.L. Ghormley, the commander of the ★South Pacific Area, had earlier set up his headquarters in Auckland. Censorship requirements ensured that there would be no official statement about the American presence until the following November.

Neither of the first American formations in New Zealand remained long. The 37th Division personnel began re-embarking for Fiji a fortnight after their arrival, and all had gone by the end of July. For the men of the 1st Marine Division, who left on 22 July, the stay in Wellington was a brief interlude before they launched themselves on to the beaches of Guadalcanal in the Solomon Islands on 7 August 1942. But they were soon followed by other American formations. Elements of the 2nd Marine Division also spent some

United States troops in New Zealand

American troops take a rest during a route march around Wellington's Oriental Bay in 1942 (*NZ Freelance Collection, Alexander Turnbull Library, F-28403-1/2*)

weeks in the Wellington area before going to Guadalcanal in December 1942, and the whole division returned by March 1943 at the end of that long-drawn-out campaign. They did not leave until the following October, their destination Tarawa in the Gilbert Islands, the first thrust in the main central Pacific campaign, where they were decimated in the ultimately successful landing. In Auckland the 43rd Division arrived in October 1942; it, too, stayed only a few weeks before heading for ★New Caledonia, and eventually the Solomons. It returned in March 1944 for about four months. The other American divisions to be based in the Auckland area were the 3rd Marine Division (March–July 1943) and the 25th Division (December 1943–February 1944).

American troops in New Zealand formed three main groups. First there were those, by far the majority, who were in the country for operational reasons, either training with their formations for combat or providing support. Most of the American troops were camped in the greater Wellington and Auckland areas, with Marines only in the former and both Army and Marines in the latter. The main Wellington camps straddled McKay's Crossing just north of Paekakariki, with smaller camps in Wellington and Lower Hutt cities. In Auckland, there were a number of camps between Warkworth in the north and Pukekohe in the south. The only camp outside these two metropolitan areas was at Solway showgrounds in Masterton. Apart from the divisional troops, there were numerous American support personnel who remained in the country for long periods, serving in headquarters, air force detachments, stores depots, or medical facilities. The second large group were those sick or wounded men evacuated to New Zealand for medical treatment at one of the nineteen hospitals which were built, the largest two being at Cornwall Park in Auckland and Silverstream in Wellington. The third group comprised the steady stream of Americans—soldiers, sailors, and airmen—who came to New Zealand for rest and recreation. In all about 100,000 troops were stationed in New Zealand for varying periods during the two years 1942 to 1944, with a peak of 48,200 in the country in July 1943. In addition, many thousands of American sailors and merchant seamen made usually fleeting visits aboard American warships and merchant vessels.

In the anxious times following the fall of Singapore the sudden influx of American troops was for

New Zealanders both a relief and a curiosity. Their customs and behaviour, their unfamiliar accents and courteous manners, and their free-spending habits all set the Americans apart from the rather staid, provincial wartime New Zealand community. A small minority of the visitors irritated their hosts by their arrogance and lack of sensitivity, but for the most part relations were friendly, and New Zealanders adjusted quite easily to the American presence. To meet the off-duty needs of the visitors, new facilities were built, practices and customs were altered, and arrangements for hospitality were put in place. Coffee houses and milk bars appeared. Suppliers of certain products and services such as taxi companies, florists, jewellers, and hoteliers experienced a boom. A lively nightlife developed in Auckland and Wellington. American music and dances supplanted the English fare hitherto popular in cabarets and dance halls.

With a large proportion of New Zealand's young men serving overseas, there were opportunities aplenty for American servicemen seeking entertainment with the opposite sex—a situation which caused much heartburning among the absent New Zealanders and a morale problem for 2NZEF. Most of these relationships were transient, ending with the departure of the troops or perhaps with the death of the American in combat. Some persisted, however, and altogether 1396 New Zealand women married Americans in New Zealand and went to the United States after the war as ★war brides; this figure was no doubt supplemented by others who married later in the United States or elsewhere. For some, the end of a relationship was made more traumatic by an unwanted pregnancy.

There was sometimes friction between American troops and New Zealand men, especially those in uniform. The greater spending capacity of the Americans caused resentment, as did their involvement with women already in relationships with New Zealanders fighting overseas and their reluctance on occasions to acknowledge New Zealand's substantial if distant war effort. Such irritants were reflected in fights and brawls which periodically broke out among the two countries' servicemen. Usually these outbreaks were quickly and ruthlessly suppressed by the ever-present military police, but sometimes they became quite extensive. One such occasion was the so-called Battle of Manners Street, which became the subject of much rumour. This was a series of brawls which evidently erupted from a dispute between American soldiers and some New Zealand merchant seamen, though some witnesses later maintained that the 'battle' had been precipitated by racial slurs by southern Americans against Maori. Rumours of American deaths at the time were incorrect. There was another substantial fracas in Auckland on 3 May 1943 between Maori and US sailors in which several men were stabbed.

As the focus of the Pacific War shifted northwards, the American presence in New Zealand began to run down in 1944. The infantry and marine formations departed, and were followed by the various support personnel. The Americans vacated the naval base at Devonport on 26 October 1944, and following the war the bodies of those who had died in accidents or of wounds were repatriated to the United States. A few tangible signs of the presence remained, in the form of buildings, equipment left behind, and a handful of placenames or memorial plaques. One of the marines, Leon Uris, would later recall his division's stay in Wellington in his best-selling novel *Battlecry*, published in 1954.

H. Bioletti, *The Yanks Are Coming: The American Invasion of New Zealand 1942–1944* (Century Hutchinson, Auckland, 1989); N.M. Taylor, *The Home Front*, 2 vols (Historical Publications Branch, Wellington, 1986).

Upham, Captain Charles Hazlitt (21 September 1908–22 November 1994) was one of only three men, and the only combat soldier, to win the ★Victoria Cross twice. Born at Christchurch, he attended Lincoln College and spent his early twenties as a shepherd, musterer, and farm manager. A contemporary described him as 'an experienced, educated, well-bred rough diamond'. Enlisting in 2NZEF just two weeks after the outbreak of the ★Second World War, he left New Zealand with the First Echelon in January 1940 as a private in 20th Battalion. His qualities as a natural leader were quickly recognised, and he was sent off to officer training school, from which he emerged as a junior subaltern later in the year. He drove himself hard in preparing for combat, spending hours perfecting his knowledge of the various weapons. His courage, practical common sense, sense of duty, and intense hatred of the enemy made him a formidable soldier, and an inspiration to those he led in combat, which he did for the first time as a platoon commander in ★Greece. Soon afterwards, during the unsuccessful defence of ★Crete, he won his first VC. He was conspicuous during 20th Battalion's counter-attack on Maleme airfield on the night of 21–22 May 1941, when he thrice destroyed German machine-gun posts with hand grenades. Over the next few days he disregarded wounds in the shoulder and foot as he repeatedly went forward to engage the Germans with hand grenades. On one occasion he was shot at by two Germans; pretending to be dead, he waited for the Germans to come forward before killing them. On 30 May, now exhausted from his wounds and dysentery, he and three others ambushed a German force, killing many and preventing the New Zealand rearguard from being cut off. His performance as a company com-

Lieutenant Charles Upham (centre) is congratulated by his platoon sergeant after learning of the award of his first VC (*War History Collection, Alexander Turnbull Library, F-2108-1/2-DA*)

mander during the ensuing ★North African campaign was equally outstanding. During the 2nd New Zealand Division's desperate breakout from Minqar Qaim on 28 June 1942, he again excelled in the close quarters fighting, attacking German guns and trucks with hand grenades and being wounded by fragments of his own bombs. At Ruweisat Ridge on 14–15 July 1942 he went forward in a jeep to reconnoitre the enemy positions. When his battalion was ordered to attack, he led a fierce assault on the German positions, during which he was wounded in the arm. Exhausted and suffering from blood loss, he had his wounds dressed, but returned to his men and was again badly wounded. Immobilised, he was taken prisoner when his company was overrun by German tanks later in the day. For his exploits at Ruweisat Ridge, he would be awarded a bar to his VC in 1945. Held initially as a POW in Italy, later in Germany, he made several unsuccessful attempts to escape before being sent to the infamous Oflag IVC (Colditz) camp, where he was liberated in April 1945. Quietly determined, ever confident, self-effacing, he epitomised the New Zealand soldier of the Second World War. After the war he farmed in Canterbury. A modest man, he shunned publicity despite being the most widely known of New Zealand's VC winners. A scholarship and the military sealift ship, HMNZS *Charles Upham*, were named in his honour.

K. Sandford, *Mark of the Lion: The Story of Capt. Charles Upham V.C. and Bar* (Hutchinson, London, 1962).

V

V-Force was the New Zealand Army's contingent in the United States–led coalition which sought to preserve the Republic of Vietnam (see VIETNAM WAR).

Venereal disease during wartime has until recently been seen largely as a problem of manpower 'wastage'. It has at times been a major social problem, not just for the forces but for New Zealand society as a whole. Until penicillin became available late in the ★Second World War, there was no easy way of treating syphilis and gonorrhoea. The arsenic cure for the former could be worse than the disease, while frequent urethral irrigations for the latter were painful, unreliable, and long drawn out. Syphilis was a killer disease responsible for many deaths as well as problems ranging from blindness, heart disease, and madness to miscarriage and stillbirth. Gonorrhoea, about ten times as prevalent, was less of a problem for men but a major cause of sterility in women.

When 1NZEF's Main Body landed in Egypt late in 1914, its commander, Major-General Sir Alexander ★Godley, expected to lose 10 per cent of his men to VD. He warned them on board not to consort with prostitutes, opened a wet canteen in camp so that they did not have to go to town for a drink, and marched them through Cairo's brothel district, the Wazza, during daylight. But he also went beyond these measures of 'moral prophylaxis' by instituting 'early treatment', giving medical officers syringes for urethral irrigation. As this treatment was carried out after sexual intercourse had taken place, it was not properly the prohibited 'physical prophylaxis', though it was a step in that direction. Godley made no official record of it. Initially, infected men were sent home. The first cases, arriving in April 1915, were placed on Quarantine Island in Dunedin Harbour. But the numbers involved and the potential for scandal put paid to this approach, and New Zealanders began to be treated at the Australian Dermatological Hospital.

Following the move to France, it was assumed that with men going to the United Kingdom on leave VD would not be a problem. But the rates among men going to London were so high that Prime Minister William ★Massey even complained about it at the Imperial War Conference in 1917. At the end of that year 1NZEF adopted the prophylactic kit (containing calomel ointment, Condys crystals, and condoms) which had been developed by the New Zealand anti-VD campaigner Ettie ★Rout. They were handed out on a free and compulsory basis to men going on leave. The NZMC masseur Fred Hornibrook (later Rout's husband) was appointed as official prophylaxis lecturer. The policy change had come about when the Minister of Defence, Sir James ★Allen, authorised the 1NZEF commander in the United Kingdom, Brigadier-General G.S. ★Richardson, to do whatever was necessary to deal with the problem. Although publicly funded, it was not publicised in New Zealand. This was to avoid a huge outcry, particularly from women, whose main lobby group, the Woman's Christian Temperance Union, had 'social purity' as one of its major planks and regarded prophylaxis as an attempt to 'make vice safe'.

No reliable figures exist for VD rates in the First World War. Although the medical official history gives a figure of approximately 3600 per annum, the 'moderate estimate' of a member of the NZMC was 12,000 gonorrhoea and 4000 syphilis cases. This was about one in six of the men. The large numbers of men coming back with VD in 1919 led the Public Health Department to set up clinics in the four main cities, with the Defence Department partly funding the salaries of the doctors involved.

From the outset 2NZEF used physical prophylaxis. Prophylactic kits were handed out, and ablution centres, called 'blue light' centres, were provided. The authorities went so far as to remove prostitutes from areas New Zealand soldiers were in, as occurred in Italy, and to set up controlled brothels, as in Syria, where prostitutes were examined weekly by New Zealand medical officers. The invention of sulphonamide drugs during the 1920s had greatly simplified treatment of VD, though it still consisted of ten weekly injections. Sulpha-resistant gonorrhoea proved a problem in the ★North African campaign, because men in the desert sometimes only got occasional doses of sulphapyridine. There were also difficulties in diagnosing syphilis when men could not get to treatment centres before the primary sores had healed. As a result, a mobile treatment centre was set up in 1943 to carry out tests and treatments in the forward areas. It proved useful when the New Zealanders went to Italy, where VD incidence was high and women were available for a few cigarettes. The worst areas, Pompeii and Naples, were put out of bounds to New Zealand troops in 1944. The highest rates came in northern Italy following the end of the campaign, especially in Trieste. Rates were also high among ★Jayforce in the occupation of Japan, and later in ★Kayforce during the ★Korean War; the dislocation of war and defeat made prostitutes readily available in both Japan and Korea. Nevertheless the military significance of VD had lessened, as it became easier to treat men without removing them from their units. Penicillin, which became available in 1944, provided a relatively simple cure, a course of injections for syphilis, for example, only taking a week.

On the home front there was a moral panic about VD, largely centred on American servicemen and their relationships with New Zealand women. This was especially so in Auckland, where prostitution flourished. But in fact the disease rate had risen sharply before the arrival of the Americans. In 1941 new emergency regulations meant that both men and women suspected of having VD could be examined, taken to hospital, and kept there until cured. There were also efforts to educate civilians, particularly with the film 'No Greater Sin—The Story of Syphilis', which was endorsed by the Minister of Health and the Director-General of Medical Services.

JANE TOLERTON

Veterans' associations were first formed by British soldiers who had taken their discharge in New Zealand during the ★New Zealand Wars, and were essentially for the purpose of reunions. In 1900 men who had served in imperial forces overseas formed the Empire Veterans' Association of New Zealand. Renamed the King's Empire Veterans' Association in 1910, it focused on promoting the welfare of its members and taking part in, and sometimes helping to control crowds at, ceremonial events, when a uniform of a ★lemon-squeezer and blue tunic was worn. With a view to remaining in contact, veterans of the ★Boer War also formed a number of clubs, such as that of the First Mounted Rifles Contingent. It was not until 1920, however, that the South African War Veterans' Association was formed. It held periodic reunions until 1978, when, with only seven Boer War veterans surviving, the association was wound up. Most other veterans' organisations have tended to follow this pattern of comradeship associations. After the ★Second World War a plethora of unit associations were established. There are currently about twenty representing units from that conflict. Most 2NZEF battalions and regiments have their own associations with regular reunions. Similarly specific campaigns have given rise to associations, such as the Ex-Prisoners of War Association, or the North Russian Convoy Veterans' Association, serving to preserve comradeship and assist members. Since the Second World War associations have been formed by participants in specific campaigns or deployments, such as the J-Force and BCOF Veterans' Association and the New Zealand Korea Veterans' Association. The Vietnam Services' Association has served as more than an association for comradeship; it has also been active in representing Vietnam veterans in claims for compensation for the effects of ★Agent Orange. Since 1934 former members of the Royal New Zealand Artillery have met under the auspices of the New Zealand Permanent Force Old Comrades' Association.

The most important veterans' organisation has been the New Zealand Returned Services' Association, which had its origins in the ★First World War. Former members of 1NZEF began forming returned soldier clubs as early as 1915. As the numbers of repatriated soldiers grew, the need for a national body began to be recognised. Formed on 28 April 1916, the New Zealand Returned Soldiers' Association had among its objects the guarding of the interests of men overseas and the rehabilitation of returned soldiers. By 1917 4027 men had paid their ten shillings membership fee. However, the war years were a trying time for the association. The first elected President, Captain W.T. Pitt, resigned after misappropriating RSA funds, and there was tension between the national body and provincial organisations. In 1919 a disillusioned Auckland branch demanded that the national association take an overtly political stance by endorsing a platform of employment preference, land settlement and state housing for returned soldiers, and a 'white New Zealand' policy. At a bitter special conference, it was

Veterans' associations

decided, judiciously, that the RSA would achieve greater success by remaining a 'non-political' pressure group; it would also be less likely to be internally rent by partisan strife. As a large united organisation, the RSA was able to exercise a considerable influence in mainstream politics during the rest of the century: Ministers of Defence have always been attentive to RSA deputations and many senior politicians have themselves been RSA members.

Following the First World War, the RSA was active in a wide variety of *repatriation issues, such as pressing for increases to the mufti allowance or arranging concessions for wounded soldiers at university. It was particularly concerned with the advancement of veterans' employment rights and privileges, land settlement schemes, and *war pensions. Continual agitation on behalf of returned soldiers in these areas brought useful results. The RSA was also instrumental in the emergence of *Anzac Day as a sacred day of remembrance, and its establishment as a public holiday. A 'Poppy Day' is held in the week preceding 25 April, during which members distribute artificial poppies and receive donations which are devoted to the RSA's welfare programmes.

Under the steady guidance of Ernest Boxer, the RSA President from 1918 to 1921, RSA membership increased to 57,000 by 1920. By the mid 1920s the organisation had assumed its basic structure of largely autonomous local sub-branches and branches, the branches forming provincial districts. At a national level, the RSA was administered by the Dominion Executive Council, composed of representatives of the provincial districts, which met monthly at Wellington. Policy was determined at an annual conference, which debated remits from the branches and passed resolutions. A newspaper, first published as *Quick March* in 1918, provided both a valuable link between branches and a forum for the articulation of returned soldiers' grievances. *RSA Review*, which replaced *Quick March* in 1924, is still published bi-monthly.

By the 1920s the RSA, led for most of the time by New Zealand's leading citizen soldier, Major-General Sir Andrew *Russell, was the accepted representative of returned soldiers, with the ear of returned soldiers in the government and a high level of public sympathy. However, its very success as a pressure group in assisting the rehabilitation of ex-soldiers may have made it less relevant by the mid 1920s. Membership declined, reaching a low of 6671 in 1927. However, during the 1930s the RSA began to expand again, as ageing returned soldiers sought comradeship and recognised the need for a strong lobbying organisation during troubled economic conditions. Pressure from the RSA was instrumental in alleviating the effects of cuts to war pensions in 1932 and in expanding the eligibility for such pensions in 1935. Particularly important during the Depression was the establishment, as the result of persistent lobbying by the RSA, of the Soldiers' Civil Re-establishment League, under whose auspices disabled soldiers made and sold various items. The RSA took a more assertive stance towards defence issues during the 1930s, and was openly critical of the first Labour government's defence policies.

During the Second World War, the RSA assisted the government with rehabilitation policy, many of its proposals being embodied in the Rehabilitation Act 1941. Throughout the war it was influential in gaining further concessions from the government for the rehabilitation of returned servicemen in the important areas of employment, housing, and land settlement. In war pensions, too, RSA lobbying gained increased benefits for veterans. The RSA also served as a patriotic 'ginger group', condemning *conscientious objectors and aliens (ostensibly to protect the rights of soldiers serving overseas) and advocating *conscription. In spite of public stances often critical of government policies, the RSA still took its non-political stance seriously. Its Dominion President, William Perry, resigned when appointed to the *War Cabinet in 1943. Efforts on behalf of serving New Zealand soldiers were combined with attempts to gain their membership upon their return. In this the RSA was initially successful, with three-quarters of returning soldiers joining it by 1943, but a certain restiveness among younger members was soon apparent. The RSA did its best to accommodate them, and to broaden the association's appeal to servicemen outside 2NZEF. In October 1941 its name was changed to New Zealand Returned Services' Association to signify that the RSA was more than an organisation for returned army personnel.

From 1942, the RSA had a rival—the 2nd NZEF Association. Many Second World War servicemen believed that the RSA, dominated by older First World War veterans, had little to offer them. The 2nd NZEF Association was very different from the RSA. It appealed more directly to the sentiments of young men. Far more impatient in its demands to create a 'New World' than the 'old generation' RSA, it revealed a willingness to embrace radical causes. It advocated monetary reform and, in 1949, opposed *compulsory military training. Its newspaper, the *Kiwi*, was more racy and strident in tone than the *RSA Review*. But, lacking the established structure or influence of the RSA, it was not able to expand its membership above the peak of about 10,000 achieved in the late 1940s. During the following decade it went into decline, and its members were eventually absorbed into the RSA.

In contrast to the 2nd NZEF Association's competitive approach, the New Zealand Homeservicemen's Association (NZHSA) was formed in 1943 with the assistance of the RSA. It represented those members of the armed forces who had at least six months' service in New Zealand without being sent overseas. Although in theory representing about 66,000 personnel, the NZHSA lacked the established structure of the RSA and it had only about 20,000 members by the late 1940s. Relations between the NZHSA and RSA have always been cooperative, and RSA clubs have accepted NZHSA members.

In the immediate aftermath of the Second World War, the RSA was at its strongest, with a membership of 136,000 in 1947. Of these, 92,000 had served in the just-completed conflict. Often critical of government rehabilitation schemes, the RSA was particularly frustrated by the lack of housing for returned servicemen and demanded preferential employment and low interest loans. Under the leadership of its President, the eminent 2NZEF officer Major-General Sir Howard ★Kippenberger, it was a strong advocate of CMT, a stance which went hand in hand with hostility to military defaulters and communists.

The greatest change to the RSA after the Second World War was at a local level. This derived from the organisation's much stronger and more stable level of membership, which was about 90,000 throughout the 1960s. Branches developed a 'club' atmosphere, with comfortable lounges, bar rooms, billiard rooms, and social halls. Darts, golf, and especially bowls teams added to the camaraderie. The *RSA Review* reflected the RSA's gradual move from a pressure group to a social institution, with women's, gardening, and sporting sections being added to the items on rehabilitation and branch news. Local branches also undertook important welfare work for ex-service personnel and their dependants.

With the decline in numbers of First and Second World War members through natural attrition, the RSA has undergone considerable change. Sustaining the association's clubs and services demanded the opening of membership to people who had not necessarily served overseas. Relatives of RSA members were allowed to join as house members, and from 1977 armed forces personnel could join as service members. By 1998 about half the RSA's members were ex-servicemen and women, rather than veterans of overseas campaigns. Still one of New Zealand's largest voluntary organisations, it had a membership of 126,000.

With the ageing of its membership, the RSA has suffered a steady decline in its influence as a lobby group, though it still commands much attention from the government. Since the 1960s its conservative stance on such issues as New Zealand's involvement in the ★Vietnam War, ★ANZUS, and visits by American warships has sometimes left it the target of criticism, as social attitudes change among a younger generation which has never experienced war. Angry confrontations between RSA members and protesters marked Anzac Day commemorations in the late 1960s and early 1970s. In the 1990s, however, public attitudes to ex-servicemen generally were more sympathetic, a change reflected in the warm response to the parade and reunion organised by Vietnam veterans in Wellington in 1998. The RSA continues to lobby the government of the day in favour of sustaining effective armed forces and on a range of issues relating to the health and welfare of returned servicemen and women.

R.A. Patterson, 'The RSA in Action 1943–1950' (MA thesis, University of Auckland, 1973).

VE/VJ Days The response of New Zealanders to news of the end of the war in Europe in May 1945, and then of the victory over Japan in August 1945, tells us much about the extent of social regulation and conformity a world war had produced. Germany surrendered in the early afternoon of 7 May, New Zealand time. The news became known the next morning, with screaming headlines in the morning papers. But the acting Prime Minister, Walter Nash, insisted that celebrations should wait until Winston Churchill officially announced the peace, which would not be heard in New Zealand until 1 a.m. on 9 May. So on Tuesday, 8 May, when everybody felt like celebrating, Nash told the country by radio that they should all go to work and that VE Day would be on the 9th.

In most places New Zealanders accepted the edict. They were not 'inclined to let off steam without official authorisation'. Only Dunedin bucked the trend. There the holding of the capping parade released the inhibitions. By midday the factories had downed tools, the town hall bells were rung, and the mayor organised a short ceremony in the Octagon. Even then this spontaneous celebration never exceeded the bounds of decorum.

On VE Day itself weeks of official preparation rolled into action. Citizens were woken by bells and sirens, and flags quickly appeared. In Wellington at the Government Buildings there were speeches by the Governor-General, the acting Prime Minister, and the Leader of the Opposition. The American, Soviet, and New Zealand national anthems were sung; and only then, after midday, did official local ceremonies start. These local programmes of events, which generally extended over the next day, Thursday 10 May, also a public holiday, were highly orchestrated affairs. There were bands parading, community sing-songs, thanksgiving services often held at the local war memorial, and in smaller places bonfires and sports programmes for the children and Victory Balls for the adults. In Wellington music was played at three sites, and there was a Victory Service at the Basin Reserve. In

Victoria Cross

Christchurch the Trades Council organised a People's Victory March in which 25,000 paraded from Latimer Square to Cathedral Square singing patriotic ditties.

The organised ceremonies were in part designed to 'keep the lid on' more spontaneous celebration. There was, of course, plenty of spontaneity—the pubs were full and in Wellington there was broken glass in the streets. There was singing and dancing in the streets and kissing of strangers. People joined together in crocodiles and took part in impromptu street theatre. But it never got out of hand. There was little damage to property, and in both Wellington and Auckland there was but one case brought before the courts the next day. Elsewhere citizens were complimented on their 'commendable restraint'.

VJ Day again showed public regulation at work. Again the preparation had been considerable and this time went more smoothly. The news of the Japanese surrender arrived in New Zealand at 11 a.m. on 15 August. The sirens immediately sounded, a national ceremony was held, and the local celebrations followed. Once more there were parades, bands playing, thanksgiving services, bonfires, dances, and community sports. Once more the beer flowed and there were streamers and whistles and dancing in the streets. Again there were two days' public holiday.

There were also some revealing differences. In Auckland, where there were few organised events, the city went out to enjoy itself the moment the factory whistle sounded. At first it was simply people drinking and dancing and scattering confetti. Then the 'rowdies' began throwing bottles. Windows were smashed, people were hurt. By the evening fifty-one people had been taken to hospital and fifteen tons of glass lay in the roads. The next day, although the crowds were much smaller, drunken hooligans returned, and the police arrived in numbers to restore civil peace. In Wellington inclement weather reduced the numbers in the streets—instead people crowded into the hotels—while in Christchurch another 'People's March' was less successful, with some prominent employers concerned that the unions had taken the lead. Everywhere it was noted that people in uniform attracted less adoration than in May. New Zealanders were enthusiastic about peace on VJ Day, but by comparison with VE Day the unity of war had begun to weaken, to be replaced by some of the social conflicts of peace.

N.M. Taylor, *The Home Front*, 2 vols (Historical Publications Branch, Wellington, 1986).

JOCK PHILLIPS

Victoria Cross, the highest award open to New Zealand service personnel, has its origins in recognition during the ★Crimean War that there was an inadequate means of marking the many acts of gallantry performed by British naval and military personnel irrespective of their rank. It was instituted by Queen Victoria by Royal Warrant dated 29 January 1856 for award 'to those officers or men who … in the presence of the enemy shall have then performed some signal act of valour, or devotion to their country'. Made retrospective to 1854 to cover those acts performed during the Crimean War, it was from the outset intended to be the premier award of the British Crown for acts of valour in times of war. Between 1858 and 1881 the award also covered certain acts performed in a non-combative situation. In the 'order of wear' of decorations and medals it enjoys a precedence before all other ★honours and awards from the Crown.

In 1864 the Governor, Sir George ★Grey, forwarded a recommendation for the award of the VC to two members of the New Zealand forces, Major Charles ★Heaphy, Auckland Militia, and Sergeant Kenrick, only to have it rejected by the War Office on the grounds that the Warrant did not allow the award of the VC to local forces. A lengthy and lively debate ensued in London as to whether it was appropriate to extend the eligibility for the cross. After a strong representation from New Zealand ministers, it was agreed, somewhat reluctantly, that the VC should be extended to colonial forces and that the change should be retrospective to include the recent conflict in New Zealand. The amending Warrant, which cited the war in New Zealand as the reason for the change in policy, was signed by Queen Victoria on 1 January 1867. On 8 February 1867 Heaphy became the first colonial and non-regular soldier to receive the VC. Nothing further was heard of the case of Kenrick or of two further unnamed cases, one a Maori, which Grey had intimated to the War Office he intended submitting for consideration for the VC. The run-down of British forces in New Zealand after 1866 and the continued involvement of local units in active operations led to the institution in 1869 of the ★New Zealand Cross.

By a consolidating Warrant of 22 May 1920 the criteria for the VC were redefined to read for 'most conspicuous bravery or some daring or pre-eminent act of valour or self-sacrifice or extreme devotion to duty in the presence of the enemy'. Posthumous awards had been made for the ★Boer War, but formal provision was not made for posthumous awards until this 1920 Warrant. Eligibility was also extended to include all officers and men of the armed forces of the Empire and the ★merchant marine, women of nursing and hospital services, and civilians serving with the forces. By a further amending Warrant dated 31 December 1942 the Dominion governments, including New Zealand, were able to make

Victoria Cross

recommendations direct to the sovereign for the award of the VC.

The history of the VC has been evolutionary and, like the stories of its recipients, has been complex and occasionally controversial, all of which has helped make the award, as proposed in the preamble to the instituting Warrant, so 'highly prized and eagerly sought after'. Changes to the constitutions of those Commonwealth countries of which the Queen is head of state and which have shared the various British honours and awards have led to changes in the British honours system and the development of independent systems by those countries. This has opened a new and important chapter in the history of the VC. In 1991 the Queen of Australia instituted 'the Victoria Cross for Australia', in 1993 the Queen of Canada instituted 'the Victoria Cross for Canada', and in 1999 the Queen of New Zealand instituted 'the Victoria Cross for New Zealand'. The Australian and New Zealand crosses are identical in both design and metal composition to the British VC. The criteria for each VC is similar to that of the British VC except that several words have been changed. In the case of the VC for New Zealand the criteria is 'for most conspicuous gallantry, or some daring or pre-eminent act of valour or self-sacrifice or extreme devotion to duty in the presence of the enemy or belligerents'. In other words, the VC may be awarded in those situations where New Zealand may not necessarily be at war with a country but is acting in a *peace-keeping role between two factions who are or have been at war.

The VC is a cross *paty* or *formy* (incorrectly described as a Maltese cross in the 1856 Warrant) with in the centre the Royal Crest, the crown of which is within a scroll bearing the words FOR VALOUR. The cross is suspended from the letter V attached to an oblong laureated bar through which the crimson ribbon passes. Until 1918 the ribbon was dark blue for awards to naval personnel. The bar, to denote a second award, is of the same design as the oblong laureated suspender bar. The VC is cast in gunmetal from guns captured from the Russian Army during the Crimean War. However, for a short period during and after the *First World War metal from Chinese guns was used. The metal is chemically treated to give a dark bronze finish. The rank, name, and unit or service of the recipient is engraved on the reverse of the suspender bar and the date of the act or acts for which the cross is awarded is engraved on the central portion of the reverse. In the case of a bar, details of both the recipient and the date of award are engraved on the reverse.

Since the VC's institution there have been 1350, plus three bars, awarded up to and including the two awards made in 1983 for actions during the *Falk-

Table 13 The Victoria Cross

Name, Rank, Unit or service, Place and date of act, London Gazette *(date of award)*

1 Awards to Members of New Zealand Forces

HEAPHY, Charles, Major, Auckland Rifle Volunteers, NZ Militia, Waikato, New Zealand, 11 February 1864 (8 February 1867)

HARDHAM, William James, Farrier Sergeant-Major, 4th NZ Contingent, South Africa, 28 January 1901 (4 October 1901)

BASSETT, Cyril Royston Guyton, Corporal, NZ Divisional Signals, 1NZEF, Gallipoli, 7 August 1915 (15 October 1915)

BROWN, Donald Forrester, Sergeant, 2nd Battalion, Otago Infantry Regiment, 1NZEF, France, 15 September 1916 (14 June 1917)*

FRICKLETON, Samuel, Lance-Corporal, 3rd Battalion, 3rd NZ (Rifle) Brigade, 1NZEF, Messines, Belgium, 7 June 1917 (2 August 1917)

ANDREW, Leslie Wilton, Corporal, 2nd Battalion, Wellington Infantry Regiment, 1NZEF, France, 31 July 1917 (6 September 1917)

NICHOLAS, Henry James, Private, 1st Battalion, Canterbury Infantry Regiment, 1NZEF, Belgium, 3 December 1917 (11 January 1918)

TRAVIS, Richard Charles, DCM, MM, Sergeant, 2nd Battalion, Otago Infantry Regiment, 1NZEF, France, 24 July 1918 (27 September 1918)*

FORSYTH, Samuel, Sergeant, NZ Engineers attached to 2nd Battalion, Auckland Infantry Regiment, 1NZEF, France, 24 August 1918 (22 October 1918)*

JUDSON, Reginald Stanley, DCM, MM, Sergeant, 1st Battalion, Auckland Infantry Regiment, 1NZEF, France, 26 August 1918 (30 October 1918)

CRICHTON, James, Private, 2nd Battalion, Auckland Infantry Regiment, 1NZEF, France, 30 September 1918 (15 November 1918)

LAURENT, Harry John, Sergeant, 2nd Battalion, 3rd NZ (Rifle) Brigade, 1NZEF, France, 12 September 1918 (15 November 1918)

GRANT, John Gilroy, Sergeant, 1st Battalion, Wellington Infantry Regiment, 1NZEF, France, 1 September 1918 (27 November 1918)

WARD, James Allen, Sergeant, RNZAF (attached to RAF), over Germany, 5 July 1941 (5 August 1941)

UPHAM, Charles Hazlitt, 2nd Lieutenant, 20th Battalion, 2NZEF, Crete, 22–30 May 1941 (14 October 1941)

HULME, Alfred Clive, Sergeant, 23rd Battalion, 2NZEF, Crete, 20–28 May 1941 (14 October 1941)

HINTON, John Daniel, Sergeant, 20th Battalion, 2NZEF, Greece, 28–29 April 1941 (17 October 1941)

ELLIOTT, Keith, Sergeant, 22nd Battalion, 2NZEF, North Africa, 15 July 1942 (24 September 1942)

*Posthumous award.

Victoria Cross

NGARIMU, Moana-nui-a-Kiwa, 2nd Lieutenant, 28th (Maori) Battalion, 2NZEF, North Africa, 26 March 1943 (4 June 1943)*

TRIGG, Lloyd Allen, DFC, Flying Officer, RNZAF (attached to RAF), over the Atlantic, 11 August 1943 (2 November 1943)*

UPHAM, Charles Hazlitt, VC, Captain, 20th Battalion, 2NZEF, North Africa, 14–15 July 1942 (26 September 1945)

TRENT, Leonard Henry, DFC, Squadron-Leader, RNZAF (attached to RAF), over the Netherlands, 3 May 1943 (1 March 1946)

II Awards to Persons, Born in New Zealand, While Serving with Another Force

D'ARCY, Henry Cecil Dudgeon, Captain, Frontier Light Horse, South African Forces, Zululand, 3 July 1879 (9 October 1879)

SHOUT, Alfred John, Captain, 1st Battalion, AIF, Gallipoli, 9 August 1915 (15 October 1915)*

COOKE, Thomas, Private, 8th Battalion, AIF, France, 24–25 July 1916 (9 September 1916)*

SANDERS, William Edward, Acting Lieutenant, Royal Naval Reserve, at sea, 30 April 1917 (22 June 1917)

STORKEY, Percey Valentine, Lieutenant, 19th Battalion, AIF, France, 7 April 1918 (7 June 1918)

WEATHERS, Lawrence Carthage, Lance-corporal (Temporary Corporal), 43rd Battalion, AIF, France, 2 September 1918 (26 December 1918)

III Awards to Members of the British Forces in New Zealand 1860–66

ODGERS, William, Leading Seaman, Royal Navy, Waireke, 28 March 1860 (3 August 1860)

LUCAS, John, Colour Sergeant, 40th Regiment, Te Arei, 18 March 1861 (17 July 1861)

RYAN, John, Lance-Corporal, 65th Regiment, near Cameron Town, Waikato Heads, 7 September 1863 (16 January 1864)

MacKENNA, Edward, Colour Sergeant, 65th Regiment, near Cameron Town, Waikato Heads, 7 September 1863 (16 January 1864)

MITCHELL, Samuel, Captain of the Foretop, Royal Navy, Tauranga, 29 April 1864 (23 July 1864)

McNEILL, John Carstairs, Lieutenant-Colonel, 107th Regiment, Ohaupo 30 March 1864 (16 August 1864)

DOWN, John Thornton, Ensign, 57th Regiment, Poutoko, 2 October 1863 (22 September 1864)

STAGPOOLE, Dudley, DCM, Drummer, 57th Regiment, Poutoko, 2 October 1863 (22 September 1864)

TEMPLE, William, Assistant Surgeon, Royal Artillery, Rangiriri, 20 November 1863 (22 September 1864)

PICKARD, Arthur Frederick, Lieutenant, Royal Artillery, Rangiriri, 20 November 1863 (22 September 1864)

MANLEY, William George Nicholas, Assistant Surgeon, Royal Artillery, Tauranga, 29 April 1864 (22 September 1864)

SMITH, Frederick Augustus, Captain, 43rd Regiment, Tauranga, 21 June 1864 (4 November 1864)

MURRAY, John, Sergeant, 68th Regiment, Tauranga, 21 June 1864 (4 November 1864)

SHAW, Hugh, Captain, 18th Regiment, Nukumaru, 24 January 1865 (28 November 1865)

IV Recipients who Subsequently Served with New Zealand Forces

DANIEL, Edward St John, Midshipman, Royal Navy, Crimea, 5 November 1854 and 18 June 1855 (24 February 1857). On 4 September 1861 he became the first man (of eight) to forfeit the VC for disgraceful conduct and desertion. [Taranaki Military Settlers, 1864–67, Armed Constabulary, 1867–68]

PYE, Charles [Colquhoun], Sergeant-Major, 53rd Regiment, Lucknow, India, 17 November 1857 (24 December 1858) [Colonial Defence Force, 1863–65]

O'HEA, Timothy, Private, 1st Battalion, Rifle Brigade, Quebec, Canada (non-combat award), 9 June 1866 (1 January 1867) [Armed Constabulary, 1872–73]

MARTINEAU, Horace Robert, Sergeant, Protectorate Regiment. near Mafeking, South Africa, 26 December 1899 (6 July 1900) [1NZEF, 1914–16]

FREYBERG, Bernard Cyril, DSO, Captain (Temporary Lieutenant-Colonel), Queen's Royal Regiment (West Surrey), commanding Hood Battalion, Royal Naval Division, France, 13 November 1916 (15 December 1916) [2NZEF, 1939–45]

V Recipients who had a Family or Other Association with New Zealand

DOWELL, George Dacre, Lieutenant, Royal Marine Artillery, in the Baltic Sea, 3 July 1855 (24 February 1857) [Lived and died in New Zealand]

DIAMOND, Bernard, Sergeant, Bengal Horse Artillery, Indian Army, Bolundshahur, 28 September 1857 (24 April 1858) [Lived and died in New Zealand]

RHODES-MOORHOUSE, William Barnard, 2nd Lieutenant, Special Reserve, Royal Flying Corps, France (first VC won in the air), 26 April 1915 (22 May 1915)* [Born in United Kingdom of New Zealand parents]

FREYBERG, Bernard Cyril, see IV above [Born in the United Kingdom but educated in New Zealand, Governor-General of New Zealand 1946–52]

*Posthumous award.

lands War. (See table 13.) The VC has been awarded to twenty-one New Zealand military personnel. Captain C.H. ★Upham is not only the sole New Zealand recipient of a bar but also the only one of the three recipients of a bar to receive it in combat. It was also the only bar to be awarded during the ★Second World War. Upham's family was related to that of Captain N.G. Chavasse, one of the two other recipients of a VC and bar. Heaphy was the first New Zealand serviceman to receive the VC. However, the first recipient of New Zealand birth was Captain Henry Cecil Dudgeon D'Arcy (born at Wanganui on 11 August 1850), who was awarded the VC in 1879 for an act during the Zulu Wars while serving with the Frontier Light Horse. Hardham was the first New Zealand serviceman born in New Zealand to receive the VC (which he did despite the opinion of his superior, General Ian ★Hamilton, that he merited only a DCM). During the Great War the commander of the New Zealand Division, Major-General Sir Andrew ★Russell, resolved not to forward VC recommendations for officers. As a result, some outstanding acts of valour performed by officers were recognised with lesser decorations. Thus Captain Frederick ★Starnes, Canterbury Regiment, had to be content with an immediate appointment as a DSO, rather than the VC recommended by his brigadier. New Zealand VC winners in the 1914–18 war were confined to eleven NCOs and other ranks.

Over time, the VC criteria have gradually become tighter. This is reflected in a decline in the number of awards. Whereas there were 634 for the First World War, there were only 182 in the Second World War, the same number as awarded for the Indian Mutiny (1857–59). From the outset, there have been many instances of lobbying for the VC and many cases of recommendations being rejected or being recognised with awards of lesser status.

M.J. Crook, *The Evolution of the Victoria Cross* (Midas Books, London, 1975).

PHILLIP O'SHEA

Vietnam War The Vietnam War was New Zealand's longest and most controversial military experience of the twentieth century, and the only conflict in which it did not fight alongside the United Kingdom. It had a decisive impact on subsequent policy-making and public debate about national security, even though New Zealand's troop commitment was minimal. From the outset, official views in Wellington on the Vietnam conflict were shaped by general ★Cold War concerns and alliance considerations, alongside practical qualms about becoming directly involved. During the first Indo-China War, between the communist-dominated Viet Minh and France and its local allies from 1946 to 1954, New Zealand accepted the Anglo-American view that Vietnam was a crucial point on the front line against communist expansion in Asia. New Zealand also joined its major allies in recognising the French-sponsored Bao Dai regime in 1950, but remained dubious about the strength and legitimacy of indigenous non-communist forces there. Accordingly, it confined its military contribution to sending the French two shipments of surplus weapons and ammunition. The outcome of this conflict, however, coincided with a significant shift in New Zealand's approach to regional security. Following the French withdrawal and the Geneva Conference's 'temporary' division of Vietnam at the 17th Parallel, it became a founding member of ★SEATO, which was seen principally as a means of securing a joint Anglo-American commitment to maintaining regional stability. A New Zealand security commitment in the region, most clearly articulated in the strategy of ★forward defence in South-east Asia, was now accepted, though it did not bring closer involvement in Vietnam immediately.

The second Indo-China War began as a civil war, as the regime in South Vietnam led by Ngo Dinh Diem was confronted from 1959 with an insurgency mounted by the National Liberation Front (the Viet Cong), which was backed by the government of North Vietnam under Ho Chi Minh. By late 1961, the Viet Cong were seriously threatening the southern government, to which American non-combatant military and economic assistance was increased. New Zealand resisted American pressure to make a contribution as well, partly because of doubts about the effectiveness of external intervention and fears of a wider war, possibly including China. Pragmatism and parsimony were the hallmarks of Prime Minister K.J. Holyoake's general approach to foreign policy and defence matters, and on Vietnam issues he was always especially cautious. Unlike Australia, which sent a small team of military advisers in 1962, New Zealand confined its assistance initially to a civilian surgical team; during the ensuing twelve years this team would operate quietly but effectively at Qui Nonh in Binh Dinh province. Under continuing American pressure, the government agreed during 1963 to provide a small non-combatant military force, but the deteriorating political situation in Saigon led to delays. Not until June 1964 did twenty-five Army engineers arrive in South Vietnam. Based at Thu Dau Mot, the capital of Binh Duong province, they were engaged in reconstruction projects, such as road and bridge building, until July 1965.

Meanwhile, as the United States escalated its military involvement, New Zealand and other American allies came under increased pressure to provide combat assistance. An unenthusiastic Holyoake responded to American entreaties in December 1964 by pointing

Vietnam War

Members of V Company's 6th Platoon board one of 9 Squadron RAAF's Iroquois helicopters on 23 March 1968 to return to base after an operation in Phuoc Tuy province (*Australian War Memorial, P1661.019*)

to New Zealand's commitments in Malaysia, where its forces were involved in *Confrontation. American plans to introduce ground combat forces (as opposed to the combat advisers previously deployed) were not favoured in Wellington, New Zealand again diverging from the more 'robust' approach taken by Australia. The debility of the Saigon regime left New Zealand policymakers fearful that Vietnam would become a quagmire for the Western powers, sapping their military power to little purpose. Although at first not following suit when Australia decided to send a battalion, New Zealand eventually, on 24 May 1965, agreed to provide a four-gun field artillery battery of approximately 120 men. The potential adverse effect on the *ANZUS alliance of not supporting the United States (and Australia) in Vietnam was of paramount importance, but the decision to participate was in line with New Zealand's own national interests of countering communism in South-east Asia and of sustaining a strategy of forward defence. A failure to make a token contribution to the Allied effort in Vietnam would have brought into question the basic assumptions underlying New Zealand's post-war national security policies. During the next seven years the Holyoake government strove to keep New Zealand's involvement at the minimum level deemed necessary to meet its allies' expectations, not least because it remained sceptical about the likely outcome of external military intervention in Vietnam. New Zealand's meagre military resources, the significant troop contribution in Malaysia, and the absence of any political will to use conscripts were all obstacles to a more substantial effort, as were anxieties about financial costs and domestic criticisms.

New Zealand combat involvement in Vietnam began with the arrival in Saigon of the 161st Battery, RNZA, equipped with L5 pack howitzers, in July 1965. The personnel and their equipment were conveyed to the theatre by RNZAF Hercules aircraft—the first occasion a New Zealand unit had been deployed in a war zone with full equipment by air. The gunners were based at Bien Hoa air base, where they provided support to the American 173rd Airborne Brigade, under whose operational control they were placed. After preparing facilities for them, the engineer detachment was withdrawn to New Zealand. The battery was involved in seventeen major operations, mainly around Bien Hoa but also including two sorties into Phuoc Tuy province to the south. During 1966 it was brought up to six-gun strength and, in June, passed to the operational control of 1st Australian Task Force, which was established at Nui Dat in Phuoc Tuy province. In August 1966 the gunners played a key role in assisting Australian infantry of 6th Battalion, Royal

Vietnam War

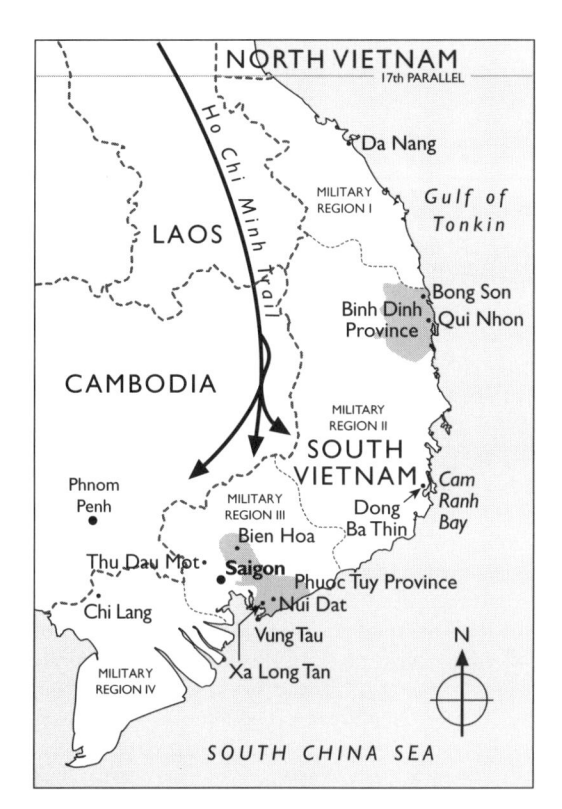

Map 26 South Vietnam, 1965–72: area of operations

Australian Regiment (RAR), during the important action at Xa Long Tan, in which 18 Australians were killed holding off a regimental sized enemy force.

Once 'Confrontation' ended and Australia decided, in December 1966, to expand 1st Australian Task Force to a brigade strength, New Zealand came under new pressure to increase its commitment. In April 1967 V Company was deployed from New Zealand's infantry battalion in west Malaysia, to be followed in December by W Company. From this time the battalion was almost exclusively focused on supporting the infantry involvement in Vietnam. The New Zealand companies operated at first under the operational control of 2nd Battalion, RAR. From March 1968 they were integrated within 2RAR to form 2RAR/NZ (Anzac) Battalion, with New Zealand personnel assuming various positions in the battalion, including that of second in command. A similar arrangement was made with 4RAR when it relieved 2RAR in May 1968, and then successively with 6RAR and 2RAR until the end of the two countries' combat commitment. Although convenient for New Zealand, given the small size of its infantry contingent, and reasonably effective in practice, the integration meant that the New Zealand identity of the units, and the artillery, tended to be overshadowed by the Australians. For the New Zealand infantrymen, the operations were a constant round of patrols or cordon and search operations. Large-scale actions were uncommon. The objective, to seize the initiative in the province, was largely achieved, and the provincial enemy forces were rendered largely ineffective without outside support.

New Zealand added several other small units and groups of personnel, including members of both the RNZN and RNZAF, to its commitment in Vietnam during the period 1967 to 1969. The 1st New Zealand Services Medical Team was deployed in April 1967 with the role of providing medical and surgical assistance to South Vietnamese civilians and encouraging the development of indigenous capacity in this field. Twenty-seven strong at its peak, it operated initially at Qui Nonh before moving north to Bong Son. In July 1967 an RNZAF pilot was made available to 9 Squadron RAAF, which operated Iroquois helicopters, and two more were provided in 1968. From December 1968 two forward air controllers served with the 7th US Air Force. The RNZAF also made a more general contribution, insofar as its transport aircraft supported the commitment in Vietnam throughout New Zealand's involvement. In January 1969 a 26-man *Special Air Service troop arrived in Vietnam, raising the strength of New Zealand's force to its peak of 543 men. It was involved in intelligence gathering operations in Phuoc Tuy province, mounting 155 patrols in all.

With the American shift of emphasis to 'Vietnamisation' of the war, New Zealand contributed an army training team of twenty-five personnel, which was deployed at the National Training Centre at Chi Lang in January 1971. A second one, of eighteen men (including two RNZN personnel), was provided in March 1972. Based at Dong Ba Thin, near Cam Ranh Bay, it assisted in the training of Cambodian battalions. As these training teams began their work, Australian and New Zealand combat forces were gradually being withdrawn, in line with reductions in American strength in Vietnam. First to go was W Company, in November 1970, and the SAS troop and artillery battery followed in February and May 1971 respectively. With the withdrawal of 1st Australian Task Force in December 1971, New Zealand's combat involvement in Vietnam was brought to an end by the withdrawal of V Company and the services medical team. One of the first acts of the Labour government led by Norman Kirk, which took office in December 1972, was to withdraw both training teams. By then, a total of 3890 New Zealand military personnel had served with *V-Force in Vietnam; 37 of them (36 Army and 1 RNZAF) had been killed and 187 wounded. All who served were regulars, or personnel who enlisted in the Regular Force for the purpose of joining V-Force. They were volunteers in the sense that they were not compelled to

Vietnam War

serve in Vietnam, though for a proportion, especially officers, choice in the matter was largely constrained by professional demands. The size of V-Force was such that New Zealand did not have to follow its American and Australian allies by introducing ★conscription.

New Zealand's limited military involvement in the Vietnam War was overshadowed by the wide-ranging debate about the conflict which erupted at home following the rise from the mid 1960s of an organised anti–Vietnam War movement. Unlike similar developments in both the United States and Australia, this protest was not given momentum by anti-conscription sentiment, though it echoed its American counterpart in terms of style and in many of its criticisms of Washington's policies. At the same time, by highlighting broader issues raised for New Zealand by the Vietnam War, the anti-war movement challenged to an unprecedented extent the alliance-based security doctrine on which official Vietnam policy was based, thereby inaugurating a new era of public debate about foreign policy. The anti-war movement also helped unsettle some prevailing orthodoxies of New Zealand domestic life, in part through its interaction with other protest causes of the late 1960s and early 1970s, such as the women's and anti-apartheid movements.

Much of the anti-war movement's critique echoed international condemnation—and especially American internal criticism—of Western intervention in Vietnam. As elsewhere, there was opposition on moral grounds for reasons ranging from pacifist convictions to objections to the weapons being used or to the undemocratic character of the South Vietnamese government. The charge was also made that the United States and its allies were interfering in a civil war. To some extent, criticisms of American policy varied according to the critic's ideological stance. Moderates were more likely to ridicule the domino theory while radicals accused the United States of outright imperialism in propping up a repressive puppet regime in Saigon and suggested that most Vietnamese desired a unified nation under some sort of socialist system. Moderates and radicals alike chastised the United States for failing to observe the 1954 Geneva accords, for using excessive force, for alleging that China was behind the war, and for denying that there was widespread support in South Vietnam for the National Liberation Front. There were also those who argued that American policy was less immoral than ill conceived and would have the counterproductive result of strengthening communism in Asia.

Of more distinct and enduring significance for New Zealand was the increasing tendency for local anti-war activists to go beyond criticising the government for supporting the United States in this particular case. Depicting the government's general alliance policies as fundamentally misguided, they rejected the strategy of forward defence, disputed the anti-communist assumptions on which it rested, and denied that communism in South-east Asia posed a threat to New Zealand. More pointedly, they called for a more 'independent' foreign policy, which was not submissive to that of the United States. Their self-consciously nationalistic critique challenged the most basic principles underpinning the country's post-war security policies.

Although this critique failed to diminish official support for American policy, rising domestic criticisms did prompt the Holyoake government to mount a detailed public defence of its stance on Vietnam. For almost a decade after first sending non-combat military assistance in 1963, the government was remarkably consistent in depicting New Zealand's Vietnam policy as a principled response within an alliance framework to a case of external communist aggression. After deciding to send combat troops, the government stressed that it was acting in conformity with treaty obligations and was upholding the principles of collective security to which New Zealand had committed itself since the ★Second World War. While taking every opportunity to express his hope for a negotiated settlement, Holyoake repeatedly argued thereafter that, as long as communist aggression persisted against South Vietnam, only military action could preserve the small nation's freedom. The Prime Minister often noted that New Zealand was acting alongside its most important allies in Vietnam, but he did not place the same emphasis in his public statements as his advisers did privately on the importance of maintaining healthy alliance relations with the United States and Australia. Nor did he ever publicly refer to his government's misgivings about the viability of the whole enterprise. He and his supporters did, however, curtly reject the anti-war movement's criticisms of official policy and vigorously defended the alliance-based policy of forward defence in South-east Asia.

It is difficult to assess which side had the better of this debate during the Vietnam War. The decision to send combat forces to Vietnam initially appeared to enjoy high levels of public support, and the National Party did not suffer unduly adverse electoral consequences, being returned to office twice—in 1966 and 1969—during the Vietnam period. Nor was the government ever sufficiently concerned by domestic criticism to change a policy it had adopted largely for alliance reasons.

On the other hand, despite having no decisive impact on official policy-making and arousing hostility from some New Zealanders, the anti-war movement drew growing support, especially during the closing stages of the Vietnam War. This support was illustrated most visibly during the 'mobilisations' of the early 1970s, when thousands marched in protest against the war in all the country's major centres. The Vietnam conflict thus brought with it a polarisation of opinion and a questioning by many New Zealanders of the government's alliance policies, especially among younger people in higher education during these years—the so-called Vietnam Generation.

Another significant domestic impact of the critique championed by the anti-war movement was that one of the two major political parties came to embrace many of its premises. The Labour Party was initially more cautious in opposing official policy on the Vietnam conflict. The party had stressed humanitarian and economic aid as more important than military action in helping to resolve Vietnam's problems from the early 1960s. Yet once New Zealand combat forces were sent, party leaders were reluctant to advocate immediate withdrawal, perhaps because of concerns about likely electoral consequences. Labour's policy on Vietnam firmed considerably after 1966. By 1969, its leader, Norman Kirk, had made an unequivocal commitment to withdraw if victorious in that year's election, but National was re-elected. Thereafter, Labour asserted its opposition more confidently, sensing it was now on the more popular side of the issue and seizing on the Americans' own progressive disengagement from Vietnam as vindication of its policy. Since almost all New Zealand troops had left Vietnam before the November 1972 election, the new Labour government's prompt withdrawal of the remaining training teams caused little controversy.

If of limited practical significance after 1973, Labour's and National's divergent policies on Vietnam symbolised wider differences about national security. National continued to accept the orthodoxies of alliance reasoning on which its Vietnam policy was based. In contrast, Labour leaders called for 'new thinking' in foreign policy that would allow New Zealand to pursue a more independent course in world affairs, that would incorporate a 'moral' dimension, and that would better reflect the country's character as a small multiracial nation in the South Pacific. Having rejected the Vietnam policy of New Zealand's major alliance partner, Labour's leaders did not repudiate ANZUS—as many anti-war activists and party members urged. Instead, they sought to sanction a position of dissent within the alliance framework, analogous to the line of argument which would later be used to justify the fourth Labour government's policy of opposing nuclear ship visits. Such qualifications notwithstanding, Labour's stance on the Vietnam War broke the previous bipartisan, Cold War consensus on foreign policy.

The Vietnam War thus marked a turning point in the evolution of New Zealand's post-war foreign and security policies. In terms of national security doctrine, combat involvement in Vietnam represented the culmination of a line of official thinking based on the primacy of the ANZUS alliance, the acceptance of stark assumptions about the menace of Asian communism, and the cogency of forward defence in South-east Asia. While privately dubious about the wisdom of a massive military effort in Vietnam, the Holyoake government showed that it was committed to the shared alliance strategy of containing communism in South-east Asia. It offered public support for American policy and contributed token combat forces in Vietnam as the price of continued participation in that strategy. The outcome of the Vietnam War, however, created a crisis for the alliance policy and several of its elements—most notably a strong forward defence posture in South-east Asia—were adjusted in the aftermath of that conflict. In large part, that readjustment was due to the re-evaluation of American regional strategy in the form of the Nixon Doctrine.

The Vietnam experience was thus also important as a test of the country's interaction with its major post-war ally. On the one hand, the National government's policy staved off any confrontation with Washington of the sort which would cause the suspension of the American security guarantee to New Zealand in the 1980s. To that extent, the Holyoake government attained the central objective of its Vietnam policy and the alliance with the United States remained intact at the end of the war. On the other hand, the alliance relationship was less firmly rooted on a popular level, with significant numbers of New Zealanders coming to oppose perceived subservience to the United States in security matters.

Those few New Zealanders who experienced combat in Vietnam at first hand were left with a searing legacy. New Zealand's Vietnam veterans, like their Australian and American counterparts, have had to adjust to various problems associated with fighting in an unpopular war. There has been much resentment within their ranks at perceived official and public indifference to the physical and psychological problems experienced by so many veterans as a result of alleged exposure to ★Agent Orange and post-traumatic stress disorders. Another source of bitterness has been the sense that, unlike Second World War veterans, they were not accorded adequate recognition for serving their country with considerable professionalism in a demanding theatre of battle. In recent years, there has been greater official sensitivity to these concerns, reflected in government assistance to Vietnam Parade 1998, a national reunion and march of veterans in Wellington in June 1998. Vietnam veterans were gratified by the generally favourable public reception of this event, though some relatively low-key protests by

Voluntary Aid Detachments

anti-war activists illustrated the continuing controversy generated by the war.

Such divisiveness has lingered because the debate precipitated by the Vietnam War was not merely about a tragic conflict in a distant Asian country or the correctness of American policy, but brought to prominence competing visions of the role New Zealand should play in the world. In that sense, New Zealand's Vietnam involvement was most significant as the catalyst for a larger ongoing debate about the relationship between national identity, national security, and 'independence' in foreign policy.

S.D. Newman, *Vietnam Gunners, 161 Battery RNZA, South Vietnam, 1965–71* (Moana Press, Tauranga, 1988); M. Subritzky, *The Vietnam Scrapbook* ('Three Feathers' Publishing Co, Papakura, 1995).

ROBERTO RABEL

Voluntary Aid Detachments (VADs) were first formed in the United Kingdom during the *First World War. When the New Zealand government proved reluctant to organise such groups in New Zealand, some untrained women keen 'to do their bit' proceeded to Great Britain to serve in British VADs. Other New Zealanders already living there also joined. Gladys Luxford was a typical example. Before the war she had never visited a hospital or learnt any first aid, but in 1917 she was allowed to go to England to serve as a VAD at Walton-on-Thames, where her father had been appointed hospital chaplain. After serving briefly as a waitress to the hospital's matron and senior sisters, she became a nursing VAD, helping to prepare the 'boys' for doctors' rounds and operations, and dressing wounds and giving sponge baths. She was one of numerous New Zealanders working, mainly as nurse aids, for the British Red Cross or the New Zealand War Contingent Association, all of whom were brought under the auspices of the New Zealand *Red Cross in 1918. During that year VADs were at last established in New Zealand as well, because of a shortage of hospital staff to deal with the *influenza pandemic. VADs staffed military hospitals and convalescent homes.

With the return to normality after the end of the war the VAD scheme lapsed. It was not until another conflict loomed in 1939 that women again began to prepare for possible VAD roles by taking first aid and home nursing courses with the Red Cross and Order of St John, the aim being to have people with some training available to assist in public hospitals during an emergency. This process was boosted by the outbreak of war, and in 1940 VAD training was extended to include motor vehicle driving, mechanical servicing, cooking, and laundry, canteen, and air raid precaution work. The first of several drafts of VADs left New Zealand to serve with Army nursing overseas, and they later became part of the Women's Auxiliary Army Corps's Medical Division. Most of the more than 10,000 VADs, who also included men, never left New Zealand, and their VAD work remained supplementary to their regular employment. In 1943 the Health Department established the Civil Nursing Reserve, consisting of registered nurses and VADs who, as a mobile group, could be assigned to hospitals as and when required.

SUSAN UPTON

Volunteer Force The New Zealand Volunteer Force was a colonial manifestation of the British tradition of voluntary military service and, in particular, the Volunteer movement which had been active in Great Britain during the late eighteenth and early nineteenth centuries and which was revived after the great invasion scare there in 1859. Volunteering's local origins lay in the Kororareka Association formed for self-defence in 1834 and the New Zealand Company Militia established in 1839.

During the early 1840s volunteer corps were established in various parts of the North Island and in Nelson in response to fears of attack by Maori. None of these units had proper legal sanction. The Kororareka corps took part in the unsuccessful defence of the town in March 1845. Following the passing of the 1845 Militia Ordinance volunteer corps were disbanded and replaced by *militia companies. The ordinance was inflexible in that it did not provide for the partial mobilisation of local manpower. The Militia Act of 1858 was more flexible and provided for the formation of volunteer units under regulations issued by each militia district. Volunteer units or corps generally had a strength of between 50 and 100 men.

Between the start of the Taranaki War in 1860 and the end of the *New Zealand Wars in 1872, the force grew from three infantry corps to 132 corps of cavalry, infantry, artillery, and engineers. During the Taranaki War, local volunteers performed usefully in a number of actions, garrisoned defensive positions, and guarded lines of communications. In Auckland and Wellington Volunteers freed regular soldiers for active service by taking over garrison duties.

Between 1860 and 1865, an amendment to the Militia Act, various regulations, and finally the Volunteer Act 1865 established a regulatory framework for the force which would largely survive until its abolition. The principal features of this regulatory framework included the following provisions. Volunteer corps were responsible for their internal organisation, the admission of members, and election of officers. Volunteers could, in normal circumstances, readily terminate their service. The government provided corps with their basic equipment. Volunteers were only paid

Volunteer Force

The Te Awamutu Cavalry Volunteers on parade at the opening of the Main Trunk railway at Puniu on 15 April 1885 (D.M. Beere Collection, Alexander Turnbull Library, G-96177-1/2)

when on actual service, but corps received an annual capitation grant for members who performed the required amount of training. Except when on actual service Volunteers could only be fined or dismissed from the force for breaches of discipline. Various incentives, including grants of land, were also introduced to encourage volunteering. Each Volunteer corps provided its own uniform. At first they tended to be of a simple practical design, but later in the century smart rather than practical ★uniforms were often preferred by corps.

During and immediately after the New Zealand Wars, Volunteer units received training assistance from the colonial forces and the British Army. Much of the training they conducted during this period was of a useful, practical nature. In the later years however, there were often not enough regular instructors and the Volunteers' conditions of service meant that they spent too much time indoors practising repetitive drills and not nearly enough time on useful field training.

The outbreak of war in the Waikato and the resumption of hostilities in Taranaki in 1863 led to the extensive employment of Volunteer units. Volunteers guarded the southern approaches to Auckland and were involved in many actions. Generally they performed reasonably well. On 17 September 1863, for example, Auckland Volunteers displayed 'steadiness and judgment' in a skirmish with a Maori raiding party near Papatoetoe. Lieutenant Charles ★Heaphy of the Auckland Rifle Volunteers was awarded the ★Victoria Cross for rescuing a wounded soldier under heavy fire on 11 February 1864. He was the first member of a non-regular colonial force to be so honoured. Auckland Volunteers objected to spending long periods on actual service because they still had their ordinary civilian employment to pursue, and much less use was made of them after the Waikato Militia became available in 1864. In Taranaki local Volunteers conducted offensive patrols, as well as assisting with garrison duties and other tasks. Volunteers comprised a significant proportion of the colonial forces employed in the later campaigns against the supporters of Pai Marire or Hauhauism, ★Te Kooti, and ★Titokowaru.

There was continuing concern in the decade following the end of the New Zealand Wars that there might be renewed conflict with disaffected Maori. Local Volunteer corps helped secure frontier areas. In April 1873, for example, Waikato and Auckland Volunteer corps were called out for actual service after a farm worker was murdered by Maori from the King Country. Nearly

567

Volunteer Force

Canterbury Engineer Volunteers practise bridge building about 1900 (The Press (Christchurch) Collection, Alexander Turnbull Library, G-8482-1/1)

1000 Volunteers from thirty-three corps supported the ★Armed Constabulary, making a 1600-strong force, in the operation in November 1881 to arrest Te Whiti o Rongomai at ★Parihaka and end his campaign of passive resistance to European settlement. Concern about a resurgence of Maori armed resistance faded away during the 1880s. As late as 1898, however, preparations were made for the employment of Volunteers against dissident Maori during the ★Dog Tax rebellion of 1898.

Volunteer corps were from the outset very much part of the local community. They were either based on a particular locality or formed as offshoots of existing organisations such as schools, parochial societies, large companies, and sporting clubs. Most commonly a small group of interested individuals would call a public meeting to discuss raising a corps; if there was enough support a formal request would be sent to the Minister of Defence to approve the formation of the new unit. The first specifically Maori corps, the Thames Native Rifle Volunteers, was formed in 1874. Individual Maori also served in the force and a few corps included special Maori sections.

Volunteer corps performed a variety of non-defence services for the community. Volunteers, for instance, occasionally assisted in the capture of criminals and in dealing with public disorder. Volunteers also helped fight fires, and naval corps, whose main role was to man coastal artillery, often provided a lifeboat service. Large crowds regularly turned out to watch the Volunteers' activities. The force also had an important role in providing military pomp and pageantry at all kinds of public events, and received a substantial amount of financial support from the community. The many bands attached to corps were an important part of Volunteering's public appeal, and the force had a pivotal role in the growth of brass bands in New Zealand.

Almost from the establishment of the first Volunteer corps in New Zealand, they had been seen as having a role in defending the colony against raids as part of a wider war between Great Britain and some other major power. After the end of the New Zealand Wars these fears, which were fanned by the *Kaskowiski* hoax in 1873 (see HOAXES), progressively became the central reason for the Volunteer Force's existence. Britain and Russia came close to war in 1878, prompting a war scare which led New Zealand to purchase twenty-two coastal defence guns and boosted the Volunteer Force.

Colonel P.H. ★Scratchley, in his 1880 report on the defences of the colony, concluded that the Volunteers were not a reliable force. He proposed that they be replaced by a smaller partly paid force, which would support a small nucleus of permanent artillerymen. Neither this recommendation nor most of the sensible proposals for reform made by a board of Volunteer officers in 1882 were put into effect.

A major Russian war scare in early 1885 led to Major-General Sir George ★Whitmore being placed in command of all New Zealand's military forces. The guns ordered in 1878 were mounted and work began on constructing a substantial system of ★coast defences at New Zealand's four main ports. Volunteer naval and garrison artillery corps now had the role of assisting the ★Permanent Militia in manning these defences. Volunteer numbers increased from 4313 in April 1884 to approximately 8000, organised into 130 corps, in June 1885. The 1886 ★Defence Act embodied the changes made to New Zealand's military forces.

Whitmore recognised that although a corps of fifty or sixty men might well be able to play a useful part in irregular warfare, it was simply too small to combat even a small raid by regular troops. Between 1885 and 1887 he progressively grouped existing corps into infantry battalions or mounted regiments. Although these battalions and regiments were largely administrative structures in which corps retained considerable independence, they were a useful initiative. Eventually Whitmore planned to improve the force's effectiveness by abolishing corps and enlisting Volunteers directly into battalions or regiments.

Volunteer officers' poor level of military knowledge was also of serious concern to Whitmore, who responded by establishing a school of instruction and a council of military education in Wellington. Both these bodies were abolished in 1887–88 as part of government cost-cutting measures. Whitmore resigned in 1888. In the following year infantry battalions and mounted regiments were abolished, largely, it appears, as a result of political pressure from Volunteer officers determined to protect the independence of their units. Similar pressures had thwarted earlier attempts to organise infantry battalions and mounted regiments.

During the late 1880s the capitation payments to Volunteers were sharply reduced and other major cuts made to defence expenditure. As a result Volunteer numbers fell significantly and morale and efficiency within the force collapsed. Both senior local officers and British Army officers brought in to report on the forces concluded that the Volunteer system should be replaced by a partly paid system.

In 1893 Colonel F.J. ★Fox, a British officer employed by the colonial government to take command of New Zealand's military forces, submitted a detailed report on the state of the forces to the Defence Minister, Richard ★Seddon. His frank comments again focused attention on the Volunteer Force's long-standing and glaring deficiencies. The force's arms and equipment were largely worn out and obsolete and needed to be replaced. There were not enough properly qualified instructors to train Volunteers. Fox attacked the election of officers and noted that such a low standard of knowledge was required in the examinations officers had to pass after being elected that they were in essence a farce. About a quarter of officers were, he considered, indifferent or bad and they became known as 'Fox's Martyrs'. Fox called for the disbandment of a substantial number of inefficient units and corps in isolated areas, which could not assist in repelling a naval raid on one of the colony's major ports. The report recommended that infantry corps be organised into battalions. Fox was highly critical of the force's training regime, which, apart from camps held at Easter, consisted largely of parades held in the evening after work. He proposed greater financial support for Volunteers and, in particular, payments to encourage them to undertake more field training. His recommendations were generally sound, but were politically unpalatable to Seddon. Little was done to implement them apart from the purchase of new Martini–Henry rifles to replace the Volunteers' obsolete Snider ★small arms.

There are three main reasons why the Volunteer Force was able to continue in existence without major reform for several decades. First, for most of the thirty years following the end of the New Zealand Wars defence was not an issue of major importance to the New Zealand public and political leaders. Second, the force was generally popular within the colony and the position of local corps was jealously guarded by their members and the local communities. Third, as Sir Julius Vogel recognised, Volunteers 'were a most important portion of the community', with considerable political influence. Whitmore noted in 1878 that 'the Volunteers have so many friends in Parliament that the least resistance to their wishes … is very difficult'.

The influence Volunteers had in the colony was in part related to the type of man attracted to the movement by its respectable, patriotic image. Volunteering also required both time and money. As a result, at least from the mid 1870s, the force contained, it seems, a disproportionate number of better paid skilled and white-collar workers. The Volunteer officer corps consisted principally of men interested in military matters who had occupations of high socioeconomic status and who were also prominent in other aspects of community life. Such men found it easier to be elected and were better able to meet the financial and other commitments entailed in holding a Volunteer commission. A small proportion of officers were politicians who saw their involvement in Volunteering as a useful means of gathering support.

Officers in the force below the rank of major were elected. During the New Zealand Wars, when there was a reasonable chance they would be called out on actual

Volunteer Force

service, corps seem to have generally elected competent men. Election, however, always caused difficulties, which were compounded by the change made in the 1886 Defence Act whereby the requirement for election was increased from a simple to a two-thirds majority. The election of officers was consistently criticised as one of the force's major failings. It was maintained until the force's abolition because it enjoyed wide support among ordinary Volunteers and politicians, who believed it to be central to the force's ethos. Contested elections could cause major divisions within units. Corps therefore generally went to considerable trouble to ensure that any man put up for election enjoyed wide support within the unit. The election system weakened the force's already mild disciplinary regime and fostered the election of men on the basis of their popularity or social position rather than military and leadership skills. NCOs were supposed to be appointed by corps commanders, but were in fact often elected.

The election of officers and NCOs was consistent with the internal organisation of Volunteer corps. Like other community organisations, Volunteer units had secretaries and treasurers, and major decisions were made at annual general meetings, at which all members had equal speaking and voting rights and were eligible to hold most administrative posts. Volunteer corps received most of their income from the government, but a substantial proportion also came from membership fees and corps's fund-raising efforts.

Volunteers were active in a wide range of team and individual sports as well as specialist military sports. By far the most important sport was rifle shooting, upon which corps lavished substantial amounts of time and money. The great emphasis on competitive shooting led corps to concentrate on producing a few marksmen and to neglect the shooting skills of most members. It also largely frustrated efforts to introduce more practical rifle training.

After 1893 Fox and to a greater extent his successor, Colonel A.P. ★Penton, managed to improve the effectiveness of the Volunteer Force. Additional military staff and training personnel were employed, new incentives were given to Volunteers to undertake more realistic outdoor training, and infantry corps were organised into battalions. Penton also endeavoured, with limited success, to create a more balanced force by encouraging the formation of engineer, transport, and medical units. In 1900 he succeeded in having a standard, practical khaki uniform adopted for all units apart from Highland corps. The ★Boer War prompted a massive expansion of the force, which grew from 4500 in 1898 to a peak of 17,057 in 1901. A large number of Volunteers served with the New Zealand forces in South Africa, where they gained useful combat experience. The war also prompted the New Zealand government to purchase a substantial amount of new equipment for the force and the introduction of more realistic training. None of these developments, however, addressed the force's fundamental weaknesses.

Under Major-General J.M. ★Babington further efforts were made to reform the force between 1902 and 1906. Two of the most important steps were the establishment of a new school of instruction and the completion of the organisation of corps into larger units. By 1905 Babington had formed the view that the Volunteer Force was 'in no sense an organised body as at present constituted. It is costly, badly equipped, and inefficient as a fighting force.' He recommended its replacement with a smaller partly paid force and in the following year supported a proposal put forward by senior regular officers for the adoption of the Swiss system of compulsory military training.

The Volunteer Force always had its critics within the community, who attacked its military effectiveness, misconduct by individual Volunteers, and the social pretensions of some members of the force. Criticism of the force became more wide-ranging and serious from about 1905 as a result of mounting concern that the British Empire was likely to become involved in a major war, in which New Zealand would need to play a part. This trend became more evident after the National Defence League of New Zealand began its campaign for the abolition of Volunteering and the introduction of ★compulsory military training.

The regular officers who sat on the Council of Defence, which took control of the defence forces in 1907, believed that the Volunteer Force had outlived its usefulness. At the government's behest, however, they tried to improve its effectiveness. Efforts were made, for instance, to improve officer education and the force's support units. Prime Minister Sir Joseph ★Ward was at first a strong supporter of the Volunteer system, but as concerns about the international situation increased and public and political support for the introduction of compulsory military training grew, he was forced to admit that the Volunteers could no longer meet New Zealand's defence requirements.

At the Imperial Defence Conference held in London in July–August 1909, Ward and other Dominion prime ministers agreed to proposals for increased cooperation in ★imperial defence, which included the Dominions being capable of providing expeditionary forces made up of units organised along the same lines as British Army units. There was no way in which even a substantially reformed Volunteer Force or a partly paid force could fulfil such a role. Ward, therefore, asked the Chief of the ★Imperial General Staff, General W.G. Nicholson, to prepare proposals for the reorganisation of the New Zealand Military Forces. Nicholson's proposals called for the establishment of a ★Territorial Force, based on compulsory military training, which could provide a 30,000-strong home defence force, from which a 10,000-man expeditionary force could easily be organised in an emergency. Ward's government accepted these proposals and they were embodied in the 1909 Defence Act. In accordance with this legislation, the Volunteer Force became the Territorial Force on 28 February 1910.

Volunteering was an important and generally popular part of the New Zealand scene for more than half a century. In 1886, for instance, about 5.4 per cent of adult males between the ages of fifteen and forty-nine were Volunteers. The force was a most unusual military organisation, whose central element, the corps, was closer in structure and ethos to other community bodies such as volunteer fire brigades than it was to conventional military units. Although Volunteers performed useful service during and immediately after the New Zealand Wars, their fate was sealed once New Zealand's national security required a better organised force capable both of home defence and overseas service.

G.J. Clayton, 'Defence not Defiance: The Shaping of New Zealand's Volunteer Force' (DPhil thesis, University of Waikato, 1990); J.A.B. Crawford, 'The Role and Structure of the New Zealand Volunteer Force 1885–1910' (MA thesis, University of Canterbury, 1986).

JOHN CRAWFORD

W

Waddell, Lieutenant-Colonel James (11 October 1872–18 February 1954), is the outstanding New Zealand soldier to have served in a foreign force. The son of a Dunedin saddler, he passed an examination for a commission in the British Army in 1895, and joined the 2nd Battalion, the Duke of Wellington's West Riding (76th) Regiment, in Natal early the following year. His enthusiasm was severely dented, however, by the hostile reception he received from his fellow junior officers, their harassment of him not ceasing until a court of inquiry had been held. While in India, to which his battalion had been posted in early 1898, he met and married a French woman who persuaded him to leave the British Army and seek a career in the French Foreign Legion. In due course, Waddell was commissioned as a second lieutenant in the Legion in April 1900, and was shortly afterwards involved in the Boxer Rebellion. During the next fourteen years, he served in its 2nd Infantry Regiment in North Africa and Indo-China. By the outbreak of the ★First World War, the diminutive New Zealander—he was only 1.6 metres tall—had risen to the rank of captain and had, in 1904, become a French citizen. At ★Gallipoli he commanded the 1st Infantry Regiment until wounded in June 1915. After his recovery, he was given command of a battalion in a reorganised Foreign Legion regiment on the ★Western Front in 1916 and took part in the Battle of the Somme. His renowned bravery in action was recognised by repeated awards of the Croix de Guerre with Palm Leaf and his appointment as a chevalier of the Legion of Honour. His service with the Foreign Legion ended with his posting, in January 1918, to the French Mission to the United States Army. In the following May he assumed command of a battalion of the French Army's 169th Infantry Regiment, a regular formation. He was appointed a commander in the Legion of Honour in 1920. Following the war he commanded a district in the French zone of occupation in Germany, and served in Tunisia before retiring in 1926. He resided in Morocco and Tunisia until 1950, when he returned to New Zealand to live with a son in Levin.

Wahawaha, Major Rapata ('Ropata') (c.1820–1 July 1897), won renown in the latter stages of the ★New Zealand Wars as a ★kupapa leader on the East Coast and, through his military prowess, emerged as the leader of the Ngati Porou. A member of Ngati Porou's Te Aowera hapu, he was enslaved as a child by the Rongowhakaata in 1828, and took the name of his captor, Rapata; later in life he liked the Pakeha pronunciation of his name, 'Ropata', under which he is now popularly known. He regained his freedom some time during the 1830s. In 1865 the spread of Pai Marire split the Ngati Porou. Ropata, an Anglican, took up arms against the Hauhau. Although the Hauhau held the advantage in early fighting, Ropata, now leader of Te Aowera, appealed for government assistance, which was duly forthcoming (especially arms and ammunition). He then led the offensive against the Hauhau, often displaying reckless courage and ruthless determination. By October 1865 the Hauhau had been driven from Ngati Porou territory. Leading a strong force of Ngati Porou kupapa, Ropata headed south, and fought at Waerenga-a-Hika in November. At Te Kopane on 13 January 1866 the Hauhau ambushed a combined Ngati Porou–Ngati Kahungunu force. Ropata rallied his men and, setting fire to the bush, routed the Hauhau. In November 1868 Ropata, perhaps partly motivated by revenge for his youthful enslavement

(Rongowhakaata was ★Te Kooti's tribe), led a force of kupapa against Te Kooti's positions at Te Karetu following the rebels' destructive raid on Poverty Bay. In December he played a prominent part in the first assault on Te Kooti's stronghold at Ngatapa. Although this attack failed, Ropata fought with such bravery that he was later awarded a ★New Zealand Cross and commissioned as a major in the New Zealand Militia. In January 1869 Ropata's kupapa (about 350 Ngati Porou), along with Te Arawa and Ngati Kahungunu kupapa and ★Armed Constabulary, surrounded Ngatapa, but Te Kooti was able to escape over a cliff. Ropata and his Ngati Porou then formed part of a column which advanced on Lake Waikaremoana. From February 1870 to December 1871 he took part in four expeditions into the Urewera in pursuit of Te Kooti and to pacify the Tuhoe. In the first he stormed Maraetahi pa, the rebels' last fortified position. On this occasion, as on several later, Te Kooti managed to elude his pursuers. In 1878 Ropata's service in the New Zealand Wars was recognised by the award to him of a sword of honour by Queen Victoria. Until 1884 he was officer in charge of the ★militia in the Ngati Porou district. He became a member of the Legislative Council in 1887.

Waikato War see NEW ZEALAND WARS

Wairau massacre was the bloodiest Maori–Pakeha clash between the signing of the Treaty of Waitangi and the outbreak of the Northern War in 1845. Its origins lay in the New Zealand Company's attempt to assert a dubious claim to ownership of land in the fertile Wairau Valley, near Blenheim. When Company surveyors began surveying the land in question even before the question of the legal title had been resolved, the Ngati Toa chiefs ★Te Rauparaha and ★Te Rangihaeata, who claimed ownership of the land by conquest in the 1820s, actively hindered them, eventually burning down their huts. A 35-strong armed party of officials and settlers led by Police Magistrate Henry Thompson and Captain Arthur Wakefield proceeded to the area from Nelson with the intention of arresting the chiefs for arson. This rash action led to an affray, on 17 June 1843, in which most of the Pakeha were quickly killed or captured. Te Rangihaeata's wife had been shot and killed at the outset of the clash, and he extracted utu by despatching many of those who had surrendered. In all twenty-two Pakeha, including Thompson and Wakefield, were killed then or later; a handful of Maori also lost their lives in the brief fight. This tragic incident led to consternation in both Nelson and Wellington, with the settlers clamouring for defences against the expected Ngati Toa attack. In the absence of any arrangements for a ★militia, ad hoc volunteers corps were formed and drilled, and some defence works were constructed. In the event, neither settlement was attacked, and the arrival at Wellington of a detachment of British troops from Auckland in July further allayed fears. When the new Governor, Robert FitzRoy, arrived in the colony later in the year, he adopted a conciliatory approach towards Te Rauparaha and Te Rangihaeata, constrained by recognition not only that military action against the well-armed Maori would be inexpedient but also that the clash had arisen because of Pakeha misconduct.

Waite, Colonel Fred (20 August 1885–29 August 1952) was the first published New Zealand official war historian. Born in Dunedin, he was a farmer when he enlisted in 1NZEF in August 1914. The *Otago Witness* engaged him to write articles for it from the front, but he only sent one before his appointment as a censor rendered such action inappropriate. He served at ★Gallipoli, and was made a DSO for rallying his men near Gaba Tepe during the night of 2–3 May 1915 when the Otago Battalion failed in its attempt to seize the Baby 700 feature. He was later adjutant of the Anzac Mounted Division's Divisional Engineers. He returned to New Zealand to take up an instructional position at Trentham in May 1917. A short descriptive account of the New Zealanders at Gallipoli which Waite wrote for historical purposes in 1918 led to his being invited to prepare the 'popular' history of New Zealand's part in that campaign. In early 1919 he assumed general oversight of the production of the four-volume series covering the whole war effort. His own volume, *The New Zealanders at Gallipoli*, was published in late 1919; a revised edition appeared two years later. It remained the standard account of the New Zealanders at Gallipoli for more than sixty years. Waite was a member of Parliament from 1925 to 1931. He was an active member of the National Historical Committee during the 1930s, and served as Commissioner of the New Zealand Patriotic Fund Board in the Middle East from 1940 to 1944. (See OFFICIAL WAR HISTORIES)

Wallingford, Air Commodore Sidney (12 July 1898–25 July 1978), was a senior RNZAF commander of the ★Second World War. Born in England, he served in the British Army and the RAF during the ★First World War, and took part in the ★Salonika and ★Sinai–Palestine campaigns. Following the war he served in the Fiji Constabulary before gaining a short-service commission in the RAF in 1924. He joined the New Zealand Permanent Air Force five years later and in January 1930 went to Western Samoa aboard HMS *Dunedin* following an affray in Apia in which anti-administration Mau demonstrators had been killed by police gunfire. During the ensuing 'war in the bush'—a largely unsuccessful attempt to round up the Mau—

Walsh brothers

Flight Lieutenant Sidney Wallingford with the Moth seaplane which he used during the operations in Samoa in early 1930 (*Penrice Collection*)

he flew an armed Moth seaplane on reconnaissance missions. This was the NZPAF's first, and only, operational activity. Between 1936 and 1941 Wallingford was in England on training and liaison duties. When he returned to New Zealand, he served on the Air Board as Member for Personnel. From March to November 1943 he commanded 1 (Islands) Air Group in the ★Solomons campaign. He subsequently occupied various staff and command posts in New Zealand, and acted as CAS for a period, until his retirement in 1954.

Walsh brothers Austin Leonard Walsh (5 February 1881–16 July 1951) and Vivian Claude Walsh (6 November 1887–3 July 1950) were founders of an important flying training school during the ★First World War. The proprietors of a mechanical engineering and motor importing business established in Auckland in the 1900s, they were excited by the new science of flight and formed the Aero Club of New Zealand. They built an aircraft, 'Manuera No. 1', which made its first successful flight in February 1911. A flying boat was completed in November 1914. In October 1915 the brothers established the New Zealand Flying School at Kohimarama, Auckland, with the intention of training pilots for the war. The British government offered £75, a first-class fare to England, and a commission in the RFC to each pilot trained by the school. Of the more than 100 pilots trained by the end of the war, sixty-eight served overseas. With peace, however, official support vanished. In 1924 the brothers closed the school and returned to engineering.

War Administration, formed on 30 June 1942, was a short-lived attempt to provide a bipartisan administration of New Zealand's war effort without establishing a formal coalition government. Essentially an 'outer War Cabinet', it comprised seven government ministers and six members of the opposition National Party, each of whom was allocated a portfolio dealing with the war effort. The ★War Cabinet was its executive body. Although clumsy, the arrangement did not prove unworkable, and for a time seemed to reflect a united war effort. It fell apart on 2 October 1942, after a disagreement over how to deal with striking miners led to the withdrawal of the National Party members.

War art The depiction of warfare dates from the very earliest inscriptions by man. The desire to record significant events or persons is perhaps an innate human trait, one with which the first inhabitants of New Zealand were certainly imbued. In creating carved images of warriors, Maori produced New Zealand's first war art. New Zealand images of warfare have since come into existence in diverse ways—by soldiers seeking to record details of terrain or structures with an operational purpose, by men seeking to distract themselves from their surroundings, to ward off boredom or to

War art

New Zealand troops moving forward in landing barges at Vella Lavella, as depicted by war artist A.B. Barns-Graham (*War History Collection, Alexander Turnbull Library, G-3953-1/4-DA*)

entertain their fellows, by artists far from the battlefield imaginatively interpreting the activities of their fellow countrymen, by artists specially commissioned to produce works related to particular campaigns, and by veterans seeking to define their experience in retrospect.

Among the earliest New Zealand works were sketches and drawings produced by amateur soldier-artists during the ★New Zealand Wars. Men like Cyprian ★Bridge, George Hyde Page, Sir Henry Warre, Edward Arthur Williams, Horatio George Robley, Gustavus von ★Tempsky, and Charles ★Heaphy left a body of work which can at best be described as technically proficient. Robley's paintings are notable for their accuracy and realism, while von Tempsky's are the most interesting and vivid depictions of the conflict in New Zealand, albeit in a typically Victorian sentimental and heroic style. This style was also in evidence during the ★Boer War. Artists in New Zealand created an imagined world of square-jawed imperial heroes battling scruffy Boers, as for instance in C.W.F. Goldie's depiction of the *Battle of New Zealand Hill* in 1900. This approach was no less evident in the portrayal by artists of events in the early part of the ★First World War. In his *Landing at Anzac, April 25 1915*, Charles Dixon, a noted maritime painter, portrayed the event as an exciting charge by colonials supported by the might of the Royal Navy. However, such an approach did not survive the growing casualty lists and the stalemate of trench warfare.

Of more lasting significance was the work of men on the spot, some of them professional artists before enlisting, who experienced the hardship and tribulations of the campaign. In sketching the landscape for HQ, Horace ★Moore-Jones followed in the tradition of the soldier-artists of the New Zealand Wars. These realistic sketches formed the basis of his collection of landscape pencil and watercolour sketches of ★Gallipoli. While exhibiting this work in Dunedin in 1917, Moore-Jones painted *The Man with the Donkey*, one of the most important New Zealand war images. The New Zealand government failed to respond to his offer to sell his works to it, and his collection was acquired by the Australian War Memorial in Canberra. Other soldier-artists included Archibald Nicoll and Francis McCracken, who sent work back to New Zealand to be exhibited in art society exhibitions, A.B. Townshend and C. Trevithick, who painted ruins on the ★Western Front, William Gummer, who painted scenes from the New Zealand camp at Ismailia, Egypt, John Weeks, and W.A.G. Penlington. Arthur Lloyd made pencil sketches and wash drawings from 1917. Two New Zealanders serving with the Australian Imperial Force, James Scott and Harold Power, became official Australian war artists.

The impulse to entertain found expression in the work of cartoonists in particular. Magazines such as *Chronicles of the N.Z.E.F.* and the annual *New Zealand at the Front* featured the work of New Zealand soldiers like Ernest Thompson, Allan Miller, Geoff Stobie, William Frederick Bell, and E.F. Hiscocks. Most of these cartoons show the stoical and cynical humour of ordinary soldiers enduring the trenches. Although some of this work was initiated by the military authorities, it was not until 1918 that war art was given serious official attention, mainly as a result of the work of the War Records Section of 1NZEF. The names of men with artistic ability were sought from among members of the force, and more than thirty nominations were received. Several soldiers were subsequently employed, including F.H. Cumberworth, G.E. Woolley, and Nugent Welch. The most prominent, Welch, was attached to the New Zealand Divisional HQ in April 1918 to make sketches and paintings. Most of his works depict a forlorn, desolate landscape in which people are conspicuously absent. Cumberworth painted scenes of the New Zealand camps in England.

The War Records Committee also commissioned artists then working in the United Kingdom. Alfred W. Pearse and George ★Butler were commissioned. Both were British-born, though Butler had lived in New Zealand for more than twenty years before 1908. Both were commissioned as honorary captains and sent to France in the closing stages of the war. Butler executed a series of watercolours, mostly landscapes depicting war's devastation. His works are dominated by deserted, shell-cratered ground and forlorn ruined buildings. Back in England, he worked on several large oil paintings and portraits of 1NZEF commanders. His most significant work was painted two years after the war: *Butte de Polygon*. 'Thy Father and I have sought thee sorrowing.' Luke II 48 portrays an old man and young woman standing over the fresh grave of a soldier amid a blasted landscape. Pearse produced a series of sketches and paintings, but his work was criticised

War art

as 'stiff and unimaginative' by the New Zealand Division commander, Major-General Sir Andrew ★Russell; none of his work is displayed in New Zealand, three of his paintings of 1918 battle scenes stored in the Dominion Museum having disappeared.

The body of war art produced by these official and unofficial artists was augmented by commissions following the war, financed by money raised by returned soldiers. Arthur Lloyd's *Soldiers of the New Zealand Division Advancing* is a rare example of a New Zealand First World War battle image. It depicts weary soldiers advancing across a landscape littered with corpses and debris as a barrage falls in the distance. Another important commissioned work was W.B. Wollen's *Fleurbaix, Christmas 1916*, which depicts a New Zealand outpost in a frozen no-man's land. Other artists turned their attention to war of their own volition: Archibald Maylett's *Assumption of the NZEF at the Wellington Carillon, 1933* has a quasi-religious theme. A completely different response to war was A. Lois White's *War Makers* in 1937, a powerful anti-war depiction of 'Financiers, money-grubbers, politicians …' and their involvement in war. William Reed produced *The Visitation* as a protest against the Italian invasion of ★Abyssinia. William Trethewey's 'Bomb Thrower' and Frank Lynch's 'Untidy Soldier' are the most prominent in a limited body of sculptured art associated with the First World War.

During the ★Second World War, soldier-art was again a feature, as men responded to the same impulses that had led their 1NZEF counterparts to take up pencil, crayon, or brush. For some, held for years in POW camps, artistic expression became a means of escape from the monotony and tedium of camp life. Nevertheless, New Zealand's Second World War art is dominated by the corpus of work produced under official auspices. The importance of war art was recognised by the New Zealand government much earlier than in the previous conflict. Its inclination to appoint Austen Deans, an artist already serving in 2NZEF, was frustrated by his capture in ★Crete. (Deans's output would be confined to a number of scenes from his POW camps in Greece and Poland.) Even before this battle, 2NZEF commander, Major-General B.C. ★Freyberg, had on his own initiative commissioned Peter ★McIntyre as war artist. The most prominent of New Zealand war artists, McIntyre painted all aspects of New Zealanders at war in the Crete, ★North African, and ★Italian campaigns. Unlike Welch or Butler, he sketched close to the action, with the result that his work possesses a sense of immediacy and tension not shared by his predecessors' efforts. This is especially the case in his work on Crete: *Parachutists Landing on Galatas, Crete* is one of the best-known images of that campaign. Throughout McIntyre's work, an empathy with the ordinary New Zealand soldier is evident. *Sargent O'Malley, Provost Corps*, a portrait of a New Zealand soldier in ★lemon-squeezer with cigarette dangling from his mouth, captures the essence of the New Zealand civilian in uniform, as does *The Kiwi*, depicting a grizzled, weary veteran of 2NZEF. His series of watercolours of Cassino are especially powerful, *Into Cassino* depicting infantry attacking into the wilderness of rubble. In another, *Wounded at Cassino*, a wounded soldier is brought out. Practically ignored by the art establishment in New Zealand after 1945, McIntyre's images of the war nevertheless struck a powerful emotional chord with veterans and ordinary New Zealanders, and contributed to his success as a peacetime artist following his demobilisation.

A number of official war artists were employed in the Pacific theatre. Russell ★Clark, an artist and illustrator, was appointed in 1943. He sketched scenes from the operations of all three services in the ★Solomons campaign in pencil, and later finished them as watercolours in New Zealand. Allan Barns-Graham, an officer in the New Zealand military forces in ★New Caledonia, was also employed as an artist. Although less proficient than Clark, he was certainly prolific, producing many images of service life in the South Pacific theatre as well as portraits of servicemen. Duncan McPhee was sent to the Solomons by the New Zealand government to produce work for an Allied exhibition. The RNZAF also appointed their own official war artist, Maurice Conly, who executed a number of paintings of air force activities in the islands.

As in the previous conflict, many soldier-artists supplemented this official work, mostly producing pencil and watercolour landscapes during and immediately after the war. In the Mediterranean theatre, they included John Snadden (who produced nearly 200 sketches of North Africa and Italy), Jack Crippen, and Robin Kay. Among the most effective were Pacific theatre soldiers James Coe and William Reed; the former's paintings are among the most disturbing images of New Zealand's war art. Reed, a medical orderly on Guadalcanal, made watercolour sketches of a Japanese POW; following the war he would paint *Guadalcanal*. Illustrators like Neville Colvin had their work published in 2NZEF's newspaper *NZEF Times*.

Since the Second World War, the RNZAF has been the most active in continuing the official art tradition. Conly, first appointed in 1941, remained the RNZAF's official artist until 1995. A commercial artist, he was responsible for designing a number of RNZAF standards (see COLOURS), and painted many pictures of RNZAF aircraft. He also visited South Vietnam in 1969 to record on canvas the activities of New Zealand troops taking part in the ★Vietnam War. More recently, Colin Wynn and Ion Brown have been commissioned by the RNZN and the ★New Zealand Army respectively as official artists.

Since 1945 non-official artists have also addressed war themes, including the ★Cold War with its threat of nuclear annihilation. Patrick Hanly's *Pintado Protest* depicts the confrontation between the visiting US warship *Pintado* and a peace flotilla. Ralph Hotere has not only addressed issues of nuclear confrontation but also, in his *Sangro, A Rosary of Olive Trees*, reflected on New Zealand's connection with the Italian campaign. Others to have incorporated war themes in their works have included Colin McCahon, Jan Nigro, Michael Shepherd, and Jacqueline Fahey.

New Zealand's war art collection has had a chequered history. In the aftermath of the First World War, it was envisaged that art works would form a significant part of the holdings of the proposed national war memorial museum. To this end various artists were commissioned to paint portraits of ★Victoria Cross winners, many from photographs. In addition to the officially initiated work of 1918, various pieces were collected, including some donated by the British government, such as a series of sixty-six lithographs by prominent British war artists. However, the war museum never got off the ground, and the collection languished in the Dominion Museum. Not until after 1945 was it brought out of storage and added to the Second World War works. About 600 images (two-thirds of them by Welch, Butler, McIntyre, Clark, and Barns-Graham) eventually passed to the National Art Gallery by way of the ★War History Branch. Although an exhibition was held in 1952, the Gallery had little interest in the collection, which fell into some disarray. Records became confused, and about a third of the works were dispersed on loan to RSA clubs, government departments, and other institutions. Some became lost, and others were damaged. Another third was loaned to the Auckland War Memorial Museum. In 1981 efforts to resuscitate the war art collection began in earnest. Responsibility for the collection was vested in the National Archives, which began the process of recalling, classifying, and restoring the works. A modest collection policy was also instituted. The National Collection of War Art now comprises more than 1500 items.

T. Martin, *New Zealand Images of War* (Dunmore Press, Palmerston North, 1990).

War brides

With more than a quarter of a million mostly single New Zealanders serving overseas during the twentieth century, it was inevitable that a proportion would become involved in relationships with local inhabitants, and would seek to marry. Although some New Zealand soldiers may have married women they met in South Africa during the ★Boer War, they had to take responsibility for bringing their brides to New Zealand. It was only during the ★First World War, with its much greater involvement of New Zealand personnel, that the government first addressed the problem of war brides. Most marriages during this conflict involved British women, whom the New Zealanders met while on leave, recuperating in hospitals, or training at various camps. Before marrying, a soldier had to have permission from his commanding officer, who in turn required a character reference for the bride, which was usually supplied by a clergyman or employer.

The government agreed to ship soldiers' wives and children to New Zealand. Although fiancées had to pay their own fare, they received a refund after they were married. During the ★Second World War the military authorities tried to dissuade servicemen from marrying foreign citizens, and many marriages were deferred until after the war. While most of the war brides that came to New Zealand were British or Irish, their numbers included Greek, French, Austrian, and Italian women, whom New Zealand soldiers had met during the Mediterranean campaigns or while being held as POWs. Loneliness, unimaginative in-laws, and the chronic housing shortage in post-war New Zealand meant that the war bride's lot was often unsatisfactory, though the process of adjustment was helped by various organisations, some of them formed by women who had themselves been war brides after the previous conflict. New Zealand women also became war brides following the Second World War, as a result of the American presence in the country during the war with Japan (see UNITED STATES TROOPS IN NEW ZEALAND). Before they departed about 1400 women who married American servicemen were lectured by Red Cross officials on the problems an immigrant wife might experience in the United States, partly to dispel any movie-inspired illusions about the nature of life there. Some of these marriages quickly collapsed, but many survived, with some couples returning to New Zealand to reside and others visiting regularly. No serving members of ★Jayforce were allowed to marry Japanese women, because they were enemy citizens until the peace settlement came into effect in 1952. After this date, ★Kayforce personnel were allowed to marry Japanese, the government having removed another barrier by relaxing immigration restrictions applying to non-Caucasian persons. In all, about fifty Japanese war brides came to New Zealand during the 1950s. Most managed to surmount especially difficult problems of adjustment resulting from cultural differences and the European orientation of New Zealand society. Since then there has been a continuing trickle of war brides, including, in 1995, a Bosnian woman who married a RNZAF officer serving in her country as a UN ★peace-keeping observer.

V. Wood, *War Brides: 'They Followed Their Hearts to New Zealand'* (Random Century, Auckland, 1991).

SUSAN UPTON

War Cabinet

War Cabinet was the key decision-making body in relation to New Zealand's war effort during most of the ★Second World War. Following the outbreak in September 1939, the Labour government resisted the idea of forming a wartime coalition administration with the only opposition party represented in Parliament, the National Party. While National and Labour cooperated over the war effort, domestic politics remained intensely partisan. The greater sense of urgency imparted by the military disasters which befell the Allies in mid 1940 led, however, to calls for a national administration. After negotiations between the two parties, the Prime Minister, Peter ★Fraser, announced on 16 July 1940 the formation of a War Cabinet of government and opposition members which would be responsible for all decisions relating to the war effort. Domestic issues remained the preserve of the full Cabinet of the Labour government. There were four Labour and two National members in the War Cabinet: Fraser, Walter Nash, Frederick ★Jones, Daniel Sullivan, Adam Hamilton, and Gordon Coates. In June 1942 the War Cabinet, which met daily except on Sundays during the early part of the war, became the 'executive' of the ★War Administration; at the same time Sidney Holland, the leader of the National Party since November 1940, joined the War Cabinet and became its deputy chairman. This arrangement lasted only three months before the National members withdrew. Coates and Hamilton thereupon defied their party by accepting an invitation to rejoin the War Cabinet as individuals. After Coates's death in 1943, his place was taken by William Perry, the President of the RSA. During 1943 the War Cabinet Secretariat, which was headed initially by C.A. ★Berendsen and later by A.D. McIntosh, took over responsibility for the duties performed by the ★Organisation for National Security. The War Cabinet operated extremely effectively. On 9 August 1945, Sullivan described it as a 'political miracle' and suggested that between all members 'there was something deeper than cooperation and understanding'. It was formally dissolved on 21 August 1945.

F.L.W. Wood, *Political and External Affairs* (War History Branch, Wellington, 1958).

War correspondents Despite the efforts of some individuals, New Zealand has not established any strong tradition of war correspondence. Most reporting of New Zealand war activities has been sponsored by the state, and, unlike in Australia, New Zealand war correspondents have been noted for their journalistic competence rather than for literary talent. The first New Zealand war reporting was carried out somewhat haphazardly during the ★New Zealand Wars. G.W. Woon, the proprietor of the *Taranaki Herald*, perhaps qualifies as the first New Zealand war correspondent: a member of a volunteer unit, he produced a journal of events in the fighting in Taranaki in 1860–61. A report on the inadequacy of New Plymouth's defences to meet a night attack led to temporary suppression of his newspaper by the military authorities. Soon afterwards the paper's editor, Richard Brown, was killed by rebels. In the later fighting newspapers assigned correspondents, such as, for example, W.D. Campbell (*Lyttelton Times*), Gustavus von ★Tempsky (*Daily Southern Cross*), and John Featon, who published a history of the Waikato campaign, *The Waikato War 1863–64*, in 1879. With the outbreak of the ★Boer War in 1899 a number of leading newspapers combined to send correspondents J.A. Shand and J.D. Moultray to South Africa with the First Contingent, though the latter soon withdrew because of illness.

Soon after the outbreak of the ★First World War the British government indicated that war correspondents were not to accompany forces in the field—mainly, it seems, because of reports that they would be shot as spies by the Germans if captured. As a result Malcolm ★Ross, who as a representative of several newspapers had accompanied the New Zealand expeditionary force dispatched to capture German Samoa in August 1914, was recalled immediately after the landing of the troops. Subsequently the authorities in London advised that one correspondent could be accredited in London, and G.H. Scholefield, the head of the New Zealand Associated Press there, was nominated. It quickly became clear, however, that he could not adequately serve the whole press in New Zealand, and the arrangement was terminated (though Scholefield continued to report on war activities for his agency, for example visiting the Grand Fleet and Ypres). Because the press themselves were not prepared to finance a correspondent, the government early in 1915 resolved, reluctantly, to appoint an official war correspondent. The New Zealand Press Association (NZPA) agreed to facilitate the distribution of the reports of this correspondent to all newspapers in the Dominion, and appointed a board of editors to advise on the appointment. This duly went to Malcolm Ross, who had been a parliamentary correspondent before the war and was a friend of Prime Minister W.F. ★Massey. Eighty-five newspapers (later reduced to seventy-four) agreed to take his reports.

After arriving in Egypt in May 1915, Ross sent his first dispatches on the basis of conversations with wounded soldiers returning from ★Gallipoli. He proceeded to Anzac Cove in the following month and remained at the front until the evacuation of the peninsula. From mid 1916 until the end of the war he was with the New Zealand Division on the ★Western Front. Far from making only occasional visits to the front, as prescribed in regulations, Ross, like his Australian counterpart C.E.W. Bean, whom he often accompanied, sought to spend as much time as possible in the vicinity of the battlefield. The arrangement was not entirely satisfactory. The needs of censorship and the ponderous method of transmission of his reports to New Zealand—he was not permitted to cable directly to Wellington and, while in France, had to deal through the High Commissioner's Office in London—led to occasional complaints in New Zealand about the lack of freshness of Ross's reports, and some newspapers withdrew from the arrangements to receive them. A more serious problem, though not one that appears to have troubled Ross, was the constraint imposed on his journalism by his status as an official correspondent and, from 1916, honorary captain in 1NZEF: his reporting was in the nature of a public relations exercise, designed to boost morale at home, and did not extend to investigating and bringing to light grievances or abuses. It was envisaged that the material he gathered would be used for the eventual preparation of the official war history, but Ross, unlike Bean in Australia, was to be excluded from this process (see OFFICIAL WAR HISTORIES).

Reporting of the activities of 2NZEF during the ★Second World War was far more extensive, though again almost exclusively within an official framework. Coverage was hindered at first by procrastination in Wellington. The government, suspicious of uncontrolled publicity and unable to decide upon suitable candidates, was determined to keep firm control through the Publicity Section of the Prime Minister's Department. As in the First World War, there was to be no direct representation by New Zealand newspapers. But no arrangements had been made by the time the first elements of 2NZEF arrived in Egypt, and ad hoc measures had to be taken to fill the gap. From February 1940 Signalman R.T. Miller acted as a de facto official war correspondent. J.H. Hall, the Assistant Director of Publicity in the Prime Minister's Department and a former editor of the *Dominion*, was appointed as official war correspondent in time to leave with the Second Echelon, but found himself diverted with it to the United Kingdom. In October 1940 the government appointed Miller as a second war correspondent. When Hall did finally arrive in the Middle East in early 1941, he became 2NZEF's public relations officer, responsible for all aspects of publicity of the force, but almost immediately was taken prisoner of war during the campaign in ★Greece. Reports on the fighting in both Greece and ★Crete were provided by Miller, who continued to serve as official war correspondent until incapacitated by illness late in 1941 (as a result of which he was repatriated to New Zealand).

The practice of employing soldiers with journalistic experience continued for the rest of the war. They wore a special correspondent's badge and (unlike Ross in the previous war) no badges of rank. From June to November 1941 W.S. Jordan (later an SOE agent in Greece and France) was the second official correspondent. Miller's place as correspondent was taken by B.L. Hewitt in December 1941. Among others to serve as correspondents in North Africa and Italy were E.G. Webber (later public relations officer, 1943–45), W.A. Brodie, C.R. Mentiplay (who later wrote the Army Board survey *One More River* on the latter stages of the ★Italian campaign), W.J. Noble, and J.A. Gasson. Their efforts were sometimes hindered by a failure within 2NZEF headquarters to recognise the specialised requirements of their role.

With the onset of the ★Pacific War, attention focused closer to home. A now-recovered Miller reported on home front activities, and from October 1942 was accredited to the US Navy in the South Pacific. He made a number of forays to the islands, including Guadalcanal. With the deployment of 2NZEF (Pacific Section) in ★New Caledonia, a public relations organisation was developed for it as well. D.W. Bain was appointed as war correspondent; he was later joined for a time by Gasson. The RNZAF also had correspondents covering its operations in the South Pacific—Clem Cave, Noel Holmes, Geoffrey Bentley, and Tom Ewart.

The activities of the many New Zealanders serving with the RAF and the Royal Navy were covered by Alan Mitchell, working for the NZPA in London. He interviewed New Zealanders and attended press briefings in London. The newspaper *Truth* obtained some firsthand material about New Zealand airmen from K.E. Hooper and Henry Bateson. In September Miller arrived in the United Kingdom as war correspondent attached to the New Zealand High Commission in London. Not until right at the end of the war was it made possible for newspapers in New Zealand to have direct representation at the front. Correspondents from three Wellington-based newspapers—A.M. Kitching (*Standard*), K.R. Hancock (*Dominion*), and Trevor Lane (*Truth*)—visited the South Pacific theatre in 1945. The end of the war forestalled the government's intention to attach an official war correspondent to the Australian forces.

New Zealand's post-war campaigns have not merited the same scale of attention. A public relations officer, S.P. ★Llewellyn, accompanied ★Kayforce to Korea. Coverage of the New Zealand forces' activities in the ★Malayan Emergency and ★Confrontation was provided by public relations officers attached to the HQ Far East Land Forces. During the ★Vietnam War a public relations officer served in ★V-Force HQ in Saigon. Groups of journalists were periodically taken up to the theatre from New Zealand.

579

War Council

A number of New Zealand journalists have made their mark as general war correspondents for overseas newspapers or agencies. Geoffrey ★Cox covered the Spanish Civil War for a London newspaper; his book, *Defence of Madrid*, was based on his observations. In 1940 he reported on the Soviet–Finnish War, about which he wrote *The Red Army Moves*, and the British Expeditionary Force's campaign in France and Belgium for the London *Daily Express*. After joining 2NZEF, he wrote several dispatches on the fighting in Crete for the *Express*, as well as briefly editing a newspaper (see SERVICE NEWSPAPERS). Freelance journalist Iris Wilkinson (Robin Hyde) visited the Sino-Japanese front in China in 1938, as did James Bertram. The latter gave an account of his experiences, including six months spent with the Chinese communist 8th Route Army, in *North China Front* (1939). Some New Zealand journalists served as war correspondents for Australian or British newspapers during the Second World War, with at least one, Keith Palmer, being killed—on Bougainville. Lachie McDonald of the *Daily Mail* reported from Tokyo even before Japan's formal surrender. He and other New Zealanders, including Ian McCrone (Australian Associated Press) and Ian Stewart (Reuters) in Korea and Nicholas Turner (Reuters) and Peter Arnett (Associated Press) in Vietnam, reported on post-war conflicts. Arnett, a Pulitzer Prize winner in 1965 for his Vietnam coverage, was responsible for reporting an anonymous US Air Force officer's February 1968 statement that 'it became necessary to destroy the town to save it', which became a favourite of anti-war activists. Arnett later covered wars in numerous other places, including Cyprus, El Salvador, Afghanistan, and Lebanon; he became internationally prominent during the 1991 ★Gulf War for his dramatic, though controversial, on-the-spot reports for the Cable News Network of the Allied bombing of Baghdad. Liam Jeory and Cameron Bennett were among a number of New Zealand journalists who covered aspects of the same conflict from Jordan; they later produced short accounts of their experience in *Foreign Correspondents* (1995). Reporting of wars in the latter part of the twentieth century, in the resolution of which New Zealand servicemen may have acted as peace-keepers, has been mainly carried out by journalists assigned by their newspaper or television channel for specific purposes, as for example Cameron Bennett's reports from Somalia in 1992. New Zealand correspondents have also reported on fighting in Bosnia–Herzegovina during the 1990s.

War Council held its first meeting on 21 June 1940. Although some form of executive role may have at first been envisaged for it, it became purely a consultative and advisory body when the ★War Cabinet was established shortly afterwards. With the National Party refusing to take part, it comprised six Cabinet ministers, a farmers' representative, an employers' representative, two trade unionists, four returned soldiers (one of whom was Maori), and an independent member of Parliament. The full Council met at intervals of about a month, but its two subcommittees, Defence and Military Affairs and Primary and Industrial Production, met more frequently. It proved a useful adjunct to the War Cabinet, to which it made recommendations on a wide range of matters. Most active in 1940, it began to falter during 1941, and by early 1942 some members were questioning its usefulness. Nevertheless it lingered on until the formation of the ★War Administration seemed to render it superfluous. Its final meeting was on 6 August 1942.

War crimes trials New Zealand first became involved in the prosecution of war criminals after the ★Second World War, when an eleven-nation International Military Tribunal for the Far East was established to try twenty-eight alleged major Japanese war criminals. This trial followed the precedent set by the Nuremberg tribunal, which on 1 October 1946 had convicted twenty-one leading Nazis of various war crimes and 'crimes against humanity'. This German trial had been preceded by considerable debate about the legality of trying Nazis for 'crimes against peace' or 'crimes against humanity', which had little or no definition under international law. Some felt, moreover, that the proceedings would be little more than a victors' show trial. Among the New Zealand public, however, there was satisfaction with the establishment of the tribunal of American, Soviet, British, and French judges to deal with the German cases, and with the outcome. Subsequent trials of Nazi war criminals were conducted by military courts of the occupying powers within Germany. New Zealand's Major-General L.M. ★Inglis was involved in this process as Chief Judge of the Control Commission Supreme Court in the British occupation zone from 1947 to 1950.

New Zealand's representative on the International Military Tribunal for the Far East was a Supreme Court Justice, Sir Erima Northcroft, while barrister R.H. Quilliam served as an associate prosecutor. (Northcroft's copy of the Tribunal papers is available in the University of Canterbury Library.) It was not an easy task for the New Zealand representatives, who found the trial to be poorly handled. Dissenting judgments after a lengthy trial did little to further the reputation of the entire process. The fact that the trial held just a few of the Japanese ruling elite responsible for war crimes also had the effect of effectively absolving the Japanese people from any moral complicity with the war crimes of their government and armed forces. Apart from these proceedings, trials of lesser figures were conducted by powers in their reoccupied territories. With no territories that had been in Japanese hands, New Zealand did not hold any such trials. Japanese who had committed crimes against New Zealanders were dealt with by British or Australian military courts.

By creating a precedent, the war crimes trials were expected to deter future aggressors and war criminals, and the establishment of an international criminal court was envisaged. The ★Cold War prevented any movement in this direction until the 1990s. In the meantime, individual countries, notably West Germany and Israel, continued to bring war criminals to justice. In Australia special war crimes legislation was passed to try suspected war criminals, but no convictions have been secured. New Zealand did not follow suit with similar legislation, preferring that alleged criminals be returned to the jurisdictions in which the acts in question took place. Claims in 1990 that forty-six alleged war criminals were living in New Zealand prompted an investigation which revealed that most had either died or gone overseas.

When during the 1990s a reinvigorated United Nations heeded calls to bring war criminals to justice, New Zealand played a substantial role in the setting up of appropriate machinery. As a member of the UN Security Council in 1993–94, it was deeply involved in the international response to atrocities which were occurring in both Rwanda, where hundreds of thousands of mainly Tutsis were slaughtered by Hutus, and Bosnia–Herzegovina. New Zealand strongly supported calls for the establishment of an international tribunal to prosecute those responsible for violations of international law in the former Yugoslavia, playing a significant part in drafting the proposed tribunal's statute and helping broker the consensus which led to its adoption in May 1993. Similarly, it took a leading role in establishing a second tribunal to deal with Rwanda. Its diplomatic efforts were important to the eventual success of this venture in November 1994. New Zealand has continued to support these two tribunals, for example providing two police officers to conduct investigations for the Yugoslavia tribunal in 1994, three years later submitting a legal brief (*amicus curiae*) to assist that tribunal in its deliberations, and, unlike some other nations at the time, ensuring that its peace-keepers cooperated with the tribunal in handing over evidence against indicted suspects. In 1998 New Zealand has also played an active role in the negotiations leading to the establishment of the statute for the International Criminal Tribunal, which will eventually provide a permanent tribunal for dealing with individuals accused of such atrocities.

R. Kay (ed), *Documents on New Zealand's External Relations, Volume II: The Surrender and Occupation of Japan* (Historical Publications Branch, Wellington, 1982).

War economy The impact of the two world wars on New Zealand was profound, and the war economy that developed at these times proved to be fundamental in shaping the evolution of the country but it did so in different ways. Both wars anchored and confirmed New Zealand's role as a key international primary commodity exporter, and dramatically enlarged the role of the state in the economy. The ★First World War, in particular, promoted extensive state control of the economy at a time of spiralling inflation yet considerable prosperity for the country. Wartime financial arrangements provided a fiscal basis for the modern state. The ★Second World War salvaged New Zealand's economy and shifted the country towards a mixed economy with accelerated industrialisation. It also cemented in place the post-war welfare state by providing the revenue necessary to fund it. The wartime stabilisation mechanisms carried over into the period of post-war prosperity.

First World War

When war came in August 1914, New Zealand had no precedent for the diversion of resources necessary to support a national war effort. Nevertheless, some action was immediately taken to put the country on to a war footing. A War Expenses Account was immediately created, while the Regulation of Trade and Commerce Act gave the government powers to fix prices, suspend industrial awards and other labour legislation, and requisition goods. In November further legislation (amended in 1915 and 1916) authorised the government to issue wide-ranging regulations in support of the war effort. After a hesitant beginning by William ★Massey's government, a National coalition ministry was formed in 1915, and Sir Joseph ★Ward, Minister of Finance, together with Arthur Myers, Minister in charge of Munitions and Supplies, largely ran the war economy.

From the outset New Zealand was determined to bear the entire cost of participation in the war itself. Between 1914 and 1919 government indebtedness doubled to £201 million, of which half was held overseas. War-related loans amounted to more than £80 million, of which two-thirds was found in New Zealand. The remainder was repaid to Great Britain for the maintenance of New Zealand troops in the field in accordance with an agreement with the British government that supplies and ammunition would be charged on a capitation basis. Ward turned to local borrowing sources as interest rates in London escalated and borrowing constraints were applied. Despite the interest rate on internal loans proving to be a minimal 0.5 per cent, such loans were usually oversubscribed. Money not required immediately was reinvested profitably in London at higher rates. While

War economy

there were compulsory provisions in legislation authorising loans in the latter part of the war, virtually all the money was raised without compulsion.

Government revenue was dramatically expanded to meet wartime expenditure needs. Ordinary government expenditure rose by nearly 60 per cent during the war. Increases in land and income tax, postage, railway charges, and stamp and death duties were made, and totalisator and amusement taxes were introduced. The rate of customs duties was raised, and duties were applied to a greater range of imports. The government saw little difficulty in demanding more revenue in the 1916 and 1917 Budgets. There was a massive increase in income tax in the former. However, Ward's attempt to impose a draconian tax on excess profits in 1916 proved a dismal failure and recourse was had instead to a more comprehensive and progressive land and income tax. Because of the rising value of imports, the level of customs revenue was maintained in spite of a decline in volume.

By the end of 1914, the containment of German naval power and the destruction of the German East Asiatic Squadron had ensured that New Zealand's shipping routes to Britain would remain open, albeit at risk of submarine attack. Its trading arrangements with Britain, long its chief market, were simplified by the conclusion of bulk purchase agreements (known as 'requisitions' or the 'commandeer') for its entire primary exports, described as 'munitions of war' by the Minister of Agriculture, W.D.S. Macdonald. These covered frozen beef, mutton, and lamb from March 1915, cheese from November 1915 (at first a third of exports), wool from November 1916, and butter from November 1917. Other items included sheep skins, hides, slipe wool, Glaxo, canned rabbits, and scheelite. The prices paid for these commodities were good and they rose as agreements were renewed.

Bulk purchase had a great impact on agriculture. The volume of primary production was maintained in spite of labour shortages, and export prices rose by about a half. Standards of inspection of products were improved. New freezing works and dairy factories were built, and freezing and cool storage was expanded tremendously as large quantities of exports had to await the availability of shipping. Exports of frozen meat, cheese, butter, and wool increased until the later years of the war when shipping shortages led to large amounts being held in store. By the end of the war, New Zealand had received £96 million under the bulk purchase arrangements, mainly for meat and wool. This was to increase to nearly £160 million by the time all requisitions had been terminated in early 1921.

Although the volume of imports remained high in the early years of the war, the increase in their value was exceeded by that of exports, with the result that New Zealand's terms of trade had never been more favourable. Later in the war import volumes declined, but this was offset by an increase in the value of goods. The proportion of imports by value from Britain declined by about 10 per cent to a little over 70 per cent of the total, while the United States doubled its contribution to just over 20 per cent.

At first the only problem confronting farmers was a lack of manpower as many of their labourers volunteered for 1NZEF, but this did not cause a decline in production. Difficulties arose in 1915 both in processing and transport. Some disorganisation blocked production in the freezing works, forcing their closure for a time. The transport problem was overcome by the requisition of all insulated space on steamers on the Australasian–Britain route. This was henceforth controlled by a Shipping Controller in London, together with representatives of overseas shipping companies in Australia and New Zealand. The re-emergence of shipping problems in 1916 led to large amounts of primary exports being held in store into the following year. Problems had resurfaced by the end of the war, by which time insulated capacity had virtually halved.

In 1914 New Zealand had the capacity to produce some of its military clothing needs and could manufacture small-arms ammunition (see INDUSTRY). Although dependent on Britain for a range of equipment for its field forces, it could not obtain the necessary supplies because of the other demands on British production. With a view to overcoming shortages, the government finally established a Department of Munitions and Supplies in August 1915. This body coordinated and organised manufacturing, built up a clothing and boot reserve, and encouraged standardisation of manufacture. By 1917 the supply situation had so improved that the Department was able to move to direct purchase rather than relying on tendering. From early 1918 New Zealand was able to ship abroad large quantities of military clothing, woollen goods, and boots. When late in the war a number of countries, including the United States and Australia, prevented exports without government sanction, the Department became busily involved in securing goods for New Zealand importers.

During the war the government had to contend with a number of difficult domestic economic issues. Perhaps the most substantial was the control of prices. Local primary commodity prices were pulled upwards by high export prices, while the cost of imports was greatly increased as a result of the shortage of shipping space and escalating freight costs. On assuming the Finance portfolio, Ward promised to tackle rising prices and profiteering. Local bodies were given powers to regulate the sale of various foodstuffs. The Cost of Living Act 1915 established a Board of Trade, which was, however, stymied by escalating costs such as freight charges. It failed to prevent the upwards spiral of inflation, which was fuelled by the high returns being received by farmers. The board investigated the prices of a wide range of commodities and in particular coal, meat, butter, wheat, flour, bread, and petrol. As a result, the price, distribution, and sale of wheat was controlled. The board also arranged for meat distribution, controlled the price of petrol and timber, and made arrangements with wholesale grocery merchants to control the price of a range of basic food items. Even so, prices continued to rise. The last year of the war was marked by industrial unrest as a gap between wages and prices opened up. Prices increased by more than a quarter during the war, though less than in other countries, according to the board's investigations.

A second major problem confronting the government related to energy. The economy was greatly dependent upon coal. Although output increased early in the war, shortages developed by 1916 and worsened in 1917–18 as output fell away and the numbers employed declined. Industrial unrest exacerbated the problem. Towards the end of the war the government was forced to introduce coal allocations and import coal from Australia and the United States.

Manpower provided another area of enduring difficulty. The outbreak of war in 1914 was followed by a jump in unemployment. This was caused by economic pessimism, coming on top of the recent strike on the waterfront. Relief works became necessary. In the early months of the war, the operations of the Arbitration Court were temporarily suspended, and hearings did not resume until April 1915. These problems proved temporary, however, as manufacturers responded to the demands of equipping 1NZEF. The enlistment of men soon eliminated unemployment. Although voluntary enlistment more than sufficed to meet military manpower requirements in the first two years of the war, it was increasingly regarded by the community as unfair. Manpower resources available for both military and industrial purposes were revealed by the registration, under the terms of the National Registration Act 1915, of all males aged seventeen to sixty. ★Conscription was introduced in 1916, and by 1918 125,000 had been mobilised. The removal of so many men from the labour force, in conjunction with shortages of materials, had a disorganising effect on local industry. To fill the gap, overtime hours were increased, particularly in clothing, boot and shoe manufacture, and biscuit and confectionery making. Major industries reduced staff to a minimum, and small employers in essential industries worked at high pressure. In addition to increased hours, the labour shortage was dealt with by the shifting of labour from non-essential to essential industries and the employment of women, retired men, and boys and girls leaving school. Women's employment expanded considerably in the public service, with many employed in the Defence Department and other wartime departments for clerical and administrative work. Numbers of women were also taken on in offices and banks for similar work. To increase the efficiency of industry generally, a National Efficiency Board was established in February 1917. It sought to achieve its objectives by classifying essential industries, ensuring the retention of workers in those industries, and organising labour generally, as well as providing assistance for the farms and businesses of those called up for military service.

The government also had to contend with industrial unrest. As wages fell behind the cost of living, there was agitation for control of inflation. Although the Arbitration Court devised a 'war bonus' scheme in 1916, this did not prevent a deterioration in industrial relations, particularly in the coal mines and on the waterfront. Regulations were issued to take control of the wharves after a protest 'go-slow' in response to the jailing of labour leaders for sedition. After miners restricted the output of coal, leaders were arrested under new regulations. Subsequent miners' strikes, protesting against conscription and demanding wage increases, resulted in government intervention and concessions. Determined to avoid confrontations in essential industries, the government took an increasingly direct role in industrial relations.

Despite these problems, New Zealand emerged from the war in good financial shape. As a result of greatly increased revenues, the government had consistently recorded surpluses, which were substantial indeed in the period 1916–19. By the end of the war, the accumulated surplus amounted to more than £15 million. While New Zealand's overall indebtedness increased, the government's revenue base had been expanded greatly and its powers of intervention had been enlarged. Thoughts turned to ★repatriation—much of the surplus went on the resettlement of discharged soldiers—and to reconstruction in the context of a post-war boom induced by the continued requisition of New Zealand's primary exports, inflation, and persistent labour shortages. Although prospects seemed good at first, the economy would have a bumpy ride in the 1920s.

Second World War

The Second World War posed a much greater threat to the New Zealand economy than had the First. Disruption of shipping and trade threatened to cut it off from its primary export market and source of essential imports. Furthermore New Zealand found that Britain could not be relied upon as a supplier of much of its military equipment. These circumstances suggested

War economy

the need for comprehensive economic planning, the development of new industries, a diversion of resources towards defence and primary industries, and extensive control of manpower.

The Labour government had been tardy in preparing for war and had failed to give a decisive lead. Nevertheless, its large public works organisation was available for ★defence construction purposes. Under the auspices of the ★Organisation for National Security, moreover, civil service bureaucrats had been quietly planning the transition to a war economy during the late 1930s. Import, exchange, and banking controls and government control of internal transport helped this process when the crisis arose. Following the outbreak of war, these powers were augmented by wide-ranging regulations and the Emergency Regulations Act. Control over supplies was crucial. A Controller was appointed, and rationing of oil and some essential foodstuffs began immediately. Over time a large number of other Controllers were appointed, but control over the supply of materials remained the critical factor until 1942.

At the outset, New Zealand secured a bulk purchase agreement with Britain for all of its exportable meat, wool, butter, and cheese, similar to those which had applied in the previous conflict. This was organised by the Marketing Department. Within the country the Department's Internal Marketing Division handled a wide range of primary produce. But in the first phase of the war there was no great pressure on primary industry to increase its output; many agricultural workers were allowed to join the armed forces.

Farming, which was already among the most efficient in the world at that time, greatly increased in efficiency during the war. Wool production increased as farmers shifted from dairying to take advantage of the good price offering for wool. This led in due course to a large stockpile, as international demand failed to keep pace with supply. Meat production also increased substantially during the war years, though butterfat declined. These gains were made largely without the imposition of draconian controls. Resistance from the Farmers' Union ensured that farming was not declared an essential industry. The Primary Industries Controller restricted his activities largely to rationing essential supplies, such as fertiliser, and to reorganising dairy production. The latter involved switching from butter to cheese production in 1941–42, in response to a request from Britain, and then back to butter in 1943. The government, again at British request, entered linen flax growing on a large scale to fill a gap in British supply, with up to 8900 hectares in crop and seventeen factories to process it at peak production in 1941–42. It also organised the Services Vegetable Production Scheme in 1942 to supply the American forces

Land girls assist with farm work during the visit to New Zealand in 1943 of Eleanor Roosevelt, President Franklin D. Roosevelt's wife, who is watching at the right (*John Pascoe Collection, Alexander Turnbull Library, F-549-1/4*)

in the Pacific, involving the establishment of dehydration and canning plants.

Mechanisation on farms, which had grown apace in the 1930s, continued during the war, with increased use of tractors and shearing machines. Electrification of power plants, including the replacement of internal combustion engines, was a feature. At the same time as farm output was increasing, labour requirements, particularly for dairying, were being reduced. This mitigated the impact of the loss of labour through manpowering. Even so, by 1942 labour shortages were adversely affecting farming. Military personnel assisted with harvesting, and eventually the reduction of the home forces enabled large numbers to return to farms. The Women's Land Service also assisted in meeting the labour demand in 1943–44 (see LAND GIRLS).

By 1943 New Zealand's role in providing food for the Allies was assuming greater importance. While still supplying Britain, New Zealand became a supply base for American forces in the Pacific. In order to increase exports domestic consumption of butter and meat was rationed in 1943 and 1944 respectively. Facing drastic shortages of food, Britain renegotiated long-term supply contracts with New Zealand in 1944 for butter, cheese, and meat at increased prices.

Because of the pre-war shortage of overseas funds and a failure to build up reserves, New Zealand's stocks of military and other supplies were low when the war began. The deterioration in the terms of trade during the war exacerbated the problem. Only with the assistance of ★Lend-Lease did the terms of trade improve substantially, from 1943. Although import prices rose considerably, volumes were lower than before the war. In addition to import controls, supplies were restricted by the lack of shipping—cargo space was reduced by a quarter during the war—and the inability of suppliers to fulfil orders. Petrol rationing had been introduced on the outbreak of war, and tea, sugar, and clothing came under similar restriction from 1942. From 1941 much of the country's essential supplies were procured in bulk by an enlarged Ministry of Supply rather than through private importing. Although domestic manufacturers were badly affected by shortages, their contribution to the goods used in New Zealand grew during the early years of the war. Imports of munitions and war stores increased to nearly half by value of all imports by 1943, while manufacturers' goods also increased substantially. On the other hand, consumer goods declined to about half the pre-war level on average during the war.

Issues of supply soon reached crisis proportions. As imports from Britain fell away because of its inability to supply, New Zealand attempted to switch to the United States but was hindered by a lack of American currency. The US Lend-Lease Act of 1941 assisted greatly with the provision of supplies, especially munitions and war stores, but also equipment needed for manufacturing and farming, in particular tractors. On the other hand, through the reciprocal aid arrangements associated with Lend-Lease, considerable pressure was put on New Zealand farming and manpower in supplying American troops. In 1943 a dramatic increase in importation of war materials from Britain, Canada, and Australia greatly reduced New Zealand's supply problems.

During the war, New Zealand managed to maintain or even exceed its pre-war volume of exports. With steadily rising prices, their value was substantially higher. In 1940 the volume rose to record levels as Britain built up food reserves, and even this was exceeded in 1942 in spite of the demands of American troops in New Zealand. Volumes fell over the next three years, however, as the American troops both in New Zealand and in the Pacific took larger quantities and as wool exports declined.

With the price of imports increasing faster than for exports, the terms of trade went against New Zealand in the period 1941–43. They would remain unfavourable for the rest of the war. However, the very slow arrival of imports ensured that a balance of payments crisis was avoided. Trade surpluses were made and overseas assets built up. From 1943 the value of imports vastly exceeded export earnings (exports having lost a third of their purchasing power by this time). When New Zealand renegotiated its bulk purchase agreement with Britain, it secured increased prices and compensation for the previous holding-down of prices. Although the situation improved in the last years of the war, the pre-war purchasing power of exports was not reached again until 1950.

The government was determined not to finance the war from overseas borrowing and to repatriate existing overseas debt. A separate War Expenses Account was established for receipts from war taxation and loans and wartime expenditure, with transfers being made from the consolidated account also. Nearly 40 per cent of war expenditure (estimated at £628 million in total) was met by internal borrowing; another 36 per cent by special war taxation; and close to 20 per cent by Lend-Lease and Canadian Mutual Aid. The cost of the war was estimated at nearly two and a half years of national income. Each year internal loans were floated, with two in 1942, dramatically increasing the proportion of public debt held internally. Only a very small amount of these funds, the first loan in 1940, was raised compulsorily. Public support for war loans proved to be high. Taxation increased in leaps and bounds: income tax and sales tax rates were raised, and a national security flat tax on incomes applied from July 1940. Government borrowing from the Reserve Bank and trading banks increased considerably.

During the peak years of 1942–43, it is estimated that half New Zealand's national income was devoted to war. By this time consumption expenditure had dropped from more than three-quarters to half of total expenditure, indicating the extent of the sacrifice made by New Zealand's population. Ordinary government expenditure increased by 60 per cent during the war.

The reduction in both imports and spending power during the war assisted New Zealand to find the £150 million in overseas funds required to fund its war effort. It also strengthened the country's overseas earnings position. This outcome was assisted by the government's determination to finance the war from internal sources by raising taxation and loans.

In the early years of the war, the mobilisation of personnel for the armed forces did not impose a great deal of strain on the labour force. Protective labour legislation was relaxed and greater use was made of women and the unemployed. The emergency conditions that followed the onset of the ★Pacific War at the end of 1941 led to the introduction of comprehensive manpower controls in January 1942. More and more elements of industry were declared essential. By March 1945 35 per cent of those in the labour force were in 'essential' undertakings.

As in the previous conflict, the withdrawal of manpower for the armed forces had a most serious impact on the economy. At its peak in September 1942, more than half of the country's males in the prime labour-force age groups (eighteen to forty-five years) were serving in the forces. As a result, it was necessary to draw into the labour force many married women, older people, and others normally outside it. During the war the public service nearly doubled in size with

War economy

large numbers of temporaries, often women, being employed. In view of the critical importance of the waterfront to the economy, a Waterfront Control Commission was established in 1940 to deal with problems and increase efficiency. Cooperative contracting was introduced gradually but did not achieve a great deal; extended hours of work contributed more to the war effort.

Some defence construction work had taken place in the 1930s, notably airfields, and public works generally had been expanded greatly. With the outbreak of war, the Public Works Department immediately embarked on a construction programme of airfields, ★air force bases, ★coast defences, ★naval bases, and mobilisation camps. With the growing threat from Japan, such work took on greater urgency. In March 1942 a Commissioner of Defence Construction was appointed to determine priorities and take control of scarce materials. The private tendering system used until then was abolished. Hours in the building industry were extended considerably, to fifty-four, but were soon reduced after proving too demanding. Defence construction reached its peak in 1942–43. House construction and other public works were almost completely halted, as military camps (for the American forces and Japanese POWs), fortifications, airfields and base expansion, anti-aircraft defences, and military road-building took precedence. During the war more than £50 million of defence works were undertaken.

With the easing of the Japanese threat, the emphasis shifted to the expansion of infrastructure for supplies such as munitions, linen flax, and processed food, and the development of hydroelectric power to overcome electricity shortages. As in the previous war, coal was an essential element in the economy, despite the strong inroads electricity had made as a source of power in factories and for domestic consumers. Intensive efforts were made to secure labour for mines, and the state took over a number of enterprises and developed open-cast mining in order to expand output.

Although there was a drastic shortage of munitions, it was particularly difficult for local manufacturing to step into the breach. New Zealand was, however, able to contribute to the supply of small arms and small-arms ammunition, tracked carriers, mortars, mortar bombs, and grenades. Labour shortages were experienced throughout the war, particularly in industries in which women could not replace men. Shift work was introduced in munitions and woollen mills and extended hours were worked in a number of other industries. Overtime hours were up to four times the pre-war level.

Manufacturing employment expanded considerably in the early years of the war and again from 1944, following the reduction in the home forces. The volume of production increased by more than a quarter during the war, but in spite of increased overtime in many industries productivity growth per unit of labour was slow because of the necessity to change production processes and direct and retrain labour.

Well over half of those in major manufacturing establishments were engaged on war contracts at the peak in 1943, with engineering virtually entirely devoted to the war effort. Heavy demands were made on metalworking for munitions, military vehicles and light tanks, and aircraft frames and parts. Clothing and footwear factories and woollen mills turned to military supplies. Shipbuilding expanded into minesweepers and patrol vessels and repairs. Food industries prepared orders for British War Office contracts. Engineering industries, which were of prime importance for munitions, expanded employment by two-thirds and developed the use of machine tools and a capacity for precision work. Later in the war, the production of radios assumed some importance. Exports of manufactured goods thus became significant during the latter part of the war.

At a time when purchasing power increasingly outstripped the availability of goods, financial stability was a vital requirement. The government was determined that inflation and wage increases should not threaten the economy. With the outbreak of war, price stabilisation was attempted, but its administration proved cumbersome and ineffective as prices continued to rise. A general wage order issued in August 1940, in combination with other pressures, tended to increase prices further. In the following month the government convened an Economic Stabilisation Conference, which recommended that wages, salaries, rents, and the prices of essential commodities be fixed. Nonetheless, the government failed to act at all until September 1941, when a narrow list of essential items was made subject to control. In the same month an Economic Stabilisation Committee was established to develop a comprehensive scheme for wages, costs, and prices. Meanwhile, the Arbitration Court rejected a further application for a general wage order by trade unions in the face of continued inflation, but this decision was reversed in January 1942.

After much work the Economic Stabilisation Committee introduced its stabilisation scheme in December 1942, to be administered by the Economic Stabilisation Commission and the Price Tribunal. By this time inflation had increased prices by 14 per cent. The list of essential items was greatly expanded. Wages, salaries, and other incomes together with rents were to be fixed subject to the movement of a special wartime prices index. The Arbitration Court's capacity to make general wage orders was restricted, and subsidies were extended and provided for shipping, coal, agriculture, essential clothing and foodstuffs, and wheat, in order to offset rising import prices. Stabilisation accounts were opened for farm produce in order to prevent increases in farm incomes adding to inflation; any money received as a result of rises in prices would be paid into these accounts, from which subsidies designed to keep down production costs would be drawn. Under the stabilisation scheme, increased costs and price rises were shifted to commodities outside the list of essential items or were to be absorbed by traders, and there was standardisation and simplification of production.

With the prices index remaining extraordinarily stable in spite of continued increases in the cost of imported goods, no further general wage orders were issued. The stabilisation policy was extremely successful—prices were held at a significantly lower level than in other Allied countries—with inflation for the whole period of the war being held to less than 20 per cent. This outcome was assisted greatly by increased taxation, which reduced the level of disposable income well below what it otherwise would have been. Controls on non-essential goods helped restrict the availability of such items, so that overall there was a good supply of essentials at stable prices and a very restricted range of luxuries at high prices. People saved rather than spent their money; for this the government was prepared with its war loans.

New Zealand came out of the Second World War with its economy in extremely good shape and wartime controls providing a platform that could be translated in peacetime into protected industrial development, full employment, and expansion of the welfare state with the aid of the much enlarged state. Of New Zealand's post-war conflicts, the only one to have any substantial impact on the economy was the *Korean War, during which a huge jump in import prices was offset by a trebling of wool prices. This latter was caused by heavy American buying for a strategic stockpile in case of war with the Soviet Union (not for use in uniforms for the forces in Korea as many then and since have assumed). The resulting rising prices for consumers was a factor in the waterfront dispute of 1951, into which the armed forces were drawn as substitute labour after a state of emergency was proclaimed (see INDUSTRIAL DISPUTES, USE OF ARMED FORCES IN).

H.T.B. Drew (ed), *The War Effort of New Zealand* (Whitcombe & Tombs, Christchurch, 1923; J.E. Martin, *Holding the Balance* (Canterbury University Press, Christchurch, 1996); J.V.T. Baker, *War Economy* (Historical Publications Branch, Wellington, 1965).

JOHN E. MARTIN

War graves are the graves of soldiers who have died on *active service or as a consequence of injury or illness from their war service. Historically, soldiers, sailors, or airmen have been buried near their place of death, often in common graves, or buried at sea. During the *New Zealand Wars many of the dead were consigned to unmarked graves to prevent looters or the enemy disinterring the bodies. Notable or wealthy officers usually received a church burial, and their ornate headstones contrast sharply with the simple wooden crosses of their dead subordinates. Just before the *First World War, responsibility for tracing and carrying out work on war graves resulting from the New Zealand Wars was assumed by the Department of Internal Affairs. By the mid 1920s its War Graves Division had identified more than a thousand graves, thanks largely to the efforts of the official inspector of old soldiers' graves, Edith Statham.

During the First World War strong public sentiment in Great Britain and elsewhere in the British Empire that the fallen be properly remembered led to the establishment of the Imperial (later Commonwealth) War Graves Commission in May 1917. All the Dominions participated in the commission, with their financial contributions being set in accordance with their relative proportions of the war dead. New Zealand's involvement was overseen by the War Graves Division, which also assumed responsibility for the maintenance of First World War servicemen's graves within New Zealand.

Three basic principles for war graves were established: that every serviceman or woman should be remembered by name on a headstone or memorial; that the headstones should be uniform, with no distinction accorded to rank, race, or creed; and that the graves and memorials should be permanent. A uniform headstone was designed of Portland stone (Coromandel granite within New Zealand) on which was cut a fernleaf, and the soldier's name, decorations (if any), rank, unit, date of death, and age. No other inscriptions were permitted on New Zealand headstones, probably to ensure equality of treatment. Great care was taken to ensure that graves were accurately inscribed, and that they were set in peaceful surroundings of trees, shrubs, and flowers, including New Zealand native plants. Unidentified corpses received the simple line 'Known Unto God' upon their headstone, while soldiers whose bodies were never found or identified had their names inscribed on memorials to the missing at the cemeteries.

New Zealand followed the principle that bodies should remain in peace. Repatriation of particular remains was seen as contrary to the principle of equality of treatment. Thus no dead from either world wars were repatriated to New Zealand. A photograph of the grave or memorial and the cemetery, and information about its location, were supplied to next of kin. In late 1939 the role of the Commission was extended to

War History Branch

The burial of Brigadier-General F.E. Johnston in Belgium in 1917 (*RSA Collection, Alexander Turnbull Library, G-12890-1/2*)

include war dead from the ★Second World War. In all 30,047 New Zealand war dead from both world wars are commemorated by the Commission. Most are buried in France (7778), Belgium (4711), Egypt (2924), and Italy (2157), and on the Gallipoli peninsula (2358). Tyne Cot, near Passchendaele in Belgium, with 520 New Zealand graves, is the largest cemetery of New Zealand war dead. The names of 1179 New Zealanders who have no known grave are also inscribed on its memorial. There are 3476 war dead buried or commemorated on memorials in New Zealand itself.

Soldiers who lost their lives serving with ★Kayforce were buried at the United Nations cemetery at Pusan. In a break with tradition thirty New Zealand dead from the ★Vietnam War were repatriated to New Zealand; the remaining seven are buried at the Terendak cemetery in Malaysia, along with those who lost their lives while serving with the New Zealand forces in the Malaysian area until 1969.

Since the 1920s all New Zealanders with war service have been eligible to be buried in a services' cemetery. Those whose death is attributable to war service are given a granite headstone or bronze plaque free of charge, while the rest receive concession rates. Plots are generally supplied free, or at a reduced rate, by the local authority. The Department of Internal Affairs pays for the structural features of these cemeteries, and makes an annual contribution towards maintenance. Local RSA branches sometimes contribute towards the cost of memorials. There are currently 172 services cemeteries in New Zealand.

War History Branch came into operation in April 1945 in the Department of Internal Affairs. The prime mover in its establishment was E.H. McCormick, 2NZEF's archivist, who headed it at first as Chief War Archivist. He oversaw a substantial programme of record collection and classification and preparation of narratives of government departments and branches, work involving more than a hundred people (including the ★Army Department's archives section) by early 1946. From 1 July 1946 Major-General H.K. ★Kippenberger headed the branch as Editor-in-Chief. He gained approval for an official war history project which ultimately resulted in the publication of nearly fifty volumes together with twenty-four booklets. At its peak the branch had a staff of about fifty.

Following Kippenberger's death in 1957, his deputy, Brigadier M.C. ★Fairbrother, became Editor-in-Chief. By this time, however, official interest in the project was waning, and a dwindling band of dedicated staff, eventually numbering seven, was left to complete the series. In 1963 the branch was redesignated the Historical Publications Branch, under whose auspices the final titles in the series were published (the last in 1986). The Second World War official history series remains the largest publishing project yet undertaken in New Zealand. (See OFFICIAL WAR HISTORIES)

War memorials Although war memorials are to be found in most societies, they are one of the more characteristic and prominent features of the New Zealand townscape, perhaps because of the importance of war to the New Zealand experience, or perhaps because of the relative absence of other public monuments.

The idea of commemorating feats of war goes back to classical times, but it was not until the mid nineteenth century in Great Britain that memorials began to be erected to ordinary soldiers, rather than to conquering generals. It was perhaps because the tradition was so recent that apart from headboards on soldiers' graves, only six war memorials were erected to the dead of the ★New Zealand Wars during the period of the wars themselves. The first of these was the remarkable monument to the ★kupapa who died in the battle of Moutoa in May 1864. The inhabitants of Wanganui were so relieved that they had been saved from invasion by the Hauhau that within 15 months of the battle, they had unveiled a statue of a weeping woman with an inscription which recalled the 'brave men' who fell 'in defence of law and order against fanaticism and barbarism'. The other memorials put up during this period were a column at Otahuhu in memory of Colonel M.G. ★Nixon; two church plaques, one of which was the famous tablet to 'the New Zealanders' at Te Awamutu; and memorials to the dead of the Wairau incident and the Battle of Ohaeawai, both erected a quarter of a century after the events.

Thereafter New Zealanders preferred to forget the New Zealand Wars, and it was not until the new century that a new effort began to commemorate the dead of that conflict. Between 1907 and 1920 more than 20 memorials were put up. This was partly because the period saw a fashion of monument-building and pioneer worship, partly because fifty-year anniversaries sparked interest, but most importantly it emerged out of the imperial jingoism following the ★Boer War and the desire to teach a new generation that others had previously died for the Empire. The prime mover in this attempt to inculcate patriotism through memorials was Edith Statham who, as secretary of the Victoria League and then after 1913 as official inspector of old soldiers' graves in the Department of Internal Affairs, toured the country inspecting graves and organising memorials largely paid for by the government. There was a further short burst of memorialising of the dead of the New Zealand Wars in the second half of the 1920s, sparked partly by James ★Cowan's history; and then in the 1960s when a number of centennial anniversary markers were put up.

Unlike the dead of the New Zealand Wars, the 229 men who died in South Africa were very quickly commemorated. All but one of the forty-four identified Boer War memorials were unveiled by 1908, and they captured in stone that enthusiasm for Empire which accompanied New Zealand's first military service overseas. Patriotism, rather than sadness, were the dominant sentiments. Significantly, one revealing image to be found on Boer War memorials is the triumphant figure of Zealandia, the daughter of Britannia, and beneath one such memorial at Waimate the inscription runs: 'In commemoration of the South African War in which New Zealand represented by her 6500 volunteers for the first time took part in the battles of Empire and assisted to maintain the prestige of the British flag'. Only belatedly do we learn that the memorial also commemorates the death of a local trooper. About a quarter of the memorials commemorate those who volunteered as well as the fallen. Much of the iconography of the memorials also shows the strength of patriotic and imperial sentiments. Oak leaves intertwine with fern leaves, Union Jacks with New Zealand ensigns, and a pride of British lions stalk around the base of memorials at Napier, Oamaru, Rotorua, Albert Park in Auckland, Westport, and Palmerston. In Christchurch the memorial to the local troopers was added to the jubilee statue of Queen Victoria. The dominant image in nine of the memorials is of a trooper and most of these are in heroic battlefield pose. Other distinctive memorials of the Boer War include drinking fountains and gas lamps.

Most Boer War memorials were initiated by local dignitaries and expressed a local as well as national pride. Nearly all towns of more than 4000 people at the turn of the century had one. But largely through the initiative of the Governor, Lord Ranfurly, there was also a national memorial which took the form of a veterans' home in Three Kings, Auckland, where 'those who had fought and won the battles of the Empire' might be looked after.

It was the Great War which made the war memorial a central icon of New Zealand life. Not counting the numerous windows and plaques in churches and schools throughout the country, there were over 500 civic monuments put up in the years following the Armistice. This time sadness was a more powerful motive. About 18,000 New Zealanders had lost their lives in the conflict. Most were buried overseas, and the grieving families, friends, lovers, and siblings had no place close by to lay their flowers. The war memorial

War pensions

functioned in part as a surrogate grave, where on *Anzac Day especially wreaths could be laid. Significantly, more of the soldier figures on the war memorials of the *First World War stand with arms reversed as at the burial of a fallen mate. But the memorials were also an expression of community pride in the achievements of 'our boys' in gaining glory in battles overseas and strengthening a sense of national identity. Great War memorials were a mixture of sorrow and pride.

Although there were a few utilitarian memorials such as bridges or clocks, the vast majority were purely ornamental, for to erect utilitarian memorials such as halls was at this stage considered derogatory to the idealism of war service; and to express the wartime spirit of sacrifice it was also considered right that most of the funding should come from voluntary giving. Government funds went only to the Soldiers' Memorial Hospital in Hastings, the Auckland War Memorial Museum, and the *National War Memorial in Wellington, the carillon, superbly designed by William Gummer, which was opened after long debate in 1932.

The most common of Great War memorials (almost a third of civic memorials) were obelisks, a form which neatly combined a traditional cemetery form with a shape which soared heavenward in triumph. Cenotaphs modelled on Edward Lutyens's Whitehall monument represented about 6 per cent of monuments and statues of soldiers constituted over 8 per cent. Most soldier figures were imported from Italy, but a number of the best were made by local sculptors. These included the famous 'untidy soldier' at Devonport sculpted by ex-digger Frank Lynch, the marble soldier nude to the waist at Cambridge which was the work of the Auckland sculptor Richard Gross, and the highly realistic New Zealand soldier at Kaiapoi. This was carved from marble by William Trethewey, who was also responsible for the finest war memorial sculpture in the country, which stands outside the Christchurch Cathedral. Arches and gates were another common form (almost 20 per cent of civic memorials), and memorial gates were frequently found at the entrance to schools where a younger generation could learn of the sacrifice of their forebears.

There are some revealing differences from memorials in other parts of the British Empire. Unlike Australian war memorials, few New Zealand memorials list those who served overseas. It is the dead who are named. Unlike British memorials, the cross is not a common form in New Zealand. However, despite the nationalism which the war is said to have engendered, New Zealand symbols are not common. Most of the iconography and many of the inscriptions draw on the symbols and language of the Bible or of British imperial culture. Rudyard Kipling's 'Lest we forget' and the biblical 'Their name liveth for evermore' are the most common. The words 'New Zealand' appear only on three memorials. The monuments were an eclectic mix of loyalties to King, God, and Country, just as they tried to combine sentiments of sadness and pride.

The war memorials of the *Second World War were very different. The Labour government was clear that there was no need for further ornaments in stone. The almost 11,000 New Zealanders who died should be commemorated this time by useful community amenities or 'living memorials'. In 1946 the government agreed to a pound-for-pound subsidy for community centres which might cater to people's recreational and cultural needs. This offer was adjusted in 1949 with a sliding scale of grants. The result was a large number of memorial projects throughout New Zealand. The majority, especially in the smaller rural townships, were memorial halls, but sports grounds, libraries, swimming pools, and marae also received support as official war memorials. The names of the Second World War fallen were often added to the local First World War memorial; and in Wellington the National War Memorial was also completed with the opening of the Hall of Memories in 1964.

The commemoration of the Second World War did not mark the end of New Zealand's memorials. The names of those who died in Korea, Malaya, or Vietnam were in places added to local war memorials; and a number of new memorials have been built, including the Queen Elizabeth II Army Memorial Museum at Waiouru, opened in 1978 as a memorial to all New Zealanders who have died in war, and the Atatürk memorial in Wellington, which honours one of New Zealand's most distinguished enemies in war. The continued vitality of the war memorial tradition is a tribute both to the deep meaning of war to New Zealanders and the important role memorials play in healing the pains and conflicts of war.

C. Maclean and J. Phillips, *The Sorrow and the Pride: New Zealand War Memorials* (GP Books, Wellington, 1990).

JOCK PHILLIPS

War pensions were first granted in New Zealand for veterans of the New Zealand Wars in 1866, when the government accepted responsibility to give financial compensation to officers and men of the colonial forces who had been disabled or the dependants of those who had been killed. Pro-government Maori (*kupapa) participants were also included. The amount paid was based on a soldier's rank and degree of disability, as well as race and whether the applicant was 'deserving' or not, the decision to award a pension being decided by a board of three doctors. While this scheme was applied to ★Boer War participants, it proved inadequate to meet the demands of the ★First World War. In 1915 a comprehensive war pensions scheme was introduced. Members of 1NZEF who had suffered a disability were entitled to a pension, the level of which was determined by a formula taking account of rank and extent of disability. War Pensions Boards, consisting of three people including a medical practitioner, were established to determine whether the death or disablement of the member of the armed forces was in fact the result of war service, and to assess the extent of the disability. The fact that veterans were not treated equally drew adverse public comment. Although high by British and Australian standards, the pension was also criticised as parsimonious, and it was increased in 1917. A representative of the NZRSA was appointed to each War Pensions Board. By the end of the First World War, more than 30,000 war pensions had been granted (including widows' pensions), costing the government £1.5 million annually.

The scheme was further amended in the 1920s. An appeal board was established in 1920 to provide for appeals from the decisions of the War Pensions Boards, and two years later the Pensions Department took responsibility from the Army for the medical treatment of veterans, such as convalescent hospital care and the provision of artificial limbs. In 1923 an 'economic pension' was created for ex-servicemen who had shown that they had been financially disadvantaged by their war service. In essence this created a second type of war pension, related not to a veteran's disability but to his economic need. That there were continual minor adjustments of the scheme and increases in amounts paid throughout the inter-war period was in no small part due to the NZRSA's vigilance and ceaseless lobbying.

To consolidate the various amendments to the legislation and to meet the changed circumstances brought about by the ★Second World War, a new Act was passed in 1943. It established the general principle that claimants should enjoy the benefit of any doubt. Henceforth War Pensions Boards could, at their discretion, grant those with severe disabilities a pension exceeding the 100 per cent disablement pension rate. At the same time, there was a move away from using the pensioner's rank as a determinant for pension rate. In 1951 war pensions were brought into line with the Social Security system in this respect, but the basic division of war pensions into compensatory payments for disability and economic pensions arising from financial need was retained. In addition, veterans were entitled to an array of allowances for free travel, cheap loans, and other benefits.

During the late 1980s the war pensions system was comprehensively overhauled. War Pensions Boards were abolished, and consideration of pension claims became the responsibility of claims panels, consisting of an officer of the Department of Social Welfare and a representative of the NZRSA. Currently there are two basic types of war pension—a war disablement pension to compensate ex-service people for disabilities due to service, and a veterans' pension to provide an income equal to New Zealand Superannuation to veterans unable to work because of disability or age. A variety of war grants for gallantry awards, clothing, funeral expenses, and education bursaries are also available.

War photography Since the 1850s the New Zealand experience of war has been documented by camera. Because of cumbersome cameras and long exposure time, early photographs were generally of troops posed on parade or for portraits. No official arrangements were made for photography during the ★Boer War. A photographer, J.D. Moultray, was sent by a group of newspapers, but soon became ill and returned home. There was similar official indifference during the ★First World War at first. No photographer accompanied 1NZEF, though many of the troops took cameras with them and recorded their experience in Egypt and at ★Gallipoli. New Zealand troops on the ★Western Front were not allowed to have cameras for security reasons. It was only in March 1917 that an official photographer, H.E. Sanders, was appointed. He photographed many of the New Zealand Division's activities. The belated steps to ensure a photographic record were repeated in the ★Second World War. Initially 2NZEF in Egypt was dependent on hired civilians, British official photographers, or photographs taken privately by soldiers. It was not until November 1940 that 2NZEF's Public Relations Service even possessed its own camera. Men were forbidden to take cameras into action, but each unit was supposed to have its own unit photographer. An official photographer was finally appointed in 1941. Harold Paton and George Kaye were the main photographers of the ★North African and ★Italian campaigns respectively. There are in all about 17,000 official Second World War photographs, the majority taken by Paton and Kaye. During the ★Korean War, the same pattern of belated attention to photographic requirements was evident. Early in 1951 Ian Mackley was assigned the task, and he and his later replacement, Peter Cooper, compiled a fine record of ★Kayforce's activities. Beginning with Peter Bush, photographers were based with New Zealand forces in Malaya from 1956, and covered

War poetry and songs

their involvement in the ★Malayan Emergency and ★Confrontation. A photographer-cum-public relations officer served with the New Zealand forces in South Vietnam throughout the ★Vietnam War. More recently the photographic record of the activities of the ★New Zealand Defence Force has been the responsibility of the public relations officers of the three services. The official war photograph collections are held by the Alexander Turnbull Library in Wellington and the Queen Elizabeth II Army Memorial Museum at Waiouru.

War poetry and songs No poetry of any importance or quality by New Zealanders emerged in either the ★Boer War or the ★First World War. However, much popular verse about the lighter aspects of military life in the 1914–18 conflict is to be found in publications like *New Zealand at the Front*, a sanitised miscellany of drawings, prose narratives, and soldiers' poems, and *The Kia Ora Coo-ee*, a newspaper for Anzacs in the Middle East theatre. Popular song was a massive industry that marketed an effusion of patriotic and romantic sentiment with lyrics like 'When You Wore a Tulip and I Wore a Big Red Rose', 'If You Were the Only Girl in the World', 'You Made Me Love You', 'The Rose of No Man's Land', 'Oh, You Beautiful Doll', 'Hello! Hello! Who's Your Lady Friend?', 'A Broken Doll', 'Good-Bye-Ee!', 'Roses of Picardy', and 'Your King and Country Need You' (subtitled 'A Woman's Recruiting Song'). This hyperbole was further inflated by dreamlike fantasies of nostalgic endurance implicit in the imagery of 'Pack Up Your Troubles in Your Old Kit-Bag', 'Little Grey Home in the West', 'It's a Long, Long Way to Tipperary', 'Keep the Home Fires Burning', and 'There's a Long, Long Trail A'Winding.' In 'One Flag, One Speech, One Empire', the occupants of New Zealand were exhorted to 'live or die for the Empire that ever guards us', and in 'Where Are the Lads of New Zealand Tonight?' they were told that 'the Nuts' we knew had taken a trip to the Dardanelles where they were facing danger gladly 'with their rifles and bayonets bright'.

But at the front it was not all grim bullets and bayonets. The New Zealand Division in France was entertained by 'The Kiwis', 'The NZ Pierrots', and 'The Tuis'. These divisional concert parties gave performances in marquees and a church hall named 'Kapai Theatre' of a pantomime called 'Achi Baba and the Forty Thieves' and 'Y Go Crook', a musical revue. The rank and file sang vulgar versions of 'Mademoiselle from Armentières' as well as traditional British Army comic refrains like 'Old King Cole' ('He called for his pipe and he called for his bowl and he called for his fiddlers three', etc.), 'The Quartermaster's Store' ('There was beer, beer, beer you couldn't get near, in the store', etc.),

'The Heroes of the Night' ('We'd rather run than fight', etc.), and the derisive 'I Don't Want to be a Soldier':

I don't want to be a soldier,
I don't want to go to war;
I'd rather hang around Piccadilly Underground, etc.

A variant of 'Fred Karno's Army' satirised W.F. ★Massey, the First World War New Zealand Prime Minister.

We are Bill Massey's Army
The ragtime infantry,
We cannot shoot, we don't salute
What bloody use are we? Etc.

Anzac soldiers in the First World War also sang 'The Lousy Lance-Corporal' to the tune of 'Villikins and His Dinah'. This was a bitter protest against those with 'soft jobs on the headquarters' staff' and an expression of anger by a Digger who had just come 'from the shambles of France'.

We're bombed on the left and we're bombed on the right,
We're shelled all the day and we're shelled all the night,
And if something don't happen and that mighty soon,
There'll be nobody left in the ——ing platoon. Etc.

Some of this output of informal song remained in circulation as an occupational folklore among the professional soldiery of the British and Commonwealth armies and was transmitted orally to subsequent generations.

In the ★Second World War the emergence of a body of serious poetic utterance about the actualities of campaigning was stimulated by the 2nd New Zealand Division's official newspaper, *NZEF Times*. Its editorial policy was to encourage original contributions from readers. These took the form mainly of cartoons, sketches, poems, and occasional prose pieces. Among the poets, Charles Smith, a First Echelon veteran who served in the division throughout the entire war, wrote with deep sensitivity about his experiences of ★Greece, ★Crete, and the desert campaign. His most widely circulated poem, 'Greece—A Year Ago', was printed in several services newspapers. It explores the close relationship that developed between New Zealand soldiers and Greek peasants during the ill-fated campaign in Greece. This and the best of the *NZEF Times* poetry is collected in *The Iron Hand* (1979).

Many of these soldier poets have a strong pastoral and rural urge to 'find another haven in these olive trees' or to imagine 'the young fresh wind that leaps with laughter from a wave I know'. Others recall the 'cynical sand of Alamein', the roar of guns, and 'the blood-spattered machinery of time'.

Poetry collections published by the Oasis Trust also include the works of 2NZEF soldier poets like Dan

War poetry and songs

★Davin, Erik de Mauny, William E. Morris, Charles Smith, Les Cleveland, and Gwenyth Hayes. The feelings of women left at home to face loneliness and anxiety are the burden of several poems by Nancy Bruce. Her 'Dawn Parade' speaks of 'Hearts that once waited, hoped, despaired and bled—hearts remembering their ever-living dead.' In her 'Returning' she invokes the familiar wartime image of the whistling train to fancy her loved one back again 'despite that far-off grave blessed by an African Star'. The stress and frustration of being a prisoner of the Japanese is articulated by James Bertram in his occasional poems. John Male, another 2NZEF infantry soldier, wrote poems that comment on the experience of soldiering in the desert and in the ★Italian campaign. His philosophic awareness of time and history enable him to see the minutiae of war in a far-reaching perspective. 'Stricken Peninsula' imagines how some roadside graves are ancient, others only day-old, while the same rivers have carried blood down to the sea 'from river crossings before ours'.

Contemporary wartime publications were subject to ★censorship. Consequently, the published poetry of the Second World War contains little that denies the requirements of security and morale. This applies also to radio, which was an important source for news, entertainment, and patriotic exhortations of wartime leaders. On the home front, radio supplied a chorus of morale-building, sentimental songs as part of a rhetoric of unity and dedication to the war effort. Much of this was derivative from American and British sources, but a few indigenous compositions added a local quality to this culture production, notably 'We Are the Boys from Way Down Under', 'Maori Battalion Marching Song', 'Blue Smoke', and a repertoire of patriotic, inspirational compositions like 'The NZ Boys Are Marching', 'Satan's Vassals', 'Sing a Song for Victory', 'Freedom's Army', 'Lads of New Zealand', 'Pilot of All', 'When You Return', and 'When We Get Back to New Zealand'.

Troops who served in Fiji became familiar with 'Isa Lei', while others were diverted by 'Ale' (a 'cheerio song and chorus'):

Ale Hitler! Ale Hitler!
Ale, ale, ale, ale, ale!
Send it to us in barrels
And we'll drink it by the pail. Etc.

An officially sponsored ★Kiwi Concert Party provided touring shows for the 2nd New Zealand Division in the Middle East and Italy, but its repertoire was mainly an export version of the homeland popular culture.

However, the most compelling utterances were those of the troops themselves in the form of informal satires, parodies, and occasional expressions of protest and disillusionment. The most radical originated in Fiji, where a garrison had been hurriedly sent in the expectation of a Japanese attack which never eventuated. In 'The Army in Fiji' (to the tune of 'The Martins and the Coys') the soldiery alleged that cases of leadhead nails had been sent by 'the old New Zealand Deadheads' for use as ammunition, because 'they'd heard the army had used them once before!' In 'Peter Fraser's Soldiers' the troops complained that they had been sent to Fiji to defend the Colonial Sugar Refinery, while in 'The C.S.R. and the Suva Snobs' they objected to oppression and injustice in the company's treatment of both them and the native labour force.

Soldiers' songs like 'The Dugout in Matruh' were a sardonic commentary on officially sponsored versions of the war in the western desert:

Oh! I'm just a greasy private in the infantry, I am;
And I've a little dugout in Matruh,
Where the flies crawl all around me
As I nestle down to sleep
In my flea-bound, bug-bound dugout in Matruh. Etc.

One of the most popular lyrics of the war was the German 'Lili Marlene', broadcast from Belgrade and listened to throughout the Middle East theatre. Parodies circulated among Allied troops and a New Zealand version was addressed to Peter ★Fraser, the wartime Prime Minister, when he toured the Italian battlefield in 1944:

Oh! Mr Fraser, won't you take us home?
We've done enough, we want no more to roam;
We've had all the sand, the sweat, the blood,
And lived in snow and rain and mud;
Oh! Won't you take us home.
Oh! Won't you take us home. Etc.

The struggle for Cassino was laconically memorialised in 'Cassino Town' to the tune of 'The Road to Gundagai'. There, the 'purple death' (a cheap wine grown in the district) is flowing and German *nebelwerfer* rockets and 88 mm shells 'go whistling by' while 'the Kiwis in their dugouts are brewing up the chai' (British 8th Army slang for tea).

In more felicitous circumstances, the Italian campaign also introduced 2NZEF to Italian popular song. Units which had acquired enough instruments to form small dance bands were able to include contemporary items like 'Tornerai', 'La Spagnola', 'Mama', 'Torna a Surriento', 'La Fiaba di Bianca Stella', 'Rive la Banda', 'Amapola', and 'Amor, Amor, Amor' in their repertoire.

In Cairo, in 1943, Arthur Wallis and Earle Taylor, two experienced performers from civilian life, joined a small group known as the Maadi Melody Makers

War trophies

where they composed and sang a series of songs that became well known throughout the division. These were 'Let's Sing', 'My Granny Smokes a Hubbly Down the Berkha', 'Mr Taylor and Mr Wallis', 'General Freyberg's Stew', 'Bomb Happy Bill the Soldier', 'Carry on, Carry on—Don't Do Your Scone', and 'Percy's on a Promise at the Pam Pam'. A further lyric, 'The Middle East Swing', circulated widely in the 8th Army owing to its catchy tune and amusing words. These describe the emergence of an imaginary Arab jazz artist who joins up with a 'singing fool' from 'the slums of Cairo' to found 'the hottest band in the Middle East', which is so good that it 'steals the show from Cab Calloway'.

They held jam sessions in low-down quarters,
A stamping ground down Maadi way,
The low-class bints and the Pasha's daughters
Went to town when they heard them play. Etc.

New Zealanders in the various wartime air services contributed to a tradition of comic song that made light of the hazards of combat flying. For instance, ★Fleet Air Arm pilots in the Royal Navy were required to submit Form A25 whenever they had an accident. The 'A25 Song' (to the tune of 'Villikins and His Dinah') satirises this procedure:

They say in the Air Force the landing's okay
If the pilot gets out and the crew walk away;
But in the Fleet Air Arm the prospects are grim
If the landing's piss-poor and the pilot can't swim!
Cracking show! I'm alive!
But I still haven't rendered my A.25. Etc.

Similarly, New Zealanders in the naval services became familiar with a long-standing repertoire of service ballads that included 'Maggie May', a composition dating from the days of transportation to Botany Bay:

How well do I remember when I first met Maggie May.
She was cruising up and down off Cannon Place;
Oh! She had a figure fine, like a clipper of the line,
Me being a sailor soon gave chase. Etc.

The inherent democratic ethos of the New Zealand rank and file surfaced in the ★Korean War in a song which expressed reservations about 'fighting for that bastard Syngman Rhee' (the dictatorial President of the Republic of Korea). But many other songs reflect regimental pride. For instance, 'The Gunner's Battle Hymn' is a spirited declaration by the Royal New Zealand Artillery's 161st Battery which saw service in both the Korean and ★Vietnam Wars to the effect that 'I wouldn't want to be in tanks or infantry, I'd rather be a gunner, like I am.' Etc.

Services songs are also an outlet for emotional anxieties, frustrations, and anger. Alarm at the American presence in New Zealand during the Second World War was displayed in a parody of the 'Marine's Hymn', which asserted that 'They're a pack of Yankee bastards' who 'think they run New Zealand, but they couldn't run latrines'. A mournful vision of an idyllic future of sexual happiness for the returning warrior also circulated throughout the Middle East and Italy entitled 'When They Send the Last Yank Home' (to the tune of 'When They Sound the Last All Clear'.)

When they send the last Yank home
How happy us Kiwis will be,
So we'll pray for the day
When they all sail away
And all of our girls will be free.
Never more we'll be alone—
We'll each have a girl of our own,
And should love still exist,
We might even be kissed
When they send the last Yank home. Etc.

L. Cleveland, *Dark Laughter: War in Song and Popular Culture* (Praeger, Westport, Conn., 1994); L. Cleveland, *The Songs We Sang* (Editorial Services, Wellington, 1959); L. Cleveland, *The Iron Hand: New Zealand Soldiers' Poems from World War Two* (Wai-te-ata Press, Wellington, 1994); C. Bollinger and N. Grange (eds), *Kiwi Youth Sings* (NZ Progressive Youth League, Wellington, 1951); V. Selwyn (ed), *The Voice of War* (Michael Joseph, London, 1995); J. Male, *Poems from a War* (Black Light Press, Wellington, 1989).

LES CLEVELAND

War trophies The classical European concept of the trophy, the civic display of enemy weaponry as a memorial to victory, was imported into colonial New Zealand by European settlers. By the late nineteenth century, obsolete cannon ornamented civic sites throughout the colony, including two genuine Russian trophy cannon captured at Sebastopol during the ★Crimean War and dispatched by the British authorities to Auckland for display. New Zealand's first war trophies were artillery and Maxim guns captured during the ★Boer War and, with the permission of the imperial authorities, shipped to New Zealand for display. The greatest war trophy activity within the British Empire occurred during the ★First World War. New Zealand's first trophies were German Colonial Service flags from the seized German colony of Samoa. The trophy tally thereafter reflected the state of the Allied campaigns in which New Zealand forces participated. Relatively few trophies were obtained during the ★Gallipoli campaign or on the ★Western Front in 1916 and 1917. During the German and Allied offensives of 1918, however, the New Zealand Division captured 145 guns, 1419 machine-guns, and two tanks. The New Zealand Mounted Rifles Brigade serving in the ★Sinai–Palestine campaign also captured significant amounts of Turkish, German, and Austrian weaponry. These trophies were supplemented by a proportion of German weapons surrendered under the terms of the Armistice in November 1918 and allocated to New Zealand by the Imperial War Trophies Committee. By 1919 approximately 200 field guns, 80 trench mortars, 2000 machine-guns, and 5000 rifles had been shipped to New Zealand. Returned servicemen hoped that the collection would form the basis of a national war museum at Wellington, the proceeds of which would be used to benefit disabled servicemen. The museum was never created, and the trophy weapons were instead distributed to local authorities, museums, and schools throughout the country for public display. They became objects of municipal pride as local authorities competed for the biggest and best items. Larger guns, unsuited to long term public display, nevertheless became temporary war memorials pending the construction of permanent monuments. Many of these trophies would be later buried or scrapped during anti-war protests in the 1930s or the invasion scares of the 1940s. Trophy Maxim guns, unsuitable for patriotic exhibits in schools and museums, were often abandoned. In 1932, amid rioting by the unemployed, the police decided that unwanted Maxim guns presented a threat to public safety and had most of them destroyed. A decade later, several German trophy Maxims were converted to fire .303 ammunition during anti-invasion preparations. During the ★Second World War practical rather than patriotic considerations underlay the official approach to trophies. Some captured weapons transported to New Zealand were for home defence and for technical evaluation and training purposes only. Similarly, trophy guns have not been repatriated for public display from any New Zealand campaigns since 1945. Many New Zealand soldiers in all of the overseas wars have been avid collectors of private trophies, especially prized items being small arms, headgear, and swords. In more recent times, many First World War trophy field guns and Maxim guns have passed into private ownership, while those few weapons which remain on public display, such as, for example, at Arrowtown and Waipawa, are finally being restored, conserved, and valued as unique relics of the 'war to end all wars'.

AARON FOX

Ward, Sergeant James Allen (14 January 1919–15 September 1941) was the first New Zealand airman to win the ★Victoria Cross. A Wanganui-born school teacher, he joined the RNZAF in July 1940 and, after training as a pilot at Wigram, departed for Great Britain for service with the RAF. From June 1941 he was a member of 75 Squadron, then flying Wellington bombers. The incident leading to his decoration occurred following an air raid on Munster on 7 July 1941. The aircraft in which he was second pilot had its starboard wing set alight by a German fighter plane. Ward got out on to the wing though a hole in the fuselage, and, spread-eagling himself, crawled to the seat of the fire, which he tried to smother with an engine cover. He later described the rush of air as 'worse than any gale I've ever known'. Although his effort failed, the fire eventually burned itself out, and the badly damaged bomber succeeded in returning to base. On 15 September 1941 Ward's aircraft was set on fire by flak while over Hamburg, and he was last seen at its controls after ordering his crew to bale out.

Ward, Sir Joseph George (26 April 1856–8 July 1930), a Liberal Party politician, was a key figure in the determination of New Zealand's defence policy in the first decade of the twentieth century. Succeeding Richard ★Seddon as Prime Minister in August 1906, he added the Defence portfolio to his responsibilities later that year. A strong imperialist, he believed that greater coordination of the resources of Great Britain and its Dominions was essential if the growing challenge to the British Empire's international position was to be resisted. At the Imperial Conference in 1911, he advanced a poorly thought-out scheme for imperial federation, including the creation of an Imperial parliament of defence. On naval defence, he accepted the principle of one navy for the Empire, and strongly supported New Zealand's existing naval policy, based upon the provision of a subsidy to the Royal Navy under the ★Australasian Naval Agreement. Resisting suggestions by the opposition Reform Party for close cooperation with Australia in developing local naval forces, he secured an increase in the subsidy to £100,000 in 1908. A naval scare in Britain over the

German guns captured during the New Zealand Division's successful attack on Messines on display in the French town of Bailleul in June 1917 (*RSA Collection, Alexander Turnbull Library, G-13389-1/2*)

Royal Navy's strength in relation to the growing German battlefleet induced him, without consulting Parliament, to make a dramatic offer to pay for 'one first-class battleship of the latest type', and if necessary another. Often depicted later as an unthinking imperialist reflex, this action was firmly grounded in New Zealand's defence interests, given the paramount importance of the British fleet for the whole system of *imperial defence upon which New Zealand depended. As a result of his initiative HMS *New Zealand was launched in 1911. In military matters, Ward was a firm supporter of the voluntary principle, and resisted pressure from his military advisers for the introduction of compulsory service as a means of lifting the standard of the *Volunteer Force. In 1909, however, he relented after being persuaded in London that a reorganisation of the forces was imperative if the essential standardisation with other imperial forces was to be achieved. Even so, he remained unenthusiastic about the *compulsory military training scheme following its introduction in 1911. After losing power in 1912, he remained Leader of the Opposition and two years later, after the outbreak of the *First World War, became deputy Prime Minister and Minister of Finance in the National coalition ministry formed by the Reform and Liberal parties. In uneasy tandem with Prime Minister W.F. *Massey, he attended Imperial War Conferences in London in 1917 and 1918, and the Paris Peace Conference in 1919. In the general election which followed the Liberal withdrawal from the coalition in 1919, he lost his seat. He returned to Parliament in 1925 and, in an unexpected and almost farcical development three years later, regained the prime ministership. In a state of increasing decrepitude, he soldiered on until finally resigning in May 1930, shortly before his death.

M. Bassett, *Sir Joseph Ward: A Political Biography* (Auckland University Press, Auckland, 1993).

Wards, Ian McLean (13 September 1920–) oversaw the completion of the official history of the Second World War. Born at Motueka, he served in 2NZEF's 36th Survey Battery from 1940 to 1944 before joining the *War History Branch in 1946. He was one of the narrators on which the *official war histories depended, and was the author of *Takrouna*, a brief account of one of the 2nd New Zealand Division's final actions in the *North African campaign. His *Shadow of the Land: A Study of British Policy and Racial Conflict in New Zealand 1832–1852* (1969) provides a well-researched account of the British Army's early involvement in New Zealand, including the fighting of 1845–46. As Chief Historian of the Historical Publications Branch from 1968 to 1982, he ensured the publication of several works on New Zealand's approach to security and edited the final volume in the Second World War series. He also initiated a documents series giving comprehensive sources on the *Australia–New Zealand Agreement, the occupation of Japan, and the *ANZUS alliance, a series of official histories of New Zealand's post-war campaigns, beginning with the *Korean War, and the *Dictionary of New Zealand Biography*, which contains entries on numerous servicemen and women.

Washbourn, Rear-Admiral Richard Everley (14 February 1910–8 August 1988) was the second New Zealander to serve as CNS. He was born and educated in Nelson, and entered the Royal Navy by special entry from New Zealand in 1927. He was attached to the *New Zealand Division of the Royal Navy while serving in HMS *Diomede* in 1933–34. After undergoing specialist instruction in gunnery in 1936–37 and serving in HMS *Excellent*, he was again seconded to the New Zealand Division, and became gunnery officer in HMS *Achilles*, in 1939. For his part in the Battle of the *River Plate, he was appointed a DSO. He reverted to the Royal Navy in 1942, and served on the battleship HMS *Anson* and at the Admiralty Gunnery Establishment before once again being loaned to New Zealand. He was successively executive officer in HMNZS *Bellona* and Commander Superintendent of the naval dockyard at Devonport. From 1950 until his retirement in 1962, he filled a number of posts in the Royal Navy, including Admiralty appointments as Director of Naval Ordnance (1956–58) and Director-General, Weapons (1960–62). He was made an OBE in 1950 and a CB in 1961. New Zealand had resisted Admiralty suggestions that he be appointed CNS in 1960; after entering the RNZN, he succeeded Peter *Phipps in the position in July 1963. The main problem with which he had to contend during his tenure, which ended in September 1965, was the composition of the new Ministry of Defence, but he revealed little grasp of the issues or forcefulness in expressing his views.

Webb, Lieutenant-General Sir Richard James Holden (21 December 1919–24 January 1990) was a leading artilleryman of the post-war *New Zealand Army. Born at Nelson, he came from a family which had already made a mark in New Zealand's military activities, his grandfather, William Holden Webb, having been secretary of the Council of Defence established in 1907. After graduating from Duntroon in 1941 and being commissioned in the RNZA, he was posted to 2NZEF, and took part in the *North African and *Italian campaigns. He attended the staff college at Haifa. After the war he occupied various staff positions in New Zealand and with *Jayforce. He also undertook an advanced artillery course at Fort Sill in the United States. He was well qualified, therefore, to be second-in-command of 16th Field Regiment, which left New Zealand in December 1950 as the major part of New Zealand's army contribution to the United Nations Command in the *Korean War. With a rather brusque temperament, he did not endear himself to the regiment's junior officers, mostly civilian volunteers, but he kept a firm grip on them. The high professional standards he demanded helped make the regiment one of the best in the theatre, and his efforts were recognised by a mention in dispatches. On his return to New Zealand he commanded 3rd Field Regiment. After attending the Joint Services Staff College in England in 1957, he was Commandant of the *Army Schools at Waiouru. From 1960 to 1968 he occupied increasingly important staff posts in New Zealand and overseas, and attended the *Imperial Defence College. He was Deputy CGS before becoming CGS in April 1970. During his brief tenure, a reorganisation of the Army was carried out: the *military districts were replaced by a more functional Field Force Command and Home Command. From 1971 he began a three-year term as CDS, during which he oversaw the withdrawal of the last New Zealand troops from Vietnam and the adjustment of New Zealand's military presence in Singapore. He was made a CBE (1970), a CB (1972), and a KBE (1974).

Weir, Major-General Sir Norman William McDonald (6 July 1893–11 July 1961) was the first post–*Second World War CGS. Born at Heathcote Valley, near Christchurch, he was one of ten New Zealand cadets who formed part of the inaugural intake of the Royal Military College at Duntroon in 1911. Following the outbreak of the *First World War, he graduated early in order to join 1NZEF. He was wounded while serving with the Auckland Battalion at *Gallipoli in 1915, and was repatriated to New Zealand. Resuming his career in the *New Zealand Staff Corps in 1917, he held a series of staff appointments, which were interrupted by command first of a military police company raised in 1930 for service in Western Samoa but not dispatched and later of the contingent sent to London for King George VI's coronation in 1937. After commanding successively the Northern and Central Military Districts, he assumed command of the Central (later 4th) Division in April 1942. From December 1942 to August 1944 he served with 2NZEF, initially in charge of administration in Egypt, and after November 1943 as commander there. Quartermaster-General and Third Military Member of the Army Board in 1944–45, he applied his administrative skills to sustaining 2NZEF in the latter stages of the war. His services were recognised by his appointment as a CBE in 1942 and a CB in 1946. As CGS from

Brigadier N.W.M. Weir, the commander of the Central Military District, inspects the Hutt Valley Battalion of the Home Guard accompanied by Captain J.W. Andrews on 5 October 1941 (*Evening Post Collection, Alexander Turnbull Library, F-159233-1/2*)

January 1946, he was confronted with the difficult tasks of demobilising 2NZEF, maintaining *Jayforce, and preparing the Army for a peacetime role. British Commonwealth discussions on Commonwealth strategy which he attended in 1946 and 1947 convinced him that New Zealand should follow, and refine, its previous approach by re-creating the *Territorial Force and reintroducing *compulsory military training. When he retired in September 1949, by which time he had been made a KBE, the Army had a firm objective based on the *Middle East commitment, a framework upon which its preparations were based for the ensuing decade.

Weir, Major-General Sir Stephen Cyril Ettrick

(4 October 1904–24 September 1969). One of New Zealand's foremost artillerymen, 'Steve' Weir—he added the name Stephen by deed poll in 1960—was born at Pukehiki, near Dunedin. His military career began as a *Territorial Force trooper in the 6th New Zealand Mounted Rifles. Appointed to a cadetship in the regular force, he undertook a two-year course at the Royal Military Academy at Woolwich in the United Kingdom in 1926–27, and was commissioned in the RNZA. Following the *Napier earthquake in 1931, he was posted to the ravaged city for five months. Weir held various appointments in the Northern Military District from 1933 until the outbreak of the *Second World War, after which he was seconded to 2NZEF. He departed from New Zealand with the Third Echelon in January 1940 as the commander of 6th Field Regiment. His efforts in *Greece in 1941 were recognised by his appointment as a DSO. During Operation Crusader (see NORTH AFRICAN CAMPAIGN) later in the year his unit suffered heavy losses, and at one point was nearly overrun by German forces. The capture of Brigadier Reginald *Miles in November 1941 opened the way for Weir to become Commander Royal Artillery at the comparatively youthful age of thirty-eight. Innovative and determined, he took advantage of the New Zealand division's deployment in Syria in 1942 to refine artillery techniques earlier developed by Miles to ensure that the fire of the Divisional Artillery could be concentrated, thereby greatly increasing its effectiveness (see ARTILLERY). The more plentiful supply of ammunition made such a development possible. Tested at Minqar Qaim in June 1942, the techniques proved so successful that they were eventually applied throughout the British artillery. Weir, who earned a bar to his DSO at the Battle of El Alamein, had established himself as one of the division's brightest stars. In February–March 1944 he commanded 10th Corps's artillery, and in the following September assumed command of 2nd New Zealand Division during Lieutenant-General Sir Bernard *Freyberg's temporary absence. This latter elevation came as an unwelcome surprise to many of his colleagues, who were conscious of his lack of seniority and limited all-arms experience and were perhaps motivated by professional jealousy. After Freyberg's return in October, Weir became the only Dominion officer to command a British division in the Second World War. During two years commanding 46th Division, he served in Italy, Austria, and Greece. Weir was appointed a CBE in 1944, and a CB in the following year. He was mentioned in dispatches six times during the war. His hopes of transferring to the British Army came to nothing, but a serious illness delayed his return to New Zealand until January 1948. He then commanded the Southern Military District (1948–49) before attending the *Imperial Defence College in 1950 and serving at the War Office in London in 1951. He was Quartermaster-General from 1952 to 1955, when he was appointed as CGS. During his five-year term, at the end of which he was promoted to a KBE, he oversaw the reorganisation of the Army, and the deployment of forces in Malaya. He was an early advocate of the establishment of a Ministry of Defence (see DEFENCE, MINISTRY OF). In 1960, to the dismay of the service *Chiefs of Staff, he assumed the somewhat anomalous position of Military Adviser to the government. A member of the Prime Minister's Department, he advised on military matters with external implications. Following his appointment as New Zealand's Ambassador to Thailand, he retired from the Army in April 1962. Cross-accredited to Vientiane and Saigon in 1962, he helped shape official attitudes to the developing *Vietnam War. He also served as New Zealand's representative at *SEATO headquarters in Bangkok until his retirement in 1967. He died at Tauranga.

GLYN HARPER

Western Front

The Western Front was the site of New Zealand's most costly military effort in terms of lives lost. The New Zealand Division was engaged there from May 1916 to the end of hostilities in November 1918. The character of the front had been long established by the time the New Zealanders were transferred to it from Egypt in April 1916. The war had begun in August 1914 with the German invasion of Belgium and France, according to precepts of the Schlieffen Plan, which provided for a great wheeling action by the German right wing that would envelop Paris and pin the French armies along the Franco-German border. At first this plan seemed to be working: the French, supported by a hastily deployed but small British Expeditionary Force, had been forced into full-scale retreat. But early in September a British and French counter-attack on the Marne had precipitated a German retreat, which was not halted until the German armies had

Western Front

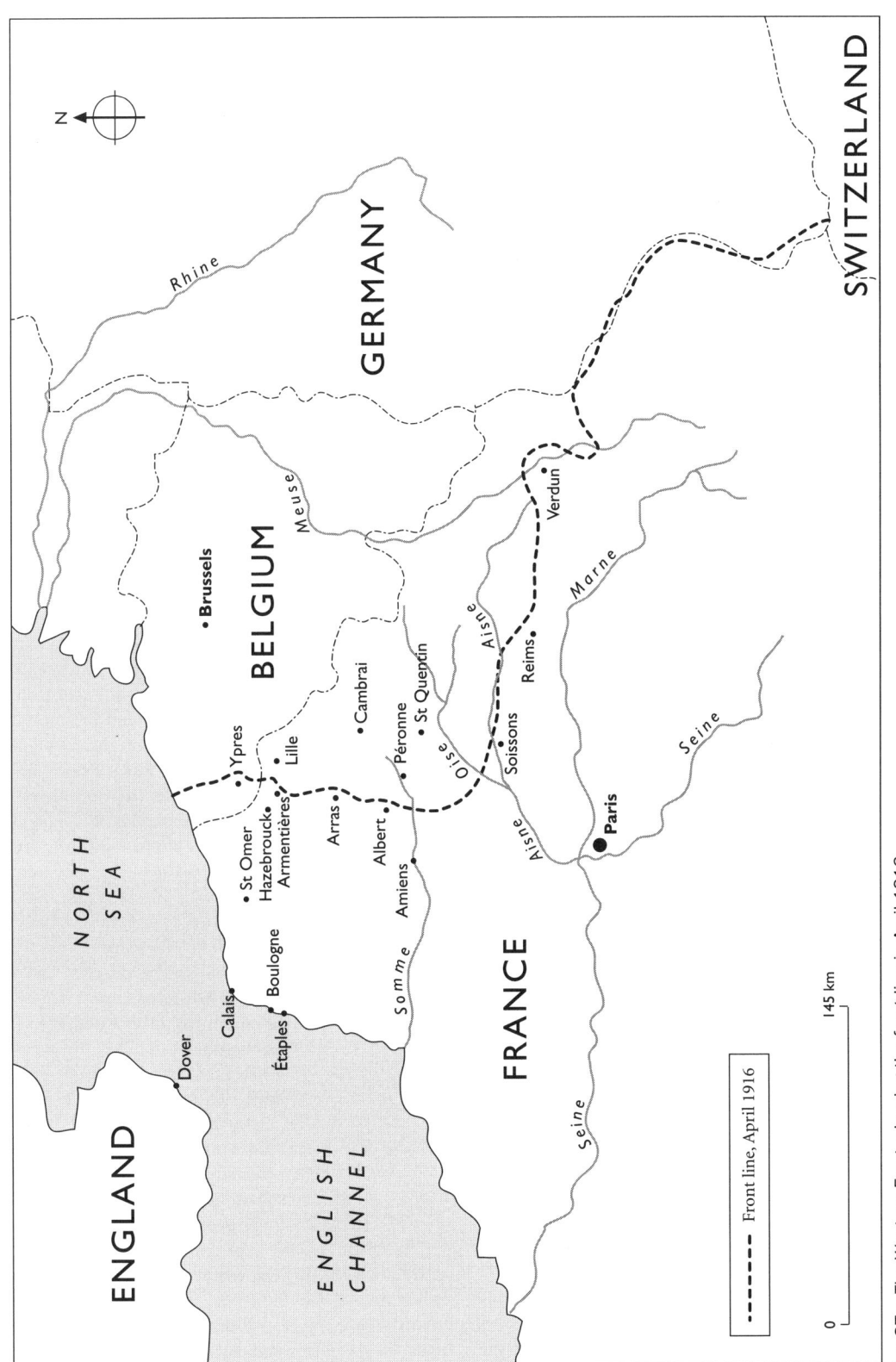

Map 27a The Western Front, showing the front line in April 1916

Western Front

fallen back to the Soissons–Rheims area. There now occurred a 'race for the sea', as both sides sought unsuccessfully to outflank each other. German attempts to capture the town of Ypres in November 1914 failed, and the Ypres salient that was formed would become one of the most hotly contested parts of the front during the next four years. As the troops entrenched themselves, a state of siege developed along a line stretching about 750 kilometres from the English Channel to Switzerland. At its northernmost extremity, the Belgian Army held a twenty-five kilometre sector. The British Expeditionary Force was responsible for that part of the line running from the Ypres salient to the River Somme, about 135 kilometres long; as reinforcements became available, including contingents from the Dominions, it would grow in size to five armies of about fifty-nine divisions—nearly 1.5 million men—by the end of 1916. The French Army held the rest of the line, a much longer extent but less densely manned, especially between Verdun and Switzerland.

The initial period of open warfare had demonstrated the killing power of the defence. The increased firepower made possible by machine-guns, supplemented by rifle fire and artillery, took a terrible toll of close-packed troops advancing in the open. The propensity of commanders on both sides towards offensive action and frontal attacks heightened the effect. Behind entrenchments—either dug below ground or, in the marshy north, breastworks or a mixture of both—the defender had the advantage, as was repeatedly demonstrated during 1915, as both sides made unsuccessful attempts to breach the opposing line. The two sides developed complex trench systems. That in the British sector generally consisted of three parallel trench lines—front, support and reserve. In the front line, about twenty metres apart, there would be a fire trench and a command trench, the former broken by buttresses to prevent enfilade fire and reduce the scope of shell blast. In front, a belt of barbed wire up to ten metres wide channelled and slowed enemy attacks. About sixty to ninety metres behind, connected by communication trenches, lay the support trench, usually also protected by wire. The reserve trench was about 350–550 metres further back, also connected by communications trenches. All three lines would be covered by strongpoints armed with machine-guns and mortars. Facing them across a no man's land usually 90 to 350 metres wide, though sometimes much less, was a German trench system of a similar nature, except that the three lines were more widely separated.

For hundreds of thousands of men trench warfare became a daily routine of 'stand-to's', small-scale patrol action, sniping, digging, and occasional artillery and mortar bombardments. The level of violence varied depending on the sector and the inclination of the units present. In some sectors, often manned by non-elite units, live and let live arrangements tended to emerge; in these circumstances, trench warfare could be a relatively untroubled existence. In others, however, the level of violence could be great indeed, as the two sides sought to dominate no man's land and constantly to harass their opponents. Elaborately planned raids punctuated the monotony, often with heavy casualties and little result. As trench warfare techniques were refined, new weapons were introduced, and centralised control was imposed, even non-active sectors were rendered more dangerous for the troops manning them. Battalions would be rotated into the front line for a period of about eight days, resting and recuperating between times in billets beyond the reserve line or more usually committed to working parties.

Trench warfare involved a steady attrition, the rate of which could be substantial in active sectors. However, it was the periodic 'big pushes' that were the large-scale killers of men on the Western Front. Troops went 'over the top' in pursuit of the mirage of the decisive breakthrough and a return to open warfare, in which the long-contained and much-vaunted cavalry would come into its own. The answer to the tactical dilemma posed by the enemy's defensive firepower seemed at first to lie in destroying it by the use of massed artillery to pulverise enemy positions before the assault. Shortages of shells precluded full implementation of this approach in 1915, but the easing of the supply problem ensured that it was a central feature of both sides' offensives the following year. Nevertheless, however heavy the bombardments, enough defenders always survived to man the machine-guns and cut down the approaching infantrymen, who were also exposed to hostile artillery in no man's land. Breaches of the enemy lines were invariably contained by counter-attacks mounted by flanking or reserve forces—and the likelihood of such a response compelled attention to consolidation of positions gained, inhibiting the troops' ability to take advantage of opportunities for further exploitation. Even the introduction by the Germans of poison gas during their attack at the Second Battle of Ypres in April 1915 failed to break the deadlock (see CHEMICAL WEAPONS). In these circumstances, there was never any prospect of the cavalry being unleashed, and even if they had they would no doubt have been relatively easily contained by enemy machine-guns to the rear.

This then was the environment that greeted the New Zealanders on their introduction to the front line in mid May 1916 in the Armentières sector, close to the Franco-Belgian border. Over the next two-and-a-half years they would participate in some of the most deadly battles of modern history. They were involved in the First Battle of the Somme, July–October 1916; Messines, June–July 1917; the Third Battle of Ypres, July–November 1917; Polderhoek, December 1917–February 1918; stemming the German spring offensive of March–April 1918; the Battle of Amiens, August 1918; breaking the Hindenburg Line, September–October 1918; and Le Quesnoy, November 1918.

The newly formed New Zealand Division was initially part of I ANZAC Corps, in the Second Army commanded by the impressively competent General Herbert Plumer. In late June it was transferred to II ANZAC Corps, which was commanded by 1NZEF's commander, Lieutenant-General Sir Alexander ★Godley, also under Plumer. The New Zealand troops, whose divisional commander for their whole period on the Western Front was Major-General Sir Andrew ★Russell, entered the line east and south-east of Armentières on the River Lys. It was a trying time as the inexperienced division adjusted to trench warfare, particularly as the New Zealanders had to cover a front of more than thirteen kilometres. They were involved in minor operations designed to keep Germans in position during the first phase of the Somme offensive. Raids on German trenches were frequent, and were sometimes costly failures. By the time it was relieved in mid August, the division had suffered 2500 casualties, including about 400 dead.

At the time of the New Zealanders' arrival in France in 1916, the Germans had embarked on an attempt to knock the heart out of the French army. At Verdun, a place of great symbolic importance to the French, the German commander, General von Falkenhayn, had deployed huge artillery resources. But the struggle, beginning in February 1916, quickly became a disaster for Germany as well, as the artillery failed to prove decisive and casualties mounted on both sides. It was partly in order to relieve pressure on the French at Verdun, and partly to utilise the rapidly growing British forces, that a joint French–British offensive was planned in the summer of 1916. The location was to be at the junction between the British and French sectors, in the Somme region. Initially the offensive was envisaged as being mainly a French affair with British flank support, but the balance shifted as French reserves were sucked into the Verdun maelstrom. The British would attack on a thirty-kilometre front north of the Somme River with the French providing flank support. The British Commander-in-Chief, General Sir Douglas Haig, aimed for a decisive breakthrough. Driving forward to seize the Thiepval–Pozières–Ginchy ridge, the infantry of General Sir Henry Rawlinson's Fourth Army (supported by a subsidiary attack on the northern flank by General Sir Edmund Allenby's Third Army) would open the way for the cavalry to burst through the German lines towards Bapaume and roll up the German front from the south. The German defenders would be overcome by a massive artillery bombardment—despite evidence at Verdun of the futility of such tactics. The reliance on cavalry to exploit was also misplaced: given the vulnerability of this arm to machine-gun fire, its chances of fulfilling its role in the battle were slender.

The British attack on 1 July 1916, after a five-day preliminary bombardment, was a disaster. About 60,000 casualties, of whom 20,000 were dead or dying, brought no significant gains of territory, or any prospect of a breakthrough. While the subsidiary attack and the northern part of the main attack were almost complete failures, some progress was made in the southern sector. The first defence line had been captured by 15 July, and Haig decided to persist in this area. A reorganisation of the British command led to the Fourth Army concentrating on the southern sector; General Sir Hubert Gough's Reserve (later Fifth) Army, which had initially been in the rear of Fourth Army, now took over the northern sector. During the next seven weeks, the second line of German defences was penetrated by the Fourth Army, and the French, on its right flank, also had some success in pushing forward. Tempted by the illusion that German resistance was on the point of cracking, Haig therefore planned a further big push for mid September. The general concept would be the same: the Fourth Army infantry would make the breach into which the cavalry would exploit and roll up the German line.

Among those earmarked for this grand attack was the New Zealand Division, which had been in a

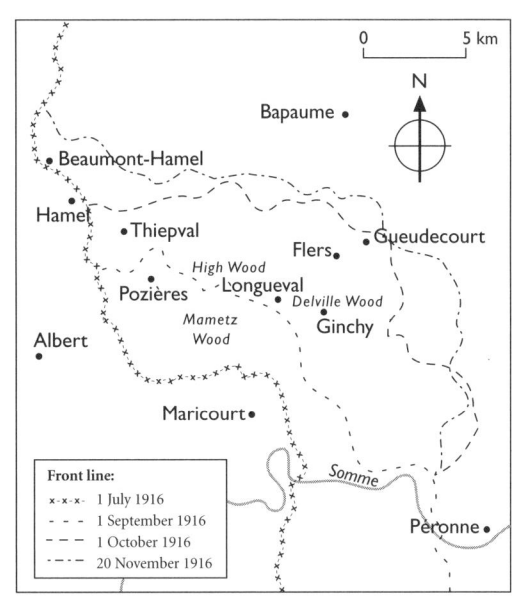

Map 27b The Somme, July–November 1916: area of operations and movement of the front line

Western Front

training area near Abbeville for a month. Now part of the Fourth Army, the New Zealanders had been practising assault tactics in preparation for their role in the coming push. The first to return to the front line were the division's field engineers and artillerymen, the latter moving into position from 5 September. The infantry followed, and the New Zealand Division took over its sector between the infamous High Wood and Delville Wood on 11 September. The objective of XV Corps, of which it was now part, was to capture the villages of Flers and Gueudecourt, an advance which would involve the seizure of three major German trench systems (the Switch Line, the Flers Line, and the Gird Line). The New Zealanders, on the left flank, had the task of capturing the trench system opposite, and establishing themselves on Grove Alley, a trench connecting the Flers and Gird systems which ran along a strip of slightly raised ground. The 2nd and 3rd (Rifle) Brigades were to make the attack with 1st Brigade in reserve.

At 6 p.m. on 14 September 1916 more than a hundred guns began pulverising the German lines opposite the New Zealanders—while others did the same right along the attack front. Against this backdrop men of the 2nd Brigade, which would lead the New Zealand advance, took up their jumping-off positions shortly before midnight. At 6.20 a.m. the advance began. In addition to their rifles, each man carried two gas helmets, two hand grenades, 220 rounds of ammunition, rations, and a shovel or pick. The New Zealanders made good progress. Within half an hour the Switch Line had been taken. The 3rd (Rifle) Brigade then came up and pushed on towards the Flers Line. While they did so, English troops on their right occupied Flers itself, though suffering heavy casualties from German shelling. The New Zealanders helped secure the village and pushed on to positions just north-west of Flers where they occupied an awkward salient. On the battlefield this day a new weapon made a portentous appearance—the tank. Although they did not arrive in time to take part in the initial attack, several intervened decisively later in the morning when part of the advance was held up (see ARMOUR). On the morning of the 16th a further assault launched by the 1st Brigade led to the capture of part of Grove Alley, but elsewhere XVth Corps was held up before Gueudecourt.

For the next twenty-three days, the New Zealanders battled on in frightful conditions, made worse by heavy rain which began in the evening of 16 September, turning the churned-up battlefield into a quagmire. In a series of vicious little clashes with bomb and bayonet, further small gains were made, positions consolidated, and German counter-attacks repelled. All the while the German guns took their toll. An improvement in weather and ground after the 19th opened the way for new British thrusts. Thrice more, on 25 September (Factory Corner–Goose Alley), 27 September (Gird Line), and 1 October (Circus Trench), the New Zealanders took part in major attacks—and each time reached their tactical objectives. But no final breakthrough had been achieved when they were relieved on 4 October 1916, by which time the spell of fine weather had broken. Allied attacks continued to be made on the Somme in atrocious conditions throughout October, and New Zealand gunners were actively engaged until 25 October, when they, too, were withdrawn. In fifty-two days they had fired half a million shells at the Germans.

In little more than three weeks' fighting, 7000 men of the New Zealand Division had become casualties—a rate far exceeding that suffered at ★Gallipoli. More than 1500 men had been killed. The battle petered out in mid November, with the Allies still far short of achieving a decisive victory. The British had suffered 400,000 casualties and the French nearly 200,000. The Germans probably lost more than half a million men during the 141 days of the Somme battle. Apart from the general attrition caused by Allied bombardments, the German tactics contributed to the scale of the casualties. In particular, the German practice of packing the forward trenches with troops ensured a high toll among the German infantry. The great bloodletting on the Somme, coming on top of that at Verdun earlier in the year, severely weakened the German armies, with important long-term consequences. In the meantime, the German high command sought to improve their exhausted troops' capacity to face a renewed Allied offensive in the spring by shortening their line. In February 1917 the Germans relinquished the Somme ground they had fought so tenaciously to defend, pulling back about thirty kilometres along a 100-kilometre front to positions that became known as the Hindenburg Line.

Following its withdrawal from the Somme, the New Zealand Division had rejoined II ANZAC Corps. On 13 October its units began occupying positions in the Sailly sector, on the right of the Second Army. But 2nd Brigade was detached to the Armentières sector until December 1916. During the winter months operations were confined to trench raids. These continued until the division was relieved in February 1917. It then moved north into Belgium, establishing its headquarters at Steenwerck. This proved to be only a temporary sojourn, for in March it moved further north. The New Zealanders deployed in the Messines sector, south of Ypres.

Far from standing on the defensive in 1917, Haig conceived a new offensive. He had long hoped to capture the ridges overlooking Ypres with a view to taking the important rail junction at Roulers and sweeping north to seize the Belgian coast and neutralise the U-boat pens there. However, these plans had to be deferred in light of the offensive strategy agreed by the British and French governments in December 1916. The new French Commander-in-Chief, General Nivelle, planned a major offensive by his armies in Champagne. This would be launched once a British attack at Arras by the Third Army on 9 April 1917, supported by the flanking First and Fifth Armies, had drawn German reserves northwards. The British initial objective—the capture of the Vimy Ridge—was successfully achieved, and pressure was maintained in accordance with the Anglo-French plan. However, when the four French armies launched their assault on 16 April, the German machine-gunners prevented any decisive breakthrough, and the French gains were confined to a small area north of the River Aisne. Although the New Zealand Division played no part in the British offensive, there was some New Zealand involvement in these operations in the form of a detachment of New Zealand pioneers and the New Zealand Tunnelling Company, which contributed to the preliminary mining operations at Arras. (See MINING OPERATIONS IN THE FIRST WORLD WAR)

With the collapse of the Nivelle offensive, Haig refocused his attention on the Ypres operation. As a preparatory step, the whole of the nearly ten-kilometre-long Messines Ridge from St Yves in the south to its junction with the salient beyond Wytschaete was to be seized, not only to secure the flank of the Ypres offensive but also to remove a German vantage point from which the preparations further north could be observed. This was to be a 'bite and hold' operation—in short, no breakout was envisaged. It was to be mounted by three corps of General Plumer's Second Army. Preparations for the attack had been going on for months, for example by the construction of railways but more especially in a vigorous mining programme. Shafts had been dug deep under the German lines and had been filled with high explosive. Troops for the assault were thoroughly trained and rested. From 21 May, the ridge had been subjected to a steadily increasing artillery bombardment. In II ANZAC Corps's sector the New Zealand Division would attack between the 3rd Australian Division and the 25th Division; its role would include the storming of the heavily fortified village of Messines itself. The final objective, the Oosttaverne Line, which lay approximately 1.5 kilometres beyond the crest, would be captured by the 4th Australian Division, pushing through the New Zealanders and 25th Division.

The attack, beginning at 3.10 a.m. on 7 June 1917, was a complete success. The explosion of the three huge mines killed many of the defenders and left the survivors dazed. Meanwhile the British artillery had so effectively disrupted its German counterpart that it

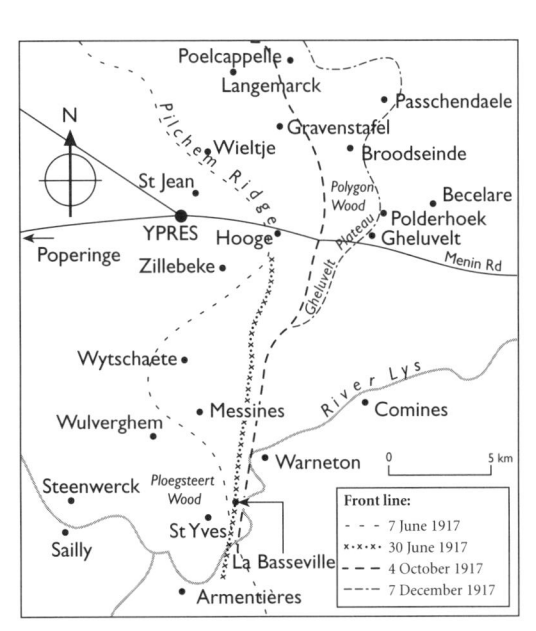

Map 27c Flanders, 1917: area of operations and movement of the front line

was ten minutes before a weak German barrage fell in no man's land. By that time, the New Zealand 2nd and 3rd (Rifle) Brigades were already across, following closely behind a meticulously planned sequence of standing and creeping barrages. The timetable was maintained, with 1st Brigade taking over and pushing beyond Messines, which was cleared by 7 a.m. The troops consolidated, as planned, just beyond the village, and at about 1.45 p.m. repulsed a German counter-attack, which crumpled under concentrated machine-gun and artillery fire. At 3.10 p.m. the 4th Australian Division launched their attack on the Oosttaverne Line; overcoming considerable resistance, the Australians had secured their final objective early the following morning. The New Zealand infantrymen, exposed on the ridge to German artillery fire, were withdrawn into reserve on the morning of the 9th, leaving their artillery to continue engaging the enemy. The attack had been a model of careful staff planning, effective preparation, and infantry–artillery coordination (though there were tragic slips, with the Australians in particular losing many men to ★friendly fire). But even successful battles were costly on the Western Front. Although light at first, the New Zealand Division's losses had risen steadily as German artillery began to shell the captured area. In all there were 3700 casualties, of whom 700 were killed. The two Australian divisions involved lost 6800 men between them. On 12 June 1917 the New Zealand Division was back in the line, pushing German outposts back to La Basseville, three kilometres south-east of

Western Front

Messines, before being relieved at the end of June. The New Zealanders were deployed back to the sector in mid July 1917, taking part in operations designed to distract the Germans from the main offensive blow further north at Ypres. As part of a feinted crossing of the River Lys, they captured La Basseville on 27 July, lost it to a counter-attack, but retook it in a renewed assault on 31 July in support of the general offensive launched that day. The division thereafter consolidated its position, in atrocious weather which reduced the trenches to a muddy swamp. The men endured miserable conditions until relieved in the latter part of August. The 3rd (Rifle) Brigade, however, remained in the Ypres salient under the command of the Second Army, engaged on digging communications.

The Third Battle of Ypres opened on 31 July with Passchendaele Ridge as the Allies' initial objective. The seven-week delay after the Messines success had allowed the Germans to strengthen their positions in the salient. In particular, they had changed their defensive tactics. To minimise the crushing weight of the British artillery the front line was now held only lightly, but the defences were constructed in great depth. They were studded with concrete 'pillboxes' and featured wide belts of barbed wire. Responsibility for the campaign fell to the Fifth Army, whose commander, General Gough, had performed poorly during the operations in April. Although the Pilckem Ridge was captured immediately, the British troops could make no headway against the commanding Gheluvelt–Passchendaele plateau. On 1 August 1917 the weather broke, and the battlefield was rapidly transformed into a morass through which the troops moved with great difficulty. The gunners were hampered in fulfilling their support role by the low cloud. Despite these adverse conditions, Gough persisted. A new attempt was made on the Gheluvelt plateau on 10 August, with disastrous results. Six days later the British troops struggled forward in a more extensive attack, but this effort too had petered out by the 24th.

Settling for more deliberate limited attacks, Haig now relegated the Fifth Army to a secondary role of flank protection, and charged Plumer's Second Army with assaulting the Gheluvelt–Passchendaele plateau. But there was a delay while better weather was awaited and preparations were completed. Not until 20 September did the Second Army attack. Plumer's approach was to apply the limited 'bite and hold' methods which had worked so effectively at Messines. The plateau would be taken by a series of short steps, the infantry advancing behind massive artillery concentrations. After each leap forward, the positions would be consolidated against the inevitable German counter-attacks. These tactics seemed to work, with the first attack on the Menin Road gaining about 1400 metres. A second attack, at Polygon Wood on 26 September, had similar results.

This was the situation that confronted Godley's II ANZAC Corps on its return to the line at the end of September 1917. After a month in the Second Army training area at Lumbres, west of St Omer, the New Zealand Division moved north and took over command of the St Jean sector on 1 October. It was earmarked to take part in Plumer's third attack, on 4 October: I ANZAC Corps would seize the heights at Broodseinde while II ANZAC Corps advanced on its left to provide flanking cover. For the New Zealanders, this would entail capturing Gravenstafel Spur, the first of two spurs from the main ridge at Passchendaele (the other was Bellevue Spur). The area was devastated and muddy, which made it unsuitable for tanks, but the attack was nonetheless successful. The British bombardment, beginning at 6 a.m., caught many Germans in the forward trenches (as a result of a change of tactics) and inflicted heavy casualties; the number of dead in the German positions encouraged the belief in the British high command that German resistance was on the point of cracking. Once they had secured their objective, the New Zealanders fell to consolidating their positions, having gained 1000 metres and taken more than a thousand prisoners. Heavy rain began to fall late on the 4th, and this exacerbated the problem posed by the destruction of the water courses in the area as a result of the constant shelling. The battlefield became a waterlogged bog. 'The mud is a worse enemy than the German,' Russell complained on 4 October.

By this time it was apparent that the strategic gains envisaged in the Ypres operation were not achievable. Far from sweeping to the coast, the British troops were still mired in the Ypres salient. Nevertheless Haig was determined to continue the assault, convinced that 'the enemy is tottering'. A new blow was planned for the two British divisions of II ANZAC Corps, on Bellevue Spur, on 9 October, to be followed by the Australians and New Zealanders taking Passchendaele on the 12th. The basis of the previously successful 'bite and hold' tactics, careful preparation and overwhelming artillery support, could not be ensured because of the short warning time and the state of the terrain. The attack on 9 October by the two British divisions was a dismal failure. Seemingly unaware of the scale of the defeat—Godley showed little disposition to ascertain at first hand the conditions in which his divisions were struggling—Haig and Plumer remained convinced they were on the verge of a breakthrough. It fell to the New Zealanders and the 3rd Australian Division to make the Second Army's next attack, while the Fifth Army launched an assault to the north. The aim would be to capture Bellevue Spur and then Passchendaele village and the ground to its north—an advance of more than

2500 metres. But once again there was insufficient time to prepare properly for the attack—or even to deal with wounded from the failed attack on the 9th, many of whom were still lying in no man's land. Conditions were awful as the men of the 2nd Brigade and 3rd (Rifle) Brigade (only recently returned to the division after six weeks of digging) prepared for the assault.

The attack, which began at 5.25 a.m. on the 12th in drizzle, was a fiasco. Because of the condition of the battlefield, the supporting artillery was not as heavy as intended. It was so muddy that many guns could not get into position, and the unstable platforms from which those that did were forced to fire affected their accuracy. In consequence the New Zealand infantrymen moved off behind a barrage that was weak and ragged, with some of the shells dropping short among them. The mud hampered their advance, and it was made worse by driving rain which set in at 6 a.m. The enemy, with an effective machine-gun barrage supported by enfilading fire, took a heavy toll of the New Zealanders, who were dismayed to find the enemy's wire still intact. Under heavy fire from German pillboxes out of reach on the other side of this impenetrable barrier, they were forced to go to ground, digging in or sheltering in shell craters from the devastating fire. Meanwhile some progress had been made on both flanks, with the Australians pushing forward about 300 metres. The New Zealanders were ordered, therefore, to renew their attack at 3 p.m., albeit with a more limited objective. Although the officers on the spot urged cancellation, these calls were at first disregarded. However, the attack was eventually postponed. The situation on the flanks had deteriorated, with the Australians held up by enfilading fire from Bellevue Spur. In the evening the men of the two divisions consolidated, but only after being withdrawn to positions not far forward of the start lines of their attack. An informal truce allowed the wounded to be evacuated, eight men being needed to carry a stretcher through the morass. Bellevue Spur was the one failure on a large scale of the New Zealand Division. More than 1500 men of 2nd Brigade had become casualties, and 1200 of 3rd Brigade. About 45 officers and 800 men lay dead or dying. In terms of lives lost on a single day, it was the greatest disaster in New Zealand history. In retrospect, the corps commander, General Godley, has borne much of the blame for this catastrophe. But this attributes to Godley more freedom of action than was available to him at the time as the commander of a corps in an operation that involved two armies. Haig and Plumer ultimately bore responsibility for the attack on 12 October 1917. Misled by the number of German casualties, they believed that the 2nd Army was on the point of a decisive breakthrough at Passchendaele in early October, and that it was foiled only by the inclement weather. But such conclusions seem unjustified: though forced back at Broodseinde, the Germans had lost none of their artillery, and had indeed brought up more pieces. They retained the capacity to resist strongly any further Allied advance, whatever the conditions, and to contain any breakthrough. At the divisional level, Russell's performance had been less than perfect; the unease of his artillery commander, Brigadier-General G.N. ★Johnston, on the eve of the attack had not induced him to check the arrangements, to his subsequent chagrin.

The Canadian Corps relieved II ANZAC Corps on 18 October, and the New Zealand Division pulled out during the next few days. It was left to the Canadians to take the Goldberg Spur by 6 November and to capture the ruins of Passchendaele, an operation which no longer had any strategic purpose. After one further attack on 10 November 1917, the offensive was closed down, having cost the Allies 100,000 casualties from 20 September. The Third Battle of Ypres had achieved no more than limited advances, and the ground was to be quickly retaken by the Germans in April 1918. In its wider aims it had been a complete failure, relieved only by the fact that German losses had also been heavy. Allied expectations were briefly raised by a successful push by the Third Army at Cambrai on 20 November, using massed tanks for the first time. However, a German counter-attack ten days later nullified the gains. With this last flurry, the exhausted troops on both sides lapsed into inactivity.

The New Zealand Division wintered in the Ypres salient in positions south of Passchendaele. An attack on Polderhoek on 3 December gained some ground, though not the objective, at considerable cost in lives. The already dispirited New Zealanders found the miserable winter conditions very trying, and their morale suffered. By the time they were relieved in late February 1918, they had lost another 3000 men, of whom nearly 500 had been killed. They went into reserve near Staple, west of Hazebrouck. On 1 January 1918 II ANZAC Corps was redesignated XXII Corps. (The end of the ANZAC connection had been dictated by the formation of the Australian Corps.) During January, there was a significant change to the structure of the New Zealand Division: the 4th Brigade was disbanded, and its men distributed within the other brigades or formed into three entrenching battalions. Unlike the British divisions at this time, which were reduced to nine battalions each because of manpower shortages, the New Zealand Division retained its twelve-battalion structure. This was made possible by the introduction of ★conscription in August 1916, which ensured a steady flow of reinforcements to the front.

Notwithstanding the disasters at Ypres, 1917 had been characterised by the increasing professionalism

Western Front

of the British forces, as they sought means of overcoming the tactical problems presented by the stalemated battlefield. Attacks were carefully planned, with an increase in both the quantity of the Allied artillery and the sophistication of its use. The creeping barrage, developed during the Somme battles of the previous year, came of age. It provided a curtain of fire in front of the advancing troops, moving forward according to a carefully timed fire plan. There was a shift of emphasis from destruction to neutralisation, the aim being to suppress enemy artillery fire. New techniques were developed for locating enemy guns, including a system known as 'sound ranging', which was based on comparing the time taken by the percussion of a gun report to reach carefully spaced detectors. Enemy batteries could be targeted for engagement at the decisive moment when the attack began. The use of aircraft as artillery spotters became more important (which placed a premium on air superiority over the front lines). Surprise was now sought by concealing the massing of artillery at the point of attack. The tank had also emerged as an effective weapon, as its reliability increased with technological development and it became available in increasing numbers. Finally, infantry tactics were also refined, to allow more flexibility during the advance. The 'waves' of advancing infantry were replaced by 'worms' of platoons and sections working their way forward with grenades, mortars, and light machine-guns. Similarly, defensive tactics emphasised an elastic defence of machine-gun posts and counter-attacks instead of trench lines. Above all, the expansion of British munitions production had now reached a stage where the weapons of trench warfare, such as machine-guns, trench mortars, and rifle grenades, were in lavish supply in comparison with those available in 1915.

Although the tactical developments of 1917 were of fundamental importance in restoring the mobility of the Allied armies, they were overshadowed early in 1918 by changes in the strategic outlook consequent on Russia's collapse. Following the Bolshevik coup in November 1917, Russia sued for an armistice and, on 3 March 1918, made peace with Germany by signing the Treaty of Brest–Litovsk. A huge accretion of strength was, as a result, available for the German armies on the Western Front, and redeployment was soon underway. To be sure, the entry to the war of the United States on the Allied side in April 1917 was a counterbalancing factor, but the arrival of American troops in France would take time to make an impact. (Because of the American insistence that their forces fight as a contingent, this would not in fact occur until September 1918.) By mid March there were forty-six fresh German divisions on the front. The German high command planned to use this new-found offensive capacity to split the British and French armies. As part of Operation Michael, as their planned offensive was titled, they would roll the British back to the coast and then deal with the French.

The prospects for this plan were enhanced by developments on the Allied side of the line. During 1917 the French Army's capacity for resistance had been undermined by a series of mutinies, and in October Haig had agreed to extend the British-held section of the line southwards to provide some relief to the beleaguered French command. Coming on top of the huge losses sustained at Ypres—the equivalent of fifteen divisions—the British found it difficult to meet this new commitment with the resources available. With Haig unwilling to weaken the forces deployed in the vital northern sector, which covered the BEF's lines of communication to Great Britain, the Fifth Army, the southernmost formation of the British front, found itself thinly stretched in its sector, with inadequate defences and few reserves. It was this sector that would bear the brunt of the German offensive.

On 21 March 1918, about sixty German divisions drove forward on a front of eighty kilometres. The Fifth Army was soon in trouble, with the Germans opening a gap between it and the Third Army, which they vigorously exploited. So great was the alarm engendered by this crisis among the Allies that they at last agreed to the appointment of a supreme commander—Marshal Foch assumed the post on 26 March 1918. The most urgent requirement was to close the yawning gap in the British line, and the New Zealand Division was among the forces hastily deployed to the Somme. It was available for this purpose because it had been out of the line for some weeks, recovering from its winter exertions and engaged in a vigorous training programme. Now part of the Third Army, it was ordered to form a line between Hébuterne and Hamel, where a critical gap of seven kilometres had opened in the British line. The New Zealanders began their move on the 24th, proceeding initially by train, then by forced marches. Contact with the enemy was made east of Mailly–Maillet, and the New Zealanders took up positions on the line held by the British before the Battle of the Somme the previous year. In often-confused fighting, they managed to stabilise the line in this area, while British and Australian infantry did the same on their flanks. On 5 April 1918 ten German divisions were thrown in between Bucquoy and Albert in an attempt to open the road to Amiens. An intense three-hour bombardment preceded the attack on the New Zealand Division's front, but the Germans made no progress. During this period more than 500 New Zealanders were killed and 1800 wounded.

The Germans now sought gains further north. On 9 April 1918 a new offensive, Operation Georgette, was

Western Front

launched on the Lys. New Zealanders were involved here too—artillery as well as XXII Corps troops. New Zealand mounted, cyclist, and entrenching troops found themselves in desperate combat as they were thrown in to close threatening gaps. In fighting at Meteren on 16 April 210 men from the 2nd Entrenching Battalion were cut off and taken prisoner, the largest number of New Zealanders captured in the First World War. Operation Georgette made about fifteen kilometres before being halted at the end of April. A further attack on the Aisne at the end of May netted another forty kilometres, but the strategic aims of the offensive were clearly beyond Germany's grasp. German gains since March had come at a terrible price—casualties exceeded 400,000, units were running short of supplies, and for the first time morale showed signs of collapse, while every advance only stretched dwindling German resources further. The situation was made worse by the outbreak of the *influenza pandemic in both German and Allied armies in June.

The Allies launched a counterstroke on 18 July with a successful attack on the Marne. For this operation, XXII Corps with four divisions was made available, and these British troops went to action in the Ardre Valley on the 19th. In this fighting New Zealand mounted troops and cyclist battalion again took part. Meanwhile the New Zealand Division had been relieved on 7 June, not returning to the line until the beginning of July. During the rest of the month the New Zealanders sought to improve the tactical position in their sector, including the elimination of the dangerous Rossignol Wood salient.

On 8 August 1918 an attack by the Canadian and Australian Corps of the Fourth Army at Amiens was described by the German commander Ludendorff as the 'blackest day of the war'. The German armies were now clearly on the defensive, and the Allied commanders determined to maintain the pressure by a series of blows. Rather than persisting in the Amiens area against reinforced and protected troops, Haig shifted the focus northwards. On 21 August IV Corps (which now included the New Zealand Division) and VI Corps of Third Army attacked on a fifteen-kilometre front. Every effort was made to ensure surprise, and the attack was successful. Grévillers was captured by the New Zealanders after another attack on 24 August, as the enemy were driven from one side of the old Somme battlefield to the other. Following a German

Troops have a meal within 200 metres of the enemy at La Signy Farm on 6 June 1918 (*RSA Collection, Alexander Turnbull Library, G-13087-1/2*)

Western Front

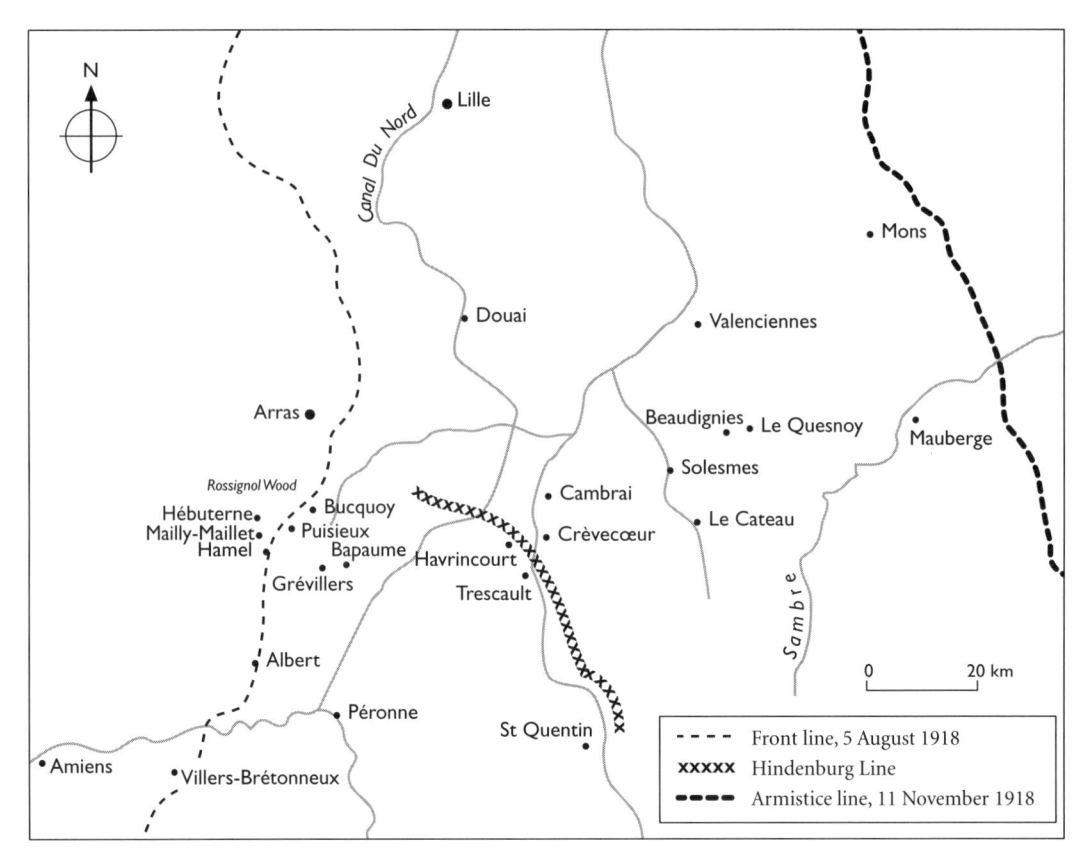

Map 27d Amiens–Arras sector, 1918: area of operations and movement of the front line

withdrawal to the Hindenburg Line, Bapaume was finally occupied by New Zealand troops on 29 August. As IV Corps followed up the German retreat, the New Zealand Division mopped up a succession of rearguards and drove the Germans off Trescault Spur after stubborn resistance. On 15 September the division was withdrawn to the Bapaume area to regroup.

By 18 September the Third and Fourth Armies had pushed up to the Hindenburg Line, a formidable fortified system 1.3 kilometres deep. The New Zealanders, still part of IV Corps, were held in reserve when the British offensive against the Hindenburg Line was launched on 27 September 1918. Not till the 29th were they committed, with 1st and 2nd Brigades both making good progress to reach the Scheldt Canal. On 1 October a fresh assault by the 1st Brigade captured Crèvecoeur on the eastern bank of the canal. By the 3rd the Fourth Army had completed the breach of the Hindenburg Line, and the German defences facing the Third Army had been turned. A German withdrawal from the Hindenburg Line was soon in evidence.

The Third and Fourth Armies lost no time in launching a new attack on 8 October. The New Zealand Division attacked eastwards from Crèvecoeur and easily secured their objective against faltering opposition. The advance continued in the following days in a series of bounds to the River Selle. The New Zealanders were relieved on the 12th after an advance of eighteen kilometres in which they had taken 1400 prisoners. Overall, the British attack had been a great success: Le Cateau and Cambrai were in British hands, along with 12,000 prisoners. However the French–American thrust had not made sufficient progress to achieve the objective of decisively defeating the Germans. An attack in Flanders now forced the Germans back in that sector as well, forcing their withdrawal from Lille and the Belgian coast. The Third Army launched its next attack on 20 October 1918, and the New Zealand infantrymen entered the fray on the 23rd. Steady progress was made in the next four days, before the attack lost its impetus against stiffening resistance in front of the historic fortified town of Le Quesnoy.

By the beginning of November, the situation confronting Germany was disastrous. Her ally, the Ottoman Empire, had sued for an armistice on 30 October 1918, and Austria–Hungary would do the same on 3 November. Her armies on the Western Front were now being forced back almost at will by the

Western Front

New Zealand and British infantrymen moving forward with Mark V tanks near Grévillers on 26 August 1918. In the background they pass captured German 4.2 inch guns (*Imperial War Museum, Q11262*)

Allies. A new blow was not long in coming, as the British sought to cut off the main avenue of escape for the German forces facing the French and Americans. A new major attack was launched on a fifty-kilometre front on 4 November by the Fourth, Third, and First Armies. During this final phase, the New Zealanders distinguished themselves by outflanking, and then capturing, Le Quesnoy, the ramparts of which were scaled in ancient fashion using ladders. On that day alone, 4 November, they advanced ten kilometres, and captured nearly 2000 prisoners and sixty field guns— in material terms, the New Zealand Division's most successful day of the whole Western Front campaign. The Allied attack finally broke the German resistance, and complete confusion was apparent as they hastily retreated.

The fighting was brought to an end with the conclusion of an armistice (in effect a German surrender), which came into effect at 11 a.m. on 11 November 1918. As the official history of the division later recorded, the news was received 'in a matter of fact way, totally devoid of any demonstration of emotion'. As part of the British occupation force, the New Zealanders marched through Belgium in December, and crossed the frontier into Germany on the 20th, with 1st Battalion, Canterbury Regiment, leading the way. The units were quartered in the various suburbs of Cologne, where they remained until concentrated at Mülheim as demobilisation proceeded. The division was finally disbanded on 25 March 1919.

The ★New Zealand Expeditionary Force's thirty-month campaign on the Western Front took the lives of 12,483 New Zealanders, and maimed thousands of others, both physically and mentally. It became, in the public mind, the epitome of military futility, a battlefield on which men struggled to survive in a hellish landscape of muddy shell holes and flooded trenches, and were sacrificed at regular intervals in pointless attacks ordered by incompetent generals safely ensconced in comfortable chateaux behind the lines. For most soldiers the experience of the Western Front was of long periods of frustrated boredom. Freezing temperatures in winter, persistent rain in autumn, and heat in summer were bad enough without the attentions of the enemy's artillery, snipers, trench mortars, and machine-guns. The prospect of random death added to the mental stress of everyday life in the trenches for the New Zealanders, as for the other troops who manned the lines on both sides. They were also sacrificed in often ill-conceived attacks in pursuit of the chimera of a strategic breakthrough, as on the Somme and at Passchendaele. Some of the generals who controlled their fate had difficulty grasping the essential reality of the battlefield: that the defensive power of artillery and machine-guns for the time being dominated and that new tactics were needed to restore offensive capability.

The New Zealand Division was recognised by the Germans as one of the elite formations in the British Expeditionary Force. That its members performed well in such a difficult environment owed much to both the quality and the quantity of its manpower. Its troops were resourceful, determined, and conspicuously reluctant to adopt live and let live tactics. On the contrary, they set out to dominate their opponents, by vigorous implementation of trench warfare techniques. This offensive predilection was also evident in the setpiece attacks, with New Zealand units readily adapting to new tactical requirements. With adequate artillery and machine-gun support, they were generally able to achieve their objectives, though casualties were invariably high. They excelled in the open fighting of the last few months of the war. As the war progressed, the New Zealand Division benefited from the regular supply of fresh reinforcements which was ensured by the introduction of conscription in August 1916. By 1918 many of the British divisions had been depleted, and those that remained in the ranks were exhausted. Because Australia had not introduced conscription, the Australian divisions were faced with increasing manpower shortages. The New Zealand Division emerged as one of the strongest divisions on the front during 1918.

H. Stewart, *The New Zealand Division 1916–1919* (Whitcombe & Tombs, Auckland, 1921).

Whaanga, Ihaka (?–14 December 1875) was an important ★kupapa leader during the ★New Zealand Wars. A Ngati Kahungunu from Mahia, he probably fought in the ★Musket Wars campaigns between Nga Puhi, Ngati Kahungunu, and invading tribes of the 1820s. By the 1840s he was known as a patron of Pakeha trade and settlement. He opposed the spread of Pai Marire, for which he received government support, including arms. In December 1865 he participated in driving Pai Marire from Wairoa, and a month later led a contingent of Ngati Kahungunu inland. At Te Kopane on 13 January 1866 his men were ambushed and he was wounded, but Ropata ★Wahawaha and his Ngati Porou kupapa counter-attacked, driving the Hauhau back. In September Hauhau established a pa near Napier at Omarunui. Whaanga and his men marched to Napier, and with the Pakeha forces of Lieutenant-Colonel G.S. ★Whitmore stormed the pa on 12 October 1866. In 1868 Whaanga led troops in the pursuit of ★Te Kooti to Makaretu and on to Ngatapa. In April 1869 he rushed south to Mohaka following Te Kooti's attack there and tried to raise the rebel's siege of Hiruharama. For his loyalty he was awarded a sword of honour by the government in 1872.

Whitmore, Major-General Sir George Stoddart (30 May 1829–16 March 1903) was perhaps both the most able and the least-loved Pakeha commander of the ★New Zealand Wars. That he 'never encumbered his mind with considerations for his men' was one of the mildest accusations levelled at him; J.C. Richmond described him as 'a capital fellow full of energy … impaired in his usefulness by incurable and extreme egotism'. Born at Malta into a military family, and educated in Edinburgh, Whitmore was commissioned in the Cape Mounted Rifles in 1847. He participated in two Kaffir Wars as well as action against the Boers in the ensuing six years. After returning to England, he was awarded a captaincy in the 62nd (Wiltshire) Regiment of Foot, with which he served in the ★Crimean War. Having graduated first in his year from the staff college at Aldershot in 1860, he was appointed Military Secretary to Lieutenant-General Duncan ★Cameron.

Finding on arrival in New Zealand that the Taranaki War was over, he resigned and acquired a sheep run at Rissington near Napier. He commanded the Napier Militia from May 1863, and in October 1866 defeated a Hauhau force at Omarunui. Meanwhile he had voluntarily reattached himself to Cameron's staff during the Waikato War of 1863–64. Early in 1868 he was appointed Commandant of the New Zealand Constabulary Force. By the end of the year he was leading mostly inexperienced troops in two separate campaigns between which he switched his forces by steamship. After pursuing ★Te Kooti and his followers inland from Poverty Bay that winter, he assumed command against ★Titokowaru on the west coast in October in time to quell a mutiny and then lose the Battle of Moturoa on 7 November. Following the 'Matawhero massacre' three days later, he rushed his best troops back to Poverty Bay, where he decisively defeated Te Kooti at Ngatapa. Returning to Wanganui in January 1869, he led 2000 men against Titokowaru at Tauranga-ika, which was abandoned before a decisive battle could occur. After a ruthless pursuit of Titokowaru's followers through inland Taranaki, he embarked for Tauranga and invaded the 'inaccessible … forests and inhospitable wilds' of the Urewera in pursuit of Te Kooti in May. Insensitive by nature, difficult to deal with, and elitist in outlook, he was nevertheless a capable military administrator who overcame logistical problems to mount effective campaigns in the two areas of conflict, albeit without securing the final defeat in battle of either adversary.

Relieved of his post by Donald *McLean in July 1869, he was made a CMG (and advanced to KCMG in 1882). He returned to farming and the Legislative Council, to which he had been appointed in 1863, becoming Colonial Secretary and Commissioner of the *Armed Constabulary in Sir George *Grey's 1877–79 ministry. In 1885, the last of the major *Russian scares led to his being promoted to the rank of major-general and given command of New Zealand's forces. He was also appointed Under-Secretary for Defence. During the next three years, he oversaw the development of the forces to man the new defences being constructed at the main ports. He resigned from both positions in 1888. His well-written if self-serving *The Last Maori War in New Zealand under the Self-Reliant Policy* was published a year before his death at Napier.

DAVID GREEN

Wigram, Sir Henry Francis (18 January 1857–6 May 1934) was the 'father of the RNZAF'. A Londoner by birth, he emigrated to New Zealand in 1883 and became a successful Christchurch businessman and active participant in community affairs. He was mayor of Christchurch from 1902 till 1904, and became a member of the Legislative Council in 1903. His interest in flying was sparked during a visit to England in 1908. After unsuccessfully urging the government to establish a flying school, he created one of his own—the Canterbury (NZ) Aviation Company—at Sockburn, Christchurch, in 1916. Three biplanes were acquired, and by February 1919 182 pilots had been trained by his company. The flying school was kept going after the war through Wigram's financial support until 1923, when the government finally took over the company after he had offered £10,000 towards the cost of buying Sockburn airfield and equipment. For his services to aviation, he was knighted in 1926. Sockburn airfield had earlier been renamed Wigram (it remained a principal RNZAF air base until 1995).

Wilkes, Group Captain Thomas Martin (24 March 1888–23 October 1958) was prominent in the development of the New Zealand air force. He was born at Thames, and became a regular soldier when he was commissioned in the *New Zealand Staff Corps in 1911. Seconded to 1NZEF, he commanded a company of the 3rd New Zealand (Rifle) Brigade in 1915; from 1916 he was staff captain of the 2nd Brigade on the *Western Front. In September 1917 he transferred to the RFC, and won an MC as an airman. Back in New Zealand, he took part in the *Fiji Expeditionary Force and became General Staff Officer for Air Services in 1920, in which capacity he also served as secretary of the short-lived Air Board. Five years later he was appointed as Director of Air Services, a position he occupied for twelve years interrupted only by a period as liaison officer at the Air Ministry in London. In 1935 he prepared an important report on air defence requirements, which took account of the possibility of delays in the implementation of the *Singapore strategy. His recommendations were useful to Group Captain R.A. *Cochrane when he arrived in the following year to report on air defences; indeed Cochrane's conclusions were not dissimilar to his own. From 1937 he was Controller of Civil Aviation. He took part in the *Pacific Defence Conference in 1939, and during the *Second World War was New Zealand's liaison officer in Melbourne. He retired after his return to New Zealand in 1946.

Williams, General Sir Guy (10 September 1881–2 February 1959) was born in India into an English military family. After graduating from the Royal Military Academy, Woolwich, he was commissioned in the Royal Engineers in 1900. During the *First World War he served on the *Western Front as an engineer and later tunnelling company commander. He was CRE of 66th Division in 1917–18, and commanded 199th Brigade in the last seven months of the war. He spent the first eighteen months of the *Second World War as GOC-in-Chief of Eastern Command in England before being appointed as military adviser to the New Zealand government. Arriving in New Zealand in June 1941, he made a close inspection of camps and defences before presenting a report, 'Appreciation of the Defence Requirements of New Zealand in the Event of War with Japan', which became the basis of New Zealand's preparations to meet a possible Japanese invasion. It was predicated on his assumption that an invasion of New Zealand was very unlikely because of the limited resources at Japan's disposal and the length of the lines of communication that would be involved. In the worst case, in which Allied naval power had been totally defeated, he foresaw the Japanese invading Fiji and launching an attack on New Zealand by a division supported by a considerable naval force, including two aircraft-carriers. As *anti-invasion measures, he advised the establishment of *coastwatchers, the reinforcement of *Fiji, and the building-up of home defence forces. He also identified the Marlborough Sounds as a spot that the Japanese might very likely select as an invasion base, with the result that heavy artillery positions were prepared and pieces installed there after his departure from New Zealand in October 1941. He retired soon after his return to the United Kingdom.

Women and the Boer War

Women and the Boer War New Zealand women actively supported their country's participation in the ★Boer War. The war gave New Zealand women, recently enfranchised, an opportunity to move into the public arena. A small number who voiced an anti-war position were labelled as 'pro-Boer', and received little support even from groups known for their anti-military views. After Wilhelmina Sheriff Bain's pacifist speech at the National Council of Women's 1900 conference, the Executive officially distanced itself from her statements. On the home front women found numerous avenues to demonstrate their support. Mothers, sisters, wives, and sweethearts personally encouraged enlistment, and some expressed their support by publishing rousing poems, songs, and music. Spurred on by the example of Queen Victoria's knitted scarves for soldiers, women created material comforts for New Zealand soldiers ranging from biscuits and other foodstuffs to pyjama suits, socks, handkerchiefs, Crimean caps (balaclavas), and cholera belts (waistbands or cummerbunds of flannel or silk believed, incorrectly, to protect against gastrointestinal ailments by keeping away the cold and damp). Working women in woollen mills and sewing shops made their contribution by manufacturing over 10,000 new uniform items. The primary channel for women's war effort was fundraising, especially in support of the Third and Fourth Contingents. Women and girls collected donations for their local More Men Fund, decorated floats and bicycles at floral fêtes, performed items, and contributed refreshments at the numerous dances and other fundraising entertainments. Maori women participated fully in well-publicised fundraising hui at Papawai, Greytown, and at the Basin Reserve, Wellington. Women of wealth and influence were prominent in arranging galas and administering garden parties attended by thousands, such as Mrs Studholme's Merivale fête, which served strawberries and champagne to two thousand people and raised £300. One influential event was Lady Douglas's Patriotic Carnival held at Government House, which attracted five thousand and was publicised in pictorial weekly newspapers throughout the country. A special feature of this carnival was the performance by a Girls' Khaki Brigade, a specially formed group of fifty young society women (including the Premier's daughter 'Sergeant' Mary Seddon) dressed in khaki uniforms with skirts and hats, and a full range of military titles. Under instruction by officers of the Kelburne Rifles, they drilled with model rifles obtained from school cadet supplies and rode decorated bicycles. Although unofficial and temporary, similar ladies' 'Contingents' were formed in many other centres and were coached in military exercises by local Volunteer officers. These, and other less formal groups, dressed in a variety of costumes, performed at local fundraising events and concerts. Images survive of the Dannevirke Huia Khaki Contingent, the Te Awamutu Amazons, the Nga Puhi Nursing Sisters, the Greymouth Khaki Corps, of groups in Wanganui, Picton, Nelson, Temuka, and Gisborne, and of a few women with the Marsden Mounted Rifles, a ★Volunteer Force unit at Maungakaramea in North Auckland. At least one girls' school cadet group existed. One Timaru woman had her picture taken with her brother, both in full uniform (including trousers) and with rifle and bandolier.

Nursing was the only sphere in which women were allowed to participate at the seat of the war. Most of the approximately thirty nurses born or trained in New Zealand who served in South Africa made their own way there from either New Zealand or Great Britain. At first the imperial government declined offers, but later officially sponsored six nurses recruited in Christchurch. A further seven from Otago and Southland were funded from public subscriptions. Nurses were stationed at military camp hospitals, most under the control of the Imperial Army Nursing Reserve. Apart from a few who served on hospital trains which came under attack, their greatest risk was from disease and their arduous duties. A few were invalided home in the first months. A group of twenty women teachers also served in South Africa. They were recruited in response to an imperial request in January 1902 to work for one year at schools in the concentration camps housing Boer women and children. Although they did not reach South Africa until after the peace treaty had been signed, they taught until the camps were broken up, and then transferred to town or Boer farm schools. With many marrying or settling in South Africa, only a few ever returned to New Zealand.

ELLEN ELLIS

Women and the First World War When war began in 1914 and men raced to join up, the role of their mothers, wives, sisters, and girlfriends was clear. They would stay behind, 'keeping the home fires burning' and knitting and sewing and raising money to provide soldiers with both 'necessaries' and 'comforts'. They would give up their menfolk to the war, though no one imagined that it would last more than four years, take away about 100,000 men, and leave more than half of them casualties, many unable to support their families in the way they had before the war.

Most New Zealand women entered wholeheartedly into the war effort, pleased to be able to do their bit for the Empire in an age of imperialism. Thousands joined the groups which sprang up within days of the outbreak of war, many of them branches of the Lady Liverpool Women's War Fund set up by the Governor's wife or women's patriotic associations. Lady Liverpool's *Knitting Book* summed up women's role:

For Empire and for Freedom
We all must do our bit;
The men go forth to battle
The women wait—and knit.

And the women certainly knitted. In Dunedin the Otago and Southland Women's Patriotic Association commandeered the Early Settlers Hall, where women packed parcels of food and other comforts. In 1915 alone they sent 47,000 articles overseas, including 3800 balaclavas, 7400 pairs of socks, and 3400 'hussifs' or sewing kits. More than 5000 Christmas parcels were dispatched and 6000 tins of jam packed. Gift packs included two pairs of socks, eucalyptus, insect powder, licorice, a cholera belt, two pairs of bootlaces, and some soap.

Jean Burt, who played a key role in the Otago and Southland association, entered herself in the Otago Queen Carnival contest to raise money. She was Queen of the Allies, representing the builders, plumbers, and merchant firms of Dunedin, who built and raffled a two-bedroom villa in St Clair to raise funds. Such carnivals were held up and down the country and the proceeds were received in kind by the soldiers overseas. Some criticised this popular effort, arguing that the government should pay for everything. But Burt replied that women's parcels included 'the human touch, that sense of love and interest which accompanies all the things we send to our boys'.

Maori women had their own organisation. Miria Woodbine Pomare, the wife of Dr Maui Pomare, set up the Maori Soldiers' Fund with Maori women's committees throughout the country to support the soldiers of the Maori contingent. They used the money raised through sales of Maori craft work, concerts, and auctions to send 1500 parcels a month to Maori soldiers and 500 to Cook Islands soldiers. These contained letters, knitted garments, personalised taniko (ornately woven flax items), and special delicacies such as strings of dried pipi (a type of shellfish) and preserved muttonbirds. Miria Pomare was appointed an OBE for her services.

Although many women wanted to play a more active role in the war effort, they found it difficult to convince the government to let them do so. When women doctors applied to be sent overseas, they were

Women sorting donated items provided by the Lady Liverpool Women's War Fund for despatch to the troops at the front (*The Press (Christchurch) Collection, Alexander Turnbull Library, G-8352-1/1*)

Women and the First World War

turned down. Dr Agnes Bennett, rejected for the Medical Corps, got herself to Egypt, where she renewed her effort to get a commission. Following a further rebuff, she worked in an infectious diseases hospital in Cairo before going to work with the Scottish Women's Hospital in *Salonika, following the lead of Dr Jessie Scott of Christchurch.

Nurses, too, were at first told they were not wanted for overseas service. The New Zealand Trained Nurses' Association urged the Minister of Defence, Colonel James *Allen, to make use of the services of its members, six hundred of whom volunteered in the first eight months of the war. Only in April 1915 was this offer taken up. The first group of fifty New Zealand Army Nursing Service nurses left for Egypt under the leadership of Hester *MacLean.

While Great Britain had its *Voluntary Aid Detachments—in which women, often from well-off families, did voluntary nurse aid and other work—there was no such organisation in New Zealand. Ettie *Rout tried to form one in mid 1915. Her New Zealand Volunteer Sisterhood was launched during an outbreak of cerebrospinal meningitis among soldiers at Trentham Camp. Although her volunteers were used during that crisis, she won no approval for her plan to take them overseas. Her initiative sparked an outcry among trained nurses and groups like the St John Ambulance Association and the *Red Cross, which gave women first aid courses. To settle this war among women for the privilege of nursing soldiers, the Minister of Public Health, G.W. Russell, held a conference, at which he reaffirmed the status of professional nurses. A year later, however, Hester MacLean asked successfully for authority to engage women to act as assistants to nurses in military hospitals.

There were attempts to set up a Women's National Reserve to mobilise women to carry out men's jobs in order to free men for overseas service, but results were piecemeal and local. The reserve, formed in Wellington in August 1915 as a branch of the men's National Reserve and sharing the aim of performing 'any available work for King and Country', urged home-front conscription of women and established a voluntary register of women. By June 1916 it had collected 850 names of Wellington women prepared to do clerical work 'for the duration'. In Christchurch women had to pay two shillings to add their names to the list. In Auckland courses were run, including not only shorthand, typing, and business methods but also gardening, shooting, and signalling. But the reserve was more written about than used, and there was no move to official centralised manpowering.

Women did move into what had been men's jobs, but this was seen as a matter of 'keeping seats warm' for soldiers while they were away. 'Smart girls could well be taken on,' editorialised the *Lyttelton Times*, 'on the understanding that when the war was over the original holder of the position would be entitled to claim it. … Should the young soldier display his gratitude to the girl who saved his billet for him by marrying her, so much the better.' Women increased their dominance in teaching during the war, and new jobs opened up in both public and private sectors for clerks, typists, stenographers, and retail staff. The trend for women to enter business life preceded the war, but was accelerated by it, with the number of female clerks and cashiers more than quadrupling and the number of female shop assistants growing about ten times between 1911 and 1921.

New Zealand women proved their worth overseas. More than 640 served as military nurses in hospitals and in *hospital ships, and seventeen lost their lives. The sinking of the *Marquette* off Salonika in October 1915 resulted in the single largest loss of life among New Zealand nurses in any conflict. Ten died and the surviving twenty-six were in the water for eight hours before being rescued. A memorial chapel was built at Christchurch Hospital to the dead nurses—the only such chapel in New Zealand dedicated to women killed on active service.

Among other New Zealand women who dedicated themselves to war work overseas was Ethel Burnett, who ran the canteen in the New Zealand Soldiers' Club in London's Russell Square from 1916 to 1919, presiding over the serving of a thousand meals per day in sittings of forty-five at a time. The club, which closed only between 7 a.m. and 9 a.m. was run by 200 'lady volunteers', many of them New Zealanders, and grew to occupy four four-storey houses, providing 220 beds. At the end of the war, Burnett was given a purse of sovereigns by Brigadier-General G.S. *Richardson and appointed a CBE. She returned to New Zealand and teaching, but went on to do similar work at Trentham Camp during the *Second World War.

Individual women, including a number on holiday in Britain when war broke out, nursed in England or joined the British VADs. Ettie Rout's Volunteer Sisterhood, though denied official sanction, went to Egypt, where some worked in the hospitals and others in the *YMCA's Esbekia Gardens canteen. One ran a military restaurant and another a British cookery school. Some later worked in the canteens Rout set up in the desert for soldiers involved in the *Sinai–Palestine campaign. Others went to London, where they worked as members of the International Women's Street Patrols in uniforms with a New Zealand badge.

While most women supported the war effort, some worked for the pacifist cause. Working-class women were involved in agitation against *conscription. In 1916 a deputation of thirty women urged Prime Minister William *Massey not to proceed with conscription, stating that as mothers of the nation they objected to bringing lives into the world to be used when they reached manhood in the interest of a class which did not represent their own interests. That year the Women's International League for Peace and Freedom (WILPF) was formed, springing from the International Committee for Women for Permanent Peace, which had been founded in the Netherlands the previous year with the aim of achieving an end to the war through a negotiated settlement and the solution of future international disputes by arbitration and conciliation. The New Zealand section is believed to have been founded in Auckland by Marian Jones and Mrs D'Arcy Hamilton. Branches were formed in the other main centres but did not survive. The league protested strongly against the dispatch of *conscientious objectors to the front in 1917, maintaining that it was 'incredible … the liberty of conscience, so dearly bought in other times by our forefathers, should be deliberately set aside'. In May 1918 the WILPF and the Auckland Women's Political League amalgamated as the Women's International and Political League to promote 'true internationalism, anti-militarism and the interests of working-class women'.

The war strengthened women's groups and brought about the resurrection of the National Council of Women, which had gone into abeyance after a ten-year life in 1907. The leading suffragist and poet Jessie Mackay sparked the revival. A preliminary meeting was held in Wellington in April 1918, and the first full conference took place in the following year.

The war years brought to the fore some of the long-standing agenda items of the women's movement, particularly in the area of alcohol, the battleground of the most powerful women's group, the Woman's Christian Temperance Union. The registration of barmaids was finally achieved and a prohibition was placed on new barmaids being taken on. Early hotel closing—at 6 p.m.—was introduced in 1916 (and would persist for more than five decades). Prohibition was nearly won in 1919, when only the soldiers' votes kept the country from going dry. The War Regulations Act 1916 gave the government wide powers to suppress prostitution, another item on the 'social purity' feminist movement's agenda.

One issue for women's groups was the treatment of a group of New Zealand women particularly disadvantaged by the war—those married to foreigners classed as enemy aliens. Controversy over the nationality of these women flared as their husbands were taken off to internment camps. For example, New Zealand–born, Maori-speaking Miriam Soljak, who was married to an immigrant who had left Austria twenty years earlier to escape conscription, was forced to register as an 'alien'; when she sought a bed at a local nursing home, she was turned away as a 'foreigner'. Women's groups campaigned on behalf of such women.

Just before the war ended, in November 1918, a killer emerged on the home front, adding to the death toll half as many again and particularly hitting Maori communities. The *influenza pandemic, believed to have arrived with a ship bringing home returning soldiers and Massey and Sir Joseph *Ward, hit Auckland first. YWCA girls trained in home nursing and ambulance work were recruited to work twelve-hour shifts tending the sick at makeshift hospitals. Auckland Girls' Grammar School head Blanche Butler organised teams of nurses, and Mary McKail Geddes established community kitchens and a door-to-door service of nursing aides and medical relief. The government's antipathy to 'untrained' women was broken down in the crisis. Women replaced men in military hospitals. They proved so much more efficient than the orderlies whose drunkenness and undisciplined behaviour had been a cause of concern that they were soon employed as part of the permanent New Zealand Medical Corps, doing the job better for a quarter of the male rate of pay.

After the war soldiers arrived home slowly, because of a shipping shortage. Men and women began the process of adjusting to peacetime life. Mothers and wives found themselves with sons and husbands suffering from *shell-shock, the effects of wounds, amputations, gassing, *venereal disease, and other problems. Many of the 18,000 men who had died left widows and children. The widow's pension, which had been introduced in 1911 but restricted to those with children, was extended during the war to those without children, the sum paid depending on the husband's rank. The war robbed many women of the chance of marriage—the principal means of survival for women. One in four women were in the paid workforce in 1919. By 1921 women made up about a quarter of the workforce, almost all of them unmarried.

One of the post-war community efforts in which women played a major role was the erection of *war memorials. Edith Statham, working with the Victoria League Graves Committee, had made the resurrection of *New Zealand Wars graves her personal mission before 1914. After the war she worked on memorials for the New Zealand soldiers who had died overseas and headstones for those who had died at home. Many other women raised money and worked voluntarily for the building of war memorials. In some communities women's patriotic societies took charge of raising money. In Wellington women made paper 'roses of remembrance' and sold them on street corners.

JANE TOLERTON

Women and the Second World War During the *Second World War New Zealand women variously worked for victory, prayed for peace, cared for their families, and attempted to live fulfilling private lives as untouched as possible by the national emergency. For

Women and the Second World War

some the war was a heady time when romance flourished and new opportunities for work and play opened up. Contemporaries believed that the war was having a profound effect on New Zealand women. 'If the war stands for anything,' wrote one magazine editor, 'it stands for the emancipation of women.' Images of women gaily dancing with soldiers by night and gallantly doing a man's job by day have become an integral part of the mythology of the war. However, it is important to balance the received images of public opportunity and private dalliance with an understanding of the hardships war brought women, and an appreciation of the continuities between women's pre- and post-war responsibilities. For many women wartime challenges came in the form of continuity with the past. Traditional female employments, domestic and non-domestic, occupied the majority of women. War or no war, children needed to be cared for, the shopping done, meals cooked, and houses cleaned; in a straitened wartime economy, with male partners frequently absent, simply maintaining a household—literally and figuratively keeping the home fires burning—was a struggle. Nor did all women in the paid workforce share equally in the war's opportunity. Relatively cheap female labour was integral to the pricing structure of many sectors of the economy. Not everyone got the chance to do a man's job or earn high wages. Being stuck in an unsatisfying and low-paid war job, single parenthood, loneliness, the deaths of friends and family members, the responsibility of assisting in the emotional and physical rehabilitation of returned servicemen, were as characteristic of women's experience of war as dancing the night away with Americans or taking a man's place on an assembly line.

Pacifism was a minority opinion in wartime New Zealand. Some singular women were involved in New Zealand pacifism, but generally women did not take public roles in the movement. Connie Jones was the only woman arrested for anti-war activity, serving three months in the Wellington women's borstal for speaking against the war. Ormond ★Burton's wife, Nell, deputised for him at public meetings and took her turn on the soap box at the Basin Reserve on Sundays. The trade unionist Helen O'Flynn and Labour Party activist Lucy Gibson spoke at public meetings opposing the war in January 1940. Two women served on the Conscientious Objectors Advisory Board, which assisted ★conscientious objectors with their appeals against military service and publicised their victimisation and ill-treatment. The wives, mothers, and daughters of objectors supported their conscientious objector kin under testing circumstances: keeping families together and dealing as best they could with poverty, social disapproval, and the uncertain prospect of peace. Janet Barrington, the wife of pacifist leader A.C. ★Barrington, wryly remembered that when her house was searched for 'subversive' literature, the police failed to find the cache of pacifist writing she hid under the baby's mattress. With help from her mother-in-law and her friends she brought up her children to be proud of their father's stand against ★conscription. At the end of the war her three children held their own victory parade, marching down the street with flags singing 'Our Daddy's coming home today from jail'.

Patriotic work, paid or unpaid, attracted many more female recruits than did anti-war protest. In the wake of New Zealand's declaration of war in September 1939 patriotic women cast about for avenues to express their support for the war. In several cities women formed quasi-military training corps, sometimes to the horror of socially conservative observers. More traditional expressions of support for the war, such as membership of the ★Red Cross, the formation of patriotic societies to provide entertainment and comforts for soldiers, and fundraising, were less controversial. Church- and marae-based women's groups also played an important part in fundraising for patriotic purposes, sustaining morale, and organising support services for military personnel and their families.

Women were urged to protect their femininity against the taint of war, even as they were encouraged to support the war effort. At their July 1940 meeting the Wellington branch of the National Council of Women listened attentively to a report from the branch president on women's war work. Despite their support for female involvement in patriotic activities, members were cautioned against too wholehearted commitment to war service along male lines. Women were expected to keep non-militaristic ideals alive even as they strove to contribute to the national struggle.

In late 1940, after strenuous lobbying by prominent women leaders, including the Prime Minister's wife,

Female munitions workers (*NZ Free Lance Collection, Alexander Turnbull Library, F-51172-1/2*)

Women and the Second World War

Janet Fraser, the government agreed to the establishment of a Women's War Service Auxiliary to coordinate women's war work. This organisation was an important precursor to the women's armed service auxiliaries, not least because it made the initial breakthrough against opposition to provision of uniforms for women war workers, overcoming Prime Minister Peter *Fraser's accusation that members were unnecessarily fixated on having a uniform. The opportunity to contribute to the war effort through an officially recognised organisation proved very popular with women. A year after its establishment the WWSA could boast 15,000 members. When at its peak strength in 1942, it claimed 75,000 women members organised through 250 district committees. Some served overseas as *Tuis. The 10,000 members of the WWSA's clerical section underwrote the country's military mobilisation by giving thousands of hours of unpaid assistance to the *Home Guard, the *Emergency Precautions Scheme, and the armed forces, including nightly attendance at army offices and service camps during the 1942 invasion scare to help clear the backlog of work and free men for civil defence duties. WWSA training classes in first aid, truck driving, vehicle maintenance, signalling, canteen operation, clerical skills, and farm work were extremely popular, with the supply of trainees often exceeding government demands for voluntary workers. The Women's Land Corps established in 1941 was initially administered by the WWSA (see LAND GIRLS). In 1941 and 1942 the WWSA assisted in the recruitment for the newly formed women's armed service auxiliaries. Many of the first members of the Women's Auxiliary Air Force, the Women's Auxiliary Army Corps, and the Women's Royal New Zealand Naval Service had been WWSA members.

Mobilising women to meet the shortfall of labour in the paid workforce was one of the most delicate tasks facing New Zealand's wartime government. The withdrawal of large amounts of manpower to the military, import restrictions, and the increase in demand for key war-related materials (most notably machinery, munitions, food, clothing, and footwear) created severe labour shortages. Women workers were part of the solution to the manpower crisis. The mobilisation of women for paid work was controversial because it implied an equivalence between male and female war service, and could be seen as endorsing women's participation in non-domestic activities. Paid work was seen as a phase in most women's life cycle, not an ongoing or important activity. Although most single New Zealand women worked for wages, social conventions dictated that once a woman married she generally gave up paid work for full-time homemaking. According to the 1936 census, less than 5 per cent of women workers were married. Combining paid work and motherhood was even rarer than combining paid work and marriage. Many New Zealanders, male and female, worried that women's increased participation in paid work would make them selfish, overly independent, and discontented with marriage and motherhood. If the government was seen to be encouraging married women and women with children to work outside the home, it ran the risk of creating opposition to the war on the grounds that it was undermining home and family life. Adding to these fears were worries that any gains women made in the paid workforce during the war would be at the expense of absentee soldiers. Conventionally, women were paid less than men, and trade unions and soldiers' advocates feared that employers would take advantage of wartime conditions and permanently replace men with cheaper female labour. The government set up a number of structures to try and minimise the threat to men's jobs. The Occupational Re-Establishment Regulations of 1940 placed a legal responsibility on employers to reinstate repatriated servicemen in their old jobs. This created a preference for using women as temporary staff on the part of some employers, including the government itself, while at the same time explicitly defining many women as temporary employees. In addition, the government set up a series of industry-specific Manpower Utilisation Councils and an Industrial Emergency Council. These bodies helped manage relations between policy-makers, unions, and employers in essential industries and advised the Minister of Labour on matters relating to the war.

A variety of other strategies were used to lessen the threat of feminisation of men's jobs and ensure any influx of women was temporary. Orders-in-Council were used to set special wage rates for women where the prevailing industrial award had failed to specify a female rate for the job, and suspend legislation that prohibited women from working long hours and late shifts, and doing heavy work. The suspension orders were deliberately short-term, valid 'for the duration only' or 'for the duration and six months'. Women were often segregated within production processes, with the more skilled, higher-status, and/or higher-paid aspects of a trade reserved for men. Generally, where a job or trade was broken up into constituent parts and some tasks given over to women workers, women were given what was regarded as lighter, less skilled, and less responsible work, with an accompanying decrease in pay. Women mail deliverers, for instance, had shorter routes than their male predecessors, female railway station workers could not signal trains, and female butchers' assistants could not cut meat. All were paid less than the men they replaced.

In a few cases where it was not possible to scale down or redefine a job, the union representatives on

Women and the Second World War

the relevant consultative committee had enough clout to insist that women received the male rate for the job, betting that if male and female labour was priced at the same level at the end of the war employers would choose to re-employ men. This strategy was used in the case of women tram conductors. Union officials saw their responsibility as protecting the interests of their male membership. Unimpressed by a suggestion from an employers' representative on the Council that 'you cannot expect the woman conductor to be as efficient a "forward" as the average man' and cope with tightly packed scrums of commuters, the Tramways Union insisted on the employment of 'conductresses' at the full male rate of pay. 'The whole crux of the question', a union official argued, 'is that if it is more economical to employ women the Tramways Authorities will employ women.' Despite its success in establishing that women could not be used to undercut male conductors' wage rates, throughout the war the Tramways Union continued to oppose the training of women drivers.

Fears that women would permanently replace men were not the only brake on the wholesale replacement of men by women. Women were part of the solution to New Zealand's manpower problem, but the New Zealand war effort would have been crippled if too many women had taken men's jobs. The shortfall of male labour had to be dealt with while at the same time ensuring a steady supply of woman workers in essential undertakings conventionally reliant on female labour. By mid 1941 an acute shortage of civilian labour had become one of the most urgent problems facing the government. Rising wages threatened its policy of controlling wartime inflation. Employers in essential industries warned that they could not guarantee to supply civilian and military necessities without a guaranteed supply of affordable, trained labour. Industrial conscription was introduced in early 1942 to try and control spiralling wages and stem the outflow of labour from essential industry. Women became liable to industrial conscription by two principal mechanisms. Most commonly women were 'manpowered' when the Minister of Industrial Manpower formally declared the industry they were working in essential. Once a 'declaration of essentiality' was issued, overtime and shiftwork allowance provisions could be overridden, and absenteeism, lateness, and carelessness subjected to penalties. Most importantly, employees lost the right to leave their job at will. By early 1943 70,000 women, approximately 35 per cent of those in the paid workforce, had come under manpower control in this manner. The secondary industries which were traditional female ghettos were among the first to be declared essential: footwear and clothing manufacture, woollen and knitting mills, and the linen flax industry. Hospitals were declared essential undertakings, as were schools. Food processing plants, food services such as hotels and restaurants, and most government departments were later added to the list. The second type of conscription affecting women was the process of registration for, and direction to, work of national importance. The registration order defined specific groups of workers, usually by age and sex, but sometimes also by occupation or residence, and required them to report to their district manpower office for an interview and possible direction to work of national importance. Although the ★National Service Department was careful to praise women for voluntarily doing their part to meet the labour shortage, officials were convinced that there was a reservoir of female labour that only compulsion could tap. They also believed that a significant number of women, though broadly supportive of the war, would remain in non-essential occupations if left to their own devices. Despite these assumptions, the department was also required to proceed cautiously in registering women. The first registration order, in March 1942, covered only women born in 1922 and 1923. By the end of the year registration had been extended to women aged twenty to thirty, and at its widest would cover women aged eighteen to forty. Marital status did not affect eligibility, but all women responsible for the care of children were automatically exempt. Proposals to make mothers liable for direction to part-time work were quickly abandoned after public and editorial opposition, as were plans for systematic government support for the establishment of day nurseries for the children of working mothers. By contrast, men were eligible for direction up to the age of sixty and irrespective of parental responsibilities.

The relative reluctance to coerce women reflected a general desire on the part of officials to avoid controversy, and a widespread conservatism about women's participation in paid work. Women who were already in an essential occupation at the time that that industry was declared essential could be said to have chosen their lot and to be responsible for the personal and professional compromises entailed. The department could be much more easily held responsible for women brought into the paid workforce by its registration orders or directed to new jobs under its auspices. In order to ensure support for its activities the department could not be seen to be coming between women and their domestic responsibilities. Nor could it risk interfering too extensively with the lives of either young or older women, as both groups were regarded as needing special care and protection. In addition, a complex set of class and ethnic prejudices shaped the manpowering of women. An industrial psychologist found that women manpowered into factories, laundries, and hospitals from other occupations, with the exception of domestic work, were generally more critical of wages and conditions than those normally working in those occupations. Maori women were frequently directed into the least desirable positions. There was a strong financial incentive for the department to choose women in low-paid jobs as transferees to other low-paid jobs, as it was required to top up wages when a worker was transferred from a high-paid job to one on lower pay. Despite exhortations to put class considerations aside in the service of the war effort, there were frequent complaints that women were being bulldozed into unsuitable occupations. Unsuitability was judged against class and ethnic criteria. As the editor of the *New Zealand National Review* put it, 'education, upbringing and individual prejudices' needed to be taken into account in directing women. Or in the words of a magistrate ruling on the case of a woman tried for breaching the manpower regulations, 'manpower officers should be fairly careful as to what class of girl they want to push into a hotel'.

By early 1943, 71,876 women had come under the control of the manpower authorities via registration orders and declarations of essentiality. Between March 1942 and the end of March 1946, when the regulations were lifted, 37,580 individual direction orders were issued to women. Industrial conscription seems to have had some success in securing labour for essential industries and temporarily increasing the number of women in paid work, but it did not represent a radical break with the past. The majority of jobs which the department was looking to fill were by definition jobs that would not be filled by voluntary labour, unglamorous and often tedious work like waitressing, sewing, hospital domestic work, and factory work. The textile and footwear industries, hospitals, hotels, and catering establishments accounted for 53 per cent of all direction orders issued to women from October 1943 to March 1945. In many ways the regulations were designed to prevent women from capitalising on wartime demands for their labour, prioritising the needs of female-dependent, and often low-paying, essential industries over the desire of individual women for new opportunities and higher wages.

The National Service Department estimated that the female labour force was 180,000 in September 1939. Under normal conditions the number of women in paid work increased by about 1000 individuals per annum. The combined effect of more extensive voluntary participation in paid work and industrial conscription produced a female labour force of 228,000 women in December 1943, which declined thereafter to 200,000 in December 1945. The war produced a series of important and far-reaching changes to the occupational structure of New Zealand's paid workforce, but few of these changes were the result of the direct substitution of women for men in stereotypically male occupations. Unsurprisingly, given the industries' historic reliance on female labour, there was an increase in the number of women employed in food processing, footwear, and textile and clothing manufacture. In a continuation of pre-war trends, the number of women working in private domestic service declined dramatically, and large numbers of women were employed in more public service occupations in restaurants, tea rooms, and hotels. Female nurses, long the backbone of hospital nursing, were in great demand for civilian health care and were a vital part of the military's medical staff. White-collar work also employed increasing numbers of women, though most of these were new jobs rather than jobs where women directly replaced men, the 16,000-woman increase in employment in finance distribution, professional service, and administration outstripping the 7000-man outflow. In the transport and communications sector 44 per cent of the 6000 new women's jobs can be accounted for by increased use of female telephonists, and another 46 per cent were post office jobs sorting and delivering mail. The high-profile and widely publicised jobs where women were visibly doing men's work, like herd testing, tram conducting, police work, and railway work, were important in drawing attention to women's potential, but statistically the number of women employed in these kinds of jobs was insignificant.

While there was no typical woman and no typical woman's war, it is possible to identify some of the overarching ideas that guided women's mobilisation and contemporary understandings of the meaning of their wartime activities. To place women's experiences of war in context, it is necessary to understand the conflicting demands the war placed on women. There was a great deal of ambivalence about the consequences of mobilising women for war. Feminine domesticity was seen as a vital part of national life, and indeed an important 'British' character trait at the heart of the value system that the war was being fought to defend. War was seen as a quintessentially masculine activity. Many people worried that participation in war work might masculinise women or encourage them to neglect their domestic responsibilities. The inauguration of the women's auxiliaries to the armed forces and the employment of small numbers of women in highly visible 'men's jobs' troubled those who feared that the war was eroding women's femininity. The Plunket Society urged its members not to abandon their infant welfare work in order to take up war work, and women were told that childbearing and rearing were important components of the struggle against Fascism and Asian expansionism. For women citizenship, patriot-

Women in the armed forces

ism, and war service were defined in deeply contradictory ways. To help King, country, and 'the boys', women were urged to contribute to the war effort like men via paid employment and the armed services, but they were also cautioned that the wartime change was 'for the duration only' and to keep the more feminine forms of national service and self-fulfilment, most notably motherhood, as their long-term goals.

Women worked for the war, but the war did not work for women. It did not remove the barriers to women's full participation in the workforce or in public life. Nor did it result in a more equitable division of household responsibilities or a recognition of the link between women's underrepresentation in politics, paid work, and public life and their disproportionate share of childrearing and domestic work. Instead, the ethos of the war privileged men in the sense that male ways of contributing to victory were seen as more fundamental and more important than female modes of war service. Women's services were recognised, but they were recognised as part of the social debt owed to the boys in return for their greater sacrifices. Women rendered sterling service, but continued to be paid less than men, were often dismissed as less competent than men and less suited for promotion, and had to struggle to find jobs that allowed them to combine paid work, marriage, and motherhood. As 'Unicorn', a businesswoman writing in the *New Zealand Woman's Weekly* in 1945, warned her sisters at the end of the war, their male workers were still more likely to regard them as frail flowers than credit them with equal abilities and equal status: 'Men have no illusions about your place in the post-war scheme ... In the war? Done a great job, yes ... Couldn't have got through without them. But load them up with extra work or hours and they cave in.' Contemporary expectations that the war would revolutionise the position of New Zealand women went largely unfulfilled.

N.M. Taylor, *The Home Front*, 2 vols (Historical Publications Branch, Wellington, 1986); D. Montgomerie, 'Man-powering Women: Industrial Conscription during the Second World War', in B. Brookes, C. Macdonald, and M. Tennant (eds), *Women in History 2* (Bridget Williams Books, Wellington, 1992); D. Montgomerie, 'Sweethearts, Soldiers, Happy Families: Gender and World War 2', in C. Daley and D. Montgomerie (eds), *The Gendered Kiwi* (Auckland University Press, Auckland, 1999).

DEBORAH MONTGOMERIE

Women in the armed forces The first women to serve in the New Zealand military forces were a contingent of the newly established New Zealand Army Nursing Service sent to Samoa in 1914, and other nurses later served in the Mediterranean and European theatres. Following the outbreak of the ★Second World War, it seemed at first that the ★First World War pattern would be repeated, and that women's participation in the armed forces would be confined to nursing. Anxious to make a contribution to the war effort, many women joined the civilian Women's War Service Auxiliary (see WOMEN AND THE SECOND WORLD WAR), but some wanted to serve more directly. Manpower shortages in the armed forces gave them the opportunity, with the emergence of women's services paralleling similar developments in the United Kingdom. Unlike their British counterparts, New Zealand women were never conscripted for service in uniform, though from March 1942 they were subjected to industrial ★conscription.

The RNZAF was the first service to accept women. The New Zealand Women's Auxiliary Air Force was formed in January 1941 under Frances ★Kain. As in the other services in due course, they quickly assumed an important role in the day-to-day running of the service. Most were employed in clerical, domestic, or medical support activities, but a proportion were employed in more specialised areas, such as parachute packing and the training of pilots in bombing techniques. Internal transport facilities were almost completely staffed by women. The service reached its peak strength of 3746 in August 1943, including a small number in Fiji. In all, 4753 women served with it during the war. Although a number of women with pilot's licences joined the WAAF, they were never used for flying duties. However, four women pilots did join the British Air Transport Auxiliary after making their own way to the United Kingdom; their duties involved ferrying aircraft between factories and aerodromes and between aerodromes. One of them, Jane Winston, was killed in 1944 when her Spitfire's engine failed on take-off.

From the outset of the war many of the positions occupied by naval ratings in the ★New Zealand Division of the Royal Navy had been taken over by women civilians. It was not until 1941, however, that attention was given to the possibility of women being allowed to don naval uniform. The formation of the Women's Royal New Zealand Naval Service (WRNZNS) was approved by the Cabinet in April 1942. Closely modelled on its British counterpart, it was commanded by Ruth ★Herrick. During the rest of the war 640 Wrens, as they were termed, served. The peak strength was 519. The first Wrens were trained in signalling, which became an important role for the service. Some Wrens worked in intelligence work, such as tracking Japanese radio traffic. Others carried out support functions, including watchkeeping and driving.

The largest of the women's services was the New Zealand Women's Auxiliary Army Corps, formed in July 1942 under the leadership of Vida ★Jowett. At its peak in July 1943, it had 4589 women in its ranks.

Women in the armed forces

WAACs operating a range finder on 21 January 1943 (*NZ Free Lance Collection, Alexander Turnbull Library, F-71988-1/2*)

Plans for it to attain a strength of 10,000 foundered as women were directed into industry. WAACs served in a multitude of tasks within New Zealand, but were especially prominent in the welfare and clerical areas. Some became drivers, radio operators, and signallers, while a number were employed in the anti-aircraft and coastal artillery defences, especially manning searchlights. More than 900 served overseas with 2NZEF, mainly in the Mediterranean theatre (see TUIS; VOLUNTARY AID DETACHMENTS). A few were deployed in the South Pacific. Many WAACs were attached to hospitals as orderlies, nursing assistants, and clerical workers, while some were employed in servicemen's clubs in Egypt and Italy. The decision to allow WAACs to serve overseas had been made with some difficulty. The possibility of their marrying while serving raised a number of issues: it was feared that married women in New Zealand would begin agitating to be allowed to serve in the Middle East as well, causing 'endless disputes, heart-burnings and arguments from both husbands and wives'. Nevertheless, the presence of WAACs was thought likely to be beneficial to the morale of 2NZEF. The success of the scheme, it was felt, depended upon getting 'capable, wise and attractive women' to take part. When the first contingent arrived in Egypt, they were told by the commander of 2NZEF, Major-General B.C. ★Freyberg, that they were there to 'supply the home touch, the atmosphere that is at present lacking' in the camps, and that the whole of 2NZEF would look up to them. A number of WAACs did enter marriages with members of the force. At least ten died while on active service.

The admission of women into the military raised a number of concerns, such as the physical safety of women in a military environment (both from the enemy and from the attentions of servicemen) and the danger of a loosening of moral standards and sexual immorality. In the event these fears proved unfounded. There were only a handful of unmarried pregnancies among the women's services, and the rate of ★venereal disease was negligible—in stark contrast to that for servicemen. Women's quarters were generally strictly segregated, and servicewomen of all ranks overseas received certain privileges, such as being admitted to officers' clubs and hotels and first-class travel. However, pay for servicewomen was substantially below that for servicemen: for example, a private in the WAACs earned two shillings a day less than her male counterpart's 7s 6d.

After the Second World War servicewomen were rapidly demobilised. By 1947 there were only 561 women in the services. Nevertheless, the women's services were retained (except, briefly, the WRNZNS). The experience of the war had shown the valuable role women could play. Furthermore, post-war conditions made the recruiting of men difficult for all three services, and ★mutinies in the RNZAF and RNZN (which

Women in the armed forces

A female soldier serving with the New Zealand contingent in the International Force East Timor in November 1999 (*NZ Army, OH99-1979-2*)

led to the re-establishment of the disbanded WRNZNS) exacerbated the situation. In August 1947 a detachment of WAACs was sent to Japan to join ★Jayforce; they were involved in welfare activities, such as running leave establishments. In 1948 the women's services were established as regular corps of their respective services, the WAACs being retitled the New Zealand Women's Army Corps (from 1952 New Zealand Women's Royal Army Corps) and the WAAFs the Women's Royal New Zealand Air Force. Nevertheless, there were problems recruiting enough women. A desperate need for clerical and communications personnel led to large numbers of servicewomen being recruited in the United Kingdom. After corps training at Burnham, members of the NZWRAC were attached to various units of the Army, mainly to carry out administrative duties. These regular servicewomen were joined, after 1974, by women who joined the ★Territorial Force.

Throughout the 1950s and 1960s the overall numbers of women in the armed forces remained relatively static at about 500, or between four and five per cent of the total regular force. While servicewomen were grouped into their own corps and came under female officers for most administrative and disciplinary matters, they were generally under the command of male officers of the units to which they were attached. Their role remained little different from that of the Second World War, encompassing mainly nursing and clerical and kitchen work. Not until the 1970s were servicewomen trained in the handling of small arms. Their pay remained substantially below that of servicemen of equivalent rank: under scales issued in 1948 it was in some cases less than half. There was a tendency to compare the pay and conditions of servicewomen with wages offered in civilian life rather than with male military personnel. Even when equal pay was introduced into the State Services in 1961, servicewomen's pay was fixed at 85 per cent of male rates on the grounds that they were not 'employed on duties requiring physical strength, endurance, discomfort or isolation'; nor were they allowed to do equal work during a national emergency. They received no additional trade pay and had reduced allowances. Only in 1965 was the percentage relationship to male rates abandoned, and servicewomen thereafter were paid according to scales set for clerical or nursing staff in the wider public service. This resulted in a further widening of the gap between men's and women's pay. Women's conditions of service were also inferior. Until the mid 1960s servicewomen were expected to be single, and were discharged from the armed forces upon marriage. Not surprisingly there was a high turnover of personnel.

The practice of having separate women's services came to an end in July 1977, a process which was accelerated by the Human Rights Act 1977. 'Within her Corps', it was now explicitly stated, 'a woman should … have the potential for a full career, to the highest possible rank, limited only by her ability; … not be restricted by policy or custom to any specific appointment(s).' Training was unified, and messing and most recreational facilities became shared. Nonetheless, women remained barred from many trades (twenty-one of eighty-five) or corps, and from employment areas involving exposure to combat or trades considered to be too physically demanding, including painter, butcher, or dental auxiliary. Another forty-four trades, including those for bandsmen, storekeepers, tailors, drivers, or mechanics, had restricted entry for women. Female naval ratings were not allowed to serve on ships, and similarly RNZAF aircrew remained a male preserve. Discrimination applied in other ways: females, for example, were not allowed entry into the prestigious officer training institutions overseas, such as the Royal Military College at Duntroon. Lacking combat or tactical training, female officers found themselves at a disadvantage with their male peers. Despite these problems, the integration of women into the mainstream armed forces in 1977 represented a major shift in attitudes towards women. Since then, servicewomen have gradually overcome the barriers to their taking an equal role. In part the need for technically proficient professionals has encouraged increasing recruitment of women and led to the opening of trades hitherto closed to them. At the same time, fears that military efficiency would be undermined and disciplinary problems created have not been borne out. In 1986 women were allowed to become non-combatant aircrew, and two years later the first New Zealand woman gained her airforce 'wings'. From 1988 women were permitted to fly combat aircraft and train for combat, though they were still barred from actually going into combat. In 1986 the RNZN allowed women to serve in HMNZS *Monowai* as part of a 'Women at Sea Pilot Study', and by 1988 they comprised 10 per cent of her crew. From 1989 women could serve in non-combatant branches and trades at sea on all ships bar the ★frigates, and this latter restriction was removed in 1993. By 1998, when a female Army officer was sent to command an artillery detachment in Bosnia–Herzegovina, every trade and branch in the armed forces except navy diving and a handful of Army combat trades were open to women, and their presence had been greatly enhanced. With 14 per cent in 1999, New Zealand had a higher proportion of women in its forces than any other Western country except the United States.

The main outstanding issue relates to the ban on women being sent into combat or occupying combat support roles. Although a 1990 report insisted that women had a basic equal right to volunteer for combat, the ★New Zealand Defence Force considered that such a situation might hinder operational efficiency. In its view the average woman's lesser physical strength, the risk of sexual harassment, and a strong natural instinct among male soldiers to protect women made women unsuitable for combat roles. Confronted with a potentially divisive issue, the government opted out, leaving it for the 'public to decide'. But the evolving nature of warfare had in any case led to a blurring of the distinction between combatant and non-combatant in combat zones. In practice the NZDF could not deploy a significant force without women serving in roles which could potentially expose them to combat. In 1999 the CDF, Air Marshal C.W. Adamson, stated that he would not use the provision in the Human Rights Act which allows the withdrawal of female soldiers, sailors, and aircrew from units that might go into combat. The restrictions on women serving in combat roles in the Army's infantry, artillery, engineers, and armoured corps, in which women previously held only command or administrative roles, were lifted from early 2000.

While the formal position of women in the services underwent substantial change in the last two decades of the twentieth century, it was not accompanied by a corresponding change in the culture of the armed forces. A comprehensive equal employment policy introduced in 1993 included 'zero tolerance' for sexual harassment. Nonetheless, a well-publicised case soon highlighted the problems faced by women serving on RNZN vessels in particular, though problems of sexual harassment and discrimination on the basis of gender were not confined to the RNZN. They have provided major barriers to the recruitment, advancement, and retention of women. A Gender Integration Audit in 1998 found the 'pervasiveness of masculine culture in the military' had prevented women from achieving

Women's Royal New Zealand Air Force

real equality. While conceding that the armed forces had embraced the concept of equality, the consultant who carried out the audit argued that it was equality based on essentially masculine terms. Greater awareness of the need to treat personnel equitably was stressed as essential. Accepting the report in its entirety, the CDF promised tough measures to eliminate harassment of women.

ELIZABETH COX

Women's Royal New Zealand Air Force see WOMEN IN THE ARMED FORCES

Women's Royal New Zealand Naval Service see WOMEN IN THE ARMED FORCES

Wynyard, Lieutenant-General Robert Henry (24 December 1802–6 January 1864) commanded the forces in New Zealand from 1851 to 1858. Born at Windsor Castle, England, into a family with a long military tradition, he began his own military career in 1819. From 1826 he held a commission in the 58th (Rutlandshire) Regiment of Foot, and assumed command of it in 1842, after service in Ireland. His regiment was dispatched to Sydney two years later, and Wynyard almost immediately proceeded with a detachment to the Bay of Islands, where they were involved in the fighting against Hone ★Heke and ★Kawiti. Wynyard took part in the storming of Ruapekapeka in January 1846. After a brief period in Sydney, he returned to New Zealand in 1847. He was Lieutenant-Governor of New Ulster from 1851 to 1853, and won elected office as Superintendent of Auckland Province in 1853 (though he resigned two years later on instruction from London). At the beginning of 1854 he became acting Governor in addition to his other offices. With news of the outbreak of the ★Crimean War, he authorised himself to undertake what were the first measures of external defence at Britomart Point in Auckland against the possibility of attack by raiding Russian warships. However, his military responsibilities were overshadowed by his key role in implementing constitutional arrangements leading to the establishment of responsible government in the colony. Not until August 1855, with the arrival of the new Governor, was he relieved of this difficult task. He left New Zealand with the 58th Regiment three years later. From 1859 to 1863 he was Officer Commanding and Lieutenant-Governor at Cape Colony in South Africa.

Y Z

Yellow peril refers to a sense of apprehension about Asia which developed in New Zealand in the late nineteenth century. It drew strength more from fears among the European population of being submerged by a tide of Asian immigration than from any sense of immediate military threat, though this emerged in the twentieth century with the rise of Japanese power (see JAPANESE THREAT). Even after the total defeat of Japan in 1945, the yellow peril remained an element in New Zealand thinking, especially in relation to China. The vision of alien hordes descending on the South Pacific was sometimes conjured by government apologists for a strong defence policy. Such anxieties faded in the later part of the twentieth century as New Zealanders' contacts with Asia and Asians broadened, and they began to see Asian economic development as presenting an opportunity for advancing their country's prosperity.

Young, Major-General Sir Robert (5 January 1877–25 February 1953), an Englishman by birth and dentist by profession, began his military career in Marton in 1901, when he joined his local ★Volunteer Force corps, the Royal Rangitikei Rifles. Enlisting in 1NZEF soon after the outbreak of the ★First World War, he left New Zealand with the Main Body in October 1914 as a company commander in the Wellington Infantry Battalion. At ★Gallipoli he commanded the Auckland Infantry Battalion from May to November 1915 before taking over the Canterbury Infantry Battalion. Following the withdrawal from the peninsula, he commanded this battalion (renamed 1st Battalion, Canterbury Regiment) on the ★Western Front. On 9 August 1917, two days after assuming command of the 3rd New Zealand (Rifle) Brigade, he suffered a severe neck wound. After recovering in England and commanding the Reserve Brigade at Sling Camp, he returned to the front line in early 1918 and commanded the 2nd Brigade until the end of the war. For his services, he was made a DSO in 1915, a CMG in 1916, and a CB in 1918. Determined to continue his military career as a regular soldier, he joined the ★New Zealand Staff Corps following his return to New Zealand in 1919, and was given command of the Canterbury Military District (later Southern Command). In December 1925 he became General Officer Commanding the New Zealand Military Forces. With an experienced officer corps and ★compulsory training scheme to ensure that units were kept up to strength, he faced a relatively straightforward task until the onset of the Depression of the early 1930s. Before retiring in March 1931, he was forced to oversee deep cuts in the forces and the suspension of the CMT scheme. From August 1940 until November 1943 Young was Director-General of the ★Home Guard.

Young Men's Christian Association (YMCA) is an international, undenominational welfare organisation. It was established in New Zealand in 1855 as an evangelical movement for young working men. In the 1900s it provided comforts such as newspapers and sweets for ★Volunteer and ★Territorial Force camps. During the ★First World War about fifty YMCA representatives went overseas to provide welfare facilities to 1NZEF. Recreational and welfare facilities such as libraries, billiard rooms, cinemas, and dry (non-alcoholic) canteens were provided for soldiers at hospitals and camps overseas and in New Zealand. YMCA clubs were established in London and Paris for soldiers on leave, offering leisure facilities. The YMCA also

Troops and staff outside a YMCA facility in France during the First World War (*Waiouru Army Museum, 1994-3345*)

operated a 'street patrol' in London to deter soldiers from associating with 'women of known disreputable character'. New Zealand troops were also served at YMCA working points ('YM Pozzies') behind the front line in dugouts, abandoned houses, and tents, distinguishable by their ubiquitous red triangle signs. Soldiers were provided cigarettes, hot drinks, toiletries, stationery, and newspapers. 'Buckshee stunts' or roadside stalls distributed hot drinks and cigarettes when soldiers left the trenches or finished a long march, and hot drinks and assistance were also provided by the YMCA at dressing stations.

In the ★Second World War the YMCA was the principal body responsible for the provision of welfare to New Zealand soldiers, though funding was provided by the National Patriotic Fund (see PATRIOTIC FUNDS). In all, 189 YMCA secretaries served overseas, most with 2NZEF in the Middle East, where a secretary was attached to each battalion or regiment. Another 406 YMCA secretaries served in New Zealand. At all the major camps both overseas and in New Zealand YMCA huts offered a dry canteen selling cigarettes, tins of fruit and milk, and toiletries. They also provided free stationery, books, and sporting equipment; bible classes and religious services were also offered. As the war dragged on, additional services were provided by the YMCA—libraries, mobile cinemas, a personal buying service for troops at the front, and a flower service for soldiers to have flowers sent to people in New Zealand. Hostels and refreshment canteens were also opened for soldiers on leave. YMCA mobile canteens in trucks followed units on campaign, distributing essential comforts, notably cigarettes and chocolate. Eight YMCA personnel were captured during the war. YMCA secretaries provided welfare services to New Zealand troops with both ★Jayforce and ★Kayforce; two secretaries accompanied the latter force.

Z Special Unit (or the Services Reconnaissance Department) was a specialist reconnaissance and sabotage unit formed in June 1942 to operate behind Japanese lines in South-east Asia. Predominantly Australian in composition, it also included British, Dutch, Timorese, Indonesians, and twenty-two New Zealanders seconded from 2NZEF—three of whom, Major D.J. ★Stott, Lieutenant R.M. Morton, and Warrant Officer L.M. Northover, had already been in action with the Special Operations Executive in Greece (see RESISTANCE IN EUROPE, NEW ZEALANDERS AND). Parties were parachuted or taken by submarine behind Japanese lines in Indonesia and Borneo to provide intelligence and conduct guerrilla warfare. Four New Zealanders lost their lives while serving with Z Special Unit.

F.A. Wigzell, 'New Zealand Army Involvement "Z" Special Unit Special Operations Australia A.I.B.' (Unpublished manuscript, Auckland, 1995).

Appendix

SENIOR OFFICERS OF THE ARMED FORCES

Chief of Defence Staff

Rear-Admiral Sir Peter *Phipps	1 July 1963	1 July 1965
Lieutenant-General Sir Leonard *Thornton	1 July 1965	15 October 1971
Lieutenant-General Sir Richard *Webb	16 October 1971	15 October 1976
Air Marshal Sir Richard Bolt	16 October 1976	15 April 1980
Vice-Admiral Sir Neil Anderson	16 April 1980	15 April 1983
Air Marshal Sir Ewan *Jamieson	16 April 1983	15 October 1986
Air Marshal David *Crooks	16 October 1986	30 November 1987
Lieutenant-General Sir John *Mace	1 December 1987	28 March 1991

Chief of Defence Force

Vice-Admiral Sir Somerford *Teagle	29 March 1991	24 February 1995
Lieutenant-General A.L. *Birks	25 February 1995	24 February 1999
Air Marshal C.W. Adamson	25 February 1999	

Navy

Naval Adviser to the New Zealand Government

Captain P.H. *Hall-Thompson RN	15 July 1914	4 August 1919
Commander T.A. Williams RN	4 August 1919	26 January 1921

Commodore Commanding NZ Station and First Naval Member

Commodore A.G. *Hotham RN	2 October 1920	24 August 1923
Commodore A.F. Beal RN	24 August 1923	9 August 1926
Commodore G.T.C.P. Swabey RN	10 August 1926	8 September 1929
Commodore Geoffrey *Blake RN	9 September 1929	16 April 1932
Rear-Admiral F. Burges Watson RN	17 April 1932	9 May 1935
Rear-Admiral the Hon E.R. Drummond RN	27 April 1935	8 June 1938

Appendix

Chief of Naval Staff and (until 1971) First Naval Member

Commodore H.E. Horan RN	8 June 1938	1 May 1940
Commodore W.E. *Parry RN	1 May 1940	1 May 1942
Commodore Sir Atwell Lake RN	1 May 1942	13 July 1945
Commodore G.H. Faulkner RN	13 July 1945	18 May 1947
Commodore G.W.G. Simpson RN	5 June 1947	25 June 1950
Commodore F.A. Ballance RN	26 June 1950	30 March 1953
Commodore Sir Charles E. Madden RN	31 March 1953	1 May 1955
Rear-Admiral J.E.H. McBeath RN	2 May 1955	26 February 1958
Rear-Admiral J.M. Villiers RN	27 February 1958	31 March 1960
Rear-Admiral Peter *Phipps	1 April 1960	1 July 1963
Rear-Admiral R.E. *Washbourn	1 July 1963	30 September 1965
Rear-Admiral J.O'C. *Ross	1 October 1965	1 July 1969
Rear-Admiral L.G. Carr	1 July 1969	30 June 1972
Rear-Admiral E.C. Thorne	1 July 1972	12 December 1975
Rear-Admiral J.F. McKenzie	13 December 1975	13 December 1977
Rear-Admiral N.D. Anderson	14 December 1977	16 April 1980
Rear-Admiral K.M. Saull	16 April 1980	16 April 1983
Rear-Admiral C.J. Steward	16 April 1983	1 February 1986
Rear-Admiral L.J. Tempero	1 February 1986	2 May 1987
Rear-Admiral D.B. Domett	11 May 1987	11 May 1989
Rear-Admiral S.F. *Teagle	12 May 1989	28 March 1991
Rear-Admiral I.A. Hunter	29 March 1991	8 April 1994
Rear-Admiral J.E.N. Welch	8 April 1994	8 April 1997
Rear-Admiral K.F. Wilson	8 April 1997	7 April 2000
Rear-Admiral P.M. McHaffie	8 April 2000	

Army

Commander of the Colonial Defence Force

Major-General T.J. *Galloway	20 September 1863	6 February 1865

Commandant, Armed Constabulary

Colonel G.S. *Whitmore	29 October 1867	28 July 1869

Commissioner, Armed Constabulary

St John Branigan	8 August 1869	21 November 1871[1]
Lieutenant-Colonel William Moule	7 December 1871	10 March 1875
Lieutenant-Colonel W.C. Lyon (acting)	11 March 1875	23 April 1876
Lieutenant-Colonel William Moule	23 April 1876	31 December 1877
Colonel G.S. Whitmore	1 January 1878	8 October 1879
Lieutenant-Colonel H.E. Reader	22 December 1879	30 June 1885
Major W.E. *Gudgeon (acting)	1 July 1885	17 November 1885
Major-General G.S. Whitmore	18 November 1885	5 January 1887

[1] Because of Branigan's committal to an asylum, Lieutenant-Colonel William Moule was temporary Commissioner from 1 June 1871.

Commander of the Forces

Major-General Sir George S. Whitmore	27 April 1885	4 April 1888
Colonel F.J. *Fox	1 January 1892	31 August 1894[2]
Major-General A.P. *Penton	1 December 1896	16 October 1901

[2] Fox's appointment as 'Commandant' was found to be *ultra vires* in 1894. From 1 September 1894 to 30 November 1896 he was Military Adviser to the New Zealand government and Inspector of the New Zealand Forces.

Appendix

Commandant

Major R.H. Owen (acting)	17 October 1901	22 January 1902
Major-General J.M. *Babington	6 December 1901	30 November 1906
Colonel W.H. Webb (acting)	22 September 1906	18 December 1906

Chief of the General Staff and First Military Member

Colonel A.W. *Robin	19 December 1906	20 December 1910

Commandant and General Officer Commanding

Major-General A.J. *Godley	7 December 1910	10 September 1914
Major-General A.W. *Robin	11 September 1914	10 December 1919
Major-General E.W.C. *Chaytor	10 December 1919	1 March 1924
Major-General C.N. *Melvill	1 May 1924	15 September 1925
Major-General Robert *Young	7 December 1925	31 March 1931
Major-General W.L.H. *Sinclair-Burgess	1 April 1931	31 March 1937

Chief of the General Staff and (until 1971) First Military Member

Major-General J.E. *Duigan	1 April 1937	31 May 1941
Major-General Sir Andrew H. *Russell (acting)	10 October 1940	28 December 1940
Lieutenant-General Edward *Puttick	1 August 1941	31 December 1945
Major-General N. McD. *Weir	1 January 1946	31 March 1949
Major-General K.L. *Stewart	1 April 1949	31 March 1952
Major-General W.G. *Gentry	1 April 1952	14 August 1955
Major General C.E. *Weir	15 August 1955	31 August 1960
Major-General L.E *Thornton	1 September 1960	31 March 1965
Major-General W.S. *McKinnon	1 April 1965	31 March 1967
Major-General R.B. Dawson	1 April 1967	31 March 1970
Major-General R.J.H. *Webb	1 April 1970	28 September 1971
Major-General L.A. Pearce	29 September 1971	30 September 1973
Major-General R.H.F. Holloway	1 October 1973	15 November 1976
Major-General R.D.P. *Hassett	15 November 1976	16 November 1978
Major-General B.M. *Poananga	16 November 1978	15 November 1981
Major-General R.G. Williams	16 November 1981	12 December 1984
Major-General J.A. *Mace	12 December 1984	30 November 1987
Major-General D.S. *McIver	1 December 1987	28 February 1989
Major-General Bruce Meldrum	1 March 1989	1 March 1992
Major-General A.L. *Birks	1 March 1992	25 February 1995
Major-General P.M. Reid	25 February 1995	25 February 1998
Major-General M.F. Dodson	26 February 1998	

Air Force

Chief of the Air Staff and (until 1971) First Air Member

Wing Commander the Hon R.A. *Cochrane RAF	1 April 1937	8 March 1939
Group Captain H.W.L. *Saunders RAF	8 March 1939	13 December 1941
Air Commodore R.V. *Goddard RAF	13 December 1941	19 July 1943
Air Vice-Marshal L.M. *Isitt	19 July 1943	15 May 1946
Air Vice-Marshal A.de T. *Nevill	16 May 1946	15 January 1951
Air Vice-Marshal D.V. Carnegie RAF	15 January 1951	23 February 1954
Air Vice-Marshal W.H. Merton	23 February 1955	5 June 1956
Air Vice-Marshal C.E. *Kay	5 June 1956	30 June 1958
Air Vice-Marshal M.F. Calder	1 July 1958	30 June 1962
Air Vice-Marshal I.G. *Morrison	1 July 1962	30 June 1966

Appendix

Air Vice-Marshal C.A. Turner	1 July 1966	30 June 1966
Air Vice-Marshal W.H. Stratton	1 July 1969	22 July 1971
Air Vice-Marshal D.F. St George	23 July 1971	7 September 1974
Air Vice-Marshal R.B. Bolt	8 September 1974	15 October 1976
Air Vice-Marshal C.L. Siegert	16 October 1986	15 October 1979
Air Vice-Marshal D.E. *Jamieson	16 October 1979	14 April 1983
Air Vice-Marshal David *Crooks	14 April 1983	15 October 1986
Air Vice-Marshal Patrick Neville	16 October 1986	15 October 1988
Air Vice-Marshal P.R. Adamson	16 October 1988	24 September 1992
Air Vice-Marshal J.S. Hosie	25 September 1992	25 September 1995
Air Vice-Marshal C.W. Adamson	26 September 1995	24 February 1999
Air Vice-Marshal D.M. Hamilton	25 February 1999	

PREMIERS AND PRIME MINISTERS

Henry Sewell	18 April 1856	20 May 1856
William Fox	20 May 1856	2 June 1856
E.W. Stafford	2 June 1856	12 July 1861
William Fox	12 July 1861	2 August 1861
Alfred Domett	6 August 1862	30 October 1863
Frederick Whitaker	30 October 1863	24 November 1864
F.A. Weld	24 November 1864	16 October 1865
E.W. Stafford	16 October 1865	28 June 1869
William Fox	28 June 1869	10 September 1872
E.W. Stafford	10 September 1872	11 October 1872
G.M. Waterhouse	11 October 1872	3 March 1873
William Fox	3 March 1873	8 April 1873
Julius Vogel	8 April 1873	6 July 1875
Daniel Pollen	6 July 1875	15 February 1876
Sir Julius Vogel	15 February 1876	1 September 1876
H.A. Atkinson	1 September 1876	13 October 1877
Sir George *Grey	13 October 1877	8 October 1879
John Hall	8 October 1879	21 April 1882
Frederick Whitaker	21 April 1882	25 September 1883
H.A. Atkinson	25 September 1883	16 August 1884
Robert Stout	16 August 1884	28 August 1884
H.A. Atkinson	28 August 1884	3 September 1884
Sir Robert Stout	3 September 1884	8 October 1887
Sir Harry Atkinson	8 October 1887	24 January 1891
John Ballance	24 January 1891	27 April 1893
R.J. *Seddon	1 May 1893	10 June 1906
William Hall-Jones	21 June 1906	6 August 1906
Sir Joseph *Ward	6 August 1906	28 March 1912
Thomas Mackenzie	28 March 1912	10 July 1912
W.F. *Massey	10 July 1912	10 May 1925
F.H.D. Bell	14 May 1925	30 May 1925
J.G. Coates	30 May 1925	10 December 1928
Sir Joseph Ward	10 December 1928	28 May 1930
G.W. Forbes	28 May 1930	6 December 1935
M.J. *Savage	6 December 1935	27 March 1940
Peter *Fraser	1 April 1940	13 December 1949
S.G. Holland	13 December 1949	20 September 1957
K.J. Holyoake	20 September 1957	12 December 1957

631

Appendix

Walter Nash	12 December 1957	12 December 1960
K.J. Holyoake	12 December 1960	7 February 1972
J.R. Marshall	7 February 1972	8 December 1972
N.E. Kirk	8 December 1972	31 August 1974
W.E. Rowling	6 September 1974	12 December 1975
R.D. Muldoon	12 December 1975	26 July 1984
D.R. *Lange	26 July 1984	8 August 1989
G.W.R. Palmer	8 August 1989	4 September 1990
M.K. Moore	4 September 1990	2 November 1990
J.B. Bolger	2 November 1990	8 December 1997
J.M. Shipley	8 December 1997	10 December 1999
H.E. Clark	10 December 1999	

MINISTERS OF DEFENCE-RELATED PORTFOLIOS

Colonial Defence

Thomas Russell	30 October 1863	24 November 1864
H.A. Atkinson	24 November 1864	16 October 1865
T.M. *Haultain	31 October 1865	28 June 1869
Donald *McLean	28 June 1869	10 September 1872

Native Affairs (also responsible for Defence)

Sir Donald *McLean	11 October 1872	7 December 1876
Daniel Pollen	18 December 1876	13 October 1877
John Sheehan	15 October 1877	8 October 1879
John Bryce	8 October 1879	21 January 1881
William Rolleston	4 February 1881	19 October 1881
John Bryce	21 April 1882	16 August 1884

Defence

John Bryce	19 October 1881	21 April 1882
John Ballance	16 August 1884	8 October 1887
Thomas Fergus	8 October 1887	17 October 1889
W.R. Russell	17 October 1889	24 January 1891
R.J. *Seddon	24 January 1891	22 June 1896
Thomas Thompson	22 June 1896	23 January 1900
R.J. Seddon	23 January 1900	10 June 1906
Albert Pitt	21 June 1906	18 November 1906
Sir Joseph *Ward	23 November 1906	28 March 1912
A.M. Myers	28 March 1912	10 July 1912
James *Allen	10 July 1912	28 April 1920
Sir Robert H. Rhodes	21 July 1920	18 January 1926
F.J. Rolleston	18 January 1926	26 November 1928
W.D. Stewart	28 November 1928	10 December 1928
T.M. Wilford	10 December 1928	10 December 1929
J.G. Cobbe	18 December 1929	6 December 1935
Frederick *Jones	6 December 1935	13 December 1949
T.L. Macdonald	13 December 1949	26 September 1957
D.J. *Eyre	26 September 1957	12 December 1957
P.G. *Connolly	12 December 1957	12 December 1960
D.J. Eyre	12 December 1960	12 December 1966
D.S. Thomson	12 December 1966	9 February 1972
Allan McCready	9 February 1972	8 December 1972

A.J. Faulkner	8 December 1972	10 September 1974
W.A. Fraser	10 September 1974	12 December 1975
Allan McCready	12 December 1975	13 December 1978
T.F. Gill	13 December 1978	21 August 1980
D.S. Thomson	22 August 1980	26 July 1984
F.D. O'Flynn	26 July 1984	24 August 1987
R.J. Tizard	24 August 1987	9 February 1990
P.W. Tapsell	9 February 1990	2 November 1990
W.E. Cooper	2 November 1990	1 March 1996
P.C. East	1 March 1996	8 December 1997
M.R. Bradford	8 December 1997	10 December 1999
R.M. Burdon	10 December 1999	

Armed Forces and War Co-ordination

J.G. Coates	30 June 1942	27 May 1943

National Service

Robert Semple	21 June 1940	30 June 1942
W.J. Broadfoot	30 June 1942	2 October 1942

Supply and Munitions

D.G. Sullivan	16 July 1940	21 August 1945

Disarmament and Arms Control

C.R. Marshall	24 August 1987	30 January 1989
F.H. Wilde	30 January 1989	2 November 1990
D.A.M. Graham	2 November 1990	16 December 1996
D.C. McKinnon	16 December 1996	10 December 1999
M.P. Robson	10 December 1999	

HEADS OF DEFENCE-RELATED GOVERNMENT DEPARTMENTS

Under-Secretary for (Colonial) Defence

William Seed[3]	17 February 1864	1 February 1865
James Holt	1 February 1865	31 July 1868
C.E. Haughton	? October 1868	? April 1869
G.S. Cooper (acting)	? July 1869	8 August 1869
St John Branigan (acting)	8 August 1869	15? October 1869
G.S. Cooper (acting)	15? October 1869	30 June 1870
G.S. Cooper	1 July 1870	6 December 1871
Lt-Col William Moule (acting)[4]	7 December 1871	10 March 1875
Lt-Col W.C. Lyon (acting)	11 March 1875	23 April 1876
Lt-Col William Moule (acting)	23 April 1876	31 December 1877
Lt-Col H.E. Reader (acting)	1 January 1878	20 March 1879
Lt-Col H.E. Reader	21 March 1879	30 June 1885[5]
Maj-Gen Sir George S. *Whitmore	18 November 1885	4 April 1888[6]
Colonel C.A. Humfrey (acting)	5 April 1888	20 October 1889
Colonel C.A. Humfrey	21 October 1889	31 March 1891
Lt-Col Arthur Hume (acting)	1 April 1891	5 June 1895
Maj Sir Arthur P. *Douglas	6 June 1895	31 March 1903
Col T.W. Porter (acting)	1 October 1904	30 June 1905
Henry Turner	10 November 1930	1 September 1937

Appendix

[3] From July to November 1863 the Colonial Defence Office appears to have been in the charge of F.D. Fenton.
[4] Although not gazetted as Acting Under-Secretary for Defence, Moule was charged with conducting 'the Correspondence of the Defence Department'.
[5] From July to October 1885 Captain C.A. Humfrey probably carried out the Under-Secretary's responsibilities.
[6] Major W.E. *Gudgeon was appointed as Acting Under-Secretary for Defence on 18 November 1885, presumably because of Whitmore's heavy workload as Commander of the Forces and Commissioner of the Armed Constabulary.

Secretary of Defence

J.K. *Hunn	8 July 1963	30 November 1965
William Hutchings (acting)	1 December 1965	31 January 1966
William Hutchings	1 February 1966	31 October 1969
J.F. *Robertson	1 November 1969	11 February 1979
D.B.G. *McLean	12 February 1979	18 November 1988
Dr B.V. Walker	5 December 1988	8 December 1989
D.J. Swallow (acting)	9 December 1989	2 September 1990
H.M. Titter	3 September 1990	2 September 1991
G.C.P. *Hensley	3 September 1991	2 September 1999
G.C. Fortune	3 September 1999	

Navy Secretary

D.A. Wraight	5 February 1951	1 April 1964

Army Secretary

Henry Turner	1 September 1937	31 December 1940
F.B. Dwyer	1 January 1941	30 April 1959
A.N.V. Dobbs	1 April 1959	1 April 1964

Air Secretary

T.A. *Barrow	1 April 1937	31 August 1954
B.R. Rae	1 September 1954	1 April 1964

Director, National Service Department

J.S. Hunter	18 June 1940	31 March 1944
H.L. Bockett	1 April 1944	31 March 1946

Index

Bold numerals indicate a main entry on the topic in question. Particular Acts, aircraft, battles, battalions, batteries, brigades, companies, government departments, divisions, expeditionary forces, naval vessels, ships, or squadrons will be found under those entries.

Abyssinia **1**, 86, 130, 364, 388, 495
active service **1**
Acts:
   Australian 135
   imperial:
      Army 134, 146, 324; Army Discipline and Regulations 323; Colonial Forces Courts-Martial 323; Colonial Naval Defence 44, 104; Foreign Enlistment 386; Mutiny 323; Naval Discipline 134, 323–4; Naval Discipline (Dominion Naval Forces) 134; Statute of Westminster 174, 233
   New Zealand:
      Air Force 135, 324, 459; Armed Constabulary 33, 103; Armed Forces Discipline 136, 324–5; Chemical Weapons (Prohibition) 86; Colonial Defence: **103**, 323; Defence: *1886*, 35, 89, 108, 134, **139**, 324, 421, 569; *1908*, 139; *1909*, 25, 89, 91, 110, 115, 135, 139, 142, 324, 364, 571; *1964*, 138–9; *1971*, 139, 239, 325; *1990*, 136, 139, 362; Discharged Soldiers'

Settlement 499; Emergency Regulations 118, 434, 584; Expeditionary Forces 135; Military Service 112, 116, 118; Militia 117, 323, 331, 566; National Military Service 112; National Registration 583; Naval Defence 129, 134, 255, 324, **353**, 362–4, 455; Naval Training Schools 316; Navy 324, 353; New Zealand Army 135, 139, 359; Nuclear Free Zone, Disarmament, and Arms Control 32; Police Force 35, 139, 324; Public Safety Conservation 91, 238, **434–5**; Registration of Aliens 158; Royal New Zealand Air Force 135, 324; Training Ships 317; Volunteer 566; War Regulations 157, 615
Adamson, Air Mshl C.W. 623
Adamson, Pte T. 361
Agent Orange **1–2**, 86, 555, 565
Air Cadet League 77
air force bases **2–4**, 40, 101, 140, 263, 281, 345, 409, 459, 462, 586, 611
Air Training Corps 76
aircraft, RNZAF **4–6**
aircraft types:
   Airtrainer 6, 240, 462, 535
   Andover 6, 419, 462, 538–9
   Anson 6, 535, 596
   Auster 5, 360, 462
   Avenger 5, 63, 461
   Avro 504K 6, 236, 535–6
   Avro 626 6, 508, 535–6
   Baffin 4, 63–4, 460, 508

   Beaver 5, 462
   Beech B2000 6, 538
   Bleriot XI–2 4
   Boeing 727 6, 463, 539
   Buffalo 5, 74, 175, 290, 406, 454
   C-47 (Dakota) 6, 14–15, 56, 292, 448, 461–2, 538–9
   Canberra 4, 63–4, 114, 292, 294, 462
   Catalina 6, 311–12, 461–2
   Consul 6, 537
   Corsair 5, 167, 256, 410, 461
   Dauntless 5, 64, 461
   DC-6 6, 539
   Devon 6, 461–2, 535–7, 540
   DH 4 5, 236, 247
   DH 50A 5, 538
   DH 9 5, 236
   Dominie 6, 535–6, 538, 540
   Dragon 6, 455, 535
   Express 5, 535
   F-16 167, 463
   Fairey III 4, 508
   Fighter 5, 236, 411
   Freighter 6, 193, 239, 292, 294, 369, 461–2, 538–9
   Friendship 6, 462, 536
   Golden Eagle 6, 538–9
   Gordon 4, 7, 536
   Grebe 5, 166, 508
   Harvard 6, 415, 462, 535–6
   Hastings 6, 187, 461, 538–9
   Hawk 5, 535
   Hercules 6, 20, 88, 161, 170, 210–11, 239, 336, 420, 463, 538–39, 562
   Hind 6, 536

Index

Hudson 5, 63–4, 166, 311, 313, 357, 461, 502, 538
Hurricane 5, 9, 15, 406
Iroquois 5, 20, 88, 91, 152, 217–18, 336, 360, 369, 462, 562
Kittyhawk/Warhawk 5, 166–7, 175, 461, 502
Lodestar 6, 461, 538
Macchi 6, 536
Magister 5, 535
Meteor 5, 166
Mosquito 5, 12, 167–8, 461, 510
Moth 6, 477, 535–7, 574
Mustang 5, 11, 166–8, 462
Orion 6, 88, 311–12, 335–6, 448, 462, 468, 534
Oxford 6, 460, 537
Rapide 6, 535–6, 538, 540
Seasprite 5, 143, 187–8, 218, 534
Singapore III 6, 312
Sioux 5, 217–18, 360
Skyhawk 3, 5, 49, 64, 129, 166, 168, 463, 536
Spitfire 14–15, 157
Stirling 52, 63
Strikemaster 6, 462, 537
Sunderland 4, 6–7, 56, 88, 311–12, 461–2, 510, 538
Tiger Moth 6, 461–2, 535–7
Vampire 5, 63, 132, 166–8, 294, 462, 537
Venom 5, 166–8, 294, 462
Ventura 5, 63, 65, 336, 461, 501
Vildebeeste 5, 14, 65, 290, 460, 495
Vincent 5, 65, 176, 460
Walrus 467
Wasp 6, 186–7, 218, 230, 467, 534
Wellington 5, 8, 63, 65–6, 73, 101, 263, 460, 507, 537
airmen, NZ, in RAF (*see also* Fleet Air Arm)
  in First World War **7–8**, 67, 73–4, 77–80, 115, 172, 247, 411, 574
  in Second World War **8–15**, 52–3, 63, 66, 73–4, 80, 85, 94, 115, 122–3, 133, 136, 154, 156–7, 160, 172, 174–5, 204, 219, 262–3, 287, 290, 336, 411–12, 431–2, 460, 540–1, 573–4, 595
Aitken, Alexander 278
Alexander, Gen Sir H. 249, 392
Alexander, Col J. 384
aliens, treatment of **157–9**, 615
Allen, A.H. 44

Allen, Col Sir J. **15–16**, 47, 202, 213, 255, 259, 297–8, 353, 362–3, 365, 400, 453, 554, 614
Allen, Col Sir S.S. **16–17**, 477
Allenby, Gen Sir E. 492, 515, 601
Alley, Rewi 280
American Civil War 36, 95, 259, 383–4
Andrew, Brig-Gen A.W. **17**
Andrew, Brig L.W. **17**, 126, 559
Anglo-Japanese Alliance **17–18**, 48, 175, 233, 235, 254–5, 258, 313, 495
Anglo-Malayan (Malaysian) Defence Agreement 72, 175, 543
animals **18–19**, 61–2
Antarctica **19–20**, 80, 89, 186, 218, 312, 354, 370, 462, 468, 480, 498, 514
anti-aircraft weapons **20–1**, 99
Anti-German League 158
anti-invasion defences **20–2**, 86, 99, 155–6, 334, 436, 461, 611
Anti-Militarist League 25
anti-nuclearism **22–3**, 30, 32, 73, 103, 140, 145, 254, 274, 287, 350, 354, 396, 427, 445, 455, 462, 468
anti-submarine warfare 10–1, **23–4**, 143, 160, 162, 185–7, 312, 437, 480, 534, 541
anti-tank weapons 24
anti-war movements **25–7**, 29, 75
Anzac Day **27–30**, 36, 75, 89, 92, 109, 198, 322, 349–50, 352, 417, 426–7, 443–5, 556–7, 590
Anzac frigate project 49, 142, 188, 240–1, 467–9
Anzac Wireless Squadron 318
ANZAM 23, **30–1**, 45, 49, 71, 438–9, 466
ANZUK **31**, 72, 175, 369, 543
ANZUS 22–3, 26, **30–2**, 49, 56, 73, 87, 92, 102–3, 129, 139, 145, 161–2, 199, 219, 234, 254, 256, 271, 274, 284, 287, 291, 318, 360, 369, 410, 417, 438, 466–8, 481–2, 484, 489, 515, 557, 562, 565, 596
appeasement 1, **32**, 56, 204, 234, 279, 282, 478, 483
Arawa Flying Column, *see* kupapa
Ardagh, Brig P.A. **32**
Armed Constabulary **32–6**, 38, 41, 48, 56, 82, 89, 96, 103, 104, 139, 165, 177–8, 210, 216, 272, 283, 294, 320, 323, 327, 329, 344, 361–2, 387, 410–11, 421, 428, 451, 506, 519, 526, 546, 560, 568, 573, 611

armed merchant cruisers **36**
Armistice Day **36**
armour **36–8**, 251–2, 388–94, 463, 602
Armstrong, Rev G. 445
Army, 8th 11, 32, 43, 161, 183, 248, 252, 265, 336, 389–95, 426, 481, 593–4
army camps 16, **38–40**, 52, 55, 80, 89, 108, 112, 140, 153, 243, 281, 345, 367, 429
Army Educational and Welfare Service **40**, 463
Army schools **40–1**
Arnett, Peter 580
artillery **41–3**, 94–100, 301, 383, 391, 470, 606
Atack, W.H. 487
atomic bomb 22, 26, **43–4**, 312, 395, 403, 410, 480
Auchinleck, Gen Sir C. 128, 389, 392
Auckland War Memorial Museum 54, 339, 358, 577, 590
Austin, Sgt S. 361
Australasian Naval Agreements **44–6**, 129, 232, 402, 455, 484, 595
Australia–New Zealand Agreement **45**, 48, 56, 409, 465, 596
Australian Auxiliary Squadron 44, **46**, 129, 402
Australian–New Zealand defence cooperation 16, **45–9**, 160–2, 202
Australians in New Zealand wars 377, **384–6**
Avery, Capt G.A. 431
Awatere, Lt-Col A. **49–50**, 311

B Force 168
Babington, Lt-Gen Sir J.M. **51**, 107, 136, 301, 337, 544, 570
Baden-Powell, Col R. 201
Bagnall, A.G. 57
Bagnold, Maj R.A. 281
Bain, D.W. 579
Bain, W.S. 25, 612
Baker, Lt-Col F. **51**, 310
Baker, Paul 321
Ballance, Rr-Ad F.A. 438
Ballance, John 484
Balneavis, Capt H.C. 136
bands **51–2**, 89, 266, 427
Bannerman Air Cdre R.B., 7, **52**
Barnes, Capt C.E. 447
Barns-Graham, A.B. 575–7
Barrington, A.C. 26, **52**, 616
Barrington, Brig B. 52
Barrington, Janet 616
Barron, Wg Cdr J.F. **52–3**

Index

Barrow, T.A. **53**, 156
Barrowclough, Maj-Gen Sir H.E. **53–4**, 148, 184, 368, 503, 507
Bartlett, Ashmead 349
Base Records **54**
Bassett, Lt-Col C.R.G. **54**, 327, 559
Batchelor, Sgt E. **54**
Bateson, Henry 579
battalions:
   Australian 269, 423, 562–3
   British 182, 193–7
   Canadian 269
   Fijian 169–70, 292, 409
   New Zealand:
      1st Bn, Auckland Regt 16, 559; 1st Bn, Canterbury Regt 263, 387, 431, 559, 609, 625; 1st Bn, NZ Scottish 528; 1st Bn, NZR 39, 52, 266, 294, 303, 465; 1st Bn, NZRB 486; 1st Bn, RNZIR 31, 39, 55, 114, 152, 242, 284, 369, 423, 465; 1st Bn, Ruahine Regt 528; 1st Bn, Wellington Regt 204, 214, 275, 559; 2nd Bn, Auckland Regt 16, 73, 75, 128, 177, 430, 559; 2nd Bn, Canterbury Regt 241, 313, 511–12; 2nd Bn, NZR 294, 423; 2nd Bn, NZRB 486, 559; 2nd Bn, Otago Regt, 73, 215, 540, 559; 2nd Bn, RNZIR 442, 464; 2nd Bn, Wellington Regt 17; 2nd Maori Bn 303, 311; 2nd/1st Bn, RNZIR 57, 161, 243, 465; 3rd Bn, NZRB 185, 436, 559; 3rd Bn, RNZIR 464; 4th Bn, NZRB 316, 436; 4th–6th Bns, RNZIR 464; 7th Bn, RNZIR 199, 465, 530; 18th 121, 280; 19th 447; 20th 74, 127, 143, 219, 264, 552–3, 559–60; 21st 126, 163, 208; 22nd 17, 124, 126, 154, 199, 391, 471, 531, 559; 23rd 54, 126, 163, 229, 497, 530–1, 559; 25th 51, 66, 345, 436; 26th 37, 163; 27th (Machine Gun) 207, 242, 253, 285; 28th (Maori) 49–51, 55, 127, 147, 163, 242, 251, 253, 266, 272, 279, 295, 307, 309–11, 387, 395, 487, 559, 593; 30th 169, 445; 37th 445; Auckland Infantry 16, 147, 241, 295, 625; Canterbury Infantry 73, 229, 241, 264, 313, 511, 624; NZ Entrenching 430, 606; NZ Machine Gun 243; NZ (Maori) Pioneer 263, 297–8, 321, 329, 367, 422–3,
506; Otago Infantry 193, 197, 241, 511; Wellington Infantry 196, 215, 241, 294–5, 316, 625
batteries, artillery:
   1st NZ 61
   161st 43, 328, 549, 562–3, 594
   34th Anti-Tank 286
   36th Survey 596
battle honours **54–5**, 70, 106, 331, 454
battles:
   Atlantic 10, 121, 187, 497, 516, 544
   Britain 9–10, 12, 136, 171, 183, 204, 350, 406, 411, 449
   Cassino 43, 66, 74, 89, 183–4, 200, 249–51, 265, 286, 311, 412
   Coral Sea 408, 502, 544
   Crusader offensive 12, 66, 147, 389–91
   Dogger Bank 357
   El Alamein 12, 43, 51, 54–5, 66, 154, 161, 183, 198, 214, 265, 281, 310, 320, 333, 335–6, 391–4, 403, 428, 592, 598
   France 9
   Gate Pa (Pukehinahina) 41, 78–9, 301, 348, 378, 384, 428, 434–5, 454, 470, 517
   Gaza 84
   Heligoland Bight 357
   Imphal 14
   Jutland 58, 107, 174, 357–8
   Kap'yong 267–9
   Kohima 14
   Kolombangara 131, 409, 502
   Krithia 195
   Messines 42, 55, 66, 73–4, 85, 147, 161, 185, 189, 202, 260, 275, 284, 316, 349, 423, 472, 595, 602–4
   Midway 408, 502, 544
   Orakau 41, 122, 171, 177, 216, 296, 326, 348, 377–8, 386, 526
   Passchendaele 16, 55, 67, 74, 85, 147, 174, 185, 202–3, 251, 260, 263, 278, 349, 423, 436, 472, 548, 604–5
   Rafa 84, 492
   Rangiriri 41, 78, 105, 377, 380, 434, 470
   River Plate 131, 134, 350, 364, 412, **451**, 465, 596
   Romani 430, 491
   Ruhr 11
   Somme 16–17, 36, 53, 66, 73–4, 85, 172, 182, 189, 215, 241,
243, 247, 260, 263–4, 266, 274, 278, 297, 313, 316, 319, 349, 423, 472, 511, 513, 601–6
   Te Ranga 78, 378, 435, 517
   Ypres 85, 202–3, 600–6
Baxter, A.M.L. **55**, 116, 278
Baxter, J.K. 55, 279–80
Beamish, F.E. 399
Beamish, Capt H. 7
Bean, C.E.W. 46, 400, 453, 579
Beatty, Adml Sir D. 358
Beauchamp, Sir H. 352
Beaufort, Chpln J.R. 83
Beazley, Kim 47
Beeby, C.E. 40
Begg, Col C.M. **55**
Belich, James 172, 301, 321, 384
Bell, A.W.D. **55**, 97
Bell, Enid 456
Bell, Maj P.H. 477
Bell, Robin 246
Bell, W.F. 575
Bennett, Agnes 614
Bennett, Cameron 580
Bennett, Lt-Col C.M. **55**, 311
Bennett, Capt G. 69
Bentley, Geoffrey 579
Berendsen, Sir C.A. **55–6**, 410, 496, 578
Berlin airlift **56**, 102, 160, 461
Bertram, James 279, 580, 593
Best, Elsdon 56
Bettington, Gp Capt A.V. 2, **56**, 67, 236, 459
bibliographies **57**
Biddle, Benjamin 361
Biggs, Maj R.C. 518
Binney, Judith 384
Biological Weapons Convention 200
Birdwood, Lt-Gen W. 27, 192, 202, 226
Birks, Lt-Gen A.L. **57**
Black, Solomon 361
black market **57–8**, 147, 481
Blake, Vice-Adml Sir G. **58**, 477
Blamey, Lt-Gen T.A. 205, 208
Bledisloe, Lord 352
Boddam, Maj T. 96
Boer War 17–18, 25, 46, 51, 54, 56, **59–63**, 66, 76, 80, 82, 84, 109, 128, 133–4, 146, 149, 171, 180, 188, 201, 213–15, 217, 224–6, 229, 232, 235–6, 260, 265, 272, 275, 277, 284, 296, 301, 313, 321, 324, 329, 332, 337, 348, 352, 364, 386–7, 399, 401, 413, 421, 424, 427–8, 430, 434, 440, 443, 446, 449, 451–2, 469, 471, 484, 486, 490, 497–8, 541, 546,

Index

549, 555, 558, 570, 575, 577–8, 589, 591–2, 594, 612
Boldrewood, Rolf 276
Bolger, J.B. 30, 32, 210, 224, 396
bomber aircraft **63–5**
Bomber Command 8–15, 66, 80, 101, 115, 154, 461, 478
bombs **65–6**
Bonifant, Brig I.L. **66**
Booth, Col H.J.P. 428
Borrie, John 279
Bosnia–Herzegovina 38, 69, 83, 106, 243, 360, 419, 426–7, 447, 462, 467, 470, 550, 580–1, 623
Bougainville conflict 167, 419, 468
Boxer, AVM Sir A.H.C. **66**
Boxer, Ernest 556
Boyle, Lt A.B. 456
Bradford, Pte G. 59
Bradford, M.R. 81
Braithwaite, Pte J. 345
Braithwaite, Brig-Gen W.G. **66–7**
Brandon, Lt-Col A. de B. 8, **67**
Branigan, St J. 33–4
Brathwaite, Errol 277, 279, 384
Brereton, C.B. 277
Bridge, Col C. **67**, 69, 372, 575
Bridges, Maj-Gen W.T. 191
Bridson, Cdr G. **67**
brigade groups 21, 106, 360, 529, 533
brigades:
    Australian 123, 191, 196, 207–8, 359, 366
    British 124, 134, 207, 270, 393, 611
    British Commonwealth 30, 215–16, 267–9, 294, **543**
    Canadian 270
    International 386
    New Zealand:
        1st (1NZEF) 73, 105, 147, 316, 605, 608; 1st Army Tank 37, 106, 412; 1st Infantry (TF) 16, 147, 423; 2nd (1NZEF) 105, 147, 241, 316, 435, 602–9, 611, 625; 2nd Infantry (TF) 163; 2nd NZ Field Artillery 412; 2nd (Wellington) Mounted Rifles 471; 3rd NZ (Rifle) 105–6, 147, 188–9, 241, 260, 274, 329–30, 435–6, 602–7, 611, 625; 4th (1NZEF) 147–8, 605; 4th (2NZEF) 37, 74, 105, 124, 148, 207, 243, 248, 389–92, 435; 4th Armoured 148, 253, 513; 5th 66, 74, 93, 124, 148, 154, 163, 207, 215, 248, 251, 264–5, 295, 335, 367, 389–91, 513; 6th 53, 66, 74, 93, 148, 198, 207, 248,

251–3, 389–90, 394, 412; 7th 281, 412; 8th 148, 169, 406, 409, 503; 9th 148, 199, 253, 256, 410, 513; 10th 124; 14th 148, 169, 407, 503; 16th 533; Fd Artillery 260; NZ Artillery 359; NZ Infantry 66, 191–8, 260, 297; NZ Mounted Rifles 18–19, 84, 106, 131, 153, 196–7, 244, 263, 297–8, 316, 320, 337, 359, 366, 429, 472, 491–4, 515, 594
    United States 562
Briggs, Lt-Gen Sir H. 291
Briggs, Mark 116
Brind, Capt W.D. 200, 340
British Army in New Zealand 38, **67–71**, 198, 327, 567
British Commonwealth Far East Strategic Reserve 30–1, **71–2**, 132, 175, 179, 234, 294, 322, 359, 445, 466, 481–2, 489, 505, 543
British Commonwealth Forces, Korea **72–3**, 107
British Commonwealth Occupation Force **72–3**, 94, 106, 132, 167, 256, 270, 322, 369, 410, 461, 538
Broad, John 279
Brodie, Cpl A. 327
Brodie, W.A., 579
Brodrick, T.N. 499
Brooke-Popham, ACM Sir R. 289
Brooker, Gary 323
Brown, Brig-Gen C.H.J. **73**
Brown, Sgt D.F. **73**, 559
Brown, Ion 576
Brown, Richard 578
Bruce, Nancy 593
Bryce, John 411
Buchanan affair 22, 32, 49, **73**, 103, 254, 274, 438
Buchanan, Ldg Smn C. 121
Buck, Maj P. 297, 422
Buckley, Air Cdre M.W. **73–4**
Buller, Sir W. 362
Bunbury, Maj T. 68
Burma campaign 14, **74**, 459–60
Burn, Lt W.W.A. 6, 74, 317, 360
Burnett, Ethel 614
Burnett, Cdre W.F. 454
Burrows, Brig J.T. **74**, 265, 279
Burt, Jean 613
Burton, Nell 616
Burton, 2Lt O.E. 26, 52, **74–5**, 278–9, 445, 616
Bush, Peter 591
Butler, Blanche 615
Butler, Capt G.E. **75**, 575–7

cadets 28, **76–7**, 110, 142
Caldicott, Helen 27
Caldwell, Air Cdre K.L. 7, **77–8**
Calliope Dock **78**, 352, 353–4, 363, 455
Cameron, Gen Sir D.A. 71, **78–9**, 87, 105, 128, 178, 209, 217, 283, 295, 327, 375, 377–9, 380, 383, 385, 435, 610
Campaign for Nuclear Disarmament 26, 142
Campbell, W.D. 578
Canadian forces 36, 269
Canberra Pact *see* Australia-New Zealand Agreement
Canterbury (NZ) Aviation Company 2, 7, 236, 611
Cape Expedition 101
Carey, Brig-Gen G.J. 377, 524–5
Carey, Maj-Gen R. **79**, 375
Cargill, Lt-Col J. 95
Carkeek, Sgt A.W. 361
Carleton, Hugh 384
Carr, Air Mshl Sir C.R. 7, **79–80**
Carroll, Sir J. 296
casualties 8, 10, 15, 63, **80**, 128, 131, 157, 208, 212, 243, 258, 270, 291–4, 297–8, 309, 311, 313, 366–8, 373–4, 378, 380, 385, 389–93, 395, 418, 430–3, 484, 486, 490–4, 503, 505, 563, 588, 601–9, 614
Cautley, Col H. 55, **80**, 96
Cave, Clem 579
censorship **80–1**, 172, 189, 210
Centre for Strategic Studies 81
Challinor, Deborah 323
Chanak crisis **82**, 85, 175, 349, 367
chaplains **82–4**, 443
Charlton, Philip 237
Chauvel, Maj-Gen H. 491–2
Chavasse, Capt N.G. 561
Chaytor, Maj-Gen Sir E.W.C. **84–5**, 110, 148, 370
Checketts, Wg Cdr J.M. **85**
chemical weapons **85–6**, 145–6, 200, 600
Chetwode, Lt-Gen Sir P. 84, 492
Chiefs of Staff:
    ANZAM 30
    Australian 30
    British 30, 112, 209, 233, 318, 412, 495–6, 505
    Joint 72
    New Zealand 21, 30, **86–7**, 131, 137–9, 141–3, 199, 230, 245, 401, 404, 407–8, 479, 489, 495, 512, 598
    US 15, 505

638

Index

Churchill, Sir W.S. 16, 31, 123, 128, 183, 190–1, 204–5, 248, 291, 350, 389, 392, 404, 408, 496, 550, 557
Chute, Gen Sir T. **87–8**, 177, 283, 379, 522, 526
civil community, assistance to **88–9**, 480
civil–military relations **91–3**, 108, 129, 174, 180, 274
civil power, aid to the **89–91**, 387, 471
Clark, Ernest 279
Clark, Gen M. 249
Clark, Lt R.S.C. **93**, 576–7
Clark-Hall, Air Mshl Sir R.H. **93**
Clements, Kevin 140
Cleveland, Les 593
Clifton, Brig G.H. **93–4**, 279
Closer Defence Relations **94**, 485
Clouston, Air Cdre A.E. **94**
Clouston, Sqn-Ldr W.G. 290
coast defences 21, 35, 38, 41, 55, 80, **94–100**, 103, 109, 129, 139–40, 148, 209–10, 258–9, 333, 351, 421, 455, 464, 470, 474, 480, 569, 586, 624
Coastal Command 8–11, 94, 121, 160, 541
coastwatchers **101**, 163, 245–6, 406, 433, 611
Coates, J.G. 233, 511, 578
Cochrane, ACM Sir R.A. 2, 53, 65, 87, 93, **101**, 459, 538, 611
Cody, J.F. 549
Coe, J.B. 576
Cohen, Gp Capt R.J. 56
Cold War 23, 26, 31–2, 56, 86, **102–3**, 110, 145, 148, 181, 230, 234, 238, 256, 267, 318, 410, 416, 428, 442, 445, 455, 461, 466, 549–50, 561, 565, 581
Cole, J.R. 278
Collett, Capt C. 7
Collins, Vice-Adml J.A. 438
Collins, Col R.J. 141
Collinson, T.B. 384
Colonial Ammunition Company 239
Colonial Conferences 160, 232, 254
Colonial Defence Committee **103**, 108–9, 143
Colonial Defence Force **103–4**, 198, 203, 283, 323, 375–6, 385, 388, 428, 560
colonial naval activities **104–5**, 385
colour patches **105–6**
colours 54, **106–7**
Colvin, Neville 426, 576
Combe, E.E. 279

command and control **107**
Commandants **107–8**, 397
commands, NZ Army **108–9**
commemorative contingents **109**, 170, 272, 452
Committee of Imperial Defence 103, **109**, 154, 214, 232–3, 401, 479, 495
Commonwealth Contingent, Korea 270
Commonwealth Liaison Mission, Korea **109**, 270
Commonwealth Trans-Antarctic Expedition 19, 498, 514
Commonwealth War Graves Commission 428, 587
companies:
  9th NZ Railway Survey 204
  10th Transport 270
  Divisional Ammunition 280
  Divisional Signal 54, 312, 318
  Light Railway Operating 320
  NZ Divisional Employment 345
  NZ Tunnelling 149, 320, 334, 603
  V 284, 562–3
  W 563
compulsory military training 16, 25–7, 39, 53, 76, 85, 92, 102, **109–13**, 115–17, 134, 139–40, 142, 146, 148, 150, 173, 181, 202, 213, 239, 265, 302, 318, 336, 348, 350, 359, 367, 369, 451–2, 461, 495, 513, 527, 531, 556, 570–1, 596, 598, 625
Confrontation 31, 80, 83, **113–14**, 132, 226, 247, 254, 284, 322, 328, 360, 423–4, 447, 462, 467, 496, 505, 543, 549, 562–3, 579, 592
Coningham, AVM Sir A. 7, 11–13, **114–15**, 133, 393
Conly, Maurice 576
Connolly, Lt-Cdr P.G. **115**
conscientious objection 26, 55, 110, **115–17**, 278–9, 330, 443, 556, 616
conscription 16, 25–8, 92, 110, **115–20**, 150, 158, 174, 180–1, 272, 281, 298, 302, 307, 321, 331, 350–1, 366, 400, 428, 443–5, 455, 478, 483, 499, 528–9, 556, 564, 583, 605, 610, 614–20
contingents, Boer War 59–63, 148, 180, 226, 272, 275, 295–6, 324, 329, 332, 337, 348, 413, 421, 424, 430, 486, 490, 497, 549
  1st 25, 59–62, 148, 229, 430, 452, 541, 578
  2nd 59–61, 452, 486

  3rd 61–2, 84, 133, 430, 452, 612
  4th 59–61, 51, 133, 188, 214, 429, 559, 612
  5th 61, 387
  6th 17, 61–2, 296, 430
  7th 62, 428
  8th 63, 84, 133
  9th 63, 215, 428
  10th 17, 63, 149, 229
convoys **120–1**, 366
Cook, Capt J. 151, 230–1, 453
Cooke, Pte T. 560
Cooper, Peter 591
Corner, F.H. 140
Corner Committee, *see* Defence Committee of Enquiry
corps:
  I ANZAC 601–4, 606
  II ANZAC 27, 46, 55, 202, 601–7
  XXII 55, 202, 605–7
  XXX 32, 93
  ANZAC **27**, 46, 191–8, 202, 359, 426
  Australian 607
  Canadian 252, 605–7
  New Zealand 251
corvettes **121**, 496
Cossgrove, Maj D. 410
Costello, Maj D.P. 246
Couchman, Gary 339
Council of Defence 86, 108, 134, 136, **139–42**, 150, 162, 180, 261, 266, 275, 325, 332, 401, 452, 467, 489, 596
Courage, James 278
Courlander, L-Cpl R.N. **121**, 387, 432–3
Coutts, Pte R. 61
Cowan, James **122**, 171, 321, 384, 399, 589
Cowell, John 343
Cox, Maj G.S. **122**, 246, 279, 487, 580
Crawford, J.A.B. 321
Crawford-Compton, AVM W.V. **122–3**
Crete 11, 16–17, 20, 46, 51, 55–6, 66, 74–5, **122–8**, 134, 147, 154, 183–4, 204, 208–9, 214–15, 229, 243, 264, 266, 278–9, 286, 295, 309, 320, 328, 368, 389, 431–2, 436–7, 447–8, 472, 487, 512–13, 530, 544, 552, 576, 579–80, 592
Crichton, Sgt J. **128**, 559
Crimean War 78, 94, **128–9**, 383, 428, 473, 480, 558–9, 594, 610, 624
Crippen, Jack 576
Crooks, Air Mshl D.M. 92, **129**
Cross, Philip 387
Crossley, PO E.D. 433

639

Index

cruisers 78, **129–32**, 176, 311, 402, 450–1, 453, 455–6, 458, 465–7, 475–6, 480, 495–6, 502, 514, 534
Crump, Brig S.H. **132**
Cullen, John 158
Culliford, F-Lt S.G. 448
Cumberworth, F.H. 575
Cunningham, Adml A.B. 127
Cunningham, Brig W.H. 168
Curnow, Allen 279
Cyprus 72, **132**, 162, 166, 168, 318, 416, 462, 539

D-Day 12–13, 32, 122, **133**, 201, 215, 251, 279, 336, 410, 413, 459
D'Arcy, Capt H.C.D. 560–1
d'Urville, Dumont 151
Dale, Stkr D.W. 199
Dalton, B.J. 321, 384
Daniel, Mdshpmn E. St J. 560
Davies, Maj-Gen R.H. 63, **133–4**, 141, 226
Davin, Maj D.M. **134**, 246, 278, 593
Davis-Goff, Cdre G.R. **134**
Dawson, Brig R.B. 543
Dawson, Lt S. 8
Deans, Austin 576
Dearing, Maj R.S. 114
death penalty 69, **134–6**, 147, 324, 344–5
declarations of war 172–3, 367, 482–3
Deere, Wg Cdr A.C. 10, **136**
defence, higher organisation of **136–7**
Defence, Ministry of 2, 40, 82, 91, **137–9**, 142–3, 161, 229, 281, 287, 356, 362, 401, 452, 486, 598
Defence Committee of Enquiry **139–40**, 423
defence construction **140**, 584, 586
Defence Council, *see* Council of Defence
Defence League 53, 110, 112
defence lobby groups **142**
defence reviews 4, **142–3**, 219, 466–7, 484–5
defence schemes 103, **143**, 178, 421
Defence Scientific Establishment 480
Defence Secretariat 87, 129, 138, **143**, 284, 489
Denvir, 2Lt J. **143**, 447
departments, NZ government:
    Air **2**, 53, 459, 479
    Army 2, **40**, 54, 312
    Civil Aviation 2
    Customs 244
    Defence 2, 40, 54, 59, 91, 108, 116, **136**, 239, 334, 399–400, 452, 479, 555, 583

    Discharged Soldiers' Information 446
    External Affairs 489
    Internal Affairs 154, 399–401, 587–8
    Labour 56, 351
    Munitions and Supplies 582–3
    National Service 86, 119, 154, 220, 273, 307, **351**, 618–19
    Navy 2, 356
    Pensions 591
    Post and Telegraph 81, 244–5, 327
    Prime Minister's 56, 138, 141, 143, 218, 489, 579
    Public Works 2, 51, 53, 55, 97, 101, 140, 219, 236, 276, 290, 368, 586
    Rehabilitation 308, 446
    Repatriation 446, 500
    Scientific and Industrial Research 166, 312, 478–80
    Supply 585
depth charges 36, 65, 73, 121, **143–4**, 176, 218
Despard, Col H. 71, **144**, 262, 372
Deverell, G.R. 36
Diamond, Sgt B. 560
Dickson, Capt E. 8
Dill, Gen Sir J. 205
disarmament 26, 86, **144–6**, 255
discipline **146–7**, 189, 252, 321–2, 481
Dittmer, Brig G. **147**, 309
divisions:
    Australian 27, 191–8, 205, 290, 603–4
    Australian/New Zealand:
        Anzac Mounted 27, 84, 148, 338, 429, 491, 515, 573; New Zealand and Australian 27, 48, 55, 66, 84, **147**, 191–8, 229, 260, 338, 360, 367, 472
    British 133–4, 182, 191–7, 201, 429, 598, 603, 611
    Commonwealth 106, 269–70, 320, 543
    German 391–2
    New Zealand:
        New Zealand (1916–19) 18, 75, 85, 105, **147**, 149, 161, 171, 179, 204, 207, 241, 243–4, 260, 278, 284, 314, 316, 320–1, 330, 359, 366, 422–3, 430, 453, 472, 505, 511–12, 540, 576, 578, 592, 594, 598–610; *1st* 21, 148; 2nd NZ 19, 24, 37, 42, 53, 93, 122–3, 132, 134, **148**, 161, 183, 205, 219, 242–3, 246, 248–53, 263–5, 278, 281,

285–6, 309, 318, 320, 338, 367–8, 388–95, 403, 408, 412, 425–6, 431, 436–7, 448, 490, 504, 512, 530–2, 553, 592, 598; *3rd* 53–4, 93, 106, **148**, 162, 184, 242, 246, 276, 285, 294, 320, 322, 328, 330, 351, 357, 368, 404, 408–9, 487, 490, 503–4, 529; *4th* 21, 148, 597; *5th* 21, 148
    Turkish 193
    United States 408, 550–1
Dixon, Charles 575
Dodecanese Islands 282, 368, 532
Dog Tax rebellion **148–9**, 387, 568
Donnithorne, D.E. 339
Dornbusch, C.E. 57
Douglas, Maj Sir A.P. **148**
Dove, Col W.W. 368
Dowding, ACM Sir H. 411
Dowell, Lt G.D. 560
Down, Ensgn J.T. 560
Doyle, Charles 280
Dreaver, Mary 273
Drew, Lt H.T.B. 400
Duder, John 228
Duigan, Maj-Gen Sir J.E. 86, **149–50**, 179, 334, 436, 473
Duigan, Sidney **150**, 447
Dulles, J.F. 31
Dunne, Brig M. 152
Dunsterforce 318, 473, 511
Duntroon, see Royal Military College
Dyer, Lt-Col H.G. 310

early Maori–European conflict **151–2**
East Coast Wars 284, 288, 379–81, 517–20, 522, 532–3, 573, 610–11
East Timor 103–4, **152**, 317, 360, 416, 419–20, 622
Edmonds, Capt A. 447
Edward VII, King 109, 272, 428
Efford, Lincoln 25
Egypt, New Zealanders in 19, 27–8, 40, 48, 51, 74, 84, 120, 123, 131–2, **153–4**, 174, 181, 183, 188, 191–6, 198–9, 202, 204, 214, 229, 241, 246–8, 264, 284, 286, 294, 296, 309–10, 313–14, 319, 330–1, 338, 345, 349, 359, 364, 366–8, 388–9, 391, 395, 397, 412, 426, 432, 436, 448, 452–3, 469–70, 475, 483, 486–7, 492–4, 506, 511–13, 531–2, 540, 542, 547, 554, 575, 578–9, 588, 591, 597–8, 613–14, 621
Elder, Rod 280

640

Index

Elizabeth II, Queen 107, 109, 132, 225, 227, 352, 362, 465
Elliott, 2nd Lt K. **154**, 229, 559
Elworthy, Mshl of RAF Sir S.C. **154**, 386
Emergency Precautions Scheme 86, 92, 119, **154–6**, 158, 220, 617
Empire Air Training Scheme 2, 8–10, 14, 53, 120, **156–7**, 247, 309, 460, 463, 478, 541
enemy operations in NZ waters **158–9**, 354, 407, 480
Ensor, Wg Cdr M.A. **159**
Epanaia Kapewhiti 379
Erebus disaster 88
Evans, H.J. 23
Ewart, Tom 579
exchanges **160**, 318
exercises **161–2**
expeditionary forces:
    1NZEF 6–7, 16–17, 27, 32, 38, 40–1, 53–6, 66, 73, 75, 82, 84, 92, 105, 110, 114, 117–18, 120, 128–9, 132, 135–6, 147, 149, 153, 158, 174, 177, 183–5, 191–2, 198, 201–4, 213–15, 226–7, 229, 240–1, 243, 247, 255, 260–1, 263, 274, 284, 287, 294, 296, 298, 312–16, 319–21, 324, 327, 330, 336–7, 345, 354, 359, **364–7**, 369, 386–7, 397, 399–400, 410–13, 422, 425, 429, 431, 435, 446, 450, 452–3, 464–5, 469, 472–3, 478, 486, 506, 511–13, 528, 531, 540–1, 547, 549, 554–5, 573, 575–6, 582–3, 590–1, 597, 602, 611, 625
    2NZEF 16–17, 20, 32, 38, 49, 52–7, 66, 74–5, 81–3, 93, 106, 110, 118–22, 128, 130, 132–5, 143, 147, 149, 153–4, 163, 169, 170–1, 180–4, 189, 198–200, 203–5, 214–15, 218–19, 227–9, 242–3, 246, 256, 266, 275, 280, 286–7, 295, 303, 307, 309, 311, 313, 319, 322, 327, 330, 336, 338, 345, 360, 364, **367–9**, 387–8, 397, 400–1, 403, 412, 423, 425–6, 431, 436, 465, 469, 470–3, 481, 483–4, 486–7, 490, 502, 506–7, 510–13, 528–32, 541–2, 549–50, 552, 555–7, 576, 579–80, 588, 591–3, 596–8, 621, 626–7
    3NZEF 359, 364, 369
Fiji **170–1**, 436, 529, 611

Samoa 56, 84, 114, 120, 129, 173, 188, 202, 213, 280, 365, 435, 452, 470, 486, 513, 578, 620
Ex-Prisoners of War Association 555
External Assessments Bureau 247
Eyre, D.J. 138, **161**

Fahey, Jacqueline 577
Fairbrother, Brig M.C. **163**, 311, 588
Falklands War **163**, 172, 187–8, 455, 467, 561
Fanning Island 81, 99, 101, 131, **163–4**, 404, 406
Featherston, I.E. 361
Featherston incident **164**, 434
Featon, John 276, 578
Fencibles 71, **164–5**, 216, 323, 325, 498
Fenian riots **165–6**
Fergusson, J.G. 44
Fielding, Gen W. 107
fighter and fighter-bomber aircraft **166–8**
Fighter Command 8–13, 219, 411
Fiji:
    coups 92, 129, **170**, 274, 346, 468, 515
    in Second World War 20, 65, 83, 99, 101, 115, 147–8, **168–70**, 313, 320, 404–9, 436, 445, 460, 478, 537, 593, 611
Fiji Expeditionary Force, *see* expeditionary forces
Fiji Military Forces, (Royal) 169–70, 406, 409, 445, 502, 532–3
films **171–2**, 384, 427
Findlay, Air Cdre J.L. **172**
First World War 7–8, **172–5**, 296–9, 455–6, 581–3, 612–15
Fisken, FO G.B. **175**
FitzRoy, Robert 209, 217, 354, 372–3, 454, 573
Five Power Defence Arrangements 31, **175–6**, 234, 543
flags 106–7, 469, 519
Fleet Air Arm 64, 121, 133, **176–7**, 409, 433, 449–50, 457–8, 496, 594
Fletcher, James 140
flotillas:
    25th Minesweeping 67, 408, 421, 453, 502
    80th and 81st Motor Launch 414
Flying Squadron 454–5
flying training 7, 101, 156–7, 176, 398, 460, 478, 574
Foch, Mshl 606
Folkes, Maj K. 220, 246
Forbes, G.W. 233

Forest Rangers 171, **177**, 276, 326, 329, 348, 376, 451, 486, 497, 505, 526
Forsyth, Sgt S. **177**, 559
Fortescue, J.W. 384
fortifications 38, **178–9**
Forward defence **179**, 255, 301, 482, 561, 564
Four Colonels' revolt 92, **179–80**
Fox, Col F.J. 41, 51, 92, 107, 139, 149, **180**, 421, 451, 484, 497, 569
Fox, William 33, 384
Fox's Martyrs 569
Frame, Janet 278
Fraser, A.A. 276
Fraser, Janet 617
Fraser, Maj J. **177**, 326, 526
Fraser, Peter 16, 43, 45, 49, 56, 110, 112, 116, 127, **180–1**, 183, 205, 209, 215, 249, 261, 275, 308, 311, 318, 345, 364, 368, 403, 409, 478, 512, 542, 549, 578, 593, 617
French, Lt-Gen Sir J. 61
French Foreign Legion 386, 572
Fresne, M. du 151
Freyberg, Lt-Gen Sir B.C. 16–17, 20, 37, 50, 53, 56, 83, 123, 125–8, 148, 153, **180–4**, 189, 195, 205, 207–9, 215, 243, 249–53, 264–6, 279, 286, 311, 322, 328, 350, 367–8, 386, 390–4, 436–7, 450, 506–7, 512, 516, 542, 544, 560, 576, 594, 598, 621
Freyberg's Charter 53, **183–4**
Frickleton, Capt S. **185**, 559
friendly fire **185**, 264, 603
frigates 24, 83, 121, 144, 176, **185–8**, 217, 230, 270, 292, 303, 318, 335, 356, 455, 466–8, 534, 537–8, 623
Fulton, Brig-Gen H.T. **188**
furlough affair 81, 147, **189**, 265, 311, 345, 369

Gallipoli 7, 16, 18, 27–30, 41, 46, 48, 54–5, 66, 73–4, 82, 84, 89, 93, 109, 115, 135, 147, 171–2, 174–5, 182, 184–5, **190–8**, 202, 204, 213, 215, 226, 228–9, 260, 263, 266, 277–8, 284, 287, 294–5, 297, 313–14, 316, 319–21, 327, 329, 336–7, 349–50, 360, 367, 400, 411, 422, 426–7, 429–30, 443, 450, 453, 472, 487, 489, 491, 494, 497, 499, 511–12, 540, 572–3, 575, 578, 588, 591, 594, 597, 602, 625
Galloway, Gen T.J. 103, **198**
Gambrill, Col R.F. 179

641

Index

Gannon, A. Te W. 296
Gardiner, Noel 279
Gardner, Pte F.M. 447
Garland, Gnr N.G. 433
Gasson, J.A. 579
Geddes, M.M. 615
Gee, Maurice 278–9
gender issues 427, 468, 623
Geneva Conventions 84, 164, 430–2, 441, 470–1
Geneva Naval Conference 144, 258
Geneva Protocol 85, 145, 199
Gentry, Maj-Gen Sir W.G. 87, **198–9**, 437
George Cross **199**, 362, 472
George IV, King 521
George V, King 172–3, 226, 272
George VI, King 109, 130, 147, 295, 460, 482, 597
George, K.D. 44
germ warfare 145–6, **199–200**
Ghormley, Vice-Adml R.L. 181, 408, 505, 550
Gibb, Rev J. 444
Gibson, E.A. 2
Gibson, Lucy 616
Gibson, Tom 384
Gilbert, Brig Sir W.H.E. **200**, 247
Gillies, Sir H.D. **200**, 285
Girls' War **200**, 340, 424
Glasgow, Lord 92, 107, 180, 484
Glover, Lt-Cdr D.J.M. 133, **201**, 279
Goddard, Air Mshl Sir R.V. **201**
Godley, Gen Sir A.J. 15, 27, 48, 69, 84, 87, 98, 108, 110, 115, 134, 136, 141, 147, 153, 161, 191, 197, **201–3**, 213, 217, 260, 275, 297, 322, 349, 359, 364–6, 399, 450, 452–3, 527, 554, 601, 604–5
Gold, Maj-Gen C.E. 69, **203**, 374
Goldie, C.W.F. 575
Goodwin, Lt R.B. 433
Gordon, Brig-Gen J.M. 48
Gore Browne, Col T. 78, 374–5
Gorst, J.E. 244, 295
Gough, Gen Sir H. 601–4
Government Communications Security Bureau 247
gradation lists **203–4**
Grant, Lt J.G. **204**, 559
Gray, Gp Capt C.F. 10, **204**
Great White Fleet 353, 455
Greece 11, 16–17, 20, 27, 46, 51, 53, 55, 66, 75, 81–2, 93, 121–4, 128, 134, 143, 147, 154, 163, 181–4, **204–9**, 214–15, 219, 246, 264, 278–9, 295, 309, 319–20, 327, 338, 350, 367–8, 388, 412, 431–2, 436, 447, 472, 475, 513,

530–1, 552, 576, 579, 592, 598, 627
Greer, Lt-Col H.H. 378
Grey, Earl 164
Grey, Sir G.E. 34–5, 69–71, 78, 95, 164–5, 172, 179, **209**, 217, 244, 276, 301, 362, 373–9, 520, 524, 558, 611
Griffiths, Capt E.N. 386
Grigg, Mary 273
Gross, Richard 590
groups:
    air 101, 80, 101, 115, 154
    1 (Islands) 73, 93, 246, 336, 461, 574; 11 9–10, 411
    army 109, 529
Grover, Ray 277
Gudgeon, Lt-Col W.E. 35, **210**
Gulf War 66, 86, 172, 200, **210–12**, 274, 362, 416, 449, 462, 467, 539, 548, 580
Gummer, William 575, 590
Gurr, Col R.M. 114

Hadfield, Octavius 444
Hague Conventions 85, 430, 471
Haig, Fd Mshl Sir D. 203, 473, 601–6
Haimona Hiroti 521
Hakaraia 381–2
Hall, D.O.W. 321, 430
Hall, J.T. 579
Hall-Thompson, Adml P.H. 199, **213**, 353, 363
Halsey, Capt L. 357
Ham, Pte W. 366
Hamilton, Adam 578
Hamilton, Mrs D. 615
Hamilton, Gen Sir I.S.M. 191–7, 202, **213–14**, 279, 472, 527, 561
Hamilton, Ian 279
Hammond, Capt J. 8
Hancock, K.R. 579
Hankey, Lt-Col Sir M.P.A. 109, **214**
Hanley, J.O. 69
Hanley, Patrick 577
Hanna, Lt S.J. 456
Hanson, Brig F.M.H. **214**
Hanson, Pte J.R. 431
Hapurona 374, 523
Hardham, Maj W.J. 61, **214–15**, 559, 561
Hardie, Jack 279
Hargest, Brig J. 17, 124, 133, 183, **215**, 279, 319, 389–90, 432
Harle Moore, J.G. 277
Harper, Glyn 322
Harris, ACM Sir A. 11, 13, 15
Harrison, Craig 280
Hart, Brig-Gen H.E. **215**
Hart, Maj I.A. 310

Haskell, D.O. 2
Hassett, Maj-Gen R.D.P. **215–16**, 339
Haultain, T.M. 33, 71, 178, **216**
Havelock, Lt-Col Sir H. 216
Hawdon, Elizabeth 277
Hayes, Gwenyth 593
Hayr, AVM Sir K. 211
Hayward, Joel 323
Hayward, Rudall 171, 384
Heaphy, Maj C. **216–17**, 558–9, 567, 575
Heard, Col E.S. 90, **217**
Heke, Hone 67, 70, **217**, 262, 271, 356, 371–3, 379, 424, 523, 624
helicopters **217–18**
Hemphill, Col H.C. 307
Henare, Maj J.C. 311
Henderson, L-Bdr J.H. **218**, 279
Henderson, Michael 280
Hensley, G.C.P. **218–19**
Henty, G.A. 384
Herford, Maj W. 385
Herrick, Lt-Cdr L.E. **219**
Herrick, Ruth **219**, 620
Hesslyn, Sqn-Ldr R.B. **219**
Hewitt, B.L. 579
Hight, Sir J. 385
Hill, L-Cpl C.T. 204
Hill, Sgt G.R. 361
Hill, Rr-Adml H.W. 220
Hillary, Sir E. 19, 514, 539
Hinton, J.D. 208, **219**, 559
Hirtzell, Lt C.A.M. 362
Hiscocks, E.F. 488, 575
Hitler, Adolf 10, 233, 253, 279, 282, 389, 393, 444, 483, 593
hoaxes 95, **219–20**, 473–4
Hobson, Capt W. 354, 454
Hogben, Lt-Cdr G.L. 133
Holland, Maj F.G.L. **220**, 409
Holland, S.G. 30, 92, 179, 238, 395, 513, 578
Holmes, Noel 579
Holt, Edgar 384
Holyoake, K.J. 22, 112, 114, 416, 561–5
Home Guard 19, 21, 92, 119, 158, **220–3**, 226, 236, 246, 274, 303, 307, 316, 351, 484, 497, 597, 617, 625
homosexuality **223**
Hong Kong 102, **223**, 292, 455, 462
Hongi Hika 217, **223–4**, 262, 338, 340, 342, 415, 424, 525–6
honours and awards 199, **224–7**, 361–2, 558
Hooper, K.E. 579
Horan, Rr-Adml H.E. 86
Horne, Pte W.M. 447
Hornibrook, Fred 554

642

Index

hospital ships **228**, 315, 441
Hotere, Ralph 577
Hotham, Adml Sir A.G. **229**, 362
Howden, Peter 349
Hudson, Sgt M.K. 199
Hughes, Pte F. 135
Hughes, Col J.G. **229**
Hull, Lt C.B. 456
Hulme, Sgt A.C. 229, 559
Hulme, Lt-Col W. 372
Hunn, J.K. 138, **229–30**
Hunt, Diane 140
Hutton, Capt F.W. 95
Hyde, Robin 278–9
hydrographic surveying **230–1**, 468–9, 498

Ihimaera, Witi 277
Imperial Air Fleet Committee 4
Imperial Camel Corps 19, 492
Imperial Conferences 174, 229, **232–4**, 255, 313, 478, 496, 595–6
imperial defence 44, 103, 107–9, 179, 214, **232–6**, 274, 313, 321–2, 327, 363–4, 404, 484–5, 527, 570, 596
Imperial Defence College 101, **235**, 247, 263, 284, 287, 336, 411, 413, 423, 436, 452–3, 510, 512, 531, 597–8
Imperial Defence Conference 232, 255, 353, 570
Imperial General Staff **235**, 400, 452, 570
Imperial gift aircraft **236**, 535
Imperial Reserve 139, 232, **235–6**, 302, 484
improvised weapons **236–7**
industrial disputes, use of armed forces in 89, 92, 186, 217, **237–9**, 402, 434, 466, 472, 539, 587
industry **239–41**, 582–6, 618–19
infantry **241–3**, 253, 600, 606
influenza pandemic **243**, 280, 288, 476, 607, 615
Inglis, Maj-Gen L.M. 124, 126, 128, **243–4**, 391, 580
intelligence 101, 123, 160, 183, **244–7**, 369, 532, 544
International Military Tribunal for the Far East 410, 580
Isitt, AVM Sir L.M. 15, 87, **247**, 410, 461
Italian campaign 12, 32, 37, 49, 57, 66, 147–8, 163, 183–5, 189, 199, 214–15, 242, 244, **248–53**, 265, 278–9, 285, 287, 311, 315, 320, 328, 333, 336, 367, 403, 412, 437, 445, 481, 497, 513, 531, 576, 579, 593, 596

Jackson, Lt W. 177, 526
Jamieson, Air Mshl Sir D.E. **254**
Japanese threat 20, 156, **254–6**, 350, 460–1, 483, 611, 625
Jayforce 57, 72, 82, 132, 227, 246, **256–8**, 275, 287, 303, 311, 322, 328–9, 350, 369, 397, 410, 423, 445, 470, 487, 502, 512–13, 531, 541, 555, 577, 596, 598, 622, 626
Jellicoe, Lord 82, 144, 168, 213, 233, 258–9, 313, 358, 362, 495
Jeory, Liam 580
Jervois, Maj-Gen Sir W.J.D. 35, 80, 95, 148, **258–9**, 480–1
J–Force and BCOF Veterans' Association 555
Johnston, Brig-Gen F.E. 191, **260**, 295, 588
Johnston, Brig-Gen G.N. **260**, 605
Joint Intelligence Bureau 247
Jolly, D.W. 387
Jones, Connie 616
Jones, Frederick 179, **260–1**, 469, 578
Jones, Marian 615
Jordan, Capt W.S. 279, 448, 579
Joseph, M.K. 278
Jowett, Lt-Col V.E. **261**, 620
Judson, Maj R.S. **261**, 559

Kain, FO E.J. **262**
Kain, Wg Offr F.I. **262**, 620
Kaskowiski 95, 219
Kawiti 67, 217, **262**, 301, 319, 338, 356, 372–3, 379, 424, 545, 624
Kay, AVM C.E. **262–3**
Kay, Robin 576
Kaye, George 591
Kayforce 74, 239, 256, **263**, 266–70, 275, 279–80, 303, 320, 328–9, 350, 359, 386, 412, 433, 437, 446–7, 462, 481, 487, 502, 507, 513, 542, 547, 555, 577, 579, 588, 591, 626
Keiha, Lt-Col K.A. 311
Kemal Atatürk 194–5, 198, 590
Kemp, Maj, *see* Te Rangihiwinui, Te K.
Kennedy, Maj D.G. 101, 246
Kenrick, Sgt 558
Kent, Capt J.R. 343, 526
Kesselring, Fd Mshl A. 248
Kidman, Fiona 280
King, Lt-Col G.A. **263**, 297, 422
King, Pte J. 135
King, Capt W.M. 337
King George V Military Hospital 387, 531

King Movement 32, 35, 209, 244, 276–7, 288, 296, 371, 374–83, 428, 435, 517, 519–20, 523–4, 526, 532
Kingi, Wiremu, *see* Te Rangitake
King's Empire Veterans' Association 555
Kingsford, Reginald 8
Kippenberger, Maj-Gen Sir H.K. 55, 124, 127, 163, 216, 249, **263–5**, 279, 322–3, 339, 350, 400–1, 433, 557, 588
Kirby, J.H. 276
Kirk, Norman 396, 563
Kitchener, Fd Mshl Lord 59–61, 110, 141, 190, 196, 202, 213, **266**, 369, 527
Kitching, A.M. 579
Kiwi, Maj A. 339
Kiwi Concert Party **266**, 330, 368, 593
Kiwikiwi 200
Knox, Elizabeth 278
Kohere, Mokena 380
Korean War 26, 31, 37, 43, 45–6, 56, 66, 72–3, 80, 83, 102, 107, 109, 134, 146, 171, 176, 181, 184–6, 210–12, 216, 219, 226, 234, 256, **266–71**, 279–80, 315, 322, 328, 333, 359–60, 386, 401, 412, 414, 416, 420, 423–4, 433, 445–6, 453, 462, 464, 466, 481, 487, 489–90, 502, 507, 513, 537, 541–3, 547, 549, 555, 587, 591, 594, 596–7
Kosovo crisis 419–20, 442, 463
Krippner, Capt 434
kupapa 33, 216, **271–2**, 288, 301, 326, 347, 362, 379–83, 428–9, 498, 517–22, 532–3, 546, 572, 589–90, 610

Laird, Capt J. 317
land girls **273**, 582, 617
Lane, Trevor 579
Lane, W. 142
Lange, D.R. 22, 32, 73, 92, 140, 170, **273–4**, 417, 445
Laurent, Lt-Col H.J. **274**, 559
Law, Col G.B.M. 324
Lawry, Walter 279
League of Nations 1, 16, 25, 32, 56, 174–5, 255, **274–5**
Lee, J.A. **275**, 278
Legion of Frontiersmen 410
lemon-squeezer 106, **275**, 294, 330, 338, 349, 426, 547, 555
Lend-Lease 166, **275–6**, 461, 538, 584–5
Lepper, Lt-Col M. 326

643

Index

Leyland, W.B. 142
Lingard, Tpr W. 361
Linklater, Joseph 277
literature 134, **276–80**
Little, Sgt K.M. 27
Liverpool, Lord 90, 92, 148, 173, 313, 329, 612
Llewellyn, Capt S.P. **279–80**, 549, 579
Lloyd, Arthur 575–6
Logan, Col R. 243, **280**, 475–6
logistics **280–1**
Long Range Desert Group 247, **281–2**, 368, 388, 532
Love, Capt E.T.W. 310
Low, Sir D.A.C. **282**
Lucas, C/Sgt J. 560
Luckie, David 95
Luckner, Cmdr F. von 159, 434
Luxford, Gladys 566
Lynch, Frank 575, 590
Lyon, W.C. 34
Lyons, J.A. 48

MacArthur, Gen Douglas 245, 257, 267, 279, 408–10
McBride, Sub-Lt T.C.G. 176
McCahon, Colin 577
McCleverty, Lt-Col W.A. 71, 374
McCormick, E.H. 400, 588
McCracken, Francis 575
McCraw, David 323
McCristell, Maj T. 243
McCrone, Ian 580
McDonald, Lachie 580
Macdonald, Lt-Cdr G.J. **283**, 458–9
Macdonald, W.D.S. 582
McDonnell, Lt-Col T. 33, 70, 165, **283–4**, 344, 361, 379–82, 522
Mace, Capt F.J. 361
Mace, Lt-Gen Sir J.A. **284**
McGavin, Maj-Gen Sir D.J. **284**
McGibbon, I.C. 321–2
McGregor, Capt M. 7
McGregor, Col R. 226
machine-guns **284–5**
McIndoe, Sir A.H. **285**, 315
McIntosh, A.D. 578
McIntyre, Maj P.D. **286**, 576–7
McIntyre, W.D. 322
McIver, Lt-Gen D.S. **286–7**, 417
Mackay, Maj-Gen I.G. 208
Mackay, Jessie 615
McKeich, Lt R. 63
MacKenna, C/Sgt E. 560
MacKenzie, Lt K. 245
Mackenzie, Sir C.N. **287**, 400, 487
Mackenzie, Sir T. 287, 357
Mackie, Charles 25
Mackie, Wg Cdr E.D. 287

McKillop, Mshpmn H.F. 104
McKinnon, Maj-Gen W.S. **287**
Mackley, Ian 591
Macky, Col N.L. 179
Maclean, Maj C. 7
McLean, Sir D. 33, 95, 284, 288, 610–11
McLean, D.B.G. **287–8**
McLean, E.P. 383
McLean, Hester **288**, 470, 614
McLeod, John 322
McNeill, Lt-Col J.C. 560
McPhee, Duncan 576
MAGIC 544
Magnusson, Tpr J.W. 199
Mair, Capt G. 288, 361, 383, 519, 546
Mair, Henry 288
Mair, William **288**, 519
Maketu 217
Malayan campaign 14, 131, 175, **289–91**, 386, 406–7, 460, 483
Malayan Emergency 19, 64, 72, 80, 83, 102, 132, 168, 226, 247, 284, **291–4**, 322, 328, 424, 445, 447, 461–2, 466, 496, 505, 531–2, 543, 549, 579, 592
Malcolm, Lt J. 164
Male, John 279, 593
Maling, Sgt C.L. 361
Malone, Lt E.L. 295
Malone, Lt-Col W.G. 275, 278, **294–5**, 541
Malta 12, 219, 228, 267, 296, 314, 388, 412
Malthus, Cecil 278
Manahi, Sgt H te R. **295**, 310–11, 395
Manhattan Project 22, 480
Maniapoto, Rewi 216, **295–6**, 347, 374, 377, 524
Maning, Frederick 384
Manley, W.G.N. 560
Maori:
    and armed forces 34–5, 109, 222, 236, 266, 271–2, **300–3**, 513, 544
    and Boer War 59, **296**
    defence works 140, **299–301**, 371–3, 383
    and First World War 105, 118, 122, 243, 272, **296–9**, 330, 349–50, 367, 422–3
    and Korean War 303, 423
    and Second World War 119, 222, 265, 272–3, 279, 294–5, 302–3, **307–11**, 331, 350, 387, 395, 406, 423–4, 560
    traditional warfare 56, **303–7**
Maori War Effort Organisation 222, **307–9**

maritime reconnaissance aircraft **311–12**
Marjouram, Sgt W. 244, 327
Marsden, Col Sir E. 43, **312–13**, 478
Marsden, Samuel 200
Marshall, Charles 343
Martineau, Sgt H.R. 560
Mason, Malcolm 279
Mason, R.A.K. 279
Mason, Rex 308
Massey, W.F. 15–16, 47, 82, 90, 92, 130, 170–1, 174, 182, 255, 258–9, 302, **313**, 330, 338, 362–5, 387, 400, 422, 450, 453, 471, 499, 501, 554, 578, 581, 592, 596, 614–15
Massey's Cossacks 90, 182, 387, 471
Matangi Hauroa, 304
Matene Rangitauira 379
Mau 16, 55, 58, 130, 459, 476, 573
Mauny, Eric de 593
Maylett, Archibald 576
Maynard, AVM F.H.M. 12
Mead, Maj-Gen O.H. **313**
medical treatment 32, 200, 284–5, **313–15**, 366, 489–90, 513
Meldrum, Brig-Gen W. **315–16**
Meldrum, Maj W.J.D. 114
Melvill, Maj-Gen Sir C.W. **316**
Mentiplay, C.R. 579
merchant marine 121, 133, 226, **316–17**, 339, 537, 558
Mesopotamia 17, 74, 129, **317–18**, 366, 470
Middle East commitment 30–1, 48, 72, 92, 102, 110, 132, 154, 181, 199, 242, **318**, 359, 364, 369, 437, 461, 466, 513, 598
Middleton, O.E. 280
Miles, Brig R. 42, 215, **319**, 432, 598
military districts 15, 148, 319, 369, 597
military engineers **319–21**
military history 263, **321–3**
military law **323–5**, 360, 481
military settlers 33, 216, 283, **325–7**, 331, 376, 486, 498
military signalling 317–18, **327–9**
military slang **329–31**
Military Studies Institute 57, 323, **331**, 463, 486
Militia 69, 82, 89, 139, 180, 301, 323, **331–2**, 337, 344, 361, 376, 428, 450, 545, 566
Militia Ordinance, 1845 319, 331
Miller, Allan 575
Miller, R.T. 579
mine countermeasures vessels **332–3**
mine tenders **334**

644

Index

mines:
  land 146, **333**, 442
  sea 129, 159, **333–4**, 480
mining operations in First World War 149, **334**, 603
missiles **335**
Mitcalfe, Barry 280
Mitchell, Alan (machine-gun designer) 237
Mitchell, Alan (war correspondent) 579
Mitchell, Samuel 560
Moir, Sgt T. 448
Moloney, Col D.W. 449
Monro, Gen Sir C. 197
Montgomerie, Deborah 322
Montgomery, Fd Mshl Lord 32, 161, 183, 248, **335–6**, 392–5
Moore, Mike 210
Moore-Jones, Spr H.M. 18, **336**, 575
Morgan, John 244
Morris, W.E. 593
Morrison, AVM I.G., 138, **336**, 462
Morrison, Muriel and John 25
mortars 20, 301, **336–7**
Mortlock, Brig R. 185, 419
Morton, Lt R.M. 448, 513, 627
Mould, Maj-Gen T.R. 178, **337**, 375
Moule, Lt-Col W. 34
Moultray, J.D. 578, 591
Mount Cook Barracks 5, 38
mounted rifles **337–8**, 442
Muldoon, R.D. 22, 27, 103, 163, 219, 273
Mulgan, Lt-Col J.A.E. 246, 278–9, **338**, 448
Multinational Force and Observers 106, 154, 218, 287, 417–18
Multinational Interception Force 467
Munich settlement 32
Murphy, Geoff 384
Murphy, W.E. 323
Murray, Sgt J. 560
Murupaenga **338**, 356, 543
museums 4, 38, 215–16, **338–40**, 536, 595
Musket Wars 151, 200, 262, 338, **340–4**, 356, 371, 415, 424, 434, 442, 497, 516–18, 521, 524, 542–3, 610
mutinies **344–6**, 422, 452, 466
Mutual Assistance Programme 170, 176, **346**, 530
Myers, Arthur 239, 581

N Force **347**
Nalder, C.N. 277
Napier earthquake 88, 130, **347–8**, 364, 496, 598

Nash, Walter 112, 115, 482, 557, 578
National Airways Corporation 461, 540
National Collection of War Art 577
National Council of Churches 444–5
National Council of Women 612, 615–16
National Defence League 15, 53, 109, 142, 473
national identity 32, 172, **347–50**, 424
National Military Reserve 21, 221–2, **350–1**
National Patriotic Fund Board 414, 425, 445, 626
National Peace Council 25
National War Memorial 38, 54, 316, 339, **351–2**, 590
Native Contingent, *see* Maori and First World War
Natusch, Spr R. 432
naval bases 78, 83, 129, 140, 281, 345, **352–3**, 455, 469, 586
naval personnel, NZ, in the Royal Navy:
  in First World War 340, 401, 437, **455–6**, 477–8
  in Second World War 67, 115, 201, 283, 291, 406, 421, 431–2, **456–9**, 465, 498, 530
naval shore establishments 352–3
  Creswell, HMAS 399
  Irirangi, HMNZS 328, 353
  King Alfred, HMS 457
  Philomel, HMNZS 130, 466, 537
  St Vincent, HMS 450, 457
  Tamaki, HMNZS 112, 339, 399, 422, 457
naval stations:
  America and West Indies 131, 451, 465
  Australia **44–6**, 67, 105, 362, 454–5
  China 45–6, 362
  East Indies 45, 465
  East Indies and China 46
  Far East 132, 186
  New Zealand 6, 36, 46, 78, 86, 120, 143, 229, 353, 364, **370**, 465, 496
naval vessels:
  Australian 120, 176, 188, 357, 455, 467, 475, 514
  Austrian 354
  British 36, 58, 67, 78, 80, 105, 115, 120, 143, 151, 187, 201, 219, 229–31, 266, 316, 354, 356, 401, 410, 413, 421, 433, 450–1, 453–5, 458, 466, 468, 497, 530, 541

Alligator 68, 151, 354, 454, 520; *Endeavour* 151, 323, 354; *Katoomba* 402; *Laburnum* 496; *Leith* 364, 497; *Mildura* 402; *Neptune* 457–8; *New Zealand* 98, 107, 144, 173, 258–9, **357–8**, 362, 454–6, 463–4, 477, 490, 529, 542, 596; *Orpheus* 454; *Pioneer* 105, 385, 402; *Prince of Wales* 83, 290, 407, 455, 458, 496; *Prize* 477; *Psyche* 90, 353, 354, 402, 475; *Pyramus* 90, 353, 402, 455, 496; *Ramillies* 120, 165, 455, 541; *Repulse* 290, 407, 496; *Resolution* 230–1, 468; *Ringarooma* 402; *Sparrow* 317, 537; *Tauranga* 402; *Torch* 537, 353; *Veronica* 496; *Wallaroo* 46, 402; *Wellington* 497; *Zealandia* 357
  French 354, 356, 475
  German 36, 159, 163, 312, 458, 475, 477, 496, 541
    Adjutant 100, 159; *Admiral Graf Spee* 245, 413, 451, 465; *Emden* 120, 354; *Komet* 159, 176, 317; *Orion* 159, 176, 317, 334; *Seeadler* 159, 434; *Tirpitz* 101, 176, 450, 458; *U-862* 100, 160; *Wolf* 129, 159, 199, 213, 332, 334
  Italian 131
  Japanese 67, 92, 120–1, 159, 255, 354–5, 421
  New Zealand:
    Achilles 1, 10, 36, 130–2, 134, 159, 311, 340, 350, 353, 357, 364, 406–8, 412, 451, 453, 457, 465, 479, 502, 549, 596; *Arabis* 121, 143, 421; *Arbutus* 121, 345, 465–6; *Bellona* 130–2, 134, 239, 345, 422, 453, 465–6, 596; *Black Prince* 130–2, 185, 453, 466, 534; *Blackpool* 144, 187, 467; *Canterbury* 22–4, 144, 152, 163, 170, 187–8, 212, 396, 467–8, 526, 534; *Charles Upham* 281, 469, 515, 542; *Chatham* 130, 229, 313, 363, 455, 518, 534, 537; *Diomede* 1, 130, 347, 363, 476; *Dunedin* 16, 58, 61, 130–1, 347, 363–4, 455, 459, 466, 476–7, 514, 536, 573; *Echuca* 332; *Endeavour* 19–20, 55, 152, 230, 281, 364, 514–15; *Gambia* 130–1, 134, 409–10, 465, 534; *Hautapu* 345, 466; *Hawea* 134, 185–6, 270, 448, 466, 537; *Hickleton*

645

Index

114, 332, 467; *Hinau* 467; *Inverell* 332, 448, 537; *Isa Lei* 514; *Kaniere* 185–7, 270, 537; *Kiama* 332, 537; *Kiwi* (corvette) 67, 121, 408, 502, 537; *Kiwi* (inshore patrol craft) 415, 467; *Koura* 448; *Kupara* 448; *Lachlan* 230, 231, 239, 395, 468; *Leander* 120, 130–1, 134, 163, 187, 217, 311, 335, 345, 364, 407–9, 465; *Mako* 448; *Manawanui* 333, 467–8; *Manga* 448, 526; *Mata* 421; *Matai* 434, 453; *Matai Junior* 434; *Moa* (corvette) 67, 115, 121, 408, 421, 502, 537; *Moa* (inshore patrol craft) 415, 467; *Monowai* (survey ship) 88, 170, 230–1, 332, 468, 623; *Monowai* (armed merchant cruiser) 36, 541; *Ngapona* 414; *Nucula* 130, 514; *Otago* 22–3, 86, 144, 187, 396, 452, 466–7, 534; *Paea* 230, 448; *Philomel* 16, 83, 120, 130, 213, 339, 345, 352–4, 362–3, 402, 422, 453, 455–6, 465, 475, 534, 537; *Pukaki* 185–7, 219, 267, 270, 292, 396, 415, 448, 455, 466, 468; *Puriri* 317, 332; *Rotoiti* 185–7, 270, 396, 448, 455, 466, 468, 517, 538; *Royalist* 130–2, 422, 453, 466–7, 514, 534; *Santon* 114, 332, 467; *South Sea* 332; *Southland* 24, 187, 335, 467, 534; *Stawell* 332, 537; *Takapu* 230, 468; *Tangaika* 434; *Taranaki* 23, 114, 144, 187, 466–7, 526, 534; *Tarapunga* 230, 468; *Taupo* 185–7, 239, 270, 448, 466, 537; *Tawhai* 332; *Te Kaha* 152, 188, 212, 467; *Te Mana* 188, 467; *Tui* 23–4, 231, 396, 468, 537; *Tutira* 185–7, 267, 270, 453, 466; *Waikato* 24, 163, 186–8, 288, 332, 356, 466–7, 515; *Wakakura* 332, 415, 453, 467, 537; *Wellington* 170, 187–8, 212, 364, 468, 515
United States 73, 248, 354, 410, 489, 514
Victorian 385, 541
naval visits **353–6**
Navy League 15, 76–7, 142
Nazi–Soviet Non-Aggression Pact 256, 483
Nelson, Maj T. 374

Nene, Tamati Waka 144, 217, 271, 338, **356**, 371, 415, 523, 543
Nevill, AVM Sir A. de T. **356**
New Caledonia 53, 99, 148, 255, 320, **356–7**, 368, 404, 408–9, 503–5, 529, 551, 576, 579
New Zealand, HMS, *see* warships, British
New Zealand Air Board 52, 87, 142, 247, 263, 356, 459, 574, 611
New Zealand Air Force 8
New Zealand Armoured Corps 338
New Zealand Army 25, 27, 39–40, 52, 54, 57, 70, 83–4, 86, 94, 106, 108, 122, 152, 185, 202, 227, 247, 264, 272, 275, 281, 285–6, 288, 292, 294, 303, 319, 324, 329, 335, 337–9, 346, 350, **359–60**, 362, 369, 417, 423, 437, 440, 442, 445, 449, 462–5, 469–70, 486, 490–1, 497–8, 505, 507, 532, 547, 554, 576, 596, 614, 620
New Zealand Army Board 40, 86, 142, 163, 214, 238, 313, 359, 436, 486, 513, 579, 597
New Zealand Army Air Corps **360**
New Zealand Army Legal Service **360**
New Zealand Army Medical Corps 312
New Zealand Army Nursing Service 288, 309, 470, 531, 547, 614
New Zealand Army Pay Corps **360**
New Zealand Army Physical Training Corps **360–1**
New Zealand Company 216, 522, 566, 573
New Zealand Cross 199, 225, 284, 288, **361–2**, 558, 573
New Zealand Defence Force, 81, 84, 109, 136, 139, 147, 162, 176, 211, 225, 227, 280–1, 331, 346, **362**, 401, 417–20, 438, 449, 526, 544, 550, 592, 623
New Zealand Division of the Royal Navy 1, 52, 58, 83, 86, 129, 134, 136, 176, 229, 258, 345, 356, **362–4**, 370, 404, 413, 451, 456, 465, 514, 537, 547, 596, 620
New Zealand Expeditionary Force, *see* expeditionary forces
New Zealand Flying School 7, 574
New Zealand Force East Timor 152, 622
New Zealand Force South East Asia 31, 106, 176, 284, 287, **369**, 466, 543

New Zealand Homeservicemen's Association 556–7
New Zealand Intelligence Corps **369**
New Zealand Korea Veterans' Association 555
New Zealand Medical Corps 55, 314, 463, 614–15
New Zealand Militia 385, 522
New Zealand Naval Board 58, 86, 120–1, 142, 229, 317, 332, 353, 356, 362, 413, 422, 453, 456–7, 465–8
New Zealand Permanent Air Force 2, 172, 236, 360, 459–60, 477, 534, 574
New Zealand Permanent Force Old Comrades' Association 555
New Zealand Permanent Staff **369**, 445
New Zealand Press Association 578
New Zealand Returned Services' (Soldiers') Association 28–9, 30, 66, 77, 112, 116, 118, 142, 215, 218, 265, 350, 446, 453, 473, 512, 555–7, 578, 588, 591
New Zealand Services Medical Team 462
New Zealand Staff Corps 17, 73–4, 93, 132, 147, 182, 185, 229, 261, 263, 265, 280, 313, 316, 332, **369–70**, 421, 436, 450, 472, 494, 510, 512, 597, 611, 625
New Zealand Veterinary Corps 18–19
New Zealand War Contingent Association 487, 566
New Zealand War Services Association 531
New Zealand Wars 18, 33, 38, 41, 46, 70, 78, 82, 87, 94, 96, 103–4, 117, 122, 140, 171–2, 209, 216, 226, 244, 271–2, 276–7, 283, 288, 297, 301–2, 307, 319, 321, 323, 325, 329, 331–2, 336–7, 339, 344, 347–8, 354, 360, **370–86**, 388, 399, 410–11, 424, 428–9, 434–5, 454, 470, 485, 497–9, 517–18, 520–3, 524, 541, 546, 555, 566–8, 569, 571, 573, 575, 578, 587, 589–90, 610, 615
New Zealanders with other nations' forces **386–7**
Newall, Col S. 90, 148, **387**
Newman, S.D. 323
Nga Puhi 41, 51, 200, 217, 223–4, 262, 271–2, 276, 298, 300, 338, 340, 342–3, 344, 356, 371, 379, 415, 424, 517, 521, 523–6, 543, 610, 612

Index

Nga Ruahine 381, 522, 532
Ngai Tahu 342–4, 516, 521, 522–3
Ngai Te Rangi 41, 342–3, 380, 428, 435, 517
Ngarimu, Lt M. 295, 310, **387**, 395, 560
Ngata, Sir A. 299, 308, 311
Ngati Apa 521–2, 525
Ngati Haua 301, 343, 415, 420, 429, 524
Ngati Kahungunu 271, 272, 303, 306, 342–3, 380–3, 424, 517–21, 525, 533, 543, 572–3, 610
Ngati Maniapoto 276, 295, 342–3, 518, 521, 523, 525
Ngati Maru 224, 342–4, 517–18, 524, 532
Ngati Paoa 224, 342–3, 415
Ngati Porou 49, 222, 271–2, 295, 380–3, 387, 423–4, 428, 572
Ngati Pukeko 343, 521
Ngati Raukawa 306, 338, 340, 342–3, 373, 517–18, 520, 521–3, 525, 543
Ngati Ruanui 283, 375, 380, 522, 532
Ngati Tama 516, 521–2
Ngati Toa 271, 277, 338, 340, 343, 373, 516, 521–5, 543, 573
Ngati Tuwharetoa 342–3, 382, 423, 517–18, 521, 525
Ngati Whatua 223–4, 262, 296, 338, 340, 342, 356, 415
Nicholas, Sgt H.J. **387**, 559
Nicholson, Gen W.G. 110, 570
Nicoll, Archibald 575
Nigro, Jan 577
Nihoniho, Tuta 296
Nimmo, R.R. 43
Nimot, Pte W.P. 158
Nixon, Maj J. 362
Nixon, Col M.G. 216, 283, 337, **387–8**, 589
No More War Movement 25
Noble, W.J. 579
Norfolk Is. 3, 47, 101, 166, 347, 408, 529, 538, 540
North African campaign 8, 11–12, 17, 32, 42, 46, 49, 53–5, 66, 93, 115, 132, 154, 176, 183, 198, 214, 218, 243, 248, 264, 278, 295, 310, 315, 320, 335, 338, 367, **387–95**, 412, 431, 458, 472, 531–2, 544, 553, 555, 576, 596, 598
North Russian Convoy Veterans' Association 555
North Russian Relief Force 79, 473
Northcott, Lt-Gen J. 72

Northcroft, Sir E. 580
Northcroft, Ensgn H.W. 361
Northern War 41, 144, 209, 217, 236, 262, 271, 276, 371–4, 377, 383–4, **395**, 424, 526, 573, 624
Northover, WO L.M. 627
nuclear weapons testing 22, 26, 102–3, 145, 234, **395–6**, 438, 455, 468, 514
nurses 63, 82, 219, 288, 312, 387, 441–2, 469–70, 500–2, 531, 614–15

O'Brien, Terence 81
O'Connor (Connors), Michael 362
O'Connor, P.S. 321
O'Flynn, Helen 616
O'Hea, Pte T. 560
Odgers, Ldg Smn W. 560
officer training **397–9**
official war histories 122, 134, 163, 263, 280, 321–2, **399–401**, 429, 436, 512–13, 588–9, 596
Olphert, Lt-Cdr W. **401**, 437
Operation Deep Freeze 19–20
Orange, Vincent 323
Organisation for National Security 48, 87, 141, 158, 245, **401**, 489, 512, 578, 584

'P' class cruisers **402**
Pacific Defence Conference 48, 56, **402–4**, 460, 478, 496, 611
Pacific Islands dispute **403**
Pacific versus Mediterranean 256, **403**, 483, 550
Pacific War 14, 20–2, 44, 53, 63–4, 74, 78, 86, 99, 101, 119–20, 131, 140, 156, 159, 166, 176, 181, 201, 220, 222, 240, 248, 279, 320, 351, 357, 391, 398, **403–10**, 412–13, 432, 433, 436, 460, 471, 483, 495–6, 502, 504, 508, 529, 533, 538, 544, 550, 552, 579, 585, 627
pacifism 25–6, 52, 55, 57, 74–5, 82, 116, 278, 350, 444–5, 532, 564, 616
Page, Alfred 25
Page, G.H. 575
Page, S.S. 25
Paikea, Paraire 307
Palmer, Keith 580
Papagos, Gen A. 205
paramilitary groups **410–11**
Parihaka 35, 56, 178, 210, 387, **411**, 452, 532, 568
Paris Peace Conference 75, 596

Park, ACM Sir K.R. 7, 9–10, 12, 15, 74, 94, 114, 172, 312, 386, **410–12**
Park, Brig R.S. **412**
Parkinson, Maj-Gen G.B. 251, 412
Parr, Alison 322
Parris, Robert 244
Parry, Adml Sir W.E. 407, **412–13**, 451
Patohe 379
Paton, Harold 591
patriotic funds **413–14**, 446
patrol craft 143, **414–15**, 468
Patuone 338, 342, 356, **415**, 523, 542–3
Paul, J.T. 81
Payne, Capt 343
Peace Pledge Union 26
peace-keeping 83, 106, 132, 152, 317, 321, 329, 360, **416–20**, 426–7, 462, 467, 490, 550
Pearce, Sir G. 48
Pearse, A.W. 575–6
Pendjeh crisis 148, 259, 301, **420**, 474
Pene Taka 319, 435
Penlington, W.A.G. 575
Penny, Victor 478
Penton, Maj-Gen A.P. 51, 107, 301, **420–1**, 452, 497, 546, 570
Perceval, Lt J.S. 386
Percival, Lt-Gen A.E. 289–91
Pere, Wi 296, 298
Perham, Frank 277
Perkins, Sgt D.C. 448
Permanent Militia 38, 89, 149, 387, 397, **421**, 452, 464, 470, 533, 569
Perry, William 222, 556, 578
Phelps, J.S. 386
Philip, Prince 439
Phillips, Adml Sir T. 407, 496
Philpott, Lt H. 245
Phipps, Vice-Adml Sir P. 87, 121, 138, 410, **421**, 467, 468, 596
Pickard, Lt A.F. 560
pilot training 8, 574
Pioneers 297, **422–3**
Pitt, Lt-Col G.D. (NZ Militia) 385
Pitt, Maj-Gen George Dean 68, **423**
Pitt, William 296
Pitt, Capt W.T. 555
Plugge, Lt-Col A. 506
Plumer, Gen Sir H. 201, 203, 601–5
Plunket Society 619
Poananga, Maj-Gen B.M. 140, 272, 303, **423**
Pohe, FO P.P. 309, **423–4**
Police 16, 33–5, 88–91, 115, 132, 139, 170, 210, 220, 244, 246–7, 297,

647

Index

347, 417–18, 421, 476–7, 511, 540, 558, 573, 581, 595, 616, 619
Pomare I **424**, 517, 525
Pomare II 372, **424**
Pomare, Sir M. 298, 349, 613
Pomare, M.W. (Lady) 299, 613
popular culture **424–8**
Pore, Heni **428**
Porter, Col T.W. **428–9**
Potae, Henare 380
Potter, Brig L. 256
Power, Harold 575
Powles, Col C.G. 400, **428–9**
Pratt, Gen T.S. 79, 178, 203, 337, 374–6, **429**
Preece, Capt G.A. 288, 361
Preston, Gaylene 172
prisoners of war 50, 59, 82, 93–4, 101, 105, 121, 127, 147, 164, 176, 184, 208, 215, 218, 246, 264–6, 267, 270, 279, 291, 309, 319, 322, 330, 379–80, 423, 425, **430–5**, 441, 447, 458, 470–2, 480–1, 513, 553, 576, 607
prize ships **434**
Pugsley, Christopher 295, 321, 384
Puhirake, Rawiri 378, **435**
Puttick, Lt-Gen Sir E. 123, 170, 189, **435–6**, 486
Pye, Sgt C. 560

Q-ships 340, 401, **437**, 477
Queen Elizabeth II Army Memorial Museum 39, 215–16, 263, 331, 339, 427, 590, 592
Queen Mary's Military Hospital 490
Queree, Brig R.C. **437**
Quilliam, R.H. 580

Rabel, Roberto 323
Rabuka, Lt-Col S. 170
Radford, Adml A.W. 438
Radford–Collins agreement 30, **438–9**
Rainbow Warrior affair 22, 88, **438**, 467
Rakai-moari 306
Ranfurly, Lord 589
Ranger Squadron SAS, 1st 114
Rangiihu, Chpln R.H. 302
ranks **438–9**
rations **440–1**
Rawlinson Gen Sir H., 601
Ray, Robert 49
Reader, Col H.E. 34
Ready, Patrick 362
Red Cross 28, 88, 150, 155, 200, 225, 243, 330, 333, 414, 425, 431, 433, **441–2**, 447, 453, 531, 566, 577, 614, 616

Reed, William 576
Reeves, Sir P. 2, 396
refugees 347, 417–18, 428, **441–2**
regimental alliances **442**
regiments:
 British:
  12th 70, 374; *14th* 70, 78, 374; *17th* 144; *18th* 70, 560; *22nd SAS* 114, 294; *26th* 429; *39th* 387; *40th* 70, 79, 216, 374, 560; *42nd* 423; *43rd* 70, 560; *50th* 67, 70; *56th* 429; *57th* 70, 374, 560; *58th* 67–8, 70, 371, 472, 624; *65th* 70, 374, 545, 560; *68th* 70, 560; *70th* 70, 87, 198; *80th* 70; *96th* 68, 70, 371, 423; *99th* 70, 144, 371; King's Oversea Dominion 386
 New Zealand:
  1st Waikato Militia 288, 325–6, 385; 2nd Waikato Militia 216, 325–6, 385; 3rd Field 597; 3rd Waikato Militia 325–6, 385, 434; 4th Field 208, 412, 437; 4th Waikato Militia 326, 385; 4th Wellington (East Coast) Mounted Rifles Volunteers 471; 5th Field 215; 5th (Wellington) 67; 6th Field 200, 345, 598; 6th (Hauraki) 16; 7th Anti-Tank 25, 437; 9th Heavy 100; 10th Heavy 100; 11th Heavy 100; 11th (Taranaki Rifles) 275, 294; 13th Heavy 100; 15th (North Auckland) 435; 16th Field 216, 267–9, 302–3, 596; 16th (Waikato) 494; Auckland 16, 32, 75, 128, 261, 430; Auckland Mounted Rifles 337, 430; Canterbury 73, 263, 298, 313, 387, 431, 609, 625; Canterbury Mounted Rifles 337; Divisional Cavalry 37, 66, 124, 207, 242, 253, 281, 303, 311; Hawke's Bay 163; New Zealand Infantry 294, 369, 426, 465; New Zealand Scottish 528; Otago 73, 471, 540; Otago Mounted Rifles 197, 215, 297, 338, 422, 540; Queen Alexandra's Armoured 37; Royal New Zealand Infantry 114, 242, 426, **464–5**, 529; Wellington 106, 204, 275, 440, 473; Wellington Mounted Rifles 197, 287, 295, 315, 337

rehabilitation 40, 51, 298–9, 308, 330, 351, 446–7, 556, 583, 617
religion 25, 75, 82–4, 116, 330, **442–5**
Rennie, Col F. 294, 445
repatriation 51, 299, 351, 366, **446–7**, 541, 556, 583, 617
resistance in Europe 85, 127, 143, 150, 279, 338, **447–8**, 627
resource protection 448, **468**
Reston, Capt R.M. 386
revolution in military affairs **448–9**
Rhodes-Moorhouse, 2Lt W.B. **449**, 560
Rhodesian Monitoring Force 417, **449**
Richards, A.M. 444
Richardson, Lt-Cdr A. 176, **449–50**, 458
Richardson, Maj-Gen G.S. 16, 182, 226, 235, 366, **450**, 476, 531, 554, 614
Richmond, J.C. 610
Richmond, Maj M. 68
Ridgway, Gen M. 267
Ridling, Lt R.G. 199
rifle clubs **450–1**
Roberts, Air Cdre G.N. 410
Roberts, Lt-Col J.M. 34, 361, 421, **451–2**
Roberts, Fd Mshl Lord 61, 266, 295
Robertson, Lt-Gen Sir H.C.H. 72, 270
Robertson, Sir J.F. 138, 287, **452**
Robin, Maj-Gen Sir A.W. 59, 86, 136, 141, 235, 246, 278, 399–400, **452**
Robley, H.G. 69, 575
Robson, Chpln G.T. 83
Rodriquez de Sardinia, Tpr A. 361
Rogers, Maj L.S. 279, 447
Rommel, Fd Mshl E. 12, 93–4, 265, 281, 310, 389–94
Rongowhakaata 271–2, 382
Roosevelt, President F.D. 248, 408, 582
Ropata, *see* Wahawaha
Ross, Capt J.C. 354
Ross, Rr-Adml J.O'C. **453**
Ross, Malcolm 277, 399–400, **452–3**, 578
Ross, S.G. 220
Roth, H.O. 57
Rout, E.A. 322, **453**, 614
Royal Air Force 2, 6–15, 55–6, 65–6, 73–4, 79–80, 93–4, 101, 115, 121–5, 133, 135–6, 154, 156–7, 160, 166–8, 172, 201, 204–5, 208, 211, 219, 226–7, 247, 254, 262–3, 287, 290–2, 309, 312, 324, 336, 356, 386, 395, 398, 406, 410–12, 423, 426, 431–3,

Index

448, 457–63, 473, 478, 483, 506–8, 510, 536–7, 539–41, 549, 573, 579, 595
Royal Australian Air Force 175, 239, 270, 312, 398, 462, 510, 536, 562–3, 595
Royal Australian Naval College 47
Royal Australian Navy 16, 23, 46, 49, 129, 168, 176, 239, 245–6, 353–4, 362, 364, 399, 462, 467–8
Royal College of Defence Studies, *see* Imperial Defence College
Royal Flying Corps 6–8, 52, 57, 67, 74, 77, 115, 172, 247, 411, 449, 459, 478, 574, 611
Royal Military College, Duntroon 48–9, 93, 198, 200, 214–15, 265, 284, 286, 319, 356, 369, 397, 412, 423, 511–12, 531, 596–7, 623
Royal Naval Air Service 7–8, 73, 79, 93, 101, 201, 455–6
Royal Naval Reserve 45, 455
Royal Naval Volunteer Reserve 67, 115, 283, 290–1, 401, 421, 453, 456–8
Royal Navy 10, 23, 45, 55, 58, 67–8, 78, 83, 93, 101, 104, 107, 114–15, 121, 128, 129–31, 133, 135, 142–3, 146, 148, 160, 163, 165, 176, 185–7, 201, 207–8, 213, 219, 227, 229–30, 232–3, 235, 245–6 248, 254, 258, 290–3, 316, 318, 321, 324, 332, 340, 352–4, 357, 362–4, 386, 399, 402, 407, 413, 428, 434, 437, 450–1, **453–9**, 465–8, 477–8, 483, 496, 510, 514, 516, 526, 530, 534, 541, 547, 575, 579, 594–6
Royal New Zealand Air Force 2–5, 14–15, 19–20, 24, 31, 40, 52–7, 63–5, 72–4, 76, 78, 83–5, 87–9, 91, 93–4, 101, 107, 112, 114, 129, 132, 143, 152, 160–1, 166–8, 175–6, 201, 210–12, 217–19, 223, 227, 238–40, 245–8, 254, 256, 263, 275, 281, 287, 290, 292, 294, 303, 309, 311–13, 318, 324–5, 328, 335–6, 339, 347, 353, 356–7, 359–60, 362, 369, 395–6, 399, 406, 409, 417–20, **459–63**, 490, 534–5, 538–41, 623
Royal New Zealand Armoured Corps 463, 465
Royal New Zealand Army Education Corps 40, **463**
Royal New Zealand Army Logistic Regiment 281, 426, **463**

Royal New Zealand Army Medical Corps **464**
Royal New Zealand Army Ordnance Corps 463–4
Royal New Zealand Army Service Corps 463
Royal New Zealand Corps of Signals **464**
Royal New Zealand Dental Corps **464**
Royal New Zealand Electrical and Mechanical Engineers 463–4
Royal New Zealand Engineers 421, **464**
Royal New Zealand Infantry Regiment, *see* regiments
Royal New Zealand Logistics Regiment 426
Royal New Zealand Military Police **465**
Royal New Zealand Naval Volunteer Reserve 83, 112, 121, 201, 227, 281, 317, 333, 399, 415, 466, 530, 537
Royal New Zealand Navy 4, 23–4, 40, 52, 54–5, 67, 83–4, 86–9, 107, 112, 120–1, 129, 131, 134, 143–4, 160, 162, 176, 185–8, 199, 217–19, 222, 227, 230–1, 238–40, 245, 247, 270, 281, 292, 294, 303, 309, 318, 324–5, 328, 332, 334–5, 339, 346, 353, 356, 362, 364, 396, 399, 407, 409, 414–15, 417–19, 421, 434, 455–6, **465–9**, 490
Royal New Zealand Nursing Corps **469–70**
Royal Regiment of New Zealand Artillery 106, **470**
Roydhouse, Garth 487
RSA, *see* New Zealand Returned Services' Association
rules of war **470–1**
Russell, Maj-Gen Sir A.H. 71, 75, 90, 142, 147–8, 179, 196, 260, 322, 359, 366, **472–3**, 511, 540, 556, 561, 576, 601–10
Russell, L-Cpl D. 199, 432, **471**
Russell, G.W. 614
Russell, W.R. 180
Russian intervention 8, 79, 456, **473**
Russian scares 34, 41, 55, 80, 95, 129, 148, 210, 239, 301, 323, 332, 420, 455, 464, **473–4**, 568, 611
Russo-Japanese War 109, 213, 474
Rutherford, Lord 22, 43, 312
Ryan, L-Cpl J. 560

Salmond, Sir J. 144

Salonika 220, 284, 312, 366, 450, 470, **475**, 487, 513, 573, 614
Samoa 364, 450, 459, **475–7**, 536, 573, 594
Sanders, Lt H.E. 591
Sanders, Lt-Cdr W.E. 340, 437, 456, **477–8**, 560
Satchell, William 276, 384
Saull, Rr-Adml K.M. 339
Saunders, ACM Sir H.W.L. 156, **478**
Savage, M.J. 180, 184, 350, **478**, 528
Scannell, Sgt-Maj D. 362
Schofield truck-tank 237
Scholefield, G.H. 487, 578
science 312, 468, **478–80**
Scott, Arch 279
Scott, James 575
Scott, Robert 276
Scott Base, 19
Scratchley, Maj-Gen Sir P.H. 35, 80, 95, **480**, 533, 533, 568
scrounging **481**
SEATO, *see* South East Asian Treaty Organisation
Second NZEF Association 556
Second World War 8–15, 307–11, 456–9, **482–4**, 583–7, 615–20
Security Intelligence Service 200, 247, 287
Seddon, R.J. 46, 51, 59, 63, 92, 107–8, 136, 149, 180, 232, 236, 254–5, 296, 302, 348, 399, 421, **484–5**, 497, 569, 595, 612
Seed, William 136
self-reliance in partnership **484–5**
self-reliant policy 216, **485–6**
Semple tank 236–7
Senussi campaign 188, 366, **486**
Serjeant, Ab Smn H. 386
service journals 287, **486**
service newspapers 426, **486–9**, 592
Shadbolt, Maurice 277–9, 295, 322, 384
Shanagan, James 362
Shanahan, Foss 87, 138, 143, 401, **489**
Shanahan, Lt P. 387, **489**
Shand, J.A. 401, 578
Sharpe, Maureen 322
Shaw, Capt H. 560
Sheehan, John 34
shell-shock 135, 215, 278, 314, **489–90**, 615
Shepherd, Michael 577
Shepherd, Sgt R. 361
ships (*see also* naval vessels; troopships)
   Amokura 317, 537
   Aparima 317, 541
   Boyd 151

649

Index

Caroline 104, 316
Elizabeth 151, 523
Ellen Ballance 334
Harriet 151, 454
Holmwood 159, 317
Janie Seddon 334
Maheno 228, 441
Marama 228, 441
Marquette 312, 469, 475, 513, 614
Nankin 245
Niagara 159, 317
Nora Niven 332
Parramatta 151
Port Kembla 159, 332
Rangitane 159, 176, 317, 480, 525
Rifleman 316, 382, 518
Simplon 332
Sophia 151, 516
Turakina 159, 317
Tutanekai 170, 477
Wahine 88, 317
Wimmera 158, 332
Shirley, Maj J. 328
shoulder titles 426, **490–1**
Shout, Capt A.J. 560
Simpson, Tony 384
Simpson, Cdre G.W.G. 185
Sinai–Palestine campaign 18, 27, 46, 132, 148, 153, 174, 298, 314, 316, 320–1, 327, 338, 366, 400, 428, 430, 453, 487, **491–4**, 515, 573, 594, 614
Sinclair, Sir K. 321, 384
Sinclair-Burgess, Maj-Gen Sir W.L.H. 355, **494–5**
Singapore strategy 1, 48, 56, 101, 144, 214, 233–4, 255, 258, 289–90, 313, 364, 402–4, 478, 483, **495–6**, 611
Sino-Japanese War 254
Slatter, Gordon 278
Slessor, ACM Sir J. 15
Slim, Fd Mshl Lord 74
sloops **496–7**
small arms **497–8**, 569
Smith, Angus 361
Smith, Charles 592–3
Smith, Capt F.A. 560
Smith, Lyndon 352
Smith, Cdr W.J.L. **498**
Snadden, John 576
soldier settlement **498–502**
Soldiers' Civil Re-establishment League 556
Soljak, Miriam 615
Solomons campaign 15, 19, 20, 37, 53, 63–4, 67, 73, 93, 121, 131, 148, 166–7, 184, 201, 242, 246, 248, 285, 287, 311, 320, 328, 336, 351–2, 357, 368, 408, 414, 421, 434, 445, 452–3, 461, 479, **502–5**, 533, 537, 574, 576

Somers, Sir E. 135
South East Asian Treaty Organisation 31, 49, 72, 87, 102–3, 179, 360, 466, **481–2**, 489, 505, 530–1, 543, 561, 598
South Pacific Area 120, 407, **504–5**, 550
South Pacific Nuclear Weapon Free Zone 145
Spanish–American War 36, 489
Spanish Civil War 122, 386–7, 580
Special Air Service 40, 109, 170, 212, 247, 281, 292, 440, 445, **505–6**, 530, 550, 563
Special Operations Executive 338, 447, 513, 625
Spencer, Pte V. 135
Spiller, Tom 386
sport 265, 426, **506–7**
Spragg, Col C.R. 179
squadrons, air:
    Fleet Air Arm 176
    RAAF 462, 563
    RAF 7, 14, 52–3, 57, 66, 74, 77, 79, 85, 94, 115, 122, 136, 154, 160, 172, 204, 219, 262, 287, 290, 411, 423, 449, 540–1
    75 (NZ) 8–9, 11–15, 63, 73, 157, 263, 336, 460, 507–8, 510; *243* 175, 287, 290–1, 406; *485 (NZ)* 11, 13, 85, 133, 157, 287, 510; *486 (NZ)* 11, 13, 133, 157, 510; *487 (NZ)* 12–13, 133, 157, 167, 510, 540; *488 (NZ)* 13, 133, 157, 510; *489 (NZ)* 10–15, 157, 510; *490 (NZ)* 10, 157, 510
    RNZAF:
    General reconnaissance, 507–8; *1* 65, 507–8, 538; *1 Airfield Construction* 14, 290, 407, 460, 502; *2* 168, 406, 462, 507–8; *3* 186, 336, 360, 461, 507–8; *4* 507–8; *5* 85, 88, 311, 462, 508; *6* 311, 461–2, 509; *7, 8* 509; *9* 357, 509; *14* 63–4, 72, 114, 129, 132, 162, 166–8, 175, 256–8, 294, 318, 461–3, 509, 536, 539; *15* 461, 502, 509; *16–19* 509; *20* 167, 509; *21–24* 509; *25* 64, 509; *26* 509; *30* 31, 63, 509; *40* 65, 211, 461–2, 510, 538–40; *41* 31, 56, 72, 223, 292, 294, 369, 461–2, 510, 538–9; *42* 7, 167, 510, 538, 540; *43* 539; *75* 5, 55, 63–4, 73, 166–8, 176, 254, 292, 294, 462–3, 507–8, 510,

549; *488* 6, 14, 291, 406, 460, 510
squadrons, RNZAF **507–10**
staff colleges **510**
Stafford, Edward 216, 380
Stagpoole, Drmr D. 560
Stark, Pte J.D. 278, **511**
Starnes, Maj F. 473, **511**, 561
Statham, Edith 587, 589, 615
Stead, C.K. 280
Stevens, Maj-Gen W.G. 48, 368, 398, 401, **511–12**
Stewart, Capt 523
Stewart, Lt-Col H. 400, **512**
Stewart, Ian 580
Stewart, Maj-Gen Sir K.L. 92, 199, 256, 303, **512–13**
Stobie, Geoff 575
Stoney, H.B. 276
Storkey, Lt P.V. 560
Stott, Maj D.J. 448, **513**, 627
Stout, Sir R. 420, 513
Stout, Col T.D.M. **513**
Student, Gen K. 124, 128
Suez crisis 132, 154, 322, 416, 422, **513–14**, 540
Sukanaivalu, Cpl S. 170
Sullivan, Daniel 578
supply ships **514–15**
Surafend massacre 338, 494, **515**
Swabey, Cdre G.T.C.P. 476
Sweeney, Pte J.J. 135

Taiaroa, Te M. 343, **516**
Tait, Adml Sir A.G. 386, **516**
Takamoana, Karaitiana **517**, 533
Tamahore 521
Tama-i-hara-nui 523
Tama-i-waho 305
Tamaikowha, Eru 380
Tamasese Leolofi III 16, 476
Tamehana Te Aewa 521
Tamehana, Hote 301, 420
Tamihana, Wiremu, *see* Te Waharoa, W.T.T.
Tangiwai disaster 88
Tapsell, Peter 518
Tapu-wae 306
Tara 340
Taraia, N. te T. 306, **517**
Taranaki Military Settlers 326, 376, 385, 560
Taranaki Wars 79, 103–4, 203, 271, 276–7, 288, 327, 331, 337, 371, 374–5, 377, 383–5, 388, 429, 443, **516–18**, 524, 532, 566, 578, 610
Taranui, Maj Te P. 362, **517**
Taratoa, H.W. 435, **517**
Tasman, Abel 151

Index

Tate, Col R.W. 476
Tawhana Tikaokao 374, 377
Tawhiao 272, 518
Taylor, Earle 593
Taylor, Chpln H. 83
Te Ahururu, H.K. 361
Te Arawa 55, 224, 271–2, 288, 295–6, 306, 310, 338, 376, 380, 424, 428, 517–19, 521, 523–5, 573
Te Ati Awa 271, 288, 295, 340, 343, 374, 443, 517–18, 522–3, 525–6
Te Hapuku 303, 533
Te Heuheu Tukino, T. 357
Te Heuheu Tukino, H. 305, **517–18**, 521
Te Heuheu Tukino, M. 343, **518**, 520, 525, 543
Te Kirikumara, I. **518**
Te Kooti 33, 106, 171, 210, 216, 271, 272, 277, 284, 288, 296, 381–4, 387, 428, 434–5, 452, 470, **517–20**, 522, 532–3, 546, 567, 573, 610
Te Maitaranui 304
Te Mamaku, H.T. 209, 373–4, **520**, 524
Te Matakatea, W.K.M. 288, **520**
Te Matauawa, H. 546
Te Pareihe 518, **520–1**, 525
Te Pehi Kupe **521**, 343
Te Pokiha, see Taranui
Te Puhi 340
Te Puoho-o-te-rangi 516, **521**, 524
Te Purewa **521**
Te Rangi Paetahi, M.K. **521**
Te Rangihaeata 104, 209, 373, **520–2**, 524, 573
Te Rangihiwinui, Maj Te K. 272, 283, 382, **522**
Te Rangitake, W.K. 277, 374, 518, 520, **523**
Te Rangiwinui 361
Te Rau, Kereopa 379, **523**
Te Rauparaha 151, 209, 277, 305, 338, 342–3, 347, 356, 373, 415, 516–18, **520–5**, 542, 573
Te Rehunga 305
Te Rei Hanataua 374
Te Roroa 342
Te Ua Haumene 379, 523, 532
Te Waharoa **524**
Te Waharoa, W.T.T. 295, 343, 377, 415, 428, **524–5**
Te Wera Hauraki 338, 340, 424, 521, **524–5**
Te Whakataupuka 343
Te Whakatohea 517, 521
Te Wharepu, P.P. 377
Te Whatanui 520, **525**

Te Wherowhero, Potatau 295, 342–3, 517, 520, 523–6
Te Whiti 35, 411
Teagle, Vice-Adml Sir S.F. **526**
Tedder, Air Mshl Sir A. 11–12, 15
Teira 374
Temple, Asst Surg W. 560
Templer, Gen Sir G. 292
Templeton, M.J.C. 322
Templeton, Natasha 278
Tempsky, G.F. von 177, 276, 283, 345, 348, 381, 451, **526–7**, 575, 578
Territorial Force 15–16, 21, 32, 38–9, 51–4, 66–7, 69, 74, 76, 79, 82, 85, 90, 92–3, 106, 108, 110, 112, 115, 117, 119, 132, 139, 146, 150, 154, 163, 179, 181, 202, 213, 215, 217, 219, 222–3, 241, 243, 247, 264–5, 275, 281, 294, 302–3, 307, 313, 319, 324, 331, 336–7, 350–1, 359, 360, 365, 367, 369–70, 397, 435, 442, 464, 470, 472, 486, 490, 505, 512, **527–31**, 547, 549, 571, 598, 622, 625
Thailand 496, **530**
Thode, Lt-Cdr C.P. **530**
Thomas, Maj-Gen W.B. 279, 432, **530–1**
Thompson, Claude 279
Thompson, Ernest 575
Thompson, Henry 373, 573
Thompson, R.H. 279
Thomson, David 172
Thornton, Lt-Gen Sir L.W. 139, 172, 322, 452, 482, **531**
Thurston, Matron M. **531**
Tinker, Lt-Col R.A. 293, **532**
Titokowaru 33, 178, 210, 216, 244, 272, 277, 283, 288, 319, 381–4, 387, 428, 452, 518, 522, **532–3**, 567, 610
Tizard, R.J. 47
Tokohihi, Epiha 374
Tolerton, J. 321
Tomoana, Henare 296, 383, **532**
Tonga 99, 101, 408, 448, 459, 529, **533**
Tonga Defence Force 346, 533
Tonkin-Covell, John 322
torpedo boats, spar 95, 105, 455, 480, **533**
torpedoes 24, 144, 218, 335, 467, **533–4**
Townshend, A.B. 575
training aircraft **534–7**
training ships 402, **537–8**
transport aircraft **538–40**
Travis, Sgt R.C. **540**, 559
Treadwell, C.A.L. 278

treaties:
  Brest-Litovsk 606
  Comprehensive Test Ban 145
  Four Power 17, 255
  Japanese Peace 56, 234, 256, 410
  Manila 31, 481–2
  North Atlantic 31, 234
  Nuclear Non-Proliferation 22, 145
  Nuclear Test Ban 26
  Ottawa Landmines 333
  Pacific Security (ANZUS) 31, 56, 234, 256
  Sèvres 82
  Versailles 174, 277, 313
  Waitangi 30, 68, 217, 262, 298, 344, 354, 356, 371, 374, 424, 454, 516–18, 522, 524, 526, 543, 573
Trent, K.L. 277
Trent, Gp Capt L.H. **540**, 560
Trethewey, William 575, 590
Trevithick, C. 575
Trieste 122, 184, 253, 279, 311, 425
Trigg, FO L.A. **541**, 560
troopships 6, 36, 40, 92, 120, 199, 228, 243, 266, 269–70, 298, 315, 317, 345, 365, 424, 469, 475, 477, 486–7, **541–2**
Trotter, A.A. 322
Tryon, Rr-Adml Sir G. 44
Tuhawaiiki 343
Tuhoe 272, 288, 297, 342–3, 380–2, 517, 519–23, 573
Tuis 330, **542**, 621
Tukorehu 521
Tulloch, Col A.M. 164
Turner, Henry 136
Turner, Nicholas 580
Turner, P. 69
Turoa, Te Paehi 518–20, 522, **542–3**
Tu-te-pouri-rangi 305
Tuwhare 338, 340, 342, 356, 415, 523, **542–3**
Tuwhare, Hone 280
Twistleton, F.M. 277
Tyrell-Baxter, J.A. 386

ULTRA 123, 127–8, 183, 245, 393, **544**
uniforms 146, 275, 426, 481, 490, **544–8**
unit diaries **548**
unit histories **548–9**
United Nations 56, 72–3, 86, 102, 106, 109, 131, 145, 152, 181, 210, 212, 263, 275, 322, 329, 386, 416–20, 466, 483, 514, 543, **549–50**

Index

Upham, Capt C.H. 127, 219, 350, 432, **552–3**, 559–61
US troops in NZ 276, 428, 502, 547, **550–2**, 555, 570

V-Force 423, 462, **554**, 563, 579
Vancouver, George 230
Vasey, Brig G.A. 124, 127
VE Day **557–8**
venereal disease 153, 202, 258, 298, 322, 453, **554–5**, 615
Vercoe, Capt H.R. 296, 298
veterans' organisations 142, **555–7**
Victoria Cross 17, 54, 61, 73, 78, 126, 128, 154, 170, 176–7, 182, 184, 199, 204, 208, 214, 216, 219, 224–5, 229, 261, 274, 295, 310–11, 319, 327, 360, 387, 449–50, 454, 456, 464, 477, 498, 511, 513, 540–1, 552–3, **558–61**, 567, 577, 595
Victoria, Queen 61, 109, 232, 272, 361, 573, 612
Victory Contingent 17, 54
Victory Parade 50, 56, 436
Vietnam Services' Association 555
Vietnam War 1, 26–7, 29, 31, 43, 46, 72, 80, 83, 92, 102, 142, 162, 172, 179, 185, 210, 226, 230, 243, 247, 266, 280, 284, 287, 294, 315, 323, 328, 333, 350, 352, 401, 416, 424, 427, 442–3, 445, 447, 462, 464, 467, 470, 482, 490, 498, 505, 548, 549, 554–5, 557, **561–6**, 576, 579, 588, 592, 594, 597–8
VJ Day 187, 350, 461, **557–8**
Vogel, Sir J. 33, 95, 140, 259, 569
Volkner, C.S. 244, 276, 379, 517, 522–3
Voluntary Aid Detachments 441, **566**, 614, 621
Volunteer Force 15, 17, 38, 40–1, 51, 59, 61, 67, 82, 84, 89, 92, 106, 108–9, 133, 139, 146, 149, 160, 166, 214–15, 229, 236, 241, 263, 272, 280, 284, 296, 301, 314–15, 323, 327, 332, 337, 361, 397, 421, 451–2, 469, 484–5, 490, 494, 527, 546–7, **566–71**, 596, 612, 625

Waddell, Lt-Col J. 386, **572**
Wahawaha, Maj R. 272, 361, 379–82, 428, 471, 519, 522, 546, 572, 610
Waikato War, 78, 80, 104–5, 198, 209, 271, 276, 295, 327, 331, 371, 375, 379, 380–1, 385, 434, 524, **573**, 610

Waikato, the 296, 298, 342, 374–6, 381, 526, **543**
Wairau massacre 373, 516, 522, 524, **573**
Waite, Col F. 400, 573
Wake, Nancy 447
Wakefield, Capt A. 371, 373, 573
Wakefield, E.G. 164
Wales, Col J.G.C. 169
Walker, Asst-Surg S. 361
Walker, Maj-Gen Sir W. 113
Wallingford, Air Cdre S. 477, **573–4**
Wallis, Arthur 593
Wallis-Wells, Pte H. 431
Walsh brothers 2, 7, 52, 77, **574**
War Administration **574**, 580
war art 67, 75, 93, 286, 336, **574–7**
War Book 245, 401
war brides 256, 552, **577**
War Cabinet 43, 189, 214, 220, 226, 234, 237, 261, 313, 401, 483, 489, 556, 574, **578**, 580
war cartoonists 282, 426, 575
war correspondents 122, 277, 385, 452–3, 487, 526, **578–80**
War Council 222, 473, 489, **580**
war crimes 50, 101, 309, 391, 406, 423–4, 430, 432–3
war crimes trials 410, **580–1**
war economy 174, 240, 270, 276, 484, **581–7**
war graves 428, **587–8**
War History Branch 55, 163, 184, 218, 280, 400–1, 436, 513, 549, 577, **588–9**, 596
war memorials 28, 348, 351, 428, 443, **589–90**, 615
war pensions 1, 499, **590–1**
war photography **591–2**
war poetry and songs **592–4**
war surgery 200, 285, 315
war trophies 339, **594**
Ward, Sgt J.A. 559, **595**
Ward, Sir J.G. 16, 47, 110, 134, 141, 255, 259, 313, 357, 422, 444, 452, 570–1, 581–3, **595–6**, 615
Wards, I.McL. 321, **596**
Warre, Sir H. 575
Warren, Miles 339
warships, see naval vessels
Washbourn, Rr-Adml R.E. 138, **596**
Washington Conference 144, 168, 358
Watson-Munro, C.N. 44
Wavell, Fd Mshl Lord 123–4, 127–8, 205, 389
Weathers, Cpl L.C. 560
Webb, Lt-Gen Sir R.J.H. **596–7**
Webb, Col W.H. 141, 596

Webber, E.G. 487, 579
Weeks, John 575
Weir, Maj-Gen Sir N.W.M. **597**
Weir, Maj-Gen Sir S.C.E. 43, 87, 278, 302, 412, **598**
Welch, Nugent 575–7
Weld, F.A. 216, 526, 486
Wellington, Duke of 71
Western Front 7, 16–19, 24, 27, 32, 36, 41, 46, 52–5, 66, 73, 75, 77–8, 85, 105, 115, 117–18, 128, 132, 147, 149, 171–2, 174–5, 182, 184–5, 188, 190, 197–8, 200, 202, 204, 207, 214–15, 243, 251, 260–1, 263–4, 266, 270, 274, 277–8, 295, 297–8, 312–14, 316, 318, 320, 327, 329, 334, 337–8, 366, 383, 387, 400, 411–12, 422, 430–1, 440, 453, 456, 472, 475, 478, 487, 489, 492, 494, 497, 511–13, 540, 547, 572, 575, 578, 591, 594, **598–611**, 625
Weston, C.H. 277
Weston, Maj-Gen E.C. 124
Westrup, Capt C. 177
Whaanga, Ihaka **610**
White, A.L. 576
White, J.C. 325, 437
Whiteley, Rev J. 82, 244
Whitmore, Maj-Gen Sir G.S. 33, 210, 284, 288, 361, 381–2, 517, 532, 569, **610–11**
Whitney, Maj J. 239
Wigram, Sir H.F. 2, 7, **611**
Wilder, Col A.S. 179
Wilding, Anthony 456
Wilkes, Gp Capt T.M., 247, **611**
Wilkie, Maj A.H. 400
Wilkinson, Iris (Robin Hyde) 580
Williams, Lt-Col E.A. 69
Williams, Gen Sir G. 21, 99, 222, 436, **611**
Williams, Henry 200
Williams, L-Sgt J. 69, 371
Willimoff, Sqn-Ldr J.J. 257
Willoughby, Howard 385
Wills, Lt E. 473
Wilson, Guthrie 278
Wilson, Gen Sir H.M. 207
Wilson, Phillip 279
Wipiti, Sgt B.S. 309, 406
Wiseman, Sir W. 105
Wollen, W.B. 576
Woman's Christian Temperance Union 554, 615
women:
    and the armed forces 83, 427, 466, 469–70, **620–4**

Index

and Boer War 469, **612**
and First World War 453, 469, 531, 542, 566, **612–15**
and Second World War 261–2, 273, 427, 441, 461, 469–70, 484, 547, 566, **615–20**
Women's Auxiliary Air Force 262, 461, 547, 617, **620**
Women's Auxiliary Army Corps 261, 330, 470, 542, 566, 617, **620–1**
Women's International League for Peace and Freedom 25–6, 615

Women's Land Corps (Service) 273, 584, 617
Women's Royal New Zealand Air Force **624**
Women's Royal New Zealand Naval Service 219, 466, 469, 547, 617, 620, **624**
Women's War Service Auxiliary 220, 261, 273, 542, 617, 620
Woolley, G.E. 575
Woon, G.W. 578
World Health Organization 23
Worsley, Lt-Cdr F. 437
Wrigg, H.C.W. 361

Wynn, Colin 576
Wynyard, Lt-Gen R.H. 129, 301, **624**

yellow peril 109, 254, **625**
Yeoman, Allan 279
YMCA (Young Men's Christian Association) 40, 82–3, 413–14, 425, 444, 487, 614–15, **625–7**
Young, Maj-Gen Sir R. 220, **625**
Young, Maj R.R.T. 311
Young, W.W. 44

Z Special Unit 513, **627**
Zedlitz, G.W. von 158

653